Directory of Federal Libraries

Edited by William R. Evinger

ORYX PRESS
1987

The rare Arabian Oryx is believed to have inspired the myth of the unicorn. This desert antelope became virtually extinct in the early 1960s. At that time several groups of international conservationists arranged to have 9 animals sent to the Phoenix Zoo to be the nucleus of a captive breeding herd. Today the Oryx population is over 400, and herds have been returned to reserves in Israel, Jordan, and Oman.

Copyright © 1987 by
William R. Evinger
P.O. Box 6826
Arlington, VA 22206

Published simultaneously in Canada

Printed and Bound in the United States of America

Library of Congress Cataloging-in-Publication Data

Evinger, William R., 1943–
    Directory of federal libraries.

    Includes index.
    1. Libraries, Governmental, administrative, etc.—
United States—Directories. 2. Libraries and state—
United States—Directories. 3. Federal government—
United States—Information. 4. Federal aid to
libraries—United States—Directories. I. Title.
Z731.E93   1987   027.5′025′73   86-42744
ISBN 0-89774-244-3

Table of Contents

Introduction

The *Directory of Federal Libraries* identifies more than 2,400 libraries serving the Federal Government throughout the United States and overseas. This *Directory* is the only directory containing such a comprehensive listing of Federal libraries. In addition to serving as a unique source for locating Federal libraries, this *Directory* contains information about the resources and services available in the Federal library and information community. It is hoped that this *Directory* will contribute to more effective use of these resources and facilities.

Scope and Coverage

This *Directory* includes libraries located in all branches of the Federal Government, as well as in independent agencies and other Federal Government organizations. The organizational arrangement essentially follows the order of the departments and agencies as listed in the *United States Government Manual 1986/87*. Within the cabinet department listings, agencies are in alphabetical order, as are the names of the libraries within each agency. Within an agency listing, libraries located in the continental United States, Hawaii, and Alaska precede entries for any overseas libraries.

For the purpose of this *Directory* a Federal library is a library serving any agency of the Federal Government, including boards, committees, commissions, and/or quasi-official agencies. It is concerned with selecting, acquiring, organizing, recording, preserving, retrieving, and disseminating informational materials (printed books, periodicals, graphic, or audiovisual materials). It includes the services of a staff (in many small libraries this is limited to a single individual) to provide and facilitate the use of such materials in meeting the information, research, educational, and/or recreational needs of its users. The library may be a single unit, or it may be a multi-unit organization having branches and other outlets administered by a single director.

With the help of the Federal Library and Information Center Committee and the Federal agency librarians, a concerted effort was made to identify and locate all Federal libraries not only in the headquarters offices in the Washington, D.C. area but also in the field and district offices and overseas. The libraries were sent a brief questionnaire in February 1986 and a follow-up mailing was done in July 1986. Even though some libraries did not respond, they are included in the *Directory* as long as a reasonable identification as a Federal library could be made. A continuing effort will be made to add to and expand this listing as additional libraries are identified and more information about the listed libraries is added.

The Federal libraries listed in the *Directory* range in size from the national libraries—the Library of Congress, the National Library of Medicine, and the National Agricultural Library—to the small holdings of the penal libraries in Federal correctional institutions, Indian schools, National Park libraries, Veterans Administration patients' libraries, and Army law libraries.

Because of their importance to the library activities of their agency, the *Directory* also includes offices that are not themselves libraries but rather the administrative headquarters for the agency's library activities.

Content of Each Entry

The information listed for each library is based on its responses to the questionnaire, descriptive information that it submitted, or information provided in response to telephone inquiries. Depending on the size of the library and the degree to which it is automated, not all libraries had information to report for all items on the questionnaire (for example, on special collections, automated bibliographic retrieval systems, or electronic mail systems).

In addition to the official name, address, and telephone number (including FTS and AUTOVON where available), the libraries were asked for as current information as possible on the following:

Library Staff—For the purpose of facilitating contact with the library and the use of its resources, libraries were asked to provide the name of the administrator in charge of the collection or head librarian, plus the name(s) of the person(s) in charge of acquisitions, reference, and interlibrary loans. The person in charge of the library may not be a professional librarian, as is the case of some Army law libraries and some other agency law libraries in field offices (e.g. Department of the Interior), some National Park libraries, and the Bureau of Indian Affairs school libraries. In many instances a person will perform more than one function. The *Directory* only includes the names of library staff reported on the questionnaire or those verifiable through telephone inquires.

Type of Library—Based on the following definitions, the libraries were asked to select the type(s) of library that best describe(s) their collection of materials. Essentially the information was recorded as reported by the library, but some editing was done for consistency, for example, military base libraries are treated as general libraries and National Park libraries as special libraries.

> **Presidential Libraries** specialize in the official records, memorabilia, literature, and other materials concerning the affairs of a specific President of the United States.

> **National Libraries** have government-wide responsibilities and missions which include concern for both national and international matters (e.g., Library of Congress, National Li-

brary of Medicine, National Agricultural Library).

Academic Libraries include those intended to serve the faculty and students in colleges, universities, graduate, and postgraduate schools.

Health and Medicine Libraries have collections that are predominantly devoted to medicine and the health sciences.

Law Libraries house collections of predominantly legal materials.

Engineering and Science Libraries are those with collections devoted predominantly to engineering and the sciences.

General Libraries provide service to meet cultural, information, educational, and recreational needs of a defined clientele (e.g., libraries on military bases and US Information Agency libraries).

Hospital (Patients') Libraries include those autonomous service units which are located in hospital facilities and are operated primarily to serve library needs of patients in the facility, but which are not part of post or base library systems.

Penal Libraries are defined as those libraries which serve penal institutions (e.g., U.S. Penitentiaries, Federal Correctional Institutions). Military libraries which provide this service to the military are not included in this category unless they are operated separately from a base or post library system.

Elementary, Intermediate, or Secondary School Libraries provide school library services on Indian reservations.

Training Center and/or Instructional (Technical) School Libraries support non-degree-granting educational (vocational) centers. Included in this group are those military libraries which support an instructional mission.

Special Libraries are those special or technical libraries whose collections support a mission plan but are not predominantly devoted to engineering and science, health and medicine, or law.

Special Subjects and Special Collections—The character and subject-matter focus of a Federal library's collection are influenced by the mission and function of the agency in which it is located. As a whole, the Federal libraries cover a wide variety of subjects. The libraries were asked to list the important subjects represented in their collections (e.g., economics, foreign relations, trade). In addition, libraries were asked to list any collections that represent areas of exceptional strength. These special collections are usually separately grouped holdings that are unusual or of notable interest and are identifiable by subject, form, name of donor, or other distinct name. Libraries were also asked to identify any in-house files that are made available through the library, as distinguished from those available through commercial sources. It is hoped that by identifying these special subjects and collections, users of the *Directory* can more easily locate materials to meet their specific information and research needs.

Depository Library Designations—The Federal libraries were asked to indicate the types of depository programs in which they participate. In some cases they are among the more than 1,380 libraries designated as depositories for documents issued by the U.S. Government Printing Office (GPO). Such libraries participate in the Federal Depository Library Program, established by Congress. They receive Federal agency publications from the GPO and provide the public free access to them. To supplement the Federal Depository Library Program, other Federal agencies (e.g., Bureau of the Census or National Aeronautics and Space Administration) and international organizations (e.g., United Nations) have designated selected libraries to receive their materials. Libraries were also asked if they participated in these other depository arrangements. For example, to ensure that a collection of Bureau of the Census reports is available for reference and research at reasonably convenient locations, the Bureau has designated libraries, such as the Federal Trade Commission library, as Census depository libraries.

Automated Operations—In view of the growing importance of automation for accessing and sharing information resources, libraries were asked to provide the following: (1) the names of the online commercial data bases they are able to access (not all of these are available to users of the library); (2) the shared cataloging network(s) in which they participate; (3) membership in library networks and consortia for sharing resources on the local, regional, or national levels; and (4) participation in any electronic mail network.

Availability of Library Services—The libraries indicated the extent to which their circulation and reference services are available to other Federal agencies, other libraries, and the general public, as well as any restrictions that might apply.

Acknowledgments

The cooperation of the Federal Library and Information Center Committee, the Federal libraries, and other persons who provided information for this *Directory* is greatly appreciated. In addition, the author is grateful for the support for this project provided by Sam Mongeau and the other members of The Oryx Press staff.

The editor of this *Directory* has made every effort to identify and list as many Federal libraries as possible. Since not every library responded or furnished complete information, the editor will be constantly updating and expanding the database. Users of the *Directory* are urged to notify the editor of additional information which will update the files and help complete the inventory of Federal libraries. Succeeding editions will feature these additional listings, as well as expanded entries with more detailed information for each facility.

While every effort has been made to ensure that all information is both accurate and current within the confines of format and scope, the publisher does not assume and hereby disclaims any liability to any party for loss or damage caused by errors or omissions in the *Directory of Federal Libraries,* whether such errors or omissions resulted from negligence, accident, or any other cause. In the event of a publication error, the sole responsibility of the publisher will be the entry of corrected information in succeeding editions. Please direct such information to: The Editor, *Directory of Federal Libraries,* The Oryx Press, 2214 North Central at Encanto, Phoenix, Arizona 85004-1483.

List of Abbreviations

AAF	Army Air Field		Jct	Junction
Acq	Acquisition		lib	librarian, libraries, library
admin'	administration		Ln	Lane
AFB	Air Force Base		med	medical, medicine
assoc	association		Metro	Metropolitan
asst	assistant		mgr	manager
ATTN:	attention		Mt	Mount
Ave	Avenue		N	North
bks	barracks		NAS	Naval Air Station
bldg	building		NSB	Naval Submarine Base
Blvd	Boulevard		NPS	National Park Service
ca	circa		Pkwy	Parkway
Cir	Circle		Pl	Place
coord	coordinator		PO Box	Post Office Box
corp	corporate, corporation		Pres	President
Ct	Court		prof	professor
ctr	center		pub	public
dept	department, departmental		Rm	Room
dir	director		Rd	Road
div	division, divisional		RR	Rural Route
DoD	Department of Defense		Rte	Route
Dr	Doctor, Drive		S	South
E	East		St	Saint, Street
eng	engineering		Stn	Station
ext	extension		Sq	Square
Fl	Floor		supt	superintendent
FL	Flight		Supv	Supervisor
Ft	Fort		tech	technical
gen	general		tnpk	turnpike
HQ	Headquarters		topo	topographic
Hwy	Highway		univ	university
ILL	Inter Library Loan		US	United States
info	information		W	West
inst	institute, institutional			

LEGISLATIVE BRANCH

Congress

1. US House of Representatives Library
Cannon Bldg, B-18, Washington, DC 20515 (202) 225-0462
Admin E Raymond Lewis (Chief Librarian); Robert LaForce (Asst Chief Librarian).
Lib Type Special.
Spec Collecs Printed documents & materials produced by the House of Representatives.
Circ Servs Avail Not open to the general public; restricted to staff use.
Ref Servs Avail Restricted to use by general public on limited basis.

2. US Senate Library
Ste S-332, The Capitol, Washington, DC 20510 (202) 224-7106
Admin Roger K Haley. *Ref Lib* Greg Harness. *Acq Lib* Thea Koehler.
Lib Type Special.
Spec Subs Legislation; political science & American government; American political history. *Spec Collecs* Legislative materials (bills & resolutions, hearings, reports, debates, etc). *In-house Files* Computer files: LEGIS (status of legislation, Presidential nominations, & treaties); on-line catalog of Senate Library collection; SCORPIO (Library of Congress in-house data bases).
Lib Deposit Designation GPO Depository Library.
Info Ret Servs DIALOG; NEXIS; LEXIS; VU/TEXT. *Shared Catalog Nets* OCLC. *Coop Lib Nets* FLICC.
Circ Servs Avail Not open to the general public; restricted to Senators & Senate Staff.
Ref Servs Avail Not open to the general public; restricted to Senators & Senate Staff.

Architect of the Capitol

3. Architect of the Capitol, Art & Reference Division
SB 15, US Capitol, Washington, DC 20515 (202) 225-1222
Admin Florian H Thayn.
Lib Type Special.
Spec Subs Art & history of the Capitol & early public buildings under the jurisdiction of the Architect of the Capitol. *Spec Collecs* Files on Statuary Hall, Speakers' portraits, busts of vice presidents, & artists represented in the Capitol. *In-house Files* Construction & maintenance of all legislative buildings.
Ref Servs Avail To other Federal libraries; to other libraries; to the general public.

United States Botanic Garden

4. US Botanic Garden Library
245 1st St, SW, Washington, DC 20024 (202) 225-8333
Lib Type Special.
Spec Subs Botany; horticulture; garden history.
Ref Servs Avail To other Federal libraries; not open to the general public.

General Accounting Office

5. General Accounting Office, Office of Library Services
441 G St NW, Washington, DC 20548 (202) 275-3691; FTS 275-3691; 275-2972 (Law Lib); 275-5180 (Tech Lib); 275-0662 (Tech Svcs Branch)
Admin Phyllis R Christenson (Dir); Larry Boyer (Law Lib); Maureen Canick (Tech Lib); Ronnie Mueller (Tech Svcs).
Lib Type Law; General.
Spec Subs Accounting; auditing; defense; law; procurement; program evaluation; public administration; information technology. *Spec Collecs* Federal military & civilian regulations; GAO history; legislative histories.
Lib Deposit Designation GPO Depository Library; Canadian Documents Depository.
Info Ret Servs DIALOG; BRS; SDC; JURIS; WESTLAW; LEXIS; HOUSE LEGIS; SCORPIO; DRI; NEXIS; GAO DOCUMENTS. *Shared Catalog Nets* OCLC; RLIN; WLN. *Coop Lib Nets* FLICC/FEDLINK. *Elec Mail Nets* GAO internal electronic mail.
Circ Servs Avail To other Federal libraries; to other libraries.
Ref Servs Avail Restricted to GAO.

6. General Accounting Office, Philadelphia Technical Information Center
11th Fl, 434 Walnut St, Philadelphia, PA 19106 (215) 597-7360; FTS 597-7360
Lib Type General.
Spec Collecs Decisions of the Comptroller General.
Circ Servs Avail To other libraries.
Ref Servs Avail Not open to the general public; restricted to staff only, others by appointment.

Library of Congress

7. Congressional Research Service, Library of Congress
10 1st St, SE, Washington, DC 20540 (202) 287-5700
Admin Joseph E Ross (Dir). *Ref Lib* Catherine A Jones (Chief, Congressional Reference Div). *ILL* Olive Jones (Chief, LC Order Div). *Acq Lib* Jack McDonald, Jr (Chief, Library Services Div).
Lib Type Special.
Spec Subs Public policy focused materials.
Lib Deposit Designation GPO Depository Library.
Info Ret Servs DIALOG; BRS; SDC; NEXIS. *Coop Lib Nets* Library of Congress. *Elec Mail Nets* E-Mail (House of Representatives).
Circ Servs Avail Not open to the general public; restricted to US Congress.
Ref Servs Avail Not open to the general public; restricted to US Congress.

8. John F Kennedy Center Performing Arts Library
Washington, DC 20566 (202) 254-9803
Admin Peter J Fay. *Ref Lib* Walter Zvonchenko; Vicky Wulff.
Lib Type Special.
Spec Subs All areas of the performing arts, including broadcasting & films. A Joint Project of the Library of Congress & John F Kennedy Center for the Performing Arts. *Spec Collecs* Video tapes of Kennedy Center honors programs; souvenir programs & playbills.

Ref Servs Avail To other Federal libraries; to other libraries; to the general public.

9. Library of Congress
101 Independence Ave, SE, Washington, DC 20540 (202) 287-6500
Admin Daniel J Boorstin. *Ref Lib* John C Broderick. *ILL* Olive James. *Acq Lib* Robert Sullivan.
Lib Type National.
Spec Subs The book collections, encyclopedic in content, are strongest in history, public law & legislation, public documents of the US & foreign governments, the political & social sciences, literature & language, science & technology, bibliography, & library science. The library's collections, according to the latest figures published in 1984, totaled more than 81 million items in the following categories: 21,765,720 volumes & pamphlets; 44,947 bound volumes of newspapers; 35,282,898 manuscripts; 3,840,454 maps; 3,693,666 items of music; 1,021,542 phonographic discs, tapes & wires; 8,737,055 photographic negatives, prints, & slides; 239,157 prints & drawings; 321,410 motion picture reels; 1,731,988 reels & strips of microfilm, & reels of newspapers on microfilm; & many other items such as microcards, micro-opaques, photostats, & posters. In addition, hundreds of thousands of single issues of current newspapers & periodicals are available for reference. Under the operation of the copyright law (chiefly since 1870) the most comprehensive collection in existence of products of the American press has been brought together by the transfer to the library of a careful selection of those works deemed worthy of preservation & inclusion in the library's collections. *Spec Collecs* The special collections include the Library of Thomas Jefferson; the Peter Force Collection of Americana, 60,000 books & pamphlets; the Toner Collection of medicine & American local history, presented by the Washington physician & antiquarian Joseph M Toner, consisting of over 29,000 books & 12,000 pamphlets & periodicals; the Yudin Collection, acquired in 1906, consisting of 80,000 volumes, chiefly in the Russian language, particularly valuable for the history of Russia, Siberia, & Alaska; the Lessing J Rosenwald Collection of manuscripts & examples of fine printing & book illustration from the 12th century to the present; more than 5,600 incunabula (books printed in the 15th century), including a perfect copy of the Gutenberg Bible; a collection of items from Justice Oliver Wendell Holmes's library; the Hans P Kraus Collection of Spanish-American manuscripts; & the papers of most presidents of the US. The following were recently acquired: a series of television productions, such as "Nicholas Nickleby," "Brideshead Revisited," & "The Jewel in the Crown"; 1300 aluminum disc recordings from the 1930s, given by the American Dialect Society & documenting regional speech habits of the era, & 13 Bettini wax cylinder recordings, among the rarest of audio formats; the Music Division acquired the holograph music manuscript of Victor Herbert's *Suite of Serenades,* composed especially for Paul Whiteman's famous Aeolian Hall jazz concert in 1924; Important manuscripts of Sigmund Freud were received from the estate of his daughter, Anna Freud; papers of the late Patricia Roberts Harris, educator, diplomat, & cabinet officer, along with some of the earliest Walt Whitman letters were added to the Manuscript Division's collections; Original drawings of the Vietnam Memorial competition, including Maya Lin's winning design are among the notable additions to the Prints & Photographs Division.
Lib Deposit Designation GPO Depository Library; United Nations; Department of Energy reports; Department of Defense technical reports; NASA reports; ERIC microfiche.
Info Ret Servs DIALOG; BRS; SDC; NASA/RECON; DOE/RECON; DTIC; OCLC; MARC tape distribution service. *Shared Catalog Nets* Linked Systems Project (LSP) for Authorities Application. *Coop Lib Nets* The Library of Congress participates in Network Advisory Committee (NAC), Federal Library & Information Network, & Assoc of Research Libraries (ARL). The library's divisions & their participation are as follows: Afr/ME—Cooperative Africana Microform Project (CAMP); European—Univ of Illinois Library Academic Search Service, American Assoc for the Advancement of Slavic Studies - Bibliography & Documentation Committee, American Library Assoc - West European Studies Section, Modern Greek Studies Assoc; GRR - Washington Metro Area Council of Governments, Librarians Technical Committee; G&M - FEDLINK; Hispanic - Seminar for the Acquisition of Latin American Library Materials (SALALM), Assoc of Caribbean Univ Research & Institutional Libraries (ACURIL); M/B/RS - Film/Television Archives Advisory Committee (FAAC/TAAC), Federation International des Archives du Film (FIAF), International Federation of Television Archives (FIAF/IFTA), Society of Motion Picture & Television Engineers (SMPTE), Assoc for Recorded Sound Collections (ARSC), International Assoc of Music Libraries/International Assoc of Sound Archives (IAML/IASA); Preservation - Research Libraries Group (RLG) Preservation Program Committee, International Federation of Library Assoc & Institutions (IFLA), Core Program on Preservation & Conservation (PAC), Conference of Cooperation Preservation Programs; P&P - Historic American Buildings Survey/Historic American Engineering Record (HABS/HAER); Ser - Organization of American States (OAS), South Pacific Commission, European Communities (EC), & United Nations: UNESCO, Food & Agriculture Organization (FAO), General Agreement on Tariffs & Trade (GATT), World Intellectual Property Organization (WIPO), United Nations University.
Circ Servs Avail To other Federal libraries; to other libraries; to the general public.
Ref Servs Avail To other Federal libraries; to other libraries; to the general public.

10. National Library Service for the Blind & Physically Handicapped, Library of Congress
1291 Taylor St NW, Washington, DC 20542 (202) 287-5100; FTS 287-5100
Admin Frank Kurt Cylke (Dir). *Ref Lib* Hylda Kamisar, (ILL) (print material). *ILL* Thomas J Martin (braille & recorded). *Acq Lib* Mona M Werner.
Lib Type National.
Spec Subs Handicapping conditions (print ref collection). *Spec Collecs* Braille & recorded books & magazines on all subjects on loan to US residents who are unable to read standard print materials due to physical or visual impairment.
Info Ret Servs DIALOG; BRS. *Shared Catalog Nets* National network of libraries serving blind & physically handicapped persons. *Coop Lib Nets* National network of libraries serving blind & physically handicapped persons.
Circ Servs Avail Restricted to eligible blind & physically handicapped persons.
Ref Servs Avail To other Federal libraries; to other libraries; to the general public.

Office of Technology Assessment

11. Office of Technology Assessment Information Center
Washington, DC 20510 (202) 226-2160
Admin Martha M Dexter (Mgr, Info Svcs). *Ref Lib* Gail M Kouril (ILL, Acq).
Lib Type Special.
Spec Subs Technology assessment; technology forecasting; technology transfer; futures research; policy analysis; congressional operations & decision-making; science policy.
Info Ret Servs DIALOG; MEDLARS; HIS; LOCIS. *Coop Lib Nets* FEDLINK. *Elec Mail Nets* CLASS.
Circ Servs Avail To other libraries; not open to the general public.
Ref Servs Avail To other libraries; not open to the general public.

Congressional Budget Office

12. Congressional Budget Office Library
House Annex #2 Rm 472 2nd & D Sts, SW, Washington, DC 20515 (202) 226-2635
Admin Jane T Sessa (Ref). *Ref Lib* Lynn Newbill (ILL, Acq).
Lib Type General.
Spec Subs Federal budget; budget process; economics.
Info Ret Servs DIALOG; BRS; NEXIS; LEXIS; Dow Jones; SCORPIO. *Coop Lib Nets* Faxon; Washington Metropolitan Library Council; Special Library Assoc.
Circ Servs Avail To other Federal libraries; to other libraries.
Ref Servs Avail To other Federal libraries; to other libraries.

JUDICIAL BRANCH

Supreme Court of the United States

13. Supreme Court of the United States Library
1st St, NE, Washington, DC 20543 (202) 252-3175; FTS 989-3177
Admin Stephen G Margeton. *Ref Lib* Martha Byrnes. *Acq Lib* Rosalie Sherwin.
Lib Type Law.
Lib Deposit Designation GPO Depository Library.
Info Ret Servs DIALOG; LEXIS; WESTLAW; JURIS. *Shared Catalog Nets* OCLC. *Coop Lib Nets* FEDLINK. *Elec Mail Nets* MCI Mail.
Circ Servs Avail Restricted to records & briefs collection to be used on premises.
Ref Servs Avail Not open to the general public.

United States Courts of Appeals

14. US Court of Appeals 2nd Circuit Library
2801 US Courthouse, Foley Sq, New York, NY 10007-1595 (212) 791-1052; FTS 662-1052
Admin Margaret J Evans. *Ref Lib* Philip N Becker. *ILL* Sally C Hand. *Acq Lib* Charlotte B Sullivan.
Lib Type Law.
Spec Subs Law; judiciary. *In-house Files* Briefs of 2nd Circuit.
Lib Deposit Designation GPO Depository Library.
Info Ret Servs WESTLAW; LEXIS. *Shared Catalog Nets* OCLC. *Coop Lib Nets* Law Library Microform Consortium (LLMC).
Circ Servs Avail Restricted to court personnel.
Ref Servs Avail To other Federal libraries; to other libraries; restricted to the general public by appointment.

15. US Court of Appeals, Branch Library
Box 43, US Courthouse, 844 King St, Wilmington, DE 19801 (302) 573-6178; FTS 487-6178
Admin Shirley Harrison.
Lib Type Law.

16. US Court of Appeals 3rd Circuit Library
22409 US Courthouse, 601 Market St, Philadelphia, PA 19106 (215) 597-2009; FTS 597-2009
Admin Dorothy Cozzolino.
Lib Type Law.
Spec Subs Judicial administration.

17. US Court of Appeals 6th Circuit Library
617 US Courthouse & Post Office Bldg, Cincinnati, OH 45202 (513) 684-2678
Lib Type Law.
Spec Collecs Anglo-American Legal Collection.
Info Ret Servs LEXIS; Westlaw. *Shared Catalog Nets* OCLC.
Circ Servs Avail Not open to the general public.
Ref Servs Avail Not open to the general public.

18. US Court of Appeals First Circuit Library
1208 J W McCormack Post Office & Courthouse, Boston, MA 02109 (617) 223-2891; FTS 223-2891
Admin Karen M Moss. *Ref Lib* Judy A Lavine (ILL).
Lib Type Law.

Spec Subs US law; selective government documents. *Spec Collecs* Agency reports; state law material for MA, ME, NH, RI, PR; Spanish civil law material; superseded federal statutes. *In-house Files* Slip opinions from the 11 circuits & the federal circuit.
Lib Deposit Designation GPO Depository Library.
Info Ret Servs DIALOG; LEXIS; WESTLAW. *Shared Catalog Nets* OCLC.
Circ Servs Avail Not open to the general public; restricted to court & lawyers for federal agencies in Boston.
Ref Servs Avail To other Federal libraries; not open to the general public; restricted to court.

19. US Court of Appeals for the 4th Circuit Charleston Branch Library
US Courthouse & Federal Bldg, Rm 4403, 500 Quarrier St, Charleston, WV 25301 (304) 347-5295; FTS 930-5295
Admin Ann Shetzer.
Lib Type Law.
Info Ret Servs WESTLAW; LEXIS. *Shared Catalog Nets* OCLC (thru the 4th Circuit in Richmond).
Circ Servs Avail Not open to the general public; restricted to West Virginia's federal courts.
Ref Servs Avail Not open to the general public.

20. US Court of Appeals for the 4th Circuit Library
US Courthouse, 10th & Main Sts, Richmond, VA 23219-3598 (804) 771-2210, 771-2219; FTS 925-2210, 925-2219
Admin Peter A Frey.
Lib Type Law.
Lib Deposit Designation GPO Depository Library.
Info Ret Servs WESTLAW; LEXIS; NEXIS. *Shared Catalog Nets* OCLC.
Circ Servs Avail Not open to the general public; restricted to judicial officers & practicing attorneys.
Ref Servs Avail Not open to the general public; restricted to judicial officers.

21. US Court of Appeals for the District of Columbia Circuit Judges' Library
US Courthouse, Rm 5518, Washington, DC 20001 (202) 535-3401; FTS 535-3400
Admin Nancy Lazar. *Ref Lib* Theresa Sautella (ILL). *Acq Lib* William Stockey.
Lib Type Law.
Lib Deposit Designation GPO Depository Library.
Info Ret Servs DIALOG; Dow Jones; LEXIS; WESTLAW. *Shared Catalog Nets* OCLC. *Coop Lib Nets* FEDLINK.
Circ Servs Avail To other Federal libraries; to other libraries.
Ref Servs Avail To other Federal libraries; restricted to members of a bar association.

22. US Court of Appeals for the 5th Circuit Library
515 Rusk Ave, Rm 10017, Houston, TX 77008 (713) 221-9696; FTS 527-0696
Admin Barbara Kalman Whitsett. *ILL* Chou-Shia Y Tseng.
Lib Type Law.
Info Ret Servs WESTLAW; LEXIS. *Shared Catalog Nets* OCLC. *Elec Mail Nets* RAPICOM.
Circ Servs Avail To other Federal libraries; to other libraries; not open to the general public; restricted to members of the bar, court, & government agencies.

Ref Servs Avail To other Federal libraries; to other libraries; not open to the general public; restricted to members of the bar, court, & government agencies.

23. US Court of Appeals for the 5th Circuit Library
600 Camp St, Rm 106, New Orleans, LA 70130 (504) 589-6510; FTS 682-6510
Admin Maxwell G Dodson. *Ref Lib* Kay Duley. *ILL* Lisa Whitley. *Acq Lib* Jo Ann Eiserloh.
Lib Type Law.
Spec Subs US statute & case law; Louisiana, Texas, & Mississippi law. *Spec Collecs* Government documents & law reviews.
Lib Deposit Designation GPO Depository Library.
Info Ret Servs WESTLAW; LEXIS. *Shared Catalog Nets* OCLC. *Coop Lib Nets* New Orleans Assoc of Law Libraries (NOALL); SEALL (Southeastern); AALL (American); Law Library Microform Consortium (LLMC).
Circ Servs Avail To other Federal libraries; to other libraries.
Ref Servs Avail To other Federal libraries; to other libraries; to the general public.

24. US Court of Appeals for the 8th Circuit Branch Library
306 US Courthouse, Des Moines, IA 50309 (515) 284-6228; FTS 862-6228
Admin Glenda L McKnight.
Lib Type Law.
Info Ret Servs WESTLAW; LEXIS. *Shared Catalog Nets* OCLC. *Coop Lib Nets* FEDLINK.
Circ Servs Avail To other Federal libraries; not open to the general public.
Ref Servs Avail To other Federal libraries; not open to the general public; restricted to in-house use by court personnel, government agencies & lawyers with cases in the bldg.

25. US Court of Appeals for the 8th Circuit Branch Library
600 W Capitol, Rm 220, Little Rock, AR 72201 (501) 378-5039; FTS 740-5039
Admin Allison P Mays.
Lib Type Law.
Info Ret Servs WESTLAW; LEXIS. *Shared Catalog Nets* OCLC.
Circ Servs Avail Not open to the general public; restricted to court personnel.
Ref Servs Avail To other Federal libraries; to other libraries; not open to the general public.

26. US Court of Appeals for the 8th Circuit, Fargo Branch Library
657 2nd Ave N, Rm 247, Fargo, ND 58102 (701) 232-1326; FTS 783-5175
Admin Suzanne Morrison.
Lib Type Law.
Info Ret Servs WESTLAW; LEXIS. *Shared Catalog Nets* OCLC (thru the 8th Circuit in St Louis).
Circ Servs Avail To other Federal libraries; restricted to courts.
Ref Servs Avail To other Federal libraries; to other libraries; to the general public.

27. US Court of Appeals for the 8th Circuit Library
9401 Federal Bldg, Omaha, NE 68102 (402) 221-4768; FTS 864-4768
Admin Mary Urban Hough.
Lib Type Law.

28. US Court of Appeals for the 6th Circuit Grand Rapids Branch Library
340 Federal Bldg, Grand Rapids, MI 49503 (616) 456-2363; FTS 372-2363
Admin Dianne Zandbergen.
Lib Type Law.
Info Ret Servs LEXIS; WESTLAW. *Shared Catalog Nets* OCLC.
Circ Servs Avail To other Federal libraries; not open to the general public; restricted to judges & their clerks.
Ref Servs Avail To other Federal libraries; not open to the general public; restricted to judges & their clerks.

29. US Court of Appeals for the 6th Circuit Memphis Branch Library
1125 Federal Courthouse Bldg, Memphis, TN 38103 (901) 521-4170; FTS 222-4170
Admin Barbara Zimmerman.
Lib Type Law.
In-house Files Vertical file of information pertaining to local court matters & background material relevant to future litigation.
Shared Catalog Nets OCLC. *Coop Lib Nets* Memphis Law Librarians Forum; 6th Circuit Librarians Network; Memphis Library Council; American Assoc of Law Libraries (past member).
Circ Servs Avail To other Federal libraries; to other libraries; not open to the general public; restricted to members of Memphis Federal Bar Assoc Courts.
Ref Servs Avail To other Federal libraries; to other libraries; not open to the general public; restricted to US courts & Memphis Federal Bar Assoc.

30. US Court of Appeals for the 10th Circuit Albuquerque Branch Library
PO Box 2066, Albuquerque, NM 87103 (505) 766-8489; FTS 474-8489
Admin Pamela M Dempsey.
Lib Type Law.
Info Ret Servs LEXIS; WESTLAW. *Shared Catalog Nets* OCLC (thru the 10th Circuit in Denver).
Circ Servs Avail Restricted to court personnel.
Ref Servs Avail To other Federal libraries; to other libraries; to the general public.

31. US Court of Appeals for the 10th Circuit Tulsa Branch Library
4-520 US Courthouse, Tulsa, OK 74103 (918) 581-7498; FTS 745-7498
Admin Caralinn Cole.
Lib Type Law.
Info Ret Servs WESTLAW; LEXIS. *Shared Catalog Nets* OCLC (thru the 10th Circuit in Denver).
Circ Servs Avail Not open to the general public; restricted to court personnel.
Ref Servs Avail To other Federal libraries; to other libraries; not open to the general public.

32. US Court of Appeals for the 11th Circuit Library
56 Forsyth St, Atlanta, GA 30303 (404) 331-2510; FTS 242-2510
Admin Elaine P Fenton. *Ref Lib* Sue Lee. *ILL* Sara Straub.
Lib Type Law.
Lib Deposit Designation GPO Depository Library.
Info Ret Servs LEXIS; WESTLAW. *Shared Catalog Nets* OCLC. *Coop Lib Nets* FEDLINK.
Circ Servs Avail Restricted to OCLC/ILL.
Ref Servs Avail Restricted to court users.

33. US Court of Appeals for the 9th Circuit Library
US Courthouse, 10th Fl, 1010 5th Ave, Seattle, WA 98104-1129 (206) 442-4475; FTS 399-4475
Admin Deborah Norwood. *Ref Lib* Jean Pasche. *ILL* Jan Olson.
Lib Type Law.
Spec Collecs Bankruptcy.
Lib Deposit Designation GPO Depository Library.
Circ Servs Avail To other Federal libraries; restricted to Seattle area.
Ref Servs Avail To other Federal libraries; to other libraries.

34. US Court of Appeals for the 9th Circuit Library
Pioneer Courthouse, 555 SW Yamhill, Portland, OR 97204-1494 (503) 221-2124; FTS 423-2124
Admin Scott McCurdy.
Lib Type Law.
Info Ret Servs WESTLAW; LEXIS.
Circ Servs Avail To other Federal libraries; to other libraries; not open to the general public.
Ref Servs Avail To other Federal libraries; to other libraries; restricted to telephone inquiries by general public.

35. US Court of Appeals for the 9th Circuit Los Angeles Branch Library
1702 US Courthouse, 312 N Spring St, Los Angeles, CA 90012 (213) 894-3636; FTS 798-3636
Admin Joanne Mazza.
Lib Type Law.
Lib Deposit Designation GPO Depository Library.
Circ Servs Avail Restricted to judges & staff.
Ref Servs Avail To other Federal libraries; to other libraries; to the general public; restricted to help given as time permits.

36. US Court of Appeals Library
US Courthouse, Rm C-411, Denver, CO 80294 (303) 844-3591; FTS 564-3591
Admin J Terry Hemming. *Ref Lib* Catherine McGuire Eason. *ILL* Carol Minor. *Acq Lib* Inez K Larson.
Lib Type Law.
Lib Deposit Designation GPO Depository Library.
Info Ret Servs LEXIS; WESTLAW. *Shared Catalog Nets* OCLC. *Coop Lib Nets* Central Colorado Library System (CCLS); FED-LINK.
Circ Servs Avail Restricted to court personnel.
Ref Servs Avail To other Federal libraries; to other libraries; to the general public; restricted to court personnel for LEXIS & WESTLAW.

37. US Court of Appeals Library
1114 Market St, Rm 503, Saint Louis, MO 63101 (314) 425-4930; FTS 279-4930
Admin Ann T Fessenden. *Ref Lib* Kirk Gregory (ILL). *Acq Lib* Mary Kay Jung.
Lib Type Law.
Spec Subs Federal law. *In-house Files* Index of 8th Circuit slip opinions.
Lib Deposit Designation GPO Depository Library.
Info Ret Servs LEXIS; WESTLAW. *Shared Catalog Nets* OCLC. *Coop Lib Nets* FEDLINK.
Circ Servs Avail To other Federal libraries; to other libraries; restricted to on-site use only for general public.
Ref Servs Avail Restricted to limited reference help for non-judiciary users.

38. US Court of Appeals Newark Branch Library
425 Post Office & Courthouse, Newark, NJ 07101 (201) 645-3034; FTS 341-3043
Admin Andrea Battel.
Lib Type Law.
Shared Catalog Nets OCLC.
Circ Servs Avail Not open to the general public; restricted to federal judges.
Ref Servs Avail Not open to the general public; restricted to attorneys & pro se patrons.

39. US Court of Appeals 9th Circuit Library
PO Box 5731, 7th & Mission Sts, San Francisco, CA 94101 (415) 556-6129; FTS 556-6129
Admin Francis Gates (Circuit Lib). *Ref Lib* Sue Welsh. *ILL* Deborah Celle (Acq).
Lib Type Law.
Spec Subs Court administration.
Lib Deposit Designation GPO Depository Library.
Info Ret Servs DIALOG; LEXIS; WESTLAW. *Shared Catalog Nets* OCLC; RLIN (search only). *Coop Lib Nets* CLASS; BARC; Bay Area Online Users Group (FG Membership).
Circ Servs Avail To other Federal libraries; to other libraries.
Ref Servs Avail To other Federal libraries; to other libraries; to the general public.

40. US Courts 2nd Circuit Library
US Courthouse, Uniondale Ave & Hempstead Tnpk, Uniondale, NY 11553
Admin Christian Rattiner.
Lib Type Law.

41. US Courts Branch Library
560 US Courthouse, 110 S 4th St, Minneapolis, MN 55401 (612) 349-3263; FTS 787-3263
Admin Cynthia R Snyder.
Lib Type Law.
Info Ret Servs WESTLAW; LEXIS. *Shared Catalog Nets* OCLC. *Coop Lib Nets* 8th Circuit Court of Appeals Library.
Circ Servs Avail Not open to the general public; restricted to judges & law clerks.
Ref Servs Avail To other Federal libraries; to other libraries; not open to the general public; restricted to primarily judges & law clerks.

42. US Courts William J Campbell Library
219 S Dearborn St, Rm 1448, Chicago, IL 60604 (312) 435-5660; FTS 387-5660
Admin Janet Wishinsky. *Ref Lib* Barry Herbert. *ILL* Peter Young.
Lib Type Law.
Lib Deposit Designation GPO Depository Library.
Info Ret Servs WESTLAW; LEXIS; NEXIS. *Shared Catalog Nets* OCLC. *Coop Lib Nets* FEDLINK.
Circ Servs Avail Restricted to federal courts & local federal agencies.
Ref Servs Avail To other Federal libraries; to other libraries; to the general public.

43. US Courts Library
805 US Courthouse, 811 Grand Ave, Kansas City, MO 64106 (816) 374-2937; FTS 758-2937
Admin M Tranne Pearce.
Lib Type Law.
Info Ret Servs WESTLAW; LEXIS. *Shared Catalog Nets* OCLC.
Circ Servs Avail To other Federal libraries; not open to the general public; restricted to members of federal bar.
Ref Servs Avail To other Federal libraries; not open to the general public; restricted to court personnel.

44. US Courts Library
482 Federal Bldg, 517 E Wisconsin Ave, Milwaukee, WI 53202 (414) 291-1698; FTS 387-5661
Admin Mary B Jones.
Lib Type Law.
Shared Catalog Nets OCLC.
Circ Servs Avail To other Federal libraries.
Ref Servs Avail To other Federal libraries; to other libraries; to the general public.

45. US Courts Library
Rm 4-520, US Courthouse, Oklahoma City, OK 73101 (405) 232-7441; FTS 745-7498
Admin Annie Seward.
Lib Type Law.

46. US Courts Library
PO Box 1873, US Courthouse, 10th & E Elizabeth Sts, Brownsville, TX 78520 FTS 529-2209
Admin Irene Maly.
Lib Type Law.

47. US Courts Library
Rm 259, US Courthouse, 350 S Main St, Salt Lake City, UT 84101 (801) 582-4090; FTS 588-3505
Admin Pat Hummell.
Lib Type Law.

48. US Courts Library
US Courthouse, Rm 220, 55 E Broadway, Tucson, AZ 85701 (612) 792-6552; FTS 762-6552
Admin Deo Maynard.
Lib Type Law.

49. US Courts Library
US Courthouse, 940 Front St, San Diego, CA 92189 (714) 293-5066; FTS 895-5066
Admin Winifred Boyle.
Lib Type Law.

50. US Courts Library
US Courthouse, Rm 6434, 230 N 1st Ave, Phoenix, AZ 85025-0074 (602) 261-3879; FTS 261-3879
Admin D Daniels. *Acq Lib* Richard Wiebelhaus.
Lib Type Law.
Spec Subs Federal practice & procedure.
Lib Deposit Designation GPO Depository Library.
Info Ret Servs LEXIS; WESTLAW. *Shared Catalog Nets* OCLC.
Circ Servs Avail To other Federal libraries; to other libraries; to the general public; restricted to types of materials.
Ref Servs Avail To other Federal libraries; to other libraries; to the general public.

51. US Courts Library
590 Federal Courts Bldg, 316 N Robert St, St. Paul, MN 55101 (612) 725-7177; FTS 725-7177
Admin Kathryn C Kratz.
Lib Type Law.
Info Ret Servs WESTLAW; LEXIS. *Shared Catalog Nets* OCLC.
Circ Servs Avail To other Federal libraries; to other libraries.
Ref Servs Avail To other Federal libraries; to other libraries; to the general public.

52. US Courts Branch Library
805 US Courthouse, 811 Grand Ave, Kansas City, MO 64106 (816) 374-2937
Lib Type Law.
Spec Collecs Legal.
Info Ret Servs WESTLAW; LEXIS.

United States Court of Appeals for the Federal Circuit

53. US Court of Appeals for the Federal Circuit Library
717 Madison Pl NW, Rm 218, Washington, DC 20439 (202) 633-5871; FTS 633-5871
Admin Patricia M McDermott. *Ref Lib* David Lockwood (ILL).
Lib Type Law.
Spec Subs Patent & trademark law; government contracts; taxation; federal employment; Indians.
Info Ret Servs LEXIS; NEXIS; WESTLAW. *Shared Catalog Nets* OCLC. *Coop Lib Nets* FEDLINK.
Circ Servs Avail To other Federal libraries; to other libraries; not open to the general public; restricted to members of the bar of Federal Circuit & US Claims Courts.
Ref Servs Avail To other Federal libraries; to other libraries.

United States District Courts

54. US District Court Eastern District of New York Library
225 Cadman Plaza E, Brooklyn, NY 11201 (718) 330-7483; FTS 656-7483
Lib Type Law.
Spec Subs Federal & state law.
Info Ret Servs Westlaw.
Ref Servs Avail Restricted to staff & attorneys practicing in Court.

55. US District Court Library
Box 36060, 450 Golden Gate Ave, San Francisco, CA 94102 (415) 556-7979; FTS 556-7979
Admin Lynn E Lundstrom.
Lib Type Law.
Info Ret Servs WESTLAW; LEXIS.
Circ Servs Avail To other Federal libraries; to other libraries; not open to the general public.
Ref Servs Avail To other Federal libraries; to other libraries; not open to the general public.

56. US District Court Library
PO Box 50128, 300 Ala Moana Blvd, Honolulu, HI 96850 (808) 546-3163; FTS 546-3163
Admin Isabel T Anduha.
Lib Type Law.
Info Ret Servs WESTLAW; LEXIS. *Coop Lib Nets* American Assoc of Law Libraries (AALL).

Circ Servs Avail To other libraries; restricted to court personnel.
Ref Servs Avail To other libraries; restricted to court personnel.

57. US District Court Library
PO Box 4, 701 C St, Anchorage, AK 99513 (907) 271-5655; FTS 271-5655
Admin Alice W Hobson.
Lib Type Law.
Spec Collecs Compiled legislative histories; Alaska Native Claims Settlement Act (ANCSA) & Alaska National Interest Lands Conservation Act (ANILCA) legislative histories.
Lib Deposit Designation GPO Depository Library.
Info Ret Servs WESTLAW; LEXIS. *Coop Lib Nets* Alaska Library Network (ALN); Alaska Library Assoc (AKLA).
Circ Servs Avail To other Federal libraries; to other libraries.
Ref Servs Avail To other Federal libraries; to other libraries; to the general public.

58. US District Court Library
213 US Courthouse, 620 SW Main St, Portland, OR 97205 (503) 221-6042; FTS 423-6042
Admin Scott McCurdy.
Lib Type Law.
Info Ret Servs WESTLAW; LEXIS.
Circ Servs Avail To other Federal libraries; to other libraries; not open to the general public.
Ref Servs Avail To other Federal libraries; to other libraries; restricted to telephone inquiries from general public.

59. US District Courts & Alaska Court System Law Library
Nome, AK 99762 (907) 443-5216
Admin Charles R Tunley (Superior Court Judge). *Acq Lib* Kathy Clark (Anchorage Law Lib).
Lib Type Law.
Lib Deposit Designation GPO Depository Library.
Coop Lib Nets Alaska Court System Law Library System. *Elec Mail Nets* Telefax.
Circ Servs Avail Restricted to local attorneys.
Ref Servs Avail To the general public.

United States Court of International Trade

60. US Court of International Trade Library
One Federal Pl, New York, NY 10007 (212) 264-2816
Admin Joseph J Mattera. *ILL* Ella Lidsky (Acq).
Lib Type Law.
Spec Subs Customs law; international trade: imports; science-technology. *In-house Files* Legislative histories of various trade & tariff acts.
Info Ret Servs LEXIS; NEXIS. *Shared Catalog Nets* OCLC.
Circ Servs Avail To other Federal libraries; to other libraries; not open to the general public; restricted to the court & members of the bar.
Ref Servs Avail To other Federal libraries; to other libraries; not open to the general public; restricted to the court & members of the bar.

United States Court of Military Appeals

61. US Court of Military Appeals Library
450 E St NW, Washington, DC 20442-0001 (202) 272-1466
Admin Mary S Kuck. *ILL* Agnes Kiang (Acq).
Lib Type Law.
Spec Subs Federal, criminal, & military law. *Spec Collecs* Military justice.
Circ Servs Avail To other Federal libraries; to other libraries; not open to the general public; restricted to attorneys or law students.
Ref Servs Avail To other Federal libraries; to other libraries; not open to the general public; restricted to attorneys or law students.

United States Tax Court

62. US Tax Court Library
400 2nd St NW, Washington, DC 20217 (202) 376-2707; FTS 376-2707
Admin Jeanne R Bonynge. *ILL* Deborah Latta.
Lib Type Law.
Spec Subs Taxation. *Spec Collecs* Federal tax law; bound legislative histories of revenue acts & amendments to 1939 & 1954 Internal Revenue Codes. *In-house Files* Card index—digest of published Tax Court opinions & US District Court, US Claims Court, Appellate Court, & US Supreme Court opinions in the federal tax field.

Info Ret Servs LEXIS; WESTLAW; PHINET; Washington Alert; ABANET. *Shared Catalog Nets* OCLC. *Coop Lib Nets* FEDLINK. *Elec Mail Nets* ABANET.
Circ Servs Avail To other libraries; not open to the general public; restricted to court personnel.
Ref Servs Avail To other Federal libraries; to other libraries; restricted to the general public with special permission.

Federal Judicial Center

63. Federal Judicial Center, Information Service Library
1520 H St NW, Washington, DC 20005 (202) 633-6365
Admin Leonard Klein.
Lib Type Law.

EXECUTIVE OFFICE OF THE PRESIDENT

Departmental

64. Executive Office of the President Library
726 Jackson Pl NW, Washington, DC 20503 (202) 395-3654
Admin Adrienne Kosciusko Gillen.
Lib Type Special.
Spec Subs US budget; public administration; political science; presidency; economics; federal legislation; federal government appropriations.
Info Ret Servs DIALOG; BRS; SDC; NEXIS; LEXIS; VU-TEXT; DataTimes; Legi-Slate; WESTLAW. *Coop Lib Nets* FEDLINK; Metropolitan Library Council.
Circ Servs Avail To other Federal libraries; restricted to DC vicinity.
Ref Servs Avail Restricted to EOP staff.

65. White House Law Library
Rm 528, Old Executive Office Bldg, Washington, DC 20500 (202) 395-3397
Admin Vacant (Librarian); Emily Carr (Library Technician).
Lib Type Law.

Spec Collecs U.S. Code, Statutes-At-Large, Federal case law books, legal treatises, & horn books, Congressional hearings, select loose-leaf services, & the *Federal Register*.
Info Ret Servs WESTLAW; LEXIS.
Circ Servs Avail Restricted to EOP staff.
Ref Servs Avail Restricted to EOP staff.

66. White House Library & Research Center
Rm 308, Old Executive Office Bldg, Washington, DC 20500 (202) 456-7000
Admin Martha Brown (Supv). *Ref Lib* Ann Dickenson; Sandra McCoy Larson; Jacqueline Cragg.
Lib Type Special.
Info Ret Servs Over 150 bibliographic & statistical data bases.
Circ Servs Avail Restricted to EOP staff.
Ref Servs Avail Restricted to EOP staff.

DEPARTMENT OF AGRICULTURE

Departmental

67. USDA National Finance Center Library
PO Box 60000, New Orleans, LA 70160 (504) 255-5516; FTS 680-5516
Admin Myrna Green.
Lib Type Special.

Agricultural Research Service

68. Agricultural Research Service, SW Watershed Research Center Library
USDA, 2000 E Allen Rd, Tucson, AZ 85719 (602) 629-6381; FTS 762-6381
Admin E Sue Anderson.
Lib Type Special.

69. Agricultural Research Service, Western Region Library
USDA, PO Box E, Ft Collins, CO 80522 (303) 482-5733; FTS 323-5201
Admin Christine L Evans.
Lib Type Special.

70. Animal Science Institute Library
Agricultural Research Service, USDA, BARC-East Bldg 200, Rm 100, Beltsville, MD 20705 (301) 344-3431; FTS 344-3431
Lib Type Special.

71. Beltsville Human Nutrition Research Center
Agricultural Research Service, USDA, BARC-East Bldg 308, Rm 219, Beltsville, MD 20705 (301) 344-2530; FTS 344-2530
Lib Type Special.

72. Biological Control of Insects Laboratory, Library
Agricultural Research Service, USDA, PO Box A, Columbia, MO 65205 (314) 875-5361; FTS 276-5361
Admin Dolores Reddick (Secretary).
Lib Type Special.

73. Carl Hayden Bee Research Center Library
2000 E Allen Rd, Tucson, AZ 85719 (602) 629-6380; FTS 762-6380
Admin M D Levin (Ctr Dir); Sari Lovell (Lib).
Lib Type Special.
Spec Subs Agriculture; apiculture. *Spec Collecs* Bee research & crop pollination. *In-house Files* Reprints pertaining to scientific studies of bee research & crop pollination.
Coop Lib Nets National Agricultural Library (NAL).
Circ Servs Avail Not open to the general public.
Ref Servs Avail Not open to the general public.

74. Horticultural Research Laboratory Library
2120 Camden Rd, Orlando, FL 32803 (305) 898-6791; FTS 822-9301
Admin David T Kaplan.
Lib Type Special.
Spec Subs Citrus.
Elec Mail Nets Telex.
Ref Servs Avail To other Federal libraries; to other libraries.

75. Roman L Hruska US Meat Animal Research Center Library
PO Box 166, Clay Center, NE 68933 (402) 762-3241
Admin Patricia L Sheridan.
Lib Type Special.
Spec Subs Meats research; nutrition; reproduction; agricultural engineering; breeding & genetics.
Info Ret Servs DIALOG. *Shared Catalog Nets* OCLC. *Coop Lib Nets* FEDLINK.
Circ Servs Avail To other Federal libraries; to other libraries; to the general public.
Ref Servs Avail To other Federal libraries; to other libraries; to the general public.

76. National Animal Disease Center Library
PO Box 70, Ames, IA 50010 (515) 239-8271; FTS 862-8271
Admin Janice K Eifling.
Lib Type Special.
Spec Subs Microbiology; immunology; biochemistry; veterinary medicine.
Info Ret Servs DIALOG.
Circ Servs Avail To other Federal libraries; to other libraries.
Ref Servs Avail To other Federal libraries; to other libraries.

77. National Soil Dynamics Laboratory Library
PO Box 792, Auburn, AL 36831-0792 (205) 887-8596; FTS 534-4515
Admin E Rome.
Lib Type Special.
Spec Subs Soil dynamics; tillage; traction; soil-machine relations; soil reactions. *Spec Collecs* Translations of foreign technical publications. *In-house Files* NSDL publications.
Coop Lib Nets National Agricultural Library.
Circ Servs Avail Not open to the general public.
Ref Servs Avail Not open to the general public.

78. Northwest Watershed Research Center
270 S Orchard, Boise, ID 83705 (208) 334-1363; FTS 554-1363
Ref Lib Clifton Johnson. *ILL* Glenna Wilson (Acq).
Lib Type Engineering & Science.
Spec Subs Hydrology; sedimentation; precipitation; geology.
Circ Servs Avail To other Federal libraries.
Ref Servs Avail To other Federal libraries.

79. Plum Island Animal Disease Center Library
PO Box 848, Greenport, NY 11935 (516) 323-2500 ext 235; FTS 649-9235
Admin Stephen E Perlman. *ILL* Joan Schneider.
Lib Type Special.
Spec Subs Foreign animal diseases exotic to the US, such as foot-and-mouth disease, African Swine Fever, Rinderpest. *Spec Collecs* Virology; microbiology; immunology; veterinary medicine; molecular biology.
Lib Deposit Designation National Agricultural Library.
Info Ret Servs DIALOG. *Shared Catalog Nets* OCLC. *Coop Lib Nets* FEDLINK; Long Island Library Resource Council (LILRC); Medical & Scientific Libraries of Long Island (Medli). *Elec Mail Nets* Telex.
Circ Servs Avail To other Federal libraries; to other libraries; to the general public.
Ref Servs Avail To other Federal libraries; to other libraries; to the general public; restricted to on-site use by special permission.

80. Russell Research Center Library

PO Box 5677, Athens, GA 30613 (404) 546-3314; FTS 250-3314
Admin Benna Brodsky Thompson. *ILL* Barbara Gazda.
Lib Type Engineering & Science.
Spec Subs Natural products; toxicology; animal reproduction; microbiology; field & horticultural crops.
Info Ret Servs DIALOG; CAS; Pergamon; RECON; Questel. *Shared Catalog Nets* OCLC. *Coop Lib Nets* Southeast Area Medical Libraries. *Elec Mail Nets* CLASS.
Circ Servs Avail To other Federal libraries; to other libraries; not open to the general public.
Ref Servs Avail To other Federal libraries; to other libraries; to the general public.

81. Southern Regional Research Center Library

PO Box 19687, New Orleans, LA 70179 (504) 589-7072; FTS 682-7072
Admin Dorothy B Skau.
Lib Type Special.
Spec Subs Chemistry; textiles; biochemistry; food & nutrition.
Info Ret Servs DIALOG. *Shared Catalog Nets* FEDLINK. *Coop Lib Nets* FEDLINK.
Circ Servs Avail To other Federal libraries; to other libraries.
Ref Servs Avail To other Federal libraries; to other libraries; to the general public.

82. Stored Product Insects Research & Development Library

PO Box 22909, Savannah, GA 31403 (912) 233-7981; FTS 248-4408
Admin M Harriet Winiger.
Lib Type Engineering & Science.
Spec Subs Stored-product insect control; insect rearing; chemistry; biology; entomology; insect-resistant packaging. *Spec Collecs* USDA publications; extensive reprint file of journal articles on insects. *In-house Files* Reprint copies of papers written by our scientists.
Info Ret Servs Current Awareness Literature Service (CALS). *Coop Lib Nets* National Agricultural Library; Russell Research Center (RRC); USDA Document Delivery System thru UGA. *Elec Mail Nets* Telex.
Circ Servs Avail To other Federal libraries; not open to the general public.
Ref Servs Avail To other Federal libraries; not open to the general public.

83. US Citrus & Subtropical Products Laboratory Library

PO Box 1909, 600 Ave S, NW, Winter Haven, FL 33881-2118 (813) 293-4133
Admin Robert E Berry (Lab Dir). *Ref Lib* Cynthia D Glasscock (ILL, Acq).
Lib Type Special.
Circ Servs Avail Not open to the general public.
Ref Servs Avail Restricted to on-site technical use.

84. USDA, Agricultural Research Service, Eastern Regional Research Center Library

600 E Mermaid Ln, Philadelphia, PA 19118 (215) 233-6602; ILL 233-6660; FTS 489-6602/6604
Admin Wendy H. Kramer.
Lib Type Special.
Spec Subs Agriculture; biochemistry; chemistry; food technology; hides & leather; industrial wastes; polymers & polymerization; plant science.
Info Ret Servs DIALOG; SDC. *Shared Catalog Nets* OCLC. *Coop Lib Nets* FEDLINK; Greater NE Regional Medical Library Program; Interlibrary Delivery Service of PA; USDA Field Library.

85. USDA, Agricultural Research Service, Snake River Conservation Research Service

Rte 1, PO Box 186, Kimberly, ID 83341 (208) 423-5582 ext 25; FTS 554-6578
Admin Aartje Smith.
Lib Type Special.
Spec Subs General agriculture; irrigation; plants; pollution; soils; water.
Circ Servs Avail Not open to the general public; restricted to staff.

Ref Servs Avail To the general public.

86. USDA, Agricultural Research Service, Water Conservation Research Library

4331 E Broadway, Phoenix, AZ 85040 (602) 261-4356; FTS 261-4356
Lib Type Special.
Spec Subs Agriculture; chemistry; engineering; evaporation; evapotranspiration; guayule (a woody plant or shrub of the SW US); hydraulics; irrigation; land treatment of sewage effluent; microbiology; plant physiology; remote sensing; salinity; soil; soil-moisture; water.
Circ Servs Avail Not open to the general public.
Ref Servs Avail To other Federal libraries; to other libraries; to the general public.

87. USDA Northern Regional Research Center Library

Agricultural Research Service, 1815 N University St, Peoria, IL 61604 (309) 685-4011; FTS 360-4525
Admin Donald L Blevins.
Lib Type Special.
Spec Subs Organic chemistry; plant physiology & chemistry; vegetable oils & fats; microbiology & biotechnology.
Info Ret Servs DIALOG. *Shared Catalog Nets* OCLC. *Coop Lib Nets* Illinois Valley Library System (IVLS); Illinois Info Network (ILLNET); FEDLINK.
Circ Servs Avail To other Federal libraries; to other libraries.
Ref Servs Avail To other Federal libraries; to other libraries; to the general public.

88. USDA Sedimentation Laboratory Library

Agricultural Research Service, Mid-South Area, Box 1157, Oxford, MS 38655 (601) 234-4121 ext 36
Admin N L Coleman (Lab Dir); Bettie Sneed (Lib).
Lib Type Engineering & Science.
Spec Subs Sedimentation research for soil & water conservation, soil erosion causes & control. *Spec Collecs* Approximately 20,000 titles (books, scientific journals & periodicals & government documents) relating to sedimentation research. *In-house Files* Extensive vertical file of material relating to sedimentation & soil erosion, including reprints of all papers authored by the staff.
Coop Lib Nets NAL Current Awareness Literature Service.
Circ Servs Avail To other Federal libraries; to other libraries; not open to the general public; restricted to education & research studies.
Ref Servs Avail To other Federal libraries; to other libraries; not open to the general public; restricted to education & research studies.

89. USDA Western Regional Research Center Library

Agricultural Research Service, Berkeley, CA 94710 (415) 486-3351; FTS 449-3351
Admin Rena Schonbrun.
Lib Type Engineering & Science.
Info Ret Servs DIALOG. *Shared Catalog Nets* OCLC. *Coop Lib Nets* FEDLINK.
Circ Servs Avail To other libraries.
Ref Servs Avail To other Federal libraries; to other libraries; to the general public; restricted to by appointment.

90. US Grain Marketing Research Laboratory Library

1515 College Ave, Manhattan, KS 66502 (913) 776-2760; FTS 752-4760
Admin Diane LaBarbera.
Lib Type Engineering & Science.
Spec Subs Cereal science.
Circ Servs Avail Not open to the general public; restricted to in-house researchers & staff use.
Ref Servs Avail To other Federal libraries; to other libraries; to the general public; restricted to telephone help.

91. US National Arboretum Library

3501 New York Ave NE, Washington, DC 20002 (202) 475-4828; FTS 475-4828
Admin Susan C Whitmore.
Lib Type Special.

Spec Subs Horticulture; botany; plant taxonomy; gardening; plant breeding & bonsai. *Spec Collecs* Bonsai; nursery & seed trade catalogs; Ikebana; early photographs of USDA plant exploration trips; photographs of agricultural practices of early 20th century; Carlton R Ball collection on Salix; Arie F den Boer manuscripts on crabapples.
Info Ret Servs DIALOG; BRS. *Shared Catalog Nets* OCLC. *Coop Lib Nets* National Agricultural Library of the USDA.
Circ Servs Avail Restricted to National Agricultural Library.

92. Western Regional Research Center Library
Berkeley, CA 94710 (415) 486-3351; FTS 449-3351
Admin Rena Schonbrun.
Lib Type Special.
Spec Subs Cereals, fruits, vegetables, food technology, chemistry, nutrition, field crops, microbiology, & pharmacology.
Info Ret Servs DIALOG. *Shared Catalog Nets* OCLC. *Coop Lib Nets* FEDLINK; USDA Document Delivery System.
Circ Servs Avail To other Federal libraries; to other libraries.
Ref Servs Avail To other Federal libraries; to other libraries; restricted to public use by special arrangement.

Animal & Plant Health Inspection Service

93. APHIS Plant Protection & Quarantine Library
Rm 628A, Federal Ctr Bldg, 6505 Belcrest Rd, Hyattsville, MD 20782 (301) 436-5240; FTS 436-5240
Admin Eileen Welch.
Lib Type Special.
Spec Subs Plant pathology & entomology; pesticides, toxicology & use.

94. APHIS Plant Protection & Quarantine Training Center Library
195 Thomas Johnson Dr, Frederick, MD 21701 (301) 933-1270; FTS 933-1270
Lib Type Special.

95. Denver Wildlife Research Center
Bldg 16, Denver Federal Center, Denver, CO 80225 (303) 236-7873; FTS 776-7873
Admin Diana L Dwyer. *ILL* Judith L Kayser.
Lib Type Engineering & Science.
Spec Subs Animal & bird damage control on international basis; predators; big game. *Spec Collecs* Food habits collection. *In-house Files* Predator-prey data base; bird damage data base; library reprint data base.
Info Ret Servs DIALOG; BRS; NLM; CAS Online; NPIRS; CIS. *Shared Catalog Nets* OCLC. *Coop Lib Nets* FEDLINK; Central Colorado Library System (CCLS). *Elec Mail Nets* ITT DIAL-COM.
Circ Servs Avail To other Federal libraries; to other libraries.
Ref Servs Avail To other Federal libraries; to other libraries; to the general public.

Economic Research Service

96. Economic Research Service Reference Center
1301 New York Ave, NW, Rm 28B, Washington, DC 20005-4788 (202) 786-1724/1725
Admin D J Fusonie.
Lib Type Special.
Spec Subs Agricultural economics. *Spec Collecs* American Agricultural Economics Documentation Center. *In-house Files* Economic Research Service & US Economics, Statistics & Cooperatives Service publications.
Info Ret Servs DIALOG.
Circ Servs Avail Not open to the general public; restricted to xeroxing for other Federal agencies.
Ref Servs Avail To other Federal libraries; to other libraries open to general public by permission.

Food & Nutrition Service

97. Food & Nutrition Service Reference Center
3101 Park Center Dr, Alexandria, VA 22302 (703) 756-3808; FTS 756-3808/3115
Admin Richard A Dengrove.
Lib Type Special.
Spec Subs Poverty; food stamps; school lunch program. *In-house Files* Older agency publications, reports & studies.
Circ Servs Avail To other Federal libraries; to other libraries; to the general public; restricted to agency first priority.
Ref Servs Avail To other Federal libraries; to other libraries; to the general public; restricted to agency first priority.

Food Safety & Inspection Service

98. Food Safety & Inspection Service, Science Administration Library
USDA, Rm 405, Annex Bldg, SW, Washington, DC 20250 (202) 447-7623; FTS 447-4382
Admin Arlene Aikens.
Lib Type Special.

Forest Service

99. Bridger-Teton National Forest Library
Kemmerer Ranger District, PO Box 31, Kemmerer, WY 83101 (307) 877-4415
Admin Jimmie Ann Wideman.
Lib Type Special.

100. Clearwater National Forest Library
12730 Hwy 12, Forest Service, USDA, Orofino, ID 83544 (208) 476-4541
Admin Office Services Supervisor.
Lib Type Special.

101. Engineering Technical Information Center
Forest Service, Rm 1113 RP-E, PO Box 2417, Washington, DC 20013 (703) 235-3111; FTS 235-3111
Admin Constance A Connolly.
Lib Type Engineering & Science.
Spec Subs Low-volume roads. *Spec Collecs* Low-volume roads.
Info Ret Servs DIALOG. *Shared Catalog Nets* OCLC. *Coop Lib Nets* FLICC/FEDLINK; FSINFO. *Elec Mail Nets* FS Network on Data General.
Circ Servs Avail To other Federal libraries; to other libraries; restricted to FS engineering materials.
Ref Servs Avail To other Federal libraries; to other libraries; to the general public; restricted to FS engineering information.

102. Engineering Technical Information Center, Forest Service
PO Box 2417, 12th & Independence Ave, SW, Washington, DC 20013 (703) 235-3111; FTS 235-3111
Admin Constance A Connolly (Tech Info Specialist).
Lib Type Engineering & Science.
Spec Subs Civil engineering; forest engineering. *Spec Collecs* Low volume roads.
Info Ret Servs DIALOG. *Shared Catalog Nets* OCLC. *Coop Lib Nets* FLC/FEDLINK. *Elec Mail Nets* ITT DIALCOM.
Circ Servs Avail To other Federal libraries; to other libraries.
Ref Servs Avail To other Federal libraries; to other libraries; to the general public.

103. Equipment Development Center Library
444 E Bonita Ave, San Dimas, CA 91773 (213) 332-6231; FTS 793-8000
Admin Anita Richardson.
Lib Type Engineering & Science.
Spec Subs Engineering field notes; project records; Missoula papers; equipment tips. *Spec Collecs* Historical section, Forest Service; 1940-1986 clipping photos; memoirs-diary of Gifford Pinchot, 1913-1931. *In-house Files* 51 subscription periodicals; 8 tabloids; foreign papers; SAE, ASAE, ASTM membership; fire

control records for 18 regional offices; 20 newsletters; aviation advisory circulars; FAA manuals; 36 helicopter manuals; NASA, DOT, DIT, GPO, DTIC, & WESTFORNET publications.
Circ Servs Avail Restricted to center personnel.
Ref Servs Avail Restricted to center personnel.

104. Equipment Development Center Library
Forest Service, USDA, Bldg 1, Ft Missoula, Missoula, MT 59801 (406) 329-3900; FTS 585-3900
Lib Type Special.

105. Forest Hydrology Laboratory Library
Forest Service, USDA, PO Box 947, Oxford, MS 38655 (601) 234-2744
Admin Sarah S Knight (Secretary).
Lib Type Special.

106. Forest Products Laboratory Library
One Gifford Pinchot Dr, Madison, WI 53705 (608) 264-5711; FTS 364-5711
Admin Roger Scharmer. *Ref Lib* Judy Kessenich. *ILL* Elaine Thompson. *Acq Lib* Rosemary Bishop.
Lib Type Engineering & Science.
Spec Subs Wood products utilization.
Info Ret Servs DIALOG. *Shared Catalog Nets* OCLC. *Coop Lib Nets* FS INFO. *Elec Mail Nets* ITT DIALCOM.
Circ Servs Avail To other Federal libraries; to other libraries.
Ref Servs Avail To other Federal libraries; to other libraries; to the general public.

107. Forest Sciences Laboratory
PO Box 152, Princeton, WV 24740 (304) 425-8106 ext 263; FTS 923-4555
Admin Diana L Donahue.
Lib Type Special.
Spec Subs Forestry; forest products.
Circ Servs Avail To other Federal libraries; to other libraries; to the general public.
Ref Servs Avail To other Federal libraries; to other libraries; to the general public.

108. Forest Service, Equipment Development Center Library
USDA, 444 E Bonita Ave, San Dimas, CA 91773 (213) 332-6231; FTS 793-8254
Admin Ralph T Lewallen.
Lib Type Special.

109. Forest Service Information, Northwest
AQ-15, University of Washington, Seattle, WA 98195 (206) 543-7484; FTS 399-1076
Admin Charles Lord.
Lib Type Special.
Info Ret Servs DIALOG; BRS; SDC. *Elec Mail Nets* ITT DIALCOM.
Circ Servs Avail To other Federal libraries; to other libraries; restricted to Forest Service & Bureau of Indian Affairs.
Ref Servs Avail To other Federal libraries; to other libraries; restricted to Forest Service & Bureau of Indian Affairs.

110. Forest Service, Pacific NW Forest & Range Experimental Station
USDA, PO Box 3890, Portland, OR 97208 (503) 231-2078; FTS 429-2078
Admin Louise Parker.
Lib Type Special.

111. Forest Service, Region 6 Information Office
USDA, PO Box 3623, Portland, OR 97208 (503) 423-2971; FTS 423-2971
Admin Paul Hansen.
Lib Type Special.

112. Forest Service, Rogue River National Forest Library
USDA, PO Box 520, Medford, OR 97501 (503) 776-3601; FTS 424-3601
Lib Type Special.

113. Forestry Sciences Laboratory Library
PO Box 909, Juneau, AK 99802 (907) 586-8811; FTS 586-8811
Admin Carol A Ayer.
Lib Type Special.
Spec Subs Forestry; fisheries; wildlife; recreation. *Spec Collecs* USDA Forest Service Research Station publications.
Info Ret Servs DIALOG. *Coop Lib Nets* FS INFO. *Elec Mail Nets* ITT DIALCOM.
Circ Servs Avail To other Federal libraries; to other libraries; to the general public; restricted to priority to Forest Service personnel.
Ref Servs Avail To other Federal libraries; to other libraries; to the general public.

114. Institute of Tropical Forestry Library
PO Box 21390, Rio Piedras, PR 00928 (809) 753-4335; FTS 753-4335
Admin JoAnne Feheley.
Lib Type Special.
Spec Subs Tropical forestry.
Info Ret Servs DIALOG. *Shared Catalog Nets* FS INFO. *Coop Lib Nets* FS INFO.
Circ Servs Avail Restricted to institute personnel.
Ref Servs Avail To other Federal libraries; to other libraries; to the general public.

115. International Forestry Staff Library
Forest Service, USDA, Rm 809-RP-E, Rosslyn, VA 22209 (202) 447-2050; FTS 447-2050
Admin Chris Johnson.
Lib Type Special.

116. North Central Forest Experiment Station Library
University of Minnesota, 1992 Folwell Ave, Saint Paul, MN 55108 (612) 642-5257; FTS 784-0257
Admin Floyd L Henderson. *ILL* Laura Hutchinson. *Acq Lib* Lois Corpe.
Lib Type Special.
Spec Subs Forestry; natural environment; wildlife. *Spec Collecs* FIREBASE. *In-house Files* US Forest Service Experiment Station publications.
Info Ret Servs DIALOG; BRS. *Shared Catalog Nets* OCLC. *Coop Lib Nets* FEDLINK; MINITEX. *Elec Mail Nets* ITT DIALCOM.
Circ Servs Avail To other Federal libraries; to other libraries; not open to the general public.
Ref Servs Avail To other Federal libraries; to other libraries; to the general public.

117. Pacific Southwest Forest & Range Experiment Station Library
Berkeley Service Ctr, PO Box 245, 1960 Addison St, Berkeley, CA 94701-0245 (415) 486-3173; FTS 449-3686
Lib Type Special.
Spec Subs Forest & wildlife management; forest pathology & injury.
Lib Deposit Designation US Forest Service Documents.
Info Ret Servs DIALOG; BRS; SDC Info Services. *Shared Catalog Nets* OCLC; RLIN. *Coop Lib Nets* Western Forestry Info Network.
Circ Servs Avail Restricted to by appointment use by general public.

118. Rocky Mountain Forest & Range Experiment Station Library
240 W Prospect St, Ft Collins, CO 80526 (303) 224-1268; FTS 223-1268
Admin Frances J Barney. *Ref Lib* Robert Dana.
Lib Type Special.
Spec Subs All aspects of forestry. *Spec Collecs* Avalanches; snow management; fire control & management. *In-house Files* Forest diseases.
Info Ret Servs DIALOG; BRS. *Shared Catalog Nets* OCLC. *Coop Lib Nets* FS INFO. *Elec Mail Nets* ITT DIALCOM.
Circ Servs Avail To other Federal libraries; to other libraries; not open to the general public.

Ref Servs Avail To other Federal libraries; to other libraries; to the general public.

119. Southern Forest Experiment Station Library
701 Loyola Ave, Rm T-10210, New Orleans, LA 70113 (504) 589-3935; FTS 682-3935
Admin Aleta Hayden.
Lib Type Special.
Info Ret Servs DIALOG. *Shared Catalog Nets* OCLC. *Elec Mail Nets* ITT DIALCOM.
Circ Servs Avail To other Federal libraries; to other libraries.
Ref Servs Avail Not open to the general public; restricted to employees.

120. SOUTHFORNET Science Library
University of Georgia, Athens, GA 30602 (404) 546-2477; FTS 250-2477
Admin Virginia L Rutherford. *Ref Lib* Sid Frederick. *ILL* Cecile Nepote.
Lib Type Special.
Spec Subs Forestry; forest products; natural resources.
Info Ret Servs DIALOG; BRS; FIREBASE. *Shared Catalog Nets* OCLC; RLIN. *Coop Lib Nets* Forest Service Information Network (FSIN). *Elec Mail Nets* ITT DIALCOM; Forest Service Data General System.
Circ Servs Avail Restricted to Forest Service & subscribers.
Ref Servs Avail To the general public; restricted to Forest Service & subscribers, except FIREBASE searches to the general public.

121. US Forest Service Library
370 Reed Rd, Broomall, PA 19008 (215) 461-3105; FTS 489-3105
Lib Type Special.
Spec Subs Forestry.
Ref Servs Avail To the general public.

122. WESTFORNET/FS-INFO Intermountain Research Station
324 25th St, Ogden, UT 84401 (801) 625-5444; FTS 586-5444
Admin Elizabeth G Close. *Ref Lib* Ruth Hyland (Acq).
Lib Type Special.
Spec Subs Forestry; Western land management; wildlife; watershed; range management; recreation (back country).
Info Ret Servs DIALOG; BRS; SDC. *Shared Catalog Nets* OCLC; FS INFO. *Coop Lib Nets* FS INFO; Forestry Online. *Elec Mail Nets* ITT DIALCOM.
Circ Servs Avail To other libraries; restricted to Forest Service employees for direct use.
Ref Servs Avail To other Federal libraries; to other libraries; to the general public.

National Agricultural Library

123. Food & Nutrition Information Center
National Agricultural Library, Rm 304, Beltsville, MD 20705 (301) 344-3719; FTS 344-3719
Admin Robyn C Frank. *Ref Lib* Jim Krebs-Smith. *ILL* Eva Kelly. *Acq Lib* Janet Harland.
Lib Type National.
Spec Subs Human nutrition research & education; food service management; food irradiation. *Spec Collecs* National depository of nutrition, education & training materials; national depository of women, infants & children nutrition education materials; food irradiation special collections.
Lib Deposit Designation USDA, Food & Nutrition Service.
Info Ret Servs DIALOG; BRS. *Shared Catalog Nets* OCLC. *Coop Lib Nets* FEDLINK. *Elec Mail Nets* ITT DIALCOM.
Circ Servs Avail To other Federal libraries; to other libraries; restricted to state government agencies; university & college faculty; federal, state, county cooperative extension services; research institutions; national officers of professional societies; school districts & individual schools, including food service personnel; Nutrition Education & Training Program (NET)

staffs; Head Start personnel; day care personnel; Supplemental Food Program for Women, Infants & Children (WIC) personnel; & Commodity Supplemental Food (CSF) Program personnel.
Ref Servs Avail To other Federal libraries; to other libraries; to the general public.

124. National Agricultural Library
10301 Baltimore Blvd, Beltsville, MD 20705 (301) 344-3755; FTS 344-3755
Admin Joseph H Howard. *Ref Lib* Jennie Brogdon (Economics & Marketing); Elizabeth Goldberg (Farming & Forestry). *ILL* Carol Ditzler. *Acq Lib* Victoria Reich.
Lib Type National.
Spec Subs Botany; chemistry; entomology; forestry; food & nutrition; water resources; economics. *Spec Collecs* The library contains historical research materials, many of which possess a unique and/or archival character & focus upon a certain subject area which lies within a particular period of time or which has been gathered together to serve a certain scientific discipline. Materials include rare books, manuscripts, oral history transcripts, seed trade catalogs & the donated private libraries of James M Gwin, poultry scientist, & Charles E Kellog, soil scientist. The library has an extensive collection of pre-Linneana imprints relating to the description of plants, as well as works by or about Carl Linneaus; the personal papers of Julian N Friant & Charles E North; the Mary Cokely Wood Japanese Classical Flower Arrangement rare book collection; the organizational records of the Prince Family Nursery as well as the American Association of Agricultural College Editors. Large sets of microforms include documents of the United Nations, the Food & Agriculture Organization of the UN, Dept of Agriculture, & US Geological Survey; papers of the American Society of Agricultural Engineers since 1968; environmental impact statements since 1970; & all documents cited in American Statistics Index, 1974-78.
Lib Deposit Designation GPO Depository Library.
Info Ret Servs DIALOG; BRS. *Shared Catalog Nets* OCLC. *Coop Lib Nets* AGLINET; USDA Regional Document Delivery System; FEDLINK; OCLC. *Elec Mail Nets* ITT DIALCOM; Telex.
Circ Servs Avail To other Federal libraries; to other libraries; to the general public.
Ref Servs Avail To other Federal libraries; to other libraries; to the general public.

125. National Agricultural Library, DC Reference Center
Rm 1052, S Bldg, Washington, DC 20250 (202) 447-3434
Admin Mary Lassanyi.
Lib Type National.

Office of General Counsel

126. Office of the General Counsel Law Library, Department of Agriculture
S Bldg, Rm 1406, Washington, DC 20250 (202) 447-7751
Admin Edward S Billings.
Lib Type Law.
Info Ret Servs DIALOG; LEXIS; WESTLAW.
Circ Servs Avail Restricted to other law libraries.
Ref Servs Avail To other Federal libraries.

Office of International Cooperation & Development

127. Office of International Cooperation & Development (OICD), Technical Inquiries
4300 Auditors Bldg, Washington, DC 20250 (202) 447-2893; FTS 447-2893
Admin Patricia A Wetmore.
Lib Type Special.

DEPARTMENT OF COMMERCE

Departmental

128. Department of Commerce, District Office Library
450 Main St, Hartford, CT 06103 (203) 722-3197; FTS 244-3197
Admin Eric B Outwater. *Ref Lib* Robert Orr (ILL, Acq).
Lib Type Special.
Spec Subs International trade; exporting information; US Government statistics on exports & imports. *Spec Collecs* US Government statistics—FT410, FT445, FT135, FT990; export statistics profiles; industry trade lists; country market surveys; foreign economic trends; overseas business reports; US Department of Commerce publications. *In-house Files* Country files; industry files for export information uses.
Circ Servs Avail Restricted to approval of district office.
Ref Servs Avail To other Federal libraries; to other libraries; to the general public.

129. Department of Commerce, Field Services Library
Rm 340, Salt Lake City, UT 84101 (801) 524-5117
Lib Type Special.

130. Department of Commerce, Houston Field Office Library
Rm 2625, Federal Bldg, 515 Rusk Ave, Houston, TX 77002 (713) 229-2578
Lib Type Special.

131. Department of Commerce, Law Library
Rm 1894, Main Commerce Bldg, 14th St & Constitution Ave, NW, Washington, DC 20230 (202) 377-5517
Admin W Allan Fulton.
Lib Type Law.
Spec Subs Government procurement; international trade law; antitrust law.
Circ Servs Avail To other Federal libraries; to other libraries.
Ref Servs Avail To other Federal libraries; to other libraries; to the general public.

132. Department of Commerce Library
Rm 7064, 14th St & Constitution Ave, Washington, DC 20230 (202) 377-5511 Main Reading Room; 377-1916 Periodical Reading Room; 377-2161 Reference; 377-5517 Law Library
Admin Stanley J Bougas.
Lib Type General.
Info Ret Servs DIALOG; SDC ; Dow Jones News Retrieval; NEXIS. *Shared Catalog Nets* OCLC.

133. Department of Commerce, Miami District Office Library
821 City National Bank, 25 W Flagler St, Miami, FL 33130 (305) 350-5267
Lib Type Special.
Spec Subs Business & management; foreign & domestic trade.

134. Department of Commerce, Office of Field Services Library
Rm 3000, New Federal Office Bldg, 500 Quarrier St, Charleston, WV 25301 (304) 343-6181; FTS 924-1375
Lib Type Special.

135. Department of Commerce, St Louis District Office Library
Ste 400, 120 S Central Ave, Saint Louis, MO 63105 (314) 425-3302; ILL 425-3304
Lib Type Special.

Bureau of the Census

136. Bureau of the Census, Atlanta Regional Office Library
1365 Peachtree St NE, Atlanta, GA 30309 (404) 881-2274; FTS 257-2274
Admin Joe Reilly.
Lib Type General.
Spec Subs Census: population, housing, economic, construction, maps.
Circ Servs Avail To other Federal libraries; not open to the general public.
Ref Servs Avail To other Federal libraries; to other libraries; to the general public.

137. Bureau of the Census, Charlotte Regional Office Library
230 S Tryon St, Suite 800, Charlotte, NC 28202 (704) 371-6144; FTS 672-6144
Admin Ken Wright.
Lib Type Special.
Spec Collecs Decennial censuses of population & housing.
Ref Servs Avail To other Federal libraries; to other libraries; to the general public.

138. Bureau of the Census, Dallas Regional Office Library
1100 Commerce St, Rm 3C54, Dallas, TX 75242 (214) 767-0625; FTS 729-0625
Admin Information Services Program Staff.
Lib Type Special.
Spec Collecs Decennial Census; economic censuses; current population reports (income, poverty, general statistics).
Circ Servs Avail To other Federal libraries; to other libraries; to the general public.
Ref Servs Avail To other Federal libraries; to other libraries; to the general public.

139. Bureau of the Census, Denver Regional Office Reference Center
PO Box 26750, 7655 W Mississippi Ave, Denver, CO 80226 (303) 236-2200; FTS 776-2200
Admin Pat Rodriguez. *Ref Lib* Kendrick J Ellwanger.
Lib Type Special.
Spec Subs US Bureau of the Census publications.
Ref Servs Avail To other Federal libraries; to the general public.

140. Bureau of the Census, Information Service Program, Boston Regional Office
10 Fl, 441 Stuart St, Boston, MA 02116 (617) 223-0226
Lib Type Special.
Ref Servs Avail To the general public.

141. Bureau of the Census, Information Services Program, Detroit Regional Office Information Center
Rm 565, 231 W Lafayette Blvd, Detroit, MI 48226 (313) 226-4675
Lib Type Special.

142. Bureau of the Census, Information Services Program Library
600 Arch St, Rm 9226, Philadelphia, PA 19106 (215) 597-8314; FTS 597-8314
Admin Dave Lewis. *Ref Lib* Linda Washington (ILL, Acq).
Lib Type Special.
Spec Subs US Census published & unpublished data. *Spec Collecs* Expanded unpublished data covering DE, MD, NJ, PA, & WV. *In-house Files* Special training on access & use of census data.
Info Ret Servs US Census covering DE, MD, NJ, PA, & WV.
Ref Servs Avail To other Federal libraries; to other libraries; to the general public.

143. Bureau of the Census Library
Administrative Services Div, Library & Information Services Branch, FB 3, Rm 2449, Washington, DC 20233 (301) 763-5040
Admin Betty Baxtresser. *Ref Lib* Grace T Waibel. *ILL* Doris Brown. *Acq Lib* Charles T Weaver.
Lib Type Special.
Spec Subs Statistical methodology; demography; business; economics; state fiscal documents. *Spec Collecs* US Census publications, 1790 to date; foreign censuses & statistics publications; survey methodology; legislative; annual reports; college catalogs.
Info Ret Servs DIALOG; BRS; SDC; NEXIS; LEXIS; USATODAY. *Shared Catalog Nets* OCLC; Faxon DATALYNX. *Coop Lib Nets* FEDLINK.
Circ Servs Avail To other Federal libraries; to other libraries; not open to the general public.
Ref Servs Avail To other Federal libraries; to other libraries; to the general public.

144. Bureau of the Census, New York Regional Office Library
37-100 Jacob K Javits Federal Bldg, New York, NY 10278 (212) 264-4730; FTS 264-4730
Admin Henry L Palacios (Coordinator).
Lib Type Special.
Spec Subs US Census data: decennial, population & housing, & economic censuses; intercensal population, housing & economic reports.
Info Ret Servs CENDATA.
Ref Servs Avail To other Federal libraries; to other libraries; to the general public; restricted to use on premises.

Bureau of Economic Analysis

145. Bureau of Economic Analysis, Research Resource Center
Dept of Commerce, Washington, DC 20230 (202) 523-0595
Admin Susan Randolph.
Lib Type Special.
Spec Subs Statistical materials.
Circ Servs Avail To other Federal libraries; to other libraries; not open to the general public.
Ref Servs Avail To other Federal libraries; not open to the general public.

Economic Development Administration

146. Economic Development Administration, Seattle Regional Office Library
1700 Westlake Ave, N, Suite 500, Seattle, WA 98109 (206) 442-0596 442-8425
Admin James J Sullivan.
Lib Type Law.
Spec Subs State codes: AK, WA, OR, ID, AZ, NV, CA, & HI. *Spec Collecs* Code of federal regulations.

Circ Servs Avail Not open to the general public; restricted to Commerce Dept.
Ref Servs Avail Not open to the general public; restricted to Commerce Dept.

International Trade Administration

147. Industry & Trade Administration Library
US Dept of Commerce, Suite 600, 1365 Peachtree St, NE, Atlanta, GA 30309 (404) 881-7000; FTS 257-7000
Lib Type Special.

148. International Trade Administration, Chicago Field Office Library
55 E Monroe St, Rm 1406, Chicago, IL 60603 (312) 353-4450
Admin Bernadine C Roberson.
Lib Type Special.
Spec Subs Exporting; international trade.
Lib Deposit Designation US Dept of Commerce.
Info Ret Servs DIALOG. *Elec Mail Nets* CompuServ.
Circ Servs Avail To other Federal libraries; to other libraries; to the general public.

149. International Trade Administration District Office, US & FCS Commercial Library
PO Box 1950, 324 W Market St, Greensboro, NC 27402 (919) 333-5345; FTS 699-5345
Admin Jack F Whitley (Deputy Dir). *Ref Lib* Alice Brumfield (ILL, Acq).
Lib Type Special.
Spec Subs Foreign trade reports from Bureau of Census; foreign trade directories; ITA trade promotion; domestic census reports. *In-house Files* Computerized listing of NC firms engaged in international trade.
Info Ret Servs DIALOG. *Elec Mail Nets* Compuserve.
Ref Servs Avail To other Federal libraries; to other libraries; to the general public.

150. International Trade Administration, International Marketing Center Library
Box 36013, 450 Golden Gate Ave, San Francisco, CA 94102 (415) 556-7501
Admin Janet Ashley.
Lib Type Special.
Spec Subs International trade; exporting.
Info Ret Servs DIALOG; NIH. *Elec Mail Nets* MCI Mail; Telex.
Circ Servs Avail To the general public.
Ref Servs Avail To the general public.

151. International Trade Administration Library
9448 Federal Bldg, 600 Arch St, Philadelphia, PA 19106 (215) 597-2850
Lib Type General.

152. International Trade Administration Library
210 Walnut St, Rm 817, Des Moines, IA 50309 (515) 284-4222; FTS 862-4222
Admin Sondra Raper.
Lib Type Special.
Ref Servs Avail To the general public.

153. International Trade Administration Library
441 Stuart St, Boston, MA 02116 (617) 223-2381
Lib Type Special.

154. International Trade Administration, Richmond District Office Library
8010 Federal Bldg, 400 N 8th St, Richmond, VA 23240 (804) 771-2246; FTS 925-2246
Admin Edna P Parent; Janie J Preston.
Lib Type Special.
Circ Servs Avail Restricted to Commerce Dept.
Ref Servs Avail Restricted to providing Commerce Dept data.

National Bureau of Standards

155. National Bureau of Standards Research Information Center
Gaithersburg, MD 20899 (301) 921-3405
Admin Patricia W Berger. *Ref Lib* Sami Klein. *ILL* Teresa Radcliffe. *Acq Lib* Marvin Bond.
Lib Type Engineering & Science.
Spec Subs Meteorology; physics; chemistry; engineering; mathematics; statistics; computer science; materials science. *Spec Collecs* Intergovernmental affairs collection; rare books collection which documents history of meteorology; museum with NBS artifacts. *In-house Files* Oral histories of NBS programs & scientists; historical information files; papers of former NBS Directors.
Info Ret Servs DIALOG; BRS SDC; DTIC; GIDEP; Mead-Data; NASA/RECON; OCLC; DOE/RECON; Occupational Health Services; Pergamon; Questel; National Library of Medicine; NTIS. *Shared Catalog Nets* OCLC. *Coop Lib Nets* FEDLINK; IUA. *Elec Mail Nets* ALANET.
Circ Servs Avail To other Federal libraries; to other libraries.
Ref Servs Avail To other Federal libraries; to other libraries.

156. National Center for Standards & Certification Information
Administration Bldg, Rm A629, Gaithersburg, MD 20899 (301) 921-2587; FTS 921-2587
Admin JoAnne Overman.
Lib Type Special.
Spec Subs Domestic, foreign, & international standards & certification information; trade related standards information. *Spec Collecs* Microform & hard-copy collection of foreign standards. *In-house Files* Key-word-in-context index of US Voluntary Engineering Standards.
Ref Servs Avail To other Federal libraries; to other libraries; to the general public.

National Oceanic & Atmospheric Administration

157. Atmospheric Turbulence & Diffusion Laboratory Library
PO Box E, Oak Ridge, TN 37831 (615) 576-1235; FTS 626-1235
Admin Ruth A Green. *Ref Lib* Carol Thompson (ILL, Acq).
Lib Type Special.
Spec Subs Atmospheric turbulence, diffusion, & deposition; transport of environmental pollution; air/surface interaction. *In-house Files* Reports & reprints published by division staff.
Circ Servs Avail To other Federal libraries; to other libraries; not open to the general public.
Ref Servs Avail To other Federal libraries; to other libraries; not open to the general public.

158. Auke Bay Fisheries Laboratory Library
PO Box 210155, Auke Bay, AK 99821 (907) 789-6009; 789-6010
Admin Paula Johnson.
Lib Type Special.
Spec Subs Fisheries; marine biology; ecology; physiology; marine pollution; computer sciences; biometrics; aquaculture. *Spec Collecs* Baker Collection—historical collection of fisheries reprints. *In-house Files* MRF manuscript report file—gray literature.
Info Ret Servs DIALOG. *Coop Lib Nets* Alaska Library Network (ALN). *Elec Mail Nets* Univ of Alaska Computer Network VAX mail system (UACN).
Circ Servs Avail To other Federal libraries; to other libraries; to the general public.
Ref Servs Avail To other Federal libraries; to other libraries; to the general public.

159. Coastal Zone Information Center
3300 Whitehaven St NW, Washington, DC 20235 (202) 634-4255; FTS 634-4255
Admin Sallie P Cauchon. *Acq Lib* Janice Beers.
Lib Type Special.

Spec Subs Books & documents directly relating to coastal zone management. *Spec Collecs* State coastal zone management work products; state coastal zone management plans; draft & final environmental impact statements; books & documents directly related to coastal zone management; reference materials; Congressional Record; reports; state maps & atlases. *In-house Files* Vertical file with subjects relating to coastal zone management.
Circ Servs Avail To other Federal libraries; to other libraries; to the general public.
Ref Servs Avail To other Federal libraries; to other libraries; to the general public.

160. Geophysical Fluid Dynamics Laboratory Library
PO Box 308, Princeton, NJ 08542 (609) 452-6550; FTS 452-6550
Admin Phil Fraulino.
Lib Type Engineering & Science.
Spec Subs Meteorology; oceanography; science; technology. *Spec Collecs* Films & microforms; technical reports.
Lib Deposit Designation Dept of Energy (limited); NOAA.
Info Ret Servs DIALOG; BRS; SDC. *Shared Catalog Nets* OCLC. *Coop Lib Nets* FEDLINK.
Circ Servs Avail To other Federal libraries; to other libraries; to the general public.
Ref Servs Avail To other Federal libraries; to other libraries; to the general public.

161. Gloucester Technical Library
National Marine Fisheries Service, 30 Emerson Ave, Gloucester, MA 01930 (617) 281-3600; FTS 837-9276
Admin Judith Krzynowek.
Lib Type Special.
Spec Subs Fishery technology, not marine biology.
Info Ret Servs DIALOG. *Coop Lib Nets* Woods Hole NMFS Library.
Circ Servs Avail Not open to the general public.
Ref Servs Avail Not open to the general public.

162. Library & Information Services Division, Camp Springs Center
World Weather Bldg, 6th Fl, 5200 Auth Rd, Camp Springs, MD 20233 (301) 763-8266/8267
Admin Jeanne May.
Lib Type Engineering & Science.
Spec Subs Geography; social sciences; science; physics; technology, weather analysis. *Spec Collecs* Special weather reports.
Shared Catalog Nets OCLC.
Circ Servs Avail To other Federal libraries; to other libraries; not open to the general public; restricted to NOAA affiliations.
Ref Servs Avail Not open to the general public; restricted to in-house use only.

163. Map Library & Information Service Library
Riverdale Bldg, 6501 Lafayette Ave, Riverdale, MD 20840 (301) 436-6978; FTS 436-6978
Admin Samuel H Walinsky.
Lib Type Special.
Spec Collecs National Ocean Service nautical charts; Great Lakes nautical charts; topographic quadrangle maps of the US Geological Survey on current issue; Central Intelligence Agency (CIA) maps of foreign countries; National Geographic Society publications; current state & county highway maps.
Ref Servs Avail To other Federal libraries; to other libraries; to the general public; restricted to specialized cartographic research to all federal government users & to the general public.

164. Miami Laboratory Library
National Marine Fisheries Service, Southeast Fisheries Center, 75 Virginia Beach Dr, Miami, FL 33149 (305) 361-4229; FTS 350-1229
Admin Julianne Josiek. *ILL* Suzanne E Burns.
Lib Type Engineering & Science.
Spec Subs Fisheries; marine biology; ecology. *Spec Collecs* Over 7,000 reprints covering fish eggs, larvae, systematics.
Info Ret Servs DIALOG. *Shared Catalog Nets* OCLC.
Circ Servs Avail To other Federal libraries; to other libraries.
Ref Servs Avail To other Federal libraries; to other libraries; to the general public.

165. Milford Laboratory Library
National Marine Fisheries Service, Northeast Fisheries Center, 212 Rogers Ave, Milford, CT 06460 (203) 783-4234; FTS 783-4234
Admin Barbara D Sabo.
Lib Type Engineering & Science.
Spec Subs Aquaculture; pollutant effects on fish. *In-house Files* Staff publications.
Info Ret Servs DIALOG.
Circ Servs Avail To other Federal libraries; to other libraries.
Ref Servs Avail To other Federal libraries; to other libraries; to the general public.

166. National Marine Fisheries Service, Honolulu Laboratory Library
Box 3830, 2570 Dole St, Honolulu, HI 96812 (808) 943-1221
Lib Type Special.

167. National Marine Fisheries Service, Southeast Fisheries Center Library
PO Box 12607, Charleston Laboratory, Charleston, SC 29412 (803) 762-1200; FTS 677-4760
Admin Lois F Winemiller.
Lib Type Special.
Spec Subs Food science; chemistry; food technology; nutrition; biology; microbiology. *Spec Collecs* Collection of materials on the processing & analysis of fish & fishery products for use by humans & animals; fish development; microconstituents in fish & fishery products; chemical composition of fish & fishery products; shellfish sanitation.
Circ Servs Avail To other Federal libraries; to other libraries.
Ref Servs Avail To other Federal libraries; to other libraries; to the general public; restricted to general public upon request for on site use.

168. National Marine Mammal Library
National Marine Fisheries Service, Bldg 4, 7600 Sand Point Way NE, Seattle, WA 98115-0070 (206) 526-4013
Admin Sherry Pearson.
Lib Type Special.
Spec Subs Marine mammals: whales, seals, sea lions. *Spec Collecs* International Whaling Commission Archives.
Circ Servs Avail To other Federal libraries; not open to the general public.
Ref Servs Avail To other Federal libraries.

169. NOAA, Coral Gables Center Library
Rm 629, Gables 1 Tower, 1320 S Dixie Hwy, Coral Gables, FL 33146 (305) 666-4613; FTS 350-5547
Admin Robert Ting (Acting).
Lib Type Special.
Spec Subs Tropical meteorology & climatology. *Spec Collecs* In-house & foreign technical reports; microfilm collection of surface maps, upper air maps, & hurricane reconnaissance flights.
Circ Servs Avail To other Federal libraries; to other libraries; not open to the general public; restricted to NOAA personnel.
Ref Servs Avail To other Federal libraries; to other libraries; to the general public; restricted to NOAA staff for free literature search of data bases.

170. NOAA, Great Lakes Environmental Research Laboratory Library
2300 Washtenaw Ave, Ann Arbor, MI 48104 (313) 668-2242; FTS 378-2242
Admin Barbara J. Carrick.
Lib Type Special.
Spec Subs Climatology; fresh water; Great Lakes; hydrology; limnology; meteorology; oceanography; sedimentation; toxic organics; nutrients.
Shared Catalog Nets OCLC. *Coop Lib Nets* FEDLINK; Washtenaw-Livingston Library Network.

171. NOAA, Miami Library
4301 Rickenbacker Causeway, Miami, FL 33149 (305) 361-4428; FTS 305-4428
Admin Robert N Ting.
Lib Type Engineering & Science.

Spec Subs Oceanography; tropical meteorology; hurricane research & data; ocean biology; ocean chemistry; underwater acoustics; applied mathematics. *Spec Collecs* Coast & Geodetic Survey Report, 1851-1934.
Info Ret Servs DIALOG; BRS. *Shared Catalog Nets* OCLC. *Coop Lib Nets* NOAA Southeastern Area Resources Council (NOAASARC).
Circ Servs Avail To other Federal libraries; to other libraries; not open to the general public.
Ref Servs Avail To other Federal libraries; to other libraries; to the general public.

172. NOAA, Mountain Administrative Support Center
325 Broadway, Boulder, CO 80303 (303) 497-3271; ILL 497-5570 FTS 320-3271
Lib Type Special.
Spec Subs Electronics; engineering; mathematics; oceanography; aeronomy; computer science; cryogenics; geophysics; meteorology; telecommunications. *Spec Collecs* Radio Science & Physics (Technical Reports 1940-1970).
Info Ret Servs DIALOG; BRS; DOE/Recon; NASA Library Network; SDC Information Services; DROLLS. *Coop Lib Nets* FEDLINK; Central Colorado Library System.
Circ Servs Avail Not open to the general public.
Ref Servs Avail To the general public.

173. NOAA, National Climatic Data Center Library
Federal Bldg, Asheville, NC 28801-2696 (704) 259-0677; FTS 672-0677
Admin Linda D Preston.
Lib Type Engineering & Science.
Spec Subs Climatic data for ocean & land areas. *Spec Collecs* Center publications; climatic atlases. *In-house Files* Inhouse newsletter & photofile.
Info Ret Servs DIALOG; BRS; SDC. *Shared Catalog Nets* OCLC; NALIS (NOAA online catalog from OCLC holdings).
Circ Servs Avail To other libraries.
Ref Servs Avail Restricted to selected researchers.

174. NOAA, Scientific Services Division
National Weather Service, Federal Bldg, 125 S St, Salt Lake City, UT 84147 (801) 524-5131; FTS 588-5131
Admin Lavonne Doubek.
Lib Type Special.

175. NOAA, Seattle Center Library
Library & Information Services Division, Bin C-15700, 7600 Sand Point Way NE, Seattle, WA 98115 (206) 526-6241; FTS 392-6241
Admin Bruce L Keck. *Ref Lib* Martha B Thayer (ILL).
Lib Type Engineering & Science.
Spec Subs Oceanography; meteorology; pollution; marine chemistry; atmospheric chemistry; polar studies.
Info Ret Servs DIALOG; BRS; SDC. *Shared Catalog Nets* OCLC; NOAA Automated Library & Information System (NALIS). *Coop Lib Nets* NOAA Library & Information Network (NLIN). *Elec Mail Nets* BRS.
Circ Servs Avail To other Federal libraries; to other libraries.
Ref Servs Avail To other Federal libraries; to other libraries; to the general public.

176. NOAA, Southeast Fisheries Center, Galveston Laboratory Library
4700 Ave U, Galveston, TX 77550 (409) 766-3500
Lib Type Engineering & Science.
Spec Subs Aquaculture; ecology; fish biology; fisheries; ichthyology; marine chemistry; marine science; oceanology; physiology; zoology.

177. NOAA World Data Center A, Oceanography
2001 Wisconsin Ave NW, Washington, DC 20235 (202) 634-7249; FTS 634-7249
Admin Ronald E Moffatt (Assoc Dir).
Lib Type Engineering & Science.
Circ Servs Avail Restricted to availability of 2nd copy.
Ref Servs Avail To other Federal libraries; to other libraries; to the general public.

178. National Severe Storms Laboratory Library
1313 Halley Cir, Norman, OK 73069 (405) 360-3620; FTS 736-4916
Admin Mary Meacham.
Lib Type Engineering & Science.
Spec Subs Thunderstorms; weather forecasting; meteorological radar; tornadoes; hail; atmospheric models.
Circ Servs Avail To other Federal libraries; to other libraries; not open to the general public.
Ref Servs Avail To other Federal libraries; to other libraries; to the general public.

179. National Weather Service, Central Region Library
601 E 12th St, Rm 1836, Kansas City, MO 64106-2477 (816) 374-5672; FTS 758-5672
Admin Beverly D Lambert.
Lib Type Special.
Spec Subs Meteorology; hydrology; climatology. *Spec Collecs* Climatological data; meteorological journals & books. *In-house Files* Technical memorandums; computer programs.
Lib Deposit Designation National Weather Service Central Region Documents.
Ref Servs Avail To other Federal libraries; to other libraries; to the general public.

180. National Weather Service, Southern Region Headquarters Library
Rm 10A29, 819 Taylor St, Fort Worth, TX 76102 (817) 334-2671; FTS 334-2671
Admin Linda Shearin.
Lib Type Special.
Spec Subs Meteorology; hydrology; climatology.
Circ Servs Avail Not open to the general public; restricted to staff.
Ref Servs Avail Not open to the general public; restricted to staff.

181. National Weather Service, Weather Service Nuclear Support Office Library
PO Box 14985, Las Vegas, NV 89114 (702) 295-1232
Lib Type Special.
Spec Subs Diffusion; meteorology; nuclear science; radioactivity.

182. NOAA, Library & Information Services Division
6009 Executive Blvd, Rockville, MD 20852 (301) 443-8358; FTS 443-8287
Admin Laurie E Stackpole (Act Lib Dir). *Ref Lib* Joan M McKean. *ILL* Barbara Thompson. *Acq Lib* Ida M Lewis.
Lib Type Engineering & Science.
Spec Subs Meteorology; mathematics; geodetic astronomy; nautical & aeronautical cartography; hydrographic surveying; photogrammetry; geophysics; marine biology & fisheries. *Spec Collecs* Rare book room with historical documents which reflect the development of the agency; classic works in atmospheric science; large selection of foreign meteorological & climatological data publications. *In-house Files* NOAA scientific series.
Info Ret Servs DIALOG; BRS; SDC; NEXIS; CIS; NASA/RECON; VU/TEXT. *Shared Catalog Nets* OCLC. *Coop Lib Nets* FEDLINK; NOAA Library Information Network (NLIN). *Elec Mail Nets* ITT DIALCOM.
Circ Servs Avail To other Federal libraries; to other libraries; not open to the general public.
Ref Servs Avail To other Federal libraries; to other libraries; to the general public.

183. Northwest & Alaska Fisheries Center Library
National Marine Fisheries Service, 2725 Montlake Blvd E, Seattle, WA 98112 (206) 442-7795; FTS 399-7795
Admin Patricia Cook.
Lib Type Engineering & Science.
Spec Subs Marine biology; fisheries; food technology; biological oceanography; biochemistry. *Spec Collecs* Over 3,000 fishery translations.
Info Ret Servs DIALOG. *Shared Catalog Nets* OCLC. *Coop Lib Nets* International Assoc of Marine Science Libraries & Information Centers (IAMSLIC).
Circ Servs Avail Not open to the general public.

Ref Servs Avail To other Federal libraries; to other libraries; to the general public.

184. Oxford Laboratory Library
National Marine Fisheries Service, Oxford, MD 21654-0279 (301) 226-5193
Admin Susie Hines.
Lib Type Special.
Spec Subs Pathobiology; fisheries; habitat & resource conservation; ecology. *In-house Files* Over 30,000 reprints on file.
Info Ret Servs DIALOG. *Shared Catalog Nets* OCLC. *Coop Lib Nets* Eastern Shore Library Consortium (ESLC); Maryland Assoc of Health Science Libraries (MAHSL).
Circ Servs Avail To other Federal libraries; to other libraries; to the general public.
Ref Servs Avail To other Federal libraries; to other libraries; to the general public.

185. Panama City Laboratory Library
National Marine Fisheries Service, Southeast Fisheries Center, 3500 Delwood Beach Rd, Panama City, FL 32407 (904) 234-6541
Admin Rosalie N Vaught.
Lib Type Engineering & Science.
Spec Subs Fisheries; marine biology; oceanography; ecology.
Info Ret Servs DIALOG. *Coop Lib Nets* NOAA Library & Information Network (NLIN).
Circ Servs Avail To other Federal libraries; to other libraries; to the general public.
Ref Servs Avail To other Federal libraries; to other libraries; to the general public.

186. Pascagoula Laboratory Library
National Marine Fisheries Service, PO Drawer 1207, 3209 Frederic St, Pascagoula, MS 39568-1207 (601) 762-4591; FTS 499-4251
Admin Jon Martin.
Lib Type Engineering & Science.
Spec Subs Marine science; oceanography; fishing gear. *In-house Files* Over 3,500 reprints.
Info Ret Servs DIALOG. *Shared Catalog Nets* OCLC. *Coop Lib Nets* NOAA Library Network; SLA; IAMSLIC.
Circ Servs Avail To other Federal libraries; to other libraries; to the general public.
Ref Servs Avail To other Federal libraries; to other libraries; to the general public.

187. Rice Library
National Marine Fisheries Service, Beaufort, NC 28516-9722 (919) 728-3595; FTS 670-8713/8714
Admin Ann Bowmann Manooch.
Lib Type Engineering & Science.
Spec Subs Fishes & fisheries; marine biology; oceanography.
Info Ret Servs DIALOG; BRS; SDC. *Shared Catalog Nets* OCLC.
Circ Servs Avail To other Federal libraries; to other libraries; to the general public.
Ref Servs Avail To other Federal libraries; to other libraries; to the general public.

188. Southwest Fisheries Center Library
National Marine Fisheries Service, PO Box 271, La Jolla, CA 92038 (619) 453-2820; FTS 893-6243
Admin Debra A Losey.
Lib Type Special.
Spec Subs Fishery biology; population dynamics of fish; marine aquaculture; oceanography. *Spec Collecs* Inter-American Tropical Tuna Commission Collection; Stanford Ocean Research Laboratory Collection.
Info Ret Servs DIALOG; BRS. *Shared Catalog Nets* OCLC. *Coop Lib Nets* FEDLINK. *Elec Mail Nets* Telex (#9103371271).
Circ Servs Avail To other Federal libraries; to other libraries; to the general public.
Ref Servs Avail To other Federal libraries; to other libraries; to the general public.

189. W F Thompson Memorial Library
NW & AK Fisheries Center, National Marine Fisheries Service, PO Box 1638, Kodiak Investigations—Research, Kodiak, AK 99615 (907) 487-4961
Admin Charmaine Swann.
Lib Type Engineering & Science.
Spec Subs Fisheries science; aquatic biology; aquaculture. *Spec Collecs* Alaska Harriman Series.
Info Ret Servs DIALOG; NALIS. *Elec Mail Nets* NW & AK Fisheries Center, Seattle.
Circ Servs Avail To other Federal libraries; to other libraries.
Ref Servs Avail To other Federal libraries; to other libraries; to the general public.

190. Tiburon Laboratory Library
National Marine Fisheries Service, Southwest Fisheries Center, 3150 Paradise Dr, Tiburon, CA 94920 (415) 435-3149; FTS 556-0566
Admin Maureen Leet.
Lib Type Engineering & Science.
Spec Subs Marine science; fishery science; aquaculture; commercial fishing methods. *Spec Collecs* Dr V L Loosanoff Collection on commercial shellfish; Shark Taxonomy Reprint Collection.
Info Ret Servs DIALOG; BRS; SDC. *Shared Catalog Nets* OCLC. *Elec Mail Nets* FEDLINK.
Circ Servs Avail To other Federal libraries; to other libraries; to the general public.
Ref Servs Avail To other Federal libraries; to other libraries; to the general public.

191. Lionel A Walford Library
Sandy Hook Laboratory, Highlands, NJ 07732 (201) 872-0200 ext 234,235; FTS 342-8235
Admin Claire L Steimle. *ILL* Judith Berrien.
Lib Type Special.
Spec Subs Marine biology; fisheries; oceanography.
Info Ret Servs DIALOG. *Shared Catalog Nets* OCLC. *Coop Lib Nets* NOAA Library Network; NJ Library Network; Region V Library Cooperative.

Circ Servs Avail To other Federal libraries; to other libraries; not open to the general public; restricted to organizations with cooperative agreements with NOAA.
Ref Servs Avail To other Federal libraries; to other libraries; to the general public.

192. Woods Hole Laboratory Library
National Marine Fisheries Service, Woods Hole, MA 02543 (617) 548-5123 ext 260; FTS 840-1260
Admin Judith Brownlow.
Lib Type Special.
Spec Subs Fisheries. *Spec Collecs* International Council for the Exploration of the Sea C M Documents. *In-house Files* Woods Hole Laboratory Reference Documents.
Info Ret Servs DIALOG. *Shared Catalog Nets* OCLC.
Circ Servs Avail To other Federal libraries; to other libraries; to the general public.
Ref Servs Avail To other Federal libraries; to other libraries; to the general public.

Patent & Trademark Office

193. Patent & Trademark Office, Law Library
Dept of Commerce, Washington, DC 20231 (703) 557-4052
Lib Type Law.

194. Patent & Trademark Office Scientific Library
Washington, DC 20231 (703) 557-3428; FTS 557-2957
Admin Henry Rosicky. *Ref Lib* Dora D Weinstein (ILL). *Acq Lib* Jesse Gibson.
Lib Type Engineering & Science.
Spec Subs Science & technology. *Spec Collecs* Foreign patents.
Info Ret Servs DIALOG; BRS; SDC; CAS Online; MEAD; DOD; DTIC; INPADOC. *Shared Catalog Nets* OCLC. *Coop Lib Nets* FEDLINK; OCLC. *Elec Mail Nets* FAX.
Circ Servs Avail To other Federal libraries; to other libraries; restricted to staff.
Ref Servs Avail To other Federal libraries; to other libraries; to the general public.

DEPARTMENT OF DEFENSE

Department of the Air Force—Domestic

195. Air Force Accounting & Finance Center Library/FL 7040
Bldg 444, Denver, CO 80279-5000 (303) 370-7566; AUTOVON 926-7566
Admin Alreeta Eidson. *Ref Lib* Wilma A Daane (ILL).
Lib Type Special.
Spec Subs Accounting; data processing; management; statistics.
Info Ret Servs DIALOG; BRS; SDC; WILSONLINE. *Shared Catalog Nets* OCLC.
Circ Servs Avail To other Federal libraries; to other libraries; not open to the general public.
Ref Servs Avail To other Federal libraries; to other libraries; not open to the general public.

196. Air Force Engineering & Services Center Technical Library/FL 7050
Bldg 1120/Stop 21, Tyndall AFB, FL 32403-6001 (904) 283-6282/6285; FTS 970-6449; TTY (904) 283-6449; AUTOVON 970-6282/6285
Admin Andrew D Poulis. *ILL* Lola Fletcher.
Lib Type Engineering & Science.
Spec Subs Civil engineering; environmental engineering readiness; environmental planning; construction costs; information management. *Spec Collecs* Rapid runway repair; air-bird strikes; fire technology; soil mechanics; pavements. *In-house Files* Air-bird strikes; rapid runway repair.
Lib Deposit Designation NASA (partial); DTIC; NTIS; GAO.
Info Ret Servs DIALOG; BRS; DTIC/DROLS; NASA/RECON; DOE/RECON. *Shared Catalog Nets* OCLC; DTIC/SBIN. *Coop Lib Nets* FLIN; GOAL; SLA Florida Chapter; DTIC Users Group.
Circ Servs Avail To other Federal libraries; to other libraries; not open to the general public.
Ref Servs Avail Restricted to HQ AFESC.

197. Air Force Flight Test Center, Technical Library/FL 2806
6520 TEST G-ENXL, Edwards AFB, CA 93523-5000 (805) 277-3606
Lib Type Special.
Spec Subs Aeronautics; chemistry; mathematics; missiles & rockets; propulsion systems; electrical & electronic engineering; physics.
Info Ret Servs DIALOG; Defense Technical Info Ctr (DTIC). *Shared Catalog Nets* OCLC.
Circ Servs Avail Restricted to staff only.
Ref Servs Avail Restricted to staff only.

198. Air Force Geophysics Laboratory Research Library
AFGL/SULL, Hanscom AFB, MA 01731 (617) 861-4895; AUTOVON 478-4895
Admin Ruth K Seidman. *Ref Lib* Ellen Dobi. *ILL* Nina Lanzetta. *Acq Lib* Lee McLaughlin.
Lib Type Engineering & Science.
Spec Subs Physics; geophysics; meteorology; math & computer sciences; electronics; materials science. *Spec Collecs* Rayleigh Collection (original manuscripts of 3rd & 4th Lords Rayleigh); early science monographs.
Info Ret Servs DIALOG; BRS. *Shared Catalog Nets* OCLC.
Circ Servs Avail Restricted to ILL to other libraries.

Ref Servs Avail To other Federal libraries; to other libraries; to the general public.

199. Air Force Human Resources Laboratory, Technical Library/FL 2870
Brooks AFB, TX 78235-5601 (512) 536-2651; AUTOVON 240-2651
Admin Orrine L Woinowsk. *ILL* Mildred A Jones (Acq).
Lib Type Special.
Spec Subs Psychology; mathematical statistics; computer sciences. *In-house Files* AFHRL technical reports.
Info Ret Servs DIALOG; DROLS. *Shared Catalog Nets* OCLC. *Coop Lib Nets* AMIGOS; CORAL; HOLSA.
Circ Servs Avail To other Federal libraries; to other libraries; not open to the general public; restricted to local military & civilian personnel.
Ref Servs Avail To other Federal libraries; to other libraries; not open to the general public; restricted to local military & civilian personnel.

200. Air Force Institute of Technology Academic Library/FL 3319
Bldg 640 Area B, Wright-Patterson AFB, OH 45433-6583 (513) 237-9657; AUTOVON 785-5894
Admin James T Helling. *Ref Lib* Pam McCarthy (ILL)(Main Lib); Ron Lundquist (ILL)(Branch Lib). *Acq Lib* Mary Browning (Main Lib); Chris Cupp (Branch Lib).
Lib Type Academic.
Spec Subs Engineering; aeronautics; logistics.
Lib Deposit Designation Rand Corporation.
Info Ret Servs DIALOG. *Shared Catalog Nets* OCLC. *Coop Lib Nets* Southwestern Ohio Council for Higher Education (SOCHE).
Circ Servs Avail To other Federal libraries; not open to the general public.
Ref Servs Avail To other Federal libraries; not open to the general public.

201. Air Force Institute of Technology Library
Bldg 215, Grand Forks AFB, ND 58205 (701) 594-6366
Lib Type Special.
Spec Subs Business & management; economics.

202. Air Force Logistics Management Center, Technical Library
Bldg 205, Gunter Air Force Station, AL 36114-6693 (205) 279-4830; AUTOVON 446-4830
Admin Ernest P Laseter; Judith A Osborne (Lib Tech).
Lib Type Special.
Spec Subs Air force base level logistics systems. *In-house Files* Logistics studies research program (automated database).
Info Ret Servs DROLS (DTIC).
Circ Servs Avail Not open to the general public; restricted to DoD.
Ref Servs Avail Not open to the general public; restricted to DoD.

203. Air Force Occupational & Environmental Health Laboratory, Technical Library/FL 2817
Bldg 140, Brooks AFB, TX 78235-5501 (512) 536-3421; AUTOVON 240-3421
Admin Ann Russell Potter. *ILL* Evelyn Garcia-Gonzalez.
Lib Type Health & Medicine.

Spec Subs Environmental health; occupational medicine; radiation safety.
Info Ret Servs DIALOG; Chemical Info System; NLM; DTIC. *Shared Catalog Nets* OCLC. *Coop Lib Nets* Health Oriented Libraries of San Antonio (HOLSA).
Circ Servs Avail To other Federal libraries; to other libraries.
Ref Servs Avail To other Federal libraries; to other libraries.

204. Air Force Office of Scientific Research Library/FL 2819
Bolling AFB, DC 20332 (202) 767-4910; AUTOVON 297-4910
Admin Anthony G Bialecki.
Lib Type Engineering & Science.
Spec Subs Physics; chemistry; mathematics; life sciences.
Info Ret Servs DIALOG.
Circ Servs Avail To other Federal libraries; to other libraries; not open to the general public.
Ref Servs Avail To other Federal libraries; to other libraries; not open to the general public.

205. Air Force Officer Training School Library/FL 3050
OTS/MTDL, Bldg 147, Lackland AFB, TX 78236-5000 (512) 671-4316; AUTOVON 473-4316
Admin Beulah Phillips. *ILL* Gwendolyn Morgan.
Lib Type Training Center.
Spec Subs Military science; technology; engineering; leadership; management; communicative skills.
Circ Servs Avail To other Federal libraries; restricted to students & staff.
Ref Servs Avail To other Federal libraries; restricted to students & staff.

206. Air Force School of Aerospace Medicine, Strughold Aeromedical Library/FL 2855
Brooks AFB, TX 78235-5301 (512) 536-3321; AUTOVON 240-3321
Admin Fred W Todd. *Ref Lib* Bonnie J Fridley. *Acq Lib* Olive Brewster.
Lib Type Health & Medicine.
Spec Subs Aviation & space medicine; military medicine; biomedical & human engineering; radiology. *Spec Collecs* Personal collection, Hubertus Strughold, MD, PhD. *In-house Files* Selected archives, AF School of Aerospace Medicine.
Lib Deposit Designation NASA.
Info Ret Servs DIALOG; BRS; SDC; MEDLARS; NPIRS; NASA/RECON; DOE/RECON; CIS; DTIC. *Shared Catalog Nets* OCLC. *Coop Lib Nets* TALON Regional Medical Library Network; Council of Research & Academic Libraries of San Antonio (CORAL); Health-Oriented Libraries of San Antonio (HOLSA). *Elec Mail Nets* OPTIMIST; CLASS.
Circ Servs Avail To other Federal libraries; to other libraries; not open to the general public; restricted to special permission.
Ref Servs Avail To other Federal libraries; to other libraries; not open to the general public; restricted to special permission.

207. Air Force Space Command Library/FL 2508
HQ AFSPACECOM/MPSL, Peterson AFB, CO 80914-5001 (303) 591-7462; AUTOVON 692-3495
Admin Judy A Hawthorne. *ILL* Jean Lockett.
Lib Type Engineering & Science.
Spec Subs Space sciences; aerospace; computer sciences; military science.
Lib Deposit Designation NASA & DTIC.
Info Ret Servs DIALOG; DROLS; NASA/RECON; Aerospace Online; LEXIS; NEXIS CQ; Washington Alert. *Shared Catalog Nets* OCLC. *Coop Lib Nets* FEDLINK.
Circ Servs Avail To other libraries.
Ref Servs Avail To other libraries.

208. Air Force Systems Command Technical Information Center
HQ AFSC/MPSLT, Andrews AFB, DC 20334-5000 (301) 981-3551; AUTOVON 858-2019
Admin Yvonne Kinkaid.
Lib Type Special.
Spec Subs Aerospace; weapons systems; radar; management.

Info Ret Servs DIALOG; DROLS (DTIC). *Shared Catalog Nets* OCLC. *Coop Lib Nets* FEDLINK.
Circ Servs Avail To other Federal libraries; to other libraries; restricted to DoD personnel.
Ref Servs Avail To other Federal libraries; to other libraries; restricted to DoD personnel.

209. Air Force Weapons Laboratory Technical Library/FL 2809
AFWL/SUL, Kirtland AFB, NM 87117-6008 (505) 844-7449; AUTOVON 224-7449
Admin Barbara I Newton. *Ref Lib* Virginia K King. *ILL* Donna E Cromer. *Acq Lib* Carol A Cahn.
Lib Type Engineering & Science.
Spec Subs Physical sciences; engineering; lasers; nuclear weapons; space.
Info Ret Servs DIALOG; BRS; DTIC; STN; NASA/RECON; DOE/RECON. *Shared Catalog Nets* OCLC. *Coop Lib Nets* FEDLINK.
Circ Servs Avail To other Federal libraries; to other libraries; not open to the general public; restricted to unclassified materials on ILL.
Ref Servs Avail To other Federal libraries; to other libraries; not open to the general public; restricted to base personnel.

210. Air Force Western Space & Missile Center, Technical Library/FL 2827
WSMC/PMET, Vandenberg AFB, CA 93437 (805) 866-9745; FTS 986-9745; AUTOVON 276-9745
Admin Paula K Turley. *Ref Lib* Cheryl Koss. *ILL* M Suzanne Stanton.
Lib Type Special.
Spec Subs Computers; radar; guided missiles; aerospace sciences.
Info Ret Servs DIALOG; SDC; DROLS; NASA/RECON. *Shared Catalog Nets* OCLC. *Coop Lib Nets* CLASS; Total Interlibrary Exchange (TIE).
Circ Servs Avail To other Federal libraries; to other libraries; restricted to government, military & civilian employees on base.
Ref Servs Avail To other Federal libraries; to other libraries; restricted to government, military & civilian employees on base.

211. Air University Library/FL 3368
Maxwell AFB, AL 36112 (205) 293-2888; AUTOVON 875-2888
Admin Robert B Lane. *Ref Lib* Helen Talisfforro. *ILL* Marie Harper. *Acq Lib* Karin Johns.
Lib Type Academic.
Spec Subs Military science & history. *Spec Collecs* The Air Univ Collection: rare books on the history of flight.
Lib Deposit Designation GPO Depository Library.
Info Ret Servs DIALOG. *Shared Catalog Nets* OCLC. *Coop Lib Nets* SOLINET.
Circ Servs Avail To other Federal libraries; to other libraries.
Ref Servs Avail To other Federal libraries; to other libraries; to the general public.

212. Air Weather Service Technical Library/FL 4414
Scott AFB, IL 62225-5438 (618) 256-2625/4044; WATS (800) 638-2625
Lib Type Special.
Spec Subs Astrogeophysics; geophysics; meteorology. *Spec Collecs* Meteorology (Climatic Data Summaries); Meteorology MESS, DTIC, TFRN's & AWS Historic Collection.
Info Ret Servs DIALOG; BRS; SDC; DTIC. *Shared Catalog Nets* OCLC.

213. Alaskan Air Command, Library Service Center/FL 5001
Elmendorf AFB, AK 99506 (907) 752-5230; AUTOVON (317) 552-5230
Admin Laurel Langenwalter.
Lib Type General.

214. Alert Facility Base Level Library
Box 26, Grand Forks AFB, ND 58205 (701) 594-6681
Lib Type Special.

215. Altus AFB, Base Library/FL 4419
443ABGp/SSL, Altus AFB, OK 73523-5985 (405) 482-8670; AUTOVON 866-6302
Admin Bruce Gaver. *Ref Lib* Bessie Hoffman. *ILL* Connie Grinston. *Acq Lib* Virginia Carlucci.
Lib Type General.
Circ Servs Avail To other Federal libraries; to other libraries; restricted to DoD employees.
Ref Servs Avail To other Federal libraries; to other libraries; restricted to DoD employees.

216. Andrews AFB Base Library/FL 4425
Bldg 1642, Andrews AFB, DC 20331-5984 (301) 981-6454
Admin Linn Landis. *ILL* Linda Edwards (Acq).
Lib Type General.
Circ Servs Avail Restricted to military personnel, dependents, & base DoD employees.
Ref Servs Avail Restricted to military personnel, dependents, & base DoD employees.

217. Armament Division Technical Library/FL 2825
Elgin AFB, FL 32542-5438 (904) 882-3212; AUTOVON 872-3212
Admin June C Stercho. *Ref Lib* Mary A Murphy (Acq). *ILL* Betty Downs.
Lib Type Engineering & Science.
Spec Subs Chemistry; physics; aeronautics; mathematics; computer science; management; environics.
Info Ret Servs DIALOG. *Shared Catalog Nets* OCLC. *Coop Lib Nets* FEDLINK. *Elec Mail Nets* DTIC.
Circ Servs Avail To other Federal libraries; to other libraries; not open to the general public.
Ref Servs Avail To other Federal libraries; to other libraries; not open to the general public.

218. Arnold Engineering Development Center Technical Library/FL 2804
Mail Stop 100, Arnold Air Force Station, TN 37389-9998 (615) 454-5431, Tech 454-5462; AUTOVON 340-5431, Tech 340-5462
Admin Gay D Goethert. *ILL* Della Burch (Open Lit)(ILL); Effie Boyd (Tech)(ILL).
Lib Type Engineering & Science.
Spec Subs Aerodynamics; aerospace sciences; aircraft propulsion; astronomy; chemistry; mathematics; optics; physics; pollution. *Spec Collecs* NACA & NASA Reports (complete sets); NACA technical reports after 800; NACA wartime reports (all but 40).
Info Ret Servs DIALOG; WILSONLINE. *Shared Catalog Nets* OCLC. *Coop Lib Nets* Southeastern Library Network (SOLINET).
Circ Servs Avail To other Federal libraries; to other libraries; not open to the general public.
Ref Servs Avail To other Federal libraries; not open to the general public.

219. Barksdale AFB, Base Library/FL 4608
2 CSG/SSL, Barksdale AFB, Shreveport, LA 71110-5000 (318) 456-4101; AUTOVON 781-4182
Admin Julienne L Wood. *ILL* Joanna Hansen.
Lib Type General.
Spec Subs Louisiana. *Spec Collecs* Project Warrior.
Circ Servs Avail To other Federal libraries; to other libraries; restricted to base community & other AF libraries.
Ref Servs Avail To other Federal libraries; to other libraries; restricted to base community & other AF libraries.

220. Beale AFB, Base Library/FL 4686
Bldg 2439, Beale AFB, CA 95903-5000 (916) 634-3706; AUTOVON 368-2706
Admin Sylvia J Sefcik.
Lib Type General.
Spec Subs Aeronautics & military science. *Spec Collecs* California.
Circ Servs Avail To other Federal libraries; restricted to base personnel.
Ref Servs Avail To other Federal libraries; restricted to base personnel.

221. Bergstrom AFB, Base Library/FL 4857
Bergstrom AFB, TX 78743 (512) 479-3740; AUTOVON 685-3739
Admin Louise St John. *ILL* Hope Garcia. *Acq Lib* Efigenia Valdez.
Lib Type General.
Spec Subs Aeronautics; AF history; electronics; foreign affairs; women; race relations. *Spec Collecs* Video movies; video cassettes on management; training files for AF MWR programs & speed reading.
Circ Servs Avail To other libraries; restricted to military & civilian personnel.
Ref Servs Avail To other libraries; not open to the general public; restricted to use in library.

222. Blytheville AFB, Base Library/FL 4634
Blytheville AFB, AR 72317-5225 (501) 762-7286; AUTOVON 634-7286
Admin Bethry J Becker. *ILL* Martha Best.
Lib Type General.
Circ Servs Avail Not open to the general public.
Ref Servs Avail Not open to the general public.

223. Bolling AFB Base Library/FL 7058
HQ USAF/CHOR, Bldg 5681, Bolling AFB, Washington, DC 20332 (202) 767-5088; AUTOVON 297-5088
Admin Sue Cober.
Lib Type General.

224. Bolling AFB, Base Library/FL 4400
Bldg 409, Bolling AFB, DC 20332-5000 (202) 767-5578/4251; TTY 767-6067; AUTOVON 297-5578
Admin Gloria G P Guffey. *Ref Lib* Pearline Seals (ILL). *Acq Lib* Eileen G Mayhem.
Lib Type General.
Spec Subs Aeronautics; military history; Black history. *Spec Collecs* Large print books; cassettes for the blind.
Circ Servs Avail To other Federal libraries; to other libraries; restricted to military & dependents.
Ref Servs Avail To other Federal libraries; to other libraries; restricted to military & dependents.

225. Bolling AFB Office of the Judge Advocate General Library
Bldg 5683, HQ USAF/JAESP, Washington, DC 20332-6128 (202) 767-1520; AUTOVON 297-1520
Admin J Conley Meredith. *Ref Lib* William J Zschunke (ILL). *Acq Lib* Linda G Detz.
Lib Type Law.
Shared Catalog Nets JURIS. *Elec Mail Nets* d.
Ref Servs Avail To other Federal libraries; to other libraries; to the general public.

226. Brooks AFB, Base Library/FL 2857
6570 ABG/SSL, Brooks AFB, TX 78235 (512) 536-2205/2634; AUTOVON 240-2205/2634
Admin Marion D Fontish. *ILL* Alice Serafin. *Acq Lib* Joan Pattison.
Lib Type General.
Circ Servs Avail To other Federal libraries; to other libraries; not open to the general public; restricted to active duty & retired military & dependents & civilians employed on base.
Ref Servs Avail To other Federal libraries; to other libraries; to the general public.

227. I G Brown Professional Military Education Center Library/FL 6599
Det 10, ANGSC, Box 9110, Alcoa, TN 37701 (615) 970-3077 ext 290; AUTOVON 599-8293
Admin Paul Goldman (Librarian); Carol Maples (Asst).
Lib Type Academic.

228. Cannon AFB, Base Library/FL 4855
Cannon AFB, NM 88103-5000 (505) 784-3311 ext 2786; AUTOVON 681-2786
Admin Carol J Davidson.
Lib Type General.
Circ Servs Avail Restricted to DoD personnel & retirees.

Ref Servs Avail To other libraries; restricted to DoD personnel & retirees.

229. Carswell AFB Base Library/FL 4689
Carswell AFB, TX 76127 (817) 735-5230
Lib Type General.
Spec Subs Aeronautics.

230. Castle AFB, Baker Library/FL 4672
Castle AFB, CA 95342 (209) 726-2630; AUTOVON 347-2630
Admin Beatrice Alger.
Lib Type General.
Spec Subs Air Force history; aeronautics; WWII; business; public administration.
Coop Lib Nets 49-99 Library Cooperative Services.
Circ Servs Avail To other libraries; not open to the general public; restricted to military, dependents, retirees, & DoD employees.
Ref Servs Avail To other Federal libraries; to other libraries; to the general public.

231. Chanute AFB, Base Library/FL 3018
Chanute AFB, IL 61868 (217) 495-3193; AUTOVON 862-3193
Admin James Lee Clark. *ILL* Sheila Roberts.
Lib Type General.
Spec Subs Air Force history; business & management; aeronautics.
Coop Lib Nets Lincoln Trails Library System Online CLSI.
Circ Servs Avail To other libraries; restricted to military & DoD civilian personnel.
Ref Servs Avail To other Federal libraries; to other libraries; to the general public.

232. Charleston AFB, Base Library/FL 4418
437 ABG/SSL, Charleston AFB, SC 29404-5225 (803) 554-3134; AUTOVON 583-3164
Admin William Darcy. *Ref Lib* Cynthia Marsh (ILL). *Acq Lib* Annie Davis.
Lib Type General.
Circ Servs Avail To other libraries; not open to the general public; restricted to valid DoD ID.
Ref Servs Avail To other Federal libraries; to other libraries; not open to the general public; restricted to valid DoD ID.

233. Columbus AFB, Base Library/FL 3022
Columbus AFB, MS 39701-5000 (601) 434-7762/7858; AUTOVON 742-7762/7858
Admin Gloria Zumberge. *ILL* Linda Foster.
Lib Type General.
Spec Subs Military history; aircraft & flying.
Circ Servs Avail Restricted to base personnel & dependents.
Ref Servs Avail To the general public.

234. Davis-Monthan AFB, Base Library/FL 4877
Davis-Monthan AFB, AZ 85707 (602) 748-4381
Lib Type General.

235. Defense Institute of Security Assistance Management Library/FL 2301
Bldg 125, Area B, Wright-Patterson AFB, OH 45433 (513) 255-5567
Lib Type Special.
Spec Subs Foreign military sales; intercultural studies; military & security assistance; political science; area studies; management of security assistance.
Info Ret Servs DIALOG. *Shared Catalog Nets* OCLC. *Coop Lib Nets* FEDLINK.

236. Dover AFB, Base Library/FL 4497
Bldg 443, 436 ABG/SSL, Dover AFB, DE 19902-5225 (302) 678-6246; AUTOVON 455-6246/7356
Admin Harry Brooks.
Lib Type General.
Spec Subs Military aviation. *Spec Collecs* Computer software swap.
Shared Catalog Nets USAF Libraries (MARCIVE). *Coop Lib Nets* Kent Lib Network (KLN).
Circ Servs Avail To other Federal libraries; to other libraries; restricted to US government ID holders.

Ref Servs Avail To other Federal libraries; to other libraries; not open to the general public.

237. Dyess AFB, Base Library/FL 4661
Dyess AFB, TX 79607-5000 (915) 696-2618; AUTOVON 461-5002
ILL Lesa Dunn. *Acq Lib* Connie Leetsch.
Lib Type General.
Spec Collecs Texas.
Coop Lib Nets Texas St Lib Communications Network (TSLCN).
Circ Servs Avail To other Federal libraries; to other libraries; not open to the general public; restricted to base personnel & area retirees.
Ref Servs Avail To other Federal libraries; to other libraries; not open to the general public; restricted to base personnel & area retirees.

238. Eastern Space & Missile Center Technical Library/FL 2828
ESMC/PAECL, Patrick AFB, FL 32925 (305) 494-6638; AUTOVON 854-6638
Admin Robert L Allen. *Ref Lib* Judith S Sauder. *ILL* M Kathleen Burgess. *Acq Lib* Dottie Pantones.
Lib Type Special.
Spec Subs Engineering; science; business. *Spec Collecs* Eastern Space & Missile Center operations & maintenance manuals for range instrumentation, data handling & communications.
Info Ret Servs DIALOG. *Shared Catalog Nets* OCLC.
Circ Servs Avail To other libraries; not open to the general public; restricted to ILL.
Ref Servs Avail Not open to the general public; restricted to military & civilian personnel.

239. Edwards AFB, Base Library/FL 2805
6510 ABG/SSL, Stop 115, Edwards AFB, CA 93523-5000 (805) 277-2375; AUTOVON 350-4881
Admin O M Moyer. *ILL* Elizabeth Arce.
Lib Type General.
Shared Catalog Nets OCLC; FEDLINK.
Circ Servs Avail To other Federal libraries; to other libraries; not open to the general public.
Ref Servs Avail To other Federal libraries; to other libraries; to the general public.

240. Eielson AFB, Base Library/FL 5004
343 CSG/SSL, Eielson AFB, AK 99702-5000 (907) 377-3174
Lib Type General.
Spec Subs Arctic Collection; Gold Prospecting Collection; Project Warrior.
Circ Servs Avail Restricted to active & retired military & base civilians.
Ref Servs Avail Restricted to active & retired military & base civilians.

241. Electronic Security Command, General Library/FL 7046
6923 SS/SSL, San Antonio, TX 78243-5000 (512) 925-2617; AUTOVON 945-2617
Admin Dale T Ogden.
Lib Type General.
Spec Subs Electronics; electronic warfare.
Circ Servs Avail To other Federal libraries; to other libraries; restricted to military ID card holders.
Ref Servs Avail To other Federal libraries; to other libraries; restricted to military ID card holders.

242. Elgin AFB, Base Library/FL 2823/SSL
Elgin AFB, FL 32542-5100 (904) 882-5088/5016/2460; AUTOVON 872-5088
Admin F P Morgan. *Ref Lib* Carole B Steele (Acq). *ILL* Betty J Powell.
Lib Type General.
Spec Subs Military history; business & public administration.
Info Ret Servs DIALOG. *Shared Catalog Nets* OCLC.
Circ Servs Avail To other Federal libraries; to other libraries; not open to the general public.

Ref Servs Avail To other Federal libraries; not open to the general public.

243. Ellsworth AFB, Base Library/FL 4690
Ellsworth AFB, SD 57706-5000 (605) 399-7965
Lib Type General.
Spec Subs Military science; aeronautical sciences; astronautics; electronics.
Circ Servs Avail Not open to the general public.
Ref Servs Avail Not open to the general public.

244. Elmendorf AFB, Base Library
Bldg 6-92D, Elmendorf AFB, AK 99506 (907) 552-3787; FTS 552-3787; AUTOVON 552-2700
Admin Laurel B Langenwalter. *Ref Lib* Wanda Schnatterly. *ILL* Patricia Richards.
Lib Type General.
Spec Subs Military history; Project Warrior. *Spec Collecs* Alaskana.
Coop Lib Nets Alaska Lib Network (ALN).
Circ Servs Avail To other Federal libraries; to other libraries; not open to the general public; restricted to military & dependents.
Ref Servs Avail To other Federal libraries; to other libraries; not open to the general public; restricted to military & dependents.

245. Elmendorf AFB, Medical/Patients' Library
USAF Regional Hospital Elmendorf/SGQAL, Elmendorf AFB, AK 99506-5300 (907) 552-5328 552-3383; AUTOVON 552-5328
Admin Jeraldine J van den Top. *Ref Lib* Betty J Helms (ILL, Acq).
Lib Type Health & Medicine; Hospital (Patients).
Spec Subs Consumer health education.
Info Ret Servs National Library of Medicine Medlars. *Shared Catalog Nets* WLN, Recon member from Alaska. *Coop Lib Nets* Alaska Library Network (ALN); NLM (Region 6).
Circ Servs Avail To other Federal libraries; to other libraries; restricted to hospital personnel, military & dependents.
Ref Servs Avail To other Federal libraries; to other libraries; to the general public.

246. England AFB, Base Library/FL 4805
Bldg 1213, England AFB, LA 71311 (318) 448-5621
Lib Type General.
Ref Servs Avail Not open to the general public; restricted to base personnel.

247. Fairchild AFB, Base Library/FL 4620
Fairchild AFB, WA 99001-5000 (509) 247-5556/5228; AUTOVON 352-5556/5228
Admin Nancy M Bemis. *ILL* Sharon Brown.
Lib Type General.
Spec Subs Military history; strategy; foreign relations; aviation.
Circ Servs Avail To other libraries; restricted to military & civilian personnel & dependents.
Ref Servs Avail To other libraries; restricted to military & civilian personnel & dependents.

248. Foreign Technology Division Technical Library/FL 2830
Bldg 856, Area A, Wright-Patterson AFB, OH 45433 (513) 257-3531
Lib Type Special.

249. George AFB, Base Library/FL 4812
George AFB, CA 92394-5000 (619) 269-3228; AUTOVON 353-3228
Admin Celia Pamintuan. *ILL* Priscilla McGill.
Lib Type General.
Spec Collecs Social science; business & management; education; military science & history.
Coop Lib Nets San Bernardino, Inyo, Riverside Counties United Lib Services (SIRCULS).
Circ Servs Avail To other Federal libraries; to other libraries; not open to the general public.
Ref Servs Avail To other Federal libraries; to other libraries; to the general public.

250. Goodfellow AFB, Base Library/FL 3030
3480 ABG/SSL, Goodfellow AFB, TX 76908-5000 (915) 653-3231 ext 2412; AUTOVON 477-3045
Admin Elaine C Penner. *ILL* Judy L Rowey. *Acq Lib* John L Mullen.
Lib Type General.
Spec Subs Military arts & sciences; cryptology; foreign languages.
Circ Servs Avail To other Federal libraries; restricted to military & civilian personnel & dependents.
Ref Servs Avail To other Federal libraries; to other libraries; to the general public.

251. Grand Forks AFB, Base Library/FL 4659
321 CGS/SSL, Grand Forks AFB, ND 58205-5000 (701) 594-6725/3523; AUTOVON 362-6725/3523
Admin Bruce B Brown.
Lib Type General.
Circ Servs Avail To other Federal libraries; to other libraries; restricted to DoD military & civilian personnel & dependents.
Ref Servs Avail To other Federal libraries; to other libraries; restricted to DoD military & civilian personnel & dependents.

252. David Grant USAF Medical Center, Medical Library/SGEL
Travis AFB, CA 94535-5300 (707) 438-5254
Admin V Kay Hafner. *ILL* Elizabeth Hosler.
Lib Type Health & Medicine.
Spec Subs Medicine; nursing; hospital administration.
Info Ret Servs BRS; MEDLINE. *Shared Catalog Nets* OCLC. *Coop Lib Nets* MML; Northern California & Nevada Medical Lib Group (NCNMLG). *Elec Mail Nets* CLASS.
Circ Servs Avail Not open to the general public.
Ref Servs Avail Not open to the general public.

253. Griffiss AFB, Base Library/FL 4616
Griffiss AFB, NY 13441-5000 (315) 330-7607; AUTOVON 587-7030
Admin Mary Klingelhoeffer. *ILL* Deborah Melnick.
Lib Type General.
Spec Subs Electronics; aircraft; military history.
Coop Lib Nets Central New York Libraries Resources Council (CENTRO).
Circ Servs Avail To other Federal libraries; to other libraries; restricted to base personnel.
Ref Servs Avail To other Federal libraries; to other libraries; to the general public.

254. Grissom AFB, Base Library/FL 4654
Bldg 575, 305 CSG/SSL, Grissom AFB, IN 46971-5000 (317) 689-2056; AUTOVON 928-2056
Lib Type General.
Spec Subs Aircraft; avionics; business/management.
Coop Lib Nets Walbash Valley Area Lib Services Authority.
Circ Servs Avail To the general public.
Ref Servs Avail To the general public.

255. Malcolm Grow Medical Center Library
Box 3097, Andrews AFB, Washington, DC 20331 (301) 981-2354
Lib Type Health & Medicine.
Info Ret Servs MEDLINE. *Shared Catalog Nets* OCLC.
Circ Servs Avail Not open to the general public; restricted to staff.
Ref Servs Avail Not open to the general public; restricted to researchers by appointment.

256. Gunter AFB, Base Library/FL 3370
Bldg 850, Gunter AFB, AL 36114-5000 (205) 279-3179; 279-4732
Lib Type General.
Spec Collecs Career & occupational study guides; foreign language records & tapes.
Circ Servs Avail Restricted to base personnel, DoD civilians on base, & retired military.
Ref Servs Avail Restricted to base personnel, DoD civilians on base, & retired military.

257. Gunter AFB, Technical Library/FL 3100
AFDSDC/DAPL, Gunter AFB, AL 36114 (205) 279-4749; AUTO-
VON 921-4749
Admin Shirley Martin.
Lib Type General.

258. Hanscom AFB, Base Library/FL 2835
Hanscom AFB, MA 01731-5000 (617) 377-2177; AUTOVON 478-
2177
Admin Gerald T Griffin. *Ref Lib* Susan L Benzer (ILL).
Lib Type General.
Spec Subs Military aviation. *Spec Collecs* Air War College; Project
Warrior.
Shared Catalog Nets OCLC. *Coop Lib Nets* FEDLINK.
Circ Servs Avail Restricted to base personnel.
Ref Servs Avail To other Federal libraries; to other libraries; to the
general public.

259. HQ Air Force Systems Command Library Division
HQ AFSC/MPSL, Andrews AFB, DC 20334-5000 (301) 981-2598;
AUTOVON 858-2598
Admin Frances Quinn Deel.
Lib Type Special.
Spec Subs This is the administrative office responsible for devel-
oping & directing the Air Force Systems Command (AFSC)
library program & supervising the HQ AFSC Technical In-
formation Center.

260. HQ Tactical Air Command/FL 4899
HQ TAC/DPSRL, Langley AFB, VA 23669 (804) 764-3584;
AUTOVON 574-2466
Admin Alice R Roy.
Lib Type Special.
Spec Subs This is the administrative headquarters for Tactical Air
Command libraries.

261. Hickam AFB, Base Library/FL 5260
15th Air Base Wing (SSL), Hickam AFB, HI 96853-5000
(808) 449-6285/2831; AUTOVON 430-0111
Admin Stella K Watanabe. *ILL* Louise Clark.
Lib Type General.
Spec Subs World War II.
Info Ret Servs DIALOG. *Shared Catalog Nets* OCLC. *Coop Lib
Nets* PACAT.
Circ Servs Avail To other Federal libraries; not open to the general
public.
Ref Servs Avail To other Federal libraries; not open to the general
public.

262. Hickam AFB, Library Service Center/FL 5239
Pacific Air Forces, Hickam AFB, HI 96853 (808) 449-2209/2110;
AUTOVON (315) 449-2209/2110
Admin Christian Cupp (Librarian); Deborah A Thompson (Asst).
Lib Type General.

263. Hill AFB, Gerrity Memorial Library/FL 2020
Bldg 440, Hill AFB, UT 84056 (801) 777-2533; AUTOVON 458-
2533
Admin Pamela Duett.
Lib Type General.
Circ Servs Avail Restricted to military & civilian DoD personnel
& dependents.
Ref Servs Avail Restricted to military & civilian DoD personnel &
dependents.

264. Holloman AFB, Base Library/FL 4801
Holloman AFB, NM 88330 (505) 479-6511 ext 3501
Lib Type General.
Spec Subs Aerospace; business & management; foreign relations;
military; Southwest.
Coop Lib Nets New Mexico Information Systems.

265. Holloman AFB, Hospital Library/AFM 4801
Bldg 15, Holloman AFB, NM 88330 (505) 479-6511 ext 3777
Lib Type Health & Medicine.

266. Homestead AFB, Base Library/FL 4829
Homestead AFB, FL 33039-5000 (305) 257-8184; AUTOVON
791-8184/8185
Admin Bettylou Rosen.
Lib Type General.
Spec Collecs Florida; Project Warrior.
Info Ret Servs DIALOG. *Coop Lib Nets* FEDLINK.
Circ Servs Avail To other Federal libraries; to other libraries;
restricted to military & DoD civilian personnel & dependents.
Ref Servs Avail To other Federal libraries; to other libraries; re-
stricted to military & DoD civilian personnel & dependents.

267. Hurlburt AFB, Base Library/FL 4417
834 CSG/SSL, Hurlburt Field, FL 32544-5000 (904) 884-6947/
7143; AUTOVON 872-6947/7143
Admin Jimmie S Norton. *ILL* Myra E Carpenter.
Lib Type General.
Circ Servs Avail To other Federal libraries; to other libraries;
restricted to military & civilian personnel & dependents.
Ref Servs Avail To other Federal libraries; to other libraries; restricted to military & civilian personnel & dependents.

268. Seymour Johnson AFB, Base Library/FL 4809
Seymour Johnson AFB, NC 27531-5725 (919) 736-5707; AUTO-
VON 488-5707/5739
Admin Blanchella K L Casey. *ILL* Judith G King. *Acq
Lib* MaryAnn P Brewer.
Lib Type General.
Spec Collecs Project Warrior (military).
Coop Lib Nets Wayne Co Library Assoc.
Circ Servs Avail To other Federal libraries; to other libraries;
restricted to military & DoD civilian personnel & dependents.
Ref Servs Avail To other Federal libraries; to other libraries; not
open to the general public; restricted to telephone reference by
the general public.

269. Keesler AFB, Academic Library/FL 3011
Bldg 2818, Rm 108, Keesler AFB, MS 39534-5000 (601) 377-
4295; AUTOVON 868-4295
Admin Verna M Westerburg.
Lib Type Academic.
Spec Subs Communications; telecommunications; electronics; com-
puters.
Circ Servs Avail To other Federal libraries; to other libraries; not
open to the general public; restricted to base personnel & DoD
civilians.
Ref Servs Avail To other Federal libraries; to other libraries; to the
general public.

270. Keesler AFB, Medical Library/SGAL
USAF Medical Center, Keesler AFB, MS 39534-5300 (601) 377-
6249/6042; AUTOVON 868-6249/6042
Admin Sherry N Nave. *ILL* Phyllis Harper.
Lib Type Health & Medicine.
Spec Subs Medicine, nursing, & allied health.
Info Ret Servs DIALOG; NLM. *Coop Lib Nets* Gulf Coast
Biomedical Library Consortium; Mississippi Biomedical Library
Consortium; Southeastern Regional Medical Library Program.
Circ Servs Avail To other Federal libraries; to other libraries; not
open to the general public.
Ref Servs Avail To other Federal libraries; to other libraries; to the
general public.

271. Kelly AFB, Base Library/FL 2051
Bldg 171, SA-ALC/MMEDO, Kelly AFB, TX 78241 (512) 925-
5636/5759; AUTOVON 945-5636/5759
Admin Rose Moorhouse.
Lib Type General.

272. Kelly AFB, Base Library/FL 2050
Bldg 1650, Kelly AFB, TX 78241-5000 (512) 925-3214/4116;
AUTOVON 945-3214/4116
Admin Elizabeth Louise Brown. *ILL* Marie Gonzales. *Acq
Lib* Mary Lavender.
Lib Type General.

Spec Subs Military arts & sciences. *Spec Collecs* Texana; Project Warrior; Hispanic culture; auto repair manuals; test tutor books.
Circ Servs Avail To other Federal libraries; to other libraries; restricted to military & civilian personnel & dependents.
Ref Servs Avail To other Federal libraries; to other libraries; restricted to military & civilian personnel & dependents.

273. Kirtland AFB, Base Library/FL 4469
Kirtland AFB, NM 87117-5000 (505) 844-0795; AUTOVON 822-0795/7320
Admin Martha K Sumpter. *Ref Lib* Robert C Mathews (ILL, Acq).
Lib Type General.
Spec Subs Military arts & sciences; educational materials. *Spec Collecs* Southwestern books. *In-house Files* Base brochures.
Circ Servs Avail To other Federal libraries; to other libraries; not open to the general public.
Ref Servs Avail To other Federal libraries; to other libraries; to the general public.

274. Kirtland AFB, Medical Library/SGAL
USAF Hospital Kirtland, Kirtland AFB, NM 87111-5300 (505) 844-1086; AUTOVON 844-1086
Admin Alice T Lee.
Lib Type Health & Medicine.
Spec Subs Surgery; obstetrics & gynecology; ophthalmology; pediatrics; orthopedics. *Spec Collecs* Patient education: audio-visual & software. *In-house Files* Monographs & journals.
Info Ret Servs Medlars. *Coop Lib Nets* New Mexico Consortium of Biomedical Libraries.
Circ Servs Avail Not open to the general public; restricted to AF personnel & NM consortium members.
Ref Servs Avail To other libraries; not open to the general public; restricted to AF personnel & NM consortium members.

275. Lackland AFB, Base Library/FL 3047
Bldg 6114, Lackland AFB, TX 78236-5000 (512) 671-4316; AUTOVON 473-3610
Admin Iris Varela. *Ref Lib* Katherine S Black. *ILL* Kathy Valdez.
Lib Type General.
Circ Servs Avail To other libraries; restricted to military & civilian personnel.
Ref Servs Avail To other libraries; to the general public.

276. Lackland AFB, Wilford Hall Medical Center Library/FL 2879
Lackland AFB, TX 78236-5300 (512) 670-7204
Lib Type General.
Spec Subs Clinical medicine; dentistry.
Info Ret Servs MEDLINE. *Shared Catalog Nets* OCLC.
Circ Servs Avail Not open to the general public.
Ref Servs Avail Not open to the general public.

277. Langley AFB, Base Library/FL 4800
Langley AFB, VA 23665-5725 (804) 764-2906
Lib Type General.
Spec Subs Aeronautics; foreign affairs; military history; SE Asia.
Info Ret Servs DIALOG. *Shared Catalog Nets* OCLC.

278. Laughlin AFB, Base Library/FL 3099
Bldg 257, Laughlin AFB, TX 78840-5000 (512) 298-5119; AUTOVON 732-5119
Admin Carlton Moyers.
Lib Type General.
Coop Lib Nets Texas State Library Communications Network (TSLCN).
Circ Servs Avail To other Federal libraries; not open to the general public.
Ref Servs Avail To other Federal libraries; not open to the general public.

279. Laughlin AFB Hospital, Medical Library
Laughlin AFB, TX 78843 (512) 298-2317
Lib Type Health & Medicine.

280. Little Rock AFB, Base Library/FL 4460
Little Rock AFB, AR 72099-5000 (501) 988-6979; AUTOVON 731-6979
Admin Lee Missavage.
Lib Type General.
Spec Subs Military history & technology.
Circ Servs Avail To other libraries; not open to the general public.
Ref Servs Avail To other libraries; not open to the general public.

281. Loring AFB, Base Library/FL 4678
Loring AFB, ME 04751-5000 (207) 999-2416; AUTOVON 920-2416
Admin Mary E Bushey.
Lib Type General.
Spec Subs Military history; aeronautics; space exploration. *Spec Collecs* Maine & New England area history & travel.
Coop Lib Nets Maine Library Assoc; New England Library Assoc.
Circ Servs Avail Restricted to military personnel & dependents.
Ref Servs Avail Restricted to military personnel & dependents.

282. Lowry AFB, Base Library/FL 3059
Lowry AFB, CO 80230-5000 (303) 370-3093/3836; AUTOVON 936-3093/3836
Admin Helen McClaughry. *Ref Lib* Eileen Hogan. *ILL* Joan Roush.
Lib Type General.
Spec Subs Electronics; military; aeronautics; photography; intelligence; space; education. *Spec Collecs* Colorado; Project Warrior; Air War College; CLEP & civil service test books. *In-house Files* Base brochure files.
Info Ret Servs DIALOG; BRS; SDC. *Coop Lib Nets* Central Colorado Library System.
Circ Servs Avail To other Federal libraries; to other libraries; restricted to military & civilian base personnel & dependents.
Ref Servs Avail To other Federal libraries; to other libraries; to the general public.

283. Luke AFB, Base Library/FL 4887
Luke AFB, AZ 85309-5725 (602) 935-6301/7191; AUTOVON 853-6301
Admin Katheryn Kessler. *Ref Lib* Dulcie Geske. *ILL* Francis Lukasik. *Acq Lib* Roberta Kwiatkowski.
Lib Type General.
Spec Subs AF & military history; foreign relations. *Spec Collecs* Project Warrior; Arizona.
Info Ret Servs DIALOG. *Coop Lib Nets* FEDLINK.
Circ Servs Avail To other Federal libraries; to other libraries; restricted to military & DoD civilian personnel & dependents.
Ref Servs Avail To other Federal libraries; to other libraries; restricted to military & DoD civilian personnel & dependents.

284. MacDill AFB, Base Library/FL 4814
MacDill AFB, FL 33608-5000 (813) 830-2349; 830-3607; AUTOVON 968-2349; 968-3607
Admin Jean Jacob Phillips. *ILL* Susan Morgan.
Lib Type General.
Spec Subs Southwest Asia (Middle East); Central America; military leadership; military strategy & history.
Info Ret Servs DIALOG; NEXIS. *Shared Catalog Nets* OCLC. *Coop Lib Nets* FEDLINK; Tampa Bay Library Consortium (TBLC).
Circ Servs Avail To other Federal libraries; to other libraries; not open to the general public; restricted to base personnel, DoD civilians on base, & retired military.
Ref Servs Avail To other Federal libraries; to other libraries; not open to the general public; restricted to base personnel, DoD civilians on base, & on-base students, including PME.

285. MacDill AFB, Office of the Staff Judge Advocate, HQ, US Central Command, Law Library
MacDill AFB, FL 33608-7001 (813) 830-6422; AUTOVON 968-6422
Lib Type Law.
Circ Servs Avail Not open to the general public.
Ref Servs Avail Not open to the general public.

286. Malmstrom AFB, Base Library/FL 4626
Malmstrom AFB, MT 59402-5000 (406) 731-2748; AUTOVON 632-2748
Admin David English.
Lib Type General.
Spec Collecs College level exam program.
Circ Servs Avail To other Federal libraries; to other libraries; restricted to AF affiliation.
Ref Servs Avail To other Federal libraries; to other libraries; restricted to AF affiliation.

287. March AFB, Base Library/FL 4664
Bldg 938, March AFB, CA 92518-5000 (714) 655-2203
Lib Type General.
Spec Subs Aeronautics; art & architecture; business & management; history; scientific-technical; sociology & behavioral science. *Spec Collecs* Air War College Collection; Caldeco H. Newbery Collection; International Relations Collection; Embry Riddle Aeronautical Univ; Southern IL Univ-Occupational Education; Aviation Management.
Coop Lib Nets San Bernadino, Inyo, Riverside Counties United Library Services.
Circ Servs Avail Not open to the general public.
Ref Servs Avail Not open to the general public.

288. Mather AFB, Base Library/FL 3067
Bldg 1705, Mather AFB, CA 95655-5000 (916) 364-4759; AUTO-VON 828-4759
Admin Mary Kay Briggs. *ILL* Patti Kirsch.
Lib Type General.
Spec Subs Military history; foreign relations; management.
Circ Servs Avail To other Federal libraries; not open to the general public.
Ref Servs Avail To other Federal libraries; to other libraries; not open to the general public.

289. Maxwell AFB, Base Library/FL 3300
Bldg 28, Maxwell AFB, AL 36112-5000 (205) 293-6484; AUTO-VON 875-6484
Admin Rebecca Ware Howze.
Lib Type General.
Coop Lib Nets HQ/AF AUL.
Circ Servs Avail Not open to the general public.
Ref Servs Avail Not open to the general public.

290. Maxwell AFB, USAF Regional Hospital
Professional Medical Library, Maxwell AFB, AL 36112-5304 (205) 293-6206; AUTOVON 875-6206
Admin Patricia A Kuther.
Lib Type Health & Medicine.
Circ Servs Avail To other Federal libraries; to other libraries; not open to the general public; restricted to medical personnel.
Ref Servs Avail To other Federal libraries; to other libraries; not open to the general public; restricted to medical personnel.

291. McBride Library/FL 3010
Bldg 2222, Larcher Blvd, Keesler AFB, MS 39534-5225 (607) 377-2181; AUTOVON 868-2181/2604
Admin Elizabeth A DeCoux (Admin Lib); Jack Freedman (Tech Lib). *Ref Lib* Beth McConitas. *ILL* Alice Dubaz. *Acq Lib* Cheryl Sheehan.
Lib Type Training Center; General.
Spec Subs Warrior Wisdom, emphasis on the American way of war & personal narratives on war. *Spec Collecs* Military science; management & communications; computer science.
Info Ret Servs OCLC; DTIC. *Shared Catalog Nets* OCLC. *Coop Lib Nets* FEDLINK.
Circ Servs Avail To other Federal libraries; to other libraries; to the general public; not open to the general public; restricted to appropriate ID.
Ref Servs Avail To other Federal libraries; to other libraries; to the general public; not open to the general public; restricted to appropriate ID.

292. McClellan AFB, Base Library/FL 2040
2852 ABG/SSL, McClellan AFB, CA 95652-5000 (916) 643-4640; AUTOVON 633-4640
Admin Weldon B Champneys. *ILL* Olive E Claffey.
Lib Type General.
Spec Subs Military studies. *Spec Collecs* Project Warrior; California collection: history, description & travel. *In-house Files* File of military bases.
Circ Servs Avail To other Federal libraries; to other libraries; restricted to DoD personnel & dependents.
Ref Servs Avail To other Federal libraries; to other libraries; not open to the general public; restricted to DoD personnel & dependents.

293. McConnell AFB, Base Library/FL 4621
McConnell AFB, KS 67221-5000 (316) 681-5414; AUTOVON 743-5414
Admin Ann D Moore.
Lib Type General.
Spec Collecs Military arts & sciences; Kansas collection; Project Warrior Collection.
Coop Lib Nets South Central Kansas Library System (SCKLS).
Circ Servs Avail To other Federal libraries; to other libraries; restricted to military & personnel & dependents.
Ref Servs Avail To other Federal libraries; to other libraries; restricted to military & personnel & dependents.

294. McCord AFB, Base Library/FL 4479
Bldg 765, McCord AFB, WA 98438 (206) 984-3454; AUTOVON 976-3454
Admin Margaret Ono.
Lib Type General.

295. McGuire AFB, Base Library/FL 4484
McGuire AFB, NJ 08641 (609) 724-2079/4319; AUTOVON 440-724-2079
Admin Barbara-Ann Bomgardner.
Lib Type General.
Circ Servs Avail To other Federal libraries; to other libraries; restricted to military & civilian personnel & dependents.
Ref Servs Avail To other Federal libraries; to other libraries; not open to the general public.

296. Military Airlift Command Library/FL 4401
HQ MAC/DPSRL, Scott AFB, IL 62225-5001 (618) 256-3228
Lib Type General.
Spec Subs General military. *Spec Collecs* Professional military education collection; Project Warrior.
Shared Catalog Nets OCLC. *Coop Lib Nets* Responsible for the administration of the Military Air Command (MAC) Library System; FEDLINK.

297. Minot AFB, Base Library/FL 4528
Minot AFB, ND 58705-5000 (701) 727-3344/3406; AUTOVON 344-3344/3406
Admin William R Province.
Lib Type General.
Spec Subs Military science. *Spec Collecs* Military science; Project Warrior; Air War College test tutor. *In-house Files* DTIC documents; Defense Logistics Studies Info Exchange Documents (DLSIE).
Circ Servs Avail To other Federal libraries; to other libraries; restricted to military & civil service personnel.
Ref Servs Avail To other Federal libraries; to other libraries; restricted to military & civil service personnel.

298. Moody AFB, Base Library/FL 4830
Moody AFB, Valdosta, GA 31699-5000 (912) 333-3539
Lib Type General.
Circ Servs Avail Not open to the general public; restricted to AF military, dependents, & civilian personnel.
Ref Servs Avail Not open to the general public; restricted to AF military, dependents, & civilian personnel.

299. Mountain Home AFB, Base Library/FL 4897
Mountain Home AFB, ID 83648-5000 (208) 828-2544; AUTO-VON 828-2544/2326
Admin Nancy L Lomen.
Lib Type General.
Spec Subs Military history; foreign policy; Warrior materials. *Spec Collecs* Idaho history; base history.
Shared Catalog Nets OCLC. *Coop Lib Nets* WLN.
Circ Servs Avail Restricted to military & civilian personnel & dependents.
Ref Servs Avail To the general public use in library.

300. Myrtle Beach AFB, Base Library/FL 4806
Myrtle Beach AFB, SC 29579-5000 (803) 238-7195; AUTOVON 748-7195
Admin Jean L Cady. *ILL* Pearl Flores. *Acq Lib* Patricia Willis.
Lib Type General.
Spec Subs Electronics; military leadership; military science; aviation; history of flying; history of Air Force; management; aeronautics; mathematics. *Spec Collecs* South Carolina; Project Warrior; Air War College.
Circ Servs Avail To other Federal libraries; to other libraries; restricted to military & civilian personnel & dependents & civilians taking base courses.
Ref Servs Avail To other Federal libraries; to other libraries; restricted to military & civilian personnel & dependents & civilians taking base courses.

301. Nellis AFB, Base Library/FL 4852
Nellis AFB, NV 89191-5000 (702) 643-2280; AUTOVON 682-4484
Admin Dorothy Hart. *ILL* Ann J Brush.
Lib Type General.
Spec Subs Aeronautics; business; management. *Spec Colles* Audio-visual (VHS) cassettes.
Info Ret Servs DIALOG. *Coop Lib Nets* Nevada Network.
Circ Servs Avail To other Federal libraries; to other libraries.
Ref Servs Avail To other Federal libraries; to other libraries; to the general public.

302. Norton AFB, Base Library/FL 4448
Norton AFB, CA 92409-5985 (714) 382-7119
Lib Type General.
Spec Subs Aeronautics; business & management; military.
Circ Servs Avail Not open to the general public; restricted to base personnel.
Ref Servs Avail Not open to the general public; restricted to base personnel.

303. Offutt AFB, Base Library/FL 4600
Offutt AFB, NE 68113-5000 (402) 294-2533; AUTOVON 271-2533
Admin Margaret Byrne.
Lib Type General.
Circ Servs Avail Restricted to military & civilian personnel & dependents.
Ref Servs Avail Restricted to military & civilian personnel & dependents.

304. 119 Fig Field Library
PO Box 5536, State University Station, Fargo, ND 58105-5536 (701) 237-6030
Lib Type Special.

305. Patrick AFB, Base Library/FL 2829
6550 Air Base Group/SSL, Patrick AFB, FL 32925-6625 (305) 494-6881; AUTOVON 854-6881
Admin Suzanne M Lomanno.
Lib Type General.
Spec Subs Military history.
Circ Servs Avail Restricted to military & civilian personnel & dependents.
Ref Servs Avail Restricted to military & civilian personnel & dependents.

306. Pease AFB, Base Library/FL 4623
Pease AFB, NH 03803-5000 (603) 436-3734; AUTOVON 852-3734
Admin Teresa Hathaway. *ILL* Linda Prusak.
Lib Type General.
Spec Subs Military & Air Force history.
Circ Servs Avail To other Federal libraries; to other libraries; restricted to base personnel & dependents.
Ref Servs Avail To other Federal libraries; to other libraries; to the general public.

307. Peterson AFB, Base Library/FL 2500
Stop 60, Peterson AFB, CO 80914-5000 (303) 591-7462; AUTOVON 692-7462
Admin Barbara Coleman Ref. *ILL* Diane Jacobsen. *Acq Lib* C Fern Riegle.
Lib Type General.
Spec Subs Aeronautics; astronautics; business & management. *Spec Collecs* Space law; space management.
Info Ret Servs DIALOG; Penrose Public Library. *Coop Lib Nets* Plains & Peaks Regional Library System (PPRLS).
Circ Servs Avail To other Federal libraries; to other libraries; not open to the general public.
Ref Servs Avail To other Federal libraries; to other libraries; not open to the general public.

308. Plattsburgh AFB, Base Library/FL 4615
Plattsburgh AFB, NY 12903 (518) 563-7046; AUTOVON 689-7613
Admin Edward F Ruddy.
Lib Type General.
Spec Collecs Northern New York State region.
Coop Lib Nets Clinton-Essex-Franklin Library System for ILL.
Circ Servs Avail To other libraries; restricted to base personnel.
Ref Servs Avail To other libraries; restricted to base personnel.

309. Pope AFB, Base Library/FL 4488
Pope AFB, NC 28308 (919) 394-2791; AUTOVON 486-2791
Admin Jean L Hort. *ILL* Brenda Smith. *Acq Lib* Emily Borland.
Lib Type General.
Circ Servs Avail To other Federal libraries; to other libraries; restricted to military & civilian personnel & dependents.
Ref Servs Avail To other Federal libraries; to other libraries; restricted to military & civilian personnel & dependents.

310. Randolph AFB, Base Library/FL 3000
HQ ATC/DPSOL, Randolph AFB, TX 78150 (512) 652-3410/2438; AUTOVON 487-3410/2438
Admin Duane Johnson.
Lib Type General.

311. Randolph AFB, Base Library/FL 3089
Randolph AFB, TX 78150-5000 (512) 652-2617; AUTOVON 487-2617
Admin Michael Lazor. *ILL* Ruth Francis (Acq). *Acq Lib* Mary Susan.
Lib Type General.
Coop Lib Nets Council of Research & Academic Libraries (CORAL).
Circ Servs Avail To other Federal libraries; to other libraries; restricted to base military & civilian personnel.
Ref Servs Avail To other Federal libraries; to other libraries; not open to the general public.

312. Reese AFB, Base Library/FL 3060
Reese AFB, TX 79489-5438 (806) 885-3344
Lib Type General.

313. Reese AFB, Medical Library
Reese AFB, TX 79489 (806) 885-3543
Lib Type Health & Medicine.

314. Robins AFB, Base Library/FL 2060
Robins AFB, GA 31098-5000 (912) 926-5411; AUTOVON 468-5411
Admin Carolyn M Covington. *Ref Lib* Joann Browning (ILL). *Acq Lib* Martha Scarborough.

Lib Type General.
Spec Subs Electronics; management.
Circ Servs Avail To other Federal libraries; to other libraries; to the general public.
Ref Servs Avail To other Federal libraries; to other libraries; to the general public.

315. Rome Air Development Center Technical Library/FL 2810
RADC/DOL, Griffiss AFB, NY 13441-5700 (315) 330-7607; AUTOVON 587-7607
Admin Linda R Evans. *Ref Lib* Gene Schreiner (Books/Journals); Fran Schwartz (Tech Reports). *ILL* Ann Crescenzi. *Acq Lib* Gene Schreiner (Selection); Cora Crowley (Ordering).
Lib Type Engineering & Science.
Spec Subs Electronics; communications; command & control; reliability & compatibility; information displays & processing; artificial intelligence. *Spec Collecs* IEEE periodicals.
Info Ret Servs DIALOG. *Shared Catalog Nets* OCLC. *Coop Lib Nets* Central New York Library Resources Council (CENTRO).
Circ Servs Avail Restricted to ALA ILL.
Ref Servs Avail To other Federal libraries; to other libraries; not open to the general public; restricted to identification & ordering info for RADC publications.

316. K I Sawyer AFB, Base Library/FL 4515
K I Sawyer AFB, MI 49843-5000 (906) 346-2864; AUTOVON 472-2864
Admin Margie Buchanan. *ILL* Valerie Robbins.
Lib Type General.
Spec Subs Regional Michigan; air power; aviation; military history.
Coop Lib Nets Superior Land Library Cooperative.
Circ Servs Avail To other Federal libraries; to other libraries; restricted to DoD personnel & dependents.
Ref Servs Avail To other Federal libraries; to other libraries; to the general public.

317. Scott AFB, Academic Library/FL 4499
AOS/LDT, Scott AFB, IL 62225 (618) 256-2029; AUTOVON 576-2029
Lib Type Academic.

318. Scott AFB, Base Library/FL 4407
Bldg 1940, 375 ABG/SSL, Scott AFB, IL 62225 (618) 256-5100; ILL 256-3028
Lib Type General.
Spec Subs Educational activities; recreational reading; military history.
Shared Catalog Nets OCLC. *Coop Lib Nets* Kaskasia Library System.
Ref Servs Avail Not open to the general public; restricted to military & base civilian personnel.

319. Scott AFB, Base Library/FL 3114
375 ABG/SSL, Scott AFB, IL 62225-5225 (618) 256-4437/3228; AUTOVON 576-5100
Admin Diane M Gordon. *ILL* Theresa Widman (Acq).
Lib Type General.
Shared Catalog Nets OCLC. *Coop Lib Nets* ILINET; MALNET.
Circ Servs Avail To other Federal libraries; to other libraries.
Ref Servs Avail To other Federal libraries; to other libraries.

320. Shaw AFB, Base Library/FL 4803
Shaw AFB, SC 29152 (803) 668-3084
Lib Type General.

321. Sheppard AFB, Base Library/FL 3020
Sheppard AFB, TX 76311-5000 (817) 851-2687; FTS 851-2687; AUTOVON 736-2687
Admin Linda Fryar.
Lib Type General.
Circ Servs Avail To other Federal libraries; to other libraries; not open to the general public; restricted to DoD personnel.
Ref Servs Avail To other Federal libraries; to other libraries; not open to the general public; restricted to DoD personnel.

322. Sheppard AFB Regional Hospital, Medical Library
Sheppard AFB, TX 76311-5300 (817) 851-6647
Lib Type Health & Medicine.
Spec Subs Administration; dentistry; medicine; nursing; surgery; veterinary medicine.
Coop Lib Nets South Central Regional Medical Library Program.

323. Strategic Air Command HQ Library/FL 4599
HQ SAC/DPSOL, Offutt AFB, NE 68113-5001 (402) 294-2367; AUTOVON 271-2367/2223
Admin Mary L Sauer.
Lib Type General.

324. Survival Training Reference Library/FL 3061
3636 Combat Crew Training Wing/DOTD, Fairchild AFB, WA 99011-6024 (509) 247-2597; AUTOVON 352-2597
Admin John T Milton.
Lib Type Training Center.
Spec Subs Prisoners of war; code of conduct; survival training. *Spec Collecs* Prisoners of war; code of conduct; survival training. *In-house Files* Prisoners of war; code of conduct; survival training.
Circ Servs Avail To other Federal libraries.
Ref Servs Avail To other Federal libraries.

325. Tinker AFB, Base Library/FL 2030
Bldg 5702, Tinker AFB, OK 73145 (405) 734-3083
Lib Type General.
Spec Subs Aeronautical engineering; management; recreational.

326. Tinker AFB, Medical Library
USAF Hospital Tinker, Tinker AFB, OK 73145-5300 (405) 734-8443; AUTOVON 884-8443
Admin Mary B Mills.
Lib Type Health & Medicine.
Circ Servs Avail To other Federal libraries; to other libraries; not open to the general public.
Ref Servs Avail To other Federal libraries; to other libraries; not open to the general public.

327. Travis AFB, Mitchell Memorial Library/FL 4427
60 ABG/SSL, Travis AFB, CA 94535-5000 (707) 438-5254; AUTOVON 837-5254
Admin Nina Jacobs. *ILL* Hatsu Spivey.
Lib Type General.
Shared Catalog Nets CENCARD. *Coop Lib Nets* North Bay Cooperative Library System.
Circ Servs Avail To other Federal libraries; to other libraries; not open to the general public.
Ref Servs Avail To other Federal libraries; to other libraries; not open to the general public.

328. Tyndall AFB, Base Library/FL 4819
325 CSG/SSL/45, Tyndall AFB, FL 32403-5000 (904) 283-4287; AUTOVON 970-4287
Admin Sheila Ray.
Lib Type General.
Spec Subs Military history.
Info Ret Servs DIALOG.
Circ Servs Avail To other Federal libraries; restricted to military & DoD civilian personnel & dependents.
Ref Servs Avail To other Federal libraries; to other libraries.

329. US Air Force Academy, Community Library/FL 7000
HQ USAFA/COMLIB, USAF Academy, Colorado Springs, CO 80840-5731 (303) 472-2590/4406/4749; AUTOVON 259-4665
Admin Marie L Nelson.
Lib Type General.
Coop Lib Nets Plains & Peaks Regional Library System.
Circ Servs Avail Restricted to military & DoD civilian personnel of AF Academy.
Ref Servs Avail To other Federal libraries; to other libraries; to the general public.

330. US Air Force Academy, Law Library
Fairchild Hall, USAF Academy, Colorado Springs, CO 80840-5731 (303) 472-3680; AUTOVON 259-3680
Admin H C Manson.
Lib Type Law.
Circ Servs Avail Not open to the general public; restricted to cadets & faculty.
Ref Servs Avail To other Federal libraries; not open to the general public.

331. US Air Force Academy Library/FL 7000
DFSEL, Colorado Springs, CO 80840-5701 (303) 472-2590; AUTOVON 259-2590
Admin Reiner H Schaeffer. *Ref Lib* Betsy C Kysely. *ILL* Sharon Johnson. *Acq Lib* Mary Ellen Haug.
Lib Type Academic.
Spec Subs Aeronautics & aeronautics history; military & military history. *Spec Collecs* US Air Force Academy Archives; Col Richard Gimbel Aeronautics History Collection.
Lib Deposit Designation GPO Depository Library.
Info Ret Servs DIALOG; BRS; SDC; OCLC. *Shared Catalog Nets* OCLC. *Coop Lib Nets* Bibliographic Center for Research (BCR); FEDLINK; Plains & Peaks Regional Library System.
Circ Servs Avail Not open to the general public; restricted to ILL.
Ref Servs Avail To other Federal libraries; to other libraries; not open to the general public.

332. US Air Force Academy, Medical Library/SGAL
Colorado Springs, CO 80840-5300 (303) 472-5107
Lib Type Health & Medicine.

333. USAF Central Visual Information Library
Bldg 248, 1352 AVS/DOSL, Norton AFB, CA 92409-5996 (714) 382-2393; AUTOVON 876-2393
Admin Donald J Carroll (Chief). *ILL* Richard A McKelvey. *Acq Lib* Edward T Collins.
Lib Type Special.
Circ Servs Avail To other Federal libraries.

334. US Air Force Historical Research Center
USAFHRC, Maxwell Air Force Base, AL 36112-6678 (205) 293-5958
Lib Type Special.
Spec Subs Complete history of the US Air Force. *Spec Collecs* Histories of Air Force organizations; personal papers of Air Force personnel; historical monographs; end of tour reports; USAF individual aircraft record card collection; German Air Force (Karlsruhe Document Collection) & GAF Monograph Series; Oral history.

335. US Air Force Military Personnel Center, Directorate of Morale, Welfare, & Recreation, Library/FL 1000
Administrative HQ, AF Library Program, AFMPC/DPMSRL, Randolph AFB, TX 78150-6001 (512) 652-4589/3037
Lib Type General.
Spec Subs This system services the general, technical, & academic libraries of the US Air Force in the US & overseas.

336. US Air Force Regional Hospital, Carswell (SAC), Medical Library
SGEL, Carswell AFB, TX 76127 (817) 735-7579
Lib Type Health & Medicine.
Spec Subs Medicine; surgery.

337. USAF School of Health Care Science, Academic Library/FL 3021
Bldg 1900, Sheppard AFB, TX 76311 (817) 851-4471
Lib Type Academic.
Spec Subs Dentistry; hospital administration; medicine; nursing.

338. Vance AFB, Base Library/FL 3029
Vance AFB, OK 73705-5000 (405) 249-7368
Lib Type General.

339. Vandenberg AFB, Base Library/FL 4610
Bldg 10343-A, Vandenberg AFB, CA 93437-5000 (805) 866-9745; AUTOVON 276-6414
Admin Joseph L Buelna. *ILL* Marilyn Bess.
Lib Type General.
Spec Subs Aerospace research & development. *Spec Collecs* Central California.
Coop Lib Nets Black Gold Library Cooperative.
Circ Servs Avail To other Federal libraries; to other libraries; restricted to base personnel.
Ref Servs Avail To other Federal libraries; to other libraries; to the general public.

340. F E Warren AFB, Base Library/FL 4613
Bldg 213, F E Warren AFB, WY 82005-5225 (307) 775-3416; AUTOVON 481-3416
Admin Ellen S Tarbell. *Ref Lib* Marjorie Brand.
Lib Type General.
Spec Collecs Aeronautics.
Circ Servs Avail Restricted to base personnel.
Ref Servs Avail Restricted to base personnel.

341. Wheeler AFB, Base Library/FL 5296
15 ABS/SSL, Wheeler AFB, HI 96854 (808) 655-1867
Admin Joanne M Okuma.
Lib Type General.
Circ Servs Avail Restricted to military & DoD civilian personnel & dependents.
Ref Servs Avail To other Federal libraries; to other libraries; to the general public.

342. Whiteman AFB, Base Library/FL 4625
Whiteman AFB, MO 65305-5000 (816) 687-3089; AUTOVON 975-3089
Admin Karen Highfill. *ILL* Lucille McClure.
Lib Type General.
Spec Subs Project Warrior.
Circ Servs Avail Restricted to military libraries.
Ref Servs Avail Restricted to military libraries.

343. Williams AFB, Base Library/FL 3044
Williams AFB, AZ 85224 (602) 988-2611 ext 5279
Lib Type General.
Spec Subs American Indians; World War II.
Ref Servs Avail Restricted to base personnel.

344. Wright-Patterson AFB, Base Library/FL 2300
2750 ABW/SSL, Bldg 1044, Kittyhawk Center, Wright-Patterson AFB, OH 45433 (513) 257-4815/2302; AUTOVON 787-4815
Admin Mary E Rinas. *Ref Lib* David Ryans. *Acq Lib* Mildred I Crowe.
Lib Type General.
Spec Subs Military history; business. *Spec Collecs* Ohio; Project Warrior.
Circ Servs Avail To other Federal libraries; to other libraries; not open to the general public; restricted to DoD personnel.
Ref Servs Avail To other Federal libraries; to other libraries; not open to the general public; restricted to DoD personnel.

345. Wright-Patterson AFB, Technical Library/FL 2802
AFWAL/GLISL, Bldg 22, Area B, Wright-Patterson AFB, OH 45433 (513) 255-5511
Lib Type Special.
Spec Subs Aeronautical research; avionics; flight dynamics; propulsion; aerospace medicine; computer science; physical science & engineering. *Spec Collecs* Lahm-Chandler Collection of Aeronautica.
Info Ret Servs DIALOG; BRS; NEXIS; DTIC. *Shared Catalog Nets* OCLC. *Coop Lib Nets* FEDLINK; National Library of Medicine; SW Ohio Council for Higher Education.

346. Wright-Patterson AFB, Area A Technical Library
B266 R207 P203I, Wright Patterson AFB, OH 45433 (513) 257-2560
Admin David A Ryans. *Ref Lib* Maria Overholt. *ILL* Kathy Wilson.
Lib Type Special.

Spec Subs Business; logistics.
Circ Servs Avail Restricted to base personnel.
Ref Servs Avail Restricted to base personnel.

347. Wright-Patterson AFB, Medical Center Library
SGEL, Bldg 830A, Wright-Patterson AFB, OH 45433 (513) 257-4506
Lib Type Health & Medicine.
Spec Subs Aerospace medicine; dentistry; clinical medicine & psychology; toxicology; veterinary medicine.
Info Ret Servs BRS; MEDLINE. *Shared Catalog Nets* OCLC.
Coop Lib Nets Miami Valley Libraries.

348. Wurtsmith AFB, Base Library/FL 4585
Wurtsmith AFB, Oscoda, MI 48753-5000 (517) 739-6597; AUTOVON 623-6597
Admin Audrey Jean Marques.
Lib Type General.
Circ Servs Avail Restricted to military & dependents.
Ref Servs Avail Restricted to military & dependents.

Department of the Air Force—Overseas

349. Alconbury Base Library/FL 5643
RAF Alconbury Base, Bldg 678, APO New York, NY 09238-5000 UK AUTOVON 223-2687
Admin Patrick D Colucci, Jr. *ILL* Brenda Y Harris. *Acq Lib* Pamela N Millen.
Lib Type General.
Spec Subs Aeronautics; Project Warrior. *Spec Collecs* Project Warrior; military studies.
Circ Servs Avail Not open to the general public.
Ref Servs Avail To other Federal libraries; to other libraries; to the general public.

350. Andersen Base Library/FL 4624
43 CSG/SSL, APO San Francisco, CA 96334-5225 Guam
Admin Geraine Krizman.
Lib Type General.
Spec Subs Guam & Micronesia; Project Warrior; Air War College. *Spec Collecs* Pacific collection.
Circ Servs Avail Restricted to DoD.
Ref Servs Avail Restricted to DoD.

351. Ankara AS Library/FL 5694
USAFE APO New York, NY 09254-5225, Ankara Turkey AUTOVON 672-3290
Admin Donna Homewood.
Lib Type General.

352. Aviano AB Library/FL 5682
USAFE APO New York, NY 09293-5000 Italy AUTOVON 632-2893
Admin Esther Sims.
Lib Type General.

353. Base Library
7217th ABG/SSL, APO New York, NY 09254-5225 Turkey AUTOVON (314) 672-3290
Admin Donna V Homewood.
Lib Type General.
Spec Collecs Turkish—culture, history, & travel.
Circ Servs Avail To other Federal libraries; to other libraries; not open to the general public; restricted to Americans working in Ankara & Turks working for AF.
Ref Servs Avail To other Federal libraries; to other libraries; not open to the general public; restricted to Americans working in Ankara & Turks working for AF.

354. Base Library/FL 5517
APO New York, NY 09240-5000 Italy AUTOVON 622-3574
Admin Wendell E James. *ILL* Maria J Acevedo.
Lib Type General.
Spec Collecs Italian collection.
Circ Servs Avail To other Federal libraries; to other libraries; to the general public.

Ref Servs Avail To other Federal libraries; to other libraries; to the general public.

355. Base Library/FL 5531
APO New York, NY 09224-5000 Izmir, Turkey 145360 ext 3440; AUTOVON 675-1110 ext 3440
Admin Jane G Crowe. *ILL* Lale Hepaguslar.
Lib Type General.
Spec Subs Military history; Turkey, history & travel; foreign relations; management.
Circ Servs Avail To other Federal libraries; to other libraries; not open to the general public; restricted to military, DoD civilians, & contractors.
Ref Servs Avail To other Federal libraries; to other libraries; not open to the general public; restricted to military, DoD civilians, & contractors.

356. Base Library/FL 5537
20 CSG/SSL, APO New York, NY 09194-5000 UK AUTOVON 263-4963
Admin Joseph A Burke. *Ref Lib* Margaret Wilson. *ILL* Jane L Johnson.
Lib Type General.
Spec Subs Great Britain. *Spec Collecs* Great Britain.
Circ Servs Avail To other Federal libraries; to other libraries; restricted to base military dependents.
Ref Servs Avail To other Federal libraries; to other libraries; restricted to base military dependents.

357. Base Library/FL 5543
APO New York, NY 09150 UK AUTOVON 266-2216
Admin Jackie Garrison.
Lib Type General.
Spec Collecs Project Warrior.
Circ Servs Avail To other libraries; restricted to military & civilian personnel & dependents.
Ref Servs Avail To other Federal libraries; to other libraries; to the general public.

358. Base Library/FL 5606
36 CSG/SSL, APO New York, NY 09132 Federal Republic of Germany AUTOVON 453-7056
Admin Tom Stubbs. *Ref Lib* Uschi Kroll. *ILL* Easter Sarnecki.
Lib Type General.
Circ Servs Avail To other Federal libraries; to other libraries; to the general public.
Ref Servs Avail To other Federal libraries; to other libraries; to the general public.

359. Base Library/FL 5620
APO New York, NY 09109-5225 Federal Republic of Germany AUTOVON (314) 450-7677
Admin Suzanne K Miller. *ILL* Gabrielle Bebbon.
Lib Type General.
Circ Servs Avail To other Federal libraries; not open to the general public.
Ref Servs Avail To other Federal libraries; not open to the general public.

360. Base Library/FL 5670
MHS, APO New York, NY 09210 UK AUTOVON 262-1110-7737
Admin Jeanne M Cahill.
Lib Type General.
Spec Subs Business management; computers; electronics; foreign relations; US history. *Spec Collecs* Business management; Great Britain: culture, travel, & history; communications technology.
Circ Servs Avail To other Federal libraries; to other libraries; not open to the general public; restricted to base personnel.
Ref Servs Avail To other Federal libraries; to other libraries; not open to the general public; restricted to base personnel.

361. Bentwaters Base Library/FL 5644
APO New York, NY 09755-5000 UK AUTOVON 225-2691
Admin Marjorie Flood.
Lib Type General.
Circ Servs Avail To other Federal libraries; to other libraries; restricted to military & civilian personnel & dependents, ILL with libraries of UK.
Ref Servs Avail To other Federal libraries; to other libraries; restricted to military & civilian personnel & dependents.

362. Camp New Amsterdam, Base Library/FL 5688
APO New York, NY 09292 Netherlands AUTOVON 2949
Admin Mary M Ezzell.
Lib Type General.
Spec Collecs Holland.
Coop Lib Nets USAFE libraries.
Circ Servs Avail To other Federal libraries; to other libraries; not open to the general public; restricted to personnel authorized on base.
Ref Servs Avail To other Federal libraries; to other libraries; not open to the general public; restricted to personnel authorized on base.

363. Chicksands Base Library/FL 5650
APO New York, NY 09193-5000 UK 0462 812571 ext 347; AUTOVON 234-2347
Admin Frances Lum.
Lib Type General.
Spec Subs British Isles.
Circ Servs Avail To other Federal libraries; restricted to base personnel.
Ref Servs Avail To other Federal libraries; restricted to base personnel.

364. Clark Base Library/FL 5251
3rd Combat Support Group/SSL, APO San Francisco, CA 96274-5000 The Philippines 49228/49159; AUTOVON 822-1201
Admin Eleanor F Ballou. *Ref Lib* Renate Giondomenica. *ILL* Eduardo L Santos; Alfreda P Ricana.
Lib Type General.
Spec Collecs Philippine Collection.
Circ Servs Avail Not open to the general public; restricted to US active duty & retired military & dependents & Filipino employees.

365. Comiso AS Base Library/FL 5541
487 CSG/SSL, APO New York, NY 09694-5000 Sicily, Italy 690-343; AUTOVON 6780
Admin Marcia D Mohn. *ILL* Eleanor Palazzolo.
Lib Type General.
Circ Servs Avail To other Federal libraries; to the general public.
Ref Servs Avail To the general public.

366. Fairford Base Library/FL 5560
7020 ABG/SSL, APO New York, NY 09125-5000 UK Cirencester (0285) 712511 ext 2938; AUTOVON 247-2938
Admin Janet G Burke.
Lib Type General.
Circ Servs Avail To other Federal libraries; to other libraries; not open to the general public; restricted to USAF military & civilian personnel & dependents.
Ref Servs Avail To other Federal libraries; to other libraries; to the general public; restricted to by phone or letter to the general public.

367. Florennes Base Library/FL 5630
APO New York, NY 09188 Belgium AUTOVON 791-3255
Admin Charlyne Van Oosbree.
Lib Type General.
Coop Lib Nets USAFE.
Circ Servs Avail To other Federal libraries; to other libraries; not open to the general public; restricted to military & civilian personnel & dependents.
Ref Servs Avail To other Federal libraries; to other libraries; not open to the general public; restricted to military & civilian personnel & dependents.

368. Hellenikon ABG Base Library/FL 5687
USAFE APO New York, NY 09223-5000, Hellenikon Greece 01-989-5579; AUTOVON 662-5579
Admin Velma R Coon. *ILL* Fani Tzivelopoulou.
Lib Type General.
Spec Collecs Greek collection.
Circ Servs Avail Not open to the general public; restricted to Military ID holders & others as approved.
Ref Servs Avail Not open to the general public; restricted to Military ID holders & others as approved.

369. Howard AB Library/FL 4810
Tactical Air Command APO Miami FL 34001 Panama AUTOVON (281) 221-4012, ext 84-6249-3006
Admin Sandra Murdoch (Librarian); Ronald Ferland (Asst).
Lib Type General.

370. Incirlik Base Library/FL 5685
APO New York, NY 09289 Turkey AUTOVON 676-6759
Admin Maggie Gordon. *ILL* Suna Gunay.
Lib Type General.
Spec Collecs Turkish from history to carpeting to juvenile readings. *In-house Files* Video: Time Life & Nova.
Lib Deposit Designation Supports & houses Univ of Maryland materials.
Circ Servs Avail To other Federal libraries; to other libraries; to the general public.
Ref Servs Avail To other Federal libraries; to other libraries; to the general public.

371. Iraklion Base Library/FL 5699
APO New York, NY 09291-5225 Crete AUTOVON 668-3851
Admin Margaret D Andrews.
Lib Type General.
Circ Servs Avail Not open to the general public; restricted to base personnel.
Ref Servs Avail Not open to the general public; restricted to base personnel.

372. Joint US Military Mission for Aid to Turkey, Library
HQ JUSMMAT/ALD-L, APO New York, NY 09254-5365 Turkey AUTOVON 672-2167
Admin Eve Skelton.
Lib Type General.
Circ Servs Avail Not open to the general public; restricted to assigned personnel.
Ref Servs Avail To the general public.

373. Kadena AFB, Base Library/FL 5270
18 CSW/SSL APO San Francisco, CA 96239-5000, Okinawa Japan AUTOVON 654-1502
Admin Nova C Maddox. *ILL* Teruko Tamanaha.
Lib Type General.
Spec Subs Okinawa; Japan. *Spec Collecs* Project Warrior; Asian collection. *In-house Files* Vertical files.
Circ Servs Avail To other Federal libraries; to other libraries; to the general public.
Ref Servs Avail To other Federal libraries; to other libraries; to the general public.

374. Kunsan AB Library/FL 5284
Pacific Air Forces APO San Francisco, CA 96264, Kunsan Korea AUTOVON 272-4817/5469
Admin Cynthia Rutledge.
Lib Type General.

375. Lajes Field, Base Library/FL 4486
Military Air Command APO New York, NY 09406-5000 Azores AUTOVON 858-1110, ask for Latjes 6253/7288
Admin Madeline Peyton.
Lib Type General.

376. Lakenheath Base Library
48 CSG/SSL, APO New York, NY 09179-5000 UK AUTOVON 226-3713
Admin Carolyn Mallalieu-Knapp. *ILL* Elizabeth Stanford.
Lib Type General.

Spec Subs Local history—East Anglia.
Info Ret Servs DIALOG.
Circ Servs Avail To other Federal libraries; to other libraries; to the general public.
Ref Servs Avail To other Federal libraries; to other libraries; to the general public.

377. Library Service Center, HQ USAFE
FL 5510, APO New York, NY 09012 Federal Republic of Germany AUTOVON 489-6752
Admin Marlow E Peters; Mary R Wallace (Tech Svcs).
Lib Type General.
Circ Servs Avail Restricted to isolated USAF sites in 17 countries.

378. Lindsey AS, Base Library/FL 5600
USAFE APO New York, NY 09633, Berlin Federal Republic of Germany AUTOVON 472-6333/3093
Admin Joan E Breen.
Lib Type General.

379. Mildenhall Base Library/FL 5518
USAFE APO New York, NY 09127 United Kingdom 712511 ext 2352; AUTOVON 238-2352
Admin Frank William Gadbois. *ILL* Peter Bowden.
Lib Type General.
Spec Subs Travel in the British Isles & Europe. *Spec Collecs* British Isles; international relations; European travel.
Circ Servs Avail To other Federal libraries; not open to the general public; restricted to base personnel.
Ref Servs Avail To other Federal libraries; not open to the general public; restricted to base personnel.

380. Misawa Base, Overstreet Memorial Library/FL 5205
APO San Francisco, CA 96519-5000 Japan AUTOVON 226-3068
Admin Garth Elmore.
Lib Type General.
Spec Collecs Japan; China; Korea.
Coop Lib Nets USAF/PACAF Command.
Circ Servs Avail To other Federal libraries.
Ref Servs Avail To other Federal libraries.

381. Osan Base Library/FL 5294
51st Combat Support Group, APO San Francisco, CA 96570-5000 Korea AUTOVON 284-6611/4892
Admin Judson L Erwin. *Ref Lib* Hyong Sop Kim. *ILL* Hyon Sun Chang. *Acq Lib* Hyong Ui Yi.
Lib Type General.
Spec Collecs Project Warrior.
Circ Servs Avail To other Federal libraries; to other libraries; not open to the general public.
Ref Servs Avail To other Federal libraries; to other libraries; not open to the general public.

382. Ramstein Library/FL 5612
APO New York, NY 09012 Federal Republic of Germany 06371-47-7409; AUTOVON 480-7409
Admin Eileen Grady Diel. *Ref Lib* Mary Jane Petrowski.
Lib Type General.
Spec Subs Social sciences; international relations; military affairs.
Circ Servs Avail To other Federal libraries; to other libraries; to the general public.
Ref Servs Avail To other Federal libraries; to other libraries; to the general public.

383. Rhine-Main Base Library/FL 4420
435 CSG/SSL, APO New York, NY 09057 Federal Republic of Germany AUTOVON (314) 330-6494/7373
Admin Sharron Cooper.
Lib Type General.
Circ Servs Avail To other Federal libraries; to other libraries; to the general public.
Ref Servs Avail To other Federal libraries; to other libraries; to the general public.

384. Sembach AB Library/FL 5604
USAFE APO New York NY 09130 Federal Republic of Germany AUTOVON 496-7895
Admin John Medeiros.
Lib Type General.

385. Spangdahlem Base Library/FL 5621
APO New York, NY 09123 Federal Republic of Germany AUTOVON 452-6203
Admin William L Confer.
Lib Type General.
Circ Servs Avail To other Federal libraries; to other libraries; not open to the general public; restricted to US military & civilian employees & dependents.
Ref Servs Avail To other Federal libraries; to other libraries; not open to the general public; restricted to US military & civilian employees & dependents.

386. Suwon Base Library/FL 5261
APO San Francisco, CA 96461-5000 Korea AUTOVON 288-5553
Admin Nancy M Bemis.
Lib Type General.
Spec Subs Military history; Korea.
Circ Servs Avail Restricted to military & DoD civilian personnel & dependents.
Ref Servs Avail Restricted to military & DoD civilian personnel & dependents.

387. Templehof Airport, Base Library/FL 5622
USAFE APO New York, NY 09611, Berlin Federal Republic of Germany AUTOVON 442-5359/5059
Lib Type General.

388. Thule Base Library/FL 2507
1012 ABG/SSL, APO New York, NY 09023-5000 Greenland
Admin Vibeke Sloth Jakobsen.
Lib Type General.
Spec Subs Greenland. *Spec Collecs* Greenland; Project Warrior.
Circ Servs Avail To other Federal libraries.
Ref Servs Avail To other libraries.

389. Torrejon Base Library/FL 5573
APO New York, NY 09283 Spain AUTOVON 7223-5168/3177
Admin Wynne A Tysdal. *ILL* Nancy J Pagel.
Lib Type General.
Spec Collecs Spanish history, language, & culture.
Coop Lib Nets USAFE.
Circ Servs Avail To other Federal libraries; to other libraries; not open to the general public; restricted to military & civilian personnel & dependents.
Ref Servs Avail To other Federal libraries; to other libraries.

390. Vogelweh Base Library/FL 5500
APO New York, NY 09012 Federal Republic of Germany AUTOVON 499-7665
Admin Faye B Matlock.
Lib Type General.
Coop Lib Nets USAFE.
Circ Servs Avail Not open to the general public; restricted to military & civilian personnel.
Ref Servs Avail Not open to the general public; restricted to military & civilian personnel.

391. Vogelweh Ramstein AB Library FL/5530
86 CSG/KSSL, USAFE APO New York, NY 09012 Federal Republic of Germany AUTOVON 499-7665
Admin Faye B Matlock.
Lib Type General.

392. Warrior Preparation Center, Library/FL 5649
APO New York NY 09012, Einsiedlerhof AS GE Federal Republic of Germany
Lib Type Special.

393. Yokota AB, Base Library/FL 5209
Pacific Air Forces, APO San Francisco, CA 96328 Japan AUTO-VON 225-7490
Admin Rodney M M Heines. *Ref Lib* E R Godbey. *ILL* N Iwai.
Lib Type General.
Coop Lib Nets Pacific Air Forces Command Library Network (PACAF).
Circ Servs Avail To other Federal libraries; to other libraries; not open to the general public; restricted to military & base civilians.
Ref Servs Avail To other Federal libraries; to other libraries; not open to the general public.

394. Zaragoza Base Library/FL 5571
APO New York, NY 09286-5000 Spain AUTOVON 724-2052
Admin Thelma R Hall. *ILL* Karen Jernigan.
Lib Type General.
Spec Subs Aeronautics; management; public administration; geography. *Spec Collecs* Spain; video cassettes; laser discs; talking books; audio cassettes.
Circ Servs Avail To other Federal libraries; to other libraries; restricted to military & DoD civilian personnel & dependents.
Ref Servs Avail To other Federal libraries; to other libraries.

395. Zweibrucken Air Base Library/FL 5529
26 CSG/SSL, APO New York, NY 09860 Federal Republic of Germany 1-06332-44041-2327; AUTOVON 498-2327
Admin Margaret Whitehill. *ILL* Rebecca Byrns.
Lib Type General.
Circ Servs Avail Not open to the general public.
Ref Servs Avail Not open to the general public.

Department of the Army—Domestic

396. Aberdeen Proving Ground, Kirk US Army Health Clinic, Medical Library
Aberdeen Proving Ground, MD 21005-5131 (301) 278-4088; AUTOVON 298-4088
Admin Gerald M Torba. *Ref Lib* Gladys Cereghin (ILL, Acq).
Lib Type Health & Medicine.
Shared Catalog Nets OCLC.
Circ Servs Avail To other Federal libraries.
Ref Servs Avail To other libraries.

397. Aberdeen Proving Ground, Office of the Staff Judge Advocate, Army Law Library
US Army Garrison, Aberdeen Proving Ground, MD 21005 (301) 278-5281
Lib Type Law.

398. Aberdeen Proving Ground, Ordnance Center & School Library
Bldg 3071, Aberdeen Proving Ground, MD 21005-5201 (301) 278-4991; ILL 278-5615
Lib Type Special.
Spec Subs Business & management; education; history; military arts & science; military equipment & maintenance; ordnance. *Spec Collecs* Military publications.
Info Ret Servs DIALOG; DTIC. *Shared Catalog Nets* OCLC. *Coop Lib Nets* FEDLINK.
Ref Servs Avail Restricted to prior approval for general public.

399. Aberdeen Proving Ground, Ordnance Center & School Museum Library
Bldg 2601, Aberdeen Proving Ground, MD 21005 (301) 278-3602
Lib Type Special.
Spec Subs Archival type materials in support of assigned ordnance & chemicals. *Spec Collecs* Army historical properties.

400. Anniston Army Depot, Office of the Post Judge Advocate, Army Law Library
Anniston, AL 36201 (205) 238-6773
Lib Type Law.

401. Arlington Hall Station, Post Legal Office, Army Law Library
Arlington, VA 22212 AUTOVON 80-692-6397
Lib Type Law.

402. Arlington Hall Station, Post Library
Arlington, VA 22212 (703) 692-5236; AUTOVON 222-2688
Admin Dale B Ram.
Lib Type General.
Shared Catalog Nets OCLC.
Circ Servs Avail To other Federal libraries; to other libraries; not open to the general public.
Ref Servs Avail To other Federal libraries; to other libraries; not open to the general public.

403. Arlington Hall Station, Staff Judge Advocate, Army Law Library
HQS INSCOM, Arlington, VA 22212 (703) 692-5245; AUTOVON 222-5245/5249
Admin Dolores Hawks.
Lib Type Law.
Info Ret Servs WESTLAW.
Circ Servs Avail Restricted to USAINSCOM.
Ref Servs Avail Restricted to USAINSCOM.

404. Armament, Munitions, & Chemical Command HQ, Technical Library
ATTN: SMCAR-ESP-L, Rock Island, IL 61299-7300 (309) 794-5031; AUTOVON 793-5031
Admin Philip E Krouse. *ILL* Sandra Paul.
Lib Type Engineering & Science.
Info Ret Servs DIALOG. *Coop Lib Nets* Riverbend Library System.
Circ Servs Avail To other Federal libraries.
Ref Servs Avail To other Federal libraries.

405. Armed Forces Institute of Pathology, Ash Library
Bldg 54 Rm 4077, Washington, DC 20306-6000 (202) 576-2983
Admin Patricia C Patel. *ILL* Darlene J Butler.
Lib Type Health & Medicine.
Spec Subs Pathology. *Spec Collecs* Yakolev Collection (neurology/pathology of cerebral functions), Mr. Halem (Curator), 576-2692; Audio-visual collection (microscopic slides).
Info Ret Servs DIALOG. *Shared Catalog Nets* OCLC; RLIN. *Coop Lib Nets* WRAMC Cooperative Integrated Library system (ILS)—WRC, WRA, WRD.
Circ Servs Avail To other Federal libraries; to other libraries; to the general public; restricted to ILL.
Ref Servs Avail To other Federal libraries; to other libraries; to the general public; restricted to on-site collection usage.

406. Armed Forces Institute of Pathology, Legal Library
Washington, DC 20315 AUTOVON 80-576-2439
Lib Type Law.

407. Army Audit Agency, Army Law Library
Chief Legal Branch, 3101 Park Center Dr, Alexandria, VA 22302 (703) 756-2806
Lib Type Law.

408. Army Materiel Command Headquarters, Technical Library
ATTN: AMCDMA-ML, 5001 Eisenhower Ave, Alexandria, VA 22333-0001 (202) 274-8152; FTS 274-8152; AUTOVON 284-8152
Admin David J Monroe. *ILL* Carol Watkin. *Acq Lib* Janice M Haines.
Lib Type Special.
Spec Subs Computer science; management; military studies; international affairs.
Info Ret Servs DIALOG. *Shared Catalog Nets* OCLC. *Coop Lib Nets* FEDLINK.
Circ Servs Avail To other Federal libraries; to other libraries; not open to the general public; restricted to HQ, AMC employees.
Ref Servs Avail To other Federal libraries; to other libraries; not open to the general public; restricted to DoD employees.

409. Auto Log Management Systems Activity, Technical Library
ATTN: AMXAL-AAG, St Louis, MO 63188
Lib Type Engineering & Science.

410. Aviation Applied Technology Directorate, Technical Library
USAARTA (AVSCOM) Bldg 401, Fort Eustis, VA 23604-5577 (804) 878-4377/2963; AUTOVON 927-4377/2963
Admin David J Arola. *Ref Lib* Edwin P Knihnicki.
Lib Type Engineering & Science.
Spec Subs Army aircraft; low-speed aeronautics; composite structures; aviation safety; gas turbines; propulsion systems; rotary wing aircraft.
Info Ret Servs DROLS. *Shared Catalog Nets* SBIN.
Circ Servs Avail To other Federal libraries; not open to the general public; restricted to government agencies & contractors.
Ref Servs Avail To other Federal libraries; not open to the general public; restricted to government agencies & contractors.

411. Aviation Systems Command, Library & Information Center
AMSAV-DIL, 4300 Goodfellow St, Saint Louis, MO 63120-1798 (314) 263-2345
Lib Type Special.
Spec Subs Aeronautics; aircraft procurement & maintenance; aviation.
Coop Lib Nets FEDLINK.

412. Ballistic Defense System Command, Office of the Staff Judge Advocate, Army Law Library
PO Box 1500, Huntsville, AL 35807 (205) 895-4520
Lib Type Law.

413. William Beaumont Army Medical Center Library
Bldg 7777, El Paso, TX 79920-5001 (915) 569-2537/2580
Lib Type Health & Medicine.
Info Ret Servs DIALOG; Medlars. *Shared Catalog Nets* OCLC.

414. William Beaumont Army Medical Center, Office of the Judge Advocate, Army Law Library
El Paso, TX 79920 (915) 569-2280
Lib Type Law.

415. William Beaumont Army Medical Center, Patients' Library
Bldg 7777, Rm 1-187, El Paso, TX 79920-5001 (915) 569-2314; AUTOVON 979-2314
Admin Alice White.
Lib Type Hospital (Patients).
Circ Servs Avail Restricted to patients & staff.
Ref Servs Avail Restricted to patients & staff.

416. Benet Weapons Laboratory, Technical Library
Armament Research & Development Center, SNCSR-LCB-TL, Watervliet Arsenal, Watervliet, NY 12189-4050 (518) 266-5613
Lib Type Special.
Spec Subs Artillery; mathematics; science; physical science.
Ref Servs Avail To the general public; restricted to certain types of requests.

417. Carlisle Barracks, Office of the Staff Judge Advocate, Army Law Library
Carlisle Barracks, PA 17013 (717) 245-4940
Lib Type Law.

418. Carlisle Barracks, Post Library
Bldg 46, Carlisle, PA 17013-5002 (717) 245-3718; AUTOVON 242-3718
Admin Theresa G Munson. *ILL* Anne C Hurst.
Lib Type General.
Spec Subs Military family. *Spec Collecs* Pennsylvania collection.
Info Ret Servs DIALOG. *Shared Catalog Nets* OCLC; TRALINET. *Coop Lib Nets* TRALINET. *Elec Mail Nets* OPTIMIS.

Circ Servs Avail To other Federal libraries; to other libraries; not open to the general public; restricted to military, dependents & civilian employees.
Ref Servs Avail To other Federal libraries; to other libraries; not open to the general public; restricted to military, dependents & civilian employees.

419. Chemical Research & Development Center, Technical Library
Aberdeen Proving Ground, MD 21010-5423 (301) 671-2934; FTS 671-2936; AUTOVON 584-2934
Admin Concetta R Anaclerio. *Ref Lib* Donna C Smith. *ILL* Mary L D'Eramo.
Lib Type Engineering & Science.
Info Ret Servs DIALOG; BRS. *Shared Catalog Nets* OCLC. *Coop Lib Nets* FEDLINK.
Circ Servs Avail Not open to the general public.
Ref Servs Avail Not open to the general public.

420. Combat Developments Experimentation Center, Technical Information Center
Bldg 2925, Fort Ord, CA 93941-7000 (408) 242-3618/4706
Lib Type Special.
Spec Subs Automatic data processing & computer systems; experimental design; human factors; simulation models; weapons systems & equipment.
Info Ret Servs DIALOG; Defense Technical Info Ctr (DTIC). *Shared Catalog Nets* OCLC.
Circ Servs Avail Not open to the general public.
Ref Servs Avail Not open to the general public.

421. Combat Studies Institute Library
US Army Command & General Staff College, ATTN: ATZL-SWI-A (Lib), Fort Leavenworth, KS 66027-6900 (913) 684-4110/3904; AUTOVON 552-4110/3904
Admin Elizabeth R Snoke.
Lib Type Special.
Spec Collecs Military history reference collection.
Ref Servs Avail To other Federal libraries; to other libraries; to the general public; restricted to mail requests for military history information on a limited basis.

422. Combined Arms Research Library
US Army Command & General Staff College, ATZL-SWS-L, Fort Leavenworth, KS 66027-6900 (913) 684-4035; FTS 753-4035; AUTOVON 552-4035
Admin JoAn I Stolley. *Ref Lib* Bertina Byers. *ILL* Carol Ramkey. *Acq Lib* Alice Blaser.
Lib Type Academic.
Spec Subs Military arts & sciences; World War II; US foreign policy & international relations. *Spec Collecs* Archives.
Info Ret Servs DIALOG; BRS; NEXIS. *Shared Catalog Nets* OCLC. *Coop Lib Nets* FEDLINK; TRALINET. *Elec Mail Nets* OPTIMIS.
Circ Servs Avail To other Federal libraries; to other libraries; to the general public.
Ref Servs Avail To other Federal libraries; to other libraries; to the general public.

423. Communications Electronics Command, Technical Library
ATTN: AMSEL-ME-PSL, Fort Monmouth, NJ 07703-5007 (201) 532-1298; AUTOVON 992-1298
Admin Regina Sieben (Ref). *ILL* Jean Hurley. *Acq Lib* Marion Clinton.
Lib Type Special.
Spec Subs Electronic & communication equipment.
Info Ret Servs BRS. *Shared Catalog Nets* OCLC. *Coop Lib Nets* FEDLINK.
Circ Servs Avail Not open to the general public.
Ref Servs Avail To other Federal libraries; to other libraries.

424. Corpus Christi Army Depot, Office of the Command Judge Advocate, Army Law Library
Corpus Christi, TX 78419 (512) 939-3324
Lib Type Law.

425. Corpus Christi Army Depot, Reference & Research Library
Stop 6, NAS Bldg 8, Corpus Christi, TX 78419-6020 (512) 939-3324
Lib Type General.
Spec Subs Administration & management; chemistry; helicopter maintenance.

426. Darnall Army Community Hospital, Medical Library
Bldg 36000, Fort Hood, TX 76544-5063 (817) 288-8368; ILL 288-8367
Lib Type Health & Medicine.
Spec Subs Basic science; dentistry; specialties & surgical.
Info Ret Servs DIALOG; BRS; National Library of Medicine. *Shared Catalog Nets* OCLC. *Coop Lib Nets* South Central Regional Library Program.

427. Defense Depot, Morale Welfare & Recreation Library
500 W 12th St, Ogden, UT 84401-5000 (801) 399-7239
Admin Muriel H Rhodes.
Lib Type General.
Circ Servs Avail To other Federal libraries; not open to the general public.

428. Dewitt Army Hospital, Medical Library
Fort Belvoir, VA 22060 (703) 664-4482; AUTOVON 354-4482
Lib Type Health & Medicine.

429. Dugway Proving Ground, Office of the Judge Advocate, Army Law Library
Dugway, UT 84022 AUTOVON 80-582-3333
Lib Type Law.

430. Dugway Proving Ground, Post Library
Dugway, UT 84022-5000 (801) 522-2178
Lib Type General.

431. Dugway Proving Ground, Technical Library
Commander, US Army Dugway Proving Ground, ATTN: Technical Library, Dugway, UT 84022-5000 (801) 831-3565; AUTOVON 789-3565
Admin Duane E Williamson. *Ref Lib* Erica Salomon. *ILL* Reed Carlson. *Acq Lib* Hazel Solomon.
Lib Type Special.
Spec Subs Chemical warfare; biological defense systems; flame & incendiary systems. *Spec Collecs* Unclassified & classified test reports/documentation dealing with above special subjects (limited access).
Info Ret Servs DIALOG; DTIC.
Circ Servs Avail Restricted to DoD & government contractors with verified need-to-know.
Ref Servs Avail Restricted to DoD & government contractors with verified need-to-know.

432. Dunham Army Health Clinic, Medical Library
Carlisle Barracks, PA 17013-5050 (717) 245-4112; AUTOVON 242-4112
Lib Type Health & Medicine.

433. Eastern Area, Office of the Staff Judge Advocate, Army Law Library
Eastern Area M1C MOT, Bayonne, NJ 07002 AUTOVON 339-7126
Lib Type Law.

434. XVIII Airborne Corps & Ft Bragg, Office of the Staff Judge Advocate, Army Law Library
Fort Bragg, NC 28307 AUTOVON 80-675-4408
Lib Type Law.

435. 82nd Airborne Division, Office of the Staff Judge Advocate, Army Law Library
Fort Bragg, NC 28307 (919) 396-0730
Lib Type Law.

436. Eisenhower Army Medical Center, Health Sciences Library
Fort Gordon, GA 30905-5656 (404) 791-4238/6765; FTS 240-4238; AUTOVON 780-4238
Admin Judy M Krivanek.
Lib Type Health & Medicine.
Spec Subs Clinical medicine.
Info Ret Servs DIALOG; BRS; MEDLINE. *Shared Catalog Nets* OCLC. *Coop Lib Nets* Southeastern/Atlantic Regional Medical Library Program (NLM-Region 2).
Circ Servs Avail To other Federal libraries.
Ref Servs Avail To other Federal libraries.

437. ERADCOM, Army Law Library
2800 Powder Mill Rd, Adelphi, MD 20783 AUTOVON 80-394-1070
Lib Type Law.

438. 5th United States Army, Office of the Staff Judge Advocate, Army Law Library
Fort Sam Houston, TX 78234 AUTOVON 80-746-5014
Lib Type Law.

439. 1st Cavalry Division, Office of the Staff Judge Advocate, Army Law Library
Fort Hood, TX 76545 (817) 747-6060
Lib Type Law.

440. Fitzsimons Army Medical Center, Medical Technical Library
Aurora, CO 80045-5000 (303) 361-8918; FTS 337-1101; AUTOVON 943-1101
Admin Sharon Johnson. *Ref Lib* Jeanne Durocher. *ILL* Dorothy Phillips. *Acq Lib* Marilyn Monahan.
Lib Type Health & Medicine.
Spec Collecs History of medicine collection.
Info Ret Servs BRS; MEDLINE. *Shared Catalog Nets* OCLC. *Coop Lib Nets* Colorado Council of Medical Librarians (CCML). *Elec Mail Nets* OPTIMIS; ARCONS; OCTANET.
Circ Servs Avail Restricted to active duty personnel.

441. Fitzsimons Army Medical Center, Office of the Judge Advocate, Army Law Library
Aurora, CO 80240 (303) 361-1212
Lib Type Law.

442. Fitzsimons Army Medical Center, Post-Patients' Library
Aurora, CO 80045-5300 (303) 361-8104; FTS 337-8104; AUTOVON 943-8104
Admin Cynthia A Banicki.
Lib Type Hospital (Patients).
Spec Subs Medical self-help; patient education; military history.
Info Ret Servs DIALOG. *Shared Catalog Nets* OCLC. *Coop Lib Nets* FEDLINK; BCR. *Elec Mail Nets* OPTIMIS.
Circ Servs Avail To other Federal libraries; to other libraries; not open to the general public.
Ref Servs Avail Restricted to US Army libraries.

443. Ft Belvoir, Staff Judge Advocate, Army Law Library
US Army Engineering Center, Fort Belvoir, VA 22060 (703) 664-4026; FTS 664-4026; AUTOVON 354-4026
Admin Thomas E Chilton. *Ref Lib* Franklin Henson.
Lib Type Law.
Info Ret Servs WESTLAW. *Coop Lib Nets* WESTLAW.
Circ Servs Avail Not open to the general public.
Ref Servs Avail Not open to the general public.

444. Ft Benning, Sayers Memorial Library
Bldg 93, Fort Benning, GA 31905-5226 (404) 545-1769/4911/7141; AUTOVON 835-1769
Admin Gwendolyn I Lewis. *Ref Lib* Lois Booth (ILL).
Lib Type General.
Info Ret Servs DIALOG. *Shared Catalog Nets* TRALINET. *Coop Lib Nets* GLIN; TRALINET. *Elec Mail Nets* OPTIMIS.

Circ Servs Avail To other Federal libraries; to other libraries; restricted to military, dependents, & local DoD civilians.
Ref Servs Avail To other Federal libraries; to other libraries.

445. Ft Bliss, Center Library
Bldg 21, Fort Bliss, TX 79916 (915) 568-2489; AUTOVON 978-7705
Admin Christel G Marton. *Ref Lib* Doris Martinez (ILL).
Lib Type General.
Spec Subs Investments; business administration; military history. *Spec Collecs* History of the southwest; military history. *In-house Files* Vertical files; periodicals on microfilm.
Info Ret Servs DIALOG. *Shared Catalog Nets* OCLC. *Coop Lib Nets* TRALINET. *Elec Mail Nets* OPTIMIS.
Circ Servs Avail To other libraries; restricted to military & dependents, retirees, DACS.
Ref Servs Avail To other libraries; restricted to military & dependents, retirees, DACS.

446. Ft Bliss, Valent Learning Resources Center Library
US Army Sergeants Major Academy, Fort Bliss, TX 79918-5000 (915) 568-8176/8614; FTS 478-8176; AUTOVON 978-8176
Admin Marijean Murray. *Ref Lib* Linda Gaunt; Melissa Cooper (ILL).
Lib Type Academic.
Spec Subs Military history & science; management; leadership; psychology. *Spec Collecs* Army unit histories; autographed collection. *In-house Files* Noncommissioned officer history datafile.
Info Ret Servs DIALOG. *Coop Lib Nets* TRALINET. *Elec Mail Nets* OPTIMIS.
Circ Servs Avail To other Federal libraries; to other libraries; restricted to appropriate DoD members & employees.
Ref Servs Avail To other Federal libraries; to other libraries; restricted to appropriate DoD members & employees.

447. Ft Bragg Command Reference Center & Main Post Library
ATTN: AFZA-PA-R, Fort Bragg, NC 28307-5000 (919) 396-3526; FTS 675-3523; AUTOVON 236-3523
Admin Barbara A Eller (Chief Lib Branch); Beverly D Wood (Main Post Lib). *Ref Lib* Nancy L Kutula. *ILL* Paul Y Fritts. *Acq Lib* Patricia Javaher.
Lib Type General.
Spec Subs Military history; education; social sciences; genealogy; international affairs. *Spec Collecs* Microforms collection; CIS; books for college libraries; library of American civilization; genealogy & local history; ERIC.
Info Ret Servs DIALOG. *Shared Catalog Nets* OCLC. *Coop Lib Nets* FEDLINK.
Circ Servs Avail To other Federal libraries; to other libraries; restricted to military & dependents of Ft Bragg & Pope AFB.
Ref Servs Avail To other Federal libraries; to other libraries; to the general public.

448. Ft Bragg, Office of the Staff Judge Advocate, Army Law Library
1st Special Operations Command (Airborne), Fort Bragg, NC 28307-5000 (919) 396-4820 396-6609; FTS 675-4820; AUTOVON 236-4820
Admin Christian L Hurst.
Lib Type Law.
Circ Servs Avail Restricted to Dept of the Army.
Ref Servs Avail Restricted to Dept of the Army.

449. Ft Bragg, Womack Army Community Hospital, Medical Library
Fort Bragg, NC 28307-5000 (919) 396-1819/5076; FTS 675-1819/5076; AUTOVON 236-1819/5076
Admin Cecilia C Edwards. *ILL* Irene M Walker.
Lib Type Health & Medicine.
Spec Subs Medicine; dentistry; nursing; allied health; hospital administration.
Info Ret Servs MEDLARS; MEDLINE. *Shared Catalog Nets* OCLC. *Coop Lib Nets* Military Medical Libraries; Cape Fear Health Sciences Consortium; North Carolina Union List of Serials; Region 2 List of Serials. *Elec Mail Nets* OPTIMIS.

Circ Servs Avail To other Federal libraries; to other libraries; not open to the general public; restricted to MEDDAC personnel.
Ref Servs Avail To other Federal libraries; to other libraries; not open to the general public; restricted to students of institutions part of consortium.

450. Ft Campbell, Blanchfield Army Community Hospital, Medical Library
Fort Campbell, KY 42223-1498 (502) 798-8015; FTS 798-8014; AUTOVON 635-8014
Admin Ina L Nesbitt. *Acq Lib* Deborah Dube.
Lib Type Health & Medicine.
Spec Subs Clinical medicine; preventive medicine; veterinary medicine.
Info Ret Servs DIALOG; MEDLARS. *Coop Lib Nets* Greater Midwest Regional Medical Library Network (GMRMLN); USA Regional Medical Libraries. *Elec Mail Nets* OPTIMIS.
Circ Servs Avail To other libraries; not open to the general public; restricted to medical staff.
Ref Servs Avail To other libraries; not open to the general public; restricted to medical staff.

451. Ft Campbell, 101st Airborne Division (Air Assault), Office of the Staff Judge Advocate, Army Law Library
Fort Campbell, KY 42223 (502) 356-2733
Lib Type Law.

452. Ft Campbell, R F Sink Library
Bldg 38, Fort Campbell, KY 42223-5000 (502) 798-5729; AUTOVON 635-4827
Admin Mary H Wooten. *Ref Lib* Janet Daugherty. *ILL* Sherry Miller. *Acq Lib* Anna B Cole.
Lib Type General.
Spec Subs History of the 101st Airborne Div. *Spec Collecs* Military science; World War II; crafts & home improvement; educational study guides; family relationships.
Shared Catalog Nets OCLC.
Circ Servs Avail To other libraries; not open to the general public; restricted to military, dependents, & DA civilians.
Ref Servs Avail To other Federal libraries; to other libraries; not open to the general public; restricted to military, dependents, & DA civilians.

453. Ft Carson, Evans US Army Community Hospital, Medical Library
USAH MEDDAC/ATTN: Medical Library, Fort Carson, CO 80913-5207 (303) 579-3209/2196; AUTOVON 691-2196
Admin Alfreda H Hanna. *Acq Lib* Roma A Marcum.
Lib Type Health & Medicine.
Spec Subs Dentistry; medicine; nursing; orthopedics; patient education; pharmaceutics; physical therapy; veterinary medicine; mental hygiene. *Spec Collecs* Patient information.
Info Ret Servs DIALOG; MEDLARS. *Shared Catalog Nets* OCLC. *Coop Lib Nets* Colorado Council of Medical Librarians (CCML); Plains & Peaks Regional Library System; Peaks & Valleys Library Consortium. *Elec Mail Nets* OPTIMIS; OC-TANET; OCLC; Mile High Media.

454. Ft Carson Post Library
Grant Library, Fort Carson, CO 80913 (303) 279-2842; AUTOVON 691-2842
Admin Barbara E Stevens. *ILL* Katherine Turner. *Acq Lib* Judy Newell.
Lib Type General.
Spec Collecs Colorado.
Shared Catalog Nets OCLC. *Coop Lib Nets* Peaks & Plains Regional Library System.
Circ Servs Avail To other libraries.
Ref Servs Avail To other libraries.

455. Ft Chaffee Post Library
Bldg 1318 USAG, Fort Chaffee, AR 72905 (501) 484-2550; AUTOVON 962-2550
Admin Keith Burton.
Lib Type General.
Circ Servs Avail To other Federal libraries; not open to the general public; restricted to Army.

Ref Servs Avail To other Federal libraries; not open to the general public; restricted to Army.

456. Ft Detrick, Office of the Staff Judge Advocate, Army Law Library
Bldg 715, Fort Detrick, MD 21701-5000 (301) 663-2807; FTS 935-2643; AUTOVON 343-2643
Admin Patricia J Goodrich.
Lib Type Law.
Circ Servs Avail Restricted to Office only.
Ref Servs Avail Restricted to Office only.

457. Ft Detrick Post Library
Bldg 917, Frederick, MD 21701-5000 (301) 663-2806; FTS 935-2806
Lib Type General.

458. Ft Devens, Davis Library
Bldg 2001, Fort Devens, MA 01433-5350 (617) 796-2431
Admin Josephine Weaver (Acq). *Ref Lib* Karen Olender (ILL).
Lib Type General.
Spec Collecs Military affairs.
Info Ret Servs DIALOG *Shared Catalog Nets* OCLC.
Circ Servs Avail To other Federal libraries; to other libraries; to the general public.
Ref Servs Avail To other Federal libraries; to other libraries; to the general public.

459. Ft Devens Medical Library
Cutler Army Community Hospital, Fort Devens, MA 01433-6401 (617) 796-6750; AUTOVON 256-6750
Admin Leslie R Seidel.
Lib Type Health & Medicine.
Coop Lib Nets Northeastern Consortium for Health Information (NECHI).

460. Ft Devens, Office of the Post Judge Advocate, Army Law Library
US Army Garrison, Fort Devens, MA 01433 (617) 796-2255
Lib Type Law.

461. Ft Dix, Office of the Staff Judge Advocate, US Army Training Center & Ft Dix, Law Library
Bldg 5402, Fort Dix, NJ 08640 (609) 562-4858/3587; FTS 944-2498
Admin Ann S Johnson.
Lib Type Law.
Circ Servs Avail Not open to the general public; restricted to Staff Judge Advocate Office.
Ref Servs Avail Not open to the general public; restricted to Staff Judge Advocate Office.

462. Ft Dix, US Army Training Center & Post Library
Bldg 6501, Pennsylvania Ave, Fort Dix, NJ 08640-5111 (609) 562-4858/3587
Lib Type General.
Spec Subs Recreational; military science.
Info Ret Servs DIALOG; BRS. *Shared Catalog Nets* OCLC.
Circ Servs Avail Not open to the general public; restricted to base military.
Ref Servs Avail Not open to the general public; restricted to military.

463. Ft Dix, Walson Army Community Hospital, Medical Library
Fort Dix, NJ 08640 (609) 562-5741/2664; AUTOVON 944-5741
Lib Type Health & Medicine.
Spec Subs Dentistry; medicine; mental hygiene; nursing; preventative medicine; surgery.

464. Ft Drum, Office of the Post Judge Advocate, Army Law Library
Bldg T-102, Fort Drum, NY 13602 AUTOVON 953-3220
Lib Type Law.

465. Ft Drum Post Library
Fort Drum, NY 13602-5000 (315) 772-5929; FTS 775-5929; AUTOVON 341-5929
Admin Nikki Hathaway. *ILL* Kathy Delong.
Lib Type General.
Spec Subs New York State, with emphasis on North Country. *Spec Collecs* New York State.
Shared Catalog Nets OCLC. *Coop Lib Nets* FEDLINK; North Country.
Circ Servs Avail To other Federal libraries; to other libraries; not open to the general public; restricted to military & DoD civilians, ILL to local schools.
Ref Servs Avail To other Federal libraries; to other libraries.

466. Ft Eustis, McDonald US Army Community Hospital, Medical Library
Fort Eustis, VA 23604-5549 (804) 878-2897; FTS 988-5251; AUTOVON 927-2897
Admin Helen O Hearn.
Lib Type Health & Medicine.
Spec Subs Medicine; nursing.
Coop Lib Nets Tidewater Health Sciences Librarians.
Circ Servs Avail To other Federal libraries; to other libraries.
Ref Servs Avail To other Federal libraries; to other libraries.

467. Ft Eustis, Office of the Staff Judge Advocate, Army Law Library
US Army Transportation Center & Ft Eustis, Fort Eustis, VA 23604-5000 (804) 878-5017; AUTOVON 927-5286
Admin Dennis Pilkington.
Lib Type Law.
Circ Servs Avail Not open to the general public.
Ref Servs Avail To the general public.

468. Ft Gillem, Army Law Library
HQ 2nd Army, Forest Park, GA 30050 (404) 362-3343
Lib Type Law.

469. Ft Gordon, Main Post Library
Bldg 33500, Fort Gordon, GA 30905 AUTOVON 780-3922
Lib Type General.

470. Ft Gordon, Morale Support Activities Library Branch, Patients' Library
Bldg 33500, Fort Gordon, GA 30905-5020 (404) 791-2449
Lib Type Hospital (Patients).
Spec Subs Contemporary military; foreign languages; young people & children's literature. *Spec Collecs* USAFI Collection.
Info Ret Servs DIALOG.

471. Ft Gordon, Office of the Staff Judge Advocate, Army Law Library
Fort Gordon, GA 30905 (404) 791-4454; AUTOVON 80-791-4454
Lib Type Law.

472. Ft Greeley, Office of the Post Judge Advocate, 6th Infantry Division (Light), Army Law Library
Fort Greely, APO Seattle, WA 98733 AUTOVON (317) 873-4202
Admin Victor L Horton.
Lib Type Law.
Spec Subs Military law.
Shared Catalog Nets Army Law Library Service. *Coop Lib Nets* Army Law Library Service. *Elec Mail Nets* Army Law Library Service.
Circ Servs Avail Not open to the general public.
Ref Servs Avail Not open to the general public.

473. Ft Greely Post Library
Bldg 663, APO Seattle, WA 98733 (907) 873-4117; AUTOVON 873-3217
Admin Bonnie Ricks. *ILL* Betty Phillips.
Lib Type General.
Spec Subs Arctic; applied science.
Info Ret Servs WLN. *Shared Catalog Nets* WLN. *Coop Lib Nets* Alaska Library Network (ALN).

Circ Servs Avail To other Federal libraries; to other libraries; to the general public.
Ref Servs Avail To other Federal libraries; to other libraries; to the general public.

474. Ft Hamilton, Morale Support Activities, Post Library
Bldg 404, Fort Hamilton, NY 11252-5155 (718) 630-4875
Lib Type General.
Spec Subs Military history, science & tactics. *Spec Collecs* New York City & state history (New Yorkana Collection).
Info Ret Servs DIALOG. *Shared Catalog Nets* OCLC. *Coop Lib Nets* Telecommunications Library Information Network.
Circ Servs Avail Not open to the general public; restricted to ILL.
Ref Servs Avail Not open to the general public; restricted to Active & retired military & dependents.

475. Ft Hamilton, Office of the Staff Judge Advocate, Army Law Library
NYAC & Ft Hamilton, Brooklyn, NY 11252 (718) 630-4562; FTS 630-4562; AUTOVON 232-4562
Admin Cecilia A Kampsula.
Lib Type Law.
Spec Collecs Military justice texts.
Coop Lib Nets US Army Law Library Service.
Circ Servs Avail Restricted to SJA office.
Ref Servs Avail To other Federal libraries; not open to the general public.

476. Ft Hancock Post Library
Fort Hancock, Highlands, NJ 07732
Lib Type General.

477. Ft Benjamin Harrison, Academic & Media Center
Bldg 400, Rm 255, Fort Benjamin Harrison, IN 46216-5100 (317) 542-4956; AUTOVON 699-4956
Lib Type General.

478. Ft Benjamin Harrison, Post Library
Bldg 31, Fort Benjamin Harrison, IN 46216 (317) 542-4958
Lib Type General.
Info Ret Servs DIALOG; DTIC. *Shared Catalog Nets* OCLC; TRADOC.

479. Ft Benjamin Harrison, Soldiers' Support Center Library
Bldg 400, Rm 205, Fort Benjamin Harrison, IN 46216 (317) 542-4958
Lib Type General.
Spec Subs Broadcasting; education; mass communications management; military history; public relations.
Info Ret Servs DIALOG; DTIC.

480. Ft Hood, Language Training Facility Library
ATTN: AFZF-DPT-TS-ED, Fort Hood, TX 76544-5056 (817) 287-7506
Admin Else B d'Emery.
Lib Type Training Center.
Spec Collecs Bible Collection (132 languages & dialects).
Circ Servs Avail To other Federal libraries; to other libraries; restricted to military, dependents, DoD civilians, National Guard & Reserve.
Ref Servs Avail Restricted to in-house use.

481. Ft Hood Library System
Bldg 1850, DPCA-MSA, Fort Hood, TX 76544-5056 (817) 287-6011; AUTOVON 737-6011
Admin Gordon Cheatham (Lib Coord); Mary Rogerson (Supv Lib, Casey Memorial Lib). *Ref Lib* Alice Sheplar; Joseph Page (ILL). *Acq Lib* Patsy Shields.
Lib Type General.
In-house Files POSTDATES—online reference system of community services.
Info Ret Servs DIALOG. *Shared Catalog Nets* OCLC.
Circ Servs Avail To other libraries; not open to the general public; restricted to military, dependents, & DoD civilians.
Ref Servs Avail To other Federal libraries; to other libraries; to the general public.

482. Ft Hood, Office of the Staff Judge Advocate, HQ III Corps & Ft Hood, Army Law Library
Fort Hood, TX 76544 (817) 287-2499; FTS 287-2499; AUTOVON 734-2499
Admin Charles H Allred.
Lib Type Law.
Spec Subs General & military law.
Circ Servs Avail To other Federal libraries; restricted to use by the general public on request.
Ref Servs Avail To other Federal libraries; restricted to use by the general public on request.

483. Ft Hood, Office of the Staff Judge Advocate, 2nd Armored Division, Law Library
Account J-418, Fort Hood, TX 76546 (817) 287-7338; FTS 747-4912; AUTOVON 737-4912
Admin Paul C Renfro.
Lib Type Law.
Coop Lib Nets ALLS.
Circ Servs Avail To other Federal libraries; not open to the general public.
Ref Servs Avail To other Federal libraries; not open to the general public.

484. Ft Sam Houston, Academy of Health Sciences, Stimson Library
Bldg 2840, Fort Sam Houston, TX 78234-6100 (512) 221-5932; FTS 221-5932; AUTOVON 471-5932
Admin Norma L Sellers. *Ref Lib* Bertha Huber (Acq). *ILL* John Grayer.
Lib Type Academic; Health & Medicine.
Spec Subs Military medicine; health care administration & management; physical therapy; psychology; sociology; public health; nursing.
Info Ret Servs DIALOG; MEDLINE; DROLS. *Shared Catalog Nets* OCLC. *Coop Lib Nets* Council of Research & Academic Libraries (CORAL); Health Oriented Libraries of San Antonio (HOLSA). *Elec Mail Nets* OPTIMIS.
Circ Servs Avail Not open to the general public.
Ref Servs Avail To other libraries.

485. Ft Sam Houston, Brooke Army Medical Center, Medical Library
Fort Sam Houston, TX 78234-6200 (512) 221-4119/7782; AUTOVON 471-7182
Admin Kimmie Yu. *ILL* Martin Perez. *Acq Lib* Geraldine Trumbo.
Lib Type Health & Medicine; Hospital (Patients).
Spec Subs Medical; dental; nursing; biomedical.
Info Ret Servs DIALOG; MEDLARS. *Shared Catalog Nets* OCLC. *Coop Lib Nets* HSC (Union List of Serials); CORAL; HOLSA (Union List of Serials). *Elec Mail Nets* GTE Telemail.
Circ Servs Avail Restricted to Brooke Army Installation.
Ref Servs Avail Restricted to Brooke Army Installation.

486. Ft Sam Houston, Morale Support Activities, Library System
Bldg 2242, Fort Sam Houston, TX 78234-5000 (512) 221-2017
Lib Type Health & Medicine; General; Hospital (Patients).
Spec Subs Post library, hospital patients' library, hospital medical trainees' library, & library service center.
Shared Catalog Nets OCLC. *Coop Lib Nets* FEDLINK.
Circ Servs Avail Not open to the general public; restricted to military & dependents.
Ref Servs Avail Not open to the general public; restricted to military & dependents.

487. Ft Sam Houston, Office of the Staff Judge Advocate, Army Law Library
Fort Sam Houston, TX 78234 AUTOVON 80-746-3400
Lib Type Law.

488. Ft Sam Houston, Office of the Staff Judge Advocate, Army Law Library
Health Services Command, Fort Sam Houston, TX 78234-6000 (512) 221-3400; AUTOVON 471-3400
Admin Ann M Lewis. *Ref Lib* Tae K Sture (ILL).
Lib Type Law.
Spec Subs Medical/Legal.
Info Ret Servs WESTLAW.
Circ Servs Avail Not open to the general public; restricted to attorneys.
Ref Servs Avail Not open to the general public; restricted to attorneys.

489. Ft Sam Houston, US Army Library Service Center
Bldg 2242, Fort Sam Houston, TX 78234-5000 AUTOVON 471-2387
Lib Type Special.

490. Ft Huachuca, Raymond W Bliss Army Community Hospital, Medical Library
Fort Huachuca, AZ 85613-7040 (602) 538-5668; AUTOVON 879-5668
Admin Ann E Nichols.
Lib Type Health & Medicine.
Spec Subs Medicine; nursing; dentistry; veterinary. *Spec Collecs* Military medical history.
Coop Lib Nets Health Services Command (HSC); Pacific Southwest Region Medical Library Service (PSRMLS).
Circ Servs Avail To other Federal libraries; to other libraries; not open to the general public; restricted to staff.
Ref Servs Avail To other Federal libraries; to other libraries; to the general public; restricted to regular hours for general public & no ILL requests.

491. Ft Huachuca Library Division
US Army Garrison, Fort Huachuca, AZ 85613-6000 (602) 538-3041; AUTOVON 879-3041
Admin Dorothy C Tompkins. *Ref Lib* Natalie Danforth. *ILL* Georgette Bordine. *Acq Lib* Katharine Ferguson.
Lib Type General.
Spec Subs Military affairs, Southwest.
Info Ret Servs DIALOG. *Shared Catalog Nets* OCLC. *Coop Lib Nets* FEDLINK.
Circ Servs Avail To other Federal libraries; to other libraries; not open to the general public; restricted to military, dependents, & DoD civilians.
Ref Servs Avail To other Federal libraries; not open to the general public; restricted to military, dependents, & DoD civilians.

492. Ft Huachuca, Procurement Division IOD, Army Law Library
PO Box 784, Fort Huachuca, AZ 85613 (602) 538-5519
Lib Type Law.

493. Ft Huachuca Technical Library
US Army Garrison, Fort Huachuca, AZ 85613-6000 (602) 538-6304; AUTOVON 879-6304
Admin Dorothy C Tompkins. *ILL* Priscilla Linden. *Acq Lib* Katharine Ferguson.
Lib Type Engineering & Science.
Spec Subs Electrical engineering; telecommunications; computer science; business management. *Spec Collecs* VSMF & IEEE.
Lib Deposit Designation AG publications.
Info Ret Servs DIALOG. *Shared Catalog Nets* OCLC. *Coop Lib Nets* FEDLINK.
Circ Servs Avail To other Federal libraries; to other libraries; not open to the general public; restricted to military, DoD civilians, & government contractors.
Ref Servs Avail To other Federal libraries; not open to the general public; restricted to military, DoD civilians, & government contractors.

494. Ft Huachuca, Technical Processing Library
ATTN: ASH-PCA-LO, Fort Huachuca, AZ 85613 (602) 538-3301
Lib Type General.
Shared Catalog Nets OCLC.

495. Ft Huachuca, US Army Intelligence Center & School, Library
ATSI-TD-SFL, Fort Huachuca, AZ 85613-7000 (602) 538-7930; AUTOVON 879-7930
Admin Sylvia J Webber. *Ref Lib* Pauline Spanabel (ILL). *Acq Lib* Esther A Wruck.
Lib Type Academic.
Spec Subs Military intelligence. *Spec Collecs* Military history. *In-house Files* Advanced course student papers, 1973-.
Info Ret Servs DIALOG. *Shared Catalog Nets* OCLC. *Coop Lib Nets* TRALINET. *Elec Mail Nets* OPTIMIS.
Circ Servs Avail To other Federal libraries; to other libraries; not open to the general public.
Ref Servs Avail To other Federal libraries; to other libraries; not open to the general public.

496. Ft Stewart, Hunter AAF Library System
Bldg 411, Fort Stewart, GA 31314 (912) 767-2260; FTS 767-2260; AUTOVON 870-2828
Admin Richard D Boyce. *Ref Lib* Fred A Berg (ILL). *Acq Lib* Cheryl Weidner.
Lib Type General.
Shared Catalog Nets OCLC. *Coop Lib Nets* FEDLINK; GLIN.
Circ Servs Avail To other Federal libraries; to other libraries; not open to the general public; restricted to DoD.
Ref Servs Avail To other Federal libraries; to other libraries; to the general public.

497. Ft Indiantown Gap Post Library
Indiantown Gap Military Reservation, Annville, PA 17003 (717) 865-5444 ext 2030; FTS 865-5444
Admin Joanna I DeHart.
Lib Type General.
Circ Servs Avail To other Federal libraries; to other libraries; not open to the general public; restricted to area military, dependents, & civilian employees.
Ref Servs Avail To other Federal libraries; to other libraries; not open to the general public; restricted to military, dependents, & civilian employees.

498. Ft Irwin Post Library
National Training Center, Fort Irwin, CA 92310-5000 (619) 386-3462
Lib Type Training Center.
Spec Subs Military history & science.
Coop Lib Nets San Bernadino, Inyo, Riverside County United Library Services.

499. Ft Irwin, Weed Army Community Hospital, Medical Library
USA MEDDAC, Fort Irwin, CA 92310-5065 (619) 386-3143; AUTOVON 470-3143
Admin Vicky J Chee.
Lib Type Health & Medicine.
Spec Subs Health care.
Circ Servs Avail To other Federal libraries; to other libraries; not open to the general public.
Ref Servs Avail To other Federal libraries; to other libraries; not open to the general public.

500. Ft Jackson Thomas E Hall Post Library
Recreation Services Division, Fort Jackson, SC 29207-5170 (803) 751-4816/5589; AUTOVON 734-4816/5589
Admin Marilyn M Mancuso. *Ref Lib* Fred Bush (Acq). *ILL* Doris Cromartie.
Lib Type General.
Spec Subs Military science; military history.
Info Ret Servs DIALOG; BRS; WILSONLINE. *Shared Catalog Nets* OCLC. *Coop Lib Nets* TRADOC Library & Information Network (TRALINET). *Elec Mail Nets* OPTIMIS.
Circ Servs Avail To other Federal libraries; to other libraries; not open to the general public; restricted to military, active & retired, dependents, base employees & dependents.
Ref Servs Avail To other Federal libraries; to other libraries; to the general public.

501. Ft Jackson, Office of the Staff Judge Advocate, Army Law Library
Fort Jackson, SC 29207 (803) 751-6811; AUTOVON 80-751-6811
Lib Type Law.

502. Ft Knox, Barr Memorial Library
400 Quartermaster St, Fort Knox, KY 40121-5000 (502) 624-1232; FTS 354-1232; AUTOVON 464-1232
Admin William F Nichols. *Ref Lib* Nancy O'Hare (ILL).
Lib Type General.
Spec Subs Armor; cavalry; Ft Knox history; US Bullion Depository history.
Info Ret Servs DIALOG. *Shared Catalog Nets* OCLC. *Coop Lib Nets* TRADOC Library & Information Network (TRALINET). *Elec Mail Nets* OPTIMIS.
Circ Servs Avail To other Federal libraries; to other libraries; to the general public.
Ref Servs Avail To other Federal libraries; to other libraries; to the general public.

503. Ft Knox, Community Recreation Division, Library Branch
Fort Knox, KY 40121-5000 (502) 624-5351
Lib Type General.

504. Ft Knox, Emert L Davis Memorial Library
PO Box 208, Patton Museum of Cavalry & Armor, Fort Knox, KY 40121-0208 (502) 624-6350 624-3812; FTS 354-6350 354-3812; AUTOVON 464-6350 464-3812
Admin David A Holt.
Lib Type Special.
Spec Subs Armored fighting vehicles; history of armor & mechanized cavalry. *Spec Collecs* Col Robert J Icks Collection of photographs & papers on armored fighting vehicles & their history.
Coop Lib Nets Kentucky Union List of Serials (KULS).
Circ Servs Avail To other Federal libraries; to other libraries; restricted to persons with research interest in armor/mechanized cavalry by appointment.
Ref Servs Avail To other Federal libraries; to other libraries; restricted to persons with research interest in armor/mechanized cavalry by appointment.

505. Ft Knox, Educational Development Library
1174 Dixie St, Fort Knox, KY 40121 (502) 624-5344
Lib Type General.

506. Ft Knox, Ireland Army Hospital, Medical Library
Bldg 851, Fort Knox, KY 40121 (502) 624-9550
Lib Type Health & Medicine.
Info Ret Servs National Library of Medicine.
Circ Servs Avail Not open to the general public; restricted to staff.
Ref Servs Avail Not open to the general public; restricted to staff.

507. Ft Knox, Ireland Army Hospital, Patients' Library
Bldg 851, Fort Knox, KY 40121 (502) 624-9929
Lib Type Hospital (Patients).

508. Ft Knox, Staff Judge Advocate, Army Law Library
Fort Knox, KY 40121 (502) 624-5449; FTS 354-4628; AUTOVON 464-4628
Admin William H Weaver.
Lib Type Law.
Info Ret Servs LEXIS; NEXIS; WESTLAW.
Circ Servs Avail To other Federal libraries; not open to the general public.
Ref Servs Avail To other Federal libraries; not open to the general public.

509. Ft Leavenworth, Munson Army Community Hospital, Medical Library
Fort Leavenworth, KS 66027-5400 (913) 684-5401 ext 24; FTS 753-5401; AUTOVON 552-5401
Admin Judy Ronk.
Lib Type Health & Medicine.
Spec Subs Medical subjects only.

Coop Lib Nets UMKC.
Circ Servs Avail To other Federal libraries; to other libraries; not open to the general public.
Ref Servs Avail To other Federal libraries; to other libraries; not open to the general public.

510. Ft Leavenworth Post Library
Bldg 275, Fort Leavenworth, KS 66027-5093 (913) 684-3569; FTS 684-3569; AUTOVON 552-3569
Admin Wanda C Holder. *ILL* Jerry Bradley. *Acq Lib* Mary Lou Hoffman.
Lib Type General.
Shared Catalog Nets OCLC.
Circ Servs Avail Restricted to military & dependents.
Ref Servs Avail To other libraries.

511. Ft Leavenworth Staff Judge Advocate, Army Law Library
Fort Leavenworth, KS 66027-5060 (913) 684-4941; FTS 753-4941; AUTOVON 552-4941
Admin Mike Taylor.
Lib Type Law.
Info Ret Servs WESTLAW. *Coop Lib Nets* Army Library Service.
Circ Servs Avail Not open to the general public.
Ref Servs Avail Not open to the general public.

512. Ft Leavenworth, US Army Disciplinary Barracks Library
Drawer A, Fort Leavenworth, KS 66027 (913) 684-8480; FTS 684-8480; AUTOVON 552-8480
Admin Linda B Cook.
Lib Type Penal.
Coop Lib Nets TRALINET.
Circ Servs Avail Restricted to inmates.
Ref Servs Avail Restricted to inmates.

513. Ft Lee, Kenner Army Community Hospital, Medical Library
Fort Lee, VA 23801-5260 (804) 734-1339
Lib Type Health & Medicine.

514. Ft Lee, Post Library & Quartermaster Center
Bldg 9023, Fort Lee, VA 23801-5142 (804) 734-2322
Lib Type General.
Info Ret Servs DIALOG; BRS; DTIC. *Shared Catalog Nets* OCLC; TRALINET.
Circ Servs Avail Not open to the general public; restricted to military community.
Ref Servs Avail To the general public.

515. Ft Lewis Military Museum, Research Library
Main St, Bldg T 4320, Fort Lewis, WA 98433
Lib Type Special.

516. Ft Lewis, Office of the Staff Judge Advocate, Army Law Library
HQ, 9th Infantry Division, Fort Lewis, WA 98433-6000 (206) 967-5945 967-5314; AUTOVON 357-5945
Admin William T Gardner.
Lib Type Law.
Spec Subs Criminal law.
Coop Lib Nets US Army Law Library Services.
Circ Servs Avail Not open to the general public.
Ref Servs Avail Not open to the general public.

517. Ft Lewis, Office of the Staff Judge Advocate, I Corps & Ft Lewis, Army Law Library
Fort Lewis, WA 98433-5000 (206) 967-6153; FTS 967-6153; AUTOVON 357-6153
Admin Sidney L Coleman. *Ref Lib* Hilda Zielinski.
Lib Type Law.
Circ Servs Avail Not open to the general public.
Ref Servs Avail To other Federal libraries; not open to the general public.

518. Ft Hunter Liggett, Post Library
Jolon, CA 93928
Lib Type General.

519. Ft Mason, Main Post Library
Bldg 386, Presidio of San Francisco, CA 94129-5123 (415) 561-3448/5037; AUTOVON 586-3448
Admin Juanita W Taylor. *Ref Lib* Andrew Minjiras (ILL, Acq).
Lib Type General.
Spec Subs Military & California history.
Circ Servs Avail To other Federal libraries; to other libraries; not open to the general public; restricted to military.
Ref Servs Avail To other Federal libraries; to other libraries; not open to the general public; restricted to military.

520. Ft McClellan, Abrams Library
Bldg 2102, Fort McClellan, AL 36205-5000 (205) 238-3715; AUTOVON 865-3715/4151
Admin Joyce A Waybright. *ILL* Cheryl B Fuller. *Acq Lib* Candace L Fuller.
Lib Type General.
Info Ret Servs DIALOG. *Shared Catalog Nets* OCLC; TRALINET. *Coop Lib Nets* FEDLINK; TRALINET. *Elec Mail Nets* OPTIMIS.
Circ Servs Avail To other Federal libraries; to other libraries; not open to the general public.
Ref Servs Avail To other Federal libraries; to other libraries; not open to the general public.

521. Ft McClellan, Medical Library
USA MEDDAC, Bldg 292, Fort McClellan, AL 36205 (205) 238-2411
Admin Kathryn S Aide.
Lib Type Health & Medicine.
Coop Lib Nets HSC.
Circ Servs Avail To other Federal libraries; restricted to photocopies.

522. Ft McClellan, Office of the Staff Judge Advocate, Army Law Library
HQ, USACML & MPCEN&FM, Fort McClellan, AL 36205-5000 (205) 238-5435; FTS 538-5435; AUTOVON 865-5435
Admin Joseph M Perdue.
Lib Type Law.
Circ Servs Avail Not open to the general public.

523. Ft McCoy, Office of the Judge Advocate, Army Law Library
Bldg 1347, Fort McCoy, Sparta, WI 54656-5000 (608) 388-2304; FTS 780-2304; AUTOVON 280-2304
Admin Michael A Burke.
Lib Type Law.
Circ Servs Avail Not open to the general public; restricted to office staff.
Ref Servs Avail Not open to the general public; restricted to office staff.

524. Ft Lesley J McNair Post Library
Bldg 41, 4th & P Sts, SW, Washington, DC 20319 (202) 693-8622
Admin Carol K Norton.
Lib Type General.
Shared Catalog Nets OCLC.
Circ Servs Avail Not open to the general public; restricted to army & dependents, & post civilian employees.

525. Ft Lesley J McNair, Staff Judge Advocate, Army Law Library
HQ Military District of Washington, Ft Lesley J McNair, Washington, DC 20319 (202) 693-8622; AUTOVON 335-1455
Admin Gibson W Gahan.
Lib Type Law.
Spec Subs Military reference.
Info Ret Servs LEXIS; NEXIS. *Coop Lib Nets* TJAGSA.
Circ Servs Avail To other Federal libraries; to other libraries; to the general public.
Ref Servs Avail To other Federal libraries; to other libraries; to the general public.

526. Ft McPherson Library System
Bldg T-44, Fort McPherson, GA 30330-5000 (404) 752-2528; FTS 752-3218; AUTOVON 588-3218
Admin Helen T Kiss. *Ref Lib* Janet Hansen (ILL).
Lib Type General.
Spec Subs Military arts & sciences. *Spec Collecs* DoD & Dept of the Army publications.
Info Ret Servs DIALOG. *Shared Catalog Nets* OCLC. *Coop Lib Nets* FEDLINK.
Circ Servs Avail To other Federal libraries; to other libraries.
Ref Servs Avail To other Federal libraries; to other libraries; to the general public.

527. Ft McPherson, Staff Judge Advocate, HQ US Army Forces Command Law Library
J-301, Fort McPherson, GA 30330 (404) 752-2528/3055; FTS 256-3113; AUTOVON 588-2453
Admin Ray E Rauschenberg.
Lib Type Law.
Spec Subs Contracts.
Circ Servs Avail Not open to the general public.
Ref Servs Avail Not open to the general public.

528. Ft McPherson, Staff Judge Advocate, 3rd US Army Law Library
ATTN: AFRD-JA, Bldg 65, Fort McPherson, GA 30330-6000 (404) 752-2528; FTS 256-3836; AUTOVON 588-3836
Admin John W Doriety. *Acq Lib* Paul Stephens.
Lib Type Law.
Spec Subs Islamic law; laws of the Middle East & northeast African countries; military operations.
Info Ret Servs WESTLAW.
Circ Servs Avail Restricted to military.
Ref Servs Avail Restricted to military.

529. Ft McPherson, US Army Clinic, Medical Library
Fort McPherson, GA 30330 (404) 752-3409; AUTOVON 588-3409
Lib Type Health & Medicine.

530. Ft McPherson, US Army Forces Command Library
AFPR-CFA, Fort McPherson, GA 30330-5000 (404) 362-3100; AUTOVON 797-3100
Lib Type General.

531. Ft McPherson, US Army Garrison, Army Law Library
Fort McPherson, GA 30330 (404) 752-2574/4159; AUTOVON 80-752-2574/4159
Lib Type Law.

532. Ft George G Meade, Kimbrough Army Community Hospital, Medical Library
Fort George G Meade, MD 20755-5800 (301) 677-4228; AUTOVON 923-4228
Lib Type Health & Medicine.
Spec Subs Water resources; locks & dams.
Coop Lib Nets MAHSL, Region 2; Military Union List Region 4.
Circ Servs Avail To other Federal libraries; to other libraries; not open to the general public.
Ref Servs Avail To other Federal libraries; to other libraries; not open to the general public.

533. Ft George G Meade, Language Training Facility Library
c/o US Army Education Ctr, Bldg 393, Fort George G Meade, MD 20755 (301) 677-7255
Lib Type Special.
Spec Collecs Books from behind the Iron Curtain Collection; Foreign Language; (Books from the War Dept, pre-1945); Foreign Language Typewriters Collection; international newspapers & magazines; reading & study materials in 49 languages.

534. Ft George G Meade, Office of the Staff Judge Advocate, HQ, Fort George G Meade Law Library
Fort George G Meade, MD 20755 (301) 677-4509; FTS 938-2337; AUTOVON 923-2337
Admin Sponce A Cade.
Lib Type Law.
Circ Servs Avail To other Federal libraries; not open to the general public.
Ref Servs Avail To other Federal libraries; not open to the general public.

535. Ft George G Meade, Post Library
Bldg 4418, Fort George G Meade, MD 20755-5068 (301) 677-4509
Lib Type General.
Spec Subs Material in support of college & graduate study; foreign language; management; military science.
Info Ret Servs DIALOG. *Shared Catalog Nets* OCLC.

536. Ft George G Meade, Staff Judge Advocate, Army Law Library
1st US Army, Fort George G Meade, MD 20755-7000 (301) 677-5572/2319; FTS 938-5572/2319; AUTOVON 923-5572/2319
Admin James M Ochoa.
Lib Type Law.
Coop Lib Nets Army Law Library Service.
Circ Servs Avail Not open to the general public; restricted to US Army.
Ref Servs Avail Not open to the general public; restricted to US Army.

537. Ft Monmouth, Patterson Army Community Hospital, Medical & Patients' Library
ATTN: HSXS-A-ML, Fort Monmouth, NJ 07703-5504 (201) 532-4277; FTS 532-4277; AUTOVON 992-4277
Admin E Elizabeth Butler.
Lib Type Health & Medicine; Hospital (Patients).
Spec Subs Health; medicine; preventive medicine; environmental.
Circ Servs Avail Not open to the general public.
Ref Servs Avail Not open to the general public.

538. Ft Monroe, General Library & Intern Training Center
Bldg 7, ATLS-LP, Fort Monroe, VA 23651-5123 (804) 727-2909/2797/2451; FTS 931-2909; AUTOVON 680-2909/2797
Admin Janet M Scheitle.
Lib Type General.
Spec Subs Management; Army family; Army life.
Info Ret Servs DIALOG; BRS; OCLC (ILL only). *Shared Catalog Nets* OCLC; TRALINET. *Coop Lib Nets* FEDLINK; TRALINET. *Elec Mail Nets* OPTIMIS; BRS.
Circ Servs Avail To other Federal libraries; to other libraries; not open to the general public; restricted to area military, dependents & DoD civilian employees.
Ref Servs Avail To other Federal libraries; to other libraries; not open to the general public; restricted to area military, dependents & DoD civilian employees.

539. Ft Myer Post Library
Bldg 469, Fort Myer, VA 22211-5050 (202) 692-9650; AUTOVON 226-3555
Admin Barbara S Christine. *Ref Lib* Lily Waters. *ILL* Phyllis Mauger. *Acq Lib* Gloria Holland.
Lib Type General.
Spec Subs Military science; business & public administration; computer science.
Shared Catalog Nets OCLC.
Circ Servs Avail Restricted to military & civilian personnel in Military District of Washington (MDW).
Ref Servs Avail Restricted to military & civilian personnel in Military District of Washington (MDW).

540. Ft Ord, Silas B Hayes Army Community Hospital, Medical Library
Fort Ord, CA 93941-5800 (408) 242-2023/6607
Lib Type Health & Medicine.

541. Ft Ord, Library Service Center
Bldg 4275, Fort Ord, CA 93941-5605 (408) 242-3618/4706; AUTOVON 929-7209
Admin Demaris B Klika. *Ref Lib* Carol Norton. *ILL* Marie James. *Acq Lib* Wendy S Hill.
Lib Type General.
Shared Catalog Nets OCLC. *Coop Lib Nets* Monterey Bay Area Cooperative (MOBAC).
Circ Servs Avail To other Federal libraries; to other libraries; restricted to military & authorized civilians.
Ref Servs Avail To other Federal libraries; to other libraries; restricted to military & authorized civilians.

542. Ft Polk, Bayne-Jones Army Community Hospital, Medical Library
Fort Polk, LA 71459-6000 (318) 535-3725/3736; FTS 528-3726; AUTOVON 863-3726
Admin Cecelia B Higginbotham. *ILL* Mary K Bradford.
Lib Type Health & Medicine.
Info Ret Servs MEDLINE. *Coop Lib Nets* HSC Union List of Serials; Health Science Library Assoc List of Serials. *Elec Mail Nets* OPTIMIS.
Circ Servs Avail To other Federal libraries; to other libraries; not open to the general public; restricted to staff.
Ref Servs Avail To other Federal libraries; to other libraries; restricted to staff.

543. Ft Polk, Morale Support Activities Library
Bldg 1801, Fort Polk, LA 71459 (318) 535-4212
Lib Type General.
Spec Subs Louisiana; military history.

544. Ft Polk, Office of the Staff Judge Advocate, HQ, 5th Infantry Division (Mech), Law Library
Fort Polk, LA 71459-5000 (318) 535-7231; FTS 528-2019; AUTOVON 863-2019
Admin A G Barber.
Lib Type Law.
Spec Subs Federal Reporter & supplements. *Spec Collecs* Louisiana & Texas case law.
Info Ret Servs WESTLAW.
Circ Servs Avail Restricted to office employees.
Ref Servs Avail Restricted to federal employees.

545. Ft Richardson, Post Library
Bldg 636, Fort Richardson, AK 99505-5100 AUTOVON 862-9188/0201
Lib Type General.

546. Ft Riley, Irwin Army Hospital, Medical Library
Bldg 485, Fort Riley, KS 66442-5036 (913) 239-7874; AUTOVON 856-7874
Admin Phyllis J Whiteside.
Lib Type Health & Medicine.
Spec Subs Medicine.
Info Ret Servs DIALOG. *Coop Lib Nets* Midcontinental Regional Medical Library Group; Health Service Command Journal Holdings. *Elec Mail Nets* OPTIMIS.
Circ Servs Avail To other Federal libraries; to other libraries; not open to the general public.
Ref Servs Avail Not open to the general public.

547. Ft Riley, Law Library
ATTN: AFYA-L (SRA-502), Fort Riley, KS 66442 (913) 239-2322; AUTOVON 856-6233/3670
Admin J D Sanders.
Lib Type Law.
Info Ret Servs WESTLAW.
Circ Servs Avail Restricted to Army personnel.
Ref Servs Avail Restricted to Army personnel.

548. Ft Riley, Main Post Library
Fort Riley, KS 66442-6416 (913) 239-2392; ILL 239-2460
Lib Type General.
Spec Subs Military history.
Circ Servs Avail Not open to the general public; restricted to military & dependents.

Ref Servs Avail Not open to the general public; restricted to military & dependents.

549. Ft Riley, Office of the Staff Judge Advocate, Law Library
1st Inf Div (M) & Fort Riley, ATTN: AFZN-JA, Fort Riley, KS 66442-5017 (913) 239-2217/3214; AUTOVON 856-2217/3214
Admin John A Burton.
Lib Type Law.
Info Ret Servs WESTLAW.
Circ Servs Avail To other Federal libraries; not open to the general public.
Ref Servs Avail To other Federal libraries; not open to the general public.

550. Ft Ritchie, Robert F Barrick, Memorial Library
Fort Ritchie, MD 21719 (301) 878-5060; AUTOVON 277-5060
Admin Rosemary M Knold.
Lib Type General.
Circ Servs Avail To other Federal libraries; to other libraries; not open to the general public; restricted to military & employees on post.
Ref Servs Avail To other Federal libraries; to other libraries; not open to the general public; restricted to military & employees on post.

551. Ft Rucker, Medical Library
Lyster Army Hospital, Bldg 301, Fort Rucker, AL 36362-5333 (205) 255-7350 255-7349; FTS 533-7350; AUTOVON 558-7350
Admin Jeanette A Chambers.
Lib Type Health & Medicine.
Spec Subs Clinical medicine; aviation medicine; dental, nursing, & veterinary medicine.
Shared Catalog Nets SEARMLS.
Circ Servs Avail To other Federal libraries; to other libraries; not open to the general public; restricted to in-house use.
Ref Servs Avail To other Federal libraries; to other libraries; to the general public.

552. Ft Shafter, Office of the Staff Judge Advocate, Law Library
SRA J-P5, US Army Western Command, Fort Shafter, HI 96858-5100 AUTOVON 438-9470
Admin Joseph C Nawahine.
Lib Type Law.
Spec Subs Medical malpractice. *Spec Collecs* Hawaiian law.
Circ Servs Avail Not open to the general public; restricted to in-house use only.
Ref Servs Avail Not open to the general public; restricted to DoD agencies, primarily Armed Forces.

553. Ft Shafter, Office of the Staff Judge Advocate, USASCH, Army Law Library
Bldg 718, Fort Shafter, HI 96858 AUTOVON (808) 438-2671
Admin Teresa A Houk.
Lib Type Law.
Circ Servs Avail To other libraries.
Ref Servs Avail To other Federal libraries; to other libraries.

554. Ft Sheridan, Law Library
ATTN: AFZO-JA, Fort Sheridan, IL 60037-5000 (312) 926-3188; AUTOVON 459-2605
Admin Bettie L Smith; David T Henry. *Acq Lib* David T Henry.
Lib Type Law.
Coop Lib Nets WESTLAW.
Circ Servs Avail Not open to the general public.
Ref Servs Avail Not open to the general public.

555. Ft Sheridan Post Library
Bldg 1, Bradley Loop, Fort Sheridan, IL 60037-5000 (312) 926-3188; FTS 926-5526; AUTOVON 459-5526
Admin Patricia Ann Reeves. *Ref Lib* Kaye Tocci (ILL).
Lib Type General.
Spec Subs Military arts & sciences; World Wars I & II; art; business.
Coop Lib Nets NSLS.
Circ Servs Avail To other Federal libraries; to other libraries.

Ref Servs Avail To other Federal libraries; to other libraries; to the general public; restricted to in-library use only.

556. Ft Sill, Nye Library
1640 Randolph Rd, Fort Sill, OK 73503-5100 (405) 351-3150; AUTOVON 639-5111
Admin Carolyn J Pate. *Ref Lib* Arlene Shaw. *ILL* Debora Kiehart. *Acq Lib* Darlene Wilson.
Lib Type General.
Spec Subs World War II; family affairs. *Spec Collecs* Webster University Deposit Collection. *In-house Files* Guides to military installations.
Info Ret Servs DIALOG. *Shared Catalog Nets* OCLC; TRALINET. *Coop Lib Nets* TRALINET. *Elec Mail Nets* OPTIMIS.
Circ Servs Avail To other Federal libraries; to other libraries; to the general public.
Ref Servs Avail To other Federal libraries; to other libraries; to the general public; restricted to on-site.

557. Ft Sill, Reynolds Army Hospital, Medical Library
Fort Sill, OK 73503-6400 (405) 351-5815; AUTOVON 639-3281
Lib Type Health & Medicine.

558. Ft Sill, Morris Swett Technical Library
Asst Commandant, USAFAS, Fort Sill, OK 73503-0312 (405) 351-4525/4477; AUTOVON 639-4525
Admin Lester Miller. *ILL* Martha Relph.
Lib Type Training Center.
Spec Subs Artillery; military science. *Spec Collecs* Indexes; rare books; computer video war coverage; unit histories. *In-house Files* Bibliographies; indexes; analytical files; vertical files.
Info Ret Servs DIALOG; BRS. *Shared Catalog Nets* OCLC; TRADOC. *Coop Lib Nets* OKULS; ODL. *Elec Mail Nets* OPTIMIS.
Circ Servs Avail To other Federal libraries; to other libraries; restricted to authorized users, interlibrary loan to all others.
Ref Servs Avail To other Federal libraries; to other libraries; to the general public.

559. Ft Stewart, Office of the Staff Judge Advocate, Army Law Library
ATTN: AFZP-JA, Fort Stewart, GA 31314 (912) 767-2952 767-2954; AUTOVON 870-2952 870-2954
Admin Julie W Walker. *ILL* Ronald H Johnson.
Lib Type Law.
Info Ret Servs WESTLAW.
Circ Servs Avail Not open to the general public; restricted to DoD & lawyers with need to use.
Ref Servs Avail Not open to the general public; restricted to DoD & lawyers with need to use.

560. Ft Stewart, Winn Army Community Hospital, Medical Library
USA Meddac, Bldg 302, Fort Stewart, GA 31314 (912) 767-6542
Lib Type Health & Medicine.

561. Ft Story Post Library
Bldg T-530, Fort Story, VA 23459-5067 (804) 422-7548; FTS 925-0548; AUTOVON 927-9548
Admin Leslie Smail. *ILL* Jacqueline Hite.
Lib Type General.
Spec Subs Military (Army); World War II. *Spec Collecs* Contemporary military reading; professional development reading; vocational & career materials; automotive repair & maintenance.
Info Ret Servs DIALOG. *Shared Catalog Nets* OCLC; TRALINET. *Coop Lib Nets* TRALINET. *Elec Mail Nets* OPTIMIS.
Circ Servs Avail To other Federal libraries; to other libraries; restricted to military & dependents.
Ref Servs Avail To other Federal libraries; to other libraries; restricted to military & dependents.

562. Ft Tilden Post Library
Fort Tilden, NY 11695
Lib Type General.

563. Ft Wainwright, Basset Army Hospital, Medical Library

Fort Wainwright, AK 99703-7300 (907) 353-8194; AUTOVON 353-5194
Admin Charles M Casterline. *Acq Lib* Ltc Waldman.
Lib Type Health & Medicine.
In-house Files Alaskan information.
Lib Deposit Designation NLM; ALN.
Shared Catalog Nets Madigan Medical Center, Tacoma, WA. *Coop Lib Nets* Alaska Library Network (ALN); Western Library Network (WLN).
Circ Servs Avail To other Federal libraries; to other libraries; restricted to hospital staff.
Ref Servs Avail To other Federal libraries; to other libraries; restricted to hospital staff except ILL or on approval of lib dir.

564. Ft Wainwright, Office of the Judge Advocate, Army Law Library

HQ, Fort Wainwright, AK 99703 (907) 353-7204; AUTOVON (317) 353-7204
Admin Lee Young. *Ref Lib* David Arcuri.
Lib Type Law.
Circ Servs Avail Not open to the general public; restricted to office staff.
Ref Servs Avail Not open to the general public; restricted to office staff.

565. Ft Wainwright Post Library

Bldg 3717, Fort Wainwright, AK 99703-5100 (907) 353-6114; AUTOVON (317) 353-6114
Admin Isabelle Mudd. *Ref Lib* Alfred Preston. *ILL* Betty Garrett. *Acq Lib* Judy Newton.
Lib Type General.
Shared Catalog Nets WLN. *Coop Lib Nets* Alaska Library Network (ALN). *Elec Mail Nets* Univ of Alaska VAX.
Circ Servs Avail To other Federal libraries; to other libraries.
Ref Servs Avail To other Federal libraries; to other libraries; to the general public.

566. Ft Leonard Wood, Gen Leonard Wood Army Community Hospital, Medical Library

Bldg 310, Fort Leonard Wood, MO 65473-5700 (314) 368-9110; FTS 270-9110; AUTOVON 581-9110
Admin Marian B Strang.
Lib Type Health & Medicine.
Spec Subs Medicine.
Info Ret Servs MEDLINE. *Coop Lib Nets* OCTANET. *Elec Mail Nets* OPTIMIS.
Circ Servs Avail To other Federal libraries; to other libraries; not open to the general public; restricted to hospital staff.
Ref Servs Avail To other Federal libraries; to other libraries; not open to the general public; restricted to hospital staff.

567. Ft Leonard Wood, Library Service Center

Bldg 384, Community Recreation Division, Fort Leonard Wood, MO 65473-5000 (314) 368-5431; FTS 368-5431; AUTOVON 581-5431
Admin Christine M Reser. *Ref Lib* Belenda Wilkerson (ILL).
Lib Type General.
Spec Subs Military arts & science. *Spec Collecs* Videos.
Info Ret Servs DIALOG; BRS; OCLC. *Shared Catalog Nets* OCLC. *Coop Lib Nets* Southwest Missouri Library Network. *Elec Mail Nets* OPTIMIS.
Circ Servs Avail To other Federal libraries; to other libraries; restricted to the military community.
Ref Servs Avail To other Federal libraries; to other libraries; restricted to the military community.

568. Ft Leonard Wood, Office of the Staff Judge Advocate, Army Field Law Library

Fort Leonard Wood, MO 65473-5000 (314) 368-2133; AUTOVON 581-2133
Admin John E White.
Lib Type Law.

Spec Subs Missouri law; federal law. *Spec Collecs* Federal Reporter; federal supplement; ALR's; Missouri state statutes & reporters; SW Reporter; CCH labor law library; CFR; Federal Register.
Info Ret Servs WESTLAW; NEXIS; LEXIS. *Coop Lib Nets* ALLS.
Ref Servs Avail To other Federal libraries; not open to the general public; restricted to use by local & visiting attorneys & the colleges on site.

569. Ft Leonard Wood Post Library

Bldg 1607, Fort Leonard Wood, MO 65473-5000 (314) 368-5431; FTS 368-5431; AUTOVON 581-5431
Admin Christine M Reser. *Ref Lib* Belenda Wilkerson (ILL).
Lib Type General.
Spec Subs College catalogs on fiche; Black literature; Military arts & science; management & business administration. *Spec Collecs* Telephone directories on microfiche; foreign language collection.
Info Ret Servs DIALOG; BRS; DTIC. *Shared Catalog Nets* OCLC. *Coop Lib Nets* TRALINET; Southwest Missouri Library Network. *Elec Mail Nets* OPTIMIS.
Circ Servs Avail To other Federal libraries; to other libraries; to the general public.
Ref Servs Avail To other Federal libraries; to other libraries; to the general public.

570. 4th Army, Office of the Staff Judge Advocate, Army Law Library

Fort Sheridan, IL 60037 (512) 221-2208
Lib Type Law.

571. 4th Infantry Division (Mech), Office of the Staff Judge Advocate, Army Law Library

Fort Carson, CO 80913 (303) 579-3012
Lib Type Law.

572. Hawley Army Health Clinic Library

Bldg 300, Fort Benjamin Harrison, IN 46216 (317) 542-5196
Lib Type Health & Medicine.
Coop Lib Nets Central Indiana Health Science Library Consortium.

573. HQ Army COMMO Command, Army Law Library

ACC-SJA, Fort Huachuca, AZ 85613 AUTOVON 80-761-2151
Lib Type Law.

574. HQ Military Traffic Management Command (MTMC), Office of the Staff Judge Advocate, Army Law Library

NASSIF Bldg, Falls Church, VA 22041 AUTOVON 80-756-1580
Lib Type Law.

575. HQ 7th Signal Command & Ft Ritchie, Office of the Command Judge Advocate, Army Law Library

Fort Ritchie, MD 21719 AUTOVON 80-650-5771/5731
Lib Type Law.

576. HQ 3rd Reg US Army Criminal Investigation Command (USACIDC), Office of the Judge Advocate, Army Law Library

Fort Gillem, Forest Park, GA 30050 (404) 678-6811/7323
Lib Type Law.

577. HQ TRADOC Combined Arms Test Activity (TCATA), Technical Library

Fort Hood, TX 76544 (817) 288-9004; FTS 788-9004; AUTOVON 738-9004
Lib Type Special.
Spec Subs Computer science; military technology.
Info Ret Servs DTIC. *Coop Lib Nets* TRALINET.
Circ Servs Avail Not open to the general public; restricted to DoD personnel.
Ref Servs Avail Not open to the general public; restricted to DoD personnel.

578. HQ US Army Computer System Command, Army Law Library
Legal Office, STOP C-8, Fort Belvoir, VA 22060 (703) 664-4083
Lib Type Law.

579. HQ US Army Criminal Investigation Command (USACIDC), Office of the Staff Judge Advocate, Army Law Library
5611 Columbia Pike, Falls Church, VA 22041 AUTOVON 80-756-2281
Lib Type Law.

580. HQ, US Army Materiel Command
ATTN: AMCIM-RF, 5001 Eisenhower Ave, Alexandria, VA 22333-0001 (202) 274-8087; AUTOVON 284-8087
Admin Ingjerd O Omdahl.
Spec Subs This is the administrative office with the responsibility for 42 general & technical libraries within the command.
Elec Mail Nets OPTIMIS; ARPANET.

581. HQ US Army Training & Doctrine Command, Technical Library
Bldg 133 (ATLS-LT), Fort Monroe, VA 23651-5123 (804) 727-2821; FTS 931-2821; AUTOVON 680-2821
Admin Frances M Doyle. *Ref Lib* Areena J Lowe.
Lib Type Special.
Spec Subs Military science; military history. *Spec Collecs* Obsolete field manuals & Army regulations.
Info Ret Servs DIALOG; OCLC(loar subsystem); BRS; NASA RECON; DTIC; DROLS. *Shared Catalog Nets* OCLC; TRALINET. *Coop Lib Nets* FEDLINK; TRALINET. *Elec Mail Nets* OPTIMIS; BRS.
Circ Servs Avail To other Federal libraries; to other libraries; not open to the general public; restricted to US Government or ILL.
Ref Servs Avail To other Federal libraries; to other libraries; not open to the general public; restricted to US Government or interlibrary request.

582. HQ Western Area, Office of the Staff Judge Advocate, Law Library
HQ MTMC-WA OAB, Oakland, CA 94626 (415) 466-2921; FTS 466-2921; AUTOVON 859-2921
Admin Winston J Jackson, Jr.
Lib Type Law.
Spec Subs Military Justice Reporter; decisions of the Comptroller General. *Spec Collecs* Army Lawyer.
Info Ret Servs WESTLAW.
Circ Servs Avail Restricted to command staff group.
Ref Servs Avail Restricted to command staff group.

583. The Institute of Heraldry Library
Army Adjutant General Ctr, Bldg 15, Cameron Station, 5010 Duke St, Alexandria, VA 22304-5050 (202) 274-6544
Lib Type Special.
Spec Subs Art; flags; heraldry; insignia; military history; medals; medallic art; seals; symbols & symbolism; uniforms.
Ref Servs Avail Not open to the general public; restricted to use by special permission.

584. The Judge Advocate General's School, Army Law Library Service, Army Law Library
Charlottesville, VA 22901 (804) 293-4382
Admin Helena Daidone.
Lib Type Law.

585. Letterkenny Post Library
Letterkenny Army Depot, Chambersburg, PA 17201 (717) 267-8875; AUTOVON 238-8875
Admin Judith Moore.
Lib Type General.
Circ Servs Avail To other Federal libraries; not open to the general public; restricted to military & dependents.
Ref Servs Avail To other Federal libraries; not open to the general public; restricted to military & dependents.

586. Letterman Army Institute of Research, Medical Research Library
Presidio of San Francisco, CA 94129-6800 (415) 561-2600; AUTOVON 586-2600
Admin Cynthia Matison. *ILL* Phyllis Schweitzer. *Acq Lib* Richard Kempton.
Lib Type Health & Medicine.
Spec Subs Blood research; insect repellents; combat casualty studies (military trauma); lasers (ocular hazards); toxicology; veterinary medicine. *In-house Files* Institute reports & reprints.
Info Ret Servs DIALOG; MEDLARS; DROLS (DOD/DTIC). *Shared Catalog Nets* OCLC. *Coop Lib Nets* SFBLN; NCNMLG; OPTIMIS/Army Libraries (HSC). *Elec Mail Nets* OPTIMIS; Ontyme; DOCLINE.
Circ Servs Avail Not open to the general public.
Ref Servs Avail Not open to the general public.

587. Letterman Army Medical Center, Medical Library
Bldg 1100 Rm 338, Presidio of San Francisco, CA 94129-6700 (415) 561-3124; AUTOVON 586-3124
Admin Dixie Meagher. *Ref Lib* Anne Ludvik.
Lib Type Health & Medicine.
Info Ret Servs DIALOG; MEDLARS. *Shared Catalog Nets* OCLC. *Coop Lib Nets* San Francisco Biomedical Library Network (SFBLN); Northern California & Nevada Medical Library Group (NCNMLG). *Elec Mail Nets* OnTyme; OPTIMIS.
Circ Servs Avail Not open to the general public; restricted to staff.
Ref Servs Avail Not open to the general public; restricted to staff.

588. Letterman Army Medical Center, Office of the Judge Advocate, Army Law Library
San Francisco, CA 94129 (415) 561-4932
Lib Type Law.

589. Lexington Bluegrass Army Depot, Division of Quality Assurance, Technical Library
SDSLB-QAQ, Lexington, KY 40511-5030 (606) 293-3891
Lib Type General.
Spec Subs Technical data filing & research for repair, testing, & storage of electronic & other army equipment.

590. Lexington Bluegrass Army Depot, Law Library
Lexington, KY 40511-5003 (606) 293-3932; AUTOVON 745-3932
Admin Mary C Ledford.
Lib Type Law.
Spec Subs Legal reference.
Circ Servs Avail Not open to the general public.
Ref Servs Avail Not open to the general public.

591. Madigan Army Medical Center, Medical Library
Box 375, Tacoma, WA 98431-5375 (206) 967-6782; AUTOVON 357-6782
Admin Elizabeth C Bolden. *ILL* Robert L Clark.
Lib Type Health & Medicine.
Info Ret Servs NLM. *Shared Catalog Nets* OCLC. *Elec Mail Nets* OPTIMIS; CLASS.
Circ Servs Avail To other Federal libraries; to other libraries; not open to the general public.
Ref Servs Avail To other Federal libraries; to other libraries; not open to the general public.

592. Madigan Army Medical Center, Medical Technical Library
Tacoma, WA 98431-5068 (206) 967-7082; FTS 967-6737; AUTOVON 357-6737
Admin S A Davidson. *Ref Lib* Ted McKenna.
Lib Type Law.
Lib Deposit Designation JAG Corps.
Circ Servs Avail To other libraries; not open to the general public.
Ref Servs Avail To other libraries; not open to the general public.

593. Madigan Army Medical Center, Morale Support Library
Box 263, Tacoma, WA 98431-5263 (206) 967-6198
Admin Marganne Weathers.
Lib Type Hospital (Patients).
Spec Subs Patient education.
Shared Catalog Nets OCLC.
Circ Servs Avail To other Federal libraries; to other libraries; restricted to military ID card holders.
Ref Servs Avail To other Federal libraries; to other libraries; restricted to military ID card holders.

594. Martin Army Hospital, Professional & Patients' Library
Bldg 9200, HSXB-B-L, Fort Benning, GA 31905-6100 (404) 544-1341
Lib Type Health & Medicine.

595. McAlester Army Ammunition Plant, Army Law Library
Legal Counsel, SARMC-CC, McAlester, OK 74501 (918) 731-3145, ext 2438
Lib Type Law.

596. Mechanicsburg Defense Depot, Base Library
Mechanicsburg, PA 17055
Lib Type General.

597. Medical Research Institute for Infectious Diseases Library
Fort Detrick, Frederick, MD 21701 (301) 663-2720
Lib Type Health & Medicine.

598. Medical Research Institute of Chemical Defense, Wood Technical Library
Aberdeen Proving Ground, MD 21010-5425 (301) 671-4135
Lib Type Health & Medicine.
Spec Subs Neurosciences; toxicology.
Info Ret Servs DIALOG; MEDLINE. *Shared Catalog Nets* OCLC. *Coop Lib Nets* FEDLINK.

599. Military Ocean Terminal Post Library
Bldg 61B, MTMC EA ATTN:MTE-BY-ISM, Bayonne, NJ 07002-5301 (201) 823-6203; AUTOVON 247-6203
Admin E Estelle Reid.
Lib Type General.
Circ Servs Avail To other Federal libraries; to other libraries; restricted to DoD base personnel.
Ref Servs Avail To other Federal libraries; to other libraries; to the general public.

600. Moncrief Army Hospital, Medical Library
Fort Jackson, SC 29207 (803) 751-2293; AUTOVON 734-2293
Lib Type Health & Medicine.

601. New Cumberland Army Depot, Law Library
Legal Office, New Cumberland, PA 17070 (717) 782-6310; FTS 589-6310; AUTOVON 977-6310
Admin James F Toms (Chief Counsel).
Lib Type Law.
Info Ret Servs LEXIS.
Circ Servs Avail Not open to the general public.
Ref Servs Avail Restricted to Depot & tenant agencies.

602. New Cumberland Army Depot Post Library
New Cumberland, PA 17070-5001 (717) 782-6011; AUTOVON 977-7121
Admin Sharon J Kauffman.
Lib Type General.

603. Oakland Army Base Post Library
Bldg 726, Oakland, CA 94626-5000 (415) 466-2906
Lib Type General.
Spec Subs Military science.
Circ Servs Avail Not open to the general public; restricted to base personnel.

Ref Servs Avail Not open to the general public; restricted to base personnel.

604. Pentagon Law Library
Rm 1A518, The Pentagon, Washington, DC 20310-6000 (202) 695-2957
Admin Dorothy Cross (Dir). *Ref Lib* A L Hardin.
Lib Type Law.
Spec Subs Military law; defense procurement.
Circ Servs Avail To other Federal libraries; to other libraries; not open to the general public.
Ref Servs Avail To other Federal libraries; to other libraries; restricted to those with access to the Pentagon.

605. Pentagon Library
Pentagon, Rm 1A518, Washington, DC 20310-6000 (202) 697-4301; AUTOVON 227-4301
Admin Dorothy A Cross; Clarence Hardin (Law). *Ref Lib* Gene Kubal. *ILL* Carol Bursik. *Acq Lib* Menandra Whitmore.
Lib Type Special.
Spec Subs Law; management; international affairs; military science. *Spec Collecs* Army regulations.
Lib Deposit Designation GPO Depository Library.
Info Ret Servs DIALOG; NEXIS; LEXIS; WESTLAW; LEGISLATE; DMS. *Shared Catalog Nets* OCLC. *Coop Lib Nets* FEDLINK; FLICC. *Elec Mail Nets* OPTIMIS.
Circ Servs Avail To other Federal libraries; to other libraries; not open to the general public; restricted to DoD—Pentagon.
Ref Servs Avail Not open to the general public; restricted to DoD—Pentagon.

606. Pine Bluff Arsenal, Office of the Post Judge Advocate, Army Law Library
Pine Bluff, AR 71611 (501) 740-5892
Lib Type Law.

607. Presidio Army Museum Library
Bldg 2, Presidio of San Francisco, CA 94129-5502 (415) 561-4115
Lib Type Special.
Spec Subs 19th century; Spanish-American War. *Spec Collecs* History of San Francisco; History of the West; Indian Wars; Presidio History of San Francisco; Women of War; US Army History, World War I & II, Korea, Vietnam.
Ref Servs Avail Not open to the general public; restricted to staff & researchers by appointment.

608. Presidio of San Francisco, Office of the Staff Judge Advocate, Army Law Library
HQ, 6th Region USACIDC, San Francisco, CA 94129 (415) 561-3812; AUTOVON 586-3812
Admin Stephen Nypaver III.
Lib Type Law.

609. Presidio of San Francisco, Post Library
Bldg 386, Presidio of San Francisco, CA 94129-5000 AUTOVON 586-3448
Lib Type General.

610. Presidio of San Francisco, 6th US Army, Office of the Staff Judge Advocate, Army Law Library
Presidio San Francisco, San Francisco, CA 94129 (415) 561-5146
Lib Type Law.

611. Presidio San Francisco, Office of the Post Judge Advocate, Army Law Library
San Francisco, CA 94129 (415) 561-5591
Lib Type Law.

612. Red River Army Depot, Army Law Library
Legal Officer, Texarkana, TX 75501 AUTOVON 80-730-3258
Lib Type Law.

613. Red River Army Depot, School of Engineering & Logistics, Technical Library

Red River Army Depot, Texarkana, TX 75507-5000 (214) 838-2817/3430; FTS 730-3430; AUTOVON 829-3430

Admin Lelia K Vollman. *Ref Lib* Reference. *ILL* Mary Weeks (Acq).

Lib Type Training Center.

Spec Subs Engineering production, safety, maintainability & quality/reliability; supply & maintenance management fields; computer science; management; military history. *Spec Collecs* Reports by former students.

Info Ret Servs NTIS; DTIC; DLSIE.

Circ Servs Avail To other Federal libraries; to other libraries; not open to the general public.

Ref Servs Avail To other Federal libraries; not open to the general public; restricted to DoD agencies.

614. Redstone Arsenal, Fox Army Community Hospital, Medical Library

Redstone Arsenal, AL 35809

Lib Type Health & Medicine.

615. Redstone Scientific Information Center

Redstone Arsenal, AL 35898-5241 (205) 876-3251; FTS 876-3251; AUTOVON 746-3251

Admin Jane F Cooney. *Ref Lib* Joyce B Plaster. *ILL* Joyce M Kelly. *Acq Lib* Dorothy S Ward.

Lib Type Engineering & Science.

Spec Subs Aeronautics; astronomy & astrophysics; atmospheric sciences; chemistry; electronics & electrical engineering; mathematical & computer sciences; mechanical & industrial engineering; military sciences; missile technology, communication, detection, & countermeasures; nuclear science & technology; ordnance; physics; propulsion & fuels; space technology.

Lib Deposit Designation DoD; NASA.

Info Ret Servs DIALOG; BRS; SDC. *Coop Lib Nets* ALEX; NAAL.

Circ Servs Avail To other Federal libraries; to other libraries; restricted to registered patrons.

Ref Servs Avail To other Federal libraries; to other libraries; to the general public.

616. Walter Reed Army Institute of Research Library

Walter Reed Army Medical Center, Bldg 40 Rm 1062, Washington, DC 20307-5100 (202) 576-2417; AUTOVON 291-2417

Admin V Lynn Gera. *Ref Lib* James E Tolliver, Jr (ILL). *Acq Lib* Rae E Dubois.

Lib Type Special.

Info Ret Servs DIALOG; BRS. *Shared Catalog Nets* OCLC.

Circ Servs Avail To other Federal libraries; to other libraries; to the general public.

Ref Servs Avail To other Federal libraries; to other libraries; to the general public.

617. Walter Reed Army Medical Center, Post/Patients' Library

Bldg 2 Rm 3D01, Washington, DC 20307-5001 (202) 576-1314; AUTOVON 291-1314

Admin Gail M Henderson.

Lib Type General; Hospital (Patients).

Spec Subs Cancer & AIDS.

Shared Catalog Nets OCLC. *Coop Lib Nets* FEDLINK. *Elec Mail Nets* OPTIMIS.

Circ Servs Avail To other Federal libraries; to other libraries.

Ref Servs Avail To other Federal libraries; to other libraries.

618. Sacramento Army Depot, Law Library

Commander, Legal & Claims Office, AHN: SDSSA-ALO, Sacramento, CA 95813-5020 (916) 388-3274

Admin Larry Bergdahl. *Ref Lib* Clifford J Moy (Chief Counsel).

Lib Type Law.

Circ Servs Avail Not open to the general public; restricted to office lawyers.

Ref Servs Avail Not open to the general public; restricted to office lawyers.

619. Sacramento Army Depot, Technical Library

ATTN: SDSSA-QSM-4, Sacramento, CA 95813-5027 (916) 388-2211; AUTOVON 839-2467/2756

Admin L Connie Maynard. *Ref Lib* Jarrett Richie (ILL, Acq).

Lib Type Training Center.

Spec Subs Operator's, organizational, & direct support maintenance manuals. *In-house Files* SAAD final performance checks; SAAD suggestions.

Ref Servs Avail To other Federal libraries; not open to the general public.

620. St Louis Area Support Center, Recreational Library

Bldg 183, Granite City, IL 62040 (618) 452-4332; AUTOVON 892-4332

Lib Type General.

Spec Subs Illinois & Missouri. *Spec Collecs* Military science.

Ref Servs Avail Not open to the general public; restricted to military, dependents, & post civilians.

621. Schofield Barracks, Office of the Staff Judge Advocate, 25th Infantry Division, Army Law Library

Schofield Barracks, HI 96857 (808) 655-9269; AUTOVON 455-4885

Admin Michael Parker.

Lib Type Law.

Info Ret Servs LEXIS. *Elec Mail Nets* LEXIS.

Circ Servs Avail Restricted to military.

Ref Servs Avail Restricted to military.

622. Schofield Barracks, Sgt Yano Library

Bldg 362, Schofield Bks, HI 96857-5000 (808) 655-0145

Admin William R Ranger. *ILL* June Kniery.

Lib Type General.

Spec Collecs Hawaiiana; US Army in the Pacific. *In-house Files* Photo collection; vertical file materials on US Army in Hawaii.

Info Ret Servs DIALOG; WILSONLINE. *Shared Catalog Nets* OCLC. *Coop Lib Nets* Informal network between Army & Pacific Air Force (PACAF) Library systems; informal arrangement with other armed forces libraries, the Univ of Hawaii, & the state library systems.

Circ Servs Avail To other Federal libraries; to other libraries.

Ref Servs Avail To other Federal libraries; to other libraries; to the general public.

623. Scientific & Technical Information Division Library

Information Management Directorate, Bldg 59, Dover, NJ 07801 (201) 724-2914; FTS 724-2914; AUTOVON 880-2914

Admin Normand L Varieur. *Ref Lib* Ismail Haznedari (Reports); Ruth Rudisill (Books & Serials, ILL). *Acq Lib* Diana Seville.

Lib Type Engineering & Science.

Spec Subs Explosives; propellants; pyrotechnics; armament; fire control (weaponry). *Spec Collecs* Archives of Picatinny Arsenal, Dover, NJ; Frankford Arsenal, Philadelphia, PA; Rodman Research Lab, Rock Island, IL.

Info Ret Servs DIALOG; BRS. *Shared Catalog Nets* OCLC; SBIN. *Coop Lib Nets* OCLC; FLICC; NJ Regional Library Cooperative.

Circ Servs Avail To other libraries; restricted to Picatinny personnel.

Ref Servs Avail To other Federal libraries; to other libraries; to the general public.

624. Selfridge ANG Base Library

Bldg 169, US Army Support Activity, Wagner & George Sts, Selfridge ANG Base, MI 48045 (313) 466-5088/5238

Lib Type General.

Spec Subs Military history.

Circ Servs Avail Not open to the general public; restricted to military, dependents, & base civilian employees.

Ref Servs Avail Not open to the general public; restricted to military, dependents, & base civilian employees.

625. Seneca Post Library
Seneca Army Depot, ATTN: SDSSE-TR, Romulus, NY 14541 (607) 869-0548; FTS 869-0548; AUTOVON 78-489-8548
Admin Margaret A Brewer.
Lib Type General.
Spec Subs Military arts & sciences; police; criminology; NY Finger Lakes region; women's history.
Circ Servs Avail To other Federal libraries; not open to the general public; restricted to military, dependents, & civilian employees.
Ref Servs Avail To other Federal libraries; not open to the general public; restricted to military, dependents, & civilian employees.

626. Sharpe Army Depot, Installation Library
ATTN: SDSSH-AMW-MSA, Lathrop, CA 95331-5214 (209) 982-2656; AUTOVON 462-2656
Admin Sheila White.
Lib Type General.
Coop Lib Nets CAL Cooperative Library (49-99).
Circ Servs Avail Restricted to military & DoD employees.
Ref Servs Avail Restricted to military & DoD employees.

627. Sharpe Army Depot, Law Library
Bldg S-4, Legal & Claims Office, Lathrop, CA 95331-5120 (209) 982-2404/2419; FTS 623-2442; AUTOVON 462-2441/2442
Admin Donna M Mizar.
Lib Type Law.
Spec Subs Government contracts; merit system protection board; federal labor relations; equal employment.
Coop Lib Nets Army Law Library, Charlottesville, VA.
Circ Servs Avail To other Federal libraries; not open to the general public.
Ref Servs Avail To other Federal libraries; not open to the general public.

628. Sierra Army Depot, Law Library
Herlong, CA 96113 (916) 827-2111; AUTOVON 830-9548
Admin Jerry Lawson.
Lib Type Law.
Circ Servs Avail To other Federal libraries; not open to the general public.
Ref Servs Avail To other Federal libraries; not open to the general public.

629. SW Region Recruiting Command, Office of the Judge Advocate, Army Law Library
PO Box 8277, Wainwright St, San Antonio, TX 78293 AUTOVON 80-746-6302
Lib Type Law.

630. Stewart Subpost Library
Stewart Army Subpost, Newburgh, NY 12550-9999 (914) 564-1253; AUTOVON 247-3501
Admin Florence K Irons.
Lib Type General.
Circ Servs Avail To other Federal libraries; not open to the general public; restricted to Armed Forces & DACs.
Ref Servs Avail To other Federal libraries; to other libraries; not open to the general public; restricted to Armed Forces & DACs.

631. TECOM, HQ Library
ATTN: DRSTE-TO-F, Aberdeen, MD 21005 (301) 278-5517; AUTOVON 283-5517/5323
Lib Type General.

632. Thayer Engineering Library
Bldg 270, Fort Belvoir, VA 22060-5261 (703) 664-2524; FTS 664-2524; AUTOVON 354-2524
Admin William F Tuceling. *Ref Lib* Roberta Babbitt (ILL).
Lib Type Engineering & Science.
Spec Subs Civil & military engineering, American & military history. *Spec Collecs* Rare book room (18th-20th century).
Info Ret Servs DIALOG; DTIC. *Shared Catalog Nets* OCLC. *Coop Lib Nets* TRALINET. *Elec Mail Nets* OPTIMIS.
Circ Servs Avail To other Federal libraries; to other libraries; not open to the general public.

633. Tobyhanna Army Depot, Post Library
Tobyhanna, PA 18466-5099 (717) 894-7316
Lib Type General.
Info Ret Servs BRS. *Shared Catalog Nets* OCLC. *Coop Lib Nets* FEDLINK.

634. Tobyhanna Army Depot, Technical Library
ATTN: SDSTO-TM, Tobyhanna, PA 18466-5097 AUTOVON 795-7679
Lib Type General.

635. Tripler Army Medical Center, Hospital Library
Tripler AMC, HI 96859-5000 (808) 433-6968/6745
Admin Charles W Walton. *ILL* Dennis Halbert.
Lib Type Hospital (Patients).
Spec Subs Health; military history. *Spec Collecs* Hawaiiana.
Info Ret Servs DIALOG. *Shared Catalog Nets* OCLC. *Coop Lib Nets* Oahu Library Network (OLN). *Elec Mail Nets* Telex.
Circ Servs Avail To other Federal libraries; to other libraries; not open to the general public; restricted to active duty military & retirees & dependents.
Ref Servs Avail To other Federal libraries; to other libraries; not open to the general public; restricted to active duty military & retirees & dependents.

636. Tripler Army Medical Center, Medical Library
US Army Health Services Command, Tripler AMC, HI 96859-5000 (808) 433-6391/6917
Admin Marilyn A Requena. *Ref Lib* Janice V Nakagawara (Acq). *ILL* Alma Yee.
Lib Type Health & Medicine.
Spec Subs Urology; psychiatry; neurology; military medicine.
Info Ret Servs DIALOG; MEDLARS. *Shared Catalog Nets* OCLC. *Coop Lib Nets* FEDLINK/FLICC; Medical Library Group of Hawaii (MLGH Union list); Health Services Command (HSC Union List); Regional Medical Library Network (RML). *Elec Mail Nets* OPTIMIS.
Circ Servs Avail To other Federal libraries; to other libraries; not open to the general public.
Ref Servs Avail To other Federal libraries; to other libraries; not open to the general public.

637. Umatilla Depot Activity, Reference Library
Bldg 1, Hermiston, OR 97838 (503) 567-6421 ext 230; AUTOVON 790-5230
Admin Sondra Fortney.
Lib Type General.
Spec Subs Army regulations; pamphlets; training manuals.
Circ Servs Avail Not open to the general public; restricted to government use.
Ref Servs Avail Not open to the general public; restricted to government use.

638. US Army Aberdeen Proving Ground Post Library
Bldg 3320, Aberdeen, MD 21005 AUTOVON 283-3417
Lib Type General.

639. US Army Aeromedical Research Laboratory, Medical Library
Bldg 301, USAAMC, Aeromedical Center-Lyster US Army Community Hospital, Fort Rucker, AL 36362-5333 (205) 255-7350
Lib Type Health & Medicine.
Spec Subs Clinical medicine; pathology; dentistry; aviation medicine; veterinary medicine.

640. US Army Air Defense Artillery Center, Office of the Staff Judge Advocate, Army Law Library
Fort Bliss, TX 79916 (915) 568-5504
Lib Type Law.

641. US Army Air Defense Artillery School Library
Bldg 2 Wing E Rm 181, Fort Bliss, TX 79916-7027 (915) 568-2489; FTS 478-5781; AUTOVON 978-5781
Admin Delfina C Galloway. *Ref Lib* Dorothy R LeBorious (ILL).
Lib Type Training Center.
Spec Subs Air defense; artillery; education; technology; military history. *Spec Collecs* Southwest collection; archives collection.

Info Ret Servs DIALOG. *Shared Catalog Nets* OCLC. *Coop Lib Nets* FEDLINK. *Elec Mail Nets* OPTIMIS.
Circ Servs Avail To other Federal libraries; to other libraries.
Ref Servs Avail To other Federal libraries; to other libraries; to the general public.

642. US Army & Air Force Exchange Service, Army Law Library
Office of Counsel, Dallas, TX 75222 (214) 738-3642
Lib Type Law.

643. US Army Armament Research & Development Center, Plastics Technical Evaluation Center
SMCAR-AET-O, Dover, NJ 07801-5001 (201) 724-2778; FTS 724-2778; AUTOVON 880-2778
Admin Harry E Pebly (Dir). *Ref Lib* Suseela Chandrasekar.
Lib Type Special.
Spec Subs Plastics; reinforced plastics; adhesives; applications of plastics; filament winding; NDT—plastics; processing plastics; weathering plastics. *Spec Collecs* Military specifications & standards; handbooks on plastics. *In-house Files* Reports published on above subjects.
Info Ret Servs DIALOG; DTIC. *Shared Catalog Nets* OCLC.
Circ Servs Avail To other Federal libraries; restricted to Center patrons.
Ref Servs Avail To other Federal libraries; restricted to Center patrons.

644. US Army Armor School Library
ATSB-DOTD-L, Bldg 2369, Fort Knox, KY 40121-5200 (502) 624-6231; FTS 354-6231; AUTOVON 464-6231
Admin William H Hansen. *Ref Lib* Freeman F Shell, Jr. *ILL* Lorraine M Tilton. *Acq Lib* Judy C Stephenson.
Lib Type Training Center.
Spec Subs Armored warfare; history & role of armor; military history. *Spec Collecs* Student papers; after action-reports; armor units in World War II. *In-house Files* School academic archives.
Lib Deposit Designation US Army Armor School.
Info Ret Servs DIALOG; BRS; DROLS. *Shared Catalog Nets* OCLC. *Coop Lib Nets* TRALINET; KLN. *Elec Mail Nets* OPTIMIS.
Circ Servs Avail To other Federal libraries; to other libraries.
Ref Servs Avail To other Federal libraries; to other libraries; to the general public.

645. US Army Arms, Munitions & Chemical Command, Army Law Library
Legal Office, DRSMC-GC (R), Rock Island, IL 61299 AUTOVON 80-794-4051
Lib Type Law.

646. US Army Aviation Center Library
Community Activities Program, Bldg 212, Novosel Rd & 5th Ave, Fort Rucker, AL 36362 (205) 255-5010
Lib Type General.
Spec Subs Support for undergraduate degree courses offered on post. *Spec Collecs* Jackson Aviation Collection.
Shared Catalog Nets OCLC.
Circ Servs Avail Restricted to military, dependents & retirees.
Ref Servs Avail Restricted to military, dependents & retirees.

647. US Army Aviation Center, Office of the Staff Judge Advocate, Army Law Library
Fort Rucker, AL 36362 (205) 255-5491
Lib Type Law.

648. US Army Aviation System Command (AVSCOM), AMSAV-JR, Army Law Library
Legal Office, 4300 Goodfellow Blvd, Saint Louis, MO 63120 AUTOVON 80-273-3391
Lib Type Law.

649. US Army Aviation Technical Library
Fort Rucker, AL 36362-5000 (205) 255-5018; FTS 533-5018; AUTOVON 558-5018
Admin Anne P Foreman. *Ref Lib* Beverly Hall/Beverly McMaster (ILL). *ILL* Beverly McMaster. *Acq Lib* James Lee.
Lib Type Training Center.
Spec Subs Aviation & military history. *Spec Collecs* Army aviation. *In-house Files* Army regulations & publications, military standards.
Info Ret Servs DIALOG; BRS; NASA/RECON; NEXIS; LEXIS; DTIC; WILSONLINE. *Coop Lib Nets* OCLC; TRADOC Library & Information Network (TRALINET). *Elec Mail Nets* OPTIMIS.
Circ Servs Avail To other Federal libraries; to other libraries; to the general public.
Ref Servs Avail To other Federal libraries; to other libraries; to the general public; restricted to manual reference questions, no extensive research or computer searches.

650. US Army Ballistics Research Laboratory, Scientific & Technical Information Center
AMXBR-OD-ST, Aberdeen, MD 21005-5066 (301) 671-6841; AUTOVON 298-6839
Admin Louise LeTendre.
Lib Type General.

651. US Army Belvoir Research Development & Engineering Technical Library
Bldg 315, Fort Belvoir, VA 22060-5606 (703) 664-5179; AUTOVON 354-5179
Admin Gloria R James. *Ref Lib* Lois Carey. *ILL* Sonia Smith. *Acq Lib* Lois McCown.
Lib Type Engineering & Science.
Spec Subs Electronics; countermine; counterintrusion; fuels; lubricants; bridging; robotics; energy; engines.
Info Ret Servs DIALOG. *Shared Catalog Nets* OCLC.
Circ Servs Avail To other Federal libraries; to other libraries; not open to the general public.
Ref Servs Avail To other Federal libraries; to other libraries.

652. US Army Center of Military History Library
20 Massachusetts Ave NW, Washington, DC 20314-0200 (202) 272-0321; AUTOVON 285-0321
Admin Hannah Zeidlik. *Ref Lib* Mary L Sawyer (ILL, Acq).
Lib Type Special.
Spec Subs History of the US Army & related activities. *Spec Collecs* Army unit histories; War Dept/Dept of the Army publications; Army directories & strength reports.
Shared Catalog Nets OCLC. *Coop Lib Nets* FEDLINK.
Circ Servs Avail Restricted to CMH employees.
Ref Servs Avail To other Federal libraries; to other libraries; to the general public.

653. US Army Chaplain Center & School Library
Fort Monmouth, NJ 07703-5511 (201) 532-3082
Lib Type Academic.

654. US Army Chemical School, Fisher Library
Bldg 2262, Fort McClellan, AL 36205-5020 (205) 238-4414; FTS 238-4414; AUTOVON 865-4414
Admin Sybil P Parker. *Ref Lib* Mary N Russell (ILL). *Acq Lib* Martha W Boshell.
Lib Type Academic.
Spec Subs Military; science.
Info Ret Servs DIALOG; DTIC. *Shared Catalog Nets* OCLC. *Elec Mail Nets* OPTIMIS.
Circ Servs Avail To other Federal libraries; to other libraries; not open to the general public.
Ref Servs Avail To other Federal libraries; to other libraries; not open to the general public.

655. US Army Claims Service, Office of the Post Judge Advocate, Army Law Library
Fort George G Meade, MD 20755 AUTOVON 938-5336
Lib Type Law.

656. US Army Cold Region Research & Engineering Laboratory Library
72 Lyme Rd, Hanover, NH 03755-1290 (603) 646-4221; FTS 836-4221; AUTOVON 684-4221
Admin Nancy C Liston.
Lib Type Engineering & Science.
Spec Subs Engineering; hydrology; climatology; Antarctica; the arctic including Alaska. *Spec Collecs* Bibliography on Cold Regions Science & Technology. *In-house Files* Bibliography on-line with SDC as file COLD available.
Info Ret Servs DIALOG; SDC; DTIC. *Shared Catalog Nets* OCLC. *Coop Lib Nets* Corps of Engineers.
Circ Servs Avail To other Federal libraries; to other libraries.
Ref Servs Avail To other Federal libraries; to other libraries; to the general public.

657. US Army Comp Sys Sel Acq Agency, Library
ACSA-TD-R, 2461 Eisenhower Ave, Rm 280, Hoff 1, Alexandria, VA 22331
Lib Type General.

658. US Army Construction Engineering Research Laboratory Library
PO Box 4005, Champaign, IL 61820-1305 (217) 373-7217; FTS 958-7217
Admin Martha A Blake.
Lib Type Engineering & Science.
Spec Subs Construction management; environmental engineering. *In-house Files* US Army CERL reports.
Info Ret Servs DIALOG; Pergamon Infoline. *Shared Catalog Nets* OCLC. *Coop Lib Nets* ILLINET; Corps of Engineers Network.
Circ Servs Avail To other Federal libraries; to other libraries; to the general public.
Ref Servs Avail To other Federal libraries; to other libraries; to the general public.

659. US Army Corps of Engineers, Albuquerque District Library
PO Box 1580, 517 Gold Ave SW, Albuquerque, NM 87103-1580 (505) 766-8028; FTS 474-8028
Admin Judy A Sena.
Lib Type Engineering & Science.
In-house Files Civil engineering; environmental studies; flood operations; parks & recreation.
Info Ret Servs DIALOG. *Shared Catalog Nets* OCLC.
Circ Servs Avail To other Federal libraries; to other libraries; to the general public.
Ref Servs Avail To other Federal libraries; to other libraries; to the general public.

660. US Army Corps of Engineers, Baltimore District Library Branch
PO Box 1715, Baltimore, MD 21203-1715 (301) 962-3423; FTS 922-3423
Ref Lib Stephen L Brooks; Shirley Fisher (Law Lib).
Lib Type Law; Engineering & Science.
Spec Subs Science technical books; EEO literature; management; military & Corps of Engineers history; regional law reporters for Baltimore District. *Spec Collecs* Rivers & harbors; House Documents; technical reports; Congressional Documents, 1970-present. *In-house Files* Planning an in-house data base index to technical report collection & computerized catalog of the science technical book collection.
Info Ret Servs DIALOG; BRS. *Shared Catalog Nets* OCLC.
Circ Servs Avail To other Federal libraries; to other libraries.
Ref Servs Avail To other Federal libraries; to other libraries; to the general public.

661. US Army Corps of Engineers, Buffalo District Technical Library
1776 Niagara, Buffalo, NY 14207-3199 (716) 876-5454; FTS 473-2114
Admin Thomas Van Wart.
Lib Type Engineering & Science.

Spec Subs Chemical; construction; economics; engineering; environmental studies; geology; hydrology; water resources development. *Spec Collecs* Aerial photography; government documents; Great Lakes research; nuclear waste disposal; microcomputer software bank.
Info Ret Servs DIALOG. *Shared Catalog Nets* OCLC. *Coop Lib Nets* FEDLINK.

662. US Army Corps of Engineers, Charleston District Law Library
PO Box 919, Charleston, SC 29402-0919 (803) 724-4517; FTS 677-4517
Admin Barbara D Britz.
Lib Type Law.
Coop Lib Nets Army Law Library Service (ALLS). *Elec Mail Nets* Ontyme.
Circ Servs Avail Not open to the general public.
Ref Servs Avail To other Federal libraries; not open to the general public.

663. US Army Corps of Engineers, Detroit District Law Library
PO Box 1027, Detroit, MI 48231 AUTOVON 80-226-6821
Lib Type Law.

664. US Army Corps of Engineers, Detroit District Technical Library
PO Box 1027, Detroit, MI 48231-1027 (313) 226-6231; FTS 226-6231
Admin Monica Moffa.
Lib Type Engineering & Science.
Spec Subs Engineering; earth sciences; Great Lakes water resources. *Spec Collecs* District projects slide collection.
Info Ret Servs DIALOG. *Shared Catalog Nets* OCLC. *Coop Lib Nets* FEDLINK.
Circ Servs Avail To other libraries; restricted to ILL.
Ref Servs Avail To other libraries; to the general public.

665. US Army Corps of Engineers, Ft Worth District Law Library
PO Box 17300, Fort Worth, TX 76102 AUTOVON 80-334-4820
Lib Type Law.

666. US Army Corps of Engineers, Ft Worth District, Technical Library
PO Box 17300, 819 Taylor, Fort Worth, TX 76102-0300 (817) 334-4884; FTS 334-4884
Admin Sue L Raymond. *ILL* Barbara Norman.
Lib Type Engineering & Science.
Spec Subs Hydrology/hydraulic engineering; Texas law; military, federal, industry specifications & standards; construction; Army engineering regulations & guidance; water resources & supply; soils; geology; archeology. *Spec Collecs* Ft Worth District design memoranda for dam construction sites.
Info Ret Servs DIALOG. *Shared Catalog Nets* OCLC. *Coop Lib Nets* FEDLINK.
Circ Servs Avail To other Federal libraries; to other libraries; not open to the general public.
Ref Servs Avail To other Federal libraries; to other libraries; to the general public; restricted to as needed.

667. US Army Corps of Engineers, Galveston District Technical Library
PO Box 1229, Galveston, TX 77553-1229 (409) 766-3196; FTS 527-6196
Admin Larry L Castleman.
Lib Type Engineering & Science.
Spec Subs Coastal engineering; law; ecology; dredging technology.
Info Ret Servs DIALOG; Corps of Engineers LS/2000. *Shared Catalog Nets* OCLC. *Coop Lib Nets* AMIGOS. *Elec Mail Nets* Ontyme.
Circ Servs Avail To other Federal libraries; to other libraries; to the general public.
Ref Servs Avail To other Federal libraries; to other libraries; to the general public.

668. US Army Corps of Engineers, Headquarters Library
HQDA-DAEN-IMS-L, Rm 3119, 20 Massachusetts Ave NW, Washington, DC 20314 (202) 272-0455; TTY 272-0455; AUTOVON 272-0455
Admin Sarah A Mikel. *Ref Lib* Ann (Penny) Crumpler. *ILL* Jacqueline Patterson. *Acq Lib* Vivian Fisher.
Lib Type Engineering & Science.
Spec Subs Engineering; congressional. *Spec Collecs* Depository for Corps of Engineers technical publications & historical materials. *In-house Files* LS/2000—the master bibliography contains the cumulative holdings of the Corps of Engineers Library Program (48 sites).
Info Ret Servs DIALOG; OCLC; LEGI-SLATE; CQ Washington Alert; DTIC; LEXIS; NEXIS. *Shared Catalog Nets* OCLC. *Coop Lib Nets* FEDLINK. *Elec Mail Nets* LS/2000 System.
Circ Servs Avail To other libraries; not open to the general public.
Ref Servs Avail To other Federal libraries; to other libraries; to the general public.

669. US Army Corps of Engineers, Huntington District Law Library
502 8th St, Huntington, WV 25701-2070 (304) 529-5261; FTS 924-5261
Admin Geneva A Lares.
Lib Type Law.
Spec Collecs Federal statutes & regulations (CFR, codes, etc); Supreme Court Reporter; State codes & reports for WV, KY, PA, OH, & VA.
Info Ret Servs LEXIS; WESTLAW; JURIS. *Elec Mail Nets* Ontyme.
Circ Servs Avail Restricted to District Corps of Engineers.
Ref Servs Avail To other Federal libraries; not open to the general public.

670. US Army Corps of Engineers, Huntington District, Technical Library
502 8th St, Huntington, WV 25701-2070 (304) 529-5435/5713; FTS 924-5435
Admin Sandra V Morris. *Acq Lib* Judy Daniels.
Lib Type Engineering & Science.
Spec Subs Civil engineering; environment. *Spec Collecs* Water quality; oral histories of key retired personnel.
Info Ret Servs DIALOG; LEXIS; NEXIS. *Shared Catalog Nets* OCLC. *Coop Lib Nets* FEDLINK. *Elec Mail Nets* Ontyme.
Circ Servs Avail To other Federal libraries; to other libraries.
Ref Servs Avail To other Federal libraries; to other libraries; to the general public.

671. US Army Corps of Engineers Huntsville Division, Law Library
PO Box 1600, W Stn, Huntsville, AL 35807 (205) 805-5581
Lib Type Law.

672. US Army Corps of Engineers, Huntsville Division, Technical Information Center
1600 Wynn Dr, Huntsville, AL 35805-4301 (205) 895-5621; FTS 873-5621; AUTOVON 742-5621
Admin Samuel Bowen. *Ref Lib* Daniel Talbott (ILL). *Acq Lib* Martha Barrett.
Lib Type Engineering & Science.
Info Ret Servs DIALOG. *Elec Mail Nets* OnTyme.
Circ Servs Avail To other Federal libraries; not open to the general public.
Ref Servs Avail To other Federal libraries; not open to the general public.

673. US Army Corps of Engineers, Hydrologic Engineering Center Library
609 2nd St, Davis, CA 95616 (916) 756-1104, ext 36; FTS 448-2105
Lib Type Engineering & Science.
Spec Subs Hydraulic & hydrologic engineering; water resources planning & management.
Info Ret Servs DIALOG. *Shared Catalog Nets* OCLC. *Coop Lib Nets* FEDLINK.

674. US Army Corps of Engineers, Jacksonville District Law Library
PO Box 4970, Jacksonville, FL 32201 AUTOVON 80-791-3762
Lib Type Law.

675. US Army Corps of Engineers, Jacksonville District Technical Library
PO Box 4970, Jacksonville, FL 32232-0019 (904) 791-3643; FTS 946-3643
Admin Oriana B West.
Lib Type Engineering & Science.
Spec Subs Engineering; beach erosion control; fish & wildlife. *Spec Collecs* Central & southern Florida flood control.
Info Ret Servs DIALOG; BRS; SDC. *Shared Catalog Nets* OCLC. *Elec Mail Nets* Ontyme.
Circ Servs Avail To other Federal libraries; to other libraries; not open to the general public.
Ref Servs Avail To other Federal libraries; to other libraries; not open to the general public; restricted to engineers.

676. US Army Corps of Engineers, Kansas City District Library
Rm 700, New Federal Office Bldg, 601 E 12th St, Kansas City, MO 64106 (816) 374-3896
Lib Type Engineering & Science.

677. US Army Corps of Engineers, Kansas City District, Office of Counsel Law Library
601 E 12th St, Kansas City, MO 64106 (816) 374-3896; FTS 758-2375
Admin Tonja Nero. *ILL* Homer King (Acq).
Lib Type Law.
Spec Subs Federal regulations; labor & management.
Circ Servs Avail Not open to the general public; restricted to COE employees.
Ref Servs Avail To other Federal libraries.

678. US Army Corps of Engineers, Little Rock District Technical Library
PO Box 867, Little Rock, AR 72203-0867 (501) 378-6107; FTS 740-6167
Admin Judy Lester.
Lib Type Engineering & Science.
Spec Subs Engineering materials; waterway projects.
Info Ret Servs DIALOG. *Shared Catalog Nets* OCLC.
Circ Servs Avail To other Federal libraries; to other libraries.

679. US Army Corps of Engineers, Los Angeles District Law Library
PO Box 2711, Los Angeles, CA 90053 (213) 688-5390
Lib Type Law.

680. US Army Corps of Engineers, Los Angeles District Technical Library
PO Box 2711, Los Angeles, CA 90053 (213) 894-5313; FTS 798-5313
Admin Connie Castillo.
Lib Type Engineering & Science.
Spec Subs Engineering. *Spec Collecs* Technical reports of the Corps of Engineers.
Info Ret Servs DIALOG; OCLC. *Shared Catalog Nets* OCLC. *Coop Lib Nets* PACNET.
Circ Servs Avail To other Federal libraries; to other libraries; to the general public.
Ref Servs Avail To other Federal libraries; to other libraries; to the general public.

681. US Army Corps of Engineers, Louisville District Law Library
PO Box 59, Louisville, KY 40201 (502) 352-5678
Lib Type Law.

682. US Army Corps of Engineers, Louisville District Technical Library
PO Box 59, Rm 822B 600 Federal Pl, Louisville, KY 40201 (502) 582-6427; FTS 352-6427
Admin Douglas S Blunk. *Ref Lib* Wanda Stoffregen.
Lib Type Engineering & Science.
Info Ret Servs DIALOG. *Shared Catalog Nets* OCLC. *Coop Lib Nets* FEDLINK.
Circ Servs Avail To other Federal libraries; to other libraries.
Ref Servs Avail To other Federal libraries; to other libraries; to the general public.

683. US Army Corps of Engineers, Mississippi River Commission Technical Library
PO Box 80, 1500 Walnut St, Vicksburg, MS 39180 (601) 634-5880; ILL 634-5881; FTS 542-5880
Lib Type Special.
Spec Subs Geology; harbors; hyrdaulics; inland waterways; rivers; soils; law. *Spec Collecs* Archives, Mississippi River Commission.
Info Ret Servs DIALOG; Legislate; LEXIS; NEXIS. *Shared Catalog Nets* OCLC.

684. US Army Corps of Engineers, Missouri River Division, Omaha District Technical Library
215 N 17th St, Omaha, NE 68102-4978 (402) 221-3229; FTS 864-3230
Lib Type Engineering & Science.
Spec Subs Engineering; law.

685. US Army Corps of Engineers, Mobile District Law Library
PO Box 2288, Mobile, AL 36628 AUTOVON 80-534-2491
Lib Type Law.

686. US Army Corps of Engineers Nashville District Law Library
PO Box A643 Federal Annex Bldg, Nashville, TN 37202 AUTOVON 80-852-5687
Lib Type Law.

687. US Army Corps of Engineers, Nashville District Technical Library
PO Box 1070, Nashville, TN 37202-1070 (615) 736-5641; FTS 852-5641
Admin James T Siburt.
Lib Type Engineering & Science.
Spec Subs Engineering; hydraulics & hydrology; environmental science.
Info Ret Servs DIALOG. *Shared Catalog Nets* OCLC. *Coop Lib Nets* FEDLINK. *Elec Mail Nets* Ontyme.
Circ Servs Avail To other libraries; not open to the general public.
Ref Servs Avail To other Federal libraries; to other libraries; not open to the general public.

688. US Army Corps of Engineers, New England Division Law Library
424 Trapelo Rd, Waltham, MA 02154 (617) 647-8250
Lib Type Law.

689. US Army Corps of Engineers, New England Division Technical Library
424 Trapelo Rd, Waltham, MA 02154-9149 (617) 647-8118; FTS 839-7349; ILL 647-8701
Lib Type Engineering & Science.
Spec Subs Civil engineering; coastal studies; dredging; ecology; flood plain management; hydrology; hydropower; natural science; real estate; structural engineering; water resources; wildlife studies; water resource management.
Info Ret Servs DIALOG; SDC; LEXIS; NEXIS. *Shared Catalog Nets* OCLC. *Coop Lib Nets* FEDLINK.

690. US Army Corps of Engineers, New Orleans District Law Library
Office of Council, New Orleans, LA 70160 (504) 838-2824
Lib Type Law.

691. US Army Corps of Engineers, New Orleans District Technical Library
PO Box 60267, New Orleans, LA 70160-0267 (504) 862-2558
Admin Barbara J Fox. *ILL* Kelly Laslie. *Acq Lib* Edwin Betbeze.
Lib Type Engineering & Science.
Spec Subs Civil engineering; hydrology; environment.
Info Ret Servs DIALOG; BRS. *Shared Catalog Nets* OCLC. *Coop Lib Nets* FEDLINK. *Elec Mail Nets* FEDLINK.
Circ Servs Avail To other Federal libraries; to other libraries.
Ref Servs Avail To other Federal libraries; to other libraries; to the general public.

692. US Army Corps of Engineers, New York District Law Library
26 Federal Plaza, New York, NY 10007 AUTOVON 264-0234
Lib Type Law.

693. US Army Corps of Engineers, New York District Technical Library
26 Federal Plaza, Rm 1802, New York, NY 10278-0090 (212) 264-0234; FTS 264-0234; AUTOVON 796-0234
Admin Louise A Heller.
Lib Type Engineering & Science.
Spec Subs Engineering & allied fields. *Spec Collecs* Port of New York.
Info Ret Servs DIALOG. *Shared Catalog Nets* OCLC. *Coop Lib Nets* FEDLINK.
Circ Servs Avail To other libraries.
Ref Servs Avail To the general public.

694. US Army Corps of Engineers, Norfolk District Technical Library
803 Front St, Norfolk, VA 23510-1096 (804) 441-3562; FTS 827-3562; AUTOVON 680-9562
Admin Lane Killam.
Lib Type Engineering & Science.
Info Ret Servs DIALOG. *Shared Catalog Nets* OCLC. *Coop Lib Nets* FEDLINK.
Circ Servs Avail To other libraries.
Ref Servs Avail To other libraries.

695. US Army Corps of Engineers, North Atlantic Division Law Library
90 Church St, New York, NY 10007 (212) 264-7645; FTS 264-7645
Admin Thomas J Doherty.
Lib Type Law.
Circ Servs Avail Not open to the general public.
Ref Servs Avail Not open to the general public.

696. US Army Corps of Engineers, North Atlantic Division Technical Library
90 Church St, New York, NY 10007-2979 (212) 264-7698; FTS 264-7698
Admin Susan Tu Lin.
Lib Type Engineering & Science.
Spec Subs Water resources; locks & dams.
Info Ret Servs DIALOG; OCLC; LEXIS; NEXIS; CQ Washington Alert. *Shared Catalog Nets* OCLC; Corps of Engineers Network, LS/2000.
Circ Servs Avail Not open to the general public.
Ref Servs Avail Not open to the general public.

697. US Army Corps of Engineers, North Central Division Law Library
536 S Clark St, Chicago, IL 60605 AUTOVON 80-353-6337
Lib Type Law.

698. US Army Corps of Engineers, North Central Division Library
536 S Clark St, Chicago, IL 60605-1592 (312) 353-5038
Lib Type Engineering & Science.
Spec Subs Civil engineering; dams; energy; environmental studies; navigation; public works; waterways. *Spec Collecs* Congressional documents series; US Board of Engineers for Rivers & Harbors; US Waterways Experiment Station; other Corps of Engineer's Laboratory reports.
Coop Lib Nets FEDLINK; Chicago Library System.

699. US Army Corps of Engineers, North Pacific Law Library
PO Box 2870, Portland, OR 97208-2870 (503) 221-3892; FTS 423-3892
Admin Rebecca B Ransom. *Ref Lib* T J French (ILL, Acq).
Lib Type Law.
Spec Subs Comptroller General decisions.
Elec Mail Nets Ontyme.
Circ Servs Avail Not open to the general public.
Ref Servs Avail To other Federal libraries; not open to the general public.

700. US Army Corps of Engineers, Ohio River District Technical Library
PO Box 1159, 550 Main St, Cincinnati, OH 45201-1159 (513) 684-3040; FTS 684-3040
Lib Type Special.
Spec Collecs Water resources development & engineering.
Shared Catalog Nets OCLC. *Coop Lib Nets* FEDLINK.
Ref Servs Avail Not open to the general public; restricted to staff & other by application.

701. US Army Corps of Engineers, Ohio River Division, Law Library
PO Box 1159, Cincinnati, OH 45201 (513) 684-3083
Lib Type Law.

702. US Army Corps of Engineers, Omaha District Library
1612 US Post Office & Courthouse, Omaha, NE 68102-4978 (402) 221-3230/3229; FTS 864-3230
Admin Mary E Peters. *ILL* Karen S Shafer. *Acq Lib* Jeanne E Cummins.
Lib Type Law; Engineering & Science.
Spec Collecs MDR Sediment Series; design memorandums of Omaha District projects. *In-house Files* Army & engineering regulations.
Info Ret Servs DIALOG. *Shared Catalog Nets* OCLC. *Elec Mail Nets* OnTyme.
Circ Servs Avail To other Federal libraries; to other libraries.
Ref Servs Avail To other Federal libraries.

703. US Army Corps of Engineers, Omaha District Technical Library
6014 US Post Office & Courthouse, Omaha, NE 68102-4978 (402) 221-3229; FTS 864-3230
Admin Mary E Peters. *ILL* Karen Shafer. *Acq Lib* Jeanne Cummins.
Lib Type Law; Engineering & Science.
Spec Subs Water; engineering; architecture. *In-house Files* MRD sediment series; Omaha District design memorandums.
Info Ret Servs DIALOG. *Shared Catalog Nets* OCLC.
Circ Servs Avail To other Federal libraries; to other libraries.
Ref Servs Avail To other Federal libraries; to other libraries.

704. US Army Corps of Engineers, Pacific Ocean Division Law Library
Bldg 230, Fort Shafter, HI 96858 (808) 438-1064/2423
Lib Type Law.

705. US Army Corps of Engineers, Pacific Ocean Division, Technical Library
Bldg 230, Fort Shafter, HI 96858 (808) 438-9496
Lib Type Engineering & Science.

706. US Army Corps of Engineers, Pittsburgh District Law Library
Office of Counsel, Federal Bldg, 1000 Liberty Ave, Pittsburgh, PA 15222 (412) 644-6924; FTS 722-6887
Admin Carol Wise; George H Craig, Jr.
Lib Type Law.
Coop Lib Nets WESTLAW; JURIS.

707. US Army Corps of Engineers, Pittsburgh District Technical Library
1802 Federal Bldg, 1000 Liberty Ave, Pittsburgh, PA 15222
Lib Type Engineering & Science.

708. US Army Corps of Engineers, Portland District Law Library
PO Box 2946, Portland, OR 97208-2946 (503) 221-6021; FTS 423-6027
Admin Janice Webster. *Acq Lib* Chris Hurd.
Lib Type Law.
Circ Servs Avail Restricted to Corps use.
Ref Servs Avail Restricted to Corps use.

709. US Army Corps of Engineers, Portland District Technical Library
PO Box 2946, Portland, OR 97208 (503) 221-6016; FTS 423-6016
Admin Chris Hurd. *ILL* Jan Hayden.
Lib Type Engineering & Science.
Spec Subs Dredging; water resource development. *Spec Collecs* Portland District reports.
Info Ret Servs DIALOG; BRS. *Shared Catalog Nets* OCLC.

710. US Army Corps of Engineers, Rock Island District Technical Library
PO Box 2004, Clock Tower Bldg, Rock Island, IL 61204-2004 (309) 788-6361, ext 576; FTS 386-6576
Admin Nancy J Larson-Bloomer.
Lib Type Engineering & Science.
Spec Subs Concrete; civil engineering; environment; hydraulics & soil mechanics.
Info Ret Servs DIALOG; LS/2000; DTIC. *Shared Catalog Nets* OCLC. *Coop Lib Nets* FEDLINK; River Bend Library System.
Circ Servs Avail To other Federal libraries; to other libraries; not open to the general public.
Ref Servs Avail To other Federal libraries; to other libraries; restricted to general public by appointment.

711. US Army Corps of Engineers, Sacramento District Law Library
650 Capitol Mall, Sacramento, CA 95814-4794 (916) 440-3404; FTS 460-2423
Lib Type Law.
Circ Servs Avail Not open to the general public.
Ref Servs Avail To other Federal libraries.

712. US Army Corps of Engineers, Sacramento District Technical Library
650 Capitol Mall, Sacramento, CA 95814-4794 (916) 440-3404; FTS 460-2456
Admin Deborah A Newton. *Ref Lib* Fran Sweeney. *ILL* Maria Perez. *Acq Lib* Gretchen Fau.
Lib Type Engineering & Science.
Spec Subs Hydrology; hydraulics; construction; environmental planning; water resources planning.
Info Ret Servs DIALOG; BRS; SDC. *Shared Catalog Nets* OCLC. *Coop Lib Nets* FEDLINK.
Circ Servs Avail To other Federal libraries; to other libraries.
Ref Servs Avail To other libraries.

713. US Army Corps of Engineers, St Louis District Technical Library
210 Tucker Blvd N, Saint Louis, MO 63101 (314) 263-5675; FTS 273-5675; AUTOVON 693-5675
Admin Katharine Hayes. *ILL* Hazel Schnatzmeyer (Acq).
Lib Type Engineering & Science.

Spec Subs Civil engineering; business & management; forestry; outdoor recreation; urban planning; wildlife management.
Info Ret Servs DIALOG; CQ Washington Alert. *Shared Catalog Nets* OCLC. *Coop Lib Nets* Missouri Union List of Serials. *Elec Mail Nets* Ontyme.
Circ Servs Avail To other Federal libraries; to other libraries; to the general public.
Ref Servs Avail To other Federal libraries; to other libraries; to the general public.

714. US Army Corps of Engineers, St Paul District Technical Library
1135 USPO & Customs House, Saint Paul, MN 55101-1479 (612) 725-5921; FTS 725-5921
Admin Jean M Schmidt.
Lib Type Engineering & Science.
Spec Subs River engineering & navigation; environmental aspects; industrial mobilization. *Spec Collecs* Waterways experiment station reports; waterborne commerce statistics; history of military engineering.
Info Ret Servs DIALOG. *Shared Catalog Nets* OCLC. *Coop Lib Nets* FEDLINK; METRONET.
Circ Servs Avail To other Federal libraries; to other libraries.
Ref Servs Avail To other Federal libraries; to other libraries; to the general public.

715. US Army Corps of Engineers, San Francisco District Law Library
211 Main St, San Francisco, CA 94105 (415) 556-5320
Lib Type Law.

716. US Army Corps of Engineers, Savannah District Law Library
PO Box 889, Savannah, GA 31402 (803) 751-6811; AUTOVON 80-751-6811
Lib Type Law.

717. US Army Corps of Engineers Savannah District, Technical Library
PO Box 889, Savannah, GA 31402 (912) 944-5462
Lib Type Engineering & Science.

718. US Army Corps of Engineers, Seattle District Library
PO Box C-3755, Seattle, WA 98124 (206) 764-3728; FTS 399-3728
Admin Pat J Perry.
Lib Type Engineering & Science.
Spec Subs Dam safety; hospital planning & construction; archeological surveys, Pacific NW; NTIS microfiche; engineering & water projects. *Spec Collecs* Paper copies of waterways experimental station reports.
Info Ret Servs DIALOG; BRS; DTIC; DROLS. *Shared Catalog Nets* OCLC. *Coop Lib Nets* OCLC; Corps of Engineers LS/2000; FEDLINK. *Elec Mail Nets* Ontyme; Class; Western Union Easylink.
Circ Servs Avail To other Federal libraries; to other libraries; not open to the general public.
Ref Servs Avail To other Federal libraries; to other libraries; to the general public.

719. US Army Corps of Engineers, South Atlantic Division Law Library
431 Title Bldg, 30 Pryor St SW, Atlanta, GA 30335-6801 (404) 221-6620; FTS 242-6620
Lib Type Law.
Spec Subs Labor law.
Info Ret Servs JURIS; WESTLAW.
Circ Servs Avail Not open to the general public.
Ref Servs Avail Not open to the general public.

720. US Army Corps of Engineers, South Atlantic Division Technical Library
426 Title Bldg, 30 Pryor St SW, Atlanta, GA 30335-6801 (404) 221-6620; FTS 242-6620
Admin James Chestnut.
Lib Type Engineering & Science.

Spec Subs Civil engineering.
Info Ret Servs DIALOG. *Shared Catalog Nets* OCLC. *Coop Lib Nets* FEDLINK; GLIN.
Circ Servs Avail To other Federal libraries; to other libraries.
Ref Servs Avail To other Federal libraries; to other libraries; to the general public.

721. US Army Corps of Engineers, South Pacific Division Law Library
Rm 1216, 630 Sansome St, San Francisco, CA 94111 AUTOVON 80-415-556-5320
Lib Type Law.

722. US Army Corps of Engineers, South Pacific Division Technical Library
630 Sansome St, Rm 1216, San Francisco, CA 94111 (415) 556-5320; FTS 556-5320
Admin Mary G Anderson.
Lib Type Engineering & Science.
Spec Collecs Hydrology; civil engineering; geotechnical.
Info Ret Servs DIALOG. *Shared Catalog Nets* OCLC. *Coop Lib Nets* FEDLINK. *Elec Mail Nets* OnTyme.
Circ Servs Avail To other Federal libraries; to other libraries.
Ref Servs Avail To other Federal libraries; to other libraries; to the general public.

723. US Army Corps of Engineers, Southwest Division Technical Library
1114 Commerce St, Dallas, TX 75242 (214) 767-2325; FTS 729-2325
Admin Valetta Sharp. *Ref Lib* Jim Quevedo (ILL, Acq).
Lib Type Law; Engineering & Science.
Spec Subs Engineering; water resources; congressional materials; law. *Spec Collecs* Texas Dept of Water Resources Reports; superseded/rescinded Corps of Engineers publications.
Info Ret Servs DIALOG; BRS. *Shared Catalog Nets* OCLC. *Coop Lib Nets* FEDLINK.
Circ Servs Avail To other Federal libraries; to other libraries.
Ref Servs Avail To other Federal libraries; to other libraries; to the general public.

724. US Army Corps of Engineers, Tulsa District Law Library
PO Box 61, Tulsa, OK 74102 (918) 748-7295
Lib Type Law.

725. US Army Corps of Engineers, Walla Walla District Technical & Law Library
Bldg 602, City-County Airport, Walla Walla, WA 99362-9265 (509) 522-6444/6441/6443/6445; FTS 434-6444
Admin Nancy Fitzsimmons. *ILL* Angela Camarillo. *Acq Lib* Rose Marie Moore.
Lib Type Law; Engineering & Science.
Spec Subs Engineering; law; water resources development; fish & wildlife. *Spec Collecs* Law collection; Corps of Engineers lab reports; Walla Walla District reports.
Info Ret Servs DIALOG. *Shared Catalog Nets* OCLC. *Coop Lib Nets* PACNET (OCLC). *Elec Mail Nets* CLASS.
Circ Servs Avail To other Federal libraries; to other libraries; to the general public.
Ref Servs Avail To other Federal libraries; to other libraries; to the general public.

726. US Army Corps of Engineers, Wilmington District Law Library
308 Federal Bldg, US Courthouse, Wilmington, NC 28401 AUTOVON 80-671-4644
Lib Type Law.

727. US Army Criminal Investigation Command (USACIDC), First Region, Office of the Region Judge Advocate, Army Law Library
Fort George G Meade, MD 20755 (301) 677-7435; AUTOVON 80-922-3311
Lib Type Law.

728. US Army Engineer Center & Ft Belvoir, Van Noy Library
Bldg 1024, Fort Belvoir, VA 22060-5000 (703) 664-6255
Lib Type Special.
Spec Subs Military history & science; social & political science.
Shared Catalog Nets OCLC.

729. US Army Engineer Division, LMV, Technical Library
PO Box 80, Vicksburg, MS 39180 (601) 634-5880
Admin Sherrie L Moran. *Ref Lib* Bettie Wiley. *ILL* Mary Hall (Acq).
Lib Type Engineering & Science.
Spec Subs River & harbor documents; congressional documents; river engineering; Mississippi River; geology. *Spec Collecs* Historical collection of records on the Mississippi River. *In-house Files* Technical reports; flood control data; stage & discharge records.
Info Ret Servs DIALOG; BRS. *Shared Catalog Nets* OCLC. *Coop Lib Nets* FEDLINK.
Circ Servs Avail To other Federal libraries; to other libraries; not open to the general public.
Ref Servs Avail To other Federal libraries; to other libraries; to the general public.

730. US Army Engineer Division, Memphis District, Law Library
ATTN: LMMOC, B-202 Clifford Davis Federal Bldg, Memphis, TN 38103-1894 (901) 521-3608; FTS 222-3608
Admin Janice L Esposito (Asst Dist Counsel).
Lib Type Law.
Spec Subs Federal contracts; labor law. *Spec Collecs* State codes & digests for AR, MS, MO, & TN; US CODE; Code of Federal Regulations.
Info Ret Servs WESTLAW; JURIS; LEXIS. *Coop Lib Nets* US Army Law Library Service. *Elec Mail Nets* CLASS.
Circ Servs Avail Not open to the general public.
Ref Servs Avail Not open to the general public.

731. US Army Engineering District, Technical Library
US Army Corps of Engineers, US Customs House, 2nd & Chestnut Sts, Philadelphia, PA 19106-2991 (215) 597-3610; FTS 597-3610
Admin Jeannemarie Faison.
Lib Type Engineering & Science.
Spec Subs Civil engineering; water resources development. *Spec Collecs* Waterways experiment station technical reports. *In-house Files* Corps of Engineers Philadelphia District, documents & reports.
Info Ret Servs DIALOG. *Shared Catalog Nets* OCLC.
Circ Servs Avail To other Federal libraries; to other libraries; not open to the general public; restricted to COE employees.
Ref Servs Avail To other Federal libraries; to other libraries; to the general public.

732. US Army Engineering Topographic Laboratories Scientific & Technical Information Center
Fort Belvoir, VA 22060-5546 (703) 664-3834; TTY 355-2656; AUTOVON 345-2656
Admin Mildred L Stiger. *ILL* Dot Murphy.
Lib Type Engineering & Science.
Spec Subs Mapping; remote sensing; photogrammetry; charting; geodesy; artificial intelligence.
Info Ret Servs DIALOG; BRS; DTIC. *Shared Catalog Nets* OCLC. *Coop Lib Nets* FEDLINK. *Elec Mail Nets* OPTIMIS.
Circ Servs Avail Not open to the general public.
Ref Servs Avail Not open to the general public.

733. US Army Environmental Hygiene Agency Library
US Army Health Services Command, APG Edgewood Arsenal, Aberdeen Proving Ground, MD 21010-5422 (301) 671-4236; FTS 671-4236; AUTOVON 584-4236
Admin Krishan S Goel.
Lib Type Special.
Spec Subs Toxicology; health physics; waste disposal; pesticides; bioacoustics; occupational medicine; water quality. *Spec Collecs* NIOSH & EPA documents.

Info Ret Servs DIALOG; MEDLARS. *Shared Catalog Nets* OCLC. *Coop Lib Nets* NLM Region 2. *Elec Mail Nets* OPTIMIS.
Circ Servs Avail Not open to the general public.
Ref Servs Avail Not open to the general public.

734. US Army ERADCOM, Army Library
DELSD-L, Fort Monmouth, NJ 07703 AUTOVON 995-2236
Lib Type General.

735. US Army Facilities Engineering Support Agency, Technical Library
Bldg 358, Fort Belvoir, VA 22060 (703) 664-2871
Lib Type General.

736. US Army Field Artillery Center & Ft Sill, Office of the Staff Judge Advocate, Army Law Library
Fort Sill, OK 73503 (744) 3311/2685
Lib Type Law.

737. US Army Finance & Accounting Center, Legal Office Law Library
Indianapolis, IN 46249-0160 (317) 542-2154; FTS 335-2154; AUTOVON 699-2154
Admin Nelda Armstrong.
Lib Type Law.
Coop Lib Nets WESTLAW.
Circ Servs Avail Not open to the general public.
Ref Servs Avail Not open to the general public.

738. US Army Foreign Science & Technical Center
ATTN: AIAST-IM-IS3L, 220 7th St, NE, Charlottesville, VA 22901-5396
Lib Type Special.

739. US Army Health Services Command
USA HQ, HSC/HSCL-C, Fort Sam Houston, TX 78234-6000 (512) 221-3702; FTS 746-6984; AUTOVON 221-6984
Admin Judith A Arnn.
Lib Type Health & Medicine.
Spec Subs This office serves as a consultant for HSC libraries (primarily medical).
Elec Mail Nets OPTIMIS, Dept of the Army.

740. US Army Infantry School, Donovan Technical Library
Bldg 4, Infantry Hall, Fort Benning, GA 31905-5452 (404) 544-4053; FTS 544-4053; AUTOVON 784-4053
Admin Vivian S Dodson. *Ref Lib* Dianne Tapley (ILL). *Acq Lib* Betty Collins.
Lib Type Training Center.
Spec Subs Infantry. *Spec Collecs* Anti-terrorism collection; professional development collection for students/faculty. *In-house Files* History of the infantry school; staff studies/monographs; after-action reports of the wars.
Info Ret Servs DIALOG; DTIC. *Shared Catalog Nets* OCLC. *Coop Lib Nets* GLIN; TRALINET. *Elec Mail Nets* OPTIMIS.
Circ Servs Avail To other Federal libraries; to other libraries; not open to the general public.
Ref Servs Avail To other Federal libraries; to other libraries; not open to the general public.

741. US Army Information Engineering Command Software Support
AISEC-PE (Annex), Stop H-9, Fort Belvoir, VA 22060 (703) 756-5497
Lib Type Special.
Spec Subs Automatic data processing; computer languages; computer science; programming.

742. US Army Institute of Surgical Research, Library Branch
Fort Sam Houston, Bldg 2653, San Antonio, TX 78234-6200 (512) 221-4559; FTS 746-4559; AUTOVON 471-4559
Admin Janice M Duke.
Lib Type Health & Medicine.
Spec Subs Burns & trauma. *In-house Files* Institute's annual reports; reprints of institute's publications.

Info Ret Servs DIALOG. *Shared Catalog Nets* OCLC. *Coop Lib Nets* FEDLINK. *Elec Mail Nets* OPTIMIS (Operation Management Information System).
Circ Servs Avail To other libraries.
Ref Servs Avail To other Federal libraries; to other libraries.

743. US Army Intelligence & Security Command (INSCOM) CONUS MIGP, Army Law Library
Legal Assistance Office, Fort George G Meade, MD 20755 (301) 688-6533
Lib Type Law.

744. US Army Intelligence & Security Command, Post Library
Vint Hill Farms Stn, Warrenton, VA 22186-5072 (703) 347-6466
Lib Type General.
Spec Subs General recreational reading; military arts & science; military history.

745. US Army Intelligence & Threat Analysis Center, Information Service Branch
ATTN: AIAIT-HI, Washington Navy Yard, Bldg 203, Washington, DC 20374-2136 (202) 692-6381; FTS 335-2606
Admin Dean A Burns. *Ref Lib* Deane Pinckard. *ILL* Margaret Nicholas. *Acq Lib* Anita Parins.
Lib Type Special.
Spec Subs Military intelligence.
Info Ret Servs DIALOG; BRS; SDC; NEXIS. *Shared Catalog Nets* OCLC. *Coop Lib Nets* FEDLINK. *Elec Mail Nets* OPTIMIS.
Circ Servs Avail Not open to the general public; restricted to need to know.
Ref Servs Avail Not open to the general public.

746. US Army, Keller Army Community Hospital Library
West Point, NY 10996-1197 (914) 938-2722; AUTOVON 688-2722
Admin Manja Yirka.
Lib Type Health & Medicine.
Spec Subs Medicine; nursing; sports medicine; clinical medicine.
Info Ret Servs DIALOG *Coop Lib Nets* SENYRLC; HILOW.
Circ Servs Avail To other libraries; restricted to US Military Academy community.
Ref Servs Avail To other libraries; restricted to US Military Academy community.

747. US Army John F Kennedy Special Warfare Center, Marquat Memorial Library
Kennedy Hall, Rm 140, Fort Bragg, NC 28307-5000 (236) 396-9222/6503
Admin Frank London. *Ref Lib* Fred Fuller. *ILL* Mary Grooms. *Acq Lib* Roberta Straight.
Lib Type Academic.
Spec Subs International relations; political science; unconventional warfare; terrorism; geopolitics.
Info Ret Servs DIALOG; BRS. *Shared Catalog Nets* OCLC. *Coop Lib Nets* TRALINET. *Elec Mail Nets* OPTIMIS.
Circ Servs Avail To other libraries; not open to the general public.
Ref Servs Avail To other libraries; not open to the general public.

748. US Army Laboratory Command, Human Engineering Laboratory Library
Bldg 459, Aberdeen Proving Ground, MD 21005-5001 (301) 278-5899; FTS 939-5899; AUTOVON 298-5899
Admin Joyce C Watlington.
Lib Type Engineering & Science.
Spec Subs Human factors engineering; psychology; acoustics; robotics.
Info Ret Servs DIALOG; BRS; SDC.
Circ Servs Avail To other Federal libraries; to other libraries.
Ref Servs Avail To other Federal libraries; to other libraries.

749. US Army Laboratory Command, Technical Information Branch (SLCIS-IM-TL)
Harry Diamond Laboratories, 2800 Powder Mill Rd, Adelphi, MD 20783-1197 (202) 394-2536; AUTOVON 290-2536
Admin Barbra L McLaughlin. *Ref Lib* Norman Brandt (Acq). *ILL* Patrick Dore.
Lib Type Special.
Info Ret Servs DIALOG; SDC. *Shared Catalog Nets* OCLC.
Circ Servs Avail To other Federal libraries; to other libraries; not open to the general public.
Ref Servs Avail To other Federal libraries; to other libraries.

750. US Army Legal Services Agency, Law Library
5611 Columbia Pike, Falls Church, VA 22041-5013 (202) 756-2234; TTY 756-1806; AUTOVON 289-2234
Admin Maxine M Ellis.
Lib Type Law.
Spec Subs Military law; contract law; public utilities; patent law.
Spec Collecs Rare books on military law.
Info Ret Servs DIALOG; LEXIS; WESTLAW.
Circ Servs Avail To other Federal libraries; not open to the general public.

751. US Army Logistics Library
Bunker Hall, Bldg P-12500, Fort Lee, VA 23801-6047 (804) 734-1797/4286; FTS 927-4286/1797; AUTOVON 687-4286/1797
Admin Raymon Trisdale. *Ref Lib* Kenneth A Grabach. *ILL* Nola J Parham.
Lib Type Special.
Spec Subs Logistics; management; military history; military science; government procurement & supply; food.
Lib Deposit Designation US Army & DoD.
Info Ret Servs DIALOG; BRS; DTIC/DROLS. *Shared Catalog Nets* OCLC. *Coop Lib Nets* FEDLINK; TRALINET. *Elec Mail Nets* OPTIMIS; DDN.
Circ Servs Avail To other Federal libraries; to other libraries; to the general public.
Ref Servs Avail To other Federal libraries; to other libraries; to the general public.

752. US Army Logistics Management Center, Army Law Library
Fort Lee, VA 23801 AUTOVON 734-1787/4286
Lib Type Law.

753. US Army Materials & Mechanics Research Center, Technical Library
AMXMR-PL, Watertown, MA 02172-0001 (617) 923-5460
Lib Type Special.
Info Ret Servs DIALOG; BRS; DTIC; NASA/Recon. *Shared Catalog Nets* OCLC. *Coop Lib Nets* FEDLINK; Nelinet.
Ref Servs Avail Not open to the general public; restricted to DoD & contractors.

754. US Army Materiel R&D Command, Army Law Library
Command Counsel, 5001 Eisenhower Ave, Alexandria, VA 22333 AUTOVON 80-274-8885
Lib Type Law.

755. US Army Medical R&D Command, Office of the Judge Advocate, Army Law Library
SGO Fort Detrick, Frederick, MD 21701 AUTOVON 80-935-2065
Lib Type Law.

756. US Army Medical Research Institute of Infectious Diseases Library
Bldg 1425, Fort Detrick, MD 21701-5000 (301) 663-2720
Lib Type Health & Medicine.
Circ Servs Avail Not open to the general public.
Ref Servs Avail Not open to the general public.

757. US Army Military History Institute Library
Carlisle Barracks, PA 17013-5008 (717) 245-3611/4139; AUTO-VON 242-3611/4139
Admin Nancy L Gilbert. *Ref Lib* John J Slonaker. *ILL* Judith A Meck. *Acq Lib* Kathryn E Davis.
Lib Type Special.
Spec Subs Military history; Civil War; Spanish-American War; World War I; World War II; Vietnam War; US history. *Spec Collecs* Unit histories.
Shared Catalog Nets OCLC. *Coop Lib Nets* FLICC.
Circ Servs Avail To other Federal libraries; to other libraries.
Ref Servs Avail To other Federal libraries; to other libraries; to the general public.

758. US Army Military Personnel Center, Army Law Library
Commander DAPAC, 200 Stoval St, Alexandria, VA 22332 (202) 325-8855
Lib Type Law.

759. US Army Military Police School, Ramsey Library
Bldg 3181 Rm 10, Fort McClellan, AL 36205 (205) 238-3737; FTS 538-3737; AUTOVON 865-3737
Admin Bernice Z Parks. *Ref Lib* Martha Morgan (Acq).
Lib Type Training Center.
Spec Subs Law enforcement; psychology; education; military science; military history. *Spec Collecs* Military Police historical collection.
Info Ret Servs DIALOG; DTIC. *Shared Catalog Nets* OCLC. *Coop Lib Nets* TRALINET. *Elec Mail Nets* OPTIMIS.
Circ Servs Avail To other libraries.
Ref Servs Avail To other Federal libraries; to other libraries; to the general public.

760. US Army Missile & Space Intelligence Center Library
ATTN: AIAMS-YDL, Redstone Arsenal, AL 35898-5500 (205) 876-4412; FTS 876-4412; AUTOVON 746-4412
Admin Marcile L Bagley. *Ref Lib* Daniel Gregg; Judy Kennedy; Lee South. *ILL* Helen Gudaitis (Acq).
Lib Type Engineering & Science.
Spec Subs Foreign scientific & technical data. *Spec Collecs* Books, reports, analogs, magnetic & video tapes, maps, journals, periodicals, & microfiche. *In-house Files* Collateral (Uncla thru T S, NATO & special collections); Sensitive Compartmented Information (SCI); Central Information Reference & Control (CIRC II).
Info Ret Servs DIALOG. *Shared Catalog Nets* CIRC II. *Coop Lib Nets* Central Information Reference & Control (CIRC II); Department of Defense Scientific & Technical Intelligence Information Services Program (DOD STIISP); Defense Intelligence Agency On-Line Community Intelligence System (DIAOLS/COINS). *Elec Mail Nets* In-House Electronic Mail Secure System.
Circ Servs Avail Restricted to special authorization.
Ref Servs Avail Restricted to special authorization.

761. US Army Missile Command, Legal Office Library
Redstone Arsenal, AL 35898-5120 (205) 876-2251; AUTOVON 746-2251
Admin Doris Kirkpatrick.
Lib Type Law.
Spec Subs Contract law.
Info Ret Servs LEXIS. *Coop Lib Nets* Army Library, The Judge Advocate General's School, Charlottesville, VA.
Circ Servs Avail Not open to the general public; restricted to attorneys in office.
Ref Servs Avail To other Federal libraries; to other libraries; not open to the general public.

762. US Army Missile Command (SUPT), Post Library
Redstone Arsenal, AL 35898-5355
Lib Type General.

763. US Army Mobility R&D Command, Army Law Library
Office of Counsel, Fort Belvoir, VA 22060 (404) 752-5411
Lib Type Law.

764. US Army Museum Library
ATTN: AFZW-DPT-P, Presidio of Monterey, CA 93944 (408) 647-5414; AUTOVON 878-5414
Admin Margaret B Adams (Chief Curator); Victor D McNamara (Museum Tech).
Lib Type Special.
Spec Subs Defense Language Institute; Cavalry & Field Artillery, 1900-1940; Presidio of Monterey (history). *Spec Collecs* Reference files pertaining to the special subjects & microfiche pertaining to general US Army materials/history.
Ref Servs Avail To other Federal libraries; to other libraries; to the general public; restricted to on-site use only.

765. US Army Natick R&D Command, Chief Legal Office, Army Law Library
Natick, MA 01760 (617) 651-4248
Lib Type Law.

766. US Army Natick Research, Development, & Engineering Center, Technical Library
Natick, MA 01760-5000 (617) 651-4248; AUTOVON 256-4248
Admin Carol J Bursik. *Ref Lib* Patricia B Olstead. *ILL* Patricia E Bremner.
Lib Type Engineering & Science.
Spec Subs Air drop; biology; food science & technology; packaging; environmental medicine; textile technology; chemistry.
Info Ret Servs DIALOG; BRS; SDC; DTIC; TECH DATA. *Shared Catalog Nets* OCLC. *Coop Lib Nets* FEDLINK; NELINET. *Elec Mail Nets* ARPANET.
Circ Servs Avail To other Federal libraries; to other libraries; not open to the general public.
Ref Servs Avail To other Federal libraries; to other libraries; to the general public.

767. US Army Operational Test & Evaluation Agency, Technical Library
5600 Columbia Pike, Falls Church, VA 22041-5115 (202) 576-2234; AUTOVON 289-2234
Admin Ava D Headley. *ILL* Linda Gross. *Acq Lib* Marjorie Rust.
Lib Type Special.
Spec Subs Science & technology; military science; test & evaluation. *Spec Collecs* DoD & Dept of Army official publications. *In-house Files* OTEA publications available from DTIC only.
Info Ret Servs DIALOG; DROLS (DTIC).
Circ Servs Avail To other libraries; restricted to DoD agencies.
Ref Servs Avail To other Federal libraries; not open to the general public; restricted to DoD libraries.

768. US Army Ordnance Center & School Library
Bldg 3071, Simpson Hall, Aberdeen Proving Ground, MD 21005-5201 (301) 278-4991/5615; FTS 939-4991; AUTOVON 298-4991/5615
Admin Janice C Weston. *Ref Lib* Tracy Landfried. *ILL* Helen Crouse.
Lib Type Academic; Training Center.
Spec Subs Education; military arts & sciences; military history; business; science & technology.
Info Ret Servs DIALOG; DTIC. *Shared Catalog Nets* OCLC. *Coop Lib Nets* TRALINET. *Elec Mail Nets* OPTIMIS.
Circ Servs Avail To other libraries; not open to the general public; restricted to ILL & local agency.
Ref Servs Avail To other Federal libraries; to other libraries; not open to the general public.

769. US Army Ordnance Missile & Munitions Center & School, Technical Library
ATTN: ATSK-AB, Bldg 3323, Redstone Arsenal, AL 35897-6280 (205) 876-7425; FTS 876-7425; AUTOVON 746-7425/4524
Admin Eleanore Zeman.
Lib Type Academic.
Spec Subs Education; electronics; technology; general; physics; management; psychology. *Spec Collecs* College catalogs; city telephone directories.
Info Ret Servs DIALOG; BRS; DTIC. *Shared Catalog Nets* OCLC.
Circ Servs Avail Not open to the general public.
Ref Servs Avail Not open to the general public.

770. US Army Physical Disability Agency, Office of the Judge Advocate, Army Law Library
Forest Glen Section (WRAMC), Washington, DC 20307 AUTO-VON 80-427-5171
Lib Type Law.

771. US Army Recruiting Command, Army Law Library
Command Legal Counsel, Bldg 48E, Fort Sheridan, IL 60037 (312) 926-2151; AUTOVON 80-926-2151
Lib Type Law.

772. US Army Research Institute of Environmental Medicine, Medical Library
Natick, MA 01760 (617) 651-4000
Lib Type Health & Medicine.

773. US Army Research Institute, Technical Information Center
ATTN: PERI-POT-I, 5001 Eisenhower Ave, Alexandria, VA 22333-5600 (202) 274-8653; AUTOVON 284-8653
Admin Arlene D Blose. *ILL* Mary Caswell.
Lib Type Special.
Spec Subs Psychology.
Info Ret Servs DIALOG; BRS; DROLS. *Shared Catalog Nets* OCLC.
Circ Servs Avail To other Federal libraries; to other libraries; not open to the general public.
Ref Servs Avail To other Federal libraries; to other libraries; not open to the general public.

774. US Army Research Office, Army Law Library
Legal Office, PO Box 12211, Research Triangle Park, NC 27709 (919) 549-0641
Lib Type Law.

775. US Army Reserve Components Personnel & Administration Center, Office of the Judge Advocate, Army Law Library
9700 Page Blvd, Saint Louis, MO 63132 (314) 263-7533
Lib Type Law.

776. US Army School of the Americas Library
ATTN: ATZL-SA-S-L, Bldg 35, Rm 309, Fort Benning, GA 31905-6245 (404) 545-4631; AUTOVON 835-4631
Lib Type Academic.

777. US Army, Sierra Army Depot, Post Library
Herlong, CA 96113-5001 (916) 827-4157; AUTOVON 830-9157
Lib Type General.

778. US Army Signal Center, Conrad Technical Library
Fort Gordon, GA 30905 (404) 791-3922; FTS 791-3922; AUTO-VON 780-3922
Admin Margaret H Novinger. *Ref Lib* Linda L Orne.
Lib Type Training Center.
Spec Subs Communications—electronics; artificial intelligence; expert systems; Signal Corps history.
Info Ret Servs DIALOG; BRS; DTIC. *Shared Catalog Nets* OCLC; TRALINET. *Coop Lib Nets* TRALINET; GLIN. *Elec Mail Nets* OPTIMIS.
Circ Servs Avail To other Federal libraries; to other libraries.
Ref Servs Avail To other Federal libraries; to other libraries.

779. US Army 6th Recruiting Brigade (Western), Law Library
Presidio of San Francisco (Fort Baker), CA 94129-7600 (415) 561-3448; FTS 556-2454; AUTOVON 586-7685
Admin Margaret M Hammer. *Ref Lib* Kimball J P Sargeant.
Lib Type Law.
Circ Servs Avail Restricted to Brigade.
Ref Servs Avail Restricted to Brigade.

780. US Army Soldier Support Center, Office of the Staff Judge Advocate, Army Law Library
ATZI-JA 3, Fort Benjamin Harrison, IN 46216 AUTOVON 80-335-3215
Lib Type Law.

781. US Army Strategic Defense Command, Huntsville, Library
PO Box 1500, Huntsville, AL 35807-3801 (205) 895-3877; FTS 872-3877; AUTOVON 742-3877
Admin Anna B Dumas. *Ref Lib* Aileen Moon. *ILL* Lornette Stokes (Acq).
Lib Type Engineering & Science.
Spec Subs Antimissile defense; laser technology; radar technology; physics; defense systems; communications; engineering. *Spec Collecs* Science & technology; weapons systems.
Info Ret Servs DROLS. *Shared Catalog Nets* SBIN.
Circ Servs Avail Not open to the general public; restricted to US government/DoD.
Ref Servs Avail Not open to the general public; restricted to US government/DoD.

782. US Army Support Command, Hawaii Library System
ATTN: APZV-PAR-L, Fort Shafter, HI 96858-5000 AUTOVON (808) 655-9269
Admin Arlene Tibayan. *Ref Lib* William R Ranger. *ILL* Jean S Matsushige. *Acq Lib* Amy E Nogami.
Lib Type General.
Spec Subs US Army in Hawaii; Hawaiian resources. *Spec Collecs* Video cassette library: general subject areas to support MWR activities; microfiche: newsbank, college catalogs; phonefiche. *In-house Files* Picture history of Schofield Barracks.
Info Ret Servs DIALOG; WILSONLINE. *Shared Catalog Nets* OCLC.
Circ Servs Avail To other Federal libraries; to other libraries; to the general public.
Ref Servs Avail To other Federal libraries; to other libraries; to the general public.

783. US Army Tank-Automotive Command, Technical Library
ATTN: DRSTA-TSL, Warren, MI 48090 (313) 574-6543
Lib Type Engineering & Science.

784. US Army Tank-Automotive Matter Readiness Command, Army Law Library
Chief Counsel, DRSTA-l, Warren, MI 48090 AUTOVON 80-973-5970
Lib Type Law.

785. US Army TRADOC Systems Analysis Activity TRASANA, Technical Library
ATTN: ATOR-TSL, White Sands Missile Range, NM 88002-5502 (505) 678-3135; FTS 898-3135; AUTOVON 258-3135
Admin Julie A Gibson. *ILL* Evelyn Jones.
Lib Type Special.
Spec Subs Computer science; mathematics; operations research; statistics; military. *Spec Collecs* DMA maps; DTIC technical reports.
Lib Deposit Designation NATO.
Info Ret Servs DIALOG; BRS. *Shared Catalog Nets* OCLC. *Coop Lib Nets* FEDLINK; AMIGOS. *Elec Mail Nets* OPTIMIS.
Circ Servs Avail To other libraries; not open to the general public.
Ref Servs Avail To other libraries; not open to the general public.

786. US Army Training & Doctrine Command (TRADOC), Command Staff Judge Advocate, Army Law Library
Fort Monroe, VA 23651 AUTOVON 931-4363
Lib Type Law.

787. US Army Training & Doctrine Command, Technical Library
HQ TRADOC, Bldg 133, Fort Monroe, VA 23651-5123 (804) 727-2821; FTS 931-2821; AUTOVON 680-2821
Admin Frances M Doyle. *Ref Lib* Areena J Lowe.
Lib Type Special.

Spec Subs Military science & history.
Info Ret Servs DIALOG; BRS; NASA RECON; LEXIS; NEXIS. *Shared Catalog Nets* TRALINET. *Coop Lib Nets* TRADOC Library & Information Network (TRALINET). *Elec Mail Nets* OPTIMIS (Pentagon).
Circ Servs Avail To other Federal libraries; to other libraries; not open to the general public.
Ref Servs Avail To other Federal libraries; to other libraries; not open to the general public.

788. US Army Transportation & Aviation Logistics Schools, Information Center

Bldg 705, Rm 36, Fort Eustis, VA 23604-5450 (804) 878-5563; FTS 988-4126; AUTOVON 927-4126/5563
Admin Jerri Knihnicki. *Ref Lib* Valerie D Fashion. *ILL* Nancy Reinfeld. *Acq Lib* Dianne Forbès.
Lib Type Training Center.
Spec Subs Transportation (air, water, rail, highway); management; leadership education.
Info Ret Servs DIALOG; BRS; DTIC. *Coop Lib Nets* TRALINET. *Elec Mail Nets* OPTIMIS.
Circ Servs Avail To other Federal libraries; to other libraries; to the general public.
Ref Servs Avail To other Federal libraries; to other libraries; to the general public.

789. US Army Transportation Center, Groninger Library

Bldg 1313, Fort Eustis, VA 23604-5107 (804) 878-5017
Lib Type General.
Spec Subs Military science; transportation; local history.
Info Ret Servs DIALOG; BRS. *Shared Catalog Nets* OCLC; TRALINET.

790. US Army War College Library

Carlisle Barracks, PA 17013 (717) 245-3660; AUTOVON 242-3660
Admin Barbara E Stevens. *Ref Lib* Bohdan Kohutiak. *ILL* Patsy Myers. *Acq Lib* Joan Hench.
Lib Type Academic.
Spec Subs Military science, especially strategy; international relations; area studies; economics.
Info Ret Servs DIALOG. *Shared Catalog Nets* OCLC. *Coop Lib Nets* FEDLINK. *Elec Mail Nets* OPTIMIS.
Circ Servs Avail To other Federal libraries; to other libraries; not open to the general public.
Ref Servs Avail To other Federal libraries; to other libraries; not open to the general public.

791. US Army Waterways Experiment Station, Technical Library

PO Box 631, Vicksburg, MS 39180-0631 (601) 634-2542; FTS 542-2542
Admin Bernice B Black (Chief Library Branch). *Ref Lib* Carol L McMillin. *ILL* Kathleen B Wilson. *Acq Lib* Deborah J Carpenter.
Lib Type Engineering & Science.
Spec Subs Civil engineering. *Spec Collecs* Design memos.
Info Ret Servs DIALOG. *Shared Catalog Nets* OCLC. *Coop Lib Nets* DTIC. *Elec Mail Nets* Ontyme.
Circ Servs Avail To other libraries.
Ref Servs Avail To other libraries.

792. US Disciplinary Barracks, Army Command Judge Advocate, Law Library

Fort Leavenworth, KS 66027-7100 (913) 684-3348; FTS 684-3348; AUTOVON 552-3348
Admin Alfred A Smith.
Lib Type Law.
Info Ret Servs WESTLAW. *Elec Mail Nets* Army Law Library Services (ALLS).
Circ Servs Avail Not open to the general public; restricted to US Army.
Ref Servs Avail Not open to the general public; restricted to US Army.

793. US Military Academy, Department of Law Library

West Point, NY 10996-1794 (914) 938-2312/3510; FTS 688-938-2312
Admin James C Gibson, Jr; Linda Tomasi.
Lib Type Academic; Law.
Lib Deposit Designation GPO Depository Library.
Circ Servs Avail Not open to the general public.
Ref Servs Avail Not open to the general public; restricted to West Point community.

794. US Military Academy Library

West Point, NY 10996-1799 (914) 938-2230; AUTOVON 688-2209
Admin Egon A Weiss. *Ref Lib* Robert D Adamshick. *ILL* Charlotte R Snyder. *Acq Lib* Rose M Robischon; Joseph M Barth (Collection Development).
Lib Type Academic.
Spec Subs Military history; military engineering & arts; engineering; science. *Spec Collecs* US Army history; West Pointiana; Hudson Highlands history; military arts; USMA archives; Omar M Bradley papers; Orientalia; papers & writings of Academy graduates; cadet textbooks; chess collection. *In-house Files* Academy archives.
Lib Deposit Designation GPO Depository Library.
Info Ret Servs DIALOG. *Shared Catalog Nets* OCLC. *Coop Lib Nets* FEDLINK; SE New York Library Resources Council; SUNY/OCLC. *Elec Mail Nets* OPTIMIS.
Circ Servs Avail To other Federal libraries; to other libraries; not open to the general public; restricted to cadets, faculty, & approved researchers.
Ref Servs Avail To other Federal libraries; to other libraries; restricted to cadets & faculty.

795. US Military Academy, Office of the Staff Judge Advocate, Army Law Library

West Point, NY 10996 (914) 938-2781/4570
Lib Type Law.

796. US Military Academy, Preparatory School Library

Fort Monmouth, NJ 07703 (201) 532-5307
Lib Type Academic.

797. US Readiness Command, Law Library

USREDCOM/RCJA, MacDill AFB, FL 33608-6001 (813) 830-3252; AUTOVON 968-3252
Admin Carrie Stacha.
Lib Type Law.
Circ Servs Avail Restricted to Office of Staff Judge Advocate.
Ref Servs Avail Restricted to Office of Staff Judge Advocate.

798. US ACOM, Army Library

Commander, DELSD-L, Fort Monmouth, NJ 07703
Lib Type General.

799. Van Deusen Post Library

Bldg 502, ATTN: SELHI-CS-R, Fort Monmouth, NJ 07703-5118 (201) 532-3172; AUTOVON 992-3172
Admin Brenda W Shanholtz. *Ref Lib* Jean Hurley. *ILL* Mary Sandilos.
Lib Type General.
Spec Collecs Military history.
Info Ret Servs DIALOG. *Shared Catalog Nets* OCLC. *Coop Lib Nets* FEDLINK; NJ Union List of Serials. *Elec Mail Nets* Dialnet.
Circ Servs Avail To other Federal libraries; to other libraries; not open to the general public; restricted to military, retirees, & DoD civilians.
Ref Servs Avail To other Federal libraries; to other libraries; restricted to military, retirees, & DoD civilians.

800. Vint Hill Farms Station, Office of the Post Judge Advocate, Army Law Library

Warrenton, VA 22186 (703) 341-6380
Lib Type Law.

801. Walter Reed Medical Center, Office of the Center Advocate, Army Law Library
Washington, DC 20307 AUTOVON 80-576-3292
Lib Type Law.

802. Watervliet Arsenal, Legal Office
Watervliet, NY 12189 AUTOVON 568-5141
Lib Type Law.

803. West Point Post Library
Bldg 622, West Point, NY 10996-1981 (914) 938-2974; AUTOVON 688-2974
Admin Suzanne Moskala.
Lib Type General.
Spec Subs West Point; Hudson Valley local history.
Info Ret Servs Access to USMA Cadet Library's GEAC system.
Circ Servs Avail Restricted to USMA military & civilian employees & families.
Ref Servs Avail Restricted to USMA military & civilian employees & families.

804. White Sands Missile Range, McAfee US Army Health Clinic Library
White Sands Missile Range, NM 88002-5520 (505) 678-1138; FTS 898-1138; AUTOVON 258-1138
Admin M Dolores Esparza.
Lib Type Health & Medicine.
Circ Servs Avail Restricted to McAfee USAHC.
Ref Servs Avail Restricted to McAfee USAHC.

805. White Sands Missile Range, Post Library
Bldg 464, White Sands Missile Range, NM 88002-5039 (505) 678-5820/1556; AUTOVON 258-5820
Admin Eula B Curtsinger. *Ref Lib* Rita L Smith. *ILL* Mazie M Kassim. *Acq Lib* Gloria S Espinoza.
Lib Type General.
Spec Subs Management; automatic data processing; American history; military history; cookery; minority literature (Black & Hispanic). *Spec Collecs* Southwest literature; Spanish literature. *In-house Files* Local history.
Shared Catalog Nets OCLC. *Coop Lib Nets* OCLC.
Circ Servs Avail To other Federal libraries; to other libraries; to the general public.
Ref Servs Avail To other Federal libraries; to other libraries; to the general public.

806. White Sands Missile Range, Technical Library
STEWS-TE-TL, White Sands Missile Range, NM 88002-5029 (505) 678-1317; FTS 898-1317; AUTOVON 258-1317
Admin Laurel B Saunders. *Ref Lib* Ruth Van Liew; Amelia Sutton (Documents). *ILL* Richard Farmer. *Acq Lib* Kathleen Hogan.
Lib Type Engineering & Science.
Spec Subs Electrical & electronic engineering; missiles; physics; computers. *Spec Collecs* Industrial standards; military specifications & standards.
Info Ret Servs DIALOG; BRS; DTIC; WSDM. *Shared Catalog Nets* OCLC. *Elec Mail Nets* MISER.
Circ Servs Avail To other libraries; not open to the general public; restricted to ILL.
Ref Servs Avail To other libraries; not open to the general public; restricted to ILL & computer printouts.

807. White Sands Missle Range, Office of the Staff Judge Advocate, Army Law Library
Bldg 1870, White Sands Missile Range, NM 88002 (505) 678-6218
Lib Type Law.
Ref Servs Avail Not open to the general public; restricted to staff.

808. Yakima Firing Center, Field Library
Yakima, WA 98901 (509) 454-8291
Admin Patty Louderback. *Ref Lib* Edye Pinheiro (ILL). *Acq Lib* Elsa Largen.
Lib Type Training Center.
Spec Subs Military history; arts, crafts & hobbies.
Coop Lib Nets Ft Lewis Library System.
Circ Servs Avail Restricted to military, civilian employees & dependents.

Ref Servs Avail Restricted to military, civilian employees & dependents.

809. Yuma Proving Ground, Post Library
STEYP-IM-AL, Yuma Proving Ground, AZ 85365-9102 (602) 328-2545
Admin B Miller.
Lib Type General.
Shared Catalog Nets OCLC. *Elec Mail Nets* DIALOG.
Circ Servs Avail To other Federal libraries; to other libraries; to the general public.
Ref Servs Avail To other Federal libraries; to other libraries; to the general public.

810. Yuma Proving Ground, Technical Library
STEYP-IM-AT, Yuma, AZ 85365-9103 (602) 328-2527; FTS 765-2527; AUTOVON 899-2527
Admin Jean McCall.
Lib Type Special.

Department of the Army—Overseas

811. AFCENT, US Army Library
Attn: AERAN-DA-MS APO New York, NY 09011, Brunsum Netherlands
Lib Type General.

812. Army Community Recreation Library
20th Support Group, APO San Francisco, CA 96218-0074 Korea
Admin Samuel C Bourke.
Lib Type General.

813. Army Law Library, Legal Advisor
AF South Box 130, APO New York, NY 09524 Naples, Italy
Lib Type Law.

814. Baumholder Military Community, US Army Library
APO New York, NY 09034 06783-6-7229
Admin Daniel C Norum.
Lib Type General.
Circ Servs Avail To other Federal libraries; to other libraries; restricted to military ID card holders.
Ref Servs Avail To other Federal libraries; to other libraries; restricted to military ID card holders.

815. Camp Darby Post Library
8th Support Group, USASETAF APO New York, NY 09019, Livorno Italy (050) 37363-7623; AUTOVON 633-7623
Admin Belinda J Pugh. *Ref Lib* Daniela Battalini. *ILL* Dorene Albury.
Lib Type General.
Spec Collecs Books in Italian.
Circ Servs Avail To other libraries; not open to the general public; restricted to military & DoD Civilians.
Ref Servs Avail To other libraries; not open to the general public; restricted to military & DoD Civilians.

816. Camp Ederle, US Army Library
USASETAF APO New York, NY 09221, Vicenza, Italy
Admin Marian Nance.
Lib Type General.

817. Camp Humphreys Legal Center
HQ, 23rd Support Group, APO San Francisco, CA 96271 Pyong-taaek, Korea AUTOVON 253-8045/8046/8047
Admin Henry Winbush.
Lib Type Law.
Spec Subs Law, especially immigration & administrative law.
Circ Servs Avail Restricted to US military.
Ref Servs Avail Restricted to US military.

818. Camp Market Army Library
APO San Francisco, CA 96483-0074 Korea AUTOVON 262-1101-2923-344
Admin Patricia S Vanderburg.
Lib Type General.

Circ Servs Avail To other Federal libraries; to other libraries; restricted to authorized ID card holders.
Ref Servs Avail To other Federal libraries; to other libraries; restricted to authorized ID card holders.

819. Camp Mercer Army Library
APO San Francisco, CA 96483-0074 Korea AUTOVON 262-1101-2923-344
Admin Patricia S Vanderburg.
Lib Type General.
Circ Servs Avail To other Federal libraries; to other libraries; restricted to authorized ID card holders.
Ref Servs Avail To other Federal libraries; to other libraries; restricted to authorized ID card holders.

820. Camp Nainhof Hohenfels, US Army Library
APO New York, NY 09173 West Germany
Admin Michael von Barfuss.
Lib Type General.
Info Ret Servs DIALOG.
Circ Servs Avail To other Federal libraries; to other libraries; to the general public.
Ref Servs Avail To other Federal libraries; to other libraries.

821. Camp Red Cloud Army Library
HQ Special Troops Combined Field Army (ROK/US), APO San Francisco, CA 96358-0074 Korea AUTOVON 299-6723
Admin Frank Ducic. *Ref Lib* Audrey J Thomas (ILL, Acq).
Lib Type General.
Spec Subs Military history. *Spec Collecs* Korean language material.
Coop Lib Nets FEDLINK.
Circ Servs Avail To other Federal libraries; restricted to military personnel & dependents.
Ref Servs Avail To other Federal libraries; restricted to military personnel & dependents.

822. Command Judge Advocate, Army Law Library
Commander, HQ, 56th FA CMD APO New York, NY 09281-6321 Federal Republic of Germany 07171-39220
Admin Rejeanne T Ridgeway.
Lib Type Law.
Spec Subs Federal tapes; federal statutes; state law.

823. Community Library
Community Recreation Division, USMCA Bamberg APO New York, NY 09139-0033, Bamberg, Federal Republic of Germany AUTOVON 2652-8875
Admin Andrea Freeman. *Ref Lib* Thomas Fisher. *ILL* Linda Cullen.
Lib Type General.
Info Ret Servs PALS. *Coop Lib Nets* USAREUR Library Program.
Circ Servs Avail Not open to the general public; restricted to military community & dependents.
Ref Servs Avail Not open to the general public; restricted to military community & dependents.

824. Cooke Barracks, US Army Library
APO New York, NY 09454, Goeppingen, Federal Republic of Germany
Admin Ericka Lozo.
Lib Type General.

825. Darmstadt MILCOM, US Army Library
APO New York, NY 09175 West Germany Civilian 06151-69-6272/7233; European military 348-6272/7233; AUTOVON 995-6272/7233
Admin Candice K Case. *Ref Lib* Liza Allenbach (ILL).
Lib Type General.
Circ Servs Avail To other Federal libraries; to other libraries; restricted to US Army, civilian employees & dependents.

826. Defense Attache Office, Chief Legal Section, Army Law Library
APO New York, NY 09777 Paris, France AUTOVON 296-1202
Lib Type Law.

827. 8th Infantry Division, Baumholder Branch, Staff Judge Advocate, Law Library
ATTN: AETHJA-BHR-LA APO New York, NY 09034 Federal Republic of Germany 011-49-06783-6-6506/7246; ETS 485-6506/7246
Admin Scott R Morris.
Spec Subs Army regulations; USAREUR regulations.
Circ Servs Avail To other Federal libraries; to the general public.
Ref Servs Avail To other Federal libraries; to the general public.

828. 8th Infantry Division, Office of the Judge Advocate, Army Law Library
APO New York, NY 09111 Bad Kreuznach, Federal Republic of Germany AUTOVON 493-6412/8317
Lib Type Law.

829. V Corps, Office of the Staff Judge Advocate, Army Law Library
V Corps, Wiesbaden Branch Office, APO New York, NY 09457 Federal Republic of Germany AUTOVON 337-5128
Admin Larry D Vick. *Ref Lib* Gary Flanders (ILL, Acq).
Lib Type Law.
Spec Subs Military justice. *In-house Files* Army regulations & DoD directives.
Ref Servs Avail To other Federal libraries; to other libraries.

830. 5th Corps, Office of the Staff Judge Advocate, Army Law Library
APO New York, NY 09079 Frankfurt, Federal Republic of Germany
Lib Type Law.

831. 5th General Hospital, Medical Library
APO New York, NY 09154, Bad Canstatt-Stuttgart, Federal Republic of Germany
Lib Type Health & Medicine.

832. 54th Area Support Group, Office of the Group Judge Advocate, Army Law Library
APO New York, NY 09712 Rheinburg, Federal Republic of Germany
Lib Type Law.

833. 1st Armored Division, Office of the Staff Judge Advocate, Army Law Library
Nurenberg Law Center, APO New York, NY 09696 Federal Republic of Germany
Lib Type Law.

834. 1st Infantry Division Forward, Office of the Judge Advocate, Army Law Library
APO New York, NY 09137-5708 AUTOVON 425-3724/3454
Admin Dwight Landen.
Lib Type Law.
Coop Lib Nets ALLS.
Circ Servs Avail Restricted to official use.
Ref Servs Avail To other Federal libraries; to other libraries; restricted to official use.

835. 1st Infantry Division Forward, Office of the Staff Judge Advocate, Army Law Library
Neu Ulm Branch, APO New York, NY 09035 Federal Republic of Germany
Lib Type Law.

836. 1st Infantry Division Forward, Office of the Staff Judge Advocate, Army Law Library
Boblingen Branch Office, APO New York, NY 09046 Federal Republic of Germany
Lib Type Law.

837. Ft Buchanan Post Library
Bldg 399, Fort Buchanan, PR 00934 (809) 783-2424; FTS 783-2424; AUTOVON 894-1490
Admin John R Tejera.
Lib Type General.
Spec Subs Children's education; Caribbean.
Circ Servs Avail To other Federal libraries; to other libraries; to the general public.
Ref Servs Avail To other Federal libraries; to other libraries; to the general public.

838. Ft Clayton Post Library
Drawer 933, APO Miami, FL 34004 Panama
Admin John D Paulding. *Ref Lib* Mary Threadgill.
Lib Type General.
Spec Subs Panama Canal. *Spec Collecs* Panama.
Circ Servs Avail To other Federal libraries; to other libraries; restricted to DoD & other US government employees & dependents.
Ref Servs Avail To other Federal libraries; to other libraries; to the general public.

839. Frankfurt Army Regional Medical Center, Medical Library
APO New York, NY 09757-3398 West Germany AUTOVON 325-7572
Admin Gillian C Oliver.
Lib Type Health & Medicine.
Info Ret Servs DIMDI. *Coop Lib Nets* 7th Medical Command Medical Libraries.
Circ Servs Avail Restricted to FARMC service members.
Ref Servs Avail To other Federal libraries; to other libraries.

840. Fulda MILCOM, US Army Library
Downs Bks APO New York, NY 09146, Fulda, Federal Republic of Germany
Admin John D Pauling; Nancy Strachen.
Lib Type General.

841. Gorgas Army Hospital, S T Darling Library
APO Miami, FL 34004 Panama
Admin Fawn Walker.
Lib Type Health & Medicine.
Circ Servs Avail To other Federal libraries; to other libraries; restricted to MEDDAC.
Ref Servs Avail To other Federal libraries; to other libraries; restricted to MEDDAC.

842. Hannam Village Army Library
CFSSCK-C-Korea, APO San Francisco, CA 96301 Korea
Admin Jeanne A Bynum.
Lib Type General.
Circ Servs Avail Restricted to military, civilian employees & dependents.
Ref Servs Avail Restricted to military, civilian employees & dependents.

843. HQ 5th Corps, Office of the Judge Advocate, Army Law Library
Fulda Branch, APO New York, NY 09146 Federal Republic of Germany
Lib Type Law.

844. HQ 5th Signal Command, Office of the Staff Judge Advocate, Army Law Library
APO New York, NY 09056 Worms, Federal Republic of Germany
Lib Type Law.

845. HQ, 19th SUPCOM, Office of the Staff Judge Advocate, Army Field Law Library SRA P-50
Box 2278, APO San Francisco, CA 96212-0171 Taego, Korea AUTOVON 262-1101, ask for 268-7206/7692
Admin D C Boulanger.
Lib Type Law.
Info Ret Servs WESTLAW; LEXIS. *Coop Lib Nets* OPTIMIS. *Elec Mail Nets* DDN.

Circ Servs Avail To other Federal libraries; to the general public.
Ref Servs Avail To other Federal libraries; to the general public.

846. HQ 193rd INF BDE (Panama), Office of the Staff Judge Advocate, Army Law Library
APO Miami, FL 34004 Panama (313) 287-5168
Lib Type Law.

847. HQ 2nd Armored Division Forward, Office of the Staff Judge Advocate, Army Law Library
Legal Service Center, APO New York, NY 09355 Garlstedt, Federal Republic of Germany
Lib Type Law.

848. HQ, VII Corps, Staff Judge Advocate, Army Law Library
HQ VII Corps, Heilbronn Branch Office APO New York, NY 09176, Heilbronn, Federal Republic of Germany 07131-532775; AUTOVON 4262-775
Admin Marianne Odle.
Lib Type Law.
Spec Subs Criminal, administrative, & military law. *Spec Collecs* Military Justice Reporter; court martial reports; JSC collection.
Circ Servs Avail Not open to the general public; restricted to Staff Judge Advocate.
Ref Servs Avail Not open to the general public; restricted to Staff Judge Advocate.

849. HQ, 10th Area Support Group (Prov), Office of the Staff Judge Advocate, Army Law Library
APO San Francisco, CA 96331-0008 Okinawa, Japan FTS 637-4107
Admin Steven S Rowland. *Ref Lib* Joseph J Switzer.
Lib Type Law.
Spec Subs Military law. *Spec Collecs* Taxes.
Circ Servs Avail To the general public.
Ref Servs Avail To the general public.

850. HQ 3rd Infantry Division, Office of the Staff Judge Advocate, Army Law Library
APO New York, NY 09031 Kitzingen, Federal Republic of Germany
Lib Type Law.

851. HQ 23rd Support Group, Army Library
APO San Francisco, CA 96271-0074 Pyongtaaek, Korea AUTOVON 253-8818
Admin Robert S Wood.
Lib Type General.
Spec Subs Korea. *Spec Collecs* Korean language general collection.
Coop Lib Nets Army Libraries Korea.
Circ Servs Avail To other libraries.
Ref Servs Avail To other libraries; to the general public.

852. HQ, US Army Element, LANDSOUTHEAST, Office of the Staff Judge Advocate, Army Law Library
APO New York, NY 09224 AUTOVON 675-1110 ext 3218
Admin Mark Graham.
Lib Type Law.
Circ Servs Avail To other Federal libraries.
Ref Servs Avail To other Federal libraries.

853. HQ, US Army Japan/9th Corps, Office of the Staff Judge Advocate, Army Field Law Library
APO San Francisco, CA 96343-0054 Zama, Japan AUTOVON 233-3013/4041
Admin Y Suzuki; D D Hughes, Jr (Lib Accountable Officer).
Lib Type Law.
Spec Subs Supreme Court cases; public laws; federal tax; court-martial cases. *Spec Collecs* US Code; Supreme Court reports; court-martial reports; American jurisprudence; federal tax reporters.
Ref Servs Avail To the general public.

854. HQ US Army Materiel Command-Europe, Office of the Staff Judge Advocate, Army Law Library
APO New York, NY 09333 Seckenheim, Federal Republic of Germany
Lib Type Law.

855. HQ US EUCOM, Army Law Library
APO New York, NY 09128 Vaihingen, Federal Republic of Germany
Lib Type Law.

856. Patrick Henry Village, US Army Library
US Military Command ACTV, APO New York, NY 09102 Heidelberg, West Germany AUTOVON 370-6369
Admin Wesley R Wilson. *Ref Lib* Mary Ruth Duncan. *ILL* Anita Stovall.
Lib Type General.
Shared Catalog Nets PALS. *Coop Lib Nets* PALS.
Circ Servs Avail To other Federal libraries; to other libraries; to the general public.
Ref Servs Avail To other Federal libraries; to other libraries; to the general public.

857. Hindenburg Kaserne, US Army Library
APO New York, NY 09177, Ansbach, Federal Republic of Germany
Admin John Cook.
Lib Type General.

858. Karlsruhe Legal Center, US Army Law Library
c/o 79th Engineering Battalion, APO New York, NY 09360 West Germany
Admin Michael Rogus.
Lib Type Law.
Spec Subs Law.
Circ Servs Avail Restricted to employees.
Ref Servs Avail Restricted to employees.

859. Landstuhl Army Medical Center, Medical Library
Box 38, LARMC APO New York, NY 09180 Federal Republic of Germany 486-7111/8204
Admin Lillian G Graham (Medical Librarian). *ILL* Peter Kleinz. *Acq Lib* Kathy Koga.
Lib Type Health & Medicine.
Info Ret Servs MEDLARS. *Coop Lib Nets* 7th Army Command Libraries.
Circ Servs Avail Not open to the general public.
Ref Servs Avail Not open to the general public.

860. Ledward Barracks, US Army Library
APO New York, NY 09033, Schweinfurt, Federal Republic of Germany
Admin Richard M Barone.
Lib Type General.

861. Lee Barracks, US Army Library
APO New York, NY 09185, Mainz, Federal Republic of Germany
Admin William P Price.
Lib Type General.

862. Leighton Barracks, US Army Library
ATTN: AETSWRZ-AM-L, APO New York, NY 09801 West Germany AUTOVON 350-2321-6372
Admin Marcia W Hampton. *Ref Lib* Vera Goran. *ILL* Nancy Martin (Acq).
Lib Type General.
Coop Lib Nets PALS.
Circ Servs Avail To other Federal libraries; to other libraries; restricted to US military, DoD civilians & dependents.
Ref Servs Avail To other Federal libraries; to other libraries; to the general public.

863. Mainz Detachment, Office of the Staff Judge Advocate, Law Library
APO New York, NY 09185-4349 Federal Republic of Germany 06131-48-7580/8158; AUTOVON (ETS) 334-7580/8158
Admin John W Bearden.
Lib Type Law.
Spec Subs Administrative law; litigation; claims; criminal law.
Spec Collecs Military Justice Reporters; US Code annotated; Criminal Law Reporter; Law Week; Legal Assistance Reporter.
Coop Lib Nets Army Law Library Service (ALLS).
Ref Servs Avail To the general public.

864. Mannheim Community Library
USMCA Mannheim, APO New York, NY 09086-3877 West Germany AUTOVON 380-7206
Admin M Ann Parham. *Ref Lib* Sherrie Bingham (ILL).
Lib Type General.
Spec Subs Military science.
Coop Lib Nets PALS.
Circ Servs Avail Restricted to military & dependents.
Ref Servs Avail To the general public.

865. Mannheim Law Center, US Army Law Library
APO New York, NY 09086 West Germany Mannheim Military 2131-8226/7286; AUTOVON 380
Admin Baxter S Simpson.
Lib Type Law.
Spec Subs Military & federal law publications.
Circ Servs Avail To other Federal libraries; not open to the general public.
Ref Servs Avail To other Federal libraries; not open to the general public.

866. McGraw Kaserne, US Army Library
APO New York, NY 09407-0010 Munich, West Germany AUTOVON 440-6533
Admin Rosemary C Marlowe. *Ref Lib* Ralph Vicente. *ILL* Eleanore Spears. *Acq Lib* Sandra DiRocco.
Lib Type General.
Circ Servs Avail Restricted to US Army personnel & DA civilians.
Ref Servs Avail To other Federal libraries; to other libraries; to the general public.

867. McNair Kaserne Hoechst, US Army Library
Attn: Technical Services APO New York, NY 09102 Federal Republic of Germany
Lib Type General.

868. NATO SUPACT (US), US Army Library (Main)
ATTN: AERSH-N-MS, APO New York, NY 09667-5003 Brussels, Belgium 02 720 9015 ext 51
Admin Anne V Wallace. *ILL* Essie Roberts.
Lib Type General.
Coop Lib Nets USAREUR Library Program.
Circ Servs Avail To other Federal libraries; to other libraries; to the general public.
Ref Servs Avail To other Federal libraries; to other libraries; to the general public.

869. NATO/SHAPE, Office of the Staff Judge Advocate, Army Law Library
NATO/SHAPE Support (US), APO New York, NY 09088 Chievres, Belgium
Lib Type Law.

870. Office of the Staff Judge Advocate, Army Law Library
APO New York, NY 09742 Berlin, Federal Republic of Germany
Lib Type Law.

871. 196th Hospital SHAPE, Medical Library
Dept Act APO New York, NY 09055, Mons, Belgium
Lib Type Health & Medicine.

872. 130th General Hospital, Medical Library
APO New York, NY 09105, Nurnburg, Federal Republic of Germany
Lib Type Health & Medicine.

873. 130th Station Hospital, Medical Library
APO New York, NY 09102, Heidelberg, Federal Republic of Germany
Lib Type Health & Medicine.

874. 121st Evacuation Hospital, Army Library
APO San Francisco, CA 96301-0074 Korea AUTOVON 262-1101-293-5335/5471
Admin Patricia S Vanderburg.
Lib Type Hospital (Patients).
Circ Servs Avail To other Federal libraries; to other libraries; restricted to authorized ID card holders.
Ref Servs Avail To other Federal libraries; to other libraries; restricted to authorized ID card holders.

875. Patch Barracks, US Army Library
Vaihingen, APO New York, NY 09131 AUTOVON 430-7138
Admin Nancy E Klein.
Lib Type General.
Spec Subs International relations; feminist literature.
Coop Lib Nets PALS.
Circ Servs Avail To other Federal libraries; to other libraries; to the general public.
Ref Servs Avail To other Federal libraries; to other libraries; to the general public.

876. Pendleton Barracks, US Army Library
APO New York, NY 09169, Giessen, Federal Republic of Germany
Admin Geraldine A Smith.
Lib Type General.

877. Pirmasens Legal Services Center, Office Library
USMCA-P, APO New York, NY 09189-3754 Federal Republic of Germany 06331-99506
Admin Kenneth Allen.
Lib Type Law.
Coop Lib Nets Army Law Library Service (ALLS).
Circ Servs Avail Not open to the general public.
Ref Servs Avail To other Federal libraries; not open to the general public.

878. Robinson Barracks, US Army Library
APO New York, NY 09154-0010 Stuttgart, West Germany AUTOVON 420-6424/7385
Admin Billie K Portmann.
Lib Type General.
Spec Subs European travel; military history. *Spec Collecs* Genealogy.
Coop Lib Nets PALS.
Circ Servs Avail To other Federal libraries; to other libraries; not open to the general public.
Ref Servs Avail To other Federal libraries; to other libraries; not open to the general public.

879. Rose Barracks, US Army Library
APO New York, NY 09252, Bad Kreuznach, Federal Republic of Germany
Admin Cheryl Hunter.
Lib Type General.

880. 2nd Region US Army Criminal Investigation Command (USACIDC), Region Judge Advocate, Army Law Library
APO New York, NY 09102 Heidelberg, Federal Republic of Germany
Lib Type Law.

881. 7th Corps, Office of the Staff Judge Advocate, Army Law Library
North Stuttgart Branch, APO New York, NY 09154 Stuttgart, Federal Republic of Germany
Lib Type Law.

882. 7th Corps, Office of the Staff Judge Advocate, Army Law Library
Augsburg Branch Office, APO New York, NY 09178 Federal Republic of Germany
Lib Type Law.

883. 7th Corps, Office of the Staff Judge Advocate, Army Law Library
Munich Branch, APO New York, NY 09407 Federal Republic of Germany
Lib Type Law.

884. VII Corps, Office of the Staff Judge Advocate, Army Law Library
APO New York, NY 09107 Stuttgart, West Germany 0711-7292-817; AUTOVON 421-2817
Lib Type Law.
Spec Subs Army regulations.
Circ Servs Avail Not open to the general public.
Ref Servs Avail Not open to the general public.

885. 7th Medical Command, Command Judge Advocate, Army Law Library
APO New York, NY 09102 Heidelberg, Federal Republic of Germany
Lib Type Law.

886. Smiley Barracks, US Army Library
APO New York, NY 09164, Karlsruhe, Federal Republic of Germany
Admin Nancy Hahn; Catherine Sheedy. *ILL* Mary Cecil.
Lib Type General.
Spec Collecs Books on the cities & regions of Germany.
Circ Servs Avail To other libraries; to the general public.
Ref Servs Avail To other libraries; to the general public.

887. SHAPE Community Library
A & R Branch IHSC APO New York, NY 09055, Casteau, Belgium
Lib Type General.

888. Task Force Judge Advocate Army Law Library
US Battalion, MFO South Camp, APO New York, NY 09679 Sinai, Egypt 1-011-972-3-622-316 ext 4631
Admin Task Force Judge Advocate.
Lib Type Law.
Spec Collecs Military Justice Reporters; Selected Army regulations & publications.
Ref Servs Avail Restricted to members of the Command & Staff of the US Battalion & Logistical Support Unit of the Multinational Force & Observers.

889. 3rd Armored Division, Army Law Library, Legal Library
Giessen Legal Center, APO New York, NY 09169 Federal Republic of Germany
Lib Type Law.

890. 3rd Armored Division, Office of the Staff Judge Advocate, Army Law Library
Butzbach Branch, APO New York, NY 09077 Federal Republic of Germany
Lib Type Law.

891. 3rd Armored Division, Office of the Staff Judge Advocate, Army Law Library
Gelnhausen Legal Service Center, APO New York, NY 09091 Federal Republic of Germany
Lib Type Law.

892. 3rd Armored Division, Office of the Staff Judge Advocate, Army Law Library
Hanau Branch, APO New York, NY 09165 Federal Republic of Germany
Lib Type Law.

893. 3rd Infantry Division, Office of the Staff Judge Advocate, Army Law Library
APO New York, NY 09036 Wurzburg, Federal Republic of Germany
Lib Type Law.

894. 3rd Infantry Division, Office of the Staff Judge Advocate, Army Law Library
APO New York, NY 09162 Aschaffenburg, Federal Republic of Germany
Lib Type Law.

895. 3rd Infantry Division, Office of the Staff Judge Advocate, Army Law Library
APO New York, NY 09701 Schweinfurt, Federal Republic of Germany
Lib Type Law.

896. 32nd Army Air Defense Command, Office of the Staff Judge Advocate, Army Law Library
APO New York, NY 09175 Darmstadt, Federal Republic of Germany
Lib Type Law.

897. Torii Station Library, DPCA, MSAD
US Dept of the Army, 10th Area Support Group (PROV)(USAGO), APO San Francisco, CA 96331-1040 Okinawa, Japan 631-4468 (on base)
Admin Helen G Hopkins.
Lib Type General.
Spec Collecs Japan; Okinawa.
Coop Lib Nets Union List of Periodicals in the Pacific Area, prepared by PACAF Library Service Center.
Circ Servs Avail To other Federal libraries; not open to the general public; restricted to military, dependents & civilian employees.
Ref Servs Avail To other Federal libraries; not open to the general public; restricted to military, dependents & civilian employees.

898. 21st SUPCOM, Law Library
Northern Law Center, Schinnen Branch APO New York, NY 09011, Brunssom, Netherlands 0031-4493-3905; ETS 360-7235
Admin Elek A Fenyes. *Ref Lib* Roger D Vian (ACQ).
Lib Type Law.
Spec Collecs Complete set of Dutch legal reference material.
Circ Servs Avail To other Federal libraries.

899. 21st Support Command, Office of Staff Judge Advocate, Law Library
Kaiserslautern, APO New York, NY 09325 Federal Republic of Germany 49-631-411-8304
Admin Jerry E Shiles.
Lib Type Law.
Spec Subs Military justice; estate planning; international law; federal & state taxation; administration law.
Circ Servs Avail To other Federal libraries; to other libraries; not open to the general public.
Ref Servs Avail To other Federal libraries; to other libraries; to the general public.

900. 279th Station Hospital, Medical Library
MEDDAC APO New York, NY 09742, Berlin, Federal Republic of Germany
Lib Type Health & Medicine.

901. US Army & Air Force Exchange Service (USAAFES), Office of the Counsel, Army Law Library
APO New York, NY 09245 Munich, Federal Republic of Germany
Lib Type Law.

902. US Army Arctic Test Center, Technical Library
Ft Greely APO Seattle, WA 98733, AK
Lib Type General.

903. USAB Library System
MSAD, Main Library APO New York, NY 09742, Berlin, Federal Republic of Germany
Admin Joe Chicarella.
Lib Type General.

904. US Army Claims Office, Army Law Library
APO New York, NY 09667 Brussels, Belgium
Lib Type Law.

905. US Army Claims Service Europe, Law Library
APO New York, NY 09166-5346 AUTOVON 380-6485/7146
Admin Michael T Ringstad.
Lib Type Law.
Circ Servs Avail Not open to the general public.
Ref Servs Avail Not open to the general public.

906. US Army Contracting Agency Europe, Office of Counsel, Army Law Library
APO New York, NY 09710 Frankfurt, Federal Republic of Germany
Lib Type Law.

907. US Army Contracting Agency Korea, Office of Counsel, Law Library
EAKC-OC APO San Francisco, CA 96301-0062, Yongsan, Korea AUTOVON 262-1101, EXT 294-7515
Admin Mat Duffy.
Lib Type Law.
Spec Subs Contract law.
Circ Servs Avail Not open to the general public; restricted to Agency personnel.
Ref Servs Avail Not open to the general public; restricted to Agency personnel.

908. US Army Engineer Division Europe, Technical Library
ATTN: EUDAS-L, APO New York, NY 09757 West Germany 49 69 151 5385; FTS 320-5385
Admin Inga Rafatjah.
Lib Type Engineering & Science.
Spec Subs Construction. *Spec Collecs* German building materials.
Circ Servs Avail Restricted to EUD.
Ref Servs Avail To other Federal libraries; to other libraries.

909. US Army Engineer Division Europe, Technical Library
Attn: EUDAS-L APO New York, NY 09757 Federal Republic of Germany 049-69-151-5385; FTS GE-320-5385; AUTOVON 314-320-5385
Admin Inga B Rafatjah.
Lib Type Law; Engineering & Science.
Spec Subs Engineering; law. *Spec Collecs* German building regulations.
Circ Servs Avail Not open to the general public; restricted to Corps of Engineers.
Ref Servs Avail To other Federal libraries; to other libraries; not open to the general public.

910. USAREUR Judge Advocate's Law Library
APO New York, NY 09403 Heidelberg, Federal Republic of Germany 06221-576655
Admin Linda L Powell.
Lib Type Law.
Info Ret Servs DIALOG.
Circ Servs Avail To other Federal libraries; not open to the general public.
Ref Servs Avail To other Federal libraries; not open to the general public.

911. USAREUR Library & Resource Center
ATTN: AEAIM-DL-L, HQ USAREUR & 7th Army, APO New York, NY 09403 Heidelberg, Federal Republic of Germany 011-49-6221-57-7430/8129/8239; AUTOVON 370-7430/8129/8239
Admin Duane G Nahley. *Ref Lib* George Patail. *ILL* Phyllis Kelly. *Acq Lib* Martha A Davis.
Lib Type General.
Spec Subs Military art & science; foreign affairs; European history; economics; business. *Spec Collecs* ERIC; BCL; LEL; CIS; Evans collection; genealogy & local history; Cox library; Marburger Index. *In-house Files* US Army in WW II & unit history pamphlet files.
Info Ret Servs DIALOG. *Shared Catalog Nets* PALS (GEAC). *Coop Lib Nets* Interlibrary Loan Fee Payment Pilot Project. *Elec Mail Nets* USAREUR-EM.
Circ Servs Avail To other Federal libraries; to other libraries; to the general public.
Ref Servs Avail To other Federal libraries; to other libraries; to the general public.

912. US Army Field Station, Augsburg, Office of the Judge Advocate, Army Law Library
APO New York, NY 09458 Federal Republic of Germany
Lib Type Law.

913. US Army Field Station, Command Judge Advocate, Diogenes Station Law Library
USAFS APO New York, NY 09133, Sinop, Turkey 1-011-90-3761-5431/5432, ext 249
Admin John M Fomous. *Ref Lib* Barry N Dalton.
Lib Type Law.
Circ Servs Avail Not open to the general public.
Ref Servs Avail Not open to the general public.

914. US Army Hospital, Medical Library
APO New York, NY 09069, Bremerhaven, Federal Republic of Germany
Lib Type Health & Medicine.

915. US Army Hospital, Medical Library
APO New York, NY 09178, Augsburg, Federal Republic of Germany
Lib Type Health & Medicine.

916. US Army Hospital, Medical Library
APO New York, NY 09221, Vicenza, Italy
Lib Type Health & Medicine.

917. US Army Hospital, Wurzburg, Medical Library
APO New York, NY 09801, Wurzburg, Federal Republic of Germany
Lib Type Health & Medicine.

918. US Army Law Library, Vilseck-Grafenwoehr
Legal Division CTMD-7A CATC APO New York, NY 09114 Federal Republic of Germany
Admin M Stevens.
Lib Type Law.
Spec Subs Military law.
Circ Servs Avail To other libraries; to the general public.
Ref Servs Avail To other libraries; to the general public.

919. US Army Library
USMCA Augsburg (AETS-AUG-DPCA-CRD-L), APO New York, NY 09458 Federal Republic of Germany 0821-448-6380; FTS 434-6380; AUTOVON 434-6380
Admin Dolores R Allen. *Ref Lib* Kathryn Mayall (ILL).
Lib Type General.
Info Ret Servs DIALOG.
Circ Servs Avail To other Federal libraries; restricted to registered patrons of the Augsburg Military Community.
Ref Servs Avail To other Federal libraries; to the general public.

920. US Army Library
APO New York, NY 09114, Grafenwoehr, Federal Republic of Germany
Admin Mary T McCullugh.
Lib Type General.

921. US Army Library Service Center
Camp Market, APO San Francisco, CA 96483-0074 Republic of Korea AUTOVON 262-1101 ext 2923-811/824
Admin Jewel A Player.
Spec Subs This is the centralized technical service facility providing all acquisitions & cataloging/processing functions for all 35 US Army libraries in the Republic of Korea.
Coop Lib Nets FEDLINK. *Elec Mail Nets* Defense Data Network (DDN).
Ref Servs Avail Not open to the general public.

922. US Army Library System, Norddeutschland
APO New York, NY 09069 West Germany AUTOVON 342-8578
Admin Richard D Hanusey; Hilde L Neuschaefer (Bremerhaven); J Michael Morrison (Garlstedt).
Lib Type General.
Spec Subs North Federal Republic of Germany: history, area collections. *Spec Collecs* European travel; languages. *In-house Files* Travel maps; guides; railway time tables; language aids.
Info Ret Servs DIALOG. *Coop Lib Nets* PALS. *Elec Mail Nets* DDN (access thru PALS).
Circ Servs Avail To other Federal libraries; to other libraries; restricted to NATO/US military.
Ref Servs Avail To other Federal libraries.

923. US Army Library, Wharton Barracks
APO New York, NY 09176, Heilbronn, Federal Republic of Germany AUTOVON 4262/504
Admin Patricia Ames.
Lib Type General.

924. US Army Library, Worms
Attn: AERWP-RL APO New York, NY 09058-3879 Federal Republic of Germany 06241-487210; AUTOVON 383-7210
Admin Carlton Dempfle.
Lib Type General.
Coop Lib Nets USAREUR.
Circ Servs Avail Not open to the general public; restricted to US military personnel, civilian employees, & dependents.
Ref Servs Avail Not open to the general public; restricted to US military personnel, civilian employees, & dependents.

925. US Army PPCE, Remote Site Center Library
Attn: AEAAG-ALR APO New York, NY 09090, Roedeheim, Federal Republic of Germany
Lib Type General.

926. US Army Real Estate Agency Europe, Office of the Staff Judge Advocate, Army Law Library
APO New York, NY 09710 Frankfurt, Federal Republic of Germany
Lib Type Law.

927. US Army Russian Institute, Research Library
APO New York, NY 09053, Garmisch, Federal Republic of Germany (0498821)-750720; AUTOVON 4440-1110, 720 or 796
Admin Germaine K Pavlova. *Ref Lib* D French; I Gorshenin. *ILL* Tracy McLaughlin.
Lib Type Academic; Training Center.
Spec Subs Russian language & literature; Russian/Soviet military, economic, political, historical, sociological, & cultural affairs. *Spec Collecs* Newspapers, maps, microfilms, & microfiche collections; documents from NTIS & DTIS. *In-house Files* Alphabetical catalogue & files.
Circ Servs Avail To other Federal libraries; not open to the general public.
Ref Servs Avail To other Federal libraries; not open to the general public.

928. US Army Southern European Task Force & 5th Support Command, Army Law Library
ATTN: AESE-JAS, APO New York, NY 09168 Vicenza, Italy AUTOVON 634-7818
Admin Clarence H Thompson.
Lib Type Law.
Spec Subs General law effecting the military & civilian legal assistance program. *Spec Collecs* Italian laws & penal codes.
Circ Servs Avail To other Federal libraries; to the general public.
Ref Servs Avail To other Federal libraries; to the general public.

929. US Army Support Group, Legal Services Center, Army Law Library
NDL, APO New York, NY 09069 Bremerhaven, Federal Republic of Germany
Lib Type Law.

930. US Army Tropic Test Center, Technical Information Center
Drawer 942, APO Miami, FL 34004-5000 011-507-85-5910; AUTOVON (313) 285-5910
Admin Ann Guerriero. *Acq Lib* Arlene Sollas.
Lib Type Special.
In-house Files Tropic test reports.
Circ Servs Avail To other Federal libraries; not open to the general public.
Ref Servs Avail To other Federal libraries; not open to the general public.

931. USMCA, Garmisch, Army Library
USMCA APO New York, NY 09053, Garmisch, Federal Republic of Germany
Lib Type General.

932. USMCA, Jaeger Kaserne, US Army Library
APO New York, NY 09054, Aschaffenburg, Federal Republic of Germany
Lib Type General.

933. USMCA, Pirmasens, Army Library
Husterhoeh Kaserne, HQS USMCA APO New York, NY 09189, Pirmasens, Federal Republic of Germany
Admin Barbara Jordan.
Lib Type General.

934. USMCA, Rheinburg, Army Library
USMCA APO New York, NY 09712, Rheinburg, Federal Republic of Germany
Lib Type General.

935. USMCA, Zweibruecken, Army Library
APO New York, NY 09052, Kreuzberg Kaserne, Zweibruecken, Federal Republic of Germany
Admin Patricia S Larrabee; Mary Chinn.
Lib Type General.

936. US Southern Command, Office of the Staff Judge Advocate
APO Miami, FL 34003, Quarry Heights, Panama (507) 82-4605; AUTOVON 282-4605
Admin Terry G Kemp. *Acq Lib* Giovanni E Ortiz.
Lib Type Law.
Circ Servs Avail Not open to the general public.
Ref Servs Avail Not open to the general public.

937. Wiesbaden US Army Library
USMCA Wiesbaden, APO New York, NY 09457 West Germany AUTOVON 337-5951
Admin Ann C Sullivan. *ILL* Sharon Primus.
Lib Type General.
Circ Servs Avail To other libraries; restricted to military & DoD.
Ref Servs Avail To other libraries; restricted to military & DoD.

938. Wildflecken Military Community, Office of the Staff Judge Advocate, US Army Law Library
APO New York, NY 09026 Federal Republic of Germany
Lib Type Law.

939. Wildflecken US Military Community, Army Library Program
APO New York, NY 09026 Federal Republic of Germany
Admin Barbara Oslizly.
Lib Type General.

940. Wiley Barracks, US Army Library
APO New York, NY 09035, Neu-Ulm, Federal Republic of Germany
Admin Ronald W Argen.
Lib Type General.

941. Wolfgang Pioneer Kaserene, US Army Library
APO New York, NY 09165 West Germany ETS 322-8715
Admin Sharon A McKinley. *ILL* Marie Routhier.
Lib Type General.
Circ Servs Avail To other libraries; to the general public.
Ref Servs Avail To the general public.

942. Yongsan Library
Community Recreation Region Central, CFSSCK, APO San Francisco, CA 96301-0074 Korea AUTOVON 262-1101-7300
Admin Arlene C Hahn. *Ref Lib* Roselle C Dill. *ILL* Myung Ja Lee.
Lib Type General.
Spec Subs Koreana; military arts & sciences education; business. *Spec Collecs* Koreana.
Circ Servs Avail To other Federal libraries; to other libraries; to the general public.
Ref Servs Avail To other Federal libraries; to other libraries; to the general public.

943. Zama Library
USAGH DPA-CRL, APO San Francisco, CA 96343-0068 Zama, Japan AUTOVON 233-3517
Admin Pamela A Shelton. *Acq Lib* Ebtisam Habek.
Lib Type General.
Spec Subs Military history. *Spec Collecs* Japan.
Circ Servs Avail To other Federal libraries; to other libraries; to the general public.
Ref Servs Avail To other Federal libraries; to other libraries; to the general public.

Department of the Navy—Domestic

944. Alameda Naval Air Station Library
Bldg 2 Wing 3, Alameda, CA 94501-5051 (415) 869-2519; AUTOVON 686-3504/3505
Admin Barbara A Arnott. *ILL* Diane J McDermott.
Lib Type General.
Spec Collecs California; women; minorities; careers & education.
Coop Lib Nets Bay Area Library & Information System (BALIS).
Circ Servs Avail To other Federal libraries; to other libraries; not open to the general public.
Ref Servs Avail To other Federal libraries; to other libraries; restricted to use by the general public by appointment.

945. Annapolis Naval Station Library
Annapolis, MD 21402-5054 (301) 267-2311; AUTOVON 281-2311
Admin G E Buckley.
Lib Type General.
Circ Servs Avail Restricted to Navy personnel.
Ref Servs Avail Restricted to Navy personnel.

946. Armed Forces Radiobiology Research Institute Library
Naval Medical Command, National Capitol Region, Bldg 42, Bethesda, MD 20814 (202) 295-4028
Admin Ilse Vada.
Lib Type Health & Medicine.
Spec Subs Medical effects of radiation.

Circ Servs Avail To other libraries.
Ref Servs Avail To other Federal libraries; to other libraries; to the general public.

947. Atlanta Naval Air Station Library
Marietta, GA 30060 (404) 429-5000
Lib Type General.

948. Bangor Naval Submarine Base Library
Bldg 2500, NSB Bangor, WA 98315 (206) 779-9724
Admin Gail L Goodrick. *ILL* Handled at Kitsap Regional Library, Bremerton, WA. *Acq Lib* Gail Goodrick (Adult); Kathy Hayes (Children's).
Lib Type General.
Spec Collecs US Naval history.
Shared Catalog Nets WLN. *Coop Lib Nets* Washington Library Film Circuit.
Circ Servs Avail To other Federal libraries; to other libraries; to the general public.
Ref Servs Avail To other Federal libraries; to other libraries; to the general public.

949. Barbers Point Naval Air Station Library
Barbers Point, HI 96862-5050 (808) 684-5217/4222
Admin Marsha Dreier.
Lib Type General.
Circ Servs Avail To other Federal libraries; to other libraries; not open to the general public; restricted to military & dependents.
Ref Servs Avail To other Federal libraries; to other libraries; not open to the general public; restricted to military & dependents.

950. Beaufort Naval Hospital, Medical Library
Beaufort, SC 29902 (803) 525-5551
Lib Type Health & Medicine.

951. Beeville Naval Air Station Library
Beeville, TX 78103 (512) 354-5301; AUTOVON 354-5301
Admin John L Sullivan.
Lib Type General.
Spec Collecs Naval War College Collections.
Lib Deposit Designation Department of Defense.
Circ Servs Avail To other Federal libraries; to other libraries; not open to the general public; restricted to DoD.
Ref Servs Avail To other Federal libraries; not open to the general public; restricted to DoD.

952. Bethesda Naval Hospital, General Library
NMC NCR, Bldg 2, Rm 1402, Bethesda, MD 20814-5011 (202) 295-0993; AUTOVON 295-0993
Admin Patricia W Simmons.
Lib Type Hospital (Patients).
Circ Servs Avail Not open to the general public; restricted to patients & staff.
Ref Servs Avail Not open to the general public; restricted to patients & staff.

953. Bethesda Naval Hospital, Edward Rhodes Stitt Library
Naval Medical Command, National Capital Region, Bethesda, MD 20814-5011 (202) 295-1184; AUTOVON 295-1184
Admin Jerry Meyer. *Ref Lib* Cindy Brancato. *ILL* Lois Springirth. *Acq Lib* Barbara Haley.
Lib Type Health & Medicine.
Spec Subs Medicine; surgery; nursing; dentistry; allied health sciences; US Surgeon General's Library. *Spec Collecs* History of medicine; pastoral care.
Info Ret Servs BRS; MEDLINE thru NTIS.
Circ Servs Avail Restricted to Navy medical dept personnel.
Ref Servs Avail Restricted to Navy medical dept personnel.

954. Bethesda Naval Medical Research Institute, Information Services Branch
Bethesda, MD 20814-5055 (202) 295-2186; AUTOVON 295-2186
Admin Rosemary Coskey. *Ref Lib* Susan Humphrey (ILL). *Acq Lib* Aletha Holser.
Lib Type Health & Medicine.

Spec Subs Hyperbaric medicine; transplantation; immunology; infectious disease; experimental surgery; casualty care; environmental stress. *In-house Files* NMRI technical reports.
Info Ret Servs DIALOG; BRS. *Shared Catalog Nets* OCLC. *Coop Lib Nets* IUA; FEDLINK.
Circ Servs Avail To other libraries; restricted to thru ILL.
Ref Servs Avail To other libraries; restricted to Navy personnel; scientific researchers with approval.

955. Bremerton Naval Hospital, Medical Library
Boone Rd, Bremerton, WA 98312-1898 (206) 478-9316; AUTOVON 439-9316
Admin Jane Easley.
Lib Type Health & Medicine.
Info Ret Servs MEDLARS. *Coop Lib Nets* Washington Medical Librarians Assoc (WMLA). *Elec Mail Nets* CLASS.
Circ Servs Avail To other Federal libraries; to other libraries; not open to the general public.
Ref Servs Avail Restricted to hospital & regional medical staff.

956. Brunswick Naval Air Station Library
Box 21, Brunswick, ME 04011-5000 (207) 921-2639; AUTOVON 476-2639
Admin Judy Schwartz.
Lib Type General.
Coop Lib Nets Maine Library Assoc; Special Libraries Group (SLG).
Circ Servs Avail To other Federal libraries; to other libraries; not open to the general public; restricted to active duty military, retired, dependents, & base civilians.
Ref Servs Avail To other Federal libraries; to other libraries; not open to the general public.

957. Camp Lejeune Naval Hospital, Medical & General Libraries
Camp Lejeune, NC 28542-5008 (919) 451-4076; AUTOVON 484-4076
Admin Betty Frazelle.
Lib Type Health & Medicine; Hospital (Patients).
Spec Subs Medicine; surgery; ENT; nursing; dental.
Circ Servs Avail Restricted to staff & patients.
Ref Servs Avail Restricted to staff & patients.

958. Camp Pendleton Naval Hospital, Crew's Library
PO Box 541, Bldg H-100, Camp Pendleton, CA 92055-5008 (619) 725-1229; AUTOVON 365-1229
Admin Kathleen Dunning-Torbett.
Lib Type General; Hospital (Patients).
Circ Servs Avail Not open to the general public; restricted to patients, staff, & dependents.
Ref Servs Avail To other Federal libraries; not open to the general public; restricted to patients, staff, & dependents.

959. Camp Pendleton Naval Hospital Library
Camp Pendleton, CA 92069-5008 (619) 725-1322; FTS 725-1322; AUTOVON 993-1322
Admin Deborah Batey. *ILL* Manie Washington.
Lib Type Health & Medicine.
Spec Subs Medicine; nursing; dentistry.
Info Ret Servs MEDLINE (NLM). *Coop Lib Nets* Pacific Southwest Regional Medical Library Service (PSRMLS).
Circ Servs Avail To other Federal libraries; to other libraries; not open to the general public; restricted to hospital staff personnel.
Ref Servs Avail To other Federal libraries; to other libraries; to the general public.

960. Cecil Field Naval Air Station Library
Box 104, Cecil Field, FL 32215-0104 (904) 778-5311
Lib Type General.

961. Charleston Naval Hospital, Medical Library
Charleston, SC 29408 (803) 743-6913
Admin J M Griffin.
Lib Type Health & Medicine.
Shared Catalog Nets SCHIN.
Circ Servs Avail To other Federal libraries; not open to the general public; restricted to staff.

Ref Servs Avail To other Federal libraries; not open to the general public; restricted to staff.

962. Charleston Naval Shipyard, Technical Library
Code 202.3, Charleston, SC 29408 (803) 743-3843; AUTOVON 563-3843
Admin Leola Gadsden. *ILL* Carole Venning (Acq).
Lib Type Special.
Circ Servs Avail To other Federal libraries; not open to the general public.
Ref Servs Avail To other Federal libraries; not open to the general public.

963. Charleston Naval Station Base Library
Bldg 46, Charleston, SC 29408-5000 (803) 743-5399
Lib Type General.
Circ Servs Avail Not open to the general public; restricted to military & dependents.
Ref Servs Avail Not open to the general public; restricted to military & dependents.

964. Charleston Naval Station, Brig Library
Bldg 648, Charleston, SC 29408 (803) 743-6490
Lib Type General.

965. Charleston Naval Station, Naval Hospital, Regional Medical Center, General Library
Charleston, SC 29408 (803) 743-6172
Lib Type Health & Medicine.

966. Cheltenham Station Library, Naval Communication Unit
Bldg 13, Washington, DC 20390 (202) 238-2201/2202
Lib Type Special.

967. CINCLANTFLT Library, HSA
Bldg NH-30, Norfolk, VA 23511-6689 (804) 444-6262; AUTOVON 564-6262
Admin Beulah M Mull.
Lib Type General.
Circ Servs Avail To the general public.
Ref Servs Avail To the general public.

968. Colts Neck Naval Weapons Station, Earle Library
Bldg C-29, Colts Neck, NJ 07722 (201) 577-2103; AUTOVON 449-1103
Admin Nancy Sheppard.
Lib Type General.
Circ Servs Avail Restricted to military, DoD civilians & dependents.
Ref Servs Avail Restricted to military, DoD civilians & dependents.

969. Concord Naval Weapons Station Library
Bldg I-A10, Code 014, Concord, CA 94520 (415) 671-5851; AUTOVON 253-5851
Admin Celie Simmons.
Lib Type General.
Circ Servs Avail To other Federal libraries; to other libraries; restricted to military, dependents, & employees.

970. Coos Head Naval Station Library
Coos Head Naval Facility, Charleston, OR 97420 (503) 888-3221; AUTOVON 355-2011
Lib Type General.
Circ Servs Avail Not open to the general public; restricted to active duty personnel.
Ref Servs Avail Not open to the general public; restricted to active duty personnel.

971. Corpus Christi Naval Air Station Library
Bldg 5, Corpus Christi, TX 78419 (512) 939-3574
Lib Type General.

972. Dallas Naval Air Station Library
Dallas, TX 75211-9501 (214) 266-6132; AUTOVON 874-6132/6340
Admin Linda Barnes. *Acq Lib* Virginia Byers.
Lib Type General.
Circ Servs Avail To other Federal libraries; not open to the general public.
Ref Servs Avail To other Federal libraries; not open to the general public.

973. El Centro Naval Air Facility General Library
El Centro, CA 92243 (619) 339-2461
Lib Type General.
Circ Servs Avail To the general public.
Ref Servs Avail To the general public.

974. Electronic Warfare Department, Tactical Publication Library
Bldg 516, Code 330L, NTTC Corry Station, Pensacola, FL 32511 (904) 452-6308/6309; AUTOVON 922-6308/6309
Admin Jeanne M Fillingim.
Lib Type Training Center.
Circ Servs Avail Not open to the general public.
Ref Servs Avail Not open to the general public.

975. Fallon Naval Air Station Library
Bks 2, Fallon, NV 89406 (702) 426-5161, ext 2599
Lib Type General.

976. Fleet & Mine Warfare Training Center
Naval Base, Charleston, SC 29408-5200 (803) 743-4733; FTS 573-4722; TTY 743-4722; AUTOVON 563-4722
Admin Iris G Rubio.
Lib Type Training Center.
Spec Subs Mine warfare & mine counter-measures; mine warfare repository. *Spec Collecs* Defense intelligence publications.
Circ Servs Avail To other Federal libraries; not open to the general public.
Ref Servs Avail To other Federal libraries; not open to the general public.

977. Fleet Anti-Submarine Warfare Training Center, Pacific, Technical Library
San Diego, CA 92147-5000 (619) 225-4238; AUTOVON 957-4238
Admin David L Jones.
Lib Type Training Center.
Spec Subs Naval Warfare Publications Library (NWPL). *Spec Collecs* Technical publications associated with anti-submarine warfare training & associated equipment.
Circ Servs Avail Not open to the general public.
Ref Servs Avail Not open to the general public; restricted to need to know with proper security clearance.

978. Fleet Combat Direction Systems, Support Activity
Data Resource Ctr, San Diego, CA 92147 (619) 225-2950; AUTOVON 933-2950
Admin Marilyn Soldwisch.
Lib Type General.

979. Fleet Combat Training Center Library
Atlantic Dam Neck, Virginia Beach, VA 23461 (804) 433-6565
Admin Max E Dunks.
Lib Type Training Center.
Circ Servs Avail Not open to the general public.
Ref Servs Avail Not open to the general public.

980. Fleet Intelligence Center, Europe & Atlantic, Library
Code 113, Norfolk, VA 23511-6690 (804) 444-6262; FTS 444-6515; AUTOVON 564-6515
Admin Millie King; Ens Cerovsky.
Lib Type General.
Spec Subs Foreign relations; military intelligence; country studies; military weapons; military forces. *Spec Collecs* Government series; monographs.
Info Ret Servs In house service (Fleet Intelligence Production System).
Circ Servs Avail To other Federal libraries; restricted to local.

Ref Servs Avail To other Federal libraries; restricted to local.

981. Fleet Intelligence Center, Pacific, Library
Box 500, Pearl Harbor, HI 96860 (808) 474-6122
Admin M T Black.
Lib Type General.

982. Glenview Naval Air Station Library
Bldg 10, Glenview, IL 60026
Lib Type General.

983. Great Lakes Naval Hospital, General Library
Bldg 200-H, Great Lakes, IL 60088
Lib Type Hospital (Patients).

984. Great Lakes Naval Hospital, Medical Library
Bldg 200-H, Great Lakes, IL 60088 (312) 688-4601
Lib Type Health & Medicine.
Spec Subs Clinical medicine.
Coop Lib Nets Lake County Consortium.

985. Great Lakes Naval Training Station Center Library
Bldg 3, Great Lakes, IL 60088-5100 (312) 688-4617; FTS 688-3742; AUTOVON 792-3742
Admin Mary M Dobnikar; Linda Nix (Asst).
Lib Type General.
Spec Subs Naval & military history. *Spec Collecs* Jane's Fighting Ships.
Coop Lib Nets North Suburban Library System (NSLS).
Circ Servs Avail To other Federal libraries; to other libraries; not open to the general public; restricted to qualified users.
Ref Servs Avail To other Federal libraries; to other libraries; not open to the general public; restricted to qualified users.

986. Great Lakes Training Center Library
Bldg 3, Great Lakes, IL 60088 (312) 688-4617
Lib Type Training Center.
Ref Servs Avail Not open to the general public; restricted to military personnel & staff.

987. Hull, Machinery & Electrical Technical Library
Philadelphia Naval Shipyard, Philadelphia, PA 19112 (215) 755-4778; AUTOVON 433-3864
Admin Ruth Young.
Lib Type General.

988. Jacksonville Naval Air Station Library
Bldg 930, Box 52, Jacksonville, FL 32212-5000 (904) 772-3415; AUTOVON 942-3433
Admin Maytag Aircraft Corp (on contract).
Lib Type General.
Circ Servs Avail Not open to the general public.
Ref Servs Avail To other Federal libraries; to other libraries.

989. Key West Naval Air Station Library
Bldg 623, Key West, FL 33040-5000 (305) 296-3561 ext 2116; AUTOVON 483-2116
Admin Nancy Lee Cannon.
Lib Type General.
Circ Servs Avail Not open to the general public.
Ref Servs Avail Not open to the general public.

990. Key West Naval Medical Clinic, General Library
Key West, FL 33040
Lib Type General.

991. Kings Bay Base Library
Naval Submarine Base, Kings Bay, GA 31547 (912) 673-2000; FTS 970-4526; AUTOVON 860-4526
Admin Patricia C Doyle. *ILL* Shirley Holcomb.
Lib Type General.
Spec Collecs Military Family Collection.
Coop Lib Nets South Georgia Associated Libraries (SGAL).
Circ Servs Avail Not open to the general public; restricted to military & dependents, base DoD employees.

Ref Servs Avail Not open to the general public; restricted to military & dependents, base DoD employees.

992. Kingsville Naval Air Station Library
Bldg 1781, Kingsville, TX 78363 (512) 595-6212; AUTOVON 861-6271
Admin Mary Ann Naylor.
Lib Type General.
Spec Subs Aeronautics & Naval history.
Circ Servs Avail Not open to the general public.
Ref Servs Avail Not open to the general public.

993. Lemoore Naval Air Station Library
Bldg 821, Lemoore NAS, CA 93246-0001 (209) 998-3144
Lib Type General.
Spec Subs Geography; history; psychology; Vietnamese War; drugs.

994. Long Beach Naval Hospital, General Library
7500 E Carson St, Long Beach, CA 90822 (213) 420-5287; AUTOVON 873-9287
Lib Type Hospital (Patients).

995. Long Beach Naval Shipyard, Technical Library
Code 202.4, Long Beach, CA 90822 (213) 547-6515 547-7064; AUTOVON 360-7064
Admin Mari S Zeoli.
Lib Type Engineering & Science.
Spec Subs Naval art & architecture; shipbuilding; ship maintenance & repair; industrial & marine engineering; civil & chemical engineering; occupational health; management. *Spec Collecs* Military specifications; handbooks & standards; naval sea systems; command technical manuals on electronics, weapons, electrical & mechanical equipment; manufacturers' & vendors' catalogs.
Coop Lib Nets Naval shipyards libraries.
Circ Servs Avail Restricted to DoD agencies & limited number of contractors.
Ref Servs Avail To other Federal libraries; restricted to specific contractors.

996. Long Beach Naval Station Library
Bldg 398, Long Beach, CA 90822 (213) 547-7349
Lib Type General.
Spec Subs Battleship history; naval history.
Circ Servs Avail Not open to the general public; restricted to military, dependents, & civilian base personnel.
Ref Servs Avail Restricted to general public, on request.

997. Mare Island Naval Shipyard, Technical Library
Code 202.13, STOP T-4/483, Vallejo, CA 94592-5100 (707) 646-4306; AUTOVON 253-2532/4306
Admin Carol Y Wong. *ILL* Susan Miller. *Acq Lib* Janice Edwards.
Lib Type Engineering & Science.
Spec Subs Shipbuilding & repair; material sciences; occupational safety & health; nuclear & ocean engineering. *Spec Collecs* Standards & specifications; technical reports.
Info Ret Servs DIALOG; DROLS; OCLC. *Shared Catalog Nets* OCLC. *Coop Lib Nets* FEDLINK. *Elec Mail Nets* OPTIMIS; FEDLINK BBS.
Circ Servs Avail To other Federal libraries; to other libraries; to the general public.
Ref Servs Avail To other Federal libraries; to other libraries; to the general public.

998. Mare Island Naval Station, Rodman Library
Code 41B, Vallejo, CA 94592-5000 (707) 646-3338; AUTOVON 253-3338
Admin Otome Andrews. *ILL* Katherine Lake.
Lib Type General.
Spec Subs Navy history.
Circ Servs Avail To other Federal libraries; to other libraries; not open to the general public; restricted to military, DoD civilians & dependents.
Ref Servs Avail To other Federal libraries; to other libraries; not open to the general public; restricted to military, DoD civilians & dependents.

999. Matthew Fontaine Maury Oceanographic Library
Naval Oceanographic Office, Bay St Louis, National Space Technology Laboratories, NSTL, MS 39522-5001 (601) 688-4597; FTS 494-4597; AUTOVON 485-4597
Admin Katharine Wallace. *Ref Lib* Ann Loomis. *ILL* Joan Mead. *Acq Lib* Dianne Sellier.
Lib Type Special.
Spec Subs Ocean science & technology; acoustics; remote sensing. *Spec Collecs* Hydrographic Office (HO) publications; sailing directions; hydrographic/oceanographic expedition reports. *In-house Files* Technical reports.
Info Ret Servs DIALOG; BRS; SDC; DTIS. *Shared Catalog Nets* OCLC. *Coop Lib Nets* FEDLINK; Coastal Mississippi Library Consortium (CMLC).
Circ Servs Avail To other Federal libraries; to other libraries.
Ref Servs Avail To other Federal libraries; to other libraries; to the general public.

1000. Mayport Naval Air Station Library
Box 52, Bldg 930, Jacksonville, FL 32212 (904) 772-3415
Lib Type General.
Spec Subs Aviation; Naval history; World War II.

1001. Mayport Naval Hospital, Crew's Library
Box 209, Jacksonville, FL 32214 (904) 777-7530
Lib Type Hospital (Patients).
Spec Subs Recreational reading.
Circ Servs Avail Not open to the general public; restricted to staff.
Ref Servs Avail Not open to the general public; restricted to patients & staff.

1002. Mayport Naval Hospital, Medical Library
Box 209, Jacksonville, FL 32214 (904) 777-7583
Lib Type Special.
Circ Servs Avail Not open to the general public; restricted to staff.
Ref Servs Avail Not open to the general public; restricted to staff.

1003. Mayport Naval Station Library
Bldg 66, Jacksonville, FL 32228 (904) 246-5393
Admin Elizabeth K Fahnert. *ILL* Joseph F Pickett, Sr.
Lib Type General.
Spec Subs Naval history.
Circ Servs Avail To other libraries; not open to the general public; restricted to Navy personnel & dependents.
Ref Servs Avail Not open to the general public; restricted to in-house use by Navy personnel & dependents.

1004. Memphis Naval Air Station Library
Bldg S-78, Millington, TN 38054 (901) 872-5683
Lib Type General.
Spec Subs Aeronautics; electronics; mathematics; military history.

1005. Memphis Naval Regional Medical Center, General & Medical Libraries
Rm 216, Code 307, Millington, TN 38054 (901) 872-5846
Lib Type Health & Medicine; General.
Spec Subs Dentistry; medicine; nursing.

1006. Meridian Naval Air Station Library
Box 31, Meridian, MS 39309-5000 (601) 679-2623
Admin Sharon A Fales.
Lib Type General.
Circ Servs Avail To other Federal libraries; to other libraries; not open to the general public.
Ref Servs Avail To other Federal libraries; to other libraries; not open to the general public.

1007. Military Sealift Command, Technical Library
Dept of the Navy, Washington Navy Yard, Washington, DC 20390 (202) 433-0115; AUTOVON 288-0115
Lib Type Special.
Spec Subs Military reference.
Circ Servs Avail Not open to the general public; restricted to military & staff.
Ref Servs Avail To the general public; restricted to on-site use.

1008. Miramar Naval Air Station Library
Bldg M305, San Diego, CA 92145 (619) 271-3557; AUTOVON 959-3557
Admin Dorothy E Caudill.
Lib Type General.
Spec Subs Military arts & sciences; naval history; World War II; basic education; management.
Circ Servs Avail To other Federal libraries; to other libraries; not open to the general public; restricted to military.
Ref Servs Avail To other Federal libraries; to other libraries; not open to the general public; restricted to military.

1009. Moffett Field Station Library
Bldg 14, Moffett Field, CA 94035 (415) 966-5455; AUTOVON 462-5455
Admin Michele Q Drovdahl.
Lib Type General.
Circ Servs Avail Not open to the general public; restricted to military & dependents.
Ref Servs Avail Not open to the general public; restricted to military & dependents.

1010. Nautilus Memorial/Submarine Force Library & Museum
Naval Submarine Base New London, Box 571, Groton, CT 06349 (203) 449-3174; AUTOVON 241-3558
Lib Type Special.
Spec Collecs Repository for records & history of US submarine force from its beginning to present.
Ref Servs Avail Restricted to researchers only.

1011. Naval Academy Preparatory School Library
Nimitz Hall, Naval Education & Training Center, Newport, RI 02841 (401) 841-3488; AUTOVON 948-3488
Admin Richard G Flinn (English Supervisor). *Ref Lib* Eleanor Ward (ILL, Acq).
Lib Type Special.
Spec Subs All subjects for a 9-month post-secondary school library serving students entering the US Naval Academy. *In-house Files* Vertical files containing special research articles, pamphlets, photostats pertinent to students' curriculum needs.
Circ Servs Avail Not open to the general public; restricted to NAPS' & OCS Prep personnel.
Ref Servs Avail Not open to the general public; restricted to NAPS' & OCS Prep personnel.

1012. Naval Administrative Command Library
Bldg 2105, Naval Training Center, Orlando, FL 32813-5010 (305) 646-5137; FTS 946-5137; AUTOVON 791-5137
Admin D C Bowen.
Lib Type General.
In-house Files 2-4 year back issues of 244 periodicals.
Circ Servs Avail To other Federal libraries; to other libraries; not open to the general public.
Ref Servs Avail To other Federal libraries; to other libraries; not open to the general public.

1013. Naval Aerospace Medical Institute Library
Code 012, Bldg 1953, Pensacola NAS, FL 32508-5600 (904) 452-2256; FTS 968-3517; AUTOVON 922-2256
Admin Ruth T Rogers. *ILL* Ann E Chalk.
Lib Type Health & Medicine.
Spec Subs Aviation & aerospace medicine.
Info Ret Servs BRS. *Coop Lib Nets* West Florida Union List (WFUL); Florida Union List of Serials; Dept of the Navy Union List of Serials. *Elec Mail Nets* OPTIMIS.
Circ Servs Avail To other libraries; not open to the general public; restricted to staff, patrons, in-house only.
Ref Servs Avail To other libraries; not open to the general public; restricted to staff, patrons, in-house only.

1014. Naval Air Development Center, Scientific & Technical Library Branch
Code 8131, Warminster, PA 18974 (215) 441-2541; AUTOVON 441-2918
Admin Dora Huang. *Ref Lib* Mary Hellings (ILL). *Acq Lib* Kay Aydelotte.

Lib Type Engineering & Science.
Spec Subs Aeronautics; naval aviation. *Spec Collecs* NADC research reports.
Lib Deposit Designation DTIC; NASA.
Info Ret Servs DIALOG; DTIC; NASA/RECON. *Shared Catalog Nets* OCLC. *Coop Lib Nets* FEDLINK. *Elec Mail Nets* Navy.
Circ Servs Avail Not open to the general public.
Ref Servs Avail Not open to the general public; restricted to DoD—Navy & contractors.

1015. Naval Air Engineering Center, Technical Library
Code 1115, Lakehurst, NJ 08733 (201) 323-2893; AUTOVON 624-2893
Admin Linda M Kozloff. *Ref Lib* Roberta M Graves (ILL, Acq).
Lib Type Training Center.
Spec Subs Aeronautical, mechanical, & electrical engineering; cryogenics; ground support equipment; research & development; ship installation.
Circ Servs Avail To other Federal libraries; to other libraries; not open to the general public.
Ref Servs Avail Not open to the general public.

1016. Naval Air Propulsion Center, Technical Library
PO Box 7176, Trenton, NJ 08628 (609) 896-5609; FTS 346-5609; AUTOVON 442-7609
Admin Robert M Malone.
Lib Type Engineering & Science.
Spec Subs Aeronautical engineering; jet propulsion; aircraft fuels.
Circ Servs Avail To other Federal libraries; to other libraries; not open to the general public.
Ref Servs Avail To other Federal libraries; to other libraries; not open to the general public.

1017. Naval Air Rework Facility, Technical Library
624 Naval Air Station, Alameda, CA 94501 (415) 869-2871
Lib Type Special.

1018. Naval Air Systems Command, Technical Information & Reference Center
AIR-5004, Washington, DC 20361-5004 (202) 692-9006; AUTOVON 222-9006
Admin Pat Stone. *Ref Lib* Marilynn Harned (ILL). *Acq Lib* Dorothy Taylor.
Lib Type Special.
Spec Subs Aeronautics; air weapons; mathematics; management.
Info Ret Servs DIALOG; DROLS. *Shared Catalog Nets* OCLC. *Coop Lib Nets* FEDLINK; IUA.
Circ Servs Avail To other Federal libraries; to other libraries; not open to the general public.
Ref Servs Avail To other Federal libraries; to other libraries; not open to the general public.

1019. Naval Air Test Center, Technical Information Department
Technical Publications, CT 252, Bldg 405, Patuxent River, MD 20670 (301) 863-3620/3641; AUTOVON 356-3641
Admin George F Hurlburt.
Lib Type Special.

1020. Naval Amphibious Base Library
Bldg 3004, Little Creek, Norfolk, VA 23521 (804) 464-7691
Lib Type General.

1021. Naval Amphibious School Library
Bldg 401, Naval Amphibious School Coronado, San Diego, CA 92155 (619) 437-2295
Lib Type Academic.
Spec Subs Amphibious warfare; underwater demolition; intercultural relations; interpersonal relations; leadership & management; military history; foreign diplomacy.

1022. Naval Amphibious School, John Sidney McCain, Jr Amphibious Warfare Library
Little Creek, Bldg 3504, NAB, Norfolk, VA 23521-5290 (804) 464-7691; AUTOVON 680-7467
Admin Carolyn G Jones.
Lib Type Training Center.
Spec Subs Management books in support of Leadership Management education & training courses.
Circ Servs Avail To other Federal libraries; to other libraries; not open to the general public.
Ref Servs Avail To other Federal libraries; to other libraries; to the general public; restricted to in-house use by general public of unclassified documents by special arrangement.

1023. Naval Audit Service Headquarters Library
PO Box 1206, 5611 Columbia Pike, Falls Church, VA 22041-0206 (703) 756-2129; AUTOVON 289-2129
Admin Suzanne K Noss.
Lib Type Special.
Spec Collecs Audit reports; Naval instructions & notes.
Coop Lib Nets Naval Librarians of Washington DC Assoc.
Circ Servs Avail Restricted to Navy & Army.
Ref Servs Avail Restricted to Navy & Army.

1024. Naval Avionics Center, Technical Library
6000 E 21st St, Indianapolis, IN 46219-2189 (317) 353-7765
Lib Type Special.
Spec Subs Electronics; engineering; metallurgy.

1025. Naval Chaplains' School Library
Bldg 114, Naval Education & Training Ctr, Newport, RI 02841-5014 (401) 841-2557; AUTOVON 948-2557
Admin R P C Mayes. *Ref Lib* A Wayne Riggs, CHC (ILL, ACQ).
Lib Type Training Center.
Spec Subs Religious theology & reference matters. *Spec Collecs* Chaplains' thesis library. *In-house Files* CARDEX & locator file.
Circ Servs Avail Not open to the general public; restricted to staff & students.
Ref Servs Avail Not open to the general public; restricted to staff & students.

1026. Naval Civil Engineering Laboratory Library
Code L08A, Port Hueneme, CA 93043-5003 (805) 982-4252/4788
Lib Type Engineering & Science.
Spec Subs Amphibious operations; civil engineering; construction materials; corrosion; energy; environmental protection; ocean engineering; physical security; polar operations; soil mechanics.
Info Ret Servs DIALOG. *Coop Lib Nets* Total Interlibrary Exchange.
Circ Servs Avail Not open to the general public; restricted to staff.
Ref Servs Avail Restricted to use by general public by appointment.

1027. Naval Coastal Systems Center, General Library
Panama City, FL 32407 (904) 234-4232
Admin Myrtle Rhodes.
Lib Type General.
Circ Servs Avail Not open to the general public.
Ref Servs Avail Not open to the general public.

1028. Naval Coastal Systems Center, Technical Information Services Branch
Code 6120, Panama City, FL 32407 (904) 234-4321
Lib Type Special.
Spec Subs Acoustic warfare; coastal & ocean technology; inshore undersea warfare; mine countermeasures; torpedo defense; underwater sound.
Info Ret Servs DIALOG; Defense Technical Information Center.

1029. Naval Communication Area Station Library
Master Station EASTPAC, Wahiawa, HI 96786
Lib Type General.

1030. Naval Communication Station, Stockton, Base Library
Stockton, CA 95203-5000 (209) 944-7282; AUTOVON 466-7282
Admin Richard Metz.
Lib Type General.
Circ Servs Avail Not open to the general public; restricted to military, active & retired, & dependents.
Ref Servs Avail Not open to the general public; restricted to military, active & retired, & dependents.

1031. Naval Construction Battalion Center Base Library
Code 3334, Bldg 172, Gulfport, MS 39501 (601) 865-2409; AUTOVON 363-2409
Admin Doris L Mahalak; R B Beliech (Head MWR).
Lib Type General.
Circ Servs Avail To other Federal libraries; restricted to military, DoD civilians & dependents.
Ref Servs Avail To other Federal libraries; restricted to military, DoD civilians & dependents.

1032. Naval Construction Battalion Center Library
Bldg 31L, Port Hueneme, CA 93043 (805) 982-4411; AUTOVON 360-4411
Admin Nancy R Thorne. *ILL* Gene Krivenko.
Lib Type General.
Coop Lib Nets Black-Gold Cooperative.
Circ Servs Avail To other Federal libraries; to other libraries; not open to the general public; restricted to military & civilians stationed on base.
Ref Servs Avail To other Federal libraries; to other libraries; restricted to military & civilians stationed on base.

1033. Naval Dental Research Institute Library
Great Lakes, IL 60088 (312) 688-5647; AUTOVON 792-5647
Admin Myra Rouse.
Lib Type Health & Medicine.

1034. Naval Dental School, William L Darnall Library
Naval Dental Clinic, Naval Medical Command, National Capital Region, Bethesda, MD 20814-5077 (202) 295-0080; AUTOVON 295-0080
Admin Patricia A Evans.
Lib Type Health & Medicine.
Coop Lib Nets Union List, Region IV.
Circ Servs Avail To other Federal libraries.
Ref Servs Avail To other Federal libraries.

1035. Naval Education & Training Center, Main Library
Bldg 114, Newport, RI 02841-5031 (401) 841-3044/4352
Admin James F Aylward (Acq). *Ref Lib* Robert Wessells (ILL).
Lib Type Training Center.
Spec Subs Education; leadership-management; military; Naval history; technology. *Spec Collecs* Military documents; Naval training manuals.
Info Ret Servs DTIC; DLSIE. *Coop Lib Nets* Defense Logistics Studies Info Exchange; Rhode Island Interrelated Library System.
Circ Servs Avail To other Federal libraries; to other libraries; not open to the general public; restricted to military & government employees.
Ref Servs Avail To other Federal libraries; to other libraries; to the general public; not open to the general public; restricted to military & government employees.

1036. Naval Education & Training Program Development Center, General Library Services
Administrative Office, Pensacola, FL 32509 (904) 452-1380; FTS 948-1380; AUTOVON 922-1380
Lib Type Special.
Spec Subs This office is responsible for the review, selection, acquisition, & distribution of materials for the general libraries of Navy & Marine Corps activities in the US & overseas.

1037. Naval Electronic Systems Engineering Center, Portsmouth Electronic Library
PO Box 55, Portsmouth, VA 23705 (804) 396-7688
Lib Type Engineering & Science.
Spec Subs Communications; education; electronics; engineering; management.

1038. Naval Electronic Systems Engineering Center, Technical Library
Code AL, PO Box 80337, 4297 Pacific Hwy, San Diego, CA 92138-3288 (619) 260-2482/2483/2484; AUTOVON 957-2484
Admin Christine E Larsen.
Lib Type Engineering & Science.

Spec Subs Electronic engineering & computer science. *Spec Collecs* Technical manuals on Navy equipment. *In-house Files* Government documents.
Coop Lib Nets Council of Navy Scientific & Technical Libraries (CONSATL).
Circ Servs Avail To other Federal libraries; to other libraries; not open to the general public; restricted to need to know & in some cases security clearance.
Ref Servs Avail To other Federal libraries; to other libraries; not open to the general public; restricted to need to know & in some cases security clearance.

1039. Naval Electronic Systems, Security Engineering, Naval Security Station, Technical Library
3801 Nebraska Ave, NW, Washington, DC 20390 (202) 282-0435; AUTOVON 292-0435
Admin Edith A Francis.
Lib Type General.

1040. Naval Electronics Systems, Technical Library
Engineering Center, Charleston, 4600 Marriott Dr, North Charleston, SC 29418 (803) 554-5565; FTS 679-2030; AUTOVON 794-2045
Admin Claudia E Mazyck.
Lib Type Engineering & Science.
Circ Servs Avail To other Federal libraries; not open to the general public.
Ref Servs Avail To other Federal libraries; not open to the general public.

1041. Naval Environmental Prediction Research Facility/ Fleet Numerical Oceanography Center Technical Library
Monterey, CA 93943 (408) 646-2813; AUTOVON 878-2813
Admin Joanne May.
Lib Type Engineering & Science.
Spec Subs Meteorology. *In-house Files* NWRF, FNWC, EPRF, NEPRF, & FNOC technical reports.
Info Ret Servs DIALOG.
Circ Servs Avail To other Federal libraries; to other libraries; not open to the general public.
Ref Servs Avail To other Federal libraries; to other libraries; not open to the general public.

1042. Naval Explosive Ordnance Disposal Technology Center, Library
Code 604, Indian Head, MD 20640-5070 (310) 743-4738/4739; AUTOVON 364-4738/4739
Admin Bonnie D Davis. *Ref Lib* Betty L Legagneux (ILL). *Acq Lib* Peggy Taylor.
Lib Type Special.
Spec Subs Ordnance; diving; acoustics; radar.
Info Ret Servs DIALOG; BRS. *Coop Lib Nets* Metro Council of Governments. *Elec Mail Nets* DTIC.
Circ Servs Avail To other Federal libraries; to other libraries; not open to the general public; restricted to need to know.
Ref Servs Avail To other Federal libraries; to other libraries; not open to the general public; restricted to need to know.

1043. Naval Facilities Engineering Command Library
Bldg 77-L, Code 04A5-L, Philadelphia Naval Base, Philadelphia, PA 19112 (215) 897-6043; AUTOVON 443-6043
Admin Mary Crum (in charge).
Lib Type General.

1044. Naval Facilities Engineering Command, Technical Library
200 Stovall St, Alexandria, VA 22332-2300 (202) 325-8507; AUTOVON 221-8507
Admin Cynthia K Neyland.
Lib Type Engineering & Science.
Spec Subs Civil, mechanical, sanitary, electrical & structural engineering; management theory. *In-house Files* Reference copies of NAVFAC publications; Navy Civil Engineering Laboratory publications.
Info Ret Servs DIALOG. *Shared Catalog Nets* OCLC. *Coop Lib Nets* Council of Navy Scientific & Technical Libraries (CONSATL).

Circ Servs Avail To other Federal libraries; to other libraries.
Ref Servs Avail To other Federal libraries; to other libraries.

1045. Naval Facility, Centerville Beach, Station Library
Ferndale, CA 95536 (707) 786-9531, ext 216
Lib Type General.

1046. Naval Health Research Center, Wilkins Biomedical Library
PO Box 85122, San Diego, CA 92138-9174 (619) 225-6640; AUTOVON 933-6640
Admin Mary Aldous. *ILL* Betty Croft.
Lib Type Health & Medicine.
Spec Subs Medicine; psychology.
Info Ret Servs DIALOG; BRS; NLM (MEDLINE); DTIC. *Shared Catalog Nets* OCLC. *Coop Lib Nets* Medical Lib Group of Southern California & Arizona (MLGSCA). *Elec Mail Nets* CLASS.
Circ Servs Avail To other Federal libraries; to other libraries; restricted to NHRC personnel.
Ref Servs Avail To other Federal libraries; to other libraries; to the general public; restricted to NHRC personnel; on-site use only for general public.

1047. Naval Home Library
1800 E Beach Blvd, Gulfport, MS 39501
Lib Type General.

1048. Naval Hospital General Library
Bldg H-100, Corpus Christi, TX 78419-5200 (512) 939-2189
Lib Type Hospital (Patients).

1049. Naval Hospital, Medical & Crew's Libraries
Pensacola, FL 32512-5000 (904) 452-6635
Lib Type Health & Medicine; Hospital (Patients).

1050. Naval Hospital, Medical Library
Bldg 1, Newport, RI 02841-5003 (401) 841-4512
Admin Winifred M Jacome.
Lib Type Health & Medicine; Hospital (Patients).
Spec Subs Fiction; medical books & periodicals.
Coop Lib Nets Assn of RI Health Sciences Librarians (ARIHSL); UCMP Data Base—Medical Library Center of NY.
Circ Servs Avail To other Federal libraries; to other libraries; restricted to appointment only.
Ref Servs Avail To other Federal libraries; to other libraries; restricted to appointment only.

1051. Naval Hospital NW Region Medical Command, General Library
Bldg 101, Oakland, CA 94627 (415) 633-6127; AUTOVON 855-6127
Admin Robert C Bernhardi.
Lib Type General.
Spec Subs World War II.
Circ Servs Avail Not open to the general public; restricted to base military, DoD civilians & dependents.
Ref Servs Avail Not open to the general public.

1052. Naval Intelligence Support Center Library
Code 63, 4301 Suitland Rd, Washington, DC 20390 (301) 963-1604; AUTOVON 293-1606
Admin Stephanie Williams. *Ref Lib* Raymond Kee. *ILL* Jess Hawkins (Acq).
Lib Type Special.
Spec Subs Science & technology. *Spec Collecs* Russian books.
Info Ret Servs DIALOG; BRS; NEXIS; LEXIS; OCLC. *Shared Catalog Nets* OCLC.
Circ Servs Avail Not open to the general public DoD.
Ref Servs Avail Not open to the general public.

1053. Naval Medical Clinic Library
New Orleans, LA 70142 (504) 361-2418; AUTOVON 485-2400
Admin H M C Hammond.
Lib Type Health & Medicine.

1054. Naval Military Personnel Command, Technical Library
NMPC-013DD, Arlington Annex, Rm 1403, Washington, DC 20370 (703) 694-2073
Ref Lib Detra Peay (ILL).
Lib Type Special.
Spec Subs Register of officers; naval leadership; fighting ships; who's who in the military; technique microwave measurement.
Circ Servs Avail To other libraries ILL.
Ref Servs Avail To the general public.

1055. Naval Mine Warfare Engineering Activity, Library
Code 322, Yorktown, VA 23691 (804) 887-4671/4672; AUTOVON 953-4671
Admin Clyde W Whitted.
Lib Type Engineering & Science.

1056. Naval Mobile Construction Battalion Center Library
Code 31L, Bldg 65, Port Hueneme, CA 93043 (805) 982-4411
Lib Type Special.
Spec Subs Educational material at both high school & college levels; US Navy; World War II.
Circ Servs Avail Not open to the general public; restricted to military & dependents.
Ref Servs Avail Not open to the general public; restricted to military & dependents.

1057. Naval Ocean Research & Development Activity Library
Code 125L, NSTL Station, Bay Saint Louis, MS 39529 (601) 688-4739; FTS 494-4739; AUTOVON 485-4684
Admin Mary Ellen Tipper.
Lib Type Special.

1058. Naval Ocean Systems Center, Technical Libraries
San Diego, CA 92152-5000 (619) 225-6623; AUTOVON 933-6623
Admin Joan Leland Buntzen.
Lib Type Engineering & Science.
Spec Subs Physics; oceanography; artificial intelligence; ocean engineering; communication; robotics; marine sciences; the arctic; underwater ordnance; remote sensing.
Info Ret Servs DIALOG; BRS; SDC; DTIC; VU/TEXT; TECH DATA; NASA. *Shared Catalog Nets* OCLC. *Coop Lib Nets* CLASS.
Circ Servs Avail To other Federal libraries; to other libraries.
Ref Servs Avail To other Federal libraries; to other libraries.

1059. Naval Ordnance Station, Library Branch
Code 5246, Indian Head, MD 20640-5000 (301) 743-4742; AUTOVON 364-4742/4743
Admin Charles Gallagher.
Lib Type General.
Spec Subs Explosives & propellants; missiles.
Info Ret Servs DIALOG; BRS. *Shared Catalog Nets* OCLC. *Coop Lib Nets* FEDLINK.
Circ Servs Avail To other Federal libraries; to other libraries; not open to the general public.
Ref Servs Avail To other Federal libraries; to other libraries; not open to the general public.

1060. Naval Ordnance Station, Technical Library
Code 50D, Louisville, KY 40214 (502) 367-5667; FTS 355-5667; AUTOVON 989-5667
Admin L Miles.
Lib Type General.

1061. Naval Postgraduate School, Dudley Knox Library
Monterey, CA 93943-5002 (408) 646-2341; ILL 646-2485
Lib Type Academic.
Spec Subs Business & management; economics; military; science-technology; sociology & behavioral science. *Spec Collecs* Naval History & the Sea (Christopher Buckley Jr Collection).
Info Ret Servs DIALOG; BRS; NASA/RECON; NEXIS. *Shared Catalog Nets* RLIN. *Coop Lib Nets* Monterey Bay Area Cooperative Library System; South Bay Cooperative Library System. *Elec Mail Nets* CLASS.

1062. Naval Postgraduate School, Dudley Knox Library
Code 0142, Monterey, CA 93943-5002 (408) 646-2341; AUTO-VON 878-2341
Admin Paul Spinks. *Ref Lib* Roger Martin. *ILL* Ronald Rodrigues. *Acq Lib* Sharon Serzan.
Lib Type Academic.
Spec Subs Engineering; science; operations research; management; economics; military & naval science; international affairs; military history. *Spec Collecs* Buckley Collection, 8,000 volume collection of books relating to the sea & naval history. *In-house Files* SABIRS (Selected Automatic Bibliographic Information Retrieval Service), used for bibliographic control & retrieval of hard-copy technical reports & NPS theses.
Lib Deposit Designation GPO Depository Library.
Info Ret Servs DIALOG; BRS; NEXIS; WILSONLINE; NASA/RECON. *Shared Catalog Nets* RLIN. *Coop Lib Nets* Monterey Bay Cooperative Library System (MOBAC); SOUTHNET; California Library Authority for Systems & Services. *Elec Mail Nets* ONTYME.
Circ Servs Avail Restricted to School faculty, students & staff; ILL.
Ref Servs Avail To other Federal libraries; to other libraries; restricted to staff & time limitations.

1063. Naval Radio Station Library
Sugar Grove, WV 26815 (304) 249-6360
Lib Type General.
Ref Servs Avail Not open to the general public; restricted to military, dependents, & station civilian employees.

1064. Naval Regional Library, Groton
Box 52, Bldg 83, New London Submarine Base, Groton, CT 06349-5052 (203) 449-4655; FTS 648-4655; AUTOVON 241-4655
Admin Edwin E Williams.
Lib Type Special.
Spec Subs Submarines; US Navy; general recreational reading.
Coop Lib Nets SE Connecticut Library Assn (SECLA); Naval General Library Program.
Ref Servs Avail Not open to the general public; restricted to Naval general library advisory services to naval ships & shore libraries within the northeastern US, Atlantic bases, Europe, & fleet book exchange.

1065. Naval Regional Medical Center, Navy Hospital Medical Library
7500 E Carson St, Long Beach, CA 90822 (213) 420-5287
Lib Type Health & Medicine.
Spec Subs Clinical medicine.
Coop Lib Nets Medical Library Group of S CA & AZ.
Circ Servs Avail Restricted to staff.
Ref Servs Avail Restricted to staff.

1066. Naval Research Laboratory, Ruth H Hooker Technical Library
Washington, DC 20375-5000 (202) 767-2357; AUTOVON 297-2357; Reference 767-2354; ILL 767-3369
Admin Peter H Imhof.
Lib Type Engineering & Science.
Spec Subs Physical sciences & related disciplines.
Circ Servs Avail To other Federal libraries; to other libraries; not open to the general public.
Ref Servs Avail To other Federal libraries; to other libraries; not open to the general public.

1067. Naval Research Laboratory, USRD
ATTN: Code 5905.2, PO Box 568337, Orlando, FL 32856-8337 (305) 857-5238; FTS 820-5238
Admin Marge Tarnowski.
Lib Type Special.
Spec Subs Physics; acoustics; underwater sound.
Circ Servs Avail To other Federal libraries; not open to the general public; restricted to consideration of individual requests.
Ref Servs Avail To other Federal libraries; not open to the general public.

1068. Naval School, Civil Engineer Corps Officers, Moreell Library
Code C35, Port Hueneme, CA 93043-5002 (805) 982-3241; FTS 799-3241; AUTOVON 360-3241
Admin Dianne G Thompson.
Lib Type Engineering & Science.
Spec Subs Civil engineering; building construction; business administration; military & US history. *Spec Collecs* Moreell Collection: books & papers of Admiral Ben Moreell, founder of Navy Seabees.
Coop Lib Nets Total Interlibrary Exchange (TIE).
Circ Servs Avail Not open to the general public; restricted to in-house personnel.
Ref Servs Avail Not open to the general public; restricted to in-house personnel.

1069. Naval School of Health Sciences Library
Bldg 141, Bethesda, MD 20814-5033 (301) 295-0393; AUTOVON 295-0393
Admin Phyllis Blum.
Lib Type Health & Medicine.
Spec Subs Health care administration; general management; military topics.
Info Ret Servs BRS. *Shared Catalog Nets* OCLC. *Coop Lib Nets* FEDLINK.
Circ Servs Avail To other Federal libraries; to other libraries; not open to the general public.

1070. Naval Sea Support Center, Atlantic, Technical Library
Code 22.4, St Juliens Creek Annex, Portsmouth, VA 23702-5098 (804) 485-6100; AUTOVON 961-6100
Admin Sandra L Becker.
Lib Type Special.
Spec Subs Technical & engineering.
Coop Lib Nets Council of Navy, Scientific & Technical Librarians (CONSATL).
Circ Servs Avail To other Federal libraries; not open to the general public.
Ref Servs Avail To other Federal libraries; not open to the general public.

1071. Naval Sea Support Center, Pacific, Library
Technical Documentation Div (Code 14), PO Box 85548, 4297 Pacific Hwy, San Diego, CA 92138-5548 (619) 260-2122; AUTOVON 957-2122
Admin Stella A. Holfert.
Lib Type Special.
Spec Subs Naval ordnance; electronics; hull, mechanical & electrical systems.
Circ Servs Avail To other Federal libraries; not open to the general public; restricted to need to know.
Ref Servs Avail To other Federal libraries; not open to the general public; restricted to need to know.

1072. Naval Sea Systems Command, Library Documentation Branch
SEA 09B31, Washington, DC 20362-5101 (202) 692-3349; AUTOVON 222-3349
Admin Alan M Lewis. *Ref Lib* Claudia Devlin. *ILL* Elmer Long. *Acq Lib* Dolores Garrett.
Lib Type Engineering & Science.
Spec Subs Naval architecture; marine engineering; sonar; naval ordnance. *Spec Collecs* Navy technical manuals.
Info Ret Servs DIALOG; SDC; NEXIS. *Shared Catalog Nets* OCLC. *Coop Lib Nets* FEDLINK; IUA.
Circ Servs Avail Not open to the general public.
Ref Servs Avail Not open to the general public.

1073. Naval Security Group Activity, Northwest, General Library
Chesapeake, VA 23322 (804) 421-8229
Admin Candise Carpenter; Kathryn Swain.
Lib Type General.
Circ Servs Avail To other Federal libraries; not open to the general public; restricted to military, retired, & dependents.
Ref Servs Avail Not open to the general public; restricted to military, retired, & dependents.

1074. Naval Security Group Activity Station Library
Winter Harbor, ME 04693-0900 (207) 963-5534, ext 224
Lib Type Special.
Spec Subs Education; military.
Ref Servs Avail Not open to the general public; restricted to military, dependents & civilian base personnel.

1075. Naval Ship Research & Development Center, W Taylor Library
Technical Info Ctr, Annapolis, MD 21402 (301) 267-2757
Lib Type Special.
Spec Subs Environmental control; energy research & materials.

1076. Naval Ship Systems Engineering Station, Technical Library
Bldg 619, Philadelphia, PA 19112-5083 (215) 952-7078 ext 7816; AUTOVON 444-7078
Admin Pearl O Robinson. *Acq Lib* Corrinn Fields.
Lib Type Engineering & Science.
Spec Subs Mechanical, electronic, electrical, & metallurgical engineering. *Spec Collecs* Technical manuals for inservice engineering; Navy Hull; mechanical & electrical equipment.
Info Ret Servs BRS; TECH DATA.
Circ Servs Avail To other Federal libraries; not open to the general public.
Ref Servs Avail To other Federal libraries; to other libraries; not open to the general public.

1077. Naval Ship Weapons Systems, Engineering Station, Technical Library
Data Information Branch, Code 5B25, Port Hueneme, CA 93043-5007 (805) 982-4931; AUTOVON 360-4931
Admin Yvonne Miller. *Ref Lib* Betty Magdaleno (ILL). *Acq Lib* Barbara Barret; Eleanor C Berger.
Lib Type Engineering & Science.
Circ Servs Avail To other Federal libraries; to other libraries; not open to the general public; restricted to NSWSES.
Ref Servs Avail To other Federal libraries; to other libraries; not open to the general public; restricted to DoD.

1078. Naval Submarine Medical Research Laboratory, Medical Library
Box 900, Naval Submarine Base, Groton, CT 06349-5900 (203) 449-3629; FTS 449-3629; AUTOVON 241-3629
Admin Elaine M Gaucher.
Lib Type Health & Medicine.
Spec Collecs Submarine medicine. *In-house Files* Submarine & diving medicine.
Info Ret Servs BRS; DROLS. *Coop Lib Nets* Connecticut Assoc Health Sciences Libraries (CAHSL).
Circ Servs Avail To other Federal libraries; to other libraries.
Ref Servs Avail To other Federal libraries; to other libraries.

1079. Naval Supervisor of Shipbuilding, Conversion & Repair, Technical Library
Code 245.2, 495 Summer St, Boston, MA 02210-2181 (617) 451-4695; AUTOVON 955-4695
Admin Frank L Mercugliano.
Lib Type Engineering & Science.
Spec Subs Electronic & mechanical engineering; naval architecture. *In-house Files* Naval technical manuals, specifications, & standards.
Coop Lib Nets Council of Navy Scientific & Technical Librarians (CONSATL); Military Librarians' Workshop (MLW).
Circ Servs Avail Not open to the general public; restricted to Navy libraries.
Ref Servs Avail Not open to the general public; restricted to Navy libraries.

1080. Naval Supply Center Library
Box 300, Bldg 475, 2nd Fl, Central Files, ATTN: CODE 4411, Pearl Harbor, HI 96860-5300 (808) 471-9689/9631
Admin James E Smalec. *Ref Lib* Raymond Nishio.
Lib Type General.
Circ Servs Avail Restricted to Naval tenant activities.
Ref Servs Avail Restricted to Naval tenant activities.

1081. Naval Supply Center, Technical Division Library
Code 103L, Bldg 311-2-W, Oakland, CA 94625-5000 (415) 466-4423; AUTOVON 836-4423
Admin Arelene May Berry.
Lib Type Special.
Spec Subs Naval technical publications for shipboard equipment. *In-house Files* National stock numbers.
Lib Deposit Designation NAVSEA Technical Manuals & blueprints/drawings.
Circ Servs Avail To other Federal libraries; not open to the general public; restricted to DoD personnel.
Ref Servs Avail To other Federal libraries; not open to the general public; restricted to DoD personnel.

1082. Naval Supply Corps School Library
Athens, GA 30606-5000 (404) 354-7217; AUTOVON 588-7217
Admin Library Officer.
Lib Type Training Center.
In-house Files Folders on individual ships, foreign shore & US bases.
Circ Servs Avail Not open to the general public; restricted to military.
Ref Servs Avail Not open to the general public; restricted to military; resources made available on special request.

1083. Naval Support Activity Library
Bldg 24, New Orleans, LA 70142 (504) 361-2210
Admin Carmelita B Addamus.
Lib Type General.
Spec Subs War related subjects.
Circ Servs Avail To other Federal libraries; to other libraries; to the general public; not open to the general public; restricted to staff & dependents.
Ref Servs Avail To other Federal libraries; to other libraries; to the general public.

1084. Naval Support Facility, General Library
Box 1000, Thurmont, MD 21788
Lib Type General.

1085. Naval Surface Warfare Officers School Library
Commanding Officer, Surface Warfare Officers School Command, Newport, RI 02841-5012 (410) 841-4196; AUTOVON 948-4196
Admin Loretta I Silvia. *Acq Lib* Paul Dennewitz.
Lib Type Training Center.
Spec Subs US Navy ships: description, operation, & maintenance. *Spec Collecs* NAVSEA technical manuals.
Circ Servs Avail Not open to the general public; restricted to SWOSCOLCOM.
Ref Servs Avail To other Federal libraries.

1086. Naval Surface Weapons Center, General Library
Code X55, Dahlgren, VA 22448 (703) 663-3404; AUTOVON 249-7474
Admin Wendy Smith. *Ref Lib* Tammy Pryka (ILL).
Lib Type General.
Circ Servs Avail To the general public.
Ref Servs Avail To the general public.

1087. Naval Surface Weapons Center, Technical Library
White Oak Laboratory, 10901 New Hampshire Ave, Silver Spring, MD 20903-5000 (202) 394-1922; AUTOVON 290-1922
Admin J Marshall Hughes II. *Ref Lib* Catheryn Lee. *ILL* Flo Smith. *Acq Lib* Margie Gutridge.
Lib Type Engineering & Science.
Spec Subs Military sciences; weapons systems; mines; physics; chemistry; engineering.
Info Ret Servs DIALOG; BRS; SDC; DTIC; NASA; NTIS. *Shared Catalog Nets* OCLC. *Coop Lib Nets* Naval Union List of Serials; IUA.
Circ Servs Avail To other Federal libraries; to other libraries.
Ref Servs Avail To other Federal libraries; to other libraries.

1088. Naval Surface Weapons Center, Technical Library
Code E23, Dahlgren, VA 22448 (703) 663-8351; AUTOVON 249-8351
Admin J Marshall Hughes II. *Ref Lib* Patricia N Pulliam. *ILL* Margaret Perry. *Acq Lib* Martha Rollins.
Lib Type Special.
Spec Subs Weapons systems; ordnance.
Info Ret Servs DIALOG; BRS; SDC. *Shared Catalog Nets* OCLC. *Coop Lib Nets* IUA; DTIC.
Circ Servs Avail To other Federal libraries; not open to the general public.
Ref Servs Avail To other Federal libraries; not open to the general public.

1089. Naval Technical Training Center, Station Library
Bldg 502, Pensacola, FL 32511-5000 (904) 452-4362; AUTOVON 922-6394
Admin Rebecca Kessel.
Lib Type General.
Circ Servs Avail To other Federal libraries; to other libraries; not open to the general public; restricted to military, DoD civilians & dependents.
Ref Servs Avail To other Federal libraries; to other libraries; not open to the general public; restricted to military, DoD civilians & dependents.

1090. Naval Test Pilot School Library
Naval Air Test Ctr, Patuxent River, MD 20670 (301) 863-4411; AUTOVON 356-4411
Admin Robert B Richards.
Lib Type Training Center.

1091. Naval Training Systems Center
Technical Information Center, Bldg 2068, Orlando, FL 32813-7100 (305) 646-5637 646-4797; FTS 848-5637 848-4797; AUTOVON 791-4797
Lib Type Engineering & Science.
Spec Subs Simulation, training aids. *Spec Collecs* Human factors core. *In-house Files* Naval Training Systems Center (NTSC) documents.
Info Ret Servs BRS; DTIC. *Coop Lib Nets* FEDLINK.
Circ Servs Avail To other Federal libraries; not open to the general public; restricted to ILL depending on request & need to know.
Ref Servs Avail Not open to the general public; restricted to NTSC documents.

1092. Naval Underwater Systems Center, New London Laboratory, Technical Library
Rm 2065, Bldg 80, New London, CT 06320 (203) 440-4365
Lib Type Special.
Spec Subs Data processing; engineering; underwater acoustics & ordnance.
Info Ret Servs DIALOG; SDC.
Circ Servs Avail Not open to the general public; restricted to staff.
Ref Servs Avail Not open to the general public; restricted to staff.

1093. Naval Underwater Systems Center, Technical/Books & Periodicals Library
Code 02151, New London Laboratory, New London, CT 06320 (203) 440-4365; AUTOVON 636-4276
Admin David Hanna. *Ref Lib* J Ned Shaw; Charles R Logan. *ILL* Jerome J Barner. *Acq Lib* Barbara A Campbell.
Lib Type Engineering & Science.
Info Ret Servs DIALOG; BRS; SDC; DTIS. *Shared Catalog Nets* OCLC. *Coop Lib Nets* FEDLINK.
Circ Servs Avail Not open to the general public.
Ref Servs Avail Not open to the general public.

1094. Naval Underwater Systems Center, Technical Library
Bldg 103, Newport, RI 02840-4421 (401) 841-4421/4338
Lib Type Special.
Spec Subs Computers; engineering; management; underwater acoustics & ordnance.
Info Ret Servs DIALOG; BRS; SDC; DTIC.

1095. Naval War College Library
Library Department, Newport, RI 02841-5010 (401) 841-2641; AUTOVON 948-2641
Admin Earl R Schwass. *Ref Lib* Doris Ottaviano. *ILL* Sue Barker. *Acq Lib* Marilyn Curtis.
Lib Type Academic.
Spec Subs Economics; history; social & behavioral sciences; international law. *Spec Collecs* Rare books on naval military history, tactics, & strategy. *In-house Files* Naval War College authors; bibliographies compiled; chronology of Naval War College.
Lib Deposit Designation GPO Depository Library.
Info Ret Servs DIALOG. *Shared Catalog Nets* OCLC. *Coop Lib Nets* CRIARL.
Circ Servs Avail Restricted to ILL for non-Naval War College individuals.
Ref Servs Avail To other libraries.

1096. Naval Weapons Center Library
Code 3436, China Lake, CA 93555-6001 (619) 939-3278; FTS 798-5000; AUTOVON 437-3278
Admin Elizabeth Shanteler. *Ref Lib* Constance Hall-Moore. *ILL* Brenda Blowers.
Lib Type General.
Spec Subs Military history; the West; desert.
Circ Servs Avail To other Federal libraries; to other libraries; not open to the general public; restricted to military, DoD civilians & dependents.
Ref Servs Avail To other Federal libraries; to other libraries; to the general public.

1097. Naval Weapons Center, Technical Library
Code 343, China Lake, CA 93555 (619) 939-3278/2592; AUTOVON 437-2507
Admin Elizabeth Babcock. *Ref Lib* Craig Pelz (ILL). *Acq Lib* Mary-Deirdre Coraggio.
Lib Type Special.
Spec Subs Chemistry; computer science; electronics; mathematics; missiles; optics; ordnance; parachute technology; physics; propulsion systems & propellants.
Info Ret Servs DIALOG; SDC; DTIC; RLIN; NASA. *Shared Catalog Nets* RLIN. *Coop Lib Nets* CLASS; FEDLINK; Council of Navy Scientific & Technical Libraries (CONSATL). *Elec Mail Nets* RLIN.
Circ Servs Avail To other Federal libraries; not open to the general public.
Ref Servs Avail To other Federal libraries; not open to the general public.

1098. Naval Weapons Station Library
Bldg 705, Yorktown, VA 23691-5000 (804) 887-4720; AUTOVON 953-4726
Admin E Lacy Sorokatch.
Lib Type General.
Spec Subs Chemistry; electronics; US & naval history.
Coop Lib Nets OCLC-ILL.
Circ Servs Avail To other Federal libraries; to other libraries; not open to the general public; restricted to station employees, military & dependents.
Ref Servs Avail To other Federal libraries; to other libraries; not open to the general public.

1099. Naval Weapons Station, MenRiv Library
Bldg 732, Charleston, SC 29408-7000 (803) 764-7900; FTS 679-7900
Admin Joan McCrann.
Lib Type General.
Spec Collecs Social Issue Resource Series; contemporary literary criticism. *In-house Files* Mitchell Motor Manuals, South Carolina Section.
Circ Servs Avail To other Federal libraries.
Ref Servs Avail To other Federal libraries.

1100. Naval Weapons Station, Seal Beach, Scientific & Technical Library
Code 012, Seal Beach, CA 90740-5000 (213) 594-7574; AUTOVON 873-7574
Admin Rose Moorhouse.
Lib Type Engineering & Science.

Info Ret Servs DIALOG; DROLS; NASA. *Shared Catalog Nets* OCLC. *Coop Lib Nets* FEDLINK.
Circ Servs Avail To other Federal libraries; not open to the general public.
Ref Servs Avail To other Federal libraries; to other libraries; not open to the general public.

1101. Naval Weapons Station, Seal Beach, Scientific & Technical Library, Corona Site
Code C-012, Corona, CA 91720-5000 (714) 736-4467; AUTOVON 933-4467
Admin Rose Moorhouse.
Lib Type Engineering & Science.
Info Ret Servs DIALOG; DROLS; NASA. *Shared Catalog Nets* OCLC. *Coop Lib Nets* FEDLINK.
Circ Servs Avail To other Federal libraries; not open to the general public.
Ref Servs Avail To other Federal libraries; to other libraries; not open to the general public.

1102. Naval Weapons Station, Seal Beach, Scientific & Technical Library, Fallbrook Site
Code F-012, Fallbrook, CA 92028-5000 (619) 728-3444; AUTO-VON 873-3444
Admin Rose Moorhouse.
Lib Type Engineering & Science.
Info Ret Servs DIALOG; DROLS; NASA. *Shared Catalog Nets* OCLC. *Coop Lib Nets* FEDLINK.
Circ Servs Avail To other Federal libraries; not open to the general public.
Ref Servs Avail To other Federal libraries; to other libraries; not open to the general public.

1103. Naval Weapons Station, Technical Services Library
TDCC - Code 012, Seal Beach, CA 90740 (213) 594-7386; AUTO-VON 873-7386
Admin Bernice Lenaham.
Lib Type General.

1104. Naval Weapons Station, WQEC Technical Library
Code 3014, Seal Beach, CA 90740 (213) 594-7574; AUTOVON 873-7574
Admin Josephine Walsh.
Lib Type General.

1105. Naval Weapons Support Center, Technical Library
Code 016, Crane, IN 47522 (812) 854-1615; AUTOVON 482-1615
Admin Peggy Curran.
Lib Type General.

1106. Navy Department Library
Bldg 44, Washington Navy Yard, Washington, DC 20374-0571 (202) 433-4131; AUTOVON 288-4131
Admin Stanley Kalkus. *Ref Lib* Barbara Lynch. *ILL* Katherine Bowman. *Acq Lib* John Vajda.
Lib Type General.
Spec Subs Naval & military history; exploring expeditions; foreign affairs; US history. *Spec Collecs* Navy registers & directories; annual reports of the secretary of the Navy; cruisebooks; US Naval administration in World War II; 15th & 16th century works on navigation; theses & dissertations on naval subjects.
Lib Deposit Designation GPO Depository Library.
Info Ret Servs DIALOG; SDC; DROLS. *Shared Catalog Nets* OCLC. *Coop Lib Nets* FEDLINK.
Circ Servs Avail To other Federal libraries; to other libraries; restricted to Navy personnel MDW.
Ref Servs Avail To other Federal libraries; to other libraries; to the general public.

1107. Navy Disease Vector Ecology & Control Center Library
Box 43, NAS, Jacksonville, FL 32212-0043 (904) 772-3439; AUTOVON 942-2428
Admin Andrew F Beck.
Lib Type Health & Medicine.
Spec Subs Entomology; pest control technology; vector-borne disease.

Elec Mail Nets MCI Mail.
Circ Servs Avail Not open to the general public; restricted to in-house use.
Ref Servs Avail Not open to the general public; restricted to in-house use.

1108. Navy Environmental Health Center Library
Code 44, Naval Station, Bldg X-353, Norfolk, VA 23511-6695 (804) 444-4657; FTS 954-4657; TTY 4-3672; AUTOVON 564-4657
Admin Nettie Keeter.
Lib Type Health & Medicine.
Spec Subs Occupational health; preventive medicine; industrial hygiene; environmental health; toxicology; radiological health.
Info Ret Servs MEDLARS. *Coop Lib Nets* Tidewater Health Sciences Librarians (THSL); Southeastern/Atlantic Regional Medical Library Services.
Circ Servs Avail To other Federal libraries; to other libraries; restricted to NEHC, except for ILL.
Ref Servs Avail To other Federal libraries; to other libraries; to the general public.

1109. Navy Fleet Ballistic Missile Submarine Training Center, Technical Publications Library
Naval Base, Charleston, SC 29408 (803) 743-6136; FTS 743-6136; AUTOVON 794-6136
Admin Sylvia M Christopher.
Lib Type Training Center.
Spec Collecs Technical manuals related to training mission of command for SSBN & SSN personnel.
Circ Servs Avail Not open to the general public.
Ref Servs Avail Not open to the general public.

1110. Navy Personnel Research & Development Center, Technical Library
San Diego, CA 92152-6800 (619) 225-7123; AUTOVON 933-7123
Admin Marie D McDowell.
Lib Type Special.
Spec Subs Industrial & applied psychology; training, management & operation research. *Spec Collecs* Center reports.
Info Ret Servs DIALOG; BRS; DROLS. *Shared Catalog Nets* OCLC. *Coop Lib Nets* FEDLINK.
Circ Servs Avail To other Federal libraries; to other libraries; not open to the general public.
Ref Servs Avail To other Federal libraries; to other libraries; not open to the general public.

1111. Navy Regional Data Automation Center
Norfolk, VA 23511 (804) 444-2401; AUTOVON 690-2401
Lib Type Special.

1112. Navy Regional Data Automation Center, Technical Library
Code 20144, Bldg 143, Washington Navy Yard, Washington, DC 20374 (202) 433-5700/5701; AUTOVON 288-5700
Admin William H Hagen.
Lib Type General.

1113. Navy Supply Center, Inventory Control Department, Technical Library
Commanding Officer, Naval Supply Center, Code 103.2, Charleston, SC 29408-6313 (803) 743-4650; FTS 679-4650; AUTO-VON 794-4650
Admin Donna R Cash.
Lib Type Special.
Ref Servs Avail Not open to the general public; restricted to use by equipment specialists in Technical Div.

1114. Navy Tactical Support Activity Library
PO Box 1042, Silver Spring, MD 20910 (301) 394-1623; AUTO-VON 290-1623
Admin Harvey Eisenberg.
Lib Type General.

1115. New Orleans Naval Air Station Library
New Orleans, LA 70143
Lib Type General.

1116. Norfolk Naval Air Station, Branch Library
Bldg U-16, Norfolk, VA 23511-5117 (804) 444-3583; AUTOVON 690-3583
Admin John Kotecki.
Lib Type General.
Circ Servs Avail Restricted to military, DoD civilians & dependents.
Ref Servs Avail To other Federal libraries; to other libraries; not open to the general public; restricted to military, DoD civilians & dependents.

1117. Norfolk Naval Shipyard, Technical Library
Bldg 29, 2nd Fl, Planning Dept, Portsmouth, VA 23709-5000 (804) 396-5674
Lib Type General.

1118. Norfolk Naval Station Library
Bldg C-9, Norfolk, VA 23511-5117 (804) 444-2888; FTS 444-2888; AUTOVON 564-2888
Admin Jane F Sullivan.
Lib Type General.
Circ Servs Avail To other libraries; not open to the general public; restricted to station personnel.
Ref Servs Avail To other Federal libraries; to other libraries; not open to the general public; restricted to station personnel.

1119. Oakland Naval Hospital, Medical Library
8750 Mountain Blvd, Oakland, CA 94627-5000 (415) 633-5606; AUTOVON 855-5607
Admin Harriet V Cohen. *Ref Lib* Robin L Holloway.
Lib Type Health & Medicine.
Spec Subs Medicine; surgery.
Info Ret Servs National Library of Medicine Data Bases. *Coop Lib Nets* Northern California & Nevada Medical Library Group. *Elec Mail Nets* ONTYME.
Circ Servs Avail Restricted to staff.
Ref Servs Avail To other Federal libraries; to other libraries; not open to the general public.

1120. Oceana Naval Air Station Library
Bldg 416, Virginia Beach, VA 23460 (804) 433-2400/2401
Admin Karen E Pollok.
Lib Type General.
Spec Subs Military life; naval history; naval operations.
Circ Servs Avail Not open to the general public.
Ref Servs Avail Restricted to US military personnel, their dependents, & retirees.

1121. Office of Naval Research, Detachment Boston Library
495 Summer St, Boston, MA 02210 (617) 451-3184
Lib Type Special.
Spec Subs Acoustics; oceanography; optics; polymer chemistry & infrared.
Circ Servs Avail Not open to the general public; restricted to staff.
Ref Servs Avail Not open to the general public; restricted to contractor personnel.

1122. Office of the Chief of Naval Research Library
800 N Quincy St, Arlington, VA 22217-5000 (202) 696-4415; AUTOVON 226-4415
Admin Dorcas Tabor.
Lib Type Engineering & Science.
Spec Subs Naval; biological & medical sciences; physical & chemical sciences; psychological & social sciences.
Info Ret Servs DIALOG. *Shared Catalog Nets* OCLC; ILS, Integrated Library Service with NRL. *Coop Lib Nets* ILS.
Circ Servs Avail Restricted to mail or phone requests.
Ref Servs Avail Restricted to mail or phone requests.

1123. Office of the General Counsel, Law Library
Dept of the Navy, Crystal Plaza, Bldg 5 Rm 450, Washington, DC 20360-5110 (202) 692-7378; AUTOVON 222-7378
Admin Mary Kathryn Wilson.
Lib Type Law.
Info Ret Servs WESTLAW; JURIS. *Shared Catalog Nets* OCLC. *Coop Lib Nets* FEDLINK.
Circ Servs Avail To other Federal libraries; not open to the general public; restricted to authorized federal government employees.
Ref Servs Avail Not open to the general public.

1124. Office of the Judge Advocate General, Department of the Navy, Law Library
Code 64.3, 200 Stovall St, Alexandria, VA 22332-22400 (202) 325-9565; AUTOVON 221-9565
Admin Richard S Barrows. *Ref Lib* Susan S Roach (ILL).
Lib Type Law.
Info Ret Servs WESTLAW. *Shared Catalog Nets* OCLC. *Coop Lib Nets* Council of Navy Scientific & Technical Librarians.
Circ Servs Avail To other libraries.
Ref Servs Avail Restricted to DoD.

1125. Orlando Naval Hospital, Medical Library
Orlando, FL 32813-5200 (305) 646-4959; AUTOVON 646-4959
Admin Nancy Hanson.
Lib Type Health & Medicine.
Spec Subs Medicine; surgery; nursing.
Circ Servs Avail To other Federal libraries; to other libraries; not open to the general public; restricted to staff.
Ref Servs Avail To other Federal libraries; to other libraries; not open to the general public; restricted to staff.

1126. Pacific Beach Naval Facility Library
Pacific Beach, WA 98571 (206) 276-4414; AUTOVON 941-7420
Admin R E Rush.
Lib Type General.
Circ Servs Avail Not open to the general public.
Ref Servs Avail Not open to the general public.

1127. Pacific Missile Test Center, Technical Library
Code 1018, Bldg 511A, Point Mugu, CA 93042-5000 (805) 982-8156; AUTOVON 351-8156
Admin Alice Doidge.
Lib Type Engineering & Science.
Spec Subs Radar.
Coop Lib Nets Total Interlibrary Exchange (TIE).
Circ Servs Avail To other libraries; not open to the general public.
Ref Servs Avail To other libraries; not open to the general public.

1128. Pacific Naval Facilities Engineering Command Library
Commander Pacific Division, PacNavFacEngCom, Pearl Harbor, HI 96860-7300 (808) 471-9698
Admin P Moana Dillon.
Lib Type General.
In-house Files All subjects pertaining to engineering, construction, transportation, housing, & environmental engineering.
Circ Servs Avail To other Federal libraries; to other libraries; to the general public.
Ref Servs Avail To other Federal libraries; to other libraries; to the general public.

1129. Patuxent Naval Air Station Library
Bldg 407, Patuxent River, MD 20670 (301) 863-1927
Lib Type General.
Spec Subs Aviation; electricity & electronics; engineering; foreign affairs; military & naval science; physical science; US government.
Lib Deposit Designation GPO Depository Library.
Shared Catalog Nets OCLC. *Coop Lib Nets* FEDLINK.

1130. Patuxent Naval Aviation Logistics Center, Technical Library
Code 1122, Naval Aviation Logistics Center, Patuxent, MD 20670 (301) 863-3372; AUTOVON 356-3372
Admin Ramona Bradburn.
Lib Type Special.

Spec Collecs Naval Air Systems Command Publications.
Circ Servs Avail To other Federal libraries; not open to the general public.
Ref Servs Avail To other Federal libraries; not open to the general public; restricted to local activities, NAVAIRSYSCOM & all NAVAIREWORKFACS.

1131. Pearl Harbor Naval Base Library
1514 Makalapa Dr, Honolulu, HI 96818 (808) 471-8238
Admin Dorothy M Fuller. *Ref Lib* Sharron Dilay. *ILL* Harry Maglasang. *Acq Lib* Michele Mekaru.
Lib Type General.
Spec Collecs James E Wise, Jr Room of Naval history; Auxiliary Library Service Collection (ALSC) of technical & professional reading for Naval personnel, Hawaiiana, China collection.
Circ Servs Avail Restricted to military, DoD civilians.
Ref Servs Avail Restricted to military, DoD civilians.

1132. Pearl Harbor Naval Shipyard, Technical Library
Box 400, Pearl Harbor, HI 96860-5350 (808) 471-3408; AUTO-VON 8-312-471-3408
Admin Lincoln H S Yu.
Lib Type General.
Spec Subs Naval engineering & discipline & technology allied with shipbuilding. *In-house Files* Books, engineering drawings, technical manuals/publications, & reports.
Circ Servs Avail Restricted to Navy personnel.
Ref Servs Avail To other Federal libraries.

1133. Pensacola Naval Air Station Library
Bldg 633, Pensacola Naval Air Station, FL 32508 (904) 452-4362; AUTOVON 922-4362
Admin C R Moreland. *Ref Lib* Judita Walker. *ILL* Marie Baxter.
Lib Type General.
Info Ret Servs DIALOG.
Circ Servs Avail To other Federal libraries; to other libraries; not open to the general public.
Ref Servs Avail To other Federal libraries; to other libraries; to the general public; restricted to telephone requests by the general public.

1134. Pensacola Naval Hospital, Medical Library
Pensacola, FL 32512-5000 (904) 452-6635; FTS 948-6635; AUTO-VON 922-6635
Admin Juan E Terry.
Lib Type Health & Medicine; Hospital (Patients).
Circ Servs Avail Not open to the general public.
Ref Servs Avail To other libraries; not open to the general public.

1135. Philadelphia Naval Hospital, Medical & General Libraries
17th & Pattison Ave, Philadelphia, PA 19145-5199 (215) 755-8314; AUTOVON 443-8038
Admin Giovina C Cavacini.
Lib Type Health & Medicine; General.
Spec Subs Military arts & sciences; sociology; general history.
Circ Servs Avail To other Federal libraries; not open to the general public.
Ref Servs Avail To other Federal libraries; to other libraries; not open to the general public.

1136. Philadelphia Naval Shipyard, Technical Library
Philadelphia, PA 19112 (215) 897-3657
Lib Type General.
Spec Subs Electronics; marine, mechanical, & electrical engineering; mathematics & naval architecture; naval science. *Spec Collecs* Military specifications; design engineering; military standard drawings; manufacturer catalogs (Documentation Service); commercial standards; American Society for Testing & Materials Standards.
Ref Servs Avail Not open to the general public; restricted to staff only, contractors on need to know basis.

1137. Philadelphia Naval Station Library
Bldg 76, 5th Fl, Philadelphia, PA 19112-5004 (215) 897-3657; AUTOVON 443-5280
Admin David Jackson. *Ref Lib* Marilyn Schulz (ILL, Acq).
Lib Type General.
Spec Subs Military history; naval warfare; military life.
Circ Servs Avail To other Federal libraries; to other libraries; not open to the general public; restricted to military, dependents, retirees, & civil service workers.

1138. Point Mugu Naval Air Station Library
Code 6864, Bldg 221, Point Mugu, CA 93042-5000 (805) 982-7771
Lib Type General.
Spec Subs Aeronautics; astronautics; electronics; engineering; mathematics; meteorology; military history; weapons.
Coop Lib Nets Black Gold Cooperative Library System; Total Interlibrary Exchange.

1139. Portsmouth Naval Hospital, Crew's Library
Bldg 215, Portsmouth, VA 23708 (804) 398-5858
Admin Wendy E Moore.
Lib Type Hospital (Patients).
Circ Servs Avail Restricted to Navy personnel & dependents.
Ref Servs Avail Restricted to Navy personnel & dependents.

1140. Portsmouth Naval Hospital, General Library
Bldg H-1, Portsmouth, VA 23708 (804) 398-5858
Admin Wendy E Moore.
Lib Type Hospital (Patients).
Circ Servs Avail Not open to the general public; restricted to military, DoD civilians & dependents.
Ref Servs Avail Restricted to military, DoD civilians & dependents.

1141. Portsmouth Naval Hospital, Medical Library
Portsmouth, VA 23708 (804) 398-5384; FTS 827-0921; AUTO-VON 564-0111
Admin Suad Jones. *Acq Lib* Diane Ward.
Lib Type Health & Medicine; Hospital (Patients).
Info Ret Servs BRS; National Library of Medicine Data Bases. *Coop Lib Nets* Tidewater Health Sciences Librarians (THSL). *Elec Mail Nets* CLASS.
Circ Servs Avail To other Federal libraries; to other libraries; restricted to general public with approval.
Ref Servs Avail To other Federal libraries; to other libraries; not open to the general public.

1142. Portsmouth Naval Shipyard Library
Code 863, Portsmouth, NH 03804-5000 (207) 438-2769; AUTO-VON 684-2769
Admin Josephine Rafferty.
Lib Type General.
Spec Subs Engineering.
Circ Servs Avail To other Federal libraries; to other libraries; not open to the general public; restricted to military, dependents, & shipyard personnel.
Ref Servs Avail To other Federal libraries; to other libraries; not open to the general public; restricted to telephone requests from general public.

1143. Portsmouth Naval Shipyard Museum, Marshall W Butt Library
PO Box 248, 2 High St, Portsmouth, VA 23705 (804) 393-8591
Admin Alice C Hanes (Curator).
Lib Type Special.
Spec Subs History of Norfolk Naval Shipyard; City of Portsmouth; ordnance; ships; journals; diaries of early shipyard work; old engineering journals; early Secretary of the Navy reports; Civil War Rebellion books. *In-house Files* Photo copies & some original maps of the region & Norfolk Naval Shipyard (Gosport Shipyard).
Ref Servs Avail Restricted to use by appointment.

1144. Portsmouth Naval Shipyard, Supply Department, Technical Library
Code 542, Portsmouth, NH 03801 (207) 438-1670, ext 1670
Lib Type Special.
Spec Subs Electronics; hull & machinery equipment; commercial production. *Spec Collecs* American Society Testing Material; American Iron & Steel Institute; American National Standards Institute.

1145. Puget Sound Naval Shipyard, Engineering Library
Code 202.5, Bremerton, WA 98314-5000 (206) 476-2767; AUTO-VON 439-2767
Admin Carol Campbell.
Lib Type Engineering & Science.
Spec Subs Naval architecture; marine engineering; electrical engineering; naval history; other general engineering.
Info Ret Servs DIALOG.
Circ Servs Avail To other Federal libraries; to other libraries; not open to the general public.
Ref Servs Avail To other Federal libraries; to other libraries; not open to the general public.

1146. Rodman Naval Station, General Library
Code 41B, Mare Island, Vallejo, CA 94592-5000 (707) 646-3338; AUTOVON 253-3338
Admin Otome I Andrews.
Lib Type General.
Circ Servs Avail To other Federal libraries; to other libraries.
Ref Servs Avail To other Federal libraries; to other libraries.

1147. San Diego Naval Air Station Library
North Island, Box 29, Bldg 650, San Diego, CA 92135 (619) 437-7041; AUTOVON 951-7041
Admin Sharon Nelson.
Lib Type General.
In-house Files North Island history.
Coop Lib Nets Metro.
Circ Servs Avail To other Federal libraries; restricted to persons attached to or working at the base.
Ref Servs Avail To other Federal libraries; to other libraries; not open to the general public.

1148. San Diego Naval Hospital, General Library
Bldg 9-1, San Diego, CA 92134 (619) 233-2816/2804
Admin Marilyn W Schwartz.
Lib Type Hospital (Patients).
Coop Lib Nets Serra Cooperative Library System—San Diego & Imperial Counties, CA.
Circ Servs Avail To other Federal libraries; to other libraries; restricted to Naval hospital only.
Ref Servs Avail To other libraries; restricted to Navy personnel only.

1149. San Diego Naval Hospital, Thompson Medical Library
San Diego, CA 92134 (619) 233-2816; AUTOVON 987-2367
Admin Marilyn W Schwartz. *Ref Lib* Jan Dempsey. *ILL* Marjorie Knight. *Acq Lib* Judith Mueller.
Lib Type Health & Medicine.
Spec Subs Ophthalmology.
Info Ret Servs DIALOG; BRS; MEDLINE. *Shared Catalog Nets* OCLC. *Coop Lib Nets* Pacific Southwest Regional Medical Library Service (PSRMLS). *Elec Mail Nets* CLASS ONTYME.
Circ Servs Avail To other Federal libraries; to other libraries; restricted to Naval Medical Command staff.
Ref Servs Avail To other Federal libraries; to other libraries; to the general public.

1150. San Diego Naval Station Library
Box 224, San Diego, CA 92136-5224 (619) 235-1403/2420; AUTOVON 958-1403/2420
Lib Type General.
Shared Catalog Nets Naval Education Training Program Development Center.
Circ Servs Avail Not open to the general public; restricted to military, active & retired, & dependents & on-base civil service.
Ref Servs Avail Not open to the general public.

1151. San Diego Naval Submarine Base, General Library
Bldg 211, 140 Sylvester Rd, San Diego, CA 92106
Lib Type General.

1152. San Diego Naval Supply, Technical Library
937 N Harbor Dr, San Diego, CA 92132-5068 (619) 235-3237/3238; AUTOVON 958-3237
Admin Truman Nielsen. *Ref Lib* Ivy Seaberry.
Lib Type Special.
In-house Files Material for research from Naval Publication & Forms Center, Ships Part Control Center, Mechanicsburg, & other government facilities.
Circ Servs Avail To other Federal libraries.
Ref Servs Avail To other Federal libraries; to other libraries; to the general public.

1153. San Diego Naval Training Center Library
Bldg 177, San Diego, CA 92133 (619) 225-5470; FTS 893-1509; AUTOVON 957-5470
Admin Raul P Fernandez, Jr.
Lib Type General.
Circ Servs Avail Restricted to military, DoD civilians & dependents.
Ref Servs Avail To other libraries.

1154. Skaggs Island Station Library
Sonoma, CA 95476 (707) 553-3431
Lib Type General.

1155. South Weymouth Base Library
Family Service Center, Naval Air Station, South Weymouth, MA 02190-5000 (617) 786-2581 786-2583; AUTOVON 955-2581
Admin William Hill.
Lib Type General.
Circ Servs Avail To other Federal libraries; not open to the general public; restricted to military.
Ref Servs Avail To other Federal libraries; not open to the general public; restricted to military.

1156. Space & Naval Warfare Systems Command Library
Code 7053, Washington, DC 20363-5100 (202) 692-8771; AUTO-VON 442-1482
Admin Sue L Hall.
Lib Type Special.
Spec Subs Electronics; computers; management; mathematics; engineering & naval science.
Shared Catalog Nets OCLC.
Circ Servs Avail Restricted to SPA WAR personnel.

1157. Strategic Systems Program Office, Technical Library
Washington, DC 20376 (202) 697-2852; AUTOVON 227-2852
Admin June Gable.
Lib Type Special.
Spec Subs Missile technology; management.
Info Ret Servs DIALOG. *Shared Catalog Nets* OCLC.
Circ Servs Avail To other libraries; not open to the general public.
Ref Servs Avail To other libraries; not open to the general public.

1158. Strategic Weapons Facility, Pacific, Library
SPB 161, Bremerton, WA 98315 (206) 396-4811; AUTOVON 744-4811
Admin Maureen Melton.
Lib Type General.

1159. Supervisor of Shipbuilding Conversion & Repair Library
Box 119, Code 253, San Diego, CA 92136-5199 (619) 235-2455
Lib Type Special.
Spec Subs Ordnance; ship machinery & electronics.

1160. Supervisor of Shipbuilding Conversion & Repair Library
Code 241A, Drawer T, USN Mayport Naval Station, Jacksonville, FL 32228 (904) 246-5779; AUTOVON 960-5779
Admin Zelda L Clarke.
Lib Type Special.

1161. Supervisor of Shipbuilding, Conversion & Repair Library
Code 202.1, Portsmouth, VA 23705 (804) 396-5962; AUTOVON 961-5962
Admin Patricia S Holins.
Lib Type General.
Circ Servs Avail To other Federal libraries; to other libraries; not open to the general public.
Ref Servs Avail To other Federal libraries; to other libraries; not open to the general public.

1162. Supervisor of Shipbuilding Conversion & Repair Library
Code 245, San Francisco, CA 94135 (415) 641-3057; AUTOVON 799-3057
Admin Lawrence H Hoelter.
Lib Type Special.

1163. Supervisor of Shipbuilding, Conversion & Repair, SUPSHIPS Technical Library
Code 242.C, New Orleans, LA 70142 (504) 361-2580; AUTOVON 485-2580
Admin Michel Loria.
Lib Type Engineering & Science.
Spec Subs Ship construction only. *Spec Collecs* NAVSEA technical manuals for new construction & conversions.
Info Ret Servs DATA POINT 8700 System.
Circ Servs Avail To other Federal libraries.
Ref Servs Avail To other Federal libraries.

1164. Supervisor of Shipbuilding Conversion & Repair, Technical Library
Seattle, WA 98115 (206) 527-3859; AUTOVON 941-3859
Admin Mike Marion.
Lib Type General.

1165. Supervisor of Shipbuilding, Conversion & Repair, Technical Library
Flushing & Washington Ave, Brooklyn, NY 11251 (718) 834-2331 834-2338; AUTOVON 456-2331 456-2338
Admin Sylvia Wernow.
Lib Type Special.
Spec Subs Ship repair: boilers, piping, switchboards, & ordnance.
Circ Servs Avail To other Federal libraries; to other libraries; not open to the general public.
Ref Servs Avail To other Federal libraries; to other libraries; not open to the general public; restricted to contract employees.

1166. David Taylor Naval Ship R&D Center, Technical Information Center
Code 5220, Bethesda, MD 20084-5000 (202) 227-3623
Admin Michael Dankewych. *Ref Lib* Margaret Bowman. *ILL* Esdale McInnis. *Acq Lib* Norma Zimmerman.
Lib Type Engineering & Science.
Spec Subs Acoustics; hydrodynamics; structures; aerodynamics; marine engineering.
Info Ret Servs DIALOG. *Coop Lib Nets* Interlibrary User's Assoc (IUA).
Circ Servs Avail To other libraries; not open to the general public.
Ref Servs Avail To other Federal libraries; not open to the general public.

1167. Treasure Island Naval Station, General Library
Bldg 265, NAVSTA Treasure Island, San Francisco, CA 94130 (415) 765-5809; AUTOVON 869-5809
Admin James Deering.
Lib Type General.
Coop Lib Nets Bay Area Library Information System (BAYLIS).
Circ Servs Avail To other libraries; not open to the general public; restricted to NAVSTA personnel.
Ref Servs Avail To other libraries; restricted to NAVSTA personnel.

1168. Trident Refit Facility, Bangor, Library
Code 424, Bremerton, WA 98315 (206) 396-4321; AUTOVON 744-4321/6888
Admin James Hudson.
Lib Type General.

1169. US Naval Academy, Nimitz Library
Annapolis, MD 21402-1390 (301) 267-2194/2800; ILL 267-2233
Admin Richard A Evans.
Lib Type Academic.
Spec Subs History; military; science-technology; social & behavioral science; naval art & science; engineering; mathematics. *Spec Collecs* Electricity & Magnetism (Benjamin Collection); Physics (Albert A Michelson Collection); Seapower; Ambassador William Sebald Papers; Steichen Photography Collection; oral history.
Lib Deposit Designation GPO Depository Library.
Shared Catalog Nets OCLC. *Coop Lib Nets* FEDLINK.
Circ Servs Avail To other Federal libraries; to other libraries; to the general public.
Ref Servs Avail To other Federal libraries; to other libraries; to the general public.

1170. US Naval Historical Center, Operational Archives Branch
Bldg 57, Washington Navy Yard, Washington, DC 20374 (202) 433-3170
Lib Type Special.
Spec Collecs Dept of the Navy Archives (primarily from 1939); history of specific commands; naval operations; policy & strategy; officer biography.
Ref Servs Avail To the general public.

1171. US Naval Institute, Photographic & Reference Library
Annapolis, MD 21402 (301) 268-6110; 1-800-233-8764
Admin Patty M Maddocks.
Lib Type Special.
Spec Subs Proceedings, US Naval Institute Index. *Spec Collecs* Fahey photographic collection; "Our Navy" Collection.
Ref Servs Avail To other Federal libraries; restricted to members.

1172. US Naval Observatory Library
34th & Massachusetts Ave NW, Washington, DC 20390 (202) 653-1499; AUTOVON 294-1499
Admin Brenda G Corbin. *ILL* Sandra Kay.
Lib Type Engineering & Science.
Spec Subs Astronomy; mathematics; physics; navigation. *Spec Collecs* Approximately 800 rare books printed before 1800 on astronomy, mathematics, & navigation.
Info Ret Servs DIALOG. *Shared Catalog Nets* OCLC. *Coop Lib Nets* Council of Navy Scientific & Technical Libraries (CONSATL).
Circ Servs Avail To other Federal libraries; to other libraries; not open to the general public.
Ref Servs Avail To other Federal libraries; to other libraries; not open to the general public.

1173. US Navy Operational Test & Evaluation Force Library
Norfolk, VA 23511 (804) 444-5619; AUTOVON 690-5619
Admin Margaret Murphy.
Lib Type Special.

1174. US Navy Ships Parts Control Center, General Library
Code 075, Bldg 214, Mechanicsburg, PA 17055 (717) 790-2628
Lib Type General.

1175. Weapons Quality Engineering Center Library
Commanding Officer, Naval Undersea Warfare Eng Stn, ATTN: Code 3011, Keyport, WA 98345 (206) 396-2710; AUTOVON 396-2501
Admin George L McLean.
Lib Type Engineering & Science.
In-house Files Engineering test reports.

Circ Servs Avail Not open to the general public; restricted to mostly WQEC.
Ref Servs Avail Not open to the general public.

1176. Whidbey Island Naval Air Station Library
Bldg 103, Oak Harbor, WA 98278-2200 (206) 257-2702; AUTO-VON 820-2702
Admin Susan McClung.
Lib Type Special.
Coop Lib Nets Washington Library Network (WLN).
Circ Servs Avail To other Federal libraries; to other libraries; not open to the general public; restricted to military, DoD civilians & dependents.
Ref Servs Avail To other Federal libraries; to other libraries; not open to the general public; restricted to military, DoD civilians & dependents.

1177. Whiting Field Naval Air Station Library
Milton, FL 32570 (904) 623-7274
Admin Rebecca H Hall.
Lib Type General.
Circ Servs Avail Not open to the general public.
Ref Servs Avail Not open to the general public.

1178. Willow Grove Naval Air Station Library
Bldg 2, Willow Grove, PA 19090-5010 (215) 443-6095
Admin Janet Gick.
Lib Type General.
Circ Servs Avail To other Federal libraries; to other libraries; to the general public.
Ref Servs Avail To other Federal libraries; to other libraries; to the general public.

Department of the Navy—Overseas

1179. Allied Forces, South Europe, Library
Headquarters Command, Box 141, FPO New York, NY 09524
Admin Mario Petraglia.
Lib Type General.
Spec Subs Economics.
Circ Servs Avail To other libraries; not open to the general public.
Ref Servs Avail To other libraries; not open to the general public.

1180. COMFLEACT Library
US Fleet Activities, Yokosuka (Code 120), FPO Seattle, WA 98762-1100 Japan 26-1991 ext 5574; AUTOVON (218) 234-7253/5574
Admin Donald R Erickson. *ILL* Eiichi Miyazawa. *Acq Lib* Arlette Cheramie.
Lib Type General.
Spec Subs Japan; management. *Spec Collecs* Japan; Systems Management (for Univ of Southern California); university studies; paperback browsing collection. *In-house Files* Maps; holiday pamphlet handouts; subject area bibliographies; Navy & Marine Corps histories.
Circ Servs Avail To other libraries; restricted to US military, DoD civilians & dependents.
Ref Servs Avail To other libraries; restricted to US military, DoD civilians & dependents.

1181. COMNAVACTUK Library
Box 60, US Naval Activities FPO New York, NY 09510, London United Kingdom (01) 409-4556; AUTOVON 235-4556
Admin Ruth Sullivan. *Ref Lib* Katherine Bradley (ILL, ACQ).
Lib Type General.
Circ Servs Avail To other Federal libraries; to other libraries; not open to the general public; restricted to Navy & DoD civilians in London & dependents.
Ref Servs Avail To other Federal libraries; not open to the general public; restricted to Navy & DoD civilians in London & dependents.

1182. Cubi Point Naval Air Station Library
Box 1, Bldg 8280, FPO San Francisco, CA 96654 The Philippines 885-4157
Admin Tony Zolina, Jr. *Ref Lib* Johnny Ventura. *ILL* Tess Carreon. *Acq Lib* Gloria Basilio.
Lib Type General.
Spec Subs Military; naval power; naval history; hobbies; auto repair reference. *Spec Collecs* Philippine culture & history.
Coop Lib Nets CNET (Commander Naval Education & Training Program Development Center).
Circ Servs Avail To other Federal libraries; to other libraries; not open to the general public; restricted to US military, dependents, & DoD employees.
Ref Servs Avail To other Federal libraries; to other libraries; to the general public.

1183. Diego Garcia Station Library
Box 18, US Navy Support Facility, FPO San Francisco, CA 96685-2000 Diego Garcia AUTOVON 870-4601
Admin Maribel A Leomo.
Lib Type General.
Circ Servs Avail To other libraries; to the general public.
Ref Servs Avail To other libraries; to the general public.

1184. Fleet Activities, General Library
FPO Seattle, WA 98766, Sasebo Japan
Lib Type General.

1185. Guantanamo US Naval Base Library
US NAVSTA, Box 14, FPO New York, NY 09593 Guantanamo Bay, Cuba 011-53-99-4541; AUTOVON 723-4541
Admin Elizabeth L Lane.
Lib Type General.
Spec Collecs Automobile & vehicle repairs; careers & tests. *In-house Files* Caribbean Islands; Naval & Marine bases world wide.
Circ Servs Avail To other Federal libraries; to other libraries; to the general public; restricted to GTMO residents.
Ref Servs Avail To other Federal libraries; to other libraries; to the general public; restricted to GTMO residents.

1186. Kami Seya Station Library
NRRF Kami Seya, 68-A, FPO Seattle, WA 98768-1801 Japan
Admin Leland G Offret.
Lib Type General.
Spec Subs Japan & Far Eastern Asia. *Spec Collecs* Japan, history & culture.
Coop Lib Nets Naval Regional Librarian, Pearl Harbor.
Circ Servs Avail To other Federal libraries; not open to the general public; restricted to US military & dependents.
Ref Servs Avail To other Federal libraries; not open to the general public; restricted to US military & dependents.

1187. Naval Regional Medical Center, Medical Library
FPO Seattle, WA 98765, Yokosuka Japan
Admin Kathy S Bartlett.
Lib Type Health & Medicine.

1188. Naval Security Group Activity Library
Box 559 NSGA, FPO Seattle, WA 98777 (907) 592-6310
Admin Raymond A Hall. *ILL* M L Williams (Acq).
Lib Type General.
Coop Lib Nets Naval Regional Librarian, San Francisco.
Circ Servs Avail To other libraries; not open to the general public; restricted to military & dependents.
Ref Servs Avail To other libraries; to the general public.

1189. Roosevelt Roads Naval Station Library
Bldg 735, Resident Naval Mobile Construction Battalion, FPO Miami, FL 34051 Puerto Rico (809) 865-2000, ext 4353
Lib Type General.
Spec Subs American history; military arts & sciences; World War II.

1190. Subic Naval Station Library
Box 12, FPO San Francisco, CA 96651-1009 The Philippines 884-8423
Admin Margaret Johnson.
Lib Type General.
Spec Subs The Philippines.
Circ Servs Avail Not open to the general public; restricted to military, dependents, & base civilians.
Ref Servs Avail Not open to the general public; restricted to military, dependents, & base civilians.

1191. Task Force 199 Library
US Naval Support Force FPO San Francisco, CA 96601, Naval Mobile Units Pacific Antarctica
Lib Type General.

1192. US National Support Unit, General Library
COMIBERLANT FPO New York, NY 09678, Lisbon, Portugal
Lib Type General.

1193. US Naval Air Facility, General Library
APO New York, NY 09406, Terceira, Azores
Lib Type General.

1194. US Naval Air Facility Library
Box 20, FPO Seattle, WA 98767-1270 AUTOVON 228-3776
Admin Paul M Ichikawa.
Lib Type General.
Circ Servs Avail To other Federal libraries; to other libraries.
Ref Servs Avail To other Federal libraries; to other libraries.

1195. US Naval Air Station, Guam, Station Library
Box 52 FPO San Francisco, CA 96637 Guam
Lib Type General.

1196. US Naval Air Station Library
Box 43, FPO New York, NY 09571 Iceland
Admin Oskar Gudjonsson.
Lib Type General.
Spec Collecs Icelandic books in English.
Circ Servs Avail To other Federal libraries; to other libraries; to the general public.
Ref Servs Avail To other Federal libraries; to other libraries; to the general public.

1197. US Naval Air Station Main Library
Bldg 338, FPO New York, NY 09560 AUTOVON 938-6208
Admin Margo A Cannonier.
Lib Type General.
Circ Servs Avail Restricted to US Naval personnel.
Ref Servs Avail Restricted to US Naval personnel.

1198. US Naval Air Station, Sigonella, Base Library
Box 470 FPO New York, NY 09523, Sicily, Italy 39-95-56-4332; AUTOVON 624-4332
Admin Lauralee Shiere.
Lib Type General.
Spec Subs World War II; Sicily, history & travel.
Circ Servs Avail Not open to the general public; restricted to station personnel.
Ref Servs Avail Not open to the general public; restricted to station personnel.

1199. US Naval Communication Station, San Miguel, Station Library
Bldg 7377, Box 23 FPO San Francisco, CA 96656, Tarlac, Philippines
Lib Type General.

1200. US Naval Communication Station, Station Library
FPO New York, NY 09525, Nea Makri, Greece
Lib Type General.

1201. US Naval Communications Area, Station Library
Master Station, WESTPAC-GUAM, Box 108, FPO San Francisco, CA 96630-1860 Guam AUTOVON 355-5921
Admin Rose Ramon.
Lib Type General.
Circ Servs Avail To other Federal libraries; restricted to military.
Ref Servs Avail Restricted to military.

1202. US Naval Communications Station Library
United Kingdom, FPO New York, NY 09516-3000 UK AUTOVON 314-392-8556
Admin Robert Hill.
Lib Type General.
Circ Servs Avail Not open to the general public.
Ref Servs Avail Not open to the general public.

1203. US Naval Communications Station, Station Library
Box 10, FPO San Francisco, CA 96680 AUTOVON 821-1945
Lib Type General.
Coop Lib Nets Chief of Naval Education & Training (CNET).
Circ Servs Avail Not open to the general public; restricted to military (RAN, USN, USAF), DoD employees & dependents.
Ref Servs Avail Not open to the general public; restricted to military (RAN, USN, USAF), DoD employees & dependents.

1204. US Naval Facility, General Library
FPO New York, NY 09519, Brawdy, Wales United Kingdom
Lib Type General.

1205. US Naval Facility, General Library
Bldg 116, PO Box 559 FPO New York, NY 09597, Argentia, Newfoundland Canada
Lib Type General.

1206. US Naval Facility, General Library
FPO Miami, FL 34054
Lib Type General.

1207. US Naval Hospital, Medical & General Libraries
Guam, PO Box 7747, FPO San Francisco, CA 96630-1649 Guam (671) 344-9250; AUTOVON 344-9250
Admin Alice E Hadley.
Lib Type Health & Medicine; General.
Spec Subs Guam & Micronesia.
Coop Lib Nets Guam ILL Network; Pacific Southwest Regional Medical Library Service (PSRMLS).
Circ Servs Avail To other Federal libraries; to other libraries; not open to the general public; restricted to staff & patients, military & dependents & federal employees.
Ref Servs Avail To other Federal libraries; to other libraries; not open to the general public; restricted to staff & patients, military & dependents & federal employees.

1208. US Naval Hospital, Medical, Crews' & Patients' Library
FPO San Francisco, CA 96652 The Philippines
Admin Julio E Dizon Jr.
Lib Type Health & Medicine; Hospital (Patients).
Spec Subs Medicine & allied fields. *Spec Collecs* The Philippines.
Info Ret Servs MEDLARS. *Coop Lib Nets* Interlibrary loans; Photocopy cooperation with other US military hospital libraries.
Circ Servs Avail Not open to the general public; restricted to hospital staff, residents, & paramedical staff.
Ref Servs Avail To other Federal libraries; to other libraries; to the general public.

1209. US Naval Hospital, Medical Library
Box 3007, FPO Miami, FL 34051 Puerto Rico AUTOVON 831-4183/4133, ext 232
Lib Type Health & Medicine.

1210. US Naval Hospital, Okinawa, Medical Library
FPO Seattle, CA 98778 Okinawa, Japan
Admin Jane M Hall. *ILL* Sumiko Ikehara.
Lib Type Health & Medicine.
Circ Servs Avail Not open to the general public; restricted to medical personnel affiliated with US military.

Ref Servs Avail To other Federal libraries; to other libraries; not open to the general public; restricted to medical personnel affiliated with US military.

1211. US Naval Radio Transmitting Facility, Tarlac, General Library

FPO San Francisco, CA 96658 Philippines
Lib Type General.

1212. US Naval Security Group Activity, General Library

FPO Miami, FL 34053
Lib Type General.

1213. US Naval Security Group Activity, Station Library

FPO New York, NY 09518, Edzell, Scotland United Kingdom
Lib Type General.

1214. US Naval Station, Fletcher Library

Box 2 NAS FPO Seattle, WA 98791-1202, Adak, AK (907) 592-8215
Admin Sharon C Bodkin.
Lib Type General.
Circ Servs Avail Not open to the general public; restricted to base personnel.
Ref Servs Avail Not open to the general public; restricted to base personnel.

1215. US Naval Station, Guam, Station Library

Box 174 FPO San Francisco, CA 96630 Guam
Lib Type General.

1216. US Naval Station Library

Box 14, Rota, Spain, FPO New York, NY 09540 Spain AUTOVON 727-2418
Admin Rose Marie Puncke.
Lib Type General.
Circ Servs Avail To other Federal libraries; not open to the general public; restricted to US Navy & other DoD employees.
Ref Servs Avail To other Federal libraries; not open to the general public; restricted to US Navy & other DoD employees.

1217. US Naval Support Activity Detachment, Library

Code GA3 FPO New York, NY 09522-1006 Italy 039-0771-463606
Admin Ted Hodgson.
Lib Type General.
Circ Servs Avail To the general public.
Ref Servs Avail To the general public.

1218. US Naval Support Activity, General Library

FPO New York, NY 09514, Holyloch, Scotland United Kingdom
Lib Type General.

1219. US Naval Support Activity General Library

c/o Recreational Services Dept, USNAVSUPPACT Souda Bay, Crete, FPO New York, NY 09528 Crete, Greece AUTOVON 399-9489
Admin J R Temple.
Lib Type General.
Circ Servs Avail To the general public.
Ref Servs Avail To the general public.

1220. US Naval Support Activity Library

PO Box 13, FPO New York, NY 09521 AUTOVON 625-4559
Admin Kevin R Jones.
Lib Type General.
Circ Servs Avail Not open to the general public.
Ref Servs Avail To other libraries.

1221. US Navy Administrative Support Unit, General Library

FPO New York, NY 09526, Jafair, Bahrain
Lib Type General.

1222. US Navy Atlantic Fleet Weapons Training Facility

FPO Miami, FL 34051 Puerto Rico (809) 863-2000; AUTOVON 831-5312/5313
Lib Type Training Center.

1223. US Navy Office of Naval Research, Branch Office, London, Library

PO Box 39 FPO New York, NY 09510, London, United Kingdom AUTOVON 235-4511
Admin Donna L Mott.
Lib Type General.

1224. US Navy Public Works Center, Technical Library

FPO San Francisco, CA 96630-2937 AUTOVON 339-3200
Admin Joseph D L Santos.
Lib Type Engineering & Science.
Spec Subs Reports on Marianas Islands. *Spec Collecs* Microfilm & microfiche collections.
Circ Servs Avail To other Federal libraries; to other libraries; not open to the general public.
Ref Servs Avail To other Federal libraries; to other libraries; not open to the general public.

1225. US Navy Support Office Library

Box 235, NAVSUPPO, FPO New York, NY 09533 Italy AUTOVON 726-1110 ext 289
Admin Loida Ramos Canlas.
Lib Type General.
Spec Subs Italy. *Spec Collecs* Travel guides; juvenile books.
Coop Lib Nets Naval Education & Training Program Development Center.
Circ Servs Avail Restricted to military libraries, military, veterans & dependents.
Ref Servs Avail Restricted to military libraries, military, veterans & dependents.

1226. USS Ponce (LPD-15), Crew & Troop Library (804) 444-3900

Admin Lyman Smith (Library Officer). *Ref Lib* Johnny Thomas.
Lib Type General.
Coop Lib Nets Naval Education & Training Support Center, Atlantic (NAVEDTRASUPCEN).
Circ Servs Avail Not open to the general public; restricted to ship's company & embarked Marines.

United States Marine Corps—Domestic

1227. James Carson Breckinridge Library & Amphibious Warfare Facility

Education Center, MCDEC, Quantico, VA 22134-5050 (703) 640-2248; AUTOVON 278-2248
Admin D C Brown. *Ref Lib* Mary Porter (ILL). *Acq Lib* JoAnne Payne.
Lib Type Training Center.
Spec Subs Military arts & sciences; US Marine Corps; amphibious warfare. *Spec Collecs* Marine Corps history; Prof W H Russell Collection.
Lib Deposit Designation GPO Depository Library.
Shared Catalog Nets OCLC. *Coop Lib Nets* FEDLINK.
Circ Servs Avail To other Federal libraries; to other libraries.
Ref Servs Avail To other Federal libraries; to other libraries; to the general public.

1228. Camp Lejeune, Marine Corps Base Library

Bldg 63, Camp Lejeune, NC 28542 (919) 451-5724; AUTOVON 484-5724
Lib Type General.
Circ Servs Avail Not open to the general public; restricted to military, dependents, & base civilian employees.
Ref Servs Avail Not open to the general public; restricted to military, dependents, & base civilian employees.

1229. Camp Pendleton Base Library System
Marine Corps Base, Camp Pendleton, CA 92055-5000 (619) 725-5104/5669/5973; FTS 345-5104; AUTOVON 365-5104; South Mesa Branch (619) 725-2032; San Mateo Branch (619) 725-7325
Admin Patrick J Carney; Ruth Hebert (South Mesa Branch); Dan Read (Bookmobile Service). *Ref Lib* Ann L Dart.
Lib Type General.
Coop Lib Nets San Diego Greater Metro Library Council (METRO).
Circ Servs Avail To other Federal libraries; to other libraries; not open to the general public.
Ref Servs Avail To other Federal libraries; to other libraries; to the general public.

1230. Camp Smith Library
Bldg 27, Camp H M Smith, HI 96861 (808) 477-6348
Admin Evelyn Mau.
Lib Type General.
Spec Subs Recreational with leanings towards military history/science.
Circ Servs Avail To other libraries; not open to the general public; restricted to military & base personnel.
Ref Servs Avail To other libraries; to the general public.

1231. Cherry Point Marine Corps Air Station Library
Bldg 298, Cherry Point, NC 28533 (919) 466-3571/3552
Lib Type General.
Spec Collecs Federal Register, 1936-present; Library of American Civilization; New York Times, 1851-present, microfiche.
Circ Servs Avail Not open to the general public; restricted to military, dependents, & base personnel.
Ref Servs Avail Not open to the general public; restricted to military, dependents, & base personnel.

1232. Doctrine Center Library
Code C 0914, MCDEC, Quantico, VA 22134-5001 (703) 640-3387; AUTOVON 278-3387
Admin Tanny Franco.
Lib Type Special.
Spec Subs Military affairs; doctrinal history; field manuals; training circulars; operational handbooks. *Spec Collecs* Publications, regulations, reports, & studies used in developing Marine Corps doctrine. *In-house Files* Current Marine Corps operational handbook listings.
Circ Servs Avail Not open to the general public; restricted to active duty military personnel.
Ref Servs Avail Not open to the general public.

1233. El Toro Marine Corps Air Station Library
Bldg 280, El Toro Marine Base, Santa Ana, CA 92709-5007 (714) 651-2569
Lib Type General.
Spec Subs American history (especially war materials); biography; fiction; international relations; social & biological sciences; early California history; Marine Corps aviation history. *Spec Collecs* Microbook Library of American Civilization.
Coop Lib Nets Libraries of Orange County Network.
Ref Servs Avail Not open to the general public; restricted to military & dependents & base civilian dependents.

1234. Kaneohe Bay Marine Corps Air Station Library
Bldg 219, Kaneohe Bay, HI 96863
Lib Type General.

1235. Marine Corps Air Station Library
Beaufort, SC 29904 (803) 846-7682
Admin Janet Ellis.
Lib Type General.
Coop Lib Nets Library Association of Beaufort County.
Circ Servs Avail To other libraries; not open to the general public; restricted to military, dependents, retirees, & base civilians.
Ref Servs Avail To other libraries; not open to the general public.

1236. Marine Corps Development & Education Center, Special Services Library
Quantico, VA 22134-5006 (703) 640-2414; AUTOVON 278-2414
Admin Mary Lou Lesser.
Lib Type General.
Circ Servs Avail To other Federal libraries; restricted to military & dependents.
Ref Servs Avail To other Federal libraries; to other libraries; to the general public.

1237. Marine Corps Historical Center Library
Bldg 58, Washington Navy Yard, Washington, DC 20374-0580 (202) 433-3447/4253; AUTOVON 288-4253/3447
Admin Evelyn Englander (excluding special collection).
Lib Type Special.
Spec Subs Marine Corps history; history of amphibious warfare. *Spec Collecs* Personal papers; oral history; archives; historical reference. *In-house Files* Subject, biographical, & geographical files relating to USMC.
Coop Lib Nets FEDLINK.
Circ Servs Avail To other Federal libraries; to other libraries.
Ref Servs Avail To other Federal libraries; to other libraries; to the general public.

1238. Marine Corps Logistics Support Base Library
Bldg 7450, Albany, GA 31704-5000 (912) 439-5242
Lib Type General.
Circ Servs Avail Not open to the general public; restricted to military personnel & base civilians.
Ref Servs Avail Not open to the general public; restricted to military personnel & base civilians.

1239. Marine Corps Recruit Depot Library
Bldg 7, San Diego, CA 92140-5011 (619) 225-5392; AUTOVON 957-5392
Admin Dorothy C Fowlie.
Lib Type General.
Spec Subs Military History.
Coop Lib Nets Serra Regional Library Network.
Circ Servs Avail To other libraries; to the general public.
Ref Servs Avail To other libraries; to the general public; restricted to military: active, retired, dependents.

1240. New River Marine Corps Air Station Library
Jacksonville, NC 28545-5001 (919) 451-6715
Lib Type General.
Spec Subs Drug & alcohol-abuse control; human relations; juvenile books; microcomputer software, programs, & languages; military preparedness; sports.

1241. 9th Marine Corps District Library
HQ 9th Marine Corps District, 10000 W 75th St, Shawnee Mission, KS 66204-2265 (913) 236-3515/16; FTS 757-3515; AUTOVON 465-3515
Admin K J Miller (Co-Admin); Marion Lynch (Co-Admin).
Lib Type General.
Spec Subs Sales.
Circ Servs Avail Not open to the general public.
Ref Servs Avail Not open to the general public.

1242. Parris Island, Marine Corps Recruit Depot Station Library
Box 5-055, Parris Island, SC 29905 (803) 525-3261
Lib Type General.
Spec Collecs Large print collection; professional military collection; South Carolina collection.

1243. US Marine Band, Music Library
Marine Bks, 8th & I Sts SE, Washington, DC 20390 (202) 433-4298
Admin Frank Byrne.
Lib Type Special.
Spec Subs Band, orchestra, & ensemble music. *Spec Collecs* John Phillip Sousa Collection—memorabilia of former Sousa Band members. *In-house Files* Programs; historical files; photographs; Marine band memorabilia.
Circ Servs Avail Restricted to approval by director.

Ref Servs Avail Restricted to scholars & researchers.

1244. US Marine Corps Air Ground Combat Center Library
MCAGCC, Bldg 1528, Twentynine Palms, CA 92278-5001 (619) 368-6875; AUTOVON 952-6875
Admin S Kay Emerson.
Lib Type General.
Spec Subs Marine Corps; military. *Spec Collecs* Great Books of the Western World; Newsbank.
Circ Servs Avail Restricted to military & dependents.
Ref Servs Avail Restricted to military & dependents.

1245. US Marine Corps Air Station Library
Bldg 633, Yuma, AZ 85369-5000 (602) 726-2785
Lib Type General.
Circ Servs Avail Restricted to base & retired military.
Ref Servs Avail Restricted to base & retired military.

1246. US Marine Corps HQ, Judge Advocate Division, Legal Library
Code JAR, Washington, DC 20380 (202) 694-2510; AUTOVON 224-2510
Admin Adrian L Patterson.
Lib Type Law.
Info Ret Servs WESTLAW.
Circ Servs Avail Restricted to HQMC.

1247. US Marine Corps Tactical Systems Support Activity, Technical Library
Bldg 31337, Camp Pendleton, CA 92055 (619) 725-2875
Lib Type General.
Spec Subs Computer science.
Circ Servs Avail Not open to the general public.
Ref Servs Avail Not open to the general public.

1248. US Marine Corps Technical Library
HQ, Code LMA-1, Washington, DC 20380-0001 (202) 694-3185; AUTOVON 224-1997/2047
Admin Clara S Miller.
Lib Type Special.
Circ Servs Avail To other Federal libraries.
Ref Servs Avail To other Federal libraries.

United States Marine Corps—Overseas

1249. Nurenberg Base Library
ATTN: CRD (Lib Branch), APO New York, NY 09696-0010 Federal Republic of Germany 460-7114/6509
Admin Benard E Strong. *Ref Lib* Willis Benson (ILL).
Lib Type General.
Coop Lib Nets Patron Oriented Library System (PALS).
Circ Servs Avail To other Federal libraries; to other libraries; not open to the general public; restricted to US Military & DoD personnel.
Ref Servs Avail Not open to the general public; restricted to US Military & DoD personnel.

1250. Special Services Library
US Marine Corps Air Station, FPO Seattle, WA 98764 Japan 236-3078
Admin Patricia Salchert. *Ref Lib* Elizabeth Thigpen. *ILL* Irene Rasmuson.
Lib Type Special.
Circ Servs Avail To other Federal libraries; to other libraries; to the general public.
Ref Servs Avail To other Federal libraries; to other libraries; to the general public.

1251. US Marine Corps Base, Camp Smedley D Butler, Library Processing Center
FPO Seattle, WA 98773, Kawasaki, Okinawa Japan
Admin Jean Kolbeck.
Lib Type General.

Department of Defense Agencies & Joint Service Schools

1252. Armed Forces Institute of Pathology, Ash Library
Washington, DC 20306-6000 (202) 576-2983; AUTOVON 291-2983
Admin Patricia C Patel. *ILL* Darlene Butler.
Lib Type Health & Medicine.
Spec Subs Specialized areas (24) of Pathology; AIDS Registry. *Spec Collecs* Yakolev Collection, M Haleem, Curator.
Info Ret Servs DIALOG. *Shared Catalog Nets* OCLC. *Coop Lib Nets* Integrated Library System (ILS).
Circ Servs Avail To other Federal libraries; to other libraries.
Ref Servs Avail To other Federal libraries; to other libraries; to the general public; restricted to limited use by general public.

1253. Armed Forces Staff College Library
7800 Hampton Blvd, Norfolk, VA 23511-6097 (804) 444-5155; FTS 954-5155; AUTOVON 564-5155
Admin Margaret J Martin. *Ref Lib* J Gail Nicula. *ILL* Marie Harrison. *Acq Lib* Jane Kobelski.
Lib Type Academic.
Spec Subs Military & naval science; history; international relations; political science; management.
Info Ret Servs DIALOG; DROLS; WILSONLINE. *Shared Catalog Nets* OCLC. *Coop Lib Nets* FEDLINK.
Circ Servs Avail To other Federal libraries; to other libraries; not open to the general public; restricted to military.
Ref Servs Avail To other Federal libraries; to other libraries; not open to the general public; restricted to military; others by special permission.

1254. Armed Services Board of Contract Appeals, Law Library
200 Stovall St, Alexandria, VA 22332 (703) 325-9180; AUTOVON 221-9180
Admin John Lane (Admin Judge). *Ref Lib* Beverly Davis (ILL, Acq).
Lib Type Law.
Spec Subs Government contracts. *In-house Files* Historical decisions of ASBCA & WDBCA; historical superseded Armed Services procurement regulations.
Ref Servs Avail To other Federal libraries; to other libraries; to the general public.

1255. Army & Air Force Exchange Service, Law Library
919 Ala Moana, Honolulu, HI 96814 (808) 533-8421
Admin Evan Thomas.
Lib Type Law.
Spec Subs Government contracts.
Circ Servs Avail Not open to the general public.
Ref Servs Avail Not open to the general public.

1256. Defense Communications Agency, Technical & Management Information Center
Code H396, Washington, DC 20305-2000 (202) 692-2468; AUTOVON 222-2468
Admin Donald Guerriero. *Ref Lib* Margaret Martinez. *Acq Lib* Mary Jane Steele.
Lib Type Engineering & Science.
Spec Subs Telecommunications; computer science. *Spec Collecs* IEEE Proceedings.
Info Ret Servs DIALOG; BRS; SDC; DTIC; DMS. *Shared Catalog Nets* OCLC. *Elec Mail Nets* Infomail.
Circ Servs Avail Not open to the general public.
Ref Servs Avail Not open to the general public.

1257. Defense Communications Engineering Center, Information & Management Center
1860 Wiehle Ave, Reston, VA 22090-5500 (703) 437-2313; AUTOVON 364-2313
Admin Grace Aitel.
Lib Type Engineering & Science.
Info Ret Servs DIALOG; BRS. *Shared Catalog Nets* OCLC.
Circ Servs Avail To other Federal libraries; to other libraries; not open to the general public.

Ref Servs Avail To other Federal libraries; to other libraries; not open to the general public.

1258. Defense Depot, Memphis, Library
2163 Airways Blvd, Memphis, TN 38114-5297 (901) 744-5549; AUTOVON 683-4915
Admin Nancy M Denman.
Lib Type General.
Spec Subs Regulatory publications.
Ref Servs Avail Restricted to Defense Depot Memphis & tenant activities.

1259. Defense Equal Opportunity Management Institute Library
Bldg 560, Patrick AFB, FL 32925-6685 (305) 494-6881; AUTOVON 854-4917
Admin Merry V Cresswell. *Ref Lib* Diane Petitpas. *ILL* Connie Morrison.
Lib Type Training Center.
Spec Subs Social sciences & management; ethnic material. *Spec Collecs* Black Americans; Hispanic Americans; Native Americans; Asian Americans; women; equal opportunity; Jewish Americans. *In-house Files* Vertical files to support the above collections.
Info Ret Servs DIALOG. *Shared Catalog Nets* OCLC.
Circ Servs Avail To other Federal libraries; to other libraries; not open to the general public.
Ref Servs Avail To other Federal libraries; to other libraries; not open to the general public.

1260. Defense General Supply Center Library
Defense Logistics Agency, Bldg 34, Richmond, VA 23297-5000 (804) 275-3215; AUTOVON 695-3215
Admin Yvonne Oakley.
Lib Type General.
Spec Subs Management; economics; military science. *Spec Collecs* DoD, DLA, DGSC, OPM, & some Army, Air Force, & Navy regulations, handbooks, & manuals.
Info Ret Servs BRS. *Shared Catalog Nets* OCLC. *Coop Lib Nets* FEDLINK.
Circ Servs Avail To other Federal libraries; to other libraries.
Ref Servs Avail To other Federal libraries; to other libraries.

1261. Defense Industrial Supply, Technical Data Repository
700 Robbins Ave, Philadelphia, PA 19111 (215) 697-2757
Lib Type Special.
Spec Subs Engineering data; industrial hardware.

1262. Defense Institute of Security Assistance Management Library
Bldg 125, Area B, Wright-Patterson AFB, OH 45433 (513) 255-5567; AUTOVON 785-5567
Admin Theresa J Knasiak. *ILL* Michael Sizemore. *Acq Lib* Alta O'Brien.
Lib Type Training Center.
Spec Subs Foreign military sales; area studies; terrorism; human rights.
Info Ret Servs DIALOG. *Shared Catalog Nets* OCLC. *Coop Lib Nets* FEDLINK.
Circ Servs Avail To other libraries; restricted to assigned personnel.
Ref Servs Avail Restricted to assigned personnel.

1263. Defense Intelligence Agency Library
ATTN: RTS-2A, Washington, DC 20301-6111 (202) 373-3775; AUTOVON 243-3775
Admin William E Crislip. *Ref Lib* George Jupin. *ILL* Gwen Estep. *Acq Lib* Marie Hanrahan.
Lib Type Special.
Spec Subs Military affairs; area studies; foreign materials with geographic orientation.
Info Ret Servs DIALOG; SDC; NEXIS; DMS/ONLINE. *Shared Catalog Nets* OCLC.
Circ Servs Avail To other Federal libraries; to other libraries; not open to the general public; restricted to special arrangements.
Ref Servs Avail To other Federal libraries; to other libraries; not open to the general public; restricted to special arrangements.

1264. Defense Language English Language Center, Academic Library/FL 3046
DLIELC/LESSL, Lackland AFB, TX 78236-5000 (512) 671-2767; AUTOVON 473-2767
Admin Carol-Anne L Charbonneau. *ILL* Deborah A Hann.
Lib Type Training Center.
Spec Subs Teaching & learning English as a second language.
Circ Servs Avail To other libraries; restricted to DLIELC personnel.
Ref Servs Avail To other Federal libraries; to other libraries; to the general public.

1265. Defense Language Institute, Learning Resource Center
Presidio of Monterey, CA 93944-5001 (408) 647-8206
Admin Gary D Walter.
Lib Type Training Center.
Spec Subs Foreign language education.
Info Ret Servs DIALOG; BRS.
Circ Servs Avail To other Federal libraries; to other libraries.
Ref Servs Avail To other Federal libraries; to other libraries; to the general public.

1266. Defense Logistic Services Center, Learning Resources Center Library
Federal Center, 74 N Washington, Battle Creek, MI 49017-3084 (616) 962-6511 ext 6787; FTS 372-6787; AUTOVON 369-6787
Admin Anna K Winger.
Lib Type Special.
Spec Subs Management; data processing.
Info Ret Servs BRS. *Shared Catalog Nets* OCLC. *Coop Lib Nets* FEDLINK.
Circ Servs Avail To other Federal libraries; to other libraries; not open to the general public; restricted to employees.
Ref Servs Avail To other Federal libraries; to other libraries; to the general public.

1267. Defense Logistics Agency Headquarters Library
Cameron Station, Rm 4D120, Alexandria, VA 22304-6100 (703) 274-6055; AUTOVON 284-6056
Admin Barbara A Federline. *ILL* Barbara A Sable.
Lib Type Special.
Spec Subs Management; data processing; economics; military regulatory publications; military specifications & standards. *Spec Collecs* Industry standards; military specifications & standards.
Info Ret Servs DIALOG; BRS; SDC; OCLC; HAYSTACK; LEGISLATE; WESTLAW. *Shared Catalog Nets* OCLC.
Circ Servs Avail To other Federal libraries; to other libraries; restricted to general public by appointment.
Ref Servs Avail To other Federal libraries; to other libraries; restricted to general public by appointment.

1268. Defense Mapping Agency, Aerospace Center Technical Library
3200 S 2nd St, Saint Louis, MO 63118-3399 (314) 263-4268; AUTOVON 693-4268
Admin James W Tancock. *Ref Lib* Peggy Mechanic. *ILL* Bruce Brooks. *Acq Lib* Louise Hildenbrand.
Lib Type Special.
Spec Subs Mapping; charting; geodesy.
Info Ret Servs DIALOG; DTIC.
Circ Servs Avail To other Federal libraries; to other libraries; not open to the general public.
Ref Servs Avail To other Federal libraries; to other libraries; not open to the general public.

1269. Defense Mapping Agency, Hydrographic/Topographic Center Library
Washington, DC 20315-0030 (202) 227-2108; AUTOVON 287-2108
Admin New Rucker (Branch Chief). *Ref Lib* Lois Beauchamp (Inquiries).
Lib Type Special.
Spec Subs Geodetic & trigonometric record books.
Circ Servs Avail Not open to the general public; restricted to ILL.
Ref Servs Avail To the general public; restricted to limited telephone inquiries.

1270. Defense Nuclear Agency, National Naval Medical Center Library
Armed Forces Radiobiology Research Institute, Bldg 42, Bethesda, MD 20814 (301) 295-0428
Lib Type Health & Medicine.
Spec Subs Biomedical effects of radiation.
Info Ret Servs BRS. *Shared Catalog Nets* OCLC.
Circ Servs Avail To other Federal libraries; to other libraries.
Ref Servs Avail To other Federal libraries; to other libraries.

1271. Defense Nuclear Agency, Technical Library Services
Hybla Valley Federal Bldg, 6801 Telegraph Rd, Alexandria, VA 20305 (202) 325-7780
Lib Type Special.
Spec Subs Nuclear weapons effects.
Circ Servs Avail Not open to the general public.
Ref Servs Avail Not open to the general public.

1272. Defense Personnel Support Center, Directorate of Medical Material Library
Bldg 9-3-F, 2800 S 20th St, Philadelphia, PA 19101 (215) 952-2110; Reference 952-5270; ILL 952-2110
Admin Gerald J. Ziccardi.
Lib Type Health & Medicine.
Spec Subs Biology; chemistry; engineering; mathematics; medicine; physics; pharmacy. *Spec Collecs* Pharmacy - Continuing Education Program for Pharmacists from the College of Philadelphia; Information Handling Services; ASTM standards; government reports, announcements & index.
Info Ret Servs DTIC; MEDLINE.
Circ Servs Avail Not open to the general public.
Ref Servs Avail Not open to the general public; restricted to center employees.

1273. Defense Personnel Support Center Library
Philadelphia, PA 19105 (215) 952-3702
Admin Paul R Kesler.
Lib Type Special.
Spec Subs Military, also reference & general interest. *Spec Collecs* Regulations, manuals, handbooks, selected newsletters & bulletins for DPSC, DLA, DoD, & Armed Forces.
Circ Servs Avail Not open to the general public; restricted to DPSC personnel.
Ref Servs Avail Not open to the general public; restricted to DPSC personnel.

1274. Defense Systems Management College, Library
Fort Belvoir, VA 22060 (703) 664-2732; AUTOVON 354-2732
Lib Type Academic.

1275. Defense Technical Information Center, Technical Library
Cameron Station, Bldg 5, Alexandria, VA 22030 (202) 274-6833; AUTOVON 284-6833
Lib Type Special.
Spec Subs Computer; armaments.
Info Ret Servs DIALOG; BRS; SDC; OCLC. *Shared Catalog Nets* OCLC.
Circ Servs Avail To other Federal libraries; not open to the general public.
Ref Servs Avail To other Federal libraries; not open to the general public.

1276. Department of Defense Computer Institute, Technical Library
Bldg 175 Rm 37, Washington Navy Yard, Washington, DC 20374 (202) 433-3653; AUTOVON 288-3653
Admin Johnsie A Smalls.
Lib Type Training Center.
Spec Subs Computer hardware, software, & management concerns. *Spec Collecs* DataPro; Auerbach.
Circ Servs Avail Restricted to faculty & students of the institute.
Ref Servs Avail Restricted to faculty & students of the institute.

1277. Directorate of Medical Materiel Library
Defense Personnel Support Center, Bldg 9-3-F, 2800 S 20th St, Philadelphia, PA 19101 (215) 952-2110; AUTOVON 444-2110
Admin Gerald J Ziccardi.
Lib Type Health & Medicine; Engineering & Science.
Spec Subs Chemistry; medicine; pharmacy; physics; engineering. *Spec Collecs* Microfilm of military & federal specifications & ASTM standards. *In-house Files* Over 1,500 catalogs & pamphlets from manufacturers of medical, pharmaceutical, diagnostic, surgical, dental, & instrument products.
Coop Lib Nets FEDLINK.
Circ Servs Avail Not open to the general public; restricted to agency employees.
Ref Servs Avail Not open to the general public; restricted to agency employees.

1278. National Defense University Library
Fort Lesley J McNair, 4th & P Sts SW, Washington, DC 20319-6000 (202) 475-1905; ILL 475-1622
Admin J Thomas Russell.
Lib Type Academic.
Spec Subs Diplomatic history; industrial mobilization; international relations; management of resources; military history & science; national security; political science. *Spec Collecs* Personal papers of generals Maxwell Taylor, Lyman L Lemnitzer, Andrew J Goodpaster, Paul D Adams, & George S Brown; libraries of Hoffman Nickerson (military history) & Admiral Arthur Radford; library & papers of Dr Ralph L Powell (China); speeches on industrial mobilization by J Carlton Ward Jr; correspondence of Bernard Baruch & Julius A Krug; early editions of Marshall de Saxe; local history, photographs & maps; academic & institutional archives, including Hudson Institute central files on microfiche.
Info Ret Servs DIALOG; BRS; SDC; LEXIS; NEXIS; Congressional Quarterly; DTIC. *Shared Catalog Nets* OCLC. *Coop Lib Nets* FEDLINK; Research Libraries Information Network.

1279. National Security Agency, Central Security Service Libraries
9800 Savage Rd, Fort George G Meade, MD 20755-6000 (301) 688-7581; AUTOVON 235-7581
Admin Kathleen S Arnett. *Ref Lib* Charlotte Byrom. *ILL* Lucille Cooper. *Acq Lib* Ida Clayton.
Lib Type Engineering & Science.
Spec Collecs Language collection.
Info Ret Servs DIALOG; LEXIS; NEXIS. *Shared Catalog Nets* OCLC.
Circ Servs Avail To other Federal libraries; to other libraries; not open to the general public; restricted to OCLC ILL members.
Ref Servs Avail To other Federal libraries; not open to the general public.

1280. Offices of the Surgeons General, US Army - US Air Force, Joint Medical Library
Rm 1B-473, The Pentagon, Washington, DC 20310 (202) 695-5752
Admin Donna Griffiths.
Lib Type Health & Medicine.

1281. Still Media Records Center
Dept of Defense, Washington, DC 20374 (202) 433-2166; AUTOVON 288-2166
Admin Mr Rusnak (Depository Operations).
Lib Type Special.
Spec Collecs Still photographic media for all DoD services. *In-house Files* Ready access - current high use photography.
Circ Servs Avail To other Federal libraries; not open to the general public.
Ref Servs Avail To other Federal libraries; to other libraries; to the general public.

1282. Uniformed Services University of the Health Services, Learning Resource Center
4301 Jones Bridge Rd, Bethesda, MD 20814-4799 (301) 295-3356
Admin Chester J Pletzke. *Ref Lib* Judith Torrence. *Acq Lib* Janice Muller (Tech Svcs).
Lib Type Academic; Health & Medicine.

Spec Subs Medicine. *Spec Collecs* Military medicine.
Lib Deposit Designation GPO Depository Library.
Info Ret Servs Over 200 commercial data base files available. *Shared Catalog Nets* OCLC. *Coop Lib Nets* NLM/RML Program; Metropolitan Washington Library Council.
Circ Servs Avail Restricted to university personnel.
Ref Servs Avail Restricted to university personnel.

1283. US Army & Air Force Exchange Service, Central Library

3911 S Walton Walker Blvd, Dallas, TX 75236-1598 (214) 780-2011
Lib Type Special.
Spec Subs Data systems; engineering; military regulations; personnel; transportation.

1284. US Army Intelligence School Library

USAISD, ATTN: ATSI-ETD-L (Lib), Fort Devens, MA 01433-6301 (617) 796-3413; AUTOVON 256-3413
Admin Ornella L Pensyl. *Ref Lib* Susan Wawrzaszek (ILL).
Lib Type Training Center.
Spec Subs Education; electronics; computer science; current affairs; military intelligence; military science. *Spec Collecs* Electronic warfare.
Info Ret Servs DIALOG; BRS; DTIC. *Shared Catalog Nets* OCLC. *Coop Lib Nets* TRADOC Library & Information Network (TRALINET). *Elec Mail Nets* OPTIMUS.
Circ Servs Avail To other Federal libraries; to other libraries; not open to the general public; restricted to need to know.
Ref Servs Avail To other Federal libraries; to other libraries; not open to the general public; restricted to need to know.

DEPARTMENT OF EDUCATION

Departmental

1285. Gallaudet University Library
7th St & Florida Ave, NE, Washington, DC 20002 (202) 651-5566
(voice or TDD); 651-5585 (Reference/ILL); 651-5575 (TDD)
Lib Type Special.
Spec Subs Deafness; remedial speech & hearing; education of the
deaf.
Circ Servs Avail Not open to the general public; restricted to
Gallaudet College patrons & eligible consortium of universities
of the Washington metro area.
Ref Servs Avail Not open to the general public; restricted to
faculty, staff, & students; consortium; on site public use.

**1286. US Department of Education, Office of Educational
Research & Improvement Library**
555 New Jersey Ave, NW, Washington, DC 20208 (202) 357-6273;
357-6275 (ILL); 357-6260 (ACQ)
Admin Milbrey L Jones. *Ref Lib* John Blake. *ILL* Francine
O'Neil. *Acq Lib* Jo Ann Cassell.

Lib Type Special.
Spec Subs Federal role in education; educational statistics; history
of US education; library & information science; management;
psychology; elementary & secondary education. *Spec
Collecs* ERIC (Educational Resources Information Center); US
Office of Education & National Institute of Education Archives
(1976), microform; National Institute of Education Reports;
Rare Books Collection; Early American Textbook Collection;
20th Century American Textbook; US Office of Education,
1870-present; State Education Annual Reports (historical);
Newsbank, microform; William S Gray Reading Collection,
microform; Education Material Center Collection.
Info Ret Servs DIALOG. *Shared Catalog Nets* OCLC. *Coop Lib
Nets* FEDLINK.
Circ Servs Avail Not open to the general public; restricted to staff.
Ref Servs Avail To the general public; restricted to on site.

DEPARTMENT OF ENERGY

Departmental

1287. Alaska Power Administration Library
Box 50, 709 W 9th St, Juneau, AK 99802 (907) 586-7405
Lib Type Special.
Spec Subs Power related subjects. *Spec Collecs* Dept of Energy publications.

1288. Argonne National Laboratory, Argonne-West, Technical Library
PO Box 2528, Idaho Falls, ID 83403-2528 (208) 526-7237; FTS 583-7237
Lib Type Engineering & Science.
Spec Subs LMFBR technology; metallurgy; nuclear science & engineering.
Info Ret Servs DIALOG; DOE/Recon. *Shared Catalog Nets* OCLC. *Elec Mail Nets* Class.

1289. Argonne National Laboratory, Technical Information Services Department
Bldg 203 Rm C110, 9700 S Cass Ave, Argonne, IL 60439 (312) 972-4221; FTS 972-4221
Admin Hillis L Griffin. *ILL* Yvette Woell. *Acq Lib* Melissa Gregory.
Lib Type Engineering & Science.
Spec Subs Materials science; physics; chemistry; nuclear science & engineering. *Spec Collecs* AEC/ERDA/DOE scientific & technical reports.
Info Ret Servs DIALOG; BRS; SDC; DOE RECON. *Coop Lib Nets* Suburban Library System. *Elec Mail Nets* ALANET.
Circ Servs Avail To other libraries.
Ref Servs Avail To other libraries.

1290. Basalt Waste Isolation Project Library
Rockwell Hanford Operations, Richland, WA 99352 (509) 376-6898; FTS 444-6898
Admin Betty E King.
Lib Type Engineering & Science.
Spec Subs High level nuclear waste; geology; hydrology; rock mechanics; engineering. *In-house Files* Rockwell Hanford Operations documents.
Coop Lib Nets Battelle Hanford Technical Library.
Circ Servs Avail Not open to the general public; restricted to RHO & DOE.
Ref Servs Avail To other Federal libraries.

1291. Bonneville Power Administration Library
Attn: Library SSL, PO Box 3621, Portland, OR 97208 (503) 230-4171; FTS 429-4171
Admin Karen Hadman. *Ref Lib* Monte Gittings. *ILL* Florence S Simonton. *Acq Lib* Linda L Kuriger.
Lib Type Special.
Spec Subs Law; electrical engineering; energy management & conservation. *Spec Collecs* Solar & conservation material from the Western Solar Utilization Network Library (now defunct). *In-house Files* Online cataloging file; online laboratory report file.
Lib Deposit Designation GPO Depository Library.
Info Ret Servs DIALOG; BRS; SDC; MEDLARS; DOE/RECON; LEXIS.
Circ Servs Avail To other Federal libraries; to other libraries.
Ref Servs Avail To other Federal libraries; to other libraries; to the general public.

1292. Brookhaven National Laboratory, Nuclear Safeguards Library
Bldg 197C, Upton, NY 11973 (516) 282-2909; FTS 666-2909
Admin Donna M Albertus. *ILL* Kathryn J Lancaster.
Lib Type Special.
Spec Subs Nuclear safeguards; nuclear nonproliferation; arms control. *Spec Collecs* Documents of the International Atomic Energy Agency (IAEA); technical reports. *In-house Files* In-house online data base of library holdings.
Info Ret Servs DIALOG; BRS; SDC; DOE/RECON; DTIC/DROLS; LEXIS; NEXIS; VU/TEXT. *Shared Catalog Nets* OCLC.
Circ Servs Avail Not open to the general public.
Ref Servs Avail Not open to the general public.

1293. Brookhaven National Laboratory, Research Library
Bldg 477A, Upton, NY 11973 (516) 282-3485; FTS 666-3485
Admin Marilyn C Galli. *ILL* Carol Beckner. *Acq Lib* Doris Alkes.
Lib Type Special.
Spec Subs Physics: including high energy, theoretical & nuclear; chemistry: nuclear, inorganic, radiation; biology: genetics, molecular, ecology, biophysics; applied science: nuclear engineering, reactor physics; environmental science; energy; mathematics. *Spec Collecs* US Department of Energy Technical Reports.
Info Ret Servs DIALOG; BRS; SDC; DOE/RECON; C A; CSIN; WILSONLINE; SPIRES; STN. *Shared Catalog Nets* OCLC; RLIN. *Coop Lib Nets* Long Island Library Resources Council (LILRC).
Circ Servs Avail To other libraries; not open to the general public.
Ref Servs Avail Not open to the general public.

1294. Department of Energy, Grand Junction Area Office, Technical Library
PO Box 1569, Bendix Field Eng Corp, Grand Junction, CO 81502-1569 (303) 242-8621 ext 278; FTS 322-9278
Lib Type Special.
Spec Subs Chemistry; geology; geophysics; mining; physics; uranium. *Spec Collecs* US Geological Survey publications.

1295. Department of Energy, Office of General Counsel, Law Library
Rm 6A-156, 1000 Independence Ave SW, Washington, DC 20585 (202) 586-4848
Admin Oscar E Strothus. *Ref Lib* Paula Lipman (ILL, Acq).
Lib Type Law.
Spec Subs Administrative law; energy & environmental law; contracts; bankruptcy; federal procedure. *Spec Collecs* Videotapes on evidence & trial practice.
Info Ret Servs LEXIS; WESTLAW; JURIS. *Shared Catalog Nets* OCLC.
Circ Servs Avail To other Federal libraries.
Ref Servs Avail To other Federal libraries; to other libraries; to the general public.

1296. Department of Energy, Solar Research Institute, Technical Library
1617 Cole Blvd, Golden, CO 80401 (303) 231-1415; FTS 327-1415
Lib Type Engineering & Science.

Spec Subs Biomass; ocean thermal energy; materials science; photobiology; photovoltaics; solar energy; solid-state physics; wind energy. *Spec Collecs* Management Training & Development.
Info Ret Servs DIALOG; BRS; DOE/Recon; SDC Information Service. *Shared Catalog Nets* OCLC. *Coop Lib Nets* FEDLINK; Central Colorado Library Service System.
Circ Servs Avail Not open to the general public; restricted to employees.
Ref Servs Avail Not open to the general public; restricted to employees - others by appointment.

1297. Energy Information Center
San Francisco Operations Office, 1333 Broadway, Oakland, CA 94612 (415) 273-4428; FTS 536-4428
Admin Norma A Del Gaudio.
Lib Type Special.
Spec Subs Energy. *Spec Collecs* Energy research abstracts; Energy Information Administration (EIA) Reports.
Info Ret Servs RECON (US DOE), one sample search per requester.
Circ Servs Avail To other Federal libraries; to other libraries; to the general public.
Ref Servs Avail To other Federal libraries; to other libraries; to the general public.

1298. Energy Library
Forrestal Bldg, Washington, DC 20585 (202) 586-9534; FTS 586-9534
Admin Denise B Diggin.
Lib Type Engineering & Science.
Spec Subs Energy sources, statistics, resources, alternatives, & technology; environment. *Spec Collecs* International Atomic Energy Agency (IAEA) publications; Joint Committee on Atomic Energy (JCAE) legislation.
Lib Deposit Designation Department of Energy.
Info Ret Servs DIALOG; BRS; SDC; QUESTEL; NEXIS; LEXIS; NASA/RECON; NEDRES (NOAA); TEXTLINE; Dow Jones; Chase Econometrics. *Shared Catalog Nets* OCLC; RLIN. *Coop Lib Nets* FLICC/FEDLINK. *Elec Mail Nets* ITT DIALCOM.
Circ Servs Avail To other Federal libraries; to other libraries; not open to the general public; restricted to ILL.
Ref Servs Avail To other Federal libraries; to other libraries; restricted to the general public by telephone.

1299. The Energy Library, Germantown Branch
Dept of Energy, Washington, DC 20545 (301) 353-4301; FTS 233-4301
Admin Denise Diggin.
Lib Type Special.
Spec Subs Nuclear energy; fossil fuels; energy research; environmental protection; safety; emergency preparedness.

1300. Environmental Measurements Laboratory Library
376 Hudson St, New York, NY 10014 (212) 620-3606; FTS 660-3606
Admin Rita D Rosen.
Lib Type Engineering & Science.
Spec Subs Physics; chemistry; environmental & electronic engineering.
Info Ret Servs DIALOG.
Circ Servs Avail To other Federal libraries; not open to the general public.
Ref Servs Avail To other Federal libraries; not open to the general public.

1301. Fermi National Accelerator Laboratory Library
(Fermilab Library) PO Box 500, Batavia, IL 60510-5000 (312) 840-3401; FTS 370-3401
Admin May West (Acting).
Lib Type Engineering & Science.
Spec Subs High energy physics.
Info Ret Servs DIALOG. *Shared Catalog Nets* OCLC. *Coop Lib Nets* DuPage Library System (DLS).
Circ Servs Avail Not open to the general public.
Ref Servs Avail To other libraries; to the general public.

1302. Institute for Energy Analysis Library
Oak Ridge Associated Universities, PO Box 117, Oak Ridge, TN 37831 (615) 576-3199/3192; FTS 626-3199/3192
Admin J Louise Markel.
Lib Type Special.
Spec Subs Research & interests in energy policy area.
Info Ret Servs DOE/RECON.
Circ Servs Avail To other libraries; not open to the general public; restricted to IEA personnel.
Ref Servs Avail Not open to the general public; restricted to IEA personnel.

1303. Los Alamos National Laboratory Libraries
MS-P362, Box 1663, Los Alamos, NM 87545-0020 (505) 667-4448; ILL 667-4175; FTS 843-4448
Lib Type Engineering & Science.
Spec Subs Energy; engineering; physical & biomedical sciences; military & peaceful uses of nuclear energy.
Info Ret Servs DIALOG; BRS; SDC; DOE/Recon; MEDLINE; NEXIS; NASA. *Shared Catalog Nets* RLIN. *Coop Lib Nets* New Mexico Information Systems.
Ref Servs Avail To the general public; restricted to limited hours.

1304. Los Alamos National Laboratory, Medical Library
MS-M884, Box 1663, Los Alamos, NM 87545 (505) 667-2762
Lib Type Health & Medicine.
Spec Subs Biology; medicine.

1305. Manpower, Education, Research, & Training (MERT) Division Library
Oak Ridge Associated Universities, PO Box 117, Rm E-1, Bldg 2714-F, 246 Laboratory Rd, Oak Ridge, TN 37831 (615) 576-3408; FTS 626-3408
Admin Harry T Burn; Celeste Phillips (Asst).
Lib Type Special.
Spec Subs Energy education; manpower education; research & training.
Info Ret Servs DIALOG; DOE/RECON; OCLC; BRS; DROLS.
Circ Servs Avail To other libraries.

1306. Medical & Health Sciences Division Library
Oak Ridge Associated Universities, PO Box 117, Oak Ridge, TN 37831 (615) 576-3490; FTS 626-3490
Admin Rana Yalcintas (Head Librarian); Bonnie Couch (Asst).
Lib Type Health & Medicine.
Spec Subs Biochemistry; nuclear medicine; occupational & environmental medicine; radiation biology.
Info Ret Servs MEDLARS.
Circ Servs Avail To other libraries.
Ref Servs Avail Not open to the general public; restricted to researchers on site.

1307. Morgantown Energy Technology Center
PO Box 880, Morgantown, WV 26505 (304) 291-4183; FTS 923-7183
Lib Type Special.
Spec Subs Chemistry; fossil fuels; geology; petroleum. *Spec Collecs* US Bureau of Mines: reports of investigations, information circulars, & open file reports; US Dept of Energy fossil energy reports.
Info Ret Servs DIALOG; SDC; DOE/Recon.

1308. National Atomic Museum Library
PO Box 5400, Public Document Rm, Albuquerque, NM 87115 (505) 844-4378; FTS 844-4378; AUTOVON 244-4225
Admin Loretta Helling.
Lib Type Special.
Spec Subs Manhattan Project; nuclear weapons history; World War II; energy. *Spec Collecs* Waste Isolation Pilot Plant (WIPP) & Uranium Mill Tailings Remedial Action (UMTRA) public documents.
Info Ret Servs DOE/RECON.
Circ Servs Avail To other Federal libraries; to other libraries; to the general public.
Ref Servs Avail To other Federal libraries; not open to the general public.

1309. National Atomic Museum Library, Public Document Room
PO Box 5400, Albuquerque, NM 87115 (505) 844-4378; FTS 844-4378
Admin Loretta Helling.
Lib Type Special.
Spec Subs Nuclear weapons history, World War II; energy. *Spec Collecs* Waste Isolation Pilot Plant (WIPP) documents; Uranium Mill Tailings Remedial Action (UMTRA) documents.
Lib Deposit Designation GPO Depository Library.
Info Ret Servs DOE/RECON.
Circ Servs Avail To other Federal libraries; to other libraries; to the general public.
Ref Servs Avail To other Federal libraries; to other libraries; to the general public.

1310. National Institute for Petroleum & Energy Research Library
PO Box 2128, 220 NW Virginia Ave, Bartlesville, OK 74005 (918) 336-2400, ext 371; FTS 745-4371
Admin Josh H Stroman. *ILL* Bonnie Mitchell. *Acq Lib* Mildred R Marak.
Lib Type Special.
Spec Subs Liquid fossil fuels research & development; enhanced oil & gas recovery; fuel chemistry; thermodynamics; surface chemistry.
Lib Deposit Designation US Bureau of Mines; US Department of Energy.
Info Ret Servs DIALOG; SDC; DOE/RECON. *Shared Catalog Nets* OCLC. *Coop Lib Nets* FEDLINK.
Circ Servs Avail Not open to the general public; restricted to staff.
Ref Servs Avail Not open to the general public; restricted to staff.

1311. Nevada Technical Library, Department of Energy
PO Box 14100, Las Vegas, NV 89114 (702) 295-1274; FTS 575-1274
Admin Cynthia Ortiz.
Lib Type Special.
Spec Subs Nuclear explosives; radiation bioenvironmental effects; radioactive waste storage; geology; hydrology; alternate energy sources. *Spec Collecs* Peaceful uses of nuclear explosions.
Info Ret Servs DIALOG; DOE/RECON; LEXIS; NEXIS. *Coop Lib Nets* Nevada Union List of Serials (NULS).
Circ Servs Avail To other Federal libraries; to other libraries; restricted to DOE & contractor staff & ILL to general public.
Ref Servs Avail To other Federal libraries; to other libraries; restricted to prior appointment for general public with proper clearance.

1312. Office of Chief Counsel Legal Law Library, Savannah River Operations Office
Aiken, SC 29802 (803) 725-2497; FTS 239-2497
Admin Jacqueline Jones. *ILL* Pat Albertson (Acq).
Lib Type Law.
Spec Subs Environmental issues; contracts; security.
Info Ret Servs LEXIS; NEXIS.
Circ Servs Avail Not open to the general public; restricted to Savannah River Plant.
Ref Servs Avail Not open to the general public; restricted to Savannah River Plant.

1313. Sandia National Laboratories, Technical Library
Department of Energy, PO Box 969, Livermore, CA 94550 (415) 422-3035; ILL 422-2526 ; FTS 532-3053
Lib Type Special.
Spec Subs Chemistry; engineering; mathematics; metallurgy; nuclear science; physics.
Info Ret Servs DIALOG; DOE/RECON.

1314. Sandia National Laboratories, Technical Library
PO Box 5800, org 3140, Albuquerque, NM 87185 (505) 844-2869; FTS 844-2869
Admin Doug E Robertson. *Ref Lib* George R Dalphin (ILL). *Acq Lib* Sally A Landenberger.
Lib Type Engineering & Science.
Spec Subs Nuclear weapons; nuclear waste management; nuclear safety & security; electronics; explosives; materials; aerodynamics; solid-state physics; ordnance; energy research.
Info Ret Servs DIALOG; SDC; Pergamon; STN; NEXIS; DOE/RECON; DROLS; NASA/RECON. *Shared Catalog Nets* RLIN.
Circ Servs Avail Restricted to employees & DOE/Albuquerque.
Ref Servs Avail Restricted to employees & DOE/Albuquerque.

1315. Southeastern Power Administration Library
Samuel Elbert Bldg, Elberton, GA 30635 (404) 283-9911
Admin Lucille E Wells (Lib Tech Div); Karl E Tucker (Div Adm Mgmt, Tech Div); Denver L Rampey, Jr (Gen Counsel, Legal Div).
Lib Type Special.
Spec Subs Energy: power marketing, federal guidelines, hydroelectric power production, & budgetary information. *Spec Collecs* Technical division: Senate & House hearings, energy & water development appropriations; public papers of the presidents; presidential documents; budget of the US; development of water resources, TVA, Appalachia, etc; Legal division: US Code; code of federal regulations; West Federal Practice Digest; US Supreme Court Report; Government Contracts Reporter; opinions of the attorney general & comptroller general; Modern Federal Practice Digest; US Code Congressional & Administrative News; Federal Reporter; Federal Supplement.
Circ Servs Avail Restricted to SEPA employees & local attorneys.
Ref Servs Avail Restricted to SEPA employees & local attorneys.

1316. Southwestern Power Administration Library
PO Box 1619, Tulsa, OK 74101 (918) 581-7454; FTS 745-7454
Admin Elizabeth B Mohr. *Ref Lib* Brian Martin.
Lib Type Special.
Spec Subs Hydroelectric power marketing & transmission; public power.
Coop Lib Nets Tulsa Area Library Cooperative (TALC).
Circ Servs Avail To other Federal libraries; to other libraries.
Ref Servs Avail To other Federal libraries; to other libraries; to the general public.

1317. Western Area Power Administration, Office of General Counsel, Law Library
ATTN: A0200, PO Box 3402, Golden, CO 80401 (303) 231-1534; FTS 327-1534
Admin Susan I DeBelle. *ILL* Sandra L Parker (ILL, Acq).
Lib Type Law.
Spec Subs Reclamation law. *Spec Collecs* Hoover Dam documents; government procurement law. *In-house Files* Hoover Dam documents.
Info Ret Servs WESTLAW; Legislate.
Circ Servs Avail To other Federal libraries; not open to the general public.
Ref Servs Avail To other Federal libraries; to other libraries; not open to the general public.

Federal Energy Regulatory Commission

1318. Federal Energy Regulatory Commission Library
825 N Capitol St NE, Rm 8502, Washington, DC 20427 (202) 357-5479; FTS 357-5479
Admin Robert F Kimberlin, III. *Ref Lib* Robert W Harvie. *ILL* Lottie L Davis. *Acq Lib* Audrey R Lawson.
Lib Type General.
Spec Subs Law. *Spec Collecs* Studies on rivers; legislative histories on the Federal Water Power Act, Natural Gas Act, etc.
Lib Deposit Designation GPO Depository Library.
Info Ret Servs DIALOG; LEXIS; NEXIS; JURIS; WESTLAW.
Circ Servs Avail Restricted to interlibrary loan.
Ref Servs Avail To other Federal libraries; to other libraries; to the general public.

1319. Federal Energy Regulatory Commission Library
730 Peachtree St NE, Rm 800, Atlanta, GA 30308 (404) 881-4134; FTS 257-4134
Admin Aarne O Kauranen (Regional Dir).
Lib Type Engineering & Science.
Spec Subs FERC regulations.
Ref Servs Avail To other Federal libraries; to the general public.

DEPARTMENT OF HEALTH AND HUMAN SERVICES

Departmental

1320. Health & Human Services Department Library
330 Independence Ave SW, Rm G 600, Washington, DC 20201
  (202) 472-6575
Admin John R Boyle. *Ref Lib* Daniel Beam (ILL). *Acq Lib* Martha Collins.
Lib Type Health & Medicine; Law.
Spec Subs Social insurance; family & welfare; law & legislation; economic & social statistics. *Spec Collecs* DHHS archives; law; census; Office of Community Services; HHS Program Collection.
Lib Deposit Designation GPO Depository Library.
Info Ret Servs DIALOG; BRS; WILSONLINE; DHHS ONLINE CATALOG; WESTLAW; LEGI-SLATE; LEXIS; NEXIS; OCLC. *Shared Catalog Nets* OCLC. *Coop Lib Nets* FEDLINK.
Circ Servs Avail To other Federal libraries; to other libraries.
Ref Servs Avail To other Federal libraries; to other libraries; restricted to HHS programs & referrals.

Agency for Toxic Substances & Disease Registry

1321. Agency for Toxic Substances & Disease Registry Library
1600 Clifton Rd, NE, Atlanta, GA 30333 (404) 329-3291; FTS 236-3291
Lib Type Health & Medicine.

Alcohol, Drug Abuse, & Mental Health Administration

1322. National Institute of Mental Health Library, Division of Intramural Research Programs
Rm 115, Wm A White Bldg, St. Elizabeth's Hospital, 2700 Martin Luther King Ave SE, Washington, DC 20032 (202) 373-7575
Admin LaVerne Corum. *Ref Lib* Dera Tompkins (ILL).
Lib Type Health & Medicine.
Spec Subs Pharmacology; neuropharmacology; neuropsychopharmacology; neurology; neuroscience; psychopharmacology; neurochemistry; neuropsychiatry; biochemistry & psychiatry. *In-house Files* Vertical file: compilation of published scientific & medical articles by present & past division researchers.
Info Ret Servs DIALOG; NLM-Medline. *Coop Lib Nets* Federal Medline Center; Medlars Region IV; NLM.
Circ Servs Avail To other Federal libraries; to other libraries; to the general public.
Ref Servs Avail To other Federal libraries; to other libraries; to the general public.

1323. St Elizabeth's Hospital, Circulating Library
2700 Martin Luther King Jr Ave, Washington, DC 20032 (202) 373-7668
Lib Type General.
Spec Subs Alcoholism; bibliotherapy; bibliotherapy training programs; Black studies.

Circ Servs Avail Not open to the general public; restricted to staff.
Ref Servs Avail Not open to the general public; restricted to patients & staff.

1324. St Elizabeth's Hospital, Health Sciences Library
2700 Martin Luther King Ave, SE, Washington, DC 20032
  (202) 373-7175 373-7274
Admin Toby Port. *ILL* Marcella Fludd.
Lib Type Health & Medicine; Hospital (Patients).
Spec Subs Psychiatry; social work; psychology. *Spec Collecs* William Alanson White Collection.
Info Ret Servs Medline. *Coop Lib Nets* DUCHSIN; COG Hospital Council.
Circ Servs Avail To other Federal libraries; to other libraries.
Ref Servs Avail To other Federal libraries; to other libraries; restricted to interested professionals.

Centers for Disease Control

1325. Appalachian Laboratory for Occupational Safety & Health Library
National Institute for Occupational Safety & Health (NIOSH), 944 Chestnut Ridge Rd, Morgantown, WV 26505 (304) 291-4416; FTS 923-4416
Admin Colleen M Herrington. *ILL* Elizabeth DiGiustino.
Lib Type Health & Medicine.
Spec Subs Occupational lung diseases; workplace safety. *Spec Collecs* NIOSHTIC microfiche; CIS microfiche; NIOSH publications.
Lib Deposit Designation International Labor Office. International Occupational Safety & Health Information Centre. CIS microfiche collection.
Info Ret Servs DIALOG; BRS; SDC; Infoline. *Shared Catalog Nets* OCLC. *Coop Lib Nets* FEDLINK.
Circ Servs Avail To other libraries.
Ref Servs Avail To the general public.

1326. Centers for Disease Control, Chamblee Branch Library
Chamblee, GA 30333 (404) 452-4167
Lib Type Health & Medicine.

1327. Centers for Disease Control Library
1600 Clifton Rd NE, Atlanta, GA 30333 (404) 329-3396; FTS 236-3396
Admin Mary Alice Mills. *Ref Lib* Jan Stansell (ILL). *Acq Lib* Carole Dean.
Lib Type Health & Medicine.
Spec Subs Communicable diseases; epidemiology; public health; preventive medicine; laboratory medicine; microbiology; bacteriology; virology. *Spec Collecs* Public Health Service publications; CDC theses.
Info Ret Servs DIALOG; BRS. *Shared Catalog Nets* OCLC.
Circ Servs Avail To other Federal libraries; to other libraries.
Ref Servs Avail To other Federal libraries; to other libraries; to the general public.

1328. National Institute for Occupational Safety & Health Library
Taft Center C-21, 4676 Columbia Pkwy, Cincinnati, OH 45226 (513) 533-8321; FTS 684-8321
Admin Vivian Kay Morgan.
Lib Type Health & Medicine; Engineering & Science.
Shared Catalog Nets OCLC. *Coop Lib Nets* FEDLINK.
Circ Servs Avail To other Federal libraries; to other libraries.
Ref Servs Avail To other Federal libraries; to other libraries.

Food & Drug Administration

1329. Bureau of Radiological Health Library
US Public Health Service, Rm 408-T, 12720 Twinbrook Pkwy, Rockville, MD 20857 (301) 443-1038
Lib Type Health & Medicine.
Spec Subs Medical radiology; radiobiology; radiography; radiation; public health affects of radiation; microwaves; lasers.
Circ Servs Avail To other Federal libraries; to other libraries; not open to the general public.
Ref Servs Avail To other Federal libraries; to other libraries; not open to the general public; restricted to qualified researchers.

1330. Center for Devices & Radiological Health Library
HFZ-43, 12720 Twinbrook Pkwy, T-408, Rockville, MD 20857 (301) 443-1038
Admin Clarence F Smith. *Ref Lib* Daniel Larrick. *ILL* Pauline Bell.
Lib Type Health & Medicine.
Spec Subs Radiation; radiological health; nuclear medicine.
Info Ret Servs DIALOG; NLM. *Shared Catalog Nets* OCLC.
Ref Servs Avail To other Federal libraries; to other libraries.

1331. Center for Devices & Radiological Health Library
HFZ-46, 8757 Georgia Ave, Silver Spring, MD 20910 (301) 427-7755
Admin Harriet Albersheim.
Lib Type Health & Medicine.
Spec Subs Medicine; medical devices; biomaterials; bioengineering.
Spec Collecs Medical devices & in vitro diagnostic manufacturers' catalogs on microfilm.
Info Ret Servs DIALOG; NLM. *Shared Catalog Nets* OCLC. *Coop Lib Nets* FEDLINK.
Circ Servs Avail To other Federal libraries; to other libraries.
Ref Servs Avail To other Federal libraries; to other libraries; to the general public.

1332. Center for Food Safety & Applied Nutrition Library
FDA, HFF-37, 200 C St SW, Washington, DC 20204 (202) 245-1235
Admin Michele R Chatfield. *Ref Lib* Lee Bernstein. *ILL* Hilda Foster.
Lib Type Health & Medicine; Engineering & Science.
Spec Subs Food technology; nutrition; chemistry; toxicology; biology.
Info Ret Servs DIALOG; BRS; SDC; NLM. *Shared Catalog Nets* OCLC. *Elec Mail Nets* CLASS.
Circ Servs Avail To other Federal libraries; to other libraries.
Ref Servs Avail To other Federal libraries; to other libraries; to the general public.

1333. Food & Drug Administration, Medical Library
Rm 11B-40/HFN-98, 5600 Fishers Ln, Rockville, MD 20857 (301) 443-3180
Admin Elizabeth C Kelley (Dir); Carol G Assouad (Deputy Dir).
Lib Type Health & Medicine.
Spec Subs Drugs; epidemiology; food & drug law; medical devices; pharmaceutical chemistry; pharmacy; toxicology; veterinary medicine. *Spec Collecs* Adverse drug effects.
Coop Lib Nets FEDLINK.
Circ Servs Avail Not open to the general public; restricted to government personnel.
Ref Servs Avail Not open to the general public; restricted to researchers.

1334. Food & Drug Administration, Bureau of Foods Library
1090 Tusculum Ave, Cincinnati, OH 45226 (513) 684-8639
Lib Type Special.

1335. Food & Drug Administration, Dallas District Library
3032 Bryan St, Dallas, TX 75204 (214) 767-0309
Lib Type Special.
Spec Subs Analytical chemistry; drugs; microbiology.

1336. Food & Drug Administration Library
1521 W Pico Blvd, Los Angeles, CA 90015 (213) 252-7582
Lib Type Special.
Spec Subs Science literature for support of lab analysis.
Circ Servs Avail Not open to the general public; restricted to staff.
Ref Servs Avail Not open to the general public; restricted to staff.

1337. National Center for Toxicological Research Library
Jefferson, AR 72079 (501) 541-4322; FTS 790-4322
Admin Susan Laney-Sheehan.
Lib Type Special.
Spec Subs Toxicology; carcinogenicity; biochemistry; teratology.
Info Ret Servs DIALOG; BRS; SDC. *Shared Catalog Nets* OCLC. *Coop Lib Nets* TALON Regional Medical Library Assoc; FEDLINK.
Circ Servs Avail To other Federal libraries; not open to the general public.
Ref Servs Avail Restricted to NCTR personnel.

1338. Winchester Engineering & Analytical Center Library
109 Holton St, Winchester, MA 01890 (617) 729-5700; FTS 839-8728
Lib Type Engineering & Science.
Spec Subs Electronics; engineering; medicine; physics; radiology.

Health Resources & Services Administration

1339. Phoenix Indian Medical Center, Health Sciences Library
4212 N 16th St, Phoenix, AZ 85016 (602) 263-1200, ext 1774
Admin Thomas Mead. *ILL* Elaine White.
Lib Type Health & Medicine.
Spec Collecs Indian health.
Info Ret Servs BRS; MEDLARS. *Coop Lib Nets* Maricopa Biomedical Libraries (MaBL). *Elec Mail Nets* CLASS Ontyme.
Circ Servs Avail To other libraries.
Ref Servs Avail To other libraries.

National Institutes of Health

1340. Frederick Cancer Research Facility, Scientific Library
National Cancer Institute, Bldg 426, Frederick, MD 21701-1013 (301) 695-1093
Admin Susan W Wilson.
Lib Type Health & Medicine.
Spec Subs Cancer biology; carcinogenesis; biomedical research.
Shared Catalog Nets OCLC. *Coop Lib Nets* FEDLINK.
Circ Servs Avail To other Federal libraries; to other libraries; restricted to NCI—FCRF staff & inter-library loans.
Ref Servs Avail To other Federal libraries; to other libraries; not open to the general public; restricted to qualified researchers by appointment.

1341. National Clearinghouse for Alcohol Information Library
1776 E Jefferson St, Rockville, MD 20852 (301) 468-2600
Admin Jory Barone. *Ref Lib* Leonore Burts. *ILL* Carol Jelich (Acq).
Lib Type Health & Medicine.
Spec Subs Over 60,000 documents on alcohol-related topics. *In-house Files* In-house data base (free search service provided).
Info Ret Servs DIALOG; BRS. *Coop Lib Nets* Substance Abuse Librarians & Information Specialists (SALIS).

Circ Servs Avail To other Federal libraries.
Ref Servs Avail To other Federal libraries; to other libraries; to the general public.

1342. National Institute of Environmental Health Sciences Library

PO Box 12233, Research Triangle Park, NC 27709 (919) 541-3426; FTS 629-3426
Admin W Davenport Robertson. *Ref Lib* Larry Wright. *ILL* Fran Lyndon.
Lib Type Health & Medicine.
Spec Subs Toxicology; carcinogenesis; mutagenesis.
Info Ret Servs DIALOG; BRS; SDC; CAS Online; LEXIS; NEXIS; CIS; Hazardline. *Shared Catalog Nets* OCLC. *Coop Lib Nets* FEDLINK. *Elec Mail Nets* North Carolina Educational Computing Service; USENET.
Circ Servs Avail To other Federal libraries; to other libraries.
Ref Servs Avail To other Federal libraries; to other libraries.

1343. National Institute on Aging, Gerontology Research Center Library

4940 Eastern Ave, Baltimore, MD 21224 (301) 955-1729/1730
Admin Joanna Chen Lin.
Lib Type Health & Medicine.
Spec Subs Gerontology; geriatrics; clinical physiology; behavioral medicine; neuroscience; biological chemistry; inorganic chemistry; personality & cognition; molecular genetics. *Spec Collecs* Gerontology & geriatrics.
Info Ret Servs DIALOG; BRS; NLM. *Shared Catalog Nets* OCLC. *Coop Lib Nets* MAHSL; RML2.
Circ Servs Avail To other Federal libraries.
Ref Servs Avail To other Federal libraries; to other libraries.

1344. National Institutes of Health, Division of Computer Research & Technology Library

Bldg 12A Rm 3018, 9000 Rockville Pike, Bethesda, MD 20892 (301) 496-1658
Admin Ellen Moy Chu. *ILL* Anita F Coherd (Acq).
Lib Type Engineering & Science.
Spec Subs Computer science; mathematics; statistics; medical information systems; computer applications in biomedical sciences. *In-house Files* NIH computer center interface from 1968; DCRT staff publications; DCRT & NIH ADP reports.
Info Ret Servs DIALOG; BRS; NLM MEDLARS. *Shared Catalog Nets* OCLC. *Coop Lib Nets* FEDLINK; Interlibrary Users Assoc (IUA); Metropolitan Washington Library Council; OCLC. *Elec Mail Nets* NIH computer center.
Circ Servs Avail To other Federal libraries; to other libraries.
Ref Servs Avail To other Federal libraries; to other libraries; to the general public.

1345. National Institutes of Health Library

Bldg 10 Rm 1L25, 9000 Rockville Pike, Bethesda, MD 20205 (301) 496-2447 (Lib); 496-2184 (Ref)
Admin Carolyn P Brown. *Ref Lib* Elise Cerutti. *ILL* Patricia Barnes. *Acq Lib* Margarett Kunz.
Lib Type Health & Medicine.
Spec Subs Biology; medicine; chemistry; physiology; health sciences.
Info Ret Servs DIALOG; BRS; SDC; NLM; STN. *Shared Catalog Nets* OCLC. *Coop Lib Nets* Southeastern/Atlantic Regional Medical Library Services; OCLC.
Circ Servs Avail Restricted to NIH library card holders.
Ref Servs Avail Restricted to NIH personnel, other on a limited basis.

1346. National Library of Medicine

8600 Rockville Pike, Bethesda, MD 20894 (301) 496-4000
Admin Donald A B Lindberg. *Ref Lib* Eve-Marie Lacroix. *ILL* James Cain. *Acq Lib* Duane Arenales.
Lib Type National.
Spec Subs Medicine; health care.
Lib Deposit Designation GPO Depository Library.
Info Ret Servs NLM Online Services. *Shared Catalog Nets* OCLC; RLIN; UTLAS. *Coop Lib Nets* Regional Medical Library Network. *Elec Mail Nets* GTE Telemail; Telex.
Circ Servs Avail To other Federal libraries; to other libraries.

Ref Servs Avail To other Federal libraries; to other libraries; to the general public.

1347. Rocky Mountain Laboratory Library

National Institute of Allergy & Infectious Diseases, 903 S 4th St, Hamilton, MT 59840 (406) 363-3211
Admin Liza S Hamby.
Lib Type Health & Medicine.
Spec Subs Medical entomology; immunology; virology; microbiology.
Info Ret Servs MEDLARS. *Coop Lib Nets* Montana Health Sciences Information Network. *Elec Mail Nets* CLASS.
Circ Servs Avail To other Federal libraries; to other libraries; not open to the general public.
Ref Servs Avail To other Federal libraries; to other libraries; not open to the general public; restricted to limited reference by telephone.

Public Health Service

1348. Gillis W Long Hansen's Disease Center, Medical Library

Carville, LA 70721 (504) 642-7771 ext 249; FTS 687-0205
Admin Eloise F Jack. *Ref Lib* Marilyn P McManus.
Lib Type Health & Medicine.
Spec Subs Hansen's Disease. *Spec Collecs* Only institution in the continental US devoted entirely to the treatment of Hansen's Disease & to world-wide education about this disease. Unique collection of over 7,000 reprints collected from earliest times to the present; books, historical documents, newspaper clippings, scrapbooks, & bibliographies.
Info Ret Servs MEDLARS. *Coop Lib Nets* Health Sciences Library Assoc of Louisiana (HSLAL); TALON Regional Medical Library Assoc.
Circ Servs Avail Restricted to photocopies only.
Ref Servs Avail To other Federal libraries; to other libraries; to the general public.

1349. The National Family Planning Information Clearinghouse Library

HHS, PO Box 12921, 1700 N Moore St, 7th Fl, Arlington, VA 22209 (301) 770-3662
Admin Elizabeth Joseph. *Ref Lib* Judith Christrup. *ILL* Sandra Spetgang (ACQ).
Lib Type Health & Medicine.
Spec Collecs Family planning; adolescent pregnancy prevention services; adoption; reproductive health.
Circ Servs Avail To other Federal libraries.
Ref Servs Avail To other Federal libraries; restricted to use by appointment.

1350. Parklawn Health Library

Rm 1312, Parklawn Bldg, 5600 Fishers Ln, Rockville, MD 20857 (301) 443-2673
Admin Bruce Yamanski.
Lib Type Special.
Spec Subs Substance abuse; health planning & administration; mental health; crime & delinquency; psychiatry; psychology; pyschopharmacology. *Spec Collecs* Public Health Service Publications.
Info Ret Servs DIALOG; MEDLINE. *Shared Catalog Nets* OCLC.
Circ Servs Avail To other libraries.
Ref Servs Avail To other libraries.

1351. Parklawn Health Library, Prince George's Center Branch

3700 East-West Hwy, Rm 1-14, Hyattsville, MD 20782 (301) 436-6147
Admin Karen Myers Stakes. *ILL* Charlene Brock.
Lib Type Health & Medicine.
Spec Subs Health statistics; delivery of health care; health services research. *Spec Collecs* Vital statistics of the US.
Info Ret Servs DIALOG; MEDLARS. *Shared Catalog Nets* OCLC.
Circ Servs Avail To other Federal libraries; to other libraries.
Ref Servs Avail To other Federal libraries; to other libraries; to the general public.

Social Security Administration

1352. Social Security Administration, District of Columbia Branch Library
1875 Connecticut Ave NW, Rm 320-0, Washington, DC 20009 (202) 673-5532; FTS 934-5532
Admin Octavio Alvarez. *ILL* Leroy Raylor.
Lib Type Special.
Spec Subs Pensions; statistics; disability insurance; supplemental security income; income distribution; economics; retirement; poverty. *Spec Collecs* Welfare; statistics; economics; gerontology.
Info Ret Servs DIALOG; BRS. *Shared Catalog Nets* OCLC.
Circ Servs Avail To other Federal libraries; to other libraries; restricted to the general public by appointment.
Ref Servs Avail To other Federal libraries; to other libraries; to the general public.

1353. Social Security Administration Library
Information & Graphics Services Branch, Rm 570 Altmeyer Bldg, 6401 Security Blvd, Baltimore, MD 21235 (301) 594-1650; FTS 934-1650
Admin Rowena S Sadler. *Ref Lib* Mary Joyce Donohue. *ILL* Sylvia Lieberman. *Acq Lib* Barbara Giersch.
Lib Type Special.
Info Ret Servs DIALOG; BRS; JURIS; LEXIS; NEXIS; LEGISLATE/REGULATE. *Coop Lib Nets* OCLC.
Circ Servs Avail To other Federal libraries; to other libraries; not open to the general public; restricted to authorized scholarly researchers & authors.
Ref Servs Avail To other Federal libraries; to other libraries; not open to the general public; restricted to authorized scholarly researchers & authors.

DEPARTMENT OF HOUSING AND URBAN DEVELOPMENT

Departmental

1354. Department of Housing & Urban Development Library
451 7th St SW, Rm 8141, Washington, DC 20410 (202) 755-6376; FTS 755-6376
Admin Carol Watts. *Ref Lib* Barbara Worley. *ILL* Marge Lantzy. *Acq Lib* Susan Chapman.
Lib Type Special.
Spec Subs Housing; urban affairs; community development; housing law; planning; mortgage & construction finance; program data from HUD. *Spec Collecs* HUD Comprehensive Planning (701) Reports; HUD Urban Development Action Grant (UDAG) Reports; National Housing Policy Review Background Papers.
Lib Deposit Designation GPO Depository Library.
Info Ret Servs DIALOG; BRS; SDC; WESTLAW; VU/TEXT; WILSONLINE; NEXIS. *Shared Catalog Nets* OCLC; RLIN; Faxon Linx. *Coop Lib Nets* FEDLINK.
Circ Servs Avail To other Federal libraries; to other libraries.
Ref Servs Avail To other Federal libraries; to other libraries; to the general public.

Regional Office Libraries

1355. HUD, Region 1 Library
JKF Federal Bldg, Boston, MA 02203 (617) 223-4674; FTS 223-4674
Lib Type Special.
Spec Subs Housing & related subjects; law.
Coop Lib Nets FEDLINK.
Circ Servs Avail Restricted to ILL.

1356. HUD, Region 2 Library
Rm 3500F, 26 Federal Plaza, New York, NY 10278 (212) 264-8175
Admin Susan Heller.
Lib Type Special.
Spec Subs Legal & technical research on housing & urban development.
Circ Servs Avail Not open to the general public; restricted to HUD staff.
Ref Servs Avail Restricted to HUD staff & HUD clientele; reading room & stacks - no restrictions.

1357. HUD, Region 3 Library
6th & Walnut Sts, Curtis Bldg, Philadelphia, PA 19106 (215) 597-2608
Lib Type Special.
Circ Servs Avail To other libraries; not open to the general public.
Ref Servs Avail To other Federal libraries; not open to the general public.

1358. HUD, Region 4 Library
75 Spring St SW, Atlanta, GA 30303 (404) 331-4576
Lib Type General.
Spec Subs Housing & urban planning; urban development; law; land use. *Spec Collecs* Community Development Block Grant Program.

1359. HUD, Region 5 Library
300 S Wacker Dr, Chicago, IL 60606 (312) 886-3253; FTS 886-3253
Lib Type Special.
Spec Collecs 701 Comprehensive Planning Grant Reports.
Circ Servs Avail Not open to the general public; restricted to HUD staff.
Ref Servs Avail To the general public.

1360. HUD, Region 7 Library
12th Fl, Professional Bldg, 1103 Grand Ave, Kansas City, MO 64106 (816) 374-6675
Lib Type Special.
Circ Servs Avail Not open to the general public.
Ref Servs Avail Not open to the general public.

1361. HUD, Region 8 Library
27th FL, Executive Tower Bldg, 1405 Curtis St, Denver, CO 80202 (303) 837-3431
Lib Type Special.
Circ Servs Avail Not open to the general public; restricted to HUD attorneys.
Ref Servs Avail Not open to the general public; restricted to HUD attorneys.

1362. HUD Region 9 Library
PO Box 36003, 450 Golden Gate Ave, San Francisco, CA 94102 (415) 556-6484; 556-6110 (Law Library)
Lib Type Special; Law.
Circ Servs Avail Not open to the general public.
Ref Servs Avail Not open to the general public.

DEPARTMENT OF THE INTERIOR

Bureau of Indian Affairs

1363. Aneth Community School Library
Aneth, UT 84510 (801) 651-3271
Admin David C Everett.
Lib Type Elementary/High School.
Spec Subs Navajo Culture & Language.
Circ Servs Avail To the general public.
Ref Servs Avail To the general public.

1364. Baca Boarding School Library
Bureau of Indian Affairs, PO Box 509, Prewitt, NM 87045
(505) 867-2769
Admin Calvin Knight.
Lib Type Elementary/High School.

1365. Big Coulee School-Early Childhood Education Center
Bureau of Indian Affairs, RR 1, Box 118, Peever, SD 57257
(605) 938-4439
Admin Audrey Utley.
Lib Type Elementary/High School.
Circ Servs Avail To other libraries.
Ref Servs Avail To the general public.

1366. Bread Springs School Library
Box 1117, Gallup, NM 87301 (505) 778-5665
Admin Jerry V Collins.
Lib Type Elementary/High School.
Circ Servs Avail Restricted to students & staff.
Ref Servs Avail Restricted to students & staff.

1367. Brevig Mission, Day School Library
Bureau of Indian Affairs, Brevig Mission, AK 99878
Lib Type Elementary/High School.
Ref Servs Avail To the general public.

1368. Bridger Day School Library
Bureau of Indian Affairs, Howes, SD 57748 (605) 538-4313
Admin Faye Longbrake.
Lib Type Elementary/High School.
Spec Subs This library serves the community & elementary school.
Circ Servs Avail To other libraries; to the general public.
Ref Servs Avail To the general public.

1369. Brule Sioux High School Library
PO 245, Lower Brule, SD 57548-0245 (605) 473-5510
Admin Heather J O Collins.
Lib Type Elementary/High School.
Coop Lib Nets South Dakota State Library Inter-Loan.
Circ Servs Avail To the general public; restricted to primary use by students & staff.
Ref Servs Avail To the general public; restricted to primary use by students & staff.

1370. Bureau of Indian Affairs, Library/Media Center
PO Box 347, Bethel, AK 99559 (907) 543-2749
Admin Dorothy Stockwell.
Lib Type Elementary/High School.
Spec Subs A central library serving 27 Bureau of Indian Affairs' schools located in western Alaska; elementary school, media center, & professional education materials.

1371. Busby School Library
Busby, MT 59016 (406) 592-3646
Admin Helga A Smith.
Lib Type Elementary/High School.
Spec Collecs Indian collections.
Coop Lib Nets MPLA.
Circ Servs Avail To other libraries; to the general public.
Ref Servs Avail Restricted to in-school use.

1372. Canoncito Community School, Resource Center
Bureau of Indian Affairs, PO Box 438, Star Route, Laguna, NM 87026 (505) 831-6426
Admin Carrie Wahnee.
Lib Type Elementary/High School.
Spec Subs Technical data; teachers' reference books.

1373. Casa Blanca Day School Library
Bureau of Indian Affairs, Box HH, Bapchule, AZ 85221 (602) 562-3512; School 562-3489
Admin Geraldine Youngman.
Lib Type Elementary/High School.
Spec Subs Library usage; Indian & Pima culture. *Spec Collecs* Native American books; Pima & Indian culture.
Circ Servs Avail To other Federal libraries; to other libraries.
Ref Servs Avail To the general public.

1374. Chemawa Indian School, IMC
Bureau of Indian Affairs, 5495 Chugach St NE, Salem, OR 97303 (503) 393-4329
Admin Mark Peterson.
Lib Type Elementary/High School.
Spec Subs Indian history. *Spec Collecs* Indian history.

1375. Cherokee Elementary School Library
Cherokee, NC 28719 (704) 497-9131
Admin Esther M Ferguson.
Lib Type Elementary/High School.
Spec Subs Cherokee Indians.
Ref Servs Avail To the general public.

1376. Cherokee High School Library
Cherokee, NC 28719 (704) 497-5511
Admin Richard Meldrom.
Lib Type Elementary/High School.
Spec Subs American Indian.
Circ Servs Avail Restricted to students & staff.
Ref Servs Avail Restricted to students & staff.

1377. Cherry Creek School Library
Cherry Creek, SD 57622 (605) 538-4238
Admin Faye Longbrake.
Lib Type Elementary/High School.
Spec Subs Fiction.
Circ Servs Avail Restricted to students & staff.
Ref Servs Avail Restricted to students & staff.

1378. Cheyenne-Eagle Butte High School, Media Center
Eagle Butte, SD 57625 (605) 964-8755 ext 23
Admin William Donovan.
Lib Type Elementary/High School.
Spec Collecs Books/materials relating to Indian studies.

Circ Servs Avail Not open to the general public; restricted to student body.
Ref Servs Avail Restricted to student body.

1379. Chi Chil Tah School
Bureau of Indian Affairs, Zuni Route, Gallup, NM 87301 (505) 782-4758
Lib Type Elementary/High School.
Spec Subs Elementary reading.

1380. Chilchinbeto Day School Library
Bureau of Indian Affairs, PO Box 547, Kayenta, AZ 86033 (602) 697-3448
Admin George Mitchell.
Lib Type Elementary/High School.
Spec Subs Elementary school materials.

1381. Chilocco Indian School Library
Bureau of Indian Affairs, Chilocco, OK 74635 (405) 448-3800, ext 37
Lib Type Elementary/High School.
Spec Subs High school academia; Indian history.

1382. Chinle Boarding School Library
Bureau of Indian Affairs, PO Box 70, Many Farms, AZ 86538 (602) 781-6221
Admin Martha L Meredith.
Lib Type Elementary/High School.
Spec Subs Elementary school; early childhood. *Spec Collecs* Southwest Indian tribes.
Circ Servs Avail To other libraries.
Ref Servs Avail To the general public.

1383. Chitimacha Day School Library
Box 222, Rte 2, Jeanerette, LA 70544 (318) 923-4921
Admin Junius Wingate.
Lib Type Elementary/High School.
Circ Servs Avail Restricted to Chitimacha Reservation.
Ref Servs Avail Restricted to Chitimacha Reservation.

1384. Choctaw Central High School Library
Bureau of Indian Affairs, Rte 7, Box 72, Philadelphia, MS 39350 (601) 656-6702
Admin Susie Comby Alex.
Lib Type Elementary/High School.
Spec Subs Elementary thru high school materials; American Indians. *Spec Collecs* American Indians.
Circ Servs Avail To other libraries.
Ref Servs Avail To the general public.

1385. Concho School Library
Bureau of Indian Affairs, Concho, OK 73022 (405) 262-0143
Admin Delores Harragarra.
Lib Type Elementary/High School.
Spec Subs American Indians.
Circ Servs Avail To other libraries.
Ref Servs Avail To the general public.

1386. Cottonwood Day School Library
Chinle, AZ 86503 (602) 725-3235
Admin Allen K Anderson.
Lib Type Elementary/High School.
Circ Servs Avail Restricted to students & staff.
Ref Servs Avail Restricted to students & staff.

1387. Cove Day School
Bureau of Indian Affairs, PO Box 190, Shiprock, NM 87420 (505) 368-4457
Admin Lucy M Roanhorse.
Lib Type Elementary/High School.
Spec Subs Children's books.

1388. Crazy Horse School Library-Media Center
Wanblee, SD 57577 (605) 462-6511
Admin Robert L Vrchota.
Lib Type Elementary/High School.
Spec Subs Indians of North America (especially Lakota).

Circ Servs Avail Restricted to students & staff.
Ref Servs Avail To other libraries; to the general public.

1389. Crow Creek Reservation High School Library
Box 12, Stephan, SD 57346 (605) 852-5218
Admin Marsha M Fyler.
Lib Type Elementary/High School.
Spec Subs Small collection of books on & by Native Americans.
Circ Servs Avail Not open to the general public; restricted to Crow Creek Reservation.
Ref Servs Avail Not open to the general public; restricted to Crow Creek Reservation.

1390. Crownpoint Boarding School Media Center
Bureau of Indian Affairs, Box 178, Crownpoint, NM 87313 (505) 786-5342
Admin Christine L Nelson.
Lib Type Elementary/High School.
Spec Subs Support for curriculum (grades 1-8); Indian works.
Circ Servs Avail To other libraries.
Ref Servs Avail To the general public.

1391. Crystal Boarding School Library
Bureau of Indian Affairs, Navajo, NM 87328 (505) 777-2385
Admin Martha Alhman.
Lib Type Elementary/High School.
Spec Subs Elementary school.
Circ Servs Avail To other libraries.
Ref Servs Avail To the general public; restricted to limited use.

1392. Dennehotso Boarding School Library
Bureau of Indian Affairs, Box 308, Kayenta, AZ 86033 (602) 658-3210
Admin Velma Eisenberger.
Lib Type Elementary/High School.
Spec Subs Children's books; Southwest; Indians.
Circ Servs Avail To other libraries.

1393. Dilcon School Library
Star Rte, Winslow, AZ 86047 (602) 657-3225
Admin Hal Chenault.
Lib Type Elementary/High School.
Spec Subs American Indian.
Circ Servs Avail To the general public.
Ref Servs Avail To the general public.

1394. Dlo'Ay Azhi Boarding School Library
Bureau of Indian Affairs, Box 789, Thoreau, NM 87323 (505) 862-7525
Admin Amy Whitekiller.
Lib Type Elementary/High School.

1395. Dunseith Day School Library
PO Box 759, Dunseith, ND 58329 (701) 263-4636
Admin Karen J Gillis.
Lib Type Elementary/High School.
Circ Servs Avail Restricted to students & staff.
Ref Servs Avail Restricted to students & staff.

1396. Dzilth-Na-O-Dith-hle Community School Library
Bloomfield, NM 87413 (505) 325-2971; TTY (505) 632-1697
Admin D Duane Robinson (Principal); Dicksy Jane Howe (Lib).
Lib Type Elementary/High School.
Coop Lib Nets New Mexico Library Assoc.
Circ Servs Avail Restricted to students & staff.
Ref Servs Avail Restricted to students & staff of area Bureau of Indian Affairs schools.

1397. Flandreau Indian School Library
1000 N Crescent, Flandreau, SD 57028-1299 (605) 997-2451
Admin Joy R Chamley.
Lib Type Elementary/High School.
Spec Subs Native Americans.
Circ Servs Avail Restricted to students & staff.
Ref Servs Avail Restricted to students & staff.

1398. Fort Thompson Community School Library
Fort Thompson, SD 57339 (605) 245-2311 ext 220, 221
Admin Ollie Ann Yost.
Lib Type Elementary/High School.
Spec Subs Elementary reference. *Spec Collecs* Indian history.
Coop Lib Nets South Dakota State Library.
Circ Servs Avail Restricted to students & staff.
Ref Servs Avail Restricted to students & staff.

1399. Four Winds Elementary School Library
Fort Totten, ND 58335 (701) 766-4161/4634
Admin Helen Jacobs (Lib); Wayne Trottier, Jr (Principal).
Lib Type Elementary/High School.
Spec Subs General collection of about 10,000 volumes.
Circ Servs Avail Restricted to staff & students.
Ref Servs Avail Restricted to staff & students.

1400. Gila Crossing Day School Library
Bureau of Indian Affairs, Rte 1, Box 770, Laveen, AZ 85339
(602) 243-4834
Admin C M Mak.
Lib Type Elementary/High School.
Spec Subs Lower Elementary school. *Spec Collecs* Native American children's books.
Circ Servs Avail To other libraries.
Ref Servs Avail To the general public.

1401. Greasewood Boarding School Library
Bureau of Indian Affairs, Ganado, AZ 86505 (602) 654-3331
Admin Benjamin Holiday.
Lib Type Elementary/High School.
Spec Subs Serves the Navajo community & the elementary school.
Spec Collecs American Indians.
Circ Servs Avail To other libraries; to the general public.
Ref Servs Avail To the general public.

1402. Greyhills High School Library
Bureau of Indian Affairs/Tuba City Public Schools, Tuba City, AZ
86045 (602) 283-4211, ext 285
Admin Patsy R Roe.
Lib Type Elementary/High School.
Spec Subs US Southwest.
Circ Servs Avail To other libraries.
Ref Servs Avail To the general public.

1403. Haskell Indian Junior College, Learning Resource Center
Bureau of Indian Affairs, ADA 91, W 75th St, Ovland Park, KS
66204 (913) 341-2000, ext 238; FTS 752-2238
Admin Leonor Carraso.
Lib Type Academic.
Spec Subs Academia. *Spec Collecs* Indians of North America;
Frank Rinehart photo collection of the Omaha Exposition.
Circ Servs Avail To other libraries.
Ref Servs Avail To the general public.

1404. Hopi Day School Library
PO Box 42, Kykotsmovi, AZ 86039 (602) 734-2468
Admin Hugo Rivera (Principal). *Ref Lib* Gloria M Donelson
(Lib)(ILL, Acq).
Lib Type Elementary/High School.
Circ Servs Avail To the general public.
Ref Servs Avail To the general public.

1405. Institute of American Indian Arts Library
College of Santa Fe Campus, St Michael's Dr, Santa Fe, NM
87501 (505) 988-6670
Admin Karen Highfill. *Ref Lib* Bernadette Townsend.
Lib Type Academic.
Spec Subs Native American culture; fine arts of all Indian cultures. *Spec Collecs* Smithsonian Native American: photographs, art slides, music recordings, & video tape archives. *In-house Files* Native American newspapers, art catalogs, clippings, pamphlets; IAIA Archives.
Circ Servs Avail To other Federal libraries; to other libraries; to the general public.

Ref Servs Avail To other Federal libraries; to other libraries; to the general public.

1406. Intermountain Inter-Tribal School Library
Bureau of Indian Affairs, PO Box 345, Brigham City, UT 84321
(801) 734-2071; FTS 586-4346
Admin D Alexa West.
Lib Type Elementary/High School.
Spec Subs Vocational material; Indian history & literature.
Circ Servs Avail To other libraries.
Ref Servs Avail To the general public.

1407. Isleta Elementary School Library
Box 312, Isleta, NM 87022 (505) 869-3535
Admin B June DeVilliers.
Lib Type Elementary/High School.
Circ Servs Avail To other libraries; to the general public.
Ref Servs Avail To other libraries; to the general public.

1408. Kaibeto Boarding School Library
Bureau of Indian Affairs, Kaibeto, AZ 86053 (602) 673-3479
Admin Barbra Gibbs.
Lib Type Elementary/High School.
Circ Servs Avail To other libraries.
Ref Servs Avail To the general public.

1409. Kaibeto Elementary School Library
Kaibeto, AZ 86053 (602) 673-3479
Admin Shirley M Larson.
Lib Type Elementary/High School.
Spec Collecs Indian books.
Circ Servs Avail Restricted to students & staff.
Ref Servs Avail Restricted to students & staff.

1410. Kayenta Boarding School Library
Bureau of Indian Affairs, Box 188, Kayenta, AZ 86033 (602) 697-
3439
Admin Pauline Gatline.
Lib Type Elementary/High School.
Spec Subs Serves the community, high school, & elementary school.
Circ Servs Avail To other libraries; to the general public.
Ref Servs Avail To the general public.

1411. Keams Canyon Library
Bureau of Indian Affairs, PO Box 367, Keams Canyon, AZ 86034
(602) 738-2324
Admin Loren O Joseph.
Lib Type Elementary/High School.
Spec Subs Elementary & junior high school; American Indian history.
Circ Servs Avail To other libraries.
Ref Servs Avail To the general public.

1412. Kwethluk Day School
Bureau of Indian Affairs, Kwethluk, AK 99621 (907) 543-2033
(Village phone)
Admin Sophie Owens; Claudia Michael.
Lib Type Elementary/High School.
Spec Subs School & recreation.

1413. Laguna Elementary School Library
Bureau of Indian Affairs, Box 191, Laguna, NM 87026 (505) 552-
9200/6255
Admin Paula Armstrong.
Lib Type Elementary/High School.
Spec Subs Elementary school; teachers' professional literature.
Circ Servs Avail To other libraries.
Ref Servs Avail To the general public.

1414. Leupp Boarding School Library
H.C. 61, Winslow, AZ 86047 (602) 686-6211
Admin Mark W Sorensen (Principal).
Lib Type Elementary/High School.
Coop Lib Nets ASSETT.
Circ Servs Avail To other libraries; to the general public.

1415. Little Wound School Library
Bureau of Indian Affairs, Kyle, SD 57752 (605) 455-2461
Admin William J May.
Lib Type Elementary/High School.
Spec Subs School; American Indians.
Circ Servs Avail To other libraries.
Ref Servs Avail To the general public.

1416. Low Mountain Boarding School Library
Chinle, AZ 86503 (602) 725-3308
Admin Allen K Anderson.
Lib Type Elementary/High School.
Circ Servs Avail Restricted to students & staff.
Ref Servs Avail Restricted to students & staff.

1417. Lukachukai Boarding School Library
Bureau of Indian Affairs, Lukachukai, AZ 86507 (602) 787-2301
Admin Larry Tsosie.
Lib Type Elementary/High School.
Circ Servs Avail To other libraries.
Ref Servs Avail To the general public.

1418. Many Farms High School Library
Chinle Agency, Many Farms, AZ 86538 (602) 781-6338
Admin Horace Gray (Lib); Frederick S Culpepper (A-V Specialist).
Lib Type Elementary/High School.
Spec Subs Indian collection.
Circ Servs Avail To the general public.

1419. Moencopi Day School Library
PO Box 185, Tuba City, AZ 86045 (602) 283-5361
Admin Elvira J Pasena.
Lib Type Elementary/High School.
Circ Servs Avail Not open to the general public; restricted to school use.
Ref Servs Avail Not open to the general public; restricted to school use.

1420. Mt Edgecumbe High School, Library Media Center
Bureau of Indian Affairs, Mount Edgecumbe, AK 99835 (907) 966-2217
Admin Anita Jo Stevens.
Lib Type Elementary/High School.
Spec Subs High school. *Spec Collecs* Alaskan regional materials.
Circ Servs Avail To other libraries.
Ref Servs Avail To the general public.

1421. National Indian Training Center, Professional Library
Bureau of Indian Affairs, PO Box 66, Brigham City, UT 84302 (801) 734-2071, ext 514; FTS 586-4514
Admin Marlene Naranjo.
Lib Type Training Center.
Spec Subs Education; North American Indians. *Spec Collecs* ERIC microfiche on Indians.
Circ Servs Avail To other libraries.
Ref Servs Avail To the general public.

1422. Navajo Mountain Boarding School Library
Bureau of Indian Affairs, PO Box 787, Tuba City, AZ 86045 (602) 283-5320
Lib Type Elementary/High School.
Spec Subs Elementary school.
Circ Servs Avail To other libraries.
Ref Servs Avail To the general public.

1423. Nazlini Boarding School Library
Ganado, AZ 86505 (602) 755-6125
Admin Lorraine Etcitty. *Ref Lib* Kim Franklin (ILL, Acq).
Lib Type Elementary/High School.
Circ Servs Avail Restricted to students & staff.
Ref Servs Avail Restricted to students & staff.

1424. Oglala Community Elementary School
Bureau of Indian Affairs, Pine Ridge, SD 57770 (605) 867-5191, ext 45/46
Admin Christiane Plant.
Lib Type Elementary/High School.

Spec Subs Teacher training materials; American Indians.
Circ Servs Avail To other libraries.
Ref Servs Avail To the general public.

1425. Oglala Community High School Library
Bureau of Indian Affairs, Pine Ridge, SD 57770 (605) 867-5191, ext 41
Admin Barbra J Carson.
Lib Type Elementary/High School.
Spec Subs American Indians.
Circ Servs Avail To other libraries.
Ref Servs Avail To the general public.

1426. Phoenix Indian School Library
Bureau of Indian Affairs, PO Box 7188, Phoenix, AZ 85011 (602) 241-2638
Admin Nancy Carver.
Lib Type Elementary/High School.
Spec Subs Junior-senior high school; American Indians. *Spec Collecs* The Native American 1901-1939; The Red Skin, 1950-1975.
Circ Servs Avail To other libraries.
Ref Servs Avail To the general public.

1427. Pierre Indian Learning Center Library
Star Rte 3, Pierre, SD 57501 (605) 224-8661
Admin Arlo Levisen (Principal).
Lib Type Elementary/High School.

1428. Pinon Boarding School Library
Pinon, AZ 86510 (602) 725-3234
Admin Allen K Anderson.
Lib Type Elementary/High School.
Circ Servs Avail Restricted to students & staff.
Ref Servs Avail Restricted to students & staff.

1429. Porcupine Day School Library
Bureau of Indian Affairs, General Delivery, Porcupine, SD 57772 (605) 867-5337
Admin Kathryne Slock.
Lib Type Elementary/High School.

1430. Promise Day School Library
Bureau of Indian Affairs, Rte 2, Mobridge, SD 57601 (Radio) KAC 539, 733-2359
Admin Irene Ryan.
Lib Type Elementary/High School.
Spec Subs Elementary school.
Circ Servs Avail To other libraries.
Ref Servs Avail To the general public.

1431. Red Lake Day School Library
PO Box 62, Tonalea, AZ 86044 (602) 283-5324
Admin Ray Interpreter (Principal).
Lib Type Elementary/High School.
Spec Subs K-8 school library.
Circ Servs Avail Not open to the general public; restricted to students & staff.
Ref Servs Avail Not open to the general public; restricted to students & staff.

1432. Riverside Indian School Library
Rte 1, Anadarko, OK 73005 (405) 247-6673 ext 263; FTS 743-7263
Admin Clarice Garrett.
Lib Type Elementary/High School.
Spec Collecs Indian Heritage Collection of over 1200 books by & about the Indians of North America, including microfilm & microfiche reels of constitutions & newspapers.
Circ Servs Avail To other Federal libraries; restricted to students & staff.
Ref Servs Avail To other Federal libraries; to the general public.

1433. Rocky Ridge Boarding School Library
Bureau of Indian Affairs, Box 235, Tuba City, AZ 86045
(602) 283-5036
Admin Paul Lane.
Lib Type Elementary/High School.
Spec Subs Primary school & community library; American Indians.
Circ Servs Avail To other libraries; to the general public.
Ref Servs Avail To the general public.

1434. Salt River Day School Library
Box 117, Rte 1, Scottsdale, AZ 85256 (602) 241-2810; FTS 261-2810
Admin Farrell B Whitey (Principal). *Ref Lib* Miriam Lu (Lib).
Lib Type Elementary/High School.
Spec Collecs American Indian.
Circ Servs Avail Restricted to students & staff.
Ref Servs Avail Restricted to students & staff.

1435. San Felipe Elementary School Library
Box E, San Felipe Pueblo, NM 87001 (505) 867-2773
Admin Kathleen A Carlson.
Lib Type Elementary/High School.
Spec Subs Easy reading for elementary. *Spec Collecs* Native American reference collection.
Circ Servs Avail Restricted to students, staff & village.
Ref Servs Avail Restricted to students, staff & village.

1436. San Juan Day School Media Center
PO Box 1077, San Juan Pueblo, NM 87566 (505) 852-2154
Admin Juan G Casias.
Lib Type Elementary/High School.
Spec Collecs Native American Collection.
Circ Servs Avail To the general public.
Ref Servs Avail To the general public.

1437. San Simon Media Center
Bureau of Indian Affairs, Star Rte 1, Box 92, Sells, AZ 85634
(602) 383-2231
Admin Betty Sheppard.
Lib Type Elementary/High School.
Spec Subs Papago literature; Native American materials; elementary school.
Circ Servs Avail To other libraries.
Ref Servs Avail To the general public.

1438. Sanostee Boarding School Media Center
Bureau of Indian Affairs, Sanostee, NM 87461 (505) 723-2476
Admin Fred Danes.
Lib Type Elementary/High School.
Spec Subs Elementary school. *Spec Collecs* Navajo Culture Center.
Circ Servs Avail To other libraries.
Ref Servs Avail To the general public.

1439. Santa Clara Day School Library
Bureau of Indian Affairs, Rte 1, Box 471, Espanola, NM 87532
(505) 753-4406
Admin Linda Martinez; Grace Tapia.
Lib Type Elementary/High School.
Circ Servs Avail To other libraries.
Ref Servs Avail To the general public.

1440. Santa Rosa Boarding School Libraries
Sells, AZ 85634 (602) 383-2330
Admin Thomas Goff (Principal).
Lib Type Elementary/High School.
Circ Servs Avail Restricted to students & staff.
Ref Servs Avail Restricted to students & staff.

1441. Santa Rosa Elementary School Library
Bureau of Indian Affairs, Sells, AZ 85634 (602) 383-2330, ext
2276
Admin Gloria Green.
Lib Type Elementary/High School.
Spec Subs Papago literature; early elementary school.
Circ Servs Avail To other libraries; to the general public.
Ref Servs Avail To the general public.

1442. Second Mesa Day School Library
Second Mesa, AZ 86043 (602) 737-2571/2576
Admin Donald Covington (Principal); Gloria Donelson (Lib).
Lib Type Elementary/High School.
Circ Servs Avail To the general public.
Ref Servs Avail To the general public.

1443. Seneca Indian School Library
Bureau of Indian Affairs, Wyandotte, OK 74370 (918) 678-2286
Lib Type Elementary/High School.
Spec Subs Elementary school. *Spec Collecs* Indian & professional books.
Ref Servs Avail To the general public.

1444. Sequoyah High School Library
PO Box 558, Tahlequah, OK 74465 (918) 456-0631
Admin Rhonda Watson.
Lib Type Elementary/High School.
Spec Collecs Indians of North America.
Circ Servs Avail Restricted to students & staff.
Ref Servs Avail Restricted to students & staff.

1445. Shiprock Boarding School Library
Bureau of Indian Affairs, Box 966, Shiprock, NM 87420
(505) 368-5113
Admin Georgianna Watson.
Lib Type Elementary/High School.
Spec Subs Vocational & technical information.
Circ Servs Avail To other libraries; to the general public.
Ref Servs Avail To other libraries; to the general public.

1446. Shonto Elementary Library
Bureau of Indian Affairs, Shonto Boarding School, Shonto, AZ
86054 (602) 672-2340/2342
Admin J Richard Hicks.
Lib Type Elementary/High School.
Spec Subs Native American materials.
Circ Servs Avail To other libraries.
Ref Servs Avail To the general public.

1447. Southwestern Indian Polytechnic Institute Instructional Media Center
Bureau of Indian Affairs, PO Box 10146, 916 Cours NW, Albuquerque, NM 87184 (505) 766-3266; FTS 474-3266
Admin Margaret C Davis.
Lib Type Elementary/High School.
Spec Subs Indian interest materials; technical subjects (curriculum support).
Circ Servs Avail To other Federal libraries; to other libraries.
Ref Servs Avail To the general public.

1448. Standing Rock Community Elementary School Library
PO Box H, Fort Yates, ND 58538 (701) 854-3865
Admin Linda Lawrence (Principal). *Ref Lib* Kathryn Bickel (Lib) (ILL, Acq).
Lib Type Elementary/High School.
Circ Servs Avail Restricted to students & staff.
Ref Servs Avail Restricted to students & staff.

1449. Stewart Boarding School Library-Media Center
Bureau of Indian Affairs, Stewart, NV 89437 (702) 882-3411, ext
14
Lib Type Elementary/High School.
Spec Subs Junior-senior high school; American Indians. *Spec Collecs* Out-of-print & rare books.
Circ Servs Avail To other libraries.
Ref Servs Avail To the general public.

1450. Taos Day School Library
PO Drawer X, Taos, NM 87571 (505) 758-3652
Admin Roy French (Principal); Florence Mirabal (Lib).
Lib Type Elementary/High School.
Circ Servs Avail Restricted to students & staff.
Ref Servs Avail Restricted to students & staff.

1451. Teecnospos Boarding School Library
Teecnospos, AZ 86514 (602) 656-3252
Admin Melveta Walker.
Lib Type Elementary/High School.
Circ Servs Avail To other Federal libraries; to other libraries; restricted to students & staff.
Ref Servs Avail To other Federal libraries; to other libraries; to the general public.

1452. Toksook Bay School Library
Bureau of Indian Affairs, Toksook Bay, AK 99637
Admin Wilma Moore (Principal).
Lib Type Elementary/High School.
Circ Servs Avail To other libraries.
Ref Servs Avail To the general public.

1453. Toyei Boarding School Library
Bureau of Indian Affairs, Box 6, Ganado, AZ 86505 (602) 736-2508
Admin Paula Armstrong.
Lib Type Elementary/High School.
Spec Subs Library skills.
Circ Servs Avail To other libraries.
Ref Servs Avail To the general public.

1454. Tuba City Boarding School Library
Box 187, Tuba City, AZ 86045 (602) 283-4531 ext 345; FTS 762-4251
Admin Louis Brown.
Lib Type Elementary/High School.
Spec Subs Native Americans.
Circ Servs Avail To other libraries; not open to the general public.
Ref Servs Avail Not open to the general public.

1455. Turtle Mountain Community School Media Center
Belcourt, ND 58316 (701) 477-6471 ext 262
Admin Harry Belgarde. *Ref Lib* Duane Crawford. *ILL* Jean Warbitsky.
Lib Type Elementary/High School.
Spec Subs Chippewa & Michif (Metis) Cultures. *Spec Collecs* Indian materials. *In-house Files* North Dakota materials; local communities; contemporary history books.
Circ Servs Avail To other libraries; restricted to students & staff.
Ref Servs Avail To other Federal libraries; to other libraries; restricted to students & staff.

1456. Twin Buttes School Library
Bureau of Indian Affairs, Halliday, ND 58636 (701) 938-4396
Admin Betsey Kasper.
Lib Type Elementary/High School.
Spec Subs Sports; mysteries; animals; Indian culture.
Ref Servs Avail To the general public.

1457. Wahpeton Indian School Media Center
Wahpeton, ND 58075 (701) 642-4301
Admin Jeanne Swartz.
Lib Type Elementary/High School.
Spec Subs Indian culture.
Coop Lib Nets North Dakota State Library.
Circ Servs Avail To other Federal libraries; to other libraries; restricted to students & staff.
Ref Servs Avail Restricted to students & staff.

1458. White Horse School Library
Bureau of Indian Affairs, PO Box 7, White Horse, SD 57661 (605) 733-2183
Admin A C Whitlacth.
Lib Type Elementary/High School.
Spec Subs Fiction; reference.

1459. White Shield School Library
Bureau of Indian Affairs, Roseglen, ND 58775 (701) 743-4350
Admin Karen Woolard.
Lib Type Elementary/High School.
Spec Subs Elementary thru senior high school.
Circ Servs Avail To other libraries.
Ref Servs Avail To the general public.

1460. Wide Ruins Boarding School
Bureau of Indian Affairs, Wide Ruins, AZ 86502 (602) 652-3251
Admin Larry Tsosie.
Lib Type Elementary/High School.
Circ Servs Avail To other libraries.
Ref Servs Avail To the general public.

1461. Wide Ruins School Library
Bureau of Indian Affairs, Chambers, AZ 86502 (602) 652-3251
Admin Lena Mae Jim (Principal).
Lib Type Elementary/High School.
Spec Subs School curriculum subjects; professional books for teachers.
Circ Servs Avail To other libraries.
Ref Servs Avail To the general public.

1462. Wingate Elementary School Library
Bureau of Indian Affairs, PO Box 1, Fort Wingate, NM 87316 (505) 488-5584/5591
Admin Patricia Hall.
Lib Type Elementary/High School.
Spec Subs American Indians; US Southwest.
Circ Servs Avail To other libraries.
Ref Servs Avail To the general public.

1463. Wingate High School Library-Media Center
Box 2, Fort Wingate, NM 87316 (505) 488-5401
Admin Jerri Young.
Lib Type Elementary/High School.
Spec Collecs American Indians; Southwest; government documents.
Circ Servs Avail Restricted to students & staff.
Ref Servs Avail Restricted to students & staff.

1464. Wounded Knee District School Library
Manderson, SD 57756 (605) 867-5433
Admin Thomas Colhoff.
Lib Type Elementary/High School.
Spec Subs American Indian.
Circ Servs Avail Restricted to students & staff.
Ref Servs Avail Restricted to students & staff.

1465. Zia Day School Library
Bureau of Indian Affairs, San Ysidro, NM 87053 (505) 242-1051
Admin Pauline Panana.
Lib Type Elementary/High School.
Circ Servs Avail To other libraries.
Ref Servs Avail To the general public.

Bureau of Land Management

1466. Bureau of Land Management, Arizona State Office Library
2400 Valley Bank Ctr, Phoenix, AZ 85073 (602) 261-3706; FTS 261-3706
Admin Records Manager.
Lib Type Special.
Spec Subs Lands; minerals; wildlife; cultural resources; environmental control & protection; watershed; grazing; range cadstral survey; engineering; recreation. *Spec Collecs* Interior department decisions; Bureau of Land Management directives.
Circ Servs Avail Not open to the general public; restricted to AZ BLM personnel.
Ref Servs Avail Not open to the general public; restricted to AZ BLM personnel.

1467. Bureau of Land Management, Arizona Strip, District Office Library
196 E Tabernacle, Saint George, UT 84770 (801) 673-3545, ext 48
Lib Type Special.
Spec Subs Conservation; grazing; land & range; recreation; wildlife management.

1468. Bureau of Land Management, Baker District Office Library
PO Box 987, Baker, OR 97814 (503) 523-6391; FTS 421-6281
Admin Christina White.
Lib Type Special.
Spec Subs Forestry; lands & minerals; range management; watershed.
Circ Servs Avail Not open to the general public; restricted to staff.

1469. Bureau of Land Management, Bakersfield District Office Library
Rm 311, 800 Truxton Ave, Bakersfield, CA 93301 (805) 861-4191; FTS 984-1191
Admin Melba Larson.
Lib Type Special.
Spec Subs Land & range management; wildlife management; recreation; minerals; watershed; fire protection; trespass; antiquities protection.

1470. Bureau of Land Management, Bishop Resource Area Headquarters Library
Suite 201, 873 N Main St, Bishop, CA 93514 (714) 872-4881
Admin Peggy Ewing.
Lib Type Special.
Spec Subs Wildlife; land resources & minerals management; range conservation; cultural resources.
Circ Servs Avail To other libraries.
Ref Servs Avail To the general public.

1471. Bureau of Land Management, Branch of Records & Data Management
PO Box 2965, Portland, OR 97208 (503) 231-2029, ext 4158; FTS 429-2029
Admin Lois E Gee.
Lib Type Special.
Spec Subs Land management; forests; water; minerals; wildlife.
Ref Servs Avail To the general public.

1472. Bureau of Land Management, Burns District Office Library
74 S Alvord, Burns, OR 97720 (503) 573-2071
Admin Anita M Cornwall.
Lib Type Special.
Spec Subs Range; watershed; soils; wildlife; forestry; management.
Ref Servs Avail To the general public.

1473. Bureau of Land Management, California State Office Library
Rm E-2841, 2800 Cottage Way, Sacramento, CA 95825-1889 (916) 978-4754, ext 4713; FTS 468-4253
Lib Type Special.
Spec Subs Environmental statements; minerals & mining; natural resources; range; recreation; wildlife.
Circ Servs Avail Not open to the general public; restricted to ILL.
Ref Servs Avail Not open to the general public; restricted to staff use.

1474. Bureau of Land Management, Cedar City District Library
1579 N Main, Cedar City, UT 84720 (801) 586-2401
Admin Ada Palmer.
Lib Type Special.
Spec Subs Range; recreation; wildlife; mineral environmental projects.

1475. Bureau of Land Management, Coeur D'Alene District Office Library
1808 N 3rd St, Coeur D'Alene, ID 83814 (208) 765-7356
Lib Type Special.

1476. Bureau of Land Management, Colorado State Office Library
Rm 701, 1600 Broadway, Denver, CO 80202 (303) 837-2402; FTS 327-2402
Admin Wendy S Nettles.
Lib Type Special.
Spec Subs Natural resources.
Ref Servs Avail To the general public.

1477. Bureau of Land Management, Colorado State Office Library
20-20 Arapahoe, Denver, CO 80205 (303) 294-7513
Lib Type Special.
Spec Subs Natural resources. *Spec Collecs* Cultural Resources Series.
Ref Servs Avail Not open to the general public; restricted to employees.

1478. Bureau of Land Management, Coos Bay District Office Library
333 S 4th St, Coos Bay, OR 97420 (503) 269-5880
Lib Type Special.
Ref Servs Avail To the general public.

1479. Bureau of Land Management, Craig District Office Library
455 Emerson St, Craig, CO 81625 (303) 824-8261
Lib Type Special.

1480. Bureau of Land Management, District Library
PO Box 194, Battle Mountain, NV 89820 (702) 635-2376; FTS 470-5429
Admin Debra J Christensen.
Lib Type Special.
Spec Subs Land & resource management; watershed; economics; range & wildlife; recreation.
Circ Servs Avail To other libraries.
Ref Servs Avail To the general public.

1481. Bureau of Land Management, District Office Library
705 E 4th St, Winnemucca, NV 89445 (702) 623-3676
Admin Nevada Lee York.
Lib Type Special.
Spec Subs Environmental; livestock grazing; wild horses; mining & minerals; cultural resources; recreation; wildlife; land use, such as rights of way & pipelines.
Ref Servs Avail To other Federal libraries; to the general public.

1482. Bureau of Land Management, District Office Library
Suite 335, 1050 E William St, Carson City, NV 89701 (702) 882-1631; FTS 470-5612
Admin Cathryn Smith.
Lib Type Special.
Spec Subs Environment; minerals; range; wildlife; recreation planning.
Ref Servs Avail To the general public.

1483. Bureau of Land Management, Eastern States Office Library
350 S Pickett St, Alexandria, VA 22304 (703) 235-2898; FTS 235-2898
Admin Belynda B Bradshaw.
Lib Type Special.
Spec Subs Land resources management; mineral management; wildhorse & burro management; patents.
Circ Servs Avail To other Federal libraries; to other libraries.
Ref Servs Avail To the general public.

1484. Bureau of Land Management, Elko District Office Library
PO Box 831, Elko, NV 89801 (702) 738-4071; FTS 470-5437
Lib Type Special.
Spec Subs Environment; geology; geothermal energy; history of the district; land use; mineral & cadastral surveys; MT plates; oil & gas historical plats for townships in district; range management & fire rehabilitation; recreation statistics; topographic maps;

water; well logs; wild horses & burros; wildlife. *Spec Collecs* Aerial photos of Elko District lands; game harvests by NV Fish & Game (for past 13 yrs).

1485. Bureau of Land Management, Eugene Office Library
PO Box 10226, Eugene, OR 97440 (503) 687-6662; FTS 425-6662
Admin Caren T Cline.
Lib Type Special.
Spec Subs Forestry; wildlife; recreation.
Ref Servs Avail To the general public.

1486. Bureau of Land Management, Fairbanks District Office Library
1541 Gaffney Rd, Fairbanks, AK 99703 (907) 356-5340
Admin Kanza Easterly-Keill.
Lib Type Special.
Spec Subs Land law; minerals; recreation; cultural resources; biological resources; fire suppression. *Spec Collecs* BLM manuals; IBLA's; US Codes; US Statutes; CFR's; EIS's & RMP's for Alaska.
Circ Servs Avail To other Federal libraries.
Ref Servs Avail To other Federal libraries; to other libraries.

1487. Bureau of Land Management, Folsom District Office Library
63 Natoma St, Folsom, CA 95630 (916) 985-4474; FTS 448-3440
Admin Iris Hamilton.
Lib Type Special.
Spec Subs Resources; timber; minerals; forestry; range; outdoor recreation; watershed.
Ref Servs Avail Not open to the general public; restricted to staff.

1488. Bureau of Land Management, Garnet Resource Area Library
3255 Ft Missoula Rd, Missoula, MT 59801 (406) 329-3914
Lib Type Special.

1489. Bureau of Land Management, Idaho State Office Library
3380 Americana Terrace, Boise, ID 83706 (208) 334-1473; FTS 554-1473
Admin Junia Merill.
Lib Type Special.
Spec Subs Minerals; lands & resource management; wildlife & plant management. *In-house Files* BLM technical reports; EIS's & all books & reports written by BLM in Idaho.
Info Ret Servs BLM-LRS. *Shared Catalog Nets* BLM-LRS.
Circ Servs Avail To other Federal libraries; to other libraries.
Ref Servs Avail To other Federal libraries; to other libraries; to the general public.

1490. Bureau of Land Management, Kanab Office Library
PO Box 459, 320 N 1st E, Kanab, UT 84741 (801) 644-2672
Admin Gladys B Riggs.
Lib Type Special.
Spec Subs Minerals; range; forestry; recreation; wildlife; watershed management.
Ref Servs Avail To the general public.

1491. Bureau of Land Management, Lake States Office Library
125 Federal Bldg, Duluth, MN 55802 (218) 727-6692, ext 378; FTS 783-9378
Admin Marlene F Johnson.
Lib Type Special.
Spec Subs Natural resources. *In-house Files* Directories; pamphlets; reports; studies; technical notes; bulletins; impact statements.
Circ Servs Avail To other libraries.
Ref Servs Avail To the general public.

1492. Bureau of Land Management, Lakeview District Office Library
PO Box 151, 1000 S 9th St, Lakeview, OR 97630 (503) 947-2177
Admin Ellazan M Pike.
Lib Type Special.
Circ Servs Avail Not open to the general public; restricted to district employees.
Ref Servs Avail Not open to the general public; restricted to district employees.

1493. Bureau of Land Management, Las Cruces District Office Library
1800 Marquess, Las Cruces, NM 88005 (505) 525-8228
Lib Type Special.

1494. Bureau of Land Management, Las Vegas District Office Library
Box 26569, Las Vegas, NV 89126 (702) 388-6403
Lib Type Special.

1495. Bureau of Land Management Library
PO Box 25047, Denver Federal Ctr, Bldg 50, Denver, CO 80225-0047 (303) 236-6650; FTS 776-6650
Admin Sandra L Bowers. *Ref Lib* Judy Moisey. *ILL* Teresa Day. *Acq Lib* Barbara Klassen.
Lib Type Special.
Spec Subs Range management; land use; natural resources. *In-house Files* BLM—WESTFORNET Monthly Alert.
Info Ret Servs DIALOG; BRS; SDC. *Shared Catalog Nets* OCLC. *Coop Lib Nets* FEDLINK. *Elec Mail Nets* ITT DIALCOM.
Circ Servs Avail To other Federal libraries; to other libraries.
Ref Servs Avail To other Federal libraries; to other libraries; to the general public.

1496. Bureau of Land Management Library
764 Horizon Dr, Grand Junction, CO 81506 (303) 243-6552; FTS 323-0011
Admin Linda P Berkey. *Ref Lib* Paul Friedrichs (ILL, Acq).
Lib Type Special.
Shared Catalog Nets Library Reference System (LRS). *Coop Lib Nets* Denver Service Center Library (DSC Library). *Elec Mail Nets* ITT DIALCOM.
Circ Servs Avail To other Federal libraries; to other libraries; to the general public.
Ref Servs Avail To other Federal libraries; to other libraries; to the general public.

1497. Bureau of Land Management Library
951 N Poplar, Casper, WY 82601 (307) 265-5550 ext 5101; FTS 328-5591; AUTOVON 261-5591
Admin Trudy Closson.
Lib Type Special.
Spec Subs Minerals; forestry; fire; range; wildlife; soil; hydrology.
Elec Mail Nets BLM.
Circ Servs Avail Restricted to BLM.
Ref Servs Avail Restricted to BLM.

1498. Bureau of Land Management Library
Pan American Freeway, NE, Albuquerque, NM 87107 (505) 766-3675; FTS 474-3675
Lib Type Special.
Ref Servs Avail Not open to the general public; restricted to employees.

1499. Bureau of Land Management, Medford District Office Library
3040 Biddle Rd, Medford, OR 97504 (503) 778-4174 ext 308; FTS 424-4230
Admin Carol Weitgenant.
Lib Type Special.
Ref Servs Avail To other Federal libraries.

1500. Bureau of Land Management, Minerals Management Service Library
PO Box 101159, Anchorage, AK 99510 (907) 261-4435; FTS 261-4435
Admin Christine Huffaker. *Acq Lib* Mary Johnson.
Lib Type Special.
Spec Subs Geology; marine biology; environmental science. *Spec Collecs* Outer Continental Shelf Environmental Assessment Program—final reports; socio-economic technical reports; environmental impact statements for Alaska OCS.
Lib Deposit Designation DOI; MMS Reports.
Info Ret Servs DIALOG; LEXIS. *Shared Catalog Nets* OCLC. *Coop Lib Nets* FEDLINK.
Circ Servs Avail To other Federal libraries; not open to the general public; restricted to in-house use; some reports available to general public.
Ref Servs Avail To other Federal libraries; to other libraries; to the general public.

1501. Bureau of Land Management, Minerals Management Service Library
3301 N Causeing Blvd, Metairie, LA 70002 (504) 838-0521
Lib Type Special.

1502. Bureau of Land Management, Montana State Office Library
PO Box 36800, Billings, MT 59107 (406) 657-6671; FTS 585-6671
Admin Carolyn M Nelson. *ILL* Patricia J Koch (Acq).
Lib Type Special.
Spec Subs Geologic materials; wildlife; range lands; cultural resources; watershed for the MT, ND & SD areas. *Spec Collecs* Missouri River Basin reports.
Shared Catalog Nets OCLC. *Coop Lib Nets* FLICC; FEDLINK; Billings Area Health Sciences Information Consortium (BAHSIC).
Circ Servs Avail To other Federal libraries; to other libraries; to the general public.
Ref Servs Avail Restricted to employees.

1503. Bureau of Land Management, Montrose District Office Library
2465 S Townsend, Montrose, CO 81401 (303) 249-7791, ext 237
Lib Type Special.

1504. Bureau of Land Management, New Mexico State Office Central Files/Library
PO Box 1449, Santa Fe, NM 87504-1449 (505) 988-6047; FTS 476-6047
Admin Don Boyer (Chief, Office Services Section). *Ref Lib* Mae Ferne Bridgford (ILL). *Acq Lib* Monica L Martinez.
Lib Type Special.
Spec Subs Environmental statements; land decisions for New Mexico. *Spec Collecs* US statutes at large; decisions of the Dept of the Interior; Lindley on Mines, Vols I & II; Costigan on Mining Law; Mathew & Conway Digest of Land Decisions; Copp's Public Land Laws. *In-house Files* Internal general correspondence files.
Coop Lib Nets BLM Westfornet; OCLC. *Elec Mail Nets* ITT DIALCOM.
Circ Servs Avail Not open to the general public; restricted to BLM employees.
Ref Servs Avail To the general public.

1505. Bureau of Land Management, New Mexico State Office Library
Box 1449, Santa Fe, NM 87501 (505) 988-6047
Lib Type Special.

1506. Bureau of Land Management, New Orleans Outer-Continental Shelf Office Library
Suite 841, 500 Camp St, New Orleans, LA 70130 (504) 589-6541; FTS 682-6541
Admin Alice B Laforet.
Lib Type Special.
Spec Subs Sciences. *Spec Collecs* Environmental impact statements for the Gulf of Mexico & South Atlantic.

1507. Bureau of Land Management, Phillips Resource Area Office Library
PO Box B, 501 S 2nd St, Malta, MT 59538 (406) 654-1240
Lib Type Special.
Spec Subs Forestry; minerals; range land; recreation; soil; watershed; wildlife.

1508. Bureau of Land Management, Phoenix District Office Library
2929 W Clarendon Ave, Phoenix, AZ 85017 (602) 241-2501; FTS 261-2501
Admin Evelyn E Howell.
Lib Type Special.
Spec Subs Minerals; land use; wildlife; range; watershed; climate; engineering; environment; recreation; horse & burro studies; legal reference works.
Circ Servs Avail To other libraries.
Ref Servs Avail To the general public.

1509. Bureau of Land Management, Prineville District Office Library
185 E 4th St, Prineville, OR 97754 (503) 447-4115
Admin Rebecca Lemmer.
Lib Type Special.
Circ Servs Avail Not open to the general public.
Ref Servs Avail To other Federal libraries; not open to the general public.

1510. Bureau of Land Management, Rawlins District Office Library
PO Box 670, Rawlins, WY 82301 (307) 324-7171, ext 213
Admin Lynn McCarthy.
Lib Type Special.
Spec Subs Environmental impact statements.
Elec Mail Nets ITT DIALCOM.
Circ Servs Avail To other Federal libraries; not open to the general public.
Ref Servs Avail To other Federal libraries; not open to the general public.

1511. Bureau of Land Management, Research Library
PO Box 1048, 730 N Montana, Dillon, MT 59725 (406) 683-2337
Lib Type Special.
Ref Servs Avail Not open to the general public; restricted to use by the public on request.

1512. Bureau of Land Management, Richfield Office Library
150 E 900 N, Richfield, UT 84701 (801) 896-8221; FTS 584-8011
Admin Kathy Stubbs.
Lib Type Special.
Spec Subs Resources management.
Ref Servs Avail To the general public.

1513. Bureau of Land Management, Riverside District Office Library
1695 Spruce St, Riverside, CA 92507 (714) 351-6407
Lib Type Special.

1514. Bureau of Land Management, Roseburg District Office Library
777 NW Garden Valley Blvd, Roseburg, OR 97470 (503) 672-4491; FTS 422-4515
Admin Linda M Novakovich (Support Svcs Supv). *Ref Lib* Sharon A Albertson (Records Mgr). *ILL* Rosie Hansen (Acq). *Acq Lib* Jill Engeldorf.
Lib Type Special.
Spec Subs Wildlife; forestry; minerals; range management; road construction & engineering; administration; water recreation. *Spec Collecs* CFR'S; some Board of Land Appeals; US Code.
Coop Lib Nets Library Reference System with Denver service center (LRS). *Elec Mail Nets* ITT DIALCOM.
Circ Servs Avail Restricted to BLM.
Ref Servs Avail Restricted to BLM.

1515. Bureau of Land Management, Roswell District Office Library
PO Box 1397, Roswell, NM 88201 (505) 622-9042; FTS 572-0233
Admin Marjorie Cannon.
Lib Type Special.
Elec Mail Nets ITT DIALCOM.
Circ Servs Avail Not open to the general public.
Ref Servs Avail To the general public.

1516. Bureau of Land Management, Safford District Office Library
425 E 4th St, Safford, AZ 85546 (602) 428-4040; FTS 762-6384
Admin Irene Silva (Lib); Wally Ballow (Admin).
Lib Type Special.
Spec Subs Wildlife; archeology; minerals; range; watershed.
Ref Servs Avail Restricted to internal use.

1517. Bureau of Land Management, Salem District Office Library
PO Box 3227, Salem, OR 97303 (503) 399-5663; FTS 422-5663
Admin Lori Anderson.
Lib Type General.
Circ Servs Avail To other Federal libraries; not open to the general public.
Ref Servs Avail To other Federal libraries; not open to the general public.

1518. Bureau of Land Management, Salmon District Office Library
PO Box 430, Salmon, ID 83467 (208) 756-2201
Lib Type Special.
Spec Subs Land resource planning.

1519. Bureau of Land Management, Salt Lake City District Office Library
Department of the Interior, Salt Lake City, UT 84119 (801) 524-4450; FTS 588-4450
Admin Elaine Nielson; Dona Smedley.
Lib Type Special.
Spec Subs Grazing; wildlife; Northern Utah; public land administration.
Ref Servs Avail To other Federal libraries; to other libraries; to the general public.

1520. Bureau of Land Management, San Rafael-Price River Resource Area Library
PO Drawer AB, Price, UT 84501 (801) 637-4584
Admin Lavonne Orton.
Lib Type Special.
Spec Subs Land resources.

1521. Bureau of Land Management, Shoshone District Library
PO Box 2B, 400 W F St, Shoshone, ID 83352 (208) 886-2206; FTS 554-6576
Lib Type Special.

1522. Bureau of Land Management, Spokane District Office Library
Rm 551 US Courthouse, W 900 Riverside, Spokane, WA 99201 (509) 456-2570; FTS 439-2570
Admin Dorothy Derbergeron.
Lib Type Special.
Spec Subs Natural resource program.
Ref Servs Avail To the general public.

1523. Bureau of Land Management, Susanville District Office Library
PO Box 1090, Susanville, CA 96130 (916) 257-5385
Admin Carmie Ferrace.
Lib Type Special.
Spec Subs Natural resources; wildlife; range management; forestry. *Spec Collecs* Research material.
Ref Servs Avail To the general public.

1524. Bureau of Land Management, Ukiah District Office Library
555 Leslie St, Ukiah, CA 95482 (707) 462-3873
Lib Type Special.

1525. Bureau of Land Management, Utah State Office Library
136 E S Temple, Salt Lake City, UT 84111 (801) 524-5650; FTS 588-5330
Admin June Edmisten.
Lib Type Special.
Spec Subs Natural resources; wildlife; minerals; environment; engineering; statistics; economics; law. *Spec Collecs* Antiquities site inventories.
Circ Servs Avail To other Federal libraries; to other libraries.
Ref Servs Avail To the general public.

1526. Bureau of Land Management, Vernal District Office Library
170 S 500 E, Vernal, UT 84078 (801) 789-1362
Lib Type Special.

1527. Bureau of Land Management, Worland District Office Library
PO Box 119, Worland, WY 82401 (307) 347-6151; ILL 347-9871
Lib Type Special.

1528. Bureau of Land Management, Wyoming State Office Library
PO Box 1828, Cheyenne, WY 82001 (307) 778-2220, ext 2388; FTS 328-2388
Admin Lois J Carneal.
Lib Type Special.
Spec Subs Environment; land & resources management; recreation; minerals; legal works; reference material.
Circ Servs Avail To other libraries.
Ref Servs Avail To the general public.

1529. Bureau of Land Management, Yuma District Office Library
PO Box 5680, Yuma, AZ 85364 (602) 726-2612; FTS 261-2612
Admin Louise Mann.
Lib Type Special.
Spec Subs Land use; recreation.
Circ Servs Avail To other libraries.
Ref Servs Avail To the general public.

Bureau of Mines

1530. Avondale Research Center Library
4900 LaSalle Rd, Avondale, MD 20782 (301) 436-7552
Admin Hoor Siddiqui.
Lib Type Engineering & Science.
Spec Subs Metallurgy; solid waste recycling; particulate mineralogy. *In-house Files* Over 12,000 books & bound periodicals.
Info Ret Servs DIALOG.
Circ Servs Avail To other Federal libraries; to other libraries; not open to the general public.
Ref Servs Avail To other Federal libraries; to other libraries; not open to the general public.

1531. Bureau of Mines, Albany Metallurgy Research Center
PO Box 70, 1450 W Queen (503) 967-5864; FTS 420-5864
Admin Eleanor Abshire.
Lib Type Special.
Spec Subs Metallurgy; chemistry; physics; materials sciences; mineral resources & related fields. *Spec Collecs* Zirconium/Hafnium literature, key bibliographies; information circulars.
Circ Servs Avail To other libraries.
Ref Servs Avail To the general public.

1532. Bureau of Mines, Boulder City Metallurgy Library
500 Date St, Boulder City, NV 89005 (702) 293-1033; FTS 598-7441
Admin Julie Lund.
Lib Type Special; Engineering & Science.
Spec Subs Metallurgy; chemistry; chemical engineering. *Spec Collecs* Chemical abstracts.
Circ Servs Avail To other libraries.
Ref Servs Avail To the general public.

1533. Bureau of Mines, Charles W Henderson Memorial Library
Bldg 20, Federal Center, Denver, CO 80225 (303) 234-2817; FTS 776-0474
Admin Ann Elizabeth Chapel.
Lib Type Engineering & Science.
Spec Subs Mining engineering; mining economics; geology.
Info Ret Servs DIALOG. *Shared Catalog Nets* OCLC. *Coop Lib Nets* Engineering Info Network (EIN).
Circ Servs Avail To other Federal libraries; to other libraries; to the general public.
Ref Servs Avail To other Federal libraries; to other libraries; to the general public.

1534. Bureau of Mines Library
Boeing Services Int, PO Box 18070, Cochrans Mill Rd, Pittsburgh, PA 15236 (412) 675-4431; FTS 723-4431
Admin Kathleen M Stabryla.
Lib Type Special.
Spec Subs Coal; coal-chemistry; fossil energy; geology. *Spec Collecs* BOM documents.
Lib Deposit Designation GPO Depository Library.
Info Ret Servs DIALOG; BRS. *Coop Lib Nets* PRLC.
Circ Servs Avail To other Federal libraries.
Ref Servs Avail To other Federal libraries; to other libraries; to the general public.

1535. Bureau of Mines Library
Boeing Services Int., PO Box 18070, Cochrans Mill Rd, Pittsburgh, PA 15236 (412) 675-4431; FTS 723-4431
Admin Kathleen M Stabryla.
Lib Type Special.
Spec Subs Coal; fossil energy.
Lib Deposit Designation GPO Depository Library.
Info Ret Servs DIALOG. *Coop Lib Nets* PRLC.
Circ Servs Avail To other Federal libraries; to other libraries.
Ref Servs Avail To other Federal libraries; to other libraries; to the general public.

1536. Bureau of Mines Library
PO Box 550, Juneau, AK 99802 (907) 364-2111; FTS 586-7459
Admin Helen Jacobson.
Lib Type Special.
Spec Subs Alaskan geology; mining engineering; permafrost. *Spec Collecs* US Bureau of Mines documents; US Geological Survey documents on Alaska; CRREL documents, Alaska geological documents.
Coop Lib Nets Alaska Library Network (ALN).
Circ Servs Avail Restricted to ILL.
Ref Servs Avail To other Federal libraries; to other libraries; to the general public.

1537. Bureau of Mines, Metallurgy Research Center Library
1600 E 1st S, Salt Lake City, UT 84112 (801) 524-5379; FTS 588-5379
Admin Julia B Goodwin.
Lib Type Special; Engineering & Science.
Spec Subs Metallurgy research; natural resources conservation; water & power development; environmental pollution; engineering; physical sciences.
Circ Servs Avail To other Federal libraries; to other libraries.
Ref Servs Avail To the general public.

1538. Bureau of Mines, Salt Lake City Research Center Library
729 Arapeen Dr, Salt Lake City, UT 84112 (801) 524-6112; FTS 588-6112
Admin Jean B Bechstead (Lib); A B Whitehead (Research Supv).
Lib Type Engineering & Science.
Spec Subs Metallurgy; mining; chemistry.
Info Ret Servs DIALOG.
Circ Servs Avail To other Federal libraries; to other libraries; to the general public.
Ref Servs Avail To other Federal libraries; to other libraries; to the general public.

1539. Bureau of Mines, Section of Administrative Services Library
Rm 127, 2401 E St, NW, Washington, DC 20241 (202) 634-1116; FTS 634-1116
Admin Judy Jordan.
Lib Type Special.
Spec Subs Domestic & international material on mineral resources, supply & demand, & statistical data. *Spec Collecs* Annual reports of mineral industry firms; mineral statistics publications for foreign countries.
Circ Servs Avail To other Federal libraries; to other libraries.
Ref Servs Avail To the general public.

1540. Bureau of Mines, Spokane Research Center Library
E 315 Montgomery Ave, Spokane, WA 99207 (509) 484-1610; FTS 439-6880
Admin C E Peterson (Support Svcs Supv).
Lib Type Engineering & Science.
Spec Subs Mining engineering & associated topics; Bureau of Mines publications. *In-house Files* Final reports from all research contracts issued by the Bureau of Mines on open file.
Ref Servs Avail To other Federal libraries; to other libraries; to the general public; restricted to in-house use.

1541. Bureau of Mines, Twin Cities Library
PO Box 1660, Twin Cities, MN 55111 (612) 725-4503; FTS 725-4503
Admin Merle Bernstein.
Lib Type Special.
Spec Subs Mining & metallurgy. *Spec Collecs* Technical reports.
Circ Servs Avail To other Federal libraries; to other libraries.
Ref Servs Avail To the general public.

1542. Bureau of Mines, Twin Cities Research Center Library
5629 Minnehaha Ave S, Minneapolis, MN 55417 (612) 726-4503; FTS 726-4503
Admin Marilynn R Anderson; Ronald G Troop.
Lib Type Engineering & Science.
Spec Subs Mining research; metallurgy; mineral industries; conservation; industrial safety; rock mechanics; systems engineering. *Spec Collecs* Oil shale data base.
Info Ret Servs DIALOG.
Circ Servs Avail To other Federal libraries; to other libraries; to the general public.
Ref Servs Avail To other Federal libraries; to other libraries; to the general public.

1543. Bureau of Mines, Western Field Operations Center Library
E 360 3rd Ave, Spokane, WA 99202 (509) 484-1610 ext 348; FTS 439-5350
Admin Margaret Varner.
Lib Type Engineering & Science.
Spec Subs Geology; economic geology; engineering; geochemistry. *Spec Collecs* State geological collections for WA, OR, ID, MT, NV, & CA; NURE Dept of Energy documents; USBM war minerals records.
Info Ret Servs DIALOG. *Shared Catalog Nets* WLN; Northwest Information Directory. *Coop Lib Nets* Fred Neyer Charitable Trust; Library & Information Resources for the Northwest.
Circ Servs Avail To other Federal libraries; to other libraries; to the general public.

Ref Servs Avail To other Federal libraries; to other libraries; to the general public.

1544. Reno Metallurgy Research Center Library
1605 Evans Ave, Reno, NV 89520-0105 (702) 784-5391; FTS 470-5348
Lib Type Special.
Spec Subs Aluminum research; environmental sciences; metallurgy; mining engineering. *Spec Collecs* Complete Bureau of Mines publications (IC, RI, & Bulletin Collection). *In-house Files* Open file reports; technical papers & progress reports.

1545. Rolla Metallurgy Research Center, Technical Library
Hwy 66, PO Box 280, 1300 Bishop Ave, Rolla, MO 65401 (314) 364-3169; FTS 276-9210
Lib Type Special.

1546. Tuscaloosa Research Center Library
US Bureau of Mines, PO Box L, University, AL 35486 (205) 758-0491; FTS 222-0111
Admin Susan D Markham.
Lib Type Engineering & Science.
Spec Subs Mineralogy; mining; metallurgy; fine particle technology; ceramic & materials science; geology & chemistry. *Spec Collecs* All Bureau of Mines publications published 1921 to present. *In-house Files* In-house data base of Bureau of Mines publications.
Info Ret Servs DIALOG. *Coop Lib Nets* Alabama Library Exchange (ALEX); Alabama Online Users Group (AOUG).
Circ Servs Avail To other Federal libraries; to other libraries.
Ref Servs Avail To other Federal libraries; to other libraries; to the general public.

Bureau of Reclamation

1547. Bureau of Reclamation, Engineering & Research Center Library
PO Box 25007, Denver Federal Center, Denver, CO 80225 (303) 236-6963; FTS 776-6963
Admin Paul F Mulloney. *Ref Lib* Isabella Hopkins. *ILL* Marie Pederson. *Acq Lib* Gertrude Schalow.
Lib Type Engineering & Science.
Spec Subs Water resources, especially designing & building dams, pipelines, canals & other hydraulic structures; environment. *Spec Collecs* Water resources science & technology, particularly geotechnology, project management, water quality, & weed control. *In-house Files* Specialized field reports that cover all facets of dam construction, such as site control, preconstruction reports, environmental impact statements, cost/benefit ratios, & demographic studies.
Lib Deposit Designation GPO Depository Library.
Info Ret Servs DIALOG; BRS; SDC; CIS; MEDLINE; TOXLINE. *Shared Catalog Nets* OCLC. *Coop Lib Nets* Bibliographic Center for Research; FEDLINK. *Elec Mail Nets* ITT DIALCOM; Telex.
Circ Servs Avail To other Federal libraries; to other libraries; to the general public.
Ref Servs Avail To other Federal libraries; to other libraries; to the general public.

1548. Pacific Northwest Region Library
Box 43, 550 W Fort St, Boise, ID 83724-0043 (208) 334-1090; FTS 554-1090
Admin Esther Joslin.
Lib Type Special.
Spec Subs Project histories.
Ref Servs Avail To other Federal libraries; to other libraries; to the general public.

U.S. Fish & Wildlife Service

1549. Columbia National Fisheries Research Library
Rte 1, Columbia, MO 65201 (314) 875-5399; FTS 276-5399
Admin Axie Hindman.
Lib Type Engineering & Science.
Spec Subs Aquatic toxicology; environmental pollution.
Info Ret Servs DIALOG; BRS; CIS; NPIRS. *Shared Catalog Nets* OCLC. *Elec Mail Nets* ITT DIALCOM.
Circ Servs Avail To other Federal libraries; to other libraries.
Ref Servs Avail To other Federal libraries; to other libraries; restricted to on-site use by general public.

1550. Fish & Wildlife Service, Division of Biological Services Library
1612 June Ave, Panama City, FL 32401 (904) 769-5430; FTS 946-5215
Lib Type Special.
Spec Subs Biology; fishery resources; habitat preservation. *Spec Collecs* Government reports.
Circ Servs Avail Not open to the general public; restricted to staff.

1551. Fish & Wildlife Service Library
1011 E Tudor Rd, Anchorage, AK 99503 (907) 786-3358
Lib Type Special.
Spec Subs Service publications.
Info Ret Servs LEXIS; NEXIS. *Shared Catalog Nets* OCLC. *Coop Lib Nets* Alaska Library Network.

1552. Fish & Wildlife Service, Science Reference Library
Federal Bldg, Ft Snelling, Twin Cities, MN 55111 (612) 725-3576; FTS 725-3576
Admin Veronica Siedle.
Lib Type Special.
Spec Subs Environmental studies; water pollution; wildlife management.
Info Ret Servs DIALOG. *Shared Catalog Nets* OCLC.
Ref Servs Avail Not open to the general public; restricted to staff.

1553. Fish Farming Experimental Station Library
PO Box 860, Stuttgart, AR 72160 (501) 673-8761
Admin Joyce Cooper.
Lib Type Special.
Spec Subs Warm water fisheries research; fish husbandry; diseases.
Ref Servs Avail To other Federal libraries; to other libraries; to the general public.

1554. National Fisheries Center, Leetown Technical Information Services
Box 700, Kearneysville, WV 25430 (304) 725-8461; FTS 925-5212
Admin Joyce A Mann. *Ref Lib* Vi Catrow (Acq). *ILL* Lora McKenzie.
Lib Type Engineering & Science.
Spec Subs Fish diseases, health, culture; aquaculture. *Spec Collecs* 10,000 reprints on fish diseases.
Info Ret Servs DIALOG. *Shared Catalog Nets* OCLC. *Coop Lib Nets* FEDLINK. *Elec Mail Nets* ITT DIALCOM.
Circ Servs Avail To other Federal libraries; to other libraries.
Ref Servs Avail To other Federal libraries; to other libraries; to the general public; restricted to on-site use by general public.

1555. National Fishery Research & Development Laboratory Library
Box 63 RD 4, Wellsboro, PA 16901 (717) 724-3322
Admin Betty Driebelbies.
Lib Type Special.
Spec Subs Fish culture; fish biology; fish genetics; aquaculture engineering; bio-engineering; community ecology.
Shared Catalog Nets OCLC. *Coop Lib Nets* Susquehanna Library Cooperative (SLC).
Circ Servs Avail To other Federal libraries; to other libraries.
Ref Servs Avail To other Federal libraries; to other libraries; to the general public.

1556. National Fishery Research Center Library
PO Box 818, La Crosse, WI 54602-0818 (608) 783-6451; FTS 364-3210
Admin Rosalie A Schonich.
Lib Type Special.
Spec Subs Toxicology; aquatic ecology; fish culture; chemical & drug registration; pharmacology; fishery management. *Spec Collecs* Mississippi River; fishery chemicals.
Info Ret Servs DIALOG. *Coop Lib Nets* WILS. *Elec Mail Nets* ITT DIALCOM.
Circ Servs Avail To other Federal libraries; to other libraries; to the general public.
Ref Servs Avail To other Federal libraries; to other libraries; to the general public.

1557. Northern Prairie Wildlife Research Center Library
Fish & Wildlife Service, PO Box 1747, Jamestown, ND 58401 (701) 252-5363
Admin Angie Kokott.
Lib Type Special.
Spec Subs Wildlife management & research; avian biology; plant & animal ecology. *Spec Collecs* Waterfowl. *In-house Files* 8000 reprints; over 600 NPWRC publications.
Info Ret Servs DIALOG. *Shared Catalog Nets* OCLC. *Coop Lib Nets* MINITEX, North Dakota Library Assoc (NDLA); Minnesota Union List (MULS).
Circ Servs Avail To other Federal libraries; to other libraries; not open to the general public.
Ref Servs Avail To other libraries; not open to the general public.

1558. Patuxent Wildlife Research Center Library
US Fish & Wildlife Service, Laurel, MD 20708 (301) 498-0235; FTS 956-0235
Admin Lynda Garrett.
Lib Type Engineering & Science.
Spec Subs Wildlife, especially birds; biostatistics; environmental pollution. *Spec Collecs* Vertical file collection (56 drawers) of reprints on environmental pollutants, particularly pesticides & heavy metals.
Info Ret Servs DIALOG; BRS. *Shared Catalog Nets* OCLC. *Elec Mail Nets* ITT DIALCOM.
Circ Servs Avail To other Federal libraries; to other libraries.
Ref Servs Avail To other Federal libraries; to other libraries; to the general public.

1559. Tunison Laboratory of Fish Nutrition Library
3075 Gracie Rd, Cortland, NY 13045 (607) 753-9391; FTS 882-4220
Admin Kathy McCoy.
Lib Type Special.
Spec Subs Fish nutrition & culture; aquaculture.
Info Ret Servs DIALOG. *Shared Catalog Nets* OCLC. *Coop Lib Nets* FEDLINK. *Elec Mail Nets* ITT DIALCOM.
Circ Servs Avail To other Federal libraries; to other libraries.
Ref Servs Avail To other Federal libraries; to other libraries; to the general public; restricted to on-site use by general public.

1560. Van Oosten Library
1451 Green Rd, Ann Arbor, MI 48105 (313) 994-3331; FTS 378-1210
Admin Cynthia McCawley.
Lib Type Special.
Spec Subs Fisheries ecology; fish biology; Great Lakes; water pollution. *Spec Collecs* Personal reprint collections of Dr John Van Oosten & Dr James Moffett, former laboratory directors.
Info Ret Servs DIALOG; BRS. *Shared Catalog Nets* OCLC. *Coop Lib Nets* Washtenaw-Livingston Library Network (WLLN). *Elec Mail Nets* ITT DIALCOM.
Circ Servs Avail To other Federal libraries; to other libraries.
Ref Servs Avail To other Federal libraries.

Geological Survey

1561. EROS Data Center, Technical Reference Unit
USGS, Mundt Federal Bldg, Sioux Falls, SD 57198 (605) 594-6500; FTS 784-7500
Admin Susan H Lowell.
Lib Type Engineering & Science.
Spec Subs Remote sensing, airplane & satellite & related topics. *Spec Collecs* Complete collection of: 1) all Landsat scenes; 2) Skylab, Gemini, Apollo, & Shuttle scenes; 3) all USGS aerial photography including NHAP; 4) all NASA aerial photography.
Info Ret Servs DIALOG; NASA/RECON.
Circ Servs Avail Restricted to ILL.

1562. Geological Survey, Field Center Library
2255 N Gemini Dr, Flagstaff, AZ 86001 (602) 527-7008; FTS 765-7008; TTY 527-7008
Admin James R Nation.
Lib Type Engineering & Science.
Spec Subs Geology & extraterrestrial geology.
Shared Catalog Nets OCLC. *Coop Lib Nets* LS/2000 (USGS Network).
Circ Servs Avail Restricted to USGS.
Ref Servs Avail To other Federal libraries; to other libraries; to the general public.

1563. Geological Survey, Gerryan Memorial Library
PO Box 1026, 605 N Neil St, Champaign, IL 61820 (217) 398-5362; FTS 958-5362
Admin Alana Ferguson.
Lib Type Special.
Spec Subs Water resources & hydrology.
Ref Servs Avail To the general public.

1564. Geological Survey Library
12201 Sunrise Valley Dr, MS 950, Reston, VA 22092 (703) 648-4303; FTS 959-4302/4303
Admin Elizabeth J Yeates. *Ref Lib* Barbara Chappell. *ILL* Henry Zoller. *Acq Lib* Michael J Kubisiak.
Lib Type Engineering & Science.
Spec Subs In-depth collection of worldwide earth science literature. *Spec Collecs* Kunz collection. *In-house Files* Open-file reports.
Lib Deposit Designation GPO Depository Library; NASA.
Info Ret Servs DIALOG; BRS; SDC. *Shared Catalog Nets* OCLC. *Coop Lib Nets* FEDLINK.
Circ Servs Avail To other Federal libraries; to other libraries.
Ref Servs Avail To other Federal libraries; to other libraries; to the general public.

1565. Geological Survey Library
Box 25046, Mail Stop 914, Denver, CO 80225 (303) 236-1000; FTS 776-1000
Admin Robert A Bier, Jr. *Ref Lib* Jane Bonn. *ILL* Elaine Watson.
Lib Type Engineering & Science.
Spec Subs Earth sciences, including geology, mineral resources, water resources, mapping, & geophysics. *Spec Collecs* Photographic library; field records library.
Info Ret Servs DIALOG; SDC. *Coop Lib Nets* FEDLINK; Central Colorado Library System (CCLS).
Circ Servs Avail Restricted to ILL.

1566. Geological Survey Library
345 Middlefield Rd, MS 955, Menlo Park, CA 94025 (415) 323-8111 ext 2207; FTS 467-2208
Admin Eleanore E Wilkins. *Ref Lib* Jacquelyn Freeberg (ILL).
Lib Type Engineering & Science.
Spec Subs Earth sciences & related disciplines. *Spec Collecs* Geologic maps (emphasis on western states); slides & photos on geologic hazards.
Lib Deposit Designation GPO Depository Library; USGS; DOE; NASA; DMA.
Info Ret Servs DIALOG; SDC; INFOLINE. *Shared Catalog Nets* OCLC.
Circ Servs Avail To other Federal libraries; to other libraries.
Ref Servs Avail To other Federal libraries; to other libraries; to the general public.

1567. Geological Survey Library
Box 7944, Metairie, LA 70010 (504) 837-4720, ext 219; FTS 680-9219
Admin Isabella Hopkins.
Lib Type Special.
Spec Subs Offshore petroleum production & exploration; geophysics; petroleum engineering in the Gulf of Mexico.
Circ Servs Avail To other Federal libraries; to other libraries.
Ref Servs Avail To the general public.

1568. Geological Survey Library
PO Box 1669, Albany, NY 12201 (518) 472-3107; FTS 562-3107
Admin Peggy L Evans.
Lib Type Engineering & Science.
Spec Subs Hydrology; ground-water; acid precipitation; stream & flood studies; climatological data maps; water studies.
Info Ret Servs DIALOG; BRS. *Shared Catalog Nets* OCLC.
Circ Servs Avail Not open to the general public.
Ref Servs Avail To other Federal libraries; to other libraries; restricted to on-site use by general public.

1569. Geological Survey, Mineral Resources Library
656 US Courthouse, Spokane, WA 99201 (509) 456-2524; FTS 439-4677
Admin Anita W Tarbert.
Lib Type Engineering & Science.
Spec Subs Geology & related subjects.
Circ Servs Avail To other Federal libraries; restricted to geology oriented patrons.
Ref Servs Avail To other Federal libraries; to other libraries; to the general public.

1570. Geological Survey, National Cartographic Information Center
Box 25046, Stop 504, Federal Ctr, Bldg 25, Denver, CO 80225 (303) 236-5812; FTS 776-5812
Lib Type Special.

1571. Geological Survey, National Mapping Division Applications Assistance Facility Library
Bldg 3101, National Space Technology Laboratories, NSTL Station, Bay Saint Louis, MS 39529 (601) 688-3541
Lib Type Special.

1572. Geological Survey, National Water Quality Laboratory-Library
Box 25046, Mail Stop 407, Denver Federal Ctr, Denver, CO 80225 (303) 234-4992; FTS 234-4992
Lib Type Special.
Spec Subs Water quality; organic & inorganic chemistry; chemical methodology & instrumentation; quality control; automatic data processing.
Circ Servs Avail To other libraries.
Ref Servs Avail To the general public.

1573. Geological Survey, Public Inquiries Office
169 Federal Bldg, 1961 Stout St, Denver, CO 80294 (303) 837-4160; FTS 327-4169
Admin Irene Shy.
Lib Type Special.
Spec Subs Earth sciences. *Spec Collecs* Complete set of USGS documents.
Circ Servs Avail Not open to the general public.
Ref Servs Avail Not open to the general public.

1574. Geological Survey, Public Inquiries Office Library
Federal Bldg, Rm 7638, 300 N Los Angeles St, Los Angeles, CA 90012 (213) 688-2850
Lib Type Special.
Spec Collecs USGS reports, maps, & open files for seven western states.

1575. Geological Survey, Public Inquiries Office Library
8105 Federal Bldg, 125 S State St, Salt Lake City, UT 84138 (801) 524-5652
Lib Type Special.
Spec Collecs GSA journals; state geological publications for UT, AZ, ID, NV, NM, CO, WY, & MT; USGS publications.
Ref Servs Avail Restricted to reference use.

1576. Geological Survey, Public Inquiries Office Library
504 Custom House, 555 Battery St, San Francisco, CA 94111 (415) 556-5627
Lib Type General.

1577. Geological Survey, Resource Appraisal Group Library
Box 25046, Mail Stop 971, Denver Federal Ctr, Denver, CO 80225 (303) 234-3435; FTS 234-3435
Admin Jeanette Wesley.
Lib Type Special.
Spec Subs Oil & gas statistics.
Ref Servs Avail To the general public; restricted to research.

1578. Geological Survey, Water Resources Division, Colorado District Library
United States Geological Survey, Box 25046, Stop 415, Federal Ctr, Lakewood, CO 80225 (303) 776-4895; FTS 776-4895
Admin Barbara J Condron.
Lib Type Engineering & Science.
Spec Subs Water; climatic data for Colorado, 1891-present; complete set of USGS water supply papers & water resources annual data for all states, 1971-present. *Spec Collecs* Nearly complete set of Colorado district publications, from 1967-present; Corps of Engineers & FEMA flood reports for Colorado; reports on specific flood problems.
Info Ret Servs DIALOG; BRS. *Shared Catalog Nets* OCLC. *Coop Lib Nets* Central Colorado Library System (CCLS); High Plains Library System (HPLS); Peaks & Plains Library System (PPLS); Bibliograph Center for Research (BCR); FEDLINK; FIFL. *Elec Mail Nets* Geonet.
Circ Servs Avail To other Federal libraries; to other libraries; restricted to general public not having other sources.
Ref Servs Avail To other Federal libraries; to other libraries; to the general public.

1579. Geological Survey, Water Resources Division Library
1815 University Ave, Madison, WI 53705-4042 (608) 262-2110; FTS 262-2110
Admin Rachel A Lansing.
Lib Type Engineering & Science.
Spec Subs Water resources; geology; floods; low flow; lakes; wetlands; ground water; surface water.
Circ Servs Avail Not open to the general public.
Ref Servs Avail Not open to the general public.

1580. Geological Survey, Water Resources Division Library
USGS, Federal Bldg, Drawer 10076, 301 S Park, Helena, MT 59626-0076 (406) 449-5263; FTS 585-5263
Admin Cynthia J Diamond.
Lib Type Special.
Spec Subs Water resources of Montana. *Spec Collecs* USGS series, topographic maps for Montana.
Shared Catalog Nets OCLC.
Circ Servs Avail To other Federal libraries; to other libraries.
Ref Servs Avail To other Federal libraries; to other libraries; to the general public.

1581. Geological Survey, Water Resources Division Library
1819 N Meridian St, Indianapolis, IN 46202 (317) 269-7101; FTS 331-6594
Admin Patricia E Clark.
Lib Type Special.
Spec Subs Water resources & geology.
Circ Servs Avail To other Federal libraries; to other libraries; not open to the general public.
Ref Servs Avail To the general public; restricted to on site use.

1582. Geological Survey, Water Resources Division Library
505 Marquette Ave, NW, Albuquerque, NM 87102 (505) 766-1284; FTS 474-1284
Admin Jane Nelson.
Lib Type Special.
Spec Subs New Mexico & Southwest hydrology. *Spec Collecs* New Mexico water resources.
Ref Servs Avail Not open to the general public; restricted to staff.

1583. US Geological Survey, Public Inquiries Office Library
Rm 1 C45, 1100 Commerce St, Dallas, TX 75242 (214) 767-0198
Lib Type Special.

Heritage Conservation & Recreation Service

1584. Heritage Conservation & Recreation Service, Northwest Region Office Library
Rm 990, 915 2nd Ave, Seattle, WA 98174 (206) 442-4706; FTS 399-5366
Admin Karen L Barthocet.
Lib Type Special.
Spec Subs Outdoor recreation; water resources; natural resource & land use planning; urban recreation for the Pacific Northwest. *Spec Collecs* Regional Data Program (computer printout data by county); statewide comprehensive outdoor recreation plans; regional environmental impact statements; Alaska pipeline project proposal.
Ref Servs Avail To the general public.

1585. Historic American Buildings Survey Library
Heritage Conservation & Recreation Service, Washington, DC 20240 (202) 523-5474
Admin Alicia D Stamm.
Lib Type Special.
Spec Subs Architectural history & historic preservation. *In-house Files* When records have been edited, they are sent to the Prints & Photograph Div, Library of Congress.
Circ Servs Avail Not open to the general public; restricted to staff.
Ref Servs Avail To the general public.

1586. Interagency Archeological Services Library
Heritage Conservation & Recreation Service, PO Box 2537, Denver Federal Ctr, Denver, CO 80225 (303) 234-2560; FTS 234-2560
Admin Carolyn Pierce.
Lib Type Special.
Spec Subs Archeology.
Ref Servs Avail To the general public.

1587. Lake Central Regional Office Library
Heritage Conservation & Recreation Service, Federal Bldg, Ann Arbor, MI 48107 (313) 668-2019; FTS 378-2019
Admin James M Grasso.
Lib Type Special.
Spec Subs Outdoor recreation planning. *Spec Collecs* Statewide comprehensive outdoor recreation plans (prepared by the state). *In-house Files* Studies of various outdoor recreation resources.
Circ Servs Avail To other libraries.
Ref Servs Avail To the general public.

1588. Mid-Continent Region Library
Heritage Conservation & Recreation Service, PO Box 25387, Denver, CO 80225 (303) 234-6468; FTS 234-6462
Admin Jo Ann Bush.
Lib Type Special.
Spec Subs Outdoor recreation; river basin & land use planning.
Ref Servs Avail To the general public.

1589. National Register of Historic Places Library
Heritage Conservation & Recreation Service, Washington, DC 20240 (202) 523-5480, ext 6221
Admin Lisa Soderberg.
Lib Type Special.

Spec Subs Historic preservation; American history; architectural history; preservation planning; archeology. *In-house Files* State historic preservation plans.
Circ Servs Avail Not open to the general public; restricted to staff.
Ref Servs Avail Not open to the general public; restricted to staff.

1590. Pacific Southwest Regional Office Library
Heritage Conservation & Recreation Service, Box 36062, 450 Golden Gate Ave, San Francisco, CA 94102 (415) 556-8580; FTS 556-8313
Admin Irene Stachura.
Lib Type Special.
Spec Subs Recreation; water resources; natural resource management. *Spec Collecs* Environmental impact statements; outdoor recreation plans.
Ref Servs Avail To the general public.

Minerals Management Service

1591. Minerals Management Service Library
PO Box 101159; Department of the Interior, Anchorage, AK 99510 (907) 261-4621
Lib Type Special.

National Park Service

1592. Acadia National Park Library
PO Box 177, Bar Harbor, ME 04609 (207) 288-3338; FTS 833-7485/7486
Admin Robert Rothe. *Ref Lib* Judith Hazen (Acq).
Lib Type Special.
Spec Subs Acadia National Park & associated flora & fauna; management plans; subjects related to natural history interpretation. *In-house Files* Vertical files Acadia National Park & flora & fauna.
Circ Servs Avail Restricted to park employees.
Ref Servs Avail Restricted to park employees.

1593. Adams National Historic Site, Stone Library
PO Box 531, 135 Adams St, Quincy, MA 02169 (617) 773-1177
Lib Type Special.
Spec Collecs This library is a historic structure containing the original books owned & used by President John Quincy Adams.

1594. Horace M Albright Training Center Library
PO Box 477, Grand Canyon, AZ 86023 (602) 638-2691
Lib Type Special.
Spec Subs Natural history; law enforcement; humanities; National Parks.
Ref Servs Avail To the general public.

1595. Allegheny Portage Railroad National Historic Site Library
PO Box 247, Cresson, PA 16630 (814) 886-8176; FTS 727-4501
Admin Larry Trombello.
Lib Type Special.
Spec Subs Allegheny Portage Railroad; Johnstown Flood of 1889.

1596. American Museum of Immigration Library
Statue of Liberty National Monument, Liberty Island, NY 10004 (212) 732-1236
Admin Won H Kim.
Lib Type Special.
Spec Subs Statue of Liberty & Ellis Island National Monument; immigration; ethnic groups. *Spec Collecs* Historic photographs of the Statue of Liberty & Ellis Island; Augustus F Sherman Collection (photographs of immigrants at Ellis Island); oral history collections of Ellis Island immigrants; films; slides.
Circ Servs Avail Not open to the general public.
Ref Servs Avail To other Federal libraries; to the general public.

1597. Andersonville National Historic Site Library
Andersonville, GA 31711 (912) 924-0343
Admin John N Tucker (Supt). *Ref Lib* Steve Jarrell (ILL, Acq).
Lib Type Special.
Spec Subs Prisoners of war, especially Civil War. *Spec Collecs* Woman's Relief Corps Journal, 1896-1985.
Lib Deposit Designation American Ex-prisoner of War Assoc.
Coop Lib Nets NPS. *Elec Mail Nets* NPS.
Circ Servs Avail Restricted to on-site use.
Ref Servs Avail Restricted to on-site use.

1598. Antietam National Battlefield Library
PO Box 158, Sharpsburg, MD 21782 (301) 432-5124
Admin Betty J Otto (Park Ranger).
Lib Type Special.
Spec Subs Civil War military personalities; biographies; regimental military histories; Civil War general stories. *Spec Collecs* Regimental military histories engaged in the battles of South Mountain, Antietam (Sharpsburg), & Monocacy; Henry Kyd Douglas; Civil War photographic histories. *In-house Files* Civil War letters (originals/copies); limited collection of Civil War diaries (originals/copies); battle recollections; maps; photographs; slides; motion pictures; museum artifacts; park history.
Coop Lib Nets Library, Dept of the Interior. *Elec Mail Nets* Interior Library.
Circ Servs Avail Restricted to NPS & Interior.
Ref Servs Avail Restricted to educational, writers, researchers, news media on-site use.

1599. Apostle Islands National Lakeshore Library
Box 4, Rte 1, Bayfield, WI 54814 (715) 779-3397
Admin Pat H Miller (Supt).
Lib Type Special.
Spec Subs Natural & cultural history of Apostle Islands National Lakeshore; NPS area & planning documents. *Spec Collecs* Apostle Islands National Lakeshore biological & historical research reports. *In-house Files* Natural & cultural history of Apostle Islands National Lakeshore; NPS areas.
Coop Lib Nets Northwest Wisconsin Library System.
Circ Servs Avail To other Federal libraries; to other libraries; not open to the general public.
Ref Servs Avail To other Federal libraries; to other libraries; to the general public.

1600. Appomattox Court House National Historic Park Library
PO Box 218, Appomattox, VA 24522 (804) 352-8987
Admin Ronald G Wilson.
Lib Type Special.
Spec Subs Civil War & Appomattox campaign. *Spec Collecs* Over 1325 photographs documenting the history & preservation of the village of Appomattox Court House. *In-house Files* Special studies on the structure & history of Appomattox Court House.
Coop Lib Nets Office of Library & Archival Service, Harpers Ferry Center, NPS.
Circ Servs Avail Restricted to reference only.
Ref Servs Avail To other Federal libraries; to other libraries; to the general public; restricted to use by reservation only.

1601. Arches National Park Library
125 W 200 S, Moab, UT 84532 (801) 259-8161
Admin Tracey Morse.
Lib Type Special.
Spec Subs Geology; natural history; archeology. *Spec Collecs* Glen Canyon Archeological Survey; SE Utah regional history; Wolfe Ranch National Historic District.
Circ Servs Avail To other Federal libraries; to the general public.
Ref Servs Avail To other Federal libraries; to the general public.

1602. Arlington House, The Robert E Lee Memorial Library
George Washington Memorial Pkwy, McLean, VA 22101 (703) 557-0613
Admin Ann Fuqua (Site Supv); Agnes Mullins (Curator).
Lib Type Special.
Spec Subs Robert E Lee & family; Arlington House; the Custis family. *In-house Files* Historical research notes: Dr Murray H Nelligan.
Ref Servs Avail To the general public; restricted to by appointment.

1603. Assateague Island National Seashore Library
Rt 2, Box 294, Berlin, MD 21811 (301) 641-1441
Lib Type Special.
Spec Subs Natural history of ocean & seashore environments. *Spec Collecs* Assateague Island Seashore, slides.
Circ Servs Avail Restricted to on site use.
Ref Servs Avail Restricted to researchers & students.

1604. Aztec Ruins National Monument Library
Box U, Aztec, NM 87410 (505) 334-6174
Admin William L Schart.
Lib Type Special.
Spec Subs Southwest archaeology; Aztec Ruins. *In-house Files* Ruins stabilization reports.
Circ Servs Avail To other libraries.
Ref Servs Avail To the general public.

1605. Badlands National Park Library
PO Box 6, Interior, SD 57750 (605) 433-5361
Admin Midge Johnston.
Lib Type Special.
Spec Subs Geology; paleontology; mammals; South Dakota history; Sioux & North American Indians; homesteading.
Circ Servs Avail Not open to the general public.
Ref Servs Avail Not open to the general public.

1606. Bandelier National Monument Library
Los Alamos, NM 87544 (505) 672-3861
Admin John Hunter.
Lib Type Special.
Spec Subs Archaeology of Pajarito Plateau; southwest, natural resources & history. *In-house Files* Stabilization & other related reports.
Ref Servs Avail To the general public; restricted to by arrangement.

1607. Bent's Old Fort National Historic Site Library
35110 Hwy 194 E, La Junta, CO 81050-9523 (303) 384-2596
Admin Derek O Hambly. *Ref Lib* James O'Barr (Acq).
Lib Type Special.
Spec Subs Rocky Mountain fur trade; Santa Fe Trail; the Bent-St Vrain Company; Cheyenne-Arapaho trade; the Army of the West; Mexican-American War; general time period 1828-1850; Charles Bent; William Bent; Ceran St Vrain. *In-house Files* Staff research associated with above topics.
Circ Servs Avail Not open to the general public; restricted to staff.
Ref Servs Avail To other Federal libraries; to other libraries; to the general public.

1608. Big Bend National Park Library
Big Bend National Park, TX 79834 (915) 477-2251
Admin Ramon Olivas.
Lib Type Special.
Spec Subs West Texas geology.
Shared Catalog Nets In house, NPS.
Circ Servs Avail To other Federal libraries; to other libraries; to the general public.
Ref Servs Avail To other Federal libraries; to other libraries; to the general public; restricted to Mon-Fri, 8-5:00 if staff is available.

1609. Big Hole National Battlefield Library
Box 237, Wisdom, MT 59761 (406) 689-3155
Admin Alfred W Schulmeyer.
Lib Type Special.
Spec Subs Indians; Nez Perce-White conflict; 19th century US military history. *Spec Collecs* Battle of the Big Hole, August 9-10, 1877.
Circ Servs Avail Restricted to staff.
Ref Servs Avail Restricted to staff.

1610. Big Thicket National Preserve Library
PO Box 7408, Beaumont, TX 77706 (713) 838-0271, ext 373; FTS
527-2373/2375
Admin David D Dunatchik.
Lib Type Special.
Spec Subs Big Thicket natural history, plants, animals, & petroleum.
Circ Servs Avail To other libraries.
Ref Servs Avail To the general public.

1611. Bighorn Canyon National Recreation Area Library
Box 458, Fort Smith, MT 59035 (406) 666-2412
Admin James E Staebler.
Lib Type Special.
Spec Subs National Park Service; National Park areas; natural &
cultural history (including Crow Indians) of the Bighorn Canyon
area.
Circ Servs Avail To the general public.
Ref Servs Avail To the general public.

1612. Blue Ridge Parkway Library
PO Box 9098, Ashville, NC 28815 (704) 672-0701; FTS 672-0701
Admin Mary Ann Peckham (On-site Supv).
Lib Type Special.
Spec Subs Southern Appalachian cultural & natural history; Blue
Ridge parkway history. *In-house Files* Technical & vertical files
on southern Appalachian cultural & natural history; Blue Ridge
Parkway history.
Circ Servs Avail Restricted to NPS employees.
Ref Servs Avail To other Federal libraries; to other libraries; to the
general public.

1613. Bryce Canyon National Park Library
Bryce Canyon National Park, UT 84717 (801) 834-5322
Admin Margaret Littlejohn (Supv Park Ranger).
Lib Type Special.
Spec Subs Papers dealing with Bryce Canyon National Park, especially geology.
Circ Servs Avail Not open to the general public; restricted to
researchers.
Ref Servs Avail Not open to the general public; restricted to
researchers.

1614. Buck Island Reef National Monument Library
Christiansted National Historic Site, PO Box 160, Christiansted,
St Croix, VI 00820 (809) 773-2107
Admin William F Cissel.
Lib Type Special.
Spec Subs Terrestial & marine flora & fauna particularly relating
to Buck Island Reef. *In-house Files* Management reports.
Circ Servs Avail Restricted to NPS staff.
Ref Servs Avail Restricted to scholars upon application.

1615. Buffalo National River Library
PO Box 1173, Harrison, AR 72602-1173 (501) 741-5443
Admin Richard E McCamant.
Lib Type Special.
Spec Subs Natural history; history; Ozark culture; recreation.
Circ Servs Avail Not open to the general public.
Ref Servs Avail To other Federal libraries; to the general public.

1616. Cabrillo National Monument Library
PO Box 6670, San Diego, CA 92106 (619) 293-5450; FTS 895-
5450
Admin Edmond Roberts. *Ref Lib* Lorenza Fong.
Lib Type Special.
Spec Subs History: European exploration, military history, California; Natural History: Chaparral ecology, marine life ecology, &
resource management publications. *Spec Collecs* NPS history,
policies, & guidelines. *In-house Files* Research studies pertaining to site.
Circ Servs Avail To other Federal libraries; to the general public.
Ref Servs Avail To other Federal libraries; to the general public;
restricted to on-site use for general public.

1617. Canaveral National Seashore Park Library
PO Box 6447, Titusville, FL 32782 (305) 867-4675; FTS 823-0634
Admin Richard H Helman (Chief of Interpretation). *Ref
Lib* Sandra Hines (ILL). *Acq Lib* Richard Helman.
Lib Type Special.
Spec Subs Natural & cultural resources related to Canaveral National Seashore. *In-house Files* Audio-visual (slide) file; administrative photo file.
Circ Servs Avail To other Federal libraries.
Ref Servs Avail To other Federal libraries; to other libraries; to the
general public.

1618. Canyon de Chelly National Monument Library
PO Box 588, Chinle, AZ 86503 (602) 674-5436
Admin Nancy G Pierce.
Lib Type Special.
Spec Subs Natural history; Indian history & culture. *In-house
Files* Archeological research.
Circ Servs Avail Not open to the general public; restricted to NPS.
Ref Servs Avail Not open to the general public; restricted to NPS.

1619. Cape Cod National Seashore Library
South Wellfleet, MA 02663 (617) 349-3785
Admin Mary Saunders.
Lib Type Special.
Spec Subs Natural history; ecology; local history. *Spec
Collecs* Annual reports of the US Life Savings Services, 1889-
1914 (predecessor agency of the Coast Guard); The Plymouth
Records, 1620 to circa 1700 & an 1861 edition.
Circ Servs Avail To other Federal libraries; to other libraries.
Ref Servs Avail To the general public.

1620. Cape Hatteras National Seashore Library
Box 675, Rte 1, Manteo, NC 27954 (919) 473-2111; FTS 827-
3014
Admin Penny Ambrose. *Ref Lib* Thomas L Hartman.
Lib Type Special.
Spec Subs Natural & historic resources of coastal NC.
Circ Servs Avail Restricted to ILL.
Ref Servs Avail Restricted to on-site use.

1621. Cape Lookout National Seashore Library
PO Box 690, Beaufort, NC 28516 (919) 728-2121
Admin Bruce E Weber.
Lib Type Special.
Spec Subs Barrier island ecology; maritime history.
Circ Servs Avail Not open to the general public; restricted to
employees.
Ref Servs Avail Not open to the general public; restricted to
employees & researchers.

1622. Capitol Reef National Park Library
Torrey, UT 84775 (801) 425-3871
Admin William S Gleason.
Lib Type Special.
Spec Subs Utah history; natural history.
Circ Servs Avail Not open to the general public.
Ref Servs Avail Not open to the general public.

1623. Capulin Mountain National Monument Library
Capulin, NM 88414 (505) 278-2201
Admin Superintendent.
Lib Type Special.
Spec Subs Geology, flora, fauna, & history of immediate area.
Circ Servs Avail To other Federal libraries.
Ref Servs Avail To other Federal libraries; to the general public.

**1624. Carlsbad Caverns & Guadalupe Mountains National
Parks Headquarters Library**
3225 National Parks Hwy, Carlsbad, NM 88220 (505) 885-8884;
FTS 476-9242
Admin Katie Bridwell.
Lib Type Special.
Spec Subs Geology; speleology; archeology; botany; birds; mammals (especially bats); history; national parks; paleontology. *In-house Files* Theses on geology; speleology; archeology.
Circ Servs Avail To other Federal libraries; to other libraries.

Ref Servs Avail To other Federal libraries; to other libraries; to the general public.

1625. George Washington Carver National Monument Library
Box 38, Diamond, MO 64840 (417) 325-4151
Admin Gentry Davis (Supt). *Ref Lib* Lawrence Blake.
Lib Type Special.
Spec Subs George Washington Carver. *Spec Collecs* Collection of Carver letters & memorabilia.
Circ Servs Avail Restricted to use by special request.
Ref Servs Avail Restricted to use by special request.

1626. Castillo de San Marcos National Monument Library
1 Castillo Dr E, Saint Augustine, FL 32084 (904) 829-6506; FTS 946-3639
Admin Luis R Arana (Historian).
Lib Type Special.
Spec Subs Spanish Florida history with special emphasis on military architecture & engineering, Castillo de San Marcos & ordnance. *Spec Collecs* Photocopies of Spanish archival material related to Florida & of books on military architecture, engineering, & ordnance.
Circ Servs Avail To other Federal libraries; to other libraries; not open to the general public; restricted to use by appointment.
Ref Servs Avail To other Federal libraries; to other libraries; not open to the general public; restricted to use by appointment.

1627. Margaret Davis Cate Collection
Georgia Historical Society, 501 Whitaker St, Savannah, GA 31499 (912) 944-2128
Admin Lewis J Bellardo. *Ref Lib* Barbara S Bennett (Acq).
Lib Type Special.
Spec Collecs The Cate Collection which belongs to the National Park Service is on permanent deposit here.

1628. Catoctin Mountain Park Library
Thurmont, MD 21788 (301) 824-2574
Admin William Gray.
Lib Type Special.
Spec Subs Local natural history & folklore; National Park Service.
Ref Servs Avail To the general public; restricted to by appointment.

1629. Cedar Breaks National Monument Library
PO Box 749, Cedar City, UT 84720 (801) 586-9451
Admin Clay Alderson (Supt).
Lib Type Special.
Spec Subs Geology, plants, & animals of the southwest.
Circ Servs Avail Not open to the general public.
Ref Servs Avail Not open to the general public.

1630. Chaco Center Archives & Library, Branch of Cultural Research Library
PO Box 728, 1220 St Francis Dr S, Santa Fe, NM 87501-0728 (505) 988-6766; FTS 476-1766
Admin Judith Miles (Archeologist). *Ref Lib* Kim McLean.
Lib Type Special.
Spec Subs Archeological research, primarily San Juan Basin area. *Spec Collecs* Vivian Archives, 1920s thru 1960s; documents pertaining to archeological work at Chaco Canyon, NM. *In-house Files* Extensive archeological survey & excavation records (field notes, maps, photos) of Chaco, NM culture & Wupatki, AZ.
Shared Catalog Nets National Catalog.
Ref Servs Avail To other Federal libraries; to other libraries; to the general public.

1631. Chaco Culture National Historical Park Reference & Research Library
Box 6500, Star Rte 4, Bloomfield, NM 87413 (505) 988-6716; FTS 988-6716
Admin Chief Ranger.
Lib Type Special.
Spec Subs Chaco Canyon archeology & anthropology; natural & cultural history of the area. *Spec Collecs* Photo & slide files; ruin stabilization reports; administrative history of the site. *In-*

house Files Vertical files containing special articles & unpublished manuscripts relating to the archeology & anthropology of Chaco.
Circ Servs Avail Restricted to staff & researchers.
Ref Servs Avail To other Federal libraries; to the general public; restricted to on-site use of materials.

1632. Chamizal National Memorial Library
109 N Oregon, El Paso, TX 79901 (915) 541-7880; FTS 572-7780/ 7880
Lib Type Special.
Ref Servs Avail Restricted to on site use.

1633. Cherokee Strip Living Museum Library
PO Box 230, Arkansas City, KS 67005 (316) 442-6750
Admin Herbert D Marshall.
Lib Type Special.
Spec Subs Opening of the Cherokee Outlet in 1893; Oklahoma, Indian, & western history, 1893-1920. *Spec Collecs* Photographic collections of Pretty Man, Cornish, & Croft. *In-house Files* Oral history tapes, letters, diaries, documents, newspapers, & complete listing of land registration following Outlet Run of 1893.
Ref Servs Avail To the general public.

1634. Chesapeake & Ohio Canal National Historic Park Resource Library
Box 4, Sharpsburg, MD 21782 (301) 739-4200; FTS 739-4200
Admin Lee C Struble (Staff Curator).
Lib Type Special.
Spec Subs American & European canals; Maryland natural history. *Spec Collecs* Oral history of canal families; specifications of canal structures; early survey maps of proposed canals. *In-house Files* Local history; unpublished historical research.
Coop Lib Nets Interior Dept Library.
Ref Servs Avail Restricted to employees & researchers.

1635. Chickamauga & Chattanooga National Military Park Library
PO Box 2128, Fort Oglethorpe, GA 30742 (404) 866-9241; FTS 852-8173
Admin M Ann Belkov (Supt). *Ref Lib* Dale K Phillips.
Lib Type Special.
Spec Subs Civil War history. *Spec Collecs* Manuscripts of soldiers involved in the battles of Chickamauga & Chattanooga.
Ref Servs Avail To other Federal libraries; to other libraries; to the general public.

1636. Chiricahua National Monument Library
Dos Cabezas Star Rte, Willcox, AZ 85643 (602) 824-3560
Admin Marquetta Torres.
Lib Type Special.
Spec Subs Natural & cultural history; Indian & pioneer history. *In-house Files* Newspaper & magazine clippings.
Circ Servs Avail Not open to the general public; restricted to staff.
Ref Servs Avail To the general public.

1637. Christiansted National Historic Site Library
Christiansted, Saint Croix, VI 00820 (809) 773-2107
Admin William F Cissel.
Lib Type Special.
Spec Subs Caribbean history, especially US Virgin Islands; natural sciences pertaining to US Virgin Islands. *Spec Collecs* Danish West Indian history. *In-house Files* Historic building documents.
Circ Servs Avail Not open to the general public; restricted to NPS staff.
Ref Servs Avail Not open to the general public; restricted to scholars upon application.

1638. George Rogers Clark National Historical Park Library
401 S 2nd St, Vincennes, IN 47591 (812) 882-1776
Admin John Neal (Supt). *Ref Lib* Robert Holden.
Lib Type Special.
Spec Subs American Revolution in the West; Trans-Appalachian frontier history; War of 1812.

Circ Servs Avail Not open to the general public; restricted to agency employees.
Ref Servs Avail To other Federal libraries; to other libraries; to the general public.

1639. Colonial National Historic Park Library
Box 210, Yorktown, VA 23609 (804) 898-3400 ext 30; FTS 827-8000
Admin James N Haskett.
Lib Type Special.
Spec Subs Research on Jamestown & Yorktown sites.
Circ Servs Avail Restricted to park staff.
Ref Servs Avail Restricted to researchers by appointment.

1640. Colorado National Monument Library
Fruita, CO 81521 (303) 858-3617
Admin Richard R Walls.
Lib Type Special.
Spec Subs Natural history. *Spec Collecs* National Park Service.
Circ Servs Avail To other Federal libraries; not open to the general public; restricted to research.
Ref Servs Avail To other Federal libraries; to other libraries; not open to the general public; restricted to research.

1641. Coronado National Memorial Library
Box 126, RR 2, Hereford, AZ 85615 (602) 366-5515
Admin Laurel W Dale.
Lib Type Special.
Spec Subs 16th Century Spanish. *In-house Files* National Park Service.
Circ Servs Avail To other Federal libraries; to the general public.
Ref Servs Avail To other Federal libraries; to the general public.

1642. Coulee Dam National Recreation Area Library
PO Box 37, Coulee Dam, WA 99116 (509) 633-1360, ext 441; FTS 446-9441
Admin Jerry Rumberg.
Lib Type Special.
Spec Subs Historical data relative to Lake Roosevelt; geology; water systems.
Ref Servs Avail To the general public.

1643. Crater Lake National Park Library
PO Box 7, Crater Lake, OR 97604 (503) 594-2211; FTS 420-6980
Admin Henry M Tanski, Jr.
Lib Type Special.
Spec Subs Geology & natural sciences.
Circ Servs Avail Not open to the general public; restricted to use by appointment.
Ref Servs Avail Not open to the general public; restricted to use by appointment.

1644. Craters of the Moon National Monument Library
Box 29, Arco, ID 83213 (208) 527-3257
Admin Robert Scott (Supt). *Ref Lib* David Clark.
Lib Type Special.
Spec Subs Volcanic geology.
Circ Servs Avail Not open to the general public; restricted to on-site use.
Ref Servs Avail Not open to the general public; restricted to on-site use.

1645. Cumberland Gap National Historic Park Library
PO Box 1848, Middlesboro, KY 40965 (606) 248-2817
Admin Frank W Doughman; Daniel Brown.
Lib Type Special.
Spec Subs Pioneer era, 1750-1810.
Circ Servs Avail Restricted to use by reservation.
Ref Servs Avail Restricted to use by reservation.

1646. Curecanti National Recreation Area Library
PO Box 1040, Gunnison, CO 81230 (303) 641-2337
Admin Joseph F Alston (Supt). *Ref Lib* Donald C Hill.
Lib Type Special.
Spec Subs Local history; Colorado, especially western. *Spec Collecs* Western Colorado archeology. *In-house Files* Natural history; water based recreation; aquatic zoology & resources.

Circ Servs Avail To other Federal libraries; not open to the general public.
Ref Servs Avail To other Federal libraries; not open to the general public; restricted to park staff.

1647. Custer Battlefield National Monument Library
PO Box 39, Crow Agency, MT 59022 (406) 638-2621
Admin Mardell Plainfeather.
Lib Type Special.
Spec Subs George Armstrong Custer; Battle of Little Bighorn. *Spec Collecs* Custer collection includes correspondence, printed articles, manuscripts related to his career; Fred Dustin collection, author & historic expert on battle; 1876 7th Cavalry muster rolls. *In-house Files* Magazine files regarding Custer, battle, & other participants.
Coop Lib Nets Little Bighorn College (LBHC).
Circ Servs Avail Not open to the general public.
Ref Servs Avail Not open to the general public.

1648. Cuyahoga Valley National Recreation Area Library
PO Box 158, Peninsula, OH 44264 (216) 650-4414; FTS 293-3131
Admin Chester V Hamilton.
Lib Type Special.
Spec Subs Local area history; Ohio canal system; natural history of the Akron-Cleveland area; National Parks in Ohio.
Ref Servs Avail To the general public.

1649. John Day Fossil Beds National Monument Library
420 W Main St, John Day, OR 97845 (503) 575-0721
Admin Benjamin F Ladd (Supt). *Ref Lib* Kim E Sikoryak (ILL, Acq).
Lib Type Special.
Spec Subs Geology & paleontology, especially John Day Basin area. *Spec Collecs* Reprint collection of scientific papers related to the Monument.
Shared Catalog Nets OCLC (thru regional library in Seattle). *Coop Lib Nets* National Park Service Regional Library, Pacific Northwest Region (HQ in Seattle).
Circ Servs Avail To other Federal libraries; not open to the general public.
Ref Servs Avail To other Federal libraries; not open to the general public.

1650. De Soto National Memorial Library
75th St NW, Bradenton, FL 33529 (813) 792-0458
Admin Christopher Cruz.
Lib Type Special.
Spec Subs Spanish exploration; general exploration; NPS; Environmental education; natural history; American history; Florida history; Indian history.
Circ Servs Avail Not open to the general public.
Ref Servs Avail Not open to the general public.

1651. Death Valley National Monument Research Library
Death Valley, CA 92328 (619) 786-2331
Admin Shirley Harding (Curator/Lib).
Lib Type Special.
Spec Subs Death Valley natural sciences; archeology; ethnography; museum related publications. *Spec Collecs* Photographic materials; museum collections & archives. *In-house Files* Library & museum card catalogs; photographic finding aids & vertical files.
Circ Servs Avail To other Federal libraries; to other libraries; not open to the general public; restricted to local community.
Ref Servs Avail To other Federal libraries; to other libraries; to the general public; restricted to research requests.

1652. Delaware Water Gap Recreation Area Library
Bushkill, PA 18324 (717) 588-6637
Admin Omega East.
Lib Type Special.
Spec Subs Delaware Water Gap area.
Ref Servs Avail To the general public.

1653. Denali National Park Library
PO Box 9, Denali Park, AK 99755 (907) 683-2294
Admin East District Naturalist. *Ref Lib* Robert Butterfield.
Lib Type Special.
Spec Subs Denali (Mt McKinley) National Park & resources.
Circ Servs Avail Restricted to local use.
Ref Servs Avail Restricted to on-site use.

1654. Devils Postpile Library
PO Box 501, Mammoth Lake, CA 93546 (714) 934-2289; FTS
688-2000
Admin Wymond Eckhardt.
Lib Type Special.
Spec Subs Natural history. *Spec Collecs* Slide collection.

1655. Devils Tower National Monument Library
Administration Bldg, Devils Tower, WY 82714 (307) 467-5370
Admin Superintendent.
Lib Type Special.
Spec Subs Devils Tower geology & history.
Circ Servs Avail Restricted to researchers & NPS staff.
Ref Servs Avail Restricted to researchers & NPS staff.

1656. Dinosaur National Monument Library
Box 128, Jensen, UT 84035 (801) 789-2115
Lib Type Special.
Spec Subs Archeology; geology; local history; zoology. *Spec Collecs* Paleontology (Theodore White Collection).
Ref Servs Avail Restricted to reference only.

1657. Edison National Historic Site
Main St & Lakeside Ave, West Orange, NJ 07052 (201) 736-0550
Admin Reed Able.
Lib Type Special.
Spec Subs Career of Thomas A Edison. *Spec Collecs* 7,000 photographic negatives; 300,000 documents; phonograph recordings, uncataloged; 2,000 bound volumes of old scientific & technical journals.
Ref Servs Avail Not open to the general public; restricted to qualified researchers with prior permission.

1658. Effigy Mounds National Monument Library
Box K, McGregor, IA 52157 (319) 873-2356
Admin Thomas Munson.
Lib Type Special.
Spec Subs Archeology. *Spec Collecs* Elison Orr personal library covering archeology, history, & natural sciences of northeast Iowa.
Circ Servs Avail Not open to the general public; restricted to special loans for researchers.
Ref Servs Avail To the general public.

1659. El Morro National Monument Library
Ramah, NM 87321 (505) 783-4226
Admin Douglas Eury (Supt). *Ref Lib* Maxine Bond.
Lib Type Special.
Spec Subs History of the southwest.
Circ Servs Avail Not open to the general public; restricted to El Morro employees.
Ref Servs Avail Not open to the general public; restricted to El Morro employees.

1660. Everglades National Park Research Center Library
PO Box 279, Homestead, FL 33030 (305) 257-8184; FTS 350-4653
Admin Glenna McCowan.
Lib Type Special.
Spec Subs Hydrology; ecology; marine biology; fishery biology; wildlife biology; avian studies; botany. *Spec Collecs* Material on Everglades National Park & other south Florida park areas.
Coop Lib Nets Florida Library Information Network.
Circ Servs Avail To other Federal libraries; to other libraries; restricted to NPS & project staff of cooperating institutions.
Ref Servs Avail To the general public.

1661. Federal Hall National Memorial Library
26 Wall St, New York, NY 10005 (212) 264-4456, ext 4367; FTS
264-9467
Admin Duane Pearson.
Lib Type Special.
Spec Subs American history concerning George Washington, Theodore Roosevelt, Ulysses S Grant, & Alexander Hamilton. *Spec Collecs* New York city history; George Washington; rare books & photographs; American Revolution.
Circ Servs Avail To other Federal libraries; to other libraries.
Ref Servs Avail To the general public.

1662. Fire Island National Seashore Library
120 Laurel St, Patchogue, NY 11772 (516) 289-4810; FTS 667-1800
Admin Neal Bullington.
Lib Type Special.
Spec Subs History of Fire Island; seashore natural history.
Ref Servs Avail To other Federal libraries; to other libraries; restricted to on-site use.

1663. Florissant Fossil Beds National Monument Library
PO Box 185, Florissant, CO 80816 (303) 748-3253
Lib Type Special.
Circ Servs Avail Restricted to staff.
Ref Servs Avail Restricted to staff.

1664. Ford's Theatre National Historic Site Library
511 10th St, NW, Washington, DC 20004 (202) 426-6830 (House Where Lincoln Died & Library); TTY 426-1749
Admin Frank Hebblethwaite (Museum Tech).
Lib Type Special.
Spec Subs American history. *Spec Collecs* Biographies of Abraham Lincoln; non-fiction works on Lincoln's life, presidency, & assassination. *In-house Files* Research & photo files on Lincoln, Ford's Theatre, & the Lincoln assassination.
Circ Servs Avail To other Federal libraries; to other libraries; to the general public; restricted to the discretion of the librarian.
Ref Servs Avail To other Federal libraries; to other libraries; to the general public; restricted to the discretion of the librarian.

1665. Ft Caroline National Memorial Library
12713 Ft Caroline Rd, Jacksonville, FL 32225 (904) 641-7155; FTS 946-2011
Admin Arthur Fredricks.
Lib Type Special.
Spec Subs History of Ft Caroline.
Circ Servs Avail To other Federal libraries; to other libraries.
Ref Servs Avail To the general public.

1666. Ft Clatsop National Memorial Library
Box 604-FC, Rte 3, Astoria, OR 97103 (503) 861-2471
Admin Curt Johnson (Chief Ranger).
Lib Type Special.
Spec Subs Lewis & Clark Expedition; Indians of North America; plants & animals of the Pacific Northwest. *Spec Collecs* Lewis & Clark Expedition.
Circ Servs Avail Not open to the general public; restricted to staff & by special arrangement.
Ref Servs Avail To other Federal libraries; to other libraries; to the general public.

1667. Ft Davis National Historic Site Library
PO Box 1456, Fort Davis, TX 79734 (915) 426-3225
Admin Douglas C McChristian (Supt). *Ref Lib* Mary L Williams.
Lib Type Special.
Spec Subs Late 19th century frontier military history. *Spec Collecs* Microfilmed & xeroxed copies of Benjamin H Grierson papers (originals at Newbery Library; Illinois State Historical Library; Texas Tech Univ & Fort Concho National Historical Site, San Angelo, TX). *In-house Files* Microfilmed records of Fort Davis, 1854-91; files on fort personnel.
Coop Lib Nets Dept of the Interior Library System.
Circ Servs Avail Not open to the general public; restricted to staff, volunteers & researchers; others handled on individual basis.
Ref Servs Avail To other Federal libraries; to other libraries; to the general public; restricted to on-site use.

1668. Ft Donelson National Battlefield Library
PO Box F, Dover, TN 37058 (615) 232-5706
Admin John Stockert.
Lib Type Special.
Spec Subs Civil War history.
Ref Servs Avail To other Federal libraries; to other libraries; to the general public; restricted to on-site use by general public.

1669. Ft Frederica National Monument Library
Box 286-C, Rte 9, Saint Simons Island, GA 31522 (912) 638-3639
Admin Curtis Childs. *Acq Lib* Bob Vogel.
Lib Type Special.

1670. Ft Laramie National Historic Site Library
Fort Laramie, WY 82212 (307) 837-2221
Admin Steven Fullmer (Park Ranger); Gary K Howe (Supt).
Lib Type Special.
Spec Subs History of western expansion, fur trade, immigration, & Indian wars.
Circ Servs Avail Not open to the general public.
Ref Servs Avail To the general public; restricted to on-site use.

1671. Ft Larned National Historic Site Library
Rte 3, Larned, KS 67550 (316) 285-6911
Admin Jack Arnold (Supt). *Ref Lib* George A Elmore.
Lib Type Special.
Spec Subs Indian & military relations 1850s to 1880s. *Spec Collecs* Microfilm of Fort Larned records 1859-84.
Circ Servs Avail To other Federal libraries; to other libraries; to the general public.
Ref Servs Avail To other Federal libraries; to other libraries; to the general public.

1672. Ft McHenry National Monument & Historic Shrine Library
Baltimore, MD 21230-5393 (301) 962-4290; FTS 922-4290
Admin Terry DiMattio. *Ref Lib* Scott Sheads/Paul Plamann.
Lib Type Special.
Spec Subs History of Ft McHenry; national parks; Battle of Baltimore; War of 1812. *Spec Collecs* Holloway Papers (regarding the Star Spangled Banner being made national anthem); Walter Lord Collection (regarding his book The Dawn's Early Light).

1673. Ft Necessity National Battlefield Library
The National Pike, Box 528, RD 2, Farmington, PA 15437 (412) 329-5512
Admin Mike Greenfield. *Ref Lib* Carney Rigg (ILL, Acq).
Lib Type Special.
Spec Subs George Washington during French & Indian War; Ft Necessity; Gen Edward Braddock.
Shared Catalog Nets OCLC.
Ref Servs Avail To other Federal libraries; to other libraries; not open to the general public.

1674. Ft Point National Historic Site Library
Box 29333, Presidio of San Francisco, CA 94129 (415) 556-1693
Admin Charles S Hawkins (Site Mgr).
Lib Type Special.
Ref Servs Avail Restricted to by appointment.

1675. Ft Pulaski National Monument Library
PO Box 98, Tybee Island, GA 31328 (912) 786-5787; FTS 248-4232
Admin Daniel W Brown. *Ref Lib* Talley Kirkland. *ILL* John Beck (Acq).
Lib Type Special.
Spec Subs History of site restoration & preservation, 1924-39; museum management; Ft Pulaski history, 1829-70. *Spec Collecs* Complete set of official records (army/navy) pertaining to the War of the Rebellion. *In-house Files* Approximately 40 linear feet of files relating to historical research in GA, SC, FL, 1934-39, site management, Savannah, & Civil War.
Elec Mail Nets Southeast Region NPS EMAIL; NPS Bulletin Board Service (Washington office).
Circ Servs Avail To other Federal libraries; to other libraries.
Ref Servs Avail To other Federal libraries; to other libraries; to the general public.

1676. Ft Stanwix National Monument Library
112 E Park St, Rome, NY 13440 (315) 336-2090
Admin Beth Hagler.
Lib Type Special.

1677. Ft Sumter National Monument Library
1214 Middle St, Sullivan's Island, SC 29482 (803) 883-3123; FTS 677-4743/4740
Admin David Ruth.
Lib Type Special.
Spec Subs US coastal defense, 1776-1947. *Spec Collecs* Civil War, Revolutionary War.
Circ Servs Avail Not open to the general public.
Ref Servs Avail Not open to the general public.

1678. Ft Union National Monument Library
Watrous, NM 87753 (505) 425-8025
Admin Carol Kruse (Unit Mgr).
Lib Type Special.
Spec Subs US military & general history of the Southwest, 1800-1900. *Spec Collecs* Items pertaining to Santa Fe Trail & the history of Ft Union (1851-1891). *In-house Files* Some archival & military records on microfilm.
Ref Servs Avail Restricted to reference use on site.

1679. Ft Union Trading Post National Historic Site Library
Buford Rt, Williston, ND 58801 (701) 572-9083
Admin Paul L Hedren (Park Historian).
Lib Type Special.
Spec Subs American fur trade; Upper Missouri River history. *Spec Collecs* Research materials & photographs.
Circ Servs Avail Restricted to staff.
Ref Servs Avail To other Federal libraries; to other libraries; to the general public.

1680. Ft Vancouver National Historic Site Library
1501 E Evergreen Blvd, Vancouver, WA 98661-3897 (206) 696-7655; FTS 422-7655
Admin James M Thomson. *Ref Lib* Kent J Taylor.
Lib Type Special.
Spec Subs Pacific northwest fur trade era; Hudson's Bay Co; Fort Vancouver. *Spec Collecs* Archeological reports on old Fort Vancouver.
Shared Catalog Nets OCLC.
Circ Servs Avail Not open to the general public; restricted to staff.
Ref Servs Avail To the general public.

1681. Fossil Butte National Monument Library
PO Box 527, Kemmerer, WY 83101 (307) 877-3450
Admin Jimmie Ann Wideman.
Lib Type Special.
Spec Subs Paleontology; geology; biology; paleopathology; history.
Ref Servs Avail To the general public.

1682. Fredericksburg & Spotsylvania National Military Park Library
PO Box 679, Fredericksburg, VA 22401 (703) 373-4461; FTS 925-2023
Admin Robert K Krick (Chief Historian).
Lib Type Special.
Spec Subs Civil War in Virginia.
Circ Servs Avail Restricted to special arrangement.
Ref Servs Avail To other Federal libraries; to other libraries; to the general public; restricted to use by special arrangement.

1683. Ft Bowie National Historic Site Library
Box 158, Bowie, AZ 85605 (602) 847-2500
Admin Wilton E Hoy (Ranger-in-Charge).
Lib Type Special.
Spec Subs Western history; Fort Bowie & Apache Pass.
Circ Servs Avail To other Federal libraries; not open to the general public.
Ref Servs Avail To other Federal libraries; not open to the general public.

1684. George Washington Birthplace National Monument Library

Box 717, RR 1, Washington's Birthplace, VA 22575 (804) 224-1732

Admin Paul Carson (Interpretive Specialist).
Lib Type Special.
Spec Subs George Washington; colonial life & crafts.
Elec Mail Nets NPS Bulletin Board Service.
Circ Servs Avail Not open to the general public.
Ref Servs Avail Not open to the general public.

1685. Gettysburg National Military Park Library

Gettysburg, PA 17325 (717) 334-1124

Admin Kathleen Georg Harrison.
Lib Type Special.
Spec Subs Gettysburg campaign; Eisenhower farm. *Spec Collecs* William H Tipton photographic collection; John B Bachelder collections.
Circ Servs Avail Restricted to staff.
Ref Servs Avail To other Federal libraries; to other libraries; to the general public.

1686. Glacier Bay National Park & Preserve Library

Gustavus, AK 99826 (907) 697-2231

Admin Doris Howe (summer); Chief of Interpretation (winter). *Acq Lib* Bruce Paige.
Lib Type Special.
Circ Servs Avail Not open to the general public.
Ref Servs Avail To the general public.

1687. Glacier National Park, George C. Ruhle Library

West Glacier, MT 59936 (406) 888-5441, ext 302

Lib Type Special.
Spec Subs Botanical & zoological science; earth & life science; Glacier Park history. *Spec Collecs* Plains Indians (James Willard Schultz Collection).
Circ Servs Avail Not open to the general public; restricted to staff.
Ref Servs Avail Not open to the general public; restricted to staff.

1688. Glen Canyon National Recreation Area Library

PO Box 1507, Page, AZ 86040 (602) 645-2471/2472; FTS 261-3900

Admin Art Cloutier.
Lib Type Special.
Spec Subs Natural science & history of northern Ariz & southern Utah. *Spec Collecs* Annual reports of the Bureau of Ethnology; several early volumes of the Utah Historical Quarterly; Univ of Utah anthropological papers, 1957, during Glen Canyon Survey.
Ref Servs Avail To the general public.

1689. Grand Canyon National Park Research Library

PO Box 129, Grand Canyon, AZ 86023 (602) 638-7768; FTS 765-7768; TTY (602) 638-7772

Admin Karen Berggren.
Lib Type Special.
Spec Subs Geology & history dealing with Grand Canyon National Park; Indians of park & surrounding area; natural resources management. *Spec Collecs* Clippings file dealing with Grand Canyon. *In-house Files* Administrative documents of park.
Circ Servs Avail To other Federal libraries.
Ref Servs Avail To other Federal libraries; to other libraries; to the general public.

1690. Grand Portage National Monument Library

Box 666, 1710 W US Hwy 61, Grand Marais, MN 55604 (218) 387-2788

Admin Anthony L Andersen (Supt); Donald W Carney (Chief, Interpretation).
Lib Type Special.
Spec Subs North American fur trade, 1608-1870, with emphasis on 1730-1804; Chippewa Indian culture of the Great Lakes. *Spec Collecs* Wisconsin Historical Collection; Hudson's Bay Record Society Collection.
Coop Lib Nets North Country Library Cooperative (NCLC).
Circ Servs Avail To other Federal libraries; to other libraries; to the general public.

Ref Servs Avail To other Federal libraries; to other libraries; to the general public.

1691. Grand Teton National Park Library

PO Drawer 170, Moose, WY 83012 (307) 733-2880; FTS 584-2205

Lib Type Special.
Spec Subs Botany; geology; local & western history; zoology.
Ref Servs Avail Not open to the general public; restricted to researchers by appointment.

1692. Grant-Kohrs Ranch National Historic Site Library

PO Box 790, Deer Lodge, MT 59722 (406) 846-2070

Admin Park Ranger.
Lib Type Special.
Spec Subs Frontier cattle era history; curatorial methods; Victorian antiques; western US; site history. *Spec Collecs* Historic photographs; oral histories; some microfilms.
Ref Servs Avail To other Federal libraries; to other libraries; to the general public; restricted to on-site use by appointment.

1693. Great Sand Dunes National Monument Library

Mosca, CO 81146 (303) 378-2312

Admin Robert L Schultz (Chief Naturalist).
Lib Type Special.
Spec Subs Natural history; NPS; environmental education; sand dunes. *Spec Collecs* Sand Dunes information; local natural & cultural history. *In-house Files* Sand Dunes & other locally significant documents.
Circ Servs Avail Restricted to demonstrated need.
Ref Servs Avail Restricted to demonstrated need.

1694. Great Smoky Mountains National Park, Sugarlands Visitor Center Library

Gatlinburg, TN 37738 (615) 436-5615 ext 70; FTS 436-1296

Admin Annette Evans.
Lib Type Special.
Spec Subs Natural sciences. *Spec Collecs* Stupka collection.
Circ Servs Avail To other libraries.
Ref Servs Avail To other Federal libraries; to other libraries; to the general public.

1695. Guilford Courthouse National Military Park Library

PO Box 9806, 2332 New Garden Rd, Greensboro, NC 27429-0806 (919) 288-1776

Admin Willard W Danielson (Supt). *Ref Lib* Donald J Long.
Lib Type Special.
Spec Subs Battle of Guilford Courthouse; Southern campaign 1780-83; American Revolution. *In-house Files* Participant file (incomplete) of American soldiers who fought in the Battle of Guilford Courthouse.
Circ Servs Avail To other Federal libraries; to other libraries; to the general public; restricted to on-site use.
Ref Servs Avail To other Federal libraries; to other libraries; to the general public; restricted to on-site use.

1696. Gulf Islands National Seashore Library

PO Box 100, Gulf Breeze, FL 32561 (904) 932-0620

Admin Jerry A Eubanks (Supt).
Lib Type Special.
Circ Servs Avail Not open to the general public.
Ref Servs Avail Not open to the general public.

1697. Haleakala National Park, Library

PO Box 369, Makawao, Maui, HI 96768 (808) 572-9306

Admin Carol Beadle (Interpretive Supervisor).
Lib Type Special.
Spec Subs Natural history, human history, & geology of Haleakala; technical reports of the Univ of Hawaii covering specific aspects of flora, fauna, & geology. *Spec Collecs* Univ of Hawaii IBP & ISCU reports. *In-house Files* Pamphlet files.
Circ Servs Avail Not open to the general public.
Ref Servs Avail Restricted to on site use.

1698. Hampton National Historic Site Library
535 Hampton Ln, Towson, MD 21204 (301) 823-7054; FTS 922-3913
Admin Lynne Dakin Hasings (Curator); Adam G Karalius (Site Mgr).
Lib Type Special.
Spec Subs Ridgely family & Hampton archives. *Spec Collecs* Ridgely family papers, late 19th & early 20th century. *In-house Files* Research & reference files on Ridgely family, decorative arts & furnishings, architecture, & gardens.
Ref Servs Avail To other Federal libraries; to other libraries; to the general public; not open to the general public.

1699. Harpers Ferry Center Library
Harpers Ferry, WV 25425 (304) 535-6371 ext 264; FTS 925-6493
Admin David Nathanson. *ILL* Nancy Potts.
Lib Type Special.
Spec Subs National Parks; US history; military art & science; material culture; decorative arts; museum science. *Spec Collecs* NPS history collection; Harold L Peterson military arts & sciences collection; Ralph H Lewis museum science collection; Vera Craig decorative & useful arts collection.
Lib Deposit Designation NPS.
Info Ret Servs DIALOG; BRS. *Shared Catalog Nets* OCLC. *Coop Lib Nets* FEDLINK; West Virginia Union Catalog.
Circ Servs Avail To other Federal libraries; to other libraries; to the general public.
Ref Servs Avail To other Federal libraries; to other libraries; to the general public.

1700. Harpers Ferry National Historic Park Library
PO Box 65, Harpers Ferry, WV 25425 (304) 535-6371 ext 6563; FTS 925-6563
Admin Hilda E Staubs.
Lib Type Special.
Spec Subs John Brown; armory; Civil War; Negro education; local & general history that pertains to historic background of the park. *In-house Files* Historic structure reports & other reports on the Civil War prepared by NPS &/or park staff.
Shared Catalog Nets OCLC (thru Harpers Ferry Center Library-Nancy Potts 304-535-6371 ext 6264).
Circ Servs Avail Restricted to the general public on Mon-Fri; published work thru ILL.
Ref Servs Avail Restricted to the general public on-site when staff available.

1701. Hawaii Volcanoes National Park Library
National Park Service, Hawaii National Park, HI 96718 (808) 967-7311
Admin Thomas E. White.
Lib Type Special.
Spec Collecs Hawaiiana; Volcano House Register, 1865-1926.
Ref Servs Avail Restricted to reference only.

1702. Homestead National Monument Library
Box 47, Rte 3, Beatrice, NE 68310 (402) 223-3514
Admin Randy Baynes (Supt). *Ref Lib* Dick Williams.
Lib Type Special.
Spec Subs Homesteading; prairie; westward expansion.
Circ Servs Avail Restricted to staff.
Ref Servs Avail To other Federal libraries; to other libraries; to the general public.

1703. Herbert Hoover National Historic Site
PO Box 607, West Branch, IA 52358 (319) 643-2541
Admin Malcolm J. Berg (Supt).
Lib Type Special.
Spec Subs Herbert Hoover; 1870-80; Middle America. *In-house Files* Hoover materials.
Circ Servs Avail Not open to the general public; restricted to on site use.
Ref Servs Avail Not open to the general public; restricted to on site use.

1704. Hopewell Furnace National Historic Site Library
RD 1, Box 345, Elverson, PA 19520 (215) 582-8773
Admin Elizabeth E. Disrude (Supt).
Lib Type Special.
Spec Subs Iron-making. *Spec Collecs* Extensive 19th century document collection relating to Hopewell Furnace.
Circ Servs Avail Not open to the general public; restricted to site employees.
Ref Servs Avail To other Federal libraries; to other libraries; to the general public; restricted to on site use.

1705. Horse Bend National Military Park Library
Box 103, Rte 1, Daviston, AL 36256 (205) 234-7111
Admin Philip R Brueck (Supt). *Ref Lib* Carol L Slaughter.
Lib Type Special.
Spec Subs Creek War; War of 1812; military history; Alabama history; history of NPS.
Circ Servs Avail Restricted to other NPS areas on case-by-case basis.
Ref Servs Avail To the general public; restricted to use in park by appointment.

1706. Hot Springs National Park Library
PO Box 1860, Hot Springs, AR 71902 (501) 624-3383
Admin Mary L Smith.
Lib Type Special.
Spec Subs History; geology of the park & surrounding area. *Spec Collecs* Some rare books about the park.
Ref Servs Avail To other Federal libraries; to other libraries; to the general public.

1707. Hubbell Trading Post National Historic Site Library
PO Box 150, Ganado, AZ 86505 (602) 755-3475
Admin Constantine J Dillon.
Lib Type Special.
Spec Subs Navajo history & culture; history of the exploration & settlement of the southwest; southwest Indian cultures. *Spec Collecs* John L Hubbell & Indian trading business; Hubbell family history. *In-house Files* Hubbell papers & oral history interviews.
Lib Deposit Designation NPS.
Circ Servs Avail Not open to the general public; restricted to employees.
Ref Servs Avail To other Federal libraries; to other libraries; to the general public.

1708. Mr & Mrs John K Hulston Civil War Research Library
Wilson's Creek National Battlefield, PO Drawer C, Republic, MO 65738 (417) 732-2662; FTS 754-2762
Admin David L Lane (Supt). *Ref Lib* Richard Hatcher.
Lib Type Special.
Spec Subs Civil War; history of Missouri; Ozark regional history.
Coop Lib Nets Southwest Missouri Library Network.
Ref Servs Avail To other Federal libraries; to other libraries; to the general public.

1709. Independence National Historic Park Library
313 Walnut St, Philadelphia, PA 19106 (215) 597-8047
Admin Shirley A Mays.
Lib Type Special.
Spec Subs American history, 1774-1830; Philadelphia & Pennsylvania history; decorative arts of the 18th century. *Spec Collecs* Manuscripts; iconographic material; audio-visual training cassettes for park staff; Independence Hall Assoc papers; Judge Edwin Lewis papers.
Circ Servs Avail To other Federal libraries; not open to the general public.
Ref Servs Avail To other Federal libraries; to other libraries; to the general public.

1710. Indiana Dunes National Lakeshore Library
Rt 2, Box 139-A, Chesterton, IN 46304 (219) 926-7561; FTS 386-3601
Admin Shelley Fudge.
Lib Type Special.

Spec Subs Indiana Dunes biology & geology; Northwest Indiana history; park history; environmental education. *Spec Collecs* Illinois State Geographical Survey; Environmental Geology Notes; out-of-print books on the Indiana Dunes area; original manuscripts on *Wolves Against the Moon* by Julia Altrocchi.
Ref Servs Avail To the general public.

1711. Isle Royale National Park Library
87 N Ripley St, Houghton, MI 49931 (906) 482-3310; FTS 226-6000
Admin Robert A Huggins.
Lib Type Special.
Spec Subs Natural & human history; parks & recreation.
Circ Servs Avail To other libraries.
Ref Servs Avail To the general public.

1712. Islesford Historic Museum Library
Acadia National Park, PO Box 177, Bar Harbor, ME 04609 (207) 288-3338; FTS 833-7485/7486
Admin Robert Rothe (Chief Naturalist).
Lib Type Special.
Spec Subs Maritime Maine culture/history. *Spec Collecs* Jesuit relations.
Circ Servs Avail Not open to the general public.
Ref Servs Avail Not open to the general public.

1713. Jefferson National Expansion Memorial Library
11 N 4th St, Saint Louis, MO 63102 (314) 425-6023; FTS 279-6023
Admin Kathleen E Moenster.
Lib Type Special.
Spec Subs Westward expansion; St Louis history. *Spec Collecs* Materials on the park.
Coop Lib Nets NPS.
Circ Servs Avail Restricted to staff.
Ref Servs Avail Restricted to on-site use.

1714. Jewel Cave National Monument Library
Custer, SD 57730 (605) 673-2288; FTS 225-0250
Admin Al Hendricks.
Lib Type Special.
Spec Subs Natural history.
Ref Servs Avail To the general public; restricted to reference only.

1715. Andrew Johnson National Historic Site Library
PO Box 1088, Greeneville, TN 37744 (615) 638-3551
Admin Grady C Webb (Supt).
Lib Type Special.
Spec Subs Presidency & life of Andrew Johnson.
Circ Servs Avail Not open to the general public; restricted to employees.
Ref Servs Avail Not open to the general public; restricted to on-site use only.

1716. Lyndon B Johnson National Historical Park Library
PO Box 329, Johnson City, TX 78636 (512) 868-7521 (Lib); FTS 770-5123
Admin John T Tiff.
Lib Type Special.
Spec Subs Lyndon B Johnson; local & regional Texas history. *Spec Collecs* Oral history collection on the life & times of Lyndon B Johnson in the Texas Hill Country.
Circ Servs Avail Restricted to staff.
Ref Servs Avail To other Federal libraries; to other libraries; to the general public.

1717. Joshua Tree National Monument Library
74485 Palm Vista Dr, Twentynine Palms, CA 92277 (714) 367-7511
Admin Interpretive Specialist.
Lib Type Special.
Spec Subs Natural history; history; Indian desert cultures.
Ref Servs Avail To the general public.

1718. Katmai National Park & Preserve Library
PO Box 7, King Salmon, AK 99613 (907) 246-3305
Admin Resource Management Specialist.
Lib Type Special.
Spec Subs Natural resources, history, & archeology relevant to Katmai National Park & Preserve. *In-house Files* Research reports on research conducted in the park/preserve.
Circ Servs Avail To other Federal libraries; to other libraries; restricted to photocopies of publications for the general public.
Ref Servs Avail To other Federal libraries; to other libraries; to the general public.

1719. Kennesaw Mountain National Battlefield Park Library
Box 1167, Marietta, GA 30061 (404) 427-4686
Admin Dennis Kelly; Retha Stephens.
Lib Type Special.
Spec Subs Civil War. *Spec Collecs* Some original letters & diaries.
Ref Servs Avail To other Federal libraries; to other libraries; to the general public.

1720. Kings Mountain National Military Park Library
PO Box 31, Kings Mountain, NC 28086 (803) 936-7921
Admin James J Anderson.
Lib Type Special.
Spec Subs Revolutionary War, especially the southern campaign; Battle of Kings Mountain. *Spec Collecs* Partial collection of Lyman C Draper papers on micro-film.
Circ Servs Avail Not open to the general public.
Ref Servs Avail To the general public; restricted to during office hours.

1721. Knife River Indian Villages National Historic Site Library
Box 168, RR 1, Stanton, ND 58571 (701) 745-3309
Admin Park Ranger—Interpretation & Resource Management.
Lib Type Special.
Spec Subs Native American culture & history; Plains Indians; archeology, explorers, & traders of the Upper Missouri. *In-house Files* Management plans.
Shared Catalog Nets Library of Congress. *Coop Lib Nets* Theodore Roosevelt National Park (THRO) administrative HQ for Knife River; Fort Union National Historic Trading Post (FOUS).
Circ Servs Avail To other Federal libraries; to other libraries; to the general public.
Ref Servs Avail To other Federal libraries; to other libraries; to the general public.

1722. Jean Lafitte National Historical Park Library
423 Canal St Rm 206, New Orleans, LA 70130 (504) 589-3882; FTS 682-3882
Admin Mike Strock.
Lib Type Special.
Spec Subs Cultural diversity; Louisiana history; architecture; New Orleans history; natural resources. *In-house Files* Wetlands studies; cultural/ethnic group studies.
Circ Servs Avail Not open to the general public; restricted to park staff & contracted researchers.
Ref Servs Avail Not open to the general public; restricted to park staff & contracted researchers.

1723. Lake Mead National Recreation Area Library
601 Nevada Hwy, Boulder City, NV 89005 (702) 293-8907; FTS 598-7807
Admin Robinett R Hourie. *Ref Lib* John S Mohlhenrich (ILL, Acq).
Lib Type Special.
Spec Subs Natural & local history; animals; plants; archeology; paleontology; geology; anthropology; Indians; recreation. *Spec Collecs* archeology; slide files; historic photos; plants.
Circ Servs Avail To other Federal libraries; to other libraries; to the general public.
Ref Servs Avail To other Federal libraries; to other libraries; to the general public.

1724. Lake Meredith Recreation Area Library
Box 1438, Fritch, TX 79036 (806) 865-3874/857-3152
Admin John Wesley Phillips.
Lib Type Special.
Spec Subs Archeology; natural history; National Parks history. *Spec Collecs* Studer collection of documents pertaining to Alibates Flint Quarries National Monument. *In-house Files* NPS Areas; archeology.
Ref Servs Avail Restricted to duty hours.

1725. Lassen Volcanic National Park Library
Box 100, Mineral, CA 96063-0100 (916) 595-4444
Admin Richard L Vance.
Lib Type Special.
Circ Servs Avail Restricted to on-site use to park personnel.
Ref Servs Avail Restricted to on-site use to park personnel.

1726. Lava Beds National Monument Library
PO Box 867, Tulelake, CA 96134 (916) 667-2282
Admin Gary Hathaway (Chief, Div of Interpretation).
Lib Type Special.
Spec Subs History of the Modoc Indians & Modoc War; history of northeastern California; natural history & administrative history of Lava Beds.
Coop Lib Nets North State Cooperative Library System.
Ref Servs Avail Restricted to on-site use.

1727. Lehman Caves National Monument Library
Baker, NV 89311 (702) 234-7331
Admin Paul Thompson.
Lib Type Special.
Spec Subs Speleology.
Circ Servs Avail Not open to the general public; restricted to staff.
Ref Servs Avail To the general public.

1728. Abraham Lincoln Birthplace National Historic Site Library
Box 94, Rt 1, Hodgenville, KY 42748 (502) 358-3874
Admin Patti Reynolds.
Lib Type Special.
Spec Subs Abraham Lincoln; Lincoln family; LaRue County, KY; American history; natural resources; environmental education. *Spec Collecs* Jones collection: Lincoln Farm Assoc collection—200, 4"x5" black & white glass lantern slide of Lincoln birthplace, letters, documents, pamphlets, photographs, & subscription records; Thomas Lincoln land records—property records on holdings in Hardin (now LaRue) county, 1804-1816, taken from original courthouse records.
Ref Servs Avail To other Federal libraries; not open to the general public.

1729. Lincoln Boyhood National Memorial Library
Lincoln City, IN 47552 (812) 937-4757
Admin Gerald W Sanders (Chief of Operations).
Lib Type Special.
Spec Subs Abraham Lincoln; pioneer life; Indiana state & local history. *Spec Collecs* Abraham Lincoln (1816-1830); Spencer County, IN; local history & genealogy. *In-house Files* Lincoln history & administrative history of Lincoln Boyhood National Memorial.
Circ Servs Avail Not open to the general public.
Ref Servs Avail To the general public.

1730. Mall Operation Library
Survey Lodge, National Capital Parks Central, 1100 Ohio Drive, SW, Washington, DC 20242 (202) 426-6841/6842/6843
Admin Samuel S Coe.
Lib Type Special.
Spec Subs Biographies: Lincoln, Jefferson, Washington. *Spec Collecs* Memorial photographs; Memorial stones information; materials on construction of major memorials.
Circ Servs Avail Not open to the general public; restricted to NPS, the general public on request.
Ref Servs Avail Not open to the general public; restricted to Mall operations personnel.

1731. Mammoth Cave National Park Library
Mammoth Cave, KY 42259 (502) 758-2251
Admin Mineva B Dennison.
Lib Type Special.
Spec Subs History & natural science of the area. *Spec Collecs* Historical books, articles, pamphlets, & pictures.
Ref Servs Avail To the general public.

1732. Manassas National Battlefield Park Library
Box 1830, Manassas, VA 22110 (703) 754-7107; TTY 591-3275
Admin James Burgess.
Lib Type Special.
Spec Subs Civil War history.
Circ Servs Avail To the general public.
Ref Servs Avail To the general public.

1733. Mesa Verde Research Library
Mesa Verde National Park, CO 81330 (303) 529-4475
Admin Beverly Cunningham.
Lib Type Special.
Spec Subs Archeology—Southwest.
Shared Catalog Nets OCLC. *Coop Lib Nets* Southwest Regional Library Service System.
Ref Servs Avail Not open to the general public.

1734. Minute Man National Historical Park Library
PO Box 160, Concord, MA 01863 (617) 369-6944 or 484-6156
Admin Fredrick A Szarka (Chief of Interpretation).
Lib Type Special.
Spec Subs US history: Colonial-early federal period, Revolutionary War. *Spec Collecs* Harriett M Lothrop family papers.
Circ Servs Avail Restricted to NPS employees.
Ref Servs Avail To other Federal libraries; to other libraries; to the general public.

1735. Montezuma Castle National Monument Library
PO Box 219, Camp Verde, AZ 86322 (602) 567-3322
Admin Glen E Henderson.
Lib Type Special.
Spec Subs Sinaguan archeology.
Ref Servs Avail Restricted to research.

1736. Moores Creek National Military Park Library
PO Box 69, Currie, NC 28435 (919) 283-5591
Admin Terry H Mitchell.
Lib Type Special.
Spec Subs North Carolina colonial & revolutionary history; Highland Scots; weapons of colonial times; National Parks; natural history.
Ref Servs Avail To the general public; restricted to on site.

1737. Morristown National Historical Park Library
Washington Pl, Morristown, NJ 07960 (201) 539-2016; FTS 341-3627
Admin Janet C Wolf (Supt); Susan Kopczynski (Museum curator).
Lib Type Special.
Spec Subs American history; colonial & Revolutionary War periods. *Spec Collecs* Lloyd W Smith autograph collection; Hessian transcripts; original manuscripts. *In-house Files* Historical research files.
Circ Servs Avail Restricted to park staff.
Ref Servs Avail To other Federal libraries; to other libraries; to the general public.

1738. Mound City Group National Monument Library
16062 State Rte 104, Chillicothe, OH 45601 (614) 774-1125
Admin John Mangimeli (Park Ranger).
Lib Type Special.
Spec Subs Archeology; Native Americans; national parks.
Circ Servs Avail Not open to the general public.
Ref Servs Avail To the general public.

1739. Mount Rainier National Park Library
Longmire, WA 98397 (206) 569-2211 ext 262
Admin Chief of Interpretation. *Ref Lib* Doug Buehler.
Lib Type Special.
Spec Subs Mt Rainier natural history; history; geology.

Shared Catalog Nets OCLC.
Circ Servs Avail To other Federal libraries; to other libraries.
Ref Servs Avail To other Federal libraries; to other libraries.

1740. Mount Rushmore National Memorial Library
PO Box 268, Keystone, SD 57751 (605) 574-2523; FTS 782-1425
Admin Larry G Asher (Park Ranger).
Lib Type Special.
Spec Subs History of Mount Rushmore; South Dakota history; natural history of the Black Hills. *Spec Collecs* Oral history from sculptor Gutzon Borglum & son Lincoln Borglum. *In-house Files* Vertical file on various subjects connected with Mount Rushmore & historic photo file.
Circ Servs Avail Not open to the general public.
Ref Servs Avail Restricted to use by appointment.

1741. John Muir National Historic Site Library
4202 Alhambra Ave, Martinez, CA 94553 (415) 228-8860
Admin Phyllis Shaw (Supt). *Ref Lib* Linda Stumpff.
Lib Type Special.
Spec Subs John Muir & the conservation movement.
Circ Servs Avail Restricted to staff & volunteers.
Ref Servs Avail Restricted to Muir scholars & interested volunteers.

1742. Muir Woods National Monument, Eleanor Bello Memorial Research Library
Mill Valley, CA 94941 (415) 388-2595
Admin Mia Monroe.
Lib Type Special.
Spec Subs Redwoods; National Parks. *Spec Collecs* Redwoods; Muir Woods. *In-house Files* Muir Woods; redwood ecology.
Circ Servs Avail Not open to the general public.
Ref Servs Avail To other Federal libraries; to the general public.

1743. Natchez Trace Parkway Library
RR 1, NT-143, Tupelo, MS 38801 (601) 842-1572; FTS 222-4154
Admin John S Mohlhenrich.
Lib Type Special.
Spec Subs Natchez Trace Parkway & surrounding area history; Brices Cross Roads & Tupelo National Battlefield Sites. *In-house Files* Original research papers.
Circ Servs Avail To other Federal libraries; to other libraries.
Ref Servs Avail To the general public.

1744. National Capital Parks-East Library
1900 Anacostia Dr, SE, Washington, DC 20020 (202) 474-9227; FTS 763-1779
Admin Bruce K Kearney.
Lib Type Special.
Spec Subs Biological & earth sciences; American history. *Spec Collecs* Serves the Frederick Douglass Home, Ft Circle Parks, Ft Washington, Piscataway Park, Oxen Hill Farm, & some smaller parks.
Circ Servs Avail To other libraries.
Ref Servs Avail To the general public; restricted to on request by general public.

1745. National Maritime Museum, J Porter Shaw Library
Bldg E 3rd Fl, Fort Mason, San Francisco, CA 94123 (415) 556-9870; FTS 556-9870
Admin David A Hull. *Ref Lib* Irene Stachura (ILL). *Acq Lib* David Hull.
Lib Type Special.
Spec Subs Maritime history, especially relating to California, Pacific coast & basin. *Spec Collecs* Oral histories of seamen; logbooks & manuscripts; approximately 200,000 maritime photographs; material relating to Golden Gate National Recreation Area; San Francisco vessel arrival records, ca 1906-1965. *In-house Files* Approximately 2000 gatherings of pamphlets & ephemera relating to maritime history.
Shared Catalog Nets OCLC. *Coop Lib Nets* FEDLINK.
Circ Servs Avail To other Federal libraries; to other libraries; restricted to ILL only.
Ref Servs Avail To other Federal libraries; to other libraries; to the general public.

1746. National Park Service, Central Compliance Library
PO Box 25287, 655 Parfet St, Denver, CO 80225 (303) 234-5050
Admin Diane Rhodes.
Lib Type Special.
Spec Subs Master set of current & applicable regulations, statutes, legal decisions, federal register publications, executive orders, circulars, & revisions of the OMB, GAO, DOT, NPS, & others. *Spec Collecs* Complete up-to-date National Register of Historic Places; list of classified structures for all NPS regions. *In-house Files* The basic purpose of the collection is to provide a legal resources center & cultural resources center; in addition, distribution of relevant materials to some of the 600 employees of the Denver Service Center so that all planning documents for the NPS will be in compliance with the various laws, regulations, standards, guidelines, etc promulgated by agencies of the federal, state, & municipal governments.
Circ Servs Avail To other libraries.
Ref Servs Avail To the general public.

1747. National Park Service Library
PO Box 25287, 655 Parfet St, Denver, CO 80225 (303) 234-4443; FTS 234-4443
Admin Ruth A Larison.
Lib Type Special.
Spec Subs National Park Service areas; outdoor recreation; ecology; regional planning; natural history; architecture; American history & archeology.
Shared Catalog Nets OCLC.
Circ Servs Avail To other libraries.
Ref Servs Avail To the general public.

1748. National Park Service, Midwest Archeological Center Library
Rm 474, Federal Bldg, 100 Centennial Mall N, Lincoln, NE 68508 (402) 471-5392; FTS 867-5392
Lib Type Special.
Spec Subs American Indians; anthropology; archeology; history. *Spec Collecs* Archeology Collection.
Circ Servs Avail Not open to the general public; restricted to staff; research collection available to archeologists & anthropologists thru ILL.

1749. National Park Service Midwest Regional Library
1709 Jackson St, Omaha, NE 68102 (402) 221-3472; FTS 864-3471
Admin Elizabeth Lane.
Lib Type Special.
Spec Subs National parks & monuments. *In-house Files* Historical; architectural; restoration.
Circ Servs Avail To other Federal libraries; to other libraries; not open to the general public.
Ref Servs Avail To other Federal libraries; to other libraries; not open to the general public.

1750. National Park Service, Southeast Regional Office Library
75 Spring St, SW, Atlanta, GA 30303 (404) 221-4916; FTS 242-4916
Admin Arthur Graham.
Lib Type Special.
Spec Subs Parks & recreation; land & water resources; environmental concerns; natural history; US history.
Circ Servs Avail To other Federal libraries; to other libraries.
Ref Servs Avail To the general public.

1751. National Park Service, Southwest Regional Library
PO Box 728, Santa Fe, NM 87501 (505) 988-6838; FTS 476-1839
Admin Carmen Segura.
Lib Type Special.
Spec Subs Indian archeology.
Circ Servs Avail Not open to the general public; restricted to NPS employees.
Ref Servs Avail Not open to the general public; restricted to NPS employees.

1752. National Park Service, Western Regional Resources Library
450 Golden Gate Ave, San Francisco, CA 94102 (415) 556-4165
Lib Type Special.
Spec Subs Archeology; geology; historical architecture; history; natural history; national parks. *Spec Collecs* Oral history.

1753. Navajo National Monument Library
Box 3, H.C. 71, Tonalea, AZ 86044-9704 (602) 672-2366
Admin Marcia Stout.
Lib Type Special.
Spec Subs Pre-historic Anasazi culture; Navajo culture; Pueblo culture; southwestern archeology; ecology of the southwest. *Spec Collecs* Rare books: including publications dealing specifically with this area.
Coop Lib Nets Dept of Interior field library collection project.
Circ Servs Avail Restricted to employees.
Ref Servs Avail To other Federal libraries; to other libraries; to the general public.

1754. Nez Perce National Historic Park Library
PO Box 93, Spalding, ID 83551 (208) 843-2685
Admin Karen E Bizak; Fahy C Whitaker.
Lib Type Special.
Spec Subs Nez Perce Indian history & culture. *Spec Collecs* Historic photographs (archival collection).
Shared Catalog Nets OCLC. *Coop Lib Nets* Pacific Northwest Region of National Parks (PNR).
Circ Servs Avail To other libraries.
Ref Servs Avail Restricted to professional researchers.

1755. North Cascades National Park Library
2105 Hwy 20, Sedro Woolley, WA 98284 (206) 856-5700; FTS 396-9414
Admin John R Douglass (Staff Park Interpreter).
Lib Type Special.
Spec Subs Natural history.
Circ Servs Avail To other Federal libraries; restricted to staff, researchers & students.
Ref Servs Avail To other Federal libraries; to the general public.

1756. Ocmulgee National Monument Library
National Park Service, 1207 Emery Hwy, Macon, GA 31201 (912) 742-0447; FTS 238-0248
Lib Type Special.
Spec Subs Anthropology; archeology; environmental studies; southern history; southeastern Indian history.
Circ Servs Avail Not open to the general public; restricted to staff.
Ref Servs Avail Not open to the general public; restricted to outside researchers by appointment.

1757. Olympic National Park Library
Pioneer Memorial Museum, 3002 Mount Angeles Rd, Port Angeles, WA 98362 (206) 452-4501 ext 230; FTS 396-4230
Admin Susan Schultz (Park Historian); Bonnie Fuller (Visitor Ctr Mgr).
Lib Type Special.
Spec Subs Natural history; Pacific northwest archeology & ethnography; Olympic Peninsula history; national parks. *In-house Files* Olympic National Park administrative files, ca 1934-55; black & white photographs of Olympic National Park; slide file.
Circ Servs Avail Restricted to park staff.
Ref Servs Avail Restricted to researchers with appointments.

1758. Organ Pipe Cactus National Monument Library
Box 100, Rte 1, Ajo, AZ 85321 (602) 387-6849
Admin Interpretive specialist.
Lib Type Special.
Spec Subs Natural history of the Sonoran Desert.
Circ Servs Avail Restricted to staff.
Ref Servs Avail Not open to the general public.

1759. Ozark National Scenic Riverways Library
PO Box 490, Van Buren, MO 63965 (314) 323-4236
Admin Dorothy Belvedere.
Lib Type Special.
Spec Subs Materials dealing with Riverways management.

Circ Servs Avail To the general public.
Ref Servs Avail To the general public.

1760. Pacific Northwest Regional Library System
US National Park Service, 83 S King St, Ste 314, Seattle, WA 98104 (206) 442-5203; FTS 399-5203
Admin Ellen Traxel (Reg Lib); Richard Aroksaar (Asst Lib).
Lib Type Special.
Spec Subs National parks of the states of WA, OR, & ID. *In-house Files* Legislative histories of the National Parks in the Pacific Northwest Region; Park bibliographies for regional parks.
Info Ret Servs DIALOG; BRS; Western Library Network (WLN). *Shared Catalog Nets* OCLC; WLN. *Coop Lib Nets* Natural Resources Library Information Services (NRLIS).
Circ Servs Avail To other Federal libraries; to other libraries.
Ref Servs Avail To other Federal libraries; to other libraries; to the general public; restricted to in-house use by general public.

1761. Padre Island National Seashore Library
9405 S Padre Island Dr, Corpus Christi, TX 78418 (512) 949-8173
Admin Robert G Whistler.
Lib Type Special.
Spec Collecs Graduate study thesis on the studies made on the island on the natural & cultural resources.
Circ Servs Avail Not open to the general public.
Ref Servs Avail Restricted to on-site use.

1762. Pea Ridge National Military Park Library
Pea Ridge, AR 72751 (501) 451-8122
Admin Park Historian.
Lib Type Special.
Spec Subs Civil War.
Ref Servs Avail To the general public.

1763. Pecos National Monument Library
PO Drawer 11, Pecos, NM 87552 (505) 757-6414
Admin Darlene Romero.
Lib Type Special.
Spec Subs History & archeology. *Spec Collecs* Archeological.
Circ Servs Avail Restricted to historians & archeologists.
Ref Servs Avail Restricted to historians & archeologists.

1764. Perry's Victory & International Peace Memorial Library
PO Box 78, Put-in-Bay, OH 43456 (419) 285-2184
Lib Type Special.
Spec Subs Battle of Lake Erie; War of 1812; history of Put-in-Bay; Oliver Hazard Perry; International Peace. *Spec Collecs* Correspondence of Perry's Victory Memorial Commission on the construction & early history of the Memorial Column.
Ref Servs Avail To the general public; restricted to by appointment.

1765. Petersburg National Battlefield Library
PO Box 549, Petersburg, VA 23803 (804) 732-3531; FTS 925-7222
Admin Glenn O Clark (Supt). *Ref Lib* John R Davis, Jr.
Lib Type Special.
Spec Subs Civil War subjects, especially the siege of Petersburg, 1864-65. *In-house Files* Letters; diaries.
Ref Servs Avail Not open to the general public; restricted to on-site use.

1766. Petrified Forest National Park Library
Petrified Forest National Park, AZ 86028 (602) 524-6228
Admin L Edward Gastellum (Supt). *Ref Lib* Terry Maze.
Lib Type Special.
Spec Subs Triassic Period; Petrified wood; southwestern pre-historic & contemporary Indians.
Circ Servs Avail Not open to the general public.
Ref Servs Avail To the general public.

1767. Pictured Rocks National Lakeshore Library
PO Box 40, Munising, MI 49862 (906) 387-2607
Admin Bruce A Peterson.
Lib Type Special.
Spec Subs Natural history of the Great Lakes & the Lakeshore area; cultural history of the local & Lake Superior areas. *In-house Files* Documents pertaining to the legislation & acquisition of the Pictured Rocks National Lakeshore.
Circ Servs Avail Not open to the general public.

1768. Pinnacles National Monument Library
Conference Room, Paicines, CA 95043 (408) 389-4578
Admin Tomie Patrick Lee (East Dist Ranger). *Ref Lib* Karen McKinlay.
Lib Type Special.
Spec Subs Natural sciences; natural resources; materials especially pertaining to park.
Circ Servs Avail To other Federal libraries; not open to the general public.
Ref Servs Avail To other Federal libraries; not open to the general public.

1769. Pipe Springs National Monument Library
Moccasin, AZ 86022 (602) 643-7105
Admin William Herr (Supt).
Lib Type Special.
Spec Subs Western ranching; Arizona history; Mormon settlement. *Spec Collecs* Arizona & southwest.
Ref Servs Avail To other Federal libraries; to the general public.

1770. Point Reyes National Seashore Library
Point Reyes, CA 94956 (415) 663-1092
Admin David A Pugh (Chief of Interpretation). *Ref Lib* Marlene F Dentoni.
Lib Type Special.
Spec Subs Subjects pertaining to Point Reyes National Seashore.
Ref Servs Avail Restricted to on-site research only.

1771. Puuhonua o Honaunau National Historical Park, Library
PO Box 129, Honaunau, Kona, HI 96726 (808) 328-2326
Admin Blossom Sapp. *Ref Lib* Jerry Y Shimoda.
Lib Type Special.
Spec Subs Hawaiian history. *Spec Collecs* Flora & fauna of Hawaii. *In-house Files* Manuscripts of research done at Puuhonua o Honaunau NHP.
Circ Servs Avail Not open to the general public.
Ref Servs Avail To the general public; restricted to on site use.

1772. Redwood National Park Library
1111 2nd St, Crescent City, CA 95531 (707) 464-6101
Admin Richard A Rasp (Chief Park Interpreter). *Ref Lib* Susan Davis (ILL, Acq).
Lib Type Special.
Spec Subs Management plans; technical reports of Redwood National Park. *Spec Collecs* Technical reports generated by the park's unique forest rehabilitation program. *In-house Files* Slide files.
Circ Servs Avail To other Federal libraries; to other libraries; restricted to specific research.
Ref Servs Avail To the general public; restricted to Park use only.

1773. Richmond National Battlefield Park Headquarters Library
3215 E Broad St, Richmond, VA 23223 (804) 226-1981
Lib Type Special.
Spec Subs Civil War.

1774. Rock Creek Nature Center
5200 Glover Rd, NW, Washington, DC 20015 (202) 426-6829
Admin Albert James.
Lib Type Special.
Spec Subs Natural history; astronomy; Indians; history of Rock Creek Park, including milling activities. *Spec Collecs* Study specimens of mammal skins, birds, mushrooms, plants, & other natural history items; rock samples; photograph collection of slides & prints.

Circ Servs Avail Not open to the general public; restricted to National Capital Region employees on limited basis.
Ref Servs Avail To the general public.

1775. Rocky Mountain National Park Library
Estes Park, CO 80517 (303) 586-2371 ext 227
Admin Helen Burgener (Lib Tech).
Lib Type Special.
Spec Subs Biological & geological sciences; Indians of this area; history of Rocky Mountain National Park. *Spec Collecs* Official documents of park supt; collection of oral history tapes concerning the park. *In-house Files* Maps; reports of hearings on fire policy, boundaries.
Circ Servs Avail To other Federal libraries; not open to the general public; restricted to park personnel & researchers by appointment.
Ref Servs Avail To other Federal libraries; not open to the general public; restricted to park personnel & researchers by appointment.

1776. Franklin D Roosevelt National Historic Site Library
259 Albany Post Rd, Hyde Park, NY 12538 (914) 229-8114; FTS 883-5444
Admin William R. Emerson; Marguerite Hubbard (Curator).
Lib Type Special.
Spec Subs Franklin & Eleanor Roosevelt; American history & politics from 1913-1945; NY colonial history; Hudson River Valley history; US Naval history.
Coop Lib Nets Southeastern NY Library Resources Council.
Ref Servs Avail Restricted to use by general public by appointment.

1777. Theodore Roosevelt National Park Library
Medora, ND 58645 (701) 842-3845
Admin Susan Snow (Lib); Micki Hellickson (Chief Naturalist).
Lib Type Special.
Spec Subs Theodore Roosevelt; cowboys; Indians; natural history of North Dakota; fur trade; botany of North Dakota; US West.
Circ Servs Avail To other Federal libraries; not open to the general public; restricted to staff, Medora residents & members of the T Roosevelt Nature & History Assoc; special requests.

1778. Russell Cave National Monument Library
Box 175, Rte 1, Bridgeport, AL 35740 (205) 495-2672
Admin Dorothy H Marsh (Supt).
Lib Type Special.
Spec Subs Archeology; anthropology.
Circ Servs Avail Restricted to on-site reference.
Ref Servs Avail To the general public; restricted to on-site use.

1779. Sagamore Hill National Historic Site Library
Cove Neck Rd, Oyster Bay, NY 11771-1899 (516) 922-4447
Admin Loretta L Schmidt (Supt). *Ref Lib* Patricia J Kennedy.
Lib Type Special.
Spec Subs Collected works of Theodore Roosevelt; political studies of his presidency; general works on early 20th century American studies.
Circ Servs Avail To other Federal libraries; not open to the general public; restricted to ILL by written request.
Ref Servs Avail To other Federal libraries; to other libraries.

1780. Saguaro National Monument Library
Box 695, Rte 8, Tucson, AZ 85730 (602) 298-2036; FTS 629-6680
Admin Elnor Detlefsen; Richard Hayes.
Lib Type Special.
Spec Subs Arizona wildlife; flora & fauna.
Ref Servs Avail To other Federal libraries.

1781. St Croix National Scenic Riverway Library
PO Box 708, Saint Croix Falls, WI 54024 (715) 483-3287
Admin A L Seidenkranz.
Lib Type Special.
Spec Subs Local history.
Ref Servs Avail To the general public.

1782. Saint Gardens Library
RR No 2, Windsor, VT 05089 (603) 675-2175
Admin John H Dryfhout.
Lib Type Special.
Spec Subs Art history concentrated on late 1800's & early 1900's.
Ref Servs Avail To the general public.

1783. Salem Maritime National Historic Site Library
174 Derby St, Salem, MA 01970 (617) 744-4323
Admin Sheila Cooke-Kayser. *Acq Lib* Maureen Davi.
Lib Type Special.
Spec Subs Maritime history of New England; maritime trades; customs service; privateering in Revolutionary War.
Circ Servs Avail Not open to the general public; restricted to staff.
Ref Servs Avail To other Federal libraries; not open to the general public.

1784. Salinas National Monument Library
PO Box 496, Mountainair, NM 87036 (505) 847-2585
Lib Type Special.
Spec Subs 17th century colonial New Mexico; pre-historic people.
Circ Servs Avail Restricted to NPS employees.
Ref Servs Avail To other Federal libraries; to the general public.

1785. San Juan Island National Historical Park Library
PO Box 429, Friday Harbor, WA 98250 (206) 378-2240/2902
Admin Steven J Gobat.
Lib Type Special.
Spec Subs Military, 1860s; San Juan Water Boundary Dispute.
Shared Catalog Nets National Park Service.
Circ Servs Avail To other Federal libraries; to other libraries; not open to the general public.
Ref Servs Avail To other Federal libraries; to other libraries; to the general public.

1786. San Juan National Historic Site, Division of Visitors Services—Library
PO Box 712, Old San Juan, PR 00902 (809) 724-1992
Admin W P Crawford (Supt). *Ref Lib* Beda Velazquez (Park Ranger).
Lib Type Special.
Spec Subs Spanish & military history.
Circ Servs Avail Not open to the general public.
Ref Servs Avail Not open to the general public.

1787. Carl Sandberg Home National Historic Site Library
PO Box 395, Flat Rock, NC 28731 (704) 693-4178
Admin Benjamin Davis (Supt).
Lib Type Special.
Spec Collecs Personal working library of Carl Sandberg preserved as a museum.
Ref Servs Avail Restricted to exhibit.

1788. Saratoga National Historical Park Library
RD 2, Box 33, Stillwater, NY 12170 (518) 664-9821
Lib Type Special.
Spec Subs American Revolution; Burgoyne campaign of 1777; battles at Saratoga (Stillwater). *Spec Collecs* Neilson Collection.
Ref Servs Avail Restricted to use by appointment.

1789. Saugus Iron Works National Historic Site Library
244 Central St, Saugus, MA 01906 (617) 233-0050
Admin Jim Gott (Park Supt); Rhoda Barry (Lib).
Lib Type Special.
Spec Subs Iron manufacture: history & technology; 17th Century life-style. *Spec Collecs* Museum Collections: historic photographic collections for the iron works site; files of the First Iron Works Assoc. *In-house Files* Iron manufacture: history & technology.
Ref Servs Avail Not open to the general public.

1790. Scotts Bluff National Monument, Oregon Trail Association Library
PO Box 427, Gering, NE 69341 (308) 436-4340
Admin Robert L Burns.
Lib Type Special.
Spec Subs Oregon Trail history. *Spec Collecs* Emigrant diary transcripts; Agate Fossil Beds National Monument collection.
Circ Servs Avail Not open to the general public; restricted to members of Oregon Trail Museum Assn.
Ref Servs Avail To the general public.

1791. Sequoia & Kings Canyon National Park Library
Ash Mountain, Three Rivers, CA 93271 (209) 565-3341
Admin John J Palmer.
Lib Type Special.
Spec Subs History & natural history of the Sierra Nevada; conservation; NPS. *Spec Collecs* Inventory of Giant Sequoias of Sequoia & Kings Canyon National Parks.
Circ Servs Avail To other Federal libraries; to other libraries.
Ref Servs Avail To other Federal libraries; to other libraries.

1792. Shenandoah National Park Library
Box 292, Rte 4, Luray, VA 22835 (703) 999-2243 ext 281
Admin Dennis Carter (Chief Park Naturalist). *Ref Lib* Karen Campbell.
Lib Type Special.
Spec Subs Natural history. *In-house Files* Research carried on in or about the park.
Circ Servs Avail Not open to the general public.
Ref Servs Avail Not open to the general public.

1793. Shiloh National Monument Park Library
Shiloh, TN 38376 (901) 689-5275
Admin George A Reaves.
Lib Type Special.
Spec Subs Civil War in the West.
Circ Servs Avail To other libraries; not open to the general public.
Ref Servs Avail To other Federal libraries; to other libraries; not open to the general public.

1794. Sitka National Historic Park Library
PO Box 738, Sitka, AK 99835 (907) 747-6281; FTS 399-0150
Admin Gary Candelaria.
Lib Type Special.
Spec Subs Southeast Alaska; Alaska; Pacific Northwest Indians; history; natural history; archaeology; Northwest Coast Indians: arts, crafts, & anthropology; Russo-American history. *Spec Collecs* E W Merrill collection of approximately 200 glass plate negatives relating to the Sitka area during the late 1800's & early 1900's.
Circ Servs Avail To other libraries.
Ref Servs Avail To the general public.

1795. Southeast Archeological Center Library
National Park Service, PO Box 2416, FSU Campus, Montgomery Gym Rm 35, Tallahassee, FL 32316 (904) 222-1167
Lib Type Special.

1796. Springfield Armory National Historic Site Library
1 Armory Sq, Springfield, MA 01105 (413) 734-8551; FTS 836-9238
Admin Barbara Higgins Aubrey. *Acq Lib* Larry Lowenthal.
Lib Type Special.
Spec Subs Ordnance. *Spec Collecs* Garand & Pedersen papers. *In-house Files* Technical files on weapons development; oral history tapes.
Circ Servs Avail Not open to the general public.
Ref Servs Avail Restricted to by appointment; in-house only.

1797. Stones River National Battlefield Library
Box 495, Rte 10, Old Nashville Hwy, Murfreesboro, TN 37130 (615) 893-9501
Admin Donald E Magee (Supt).
Lib Type Special.
Spec Subs Battle of Stones River; Civil War history; military history.

Circ Servs Avail To other Federal libraries; not open to the general public.
Ref Servs Avail To other Federal libraries; not open to the general public.

1798. William Howard Taft National Historic Site Library
2038 Auburn Ave, Cincinnati, OH 45219 (513) 684-3262; FTS 684-3262
Admin Historian.
Lib Type Special.
Spec Subs William Howard Taft biographical collection. *In-house Files* William Howard Taft.
Circ Servs Avail Not open to the general public; restricted to on-site use only.
Ref Servs Avail Not open to the general public; restricted to on-site use only.

1799. Timpanogos Cave National Monument Library
RR 3, Box 200, American Fork, UT 84003 (801) 756-5238
Admin Scott W Isaacson.
Lib Type Special.
Spec Subs Speleology; local history.
Ref Servs Avail To other Federal libraries; to other libraries; to the general public.

1800. Tonto National Monument Library
PO Box 707, Roosevelt, AZ 85545 (602) 467-2241
Admin Kay Threlkeld.
Lib Type Special.
Spec Subs Southwestern archaeology; Salado Indian culture; National Park Service; anthropology.
Circ Servs Avail To other Federal libraries; not open to the general public.
Ref Servs Avail To other Federal libraries; to the general public.

1801. Travertine Nature Center Library
Chickasaw National Recreation Area, PO Box 201, Sulphur, OK 73086 (405) 622-3165
Admin Bert L Speed (Chief Park Interpreter).
Lib Type Special.
Spec Subs Natural science & US history.
Circ Servs Avail Not open to the general public; restricted to NPS staff.
Ref Servs Avail Not open to the general public; restricted to use of NPS staff.

1802. Tumacacori National Monument Library
PO Box 67, Tumacacori, AZ 85640 (602) 398-2341
Admin Joseph L Sewell.
Lib Type Special.
Spec Subs Spanish colonial history of the West & Southwest; American Indians. *In-house Files* Planning documents.
Ref Servs Avail Restricted to on-site use.

1803. Tuzigoot National Monument Library
PO Box 68, Clarksdale, AZ 86324 (602) 634-5564
Admin John Reid (Park Ranger).
Lib Type Special.
Spec Subs Archeology. *Spec Collecs* Field notes of excavation, 1933-34.
Circ Servs Avail Restricted to researchers with Supt approval.
Ref Servs Avail Restricted to researchers with Supt approval.

1804. Valley Forge National Historical Park, Horace "Vox" Willcox Library
Valley Forge, PA 19481 (215) 296-2593
Admin Ellen Weisfeld.
Lib Type Special.
Spec Subs Military history; American Revolution.
Circ Servs Avail Restricted to Park staff.
Ref Servs Avail To the general public.

1805. Martin Van Buren National Historic Site Library
Kinderhook, NY 12106 (518) 758-9689
Admin Patricia West.
Lib Type Special.
Spec Subs Martin Van Buren; Jacksonian Era; 19th century decorative arts, furniture, & architecture; conservation & museum practices. *Spec Collecs* Van Buren correspondence; prints; memorabilia.
Circ Servs Avail Restricted to the general public by appointment only.
Ref Servs Avail Restricted to the general public by appointment only.

1806. Vicksburg National Military Park Library
PO Box 349, Vicksburg, MS 39180 (601) 636-0583
Admin Nancy Miller.
Lib Type Special.
Spec Subs Civil War & military history with emphasis on the Vicksburg Campaign of 1863.
Ref Servs Avail To the general public; restricted to on site.

1807. Virgin Islands National Park Reference Library
National Park Service, Saint John, VI 00830 (809) 776-6201
Admin Chief Park Ranger. *Ref Lib* Lito Valls.
Lib Type Special.
Spec Subs Natural & cultural history. *In-house Files* Vertical files with extensive biological reprints.
Ref Servs Avail To other Federal libraries; to other libraries; to the general public.

1808. Voyageurs National Park Library
Box 50, International Falls, MN 56649 (218) 283-9821; FTS 780-5466
Admin Mary Graves (Park Ranger).
Lib Type Special.
Spec Subs Natural history & history of Voyageurs National Park area. *Spec Collecs* Oral history interviews; planning documents for Voyageurs on microfiche.
Circ Servs Avail Restricted to use by special arrangement.
Ref Servs Avail To other Federal libraries; to other libraries; to the general public.

1809. Booker T Washington National Monument Library
Box 195, Rte 1, Hardy, VA 24101 (703) 721-2094
Admin Geraldine M Bell (Supt). *Ref Lib* Eleanor C Long (Park Ranger).
Lib Type Special.
Spec Subs Booker T Washington; Afro-American history; folkcrafts; 19th century farming.
Circ Servs Avail Not open to the general public.
Ref Servs Avail To other Federal libraries; to other libraries; to the general public.

1810. Western Archeological & Conservation Center Library
PO Box 41058, Tucson, AZ 85717 (602) 629-6994; FTS 762-6501; TTY (602) 629-6501
Admin W Richard Horn.
Lib Type Special.
Spec Subs History & anthropology of Southwest. *Spec Collecs* Photographic collection, 160,000 images of national parks (late 1800s to present). *In-house Files* Archeology field notes & historic diaries of early area residents.
Info Ret Servs DIALOG; BRS. *Shared Catalog Nets* OCLC. *Coop Lib Nets* FEDLINK.
Circ Servs Avail To other Federal libraries; to other libraries.
Ref Servs Avail To other Federal libraries; to other libraries; to the general public.

1811. Whiskeytown Unit Library, National Park Service
PO Box 188, Whiskeytown, CA 96095 (916) 241-6584; FTS 450-5394
Admin Chief, Interpretive Activities.
Lib Type Special.
Spec Subs Natural history; California gold rush; gold mining; NPS history & mission.
Circ Servs Avail Not open to the general public; restricted to employees.

Ref Servs Avail To the general public.

1812. White Sands National Monument Library
PO Box 458, Alamogordo, NM 88310 (505) 437-1058
Admin Robert J Schumerth.
Lib Type Special.
Spec Subs Natural history; earth science.
Circ Servs Avail To other Federal libraries; to the general public.
Ref Servs Avail To other Federal libraries; to the general public.

1813. Whitman Mission National Historic Site Library
Box 247, Rte 2, Walla Walla, WA 99362-9699 (509) 525-5500 ext
465; FTS 434-6360
Admin Robert C Amdor (Supt). *Ref Lib* Roger Trick.
Lib Type Special.
Spec Subs Whitman Mission, ca 1830-50. *Spec Collecs* Artifacts of
the site.
Circ Servs Avail To other Federal libraries; to other libraries; to
the general public.
Ref Servs Avail To other Federal libraries; to other libraries; to the
general public.

1814. Wind Cave National Park Library
Hot Springs, SD 57747 (605) 745-4600
Admin William W Swift (Chief Naturalist).
Lib Type Special.
Spec Subs Caves; cave geology; caving; prairie ecosystems; Na-
tional Park administration & history. *Spec Collecs* Historical
park documents; some manuscripts & other material related to
the history of Wind Cave.
Circ Servs Avail To other Federal libraries; to other libraries; not
open to the general public.
Ref Servs Avail To other Federal libraries; to other libraries; not
open to the general public.

1815. Wupatki National Monument Library
Box 444A, H.C. 33, Flagstaff, AZ 86001 (602) 527-7040; FTS 765-
7040
Admin Patricia Crowley.
Lib Type Special.
Spec Subs Prehistoric Indians, especially Sinagua & Kayenta An-
asazi; southwest archeology. *Spec Collecs* Historical archeology.
Info Ret Servs DIALOG (thru DOI Natural Resource Library).
Ref Servs Avail Restricted to on-site use by researchers.

1816. Yellowstone Association Research Library
PO Box 117, Yellowstone National Park, WY 82190 (307) 344-
7381 ext 2352; FTS 585-0352
Admin Tim Manns (Park Historian).
Lib Type Special.
Spec Subs Yellowstone National Park. *Spec Collecs* Rare books &
manuscripts relating to Yellowstone.
Circ Servs Avail To other Federal libraries; to other libraries.
Ref Servs Avail Restricted to on-site use.

1817. Yosemite National Park Research Library
PO Box 577-NPS, Yosemite National Park, CA 95389 (209) 372-
0280; FTS 448-4280
Admin Mary Vocelka.
Lib Type Special.
Spec Subs Natural & human history of Yosemite; geology; Native
Americans; master plan. *Spec Collecs* Native Americans of Yo-
semite region; records of the National Park Service in Yosemite
& concessions. *In-house Files* Bibliographies of special subject
categories.
Circ Servs Avail To other Federal libraries; to other libraries; to
the general public.
Ref Servs Avail To other Federal libraries; to other libraries; to the
general public.

1818. Zion National Park Library
Springdale, UT 84767 (801) 772-3256 ext 31
Admin Roy Given (Asst Chief Park Naturalist). *Acq Lib* Victor
Jackson.
Lib Type Special.

Spec Subs Cultural & natural history of Zion National Park &
vicinity. *In-house Files* Monthly & annual reports; special studies.
Circ Servs Avail To other Federal libraries; to other libraries; to
the general public.
Ref Servs Avail To other Federal libraries; to other libraries; to the
general public.

Office of the Secretary

1819. Alaska Resources Library
Box 36, 701 C St, Anchorage, AK 99513 (907) 271-5025; FTS
271-5025
Admin Martha Shepard. *ILL* Linda Tobiska. *Acq Lib* Mary Fer-
ber.
Lib Type Special.
Spec Subs Natural resources of Alaska.
Lib Deposit Designation GPO Depository Library.
Info Ret Servs DIALOG. *Shared Catalog Nets* OCLC; WLN. *Coop
Lib Nets* Alaska Library Network.
Circ Servs Avail To other Federal libraries; to other libraries.
Ref Servs Avail To other Federal libraries; to other libraries; to the
general public.

**1820. Department of the Interior, Center for Information &
Library Services, Natural Resources Library, Law Branch**
Washington, DC 20240 (202) 343-4571; FTS 343-4571
Admin Carl Kessler.
Lib Type Law.
Spec Subs Law as it relates to the environment, land use, natural
resources, the American Indian, law of the sea, & administra-
tive law. *Spec Collecs* Tribal constitutions; Indian claims com-
mission records & briefs.
Info Ret Servs JURIS.

**1821. Department of the Interior, Center for Information &
Library Services, Natural Resources Library**
18th & C Sts, NW, Washington, DC 20240 (202) 343-5821; FTS
343-5821
Admin Phillip M Haymand. *Ref Lib* Mary E Franks. *ILL* Brenda
Graff. *Acq Lib* Sue Ellen Sloca.
Lib Type Engineering & Science.
Spec Subs US land use; parks & recreation; mines; fish & wildlife;
American Indians.
Lib Deposit Designation GPO Depository Library.
Info Ret Servs DIALOG. *Shared Catalog Nets* OCLC. *Coop Lib
Nets* FEDLINK. *Elec Mail Nets* GTE Telemail.
Circ Servs Avail To other Federal libraries; to other libraries.
Ref Servs Avail To other Federal libraries; to other libraries.

**1822. Department of the Interior, Center for Information &
Library Services, Natural Resources Library, Law Branch**
18th & C Sts, NW, Washington, DC 20240 (202) 343-4571; FTS
343-4571
Admin Carl Kessler. *Ref Lib* Dell Barnes (ILL).
Lib Type Law.
Spec Subs American Indians; natural resources; administrative
law; environmental law; Indian Claims Commission records &
briefs. *Spec Collecs* DOI secretarial orders; public land orders;
DOI administrative decisions; tribal constitutions.
Lib Deposit Designation GPO Depository Library.
Info Ret Servs DIALOG; LEXIS; WESTLAW; ELSS. *Shared Cata-
log Nets* OCLC. *Coop Lib Nets* FEDLINK.
Circ Servs Avail Restricted to in-house use only.
Ref Servs Avail To other Federal libraries.

Office of the Solicitor

**1823. Department of the Interior, Office of the Field
Solicitor, Law Library**
Box 020 US Courthouse, Boise, ID 83724 (208) 334-1911; FTS
554-1911
Admin Velva Irving.
Lib Type Law.
Spec Subs Water law.

Ref Servs Avail Not open to the general public.

1824. Department of the Interior, Office of the Regional Solicitor, Law Library
Suite 1328, 75 Spring St, SW, Atlanta, GA 30303 (404) 221-3384; FTS 242-3384
Admin Kathy Knight.
Lib Type Law.
Spec Subs Law with special emphasis on the Southeast.
Ref Servs Avail To the general public.

1825. Department of the Interior, Office of the Regional Solicitor, Law Library
Bldg D105, Rm 1480, Denver Federal Center, Denver, CO 80225 (303) 234-3175; FTS 234-3175
Admin Sally Raines.
Lib Type Law.
Circ Servs Avail To other Federal libraries.
Ref Servs Avail Not open to the general public.

1826. Department of the Interior, Office of the Regional Solicitor, Law Library
One Gateway Center, Suite 612, Newton Corner, MA 02158-2868 (617) 965-5103 ext 258; FTS 829-9258
Admin Anne Noe.
Lib Type Law.
Spec Subs Matters relating to activities of Interior Dept. *Spec Collecs* Decisions of Office of Hearings & Appeals, Dept of Interior.
Circ Servs Avail Not open to the general public; restricted to office staff.
Ref Servs Avail Not open to the general public; restricted to office staff.

1827. Department of the Interior, Office of the Regional Solicitor, Law Library
Southwest Region, PO Box 3156, Tulsa, OK 74101 (918) 581-7502; FTS 745-7502
Admin Carolyn M Jackson.
Lib Type Law.
Circ Servs Avail To other Federal libraries; to the general public.
Ref Servs Avail To other Federal libraries; to the general public.

1828. Department of the Interior, Office of the Solicitor, Field Solicitor, Law Library
686 Federal Bldg, Fort Snelling, Twin Cities, MN 55111 (612) 725-3540; FTS 725-3540
Admin Lucille M Nelson.
Lib Type Law.
Info Ret Servs WESTLAW.
Ref Servs Avail To other Federal libraries; to other libraries; to the general public.

1829. Department of the Interior, Office of the Solicitor, Field Solicitor, Law Library
Department of the Interior, PO Box 549, Aberdeen, SD 57401 (605) 225-0250, ext 254
Admin Dorothy L Johnson.
Lib Type Law.

1830. Department of the Interior, Office of the Solicitor, Field Solicitor, Law Library
Department of the Interior, PO Box 1538, Billings, MT 59103 (406) 657-6331; FTS 585-6331
Admin Donna M Rieger.
Lib Type Law.
Circ Servs Avail To other Federal libraries.
Ref Servs Avail To the general public.

1831. Department of the Interior, Office of the Solicitor, Field Solicitor, Law Library
Department of the Interior, PO Box 397, Anadarko, OK 73005 (405) 247-6673, ext 297; FTS 743-7297
Admin Carolyn Nation.
Lib Type Law.

1832. Department of the Interior, Office of the Solicitor, Field Solicitor, Law Library
Department of the Interior, c/o Osage Agency, Pawhuska, OK 74056 (918) 287-2431
Admin Cora L Harris.
Lib Type Law.
Ref Servs Avail To the general public.

1833. Department of the Interior, Office of the Solicitor, Field Solicitor, Law Library
Department of the Interior, PO Box 1508, Muskogee, OK 74401 (918) 687-2388; FTS 736-2388
Admin Harold M Shultz, Jr.
Lib Type Law.
Ref Servs Avail To the general public.

1834. Department of the Interior, Office of the Solicitor, Field Solicitor, Law Library
Department of the Interior, Valley Bank Ctr, Suite 2080, 201 N Central Ave, Phoenix, AZ 85073 (602) 261-4756
Admin Rosie Davis.
Lib Type Law.
Spec Collecs Departmental opinions & decisions.
Ref Servs Avail To the general public.

1835. Department of the Interior, Office of the Solicitor, Field Solicitor, Law Library
Department of the Interior, Window Rock, AZ 86515 (602) 871-5151; FTS 261-3900
Admin Julie A Bailey.
Lib Type Law.

1836. Department of the Interior, Office of the Solicitor, Field Solicitor, Law Library
Department of the Interior, PO Box 1696, Albuquerque, NM 87103 (505) 766-2547; FTS 474-2547
Admin Mary P Pennybacker.
Lib Type Law.
Spec Subs Law, including US, New Mexico, Colo, & Ariz statutes; Indian law; water law.
Circ Servs Avail To other Federal libraries; to the general public; restricted to local attorneys.

1837. Department of the Interior, Office of the Solicitor, Field Solicitor, Law Library
Department of the Interior, Suite 104, 3610 Central Ave, Riverside, CA 92506 (714) 787-1567; FTS 796-1567
Admin Patricia Carder.
Lib Type Law.
Ref Servs Avail To the general public.

1838. Department of the Interior, Office of the Solicitor, Field Solicitor, Law Library
Department of the Interior, Box 36064, 450 Golden Gate Ave, San Francisco, CA 94102 (415) 556-8807; FTS 556-8807
Admin Renee Breazeale.
Lib Type Law.

1839. Department of the Interior, Office of the Solicitor, Field Solicitor, Library
Department of the Interior, PO Box 1H-4393, Herring Plaza, Amarillo, TX 79101 (806) 376-2296; FTS 734-2296
Admin Ernestine Gilliam.
Lib Type Law.
Spec Subs Law, including the decisions of the Comptroller General & Attorneys General.
Circ Servs Avail To other libraries.
Ref Servs Avail Restricted to local attorneys.

1840. Department of the Interior, Office of the Solicitor, Intermountain Region, Library
6201 Federal Bldg, 125 S State St, Salt Lake City, UT 84138 (801) 524-5677; FTS 588-5677; TTY 524-5677
Admin Susan K Stone.
Lib Type Law.

Lib Deposit Designation Dept of the Interior.
Ref Servs Avail To other Federal libraries; to the general public.

1841. Department of the Interior, Office of the Solicitor, Law Library
Department of the Interior, Suite 408, 510 L St, Anchorage, AK 99501 (907) 265-5301; FTS (from continental US) 399-0150 & ask for (907) 265-5301
Admin Rita M Shiffer.
Lib Type Law.
Spec Subs Law. *Spec Collecs* Legislative history of the Alaska Native Claims Settlement Act.
Ref Servs Avail To the general public.

1842. Department of the Interior, Office of the Solicitor, Law Library
Department of the Interior, Suite 117, 331 Sandoval St, Santa Fe, NM 87501 (505) 988-6200/6201; FTS 476-1200
Admin Marguerite G Palmer.
Lib Type Law.
Circ Servs Avail To other libraries.
Ref Servs Avail To the general public.

1843. Department of the Interior, Office of the Solicitor, Regional Solicitor, Law Library
Department of the Interior, Rm E-2753, 2800 Cottage Way, Sacramento, CA 95825 (916) 484-4826; FTS 468-4216
Lib Type Law.
Ref Servs Avail To the general public.

Office of Surface Mining Reclamation & Enforcement

1844. Office of Surface Mining Reclamation & Enforcement Library
2nd Fl, 1020 15th St, Denver, CO 80202 (303) 844-2451; FTS 564-2451
Lib Type Engineering & Science.
Spec Subs Surface mining reclamation. *Spec Collecs* OSMRE publications.

Info Ret Servs DIALOG; BRS. *Shared Catalog Nets* OCLC.
Circ Servs Avail To other Federal libraries; to other libraries.
Ref Servs Avail To other Federal libraries; to other libraries; to the general public.

1845. Office of Surface Mining Reclamation & Enforcement Library
Rm 520, 46 E Ohio St, Indianapolis, IN 46204 (317) 269-2602; FTS 331-2602
Admin Mary A Berry.
Lib Type Special.
Spec Subs Coal mining & reclamation.

Water & Power Resources Service

1846. Lower Colorado Regional Library
Water & Power Resources Service, Box 427, Boulder City, NV 89005 (702) 293-8570; FTS 598-7570
Admin Frances Plyler.
Lib Type Special.
Spec Subs Water resources; geothermal information; power; irrigation; dams. *Spec Collecs* Project histories for projects within the Lower Colorado River Region.
Circ Servs Avail To other libraries.
Ref Servs Avail To the general public.

1847. Water & Power Resources Service, Regional Library
2800 Cottage Way, Sacramento, CA 95825 (916) 484-4404; FTS 468-4404
Admin Jane Biggs; Margaret Elder.
Lib Type Special.
Spec Subs Bureau of Reclamation technical publications: water, power, irrigation, agriculture, civil engineering, & electrical data.
Circ Servs Avail To other libraries.
Ref Servs Avail To the general public.

DEPARTMENT OF JUSTICE

Departmental

1848. Department of Justice Antitrust Division Library
230 S Dearborn St, Rm 3820, Chicago, IL 60604 (312) 353-7530
Admin Janice Davis.
Lib Type Law.
Circ Servs Avail Not open to the general public.
Ref Servs Avail Not open to the general public.

1849. Department of Justice Antitrust Library
10th & Pennsylvania Ave NW, Rm 3310, Washington, DC 20530
(202) 633-2431; FTS 633-2431
Admin Quinlan J Shea, Jr (Dir Lib Staff); Roger Karr (Antitrust Lib). *Ref Lib* Mary Clarity (ILL).
Lib Type Law.
Spec Subs Antitrust law; administrative law; business; industry; economics. *Spec Collecs* Legislative histories.
Lib Deposit Designation GPO Depository Library.
Info Ret Servs DIALOG; BRS; SDC; LEXIS; NEXIS; WESTLAW; JURIS; VU/TEXT; LEGI-SLATE; Dow Jones; D&B. *Shared Catalog Nets* OCLC; Internal. *Coop Lib Nets* FEDLINK; COG. *Elec Mail Nets* E-MAIL.
Circ Servs Avail To other Federal libraries; to other libraries; restricted to use by appointment.
Ref Servs Avail To other Federal libraries; to other libraries; not open to the general public.

1850. Department of Justice Civil Library
10th & Pennsylvania Ave NW, Rm 3344, Washington, DC 20530
(202) 633-3523; FTS 633-3523
Admin Quinlan J Shea, Jr (Dir Lib Staff); Evangeline N Mastriani (Civil Lib). *Ref Lib* Eileen McCarrier (ILL, Acq).
Lib Type Law.
Spec Subs Aviation & Admiralty law; bankruptcy; commercial law; intellectual property; government contracts; torts; federal practice. *Spec Collecs* Legislative histories in the indicated special areas.
Lib Deposit Designation GPO Depository Library.
Info Ret Servs DIALOG; BRS; SDC; LEXIS; NEXIS; WESTLAW; JURIS; VU/TEXT; LEGI-SLATE; Dow Jones. *Shared Catalog Nets* OCLC; Internal. *Coop Lib Nets* FEDLINK; COG. *Elec Mail Nets* E-MAIL.
Circ Servs Avail To other Federal libraries; to other libraries; restricted to use by appointment.
Ref Servs Avail To other Federal libraries; to other libraries; not open to the general public.

1851. Department of Justice Civil Rights Library
10th & Pennsylvania Ave NW, Rm 7618, Washington, DC 20530
(202) 633-4098; FTS 633-4098
Admin Quinlan J Shea, Jr (Dir Lib Staff); Kathleen T Larson (Civil Rights Lib). *Ref Lib* Gertrude Dennis (ILL).
Lib Type Law.
Spec Subs Civil Rights; civil liberties; Constitutional Law; demographics.
Lib Deposit Designation GPO Depository Library.
Info Ret Servs DIALOG; BRS; SDC; LEXIS; NEXIS; WESTLAW; JURIS; VU/TEXT; LEGI-SLATE; Dow Jones. *Shared Catalog Nets* OCLC; Internal. *Coop Lib Nets* FEDLINK; COG. *Elec Mail Nets* E-MAIL.
Circ Servs Avail To other Federal libraries; to other libraries; restricted to use by appointment.

Ref Servs Avail To other Federal libraries; to other libraries; not open to the general public.

1852. Department of Justice Criminal Library
Federal Triangle Bldg, 9th & Pennsylvania Ave NW, Rm 100, Washington, DC 20530 (202) 724-6934; FTS 724-6934
Admin Quinlan J Shea, Jr (Dir Lib Staff); Patricia A McKain (Criminal Lib). *Ref Lib* Diane Smith (ILL, Acq).
Lib Type Law.
Spec Subs Federal criminal law; procedure & evidence; crime: white collar, computer, organized; espionage; terrorism.
Lib Deposit Designation GPO Depository Library.
Info Ret Servs DIALOG; BRS; SDC; LEXIS; NEXIS; WESTLAW; JURIS; VU/TEXT; LEGI-SLATE; Dow Jones. *Shared Catalog Nets* OCLC; Internal. *Coop Lib Nets* FEDLINK; COG. *Elec Mail Nets* E-MAIL.
Circ Servs Avail To other Federal libraries; to other libraries; restricted to use by appointment.
Ref Servs Avail To other Federal libraries; to other libraries; not open to the general public.

1853. Department of Justice Lands Library
10th & Pennsylvania Ave NW, Rm 2333, Washington, DC 20530
(202) 633-2768; FTS 633-2768
Admin Quinlan J Shea, Jr (Dir Lib Staff); Adelaide Loretta Brown (Lands Lib). *Ref Lib* Edward Wolff (ILL, Acq).
Lib Type Law.
Spec Subs Civil case law material on land acquisition & title; water rights; Indian claims; hazardous wastes; public works; pollution control; marine resources; fish & wildlife; the environment.
Lib Deposit Designation GPO Depository Library.
Info Ret Servs DIALOG; BRS; SDC; LEXIS; NEXIS; WESTLAW; JURIS; VU/TEXT; LEGI-SLATE; Dow Jones. *Shared Catalog Nets* OCLC. *Coop Lib Nets* FEDLINK; COG. *Elec Mail Nets* E-MAIL.
Circ Servs Avail To other Federal libraries; to other libraries; restricted to use by appointment.
Ref Servs Avail To other Federal libraries; to other libraries; not open to the general public.

1854. Department of Justice Main Library
10th & Pennsylvania Ave NW, Rm 5400, Washington, DC 20530
(202) 633-2133; FTS 633-2133
Admin Quinlan J Shea, Jr (Dir Lib Staff); Daphne B Sampson (Chief, Reader's Svcs). *Ref Lib* Winifred M Hart. *ILL* Bozhana Kelley. *Acq Lib* Daire McCabe.
Lib Type Law.
Spec Subs Federal & state law; public administration; political science; American history; management. *Spec Collecs* Legislative histories; Supreme Court records & briefs; Department of Justice publications.
Lib Deposit Designation GPO Depository Library.
Info Ret Servs DIALOG; BRS; SDC; LEXIS; NEXIS; WESTLAW; JURIS; LEGI-SLATE; VU/TEXT; Dow Jones; CQ WASHINGTON ALERT SERVICE; WASHINGTON ONLINE; WILSONLINE; DATA TIMES. *Shared Catalog Nets* OCLC; Internal. *Coop Lib Nets* FEDLINK; COG. *Elec Mail Nets* E-MAIL.
Circ Servs Avail To other Federal libraries; to other libraries; restricted to use by appointment.
Ref Servs Avail To other Federal libraries; to other libraries; not open to the general public.

1855. Department of Justice Tax Library
10th & Pennsylvania Ave NW, Rm 4335, Washington, DC 20530 (202) 633-2819; FTS 633-2819
Admin Quinlan J Shea, Jr (Dir, Lib Staff); Jacqueline Lee (Tax Lib). *Ref Lib* Carolyn Bazarnick (ILL, Acq).
Lib Type Law.
Spec Subs Federal tax law; bankruptcy law & accounting. *Spec Collecs* Legislative histories.
Lib Deposit Designation GPO Depository Library.
Info Ret Servs DIALOG; BRS; SDC; LEXIS; NEXIS; WESTLAW; JURIS; VU/TEXT; LEGI-SLATE; Dow Jones; PHINET. *Shared Catalog Nets* OCLC; Internal. *Coop Lib Nets* FEDLINK; COG. *Elec Mail Nets* E-MAIL.
Circ Servs Avail To other Federal libraries; to other libraries; restricted to use by appointment.
Ref Servs Avail To other Federal libraries; to other libraries; not open to the general public.

1856. National Institute of Justice Library
633 Indiana Ave NW, Rm 900, Washington, DC 20531 (202) 724-5883
Admin Kyle Kramer.
Lib Type Special.
Spec Subs Criminology & criminal justice including policing, corrections, & juvenile justice. *Spec Collecs* Publications of the National Institute of Justice; Bureau of Justice Statistics; Office of Juvenile Justice & Delinquency Prevention.
Info Ret Servs DIALOG.
Circ Servs Avail Restricted to DOJ agencies.
Ref Servs Avail To other Federal libraries; to other libraries; to the general public.

1857. National Institute of Justice/National Criminal Justice Reference Service
Box 6000, Rockville, MD 20850 (800) 851-3420; (301) 251-5500
Admin Nancy J Pearse. *ILL* Nancy Broider. *Acq Lib* Teresa C Turner.
Lib Type Special; Law.
Spec Subs Criminal justice & law enforcement: police, courts, corrections, crime prevention, terrorism, white collar crime, domestic violence, dispute resolution, juvenile justice, victims, etc.
Lib Deposit Designation National Institute of Justice.
Info Ret Servs DIALOG; BRS; Custom searchers of the NCJRS Data Base, Vu-Text, Newsnet, Dow Jones, Federal Criminal Justice Research Data Base, Privatization Data Base. *Coop Lib Nets* Criminal Justice Information Exchange Group.
Circ Servs Avail Restricted to ILL.
Ref Servs Avail To other Federal libraries; to other libraries; to the general public.

Bureau of Prisons—Federal Prison System Libraries

1858. Alderson Federal Correctional Institution Library
Alderson, WV 24910 (304) 455-2901; FTS 924-3000
Admin Bobbie J Gwinn.
Lib Type Penal.

1859. Allenwood Federal Prison Camp Library
Montgomery, PA 17752 (717) 547-1641
Admin Elizabeth Skedzielewski.
Lib Type Penal.
Spec Subs Video GED Program; VT trade book library. *Spec Collecs* Books on tapes.
Shared Catalog Nets James V Brown Library. *Coop Lib Nets* James V Brown Library, Williamsport, PA; Pennsylvania Public Libraries Film Center & Video; Penn State, University Park.
Circ Servs Avail To other Federal libraries; not open to the general public.
Ref Servs Avail Not open to the general public.

1860. Ashland Federal Correctional Institution Library
Ashland, KY 41101 (606) 928-6414; FTS 924-5614
Admin Charles B Smallwood.
Lib Type Penal.

1861. Bastrop Federal Correctional Institution Library
Bastrop, TX 78602 (512) 321-3903; FTS 521-3050
Admin Jack Coble.
Lib Type Penal.

1862. Big Spring Federal Prison Camp Library
Big Spring, TX 79720 (915) 263-8304; FTS 738-9000
Admin Manuel Gomez (Supv of Education). *Ref Lib* Cruz Olague (ILL, Acq).
Lib Type Penal.
Spec Subs Post conviction & general legal references; leisure. *Spec Collecs* Encyclopedias; Great Books; Black history.
Circ Servs Avail Restricted to inmates.
Ref Servs Avail Restricted to inmates.

1863. Boron Federal Prison Camp Library
PO Box 500, Boron, CA 93516 (619) 762-5161; FTS 791-1164
Admin Dennis Hendryx.
Lib Type Penal.

1864. Butner Federal Correctional Institution Library
Box 1000, Butner, NC 27509 (919) 575-4541; FTS 629-5403
Admin E L Smith.
Lib Type Penal.
Circ Servs Avail Restricted to staff & inmates.
Ref Servs Avail Restricted to staff & inmates.

1865. Chicago Metropolitan Correctional Center Inmate Library
71 W Van Buren St, Chicago, IL 60605 (312) 353-6819
Admin Carmen Hamer.
Lib Type Penal.
Circ Servs Avail Restricted to staff & inmates.
Ref Servs Avail Restricted to staff & inmates.

1866. Danbury Federal Correctional Institution Library
Education Department, Pembroke Station, Danbury, CT 06811 (203) 743-6471; FTS 642-9071
Admin Dorothy A Baker.
Lib Type Penal.
Spec Subs World War II; business.
Circ Servs Avail Restricted to staff & inmates.
Ref Servs Avail Restricted to staff & inmates.

1867. Duluth Federal Prison Camp Library
Duluth, MN 55814 (218) 722-8634
Admin Jerome D Bauman.
Lib Type Penal.

1868. El Reno Federal Correctional Institution Library
PO Box 1000, El Reno, OK 73036 (405) 262-4875 ext 268
Admin Joseph Mendez.
Lib Type Penal.
Circ Servs Avail Restricted to inmates.
Ref Servs Avail Restricted to inmates.

1869. Elgin Federal Prison Camp Inmate Library
Elgin Air Force Base, FL 32542 (904) 882-8522
Admin Sandra Nelson.
Lib Type Penal.
Circ Servs Avail Restricted to inmates.
Ref Servs Avail Restricted to inmates.

1870. Federal Prison System Library
320 1st St NW, Rm 154, Washington, DC 20534 (202) 724-3029; FTS 724-3029
Admin Lloyd W Hooker. *ILL* Penny Doucette.
Lib Type Special.
Spec Subs Corrections; criminology; criminal justice.
Info Ret Servs OCLC. *Shared Catalog Nets* OCLC.
Circ Servs Avail To other Federal libraries.

Ref Servs Avail To other Federal libraries.

1871. Fort Worth Federal Correctional Institute Library Services
3150 Horton Rd, Fort Worth, TX 76119 (817) 535-2111 ext 190
Lib Type Penal.
Spec Subs Narcotic addiction; psychiatry; psychology.

1872. Ft Worth Federal Correctional Institution Library
Fort Worth, TX 76119 (817) 535-2111; FTS 738-4011
Admin Ruth C Creech.
Lib Type Penal.

1873. La Tuna Federal Correctional Institution Library
Anthony, NM 88021 (915) 886-3422; FTS 572-7682
Admin Art Minjarez.
Lib Type Penal.

1874. Lexington Federal Correctional Institution Library
Lexington, KY 40507 (606) 255-6812
Admin Don Reichert.
Lib Type Penal.
Circ Servs Avail Restricted to inmates.
Ref Servs Avail Restricted to inmates.

1875. Littleton Federal Correctional Institution Library
9595 W Quincy Ave, Littleton, CO 80123 (303) 985-1566; FTS 564-2881
Admin B J Bubeck (Asst Supv of Education). *Ref Lib* Jean Johnston (ILL, Acq).
Lib Type Penal.
Coop Lib Nets Central Colorado Library System (CCLS).
Circ Servs Avail Restricted to inmates.
Ref Servs Avail Restricted to inmates.

1876. Lompoc US Penitentiary Library
Lompoc, CA 93438 (805) 735-2771; FTS 960-6261
Admin Richard Kochera.
Lib Type Penal.

1877. Loretto Federal Correctional Institution Library
PO Box 1000, Loretto, PA 19540 (814) 472-4141
Admin Darlene A Mazock.
Lib Type Penal.

1878. Marion US Penitentiary Library
Marion, IL 62959 (618) 964-1441; FTS 277-5400
Admin Don Sheffer.
Lib Type Penal.

1879. Maxwell AFB, Federal Prison Camp Library
Bldg 1236, Montgomery, AL 36112 (205) 293-6591; FTS 293-6591
Admin Mark C English II. *Acq Lib* Robert L Williams.
Lib Type Penal.
Spec Subs Federal case law. *Spec Collecs* Federal Reporter; Federal Supplement; US code annotated. *In-house Files* Alabama codes; Supreme Court Digest; American Jurisprudence.
Coop Lib Nets Maxwell Air Force Base Library; Troy State University Library.
Circ Servs Avail Not open to the general public; restricted to inmates & staff.
Ref Servs Avail Not open to the general public; restricted to inmates & staff.

1880. Memphis Federal Correctional Institution Library
1101 John A Denie Rd, Memphis, TN 38134 (901) 372-2269; FTS 222-4172
Admin Palo Nesmith.
Lib Type Penal.

1881. Miami Metropolitan Correctional Center, Inmate Law Library
15801 SW 137th Ave, Miami, FL 33177 (305) 253-4400; FTS 350-6100
Admin Roberta Stewart; Arturo Blanco (Asst SOE).
Lib Type Law; Penal.

Spec Subs Law & legal materials. *Spec Collecs* Federal Reporter, 2nd Series; Federal Supplement, USCA; American Jurisprudence; Federal Practice Digest; US Supreme Court Digest.
Circ Servs Avail Not open to the general public; restricted to staff & inmates.
Ref Servs Avail Not open to the general public; restricted to staff & inmates.

1882. Milan Federal Correctional Institution Library
Arkona Rd, Milan, MI 48160 (313) 439-1571 ext 60
Lib Type Penal.
Spec Collecs Bureau of Prisons program statements & Institutions supplements; federal law books & statutes.
Coop Lib Nets Washtenaw-Livingston Library Network.
Circ Servs Avail Not open to the general public; restricted to inmates.
Ref Servs Avail Not open to the general public; restricted to inmates.

1883. Morgantown Federal Correctional Institution Library
Morgantown, WV 26505 (304) 296-4416
Admin Charles Hitchcock.
Lib Type Penal.
Spec Subs Law library with emphasis on federal correctional institutional policy & inmate rights.
Circ Servs Avail Restricted to inmates.
Ref Servs Avail Restricted to inmates.

1884. New York Metropolitan Correctional Center Library
150 Park Row, New York, NY 10007 (212) 791-9130; FTS 662-9130-9
Admin James Wall.
Lib Type Penal.

1885. Otisville Federal Correctional Institution Library
Otisville, NY 10963 (914) 386-5855; FTS 887-1055
Admin Daniel R Dunn.
Lib Type Penal.

1886. Oxford Federal Correctional Institution Library
Oxford, WI 53952 (608) 584-5511; FTS 364-2611
Admin Thomas McKnelly.
Lib Type Penal.

1887. Petersburg Federal Correctional Institution Library
Petersburg, VA 23803 (804) 733-7881; FTS 733-7881
Admin C O Jacobs. *Ref Lib* Leonard Marr. *ILL* Larry Joyner (Acq).
Lib Type Penal.
Coop Lib Nets Appomattox Regional Library.
Circ Servs Avail Restricted to inmates.
Ref Servs Avail Restricted to inmates.

1888. Phoenix Federal Correctional Institution Library
Box 1680, Black Canyon Stage I, Phoenix, AZ 85209 (602) 261-6616
Admin Gary L Walls.
Lib Type Penal.

1889. Pleasanton Federal Correctional Institution Library
5701 8th St, Dublin, CA 94568 (415) 829-3522; FTS 461-9255
Admin Ella Colley.
Lib Type Penal.

1890. Ray Brook Federal Correctional Institution Library
Ray Brook, NY 12977 (518) 891-5400; FTS 832-6717
Lib Type Penal.

1891. Rochester Federal Medical Center Library
PO Box 4600, Rochester, MN 55903 (507) 282-3242; FTS 787-1110
Admin William J Heaney.
Lib Type Penal.

1892. Safford Federal Correctional Institution Library
Box 820, RR 2, Safford, AZ 85546-9729 (602) 428-6600; FTS 762-6336
Admin Supv of Ed. *ILL* Paul Goudie (ILL, Acq).
Lib Type Penal.
Coop Lib Nets Interlibrary Loan Program, Phoenix Public Library.
Circ Servs Avail Restricted to inmates.
Ref Servs Avail Restricted to inmates.

1893. San Diego Metropolitan Correctional Center Library
San Diego, CA 92101 (619) 232-4311; FTS 891-4311
Lib Type Penal.

1894. Sandstone Federal Correctional Institution Library
Sandstone, MN 55072 (612) 245-2262; FTS 781-7400
Admin Richard L Williams.
Lib Type Penal.

1895. Seagoville Federal Correctional Institution Library
Seagoville, TX 75159 (214) 287-2911; FTS 729-8471
Admin Harry L Reynolds.
Lib Type Penal.

1896. Springfield Medical Center of Federal Prisoners Library
Springfield, MO 65802 (417) 862-7041; FTS 754-2751
Admin George E Boeringa.
Lib Type Penal.

1897. Talladega Federal Correctional Institution Library
Talladega, AL 35160 (205) 362-0410; FTS 222-1011
Admin Teddy D Sheppard.
Lib Type Penal.

1898. Tallahassee Federal Correctional Institution Library
Tallahassee, FL 32301 (904) 878-2173
Admin Virginia Warfel.
Lib Type Penal.
Circ Servs Avail Restricted to staff & inmates.
Ref Servs Avail Restricted to staff & inmates.

1899. Terminal Island Federal Correctional Institution Library
Terminal Island, CA 90731 (213) 831-8961; FTS 793-1160
Admin Carol H Hungate.
Lib Type Penal.

1900. Texarkana Federal Correctional Institution Library
Texarkana, TX 75501 (214) 838-4587; FTS 731-3190
Admin Kenneth Hoy.
Lib Type Penal.

1901. Tucson Metropolitan Correctional Center Library
8901 S Wilmot Rd, Tucson, AZ 85734 (602) 294-4404; FTS 762-6921
Lib Type Penal.

1902. US Penitentiary Legal Library, Terre Haute
Terre Haute, IN 47808 (812) 238-1531; FTS 335-0531
Admin Richard Valandingham.
Lib Type Law.
Circ Servs Avail Not open to the general public; restricted to inmates.
Ref Servs Avail Not open to the general public; restricted to inmates.

1903. US Penitentiary Library, Atlanta
601 McDonough Blvd, Atlanta, GA 30315 (404) 622-6241
Lib Type Penal.

1904. US Penitentiary Library, Leavenworth
Leavenworth, KS 66048 (913) 682-8700; FTS 758-1000
Admin Jim Spencer.
Lib Type Penal.
Circ Servs Avail Restricted to inmates.
Ref Servs Avail Restricted to inmates.

1905. US Penitentiary Resource Library, Lewisburg
Lewisburg, PA 17837 (717) 523-1251 ext 251
Admin Frederick J Glavich.
Lib Type Penal.
Circ Servs Avail Restricted to staff & inmates.
Ref Servs Avail To other Federal libraries; to other libraries; not open to the general public.

1906. US Penitentiary Reading Library, Terre Haute
Terre Haute, IN 47808 (812) 238-1531 (Penitentiary)
Admin Edward E Deischer (Asst Supv of Education); Elizabeth Robson (Lib).
Lib Type Penal.
Coop Lib Nets Stone Hills Area Library Services Authority (SHALSA).
Circ Servs Avail Restricted to inmates & staff.
Ref Servs Avail Restricted to inmates & staff.

Drug Enforcement Administration

1907. Drug Enforcement Administration Library
1405 I St NW, Washington, DC 20537 (202) 633-1369; FTS 633-1369
Admin Morton S Goren. *Ref Lib* Edith Crutchfield. *ILL* Lavonne Wienke.
Lib Type Special.
Spec Subs Drug abuse & prevention; enforcement efforts; diversion of drugs; technology. *Spec Collecs* UN drug/narcotic abuse documents.
Shared Catalog Nets OCLC. *Coop Lib Nets* FEDLINK.
Circ Servs Avail To other Federal libraries; to other libraries.
Ref Servs Avail To other Federal libraries; to other libraries; to the general public.

Federal Bureau of Investigation

1908. FBI Academy Library
Quantico, VA 22135 (703) 640-1135 ext 3042; ILL ext 3049
Admin Sandra L Coupe.
Lib Type Academic.
Spec Subs Criminal justice; police law enforcement.
Info Ret Servs DIALOG; MEDLARS; NEXIS.
Circ Servs Avail Not open to the general public; restricted to FBI Field Offices.
Ref Servs Avail Not open to the general public.

Foreign Claims Settlement Commission of the United States

1909. Foreign Claims Settlement Commission, Law Library
1111 20th St NW, Washington, DC 20579 (202) 653-5883; FTS 653-5112
Admin Robert L Maddex.
Lib Type Law.

Immigration & Naturalization Service

1910. Board of Immigration Appeals Library
5203 Leesburg Pike, Ste 1609, Falls Church, VA 22015 (703) 756-6183; FTS 756-6183
Admin April Verner.
Lib Type Law.
Spec Subs Immigration law. *Spec Collecs* Updates on immigration procedures & law (Gordon & Rosenfield).
Circ Servs Avail Not open to the general public.
Ref Servs Avail To other Federal libraries; to other libraries; to the general public; restricted to use by appointment.

1911. Immigration & Naturalization Law Library
Federal Bldg, Fort Snelling, Twin Cities, MN 55111 (612) 725-5256; FTS 725-5256
Admin Regional Counsel.
Lib Type Law.

Circ Servs Avail Not open to the general public.
Ref Servs Avail To other Federal libraries.

1912. Immigration & Naturalization Service Library
425 Eye St, NW, Ste 7048, Washington, DC 20536 (202) 633-2895; FTS 633-2895
Admin Francesco Isgro. *Ref Lib* Paul W Schmidt.
Lib Type Law.
Circ Servs Avail Not open to the general public.
Ref Servs Avail Not open to the general public.

1913. Immigration & Naturalization Service, General Counsel's Library
425 Eye St NW Rm 7048, Washington, DC 20536 (202) 633-2517; FTS 633-2517
Admin Francesco Legro.
Lib Type Law.
Spec Subs Immigration law.
Circ Servs Avail To other Federal libraries; not open to the general public.
Ref Servs Avail To other Federal libraries.

United States Attorney's Offices

1914. US Attorney's Office Camden Branch Library
Court House, 401 Market St, Camden, NJ 08102 (609) 757-5026
Lib Type Law.

1915. US Attorney's Office Library
1214 US Courthouse, 312 N Spring St, Los Angeles, CA 90012 (213) 688-2419
Lib Type Law.

1916. US Attorney's Office Library
970 Broad St, Newark, NJ 07102 (201) 645-2387
Lib Type Law.
Shared Catalog Nets OCLC.

1917. US Attorney's Office Trenton Branch Library
402 E State St, Trenton, NJ 08608 (609) 989-2190
Lib Type Law.

United States Parole Commission

1918. US Parole Commission Library
5550 Friendship Blvd, Chevy Chase, MD 20815 (301) 492-5980
Admin Ronnie Scotkin.
Lib Type Special.
Spec Subs Criminal justice; parole guidelines. *Spec Collecs* Criminal justice journals.
Circ Servs Avail To other Federal libraries.
Ref Servs Avail To other Federal libraries; to other libraries; to the general public.

DEPARTMENT OF LABOR

Departmental

1919. Department of Labor Library
200 Constitution Ave NW, Washington, DC 20210 (202) 523-6988
Admin Sabina Jacobson. *Ref Lib* Margaret Harper. *ILL* Isabelle Adams. *Acq Lib* Eileen Riley.
Lib Type Special.
Spec Subs Labor; industrial relations; trade unionism. *Spec Collecs* Labor periodicals; trade union papers (domestic & foreign).
Lib Deposit Designation Department of Labor.
Info Ret Servs DIALOG; BRS; SDC; NEXIS. *Shared Catalog Nets* OCLC. *Coop Lib Nets* FEDLINK.
Circ Servs Avail To other Federal libraries; to other libraries; restricted to the general public thru ILL.
Ref Servs Avail To other Federal libraries; to other libraries; to the general public.

Bureau of Labor Statistics

1920. Bureau of Labor Statistics Library
1515 Broadway, Ste 3400, New York, NY 10036 (212) 944-3121; FTS 265-3121
Admin Samuel M Ehrenhalt (Reg Comm). *Ref Lib* Patrica Bommicino.
Lib Type Special.
Spec Subs Employment & unemployment statistics; prices & living conditions; wages & industrial relations; productivity & technology; occupational safety & health; economic growth & employment projections.
Ref Servs Avail To other Federal libraries; to the general public.

1921. Bureau of Labor Statistics, Regional Office, Reference Library
J C Kluczynski Federal Bldg, 9th Fl, Chicago, IL 60604 (312) 353-1880
Admin Roger Sanzenbacher. *Ref Lib* Gerald Jaecks.
Lib Type Special.
Spec Subs Labor force; employment & unemployment; prices & living conditions; compensation & industrial relations; productivity; occupational safety & health; economic growth & employment projections. *Spec Collecs* Complete collections of all BLS Bulletins, Reports, & Monthly Labor Review.
Ref Servs Avail To the general public.

1922. Bureau of Labor Statistics, Regional Office, Reference Library
1603 JFK Bldg, Boston, MA 02203 (617) 565-2327
Admin Mary M Sullivan (Regional Economist).
Lib Type Special.
Spec Subs Labor statistics; consumer prices; producer prices; wages; productivity.

Ref Servs Avail To other Federal libraries; to other libraries; to the general public.

Mine Safety & Health Administration

1923. National Mine Health & Safety Academy, Learning Resource Center
PO Box 1166, Beckley, WV 25802 (304) 256-3100; FTS 924-4581
Lib Type Special.
Spec Subs Earth science; industry safety; management; mining; occupational diseases. *Spec Collecs* Mine accident reports; Bureau of Mines publications; MSHA publications.
Info Ret Servs DIALOG; SDC. *Shared Catalog Nets* OCLC. *Coop Lib Nets* FEDLINK.

Occupational Safety & Health Administration

1924. Occupational Safety & Health Administration, Region 3, Library
Gateway Bldg, Rm 14100, Philadelphia, PA 19104 (215) 596-1201; FTS 596-1201
Admin Barbara Goodman.
Lib Type Special.
Spec Subs Occupational health & OSHA safety standards; industrial hygiene; toxic substances; industrial safety.
Info Ret Servs DIALOG; MEDLARS. *Shared Catalog Nets* OCLC. *Coop Lib Nets* FEDLINK.
Circ Servs Avail Restricted to OSHA staff & affiliated safety & health professionals.
Ref Servs Avail To other Federal libraries; to other libraries; to the general public.

1925. Occupational Safety & Health Administration, Technical Data Center
200 Constitution Ave NW, Washington, DC 20210 (202) 523-9700; FTS 523-9700
Admin Thomas A Towers. *Ref Lib* James Towles. *ILL* Denise Hayes. *Acq Lib* Shirley Marshall; Robert Turnage.
Lib Type Engineering & Science.
Spec Subs Occupational safety & health; occupational medicine; toxicology; industrial hygiene; safety engineering; environmental engineering. *Spec Collecs* Rulemaking records; CIS (Geneva) microfiche collection; technical journals collection; material safety data sheets. *In-house Files* Rulemaking records; subjects files.
Info Ret Servs DIALOG; BRS; SDC; Infoline; ISI; Safety Science Abstracts. *Shared Catalog Nets* OCLC. *Elec Mail Nets* OCIS System (OSHA).
Circ Servs Avail To other Federal libraries; to other libraries.
Ref Servs Avail To other Federal libraries; to other libraries; to the general public.

DEPARTMENT OF STATE

Departmental

1926. Department of State Law Library
Office of Legal Advisor, Rm 6422, Washington, DC 20520 (202) 647-4130
Admin Helen P von Pfeil.
Lib Type Law.
Circ Servs Avail Not open to the general public.
Ref Servs Avail Not open to the general public.

1927. Department of State Library
2201 C St NW, Rm 3239, Washington, DC 20520 (202) 647-1062; FTS 647-1062
Admin Conrad P Eaton. *Ref Lib* Dan O Clemmer (ILL). *Acq Lib* Doris O Robinson-Mosley.
Lib Type Special.
Spec Subs Culture; international law; development; international relations, politics, economics. *Spec Collecs* Government gazettes of 100 countries.
Lib Deposit Designation GPO Depository Library; OECD; OAS; ILO; EEC; FAO.
Info Ret Servs DIALOG; BRS; SDC; Mead; RLIN; VU/TEXT; Dow Jones; USA TODAY; DRI. *Shared Catalog Nets* OCLC. *Coop Lib Nets* FEDLINK.
Circ Servs Avail To other Federal libraries; to other libraries; not open to the general public.

Ref Servs Avail To other Federal libraries; to other libraries; not open to the general public.

1928. Foreign Service Institute Library
Department of State, 1400 Key Blvd, Rm C2 Sa-3, Arlington, VA 22209 (703) 235-8717
Admin William W Bennett, Sr. *ILL* Joseph Erwin. *Acq Lib* Kathy B Summers.
Lib Type Academic; Training Center.
Spec Subs International relations; social sciences; linguistics; economics & finance; immigration & emigration; communication. *Spec Collecs* FSI Archives; language textbooks (FSI produced); French grade school books; special dictionaries.
Info Ret Servs DIALOG; OCLC; Mead Data Central NEXIS; UMI. *Shared Catalog Nets* OCLC. *Coop Lib Nets* FEDLINK.
Circ Servs Avail To other Federal libraries; to other libraries.
Ref Servs Avail To other Federal libraries; to other libraries; to the general public; restricted to in-house use for general public.

1929. United States Mission to the United Nations, Information Center
799 United Nations Plaza, New York, NY 10017 (212) 415-4000
Lib Type Special.
Circ Servs Avail Not open to the general public; restricted to staff use only.
Ref Servs Avail Not open to the general public; restricted to staff use only.

DEPARTMENT OF TRANSPORTATION

Departmental

1930. Department of Transportation Law Library
400 7th St SW, Rm 2215, Washington, DC 20590 (202) 366-0749
Admin Loretta A Norris. *Ref Lib* Wilbur A Smith (ILL, Acq).
Lib Type Law.
Spec Subs Transportation law; Federal law; administrative law.
Spec Collecs Legislative histories; maritime legislative collection.
Info Ret Servs JURIS; LEXIS; NEXIS. *Shared Catalog Nets* OCLC.
Circ Servs Avail To other libraries.
Ref Servs Avail To other Federal libraries; to other libraries; to the general public.

1931. Department of Transportation Library
400 7th St SW, Washington, DC 20590 (202) 366-2565
Admin Lawrence E Leonard. *Ref Lib* Mary Jo Burke. *ILL* David Vespa. *Acq Lib* William Mills.
Lib Type Engineering & Science.
Spec Subs Highways; traffic engineering; urban transportation; railroads; marine engineering; navigation; pipelines; aviation; electronics; law. *Spec Collecs* US state highway departments' maps; aviation technical & military publications; aviation technical reports. *In-house Files* Periodical index file (surface transportation) 1921-82.
Lib Deposit Designation GPO Depository Library; NASA (selected categories); DoD (selected categories).
Info Ret Servs DIALOG; BRS; OCLC; LEXIS; NEXIS; WESTLAW; JURIS; DROLS. *Shared Catalog Nets* OCLC. *Coop Lib Nets* FEDLINK.
Circ Servs Avail To other Federal libraries; to other libraries.
Ref Servs Avail To other Federal libraries; to other libraries; to the general public.

1932. Department of Transportation, Technical Reference Center
Transportation Systems Center, Kendall Sq, Cambridge, MA 02142 (617) 494-2306; FTS 837-2306
Admin Susan C Dresley. *Ref Lib* Robert Perreault (ILL). *Acq Lib* Suzanne Magnuson.
Lib Type Special.
In-house Files Archival collection of technical reports issued by the center.
Lib Deposit Designation Department of Transportation; NASA (fiche).
Info Ret Servs DIALOG. *Shared Catalog Nets* OCLC. *Coop Lib Nets* Transportation Research Information Network(TRISNET); FEDLINK.
Circ Servs Avail To other libraries; restricted to ILL requests.
Ref Servs Avail To other Federal libraries; to other libraries; to the general public.

1933. 10A Services Branch Library
Department of Transportation, FOB 10A, 800 Independence Ave SW, Rm 930, Washington, DC 20591 (202) 267-1115; 267-3174 (Law Unit)
Admin Thomas M Haggerty; Jane E Braucher (Law Unit).
Lib Type Special; Law.
Spec Subs Law; air transportation; aviation & related subjects.

Federal Aviation Administration

1934. FAA Aeronautical Center, Civil Aeromedical Institute Library (AM-101)
PO Box 25082 6500 S MacArthur, AAC-64D, Oklahoma City, OK 73125 (405) 686-4709; FTS 749-4398
Ref Lib Darrell R Goulden (ILL, Acq).
Lib Type Health & Medicine.
Spec Subs Aviation medicine; biochemistry; toxicology.
Circ Servs Avail To other Federal libraries; to other libraries; to the general public.
Ref Servs Avail To other Federal libraries; to other libraries; to the general public.

1935. FAA Central Regional Library
New Federal Office Bldg, 601 E 12th St, Rm 1556, Kansas City, MO 64106 (816) 374-3246; FTS 758-5486
Lib Type Special.
Spec Subs Aviation engineering; environment; management & sciences. *Spec Collecs* Regional Legal Collection.
Circ Servs Avail Restricted to reference use only.

1936. FAA Technical Library
(ACT 61), Atlantic City Airport, NJ 08405 (609) 484-5772; FTS 482-5772
Admin Clarence Abbott. *Ref Lib* Nancy Boylan. *ILL* Shirley Massey. *Acq Lib* Ruth Farrell.
Lib Type Engineering & Science.
Spec Subs Air traffic control; aviation safety. *Spec Collecs* Addision Johnson Memorial Collection. *In-house Files* Air traffic control.
Lib Deposit Designation NASA; DOT; FAA.
Info Ret Servs DIALOG; BRS; SDC; MEAD; RECON(NASA); DTIC. *Shared Catalog Nets* OCLC. *Coop Lib Nets* Southern New Jersey.
Circ Servs Avail To other Federal libraries; to other libraries; to the general public.
Ref Servs Avail To other Federal libraries; to other libraries; to the general public.

1937. FAA Eastern Region Library
Fitzgerald Federal Bldg, JFK International Airport, Jamaica, NY 11430 (718) 917-1116; FTS 667-1116
Admin AEA-42 Management Systems Manager.
Lib Type Special.
Circ Servs Avail Not open to the general public.
Ref Servs Avail To other Federal libraries; to other libraries; to the general public.

Maritime Administration

1938. National Maritime Research Center, Study Center Library
Maritime Admin, Dept of Transportation, Kings Point, NY 11024-1699 (516) 482-8200 ext 575 thru 578; FTS 663-8575
Admin Rayma Feldman. *Ref Lib* Elinor Haber. *ILL* Ilse E. Kagan. *Acq Lib* Herbert Loewenthal.
Lib Type Special.
Spec Subs Merchant ships; operations; shipbuilding; ship simulation. *Spec Collecs* US Maritime Admin technical reports.
Lib Deposit Designation US Maritime Admin.

Circ Servs Avail To other Federal libraries; not open to the general public; restricted to Maritime Admin.
Ref Servs Avail To other Federal libraries; to other libraries; to the general public; restricted to on a cost-recovery basis.

1939. US Merchant Marine Academy, Schyler Otis Bland Memorial Library
Kings Point, NY 11024-1699 (516) 482-8200, ILL ext 502; FTS 663-8504
Lib Type Academic.
Spec Subs Shipping; marine engineering. *Spec Collecs* Marad Technical Report Collection.
Lib Deposit Designation GPO Depository Library.
Info Ret Servs DIALOG. *Shared Catalog Nets* OCLC. *Coop Lib Nets* Long Island Library Resources Council.
Circ Servs Avail To other Federal libraries; to other libraries.
Ref Servs Avail To other Federal libraries; to other libraries; to the general public; restricted to certain collections available only upon request.

National Highway Traffic Safety Administration

1940. National Highway Traffic Safety Administration, Technical Reference Division, Library
400 7th St SW, Rm 5108, Washington, DC 20590 (202) 426-2768; FTS 426-2768
Admin Jerome A Holiber (Div Chief). *Ref Lib* Ellen Gordy. *Acq Lib* Frances Bean.
Lib Type Special.
Spec Subs Highway & motor vehicle safety. *Spec Collecs* Society of Automotive Engineers (SAE) Technical Papers.
Info Ret Servs DIALOG.
Circ Servs Avail To the general public.
Ref Servs Avail To the general public.

United States Coast Guard

1941. Coast Guard Law Library
Department of Transportation, Trans Point Bldg, 2100 2nd St SW, Rm 4407, Washington, DC 20593 (202) 267-2536
Lib Type Law.

1942. US Coast Guard Academy Library
New London, CT 06320-4195 (203) 444-8510
Admin Paul H Johnson. *Ref Lib* Mary McKenzie (ILL). *Acq Lib* Patricia Daragan.
Lib Type Academic.
Spec Subs Applied science & engineering; physical & ocean sciences; computer science; nautical science & law; economics & management; government; US Coast Guard history. *Spec Collecs* US Coast Guard history. *In-house Files* Civil engineering file: lighthouse & life-saving station plans; indices to specific Coast Guard publications; Coast Guard vertical file.
Lib Deposit Designation GPO Depository Library.
Info Ret Servs DIALOG. *Shared Catalog Nets* OCLC. *Coop Lib Nets* NELENET; GODORT/CT.
Circ Servs Avail To other libraries; not open to the general public; restricted to Coast Guard & civilian personnel.
Ref Servs Avail To other libraries; not open to the general public; restricted to Coast Guard & civilian personnel.

1943. US Coast Guard Support Center Library
Bldg 251, Governor's Island, New York, NY 10004 (212) 668-7394
Lib Type General.

1944. US Coast Guard TRACEN Library
US Coast Guard Base, Petaluma, CA 94952 (707) 765-7342; FTS 632-7342
Admin Dianna B Gerhardt.
Lib Type General.
Circ Servs Avail Restricted to military: active, retired, & dependents.
Ref Servs Avail Restricted to military: active, retired, & dependents.

DEPARTMENT OF THE TREASURY

Departmental

1945. Department of the Treasury Library
Main Treasury Bldg 1500 Pennsylvania Ave NW, Rm 5030, Washington, DC 20220 (202) 566-2069; FTS 566-2069
Admin Elizabeth S Knauff (Mgr Info Svs); Christine R Rudy (Chief, Readers Svs Branch).
Lib Type General.
Spec Collecs Congressional hearings, reports & documents.
Lib Deposit Designation GPO Depository Library.
Info Ret Servs DIALOG; CQ Washington Alert; Textline; LEXIS; NEXIS. *Shared Catalog Nets* OCLC. *Coop Lib Nets* Metropolitan Washington Council of Government's Library Council.
Circ Servs Avail To other libraries; not open to the general public.
Ref Servs Avail To other Federal libraries; to other libraries; to the general public; restricted to those able to meet on-site bldg access requirements; reference services by phone only.

Bureau of Alcohol, Tobacco, & Firearms

1946. Bureau of Alcohol, Tobacco & Firearms/National Laboratory Library
1401 Research Blvd, Rockville, MD 20850 (301) 294-0410; FTS 294-0410
Admin John Stevens. *Ref Lib* Paula Deutsch (ILL, Acqe).
Lib Type Engineering & Science.
Spec Subs Alcohol; analytical techniques; chromatography; explosives; firearms; forensic sciences; tobacco. *Spec Collecs* Technical publications of the ATF Laboratory System.
Info Ret Servs DIALOG. *Shared Catalog Nets* OCLC. *Coop Lib Nets* FEDLINK.
Circ Servs Avail To other libraries; not open to the general public.
Ref Servs Avail To other Federal libraries; to other libraries; to the general public.

1947. Bureau of Alcohol, Tobacco & Firearms Reference Library
1200 Pennsylvania Ave NW, Rm 6015, Washington, DC 20226 (202) 566-7557; FTS 566-7557
Admin Vicki R Herrmann.
Lib Type Special.
Spec Subs Regulation of the alcohol, tobacco, explosives & firearms industries. *Spec Collecs* Hearings on the repeal of Prohibition.
Circ Servs Avail To other Federal libraries; to other libraries; not open to the general public.
Ref Servs Avail To other Federal libraries; to other libraries; restricted to with special permission.

Comptroller of the Currency

1948. Comptroller of the Currency Library
490 L'Enfant Plaza SW, Washington, DC 20219 (202) 447-1843
Admin Robert A Updegrove. *ILL* Wayne Queen.
Lib Type Special.
Spec Subs Banking & banking law.
Info Ret Servs DIALOG; LEXIS; NEXIS. *Shared Catalog Nets* OCLC;.
Circ Servs Avail To other Federal libraries; to other libraries.

Ref Servs Avail To other Federal libraries.

Federal Law Enforcement Training Center

1949. Federal Law Enforcement Training Center Library
Dept of the Treasury, Bldg 262, Glynco, GA 31524 (912) 267-2320; FTS 230-2320
Lib Type Training Center.

1950. Federal Law Enforcement Training Center Library
Tom Steed Bldg, Glynco, GA 31524 (912) 267-2320; FTS 230-2320
Admin Frances Morris Johnson.
Lib Type Special.
Spec Subs Law enforcement. *Spec Collecs* Law collection. *In-house Files* Terrorism.
Info Ret Servs DIALOG (thru Main Treasury). *Shared Catalog Nets* OCLC (thru Library of Congress).
Circ Servs Avail To other Federal libraries; to other libraries; not open to the general public; restricted to ILL for all except staff & dependents, & students majoring in criminal justice.
Ref Servs Avail To other Federal libraries; to other libraries; not open to the general public; restricted to staff & dependents, & students majoring in criminal justice.

Internal Revenue Service

1951. Internal Revenue Service, Central Region, Freedom of Information Public Reading Room
201 W 2nd St, Covington, KY 41019 (606) 292-5662; FTS 778-5662
Admin George D Miller.
Lib Type Special.
Spec Subs Publications; rulings & statistics relating to federal income, employment, excise, estate, & gift taxes. *Spec Collecs* Internal Revenue Bulletins; Internal Revenue Manual. *In-house Files* IRS District Office determination letters (employee-employer relationship).
Ref Servs Avail To the general public.

1952. Internal Revenue Service Library
CC:O:SIO:LIB, 1111 Constitution Ave NW, Rm 4324, Washington, DC 20224 (202) 566-6342; FTS 566-6342
Admin Geraldine F Katz. *Ref Lib* Kathryn A Hall. *ILL* Steve Carter. *Acq Lib* Jill H Drucker.
Lib Type Law.
Spec Subs Taxation; practice & procedure of the IRS.
Info Ret Servs DIALOG; LEXIS; NEXIS; WESTLAW; Phinet; VU-TEXT; WILSONLINE; OCLC. *Shared Catalog Nets* OCLC. *Coop Lib Nets* FEDLINK.
Circ Servs Avail To other Federal libraries; not open to the general public.
Ref Servs Avail To other Federal libraries; not open to the general public.

1953. Internal Revenue Service, Office of Chief Counsel, Library
1111 Constitution Ave NW, Rm 4324, Washington, DC 20224 (202) 566-6342; FTS 566-6342
Admin Geraldine Foucault Katz (Acting Librarian). *Ref Lib* Kathryn A Hall. *ILL* Steve Carter. *Acq Lib* Jill H Drucker.
Lib Type Law.
Spec Subs Taxation; Federal law; business & finance. *Spec Collecs* Tax forms & publications—historical collection; CCH & Prentice Hall tax services—historical collection. *In-house Files* Legislative histories for all tax acts from 1913.
Info Ret Servs LEXIS; NEXIS; WESTLAW; PHINET; VU/TEXT; WILSONLINE; CQ Washington Alert. *Shared Catalog Nets* OCLC. *Coop Lib Nets* FEDLINK; Metro Washington Library Council.
Circ Servs Avail Restricted to IRS employees.
Ref Servs Avail To other Federal libraries; not open to the general public.

United States Customs Service

1954. US Customs Service, Library & Information Center
1301 Constitution Ave NW, Rm 3340, Washington, DC 20229 (202) 566-5642; FTS 566-5642
Admin Patricia M Dobrosky. *Ref Lib* Martha Glock.
Lib Type Special.
Spec Subs Legal; business & economics; scientific & technical areas; tariff & trade; cargo; shipping; navigation; law enforcement; commodities; chemical; drugs; other manufactures.
Info Ret Servs DIALOG; LEXIS; NEXIS; WESTLAW; Dun & Bradstreet; LEGI-SLATE. *Shared Catalog Nets* OCLC. *Coop Lib Nets* FEDLINK.
Circ Servs Avail To other Federal libraries; to other libraries.
Ref Servs Avail To other Federal libraries; to other libraries; to the general public.

1955. US Customs Service, New York Region, Library
6 World Trade Center, Rm 534, New York, NY 10048 (212) 466-2053/5858; FTS 668-2053
Admin Carol Hunter. *Ref Lib* Richard Cahn. *ILL* Rena Stolarsky (Ref, Acq).
Lib Type Law.
Spec Subs Customs laws, rules, regulations, & decisions; Federal laws; import/export statistics; trade information. *In-house Files* Customs Binding Rulings.
Info Ret Servs DIALOG.
Circ Servs Avail To other Federal libraries; not open to the general public.
Ref Servs Avail To other Federal libraries; not open to the general public.

1956. US Customs Service, Office of Regional Counsel, Library
423 Canal St, New Orleans, LA 70130 (504) 682-6358; FTS 682-6358
Admin James M Moster (Regional Counsel). *Acq Lib* Joyce Glorioso.
Lib Type Law.
Spec Subs US Customs decisions & materials.
Elec Mail Nets MCI Mail; Telex.
Ref Servs Avail To other Federal libraries; to other libraries; to the general public.

1957. US Customs Service, Southwest Region, Library & Information Center
5850 San Felipe, Ste 500, Houston, TX 77057 (713) 953-6855; FTS 526-9855
Admin Arlene Billings.
Lib Type Special.
Spec Subs International trade.
Info Ret Servs DIALOG; LEXIS; NEXIS. *Coop Lib Nets* Houston Area Law Librarians (HALL).
Circ Servs Avail To other Federal libraries; to other libraries.
Ref Servs Avail To other Federal libraries; to other libraries.

INDEPENDENT AGENCIES

Administrative Conference of the United States

1958. Administrative Conference of the United States, Library
2120 L St NW, Ste 500, Washington, DC 20037 (202) 254-7065
Admin Sue Judith Boley. *ILL* Carole Brown.
Lib Type Law.
Spec Subs Government regulations; administrative law & procedure. *Spec Collecs* Administrative Conference archives. *In-house Files* Administrative Conference work product & closed research files.
Lib Deposit Designation GPO Depository Library.
Info Ret Servs DIALOG; LEXIS; NEXIS. *Coop Lib Nets* FEDLINK.
Circ Servs Avail To other libraries; restricted to ILL.
Ref Servs Avail To other Federal libraries; to other libraries; to the general public.

African Development Foundation

1959. African Development Foundation Library
1724 Massachusetts Ave, NW, Washington, DC 20036 (202) 673-3916
Admin Francis Kornegay; Teixeira Nash (Public Affairs Officer).
Lib Type Special.
Spec Subs Small collection of publications on Africa.
Ref Servs Avail To the general public; restricted to Foundation publications.

Central Intelligence Agency

1960. Central Intelligence Agency, Law Library
Office of the General Counsel, Washington, DC 20505 (703) 482-6106
Lib Type Law.
Spec Subs Intelligence Law.
Circ Servs Avail Not open to the general public; restricted to limited ILL use.
Ref Servs Avail Not open to the general public; restricted to agency personnel.

1961. Central Intelligence Agency Library
Washington, DC 20505 (703) 482-5000
Lib Type Special.
Circ Servs Avail To other Federal libraries; to other libraries; not open to the general public.
Ref Servs Avail Not open to the general public; restricted to agency personnel.

Commission on Civil Rights

1962. US Commission on Civil Rights, National Clearinghouse Library
1121 Vermont Ave NW, Washington, DC 20425 (202) 376-8114
Admin Michael Williams.
Lib Type Special.
Spec Subs Aged; sex discrimination; handicapped; civil rights. *Spec Collecs* Black law school reviews; women's law reviews; Spanish speaking background law reviews & Native American law reviews; civil rights (US Commission on Civil Rights); Native American periodicals, microform; Federal Register, microform; census materials.
Info Ret Servs DIALOG. *Shared Catalog Nets* OCLC.
Circ Servs Avail Not open to the general public; restricted to ILL.
Ref Servs Avail To the general public.

1963. US Commission on Civil Rights, Western Regional Office Library
3660 Wilshire Blvd, Ste 810, Los Angeles, CA 90010 (213) 688-3437; FTS 798-3437; TTY 798-0508
Admin Philip Montez. *Ref Lib* Grace Hernandez. *ILL* Art Palacios. *Acq Lib* Sally James.
Lib Type Special.
Lib Deposit Designation US Commission on Civil Rights; Advisory Committees of AZ, CA, HI, & NV.
Coop Lib Nets Robert S Rankin Civil Rights Memorial Library.
Circ Servs Avail To other Federal libraries; to the general public.
Ref Servs Avail To other Federal libraries; to other libraries; to the general public.

Commission on Fine Arts

1964. Commission of Fine Arts Library
708 Jackson Pl NW, Washington, DC 20006 (202) 566-1066
Admin Charles Atherton (Commission Secretary). *Ref Lib* Sue Kohler.
Lib Type Special.
Spec Subs Architecture; sculpture; memorials; parks.
Circ Servs Avail Not open to the general public.
Ref Servs Avail Not open to the general public; restricted to use by written request.

Commodity Futures Trading Commission

1965. Commodity Futures Trading Commission Library
2033 K St NW, Washington, DC 20581 (202) 254-5901; FTS 254-5901
Admin John Fragale. *Ref Lib* Evelyn Parker (ILL).
Lib Type Law.
Spec Subs Futures trading; options trading. *Spec Collecs* Legislative histories related to Commodity Exchange Act & authorization & reauthorization of CFTC.
Info Ret Servs DIALOG; LEXIS; NEXIS; Dun & Bradstreet; JURIS. *Shared Catalog Nets* OCLC. *Coop Lib Nets* FEDLINK.
Circ Servs Avail To other libraries; not open to the general public; restricted to CFTC.
Ref Servs Avail Not open to the general public; restricted to CFTC.

Consumer Product Safety Commission

1966. Consumer Product Safety Commission Library
1100 Commerce, Rm 1C10, Dallas, TX 75242 (214) 767-0841;
FTS 729-0841
Admin Margaret J Cain. *Acq Lib* Elizabeth Hendricks.
Lib Type Special.
Spec Subs Law; anatomy; trade; industry; medical reference; government reference books.
Shared Catalog Nets CPSC Headquarters Library.
Circ Servs Avail Not open to the general public; restricted to office use.
Ref Servs Avail To the general public; restricted to on-site use.

1967. Consumer Product Safety Commission Library
5401 Westbard Ave, Bethesda, MD 20207 (301) 492-6544
Lib Type Special.
Spec Subs Administrative law; business & management; consumer product safety; economics; engineering; medicine; product liability; product standards; scientific-technical; technology; toxicology. *Spec Collecs* Indexed documents collection; technical standards collection.
Info Ret Servs DIALOG; NEXIS; LEXIS; MEDLINE. *Coop Lib Nets* FEDLINK.

Environmental Protection Agency

1968. Environmental Monitoring & Systems Laboratory Library
PO Box 15027, Las Vegas, NV 89114 (702) 798-2648; FTS 545-2648
Admin Doreen Wickman.
Lib Type Engineering & Science.
Spec Subs Remote sensing; hazardous waste.
Shared Catalog Nets EPA Library Network.
Circ Servs Avail To other Federal libraries; not open to the general public.
Ref Servs Avail To other Federal libraries.

1969. Environmental Protection Agency, Andrew W Breidenbach Library
26 W St Clair St, Cincinnati, OH 45268 (513) 684-7701; FTS 684-7707
Admin Jonda Byrd. *Ref Lib* Maxine Smith. *ILL* Lilian Bosworth. *Acq Lib* Joan Honeck.
Lib Type Special.
Spec Subs Water pollution; water quality; hazardous waste; environmental sciences; biochemistry; chemistry; biotechnology. *Spec Collecs* Hazardous waste collection; personal & career development. *In-house Files* Solid wastes documents.
Info Ret Servs DIALOG; BRS; OHS; STN International; NLM. *Shared Catalog Nets* OCLC; EPA Library Network. *Coop Lib Nets* EPA Library Network. *Elec Mail Nets* EPA.
Circ Servs Avail To other Federal libraries; to other libraries; restricted to ILL.
Ref Servs Avail To other Federal libraries; to other libraries; restricted to public on limited basis.

1970. Environmental Protection Agency, Central Regional Laboratory Library
839 Bestgate Rd, Annapolis, MD 21401 (301) 224-2740
Lib Type Special.
Circ Servs Avail To other Federal libraries; to other libraries; restricted to limited access for consultants, contractors, & general public.
Ref Servs Avail To other Federal libraries; to other libraries; restricted to limited access for consultants, contractors, & general public.

1971. Environmental Protection Agency, Corvallis Environmental Research Library
200 SW 35th St, Corvallis, OR 97333 (503) 757-4731; FTS 420-4731
Admin Betty M McCauley.
Lib Type Engineering & Science.
Spec Subs Pollution effects on plants & animals; acid precipitation; hazardous waste; pesticides; toxic substance; genetic engineering. *Spec Collecs* Acid precipitation.
Info Ret Servs DIALOG; RECON; CIS; NLM (limited to Toxic files). *Shared Catalog Nets* OCLC. *Coop Lib Nets* FEDLINK; EPA Network; ORULS (Oregon Union List of Serials). *Elec Mail Nets* EPA.
Circ Servs Avail To other Federal libraries; to other libraries; restricted to ILL.
Ref Servs Avail To other Federal libraries; to other libraries; to the general public.

1972. Environmental Protection Agency, Environmental Research Laboratory Library
Sabine Island, Gulf Breeze, FL 32561 (904) 932-5311; FTS 686-9011
Admin Susan M Means. *ILL* Alice Pool.
Lib Type Engineering & Science.
Spec Subs Marine ecology; microbiology; biotechnology. *Spec Collecs* Selected EPA reports. *In-house Files* Laboratory publications: comprehensive & special subject bibliographies available.
Info Ret Servs DIALOG; BRS; National Groundwater Information Center Database; NLM; CAS. *Shared Catalog Nets* OCLC. *Coop Lib Nets* FEDLINK.
Circ Servs Avail To other Federal libraries; to other libraries; not open to the general public.
Ref Servs Avail To other Federal libraries; to other libraries; to the general public.

1973. Environmental Protection Agency, Environmental Research Laboratory Library
College Station Rd, Athens, GA 30613 (404) 546-3324
Lib Type Special.
Spec Subs Aquatic biology; biology; chemistry; chromatography; engineering; microbiology; sanitary engineering; spectroscopy.
Shared Catalog Nets OCLC. *Coop Lib Nets* FEDLINK.

1974. Environmental Protection Agency Headquarters Library
PM-211A, 401 M St SW, Rm 2402, Washington, DC 20460 (202) 382-5922; FTS 382-5922
Admin Loretta Marzetti.
Lib Type Special.
Spec Subs Environmental policy management. *Spec Collecs* Hazardous waste. *In-house Files* Hazardous waste database.
Info Ret Servs DIALOG; NLM; NEXIS; LEXIS; CAS Online; CIS; NWWA. *Shared Catalog Nets* OCLC.
Circ Servs Avail Restricted to ILL requests.
Ref Servs Avail To other Federal libraries; to other libraries; to the general public; restricted to manual reference only.

1975. Environmental Protection Agency, Robert S Kerr Library
PO Box 1198, Ada, OK 74820 (405) 332-8800 ext 241; FTS 743-2241
Admin LoRene Fuller.
Lib Type Special.
Spec Subs Ground water quality & pollution; waste management; land treatment; chemistry; biology; agriculture.
Info Ret Servs DIALOG; BRS; SDC; National Ground Water Infomation Center Data Base. *Shared Catalog Nets* OCLC. *Coop Lib Nets* EPA Library Network.
Circ Servs Avail To other Federal libraries; to other libraries.
Ref Servs Avail To other Federal libraries; to other libraries; to the general public; restricted to on-site reference use for general public.

1976. Environmental Protection Agency, Law Library
LE-130L, 401 M St SW, Rm 2902, Washington, DC 20460 (202) 382-5919; FTS 382-5919
Admin Barbara Pedrini Morrison.
Lib Type Law.
Spec Subs Administrative & environmental law.
Info Ret Servs JURIS; LEXIS. *Shared Catalog Nets* OCLC. *Coop Lib Nets* FEDLINK. *Elec Mail Nets* ITT DIALCOM.

Circ Servs Avail To other Federal libraries; to other libraries.
Ref Servs Avail To other Federal libraries; to other libraries; restricted to print materials.

1977. Environmental Protection Agency Library
Mail Drop 35, Research Triangle Park, NC 27711 (919) 541-2777; FTS 629-2777
Admin Elizabeth M Smith. *ILL* Rosemary Thorne. *Acq Lib* Harriet Myers.
Lib Type Special.
Spec Subs Air pollution: effects, monitoring, & control. *Spec Collecs* Air Pollution Technical Information Center files.
Info Ret Servs DIALOG; BRS; STN CAS On-line; Newsnet. *Shared Catalog Nets* OCLC. *Coop Lib Nets* EPA Library Network. *Elec Mail Nets* ITT DIALCOM.
Circ Servs Avail To other Federal libraries; to other libraries.
Ref Servs Avail To other Federal libraries; to other libraries; to the general public.

1978. Environmental Protection Agency Library, Region 8
8M-ASL, 1860 Lincoln St, Ste 270, Denver, CO 80295 (303) 844-2560; FTS 564-2560
Lib Type Special.
Spec Subs Air pollution; energy activities; noise; pesticides; radiation; solid waste; toxic substances; water pollution; water quality.
Info Ret Servs DIALOG. *Shared Catalog Nets* OCLC. *Coop Lib Nets* FEDLINK; Central Colorado Regional Library Service System.

1979. Environmental Protection Agency, Meteorology Division Library
NOAA, MD-80, Research Triangle Park, NC 27711 (919) 541-4536; FTS 629-4536
Admin Evelyn M Poole-Kober.
Lib Type Special.
Spec Subs Atmospheric pollution. *Spec Collecs* Atmospheric pollution; weather; climate; meteorology.
Shared Catalog Nets OCLC.
Circ Servs Avail To other Federal libraries.
Ref Servs Avail To other Federal libraries; restricted to on-site use.

1980. Environmental Protection Agency, National Enforcement Investigation Center, Information Center
Box 25227, Bldg 53, Denver Federal Center, Denver, CO 80225 (303) 236-5100; FTS 776-5170
Admin Dorothy Biggs.
Lib Type Engineering & Science.
Spec Subs Environmental protection, especially environmental regulation, environmental toxicology, & air technology, including agricultural, industrial, & municipal pollution abatement. *Spec Collecs* Case files, technical reports, & data compilation on EPA-NEIC enforcement actions.
Info Ret Servs DIALOG; BRS; SDC; NLM; Compuserve; DIALOG; Dun & Bradstreet; JURIS; NEWSNET; NEXIS; NIH-EPA Chemical Information System; VU-TEXT; WESTLAW. *Shared Catalog Nets* OCLC.
Circ Servs Avail To other Federal libraries; to other libraries; to the general public; restricted to ILL requests.
Ref Servs Avail To other Federal libraries; to other libraries; to the general public.

1981. Environmental Protection Agency, National Water Quality Laboratory Library
6201 Congdon Blvd, Duluth, MN 55804 (218) 727-6692 ext 538
Lib Type Special.

1982. Environmental Protection Agency, Office of Air Quality, Planning, & Standards Library
826 Mutual Plaza, Research Triangle Park, NC 27711 (919) 541-5614
Lib Type Special.
Circ Servs Avail To other Federal libraries; to other libraries; to the general public.
Ref Servs Avail To other Federal libraries; to other libraries; to the general public.

1983. Environmental Protection Agency, Region 9 Library
215 Fremont St, San Francisco, CA 94105 (415) 974-8079; FTS 454-8079
Admin Marsha Saylor. *Ref Lib* Judith Demeter. *ILL* Lynn Fox.
Lib Type Special.
Spec Subs Environmental policies, issues, procedures, & law. *Spec Collecs* EPA Reports. *In-house Files* Fact sheets covering areas of air & water pollution & hazardous waste.
Lib Deposit Designation EPA.
Info Ret Servs DIALOG; Chemical Information Service & Occupational Health Services. *Shared Catalog Nets* OCLC. *Coop Lib Nets* FEDLINK.
Circ Servs Avail To other Federal libraries; to other libraries.
Ref Servs Avail To other Federal libraries; to other libraries; to the general public.

1984. Environmental Protection Agency, Region 1 Library
JFK Federal Bldg 2100-B, Boston, MA 02203 (212) 223-4017; FTS 223-4017
Admin Peg Nelson. *ILL* Judy Saravis.
Lib Type Special.
Spec Subs Environmental: solid & hazardous waste, air pollution; water pollution; health effects & technologies to remedy pollution. *Spec Collecs* New England materials & EPA reports.
Info Ret Servs DIALOG; BRS; Chemical Information System (CIS); NLM; NEXIS; LEXIS. *Shared Catalog Nets* OCLC. *Coop Lib Nets* FEDLINK; EPA Library Network. *Elec Mail Nets* ITT DIALCOM.
Circ Servs Avail To other Federal libraries; to other libraries.
Ref Servs Avail To other Federal libraries; to other libraries; to the general public.

1985. Environmental Protection Agency, Region 2, Field Office Library
Edison, NJ 08837 (201) 321-6762; FTS 340-6762
Admin Dorothy Szefczyk.
Lib Type Special.
Spec Subs Environmental pollution.
Info Ret Servs DIALOG. *Shared Catalog Nets* OCLC. *Coop Lib Nets* FEDLINK.
Circ Servs Avail Restricted to EPA employees.
Ref Servs Avail Restricted to EPA employees.

1986. Environmental Protection Agency, Region 2 Library
26 Federal Plaza, New York, NY 10278 (212) 264-2881; FTS 264-2881
Lib Type Special.
Spec Subs Environmental pollution.
Info Ret Servs DIALOG. *Shared Catalog Nets* OCLC. *Coop Lib Nets* FEDLINK.
Circ Servs Avail Restricted to EPA employees.
Ref Servs Avail Restricted to EPA employees.

1987. Environmental Protection Agency, Region 3 Library
841 Chestnut St, Philadelphia, PA 19107 (215) 597-0580; FTS 597-0580
Admin Diane M McCreary. *ILL* Joyce Baker.
Lib Type Law; Engineering & Science.
Spec Subs Environmental sciences; law; management. *Spec Collecs* Wetlands ecology.
Info Ret Servs DIALOG; MEDLARS; TOXNET; Chemical Information System (CIS); LEXIS; NEXIS; Ground Water Online. *Shared Catalog Nets* OCLC. *Coop Lib Nets* FEDLINK. *Elec Mail Nets* ITT DIALCOM.
Circ Servs Avail To other Federal libraries; to other libraries.
Ref Servs Avail To other Federal libraries; to other libraries; to the general public.

1988. Environmental Protection Agency, Region 4 Library
345 Courtland St NE, Atlanta, GA 30365-2401 (404) 347-4216; FTS 257-4216
Admin Gayle Alston. *ILL* Bill Marx.
Lib Type Law; Engineering & Science.
Spec Subs Hazardous wastes, air, water, & land for NC, SC, GA, AL, TN, KY, FL, & MS. *Spec Collecs* Hazardous waste; EPA reports; soil surveys for Southeast; legislative histories of environmental law.

Info Ret Servs DIALOG; CAS Online; Chemical Information. *Shared Catalog Nets* OCLC. *Coop Lib Nets* FEDLINK. *Elec Mail Nets* E-Mail.
Circ Servs Avail To other Federal libraries; to other libraries; to the general public.
Ref Servs Avail To other Federal libraries; to other libraries; to the general public.

1989. Environmental Protection Agency, Region 5 Library

230 S Dearborn St, Rm 1670, Chicago, IL 60604 (312) 353-2022; FTS 353-2022
Admin Lou W Tilley.
Lib Type Special.
Spec Subs Air pollution & air quality; drinking water; hazardous waste; pesticides; radiation; recycling & resource recovery; solid waste; toxic substances; water pollution & water quality. *Spec Collecs* EPA, Region 5 numbered reports; APTIC (air pollution) microfiche (-1978, ca 85,000 items); water resources data (midwestern states); EIC statefiche; EIS microfiche (1973 to present); over 75 video cassette tapes. *In-house Files* National priorities list dockets for Region 5 states, with comments; contract bid protest decisions, EPA.
Lib Deposit Designation EPA (paper copy &/or microfiche).
Info Ret Servs DIALOG; BRS; SDC; Chemical Infomation System (CIS); National Ground Water Infomation Ctr; LEXIS; NEXIS. *Shared Catalog Nets* OCLC; NTIS (EPS reports). *Coop Lib Nets* FEDLINK. *Elec Mail Nets* ITT DIALCOM.
Circ Servs Avail To other Federal libraries; to other libraries; to the general public.
Ref Servs Avail To other Federal libraries; to other libraries; to the general public.

1990. Environmental Protection Agency, Region 6 Library

Renaissance Tower, 1201 Elm St, Dallas, TX 75270 (214) 767-7341; FTS 729-7341
Admin Leticia Lane.
Lib Type Special.
Spec Subs Air; hazardous waste; water; toxics. *Spec Collecs* Law library; hazardous waste; soil surveys.
Lib Deposit Designation DOE; GAO.
Circ Servs Avail To other Federal libraries; to other libraries; to the general public.
Ref Servs Avail To other Federal libraries; to other libraries.

1991. Environmental Protection Agency, Region 7 Library

314 E 11th St, Kansas City, MO 64106 (913) 236-2828
Lib Type Special.
Spec Subs Agricultural, air, & water pollution; environmental law; hazardous wastes; pesticides; radiation; solid waste management; water hygiene.
Circ Servs Avail To other Federal libraries; to other libraries.
Ref Servs Avail To other Federal libraries; to other libraries; to the general public.

1992. Environmental Protection Agency, Region 10 Library

MS S41 1200 6th Ave, Seattle, WA 98101 (206) 442-1289; FTS 399-1289
Admin Julienne K Sears. *ILL* Patricia Devine.
Lib Type Special.
Spec Subs Environmental science; federal regulatory information. *In-house Files* Federal regulatory information Region 10 Reports for AK, WA, OR, & ID.
Info Ret Servs DIALOG. *Shared Catalog Nets* OCLC. *Elec Mail Nets* EPA.
Circ Servs Avail To the general public; restricted to EPA reports.
Ref Servs Avail Restricted to staff.

1993. Environmental Protection Agency, Research Laboratory Library

S Ferry Rd, Narragansett, RI 02882-1198 (401) 789-1071 ext 265; FTS 838-5087
Lib Type Special.
Spec Subs Biological oceanography; effects of pollutants on marine life; fisheries biology; marine culture systems; water/marine pollution.
Ref Servs Avail To the general public; restricted to limited use.

1994. Motor Vehicle Emission Laboratory Library

2565 Plymouth Rd, Ann Arbor, MI 48105 (313) 668-8230; FTS 374-8311
Admin Debra Talsma.
Lib Type Special.
Spec Subs Methanol use in motor vehicles; motor vehicle exhaust & emissions. *Spec Collecs* SAE papers relating to motor vehicles. *In-house Files* Technical & final reports relating to MVEL.
Shared Catalog Nets OCLC. *Elec Mail Nets* Telex.
Circ Servs Avail To other Federal libraries; to other libraries; to the general public.
Ref Servs Avail To other Federal libraries.

1995. Office of Toxic Substances, Chemical Library

401 M St SW (TS-793), Washington, DC 20460 (202) 382-3529; FTS 382-3529
Admin Geraldine D Nowak. *Ref Lib* Janette Petty. *ILL* Hattie Sykes. *Acq Lib* Betty Sterling.
Lib Type Special.
Spec Subs Chemistry; toxicology. *Spec Collecs* Office of Toxic Substances final reports.
Info Ret Servs DIALOG; BRS; SDC; NLM. *Shared Catalog Nets* OCLC. *Coop Lib Nets* FEDLINK; EPA Library System.
Circ Servs Avail To other Federal libraries; to other libraries; not open to the general public some parts of the collection do not circulate.
Ref Servs Avail To other Federal libraries; to other libraries; to the general public.

Equal Employment Opportunity Commission

1996. Equal Employment Opportunity Commission, Charlotte District Office, Law Library

5500 Central Ave, Charlotte, NC 28212 (704) 567-7115
Admin Regional Attorney. *Acq Lib* Thru main library in Washington, DC.
Lib Type Law.
Spec Subs Employment discrimination law.
Coop Lib Nets EEOC Library Network.
Circ Servs Avail Restricted to EEOC employees.
Ref Servs Avail To other Federal libraries; to the general public.

1997. Equal Employment Opportunity Commission, Cleveland District Office Library

1375 Euclid Ave, Rm 600, Cleveland, OH 44115 (216) 522-7425; FTS 942-7520
Admin Evelyn R Morson.
Lib Type Law.
Spec Subs EEOC regulations; Title VII; ADEA; EPA.
Circ Servs Avail Not open to the general public; restricted to EEOC employees.
Ref Servs Avail Not open to the general public; restricted to EEOC employees.

1998. Equal Employment Opportunity Commission, Houston District Office, Law Library

405 Main St, 6th Fl, Houston, TX 77002 (713) 226-5699; FTS 526-5699
Admin Leopoldo Fraga, Jr.
Lib Type Law.
Spec Collecs CCH—employment practice cases.
Circ Servs Avail Not open to the general public.
Ref Servs Avail Not open to the general public.

1999. Equal Employment Opportunity Commission Library

2401 E St NW, Rm 298, Washington, DC 20506 (202) 634-6990; FTS 634-6990
Admin Susan O Taylor. *Ref Lib* Minnie Sue Ripy. *ILL* Shirley Smith.
Lib Type Law.
Spec Subs Employment discrimination; federal law. *Spec Collecs* EEOC publications.
Info Ret Servs DIALOG; LEXIS; NEXIS; LEGI-SLATE. *Shared Catalog Nets* OCLC. *Coop Lib Nets* FEDLINK.

Circ Servs Avail Restricted to ILL.
Ref Servs Avail To other Federal libraries; to other libraries; to the general public.

2000. Equal Employment Opportunity Commission, Milwaukee District Office, Library
Henry S Reuss Federal Plaza, Ste 800, 310 W Wisconsin, Milwaukee, WI 53203 (414) 291-1856; FTS 362-1856
Admin Gerry Schmit (Secretary to Regional Attorney).
Lib Type Law.
Circ Servs Avail Not open to the general public; restricted to EEOC personnel.
Ref Servs Avail To other Federal libraries; not open to the general public; restricted to EEOC personnel.

2001. Equal Employment Opportunity Commission, New Orleans District Office Library
600 S Maestri Pl, Rm 535, New Orleans, LA 70130 (504) 589-2001; FTS 682-2001
Admin Michelle Mouton Goodly. *Acq Lib* Susan Taylor.
Lib Type Law.
Spec Subs Labor law.
Ref Servs Avail To other Federal libraries; to other libraries; to the general public.

Export-Import Bank of the United States

2002. Eximbank Library
811 Vermont Ave NW, Washington, DC 20571 (202) 566-8320/8894
Admin Theodora McGill. *Ref Lib* John Posniak (ILL).
Lib Type Special.
Spec Subs Banking; economics; exports; finance; trade. *Spec Collecs* OECD publications on related subjects.
Shared Catalog Nets OCLC.
Circ Servs Avail To other Federal libraries; to other libraries; not open to the general public.
Ref Servs Avail To other Federal libraries; to other libraries; not open to the general public; restricted to use by general public with permission.

Farm Credit Administration

2003. Farm Credit Administration Library
1501 Farm Credit Dr, McLean, VA 22102 (703) 883-4296
Admin Lena Phillips. *Ref Lib* Ann Brinsmead. *ILL* Ellen Crouch.
Lib Type Law.
Spec Subs Business accounting & finance; banking; law; agricultural credit. *Spec Collecs* Farm Credit Administration.
Info Ret Servs DIALOG; NEXIS; LEXIS; CQ Washington Alert. *Coop Lib Nets* FEDLINK.
Circ Servs Avail To other Federal libraries; to other libraries.
Ref Servs Avail To other libraries; not open to the general public.

Federal Communications Commission

2004. FCC Chicago District Office Library
1550 Northwest Hwy, Park Ridge, IL 60068 (312) 353-0195
Admin R D Monie (Acq). *Ref Lib* Flora Stewart; Christine Jelinek.
Lib Type Special.
Spec Subs Code of Federal Regulations, Title 47. *Spec Collecs* Incomplete files of dockets on subjects studied by the commission which appear to be of interest to the general public; commission forms distributed on request; microfiche of all classes of radio stations, including commercial & amateur individual licenses; current broadcast & cable cast year book & the television & cable fact books.
Ref Servs Avail Restricted to on-site use.

2005. FCC Library
1919 M St NW, Rm 639, Washington, DC 20554 (202) 632-7100
Admin Sheryl A Segal.
Lib Type Law.
Spec Subs Telecommunication: radio/television broadcasting; telephony. *Spec Collecs* Legislative histories, indexed. *In-house Files* Citation index; legislative history index.
Info Ret Servs DIALOG. *Shared Catalog Nets* OCLC.
Circ Servs Avail To other Federal libraries.
Ref Servs Avail To other Federal libraries; to other libraries; to the general public.

Federal Deposit Insurance Corporation

2006. FDIC Library
2345 Grand Ave, Rm 1500, Kansas City, MO 64108 (816) 472-1690
Admin Lynne Gottesburen.
Lib Type Law.
Spec Subs Banking.
Info Ret Servs WESTLAW.
Circ Servs Avail Not open to the general public.
Ref Servs Avail To other Federal libraries; not open to the general public.

2007. Federal Deposit Insurance Corporation Library
550 17th St NW, Rm 4074, Washington, DC 20007 (202) 898-3631
Admin Carole Cleland. *Ref Lib* Len Samowitz. *ILL* Ellin McNamara. *Acq Lib* Noreen Lewis.
Lib Type Law.
Spec Subs Banking. *Spec Collecs* State banking agency annual reports.
Lib Deposit Designation GPO Depository Library.
Info Ret Servs DIALOG; WESTLAW; LEXIS; NEXIS; Dow Jones. *Shared Catalog Nets* OCLC. *Elec Mail Nets* ITT DIALCOM.
Circ Servs Avail To other libraries.
Ref Servs Avail To other Federal libraries; to other libraries; to the general public; restricted to general public by appointment.

Federal Election Commission

2008. Federal Election Commission, Law Library
1325 K St NW, 4th Fl, Washington, DC 20463 (202) 523-4178
Admin Leta L Holley.
Lib Type Law.

2009. National Clearinghouse on Election Administration, Federal Election Commission Library
999 E St NW, Washington, DC 20463 (202) 376-5670
Admin Penelope Bonsall.
Lib Type Special.

Federal Emergency Management Agency

2010. Federal Emergency Management Agency Library
500 C St SW, Washington, DC 20472 (202) 646-3771; FTS 646-3771
Admin Mercedes L Emperado.
Lib Type Special.
Spec Subs Emergency management. *Spec Collecs* Civil Defense Collection; State disaster plans. *In-house Files* Technical reports, clippings, brochures on emergency management & preparedness.
Info Ret Servs DIALOG; DROLS. *Shared Catalog Nets* OCLC. *Coop Lib Nets* FEDLINK. *Elec Mail Nets* ITT DIALCOM.
Circ Servs Avail To other Federal libraries; to other libraries; restricted to ILL.
Ref Servs Avail To other Federal libraries; to other libraries; to the general public.

2011. National Emergency Training Center, Learning Resource Center
16825 S Seton Ave, Emmitsburg, MD 21727 (800) 638-1821; (301) 447-6771; FTS 652-6032
Admin Adele M Chiesa.
Lib Type Training Center.
Spec Subs Emergency management; natural hazards; hazardous materials; fire dept management; fire science; civil defense; arson. *Spec Collecs* Arson Resource Center.
Info Ret Servs DIALOG; SDC. *Shared Catalog Nets* OCLC. *Coop Lib Nets* FEDLINK; International Network Fire Information Reference Exchange (INFIRE).
Circ Servs Avail To other Federal libraries; to other libraries; to the general public No A-V servs to general public.
Ref Servs Avail To other Federal libraries; to other libraries; to the general public.

Federal Home Loan Bank Board

2012. Federal Home Loan Bank Board, Law Library
1700 G St NW, Washington, DC 20552 (202) 377-6470
Admin Joyce A Potter. *ILL* Brenda Hilliard.
Lib Type Law.
Spec Subs Banking; administrative law; corporate law; home financing; savings & loan law; securities law. *Spec Collecs* Legislative histories of banking & savings & loan assoc law since 1932.
Info Ret Servs LEXIS; NEXIS; CQ Washington Alert. *Coop Lib Nets* American Assoc of Law Libraries (AALL); Law Librarians' Society of Washington, DC (LLSDC); Federal Law Librarians (FLL).
Circ Servs Avail To other Federal libraries; not open to the general public; restricted to federal government agencies.
Ref Servs Avail To other Federal libraries; not open to the general public; restricted to federal government agencies.

2013. Federal Home Loan Bank Board, Research Library
1700 G St NW, Washington, DC 20552 (202) 377-6296; FTS 377-6296
Admin Janet B Smith. *ILL* Cheryl C Wright.
Lib Type Special.
Spec Subs Savings & loan statistics; economics; finance; real estate; housing; banking; monetary policy. *Spec Collecs* State annual reports of savings & loan assoc; historical reports of the FHLBB.
Info Ret Servs DIALOG. *Shared Catalog Nets* OCLC. *Coop Lib Nets* FEDLINK; Metro Washington Library Council.
Circ Servs Avail To other Federal libraries; to other libraries.
Ref Servs Avail To other Federal libraries; to other libraries; to the general public.

2014. Federal Home Loan Bank of Atlanta, Research Library
PO Box 56527, 260 Peachtree St, Atlanta, GA 30343 (404) 522-2450
Admin Dorothy A Lawless. *ILL* Anita Miller.
Lib Type Special.
Spec Subs Economics; thrift industry; housing; federal regulations. *In-house Files* Cost of funds, Mortgage Loan Survey, & Quarterly Statistics of FSLIC Insured S&Ls in the 4th District.
Coop Lib Nets Special Libraries (SLA); FHLB System Libraries; South Atlantic Chapter of SLA.
Circ Servs Avail Restricted to employees.
Ref Servs Avail To other Federal libraries; to other libraries; to the general public; restricted to in-house use only.

2015. Federal Home Loan Bank of Chicago Library
111 E Wacker Dr, Chicago, IL 60601 (312) 565-5700
Admin Jeanne Palermo.
Lib Type Special.
Spec Subs Finance; real estate, pertaining to home loans; mortgage interest rates; savings institutions; laws affecting savings institutions. *In-house Files* Bank Board regulations & memoranda; regulatory issues affecting savings institutions.
Coop Lib Nets Federal Home Loan Bank libraries.
Ref Servs Avail Not open to the general public; restricted to memoranda & publications sent on request.

2016. Federal Home Loan Bank of Dallas, Research & Information Library
PO Box 619026, Dallas, TX 75261 (214) 659-6477
Admin Pat Talley.
Lib Type Special.
Spec Subs Financial industry. *In-house Files* Savings institutions.
Info Ret Servs DIALOG.
Circ Servs Avail Not open to the general public; restricted to employees.
Ref Servs Avail Not open to the general public; restricted to employees.

2017. Federal Home Loan Bank of Des Moines Library
907 Walnut, Des Moines, IA 50309 (515) 243-4211; FTS 243-4211
Admin Helen Dutemple.
Lib Type Special.
Spec Subs Economics & finance.
Coop Lib Nets Federal Home Loan Bank Board libraries.
Ref Servs Avail Restricted to other FHLB libraries.

2018. Federal Home Loan Bank of Indianapolis Library
PO Box 60, Indianapolis, IN 46206-0060 (317) 236-7119
Admin Beth C Nellist.
Lib Type Special.
Spec Subs Savings associations regulations & operations.
Info Ret Servs DIALOG.
Circ Servs Avail To other libraries; restricted to internal & FHLB District 6 members.
Ref Servs Avail Restricted to internal & FHLB District 6 members.

2019. Federal Home Loan Bank of New York Library
One World Trade Center, Fl 103, New York, NY 10011 (212) 912-4829
Admin Juliette Levinton. *ILL* Linnie Hale.
Lib Type Special.
Spec Subs Housing; mortgage lending; economics; regional data for NY, NJ, & PR.
Info Ret Servs DIALOG; LEXIS; NEXIS.
Circ Servs Avail To other libraries; not open to the general public.
Ref Servs Avail To other Federal libraries; to other libraries; to the general public.

2020. Federal Home Loan Bank of San Francisco Library
PO Box 7948, San Francisco, CA 94120 (415) 393-1215
Admin Molly M Skeen. *ILL* Kurt Shuck.
Lib Type Special.
Spec Subs Savings & loan industry.
Info Ret Servs DIALOG; DRI; Telerate; Dow Jones News/Retrieval; CQ Washington Alert.
Circ Servs Avail To other Federal libraries; to other libraries.
Ref Servs Avail To other Federal libraries; to other libraries; to the general public.

Federal Labor Relations Authority

2021. Federal Labor Relations Authority Law Library
500 C St SW, Washington, DC 20424 (202) 382-0765; FTS 382-0765
Admin Patricia L Lofton.
Lib Type Law.
Spec Subs Federal service labor-management relations. *Spec Collecs* Legislative history of Civil Service Reform Act of 1978. *In-house Files* Committee reports.
Lib Deposit Designation GPO Depository Library.
Info Ret Servs WESTLAW.
Circ Servs Avail To other Federal libraries.
Ref Servs Avail To other Federal libraries; to other libraries; to the general public.

2022. Federal Labor Relations Authority, Region 2 Library
26 Federal Pl, Rm 3700, New York, NY 10278 (212) 264-4934; FTS 264-4934
Admin James E Petrucci (Regional Dir). *Ref Lib* Martha Logan-Biggs (Regional Attorney's Secretary).
Lib Type Law.

Circ Servs Avail Not open to the general public.
Ref Servs Avail To the general public.

2023. Federal Labor Relations Authority, Region 5 Library
175 W Jackson Blvd, Ste 1359A, Chicago, IL 60604 (312) 353-6306; FTS 353-6306
Admin Ernestine Harris. *Ref Lib* Saron A Bauer (ILL). *Acq Lib* Robert H Kravetz.
Lib Type Law.
Spec Subs Labor law. *In-house Files* ALI & FLRA decisions.
Ref Servs Avail To other Federal libraries; to the general public.

Federal Maritime Commission

2024. Federal Maritime Commission Library
1100 L St NW, Washington, DC 20573 (202) 523-5762
Admin Mary Ellen Daffron.
Lib Type Law.
Spec Subs Marine transportation & shipping economics.
Info Ret Servs WESTLAW; CQ Washington Alert.
Circ Servs Avail To other libraries.
Ref Servs Avail To other Federal libraries; to other libraries; to the general public.

Federal Mediation & Conciliation Service

2025. Federal Mediation & Conciliation Service, Law Library
2100 K St, NW, Washington, DC 20427 (202) 653-5290
Admin Daniel Dozier (Legal Counsel).
Lib Type Law.
Ref Servs Avail Not open to the general public.

Federal Reserve System

2026. Board of Governors of the Federal Reserve System, Law Library
21st St & Constitution Ave NW Rm B1066, Washington, DC 20551 (202) 452-3284; FTS 452-3284
Admin Judith M Weiss. *Ref Lib* Richard McKinney.
Lib Type Law.
Spec Subs Banking law. *Spec Collecs* Legislative history.
Lib Deposit Designation GPO Depository Library.
Info Ret Servs DIALOG; LEXIS; LEGI-SLATE.
Circ Servs Avail To other Federal libraries; restricted to local area.
Ref Servs Avail To other libraries.

2027. Board of Governors of the Federal Reserve System, Research Library
20th St & Constitution Ave NW, Washington, DC 20551 (202) 452-3332; FTS 452-3332
Admin Ann Roane Clary. *Ref Lib* Julia G Back (ILL). *Acq Lib* Ioana Ratesh.
Lib Type Special.
Spec Subs Banking & finance; monetary & fiscal policy; economics; credit. *Spec Collecs* History of the Federal Reserve System; foreign, central bank publications & laws.
Lib Deposit Designation GPO Depository Library.
Info Ret Servs DIALOG; BRS. *Shared Catalog Nets* OCLC thru FEDLINK. *Coop Lib Nets* FEDLINK.
Circ Servs Avail To other Federal libraries; restricted to local area.
Ref Servs Avail To other Federal libraries; to other libraries; to the general public; restricted to Thurs only for public access.

2028. Federal Reserve Bank of Atlanta, Research Library
PO Box 1731, 104 Marietta St NW, Atlanta, GA 30301 (404) 521-8867; FTS 231-8867
Admin Carolyn W Mitchell. *Ref Lib* Jerry J Donovan. *ILL* David Barros.
Lib Type Special.
Spec Subs Economics; banking; finance. *Spec Collecs* Economic working papers. *In-house Files* FRB statistical releases.

Info Ret Servs DIALOG; BRS; NEXIS. *Shared Catalog Nets* OCLC; SOLINET. *Coop Lib Nets* Committee on Library Functions, FRB.
Circ Servs Avail To other libraries.
Ref Servs Avail To other Federal libraries; to the general public; restricted to limited service.

2029. Federal Reserve Bank of Boston, Research Library
T-28, 600 Atlantic Ave, Boston, MA 02106 (617) 973-3393; ILL 973-3396
Lib Type Special.
Spec Subs Economics; finance.
Info Ret Servs BRS. *Shared Catalog Nets* OCLC.

2030. Federal Reserve Bank of Chicago Library
Box 834, 230 S LaSalle St, Chicago, IL 60690 (312) 322-5828
Lib Type Special.
Spec Subs Agricultural economics; business conditions; central banking; economics; finance; monetary policy; statistics.
Shared Catalog Nets OCLC. *Coop Lib Nets* Chicago Library System; Illinois Library & Information Network.

2031. Federal Reserve Bank of Cleveland, Research Library
PO Box 6387, 1455 E 6th St, Cleveland, OH 44101 (216) 579-2053
Admin Betty Maynard. *Ref Lib* Lynn Sniderman; Dale Riordan. *ILL* Lucy Green (Acq).
Lib Type Special.
Spec Subs Economics; banking; Federal Reserve System.
Info Ret Servs DIALOG; LEXIS; NEXIS. *Shared Catalog Nets* OCLC.
Circ Servs Avail To other libraries.
Ref Servs Avail To other libraries; not open to the general public.

2032. Federal Reserve Bank of Dallas Library
Station K, 400 S Akard St, Dallas, TX 75222 (214) 651-6391
Lib Type Special.
Spec Subs Agriculture; banking; economics; labor; petroleum; Southwest region.
Shared Catalog Nets OCLC. *Coop Lib Nets* AMIGOS.
Ref Servs Avail Restricted to reference only by appointment.

2033. Federal Reserve Bank of Kansas City, Research Library
PO Box 560, 925 Grand Ave, Kansas City, MO 64198 (816) 881-2676
Lib Type Special.
Spec Subs Agriculture; banking; economics; finance; statistics.
Shared Catalog Nets OCLC. *Coop Lib Nets* Kansas City Metropolitan Library Network.
Circ Servs Avail Not open to the general public.
Ref Servs Avail To the general public.

2034. Federal Reserve Bank of Minneapolis Library
250 Marquette Ave, Minneapolis, MN 55480 (612) 374-2292
Admin Janet Swan; Amy Hargens (Mgr of Lib & Records Serv).
Lib Type Special.
Spec Subs Economics; economic policy; regional economic conditions. *Spec Collecs* Federal Reserve System publications.
Circ Servs Avail To other libraries; not open to the general public; restricted to limited borrowing.
Ref Servs Avail To other Federal libraries; to other libraries; to the general public.

2035. Federal Reserve Bank of New York, Computer Science Library
59 Maiden Ln, 24th Fl, New York, NY 10045 (212) 791-5766
Lib Type Special.
Shared Catalog Nets OCLC.
Ref Servs Avail Not open to the general public; restricted to staff but will release software developed.

2036. Federal Reserve Bank of New York, Law Library
59 Maiden Ln, 32nd Fl, New York, NY 10045 (212) 791-5012
Lib Type Law.
Spec Subs Banking law.
Ref Servs Avail Not open to the general public; restricted to staff.

2037. Federal Reserve Bank of New York, Research Library
Federal Reserve PO Station, 33 Liberty St, New York, NY 10045
(212) 791-5670
Lib Type Special.
Spec Subs Federal Reserve System; banking; money & credit; central banking; economic & business conditions; international monetary affairs; gold; government finance.
Info Ret Servs DIALOG; NEXIS. *Shared Catalog Nets* OCLC. *Coop Lib Nets* NY Metropolitan Reference & Research Library Agency; FEDLINK.

2038. Federal Reserve Bank of Philadelphia, Information Services & Research Library
PO Box 66, 100 N 6th St, Philadelphia, PA 19105 (215) 574-6540
Admin Aileen C Boer. *Ref Lib* Deborah Naulty. *ILL* Carol Aldridge. *Acq Lib* Barbara Turnbull.
Lib Type Special.
Spec Subs Economic; banking. *Spec Collecs* Karl Bopp collection on central banking.
Info Ret Servs DIALOG; SDC; VU/TEXT. *Shared Catalog Nets* OCLC. *Coop Lib Nets* PALINET.
Circ Servs Avail To other libraries.
Ref Servs Avail To other Federal libraries; to other libraries; to the general public.

2039. Federal Reserve Bank of Richmond, Baltimore Branch Library
PO Box 1378, 502 S Sharp St, Baltimore, MD 21203 (301) 576-3392
Lib Type Special.
Spec Subs Banking; economics; Federal Reserve System; Maryland economic conditions; monetary policy; money.

2040. Federal Reserve Bank of Richmond, Research Library
PO Box 27622, 701 E Byrd St, Richmond, VA 23161 (804) 643-1250 ext 3131
Admin Ruth M E Cannon. *Ref Lib* Susan Cash. *ILL* Monique Leroux.
Lib Type Special.
Spec Subs Banking; economics; monetary policy; business. *Spec Collecs* State data on the following 5th Federal Reserve District states: VA, MD, WV, NC, & SC.
Info Ret Servs DIALOG. *Shared Catalog Nets* OCLC; FEDLINK.
Circ Servs Avail To other Federal libraries; to other libraries; restricted to general public by appointment.
Ref Servs Avail To other Federal libraries; to other libraries; restricted to Federal Reserve info.

2041. Federal Reserve Bank of St Louis, Research Library
Box 442, 411 Locust St, Saint Louis, MO 63166 (314) 444-8552; ILL 444-8551
Lib Type Special.
Spec Subs Banking; economics; money.
Shared Catalog Nets OCLC. *Coop Lib Nets* Midwest Region Library Network.

2042. Federal Reserve Bank of San Francisco, Research Library
PO Box 7702, San Francisco, CA 94120 (415) 974-3216
Admin Miriam Ciochon. *Ref Lib* Nyra Krstovich; Patricia Rea.
Lib Type Special.
Spec Subs Economics; banking. *Spec Collecs* Economic conditions of the Pacific Basin.
Info Ret Servs DIALOG; NEXIS; DataTimes. *Shared Catalog Nets* RLIN.
Circ Servs Avail To other libraries.
Ref Servs Avail To other Federal libraries; to other libraries; restricted to the general public by appointment.

Federal Trade Commission

2043. Federal Trade Commission, Atlanta Regional Office Library
1718 Peachtree St NW, Rm 1000, Atlanta, GA 30309 (404) 881-4836
Lib Type Special.
Spec Collecs Legal collection.

2044. Federal Trade Commission, Cleveland Regional Office Library
118 St Clair, Cleveland, OH 44144 (216) 522-4207
Lib Type Special.

2045. Federal Trade Commission, Dallas Regional Office Library
8303 Elmbrook Dr, Dallas, TX 75247 (214) 767-7053; FTS 729-7053
Admin Steven E Weart.
Lib Type Law.
Spec Subs Trade regulation; consumer protection; antitrust. *Spec Collecs* FTC decisions; CCH Trade Regulation Reporter. *In-house Files* FTC staff reports.
Circ Servs Avail To other Federal libraries; to other libraries.
Ref Servs Avail To other Federal libraries; to other libraries; to the general public.

2046. Federal Trade Commission, Law Library
6th & Pennsylvania Ave NW, Washington, DC 20580 (202) 523-3768; FTS 523-3768
Admin Susanne B Perella. *Ref Lib* Catherine Harman. *ILL* Estelle Hammonds. *Acq Lib* Sharon Humphries.
Lib Type Law.
Spec Subs Law; business; economics. *Spec Collecs* FTC materials.
Info Ret Servs DIALOG; LEXIS; NEXIS; WESTLAW. *Shared Catalog Nets* OCLC. *Coop Lib Nets* FEDLINK.
Circ Servs Avail To other libraries.
Ref Servs Avail To the general public.

2047. Federal Trade Commission Library
55 E Monroe St, Rm 1437, Chicago, IL 60603 (312) 353-5261; FTS 353-5261
Admin Christine Genda.
Lib Type Law.
Spec Subs Antitrust & trade regulation.
Ref Servs Avail Not open to the general public; restricted to employees.

2048. Federal Trade Commission Library
6th & Pennsylvania Ave NW, Rm 630, Washington, DC 20580 (202) 523-3871
Admin Suzanne B Perella. *Ref Lib* Catherine Harman. *ILL* Estelle Hammonds. *Acq Lib* Sharon Humphries.
Lib Type Special.
Spec Subs Law; business; economics. *Spec Collecs* FTC archives & legislative history.
Lib Deposit Designation Census.
Info Ret Servs DIALOG; LEXIS; NEXIS; WESTLAW; in-house legal research system. *Shared Catalog Nets* OCLC. *Coop Lib Nets* FEDLINK.
Circ Servs Avail To other libraries.
Ref Servs Avail To the general public.

2049. Federal Trade Commission, San Francisco Regional Office Library
PO Box 36005, 450 Golden Gate Ave, San Francisco, CA 94102 (415) 556-1270
Lib Type Special.

General Services Administration

2050. General Services Administration, Design & Construction Division Library
1500 E Bannister Rd, Kansas City, MO 64141 (816) 926-7082; FTS 926-7082
Admin Sandra S Little.
Lib Type Special.
Spec Subs Architectural; mechanical; electrical. *In-house Files* Specifications.
Circ Servs Avail To other Federal libraries; not open to the general public.
Ref Servs Avail To other Federal libraries; not open to the general public.

2051. General Services Administration Library
18th & F Sts NW, Rm 1033, Washington, DC 20405 (202) 535-7788; FTS 535-7788
Admin Gail L Kohlhorst. *Ref Lib* Darwin Koester (ILL). *Acq Lib* Nancy Mann.
Lib Type Law; Engineering & Science.
Spec Subs Law; contracts; architecture; engineering; ADP; telecommunications. *Spec Collecs* Karel Yasko collection; FAI Procurement collection.
Lib Deposit Designation GPO Depository Library.
Info Ret Servs DIALOG; NEXIS; WESTLAW; TAURUS. *Shared Catalog Nets* OCLC. *Coop Lib Nets* FEDLINK. *Elec Mail Nets* ITT DIALCOM.
Circ Servs Avail To other Federal libraries; to other libraries.
Ref Servs Avail To other Federal libraries; to other libraries; to the general public.

2052. General Services Administration, National Capitol Regional Library
7th & D Sts SW, Washington, DC 20007 (202) 472-1247
Admin Katrina E Baltimore.
Lib Type Law.
Shared Catalog Nets OCLC.
Circ Servs Avail To other Federal libraries.
Ref Servs Avail To other Federal libraries; to other libraries; to the general public.

Interstate Commerce Commission

2053. Interstate Commerce Commission Library
12th St & Constitution Ave NW, Rm 3392, Washington, DC 20423 (202) 275-7328; 275-7119 (References Services Unit)
Lib Type Special.
Spec Subs Administrative law, economic regulations; transportation law & history; statistics; valuation; finance. *Spec Collecs* Congressional Materials; US & Canada Regulatory Commissions, reports; transportation in the US; rare books & documents.
Circ Servs Avail Restricted to reference use only.
Ref Servs Avail Restricted to reference use only.

2054. Interstate Commerce Commission, Regional Library
219 S Dearborn St, Rm 1304, Chicago, IL 60614 (312) 886-6403; FTS 886-6403; TTY 886-6403
Admin Barbara J Welsch; Yvonne Anagnot.
Lib Type Law.
Spec Subs Interstate Commerce Act & regulations.
Ref Servs Avail To other Federal libraries; to other libraries; to the general public.

Merit Systems Protection Board

2055. US Merit Systems Protection Board Library
1120 Vermont Ave NW, Rm 828, Washington, DC 20419 (202) 653-7132; FTS 653-7132
Admin Kathleen P O'Sullivan.
Lib Type Law.
Spec Subs Federal personnel law. *Spec Collecs* Legislative histories on Federal personnel laws.
Lib Deposit Designation GPO Depository Library.

Info Ret Servs LEXIS. *Coop Lib Nets* Washington Metro Library Council.
Circ Servs Avail To other Federal libraries; to other libraries; not open to the general public.
Ref Servs Avail To other Federal libraries; to other libraries; to the general public.

National Aeronautics & Space Administration

2056. John F Kennedy Space Center Library
Kennedy Space Center, FL 32899 (305) 867-4540 (Lib Mgr); -3615 (Project); -2407 (Archives); -3600 (Circulation); -3613 (Documents); -2602 (Acq)
Admin H Brown (NASA/KSC); V A Rapetti (NWSI Contractor Project Mgr). *Ref Lib* Marion Rawls. *ILL* Deborah Guelzow (Acq).
Lib Type Engineering & Science.
Spec Subs Launch documents. *Spec Collecs* Archives.
Info Ret Servs DIALOG; BRS; CIS; CAS ONLINE; MEDLARS; HAZARDLINE. *Shared Catalog Nets* NASA NALNET. *Coop Lib Nets* NASA NALNET.
Circ Servs Avail To other Federal libraries; to other libraries.
Ref Servs Avail To other Federal libraries; to other libraries.

2057. Lewis Research Center Library
21000 Brookpark Rd, Cleveland, OH 44135 (216) 433-4000
Admin Dorothy Morris.
Lib Type Special.

2058. George C Marshall Space Flight Center Technical Library
ATTN: CN24L/Technical Library, Marshall Space Flight Center, AL 35812 (205) 453-1880; FTS 872-1880
Admin Annette K Tingle. *ILL* Oma Lou White.
Lib Type Special.
Lib Deposit Designation NASA.
Info Ret Servs DIALOG. *Coop Lib Nets* NASA/RECON.
Circ Servs Avail Not open to the general public.
Ref Servs Avail To other Federal libraries.

2059. NASA-AMES Research Center Library
N-202-3, Moffett Field, CA 94035-4000 (415) 694-5157; FTS 464-5157
Lib Type Special.
Spec Subs Aerospace engineering; astronomy; astrophysics; computer science & applications; fluid dynamics; mathematics.
Info Ret Servs DIALOG. *Shared Catalog Nets* NASA Library Network.

2060. NASA-AMES Research Center, Life Sciences Library
Mail Stop 239-13, Moffett Field, CA 94035 (415) 694-5387
Lib Type Engineering & Science.
Spec Subs Aviation & aerospace medicine; biomedicine; biotechnology; planetary biology; origin of life. *Spec Collecs* Biogenesis Collection; Evolution Genetics; Biochemistry (Origin of Life Collection).
Info Ret Servs DIALOG; NASA/RECON; MEDLINE. *Shared Catalog Nets* RLIN.
Ref Servs Avail Restricted to reference use only.

2061. NASA-AMES Research Center, Technical Library
Moffett Field, CA 94035 (415) 694-5157; FTS 464-5157
Admin Sarah C Dueker. *Ref Lib* Daniel Pappas. *ILL* Kathleen Ponce. *Acq Lib* Caroline Payne.
Lib Type Engineering & Science.
Spec Subs Aeronautics; astronautics; fluid mechanics; mathematics; space biology.
Info Ret Servs DIALOG; BRS. *Shared Catalog Nets* RLIN; Aerospace Research Information Network (ARIN). *Coop Lib Nets* South Bay Cooperative Library Network (SOUTHNET). *Elec Mail Nets* GTE Telemail; CLASS; OnTyme.
Circ Servs Avail Restricted to NASA.
Ref Servs Avail Restricted to NASA.

2062. NASA Dryden Flight Research Center Library
PO Box 273, Edwards AFB, CA 93523 (805) 258-3702 ext 334;
FTS 961-3702
Lib Type Special.
Spec Subs Aeronautics; aircraft; biomedical; fluid mechanics; instrumentation & data recording.
Info Ret Servs DIALOG. *Coop Lib Nets* NASA Library Network.
Ref Servs Avail Restricted to controlled admittance to center.

2063. NASA Goddard Institute for Space Studies Library
2880 Broadway, Rm 710, New York, NY 10025 (212) 678-5613;
FTS 664-5613
Lib Type Special.
Spec Subs Astronomy; astrophysics; geophysics; math; meteorology; physics; planetary atmospheres; remote sensing of environment.
Info Ret Servs DIALOG; NASA/Recon.

2064. NASA Goddard Space Flight Center Library
Library Code 252, Greenbelt Rd, Greenbelt, MD 20771 (301) 344-7000
Lib Type Special.
Spec Subs Astronomy; electronics; mathematics; physics; remote sensing; satellite communication; space science.
Coop Lib Nets NASA Library Network.

2065. NASA Goddard Space Flight Center, Wallops Flight Facility Library
Wallops Island, VA 23337 (804) 824-3411 ext 389; FTS 928-5389
Lib Type Special.
Spec Subs Aerospace; physical, mathematical, & applied science.
Coop Lib Nets NASA Library Network.

2066. NASA Lyndon B Johnson Space Center, Technical Library
Code JM2, Houston, TX 77058 (713) 483-4048; FTS 525-4048
Lib Type Engineering & Science.
Spec Subs Aeronautics; astronautics; computer science; earth resources; engineering; geosciences; life science; mathematics; physics; space science; space shuttles; space stations.
Shared Catalog Nets OCLC. *Coop Lib Nets* FEDLINK.
Circ Servs Avail Not open to the general public; restricted to NASA personnel & contractors.
Ref Servs Avail Not open to the general public; restricted to NASA personnel & contractors.

2067. NASA Langley Research Center, Technical Library
Bldg 1194, Langley AFB, Hampton, VA 23665 (804) 865-2630;
FTS 928-2786
Lib Type Special.
Spec Subs Aerospace science & technology.

2068. NASA-National Space Technology Laboratories, Research Library
NSTL, MS 39529 (601) 688-3244; FTS 494-3244
Admin Mary Bush Meighen. *Ref Lib* Michael Correro. *ILL* Doug Wills.
Lib Type Special.
Spec Subs Remote sensing; environmental sciences; ecology; cryogenics & atmospheric sciences.
Info Ret Servs DIALOG; BRS; SDC; NASA/Recon. *Shared Catalog Nets* OCLC; NASA/ARIN. *Coop Lib Nets* FEDLINK. *Elec Mail Nets* Telemail.
Circ Servs Avail To other Federal libraries; to other libraries; not open to the general public; restricted to ILL.
Ref Servs Avail To other Federal libraries; to other libraries.

2069. NASA Headquarters, S & T Library & Systems Support
Code NHS-4, 600 Independence Ave SW, Washington, DC 20546
(202) 453-8526/8545/8526; FTS 453-8545
Admin Eleanor M Burdette (Head). *Ref Lib* Barbara A Williams (On Site Project Manager; ILL, Acq).
Lib Type Special.
Spec Subs Aeronautics, astronautics & related subjects in the basic & applied physical sciences; engineering & social sciences including management, especially institutional management. *Spec*

Collecs Comprehensive collection of NASA formal publications & other reports in the NASA scientific & technical information system available in microfiche form; complete collection of formal publications of the National Advisory Committee for Aeronautics (NACA), predecessor of NASA.
Info Ret Servs DIALOG; CQ Washington Alert; Aerospace Online; DTIC/DROLS; Faxon/LINX. *Shared Catalog Nets* OCLC.
Coop Lib Nets NASA/RECON; NASA Library Network (NALNET). *Elec Mail Nets* NASAMAIL.
Circ Servs Avail To other Federal libraries; to other libraries.
Ref Servs Avail To other Federal libraries; to other libraries; to the general public; restricted to security regulations.

National Archives & Records Administration

2070. Jimmy Carter Library
One Copenhill Ave NE, Atlanta, GA 30307 (404) 331-3942; FTS 242-3942
Admin Donald B Schewe (Dir). *Ref Lib* Martin Elzy. *ILL* Robert Bohanan.
Lib Type Presidential.
Spec Subs Presidency, 1977-81. *Spec Collecs* While House files.
Info Ret Servs DIALOG; WILSONLINE. *Shared Catalog Nets* OCLC. *Coop Lib Nets* FEDLINK. *Elec Mail Nets* Datapoint E-Mail.
Circ Servs Avail Not open to the general public.
Ref Servs Avail To other Federal libraries; to other libraries; to the general public.

2071. Dwight D Eisenhower Library
SE 4th St, Abilene, KS 67410 (913) 263-4751; FTS 752-2580
Admin John Wickman. *Ref Lib* James Leyerzapf. *ILL* Bonnie Mulanax. *Acq Lib* Dwight Strandberg.
Lib Type Presidential.
Spec Subs Dwight D Eisenhower; Eisenhower administration; World War II, European theater; US Presidency.
Elec Mail Nets National presidential library system (NARA).
Circ Servs Avail Restricted to manuscript finding aids & oral history transcripts.
Ref Servs Avail To other Federal libraries; to other libraries; to the general public.

2072. Gerald R Ford Library
1000 Beal Ave, Ann Arbor, MI 48104 (313) 668-2218; FTS 378-2218
Admin Don W Wilson.
Lib Type Presidential.
Spec Subs The life & political career of President Gerald R Ford; strengths include domestic, international, & economic affairs; domestic & foreign policy issues & legislation; politics & the 1976 presidential election. *Spec Collecs* Large collection of government documents 1974-77.
Elec Mail Nets National Archives presidential library system (NARA).
Ref Servs Avail To other Federal libraries; to other libraries; to the general public.

2073. Herbert Hoover Presidential Library
234 S Downey, West Branch, IA 52358 (319) 643-5301; FTS 863-6374
Admin Robert S Wood. *Ref Lib* Mildred Mather. *ILL* Shirley Sondergard (Acq).
Lib Type Presidential.
Spec Subs 20th century history; economics & social.
Elec Mail Nets National presidential library system (NARA).
Circ Servs Avail To other Federal libraries; to other libraries; not open to the general public; restricted to researchers & staff.
Ref Servs Avail To other Federal libraries; to other libraries; to the general public.

2074. John F Kennedy Presidential Library
Columbia Point, Boston, MA 02125 (617) 929-4500; ILL 929-4543; FTS 840-4500
Admin Ronald E Whealan.
Lib Type Presidential.

Spec Subs 20th century American history; politics & government of the 1960s. *Spec Collecs* Ernest Hemingway Collection; the life & times of John F Kennedy; mid-20th century American politics & government; oral history.
Elec Mail Nets NARA E-Mail System.

2075. National Archives & Records Administration, Fort Worth Branch
PO Box 6216, 501 W Felix St, Fort Worth, TX 76115 (817) 334-5525; FTS 334-5525
Admin Kent Carter (Dir).
Lib Type Special.
Spec Collecs Record Group 21, records of US District Courts in TX, OK, AR, & LA; Record Group 75, records of the Bureau of Indian Affairs, primarily OK; Record Group 276, records of US Court of Appeals, 5th Circuit.
Lib Deposit Designation Federal agencies in 5-state area of LA, AR, TX, OK, & NM.
Elec Mail Nets Datapoint (internal system).
Ref Servs Avail To other Federal libraries; to the general public.

2076. National Archives & Records Administration, Philadelphia Branch
9th & Market Sts Rm 1350, Philadelphia, PA 19107 (215) 597-3000; FTS 597-3000
Admin Robert J Plowman (Dir). *Ref Lib* Judith Malott. *Acq Lib* Joseph J Sheehan.
Lib Type Special.
Spec Subs Legal; governmental.
Circ Servs Avail Restricted to agency creating document.
Ref Servs Avail To the general public.

2077. National Archives & Records Center, Kansas City Branch
2312 E Bannister Rd, Kansas City, MO 64131 (816) 926-7271; FTS 926-7271
Admin R Reed Whitaker (Dir). *Ref Lib* Mark Corriston.
Lib Type Special.
In-house Files Government agency files.
Lib Deposit Designation Federal Agencies (40).
Circ Servs Avail To other Federal libraries; restricted to creating agency.
Ref Servs Avail To other Federal libraries; to other libraries; to the general public.

2078. National Archives Library
Library & Printed Archives Branch (NNIL), Central Info Div, 8th & Pennsylvania Ave, NW, Washington, DC 20408 (202) 523-3218; FTS 523-3049
Admin Charles F Downs II. *Ref Lib* Trudy Dittmar-Hardcastle. *ILL* Caroline Ladiera. *Acq Lib* Veronica Williams.
Lib Type Special.
Spec Subs US history; federal government administrative history; archival science & records management. *Spec Collecs* Archival science collection (Arcol or Box collection).
Lib Deposit Designation GPO Depository Library.
Info Ret Servs DIALOG; Congress CQ Washington Alert; RLIN. *Shared Catalog Nets* OCLC. *Coop Lib Nets* FLICC/FEDLINK.
Circ Servs Avail To other Federal libraries; to other libraries; not open to the general public.
Ref Servs Avail To other Federal libraries; to other libraries; to the general public.

2079. Franklin D Roosevelt Library
259 Albany Post Rd, Hyde Park, NY 12538 (914) 229-8114; FTS 883-5444
Admin William Emerson (Dir); Sheryl Griffith (Lib, Ref, Acq). *Ref Lib* Frances Seeber (Archives). *ILL* Susan Bingler. *Acq Lib* Raymond Teichman (Archives).
Lib Type Presidential.
Spec Subs Lives & times of Franklin & Eleanor Roosevelt. *Spec Collecs* US Naval history; Hudson Valley history; early juveniles. *In-house Files* Approximately 200 manuscript collection, papers of Franklin & Eleanor Roosevelt & their associates.
Lib Deposit Designation NARA; DoD history offices.
Coop Lib Nets Southeastern NY Library Resources Council.
Circ Servs Avail Restricted to ILL limited.

Ref Servs Avail To other Federal libraries; to other libraries; not open to the general public; restricted to qualified researchers upon application.

2080. Harry S Truman Library
Independence, MO 64050 (816) 833-1400; FTS 750-1400
Admin Benedict K Zobrist. *Ref Lib* George Curtis. *ILL* Elizabeth Safly. *Acq Lib* John T Curry.
Lib Type Presidential.
Spec Subs Career of Harry S Truman; history of the Truman administration. *Spec Collecs* Papers of Harry S Truman.
Elec Mail Nets National presidential library system (NARA).
Circ Servs Avail Not open to the general public.
Ref Servs Avail To other Federal libraries; to other libraries; to the general public.

National Credit Union Administration

2081. National Credit Union Administration, General Counsel's Library
1776 G St NW, Washington, DC 20456 (202) 357-1030
Admin Lawrence Spearman.
Lib Type Law.
Spec Collecs Journals of the Credit Union National Assn (CUNA) & National Assn of Federal Credit Unions.
Circ Servs Avail To other Federal libraries.
Ref Servs Avail To other Federal libraries; to other libraries; to the general public; restricted to use by appointment.

National Foundation for the Arts & the Humanities

2082. National Endowment for the Arts Library
1100 Pennsylvania Ave NW, Washington, DC 20506 (202) 682-5485
Admin M Christine Morrison.
Lib Type Special.
Spec Subs Arts management; cultural policy; federal aid to the arts.
Coop Lib Nets Metropolitan Washington Library Council.
Circ Servs Avail To other Federal libraries; to other libraries.
Ref Servs Avail To other Federal libraries; to other libraries; restricted to the general public by appointment only.

2083. National Endowment for the Humanities Library
1100 Pennsylvania Ave NW, Rm 216, Washington, DC 20506 (202) 786-0244/0245
Admin Jeannette Coletti.
Lib Type Special.
Spec Subs Humanities; political science & current affairs. *Spec Collecs* Books resulting form NEH grants. *In-house Files* Collections of documents relating to NEH history.
Info Ret Servs DIALOG.
Circ Servs Avail To other Federal libraries; to other libraries; not open to the general public.
Ref Servs Avail To other Federal libraries; to other libraries; not open to the general public.

National Labor Relations Board

2084. National Labor Relations Board Library
1717 Pennsylvania Ave NW, Rm 900, Washington, DC 20570 (202) 254-9055
Admin Barbara W Hazelett.
Lib Type Law.
Spec Subs Labor relations law; labor history; economics & political science. *Spec Collecs* Collection includes nearly everything published by & about the NLRB & the National Labor Relations Act, as amended. *In-house Files* Legislative histories of laws of interest to the agency, including bankruptcy laws, appropriations laws, & freedom of information laws.
Info Ret Servs DIALOG; WESTLAW; Dun & Bradstreet Reports. *Shared Catalog Nets* OCLC.
Circ Servs Avail To other Federal libraries; to other libraries.

Ref Servs Avail To other Federal libraries; to other libraries; to the general public.

National Science Foundation

2085. National Science Foundation Library
1800 G St NW, Rm 245, Washington, DC 20550 (202) 357-7811
Admin Edna James-Morris. *Ref Lib* Florence Heckman (ILL). *Acq Lib* Joanne Cooper.
Lib Type Engineering & Science.
Spec Subs General works & recent research developments in the fields of astronomical, atmospheric, earth, & ocean sciences; biological, behavioral, & social sciences; mathematical, chemical, physical, & computer sciences; engineering; materials & environmental sciences; information science & technology; & polar research. *Spec Collecs* Science policy; technological innovations; current college & university catalogs on microfiche.
Info Ret Servs DIALOG. *Shared Catalog Nets* OCLC. *Coop Lib Nets* FEDLINK.
Circ Servs Avail To other Federal libraries; to other libraries; to the general public; restricted to ILL with loan form.
Ref Servs Avail To other Federal libraries; to other libraries; to the general public.

2086. National Solar Observatory, Technical Library
Sunspot, NM 88349 (505) 434-1390 ext 224; FTS 571-0224
Admin John Cornett.
Lib Type Engineering & Science.
Spec Subs Solar astronomy; physics; optics; computer science. *Spec Collecs* NSO staff publications; solar spectral atlases; stellar catalogs (magnetic tape). *In-house Files* NSO publications list; serial holdings; book acquisitions.
Info Ret Servs DIALOG. *Shared Catalog Nets* OCLC. *Coop Lib Nets* FEDLINK.
Circ Servs Avail To other Federal libraries; to other libraries; not open to the general public; restricted to professionals in solar physics.
Ref Servs Avail To other Federal libraries; to other libraries.

Nuclear Regulatory Commission

2087. Nuclear Regulatory Commission Library
Washington, DC 20555 (202) 492-7748
Admin Margaret H Conyngham. *Ref Lib* Eileen Chen. *Acq Lib* John O Redmond.
Lib Type Engineering & Science.
Spec Subs Nuclear science, engineering, & radiation; biology; energy; environmental science. *Spec Collecs* Codes & standards; International Atomic Energy Agency publications; technical reports.
Info Ret Servs DIALOG; BRS; DOE/RECON; DROLS. *Shared Catalog Nets* OCLC. *Coop Lib Nets* Interlibrary Users Assoc (IUA).
Circ Servs Avail To other Federal libraries; to other libraries; restricted to members of IUA.
Ref Servs Avail To other Federal libraries; to other libraries; to the general public.

Occupational Safety & Health Review Commission

2088. Occupational Safety & Health Review Commission Library
1825 K St NW, Rm 400, Washington, DC 20006 (202) 634-7933
Admin Roscoe J Christian.
Lib Type Law.
In-house Files OSHRC decisions.
Info Ret Servs WESTLAW. *Coop Lib Nets* FEDLINK.
Circ Servs Avail To other Federal libraries; to other libraries.
Ref Servs Avail To other Federal libraries; to other libraries; to the general public.

U.S. Office of Personnel Management

2089. US Office of Personnel Management Library
1900 E St NW, Rm 5L45, Washington, DC 20415 (202) 632-7640; 632-7640
Admin Catherine Tashjean. *Ref Lib* Leon Brody. *ILL* Edna Johnson. *Acq Lib* Phyllis Lindsey.
Lib Type Law.
Spec Subs Personnel management; public administration; civil service; management. *Spec Collecs* Ishmar Baruch Collection (position classification). *In-house Files* Personnel Management Evaluation Reports, compiled by the Compliance & Evaluation Office of OPM.
Lib Deposit Designation GPO Depository Library.
Info Ret Servs DIALOG; BRS. *Coop Lib Nets* Federal Law Librarians' Assoc; FLICC.
Circ Servs Avail To other Federal libraries; to other libraries; not open to the general public; restricted to ILL in DC metro area.
Ref Servs Avail To other Federal libraries; to other libraries; to the general public.

Peace Corps

2090. Peace Corps Information Services, Division Library
806 Connecticut Ave NW, Rm M407, Washington, DC 20526 (202) 254-3307; FTS 254-3307
Admin Rita C Warpeha. *Ref Lib* Victoria Fries (ILL).
Lib Type Special.
Spec Subs Asia; the Pacific; Africa; Latin America & the Caribbean; foreign language learning textbooks.
Info Ret Servs DIALOG. *Shared Catalog Nets* OCLC. *Coop Lib Nets* FLICC; Metro Washington Library Council.
Circ Servs Avail To other libraries.
Ref Servs Avail To other Federal libraries; to other libraries; to the general public.

Pennsylvania Avenue Development Corporation

2091. Pennsylvania Avenue Development Corporation, Law Library
1331 Pennsylvania Ave NW, Ste 1220N, Washington, DC 20004 (202) 724-9088
Admin Robert E McCally (General Counsel).
Lib Type Law.
Spec Subs Real estate; land acquisition.
Circ Servs Avail To other Federal libraries.
Ref Servs Avail To other Federal libraries; to other libraries; to the general public; restricted to use by appointment.

Pension Benefit Guaranty Corporation

2092. Pension Benefit Guaranty Corporation, Legal Department, Law Library
2020 K St NW, Ste 7200, Washington, DC 20006 (202) 956-5021
Admin Richard F Cousins.
Lib Type Law.
Spec Subs Law; pensions; employee benefits.
Lib Deposit Designation GPO Depository Library.
Circ Servs Avail Not open to the general public; restricted to PBGC staff.
Ref Servs Avail To other libraries; not open to the general public; restricted to PBGC staff.

Postal Rate Commission

2093. Postal Rate Commission Library
1333 H St NW, Washington, DC 20268-0001 (202) 789-6877
Admin Louise Voss-Goldblatt.
Lib Type Special; Law.
Spec Subs Postal Rate Commission cases. *In-house Files* Legislative & subject files related to the PRC.

Circ Servs Avail Not open to the general public.
Ref Servs Avail To other Federal libraries; to other libraries; to the general public.

Railroad Retirement Board

2094. Railroad Retirement Board Library
844 Rush St, Rm 800, Chicago, IL 60611 (312) 751-4926; FTS 387-4926
Admin Kay G Collins.
Lib Type Law.
Spec Subs Social insurance. *In-house Files* Legislative histories of Railroad Retirement Acts, Railroad Unemployment Insurance Act, & others.
Shared Catalog Nets OCLC. *Coop Lib Nets* Chicago Library System (CLS).
Circ Servs Avail To other Federal libraries; to other libraries; not open to the general public.
Ref Servs Avail To other Federal libraries; to other libraries; not open to the general public.

2095. Railroad Retirement Board Library
2000 L St, NW, Ste 558, Washington, DC 20036 (202) 653-9540
Admin David Lucci (Legislative Counsel). *Ref Lib* Margaret Stanley.
Lib Type Special.
Ref Servs Avail To other Federal libraries; restricted to use by the general public with permission.

Securities & Exchange Commission

2096. US Securities & Exchange Commission Library
Stop C-2, 450 5th St NW, Rm 1C00, Washington, DC 20549 (202) 272-2618; FTS 272-2618
Admin Charlene C Derge.
Lib Type Special.
Spec Subs Law; corporate & general finance; economics; accounting; public utilities; stock market.
Info Ret Servs LEXIS; NEXIS (for staff use only). *Shared Catalog Nets* OCLC.
Circ Servs Avail To other libraries; restricted to DC Metro area.
Ref Servs Avail To other libraries.

Selective Service System

2097. Selective Service System Law Library
National Headquarters, Washington, DC 20435 (202) 724-1167
Admin Henry N Williams.
Lib Type Law.
Circ Servs Avail Not open to the general public.
Ref Servs Avail Not open to the general public; restricted to telephone inquiries.

Small Business Administration

2098. Small Business Administration, Reference Library
1441 L St NW, Washington, DC 20416 (202) 653-6914
Admin Margaret Hickey.
Lib Type Special.
Spec Subs Small business; venture capital.
Circ Servs Avail To other Federal libraries; to other libraries.
Ref Servs Avail To other Federal libraries; to other libraries; to the general public.

Tennessee Valley Authority

2099. National Fertilizer Library
Tennessee Valley Authority, Muscle Shoals, AL 35660 (205) 386-2871; FTS 872-8871
Admin Shirley G Nichols. *Ref Lib* Marcia Bystrom. *ILL* Janice Abernathy. *Acq Lib* Earline Pollard.
Lib Type Engineering & Science.

Spec Subs Fertilizers, manufacture, use, & marketing; biomass, ethanol form cellulose. *Spec Collecs* Fertilizers; biomass; developing countries. *In-house Files* TVA, Office of Agricultural & Chemical Development publications & internal research reports.
Info Ret Servs DIALOG; BRS; SDC; CAS ONLINE; CQ Washington Alert; NLM; STN; DOE/RECON. *Shared Catalog Nets* OCLC. *Coop Lib Nets* FEDLINK; North Alabama Union List of Serials (NAULS).
Circ Servs Avail To other Federal libraries; to other libraries; to the general public.
Ref Servs Avail To other Federal libraries; to other libraries; to the general public.

2100. Tennessee Valley Authority, Land Between The Lakes Library
Golden Pond, KY 42231 (502) 924-5602; FTS 592-6281
Admin Retta Balentine.
Lib Type Special.
Spec Subs Cultural, scientific, historical, educational, & recreational information. *Spec Collecs* Documented history of Land Between The Lakes; genealogical material on former residents; file on 220 cemeteries located within Land Between the Lakes; over 200 research & special studies on Land Between the Lakes. *In-house Files* Oral history.
Info Ret Servs DIALOG; BRS; SDC. *Shared Catalog Nets* OCLC. *Coop Lib Nets* FEDLINK; FLICC.
Circ Servs Avail To other Federal libraries; to other libraries; to the general public.
Ref Servs Avail To other Federal libraries; to other libraries; to the general public.

2101. Tennessee Valley Authority, Technical Library
400 W Summit Hill Dr, Knoxville, TN 37902 (615) 632-3464; FTS 856-3464
Admin Margaret J Bull. *Ref Lib* Edwin J Best, Jr. *ILL* Debra D Mills.
Lib Type Engineering & Science.
Spec Subs Engineering; management; water resources. *Spec Collecs* TVA historical collection. *In-house Files* TVA newspaper clippings, 1933-present.
Info Ret Servs DIALOG; BRS; SDC. *Shared Catalog Nets* OCLC.
Circ Servs Avail To other Federal libraries; to other libraries; to the general public.
Ref Servs Avail To other Federal libraries; to other libraries; to the general public.

2102. Tennessee Valley Authority, Technical Library
Signal Pl 1 N, 1101 Market St, Chattanooga, TN 37402 (615) 751-4913; FTS 858-4913
Admin Dean Robinson. *Ref Lib* Barbara Reavley (ILL). *Acq Lib* Francis Bishop.
Lib Type Special.
Spec Subs Fossil, hydro, & nuclear power production, distribution & consumption; related environmental considerations. *Spec Collecs* Electric Power Research Institute reports.
Lib Deposit Designation GPO Depository Library.
Info Ret Servs DIALOG; DOE/RECON. *Shared Catalog Nets* OCLC. *Coop Lib Nets* FEDLINK.
Circ Servs Avail To other Federal libraries; to other libraries; to the general public.
Ref Servs Avail To other Federal libraries; to other libraries; to the general public.

United States Arms Control & Disarmament Agency

2103. US Arms Control & Disarmament Agency Library
320 21st St NW, Washington, DC 20451 (202) 647-1592
Admin Diane A Ferguson.
Lib Type Special.
Spec Subs Disarmament; arms control; arms treaties & agreements; arms transfer activities; international peacekeeping proposals; nonproliferation of nuclear weapons; arms transfer activities; verification of treaty compliance; strategic arms limitation talks. *Spec Collecs* Conference of the Committee on Disarmament Documents; ACDA collection of books, international

conferences documents, congressional documents, & United Nations documents is located in the Special Collections Division of The George Washington University Library, Washington, DC.
Circ Servs Avail To other Federal libraries; to other libraries; to the general public.
Ref Servs Avail To other Federal libraries; to other libraries; to the general public.

United States Information Agency

2104. US Information Agency Library
301 4th St SW, Rm 135, Washington, DC 20547 (202) 485-8947
Admin Helen Amabile. *Ref Lib* Sara C Strom (Acq). *ILL* Elizabeth Craig-Davis.
Lib Type General.
Spec Subs US culture, history, politics, government; international relations; area studies; contemporary issues. *Spec Collecs* Publications & documents by & about USIA since inception; newspaper clippings.
Lib Deposit Designation GPO Depository Library.
Info Ret Servs DIALOG; OCLC; VU/TEXT; NEXIS; LEXIS; WILSONLINE; LEGI-SLATE; EdVent/ExVent. *Shared Catalog Nets* OCLC. *Coop Lib Nets* FEDLINK. *Elec Mail Nets* ITT DIALCOM.
Circ Servs Avail To other Federal libraries; to other libraries; not open to the general public.
Ref Servs Avail To other Federal libraries; not open to the general public.

2105. USIS Library, Centre Culturel Americain, Abidjan
BP 1866, Abidjan 01; Blvd de la Rocade, Angle, Ave de l'Entente, Cocody, Abidjan Ivory Coast
Lib Type General.

2106. USIS Library, American Center, Accra
PO Box 2288; 64 Sudan Rd, Accra Ghana
Lib Type General.

2107. USIS, Regional Library Consultant, Africa
American Embassy, BP 1712, Abidjan Ivory Coast
Lib Type General.

2108. USIS, Regional Library Consultant, Africa
American Embassy, PO Box 98, Monrovia Liberia
Lib Type General.

2109. USIS, Regional Library Consultant, Africa
American Embassy, PO Box 554, Lagos Nigeria
Lib Type General.

2110. USIS, Regional Library Consultant, Africa
PO Box 2155; American Embassy, Johannesburg South Africa
Lib Type General.

2111. USIS, Regional Library Consultant, Africa
American Embassy, PO Box 3180, Harare Zimbabwe
Lib Type General.

2112. USIS Library, American Cultural Center, Alexandria
3 Pharana St, Alexandria Egypt
Lib Type General.

2113. USIS Library, American Cultural Center, Algiers
8 Rue Ali Messaoud, Hydra, Algiers Algeria
Lib Type General.

2114. USIS, Country & Regional Library Officers, American Republics
Biblioteca Benjamin Franklin, Londres 16, Col Juarez, Mexico 06600, DF Mexico
Lib Type General.

2115. USIS, Country Library Director, American Republics
SES, Lote 3, Brasilia 70403 Brazil
Lib Type General.

2116. USIS, Regional Library Consultant, American Republics
American Embassy, Santo Domingo Dominican Republic
Lib Type General.

2117. USIS, Regional Library Consultant, American Republics
Lincoln Center Library, Florida 935, Buenos Aires 1005 Argentina
Lib Type General.

2118. USIS, American Center Library, Amman
Post Box 676; Jebel Amman, Third Circle, Amman Jordan
Lib Type General.

2119. USIS Library, Amerikan Kutuphanesi, Ankara
Cinnah Caddesi No 20, Kavaklidere, Ankara Turkey
Lib Type General.

2120. USIS Library, Centre Culturel Americain, Antananarivo
BP 620; 4, Lalana Dr Razafindratandra, Antananarivo Madagascar
Lib Type General.

2121. USIS, American Library, Athens
22 Massalias St, Athens 144 Greece
Lib Type General.

2122. USIS Library, American Center, Auckland
29 Shortland St, Auckland 1 New Zealand
Lib Type General.

2123. USIS, Bibliotheque de l'Ambassade des Etats-Unis de l'Amerique, Bamako
PO Box 34; Ave Mohd V et Rue Testard, Bamako Mali
Lib Type General.

2124. USIS Library, Beirut
c/o American Embassy, Beirut Lebanon
Lib Type General.

2125. USIS Library, Americki Centar, Belgrade
Cika Ljubina 19, 11000, Belgrade Yugoslavia
Lib Type General.

2126. USIS Library, Amerika Haus, Berlin
22-24 Hardenbergstrasse, D-1000 Berlin 12 Federal Republic of Germany
Lib Type General.

2127. USIS, American Center Library, Bombay
4 New Marine Lines, Bombay 400 020 India
Lib Type General.

2128. USIS Library, American Embassy, Bonn
Deichmanns Aue 29, D-5300 Bonn 2 Federal Republic of Germany
Lib Type General.

2129. USIS Library, Casa Thomas Jefferson, Brasilia
Entrequadras 706 & 906, Brasilia 70390 DF Brazil
Lib Type General.

2130. USIS Library, Centre Culturel Americain, Brazzaville
BP 1015; Ave Foch et Malamine, Brazzaville Congo
Lib Type General.

2131. USIS, The American Library, Brussels
Square du Bastion 1c, Brussels 1050 Belgium
Lib Type General.

2132. USIS, Biblioteca Americana, Bucharest
Str Alexandru Sahia No 7-9, Bucharest 70201 Romania
Lib Type General.

2133. USIS Library, Lincoln Center, Buenos Aires
Florida 935, Buenos Aires 1005 Argentina
Lib Type General.

2134. USIS, Bibliotheque Martin Luther King, Jr, Bujumbura
BP 810; 20-22 Chaussee Prince Louis, Rwagasore, Bujumbura Burundi
Lib Type General.

2135. USIS Library, American Center, Cairo
4, Ahmed Ragheb St, Garden City, Cairo Egypt
Lib Type General.

2136. USIS, American Center Library, Calcutta
7 Jawaharlal Nehru Rd, Calcutta 700 013 India
Lib Type General.

2137. USIS, American University Library, Calcutta
1 Bidhan Sarani, Calcutta 700 073 India
Lib Type General.

2138. USIS Library, American Center, Canberra
National Press Club Bldg, Suite 1, 16 National Circuit, Barton, Canberra, Australian Capitol Territory, 2600 Australia
Lib Type General.

2139. USIS Library, American Cultural Center, Capetown
2nd Fl, Scott's Bldg, 10 Plein St, Capetown 8001 South Africa
Lib Type General.

2140. USIS, Dar America Library, Casablanca
10, Place Bel Air, Casablanca Morocco
Lib Type General.

2141. USIS Library, Cebu
Osmena Blvd, Cebu City 6401 New Zealand
Lib Type General.

2142. USIS Library, Chiang Mai
24 Rajdamnoen Rd, Chiang Mai 50000 Thailand
Lib Type General.

2143. USIS Library, American Center, Christ Church
PO Box 4221; 4th Fl, Sun Alliance Bldg, 106 Gloucester St, Christ Church New Zealand
Lib Type General.

2144. USIS Library, American Center, Colombo
Flower Rd PO Box 1245; 39 Sir Ernest de Silva Mawatha, Colombo 7 Sri Lanka
Lib Type General.

2145. USIS Library, Centre Culturel Americain, Contonou
Blvd de France Pres du Conseil de L'Entente (BP 2014), Contonou Benin
Lib Type General.

2146. USIS, American Library, Copenhagen
Dag Hammerskjolds Alle 24, DK 2100 Copenhagen Denmark
Lib Type General.

2147. USIS Library, Centre Culturel Americain, Dakar
Post Box 49; Immeuble BIAO, 2, Place de l'Independance, Dakar Senegal
Lib Type General.

2148. USIS Library, American Cultural Center, Damascus
Post Box 29; 87 Ata Ayoubi St, Malki, Damascus Syria
Lib Type General.

2149. USIS Library, American Center, Dar es Salaam
PO Box 9170; Samora Ave, Dar es Salaam Tanzania
Lib Type General.

2150. USIS Library, Davao
Davao City Chamber of Commerce Bldg, J P Laurel Ave, Davao City 9501 Philippines
Lib Type General.

2151. USIS Library, American Cultural Center, Dhaka
House No 8, Rd No 9, Dhanmondi RA, Dhaka Bangladesh
Lib Type General.

2152. USIS Library, Centre Culturel Americain, Douala
PO Box 4045; Ave du President Ahmadou Ahidjo, Douala Cameroon
Lib Type General.

2153. USIS Library, American Cultural Center, Durban
2902 Durban Bay House, 333 Smith St, Durban 4001 South Africa
Lib Type General.

2154. USIS, Country Library Officer, Library Development Office, East Asia & Pacific
American Embassy, 10-5, Akasaka 1-chome, Minato-ku, Tokyo 107 Japan
Lib Type General.

2155. USIS, Regional Library Consultant, East Asia & Pacific
American Embassy, Medan Merdeka Selatan 5, Jakarta Indonesia
Lib Type General.

2156. USIS, Regional Library Consultant, East Asia & Pacific
125 S Sathorn Rd, Bangkok 10,120 Thailand
Lib Type General.

2157. USIS, Country Library Officer, Europe
American Embassy, Deichmanns Aue, 5300 Bonn 2 Federal Republic of Germany
Lib Type General.

2158. USIS, Regional Library Consultant, Europe
Biblioteca Americana, Via Veneto 62/B, Rome 00187 Italy
Lib Type General.

2159. USIS, Regional Library Consultant, Europe
American Embassy, IX Boltmanngasse 16 A-1901, Vienna Austria
Lib Type General.

2160. USIS, Regional Library Consultant, Europe
Centre de Documentation Benjamin Franklin, 2 rue St Florentin, Paris 75001 France
Lib Type General.

2161. USIS Library, Amerika Haus, Frankfurt
1 Staufenstrasse, D-6001 Frankfurt am Main 1 Federal Republic of Germany
Lib Type General.

2162. USIS Library, American Cultural Center, Freetown
8 Walpole St, Freetown Sierra Leone
Lib Type General.

2163. USIS, American Center Library, Fukuoka
1-3-36 Tenjin, Chuo-ku, Fukuoka 810 Japan
Lib Type General.

2164. USIS, American Library, Gaborone
PO Box 90; Badiredi House, The Mall, Gaborone Botswana
Lib Type General.

2165. USIS, John F Kennedy Library, Georgetown
PO Box 10888; 34A North & King Sts, Lacytown, Georgetown Guyana
Lib Type General.

2166. USIS, Biblioteca Benjamin Franklin, Guadalajara
Apdo Postal 1-1 Bis; Av Libertad 1492, Jalisco 44100, Guadalajara Mexico
Lib Type General.

2167. USIS Library, Amerika Haus, Hamburg
Tesdorpfstrasse 1, D-2000 Hamburg 13 Federal Republic of Germany
Lib Type General.

2168. USIS Library, Amerika Haus, Hannover
Prinzenstrass 9, Postfach 440; D-3000 Hannover 1 Federal Republic of Germany
Lib Type General.

2169. USIS Library, American Cultural Center, Harare
PO Box 4010; Century House East, 38 Baker Ave, Harare Zimbabwe
Lib Type General.

2170. USIS, American Center Library, Helsinki
Kaivokatu 10A, Helsinki 00100 Finland
Lib Type General.

2171. USIS, American Library, Hong Kong
United Centre, 1st Fl, Shopping Arcade, 95 Queensway, Central, Hong Kong Hong Kong
Lib Type General.

2172. USIS, American Center Library, Hyderabad
Hospital Rd, Hyderabad Pakistan
Lib Type General.

2173. USIS Library, American Cultural Center, Ibadan
Private Mail Bag 5089; DGC Enconsult House, Bodija, Ibadan Nigeria
Lib Type General.

2174. USIS, American Center Library, Islamabad
No 60, Blue Area, Sector F-6/4, Khayaban-E-Quaid-e-Azam, Islamabad Pakistan
Lib Type General.

2175. USIS Library, Amerikan Kutuphanesi, Istanbul
104-108 Mesrutiyet Caddesi, Tepebasi, Istanbul Turkey
Lib Type General.

2176. USIS Library, Amerikan Kutuphanesi, Izmir
PO Box 404; Sehit Nevres Bey Bulvari 23A, Izmir Turkey
Lib Type General.

2177. USIS, American Cultural Center Library, Jakarta
Wisma Metropolitan II, 3rd Fl, Jalan Jendral Sudirman 29, Jakarta Indonesia
Lib Type General.

2178. USIS Library, American Cultural Center, Jerusalem
Post Box 920; 19 Keren Hayesod St, Jerusalem 94188 Israel
Lib Type General.

2179. USIS Library, American Cultural Center, Johannesburg
3rd Fl, African Life Center, 111 Commissioner St, Johannesburg 2001 South Africa
Lib Type General.

2180. USIS Library, American Cultural Center, Kaduna
Private Mail Bag 2060; 5, Ahmadu Bello Way, Kaduna Nigeria
Lib Type General.

2181. USIS Library, American Center, Kandy
17 Malabar St, Kandy Sri Lanka
Lib Type General.

2182. USIS Library, American Cultural Center, Kano
Private Mail Bag 3059; Post Office Rd, Kano Nigeria
Lib Type General.

2183. USIS, American Center Library, Karachi
Collector's Lane, 8 Abdullah Haroom Rd, Karachi Pakistan
Lib Type General.

2184. USIS, American Library, Katmandu
PO Box 58; New Rd, Katmandu Nepal
Lib Type General.

2185. USIS Library, American Center, Khartoum
Post Box 699; Plot No 2, 4G, Khartoum East, Khartoum Sudan
Lib Type General.

2186. USIS Library, American Center, Kingston
PO Box 541; 2 Oxford Rd, Kingston 5 Jamaica
Lib Type General.

2187. USIS Library, Centre Culturel Americain, Kinshasa
BP 8622; Blvd du Trente Juin, Kinshasa Republic of Zaire
Lib Type General.

2188. USIS Library, Amerika Haus, Koln
Apostelnkloster 13/15, D-5000 Cologne 1 Federal Republic of Germany
Lib Type General.

2189. USIS, Biblioteka Amerykanska, Krakow
Konsulat Stanow Zjednoczonych Ameryki, Ulica Stolarska 9, Krakow Poland
Lib Type General.

2190. USIS, Lincoln Cultural Center Library, Kuala Lumpur
181, Jalan Ampang (PO Box 35, Kuala Lumpur 01-02), Kuala Lumpur 04-07 Malaysia
Lib Type General.

2191. USIS, American Cultural Center Library, Kwangju
No 80 Hwangkum-dong, Dong-ku, 500, Kwangju Republic of Korea
Lib Type General.

2192. USIS, American Center Library, Kyoto
Higashi Monzencho 657, Sokoku-ji, Kamigyo-ku, Kyoto 602 Japan
Lib Type General.

2193. USIS Library, Whitney M Young, Jr Resource Center, Lagos
PO Box 554; 2 Broad St, Lagos Nigeria
Lib Type General.

2194. USIS, American Center Library, Lahore
20, Shahrah-e-Fatima Jinnah, Lahore Pakistan
Lib Type General.

2195. USIS Library, Centre Culturel Americain, Libreville
PO Box 2237; 16 Ave du Colonel Parant, Libreville Gabon
Lib Type General.

2196. USIS Library, American Cultural Center, Lilongwe
PO Box 30373; Old Mutual Bldg, Robert Mugabe Crescent, City Center 3, Lilongwe Malawi
Lib Type General.

2197. USIS Library, Outreach/Reference Service, Lima
Jiron Washington 1592, Lima 1 Peru
Lib Type General.

2198. USIS, American Embassy, American Library, Lisbon
Av Das Forcas Armadas, Apartado 4258, Lisbon 1507 Portugal
Lib Type General.

2199. USIS Library, Americki Centar, Ljubljana
PO Box 287; Cankarjeva 11, Ljubljana 61000 Yugoslavia
Lib Type General.

2200. USIS Library, Centre Culturel Americain, Lome
BP 852; Angle Rue Pelletier & Rue Vauban, Lome Togo
Lib Type General.

2201. USIS, The Reference Center, London
55/56 Upper Brook St, London W1A United Kingdom
Lib Type General.

2202. USIS Library, Centre Culturel Americain, Lubumbashi
Post Box 2396; 3 Ave du Moero, Lubumbashi Republic of Zaire
Lib Type General.

2203. USIS, Martin Luther King Library, American Cultural Center, Lusaka
Post Box 32053; Veritas House, Heroes Place, Lusaka Zambia
Lib Type General.

2204. USIS, American Center Library, Madras
Gemini Circle, Madras 600 006 India
Lib Type General.

2205. USIS, Biblioteca Washington Irving, Centro Cultural de los Estados Unidos, Madrid
Marques de Villamagna 8, Madrid 28001 Spain
Lib Type General.

2206. USIS Library, Thomas Jefferson Cultural Center, Manila
395 Sen Gil J Puyat Ave, Makati, Metro Manila 3117 Philippines
Lib Type General.

2207. USIS Library, Dar America Marrakech
Ave Chouhada, L'Hivernage, Marrakech Morocco
Lib Type General.

2208. USIS Library, American Cultural Center, Maseru
PO Box 573; Kingsway Rd, Maseru 100 Lesotho
Lib Type General.

2209. USIS Library, American Cultural Center, Mbabane
PO Box 199; Allister Miller St, Mbabane Swaziland
Lib Type General.

2210. USIS Library, American Center, Melbourne
PO Box 507, 24 Albert Rd, South Melbourne, 3205 Australia
Lib Type General.

2211. USIS, Biblioteca Benjamin Franklin, Mexico City
Londres 16, Col Juarez, Mexico 06600, DF Mexico
Lib Type General.

2212. USIS Library, Milan
Via Bigli 11/A, Milan 20121 Italy
Lib Type General.

2213. USIS Library, Mogadishu
PO Box 574; 433 Via Primo Luglio, Mogadishu Somalia
Lib Type General.

2214. USIS Library, American Cultural Center, Monrovia
PO Box 98; 197 Ashmun St, Monrovia Liberia
Lib Type General.

2215. USIS, Biblioteca Artigas-Washington, Montevideo
Paraguay 1217 Uruguay
Lib Type General.

2216. USIS Library, Amerika Haus, Munchen
Karolinenplatz 3, D-8000 Munich 2 Federal Republic of Germany
Lib Type General.

2217. USIS, American Center Library, Nagoya
6th Fl, Nagoya Kokusai Senta Bldg, 1-47-1 Nagono, Nakamura-ku, Nagoya 450 Japan
Lib Type General.

2218. USIS Library, American Cultural Center, Nairobi
PO Box 30143; National Bank Bldg, Harambee Ave, Nairobi Kenya
Lib Type General.

2219. USIS, American Center Library, New Delhi
24, Kasturba Gandhi Marg, New Delhi 110 001 India
Lib Type General.

2220. USIS Library, Centre Culturel Americain, Niamey
PO Box 11201; Ave de la Liberte, Niamey Niger
Lib Type General.

2221. USIS Library, The American Center, Nicosia
33B Homer Ave, Nicosia Cyprus
Lib Type General.

2222. USIS, Country Library Officer, North Africa, Near East, & South Asia
American Center Library, 24, Kasturba Gandhi Marg, New Delhi 11001 India
Lib Type General.

2223. USIS, Regional Library Consultant, North Africa, Near East, & South Asia
American Embassy, Shalkh Isa Rd, Manama Bahrain
Lib Type General.

2224. USIS, Regional Library Consultant, North Africa, Near East, & South Asia
American Embassy, PO Box 1048, Islamabad Pakistan
Lib Type General.

2225. USIS, Regional Library Consultant, North Africa, Near East, & South Asia
Centre Culturel Americain, 2, Ave de France, Tunis Tunisia
Lib Type General.

2226. USIS, American Center Library, Osaka
2-4-9 Umeda, 6th Fl, Sankei Bldg, Kita-ku, Osaka 530 Japan
Lib Type General.

2227. USIS, US Reference Center, Oslo
Drammensveien 18, 0255 Oslo 2 Norway
Lib Type General.

2228. USIS Library, Centre Culturel Americain, Ouagadougou
BP 539; Ave Binger, Ouagadougou Burkina Faso
Lib Type General.

2229. USIS, Biblioteca Amador-Washington, Panama City
Edif Gusromares, Ave Balboa y Frederico Boyd; Apartado 6959, Panama 5 Panama
Lib Type General.

2230. USIS, Centre de Documentation, Benjamin Franklin, Paris
2, Rue St Florentin, Paris 75001 France
Lib Type General.

2231. USIS Library, American Center, Perth
9th Fl, Scottish Amicable House, 246 St George's Terrace, Perth, Western Australia, 6000 Australia
Lib Type General.

2232. USIS, American Center Library, Peshawar
17 Chinar Rd, University Town, Peshawar Pakistan
Lib Type General.

2233. USIS Library, American Center, Port of Spain
PO Box 752; 21 Marli St, Port of Spain Trinidad & Tobago
Lib Type General.

2234. USIS, Biblioteka Amerykanska, Poznan
Konsulat Stanow Zjednoczonych Ameryki, Ulica Chopina 4, Poznan Poland
Lib Type General.

2235. USIS, American Cultural Center Library, Pusan
No 24, 2-ka Dae Chung Dong, Chung-ku, Pusan 600 Republic of Korea
Lib Type General.

2236. USIS, Lincoln Library, Quito
PO Box 538; American Embassy, Avda Patria No 120 y 12 de Octubre, Quito Ecuador
Lib Type General.

2237. USIS Library, Dar America Rabat
35 Ave Al Fahs, Rabat-Souissi Morocco
Lib Type General.

2238. USIS Library, American Center, Rangoon
581 Merchant St (11182), Rangoon Burma
Lib Type General.

2239. USIS, American Library, American Cultural Center, Reykjavik
Neshagi 16, 107 Reykjavik Iceland
Lib Type General.

2240. USIS Reference Library, Rio de Janeiro
Av Presidente Wilson, 147-3rd Fl Andar, 20030 Rio de Janeiro RJ Brazil
Lib Type General.

2241. USIS, American Library, Rome
Via Veneto 119a, Rome 00187 Italy
Lib Type General.

2242. USIS, Biblioteca Lincoln, Santo Domingo
Ave Abraham Lincoln No 21, Santo Domingo Dominican Republic
Lib Type General.

2243. USIS Reference Library, Sao Paulo
Rua Pe Joao Manoel, 933, 01411 Sao Paulo SP Brazil
Lib Type General.

2244. USIS, American Center Library, Sapporo
Nishi 28-chome, Oodori, Chuo-ku, Sapporo 064 Japan
Lib Type General.

2245. USIS Library, Americki Centar, Sarajevo
PO Box 82; Omladinska broj 1, Sarajevo 71000 Yugoslavia
Lib Type General.

2246. USIS, American Cultural Center Library, Seoul
(CPO 277) 63, 1-ka, Ulchi-ro, Chung-ku, Seoul 100 Republic of Korea
Lib Type General.

2247. USIS, American Library Resource Center, Singapore
30 Hill St, Singapore 0617 Singapore
Lib Type General.

2248. USIS Library, Americki Centar, Skopje
PO Box 296; Grandski Zid, blok IV, Skopje 91000 Yugoslavia
Lib Type General.

2249. USIS, American Reading Room, Soweto
c/o Johannesburg Library; Ipelegeng Community Centre, 1860 White City Jabavu, Soweto South Africa
Lib Type General.

2250. USIS, American Reference Center, Stockholm
Strandvagen 101, Stockholm 11350 Sweden
Lib Type General.

2251. USIS Library, Amerika Haus, Stuttgart
Friedrichstrasse 23A, D-7000 Stuttgart-1 Federal Republic of Germany
Lib Type General.

2252. USIS Library, American Center, Sydney
T & G Tower, 36th Fl, Hyde Park Sq, Park & Elizabeth Sts, Sydney, New South Wales, 2000 Australia
Lib Type General.

2253. USIS, American Cultural Center Library, Taegu
No 45, 2-Ka, Sam Duk Dong, Chung-ku, Taegu 630 Republic of Korea
Lib Type General.

2254. USIS Library, American Cultural Center, Tel Aviv
71 Hayarkon St, Tel Aviv 63903 Israel
Lib Type General.

2255. USIS, American Documentation Center, The Hague
2 Korte Voorhout 2, 2511 EK The Hague Netherlands
Lib Type General.

2256. USIS, American Center Library, Thessaloniki
34, Metropoleos St, Thessaloniki Greece
Lib Type General.

2257. USIS Library, Americki Centar, Titograd
Bulevar Octobarske Revolucije 100, Titograd 81000 Yugoslavia
Lib Type General.

2258. USIS, American Center Library, Tokyo
ABC Bldg, 6-3, Shiba Koen 2-chome, Minato-ku, Tokyo 105 Japan
Lib Type General.

2259. USIS Library, Centre Culturel Americain, Tunis
2, Ave de France, Tunis Tunisia
Lib Type General.

2260. USIS, American Center Library, Valletta
PO Box 510; Development House, Fl 3, St Ann St, Floriana, Valletta Malta
Lib Type General.

2261. USIS, Amerika Haus Library, Vienna
Friedrich Schmidt-Platz 2, Vienna 1010 Austria
Lib Type General.

2262. USIS, Biblioteka Amerykanska, Warszawa
Ambasada Stanow Zjednoczonych Ameryki, Aleje Ujazdowskie 29/31, Warszawa Poland
Lib Type General.

2263. USIS, American Library, Wellington
PO Box 1190; American Chancery, 29 Fitzherbert Terrace, Thorndon, Wellington 1 New Zealand
Lib Type General.

2264. USIS Library, Centre Culturel Americain, Yaounde
PO Box 817; Ave de l'Independance, Yaounde Cameroon
Lib Type General.

2265. USIS Library, Americki Centar, Zagreb
Zrinjevac 13, Zagreb 41000 Yugoslavia
Lib Type General.

United States International Development Cooperation Agency

2266. Overseas Private Investment Corporation Library
1615 M St NW, Washington, DC 20527 (202) 457-7123
Admin Myra Norton. *Ref Lib* Elizabeth A Bourg (ILL).
Lib Type Special.
Spec Subs Multinational business; foreign investment; finance. *Spec Collecs* Country collection (developing countries).
Info Ret Servs DIALOG; LEXIS; NEXIS; Citimarkets; Dun's Credit Service. *Shared Catalog Nets* OCLC. *Coop Lib Nets* FEDLINK.
Circ Servs Avail To other Federal libraries; to other libraries.
Ref Servs Avail To other Federal libraries; to other libraries.

2267. US Agency for International Development Library
105 State Annex-18, Washington, DC 20523 (703) 235-1000; FTS 235-1000
Admin Margaret S Pope. *Ref Lib* Ardith Betts (Acq). *ILL* James Harold.
Lib Type Special.
Spec Subs International development, including economic, agricultural, & social aspects. *Spec Collecs* FAO documents (on microfiche). *In-house Files* AID project documents; AID sponsored studies & monographs.
Info Ret Servs DIALOG; BRS; SDC. *Shared Catalog Nets* OCLC. *Coop Lib Nets* FEDLINK.
Circ Servs Avail To other libraries.
Ref Servs Avail To other Federal libraries; to other libraries; to the general public.

2268. US Agency for International Development Water & Sanitation for Health Project Information Center
1611 N Kent St, Rm 1002, Arlington, VA 22209 (703) 243-2605
Lib Type Special.

United States International Trade Commission

2269. US International Trade Commission, Law Library
701 E St NW, Rm 213, Washington, DC 20436 (202) 523-0333
Admin Steven Kover.
Lib Type Law.
Spec Subs Antidumping & countervailing duties; international trade law dealing with imports, patents & trademarks; tariffs. *Spec Collecs* Legislative histories dealing with trade & tariff acts.
Shared Catalog Nets OCLC.

2270. US International Trade Commission Main Library
701 E St NW, Washington, DC 20436 (202) 523-0016
Admin Barbara J Pruett.
Lib Type Special.
Spec Subs Agriculture; chemicals; commercial policy; energy; fisheries; forest products; forestry; general manufactures; international trade; leather products; machinery & equipment; metals; mineralogy; tariffs; trade statistics; textiles.
Shared Catalog Nets OCLC. *Coop Lib Nets* FEDLINK.
Circ Servs Avail Not open to the general public.
Ref Servs Avail To the general public.

United States Postal Service

2271. US Postal Service Library
475 L'Enfant Plaza W, SW, Washington, DC 20206 (202) 268-2904/2905/2906
Admin Jane F Kennedy. *Ref Lib* Catherine East. *ILL* Joseph Wojeckowski. *Acq Lib* Francene Peters.
Lib Type Law; General.

Spec Subs Postal laws & regulations; postal operations; computer science. *Spec Collecs* Congressional serial set. *In-house Files* Postal publications.
Lib Deposit Designation GPO Depository Library.
Info Ret Servs DIALOG; LEXIS; NEXIS; WESTLAW; CQ Washington Alert; Dow Jones. *Shared Catalog Nets* OCLC. *Elec Mail Nets* Dialmail; OCLC.
Circ Servs Avail To other libraries.
Ref Servs Avail To other Federal libraries; to other libraries; to the general public.

Veterans Administration

2272. James A Haley Veterans Hospital, Library Service
13000 N 30th St, Tampa, FL 33612 (813) 972-2000 ext 140; FTS 822-7531
Admin Iris A Renner. *Ref Lib* Nancy Bernal (Acq). *ILL* Diane Klein.
Lib Type Health & Medicine; Hospital (Patients).
Spec Subs Medicine; nursing.
Info Ret Servs BRS. *Coop Lib Nets* VALNET; TABAMLN. *Elec Mail Nets* CLASS.
Circ Servs Avail Restricted to staff.
Ref Servs Avail To other Federal libraries; to other libraries; not open to the general public.

2273. Louis A Johnson Veterans Administration Medical Center, Medical Library
Clarksburg, WV 26301 (304) 623-3461 ext 3435; FTS 923-3435
Admin John Package. *ILL* Mary McCloud.
Lib Type Health & Medicine.
In-house Files Government agency files.
Info Ret Servs MEDLARS. *Shared Catalog Nets* VALNET. *Coop Lib Nets* VALNET; WV Health Sciences Library Assoc; Southeastern/Atlantic Regional Medical Library Svcs, Region 2. *Elec Mail Nets* CLASS; MAILMAN.
Circ Servs Avail To other Federal libraries.
Ref Servs Avail To other Federal libraries.

2274. Royal C Johnson Veterans Memorial Medical Center, Medical & Patient's Library
PO Box 5046, Sioux Falls, SD 57117 (605) 336-3230 ext 272; FTS 782-3272
Admin Lori Klein. *Ref Lib* David Siegenthaler. *ILL* Patricia Zoerink.
Lib Type Health & Medicine; Hospital (Patients).
Spec Subs Medicine; nursing; allied health; hospital admin. *Spec Collecs* Audio-visuals; patient health education.
Info Ret Servs BRS. *Shared Catalog Nets* OCLC thru VALNET. *Coop Lib Nets* VALNET; GMRMLN; MINITEX; South Dakota Library Network. *Elec Mail Nets* CLASS; EASYLINK (Western Union).
Circ Servs Avail To other Federal libraries; to other libraries.
Ref Servs Avail To other Federal libraries; to other libraries; to the general public.

2275. John L McClellan Memorial Veterans Hospital, Health Sciences Library
4300 West 7th St, Little Rock, AR 72205 (501) 735-2044; FTS 742-2044
Admin George M Zumwalt.
Lib Type Health & Medicine.
Info Ret Servs BRS. *Shared Catalog Nets* OCLC thru VALNET. *Coop Lib Nets* VALNET. *Elec Mail Nets* BRS.
Circ Servs Avail To other Federal libraries; to other libraries.
Ref Servs Avail To other Federal libraries; to other libraries.

2276. Karl A Menninger Medical Library
Colmery O'Neil VA Medical Center, 2200 Gage Blvd, Topeka, KS 66622 (913) 272-3111 ext 271; FTS 752-5271
Admin Norma Torkelson. *Ref Lib* Nancy Vaughn. *ILL* Donna Sidel. *Acq Lib* Rosie Adkins.
Lib Type Health & Medicine.
Spec Subs Psychiatry; medicine; neurology; social work; psychology; nursing; surgery; dietetics. *Spec Collecs* Karl A Menninger's works. *In-house Files* Student papers.

Info Ret Servs BRS; MEDLINE. *Shared Catalog Nets* OCLC thru VALNET. *Coop Lib Nets* VALNET; Greater Topeka Medical Libraries; MLA; Midcontinental. *Elec Mail Nets* CLASS; OCTANET.
Circ Servs Avail To other Federal libraries; to other libraries; restricted to use in library by general public.
Ref Servs Avail To other Federal libraries; to other libraries; to the general public; restricted to quick reference for general public.

2277. William S Middleton Memorial Veterans Hospital Library Service

2500 Overlook Terrace, Madison, WI 53705 (608) 256-1901; FTS 364-1557
Admin Phyllis E Goetz.
Lib Type Health & Medicine; Hospital (Patients).
Spec Subs General medical; surgery. *Spec Collecs* Biochemistry.
Info Ret Servs MEDLINE. *Coop Lib Nets* VALNET; WHSLA; SCLS; CHARM.
Circ Servs Avail To other Federal libraries; to other libraries; not open to the general public.
Ref Servs Avail To other Federal libraries; to other libraries; not open to the general public.

2278. Mirsky Medical Library, Brentwood Division, Veterans Administration Medical Center West, Los Angeles

Los Angeles, CA 90073 (213) 478-3711; FTS 794-3711
Admin Joy J Nordhill.
Lib Type Health & Medicine.
Spec Subs Psychiatry; psychology. *Spec Collecs* Psychiatry.
Info Ret Servs DIALOG; MEDLINE. *Shared Catalog Nets* Costabile Assoc using OCLC. *Coop Lib Nets* VALNET.
Circ Servs Avail Restricted to VA.
Ref Servs Avail Restricted to VA & affiliated institutions.

2279. Audie L Murphy Memorial Veterans Hospital, Library Service

7400 Merton Minter Blvd, San Antonio, TX 78284-5701 (512) 696-9660 ext 4283; FTS 779-4283
Admin Elosia Mitchell. *Ref Lib* Marsha Murphy; Nicholas Cantu (ILL).
Lib Type Health & Medicine.
Spec Subs Medical & allied health; management. *Spec Collecs* Patient health education. *In-house Files* Univ of Texas/Dallas Internal Medicine Grand Rounds protocols.
Info Ret Servs DIALOG; BRS; MEDLARS. *Shared Catalog Nets* DOCLINE. *Coop Lib Nets* Health Oriented Libraries of San Antonio (HOLSA); San Antonio Online Users Group (SOLUG). *Elec Mail Nets* CLASS.
Circ Servs Avail To other Federal libraries; to other libraries.
Ref Servs Avail To other Federal libraries; to other libraries; to the general public.

2280. Jerry L Pettis Memorial Veterans Administration Hospital, Library Service

11201 Benton St, Loma Linda, CA 92357 (714) 825-7084 ext 2390; FTS 996-2390
Admin Kathleen M Puffer. *Ref Lib* Jean Leonard. *ILL* Chris Hensley.
Lib Type Health & Medicine.
Info Ret Servs DIALOG; BRS. *Shared Catalog Nets* Costabile Assoc using OCLC. *Coop Lib Nets* VALNET; SIRCULUS. *Elec Mail Nets* VA Mailman; Tymnet.
Circ Servs Avail To other Federal libraries.
Ref Servs Avail To other Federal libraries.

2281. Franklin Delano Roosevelt Hospital, Veterans Administration Library Service

Rte 9A, Montrose, NY 10548 (914) 737-4400; FTS 887-2578
Admin Bruce S Delman. *Ref Lib* Karl Yung (ILL, Acq).
Lib Type Health & Medicine.
Spec Subs Psychiatry; psychology; nursing; social work.
Info Ret Servs MEDLINE. *Shared Catalog Nets* OCLC thru VALNET. *Coop Lib Nets* VALNET; HILOW; METRO. *Elec Mail Nets* CLASS.
Circ Servs Avail To other Federal libraries; to other libraries.
Ref Servs Avail To other Federal libraries; to other libraries.

2282. Olin E Teague Veterans Center, Library Service

Temple, TX 76501 (817) 778-4811 ext 4111; FTS 760-4111
Admin Barbara D Coronado. *Ref Lib* Mary Kay Massay (ILL). *Acq Lib* Ruth M Hempel.
Lib Type Health & Medicine; Hospital (Patients).
Spec Subs Patient health education.
Info Ret Servs BRS; Medlars. *Shared Catalog Nets* VALNET. *Coop Lib Nets* TAMU Consortium of Medical Libraries; TALON. *Elec Mail Nets* CLASS.
Circ Servs Avail To other Federal libraries; to other libraries.
Ref Servs Avail To other Federal libraries; to other libraries; to the general public; restricted to general public in-house use only.

2283. Harry S Truman Memorial Veterans Hospital, Medical Library

800 Hospital Dr, Columbia, MO 65201 (314) 443-2511 ext 6341; FTS 276-6340
Admin Ray Starke. *Ref Lib* Mark Fleetwood (Acq). *ILL* Carmen Garcia-Otero.
Lib Type Health & Medicine.
Spec Collecs Patient education; large print; talking books.
Info Ret Servs DIALOG; BRS; MEDLARS. *Coop Lib Nets* VALNET; RMLP; MMLN. *Elec Mail Nets* CLASS; OCTNET/BRS.
Circ Servs Avail To other Federal libraries; to other libraries; to the general public.
Ref Servs Avail To other Federal libraries; to other libraries; to the general public.

2284. James E Van Zandt Veterans Administration Medical Center, Medical Library

Altoona, PA 16603 (814) 943-8164 ext 7156; FTS 727-7156
Admin Rose Altberg.
Lib Type Health & Medicine.
Spec Collecs Patient education. *In-house Files* timely subjects such as AIDS & DRGs.
Info Ret Servs BRS. *Shared Catalog Nets* Costabile Assoc using OCLC. *Coop Lib Nets* Central Pennsylvania Health Sciences Libraries. *Elec Mail Nets* Mailman.
Circ Servs Avail To other Federal libraries; to other libraries; not open to the general public.
Ref Servs Avail To other Federal libraries; to other libraries; restricted to use by general public on premises.

2285. Veterans Administration Central Office Library, Library Division

810 Vermont Ave NW, Washington, DC 20420 (202) 233-2711/3085
Admin Karen Renninger. *Ref Lib* Wendy N Carter; Margaret B O'Shea.
Lib Type Health & Medicine.
Spec Subs Health care administration; medicine; management; veterans.
Lib Deposit Designation GPO Depository Library.
Info Ret Servs DIALOG; BRS; NEXIS; National Library of Medicine. *Shared Catalog Nets* OCLC. *Coop Lib Nets* VALNET. *Elec Mail Nets* Class; MAILMAN.

2286. Veterans Administration Domiciliary Library Service

White City, OR 97503 (503) 826-2111; FTS 424-3796-3296
Admin Sarah Fitzpatrick. *ILL* Margaret Rose.
Lib Type Health & Medicine; Hospital (Patients).

2287. Veterans Administration Hospital, Health Sciences Library

555 Willard Ave, Newington, CT 06111 (203) 666-4361; FTS 643-1302
Admin Julie A Lueders.
Lib Type Health & Medicine; Hospital (Patients).
Spec Subs Medicine; nursing; patient education; surgery.
Info Ret Servs BRS. *Coop Lib Nets* VALNET; Connecticut Assn of Health Science Libraries.

2288. Veterans Administration Hospital Library
Box 4867, Barrio Monacillos, San Juan, PR 00936 (809) 758-7575, ext 323
Admin Raquel A Walters.
Lib Type Hospital (Patients).

2289. Veterans Administration Lakeside Medical Center, Library Service
333 E Huron St, Chicago, IL 60611 (312) 943-6600 ext 259; FTS 384-8259
Admin Lydia Tkaczuk. *ILL* Cheryl Kinnaird.
Lib Type Health & Medicine.
Spec Subs General clinical medicine. *Spec Collecs* Patient health education (books for laypeople on medical topics).
Info Ret Servs BRS; NLM/MEDLINE. *Shared Catalog Nets* OCLC thru VALNET. *Coop Lib Nets* VALNET; Metropolitan Consortium, Chicago. *Elec Mail Nets* CLASS.
Circ Servs Avail To other Federal libraries; to other libraries; to the general public.
Ref Servs Avail To other Federal libraries; to other libraries; to the general public.

2290. Veterans Administration Library Service, Edith Nourse Rogers Memorial Veterans Hospital
200 Springs Rd, Bedford, MA 01730 (617) 275-7500
Admin Sanford S Yagendorf.
Lib Type Health & Medicine.
Spec Subs Medicine; nursing; psychology; social work.
Coop Lib Nets VALNET. *Elec Mail Nets* CLASS.

2291. Veterans Administration Medical & Regional Office Center Library
1 N Hartland Rd, White River Junction, VT 05001 (802) 295-9363; ILL 295-9363, ext 329/330; FTS 834-1329
Admin Rick A Haver.
Lib Type Health & Medicine; Hospital (Patients).
Spec Subs Gastroenterology; hematology; general medicine; neurology.
Coop Lib Nets VALNET.

2292. Veterans Administration Medical & Regional Office Center Library Service
Togus, ME 04330 (207) 623-8411; FTS 833-5275
Admin Melda W Page. *Ref Lib* Christopher Bovie; June Roullard. *ILL* Gary Pelletier.
Lib Type Health & Medicine.

2293. Veterans Administration Medical Center & Patients' Library
54th St & 48th Ave S, Minneapolis, MN 55417 (612) 725-6308; FTS 784-6308 (Medical Library); 784-6901 (Patients' Library)
Admin Margery McNeil.
Lib Type Health & Medicine; Hospital (Patients).
Spec Collecs Medical AV collection; patient education, prints & AV.
Coop Lib Nets VALNET; Twin Cities Biomedical Consortium. *Elec Mail Nets* CLASS.

2294. Veterans Administration Medical Center, Health Sciences Library
Providence, RI 02908 (401) 273-7100, ext 3100; FTS 838-3001
Admin Lynn A Lloyd. *ILL* Beverly Lauterbad.
Lib Type Health & Medicine.
Spec Subs Cardiology; alcoholism; Vietnam veterans; hemodialysis; nursing; management.
Info Ret Servs BRS. *Shared Catalog Nets* OCLC. *Coop Lib Nets* Assn of RI Health Science Librarians (ARIHSL); North Atlantic Health Science Libraries (NAHSL). *Elec Mail Nets* Class OnTyme.
Circ Servs Avail To other Federal libraries; to other libraries; to the general public.
Ref Servs Avail To other Federal libraries; to other libraries; to the general public.

2295. Veterans Administration Medical Center, Hospital & Patients' Library
Fort Howard, MD 21052 (301) 477-1800, ext 309; FTS 922-8309
Lib Type Health & Medicine; Hospital (Patients).
Spec Subs Rehabilitation.
Coop Lib Nets VALNET. *Elec Mail Nets* CLASS; MAILMAN.

2296. Veterans Administration Medical Center, Jefferson Barracks Division, Library Service
Saint Louis, MO 63125 (314) 487-0400; FTS 276-7329
Admin Larry D Weitkemper. *Ref Lib* Katie Deberry (ILL).
Lib Type Health & Medicine; Hospital (Patients).
Spec Collecs Audiovisuals.
Lib Deposit Designation District & Regional Delivery site for VALNET networked audiovisual programs.
Info Ret Servs DIALOG; MEDLARS. *Shared Catalog Nets* OCLC (thru VA central office). *Coop Lib Nets* VALNET; St Louis Medical Librarians (SLML). *Elec Mail Nets* CLASS OnTyme.
Circ Servs Avail To other Federal libraries; to other libraries.
Ref Servs Avail To other Federal libraries; to other libraries.

2297. Veterans Administration Medical Center Learning Resource Center
Lake City, FL 32055 (904) 752-1400 ext 272/356; FTS 947-2142
Admin Shirley Mabry. *Ref Lib* Jean Johnston. *ILL* Lavonia Richardson. *Acq Lib* Julia Byrd.
Lib Type Health & Medicine; Hospital (Patients).
Spec Collecs Patient health education.
Info Ret Servs BRS; MEDLINE. *Shared Catalog Nets* OCLC thru VALNET. *Coop Lib Nets* VALNET. *Elec Mail Nets* CLASS; BRS.
Circ Servs Avail To other Federal libraries; to other libraries; not open to the general public.
Ref Servs Avail To other Federal libraries; to other libraries; to the general public.

2298. Veterans Administration Medical Center Learning Resources Center
4101 Woolworth Ave, Omaha, NE 68105 (402) 346-8800 ext 3530; FTS 860-3530
Admin Lois J Inskeep.
Lib Type Health & Medicine; Hospital (Patients).
Info Ret Servs DIALOG. *Shared Catalog Nets* OCLC thru VALNET. *Coop Lib Nets* VALNET.
Circ Servs Avail Restricted to qualified users.
Ref Servs Avail Restricted to qualified users.

2299. Veterans Administration Medical Center Learning Resources Center
Saint Cloud, MN 56301 (612) 252-1670 ext 270; FTS 783-8270 (Medical Library); 783-8291 (Patients' Library)
Admin Sanford J. Banker.
Lib Type Health & Medicine; Hospital (Patients).
Spec Subs Geriatrics; nursing; psychiatry; psychology.
Info Ret Servs MEDLINE. *Coop Lib Nets* VALNET; Central Minnesota Library Exchange.
Ref Servs Avail Not open to the general public; restricted to local medical, allied health & college communities.

2300. Veterans Administration Medical Center Learning Resources Service
Lyons, NJ 07939 (201) 647-0180 ext 491; FTS 340-4410
Admin James G Delo. *ILL* Carolyn Fellows. *Acq Lib* Marian Krugman.
Lib Type Health & Medicine; Hospital (Patients).
Spec Subs Psychology; psychiatry; geriatrics; rehabilitation. *In-house Files* VA & other government publications.
Info Ret Servs BRS; MEDLINE. *Shared Catalog Nets* OCLC thru VALNET. *Coop Lib Nets* VALNET; MEDCORE. *Elec Mail Nets* MCI Mail; Telex.
Circ Servs Avail To other Federal libraries; to other libraries; to the general public.
Ref Servs Avail To other Federal libraries; to other libraries; to the general public.

2301. Veterans Administration Medical Center Library
1000 Locust St, Reno, NV 89520 (702) 329-1051; FTS 470-1470
Admin Janet F. Monk.
Lib Type Health & Medicine.
Coop Lib Nets VALNET.

2302. Veterans Administration Medical Center Library
5901 E 7th St, Long Beach, CA 90822 (213) 494-2611; FTS 966-5463 (Medical Library); ILL 966-3686; 966-3690 (Patients' Library)
Lib Type Health & Medicine; Hospital (Patients).
Shared Catalog Nets UCLA Academic Computing. *Coop Lib Nets* VALNET.
Circ Servs Avail Not open to the general public; restricted to professional staff & employees.
Ref Servs Avail Not open to the general public; restricted to local professional persons for reference.

2303. Veterans Administration Medical Center Library
1201 NW 16th St, Miami, FL 33125 (305) 324-3187; FTS 350-3187
Admin Raissa Maurin. *Ref Lib* Thompson Cummings. *ILL* Cecilia Rowen.
Lib Type Health & Medicine.
Spec Subs Medicine; dentistry; nursing; all allied medical fields.
Info Ret Servs BRS; SDC; MEDLINE. *Shared Catalog Nets* Costabile Assoc using OCLC. *Elec Mail Nets* CLASS.
Circ Servs Avail To other Federal libraries; to other libraries; not open to the general public; restricted to staff.
Ref Servs Avail To other Federal libraries; to other libraries; not open to the general public; restricted to staff.

2304. Veterans Administration Medical Center Library
408 1st Ave, New York, NY 10010 (212) 686-7500, ext 445
Lib Type Health & Medicine.
Info Ret Servs BRS. *Coop Lib Nets* VALNET. *Elec Mail Nets* CLASS.

2305. Veterans Administration Medical Center Library
113 Holland Ave, Albany, NY 12208 (518) 462-3311, ext 349; FTS 563-9349
Admin John F. Connors.
Lib Type Health & Medicine.
Spec Subs Allied health; medicine.
Info Ret Servs MEDLINE; BRS. *Shared Catalog Nets* OCLC. *Coop Lib Nets* VALNET; Capital District Library Council for Reference $ Research Resources.

2306. Veterans Administration Medical Center Library
PO Box 12511, Castle Point, NY 12511 (914) 831-2000; FTS 882-5142
Admin William E. Kane.
Lib Type Health & Medicine.
Coop Lib Nets Southeastern New York Library Resources Council.

2307. Veterans Administration Medical Center Library
1111 E End Blvd, Wilkes-Barre, PA 18711 (717) 824-3521; FTS 592-7521; ILL 592-7423; Patients' Library 592-7421
Admin Bruce D. Reid.
Lib Type Health & Medicine.
Elec Mail Nets MAILMAN.

2308. Veterans Administration Medical Center Library
Tuskegee, AL 36083 (205) 727-3647; FTS 534-3647 (Medical Library); 534-3410 (Patients' Library)
Admin Artemisia J. Junier.
Lib Type Health & Medicine; Hospital (Patients).
Coop Lib Nets VALNET.

2309. Veterans Administration Medical Center Library
Hot Springs, SD 57747 (605) 745-4101 ext 226
Admin Carole W. Miles.
Lib Type Health & Medicine.
Spec Subs History of South Dakota; Indians; medicine.

2310. Veterans Administration Medical Center Library
2400 Gregg Ave, Big Spring, TX 79720 (915) 263-7361 ext 348; FTS 738-8348
Admin Donald D. Fortner.
Lib Type Health & Medicine.
Info Ret Servs MEDLINE. *Coop Lib Nets* VALNET.

2311. Veterans Administration Medical Center Library
2121 North Ave, Grand Junction, CO 81501 (303) 243-0731 ext 220; FTS 322-0220
Admin Lynn L. Bragdon.
Lib Type Health & Medicine.
Spec Collecs Colorado history.
Info Ret Servs BRS; National Library of Medicine. *Shared Catalog Nets* OCLC. *Coop Lib Nets* VALNET; Pathfinder Library System.

2312. Veterans Administration Medical Center Library
Arroyo Rd, Livermore, CA 94550 (415) 447-2560 ext 6363
Lib Type Health & Medicine; Hospital (Patients).
Spec Subs Medical library - health sciences; Patients library - recreational & educational materials.
Coop Lib Nets VALNET.

2313. Veterans Administration Medical Center Library
50 Irving St NW, Washington, DC 20422 (202) 745-8262; FTS 921-8262
Admin Mary M Netzow.
Lib Type Health & Medicine.
Spec Subs Clinical medicine.
Info Ret Servs BRS; National Library of Medicine. *Shared Catalog Nets* OCLC. *Coop Lib Nets* VALNET. *Elec Mail Nets* MAILMAN.
Ref Servs Avail To the general public; restricted to limited use.

2314. Veterans Administration Medical Center Library
1310 24th Ave S, Nashville, TN 37203 (615) 327-4751 ext 5524; FTS 850-5526
Admin Barbara A Meadows. *Ref Lib* Susan E Gaudet.
Lib Type Health & Medicine.
Spec Subs Medicine; surgery; dentistry; nursing.
Info Ret Servs NLM MEDLARS. *Coop Lib Nets* VALNET; NLM, Region 2; Mid-Tennessee Health Sciences Librarians Consortium. *Elec Mail Nets* VA Mailman.
Circ Servs Avail To other Federal libraries; to other libraries; not open to the general public.
Ref Servs Avail To other Federal libraries; to other libraries; not open to the general public.

2315. Veterans Administration Medical Center Library
2002 Holcombe Blvd, Houston, TX 77211 (713) 795-7471; FTS 527-7471
Admin J Barrett. *Acq Lib* C Whelton.
Lib Type Health & Medicine.
Info Ret Servs BRS; MEDLARS. *Shared Catalog Nets* VALNET. *Coop Lib Nets* VALNET; South Central Regional Medical Library Program (TALON); Houston On-line Users Council (HOLUG); Houston Health Science Library Council. *Elec Mail Nets* CLASS.
Circ Servs Avail To other Federal libraries.
Ref Servs Avail To other Federal libraries.

2316. Veterans Administration Medical Center Library
30th & Euclid, Des Moines, IA 50310 (515) 271-5824; FTS 862-5824
Admin Clare Jergens. *ILL* Diane Collett.
Lib Type Health & Medicine; Hospital (Patients).
Spec Subs Nursing; medicine; surgery. *Spec Collecs* CIBA slides; network for continuing medical education.
Info Ret Servs DIALOG; NLM-MEDLINE. *Shared Catalog Nets* VALNET. *Coop Lib Nets* VALNET; Greater Midwest Regional Medical Library Network (GMRMLN); Polk County Biomedical Consortium (PCBC).
Circ Servs Avail To other Federal libraries; to other libraries.
Ref Servs Avail To other Federal libraries; to other libraries; to the general public.

2317. Veterans Administration Medical Center Library
Hampton, VA 23667 (804) 722-9961; FTS 931-6694; 931-6695
Medical Library; 931-6326 Patients' Library
Admin Jacqueline A Bird.
Lib Type Health & Medicine.
Spec Subs Acute care; geriatrics; gerontology; patient education; rehabilitation.
Info Ret Servs BRS; MEDLINE. *Coop Lib Nets* VALNET. *Elec Mail Nets* MAILMAN; CLASS.

2318. Veterans Administration Medical Center Library
Martinsburg, WV 25401 (304) 263-0811; FTS 928-3822; ILL 940-3826; 940-4598 Patients' Library
Admin Barbara S Adams.
Lib Type Health & Medicine.
Elec Mail Nets MAILMAN.

2319. Veterans Administration Medical Center Library
1540 Spring Valley Dr, Huntington, WV 25704 (304) 429-6741; FTS 924-2261
Admin Hope S Reentsjerna.
Lib Type Health & Medicine.
Spec Subs Clinical medicine; general nursing & surgery.
Info Ret Servs MEDLINE. *Shared Catalog Nets* OCLC. *Coop Lib Nets* VALNET. *Elec Mail Nets* MAILMAN.
Circ Servs Avail Not open to the general public; restricted to staff & medical school faculty, others with permission.
Ref Servs Avail Not open to the general public; restricted to staff & medical school faculty, others with permission.

2320. Veterans Administration Medical Center Library
200 Veterans Ave, Beckley, WV 25801 (304) 255-2121, ext 4342; FTS 924-4342
Admin Shelley C Doman.
Lib Type Health & Medicine.
Elec Mail Nets MAILMAN.

2321. Veterans Administration Medical Center Library, William Jennings Bryan Dorn Veterans Hospital
Garners Ferry Rd, Columbia, SC 29201 (803) 776-4000; FTS 677-6515
Admin Charletta P Felder.
Lib Type Health & Medicine.

2322. Veterans Administration Medical Center Library-Learning Resources Center
800 Irving Ave, Syracuse, NY 13210 (315) 476-7461; Medical library 476-7284; AV library 476-7529; FTS 953-7246
Admin June M. Mitchell.
Lib Type Health & Medicine; Hospital (Patients).
Spec Subs Geriatric nursing home care; medicine; nursing; psychiatry; social work; surgery.
Coop Lib Nets VALNET; Central NY Library Resources Council.
Ref Servs Avail Not open to the general public; restricted to medical professionals.

2323. Veterans Administration Medical Center Library Service
Hines, IL 60141 (312) 343-7200 ext 2516/2517; FTS 387-2517
Admin Bill Leavens. *Ref Lib* John Cline. *ILL* Ann Novacich.
Lib Type Health & Medicine.
Info Ret Servs VALNET. *Shared Catalog Nets* OCLC. *Coop Lib Nets* VALNET; GMRNLM; Suburban Library System, Metro (Chicago) Consortium. *Elec Mail Nets* CLASS ONTYME II.
Circ Servs Avail To other libraries.
Ref Servs Avail To other Federal libraries; to other libraries.

2324. Veterans Administration Medical Center Library Service
600 S 70th St, Lincoln, NE 68510 (402) 489-3802; FTS 541-6214
Admin Ruth A Boettcher. *ILL* Lynelle McNally.
Lib Type Health & Medicine; Hospital (Patients).
Info Ret Servs MEDLARS. *Shared Catalog Nets* OCLC. *Coop Lib Nets* VALNET; Lincoln Health Sciences Library Group (consortium). *Elec Mail Nets* Octanet.
Circ Servs Avail To other Federal libraries; to other libraries.

Ref Servs Avail To other Federal libraries; to other libraries; to the general public.

2325. Veterans Administration Medical Center Library Service
Memorial Dr, Waco, TX 76703 (817) 752-6581 ext 486; FTS 334-6486
Admin Barbara H Hobbs. *Ref Lib* Niki Buettner (ILL, Acq).
Lib Type Health & Medicine; Hospital (Patients).
Spec Subs Psychiatry; psychology; nursing; rehabilitative medicine.
Spec Collecs Patient health education.
Info Ret Servs BRS. *Shared Catalog Nets* OCLC. *Coop Lib Nets* VALNET; Medical Library Program (TALON).
Circ Servs Avail To other Federal libraries; to other libraries; to the general public; restricted to ILL.
Ref Servs Avail To other Federal libraries; to other libraries.

2326. Veterans Administration Medical Center Library Service
7th St & Indian School Rd, Phoenix, AZ 85012 (602) 277-5551 ext 248/533; FTS 764-7248
Admin Diane Wiesenthal. *ILL* Jean Crosier.
Lib Type Health & Medicine; Hospital (Patients).
Spec Subs Patient health education.
Info Ret Servs BRS. *Shared Catalog Nets* VALNET. *Coop Lib Nets* VALNET; Maricopa Biomedical Libraries (MaBL). *Elec Mail Nets* CLASS.
Circ Servs Avail To other libraries; to the general public.
Ref Servs Avail To other Federal libraries; to other libraries; to the general public.

2327. Veterans Administration Medical Center Library Service
1600 Randallia Dr, Fort Wayne, IN 46805 (219) 426-5431 ext 330; FTS 333-5330
Admin Margaret O Fulsom.
Lib Type Health & Medicine.
Spec Subs Medicine; surgery.
Info Ret Servs MEDLARS. *Shared Catalog Nets* VALNET. *Coop Lib Nets* VALNET; Tri-Area Library Service Authority, Indiana (TRI-AREA).
Circ Servs Avail To other Federal libraries; to other libraries.
Ref Servs Avail To other Federal libraries; to other libraries; to the general public.

2328. Veterans Administration Medical Center Library Service
1100 N College Ave, Fayetteville, AR 72701 (501) 443-4301 ext 546/556; FTS 740-0546
Admin Jeanine B Brown. *Ref Lib* Sylvia Griffey (ILL).
Lib Type Health & Medicine.
Info Ret Servs BRS; MEDLARS. *Shared Catalog Nets* OCLC. *Coop Lib Nets* VALNET; Northwest Arkansas Shared Library.
Circ Servs Avail To other Federal libraries; to other libraries.
Ref Servs Avail To other Federal libraries; to other libraries.

2329. Veterans Administration Medical Center Library Service
Palo Alto, CA 94304 (415) 493-5000 ext 5447; FTS 449-5447
Admin C R Gallimore.
Lib Type Health & Medicine; Hospital (Patients).
Spec Subs Psychiatry; general medicine; surgery; geriatrics.
Info Ret Servs DIALOG; BRS. *Shared Catalog Nets* RLIN. *Coop Lib Nets* VALNET; CLASS; Northern California, Nevada Medical Library Group. *Elec Mail Nets* Ontyme.
Circ Servs Avail To other Federal libraries; to other libraries; not open to the general public.
Ref Servs Avail To other Federal libraries; to other libraries; not open to the general public.

2330. Veterans Administration Medical Center Library Service
University Dr, Pittsburgh, PA 15240 (412) 683-3260; FTS 726-3260
Admin Tuula I Beazell.
Lib Type Health & Medicine.
Coop Lib Nets VALNET. *Elec Mail Nets* CLASS.

2331. Veterans Administration Medical Center Library Service
150 S Huntington Ave, Boston, MA 02130 (617) 232-9500 ext 3434; FTS 839-0434
Admin Barbara W Huckins. *Ref Lib* Olga Lyczmanenko (Acq). *ILL* Ann Samson; Nancy Johnson.
Lib Type Health & Medicine; Hospital (Patients).
Spec Subs Medicine; allied health; health education.
Info Ret Servs MEDLARS. *Shared Catalog Nets* OCLC thru VAL-NET. *Coop Lib Nets* BBLC; MAHSLIN; NAHSL. *Elec Mail Nets* CLASS; MEDLINK (ALANET).
Circ Servs Avail To other Federal libraries; to other libraries; restricted to use with permission.
Ref Servs Avail To other Federal libraries; to other libraries.

2332. Veterans Administration Medical Center Library Service
940 Belmont St, Brockton, MA 02401 (617) 583-4500 ext 321/132; FTS 840-6321
Admin Suzanne N Noyes. *Ref Lib* Bruce Thornlow. *ILL* MaryEllen West. *Acq Lib* Donald Carter.
Lib Type Health & Medicine; Hospital (Patients).
Spec Subs Nursing; psychiatry; medicine; alcohol & drug abuse; social work.
Info Ret Servs DIALOG; BRS; MEDLINE. *Coop Lib Nets* BBLC; SMCL; SEMCO. *Elec Mail Nets* CLASS; MEDLINK.
Circ Servs Avail To other Federal libraries; to other libraries.
Ref Servs Avail To other Federal libraries; to other libraries; to the general public.

2333. Veterans Administration Medical Center Library Service
718 Smyth Rd, Manchester, NH 03104 (603) 624-4366 ext 333; FTS 834-3336
Admin Joan McGinnis. *ILL* Maryann Baisley.
Lib Type Health & Medicine.
Spec Subs Medicine; surgery; nursing. *Spec Collecs* Patient education audio-visual.
Info Ret Servs BRS. *Shared Catalog Nets* OCLC thru VALNET. *Coop Lib Nets* NH/VT HSL; UCMP. *Elec Mail Nets* CLASS.
Circ Servs Avail To other Federal libraries; to other libraries; not open to the general public.
Ref Servs Avail To other Federal libraries; to other libraries; not open to the general public.

2334. Veterans Administration Medical Center Library Service
Canandaigua, NY 14424 (716) 394-2000; FTS 952-9258
Admin Peter Fleming. *Ref Lib* Vikki Cecere. *ILL* DonnaLee Erti.
Lib Type Health & Medicine; Hospital (Patients).
Spec Subs Psychiatry; psychology; nursing; geriatrics.
Info Ret Servs BRS; National Lib of Medicine. *Coop Lib Nets* VALNET; RRRLC; RALIH.
Circ Servs Avail To other libraries.
Ref Servs Avail To other Federal libraries; to other libraries; to the general public.

2335. Veterans Administration Medical Center Library Service
Bath, NY 14810 (607) 776-2111 ext 223; FTS 882-1556
Admin Robert M Schnick. *Ref Lib* Sally Hillegas (ILL).
Lib Type Health & Medicine; Hospital (Patients).
Spec Subs Geriatrics; long term care.
Info Ret Servs NLM. *Shared Catalog Nets* OCLC thru VALNET. *Coop Lib Nets* VALNET; RML; STLS; South Central Research Library Council. *Elec Mail Nets* CLASS.
Circ Servs Avail To other Federal libraries; to other libraries; not open to the general public.
Ref Servs Avail To other Federal libraries; to other libraries; not open to the general public.

2336. Veterans Administration Medical Center Library Service
Coatsville, PA 19320 (215) 384-7711 ext 333; FTS 489-7245
Ref Lib Mary Lou Burton (Acq). *ILL* Lauren Honemann.
Lib Type Health & Medicine.
Spec Subs Neuropsychiatric patient health education. *Spec Collecs* Neuropsychiatric patient health education.
Info Ret Servs BRS; NLM. *Coop Lib Nets* VALNET; CHI.
Circ Servs Avail Restricted to VA medical centers & CHI libraries.
Ref Servs Avail To other Federal libraries; to other libraries.

2337. Veterans Administration Medical Center Library Service
3900 Loch Raven Blvd, Baltimore, MD 21218 (301) 467-9932 ext 5464; FTS 922-5464
Admin Deborah A Stout. *ILL* Ann Pohlhaus.
Lib Type Health & Medicine.
Spec Subs General medical; GI; cardiology.
Info Ret Servs BRS. *Coop Lib Nets* VALNET; MAHSL. *Elec Mail Nets* CLASS.
Circ Servs Avail To other libraries.
Ref Servs Avail To other libraries.

2338. Veterans Administration Medical Center Library Service
Perry Point, MD 21902 (301) 642-2411; FTS 922-0278
Admin Barbara A Schultz. *ILL* Elizabeth McMillan.
Lib Type Health & Medicine.
Spec Subs Geriatrics; psychiatry.
Info Ret Servs BRS; MEDLARS. *Coop Lib Nets* VALNET. *Elec Mail Nets* Mailman.
Circ Servs Avail To other Federal libraries; to other libraries.
Ref Servs Avail To other Federal libraries; to other libraries.

2339. Veterans Administration Medical Center Library Service
Johnson City, Mountain Home, TN 37684 (615) 926-1171 ext 7454; FTS 854-7454
Admin Nancy P Dougherty.
Lib Type Health & Medicine.
Spec Subs Medicine; gerontology.
Info Ret Servs MEDLARS. *Shared Catalog Nets* OCLC thru VAL-NET. *Coop Lib Nets* VALNET; Tri-Cities Health Sciences Libraries Consortium. *Elec Mail Nets* CLASS; VA Regional E-Mail.
Circ Servs Avail To other Federal libraries.
Ref Servs Avail To other Federal libraries; to other libraries; to the general public; restricted to no on-line searching.

2340. Veterans Administration Medical Center Library Service
1030 Jefferson Ave, Memphis, TN 38104 (901) 523-8990 ext 5657; FTS 222-5657
Admin Mary V Taylor. *Ref Lib* Lyn Melin. *ILL* Bill Johnson. *Acq Lib* Mary Taylor.
Lib Type Health & Medicine; Hospital (Patients).
Spec Subs World War I & World War II histories. *Spec Collecs* Patient education.
Shared Catalog Nets OCLC thru VALNET. *Coop Lib Nets* VALNET; AMAHSL.
Circ Servs Avail To other Federal libraries; to other libraries; not open to the general public.
Ref Servs Avail To other Federal libraries; to other libraries; not open to the general public.

2341. Veterans Administration Medical Center Library Service
800 Zorn Ave, Louisville, KY 40202 (502) 895-3401 ext 621; FTS 355-9621
Admin James F Kastner. *Ref Lib* Gene M Haynes. *ILL* Alice P Briggs.
Lib Type Health & Medicine.
Spec Subs Orthopedics; nursing; social work.
Info Ret Servs BRS; National Library of Medicine. *Shared Catalog Nets* OCLC thru VALNET. *Coop Lib Nets* VALNET; KHSLC; KULS; KLN.

Circ Servs Avail To other Federal libraries; to other libraries; not open to the general public.
Ref Servs Avail To other Federal libraries; to other libraries; not open to the general public.

2342. Veterans Administration Medical Center Library Service
3200 Vine St, Cincinnati, OH 45220 (513) 861-3100 ext 4347; FTS 773-4347
Admin Cynthia R Sterling. *ILL* Anita Jacobs.
Lib Type Health & Medicine.
Spec Subs Gerontology; Alcohol abuse; Vietnam & concerns of Vietnam veterans.
Info Ret Servs BRS; NLM. *Coop Lib Nets* CAHSLA; Miami Valley Union List.
Circ Servs Avail To other Federal libraries; to other libraries; to the general public.
Ref Servs Avail To other Federal libraries; to other libraries; to the general public.

2343. Veterans Administration Medical Center Library Service
E 38th St at Home Ave, Marion, IN 46952 (317) 674-3321 ext 200; FTS 335-9200
Admin Karen A Davis. *ILL* Kathleen Hook.
Lib Type Health & Medicine; Hospital (Patients).
Spec Subs Psychiatry; psychology; geriatrics.
Info Ret Servs BRS; MEDLARS. *Shared Catalog Nets* OCLC thru VALNET. *Coop Lib Nets* VALNET; EIALSA; EIHSLA.
Circ Servs Avail To other Federal libraries; to other libraries; not open to the general public.
Ref Servs Avail To other Federal libraries; to other libraries; to the general public.

2344. Veterans Administration Medical Center Library Service
800 Poly Pl, Brooklyn, NY 11209 (718) 836-6600 ext 525, ILL ext 278; FTS 265-6525
Lib Type Health & Medicine; Hospital (Patients).
Spec Subs Allied health; health administration; nursing; patient education; psychology.
Info Ret Servs DIALOG; BRS; MEDLINE. *Coop Lib Nets* VALNET; Medical Library Center of New York; Metro; NY State Interlibrary Loan Network.

2345. Veterans Administration Medical Center Library Service
1500 Weiss, Saginaw, MI 48602 (517) 793-2340 ext 256; FTS 374-2256
Admin Nancy R Dingman.
Lib Type Health & Medicine; Hospital (Patients).
Spec Subs Patient health education; nursing; medical. *Spec Collecs* Audio-visual software; medicine; nursing.
Info Ret Servs DIALOG; BRS; NTIS. *Shared Catalog Nets* OCLC thru VALNET. *Coop Lib Nets* VALNET; Michigan Library Consortium; White Pine Library Consortium; Michigan Health Svcs Consortium; Valley Health Svcs Consortium. *Elec Mail Nets* CLASS; Interact.
Circ Servs Avail To other Federal libraries; to other libraries; not open to the general public.
Ref Servs Avail To other Federal libraries; to other libraries; not open to the general public.

2346. Veterans Administration Medical Center Library Service
Battle Creek, MI 49016 (616) 966-5600 ext 3569; FTS 974-3569
Admin Thomas Pyles, Jr. *Ref Lib* Barbara Burhans (ILL).
Lib Type Health & Medicine; Hospital (Patients).
Spec Subs Neurology; psychiatry.
Info Ret Servs BRS. *Shared Catalog Nets* OCLC thru VALNET. *Coop Lib Nets* VALNET; Southwest Michigan Library Consortium.
Circ Servs Avail To other Federal libraries; to other libraries; not open to the general public.
Ref Servs Avail To other Federal libraries; to other libraries; not open to the general public.

2347. Veterans Administration Medical Center Library Service
Knoxville, IA 50138 (515) 842-5512; FTS 862-6063
Lib Type Health & Medicine; Hospital (Patients).
Spec Subs Psychology; psychiatry; geriatrics.
Info Ret Servs MEDLINE. *Coop Lib Nets* VALNET. *Elec Mail Nets* CLASS.
Circ Servs Avail To other Federal libraries; to other libraries; not open to the general public; restricted to employees & patients.
Ref Servs Avail To other Federal libraries; to other libraries; not open to the general public; restricted to employees & patients.

2348. Veterans Administration Medical Center Library Service
5000 W National Ave, Milwaukee, WI 53295 (414) 384-2000 ext 2353; FTS 362-7353
Admin Jeanne A Holcomb (Chief Lib). *Ref Lib* Maureen Farmer.
Lib Type Health & Medicine; Hospital (Patients).
Spec Subs Medicine; surgery; dentistry; nursing; health sciences. *Spec Collecs* Local & military history. *In-house Files* Patient education collection (print & A-V).
Info Ret Servs DIALOG; BRS; MEDLARS. *Shared Catalog Nets* OCLC thru VALNET. *Coop Lib Nets* VALNET; SWHSL. *Elec Mail Nets* CLASS.
Circ Servs Avail To other Federal libraries; to other libraries; restricted to staff & patients; ILL.
Ref Servs Avail Restricted to staff & patients.

2349. Veterans Administration Medical Center Library Service
Tomah, WI 54660 (608) 372-3971 ext 283; FTS 364-6515
Admin William E Nielsen. *ILL* Lena C Kenyon.
Lib Type Health & Medicine.
Spec Subs Geriatrics; nursing psychiatry; clinical medicine; psychology; gerontology. *Spec Collecs* Health information.
Info Ret Servs NLM. *Shared Catalog Nets* OCLC thru VALNET. *Coop Lib Nets* VALNET; Western Wisconsin Health Sciences Library Consortium.
Circ Servs Avail To other Federal libraries; to other libraries.
Ref Servs Avail To other Federal libraries; to other libraries.

2350. Veterans Administration Medical Center Library Service
Miles City, MT 59301 (406) 232-3060; FTS 585-3060
Admin Elizabeth Alme.
Lib Type Health & Medicine.
Info Ret Servs MEDLARS. *Shared Catalog Nets* OCLC thru VALNET. *Coop Lib Nets* VALNET; MONCAT; PNRHSN; Montana Health Science Lib Network.
Circ Servs Avail To other Federal libraries; to other libraries.
Ref Servs Avail To other Federal libraries; to other libraries.

2351. Veterans Administration Medical Center Library Service
Highland Dr, Pittsburgh, PA 15206 (412) 363-4900
Admin Pauline M. Mason.
Lib Type Health & Medicine; Hospital (Patients).
Info Ret Servs DIALOG; BRS; MEDLINE. *Elec Mail Nets* MAILMAN.

2352. Veterans Administration Medical Center Library Service
3350 La Jolla Village Dr, San Diego, CA 92161 (619) 453-7500 ext 3421; FTS 897-3421
Admin Constance A. Baker.
Lib Type Health & Medicine.
Spec Subs Dentistry; internal medicine; nursing; biomedical research; patient health information; psychiatry; surgery.
Info Ret Servs DIALOG; National Library of Medicine. *Coop Lib Nets* VALNET; Cooperative Library Agency for Systems & Services.
Circ Servs Avail Not open to the general public; restricted to staff & patients.
Ref Servs Avail Not open to the general public; restricted to staff & patients.

2353. Veterans Administration Medical Center Library Service
Shreveport Hwy, Alexandria, LA 71301 (318) 473-0010/2548; FTS 497-0548
Admin Nancy M Guillet. *ILL* Huey P Minor.
Lib Type Health & Medicine; Hospital (Patients).
Spec Subs Health care; management.
Info Ret Servs BRS; MEDLARS/MEDLINE. *Shared Catalog Nets* OCLC thru VALNET. *Coop Lib Nets* VALNET; HSLAL; TALON. *Elec Mail Nets* BRS.
Circ Servs Avail To other Federal libraries; to other libraries; restricted to employees, patients & volunteers.
Ref Servs Avail To other Federal libraries; to other libraries; to the general public.

2354. Veterans Administration Medical Center Library Service
4500 S Lancaster Rd, Dallas, TX 75098 (214) 376-5451 ext 214; FTS 749-5214
Admin Nancy A Clark. *Ref Lib* Shirley Campbell. *ILL* Angelina Serda. *Acq Lib* Linda Knerr.
Lib Type Health & Medicine.
Info Ret Servs BRS; NLM. *Shared Catalog Nets* OCLC thru VALNET. *Coop Lib Nets* VALNET; Dallas/Tarrant County Health Science Libraries. *Elec Mail Nets* CLASS.
Circ Servs Avail To other libraries.
Ref Servs Avail To other Federal libraries; to other libraries; to the general public.

2355. Veterans Administration Medical Center Library Service
Marlin, TX 76661 (817) 883-3511 ext 249; FTS 728-1249
Admin Edwina M Hubbard.
Lib Type Health & Medicine; Hospital (Patients).
Info Ret Servs MEDLINE. *Elec Mail Nets* CLASS.
Circ Servs Avail To other Federal libraries; to other libraries.
Ref Servs Avail To other Federal libraries; to other libraries.

2356. Veterans Administration Medical Center Library Service
Kerrville, TX 78028 (512) 896-2020; FTS 730-5070
Admin Diana F Akins. *ILL* Annette Van Ostrand.
Lib Type Health & Medicine; Hospital (Patients).
Spec Collecs Large print books & talking books.
Info Ret Servs MEDLARS. *Shared Catalog Nets* OCLC thru VALNET. *Coop Lib Nets* VALNET; HOLSA. *Elec Mail Nets* CLASS.
Circ Servs Avail To other Federal libraries; to other libraries; not open to the general public.
Ref Servs Avail To other Federal libraries; to other libraries; not open to the general public.

2357. Veterans Administration Medical Center Library Service
6010 Amarillo Blvd, W, Amarillo, TX 79106 (806) 355-9703 ext 263; FTS 735-7277
Admin Cheryl A Latham.
Lib Type Health & Medicine.
Spec Collecs Patient education; large print books.
Info Ret Servs MEDLINE. *Coop Lib Nets* VALNET.
Circ Servs Avail To other Federal libraries; to other libraries; restricted to staff & patients.
Ref Servs Avail To other Federal libraries; to other libraries; to the general public.

2358. Veterans Administration Medical Center Library Service
Sheridan, WY 82801 (307) 672-3473 ext 261
Admin Mary Curtis Kellett. *ILL* Bess Jurasek.
Lib Type Health & Medicine; Hospital (Patients).
Spec Subs Psychology.
Info Ret Servs BRS. *Shared Catalog Nets* OCLC thru VALNET. *Coop Lib Nets* VALNET; NWMLC. *Elec Mail Nets* CLASS.
Circ Servs Avail To other Federal libraries; to other libraries.
Ref Servs Avail To other Federal libraries; to other libraries; to the general public.

2359. Veterans Administration Medical Center Library Service
500 W Fort St, Boise, ID 83702 (208) 338-7206; FTS 554-7206
Admin Gordon Carlson. *ILL* Jean Stubbs.
Lib Type Hospital (Patients).
Spec Subs Internal medicine.
Info Ret Servs BRS. *Shared Catalog Nets* OCLC thru VALNET. *Coop Lib Nets* Boise Valley Health Science Lib Consortium. *Elec Mail Nets* BRS/MSGS (T7B5); CLASS.
Circ Servs Avail To other Federal libraries; to other libraries.
Ref Servs Avail To other Federal libraries; to other libraries; to the general public.

2360. Veterans Administration Medical Center Library Service
500 Foothill Blvd, Salt Lake City, UT 84148 (801) 582-1565; FTS 588-1209
Admin Cherryi M Povey. *Ref Lib* Kirk Davis. *ILL* Sharon Flaig. *Acq Lib* Barbara Windley.
Lib Type Health & Medicine; Hospital (Patients).
Info Ret Servs DIALOG; BRS. *Shared Catalog Nets* OCLC thru VALNET. *Coop Lib Nets* VALNET; Utah Health Sciences Library Consortium. *Elec Mail Nets* CLASS.
Circ Servs Avail To other Federal libraries; to other libraries; not open to the general public.
Ref Servs Avail To other Federal libraries; to other libraries; to the general public.

2361. Veterans Administration Medical Center Library Service
Tucson, AZ 85723 (602) 792-1450; FTS 765-6361
Admin Mark A Petersen. *Ref Lib* William Azevedo (Acq). *ILL* Connie Skinner.
Lib Type Health & Medicine; Hospital (Patients).
Info Ret Servs MEDLINE. *Coop Lib Nets* VALNET; SABL; MLGSCA; PSRMLS. *Elec Mail Nets* CLASS.
Circ Servs Avail To other Federal libraries; to other libraries; not open to the general public; restricted to with permission from librarian.
Ref Servs Avail To other Federal libraries; to other libraries; not open to the general public; restricted to with permission from librarian.

2362. Veterans Administration Medical Center Library Service
2100 Ridgecrest Dr, SE, Albuquerque, NM 87108 (505) 265-1711 ext 2338; FTS 572-9338
Admin Nancy E Myer. *Ref Lib* Phyllis Kregstein. *ILL* Gloria Gill.
Lib Type Health & Medicine.
Spec Subs Medicine; surgery; nursing; psychology; psychiatry.
Info Ret Servs DIALOG; MEDLARS. *Shared Catalog Nets* OCLC thru VALNET. *Coop Lib Nets* VALNET; New Mexico Consortium of Biomedical & Hospital Libraries. *Elec Mail Nets* CLASS.
Circ Servs Avail To other Federal libraries; to other libraries.
Ref Servs Avail To other Federal libraries; to other libraries.

2363. Veterans Administration Medical Center Library Service
2615 E Clinton Ave, Fresno, CA 93703 (209) 225-6100 ext 511; FTS 466-9511
Admin Cynthia K Meyer. *Ref Lib* Paul Connor. *ILL* Glenna Sprauge.
Lib Type Hospital (Patients).
Spec Subs Medicine; surgery; nursing. *Spec Collecs* Reprints on coccidioidomycosis, 1897-1972.
Info Ret Servs DIALOG; MEDLARS. *Shared Catalog Nets* OCLC thru VALNET. *Coop Lib Nets* VALNET. *Elec Mail Nets* CLASS.
Circ Servs Avail To other Federal libraries; to other libraries; not open to the general public.
Ref Servs Avail To other Federal libraries; to other libraries; not open to the general public.

2364. Veterans Administration Medical Center Library Service
Tacoma, WA 98493 (206) 582-8440; FTS 396-6357/6356/6355
Admin Dennis L Levi. *ILL* Gladys Kanz. *Acq Lib* Enid Laulicht.
Lib Type Health & Medicine.
Spec Subs Psychology; gerontology.
Info Ret Servs BRS; MEDLARS. *Coop Lib Nets* VALNET. *Elec Mail Nets* CLASS.
Circ Servs Avail To other Federal libraries; to other libraries.
Ref Servs Avail To other Federal libraries; to other libraries.

2365. Veterans Administration Medical Center Library Service
Fayetteville, AR 72701 (501) 443-4301; FTS 740-0546
Admin Jeanine B Brown. *Ref Lib* Jeannie Green. *ILL* Sylvia Griffey.
Lib Type Health & Medicine.
Spec Subs Medical; nursing.
Info Ret Servs BRS. *Coop Lib Nets* VALNET.
Circ Servs Avail To other Federal libraries; to other libraries.
Ref Servs Avail To other Federal libraries; to other libraries.

2366. Veterans Administration Medical Center Library Service
Roseburg, OR 97470 (503) 672-4411; FTS 422-4250
Admin Cathryn M Jordan. *ILL* Betty Carey.
Lib Type Health & Medicine; Hospital (Patients).
Spec Subs Medicine; nursing; consumer health.
Info Ret Servs DIALOG; BRS; MEDLARS. *Shared Catalog Nets* OCLC thru VALNET. *Coop Lib Nets* VALNET; OHSLA. *Elec Mail Nets* CLASS.
Circ Servs Avail To other Federal libraries; to other libraries.
Ref Servs Avail To other Federal libraries; to other libraries; to the general public.

2367. Veterans Administration Medical Center Library Service
1900 E Main St, Danville, IL 61832 (217) 442-8000, ext 523; FTS 951-9523
Admin Edward J. Poletti.
Lib Type Health & Medicine.
Spec Subs Paramedical; psychiatry; psychology.

2368. Veterans Administration Medical Center Library Service
1500 N Westwood Blvd, Poplar Bluff, MO 63901 (314) 686-4151, ext 309; FTS 276-8309 (Medical Library); 276-8377 (Patients' Library)
Admin Kwang H. Streiff.
Lib Type Health & Medicine; Hospital (Patients).
Info Ret Servs DIALOG; MEDLINE. *Coop Lib Nets* VALNET; Midcontinental Regional Medical Library Program.

2369. Veterans Administration Medical Center Library Service
Rt 1011, Honor Heights Dr, Muskogee, OK 74401 (918) 683-3261, ext 240; FTS 745-3240
Admin Larry L. Shea. *ILL* Allen Jestice.
Lib Type Health & Medicine; Hospital (Patients).
Info Ret Servs BRS *Shared Catalog Nets* OCLC. *Coop Lib Nets* VALNET; South Central Regional Medical Library Program; Oklahoma Health Sciences Library Association (OHSLA). *Elec Mail Nets* CLASS.
Circ Servs Avail To other Federal libraries; to other libraries.
Ref Servs Avail To other Federal libraries; to other libraries; to the general public.

2370. Veterans Administration Medical Center Library Service
PO Box 1035, Portland, OR 97207 (503) 222-9221, ext 2231; FTS 424-2231
Admin Nymah L. Trued. *Ref Lib* Sandra Brayson. *ILL* Phyllis McCulloch.
Lib Type Health & Medicine.
Spec Subs Gerontology; alcohol/drug treatment. *Spec Collecs* Patient health information.

Info Ret Servs BRS; MEDLINE. *Shared Catalog Nets* OCLC. *Coop Lib Nets* VALNET; Oregon Health Sciences Library Assn (OHSLA); Washington Medical Library Assn (WMLA). *Elec Mail Nets* CLASS.
Circ Servs Avail To other Federal libraries; to other libraries.
Ref Servs Avail To other Federal libraries; to other libraries; not open to the general public.

2371. Veterans Administration Medical Center Library Service
Batavia, NY 14020 (716) 343-7500 ext 274; FTS 473-9274
Admin Madeline Coco.
Lib Type Health & Medicine; Hospital (Patients).
Spec Subs Geriatrics & gerontology; nursing. *Spec Collecs* Patient health education; nursing.
Info Ret Servs Medline. *Shared Catalog Nets* OCLC. *Coop Lib Nets* VALNET; Western New York Library Resources Council (WNYLRC).
Circ Servs Avail To other Federal libraries; to other libraries; not open to the general public; restricted to staff, patients/outpatients, & volunteers.
Ref Servs Avail To other Federal libraries; to other libraries; to the general public.

2372. Veterans Administration Medical Center Library Service
1400 Veterans of Foreign Wars Pkwy, West Roxbury, MA 02132 (617) 323-7700 ext 5670; FTS 837-5670
Admin Suzanne N Noyes.
Lib Type Health & Medicine.
Spec Subs Allied health professions; cardiology; medicine; spinal cord injury.
Info Ret Servs BRS. *Coop Lib Nets* VALNET. *Elec Mail Nets* CLASS.

2373. Veterans Administration Medical Center Library Service
East Orange, NJ 07019 (201) 676-1000; FTS 342-1388 (Patients' Library); 342-1519 (Medical Library)
Admin Calvin A Zamarelli.
Lib Type Health & Medicine; Hospital (Patients).
Spec Subs Alcoholism; clinical needs in medicine; drug rehabilitation; neurology; nursing; psychiatry; psychology; social work.
Info Ret Servs DIALOG; BRS; MEDLINE. *Elec Mail Nets* MAILMAN.
Circ Servs Avail To other Federal libraries; not open to the general public.
Ref Servs Avail Not open to the general public; restricted to health science professionals by appointment.

2374. Veterans Administration Medical Center Library Service
2460 Wrightsboro Rd, Augusta, GA 30910 (404) 724-5116 ext 2478; FTS 251-2478
Admin Elizabeth A Northington. *Ref Lib* Anita Bell; Mary Fran Prottsman (ILL).
Lib Type Health & Medicine.
Spec Subs Psychiatry. *Spec Collecs* Patient education.
Info Ret Servs Medlars. *Shared Catalog Nets* VALNET. *Coop Lib Nets* VALNET.
Circ Servs Avail To other Federal libraries; to other libraries; to the general public.
Ref Servs Avail To other Federal libraries; to other libraries; to the general public.

2375. Veterans Administration Medical Center Library Service
10000 Brecksville Rd, Brecksville, OH 44141 (216) 525-3030 ext 6241; FTS 290-6241
Admin Nancy S Tesmer. *Ref Lib* Mary E Conway; John C White; John W Wells.
Lib Type Health & Medicine.
Spec Subs Psychiatry; mental health. *Spec Collecs* Audiovisual collection; patient health education; post-traumatic stress.
Info Ret Servs DIALOG; BRS; MEDLARS; EdVent; WILSONLINE. *Coop Lib Nets* VALNET; MLANO; O.H.I.O. *Elec Mail Nets* CLASS.

Circ Servs Avail To other Federal libraries; to other libraries; not open to the general public.
Ref Servs Avail To other Federal libraries; to other libraries; to the general public.

2376. Veterans Administration Medical Center Library Service

508 Fulton St, Durham, NC 27705 (919) 286-0411; FTS 629-6644
Admin Leola Hall Jenkins. *Ref Lib* Margaret F Clifton. *ILL* Sheila H Thompson.
Lib Type Health & Medicine; Hospital (Patients).
Spec Collecs Patient education.
Info Ret Servs BRS; NLM MEDLARS. *Shared Catalog Nets* VALNET. *Coop Lib Nets* VALNET. *Elec Mail Nets* CLASS; E-MAIL (MAILMAN).
Circ Servs Avail To other Federal libraries; to other libraries; not open to the general public.
Ref Servs Avail To other Federal libraries; to other libraries; not open to the general public.

2377. Veterans Administration Medical Center Library Service

Lexington, KY 40511 (606) 233-4511; FTS 352-3194
Admin Robert Bradley. *Ref Lib* Diane Gelarden-Cooper (Medical); Deborah Kessler (Patient's).
Lib Type Health & Medicine.
Spec Subs Leestown Div: psychiatry & geriatrics; Cooper Drive Div: geriatrics & medical-surgical.
Info Ret Servs MEDLINE. *Shared Catalog Nets* OCLC. *Coop Lib Nets* VALNET; Kentucky Health Sciences Library Consortium.
Circ Servs Avail To other Federal libraries; to other libraries; not open to the general public.
Ref Servs Avail To other Federal libraries; to other libraries; not open to the general public.

2378. Veterans Administration Medical Center Library Service

Biloxi, MS 39531 (601) 865-4798; FTS 499-5221
Admin Chris Jones. *Ref Lib* Pam Howell; Donna Locke. *ILL* Janet Chandler; Velma Jackson. *Acq Lib* Gwen Vanderfin.
Lib Type Health & Medicine.
Spec Subs General medicine; surgery; psychiatry; psychology.
Info Ret Servs BRS. *Coop Lib Nets* VALNET; Mississippi Biomedical Library Consortium. *Elec Mail Nets* OnTyme.
Circ Servs Avail To other Federal libraries; to other libraries; not open to the general public.
Ref Servs Avail To other Federal libraries; to other libraries; to the general public.

2379. Veterans Administration Medical Center Library Service

4100 W 3rd St, Dayton, OH 45428 (513) 268-6511 ext 2381; FTS 778-2381
Admin Lendell L Beverly. *Ref Lib* Robert Mohrman.
Lib Type Health & Medicine.
Spec Subs Gerontology; cardiology; gastroenterology.
Info Ret Servs DIALOG; BRS. *Coop Lib Nets* VALNET; DOCLINE; Miami Valley Assoc of Health Science Libraries (MVAHSL). *Elec Mail Nets* OnTyme II-CLASS.
Circ Servs Avail To other Federal libraries; to other libraries; not open to the general public.
Ref Servs Avail To other Federal libraries; to other libraries; to the general public; restricted to no on-line services for general public.

2380. Veterans Administration Medical Center Library Service

North Chicago, IL 60064 (312) 578-3757; FTS 384-3757
Admin Carl Worstell. *Ref Lib* Lou Ann Moore (ILL). *Acq Lib* Audrey Lyle.
Lib Type Health & Medicine; Hospital (Patients).
Spec Subs Psychiatry; psychology.
Info Ret Servs BRS. *Shared Catalog Nets* OCLC. *Coop Lib Nets* VALNET; Lake County Consortium; North Suburban Library System. *Elec Mail Nets* CLASS.
Circ Servs Avail To other Federal libraries; to other libraries; not open to the general public.

Ref Servs Avail To other Federal libraries; to other libraries; to the general public.

2381. Veterans Administration Medical Center Library Service

Prescott, AZ 86313 (602) 445-4860 ext 271; FTS 762-7271
Admin Carol Clark.
Lib Type Health & Medicine; Hospital (Patients).
Info Ret Servs BRS. *Coop Lib Nets* VALNET. *Elec Mail Nets* CLASS OnTyme.
Circ Servs Avail Restricted to hospital patients & staff.
Ref Servs Avail Restricted to hospital staff.

2382. Veterans Administration Medical Center Library Service

1201 Broad Rock Rd, Richmond, VA 23249 (804) 230-0001, ext 1763; FTS 982-1763
Lib Type Health & Medicine.

2383. Veterans Administration Medical Center Library Service

77 Wainwright Dr, Walla Walla, WA 99362 (509) 525-5200 ext 253; FTS 434-6200 ext 253
Admin Max J Merrell.
Lib Type Health & Medicine; Hospital (Patients).
Spec Subs Medical books & A-V; nursing & other health related subjects.
Info Ret Servs MEDLINE. *Shared Catalog Nets* VA central cataloging contract. *Coop Lib Nets* Washington Medical Library Assoc (WMLA); WLN, via community college. *Elec Mail Nets* CLASS.
Circ Servs Avail To other Federal libraries; to other libraries; restricted to medical personnel.
Ref Servs Avail To other Federal libraries; to other libraries; restricted to medical questions.

2384. Veterans Administration Medical Center, John L McClellan Memorial Veterans Hospital, Medical Library

4300 W 7th St, Little Rock, AR 72205 (501) 660-2044; FTS 742-2044
Admin George M Zumwalt. *Ref Lib* Michael Blanton; Jack Griffith (ILL, Acq).
Lib Type Health & Medicine.
Info Ret Servs BRS. *Shared Catalog Nets* OCLC. *Coop Lib Nets* VALNET.
Circ Servs Avail To other Federal libraries; to other libraries; restricted to staff.
Ref Servs Avail Restricted to staff.

2385. Veterans Administration Medical Center, Medical/General Library

Gainesville, FL 32602 (904) 376-1611 ext 6313; FTS 947-6313
Admin Marylyn Gresser. *ILL* Helene Petty.
Lib Type Health & Medicine.
Spec Subs Alcoholism. *Spec Collecs* Veterans. *In-house Files* Geriatrics.
Info Ret Servs BRS. *Coop Lib Nets* VALNET. *Elec Mail Nets* CLASS.
Circ Servs Avail To other libraries; not open to the general public.
Ref Servs Avail Not open to the general public; restricted to staff & community health professionals.

2386. Veterans Administration Medical Center, Medical Library

4801 Linwood Blvd, Kansas City, MO 64128 (816) 861-4700 ext 540/546; FTS 754-1540
Admin Shirley C Ting. *Ref Lib* Valerie Smith (Acq). *ILL* Herb Simon.
Lib Type Health & Medicine.
Spec Subs Medical; surgical; nursing; psychiatry. *Spec Collecs* Patient health education; management.
Info Ret Servs DIALOG; BRS. *Coop Lib Nets* VALNET; Midcontinental Regional Medical Library Program (MCRMLP); Health Sciences Library Group of Greater Kansas City (HSLGGKC). *Elec Mail Nets* GTE Telemail.
Circ Servs Avail To other Federal libraries; to other libraries; not open to the general public.

Ref Servs Avail To other Federal libraries; to other libraries; not open to the general public.

2387. Veterans Administration Medical Center, Medical Library

1660 S Columbia Way, Seattle, WA 98108 (206) 764-2065; FTS 396-2065
Admin Mary Jo Harbold (Acq). *Ref Lib* Jeanyce Almgren. *ILL* Elizabeth Miller.
Lib Type Health & Medicine.
Info Ret Servs BRS; Medline; WLN. *Shared Catalog Nets* WLN. *Coop Lib Nets* VALNET; Seattle Area Hospital Library Consortium (SAHLC).
Circ Servs Avail Not open to the general public; restricted to VA & consortium.
Ref Servs Avail To other libraries; restricted to VA & consortium.

2388. Veterans Administration Medical Center, Medical Library

West Haven, CT 06516 (203) 932-5711 ext 426/336; FTS 641-7336
Admin Fran Bernstein. *Ref Lib* Jeff Nicholas. *ILL* Gail LaScola.
Lib Type Health & Medicine.
Info Ret Servs DIALOG; BRS; MEDLARS; NLM. *Coop Lib Nets* CAHSL.
Circ Servs Avail To other Federal libraries; to other libraries.
Ref Servs Avail To other Federal libraries; to other libraries.

2389. Veterans Administration Medical Center, Medical Library

130 W Kingsbridge Rd, Bronx, NY 10468 (212) 579-1631 ext 435; FTS 663-1631
Admin Margaret M Kinney. *Ref Lib* Kathleen E O'Hogan (ILL).
Lib Type Health & Medicine.
Spec Subs Clinical medicine. *Spec Collecs* Cancer; rehabilitation medicine; spinal cord injury; dietetics.
Info Ret Servs BRS; MEDLINE. *Shared Catalog Nets* OCLC thru VALNET. *Coop Lib Nets* METRO; MLC; Manhattan-Bronx Health Sciences Libraries.
Circ Servs Avail To other Federal libraries; to other libraries; not open to the general public; restricted to health science personnel.
Ref Servs Avail Not open to the general public; restricted to health science personnel.

2390. Veterans Administration Medical Center, Medical Library

Northport, NY 11768 (516) 261-4400; FTS 663-2223
Admin Deborah M Sher. *Ref Lib* Caryl Kazen. *ILL* Magdelene Aquilino.
Lib Type Health & Medicine.
Spec Subs Geriatrics; nursing.
Info Ret Servs DIALOG; BRS; MEDLARS. *Shared Catalog Nets* OCLC thru VALNET. *Coop Lib Nets* MEDLI; LILRC. *Elec Mail Nets* CLASS.
Circ Servs Avail To other Federal libraries; to other libraries; not open to the general public.
Ref Servs Avail To other Federal libraries; to other libraries; to the general public.

2391. Veterans Administration Medical Center, Medical Library

Lebanon, PA 17042 (717) 272-6621; FTS 592-4247
Admin David E Falger. *Ref Lib* Barbara Deaven. *ILL* Suzette Flashel.
Lib Type Health & Medicine.
Spec Subs General medicine; geriatrics; psychiatry; nursing.
Info Ret Servs DIALOG; BRS; MEDLINE. *Coop Lib Nets* VALNET; Greater Northeastern Regional Medical Library Network; Central Pennsylvania Health Sciences Library Assoc. *Elec Mail Nets* Mailman.
Circ Servs Avail To other Federal libraries; to other libraries; not open to the general public.
Ref Servs Avail To other Federal libraries; to other libraries; not open to the general public.

2392. Veterans Administration Medical Center, Medical Library

1970 Roanoke Blvd, Salem, VA 24153 (703) 982-2463 ext 2380; FTS 387-2380
Admin Jean Kennedy. *Ref Lib* Jacqueline Cahill (Acq). *ILL* Velma Hardy.
Lib Type Health & Medicine.
Spec Subs Medicine; nursing; psychiatry; psychology.
Info Ret Servs MEDLARS. *Coop Lib Nets* VALNET; SWVAHILI.
Circ Servs Avail To other Federal libraries; to other libraries; not open to the general public; restricted to staff, affiliated students & community health professionals.
Ref Servs Avail To other Federal libraries; to other libraries; not open to the general public.

2393. Veterans Administration Medical Center, Medical Library

215 Perry Hill Road, Montgomery, AL 36193 (205) 272-4670; FTS 228-4128
Admin Johnette Cummins. *ILL* Susan Helms.
Lib Type Health & Medicine.
Spec Subs Medicine; nursing; pharmacy; nutrition.
Info Ret Servs MEDLARS. *Shared Catalog Nets* OCLC thru VALNET. *Coop Lib Nets* VALNET; ALHELA; MAHIC.
Circ Servs Avail To other Federal libraries; to other libraries.
Ref Servs Avail To other Federal libraries; to other libraries.

2394. Veterans Administration Medical Center, Medical Library

1481 W 10th St, Indianapolis, IN 46202 (317) 635-7401 ext 2333; FTS 332-2333
Admin Judith Alfred. *Ref Lib* Lori Klein (Acq). *ILL* Terry Brenner.
Lib Type Health & Medicine.
Spec Collecs Geriatrics; Vietnam.
Info Ret Servs BRS; NLM. *Shared Catalog Nets* OCLC thru VALNET. *Coop Lib Nets* VALNET; CIHSLC. *Elec Mail Nets* BRS; CLASS.
Circ Servs Avail To other Federal libraries; to other libraries; to the general public.
Ref Servs Avail To other Federal libraries; to other libraries; to the general public.

2395. Veterans Administration Medical Center, Medical Library

Allen Park, MI 48101 (313) 562-6000 ext 380; FTS 378-8381
Admin Arlene Devlin. *Ref Lib* Mary Jo Durivage. *ILL* Stephanie Boudreau.
Lib Type Health & Medicine.
Spec Subs Medicine; patient health; nursing.
Info Ret Servs DIALOG; BRS; MEDLARS. *Coop Lib Nets* VALNET; MDMLG; MHSLC. *Elec Mail Nets* CLASS.
Circ Servs Avail Restricted to VA staff.
Ref Servs Avail Restricted to patients & families.

2396. Veterans Administration Medical Center, Medical Library

2215 Fuller Rd, Ann Arbor, MI 48105 (313) 769-7100 ext 620; FTS 374-5620
Admin Vickie Smith (Act Chief). *ILL* Ollie Person.
Lib Type Health & Medicine.
Spec Subs Medical; patient education.
Info Ret Servs NLM. *Shared Catalog Nets* OCLC thru VALNET. *Coop Lib Nets* VALNET; MDMLG; WLN.
Circ Servs Avail To other Federal libraries; to other libraries; restricted to staff & ILL to other libraries.
Ref Servs Avail To other Federal libraries; to other libraries; to the general public.

2397. Veterans Administration Medical Center, Medical Library

Fort Meade, SD 57741 (605) 347-2511 ext 279; FTS 782-6279
Admin Gene Stevens. *ILL* Jan Olson.
Lib Type Health & Medicine.
Info Ret Servs MEDLARS (Medline). *Shared Catalog Nets* OCLC thru VALNET. *Coop Lib Nets* VALNET.

Circ Servs Avail To other Federal libraries; to other libraries; to the general public.

Ref Servs Avail To other Federal libraries; to other libraries; to the general public.

2398. Veterans Administration Medical Center Medical Library

135 E 38th St, Erie, PA 16504 (814) 868-8661 ext 157; FTS 721-2351

Admin Jeff Kager.

Lib Type Health & Medicine.

Spec Subs Medicine; mental health; nursing; surgery.

Info Ret Servs MEDLINE; BRS. *Elec Mail Nets* MAILMAN.

2399. Veterans Administration Medical Center, Medical Library

Sepulveda, CA 91343 (213) 891-7711 ext 2681; FTS 960-2681

Admin Jon Erickson (Act Chief Lib Serv). *Ref Lib* Jon Erickson (Acq). *ILL* Mariana Mirabella.

Lib Type Health & Medicine.

Spec Subs Patient health education. *Spec Collecs* Patient health education.

Info Ret Servs DIALOG; MEDLARS. *Shared Catalog Nets* OCLC thru VALNET. *Coop Lib Nets* VALNET. *Elec Mail Nets* CLASS.

Circ Servs Avail To other Federal libraries; not open to the general public.

Ref Servs Avail To other Federal libraries; not open to the general public.

2400. Veterans Administration Medical Center, Medical Library

1055 Clermont St, Denver, CO 80220 (303) 399-8020; FTS 322-2821

Admin Ruth E Gilbert.

Lib Type Health & Medicine.

Spec Subs General medicine; surgery; nursing.

Info Ret Servs BRS; MEDLARS. *Shared Catalog Nets* OCLC (thru VACO). *Coop Lib Nets* VALNET; Colorado Council Medical Librarians; Denver Area Health Sciences Libraries Consortium. *Elec Mail Nets* CLASS; Mile High Mail/Unison (Denver).

Circ Servs Avail To other Federal libraries; to other libraries.

Ref Servs Avail To other Federal libraries; to other libraries.

2401. Veterans Administration Medical Center, Medical Library

Butler, PA 16001 (412) 287-4781

Admin Dianne Hohn.

Lib Type Health & Medicine; Hospital (Patients).

Info Ret Servs BRS. *Shared Catalog Nets* OCLC. *Coop Lib Nets* VALNET. *Elec Mail Nets* CLASS Online.

Circ Servs Avail To other Federal libraries; to other libraries; to the general public; restricted to material used in library for public.

Ref Servs Avail To other Federal libraries; to other libraries; to the general public; restricted to material used in library for public.

2402. Veterans Administration Medical Center, Medical Library

Prescott, AZ 86313 (602) 445-4860; FTS 762-7271

Admin Carol A. Clark.

Lib Type Health & Medicine.

Info Ret Servs MEDLINE. *Coop Lib Nets* VALNET.

Circ Servs Avail Restricted to special arrangement.

2403. Veterans Administration Medical Center, Medical Library

2300 Ramsey St, Fayetteville, NC 28301 (919) 488-2120 ext 7072; FTS 699-7072

Admin Christine J Simpson. *ILL* Lucille Croom (Acq).

Lib Type Health & Medicine.

Spec Subs Medicine; nursing; geriatrics.

Info Ret Servs DIALOG; BRS; MEDLARS. *Shared Catalog Nets* OCLC. *Coop Lib Nets* Cape Fear Consortium. *Elec Mail Nets* Class E-Mail; VA-Mailman.

Circ Servs Avail To other Federal libraries; to other libraries; not open to the general public.

Ref Servs Avail To other Federal libraries; to other libraries; to the general public.

2404. Veterans Administration Medical Center, Medical Library

Asheville, NC 28805 (704) 298-7911 ext 5348; FTS 672-5300

Admin Sam Tucker.

Lib Type Health & Medicine; Hospital (Patients).

Info Ret Servs BRS; NLM. *Coop Lib Nets* VALNET. *Elec Mail Nets* VA-Mailman.

Circ Servs Avail To other Federal libraries; to other libraries; not open to the general public.

Ref Servs Avail To other Federal libraries; to other libraries; not open to the general public.

2405. Veterans Administration Medical Center, Medical Library

109 Bee St, Charleston, SC 29403 (803) 577-5011; FTS 236-7274

Admin Jane O Crane. *ILL* Jean Frentz.

Lib Type Health & Medicine.

Info Ret Servs NLM (Medlars). *Shared Catalog Nets* OCLC. *Coop Lib Nets* South Carolina Health Information Network (SCHIN). *Elec Mail Nets* CLASS Ontyme.

Circ Servs Avail To other Federal libraries; to other libraries.

Ref Servs Avail To other Federal libraries; to other libraries.

2406. Veterans Administration Medical Center, Medical Library

Bay Pines, FL 33504 (813) 398-9367; FTS 826-5567

Admin Ann A Conlan. *Ref Lib* Arnold Jasen. *ILL* Pauline Tucker.

Lib Type Health & Medicine.

Spec Subs Medicine; nursing. *Spec Collecs* Geriatrics.

Info Ret Servs DIALOG; BRS; MEDLINE. *Shared Catalog Nets* OCLC; VA Library Network. *Coop Lib Nets* VALNET; Tampa Bay Medical Library Network. *Elec Mail Nets* E-Mail; NLM DOCLINE.

Circ Servs Avail To other Federal libraries; restricted to medical personnel.

Ref Servs Avail To other Federal libraries; restricted to medical personnel.

2407. Veterans Administration Medical Center, Medical Library

700 S 19th St, Birmingham, AL 35233 (205) 933-8101 ext 6472; FTS 534-6472

Admin Mary Ann Knotts. *Ref Lib* Nelle Williams (ILL); Jennifer Burt (A-V). *Acq Lib* Gail Frey.

Lib Type Health & Medicine; Hospital (Patients).

Info Ret Servs DIALOG; BRS; MEDLARS. *Coop Lib Nets* Jefferson County Hospital Librarians' Assoc (JCHLA). *Elec Mail Nets* CLASS Ontyme.

Circ Servs Avail To other Federal libraries; to other libraries; not open to the general public.

Ref Servs Avail Not open to the general public.

2408. Veterans Administration Medical Center, Medical Library

Tuscaloosa, AL 35404 (205) 553-3760 ext 2355/2395; FTS 228-2355

Admin Olivia S Maniece. *Ref Lib* Betsy S Pertzog. *ILL* Ruby P Shirley.

Lib Type Health & Medicine.

Spec Subs Psychiatry; aged & aging/geriatrics; alcoholism. *Spec Collecs* Geriatrics; alcoholism; psychiatry.

Info Ret Servs MEDLINE. *Shared Catalog Nets* OCLC. *Coop Lib Nets* VALNET; Tuscaloosa Health Sciences Library Assoc (THeSLA). *Elec Mail Nets* Medical District #10 Electronic Mail System.

Circ Servs Avail To other Federal libraries; to other libraries; not open to the general public.

Ref Servs Avail To other Federal libraries; to other libraries; not open to the general public.

2409. Veterans Administration Medical Center, Medical Library

Salisbury, NC 28144 (704) 636-2351 ext 471/446; FTS 672-9471

Admin Mara R Wilhelm. *Ref Lib* Lucile Owsley; Alice Crownfield. *ILL* Brenda Seamon.

Lib Type Health & Medicine; Hospital (Patients).

Spec Subs Aging; alcoholism; drug abuse; geriatrics/gerontology; mental disorders; nursing; psychiatry; schizophrenia.

Info Ret Servs BRS; NLM. *Shared Catalog Nets* VALNET. *Elec Mail Nets* CLASS; BRS; MAILMAN.

Circ Servs Avail To other libraries; not open to the general public; restricted to staff & retirees.

Ref Servs Avail Not open to the general public; restricted to staff.

2410. Veterans Administration Medical Center, Medical Library

17273 State Rte 104, Chillicothe, OH 45601 (614) 773-1141 ext 7629; FTS 975-7692

Admin Rozelle B Webb (Act Chief). *Acq Lib* Sue Starr.

Lib Type Health & Medicine.

Spec Subs Medical & health science.

Info Ret Servs BRS. *Coop Lib Nets* VALNET.

Circ Servs Avail To other Federal libraries; to other libraries.

Ref Servs Avail To other Federal libraries; to other libraries; to the general public.

2411. Veterans Administration Medical Center, Medical Library

Iron Mountain, MI 49801 (906) 774-3300; FTS 360-3250

Admin Judith A Owen.

Lib Type Health & Medicine.

Info Ret Servs MEDLARS.

Circ Servs Avail To other Federal libraries; not open to the general public.

Ref Servs Avail To other Federal libraries; not open to the general public.

2412. Veterans Administration Medical Center, Medical Library, Library Service

4150 Clement St, San Francisco, CA 94121 (415) 221-4810; FTS 470-3302

Admin William Koch.

Lib Type Health & Medicine.

Spec Subs Biomedicine; patient education.

Info Ret Servs BRS; MEDLARS. *Shared Catalog Nets* OCLC thru VALNET. *Coop Lib Nets* VALNET; SFBLN. *Elec Mail Nets* CLASS.

Circ Servs Avail Not open to the general public.

Ref Servs Avail Not open to the general public.

2413. Veterans Administration Medical Center, Medical & Patient's Library

N Main St, Northampton, MA 01060 (413) 584-4040; FTS 836-0250/0416

Admin Marjorie S O'Brien. *Ref Lib* Marjorie C Dewey (ILL).

Lib Type Health & Medicine; Hospital (Patients).

Spec Subs Medicine; nursing; psychiatry. *Spec Collecs* Patient health education; Vietnam veterans.

Info Ret Servs BRS. *Shared Catalog Nets* OCLC thru VALNET. *Coop Lib Nets* VALNET; MAHSLIN; WMHIC. *Elec Mail Nets* CLASS; MEDLINK (ALANET-ITT based).

Circ Servs Avail To other Federal libraries; to other libraries.

Ref Servs Avail To other Federal libraries; to other libraries.

2414. Veterans Administration Medical Center, Medical & Patient's Library

3495 Bailey Ave, Buffalo, NY 14215 (716) 834-9200 ext 2694; FTS 432-2694

Admin Joyce A Kaupa. *Ref Lib* James Mendola (Acq). *ILL* Russell Hall.

Lib Type Health & Medicine; Hospital (Patients).

Spec Subs Medicine; surgery; geriatrics; cardiology; nursing; management. *Spec Collecs* Patient health education; patient recreational library. *In-house Files* Staff writings.

Info Ret Servs DIALOG; BRS; MEDLARS. *Shared Catalog Nets* OCLC thru VALNET. *Coop Lib Nets* VALNET; LCHIB; WNYLRC.

Circ Servs Avail To other Federal libraries; to other libraries; not open to the general public.

Ref Servs Avail To other Federal libraries; to other libraries; to the general public.

2415. Veterans Administration Medical Center, Medical & Patients' Library

1670 Clairmont Rd, Decatur, GA 30033 (404) 321-6111 ext 254; FTS 248-6810/6813/6816

Admin Eugenia H Abbey. *ILL* Mary Major.

Lib Type Health & Medicine; Hospital (Patients).

Info Ret Servs BRS. *Coop Lib Nets* VALNET; AHSLC; GHSLC. *Elec Mail Nets* CLASS.

Circ Servs Avail To other Federal libraries; to other libraries.

2416. Veterans Administration Medical Center, Medical & Patients' Library

Iowa City, IA 52240 (319) 338-0581 ext 274; FTS 863-6274

Admin Associate Chief of Staff for Education. *Ref Lib* Marilyn Kraus (ILL, Acq).

Lib Type Health & Medicine; Hospital (Patients).

Shared Catalog Nets OCLC thru VALNET. *Coop Lib Nets* VALNET.

Circ Servs Avail To other Federal libraries; to other libraries; not open to the general public; restricted to in-house use.

Ref Servs Avail To other Federal libraries; to other libraries; not open to the general public; restricted to staff.

2417. Veterans Administration Medical Center, Medical & Patients' Library

Marion, IL 62959 (618) 997-5311 ext 242; FTS 276-0242

Admin Arlene Dueker.

Lib Type Health & Medicine; Hospital (Patients).

Spec Subs Clinical medicine; geriatrics; Vietnam.

Info Ret Servs MEDLINE. *Shared Catalog Nets* OCLC thru VALNET. *Coop Lib Nets* Shawnee Lib Systems.

Circ Servs Avail To other Federal libraries; restricted to affiliated individuals.

Ref Servs Avail To other Federal libraries; to other libraries; to the general public.

2418. Veterans Administration Medical Center, Medical & Patients' Library

2201 N Broadwell, Grand Island, NE 68801 (308) 382-3660; FTS 864-2236

Admin Gail C Baldwin.

Lib Type Health & Medicine; Hospital (Patients).

Shared Catalog Nets OCLC thru VALNET. *Coop Lib Nets* VALNET.

Circ Servs Avail To other Federal libraries.

Ref Servs Avail To other Federal libraries.

2419. Veterans Administration Medical Center, Medical & Patients' Library

1601 Perdido St, New Orleans, LA 70146 (504) 589-5272; FTS 682-5272

Admin Wilma B Neveu. *ILL* Martha D Lepre.

Lib Type Health & Medicine; Hospital (Patients).

Spec Subs Medicine; nursing; dental; allied health.

Info Ret Servs BRS; MEDLINE. *Shared Catalog Nets* OCLC thru VALNET. *Coop Lib Nets* VALNET; VA Medical District #19; VAMCS. *Elec Mail Nets* CLASS.

Circ Servs Avail To other Federal libraries; to other libraries; not open to the general public; restricted to hospital staff & employees.

Ref Servs Avail To other Federal libraries; to other libraries; not open to the general public; restricted to hospital staff & employees.

2420. Veterans Administration Medical Center, Medical & Patients' Library

510 E Stoner Ave, Shreveport, LA 71130 (318) 221-8411; FTS 493-6036

Admin Shirley B Hegenwald. *Ref Lib* Dixie Jones (ILL).

Lib Type Health & Medicine; Hospital (Patients).

Shared Catalog Nets OCLC thru VALNET. *Coop Lib Nets* VALNET. *Elec Mail Nets* CLASS.

Circ Servs Avail To other Federal libraries; to other libraries; not open to the general public.
Ref Servs Avail To other Federal libraries; to other libraries; not open to the general public.

2421. Veterans Administration Medical Center, Medical & Patients' Library
921 NE 13th St, Oklahoma City, OK 73104 (405) 272-9876 ext 442; FTS 743-3431
Admin Verlean Delaney.
Lib Type Health & Medicine; Hospital (Patients).
Info Ret Servs BRS; MEDLINE. *Shared Catalog Nets* OCLC thru VALNET. *Coop Lib Nets* GOAL. *Elec Mail Nets* CLASS.
Circ Servs Avail To other Federal libraries; to other libraries; restricted to employees & patients.
Ref Servs Avail To other Federal libraries; to other libraries; to the general public.

2422. Veterans Administration Medical Center, Medical & Patients' Library
Fort Lyon, CO 81038 (303) 456-1260 ext 265; FTS 323-8265
Admin Helen S Bradley. *ILL* Kathy Roberts.
Lib Type Health & Medicine; Hospital (Patients).
Spec Subs Psychology; psychiatry; geriatrics; nursing.
Info Ret Servs BRS; MEDLINE. *Shared Catalog Nets* OCLC thru VALNET. *Coop Lib Nets* VALNET; AVRLSS; Peaks & Valleys.
Circ Servs Avail To other Federal libraries; to other libraries.
Ref Servs Avail To other Federal libraries; to other libraries; to the general public.

2423. Veterans Administration Medical Center, Medical & Patients' Library Wade Park & Brecksville Units
10701 East Blvd, Cleveland, OH 44106 (216) 791-3800 ext 7307; FTS 290-3800
Admin Nancy S Tesmer; Mary Nourse; Mary Conway (Medical); John C White (A-V); John Wells (Patient's).
Lib Type Health & Medicine; Hospital (Patients).
Spec Subs General medicine; surgery; psychiatry; psychology; geriatrics; nursing.
Info Ret Servs DIALOG; BRS; MEDLINE. *Coop Lib Nets* VALNET; MLANO. *Elec Mail Nets* CLASS.
Circ Servs Avail To other Federal libraries; to other libraries.
Ref Servs Avail To other Federal libraries; to other libraries.

2424. Veterans Administration Medical Center, Medical Staff Library
150 Muir Rd, Martinez, CA 94553 (415) 228-6800 ext 298; FTS 450-0298
Admin Dorothea Bennett. *ILL* Richard Phillips.
Lib Type Health & Medicine.
Info Ret Servs MEDLARS (NLM). *Shared Catalog Nets* OCLC. *Coop Lib Nets* VALNET. *Elec Mail Nets* CLASS.
Circ Servs Avail To other Federal libraries; to other libraries; not open to the general public.
Ref Servs Avail To other Federal libraries; to other libraries; not open to the general public.

2425. Veterans Administration Medical Center Patients' Library
Lebanon, PA 17042 (717) 272-6621; FTS 592-4268
Admin David E Falger. *Ref Lib* Michelle Clark (ILL, Acq).
Lib Type Hospital (Patients).
Spec Collecs Patient health education.
Info Ret Servs DIALOG; BRS; MEDLINE. *Elec Mail Nets* Mailman.
Circ Servs Avail To other Federal libraries; to other libraries; not open to the general public.
Ref Servs Avail To other Federal libraries; to other libraries; not open to the general public.

2426. Veterans Administration Medical Center Patients' Library
1970 Roanoke Blvd, Salem, VA 24153 (703) 982-2463 ext 2381; FTS 937-2380
Admin Jean Kennedy. *Ref Lib* Susan DuGrenier (ILL, Acq).
Lib Type Hospital (Patients).
Spec Subs Patient health education.

Coop Lib Nets VALNET; RVLA.
Circ Servs Avail Not open to the general public; restricted to patients & staff.
Ref Servs Avail To other Federal libraries; to other libraries; not open to the general public.

2427. Veterans Administration Medical Center Patients' Library
Leavenworth, KS 66048 (913) 682-2000 ext 223; FTS 752-0224
Admin Bennett F Lawson. *Ref Lib* Judy Gottschalk (ILL).
Lib Type Hospital (Patients).
Spec Subs Psychology; psychiatry.
Info Ret Servs DIALOG; BRS. *Shared Catalog Nets* OCLC thru VALNET. *Coop Lib Nets* VALNET; Greater Health Science Group Kansas City; Kansas City Library Network. *Elec Mail Nets* CLASS.
Circ Servs Avail To other Federal libraries; not open to the general public.
Ref Servs Avail To other Federal libraries; not open to the general public.

2428. Veterans Administration Medical Center, Carl Vinson Center Library
Dublin, GA 31021 (912) 272-1210 ext 229; FTS 259-0229 (Medical Library); FTS 259-0301 (Patients' Library)
Admin Kodel M. Thomas.
Lib Type Health & Medicine; Hospital (Patients).
Spec Subs Medical health; social science; management.
Info Ret Servs MEDLINE. *Coop Lib Nets* VALNET; Georgia Library Information Network.
Circ Servs Avail Not open to the general public; restricted to staff & patients.
Ref Servs Avail Not open to the general public; restricted to staff & patients (General Library); professionals & medical students (Medical Library).

2429. Veterans Administration Medical Library
University & Woodland Aves, Philadelphia, PA 19104 (215) 382-2400 ext 6732; Medical Library 382-6731/6693
Admin Robert S. Lyle.
Lib Type Health & Medicine.
Spec Subs General medical.
Coop Lib Nets VALNET. *Elec Mail Nets* MAILMAN.

2430. Veterans Administration Medical Library
1500 E Woodrow Wilson Dr, Jackson, MS 39216 (601) 362-4471; FTS 542-1273
Admin Carol C. Sistrunk.
Lib Type Health & Medicine.
Info Ret Servs BRS. *Coop Lib Nets* VALNET. *Elec Mail Nets* MAILMAN.

2431. Veterans Administration Medical Library, Sam Rayburn Memorial Veterans Center
Bonham, TX 75418 (214) 583-2111 ext 215; FTS 760-0215
Admin Donna S Locke. *ILL* Anna F Campbell.
Lib Type Health & Medicine.
Spec Subs General medicine. *Spec Collecs* Patient education.
Info Ret Servs MEDLARS. *Coop Lib Nets* VALNET. *Elec Mail Nets* CLASS.
Circ Servs Avail To other Federal libraries; not open to the general public.
Ref Servs Avail To other libraries.

2432. Veterans Administration Medical Library, Olin E Teague Veterans Center
Temple, TX 76501 (817) 778-4811 ext 4111; ILL ext 4113; FTS 760-4111 (Medical Library); 760-5153 (Patients' Library)
Lib Type Health & Medicine; Hospital (Patients).
Coop Lib Nets VALNET.

2433. Veterans Administration Medical & Regional Office Center Library Service
901 George Washington Blvd, Wichita, KS 67211 (316) 685-2221, 3171; FTS 752-3171
Admin Christine M Mitchell.
Lib Type Health & Medicine; Hospital (Patients).

Spec Subs Medicine; geriatrics; patient health education.
Info Ret Servs BRS; MEDLINE. *Shared Catalog Nets* OCLC thru VALNET. *Coop Lib Nets* VALNET; Wichita, Health Science Libraries Consortium. *Elec Mail Nets* CLASS; OCTANET.
Circ Servs Avail To other Federal libraries; to other libraries.
Ref Servs Avail To other Federal libraries; to other libraries.

2434. Veterans Administration Medical & Regional Office Center Medical Library

1601 Kirkwood Hwy, Wilmington, DE 19805 (302) 994-2511 ext 354/355; FTS 487-5354
Admin Don Passidomo. *Ref Lib* Helen Post (ILL).
Lib Type Health & Medicine.
Spec Subs Medicine; surgery; dentistry; nursing; patient health education; nutrition/dietetics; allied health services.
Info Ret Servs BRS; MEDLARS. *Shared Catalog Nets* OCLC thru VALNET. *Coop Lib Nets* VALNET; WABLC; LINCS. *Elec Mail Nets* Mailman.
Circ Servs Avail To other libraries; not open to the general public; restricted to staff, students & affiliated libraries.
Ref Servs Avail To other libraries; not open to the general public; restricted to staff, students & affiliated libraries.

2435. Veterans Administration Medical & Regional Office Center, Medical Library

Fargo, ND 58102 (701) 232-3241 ext 275; FTS 783-3275
Admin James M Robbins. *ILL* Joyce Nicholas.
Lib Type Hospital (Patients).
Info Ret Servs MEDLINE. *Coop Lib Nets* VALNET. *Elec Mail Nets* CLASS.
Circ Servs Avail To other Federal libraries; to other libraries.
Ref Servs Avail To other Federal libraries; to other libraries.

2436. Veterans Administration Medical & Regional Office Center, Medical & Patients' Library

Fort Harrison, MT 59636 (406) 442-6410 ext 259
Admin Maurice Knutson.
Lib Type Health & Medicine; Hospital (Patients).
Spec Subs Internal medicine; surgery.
Info Ret Servs DIALOG. *Shared Catalog Nets* OCLC thru VALNET.
Circ Servs Avail To other Federal libraries; to other libraries; not open to the general public; restricted to professionals in community.
Ref Servs Avail To other Federal libraries; to other libraries; not open to the general public; restricted to professionals in community.

2437. Veterans Administration Office of General Counsel, Law Library

810 Vermont Ave, Rm 1039 (026H), Washington, DC 20420 (202) 233-2159; FTS 233-2159
Admin Nina Kahn. *Ref Lib* Kenneth Nero (ILL, Acq).
Lib Type Law.
Spec Subs Veterans law.
Info Ret Servs LEGI-SLATE; WESTLAW.
Circ Servs Avail To other Federal libraries; not open to the general public.
Ref Servs Avail To other Federal libraries; not open to the general public.

2438. Veterans Administration Office of Technology Transfer-Reference Collection

252 7th Ave, New York, NY 10001 (212) 620-6659; FTS 660-6659
Lib Type Special.
Spec Subs Mobility devices; orthopedic implants; orthopedics; plastic surgery; prosthetics; sensory aids; spinal cord injury equipment.

Circ Servs Avail Not open to the general public; restricted to ILL.
Ref Servs Avail Not open to the general public; restricted to medical, allied health & engineering professionals.

2439. Veterans Administration Outpatient Clinic Library Service

17 Court St, Boston, MA 02108 (617) 223-2020; FTS 223-2082
Admin Carolyn Mathes. *ILL* Lucy Butler.
Lib Type Health & Medicine.
Spec Subs Psychiatry. *Spec Collecs* Patient education.
Info Ret Servs DIALOG; BRS. *Shared Catalog Nets* OCLC thru VALNET. *Coop Lib Nets* VALNET; MAHSLIN; RML1. *Elec Mail Nets* CLASS; MEDLINK.
Circ Servs Avail To other Federal libraries; to other libraries patients.
Ref Servs Avail To other Federal libraries; to other libraries; to the general public.

2440. Veterans Administration Patients' Library

1201 NW 16th St, Miami, FL 33125 (305) 324-3187; FTS 351-3622
Lib Type Hospital (Patients).
Spec Subs Patient health education; readers' services for the blind & handicapped. *Spec Collecs* Talking book program.
Circ Servs Avail Not open to the general public; restricted to staff & patients.
Ref Servs Avail Not open to the general public; restricted to staff & patients.

2441. Veterans Administration Regional Office & Medical Center

2360 E Pershing Blvd, Cheyenne, WY 82001 (307) 778-7550, ext 236; FTS 328-7550, ext 236
Admin Eric J. Kirby.
Lib Type Health & Medicine.
Info Ret Servs MEDLINE. *Coop Lib Nets* VALNET.

2442. Veterans Administration Westside Medical Center Library Service

820 S Damen Ave, Chicago, IL 60612 (312) 633-2116; FTS 388-2116
Admin Lynne D Morris. *Ref Lib* John R Cline (ILL, Acq).
Lib Type Health & Medicine; Hospital (Patients).
Spec Subs Health & medicine. *Spec Collecs* Audio-visuals: 16mm, 3/4" videotape, slides, audio cassettes.
Info Ret Servs BRS; NLM. *Shared Catalog Nets* OCLC thru VALNET. *Coop Lib Nets* VALNET; CLS; ILINET. *Elec Mail Nets* CLASS.
Circ Servs Avail To other Federal libraries; to other libraries; not open to the general public; restricted to affiliated individuals.
Ref Servs Avail To other Federal libraries; to other libraries; to the general public.

2443. Alvin C York Veterans Administration Medical Center, Library Service

3400 Lebanon Rd, Murfreesboro, TN 37130 (615) 893-1360; FTS 852-3336
Admin Joy Hunter. *Ref Lib* Marie Eubanks (ILL).
Lib Type Health & Medicine.
Spec Subs Medicine; psychiatry; geriatrics; substance abuse.
Info Ret Servs BRS. *Coop Lib Nets* VALNET. *Elec Mail Nets* CLASS.
Circ Servs Avail To other Federal libraries; to other libraries; not open to the general public.
Ref Servs Avail To other Federal libraries; to other libraries.

OTHER BOARDS, COMMITTEES, AND COMMISSIONS

Advisory Commission on Intergovernmental Relations

2444. Advisory Commission on Intergovernmental Relations Library
1111 20th St, NW, Washington, DC 20575 (202) 653-5536
Admin Lelly McManus.
Lib Type Special.
Spec Subs Intergovernmental relations. *Spec Collecs* ACIR publications.
Lib Deposit Designation GPO Depository Library.
Circ Servs Avail To other Federal libraries; to other libraries.
Ref Servs Avail To other Federal libraries; to other libraries; to the general public.

Architectural & Transportation Barriers Compliance Board

2445. Architectural & Transportation Barriers Compliance Board, Technical Library
330 C St SW, Rm 1010-2101, Washington, DC 20202 (202) 472-2700
Admin Margaret Milner (Executive Dir). *Ref Lib* David Yanchulis. *Acq Lib* Barbara Gilley.
Lib Type Special.
Spec Subs Reports on topics related to handicapped accessibility; technical accessibility; technical papers; bibliographies; state codes. *Spec Collecs* Periodicals focusing on handicaps, rehabilitation, & architecture.
Circ Servs Avail Not open to the general public.
Ref Servs Avail To other Federal libraries; to other libraries; to the general public.

Delaware River Basin Commission

2446. Delaware River Basin Commission Library
25 State Police Dr, West Trenton, NJ 08628 (609) 883-9500 ext 263; FTS 483-2063
Admin Betty A Lin.
Lib Type Engineering & Science.
Spec Subs Delaware River; water resources; water pollution; aquatic biology; geology; hydrology; flood plain management. *Spec Collecs* Topographic maps on the Delaware River Basin.
Info Ret Servs DIALOG.
Circ Servs Avail To other Federal libraries; to other libraries; not open to the general public.
Ref Servs Avail To other Federal libraries; to other libraries; to the general public; restricted to on site use by appointment.

Federal Mine Safety & Health Review Commission

2447. Federal Mine Safety & Health Review Commission Library
1730 K St NW, 6th Fl, Washington, DC 20006 (202) 653-5454; FTS 653-5454
Admin L Joseph Ferrara (Acting General Counsel). *Acq Lib* Regina M Clarke (Administrative Officer).
Lib Type Law.
Spec Subs Mine safety & health; occupational health & safety.
Lib Deposit Designation GPO Depository Library.
Circ Servs Avail To other Federal libraries; to the general public.
Ref Servs Avail To other Federal libraries; to the general public.

2448. Federal Mine Safety & Health Review Commission Library
Tremont Ctr Bldg, Rm 400, Denver, CO 80204 (303) 844-5266; FTS 564-5266
Admin John A Carlson (Administrative Law Judge in Charge).
Lib Type Law.
Spec Subs Mine safety & health law. *Spec Collecs* West's Federal Reporter; Supreme Court Reporter; BNA-MSHA & OSHA law books. *In-house Files* Decisions by the Federal Mine Safety & Health Review Commission & Occupational Health & Safety Review Commission.
Ref Servs Avail To other Federal libraries; not open to the general public; restricted to law offices & attorneys with MSHA law questions coming before judges.

Marine Mammal Commission

2449. Marine Mammal Commission Library
1625 I St NW, Rm 307, Washington, DC 20006 (202) 653-6237
Admin Robert Hofman; Phyllis Stone (Librarian).
Lib Type Special.
Spec Subs Marine mammals; polar bears. *In-house Files* Reprint files: articles on marine mammals & bibliographic file.
Circ Servs Avail To other Federal libraries; to other libraries; to the general public.
Ref Servs Avail To other Federal libraries; to other libraries; to the general public.

National Commission on Libraries & Information Science

2450. National Commission on Libraries & Information Science, Library/Information Center
GSA Bldg, 7th & D Sts SW, Ste 3122, Washington, DC 20024 (202) 382-0840
Admin Christina Carr Young.
Lib Type Special.
Spec Subs Library & information science. *In-house Files* Commission activities.
Info Ret Servs DIALOG; BRS. *Shared Catalog Nets* OCLC. *Coop Lib Nets* FEDLINK. *Elec Mail Nets* ALANET; The Source.

Circ Servs Avail Not open to the general public; restricted to in house use.
Ref Servs Avail To other Federal libraries; to other libraries; to the general public.

President's Committee on the Employment of the Handicapped

2451. President's Committee on the Employment of the Handicapped, Library
1111 20th St, NW, Rm 636, Washington, DC 20036 (202) 653-2087
Admin Larry Volin (Dir Research & Publications).
Lib Type Special.
Spec Subs Information related to the rehabilitation and employment of the handicapped.
Circ Servs Avail To other Federal libraries; to other libraries.
Ref Servs Avail To the general public.

QUASI-OFFICIAL AGENCY

Smithsonian Institution

2452. Anacostia Neighborhood Museum Library
1901 Fort Pl, 2405 Martin Luther King Jr Ave SE, Washington, DC 20020 (202) 287-3380
Admin Louise D Hutchinson (Historian).
Lib Type General.
Spec Subs Ethnic studies.

2453. Archives of American Art
AA-PG 331, 8th & G St NW, Smithsonian Institution, Washington, DC 20560 (202) 357-2781
Admin Garnett McCoy. *Ref Lib* Colleen Hennessey. *ILL* Marilyn Florek. *Acq Lib* Judy Throm.
Lib Type Special.
Spec Subs History of art in America, especially painting & sculpture.
Shared Catalog Nets SIBUS.
Ref Servs Avail To the general public.

2454. Cooper-Hewitt Museum Library
2 E 91st St, New York, NY 10028 (212) 860-6868; FTS 668-6868
Admin Katherine Martinez.
Lib Type Special.
Spec Subs Decorative arts & design. *Spec Collecs* Industrial design (Donald Deskey Archives); photographic collection; Symbols (Henry Dreyfuss Archives).
Ref Servs Avail Restricted to use by appointment.

2455. Freer Gallery of Art Library
12th & Jefferson Dr, SW, Washington, DC 20560 (202) 357-2091
Lib Type Special.
Spec Subs Near & Far Eastern Art.
Circ Servs Avail Not open to the general public; restricted to Freer Staff; no ILL except for slides.
Ref Servs Avail To other Federal libraries; to other libraries; to the general public.

2456. Hirshhorn Museum & Sculpture Garden Library
8th & Independence Ave SW, Washington, DC 20560 (202) 357-3222
Admin Anna Brooke.
Lib Type Special.
Spec Subs Modern painting & sculpture. *Spec Collecs* Samuel Murray scrapbooks. *In-house Files* Photographs & slides of works in the collection.
Info Ret Servs DIALOG.
Circ Servs Avail Not open to the general public; restricted to staff.
Ref Servs Avail To other Federal libraries; to other libraries; not open to the general public; restricted to scholars by appointment.

2457. National Air & Space Museum, Branch Library
Smithsonian Institution, 7th St & Independence Ave SW, Washington, DC 20560 (202) 357-3133
Admin Frank A Pietropaoli.
Lib Type Special.
Spec Subs Aerospace (aviation & space) history & current information; astronomy & astrophysics; earth & planetary science; geophysics. *Spec Collecs* Aerospace - Bella Landauer Sheet Music & Children's Book Collection; aerospace - Institute of Aeronautical Sciences Historical Collection, books, periodicals, &

photographs; ballooning - William A M Burden Collection, books & periodicals; rare & scarce aeronautica & astronautica - Ramsey Room; space sciences - Bellcomm, Inc.
Ref Servs Avail To the general public; restricted to special appointment for scholars only, Ramsey Room, & limited access to archives.

2458. National Gallery of Art Library
4th & Constitution Ave, NW, Washington, DC 20565 (202) 842-6511
Admin J M Edelstein. *Ref Lib* Caroline Backlund. *ILL* Lamia Doumato. *Acq Lib* Anna Rachwald.
Lib Type Special.
Spec Subs Western European art form Post-Byzantine period to present; American art. *Spec Collecs* Leonard Da Vinci; artists monographs; auction sales catalogues. *In-house Files* Vertical files of artists.
Info Ret Servs DIALOG. *Shared Catalog Nets* OCLC. *Coop Lib Nets* FEDLINK.
Circ Servs Avail To other Federal libraries; to other libraries; not open to the general public; restricted to graduate students.
Ref Servs Avail To other Federal libraries; to other libraries; to the general public.

2459. National Museum of African Art, Branch Library
Smithsonian Institution, 318 A St NE, Washington, DC 20002 (202) 287-3490
Admin Janet L Stanley.
Lib Type Special.
Spec Subs African art, sculpture, musical instruments, textiles, & artifacts, both historic & contemporary. *Spec Collecs* 100,000 Elisofon slides; memorabilia of the life & times of Frederick Douglass.

2460. National Museum of American Art & National Portrait Gallery Library
Smithsonian Institution, Washington, DC 20560 (202) 357-1886
Admin Cecelia Chin. *Ref Lib* Patricia Lynagh (ILL).
Lib Type Special.
Spec Subs Art, especially American; history; biography. *Spec Collecs* Ferdinand Perret Library of Art; Mallett Library of Art Reproductions. *In-house Files* American artists.
Info Ret Servs DIALOG; RLIN; WILSONLINE. *Shared Catalog Nets* OCLC. *Coop Lib Nets* FEDLINK.
Circ Servs Avail To other Federal libraries; to other libraries.
Ref Servs Avail To other Federal libraries; to other libraries; to the general public.

2461. National Museum of American History, Branch Library
Smithsonian Institution, 12th St & Constitution Ave NW, Washington, DC 20560 (202) 357-2414
Admin Rhoda S Ratner (Chief Librarian). *Ref Lib* Charles Berger. *ILL* James Roan.
Lib Type Special.
Spec Subs History of science & technology; social & natural history of the US. *Spec Collecs* Trade literature from the 19th & 20th centuries; expositions & world's fairs.
Shared Catalog Nets OCLC.
Circ Servs Avail To other Federal libraries; to other libraries.
Ref Servs Avail To other Federal libraries; to other libraries; to the general public; restricted to limited basis for general public.

2462. National Museum of Natural History, Branch Library
Smithsonian Institution, 10th St & Constitution Ave NW, Washington, DC 20560 (202) 357-2139
Admin Robert Maloy. *Ref Lib* Margaret Child. *ILL* Mary Clare Gray. *Acq Lib* William Neff.
Lib Type Special.
Spec Subs Anthropology, especially Native Americans; aeronautics; botany; decorative arts; entomology; geology; mineral science; oceanography; paleobiology; systematics (biological); taxonomic botany; zoology (invertebrate & vertebrate); African art. *Spec Collecs* Agrostology - Hitchcock-Chase Collection; algology - Dawson Collection; general botany - John Donnell Smith Collection; Entomology - Casey Coleoptera Collection; foraminifera - Cushman Collection; invertebrate zoology - William Copepoda Collection; physical anthropology - Hrdlicka Collection; Ornithology; History of Science & Technology - Dibner donation; commercial trade catalogs.
Info Ret Servs DIALOG. *Shared Catalog Nets* OCLC. *Coop Lib Nets* OCLC.
Circ Servs Avail To other Federal libraries; to other libraries; not open to the general public.
Ref Servs Avail To other Federal libraries; to other libraries; to the general public.

2463. National Zoological Park Library Branch
3001 Connecticut Ave NW, Washington, DC 20008 (202) 673-4771
Admin Kay Kenyon.
Lib Type Special.
Spec Subs Veterinary medicine; pathology; animal nutrition; animal behavior; wildlife conservation; care of captive animals; horticulture. *Spec Collecs* Zoo guidebooks & annual reports from zoos worldwide. *In-house Files* Zoo staff publications.
Info Ret Servs DIALOG. *Shared Catalog Nets* OCLC. *Coop Lib Nets* AAZPA Librarian Special Interest Group.
Circ Servs Avail To other libraries.
Ref Servs Avail To other Federal libraries; to other libraries; to the general public.

2464. The Phillips Collection Library
1600 21st St NW, Washington, DC 20009-1090 (202) 387-2151, ext 33
Lib Type General.
Spec Collecs Exhibition catalogues; monographs on Phillips Collection artists; monographs on 19th & 20th century European & American artists.
Circ Servs Avail Not open to the general public.
Ref Servs Avail Not open to the general public; restricted to by appointment use.

2465. Smithsonian Environmental Research Center Library, Rockville Branch
12441 Parklawn Dr, Rockville, MD 20852 (301) 249-9585
Admin Angela N Haggins.
Lib Type Engineering & Science.
Spec Subs Plant physiology; radiocarbon dating; regulatory biology; environmental biology; solar radiation.
Info Ret Servs DIALOG. *Shared Catalog Nets* OCLC & RLIN through SIL only.
Circ Servs Avail To other Federal libraries; to other libraries.
Ref Servs Avail To other Federal libraries; to other libraries; to the general public.

2466. Smithsonian Institution Archives
900 Jefferson Dr SW Rm 2135, Washington, DC 20560 (202) 357-1420
Admin William W Moss. *Ref Lib* William A Deiss.
Lib Type Special.
Spec Subs Smithsonian history; history of science. *Spec Collecs* Copies of Smithsonian Institution annual reports & other serial publications; copies of Smithsonian Press special publications; monographs.
Info Ret Servs Smithsonian Institution Bibliographic Information System (SIBIS). *Shared Catalog Nets* SIBIS. *Coop Lib Nets* SIBIS.
Circ Servs Avail Restricted to archives staff.
Ref Servs Avail To other Federal libraries; to other libraries; to the general public.

2467. Smithsonian Institution, Astrophysical Observatory Library
60 Garden St, Cambridge, MA 02138 (617) 495-7264; FTS 830-7264
Lib Type Special.
Spec Subs Astronomy; astrophysics; exobiology; geodesy; geophysics; mathematics; optics; physics; satellites; upper atmosphere.
Ref Servs Avail Restricted to use by prior arrangement.

2468. Smithsonian Institution Libraries
Natural History Bldg, Rm 24, Washington, DC 20560 (202) 357-2240; FTS 357-2240
Admin Robert Maloy.
Lib Type Special.
Spec Subs Natural Sciences; history of science & technology; design; physical sciences. *Spec Collecs* History of science & technology; air & space; natural history; design.
Info Ret Servs DIALOG; BRS;NEXIS. *Shared Catalog Nets* OCLC. *Coop Lib Nets* FEDLINK; FLICC; ARL; DCLA. *Elec Mail Nets* ALANET.
Circ Servs Avail Restricted to ILL.
Ref Servs Avail To other Federal libraries; to other libraries; restricted to general public by appointment.

2469. Smithsonian Institution Libraries, Museum Support Center Branch
(Location: 4210 Silver Hill Rd, Suitland, MD 20746), Washington, DC 20560 (202) 287-3666
Admin Karen Preslock. *ILL* Larry Baukin.
Lib Type Special.
Spec Subs Conservation of museum objects & materials & allied sciences; archeometry; instrumental analysis in regard to works of art & antiquity or museum specimens; taxonomic aspects of marine & estuarine fauna; medical entomology; related health hazards. *In-house Files* Access to reprint file of literature on conservation of materials & museum objects.
Info Ret Servs DIALOG; STN. *Shared Catalog Nets* OCLC.
Circ Servs Avail To other Federal libraries; to other libraries; restricted to ILL for general public.
Ref Servs Avail To other Federal libraries; to other libraries; restricted to general public by appointment & no on-line services.

2470. Smithsonian Institution, Museum Reference Center
A & I 2235, Washington, DC 20560 (202) 357-3101; FTS 357-3101
Admin Catherine D Scott. *ILL* Paulette Gaskins. *Acq Lib* Central Library, Smithsonian Institution.
Lib Type Special.
Spec Subs Museology; museum administration & management; fund raising & grantsmanship; exhibit design. *Spec Collecs* Subject files of museum programs; promotional material; guidebooks; educational materials.
Info Ret Servs DIALOG. *Shared Catalog Nets* OCLC.
Circ Servs Avail To other Federal libraries; to other libraries.
Ref Servs Avail To other Federal libraries; to other libraries; to the general public.

Type of Library Index

Academic

Air Force Institute of Technology Academic Library/FL 3319, 200
Air University Library/FL 3368, 211
Armed Forces Staff College Library, 1253
I G Brown Professional Military Education Center Library/FL 6599, 227
Combined Arms Research Library, 422
Defense Systems Management College, Library, 1274
FBI Academy Library, 1908
Foreign Service Institute Library, 1928
Ft Bliss, Valent Learning Resources Center Library, 446
Ft Sam Houston, Academy of Health Sciences, Stimson Library, 484
Ft Huachuca, US Army Intelligence Center & School, Library, 495
Haskell Indian Junior College, Learning Resource Center, 1403
Institute of American Indian Arts Library, 1405
Keesler AFB, Academic Library/FL 3011, 269
National Defense University Library, 1278
Naval Amphibious School Library, 1021
Naval Postgraduate School, Dudley Knox Library, 1061
Naval Postgraduate School, Dudley Knox Library, 1062
Naval War College Library, 1095
Scott AFB, Academic Library/FL 4499, 317
Uniformed Services University of the Health Services, Learning Resource Center, 1282
US Air Force Academy Library/FL 7000, 331
USAF School of Health Care Science, Academic Library/FL 3021, 337
US Army Chaplain Center & School Library, 653
US Army Chemical School, Fisher Library, 654
US Army John F Kennedy Special Warfare Center, Marquat Memorial Library, 747
US Army Ordnance Center & School Library, 768
US Army Ordnance Missile & Munitions Center & School, Technical Library, 769
US Army Russian Institute, Research Library, 927
US Army School of the Americas Library, 776
US Army War College Library, 790
US Coast Guard Academy Library, 1942
US Merchant Marine Academy, Schyler Otis Bland Memorial Library, 1939
US Military Academy, Department of Law Library, 793
US Military Academy Library, 794
US Military Academy, Preparatory School Library, 796

US Naval Academy, Nimitz Library, 1169

Elementary/High School

Aneth Community School Library, 1363
Baca Boarding School Library, 1364
Big Coulee School-Early Childhood Education Center, 1365
Bread Springs School Library, 1366
Brevig Mission, Day School Library, 1367
Bridger Day School Library, 1368
Brule Sioux High School Library, 1369
Bureau of Indian Affairs, Library/Media Center, 1370
Busby School Library, 1371
Canoncito Community School, Resource Center, 1372
Casa Blanca Day School Library, 1373
Chemawa Indian School, IMC, 1374
Cherokee Elementary School Library, 1375
Cherokee High School Library, 1376
Cherry Creek School Library, 1377
Cheyenne-Eagle Butte High School, Media Center, 1378
Chi Chil Tah School, 1379
Chilchinbeto Day School Library, 1380
Chilocco Indian School Library, 1381
Chinle Boarding School Library, 1382
Chitimacha Day School Library, 1383
Choctaw Central High School Library, 1384
Concho School Library, 1385
Cottonwood Day School Library, 1386
Cove Day School, 1387
Crazy Horse School Library-Media Center, 1388
Crow Creek Reservation High School Library, 1389
Crownpoint Boarding School Media Center, 1390
Crystal Boarding School Library, 1391
Dennehotso Boarding School Library, 1392
Dilcon School Library, 1393
Dlo'Ay Azhi Boarding School Library, 1394
Dunseith Day School Library, 1395
Dzilth-Na-O-Dith-hle Community School Library, 1396
Flandreau Indian School Library, 1397
Fort Thompson Community School Library, 1398
Four Winds Elementary School Library, 1399
Gila Crossing Day School Library, 1400
Greasewood Boarding School Library, 1401
Greyhills High School Library, 1402
Hopi Day School Library, 1404
Intermountain Inter-Tribal School Library, 1406
Isleta Elementary School Library, 1407
Kaibeto Boarding School Library, 1408
Kaibeto Elementary School Library, 1409
Kayenta Boarding School Library, 1410
Keams Canyon Library, 1411

Kwethluk Day School, 1412
Laguna Elementary School Library, 1413
Leupp Boarding School Library, 1414
Little Wound School Library, 1415
Low Mountain Boarding School Library, 1416
Lukachukai Boarding School Library, 1417
Many Farms High School Library, 1418
Moencopi Day School Library, 1419
Mt Edgecumbe High School, Library Media Center, 1420
Navajo Mountain Boarding School Library, 1422
Nazlini Boarding School Library, 1423
Oglala Community Elementary School, 1424
Oglala Community High School Library, 1425
Phoenix Indian School Library, 1426
Pierre Indian Learning Center Library, 1427
Pinon Boarding School Library, 1428
Porcupine Day School Library, 1429
Promise Day School Library, 1430
Red Lake Day School Library, 1431
Riverside Indian School Library, 1432
Rocky Ridge Boarding School Library, 1433
Salt River Day School Library, 1434
San Felipe Elementary School Library, 1435
San Juan Day School Media Center, 1436
San Simon Media Center, 1437
Sanostee Boarding School Media Center, 1438
Santa Clara Day School Library, 1439
Santa Rosa Boarding School Libraries, 1440
Santa Rosa Elementary School Library, 1441
Second Mesa Day School Library, 1442
Seneca Indian School Library, 1443
Sequoyah High School Library, 1444
Shiprock Boarding School Library, 1445
Shonto Elementary Library, 1446
Southwestern Indian Polytechnic Institute Instructional Media Center, 1447
Standing Rock Community Elementary School Library, 1448
Stewart Boarding School Library-Media Center, 1449
Taos Day School Library, 1450
Teecnospos Boarding School Library, 1451
Toksook Bay School Library, 1452
Toyei Boarding School Library, 1453
Tuba City Boarding School Library, 1454
Turtle Mountain Community School Media Center, 1455
Twin Buttes School Library, 1456
Wahpeton Indian School Media Center, 1457
White Horse School Library, 1458
White Shield School Library, 1459
Wide Ruins Boarding School, 1460

Patuxent Wildlife Research Center Library, 1558

Puget Sound Naval Shipyard, Engineering Library, 1145

Redstone Scientific Information Center, 615

Rice Library, 187

Rome Air Development Center Technical Library/FL 2810, 315

Russell Research Center Library, 80

Sandia National Laboratories, Technical Library, 1314

Scientific & Technical Information Division Library, 623

Smithsonian Environmental Research Center Library, Rockville Branch, 2465

Stored Product Insects Research & Development Library, 82

Supervisor of Shipbuilding, Conversion & Repair, SUPSHIPS Technical Library, 1163

David Taylor Naval Ship R&D Center, Technical Information Center, 1166

Tennessee Valley Authority, Technical Library, 2101

Thayer Engineering Library, 632

W F Thompson Memorial Library, 189

Tiburon Laboratory Library, 190

Tuscaloosa Research Center Library, 1546

US Army Belvoir Research Development & Engineering Technical Library, 651

US Army Cold Region Research & Engineering Laboratory Library, 656

US Army Construction Engineering Research Laboratory Library, 658

US Army Corps of Engineers, Albuquerque District Library, 659

US Army Corps of Engineers, Baltimore District Library Branch, 660

US Army Corps of Engineers, Buffalo District Technical Library, 661

US Army Corps of Engineers, Detroit District Technical Library, 664

US Army Corps of Engineers, Ft Worth District, Technical Library, 666

US Army Corps of Engineers, Galveston District Technical Library, 667

US Army Corps of Engineers, Headquarters Library, 668

US Army Corps of Engineers, Huntington District, Technical Library, 670

US Army Corps of Engineers, Huntsville Division, Technical Information Center, 672

US Army Corps of Engineers, Hydrologic Engineering Center Library, 673

US Army Corps of Engineers, Jacksonville District Technical Library, 675

US Army Corps of Engineers, Kansas City District Library, 676

US Army Corps of Engineers, Little Rock District Technical Library, 678

US Army Corps of Engineers, Los Angeles District Technical Library, 680

US Army Corps of Engineers, Louisville District Technical Library, 682

US Army Corps of Engineers, Missouri River Division, Omaha District Technical Library, 684

US Army Corps of Engineers, Nashville District Technical Library, 687

US Army Corps of Engineers, New England Division Technical Library, 689

US Army Corps of Engineers, New Orleans District Technical Library, 691

US Army Corps of Engineers, New York District Technical Library, 693

US Army Corps of Engineers, Norfolk District Technical Library, 694

US Army Corps of Engineers, North Atlantic Division Technical Library, 696

US Army Corps of Engineers, North Central Division Library, 698

US Army Corps of Engineers, Omaha District Library, 702

US Army Corps of Engineers, Omaha District Technical Library, 703

US Army Corps of Engineers, Pacific Ocean Division, Technical Library, 705

US Army Corps of Engineers, Pittsburgh District Technical Library, 707

US Army Corps of Engineers, Portland District Technical Library, 709

US Army Corps of Engineers, Rock Island District Technical Library, 710

US Army Corps of Engineers, Sacramento District Technical Library, 712

US Army Corps of Engineers, St Louis District Technical Library, 713

US Army Corps of Engineers, St Paul District Technical Library, 714

US Army Corps of Engineers Savannah District, Technical Library, 717

US Army Corps of Engineers, Seattle District Library, 718

US Army Corps of Engineers, South Atlantic Division Technical Library, 720

US Army Corps of Engineers, South Pacific Division Technical Library, 722

US Army Corps of Engineers, Southwest Division Technical Library, 723

US Army Corps of Engineers, Walla Walla District Technical & Law Library, 725

US Army Engineer Division Europe, Technical Library, 908

US Army Engineer Division Europe, Technical Library, 909

US Army Engineer Division, LMV, Technical Library, 729

US Army Engineering District, Technical Library, 731

US Army Engineering Topographic Laboratories Scientific & Technical Information Center, 732

US Army Laboratory Command, Human Engineering Laboratory Library, 748

US Army Missile & Space Intelligence Center Library, 760

US Army Natick Research, Development, & Engineering Center, Technical Library, 766

US Army Strategic Defense Command, Huntsville, Library, 781

US Army Tank-Automotive Command, Technical Library, 783

US Army Waterways Experiment Station, Technical Library, 791

USDA Sedimentation Laboratory Library, 88

USDA Western Regional Research Center Library, 89

US Grain Marketing Research Laboratory Library, 90

US Naval Observatory Library, 1172

US Navy Public Works Center, Technical Library, 1224

Weapons Quality Engineering Center Library, 1175

White Sands Missile Range, Technical Library, 806

Winchester Engineering & Analytical Center Library, 1338

General

AFCENT, US Army Library, 811

Alameda Naval Air Station Library, 944

Alaskan Air Command, Library Service Center/FL 5001, 213

Alconbury Base Library/FL 5643, 349

Allied Forces, South Europe, Library, 1179

Altus AFB, Base Library/FL 4419, 215

Anacostia Neighborhood Museum Library, 2452

Andersen Base Library/FL 4624, 350

Andrews AFB Base Library/FL 4425, 216

Ankara AS Library/FL 5694, 351

Annapolis Naval Station Library, 945

Arlington Hall Station, Post Library, 402

Army Community Recreation Library, 812

Atlanta Naval Air Station Library, 947

Aviano AB Library/FL 5682, 352

Bangor Naval Submarine Base Library, 948

Barbers Point Naval Air Station Library, 949

Barksdale AFB, Base Library/FL 4608, 219

Base Library, 353

Base Library/FL 5517, 354

Base Library/FL 5531, 355

Base Library/FL 5537, 356

Base Library/FL 5543, 357

Base Library/FL 5606, 358

Base Library/FL 5620, 359

Base Library/FL 5670, 360

Baumholder Military Community, US Army Library, 814

Beale AFB, Base Library/FL 4686, 220

Beeville Naval Air Station Library, 951

Bentwaters Base Library/FL 5644, 361

Bergstrom AFB, Base Library/FL 4857, 221

Blytheville AFB, Base Library/FL 4634, 222

Bolling AFB Base Library/FL 7058, 223

Bolling AFB, Base Library/FL 4400, 224

Brooks AFB, Base Library/FL 2857, 226

Brunswick Naval Air Station Library, 956

Bureau of Land Management, Salem District Office Library, 1517

Bureau of the Census, Atlanta Regional Office Library, 136

Camp Darby Post Library, 815

Camp Ederle, US Army Library, 816

Camp Lejeune, Marine Corps Base Library, 1228

Camp Market Army Library, 818

Camp Mercer Army Library, 819

Camp Nainhof Hohenfels, US Army Library, 820

Camp New Amsterdam, Base Library/FL 5688, 362

Camp Pendleton Base Library System, 1229

Camp Pendleton Naval Hospital, Crew's Library, 958

Camp Red Cloud Army Library, 821

Camp Smith Library, 1230

Cannon AFB, Base Library/FL 4855, 228

Carlisle Barracks, Post Library, 418

Carswell AFB Base Library/FL 4689, 229

Castle AFB, Baker Library/FL 4672, 230

Cecil Field Naval Air Station Library, 960

Chanute AFB, Base Library/FL 3018, 231

Charleston AFB, Base Library/FL 4418, 232

Charleston Naval Station Base Library, 963

Charleston Naval Station, Brig Library, 964

Cherry Point Marine Corps Air Station Library, 1231

Chicksands Base Library/FL 5650, 363

CINCLANTFLT Library, HSA, 967

Clark Base Library/FL 5251, 364

Colts Neck Naval Weapons Station, Earle Library, 968

Columbus AFB, Base Library/FL 3022, 233

COMFLEACT Library, 1180

USIS, Regional Library Consultant, North Africa, Near East, & South Asia, 2224

USIS, Regional Library Consultant, North Africa, Near East, & South Asia, 2225

USIS, American Center Library, Osaka, 2226

USIS, US Reference Center, Oslo, 2227

USIS Library, Centre Culturel Americain, Ouagadougou, 2228

USIS, Biblioteca Amador-Washington, Panama City, 2229

USIS, Centre de Documentation, Benjamin Franklin, Paris, 2230

USIS Library, American Center, Perth, 2231

USIS, American Center Library, Peshawar, 2232

USIS Library, American Center, Port of Spain, 2233

USIS, Biblioteka Amerykanska, Poznan, 2234

USIS, American Cultural Center Library, Pusan, 2235

USIS, Lincoln Library, Quito, 2236

USIS Library, Dar America Rabat, 2237

USIS Library, American Center, Rangoon, 2238

USIS, American Library, American Cultural Center, Reykjavik, 2239

USIS Reference Library, Rio de Janeiro, 2240

USIS, American Library, Rome, 2241

USIS, Biblioteca Lincoln, Santo Domingo, 2242

USIS Reference Library, Sao Paulo, 2243

USIS, American Center Library, Sapporo, 2244

USIS Library, Americki Centar, Sarajevo, 2245

USIS, American Cultural Center Library, Seoul, 2246

USIS, American Library Resource Center, Singapore, 2247

USIS Library, Americki Centar, Skopje, 2248

USIS, American Reading Room, Soweto, 2249

USIS, American Reference Center, Stockholm, 2250

USIS Library, Amerika Haus, Stuttgart, 2251

USIS Library, American Center, Sydney, 2252

USIS, American Cultural Center Library, Taegu, 2253

USIS Library, American Cultural Center, Tel Aviv, 2254

USIS, American Documentation Center, The Hague, 2255

USIS, American Center Library, Thessaloniki, 2256

USIS Library, Americki Centar, Titograd, 2257

USIS, American Center Library, Tokyo, 2258

USIS Library, Centre Culturel Americain, Tunis, 2259

USIS, American Center Library, Valletta, 2260

USIS, Amerika Haus Library, Vienna, 2261

USIS, Biblioteka Amerykanska, Warszawa, 2262

USIS, American Library, Wellington, 2263

USIS Library, Centre Culturel Americain, Yaounde, 2264

USIS Library, Americki Centar, Zagreb, 2265

US Marine Corps Air Ground Combat Center Library, 1244

US Marine Corps Air Station Library, 1245

US Marine Corps Base, Camp Smedley D Butler, Library Processing Center, 1251

US Marine Corps Tactical Systems Support Activity, Technical Library, 1247

USMCA, Garmisch, Army Library, 931

USMCA, Jaeger Kaserne, US Army Library, 932

USMCA, Pirmasens, Army Library, 933

USMCA, Rheinburg, Army Library, 934

USMCA, Zweibruecken, Army Library, 935

US National Support Unit, General Library, 1192

US Naval Air Facility, General Library, 1193

US Naval Air Facility Library, 1194

US Naval Air Station, Guam, Station Library, 1195

US Naval Air Station Library, 1196

US Naval Air Station Main Library, 1197

US Naval Air Station, Sigonella, Base Library, 1198

US Naval Communication Station, San Miguel, Station Library, 1199

US Naval Communication Station, Station Library, 1200

US Naval Communications Area, Station Library, 1201

US Naval Communications Station Library, 1202

US Naval Communications Station, Station Library, 1203

US Naval Facility, General Library, 1204

US Naval Facility, General Library, 1205

US Naval Facility, General Library, 1206

US Naval Hospital, Medical & General Libraries, 1207

US Naval Radio Transmitting Facility, Tarlac, General Library, 1211

US Naval Security Group Activity, General Library, 1212

US Naval Security Group Activity, Station Library, 1213

US Naval Station, Fletcher Library, 1214

US Naval Station, Guam, Station Library, 1215

US Naval Station Library, 1216

US Naval Support Activity Detachment, Library, 1217

US Naval Support Activity, General Library, 1218

US Naval Support Activity General Library, 1219

US Naval Support Activity Library, 1220

US Navy Administrative Support Unit, General Library, 1221

US Navy Office of Naval Research, Branch Office, London, Library, 1223

US Navy Ships Parts Control Center, General Library, 1174

US Navy Support Office Library, 1225

US Postal Service Library, 2271

USS Ponce (LPD-15), Crew & Troop Library, 1226

US ACOM, Army Library, 798

Van Deusen Post Library, 799

Vance AFB, Base Library/FL 3029, 338

Vandenberg AFB, Base Library/FL 4610, 339

Vogelweh Base Library/FL 5500, 390

Vogelweh Ramstein AB Library FL/5530, 391

F E Warren AFB, Base Library/FL 4613, 340

West Point Post Library, 803

Wheeler AFB, Base Library/FL 5296, 341

White Sands Missile Range, Post Library, 805

Whiteman AFB, Base Library/FL 4625, 342

Whiting Field Naval Air Station Library, 1177

Wiesbaden US Army Library, 937

Wildflecken US Military Community, Army Library Program, 939

Wiley Barracks, US Army Library, 940

Williams AFB, Base Library/FL 3044, 343

Willow Grove Naval Air Station Library, 1178

Wolfgang Pioneer Kaserene, US Army Library, 941

Wright-Patterson AFB, Base Library/FL 2300, 344

Wurtsmith AFB, Base Library/FL 4585, 348

Yokota AB, Base Library/FL 5209, 393

Yongsan Library, 942

Yuma Proving Ground, Post Library, 809

Zama Library, 943

Zaragoza Base Library/FL 5571, 394

Zweibrucken Air Base Library/FL 5529, 395

Health & Medicine

Aberdeen Proving Ground, Kirk US Army Health Clinic, Medical Library, 396

Agency for Toxic Substances & Disease Registry Library, 1321

Air Force Occupational & Environmental Health Laboratory, Technical Library/FL 2817, 203

Air Force School of Aerospace Medicine, Strughold Aeromedical Library/FL 2855, 206

Appalachian Laboratory for Occupational Safety & Health Library, 1325

Armed Forces Institute of Pathology, Ash Library, 405

Armed Forces Institute of Pathology, Ash Library, 1252

Armed Forces Radiobiology Research Institute Library, 946

Beaufort Naval Hospital, Medical Library, 950

William Beaumont Army Medical Center Library, 413

Bethesda Naval Hospital, Edward Rhodes Stitt Library, 953

Bethesda Naval Medical Research Institute, Information Services Branch, 954

Bremerton Naval Hospital, Medical Library, 955

Bureau of Radiological Health Library, 1329

Camp Lejeune Naval Hospital, Medical & General Libraries, 957

Camp Pendleton Naval Hospital Library, 959

Center for Devices & Radiological Health Library, 1330

Center for Devices & Radiological Health Library, 1331

Center for Food Safety & Applied Nutrition Library, 1332

Centers for Disease Control, Chamblee Branch Library, 1326

Centers for Disease Control Library, 1327

Charleston Naval Hospital, Medical Library, 961

Charleston Naval Station, Naval Hospital, Regional Medical Center, General Library, 965

Darnall Army Community Hospital, Medical Library, 426

US Army Hospital, Medical Library, 916

US Army Hospital, Wurzburg, Medical Library, 917

US Army Institute of Surgical Research, Library Branch, 742

US Army, Keller Army Community Hospital Library, 746

US Army Medical Research Institute of Infectious Diseases Library, 756

US Army Research Institute of Environmental Medicine, Medical Library, 772

US Naval Hospital, Medical & General Libraries, 1207

US Naval Hospital, Medical, Crews' & Patients' Library, 1208

US Naval Hospital, Medical Library, 1209

US Naval Hospital, Okinawa, Medical Library, 1210

James E Van Zandt Veterans Administration Medical Center, Medical Library, 2284

Veterans Administration Central Office Library, Library Division, 2285

Veterans Administration Domiciliary Library Service, 2286

Veterans Administration Hospital, Health Sciences Library, 2287

Veterans Administration Lakeside Medical Center, Library Service, 2289

Veterans Administration Library Service, Edith Nourse Rogers Memorial Veterans Hospital, 2290

Veterans Administration Medical & Regional Office Center Library, 2291

Veterans Administration Medical & Regional Office Center Library Service, 2292

Veterans Administration Medical Center & Patients' Library, 2293

Veterans Administration Medical Center, Health Sciences Library, 2294

Veterans Administration Medical Center, Hospital & Patients' Library, 2295

Veterans Administration Medical Center, Jefferson Barracks Division, Library Service, 2296

Veterans Administration Medical Center Learning Resource Center, 2297

Veterans Administration Medical Center Learning Resources Center, 2298

Veterans Administration Medical Center Learning Resources Center, 2299

Veterans Administration Medical Center Learning Resources Service, 2300

Veterans Administration Medical Center Library, 2301

Veterans Administration Medical Center Library, 2302

Veterans Administration Medical Center Library, 2303

Veterans Administration Medical Center Library, 2304

Veterans Administration Medical Center Library, 2305

Veterans Administration Medical Center Library, 2306

Veterans Administration Medical Center Library, 2307

Veterans Administration Medical Center Library, 2308

Veterans Administration Medical Center Library, 2309

Veterans Administration Medical Center Library, 2310

Veterans Administration Medical Center Library, 2311

Veterans Administration Medical Center Library, 2312

Veterans Administration Medical Center Library, 2313

Veterans Administration Medical Center Library, 2314

Veterans Administration Medical Center Library, 2315

Veterans Administration Medical Center Library, 2316

Veterans Administration Medical Center Library, 2317

Veterans Administration Medical Center Library, 2318

Veterans Administration Medical Center Library, 2319

Veterans Administration Medical Center Library, 2320

Veterans Administration Medical Center Library, William Jennings Bryan Dorn Veterans Hospital, 2321

Veterans Administration Medical Center Library-Learning Resources Center, 2322

Veterans Administration Medical Center Library Service, 2323

Veterans Administration Medical Center Library Service, 2324

Veterans Administration Medical Center Library Service, 2325

Veterans Administration Medical Center Library Service, 2326

Veterans Administration Medical Center Library Service, 2327

Veterans Administration Medical Center Library Service, 2328

Veterans Administration Medical Center Library Service, 2329

Veterans Administration Medical Center Library Service, 2330

Veterans Administration Medical Center Library Service, 2331

Veterans Administration Medical Center Library Service, 2332

Veterans Administration Medical Center Library Service, 2333

Veterans Administration Medical Center Library Service, 2334

Veterans Administration Medical Center Library Service, 2335

Veterans Administration Medical Center Library Service, 2336

Veterans Administration Medical Center Library Service, 2337

Veterans Administration Medical Center Library Service, 2338

Veterans Administration Medical Center Library Service, 2339

Veterans Administration Medical Center Library Service, 2340

Veterans Administration Medical Center Library Service, 2341

Veterans Administration Medical Center Library Service, 2342

Veterans Administration Medical Center Library Service, 2343

Veterans Administration Medical Center Library Service, 2344

Veterans Administration Medical Center Library Service, 2345

Veterans Administration Medical Center Library Service, 2346

Veterans Administration Medical Center Library Service, 2347

Veterans Administration Medical Center Library Service, 2348

Veterans Administration Medical Center Library Service, 2349

Veterans Administration Medical Center Library Service, 2350

Veterans Administration Medical Center Library Service, 2351

Veterans Administration Medical Center Library Service, 2352

Veterans Administration Medical Center Library Service, 2353

Veterans Administration Medical Center Library Service, 2354

Veterans Administration Medical Center Library Service, 2355

Veterans Administration Medical Center Library Service, 2356

Veterans Administration Medical Center Library Service, 2357

Veterans Administration Medical Center Library Service, 2358

Veterans Administration Medical Center Library Service, 2360

Veterans Administration Medical Center Library Service, 2361

Veterans Administration Medical Center Library Service, 2362

Veterans Administration Medical Center Library Service, 2364

Veterans Administration Medical Center Library Service, 2365

Veterans Administration Medical Center Library Service, 2366

Veterans Administration Medical Center Library Service, 2367

Veterans Administration Medical Center Library Service, 2368

Veterans Administration Medical Center Library Service, 2369

Veterans Administration Medical Center Library Service, 2370

Veterans Administration Medical Center Library Service, 2371

Veterans Administration Medical Center Library Service, 2372

Veterans Administration Medical Center Library Service, 2373

Veterans Administration Medical Center Library Service, 2374

Veterans Administration Medical Center Library Service, 2375

Veterans Administration Medical Center Library Service, 2376

Veterans Administration Medical Center Library Service, 2377

Veterans Administration Medical Center Library Service, 2378

Veterans Administration Medical Center Library Service, 2379

Veterans Administration Medical Center Library Service, 2380

Veterans Administration Medical Center Library Service, 2381

Veterans Administration Medical Center Library Service, 2382

Veterans Administration Medical Center Library Service, 2383

Veterans Administration Medical Center, John L McClellan Memorial Veterans Hospital, Medical Library, 2384

Veterans Administration Medical Center, Medical/General Library, 2385

Veterans Administration Medical Center, Medical Library, 2386

Veterans Administration Medical Center, Medical Library, 2387

Veterans Administration Medical Center, Medical Library, 2388

Veterans Administration Medical Center, Medical Library, 2389

Veterans Administration Medical Center, Medical Library, 2390

Veterans Administration Medical Center, Medical Library, 2391

Hospital (Patients)

Veterans Administration Medical Center Library Service, 2356

Veterans Administration Medical Center Library Service, 2358

Veterans Administration Medical Center Library Service, 2359

Veterans Administration Medical Center Library Service, 2360

Veterans Administration Medical Center Library Service, 2361

Veterans Administration Medical Center Library Service, 2363

Veterans Administration Medical Center Library Service, 2366

Veterans Administration Medical Center Library Service, 2368

Veterans Administration Medical Center Library Service, 2369

Veterans Administration Medical Center Library Service, 2371

Veterans Administration Medical Center Library Service, 2373

Veterans Administration Medical Center Library Service, 2376

Veterans Administration Medical Center Library Service, 2380

Veterans Administration Medical Center Library Service, 2381

Veterans Administration Medical Center Library Service, 2383

Veterans Administration Medical Center, Medical Library, 2401

Veterans Administration Medical Center, Medical Library, 2404

Veterans Administration Medical Center, Medical Library, 2407

Veterans Administration Medical Center, Medical Library, 2409

Veterans Administration Medical Center, Medical & Patient's Library, 2413

Veterans Administration Medical Center, Medical & Patient's Library, 2414

Veterans Administration Medical Center, Medical & Patients' Library, 2415

Veterans Administration Medical Center, Medical & Patients' Library, 2416

Veterans Administration Medical Center, Medical & Patients' Library, 2417

Veterans Administration Medical Center, Medical & Patients' Library, 2418

Veterans Administration Medical Center, Medical & Patients' Library, 2419

Veterans Administration Medical Center, Medical & Patients' Library, 2420

Veterans Administration Medical Center, Medical & Patients' Library, 2421

Veterans Administration Medical Center, Medical & Patients' Library, 2422

Veterans Administration Medical Center, Medical & Patients' Library Wade Park & Brecksville Units, 2423

Veterans Administration Medical Center Patients' Library, 2425

Veterans Administration Medical Center Patients' Library, 2426

Veterans Administration Medical Center Patients' Library, 2427

Veterans Administration Medical Center, Carl Vinson Center Library, 2428

Veterans Administration Medical Library, Olin E Teague Veterans Center, 2432

Veterans Administration Medical & Regional Office Center Library Service, 2433

Veterans Administration Medical & Regional Office Center, Medical Library, 2435

Veterans Administration Medical & Regional Office Center, Medical & Patients' Library, 2436

Veterans Administration Patients' Library, 2440

Veterans Administration Westside Medical Center Library Service, 2442

Law

Aberdeen Proving Ground, Office of the Staff Judge Advocate, Army Law Library, 397

Administrative Conference of the United States, Library, 1958

Anniston Army Depot, Office of the Post Judge Advocate, Army Law Library, 400

Arlington Hall Station, Post Legal Office, Army Law Library, 401

Arlington Hall Station, Staff Judge Advocate, Army Law Library, 403

Armed Forces Institute of Pathology, Legal Library, 406

Armed Services Board of Contract Appeals, Law Library, 1254

Army & Air Force Exchange Service, Law Library, 1255

Army Audit Agency, Army Law Library, 407

Army Law Library, Legal Advisor, 813

Ballistic Defense System Command, Office of the Staff Judge Advocate, Army Law Library, 412

William Beaumont Army Medical Center, Office of the Judge Advocate, Army Law Library, 414

Board of Governors of the Federal Reserve System, Law Library, 2026

Board of Immigration Appeals Library, 1910

Bolling AFB Office of the Judge Advocate General Library, 225

Camp Humphreys Legal Center, 817

Carlisle Barracks, Office of the Staff Judge Advocate, Army Law Library, 417

Central Intelligence Agency, Law Library, 1960

Coast Guard Law Library, 1941

Command Judge Advocate, Army Law Library, 822

Commodity Futures Trading Commission Library, 1965

Corpus Christi Army Depot, Office of the Command Judge Advocate, Army Law Library, 424

Defense Attache Office, Chief Legal Section, Army Law Library, 826

Department of Commerce, Law Library, 131

Department of Energy, Office of General Counsel, Law Library, 1295

HUD Region 9 Library, 1362

Department of Justice Antitrust Division Library, 1848

Department of Justice Antitrust Library, 1849

Department of Justice Civil Library, 1850

Department of Justice Civil Rights Library, 1851

Department of Justice Criminal Library, 1852

Department of Justice Lands Library, 1853

Department of Justice Main Library, 1854

Department of Justice Tax Library, 1855

Department of State Law Library, 1926

Department of the Interior, Center for Information & Library Services, Natural Resources Library, Law Branch, 1820

Department of the Interior, Center for Information & Library Services, Natural Resources Library, Law Branch, 1822

Department of the Interior, Office of the Field Solicitor, Law Library, 1823

Department of the Interior, Office of the Regional Solicitor, Law Library, 1824

Department of the Interior, Office of the Regional Solicitor, Law Library, 1825

Department of the Interior, Office of the Regional Solicitor, Law Library, 1826

Department of the Interior, Office of the Regional Solicitor, Law Library, 1827

Department of the Interior, Office of the Solicitor, Field Solicitor, Law Library, 1828

Department of the Interior, Office of the Solicitor, Field Solicitor, Law Library, 1829

Department of the Interior, Office of the Solicitor, Field Solicitor, Law Library, 1830

Department of the Interior, Office of the Solicitor, Field Solicitor, Law Library, 1831

Department of the Interior, Office of the Solicitor, Field Solicitor, Law Library, 1832

Department of the Interior, Office of the Solicitor, Field Solicitor, Law Library, 1833

Department of the Interior, Office of the Solicitor, Field Solicitor, Law Library, 1834

Department of the Interior, Office of the Solicitor, Field Solicitor, Law Library, 1835

Department of the Interior, Office of the Solicitor, Field Solicitor, Law Library, 1836

Department of the Interior, Office of the Solicitor, Field Solicitor, Law Library, 1837

Department of the Interior, Office of the Solicitor, Field Solicitor, Law Library, 1838

Department of the Interior, Office of the Solicitor, Field Solicitor, Library, 1839

Department of the Interior, Office of the Solicitor, Intermountain Region, Library, 1840

Department of the Interior, Office of the Solicitor, Law Library, 1841

Department of the Interior, Office of the Solicitor, Law Library, 1842

Department of the Interior, Office of the Solicitor, Regional Solicitor, Law Library, 1843

Department of Transportation Law Library, 1930

Dugway Proving Ground, Office of the Judge Advocate, Army Law Library, 429

Eastern Area, Office of the Staff Judge Advocate, Army Law Library, 433

Economic Development Administration, Seattle Regional Office Library, 146

XVIII Airborne Corps & Ft Bragg, Office of the Staff Judge Advocate, Army Law Library, 434

8th Infantry Division, Baumholder Branch, Staff Judge Advocate, Law Library, 827

8th Infantry Division, Office of the Judge Advocate, Army Law Library, 828

82nd Airborne Division, Office of the Staff Judge Advocate, Army Law Library, 435

Environmental Protection Agency, Law Library, 1976

Environmental Protection Agency, Region 3 Library, 1987

US Army Field Station, Command Judge Advocate, Diogenes Station Law Library, 913

US Army Finance & Accounting Center, Legal Office Law Library, 737

US Army Intelligence & Security Command (INSCOM) CONUS MIGP, Army Law Library, 743

US Army Law Library, Vilseck-Grafenwoehr, 918

US Army Legal Services Agency, Law Library, 750

US Army Logistics Management Center, Army Law Library, 752

US Army Materiel R&D Command, Army Law Library, 754

US Army Medical R&D Command, Office of the Judge Advocate, Army Law Library, 755

US Army Military Personnel Center, Army Law Library, 758

US Army Missile Command, Legal Office Library, 761

US Army Mobility R&D Command, Army Law Library, 763

US Army Natick R&D Command, Chief Legal Office, Army Law Library, 765

US Army Physical Disability Agency, Office of the Judge Advocate, Army Law Library, 770

US Army Real Estate Agency Europe, Office of the Staff Judge Advocate, Army Law Library, 926

US Army Recruiting Command, Army Law Library, 771

US Army Research Office, Army Law Library, 774

US Army Reserve Components Personnel & Administration Center, Office of the Judge Advocate, Army Law Library, 775

US Army 6th Recruiting Brigade (Western), Law Library, 779

US Army Soldier Support Center, Office of the Staff Judge Advocate, Army Law Library, 780

US Army Southern European Task Force & 5th Support Command, Army Law Library, 928

US Army Support Group, Legal Services Center, Army Law Library, 929

US Army Tank-Automotive Matter Readiness Command, Army Law Library, 784

US Army Training & Doctrine Command (TRADOC), Command Staff Judge Advocate, Army Law Library, 786

US Attorney's Office Camden Branch Library, 1914

US Attorney's Office Library, 1915

US Attorney's Office Library, 1916

US Attorney's Office Trenton Branch Library, 1917

US Court of Appeals 2nd Circuit Library, 14

US Court of Appeals, Branch Library, 15

US Court of Appeals 3rd Circuit Library, 16

US Court of Appeals 6th Circuit Library, 17

US Court of Appeals First Circuit Library, 18

US Court of Appeals for the 4th Circuit Charleston Branch Library, 19

US Court of Appeals for the 4th Circuit Library, 20

US Court of Appeals for the District of Columbia Circuit Judges' Library, 21

US Court of Appeals for the 5th Circuit Library, 22

US Court of Appeals for the 5th Circuit Library, 23

US Court of Appeals for the 8th Circuit Branch Library, 24

US Court of Appeals for the 8th Circuit Branch Library, 25

US Court of Appeals for the 8th Circuit, Fargo Branch Library, 26

US Court of Appeals for the 8th Circuit Library, 27

US Court of Appeals for the 6th Circuit Grand Rapids Branch Library, 28

US Court of Appeals for the 6th Circuit Memphis Branch Library, 29

US Court of Appeals for the Federal Circuit Library, 53

US Court of Appeals for the 10th Circuit Albuquerque Branch Library, 30

US Court of Appeals for the 10th Circuit Tulsa Branch Library, 31

US Court of Appeals for the 11th Circuit Library, 32

US Court of Appeals for the 9th Circuit Library, 33

US Court of Appeals for the 9th Circuit Library, 34

US Court of Appeals for the 9th Circuit Los Angeles Branch Library, 35

US Court of Appeals Library, 36

US Court of Appeals Library, 37

US Court of Appeals Newark Branch Library, 38

US Court of Appeals 9th Circuit Library, 39

US Court of International Trade Library, 60

US Court of Military Appeals Library, 61

US Courts 2nd Circuit Library, 40

US Courts Branch Library, 41

US Courts William J Campbell Library, 42

US Courts Library, 43

US Courts Library, 44

US Courts Library, 45

US Courts Library, 46

US Courts Library, 47

US Courts Library, 48

US Courts Library, 49

US Courts Library, 50

US Courts Library, 51

US Customs Service, New York Region, Library, 1955

US Customs Service, Office of Regional Counsel, Library, 1956

US Disciplinary Barracks, Army Command Judge Advocate, Law Library, 792

US District Court Eastern District of New York Library, 54

US District Court Library, 55

US District Court Library, 56

US District Court Library, 57

US District Court Library, 58

US District Courts & Alaska Court System Law Library, 59

US International Trade Commission, Law Library, 2269

US Marine Corps HQ, Judge Advocate Division, Legal Library, 1246

US Merit Systems Protection Board Library, 2055

US Military Academy, Department of Law Library, 793

US Military Academy, Office of the Staff Judge Advocate, Army Law Library, 795

US Office of Personnel Management Library, 2089

US Penitentiary Legal Library, Terre Haute, 1902

US Postal Service Library, 2271

US Readiness Command, Law Library, 797

US Southern Command, Office of the Staff Judge Advocate, 936

US Tax Court Library, 62

US Courts Branch Library, 52

Veterans Administration Office of General Counsel, Law Library, 2437

Vint Hill Farms Station, Office of the Post Judge Advocate, Army Law Library, 800

Walter Reed Medical Center, Office of the Center Advocate, Army Law Library, 801

Watervliet Arsenal, Legal Office, 802

Western Area Power Administration, Office of General Counsel, Law Library, 1317

White House Law Library, 65

White Sands Missle Range, Office of the Staff Judge Advocate, Army Law Library, 807

Wildflecken Military Community, Office of the Staff Judge Advocate, US Army Law Library, 938

National

Food & Nutrition Information Center, 123

Library of Congress, 9

National Agricultural Library, 124

National Agricultural Library, DC Reference Center, 125

National Library of Medicine, 1346

National Library Service for the Blind & Physically Handicapped, Library of Congress, 10

Penal

Alderson Federal Correctional Institution Library, 1858

Allenwood Federal Prison Camp Library, 1859

Ashland Federal Correctional Institution Library, 1860

Bastrop Federal Correctional Institution Library, 1861

Big Spring Federal Prison Camp Library, 1862

Boron Federal Prison Camp Library, 1863

Butner Federal Correctional Institution Library, 1864

Chicago Metropolitan Correctional Center Inmate Library, 1865

Danbury Federal Correctional Institution Library, 1866

Duluth Federal Prison Camp Library, 1867

El Reno Federal Correctional Institution Library, 1868

Elgin Federal Prison Camp Inmate Library, 1869

Ft Leavenworth, US Army Disciplinary Barracks, 512

Fort Worth Federal Correctional Institute Library Services, 1871

Ft Worth Federal Correctional Institution Library, 1872

La Tuna Federal Correctional Institution Library, 1873

Lexington Federal Correctional Institution Library, 1874

Littleton Federal Correctional Institution Library, 1875

Lompoc US Penitentiary Library, 1876

Loretto Federal Correctional Institution Library, 1877

Marion US Penitentiary Library, 1878

Maxwell AFB, Federal Prison Camp Library, 1879

Memphis Federal Correctional Institution Library, 1880

Miami Metropolitan Correctional Center, Inmate Law Library, 1881

Milan Federal Correctional Institution Library, 1882

Morgantown Federal Correctional Institution Library, 1883

New York Metropolitan Correctional Center Library, 1884

Otisville Federal Correctional Institution Library, 1885

Oxford Federal Correctional Institution Library, 1886

Petersburg Federal Correctional Institution Library, 1887

Phoenix Federal Correctional Institution Library, 1888

Pleasanton Federal Correctional Institution Library, 1889

Ray Brook Federal Correctional Institution Library, 1890

Rochester Federal Medical Center Library, 1891

Safford Federal Correctional Institution Library, 1892

San Diego Metropolitan Correctional Center Library, 1893

Sandstone Federal Correctional Institution Library, 1894

Seagoville Federal Correctional Institution Library, 1895

Springfield Medical Center of Federal Prisoners Library, 1896

Talladega Federal Correctional Institution Library, 1897

Tallahassee Federal Correctional Institution Library, 1898

Terminal Island Federal Correctional Institution Library, 1899

Texarkana Federal Correctional Institution Library, 1900

Tucson Metropolitan Correctional Center Library, 1901

US Penitentiary Library, Atlanta, 1903

US Penitentiary Library, Leavenworth, 1904

US Penitentiary Resource Library, Lewisburg, 1905

US Penitentiary Reading Library, Terre Haute, 1906

Presidential

Jimmy Carter Library, 2070
Dwight D Eisenhower Library, 2071
Gerald R Ford Library, 2072
Herbert Hoover Presidential Library, 2073
John F Kennedy Presidential Library, 2074
Franklin D Roosevelt Library, 2079
Harry S Truman Library, 2080

Special

Aberdeen Proving Ground, Ordnance Center & School Library, 398

Aberdeen Proving Ground, Ordnance Center & School Museum Library, 399

Acadia National Park Library, 1592

Adams National Historic Site, Stone Library, 1593

Advisory Commission on Intergovernmental Relations Library, 2444

African Development Foundation Library, 1959

Agricultural Research Service, SW Watershed Research Center Library, 68

Agricultural Research Service, Western Region Library, 69

Air Force Accounting & Finance Center Library/FL 7040, 195

Air Force Flight Test Center, Technical Library/FL 2806, 197

Air Force Human Resources Laboratory, Technical Library/FL 2870, 199

Air Force Institute of Technology Library, 201

Air Force Logistics Management Center, Technical Library, 202

Air Force Systems Command Technical Information Center, 208

Air Force Western Space & Missile Center, Technical Library/FL 2827, 210

Air Weather Service Technical Library/FL 4414, 212

Alaska Power Administration Library, 1287

Alaska Resources Library, 1819

Horace M Albright Training Center Library, 1594

Alert Facility Base Level Library, 214

Allegheny Portage Railroad National Historic Site Library, 1595

American Museum of Immigration Library, 1596

Andersonville National Historic Site Library, 1597

APHIS Plant Protection & Quarantine Library, 93

APHIS Plant Protection & Quarantine Training Center Library, 94

Animal Science Institute Library, 70

Antietam National Battlefield Library, 1598

Apostle Islands National Lakeshore Library, 1599

Appomattox Court House National Historic Park Library, 1600

Arches National Park Library, 1601

Architect of the Capitol, Art & Reference Division, 3

Architectural & Transportation Barriers Compliance Board, Technical Library, 2445

Archives of American Art, 2453

Arlington House, The Robert E Lee Memorial Library, 1602

Army Materiel Command Headquarters, Technical Library, 408

Assateague Island National Seashore Library, 1603

Atmospheric Turbulence & Diffusion Laboratory Library, 157

Auke Bay Fisheries Laboratory Library, 158

Aviation Systems Command, Library & Information Center, 411

Aztec Ruins National Monument Library, 1604

Badlands National Park Library, 1605

Bandelier National Monument Library, 1606

Beltsville Human Nutrition Research Center, 71

Benet Weapons Laboratory, Technical Library, 416

Bent's Old Fort National Historic Site Library, 1607

Big Bend National Park Library, 1608

Big Hole National Battlefield Library, 1609

Big Thicket National Preserve Library, 1610

Bighorn Canyon National Recreation Area Library, 1611

Biological Control of Insects Laboratory, Library, 72

Blue Ridge Parkway Library, 1612

Board of Governors of the Federal Reserve System, Research Library, 2027

Bonneville Power Administration Library, 1291

Bridger-Teton National Forest Library, 99

Brookhaven National Laboratory, Nuclear Safeguards Library, 1292

Brookhaven National Laboratory, Research Library, 1293

Bryce Canyon National Park Library, 1613

Buck Island Reef National Monument Library, 1614

Buffalo National River Library, 1615

Bureau of Alcohol, Tobacco & Firearms Reference Library, 1947

Bureau of Economic Analysis, Research Resource Center, 145

Bureau of Labor Statistics Library, 1920

Bureau of Labor Statistics, Regional Office, Reference Library, 1921

Bureau of Labor Statistics, Regional Office, Reference Library, 1922

Bureau of Land Management, Arizona State Office Library, 1466

Bureau of Land Management, Arizona Strip, District Office Library, 1467

Bureau of Land Management, Baker District Office Library, 1468

Bureau of Land Management, Bakersfield District Office Library, 1469

Bureau of Land Management, Bishop Resource Area Headquarters Library, 1470

Bureau of Land Management, Branch of Records & Data Management, 1471

Bureau of Land Management, Burns District Office Library, 1472

Bureau of Land Management, California State Office Library, 1473

Bureau of Land Management, Cedar City District Library, 1474

Bureau of Land Management, Coeur D'Alene District Office Library, 1475

Bureau of Land Management, Colorado State Office Library, 1476

Bureau of Land Management, Colorado State Office Library, 1477

Bureau of Land Management, Coos Bay District Office Library, 1478

Bureau of Land Management, Craig District Office Library, 1479

Bureau of Land Management, District Library, 1480

Bureau of Land Management, District Office Library, 1481

Bureau of Land Management, District Office Library, 1482

Bureau of Land Management, Eastern States Office Library, 1483

Bureau of Land Management, Elko District Office Library, 1484

Bureau of Land Management, Eugene Office Library, 1485

Bureau of Land Management, Fairbanks District Office Library, 1486

Bureau of Land Management, Folsom District Office Library, 1487

Bureau of Land Management, Garnet Resource Area Library, 1488

Bureau of Land Management, Idaho State Office Library, 1489

Bureau of Land Management, Kanab Office Library, 1490

Bureau of Land Management, Lake States Office Library, 1491

Bureau of Land Management, Lakeview District Office Library, 1492

Bureau of Land Management, Las Cruces District Office Library, 1493

Dinosaur National Monument Library, 1656

Doctrine Center Library, 1232

Drug Enforcement Administration Library, 1907

Dugway Proving Ground, Technical Library, 431

Eastern Space & Missile Center Technical Library/FL 2828, 238

Economic Research Service Reference Center, 96

Edison National Historic Site, 1657

Effigy Mounds National Monument Library, 1658

El Morro National Monument Library, 1659

Energy Information Center, 1297

The Energy Library, Germantown Branch, 1299

Environmental Protection Agency, Andrew W Breidenbach Library, 1969

Environmental Protection Agency, Central Regional Laboratory Library, 1970

Environmental Protection Agency, Environmental Research Laboratory Library, 1973

Environmental Protection Agency Headquarters Library, 1974

Environmental Protection Agency, Robert S Kerr Library, 1975

Environmental Protection Agency Library, 1977

Environmental Protection Agency Library, Region 8, 1978

Environmental Protection Agency, Meteorology Division Library, 1979

Environmental Protection Agency, National Water Quality Laboratory Library, 1981

Environmental Protection Agency, Office of Air Quality, Planning, & Standards Library, 1982

Environmental Protection Agency, Region 9 Library, 1983

Environmental Protection Agency, Region 1 Library, 1984

Environmental Protection Agency, Region 2, Field Office Library, 1985

Environmental Protection Agency, Region 2 Library, 1986

Environmental Protection Agency, Region 5 Library, 1989

Environmental Protection Agency, Region 6 Library, 1990

Environmental Protection Agency, Region 7 Library, 1991

Environmental Protection Agency, Region 10 Library, 1992

Environmental Protection Agency, Research Laboratory Library, 1993

Equipment Development Center Library, 104

Everglades National Park Research Center Library, 1660

Executive Office of the President Library, 64

Eximbank Library, 2002

FAA Central Regional Library, 1935

FCC Chicago District Office Library, 2004

FAA Eastern Region Library, 1937

Federal Emergency Management Agency Library, 2010

Federal Hall National Memorial Library, 1661

Federal Home Loan Bank Board, Research Library, 2013

Federal Home Loan Bank of Atlanta, Research Library, 2014

Federal Home Loan Bank of Chicago Library, 2015

Federal Home Loan Bank of Dallas, Research & Information Library, 2016

Federal Home Loan Bank of Des Moines Library, 2017

Federal Home Loan Bank of Indianapolis Library, 2018

Federal Home Loan Bank of New York Library, 2019

Federal Home Loan Bank of San Francisco Library, 2020

Federal Law Enforcement Training Center Library, 1950

Federal Prison System Library, 1870

Federal Reserve Bank of Atlanta, Research Library, 2028

Federal Reserve Bank of Boston, Research Library, 2029

Federal Reserve Bank of Chicago Library, 2030

Federal Reserve Bank of Cleveland, Research Library, 2031

Federal Reserve Bank of Dallas Library, 2032

Federal Reserve Bank of Kansas City, Research Library, 2033

Federal Reserve Bank of Minneapolis Library, 2034

Federal Reserve Bank of New York, Computer Science Library, 2035

Federal Reserve Bank of New York, Research Library, 2037

Federal Reserve Bank of Philadelphia, Information Services & Research Library, 2038

Federal Reserve Bank of Richmond, Baltimore Branch Library, 2039

Federal Reserve Bank of Richmond, Research Library, 2040

Federal Reserve Bank of St Louis, Research Library, 2041

Federal Reserve Bank of San Francisco, Research Library, 2042

Federal Trade Commission, Atlanta Regional Office Library, 2043

Federal Trade Commission, Cleveland Regional Office Library, 2044

Federal Trade Commission Library, 2048

Federal Trade Commission, San Francisco Regional Office Library, 2049

Fire Island National Seashore Library, 1662

Fish & Wildlife Service, Division of Biological Services Library, 1550

Fish & Wildlife Service Library, 1551

Fish & Wildlife Service, Science Reference Library, 1552

Fish Farming Experimental Station Library, 1553

Florissant Fossil Beds National Monument Library, 1663

Food & Drug Administration, Bureau of Foods Library, 1334

Food & Drug Administration, Dallas District Library, 1335

Food & Drug Administration Library, 1336

Food & Nutrition Service Reference Center, 97

Food Safety & Inspection Service, Science Administration Library, 98

Ford's Theatre National Historic Site Library, 1664

Foreign Technology Division Technical Library/FL 2830, 248

Forest Hydrology Laboratory Library, 105

Forest Sciences Laboratory, 107

Forest Service, Equipment Development Center Library, 108

Forest Service Information, Northwest, 109

Forest Service, Pacific NW Forest & Range Experimental Station, 110

Forest Service, Region 6 Information Office, 111

Forest Service, Rogue River National Forest Library, 112

Forestry Sciences Laboratory Library, 113

Ft Caroline National Memorial Library, 1665

Ft Clatsop National Memorial Library, 1666

Ft Davis National Historic Site Library, 1667

Ft Donelson National Battlefield Library, 1668

Ft Frederica National Monument Library, 1669

Ft Sam Houston, US Army Library Service Center, 489

Ft Knox, Emert L Davis Memorial Library, 504

Ft Laramie National Historic Site Library, 1670

Ft Larned National Historic Site Library, 1671

Ft Lewis Military Museum, Research Library, 515

Ft McHenry National Monument & Historic Shrine Library, 1672

Ft George G Meade, Language Training Facility Library, 533

Ft Necessity National Battlefield Library, 1673

Ft Point National Historic Site Library, 1674

Ft Pulaski National Monument Library, 1675

Ft Stanwix National Monument Library, 1676

Ft Sumter National Monument Library, 1677

Ft Union National Monument Library, 1678

Ft Union Trading Post National Historic Site Library, 1679

Ft Vancouver National Historic Site Library, 1680

Fossil Butte National Monument Library, 1681

Fredericksburg & Spotsylvania National Military Park Library, 1682

Freer Gallery of Art Library, 2455

Ft Bowie National Historic Site Library, 1683

Gallaudet University Library, 1285

General Services Administration, Design & Construction Division Library, 2050

Geological Survey, Gerryan Memorial Library, 1563

Geological Survey Library, 1567

Geological Survey, National Cartographic Information Center, 1570

Geological Survey, National Mapping Division Applications Assistance Facility Library, 1571

Geological Survey, National Water Quality Laboratory-Library, 1572

Geological Survey, Public Inquiries Office, 1573

Geological Survey, Public Inquiries Office Library, 1574

Geological Survey, Public Inquiries Office Library, 1575

Geological Survey, Resource Appraisal Group Library, 1577

National Endowment for the Humanities Library, 2083

National Fishery Research & Development Laboratory Library, 1555

National Fishery Research Center Library, 1556

National Gallery of Art Library, 2458

National Highway Traffic Safety Administration, Technical Reference Division, Library, 1940

National Institute for Petroleum & Energy Research Library, 1310

National Institute of Justice Library, 1856

National Institute of Justice/National Criminal Justice Reference Service, 1857

National Marine Fisheries Service, Honolulu Laboratory Library, 166

National Marine Fisheries Service, Southeast Fisheries Center Library, 167

National Marine Mammal Library, 168

National Maritime Museum, J Porter Shaw Library, 1745

National Maritime Research Center, Study Center Library, 1938

National Mine Health & Safety Academy, Learning Resource Center, 1923

National Museum of African Art, Branch Library, 2459

National Museum of American Art & National Portrait Gallery Library, 2460

National Museum of American History, Branch Library, 2461

National Museum of Natural History, Branch Library, 2462

NOAA, Coral Gables Center Library, 169

NOAA, Great Lakes Environmental Research Laboratory Library, 170

NOAA, Mountain Administrative Support Center, 172

NOAA, Scientific Services Division, 174

National Park Service, Central Compliance Library, 1746

National Park Service Library, 1747

National Park Service, Midwest Archeological Center Library, 1748

National Park Service Midwest Regional Library, 1749

National Park Service, Southeast Regional Office Library, 1750

National Park Service, Southwest Regional Library, 1751

National Park Service, Western Regional Resources Library, 1752

National Register of Historic Places Library, 1589

National Soil Dynamics Laboratory Library, 77

National Weather Service, Central Region Library, 179

National Weather Service, Southern Region Headquarters Library, 180

National Weather Service, Weather Service Nuclear Support Office Library, 181

National Zoological Park Library Branch, 2463

Nautilus Memorial/Submarine Force Library & Museum, 1010

Navajo National Monument Library, 1753

Naval Academy Preparatory School Library, 1011

Naval Air Rework Facility, Technical Library, 1017

Naval Air Systems Command, Technical Information & Reference Center, 1018

Naval Air Test Center, Technical Information Department, 1019

Naval Audit Service Headquarters Library, 1023

Naval Avionics Center, Technical Library, 1024

Naval Coastal Systems Center, Technical Information Services Branch, 1028

Naval Education & Training Program Development Center, General Library Services, 1036

Naval Explosive Ordnance Disposal Technology Center, Library, 1042

Naval Intelligence Support Center Library, 1052

Naval Military Personnel Command, Technical Library, 1054

Naval Mobile Construction Battalion Center Library, 1056

Naval Ocean Research & Development Activity Library, 1057

Naval Regional Library, Groton, 1064

Naval Research Laboratory, USRD, 1067

Naval Sea Support Center, Atlantic, Technical Library, 1070

Naval Sea Support Center, Pacific, Library, 1071

Naval Security Group Activity Station Library, 1074

Naval Ship Research & Development Center, W Taylor Library, 1075

Naval Supply Center, Technical Division Library, 1081

Naval Surface Weapons Center, Technical Library, 1088

Naval Underwater Systems Center, New London Laboratory, Technical Library, 1092

Naval Underwater Systems Center, Technical Library, 1094

Naval Weapons Center, Technical Library, 1097

Navy Personnel Research & Development Center, Technical Library, 1110

Navy Regional Data Automation Center, 1111

Navy Supply Center, Inventory Control Department, Technical Library, 1113

Nevada Technical Library, Department of Energy, 1311

Nez Perce National Historic Park Library, 1754

North Cascades National Park Library, 1755

North Central Forest Experiment Station Library, 116

Northern Prairie Wildlife Research Center Library, 1557

Occupational Safety & Health Administration, Region 3, Library, 1924

Ocmulgee National Monument Library, 1756

Office of International Cooperation & Development (OICD), Technical Inquiries, 127

Office of Naval Research, Detachment Boston Library, 1121

Office of Surface Mining Reclamation & Enforcement Library, 1845

Office of Technology Assessment Information Center, 11

Office of Toxic Substances, Chemical Library, 1995

Olympic National Park Library, 1757

119 Fig Field Library, 304

Organ Pipe Cactus National Monument Library, 1758

Overseas Private Investment Corporation Library, 2266

Oxford Laboratory Library, 184

Ozark National Scenic Riverways Library, 1759

Pacific Northwest Region Library, 1548

Pacific Northwest Regional Library System, 1760

Pacific Southwest Forest & Range Experiment Station Library, 117

Pacific Southwest Regional Office Library, 1590

Padre Island National Seashore Library, 1761

Parklawn Health Library, 1350

Patuxent Naval Aviation Logistics Center, Technical Library, 1130

Pea Ridge National Military Park Library, 1762

Peace Corps Information Services, Division Library, 2090

Pecos National Monument Library, 1763

Pentagon Library, 605

Perry's Victory & International Peace Memorial Library, 1764

Petersburg National Battlefield Library, 1765

Petrified Forest National Park Library, 1766

Pictured Rocks National Lakeshore Library, 1767

Pinnacles National Monument Library, 1768

Pipe Springs National Monument Library, 1769

Plum Island Animal Disease Center Library, 79

Point Reyes National Seashore Library, 1770

Portsmouth Naval Shipyard Museum, Marshall W Butt Library, 1143

Portsmouth Naval Shipyard, Supply Department, Technical Library, 1144

Postal Rate Commission Library, 2093

President's Committee on the Employment of the Handicapped, Library, 2451

Presidio Army Museum Library, 607

Puuhonua o Honaunau National Historical Park, Library, 1771

Railroad Retirement Board Library, 2095

Redwood National Park Library, 1772

Walter Reed Army Institute of Research Library, 616

Reno Metallurgy Research Center Library, 1544

Richmond National Battlefield Park Headquarters Library, 1773

Rock Creek Nature Center, 1774

Rocky Mountain Forest & Range Experiment Station Library, 118

Rocky Mountain National Park Library, 1775

Rolla Metallurgy Research Center, Technical Library, 1545

Franklin D Roosevelt National Historic Site Library, 1776

Theodore Roosevelt National Park Library, 1777

Russell Cave National Monument Library, 1778

Sagamore Hill National Historic Site Library, 1779

Saguaro National Monument Library, 1780

St Croix National Scenic Riverway Library, 1781

Saint Gardens Library, 1782

Salem Maritime National Historic Site Library, 1783

Salinas National Monument Library, 1784

San Diego Naval Supply, Technical Library, 1152

San Juan Island National Historical Park Library, 1785

San Juan National Historic Site, Division of Visitors Services—Library, 1786

Training Center

Subject Index

Acadia National Park
Acadia National Park Library, 1592

Acceleration
Fermi National Accelerator Laboratory Library, 1301

Accessibility for Handicapped
Architectural & Transportation Barriers Compliance Board, Technical Library, 2445

Accounting
Air Force Accounting & Finance Center Library/FL 7040, 195
Department of Justice Tax Library, 1855
Farm Credit Administration Library, 2003
General Accounting Office, Office of Library Services, 5
US Securities & Exchange Commission Library, 2096

Acid Precipitation
Environmental Protection Agency, Corvallis Environmental Research Library, 1971
Geological Survey Library, 1568

Acoustic Warfare
Naval Coastal Systems Center, Technical Information Services Branch, 1028

Acoustics
Matthew Fontaine Maury Oceanographic Library, 999
NOAA, Miami Library, 171
Naval Explosive Ordnance Disposal Technology Center, Library, 1042
Naval Research Laboratory, USRD, 1067
Naval Underwater Systems Center, New London Laboratory, Technical Library, 1092
Naval Underwater Systems Center, Technical Library, 1094
Office of Naval Research, Detachment Boston Library, 1121
David Taylor Naval Ship R&D Center, Technical Information Center, 1166
US Army Environmental Hygiene Agency Library, 733
US Army Laboratory Command, Human Engineering Laboratory Library, 748

Adams, John Quincy
Adams National Historic Site, Stone Library, 1593

Adams, Paul D.
National Defense University Library, 1278

Adhesives
US Army Armament Research & Development Center, Plastics Technical Evaluation Center, 643

Administrative Conference of the United States
Administrative Conference of the United States, Library, 1958

Administrative Law
Administrative Conference of the United States, Library, 1958
Camp Humphreys Legal Center, 817
Consumer Product Safety Commission Library, 1967
Department of Energy, Office of General Counsel, Law Library, 1295
Department of Justice Antitrust Library, 1849
Department of the Interior, Center for Information & Library Services, Natural Resources Library, Law Branch, 1820
Department of the Interior, Center for Information & Library Services, Natural Resources Library, Law Branch, 1822
Department of Transportation Law Library, 1930
Environmental Protection Agency, Law Library, 1976
Federal Home Loan Bank Board, Law Library, 2012
HQ, VII Corps, Staff Judge Advocate, Army Law Library, 848
Interstate Commerce Commission Library, 2053
Mainz Detachment, Office of the Staff Judge Advocate, Law Library, 863
21st Support Command, Office of Staff Judge Advocate, Law Library, 899

Admiralty Law
Department of Justice Civil Library, 1850

Adolescent Pregnancy
The National Family Planning Information Clearinghouse Library, 1349

Adoption
The National Family Planning Information Clearinghouse Library, 1349

Aerial Photography
Bureau of Land Management, Elko District Office Library, 1484
EROS Data Center, Technical Reference Unit, 1561
US Army Corps of Engineers, Buffalo District Technical Library, 661

Aerodynamics
Arnold Engineering Development Center Technical Library/FL 2804, 218
Sandia National Laboratories, Technical Library, 1314
David Taylor Naval Ship R&D Center, Technical Information Center, 1166

Aeronautical Engineering
Naval Air Engineering Center, Technical Library, 1015
Naval Air Propulsion Center, Technical Library, 1016
Tinker AFB, Base Library/FL 2030, 325

Aeronautics
Air Force Flight Test Center, Technical Library/FL 2806, 197
Air Force Institute of Technology Academic Library/FL 3319, 200
Alconbury Base Library/FL 5643, 349
Armament Division Technical Library/FL 2825, 217
Aviation Applied Technology Directorate, Technical Library, 410
Aviation Systems Command, Library & Information Center, 411
Beale AFB, Base Library/FL 4686, 220
Bergstrom AFB, Base Library/FL 4857, 221
Bolling AFB, Base Library/FL 4400, 224
Carswell AFB Base Library/FL 4689, 229
Castle AFB, Baker Library/FL 4672, 230
Chanute AFB, Base Library/FL 3018, 231
Ellsworth AFB, Base Library/FL 4690, 243
Jacksonville Naval Air Station Library, 988
Kingsville Naval Air Station Library, 992
Langley AFB, Base Library/FL 4800, 277
Loring AFB, Base Library/FL 4678, 281
Lowry AFB, Base Library/FL 3059, 282
March AFB, Base Library/FL 4664, 287
Memphis Naval Air Station Library, 1004
Myrtle Beach AFB, Base Library/FL 4806, 300
NASA-AMES Research Center, Technical Library, 2061
NASA Dryden Flight Research Center Library, 2062
NASA Lyndon B Johnson Space Center, Technical Library, 2066
NASA Headquarters, S & T Library & Systems Support, 2069
National Museum of Natural History, Branch Library, 2462
Naval Air Development Center, Scientific & Technical Library Branch, 1014
Naval Air Systems Command, Technical Information & Reference Center, 1018
Nellis AFB, Base Library/FL 4852, 301
Norton AFB, Base Library/FL 4448, 302
Peterson AFB, Base Library/FL 2500, 307

Point Mugu Naval Air Station Library, 1138

Redstone Scientific Information Center, 615

Smithsonian Institution Libraries, 2468

US Air Force Academy Library/FL 7000, 331

F E Warren AFB, Base Library/FL 4613, 340

Whiting Field Naval Air Station Library, 1177

Wright-Patterson AFB, Technical Library/FL 2802, 345

Zaragoza Base Library/FL 5571, 394

Aeronautics History

US Air Force Academy Library/FL 7000, 331

Aeronomy

NOAA, Mountain Administrative Support Center, 172

Aerospace Biology

NASA-AMES Research Center, Technical Library, 2061

Aerospace Engineering

NASA-AMES Research Center Library, 2059

Aerospace History

National Air & Space Museum, Branch Library, 2457

Aerospace Law

Peterson AFB, Base Library/FL 2500, 307

Aerospace Medicine

Air Force School of Aerospace Medicine, Strughold Aeromedical Library/FL 2855, 206

NASA-AMES Research Center, Life Sciences Library, 2060

Naval Aerospace Medical Institute Library, 1013

Wright-Patterson AFB, Technical Library/FL 2802, 345

Wright-Patterson AFB, Medical Center Library, 347

Aerospace Science

Air Force Space Command Library/FL 2508, 207

Air Force Western Space & Missile Center, Technical Library/FL 2827, 210

Arnold Engineering Development Center Technical Library/FL 2804, 218

EROS Data Center, Technical Reference Unit, 1561

Holloman AFB, Base Library/FL 4801, 264

Lowry AFB, Base Library/FL 3059, 282

NASA Goddard Institute for Space Studies Library, 2063

NASA Goddard Space Flight Center Library, 2064

NASA Goddard Space Flight Center, Wallops Flight Facility Library, 2065

NASA Lyndon B Johnson Space Center, Technical Library, 2066

NASA Langley Research Center, Technical Library, 2067

NASA-National Space Technology Laboratories, Research Library, 2068

National Air & Space Museum, Branch Library, 2457

Smithsonian Institution Libraries, 2468

US Army Missile & Space Intelligence Center Library, 760

Aerospace Technology

Air Force Systems Command Technical Information Center, 208

Air Force Weapons Laboratory Technical Library/FL 2809, 209

Eastern Space & Missile Center Technical Library/FL 2828, 238

John F Kennedy Space Center Library, 2056

Loring AFB, Base Library/FL 4678, 281

George C Marshall Space Flight Center Technical Library, 2058

NASA Langley Research Center, Technical Library, 2067

Peterson AFB, Base Library/FL 2500, 307

Redstone Scientific Information Center, 615

Smithsonian Institution Libraries, 2468

Vandenberg AFB, Base Library/FL 4610, 339

Africa

Ft McPherson, Staff Judge Advocate, 3rd US Army Law Library, 528

National Museum of African Art, Branch Library, 2459

Peace Corps Information Services, Division Library, 2090

African Art

National Museum of African Art, Branch Library, 2459

National Museum of Natural History, Branch Library, 2462

Agate Fossil Beds National Monument

Scotts Bluff National Monument, Oregon Trail Association Library, 1790

Age Discrimination

US Commission on Civil Rights, National Clearinghouse Library, 1962

Agricultural Economics

Economic Research Service Reference Center, 96

Farm Credit Administration Library, 2003

Federal Reserve Bank of Chicago Library, 2030

Agricultural Engineering

Roman L Hruska US Meat Animal Research Center Library, 75

Agriculture

Agricultural Research Service, SW Watershed Research Center Library, 68

Agricultural Research Service, Western Region Library, 69

Environmental Protection Agency, Robert S Kerr Library, 1975

Environmental Protection Agency, National Enforcement Investigation Center, Information Center, 1980

Environmental Protection Agency, Region 7 Library, 1991

Federal Reserve Bank of Dallas Library, 2032

Federal Reserve Bank of Kansas City, Research Library, 2033

Carl Hayden Bee Research Center Library, 73

National Agricultural Library, 124

National Agricultural Library, DC Reference Center, 125

Office of the General Counsel Law Library, Department of Agriculture, 126

Russell Research Center Library, 80

US Agency for International Development Library, 2267

US Citrus & Subtropical Products Laboratory Library, 83

USDA, Agricultural Research Service, Eastern Regional Research Center Library, 84

USDA, Agricultural Research Service, Snake River Conservation Research Service, 85

USDA, Agricultural Research Service, Water Conservation Research Library, 86

USDA National Finance Center Library, 67

USDA Northern Regional Research Center Library, 87

USDA Western Regional Research Center Library, 89

US Grain Marketing Research Laboratory Library, 90

US International Trade Commission Main Library, 2270

Water & Power Resources Service, Regional Library, 1847

Western Regional Research Center Library, 92

Agriculture Department

National Agricultural Library, 124

Stored Product Insects Research & Development Library, 82

US National Arboretum Library, 91

Agriculture History

US National Arboretum Library, 91

Booker T Washington National Monument Library, 1809

Agrostology

National Museum of Natural History, Branch Library, 2462

AIDS

Armed Forces Institute of Pathology, Ash Library, 1252

Walter Reed Army Medical Center, Post/Patients' Library, 617

Air Force

Air Force Institute of Technology Library, 201

Air Force Officer Training School Library/FL 3050, 205

Air Force Academy

US Air Force Academy Library/FL 7000, 331

Air Force History

Bergstrom AFB, Base Library/FL 4857, 221

Castle AFB, Baker Library/FL 4672, 230

Chanute AFB, Base Library/FL 3018, 231

Luke AFB, Base Library/FL 4887, 283

Mountain Home AFB, Base Library/FL 4897, 299

Myrtle Beach AFB, Base Library/FL 4806, 300
Pease AFB, Base Library/FL 4623, 306
US Air Force Historical Research Center, 334

Air Force Regulations

Defense General Supply Center Library, 1260

Air Pollution

Atmospheric Turbulence & Diffusion Laboratory Library, 157
Environmental Protection Agency Library, 1977
Environmental Protection Agency Library, Region 8, 1978
Environmental Protection Agency, Meteorology Division Library, 1979
Environmental Protection Agency, National Enforcement Investigation Center, Information Center, 1980
Environmental Protection Agency, Office of Air Quality, Planning, & Standards Library, 1982
Environmental Protection Agency, Region 1 Library, 1984
Environmental Protection Agency, Region 4 Library, 1988
Environmental Protection Agency, Region 5 Library, 1989
Environmental Protection Agency, Region 6 Library, 1990
Environmental Protection Agency, Region 7 Library, 1991
Motor Vehicle Emission Laboratory Library, 1994

Air Pollution Technical Information Center

Environmental Protection Agency Library, 1977

Air Traffic Control

FAA Technical Library, 1936

Air War College

Andersen Base Library/FL 4624, 350
Hanscom AFB, Base Library/FL 2835, 258
Lowry AFB, Base Library/FL 3059, 282
March AFB, Base Library/FL 4664, 287
Minot AFB, Base Library/FL 4528, 297
Myrtle Beach AFB, Base Library/FL 4806, 300

Air Weapons

Naval Air Systems Command, Technical Information & Reference Center, 1018

Air Weather Service

Air Weather Service Technical Library/FL 4414, 212

Aircraft

Arnold Engineering Development Center Technical Library/FL 2804, 218
Aviation Systems Command, Library & Information Center, 411
Columbus AFB, Base Library/FL 3022, 233
EROS Data Center, Technical Reference Unit, 1561
Griffiss AFB, Base Library/FL 4616, 253
Grissom AFB, Base Library/FL 4654, 254

NASA Dryden Flight Research Center Library, 2062
Naval Air Propulsion Center, Technical Library, 1016
US Air Force Historical Research Center, 334

Alabama

Environmental Protection Agency, Region 4 Library, 1988

Alabama History

Horse Bend National Military Park Library, 1705

Alaska

Alaska Power Administration Library, 1287
Alaska Resources Library, 1819
Bureau of Indian Affairs, Library/Media Center, 1370
Bureau of Land Management, Fairbanks District Office Library, 1486
Bureau of Land Management, Minerals Management Service Library, 1500
Bureau of Mines Library, 1536
Elmendorf AFB, Base Library, 244
Library of Congress, 9
Mt Edgecumbe High School, Library Media Center, 1420
Sitka National Historic Park Library, 1794
US Army Cold Region Research & Engineering Laboratory Library, 656

Alaska Harriman Series

W F Thompson Memorial Library, 189

Alaska History

Sitka National Historic Park Library, 1794

Alaska Law

US District Court Library, 57
US District Courts & Alaska Court System Law Library, 59

Alaska National Interest Lands Conservation Act

US District Court Library, 57

Alaska Native Claims Settlement Act

Department of the Interior, Office of the Solicitor, Law Library, 1841
US District Court Library, 57

Alaska Pipeline

Heritage Conservation & Recreation Service, Northwest Region Office Library, 1584

Alcohol Industry

Bureau of Alcohol, Tobacco & Firearms Reference Library, 1947

Alcoholism

Bureau of Alcohol, Tobacco & Firearms/ National Laboratory Library, 1946
National Clearinghouse for Alcohol Information Library, 1341
New River Marine Corps Air Station Library, 1240
St Elizabeth's Hospital, Circulating Library, 1323

Veterans Administration Medical Center, Health Sciences Library, 2294
Veterans Administration Medical Center Library Service, 2332
Veterans Administration Medical Center Library Service, 2342
Veterans Administration Medical Center Library Service, 2370
Veterans Administration Medical Center Library Service, 2373
Veterans Administration Medical Center, Medical/General Library, 2385
Veterans Administration Medical Center, Medical Library, 2408
Veterans Administration Medical Center, Medical Library, 2409
Alvin C York Veterans Administration Medical Center, Library Service, 2443

Algology

National Museum of Natural History, Branch Library, 2462

Alibates Flint Quarries National Monument

Lake Meredith Recreation Area Library, 1724

Allegheny Portage Railroad

Allegheny Portage Railroad National Historic Site Library, 1595

Allied Health Sciences

Bethesda Naval Hospital, Edward Rhodes Stitt Library, 953
Royal C Johnson Veterans Memorial Medical Center, Medical & Patient's Library, 2274
Keesler AFB, Medical Library/SGAL, 270
Audie L Murphy Memorial Veterans Hospital, Library Service, 2279
US Army Corps of Engineers, Huntington District, Technical Library, 670
US Naval Hospital, Medical, Crews' & Patients' Library, 1208
Veterans Administration Medical Center Library, 2303
Veterans Administration Medical Center Library, 2305
Veterans Administration Medical Center Library Service, 2331
Veterans Administration Medical Center Library Service, 2344
Veterans Administration Medical Center Library Service, 2367
Veterans Administration Medical Center Library Service, 2372
Veterans Administration Medical Center, Medical Library, 2410
Veterans Administration Medical Center, Medical & Patients' Library, 2419
Veterans Administration Medical & Regional Office Center Medical Library, 2434

Altrocchi, Julia

Indiana Dunes National Lakeshore Library, 1710

Aluminum

Reno Metallurgy Research Center Library, 1544

American Agricultural Economics Documentation Center

Economic Research Service Reference Center, 96

American Art

Archives of American Art, 2453
National Gallery of Art Library, 2458
National Museum of American Art & National Portrait Gallery Library, 2460
The Phillips Collection Library, 2464

American Association of Agricultural College Editors

National Agricultural Library, 124

American Dialect Society

Library of Congress, 9

American Indians

Aneth Community School Library, 1363
Badlands National Park Library, 1605
Bent's Old Fort National Historic Site Library, 1607
Big Hole National Battlefield Library, 1609
Bighorn Canyon National Recreation Area Library, 1611
Bureau of Indian Affairs, Library/Media Center, 1370
Busby School Library, 1371
Canyon de Chelly National Monument Library, 1618
Casa Blanca Day School Library, 1373
Chemawa Indian School, IMC, 1374
Cherokee Elementary School Library, 1375
Cherokee High School Library, 1376
Cherokee Strip Living Museum Library, 1633
Cheyenne-Eagle Butte High School, Media Center, 1378
Chilocco Indian School Library, 1381
Chinle Boarding School Library, 1382
Chiricahua National Monument Library, 1636
Choctaw Central High School Library, 1384
Concho School Library, 1385
Crazy Horse School Library-Media Center, 1388
Crow Creek Reservation High School Library, 1389
Crownpoint Boarding School Media Center, 1390
De Soto National Memorial Library, 1650
Defense Equal Opportunity Management Institute Library, 1259
Dennehotso Boarding School Library, 1392
Department of Justice Lands Library, 1853
Department of the Interior, Center for Information & Library Services, Natural Resources Library, Law Branch, 1820
Department of the Interior, Center for Information & Library Services, Natural Resources Library, 1821
Department of the Interior, Center for Information & Library Services, Natural Resources Library, Law Branch, 1822
Department of the Interior, Office of the Solicitor, Field Solicitor, Law Library, 1836
Dilcon School Library, 1393
Flandreau Indian School Library, 1397
Ft Clatsop National Memorial Library, 1666

Ft Laramie National Historic Site Library, 1670
Ft Larned National Historic Site Library, 1671
Fort Thompson Community School Library, 1398
Gila Crossing Day School Library, 1400
Glacier National Park, George C. Ruhle Library, 1687
Grand Canyon National Park Research Library, 1689
Grand Portage National Monument Library, 1690
Greasewood Boarding School Library, 1401
Haskell Indian Junior College, Learning Resource Center, 1403
Hubbell Trading Post National Historic Site Library, 1707
Institute of American Indian Arts Library, 1405
Intermountain Inter-Tribal School Library, 1406
Joshua Tree National Monument Library, 1717
Kaibeto Elementary School Library, 1409
Keams Canyon Library, 1411
Knife River Indian Villages National Historic Site Library, 1721
Lake Mead National Recreation Area Library, 1723
Lava Beds National Monument Library, 1726
Little Wound School Library, 1415
Many Farms High School Library, 1418
Mound City Group National Monument Library, 1738
National Archives & Records Administration, Fort Worth Branch, 2075
National Indian Training Center, Professional Library, 1421
National Museum of Natural History, Branch Library, 2462
National Park Service, Midwest Archeological Center Library, 1748
National Park Service, Southwest Regional Library, 1751
Navajo Mountain Boarding School Library, 1422
Navajo National Monument Library, 1753
Nez Perce National Historic Park Library, 1754
Ocmulgee National Monument Library, 1756
Oglala Community Elementary School, 1424
Oglala Community High School Library, 1425
Petrified Forest National Park Library, 1766
Phoenix Indian Medical Center, Health Sciences Library, 1339
Phoenix Indian School Library, 1426
Presidio Army Museum Library, 607
Riverside Indian School Library, 1432
Rock Creek Nature Center, 1774
Rocky Mountain National Park Library, 1775
Rocky Ridge Boarding School Library, 1433
Theodore Roosevelt National Park Library, 1777
Salt River Day School Library, 1434
San Felipe Elementary School Library, 1435
San Juan Day School Media Center, 1436
San Simon Media Center, 1437
Sanostee Boarding School Media Center, 1438
Seneca Indian School Library, 1443

Sequoyah High School Library, 1444
Shonto Elementary Library, 1446
Sitka National Historic Park Library, 1794
Southwestern Indian Polytechnic Institute Instructional Media Center, 1447
Stewart Boarding School Library-Media Center, 1449
Tonto National Monument Library, 1800
Tuba City Boarding School Library, 1454
Tumacacori National Monument Library, 1802
Turtle Mountain Community School Media Center, 1455
Twin Buttes School Library, 1456
US Commission on Civil Rights, National Clearinghouse Library, 1962
US Court of Appeals for the Federal Circuit Library, 53
Veterans Administration Medical Center Library, 2309
Wahpeton Indian School Media Center, 1457
Williams AFB, Base Library/FL 3044, 343
Wingate Elementary School Library, 1462
Wingate High School Library-Media Center, 1463
Wounded Knee District School Library, 1464
Wupatki National Monument Library, 1815
Yosemite National Park Research Library, 1817

American Iron and Steel Institute

Portsmouth Naval Shipyard, Supply Department, Technical Library, 1144

American National Standards Institute

Portsmouth Naval Shipyard, Supply Department, Technical Library, 1144

American Society for Testing and Materials Standards

Philadelphia Naval Shipyard, Technical Library, 1136

American Society of Agricultural Engineers

National Agricultural Library, 124

American Society Testing Material

Portsmouth Naval Shipyard, Supply Department, Technical Library, 1144

Amphibious Warfare

James Carson Breckinridge Library & Amphibious Warfare Facility, 1227
Marine Corps Historical Center Library, 1237
Naval Amphibious Base Library, 1020
Naval Amphibious School Library, 1021
Naval Amphibious School, John Sidney McCain, Jr Amphibious Warfare Library, 1022
Naval Civil Engineering Laboratory Library, 1026

Anasazi Indians

Navajo National Monument Library, 1753
Wupatki National Monument Library, 1815

Anatomy
Consumer Product Safety Commission Library, 1966

Annual Reports
Bureau of the Census Library, 143

Antarctica
US Army Cold Region Research & Engineering Laboratory Library, 656

Anthropology
Chaco Culture National Historical Park Reference & Research Library, 1631
Glen Canyon National Recreation Area Library, 1688
Lake Mead National Recreation Area Library, 1723
National Museum of Natural History, Branch Library, 2462
National Park Service, Midwest Archeological Center Library, 1748
Ocmulgee National Monument Library, 1756
Russell Cave National Monument Library, 1778
Sitka National Historic Park Library, 1794
Tonto National Monument Library, 1800
Western Archeological & Conservation Center Library, 1810

Antietam Battlefield
Antietam National Battlefield Library, 1598

Antiques
Grant-Kohrs Ranch National Historic Site Library, 1692

Antiquities
Bureau of Land Management, Bakersfield District Office Library, 1469
Bureau of Land Management, Utah State Office Library, 1525

Anti-Submarine Warfare
Fleet Anti-Submarine Warfare Training Center, Pacific, Technical Library, 977

Antitrust Law
Department of Commerce, Law Library, 131
Department of Justice Antitrust Division Library, 1848
Department of Justice Antitrust Library, 1849

Antitrust Regulations
Federal Trade Commission, Dallas Regional Office Library, 2045
Federal Trade Commission Library, 2047

Apache Pass
Ft Bowie National Historic Site Library, 1683

Apiculture
Carl Hayden Bee Research Center Library, 73

Apostle Islands
Apostle Islands National Lakeshore Library, 1599

Appalachia
Appalachian Laboratory for Occupational Safety & Health Library, 1325
Blue Ridge Parkway Library, 1612
Southeastern Power Administration Library, 1315

Appomattox Campaign
Appomattox Court House National Historic Park Library, 1600

Appomattox Court House
Appomattox Court House National Historic Park Library, 1600

Aquaculture
Auke Bay Fisheries Laboratory Library, 158
Milford Laboratory Library, 165
National Fisheries Center, Leetown Technical Information Services, 1554
National Fishery Research & Development Laboratory Library, 1555
National Fishery Research Center Library, 1556
NOAA, Southeast Fisheries Center, Galveston Laboratory Library, 176
Southwest Fisheries Center Library, 188
W F Thompson Memorial Library, 189
Tiburon Laboratory Library, 190
Tunison Laboratory of Fish Nutrition Library, 1559

Aquatic Biology
W F Thompson Memorial Library, 189

Arapaho Indians
Bent's Old Fort National Historic Site Library, 1607

Archeology
Arches National Park Library, 1601
Aztec Ruins National Monument Library, 1604
Bandelier National Monument Library, 1606
Bureau of Land Management, Safford District Office Library, 1516
Carlsbad Caverns & Guadalupe Mountains National Parks Headquarters Library, 1624
Chaco Center Archives & Library, Branch of Cultural Research Library, 1630
Chaco Culture National Historical Park Reference & Research Library, 1631
Curecanti National Recreation Area Library, 1646
Death Valley National Monument Research Library, 1651
Dinosaur National Monument Library, 1656
Effigy Mounds National Monument Library, 1658
Ft Vancouver National Historic Site Library, 1680
Interagency Archeological Services Library, 1586
Katmai National Park & Preserve Library, 1718
Knife River Indian Villages National Historic Site Library, 1721
Lake Mead National Recreation Area Library, 1723
Lake Meredith Recreation Area Library, 1724
Mesa Verde Research Library, 1733

Montezuma Castle National Monument Library, 1735
Mound City Group National Monument Library, 1738
National Park Service Library, 1747
National Park Service, Midwest Archeological Center Library, 1748
National Park Service, Southwest Regional Library, 1751
National Park Service, Western Regional Resources Library, 1752
National Register of Historic Places Library, 1589
Navajo National Monument Library, 1753
Ocmulgee National Monument Library, 1756
Olympic National Park Library, 1757
Pecos National Monument Library, 1763
Russell Cave National Monument Library, 1778
Sitka National Historic Park Library, 1794
Southeast Archeological Center Library, 1795
Tonto National Monument Library, 1800
Tuzigoot National Monument Library, 1803
US Army Corps of Engineers, Ft Worth District, Technical Library, 666
US Army Corps of Engineers, Seattle District Library, 718
Western Archeological & Conservation Center Library, 1810
Wupatki National Monument Library, 1815

Architecture
Architect of the Capitol, Art & Reference Division, 3
Architectural & Transportation Barriers Compliance Board, Technical Library, 2445
Commission of Fine Arts Library, 1964
General Services Administration, Design & Construction Division Library, 2050
General Services Administration Library, 2051
Jean Lafitte National Historical Park Library, 1722
March AFB, Base Library/FL 4664, 287
National Park Service Library, 1747
National Park Service, Western Regional Resources Library, 1752
US Army Corps of Engineers, Omaha District Technical Library, 703
Martin Van Buren National Historic Site Library, 1805

Architecture History
Historic American Buildings Survey Library, 1585
National Register of Historic Places Library, 1589

Archival Science
National Archives Library, 2078

Archives
Castillo de San Marcos National Monument Library, 1626
Combined Arms Research Library, 422
Institute of American Indian Arts Library, 1405
Marine Corps Historical Center Library, 1237
National Archives & Records Center, Kansas City Branch, 2077

US Department of Education, Office of Educational Research & Improvement Library, 1286

Arctic

Ft Greely Post Library, 473
Naval Ocean Systems Center, Technical Libraries, 1058
US Army Arctic Test Center, Technical Library, 902
US Army Cold Region Research & Engineering Laboratory Library, 656

Arctic Regions

Eielson AFB, Base Library/FL 5004, 240

Arizona

Bureau of Land Management, Arizona State Office Library, 1466
Geological Survey, Public Inquiries Office Library, 1575
Luke AFB, Base Library/FL 4887, 283
Saguaro National Monument Library, 1780

Arizona History

Glen Canyon National Recreation Area Library, 1688
Pipe Springs National Monument Library, 1769

Arizona Law

Department of the Interior, Office of the Solicitor, Field Solicitor, Law Library, 1836
Economic Development Administration, Seattle Regional Office Library, 146

Arkansas Law

Economic Development Administration, Seattle Regional Office Library, 146
National Archives & Records Administration, Fort Worth Branch, 2075
US Army Engineer Division, Memphis District, Law Library, 730

Arlington House

Arlington House, The Robert E Lee Memorial Library, 1602

Armor

Ft Knox, Barr Memorial Library, 502
Ft Knox, Emert L Davis Memorial Library, 504
US Army Armor School Library, 644

Arms Control

Brookhaven National Laboratory, Nuclear Safeguards Library, 1292
US Arms Control & Disarmament Agency Library, 2103

Army

Bent's Old Fort National Historic Site Library, 1607
Ft McPherson Library System, 526
Ft Monroe, General Library & Intern Training Center, 538
Ft Story Post Library, 561
Schofield Barracks, Sgt Yano Library, 622
US Army Center of Military History Library, 652
US Army Infantry School, Donovan Technical Library, 740
US Army Intelligence School Library, 1284

US Army John F Kennedy Special Warfare Center, Marquat Memorial Library, 747
US Army Operational Test & Evaluation Agency, Technical Library, 767
US Army Signal Center, Conrad Technical Library, 778
US Army Support Command, Hawaii Library System, 782
US Army Transportation & Aviation Logistics Schools, Information Center, 788

Army Aviation

US Army Aviation Center Library, 646
US Army Aviation Technical Library, 649

Army Chaplains

Edison National Historic Site, 1657

Army Corps of Engineers

Geological Survey, Water Resources Division, Colorado District Library, 1578
US Army Corps of Engineers, Baltimore District Library Branch, 660
US Army Corps of Engineers, Headquarters Library, 668
US Army Corps of Engineers, Los Angeles District Technical Library, 680
US Army Corps of Engineers, North Central Division Library, 698
US Army Corps of Engineers, Southwest Division Technical Library, 723
US Army Corps of Engineers, Walla Walla District Technical & Law Library, 725

Army Equipment

Lexington Bluegrass Army Depot, Division of Quality Assurance, Technical Library, 589

Army Field Manuals

HQ US Army Training & Doctrine Command, Technical Library, 581

Army History

Aberdeen Proving Ground, Ordnance Center & School Museum Library, 399
Ft Bliss, Valent Learning Resources Center Library, 446
Presidio Army Museum Library, 607
US Army Center of Military History Library, 652
US Army Military History Institute Library, 757
US Army Museum Library, 764
US Military Academy Library, 794

Army Logistics

US Army Logistics Library, 751

Army Maintenance

Sacramento Army Depot, Technical Library, 619

Army Regulations

Defense General Supply Center Library, 1260
8th Infantry Division, Baumholder Branch, Staff Judge Advocate, Law Library, 827
HQ US Army Training & Doctrine Command, Technical Library, 581
VII Corps, Office of the Staff Judge Advocate, Army Law Library, 884
Task Force Judge Advocate Army Law Library, 888

Umatilla Depot Activity, Reference Library, 637

Army Supplies

Aberdeen Proving Ground, Ordnance Center & School Museum Library, 399
US Army Materials & Mechanics Research Center, Technical Library, 753

Army Transportation

US Army Transportation Center, Groninger Library, 789

Arson

National Emergency Training Center, Learning Resource Center, 2011

Art

Architect of the Capitol, Art & Reference Division, 3
Commission of Fine Arts Library, 1964
Ft Sheridan Post Library, 555
Freer Gallery of Art Library, 2455
Hirshhorn Museum & Sculpture Garden Library, 2456
The Institute of Heraldry Library, 583
Long Beach Naval Shipyard, Technical Library, 995
March AFB, Base Library/FL 4664, 287
National Endowment for the Arts Library, 2082
National Gallery of Art Library, 2458
National Museum of African Art, Branch Library, 2459
National Museum of American Art & National Portrait Gallery Library, 2460
The Phillips Collection Library, 2464
Sitka National Historic Park Library, 1794

Art Administration

National Endowment for the Arts Library, 2082

Art History

Archives of American Art, 2453
Saint Gardens Library, 1782

Artificial Intelligence

Naval Ocean Systems Center, Technical Libraries, 1058
Rome Air Development Center Technical Library/FL 2810, 315
US Army Engineering Topographic Laboratories Scientific & Technical Information Center, 732
US Army Signal Center, Conrad Technical Library, 778

Artillery

Benet Weapons Laboratory, Technical Library, 416
Ft Sill, Morris Swett Technical Library, 558
US Army Air Defense Artillery School Library, 641
US Army Museum Library, 764

Asia

Kadena AFB, Base Library/FL 5270, 373
Kami Seya Station Library, 1186
Langley AFB, Base Library/FL 4800, 277
MacDill AFB, Base Library/FL 4814, 284
Peace Corps Information Services, Division Library, 2090

Asian Americans

Defense Equal Opportunity Management Institute Library, 1259

Asian Art

Freer Gallery of Art Library, 2455

Assateague Island Seashore

Assateague Island National Seashore Library, 1603

Astrogeophysics

Air Weather Service Technical Library/FL 4414, 212

Astronautics

Ellsworth AFB, Base Library/FL 4690, 243
NASA-AMES Research Center, Technical Library, 2061
NASA Lyndon B Johnson Space Center, Technical Library, 2066
NASA Headquarters, S & T Library & Systems Support, 2069
Peterson AFB, Base Library/FL 2500, 307
Point Mugu Naval Air Station Library, 1138

Astronomy

Arnold Engineering Development Center Technical Library/FL 2804, 218
NASA-AMES Research Center Library, 2059
NASA Goddard Institute for Space Studies Library, 2063
NASA Goddard Space Flight Center Library, 2064
National Air & Space Museum, Branch Library, 2457
National Science Foundation Library, 2085
National Solar Observatory, Technical Library, 2086
NOAA, Library & Information Services Division, 182
Redstone Scientific Information Center, 615
Rock Creek Nature Center, 1774
Smithsonian Institution, Astrophysical Observatory Library, 2467
US Naval Observatory Library, 1172

Astronomy History

US Naval Observatory Library, 1172

Astrophysics

NASA-AMES Research Center Library, 2059
NASA Goddard Institute for Space Studies Library, 2063
National Air & Space Museum, Branch Library, 2457
Redstone Scientific Information Center, 615
Smithsonian Institution, Astrophysical Observatory Library, 2467

Atlantic Ocean

Bureau of Land Management, New Orleans Outer-Continental Shelf Office Library, 1506

Atmospheric Chemistry

NOAA, Seattle Center Library, 175

Atmospheric Science

NASA-National Space Technology Laboratories, Research Library, 2068
NOAA, Seattle Center Library, 175
National Science Foundation Library, 2085
National Severe Storms Laboratory Library, 178
NOAA, Library & Information Services Division, 182
Redstone Scientific Information Center, 615
Smithsonian Institution, Astrophysical Observatory Library, 2467

Atmospheric Science History

NOAA, Library & Information Services Division, 182

Atmospheric Turbulence

Atmospheric Turbulence & Diffusion Laboratory Library, 157

Atomic Energy Commission

Argonne National Laboratory, Technical Information Services Department, 1289

Auction Sales Catalogs

National Gallery of Art Library, 2458

Audio Recordings

Library of Congress, 9
Zaragoza Base Library/FL 5571, 394

Auditing

General Accounting Office, Office of Library Services, 5

Auerbach

Department of Defense Computer Institute, Technical Library, 1276

Autographs

Morristown National Historical Park Library, 1737

Automation

Navy Regional Data Automation Center, 1111
Navy Regional Data Automation Center, Technical Library, 1112

Automotive Repair

Cubi Point Naval Air Station Library, 1182
Ft Story Post Library, 561
Guantanamo US Naval Base Library, 1185
Kelly AFB, Base Library/FL 2050, 272

Avalanches

Rocky Mountain Forest & Range Experiment Station Library, 118

Aviation

Aviation Applied Technology Directorate, Technical Library, 410
Aviation Systems Command, Library & Information Center, 411
Columbus AFB, Base Library/FL 3022, 233
Department of Transportation Library, 1931
Dover AFB, Base Library/FL 4497, 236
FAA Central Regional Library, 1935
Fairchild AFB, Base Library/FL 4620, 247
FAA Eastern Region Library, 1937
Grissom AFB, Base Library/FL 4654, 254
Hanscom AFB, Base Library/FL 2835, 258
March AFB, Base Library/FL 4664, 287
Mayport Naval Air Station Library, 1000
Myrtle Beach AFB, Base Library/FL 4806, 300
NASA-AMES Research Center, Life Sciences Library, 2060
National Air & Space Museum, Branch Library, 2457
Naval Aerospace Medical Institute Library, 1013
Naval Air Development Center, Scientific & Technical Library Branch, 1014
Naval Test Pilot School Library, 1090
Patuxent Naval Air Station Library, 1129
Patuxent Naval Aviation Logistics Center, Technical Library, 1130
K I Sawyer AFB, Base Library/FL 4515, 316
Smithsonian Institution Libraries, 2468
10A Services Branch Library, 1933
US Army Aviation Center Library, 646
US Army Aviation Technical Library, 649
Wright-Patterson AFB, Technical Library/FL 2802, 345

Aviation Engineering

FAA Central Regional Library, 1935

Aviation History

Air University Library/FL 3368, 211
El Toro Marine Corps Air Station Library, 1233
Myrtle Beach AFB, Base Library/FL 4806, 300
National Air & Space Museum, Branch Library, 2457

Aviation Law

Department of Justice Civil Library, 1850

Aviation Medicine

Air Force School of Aerospace Medicine, Strughold Aeromedical Library/FL 2855, 206
FAA Aeronautical Center, Civil Aeromedical Institute Library (AM-101), 1934
Ft Rucker, Medical Library, 551
US Army Aeromedical Research Laboratory, Medical Library, 639

Aviation Safety

Aviation Applied Technology Directorate, Technical Library, 410
FAA Technical Library, 1936

Avionics

Naval Avionics Center, Technical Library, 1024
Wright-Patterson AFB, Technical Library/FL 2802, 345

Aztec Ruins

Aztec Ruins National Monument Library, 1604

Bachelder, John B.

Gettysburg National Military Park Library, 1685

Bacteriology

Centers for Disease Control Library, 1327

Badlands
Badlands National Park Library, 1605

Ball, Carlton R.
US National Arboretum Library, 91

Ballooning
National Air & Space Museum, Branch Library, 2457

Band Music
US Marine Band, Music Library, 1243

Banking
Board of Governors of the Federal Reserve System, Research Library, 2027
Comptroller of the Currency Library, 1948
Eximbank Library, 2002
Farm Credit Administration Library, 2003
FDIC Library, 2006
Federal Deposit Insurance Corporation Library, 2007
Federal Home Loan Bank Board, Law Library, 2012
Federal Home Loan Bank Board, Research Library, 2013
Federal Home Loan Bank of Chicago Library, 2015
Federal Reserve Bank of Atlanta, Research Library, 2028
Federal Reserve Bank of Boston, Research Library, 2029
Federal Reserve Bank of Chicago Library, 2030
Federal Reserve Bank of Cleveland, Research Library, 2031
Federal Reserve Bank of Dallas Library, 2032
Federal Reserve Bank of Kansas City, Research Library, 2033
Federal Reserve Bank of New York, Computer Science Library, 2035
Federal Reserve Bank of New York, Research Library, 2037
Federal Reserve Bank of Philadelphia, Information Services & Research Library, 2038
Federal Reserve Bank of Richmond, Baltimore Branch Library, 2039
Federal Reserve Bank of Richmond, Research Library, 2040
Federal Reserve Bank of St Louis, Research Library, 2041
Federal Reserve Bank of San Francisco, Research Library, 2042

Banking Law
Board of Governors of the Federal Reserve System, Law Library, 2026
Board of Governors of the Federal Reserve System, Research Library, 2027
Comptroller of the Currency Library, 1948
Federal Home Loan Bank Board, Law Library, 2012
Federal Reserve Bank of New York, Law Library, 2036

Bankruptcy
Department of Energy, Office of General Counsel, Law Library, 1295
Department of Justice Civil Library, 1850
Department of Justice Tax Library, 1855
US Court of Appeals for the 9th Circuit Library, 33

Baruch, Bernard
National Defense University Library, 1278

Baruch, Ishmar
US Office of Personnel Management Library, 2089

Bats
Carlsbad Caverns & Guadalupe Mountains National Parks Headquarters Library, 1624

Battleships
Long Beach Naval Station Library, 996

Bees
Carl Hayden Bee Research Center Library, 73

Behavioral Medicine
National Institute on Aging, Gerontology Research Center Library, 1343

Benjamin Collection
US Naval Academy, Nimitz Library, 1169

Bent, Charles
Bent's Old Fort National Historic Site Library, 1607

Bent, William
Bent's Old Fort National Historic Site Library, 1607

Bent-St. Vrain Company
Bent's Old Fort National Historic Site Library, 1607

Bibles
Ft Hood, Language Training Facility Library, 480
Library of Congress, 9

Bibliography
Library of Congress, 9

Bibliotherapy
St Elizabeth's Hospital, Circulating Library, 1323

Big Bend
Big Bend National Park Library, 1608

Big Thicket
Big Thicket National Preserve Library, 1610

Bighorn Canyon
Bighorn Canyon National Recreation Area Library, 1611

Bioacoustics
US Army Environmental Hygiene Agency Library, 733

Biochemistry
Environmental Protection Agency, Andrew W Breidenbach Library, 1969
FAA Aeronautical Center, Civil Aeromedical Institute Library (AM-101), 1934

Medical & Health Sciences Division Library, 1306
William S Middleton Memorial Veterans Hospital Library Service, 2277
NASA-AMES Research Center, Life Sciences Library, 2060
National Animal Disease Center Library, 76
National Center for Toxicological Research Library, 1337
National Institute of Mental Health Library, Division of Intramural Research Programs, 1322
National Institute on Aging, Gerontology Research Center Library, 1343
Northwest & Alaska Fisheries Center Library, 183
Southern Regional Research Center Library, 81
USDA, Agricultural Research Service, Eastern Regional Research Center Library, 84

Bioengineering
National Fishery Research & Development Laboratory Library, 1555

Biogenesis Collection
NASA-AMES Research Center, Life Sciences Library, 2060

Biographies
Antietam National Battlefield Library, 1598
El Toro Marine Corps Air Station Library, 1233
Mall Operation Library, 1730
National Museum of American Art & National Portrait Gallery Library, 2460

Biological Warfare
Dugway Proving Ground, Technical Library, 431

Biology
Acadia National Park Library, 1592
Air Force Office of Scientific Research Library/FL 2819, 204
Brookhaven National Laboratory, Research Library, 1293
Buck Island Reef National Monument Library, 1614
Bureau of Land Management, Fairbanks District Office Library, 1486
Center for Food Safety & Applied Nutrition Library, 1332
Christiansted National Historic Site Library, 1637
Crater Lake National Park Library, 1643
Defense Personnel Support Center, Directorate of Medical Material Library, 1272
Delaware River Basin Commission Library, 2446
Environmental Protection Agency, Environmental Research Laboratory Library, 1973
Environmental Protection Agency, Robert S Kerr Library, 1975
Fish & Wildlife Service, Division of Biological Services Library, 1550
Fossil Butte National Monument Library, 1681
Glacier National Park, George C. Ruhle Library, 1687
Great Smoky Mountains National Park, Sugarlands Visitor Center Library, 1694

Indiana Dunes National Lakeshore Library, 1710

Los Alamos National Laboratory Libraries, 1303

Los Alamos National Laboratory, Medical Library, 1304

NASA-AMES Research Center, Life Sciences Library, 2060

NASA Lyndon B Johnson Space Center, Technical Library, 2066

National Capital Parks-East Library, 1744

National Institutes of Health Library, 1345

National Marine Fisheries Service, Southeast Fisheries Center Library, 167

National Museum of Natural History, Branch Library, 2462

National Science Foundation Library, 2085

Nuclear Regulatory Commission Library, 2087

Office of the Chief of Naval Research Library, 1122

Pinnacles National Monument Library, 1768

Rocky Mountain National Park Library, 1775

Smithsonian Environmental Research Center Library, Rockville Branch, 2465

Smithsonian Institution, Astrophysical Observatory Library, 2467

Stored Product Insects Research & Development Library, 82

Travertine Nature Center Library, 1801

US Army Natick Research, Development, & Engineering Center, Technical Library, 766

Biomass

Department of Energy, Solar Research Institute, Technical Library, 1296

National Fertilizer Library, 2099

Biomaterials

Center for Devices & Radiological Health Library, 1331

Biometrics

Auke Bay Fisheries Laboratory Library, 158

Biophysics

Brookhaven National Laboratory, Research Library, 1293

Biostatistics

Patuxent Wildlife Research Center Library, 1558

Biotechnology

Air Force School of Aerospace Medicine, Strughold Aeromedical Library/FL 2855, 206

Center for Devices & Radiological Health Library, 1331

Environmental Protection Agency, Andrew W Breidenbach Library, 1969

Environmental Protection Agency, Environmental Research Laboratory Library, 1972

Food & Drug Administration, Medical Library, 1333

NASA-AMES Research Center, Life Sciences Library, 2060

USDA Northern Regional Research Center Library, 87

Birds

Carlsbad Caverns & Guadalupe Mountains National Parks Headquarters Library, 1624

Everglades National Park Research Center Library, 1660

Northern Prairie Wildlife Research Center Library, 1557

Patuxent Wildlife Research Center Library, 1558

Birth Control

The National Family Planning Information Clearinghouse Library, 1349

Black Education

Harpers Ferry National Historic Park Library, 1700

Black Hills

Mount Rushmore National Memorial Library, 1740

Black History

Big Spring Federal Prison Camp Library, 1862

Bolling AFB, Base Library/FL 4400, 224

Booker T Washington National Monument Library, 1809

Black Literature

Ft Leonard Wood Post Library, 569

White Sands Missile Range, Post Library, 805

Black Studies

St Elizabeth's Hospital, Circulating Library, 1323

Blacks

Defense Equal Opportunity Management Institute Library, 1259

US Commission on Civil Rights, National Clearinghouse Library, 1962

Blood Diseases and Disorders

Letterman Army Institute of Research, Medical Research Library, 586

Blue Ridge Parkway

Blue Ridge Parkway Library, 1612

Boer, Arie F. den

US National Arboretum Library, 91

Bonsai

US National Arboretum Library, 91

Book Illustration

Library of Congress, 9

Books, History of

Library of Congress, 9

Bopp, Karl

Federal Reserve Bank of Philadelphia, Information Services & Research Library, 2038

Borglum, Gutzon

Mount Rushmore National Memorial Library, 1740

Borglum, Lincoln

Mount Rushmore National Memorial Library, 1740

Botanic Gardens

US Botanic Garden Library, 4

Botany

Acadia National Park Library, 1592

APHIS Plant Protection & Quarantine Library, 93

APHIS Plant Protection & Quarantine Training Center Library, 94

Big Thicket National Preserve Library, 1610

Buck Island Reef National Monument Library, 1614

Capulin Mountain National Monument Library, 1623

Carlsbad Caverns & Guadalupe Mountains National Parks Headquarters Library, 1624

Cedar Breaks National Monument Library, 1629

Everglades National Park Research Center Library, 1660

Glacier National Park, George C. Ruhle Library, 1687

Grand Teton National Park Library, 1691

Haleakala National Park, Library, 1697

Lake Mead National Recreation Area Library, 1723

National Agricultural Library, 124

National Museum of Natural History, Branch Library, 2462

National Museum of Natural History, Branch Library, 2462

Puuhonua o Honaunau National Historical Park, Library, 1771

Rock Creek Nature Center, 1774

Theodore Roosevelt National Park Library, 1777

Saguaro National Monument Library, 1780

Smithsonian Environmental Research Center Library, Rockville Branch, 2465

US Botanic Garden Library, 4

USDA, Agricultural Research Service, Eastern Regional Research Center Library, 84

USDA, Agricultural Research Service, Snake River Conservation Research Service, 85

USDA, Agricultural Research Service, Water Conservation Research Library, 86

USDA Northern Regional Research Center Library, 87

US National Arboretum Library, 91

Braddock, Edward

Ft Necessity National Battlefield Library, 1673

Bradley, Omar M.

US Military Academy Library, 794

Braille Materials

National Library Service for the Blind & Physically Handicapped, Library of Congress, 10

Brices Cross Roads

Natchez Trace Parkway Library, 1743

Broadcasting
Ft Benjamin Harrison, Soldiers' Support Center Library, 479
John F Kennedy Center Performing Arts Library, 8

Brown, George S.
National Defense University Library, 1278

Brown, John
Harpers Ferry National Historic Park Library, 1700

Bryce Canyon National Park
Bryce Canyon National Park Library, 1613

Buck Island Reef
Buck Island Reef National Monument Library, 1614

Buckley, Christopher Jr.
Naval Postgraduate School, Dudley Knox Library, 1061

Buckley Collection
Naval Postgraduate School, Dudley Knox Library, 1062

Budget
Congressional Budget Office Library, 12
Executive Office of the President Library, 64

Buffalo River
Buffalo National River Library, 1615

Bullion Depository
Ft Knox, Barr Memorial Library, 502

Burden, William A. M.
National Air & Space Museum, Branch Library, 2457

Burgoyne Campaign
Saratoga National Historical Park Library, 1788

Burns and Trauma
US Army Institute of Surgical Research, Library Branch, 742

Business
Bureau of the Census Library, 143
Castle AFB, Baker Library/FL 4672, 230
Danbury Federal Correctional Institution Library, 1866
Department of Justice Antitrust Library, 1849
Eastern Space & Missile Center Technical Library/FL 2828, 238
Federal Reserve Bank of Chicago Library, 2030
Federal Reserve Bank of New York, Research Library, 2037
Federal Reserve Bank of Richmond, Research Library, 2040
Federal Trade Commission, Law Library, 2046
Federal Trade Commission Library, 2048
Ft Sheridan Post Library, 555
Internal Revenue Service, Office of Chief Counsel, Library, 1953
Nellis AFB, Base Library/FL 4852, 301

USAREUR Library & Resource Center, 911
US Army Ordnance Center & School Library, 768
US Customs Service, Library & Information Center, 1954
Wright-Patterson AFB, Base Library/FL 2300, 344
Wright-Patterson AFB, Area A Technical Library, 346
Yongsan Library, 942

Business Administration
Aberdeen Proving Ground, Ordnance Center & School Library, 398
Air Force Institute of Technology Library, 201
Base Library/FL 5670, 360
Chanute AFB, Base Library/FL 3018, 231
Consumer Product Safety Commission Library, 1967
Department of Commerce, Miami District Office Library, 133
Elgin AFB, Base Library/FL 2823/SSL, 242
Ft Bliss, Center Library, 445
Ft Huachuca Technical Library, 493
Ft Myer Post Library, 539
Ft Leonard Wood Post Library, 569
George AFB, Base Library/FL 4812, 249
Grissom AFB, Base Library/FL 4654, 254
Holloman AFB, Base Library/FL 4801, 264
March AFB, Base Library/FL 4664, 287
Naval Postgraduate School, Dudley Knox Library, 1061
Naval School, Civil Engineer Corps Officers, Moreell Library, 1068
Norton AFB, Base Library/FL 4448, 302
Peterson AFB, Base Library/FL 2500, 307
US Army Corps of Engineers, St Louis District Technical Library, 713

Business, International
Department of Commerce, District Office Library, 128

Cable Television
FCC Chicago District Office Library, 2004

California
Alameda Naval Air Station Library, 944
Beale AFB, Base Library/FL 4686, 220
Bureau of Mines, Western Field Operations Center Library, 1543
Cabrillo National Monument Library, 1616
McClellan AFB, Base Library/FL 2040, 292
Vandenberg AFB, Base Library/FL 4610, 339

California History
Cabrillo National Monument Library, 1616
El Toro Marine Corps Air Station Library, 1233
Ft Mason, Main Post Library, 519
Lava Beds National Monument Library, 1726
McClellan AFB, Base Library/FL 2040, 292
National Maritime Museum, J Porter Shaw Library, 1745
Presidio Army Museum Library, 607
Sequoia & Kings Canyon National Park Library, 1791
Whiskeytown Unit Library, National Park Service, 1811

California Law
Economic Development Administration, Seattle Regional Office Library, 146

Canada
Interstate Commerce Commission Library, 2053

Canals
Bureau of Reclamation, Engineering & Research Center Library, 1547
Chesapeake & Ohio Canal National Historic Park Resource Library, 1634
Cuyahoga Valley National Recreation Area Library, 1648

Canaveral National Seashore
Canaveral National Seashore Park Library, 1617

Cancer
Frederick Cancer Research Facility, Scientific Library, 1340
Walter Reed Army Medical Center, Post/Patients' Library, 617
Veterans Administration Medical Center, Medical Library, 2389

Cape Cod
Cape Cod National Seashore Library, 1619

Cape Hatteras
Cape Hatteras National Seashore Library, 1620

Capitol
Architect of the Capitol, Art & Reference Division, 3

Capulin Mountain
Capulin Mountain National Monument Library, 1623

Carcinogenesis
Frederick Cancer Research Facility, Scientific Library, 1340
National Center for Toxicological Research Library, 1337
National Institute of Environmental Health Sciences Library, 1342

Cardiology
Veterans Administration Medical Center, Health Sciences Library, 2294
Veterans Administration Medical Center Library Service, 2337
Veterans Administration Medical Center Library Service, 2372
Veterans Administration Medical Center Library Service, 2379
Veterans Administration Medical Center, Medical & Patient's Library, 2414

Career Education
Alameda Naval Air Station Library, 944
Ft Story Post Library, 561
Guantanamo US Naval Base Library, 1185
Gunter AFB, Base Library/FL 3370, 256

Caribbean
Ft Buchanan Post Library, 837
Peace Corps Information Services, Division Library, 2090

Caribbean History
Christiansted National Historic Site Library, 1637

Carlsbad Caverns
Carlsbad Caverns & Guadalupe Mountains National Parks Headquarters Library, 1624

Carter, Jimmy
Jimmy Carter Library, 2070

Cartography
Defense Mapping Agency, Aerospace Center Technical Library, 1268
Defense Mapping Agency, Hydrographic/Topographic Center Library, 1269
Geological Survey Library, 1565
Geological Survey, National Cartographic Information Center, 1570
Geological Survey, National Mapping Division Applications Assistance Facility Library, 1571
NOAA, Library & Information Services Division, 182
US Army Engineering Topographic Laboratories Scientific & Technical Information Center, 732

Carver, George Washington
George Washington Carver National Monument Library, 1625

Case Law
Department of Justice Lands Library, 1853
Ft Polk, Office of the Staff Judge Advocate, HQ, 5th Infantry Division (Mech), Law Library, 544
Maxwell AFB, Federal Prison Camp Library, 1879
US Court of Appeals for the 5th Circuit Library, 23

Casey Coleoptera Collection
National Museum of Natural History, Branch Library, 2462

Cate, Margaret Davis
Margaret Davis Cate Collection, 1627

Catoctin Mountain
Catoctin Mountain Park Library, 1628

Cattle Ranches
Grant-Kohrs Ranch National Historic Site Library, 1692

Cavalry
Ft Knox, Barr Memorial Library, 502
US Army Museum Library, 764

Caves
Carlsbad Caverns & Guadalupe Mountains National Parks Headquarters Library, 1624
Jewel Cave National Monument Library, 1714
Lehman Caves National Monument Library, 1727
Mammoth Cave National Park Library, 1731
Russell Cave National Monument Library, 1778

Timpanogos Cave National Monument Library, 1799
Wind Cave National Park Library, 1814

Census
Bureau of the Census, Atlanta Regional Office Library, 136
Bureau of the Census, Charlotte Regional Office Library, 137
Bureau of the Census, Dallas Regional Office Library, 138
Bureau of the Census, Denver Regional Office Reference Center, 139
Bureau of the Census, Information Service Program, Boston Regional Office, 140
Bureau of the Census, Information Services Program, Detroit Regional Office Information Center, 141
Bureau of the Census, Information Services Program Library, 142
Bureau of the Census, New York Regional Office Library, 144
Health & Human Services Department Library, 1320
International Trade Administration District Office, US & FCS Commercial Library, 149

Census Bureau
Bureau of the Census Library, 143

Centers for Disease Control
Centers for Disease Control Library, 1327

Central America
MacDill AFB, Base Library/FL 4814, 284

Central Intelligence Agency
Map Library & Information Service Library, 163

Ceramic Science
Tuscaloosa Research Center Library, 1546

Cereals
US Grain Marketing Research Laboratory Library, 90
Western Regional Research Center Library, 92

Certification
National Center for Standards & Certification Information, 156

Chaco Canyon
Chaco Center Archives & Library, Branch of Cultural Research Library, 1630
Chaco Culture National Historical Park Reference & Research Library, 1631

Chaparral Ecology
Cabrillo National Monument Library, 1616

Charting
Defense Mapping Agency, Aerospace Center Technical Library, 1268
US Army Engineering Topographic Laboratories Scientific & Technical Information Center, 732

Chattanooga, Battle of
Chickamauga & Chattanooga National Military Park Library, 1635

Chemical Engineering
Bureau of Mines, Boulder City Metallurgy Library, 1532
Long Beach Naval Shipyard, Technical Library, 995

Chemical Industry
US Customs Service, Library & Information Center, 1954

Chemical Warfare
Dugway Proving Ground, Technical Library, 431

Chemicals
Aberdeen Proving Ground, Ordnance Center & School Museum Library, 399
US International Trade Commission Main Library, 2270

Chemistry
Air Force Flight Test Center, Technical Library/FL 2806, 197
Air Force Office of Scientific Research Library/FL 2819, 204
Argonne National Laboratory, Technical Information Services Department, 1289
Armament Division Technical Library/FL 2825, 217
Armament, Munitions, & Chemical Command HQ, Technical Library, 404
Arnold Engineering Development Center Technical Library/FL 2804, 218
Brookhaven National Laboratory, Research Library, 1293
Bureau of Mines, Albany Metallurgy Research Center, 1531
Bureau of Mines, Boulder City Metallurgy Library, 1532
Bureau of Mines, Salt Lake City Research Center Library, 1538
Center for Food Safety & Applied Nutrition Library, 1332
Chemical Research & Development Center, Technical Library, 419
Corpus Christi Army Depot, Reference & Research Library, 425
Defense Personnel Support Center, Directorate of Medical Material Library, 1272
Department of Energy, Grand Junction Area Office, Technical Library, 1294
Directorate of Medical Materiel Library, 1277
Environmental Measurements Laboratory Library, 1300
Environmental Protection Agency, Andrew W Breidenbach Library, 1969
Environmental Protection Agency, Environmental Research Laboratory Library, 1973
Environmental Protection Agency, Robert S Kerr Library, 1975
Food & Drug Administration, Medical Library, 1333
Food & Drug Administration, Dallas District Library, 1335
Geological Survey, National Water Quality Laboratory-Library, 1572
Morgantown Energy Technology Center, 1307
National Agricultural Library, 124
National Bureau of Standards Research Information Center, 155
National Institute on Aging, Gerontology Research Center Library, 1343
National Institutes of Health Library, 1345

National Marine Fisheries Service, Southeast Fisheries Center Library, 167
National Science Foundation Library, 2085
Naval Surface Weapons Center, Technical Library, 1087
Naval Weapons Center, Technical Library, 1097
Naval Weapons Station Library, 1098
Office of Naval Research, Detachment Boston Library, 1121
Office of the Chief of Naval Research Library, 1122
Office of Toxic Substances, Chemical Library, 1995
Redstone Scientific Information Center, 615
Sandia National Laboratories, Technical Library, 1313
Southern Regional Research Center Library, 81
Stored Product Insects Research & Development Library, 82
Tuscaloosa Research Center Library, 1546
US Army Chemical School, Fisher Library, 654
US Army Corps of Engineers, Buffalo District Technical Library, 661
US Army Natick Research, Development, & Engineering Center, Technical Library, 766
USDA, Agricultural Research Service, Eastern Regional Research Center Library, 84
USDA, Agricultural Research Service, Water Conservation Research Library, 86
USDA Northern Regional Research Center Library, 87
Western Regional Research Center Library, 92

Cherokee Indians
Cherokee Elementary School Library, 1375
Cherokee High School Library, 1376

Cherokee Strip
Cherokee Strip Living Museum Library, 1633

Chesapeake & Ohio Canal
Chesapeake & Ohio Canal National Historic Park Resource Library, 1634

Chess
US Military Academy Library, 794

Cheyenne Indians
Bent's Old Fort National Historic Site Library, 1607

Chickamauga, Battle of
Chickamauga & Chattanooga National Military Park Library, 1635

Child/Maternal Health
Food & Nutrition Information Center, 123

Children's Literature
Cove Day School, 1387
Dennehotso Boarding School Library, 1392
Ft Buchanan Post Library, 837
Ft Gordon, Morale Support Activities Library Branch, Patients' Library, 470
Gila Crossing Day School Library, 1400
National Air & Space Museum, Branch Library, 2457

New River Marine Corps Air Station Library, 1240
Franklin D Roosevelt Library, 2079
US Navy Support Office Library, 1225

China
Misawa Base, Overstreet Memorial Library/FL 5205, 380
National Defense University Library, 1278
Pearl Harbor Naval Base Library, 1131

Chippewa Indians
Grand Portage National Monument Library, 1690
Turtle Mountain Community School Media Center, 1455

Choctaw Indians
Choctaw Central High School Library, 1384

Chromatography
Environmental Protection Agency, Environmental Research Laboratory Library, 1973

Citrus Products
Horticultural Research Laboratory Library, 74
US Citrus & Subtropical Products Laboratory Library, 83

Civil Defense
Federal Emergency Management Agency Library, 2010
National Emergency Training Center, Learning Resource Center, 2011

Civil Engineering
Air Force Engineering & Services Center Technical Library/FL 7050, 196
Engineering Technical Information Center, Forest Service, 102
Long Beach Naval Shipyard, Technical Library, 995
Naval Civil Engineering Laboratory Library, 1026
Naval Facilities Engineering Command, Technical Library, 1044
Naval School, Civil Engineer Corps Officers, Moreell Library, 1068
Thayer Engineering Library, 632
US Army Corps of Engineers, Albuquerque District Library, 659
US Army Corps of Engineers, Baltimore District Library Branch, 660
US Army Corps of Engineers, Huntsville Division, Technical Information Center, 672
US Army Corps of Engineers, Kansas City District Library, 676
US Army Corps of Engineers, Louisville District Technical Library, 682
US Army Corps of Engineers, New England Division Technical Library, 689
US Army Corps of Engineers, New Orleans District Technical Library, 691
US Army Corps of Engineers, Norfolk District Technical Library, 694
US Army Corps of Engineers, North Central Division Library, 698
US Army Corps of Engineers, Pittsburgh District Technical Library, 707
US Army Corps of Engineers, Portland District Law Library, 708

US Army Corps of Engineers, Rock Island District Technical Library, 710
US Army Corps of Engineers, St Louis District Technical Library, 713
US Army Corps of Engineers, Seattle District Library, 718
US Army Corps of Engineers, South Atlantic Division Technical Library, 720
US Army Corps of Engineers, South Pacific Division Technical Library, 722
US Army Engineering District, Technical Library, 731
US Army Waterways Experiment Station, Technical Library, 791
Water & Power Resources Service, Regional Library, 1847

Civil Liberties
Department of Justice Civil Rights Library, 1851

Civil Rights
Department of Justice Civil Rights Library, 1851
US Commission on Civil Rights, National Clearinghouse Library, 1962
US Commission on Civil Rights, Western Regional Office Library, 1963

Civil Service
US Office of Personnel Management Library, 2089

Civil Service Reform Act
Federal Labor Relations Authority Law Library, 2021

Civil War
Andersonville National Historic Site Library, 1597
Antietam National Battlefield Library, 1598
Appomattox Court House National Historic Park Library, 1600
Chickamauga & Chattanooga National Military Park Library, 1635
Ft Donelson National Battlefield Library, 1668
Ft Pulaski National Monument Library, 1675
Ft Sumter National Monument Library, 1677
Fredericksburg & Spotsylvania National Military Park Library, 1682
Harpers Ferry National Historic Park Library, 1700
Mr & Mrs John K Hulston Civil War Research Library, 1708
Kennesaw Mountain National Battlefield Park Library, 1719
Manassas National Battlefield Park Library, 1732
Pea Ridge National Military Park Library, 1762
Petersburg National Battlefield Library, 1765
Portsmouth Naval Shipyard Museum, Marshall W Butt Library, 1143
Richmond National Battlefield Park Headquarters Library, 1773
Shiloh National Monument Park Library, 1793
Stones River National Battlefield Library, 1797
US Army Military History Institute Library, 757

Vicksburg National Military Park Library, 1806

Climatic Data
Air Weather Service Technical Library/FL 4414, 212
Geological Survey Library, 1568
Library & Information Services Division, Camp Springs Center, 162
NOAA, National Climatic Data Center Library, 173
National Weather Service, Central Region Library, 179
NOAA, Library & Information Services Division, 182

Climatology
Bureau of Land Management, Phoenix District Office Library, 1508
Environmental Protection Agency, Meteorology Division Library, 1979
Geological Survey Library, 1568
Geological Survey, Water Resources Division, Colorado District Library, 1578
Library & Information Services Division, Camp Springs Center, 162
NOAA, Coral Gables Center Library, 169
NOAA, Great Lakes Environmental Research Laboratory Library, 170
NOAA, National Climatic Data Center Library, 173
National Weather Service, Central Region Library, 179
National Weather Service, Southern Region Headquarters Library, 180
NOAA, Library & Information Services Division, 182
US Army Cold Region Research & Engineering Laboratory Library, 656

Coal
Bureau of Mines Library, 1534
Bureau of Mines Library, 1535
Office of Surface Mining Reclamation & Enforcement Library, 1845

Coast and Geodetic Survey Reports
NOAA, Miami Library, 171

Coast Guard
Coast Guard Law Library, 1941

Coast Guard History
US Coast Guard Academy Library, 1942

Coastal Engineering
US Army Corps of Engineers, Galveston District Technical Library, 667
US Army Corps of Engineers, Jacksonville District Technical Library, 675

Coastal Regions
Naval Coastal Systems Center, Technical Information Services Branch, 1028
US Army Corps of Engineers, New England Division Technical Library, 689

Coastal Zone Management
Coastal Zone Information Center, 159

Coccidioidomycosis
Veterans Administration Medical Center Library Service, 2363

Cold Regions
US Army Cold Region Research & Engineering Laboratory Library, 656

College Catalogs
Bureau of the Census Library, 143
Ft Leonard Wood Post Library, 569
National Science Foundation Library, 2085
US Army Ordnance Missile & Munitions Center & School, Technical Library, 769
US Army Support Command, Hawaii Library System, 782

Colonial America
Colonial National Historic Park Library, 1639
George Washington Birthplace National Monument Library, 1684
Grand Portage National Monument Library, 1690
Knife River Indian Villages National Historic Site Library, 1721
Minute Man National Historical Park Library, 1734
Moores Creek National Military Park Library, 1736
Morristown National Historical Park Library, 1737
Franklin D Roosevelt National Historic Site Library, 1776
Salinas National Monument Library, 1784
Tumacacori National Monument Library, 1802

Colorado
Bureau of Land Management, Colorado State Office Library, 1476
Bureau of Land Management, Colorado State Office Library, 1477
Colorado National Monument Library, 1640
Curecanti National Recreation Area Library, 1646
Ft Carson Post Library, 454
Geological Survey, Public Inquiries Office Library, 1575
Geological Survey, Water Resources Division, Colorado District Library, 1578
Lowry AFB, Base Library/FL 3059, 282

Colorado History
Veterans Administration Medical Center Library, 2311

Colorado Law
Department of the Interior, Office of the Solicitor, Field Solicitor, Law Library, 1836

Colorado River
Lower Colorado Regional Library, 1846

Commerce
US Army Corps of Engineers, St Paul District Technical Library, 714

Commerce Department
Department of Commerce, District Office Library, 128

Commercial Law
Department of Commerce, Law Library, 131
Department of Justice Civil Library, 1850
Federal Trade Commission, Atlanta Regional Office Library, 2043
US International Trade Commission, Law Library, 2269

Commodities
US Customs Service, Library & Information Center, 1954

Commodity Exchange Act
Commodity Futures Trading Commission Library, 1965

Commodity Futures Trading Commission
Commodity Futures Trading Commission Library, 1965

Communicable Diseases
Centers for Disease Control Library, 1327

Communication Skills
Air Force Officer Training School Library/FL 3050, 205

Communications
Base Library/FL 5670, 360
Communications Electronics Command, Technical Library, 423
Foreign Service Institute Library, 1928
Ft Benjamin Harrison, Soldiers' Support Center Library, 479
Keesler AFB, Academic Library/FL 3011, 269
McBride Library/FL 3010, 291
Naval Electronic Systems Engineering Center, Portsmouth Electronic Library, 1037
Naval Ocean Systems Center, Technical Libraries, 1058
Redstone Scientific Information Center, 615
Rome Air Development Center Technical Library/FL 2810, 315
US Army Signal Center, Conrad Technical Library, 778
US Army Strategic Defense Command, Huntsville, Library, 781

Communications Engineering
Defense Communications Engineering Center, Information & Management Center, 1257

Community Development
Department of Housing & Urban Development Library, 1354

Community Services, Office of
Health & Human Services Department Library, 1320

Comptroller General
General Accounting Office, Philadelphia Technical Information Center, 6
US Army Corps of Engineers, North Pacific Law Library, 699

Computer Crime

Department of Justice Criminal Library, 1852

Computer Languages

New River Marine Corps Air Station Library, 1240

US Army Information Engineering Command Software Support, 741

Computer Programming

US Army Information Engineering Command Software Support, 741

Computer Science

Air Force Geophysics Laboratory Research Library, 198

Air Force Human Resources Laboratory, Technical Library/FL 2870, 199

Air Force Space Command Library/FL 2508, 207

Air Force Western Space & Missile Center, Technical Library/FL 2827, 210

Armament Division Technical Library/FL 2825, 217

Army Materiel Command Headquarters, Technical Library, 408

Auke Bay Fisheries Laboratory Library, 158

Base Library/FL 5670, 360

Combat Developments Experimentation Center, Technical Information Center, 420

Defense Communications Agency, Technical & Management Information Center, 1256

Defense Technical Information Center, Technical Library, 1275

Department of Defense Computer Institute, Technical Library, 1276

Federal Reserve Bank of New York, Computer Science Library, 2035

Ft Huachuca Technical Library, 493

Ft Myer Post Library, 539

HQ TRADOC Combined Arms Test Activity (TCATA), Technical Library, 577

Keesler AFB, Academic Library/FL 3011, 269

McBride Library/FL 3010, 291

NASA-AMES Research Center Library, 2059

NASA Lyndon B Johnson Space Center, Technical Library, 2066

National Bureau of Standards Research Information Center, 155

National Institutes of Health, Division of Computer Research & Technology Library, 1344

NOAA, Mountain Administrative Support Center, 172

National Science Foundation Library, 2085

National Solar Observatory, Technical Library, 2086

Naval Electronic Systems Engineering Center, Technical Library, 1038

Naval Underwater Systems Center, Technical Library, 1094

Naval Weapons Center, Technical Library, 1097

Red River Army Depot, School of Engineering & Logistics, Technical Library, 613

Redstone Scientific Information Center, 615

Space & Naval Warfare Systems Command Library, 1156

US Army Information Engineering Command Software Support, 741

US Army Intelligence School Library, 1284

US Army TRADOC Systems Analysis Activity TRASANA, Technical Library, 785

US Coast Guard Academy Library, 1942

US Marine Corps Tactical Systems Support Activity, Technical Library, 1247

US Postal Service Library, 2271

White Sands Missile Range, Technical Library, 806

Wright-Patterson AFB, Technical Library/FL 2802, 345

Computer Software

Dover AFB, Base Library/FL 4497, 236

Ft Sill, Morris Swett Technical Library, 558

Kirtland AFB, Medical Library/SGAL, 274

New River Marine Corps Air Station Library, 1240

US Army Corps of Engineers, Buffalo District Technical Library, 661

Concrete

US Army Corps of Engineers, Rock Island District Technical Library, 710

Congress

Department of the Treasury Library, 1945

Office of Technology Assessment Information Center, 11

Southeastern Power Administration Library, 1315

US Army Corps of Engineers, Headquarters Library, 668

Conservation

Bonneville Power Administration Library, 1291

Bureau of Land Management, Arizona Strip, District Office Library, 1467

Bureau of Land Management, Bishop Resource Area Headquarters Library, 1470

Bureau of Mines, Metallurgy Research Center Library, 1537

Bureau of Mines, Twin Cities Research Center Library, 1542

Fish & Wildlife Service, Division of Biological Services Library, 1550

Heritage Conservation & Recreation Service, Northwest Region Office Library, 1584

John Muir National Historic Site Library, 1741

Oxford Laboratory Library, 184

Sequoia & Kings Canyon National Park Library, 1791

USDA Sedimentation Laboratory Library, 88

Constitutional Law

Department of Justice Civil Rights Library, 1851

Construction

Air Force Engineering & Services Center Technical Library/FL 7050, 196

Department of Housing & Urban Development Library, 1354

General Services Administration, Design & Construction Division Library, 2050

Mall Operation Library, 1730

Naval Civil Engineering Laboratory Library, 1026

Naval Construction Battalion Center Base Library, 1031

Naval School, Civil Engineer Corps Officers, Moreell Library, 1068

US Army Construction Engineering Research Laboratory Library, 658

US Army Corps of Engineers, Buffalo District Technical Library, 661

US Army Corps of Engineers, Ft Worth District, Technical Library, 666

US Army Corps of Engineers, Sacramento District Technical Library, 712

US Army Corps of Engineers, Seattle District Library, 718

US Army Engineer Division Europe, Technical Library, 908

US Army Engineer Division Europe, Technical Library, 909

Construction Census

Bureau of the Census, Atlanta Regional Office Library, 136

Consumer Prices

Bureau of Labor Statistics Library, 1920

Bureau of Labor Statistics, Regional Office, Reference Library, 1921

Bureau of Labor Statistics, Regional Office, Reference Library, 1922

Consumer Product Safety

Consumer Product Safety Commission Library, 1966

Consumer Product Safety Commission Library, 1967

Consumer Protection

Federal Trade Commission, Dallas Regional Office Library, 2045

Continuing Medical Education

Defense Personnel Support Center, Directorate of Medical Material Library, 1272

Veterans Administration Medical Center Library, 2316

Contract Law

Army & Air Force Exchange Service, Law Library, 1255

Ft McPherson, Staff Judge Advocate, HQ US Army Forces Command Law Library, 527

Sharpe Army Depot, Law Library, 627

US Army Contracting Agency Europe, Office of Counsel, Army Law Library, 906

US Army Contracting Agency Korea, Office of Counsel, Law Library, 907

US Army Engineer Division, Memphis District, Law Library, 730

US Army Legal Services Agency, Law Library, 750

US Army Missile Command, Legal Office Library, 761

Contracts

Department of Energy, Office of General Counsel, Law Library, 1295

General Services Administration Library, 2051

Office of Chief Counsel Legal Law Library, Savannah River Operations Office, 1312

Southeastern Power Administration Library, 1315

Danish West Indies History

Christiansted National Historic Site Library, 1637

Data Processing

Air Force Accounting & Finance Center Library/FL 7040, 195

Combat Developments Experimentation Center, Technical Information Center, 420

Defense Logistic Services Center, Learning Resources Center Library, 1266

Defense Logistics Agency Headquarters Library, 1267

General Services Administration Library, 2051

Geological Survey, National Water Quality Laboratory-Library, 1572

Naval Underwater Systems Center, New London Laboratory, Technical Library, 1092

Navy Regional Data Automation Center, 1111

Navy Regional Data Automation Center, Technical Library, 1112

US Army Information Engineering Command Software Support, 741

White Sands Missile Range, Post Library, 805

DataPro

Department of Defense Computer Institute, Technical Library, 1276

Dawson Collection

National Museum of Natural History, Branch Library, 2462

Deafness

Gallaudet University Library, 1285

Death Valley

Death Valley National Monument Research Library, 1651

Decorative Arts

Cooper-Hewitt Museum Library, 2454

Harpers Ferry Center Library, 1699

Independence National Historic Park Library, 1709

National Museum of Natural History, Branch Library, 2462

Martin Van Buren National Historic Site Library, 1805

Defense

Defense Communications Agency, Technical & Management Information Center, 1256

Defense Communications Engineering Center, Information & Management Center, 1257

Defense Intelligence Agency Library, 1263

Defense Technical Information Center, Technical Library, 1275

Dugway Proving Ground, Technical Library, 431

General Accounting Office, Office of Library Services, 5

US Army Air Defense Artillery School Library, 641

US Army Intelligence School Library, 1284

Defense Department

Ft McPherson Library System, 526

Still Media Records Center, 1281

US Army Operational Test & Evaluation Agency, Technical Library, 767

Defense Language Institute

US Army Museum Library, 764

Defense Technology

Combat Developments Experimentation Center, Technical Information Center, 420

Defense Industrial Supply, Technical Data Repository, 1261

HQ TRADOC Combined Arms Test Activity (TCATA), Technical Library, 577

Naval Coastal Systems Center, Technical Information Services Branch, 1028

Scientific & Technical Information Division Library, 623

US Army Strategic Defense Command, Huntsville, Library, 781

Delaware

Bureau of the Census, Information Services Program Library, 142

Delaware River

Delaware River Basin Commission Library, 2446

Delaware River Basin

Delaware River Basin Commission Library, 2446

Delaware Water Gap

Delaware Water Gap Recreation Area Library, 1652

Delinquency

Parklawn Health Library, 1350

Delinquency Prevention

National Institute of Justice Library, 1856

Demographics

Department of Justice Civil Rights Library, 1851

Demography

Bureau of the Census Library, 143

Dentistry

Bethesda Naval Hospital, Edward Rhodes Stitt Library, 953

Camp Lejeune Naval Hospital, Medical & General Libraries, 957

Camp Pendleton Naval Hospital Library, 959

Darnall Army Community Hospital, Medical Library, 426

Ft Carson, Evans US Army Community Hospital, Medical Library, 453

Ft Dix, Walson Army Community Hospital, Medical Library, 463

Ft Sam Houston, Brooke Army Medical Center, Medical Library, 485

Ft Huachuca, Raymond W Bliss Army Community Hospital, Medical Library, 490

Ft Rucker, Medical Library, 551

David Grant USAF Medical Center, Medical Library/SGEL, 252

Lackland AFB, Wilford Hall Medical Center Library/FL 2879, 276

Memphis Naval Regional Medical Center, General & Medical Libraries, 1005

Naval Dental Research Institute Library, 1033

Naval Dental School, William L Darnall Library, 1034

Sheppard AFB Regional Hospital, Medical Library, 322

USAF School of Health Care Science, Academic Library/FL 3021, 337

US Army Aeromedical Research Laboratory, Medical Library, 639

US Army Corps of Engineers, Huntington District, Technical Library, 670

Veterans Administration Medical Center Library, 2303

Veterans Administration Medical Center Library, 2314

Veterans Administration Medical Center Library Service, 2348

Veterans Administration Medical Center Library Service, 2352

Veterans Administration Medical Center, Medical & Patients' Library, 2419

Veterans Administration Medical & Regional Office Center Medical Library, 2434

Wright-Patterson AFB, Medical Center Library, 347

Deserts

Joshua Tree National Monument Library, 1717

Naval Weapons Center Library, 1096

Organ Pipe Cactus National Monument Library, 1758

Design

Cooper-Hewitt Museum Library, 2454

General Services Administration, Design & Construction Division Library, 2050

Smithsonian Institution Libraries, 2468

Design Engineering

Philadelphia Naval Shipyard, Technical Library, 1136

Deskey, Donald

Cooper-Hewitt Museum Library, 2454

Developing Countries

National Fertilizer Library, 2099

Office of International Cooperation & Development (OICD), Technical Inquiries, 127

Overseas Private Investment Corporation Library, 2266

US Agency for International Development Library, 2267

US Agency for International Development Water & Sanitation for Health Project Information Center, 2268

Devils Tower

Devils Tower National Monument Library, 1655

Dietetics

Karl A Menninger Medical Library, 2276
Veterans Administration Medical Center, Medical Library, 2389
Veterans Administration Medical & Regional Office Center Medical Library, 2434

Dinosaurs

Dinosaur National Monument Library, 1656

Disability Insurance

Social Security Administration, District of Columbia Branch Library, 1352

Disarmament

US Arms Control & Disarmament Agency Library, 2103

Dispute Resolution

National Institute of Justice/National Criminal Justice Reference Service, 1857

Diving

Naval Explosive Ordnance Disposal Technology Center, Library, 1042

Domestic Violence

National Institute of Justice/National Criminal Justice Reference Service, 1857

Douglas, Henry Kyd

Antietam National Battlefield Library, 1598

Douglass, Frederick

National Museum of African Art, Branch Library, 2459

Draper, Lyman C.

Kings Mountain National Military Park Library, 1720

Dredging

US Army Corps of Engineers, Galveston District Technical Library, 667
US Army Corps of Engineers, New England Division Technical Library, 689
US Army Corps of Engineers, Portland District Technical Library, 709

Dreyfuss, Henry

Cooper-Hewitt Museum Library, 2454

Drug Abuse

Drug Enforcement Administration Library, 1907
Fort Worth Federal Correctional Institute Library Services, 1871
Lemoore Naval Air Station Library, 993
New River Marine Corps Air Station Library, 1240
Veterans Administration Medical Center Library Service, 2332
Veterans Administration Medical Center Library Service, 2370
Veterans Administration Medical Center Library Service, 2373
Veterans Administration Medical Center, Medical Library, 2409

Alvin C York Veterans Administration Medical Center, Library Service, 2443

Drugs

Food & Drug Administration, Medical Library, 1333
Food & Drug Administration, Dallas District Library, 1335
Food & Drug Administration Library, 1336
US Customs Service, Library & Information Center, 1954

Dustin, Fred

Custer Battlefield National Monument Library, 1647

Early Childhood Education

Big Coulee School-Early Childhood Education Center, 1365
Chinle Boarding School Library, 1382

Earth Science

Geological Survey Library, 1564
Geological Survey Library, 1565
Geological Survey Library, 1566
Geological Survey, Public Inquiries Office, 1573
Glacier National Park, George C. Ruhle Library, 1687
Great Smoky Mountains National Park, Sugarlands Visitor Center Library, 1694
NASA Lyndon B Johnson Space Center, Technical Library, 2066
National Air & Space Museum, Branch Library, 2457
National Capital Parks-East Library, 1744
National Mine Health & Safety Academy, Learning Resource Center, 1923
National Science Foundation Library, 2085
US Army Corps of Engineers, Detroit District Technical Library, 664
White Sands National Monument Library, 1812

East Anglia

Lakenheath Base Library, 376

Ecology

Auke Bay Fisheries Laboratory Library, 158
Brookhaven National Laboratory, Research Library, 1293
Cabrillo National Monument Library, 1616
Cape Cod National Seashore Library, 1619
Cape Lookout National Seashore Library, 1621
Environmental Protection Agency, Environmental Research Laboratory Library, 1972
Environmental Protection Agency, Region 3 Library, 1987
Everglades National Park Research Center Library, 1660
Fish & Wildlife Service, Division of Biological Services Library, 1550
Miami Laboratory Library, 164
NASA-National Space Technology Laboratories, Research Library, 2068
National Fishery Research & Development Laboratory Library, 1555
National Fishery Research Center Library, 1556
NOAA, Southeast Fisheries Center, Galveston Laboratory Library, 176
National Park Service Library, 1747

Navajo National Monument Library, 1753
Northern Prairie Wildlife Research Center Library, 1557
Oxford Laboratory Library, 184
Panama City Laboratory Library, 185
US Army Corps of Engineers, Galveston District Technical Library, 667
US Army Corps of Engineers, New England Division Technical Library, 689
Wind Cave National Park Library, 1814

Economic Census

Bureau of the Census, Atlanta Regional Office Library, 136
Bureau of the Census, Dallas Regional Office Library, 138
Bureau of the Census, New York Regional Office Library, 144

Economic Policy

Federal Reserve Bank of Minneapolis Library, 2034
Federal Reserve Bank of Richmond, Research Library, 2040

Economic Regulations

Interstate Commerce Commission Library, 2053

Economics

Air Force Institute of Technology Library, 201
Allied Forces, South Europe, Library, 1179
Board of Governors of the Federal Reserve System, Research Library, 2027
Bureau of Economic Analysis, Research Resource Center, 145
Bureau of Labor Statistics Library, 1920
Bureau of Labor Statistics, Regional Office, Reference Library, 1921
Bureau of Land Management, District Library, 1480
Bureau of Land Management, Utah State Office Library, 1525
Bureau of the Census Library, 143
Congressional Budget Office Library, 12
Consumer Product Safety Commission Library, 1967
Defense General Supply Center Library, 1260
Defense Logistics Agency Headquarters Library, 1267
Department of Justice Antitrust Library, 1849
Department of State Library, 1927
Executive Office of the President Library, 64
Eximbank Library, 2002
Federal Home Loan Bank Board, Research Library, 2013
Federal Home Loan Bank of Atlanta, Research Library, 2014
Federal Home Loan Bank of Dallas, Research & Information Library, 2016
Federal Home Loan Bank of Des Moines Library, 2017
Federal Home Loan Bank of New York Library, 2019
Federal Reserve Bank of Atlanta, Research Library, 2028
Federal Reserve Bank of Boston, Research Library, 2029
Federal Reserve Bank of Chicago Library, 2030
Federal Reserve Bank of Cleveland, Research Library, 2031

Federal Reserve Bank of Dallas Library, 2032

Federal Reserve Bank of Kansas City, Research Library, 2033

Federal Reserve Bank of Minneapolis Library, 2034

Federal Reserve Bank of New York, Research Library, 2037

Federal Reserve Bank of Philadelphia, Information Services & Research Library, 2038

Federal Reserve Bank of Richmond, Baltimore Branch Library, 2039

Federal Reserve Bank of Richmond, Research Library, 2040

Federal Reserve Bank of St Louis, Research Library, 2041

Federal Reserve Bank of San Francisco, Research Library, 2042

Federal Trade Commission, Law Library, 2046

Federal Trade Commission Library, 2048

Gerald R Ford Library, 2072

Foreign Service Institute Library, 1928

Health & Human Services Department Library, 1320

Herbert Hoover Presidential Library, 2073

National Agricultural Library, 124

National Labor Relations Board Library, 2084

Naval Postgraduate School, Dudley Knox Library, 1061

Naval Postgraduate School, Dudley Knox Library, 1062

Naval War College Library, 1095

Social Security Administration, District of Columbia Branch Library, 1352

US Agency for International Development Library, 2267

US Army Corps of Engineers, Buffalo District Technical Library, 661

USAREUR Library & Resource Center, 911

US Army War College Library, 790

US Coast Guard Academy Library, 1942

US Customs Service, Library & Information Center, 1954

US Securities & Exchange Commission Library, 2096

Economics, International

Department of Commerce, District Office Library, 128

Education

Aberdeen Proving Ground, Ordnance Center & School Library, 398

Alameda Naval Air Station Library, 944

Canoncito Community School, Resource Center, 1372

Ft Bragg Command Reference Center & Main Post Library, 447

Ft Buchanan Post Library, 837

Ft Campbell, R F Sink Library, 452

Ft Benjamin Harrison, Soldiers' Support Center Library, 479

Ft George G Meade, Post Library, 535

George AFB, Base Library/FL 4812, 249

Kirtland AFB, Base Library/FL 4469, 273

Laguna Elementary School Library, 1413

Lowry AFB, Base Library/FL 3059, 282

Manpower, Education, Research, & Training (MERT) Division Library, 1305

Miramar Naval Air Station Library, 1008

National Indian Training Center, Professional Library, 1421

Naval Education & Training Center, Main Library, 1035

Naval Electronic Systems Engineering Center, Portsmouth Electronic Library, 1037

Naval Mobile Construction Battalion Center Library, 1056

Naval Security Group Activity Station Library, 1074

Oglala Community Elementary School, 1424

Scott AFB, Base Library/FL 4407, 318

US Army Air Defense Artillery School Library, 641

US Army Intelligence School Library, 1284

US Army Military Police School, Ramsey Library, 759

US Army Ordnance Center & School Library, 768

US Army Ordnance Missile & Munitions Center & School, Technical Library, 769

US Department of Education, Office of Educational Research & Improvement Library, 1286

Veterans Administration Medical Center Library, 2312

Wide Ruins School Library, 1461

Yongsan Library, 942

Education History

US Department of Education, Office of Educational Research & Improvement Library, 1286

Eisenhower, Dwight D.

Dwight D Eisenhower Library, 2071

Gettysburg National Military Park Library, 1685

Elections

Federal Election Commission, Law Library, 2008

National Clearinghouse on Election Administration, Federal Election Commission Library, 2009

Electric Power Research Institute

Tennessee Valley Authority, Technical Library, 2102

Electrical Engineering

Air Force Flight Test Center, Technical Library/FL 2806, 197

Bonneville Power Administration Library, 1291

Ft Huachuca Technical Library, 493

General Services Administration, Design & Construction Division Library, 2050

Hull, Machinery & Electrical Technical Library, 987

Naval Facilities Engineering Command, Technical Library, 1044

Naval Ship Systems Engineering Station, Technical Library, 1076

Philadelphia Naval Shipyard, Technical Library, 1136

Puget Sound Naval Shipyard, Engineering Library, 1145

Redstone Scientific Information Center, 615

White Sands Missile Range, Technical Library, 806

Electricity

Patuxent Naval Air Station Library, 1129

US Naval Academy, Nimitz Library, 1169

Water & Power Resources Service, Regional Library, 1847

Electronic Engineering

Air Force Flight Test Center, Technical Library/FL 2806, 197

Environmental Measurements Laboratory Library, 1300

Naval Electronic Systems Engineering Center, Technical Library, 1038

Naval Ship Systems Engineering Station, Technical Library, 1076

Naval Supervisor of Shipbuilding, Conversion & Repair, Technical Library, 1079

White Sands Missile Range, Technical Library, 806

Electronic Warfare

Electronic Security Command, General Library/FL 7046, 241

Electronic Warfare Department, Tactical Publication Library, 974

US Army Intelligence School Library, 1284

Electronics

Air Force Geophysics Laboratory Research Library, 198

Base Library/FL 5670, 360

Bergstrom AFB, Base Library/FL 4857, 221

Communications Electronics Command, Technical Library, 423

Department of Transportation Library, 1931

Electronic Security Command, General Library/FL 7046, 241

Ellsworth AFB, Base Library/FL 4690, 243

Griffiss AFB, Base Library/FL 4616, 253

Keesler AFB, Academic Library/FL 3011, 269

Long Beach Naval Shipyard, Technical Library, 995

Lowry AFB, Base Library/FL 3059, 282

Memphis Naval Air Station Library, 1004

Myrtle Beach AFB, Base Library/FL 4806, 300

NASA Goddard Space Flight Center Library, 2064

NOAA, Mountain Administrative Support Center, 172

Naval Avionics Center, Technical Library, 1024

Naval Electronic Systems Engineering Center, Portsmouth Electronic Library, 1037

Naval Electronics Systems, Technical Library, 1040

Naval Sea Support Center, Pacific, Library, 1071

Naval Weapons Center, Technical Library, 1097

Naval Weapons Station Library, 1098

Patuxent Naval Air Station Library, 1129

Philadelphia Naval Shipyard, Technical Library, 1136

Point Mugu Naval Air Station Library, 1138

Portsmouth Naval Shipyard, Supply Department, Technical Library, 1144

Redstone Scientific Information Center, 615

Robins AFB, Base Library/FL 2060, 314

Rome Air Development Center Technical Library/FL 2810, 315

Sandia National Laboratories, Technical Library, 1314

Space & Naval Warfare Systems Command Library, 1156

Supervisor of Shipbuilding Conversion & Repair Library, 1159

US Army Belvoir Research Development & Engineering Technical Library, 651

US Army Corps of Engineers, Albuquerque District Library, 659
US Army Corps of Engineers, Buffalo District Technical Library, 661
US Army Corps of Engineers, Detroit District Technical Library, 664
US Army Corps of Engineers, Galveston District Technical Library, 667
US Army Corps of Engineers, Headquarters Library, 668
US Army Corps of Engineers, Huntsville Division, Technical Information Center, 672
US Army Corps of Engineers, Jacksonville District Technical Library, 675
US Army Corps of Engineers, Kansas City District Library, 676
US Army Corps of Engineers, Little Rock District Technical Library, 678
US Army Corps of Engineers, Los Angeles District Technical Library, 680
US Army Corps of Engineers, Missouri River Division, Omaha District Technical Library, 684
US Army Corps of Engineers, Nashville District Technical Library, 687
US Army Corps of Engineers, New York District Technical Library, 693
US Army Corps of Engineers, Norfolk District Technical Library, 694
US Army Corps of Engineers, North Pacific Law Library, 699
US Army Corps of Engineers, Ohio River District Technical Library, 700
US Army Corps of Engineers, Omaha District Library, 702
US Army Corps of Engineers, Omaha District Technical Library, 703
US Army Corps of Engineers, Pittsburgh District Technical Library, 707
US Army Corps of Engineers, Portland District Law Library, 708
US Army Corps of Engineers, Seattle District Library, 718
US Army Corps of Engineers, Southwest Division Technical Library, 723
US Army Corps of Engineers, Walla Walla District Technical & Law Library, 725
US Army Engineer Division Europe, Technical Library, 909
US Army Strategic Defense Command, Huntsville, Library, 781
US Coast Guard Academy Library, 1942
USDA, Agricultural Research Service, Water Conservation Research Library, 86
US Military Academy Library, 794
US Naval Academy, Nimitz Library, 1169
Winchester Engineering & Analytical Center Library, 1338
Wright-Patterson AFB, Technical Library/FL 2802, 345

Engineering History

Portsmouth Naval Shipyard Museum, Marshall W Butt Library, 1143
US Army Corps of Engineers, Baltimore District Library Branch, 660
US Army Corps of Engineers, Headquarters Library, 668
US Army Corps of Engineers, St Paul District Technical Library, 714

Engineering Regulations

US Army Corps of Engineers, Ft Worth District, Technical Library, 666

English as a Second Language

Defense Language English Language Center, Academic Library/FL 3046, 1264

Entomology

APHIS Plant Protection & Quarantine Library, 93
Biological Control of Insects Laboratory, Library, 72
National Agricultural Library, 124
National Museum of Natural History, Branch Library, 2462
Navy Disease Vector Ecology & Control Center Library, 1107
Rocky Mountain Laboratory Library, 1347
Smithsonian Institution Libraries, Museum Support Center Branch, 2469
Stored Product Insects Research & Development Library, 82

Environmental Education

De Soto National Memorial Library, 1650
Great Sand Dunes National Monument Library, 1693
Indiana Dunes National Lakeshore Library, 1710
Abraham Lincoln Birthplace National Historic Site Library, 1728

Environmental Engineering

Air Force Engineering & Services Center Technical Library/FL 7050, 196
Environmental Measurements Laboratory Library, 1300
Occupational Safety & Health Administration, Technical Data Center, 1925
US Army Construction Engineering Research Laboratory Library, 658

Environmental Impact Statements

Bureau of Land Management, California State Office Library, 1473
Bureau of Land Management, Fairbanks District Office Library, 1486
Bureau of Land Management, Minerals Management Service Library, 1500
Bureau of Land Management, New Mexico State Office Central Files/Library, 1504
Bureau of Land Management, New Orleans Outer-Continental Shelf Office Library, 1506
Bureau of Land Management, Rawlins District Office Library, 1510
Coastal Zone Information Center, 159
Heritage Conservation & Recreation Service, Northwest Region Office Library, 1584
National Agricultural Library, 124
Pacific Southwest Regional Office Library, 1590

Environmental Law

Bureau of Land Management, Phoenix District Office Library, 1508
Bureau of Land Management, Utah State Office Library, 1525
Bureau of Land Management, Wyoming State Office Library, 1528
Department of Energy, Office of General Counsel, Law Library, 1295
Department of Justice Lands Library, 1853
Department of the Interior, Center for Information & Library Services, Natural Resources Library, Law Branch, 1820

Department of the Interior, Center for Information & Library Services, Natural Resources Library, Law Branch, 1822
Environmental Protection Agency, Law Library, 1976
Environmental Protection Agency, Region 9 Library, 1983
Environmental Protection Agency, Region 4 Library, 1988
Environmental Protection Agency, Region 6 Library, 1990
Environmental Protection Agency, Region 7 Library, 1991
Office of Chief Counsel Legal Law Library, Savannah River Operations Office, 1312

Environmental Medicine

Air Force Occupational & Environmental Health Laboratory, Technical Library/FL 2817, 203
Bethesda Naval Medical Research Institute, Information Services Branch, 954
Environmental Protection Agency, Region 1 Library, 1984
Ft Monmouth, Patterson Army Community Hospital, Medical & Patients' Library, 537
Medical & Health Sciences Division Library, 1306
National Institute of Environmental Health Sciences Library, 1342
Navy Environmental Health Center Library, 1108
US Army Environmental Hygiene Agency Library, 733
US Army Natick Research, Development, & Engineering Center, Technical Library, 766
US Army Research Institute of Environmental Medicine, Medical Library, 772

Environmental Policy

Environmental Protection Agency Headquarters Library, 1974

Environmental Programs

Bureau of Land Management, Arizona State Office Library, 1466
The Energy Library, Germantown Branch, 1299
Environmental Monitoring & Systems Laboratory Library, 1968
Environmental Protection Agency, Central Regional Laboratory Library, 1970
Environmental Protection Agency Library, Region 8, 1978
Environmental Protection Agency, National Enforcement Investigation Center, Information Center, 1980
Environmental Protection Agency, Office of Air Quality, Planning, & Standards Library, 1982
Environmental Protection Agency, Region 9 Library, 1983
Environmental Protection Agency, Region 2, Field Office Library, 1985
Environmental Protection Agency, Region 7 Library, 1991
Environmental Protection Agency, Region 10 Library, 1992
Grand Canyon National Park Research Library, 1689
National Park Service, Southeast Regional Office Library, 1750
Naval Civil Engineering Laboratory Library, 1026
Naval Ship Research & Development Center, W Taylor Library, 1075

Environmental Protection Agency

Environmental Protection Agency, Region 9 Library, 1983

Environmental Protection Agency, Region 4 Library, 1988

US Army Environmental Hygiene Agency Library, 733

Environmental Regulations

Environmental Protection Agency, National Enforcement Investigation Center, Information Center, 1980

Environmental Science

Acadia National Park Library, 1592

Armament Division Technical Library/FL 2825, 217

Brookhaven National Laboratory, Research Library, 1293

Bureau of Land Management, District Office Library, 1481

Bureau of Land Management, District Office Library, 1482

Bureau of Land Management, Elko District Office Library, 1484

Bureau of Land Management, Minerals Management Service Library, 1500

Bureau of Land Management, Phoenix District Office Library, 1508

Bureau of Land Management, Utah State Office Library, 1525

Bureau of Land Management, Wyoming State Office Library, 1528

Bureau of Reclamation, Engineering & Research Center Library, 1547

Denver Wildlife Research Center, 95

Energy Library, 1298

Environmental Protection Agency, Andrew W Breidenbach Library, 1969

Environmental Protection Agency, Region 1 Library, 1984

Environmental Protection Agency, Region 3 Library, 1987

Environmental Protection Agency, Region 10 Library, 1992

FAA Central Regional Library, 1935

Fish & Wildlife Service, Science Reference Library, 1552

NASA-National Space Technology Laboratories, Research Library, 2068

National Science Foundation Library, 2085

Naval Environmental Prediction Research Facility/Fleet Numerical Oceanography Center Technical Library, 1041

Nevada Technical Library, Department of Energy, 1311

North Central Forest Experiment Station Library, 116

Nuclear Regulatory Commission Library, 2087

Ocmulgee National Monument Library, 1756

Oxford Laboratory Library, 184

Reno Metallurgy Research Center Library, 1544

Smithsonian Environmental Research Center Library, Rockville Branch, 2465

Tennessee Valley Authority, Technical Library, 2102

US Army Corps of Engineers, Buffalo District Technical Library, 661

US Army Corps of Engineers, Nashville District Technical Library, 687

US Army Corps of Engineers, New Orleans District Technical Library, 691

US Army Corps of Engineers, North Central Division Library, 698

US Army Corps of Engineers, Rock Island District Technical Library, 710

US Army Corps of Engineers, Sacramento District Technical Library, 712

US Army Corps of Engineers, St Paul District Technical Library, 714

Epidemiology

Centers for Disease Control Library, 1327

Food & Drug Administration, Medical Library, 1333

Equal Employment

Equal Employment Opportunity Commission, Charlotte District Office, Law Library, 1996

Equal Employment Opportunity Commission, Cleveland District Office Library, 1997

Equal Employment Opportunity Commission, Houston District Office, Law Library, 1998

Equal Employment Opportunity Commission Library, 1999

Equal Employment Opportunity Commission, Milwaukee District Office, Library, 2000

Equal Employment Opportunity Commission, New Orleans District Office Library, 2001

Sharpe Army Depot, Law Library, 627

US Army Corps of Engineers, Baltimore District Library Branch, 660

Equal Employment Opportunity Commission

Equal Employment Opportunity Commission, Cleveland District Office Library, 1997

Equal Employment Opportunity Commission Library, 1999

Equal Opportunity

Defense Equal Opportunity Management Institute Library, 1259

Equipment

Equipment Development Center Library, 104

Long Beach Naval Shipyard, Technical Library, 995

US International Trade Commission Main Library, 2270

Equipment Development

Equipment Development Center Library, 103

ERIC

US Department of Education, Office of Educational Research & Improvement Library, 1286

Erosion

USDA Sedimentation Laboratory Library, 88

Espionage

Department of Justice Criminal Library, 1852

Estate Planning

21st Support Command, Office of Staff Judge Advocate, Law Library, 899

Estuaries

Smithsonian Institution Libraries, Museum Support Center Branch, 2469

Ethnic Studies

Anacostia Neighborhood Museum Library, 2452

Ethnography

Death Valley National Monument Research Library, 1651

Olympic National Park Library, 1757

Ethnology, Bureau of

Glen Canyon National Recreation Area Library, 1688

Europe

Mildenhall Base Library/FL 5518, 379

European Art

National Gallery of Art Library, 2458

The Phillips Collection Library, 2464

European History

USAREUR Library & Resource Center, 911

European Travel

Base Library/FL 5670, 360

Robinson Barracks, US Army Library, 878

US Army Library System, Norddeutschland, 922

Evaluation

General Accounting Office, Office of Library Services, 5

US Army Operational Test & Evaluation Agency, Technical Library, 767

US Navy Operational Test & Evaluation Force Library, 1173

Evaporation

USDA, Agricultural Research Service, Water Conservation Research Library, 86

Everglades National Park

Everglades National Park Research Center Library, 1660

Evolution

NASA-AMES Research Center, Life Sciences Library, 2060

Expert Systems

US Army Signal Center, Conrad Technical Library, 778

Explorers

Cabrillo National Monument Library, 1616

Castillo de San Marcos National Monument Library, 1626

De Soto National Memorial Library, 1650

Knife River Indian Villages National Historic Site Library, 1721

Explosives

Bureau of Alcohol, Tobacco & Firearms/National Laboratory Library, 1946

Naval Explosive Ordnance Disposal Technology Center, Library, 1042

Naval Ordnance Station, Library Branch, 1059
Sandia National Laboratories, Technical Library, 1314
Scientific & Technical Information Division Library, 623

Explosives Industry

Bureau of Alcohol, Tobacco & Firearms Reference Library, 1947

Exports

Department of Commerce, District Office Library, 128
Eximbank Library, 2002
International Trade Administration, Chicago Field Office Library, 148
International Trade Administration, International Marketing Center Library, 150
US Customs Service, New York Region, Library, 1955

Families

Ft Campbell, R F Sink Library, 452
Ft Sill, Nye Library, 556
Health & Human Services Department Library, 1320

Farm Credit Administration

Farm Credit Administration Library, 2003

Federal Communications Commission

FCC Chicago District Office Library, 2004

Federal Employees

Federal Labor Relations Authority Law Library, 2021
US Merit Systems Protection Board Library, 2055

Federal Energy Regulatory Commission

Federal Energy Regulatory Commission Library, 1319

Federal Home Loan Bank Board

Federal Home Loan Bank Board, Research Library, 2013

Federal Regulations

Economic Development Administration, Seattle Regional Office Library, 146

Federal Reserve System

Board of Governors of the Federal Reserve System, Law Library, 2026
Board of Governors of the Federal Reserve System, Research Library, 2027
Federal Reserve Bank of Cleveland, Research Library, 2031
Federal Reserve Bank of Minneapolis Library, 2034
Federal Reserve Bank of New York, Research Library, 2037
Federal Reserve Bank of Richmond, Baltimore Branch Library, 2039

Federal Trade Commission

Federal Trade Commission, Dallas Regional Office Library, 2045
Federal Trade Commission, Law Library, 2046
Federal Trade Commission Library, 2048

Feminism

Patch Barracks, US Army Library, 875

Fertilizers

National Fertilizer Library, 2099

Fiction

Cherry Creek School Library, 1377
COMFLEACT Library, 1180
El Toro Marine Corps Air Station Library, 1233
Naval Hospital, Medical Library, 1050
Twin Buttes School Library, 1456
White Horse School Library, 1458

Films

American Museum of Immigration Library, 1596
Geophysical Fluid Dynamics Laboratory Library, 160
John F Kennedy Center Performing Arts Library, 8
Library of Congress, 9

Finance

Air Force Accounting & Finance Center Library/FL 7040, 195
Board of Governors of the Federal Reserve System, Research Library, 2027
Eximbank Library, 2002
Farm Credit Administration Library, 2003
Federal Home Loan Bank Board, Research Library, 2013
Federal Home Loan Bank of Chicago Library, 2015
Federal Home Loan Bank of Dallas, Research & Information Library, 2016
Federal Home Loan Bank of Des Moines Library, 2017
Federal Reserve Bank of Atlanta, Research Library, 2028
Federal Reserve Bank of Boston, Research Library, 2029
Federal Reserve Bank of Chicago Library, 2030
Federal Reserve Bank of Kansas City, Research Library, 2033
Federal Reserve Bank of New York, Research Library, 2037
Federal Reserve Bank of Richmond, Baltimore Branch Library, 2039
Federal Reserve Bank of St Louis, Research Library, 2041
Foreign Service Institute Library, 1928
Internal Revenue Service, Office of Chief Counsel, Library, 1953
Interstate Commerce Commission Library, 2053
Overseas Private Investment Corporation Library, 2266
USDA National Finance Center Library, 67
US Securities & Exchange Commission Library, 2096

Finance, International

Board of Governors of the Federal Reserve System, Research Library, 2027
Federal Reserve Bank of New York, Research Library, 2037
Overseas Private Investment Corporation Library, 2266
US Agency for International Development Library, 2267

Finance Policy

Federal Reserve Bank of Chicago Library, 2030
Federal Reserve Bank of Richmond, Baltimore Branch Library, 2039

Fine Arts

Commission of Fine Arts Library, 1964
Institute of American Indian Arts Library, 1405
National Endowment for the Arts Library, 2082
Yakima Firing Center, Field Library, 808

Fire

Air Force Engineering & Services Center Technical Library/FL 7050, 196
Bureau of Land Management, Bakersfield District Office Library, 1469
Bureau of Land Management, Elko District Office Library, 1484
Bureau of Land Management, Fairbanks District Office Library, 1486
Bureau of Land Management Library, 1497
National Emergency Training Center, Learning Resource Center, 2011
Rocky Mountain Forest & Range Experiment Station Library, 118

Fire Departments

National Emergency Training Center, Learning Resource Center, 2011

Fire Island

Fire Island National Seashore Library, 1662

Firearms

Bureau of Alcohol, Tobacco & Firearms/ National Laboratory Library, 1946

Firearms Industry

Bureau of Alcohol, Tobacco & Firearms Reference Library, 1947

FIREBASE

North Central Forest Experiment Station Library, 116

Fisheries

Auke Bay Fisheries Laboratory Library, 158
Columbia National Fisheries Research Library, 1549
Environmental Protection Agency, Research Laboratory Library, 1993
Everglades National Park Research Center Library, 1660
Fish & Wildlife Service, Division of Biological Services Library, 1550
Fish & Wildlife Service Library, 1551
Fish Farming Experimental Station Library, 1553
Forestry Sciences Laboratory Library, 113
Gloucester Technical Library, 161
Miami Laboratory Library, 164
National Fisheries Center, Leetown Technical Information Services, 1554
National Fishery Research & Development Laboratory Library, 1555
National Fishery Research Center Library, 1556
National Marine Fisheries Service, Honolulu Laboratory Library, 166

National Marine Fisheries Service, Southeast Fisheries Center Library, 167
NOAA, Southeast Fisheries Center, Galveston Laboratory Library, 176
NOAA, Library & Information Services Division, 182
Northwest & Alaska Fisheries Center Library, 183
Oxford Laboratory Library, 184
Panama City Laboratory Library, 185
Rice Library, 187
Southwest Fisheries Center Library, 188
W F Thompson Memorial Library, 189
Tiburon Laboratory Library, 190
US International Trade Commission Main Library, 2270
Van Oosten Library, 1560
Lionel A Walford Library, 191
Woods Hole Laboratory Library, 192

Fishes
Department of Justice Lands Library, 1853
Department of the Interior, Center for Information & Library Services, Natural Resources Library, 1821
Fish & Wildlife Service, Science Reference Library, 1552
Fish Farming Experimental Station Library, 1553
Milford Laboratory Library, 165
National Fisheries Center, Leetown Technical Information Services, 1554
National Fishery Research & Development Laboratory Library, 1555
National Fishery Research Center Library, 1556
National Marine Fisheries Service, Southeast Fisheries Center Library, 167
NOAA, Southeast Fisheries Center, Galveston Laboratory Library, 176
Rice Library, 187
Southwest Fisheries Center Library, 188
Tunison Laboratory of Fish Nutrition Library, 1559
US Army Corps of Engineers, Jacksonville District Technical Library, 675
US Army Corps of Engineers, Walla Walla District Technical & Law Library, 725
Van Oosten Library, 1560

Fishing Industry
Pascagoula Laboratory Library, 186
Tiburon Laboratory Library, 190

Flags
The Institute of Heraldry Library, 583

Floods
Allegheny Portage Railroad National Historic Site Library, 1595
Delaware River Basin Commission Library, 2446
Geological Survey Library, 1568
Geological Survey, Water Resources Division, Colorado District Library, 1578
Geological Survey, Water Resources Division Library, 1579
US Army Corps of Engineers, Jacksonville District Technical Library, 675
US Army Corps of Engineers, New England Division Technical Library, 689

Florida
Environmental Protection Agency, Region 4 Library, 1988
Everglades National Park Research Center Library, 1660

Homestead AFB, Base Library/FL 4829, 266
US Army Corps of Engineers, Jacksonville District Technical Library, 675

Florida History
Castillo de San Marcos National Monument Library, 1626
De Soto National Memorial Library, 1650

Flower Arrangement
National Agricultural Library, 124

Fluid Dynamics
NASA-AMES Research Center Library, 2059

Fluid Mechanics
NASA-AMES Research Center, Technical Library, 2061
NASA Dryden Flight Research Center Library, 2062

Folk Art
Booker T Washington National Monument Library, 1809

Folklore
Catoctin Mountain Park Library, 1628

Food
Food & Drug Administration, Medical Library, 1333
Food & Drug Administration, Bureau of Foods Library, 1334
Food & Drug Administration, Dallas District Library, 1335
Food & Drug Administration Library, 1336
Food & Nutrition Information Center, 123
Food & Nutrition Service Reference Center, 97
Food Safety & Inspection Service, Science Administration Library, 98
National Agricultural Library, 124
National Marine Fisheries Service, Southeast Fisheries Center Library, 167
Southern Regional Research Center Library, 81
US Army Logistics Library, 751
US Army Natick Research, Development, & Engineering Center, Technical Library, 766

Food and Agriculture Organization
National Agricultural Library, 124
US Agency for International Development Library, 2267

Food Service Management
Food & Nutrition Information Center, 123

Food Stamps
Food & Nutrition Service Reference Center, 97

Food Technology
Center for Food Safety & Applied Nutrition Library, 1332
National Marine Fisheries Service, Southeast Fisheries Center Library, 167
Northwest & Alaska Fisheries Center Library, 183

US Army Natick Research, Development, & Engineering Center, Technical Library, 766
USDA, Agricultural Research Service, Eastern Regional Research Center Library, 84
Western Regional Research Center Library, 92

Force, Peter
Library of Congress, 9

Ford, Gerald R.
Gerald R Ford Library, 2072

Foreign Claims
Foreign Claims Settlement Commission, Law Library, 1909

Foreign Governments
Department of State Library, 1927

Foreign Maps
Map Library & Information Service Library, 163

Foreign Market Surveys
Department of Commerce, District Office Library, 128

Foreign Patents
Patent & Trademark Office Scientific Library, 194

Foreign Service Institute
Foreign Service Institute Library, 1928

Forensic Science
Bureau of Alcohol, Tobacco & Firearms/ National Laboratory Library, 1946

Forest Engineering
Engineering Technical Information Center, Forest Service, 102

Forest Products
Forest Products Laboratory Library, 106
Forest Sciences Laboratory, 107
SOUTHFORNET Science Library, 120

Forest Service
Equipment Development Center Library, 103
Forestry Sciences Laboratory Library, 113

Forestry
Bridger-Teton National Forest Library, 99
Bureau of Land Management, Branch of Records & Data Management, 1471
Bureau of Land Management, Eugene Office Library, 1485
Bureau of Land Management, Folsom District Office Library, 1487
Bureau of Land Management, Kanab Office Library, 1490
Bureau of Land Management Library, 1497
Bureau of Land Management, Phillips Resource Area Office Library, 1507
Bureau of Land Management, Roseburg District Office Library, 1514
Bureau of Land Management, Susanville District Office Library, 1523
Clearwater National Forest Library, 100

Engineering Technical Information Center, Forest Service, 102
Forest Sciences Laboratory, 107
Forest Service, Equipment Development Center Library, 108
Forest Service Information, Northwest, 109
Forest Service, Pacific NW Forest & Range Experimental Station, 110
Forest Service, Region 6 Information Office, 111
Forest Service, Rogue River National Forest Library, 112
Forestry Sciences Laboratory Library, 113
Institute of Tropical Forestry Library, 114
International Forestry Staff Library, 115
National Agricultural Library, 124
North Central Forest Experiment Station Library, 116
Pacific Southwest Forest & Range Experiment Station Library, 117
Redwood National Park Library, 1772
Rocky Mountain Forest & Range Experiment Station Library, 118
Southern Forest Experiment Station Library, 119
SOUTHFORNET Science Library, 120
US Army Corps of Engineers, St Louis District Technical Library, 713
US Forest Service Library, 121
US International Trade Commission Main Library, 2270
WESTFORNET/FS-INFO Intermountain Research Station, 122

Forestry History
Equipment Development Center Library, 103

Fort Bowie
Ft Bowie National Historic Site Library, 1683

Fort Caroline
Ft Caroline National Memorial Library, 1665

Fort Davis
Ft Davis National Historic Site Library, 1667

Fort Donelson
Ft Donelson National Battlefield Library, 1668

Fort Frederica
Ft Frederica National Monument Library, 1669

Fort Knox
Ft Knox, Barr Memorial Library, 502

Fort Laramie
Ft Laramie National Historic Site Library, 1670

Fort Larned
Ft Larned National Historic Site Library, 1671

Fort McHenry
Ft McHenry National Monument & Historic Shrine Library, 1672

Fort Necessity
Ft Necessity National Battlefield Library, 1673

Fort Point
Ft Point National Historic Site Library, 1674

Fort Pulaski
Ft Pulaski National Monument Library, 1675

Fort Stanwix
Ft Stanwix National Monument Library, 1676

Fort Sumter
Ft Sumter National Monument Library, 1677

Fort Union
Ft Union National Monument Library, 1678
Ft Union Trading Post National Historic Site Library, 1679

Fort Vancouver
Ft Vancouver National Historic Site Library, 1680

Fossil Energy
Bureau of Mines Library, 1534
Bureau of Mines Library, 1535
The Energy Library, Germantown Branch, 1299
Morgantown Energy Technology Center, 1307
National Institute for Petroleum & Energy Research Library, 1310
Tennessee Valley Authority, Technical Library, 2102

Fossils
John Day Fossil Beds National Monument Library, 1649
Florissant Fossil Beds National Monument Library, 1663
Scotts Bluff National Monument, Oregon Trail Association Library, 1790

Fredericksburg Battlefield
Fredericksburg & Spotsylvania National Military Park Library, 1682

French and Indian War
Ft Necessity National Battlefield Library, 1673

French Language
Foreign Service Institute Library, 1928

Freud, Sigmund
Library of Congress, 9

Friant, Julian N.
National Agricultural Library, 124

Frontier History
George Rogers Clark National Historical Park Library, 1638
Ft Davis National Historic Site Library, 1667

Grant-Kohrs Ranch National Historic Site Library, 1692
Homestead National Monument Library, 1702
Jefferson National Expansion Memorial Library, 1713

Fruits
Horticultural Research Laboratory Library, 74
Western Regional Research Center Library, 92

Fuels
Naval Air Propulsion Center, Technical Library, 1016
Redstone Scientific Information Center, 615
US Army Belvoir Research Development & Engineering Technical Library, 651

Fund Raising
Smithsonian Institution, Museum Reference Center, 2470

Fur Trade
Bent's Old Fort National Historic Site Library, 1607
Ft Laramie National Historic Site Library, 1670
Ft Union Trading Post National Historic Site Library, 1679
Ft Vancouver National Historic Site Library, 1680
Grand Portage National Monument Library, 1690
Knife River Indian Villages National Historic Site Library, 1721
Theodore Roosevelt National Park Library, 1777

Furniture
Martin Van Buren National Historic Site Library, 1805

Futures Research
Office of Technology Assessment Information Center, 11

Futures Trading
Commodity Futures Trading Commission Library, 1965

Garand Papers
Springfield Armory National Historic Site Library, 1796

Gardening
US National Arboretum Library, 91

Gardens
US Botanic Garden Library, 4

Gastroenterology
Veterans Administration Medical & Regional Office Center Library, 2291
Veterans Administration Medical Center Library Service, 2379

Genealogy

Ft Bragg Command Reference Center & Main Post Library, 447
Lincoln Boyhood National Memorial Library, 1729
Robinson Barracks, US Army Library, 878
Tennessee Valley Authority, Land Between The Lakes Library, 2100
USAREUR Library & Resource Center, 911

General Accounting Office

General Accounting Office, Office of Library Services, 5

Genetic Engineering

Environmental Protection Agency, Corvallis Environmental Research Library, 1971

Genetics

Brookhaven National Laboratory, Research Library, 1293
Roman L Hruska US Meat Animal Research Center Library, 75
NASA-AMES Research Center, Life Sciences Library, 2060
National Fishery Research & Development Laboratory Library, 1555
National Institute on Aging, Gerontology Research Center Library, 1343

Geochemistry

Bureau of Mines, Western Field Operations Center Library, 1543

Geodesy

Defense Mapping Agency, Aerospace Center Technical Library, 1268
Smithsonian Institution, Astrophysical Observatory Library, 2467
US Army Engineering Topographic Laboratories Scientific & Technical Information Center, 732

Geography

Lemoore Naval Air Station Library, 993
Library & Information Services Division, Camp Springs Center, 162
Zaragoza Base Library/FL 5571, 394

Geologic Hazards

Geological Survey Library, 1566

Geologic Maps

Geological Survey Library, 1566

Geological Survey

Department of Energy, Grand Junction Area Office, Technical Library, 1294
Geological Survey, Public Inquiries Office, 1573
Geological Survey, Public Inquiries Office Library, 1574
Geological Survey, Public Inquiries Office Library, 1575
Map Library & Information Service Library, 163
National Agricultural Library, 124

Geology

Arches National Park Library, 1601
Badlands National Park Library, 1605
Basalt Waste Isolation Project Library, 1290
Big Bend National Park Library, 1608
Bryce Canyon National Park Library, 1613
Bureau of Land Management, Elko District Office Library, 1484
Bureau of Land Management, Minerals Management Service Library, 1500
Bureau of Land Management, Montana State Office Library, 1502
Bureau of Mines, Charles W Henderson Memorial Library, 1533
Bureau of Mines Library, 1534
Bureau of Mines Library, 1536
Bureau of Mines, Western Field Operations Center Library, 1543
Capulin Mountain National Monument Library, 1623
Carlsbad Caverns & Guadalupe Mountains National Parks Headquarters Library, 1624
Cedar Breaks National Monument Library, 1629
Coulee Dam National Recreation Area Library, 1642
Crater Lake National Park Library, 1643
Craters of the Moon National Monument Library, 1644
John Day Fossil Beds National Monument Library, 1649
Delaware River Basin Commission Library, 2446
Department of Energy, Grand Junction Area Office, Technical Library, 1294
Devils Tower National Monument Library, 1655
Dinosaur National Monument Library, 1656
Fossil Butte National Monument Library, 1681
Geological Survey, Field Center Library, 1562
Geological Survey Library, 1565
Geological Survey Library, 1566
Geological Survey, Mineral Resources Library, 1569
Geological Survey, National Cartographic Information Center, 1570
Geological Survey, Public Inquiries Office, 1573
Geological Survey, Public Inquiries Office Library, 1574
Geological Survey, Public Inquiries Office Library, 1575
Geological Survey, Public Inquiries Office Library, 1576
Geological Survey, Water Resources Division Library, 1579
Geological Survey, Water Resources Division Library, 1581
Grand Canyon National Park Research Library, 1689
Grand Teton National Park Library, 1691
Haleakala National Park, Library, 1697
Hot Springs National Park Library, 1706
Indiana Dunes National Lakeshore Library, 1710
Lake Mead National Recreation Area Library, 1723
Morgantown Energy Technology Center, 1307
Mount Rainier National Park Library, 1739
NASA Lyndon B Johnson Space Center, Technical Library, 2066

National Museum of Natural History, Branch Library, 2462
National Park Service, Western Regional Resources Library, 1752
Nevada Technical Library, Department of Energy, 1311
Northwest Watershed Research Center, 78
Rocky Mountain National Park Library, 1775
Tuscaloosa Research Center Library, 1546
US Army Corps of Engineers, Buffalo District Technical Library, 661
US Army Corps of Engineers, Ft Worth District, Technical Library, 666
US Army Corps of Engineers, Mississippi River Commission Technical Library, 683
US Army Engineer Division, LMV, Technical Library, 729
US Geological Survey, Public Inquiries Office Library, 1583
Wind Cave National Park Library, 1814
Yosemite National Park Research Library, 1817

Geophysics

Air Force Geophysics Laboratory Research Library, 198
Air Weather Service Technical Library/FL 4414, 212
Department of Energy, Grand Junction Area Office, Technical Library, 1294
Geological Survey Library, 1565
Geological Survey Library, 1567
NASA Goddard Institute for Space Studies Library, 2063
National Air & Space Museum, Branch Library, 2457
NOAA, Mountain Administrative Support Center, 172
NOAA, Library & Information Services Division, 182
Smithsonian Institution, Astrophysical Observatory Library, 2467

Georgia

Environmental Protection Agency, Region 4 Library, 1988

Geotechnology

Bureau of Reclamation, Engineering & Research Center Library, 1547
US Army Corps of Engineers, South Pacific Division Technical Library, 722

Geothermal Energy

Bureau of Land Management, Elko District Office Library, 1484

Geothermal Information

Lower Colorado Regional Library, 1846

Geriatrics

National Institute on Aging, Gerontology Research Center Library, 1343
Veterans Administration Medical Center Learning Resources Center, 2299
Veterans Administration Medical Center Learning Resources Service, 2300
Veterans Administration Medical Center Library, 2317
Veterans Administration Medical Center Library-Learning Resources Center, 2322
Veterans Administration Medical Center Library Service, 2329

Veterans Administration Medical Center Library Service, 2334

Veterans Administration Medical Center Library Service, 2335

Veterans Administration Medical Center Library Service, 2338

Veterans Administration Medical Center Library Service, 2343

Veterans Administration Medical Center Library Service, 2347

Veterans Administration Medical Center Library Service, 2349

Veterans Administration Medical Center Library Service, 2371

Veterans Administration Medical Center Library Service, 2377

Veterans Administration Medical Center, Medical Library, 2390

Veterans Administration Medical Center, Medical Library, 2391

Veterans Administration Medical Center, Medical Library, 2394

Veterans Administration Medical Center, Medical Library, 2403

Veterans Administration Medical Center, Medical Library, 2406

Veterans Administration Medical Center, Medical Library, 2408

Veterans Administration Medical Center, Medical Library, 2409

Veterans Administration Medical Center, Medical & Patient's Library, 2414

Veterans Administration Medical Center, Medical & Patients' Library, 2417

Veterans Administration Medical Center, Medical & Patients' Library, 2422

Veterans Administration Medical Center, Medical & Patients' Library Wade Park & Brecksville Units, 2423

Veterans Administration Medical & Regional Office Center Library Service, 2433

Alvin C York Veterans Administration Medical Center, Library Service, 2443

German Air Force

US Air Force Historical Research Center, 334

German Construction

US Army Engineer Division Europe, Technical Library, 908

US Army Engineer Division Europe, Technical Library, 909

German History

US Army Library System, Norddeutschland, 922

Germany

US Army Library System, Norddeutschland, 922

Gerontology

National Institute on Aging, Gerontology Research Center Library, 1343

Social Security Administration, District of Columbia Branch Library, 1352

US Commission on Civil Rights, National Clearinghouse Library, 1962

Veterans Administration Medical Center Library, 2317

Veterans Administration Medical Center Library Service, 2339

Veterans Administration Medical Center Library Service, 2342

Veterans Administration Medical Center Library Service, 2349

Veterans Administration Medical Center Library Service, 2364

Veterans Administration Medical Center Library Service, 2370

Veterans Administration Medical Center Library Service, 2371

Veterans Administration Medical Center Library Service, 2379

Veterans Administration Medical Center, Medical Library, 2408

Veterans Administration Medical Center, Medical Library, 2409

Gettysburg Campaign

Gettysburg National Military Park Library, 1685

Gimbel, Richard

US Air Force Academy Library/FL 7000, 331

Glacier Bay

Glacier Bay National Park & Preserve Library, 1686

Glacier National Park

Glacier National Park, George C. Ruhle Library, 1687

Glen Canyon

Arches National Park Library, 1601

Glen Canyon National Recreation Area Library, 1688

Gold

Eielson AFB, Base Library/FL 5004, 240

Federal Reserve Bank of New York, Research Library, 2037

Ft Knox, Barr Memorial Library, 502

Gold Mining

Whiskeytown Unit Library, National Park Service, 1811

Gold Rush

Whiskeytown Unit Library, National Park Service, 1811

Golden Gate National Recreation Area

National Maritime Museum, J Porter Shaw Library, 1745

Goodpaster, Andrew J.

National Defense University Library, 1278

Government

Advisory Commission on Intergovernmental Relations Library, 2444

Consumer Product Safety Commission Library, 1966

Executive Office of the President Library, 64

Federal Reserve Bank of New York, Research Library, 2037

General Services Administration, National Capitol Regional Library, 2052

John F Kennedy Presidential Library, 2074

Library of Congress, 9

National Archives & Records Administration, Philadelphia Branch, 2076

National Archives & Records Center, Kansas City Branch, 2077

National Archives Library, 2078

Patuxent Naval Air Station Library, 1129

US Coast Guard Academy Library, 1942

US Information Agency Library, 2104

US Senate Library, 2

Government Contracts

Armed Services Board of Contract Appeals, Law Library, 1254

Army & Air Force Exchange Service, Law Library, 1255

Department of Justice Civil Library, 1850

Sharpe Army Depot, Law Library, 627

Southeastern Power Administration Library, 1315

US Army Engineer Division, Memphis District, Law Library, 730

US Court of Appeals for the Federal Circuit Library, 53

Government Procedure

Department of Energy, Office of General Counsel, Law Library, 1295

Department of Justice Civil Library, 1850

Government Procurement

Department of Commerce, Law Library, 131

Western Area Power Administration, Office of General Counsel, Law Library, 1317

Government Regulations

Administrative Conference of the United States, Library, 1958

Economic Development Administration, Seattle Regional Office Library, 146

US Army Corps of Engineers, Huntington District Law Library, 669

US Army Corps of Engineers, Kansas City District, Office of Counsel Law Library, 677

US Army Engineer Division, Memphis District, Law Library, 730

Government Specifications

Directorate of Medical Materiel Library, 1277

US Army Corps of Engineers, Ft Worth District, Technical Library, 666

Government Standards

Directorate of Medical Materiel Library, 1277

Grand Canyon

Grand Canyon National Park Research Library, 1689

Grand Teton National Park

Grand Teton National Park Library, 1691

Grant, Ulysses S.

Federal Hall National Memorial Library, 1661

Grantsmanship

Smithsonian Institution, Museum Reference Center, 2470

Olin E Teague Veterans Center, Library Service, 2282

Tripler Army Medical Center, Hospital Library, 635

Harry S Truman Memorial Veterans Hospital, Medical Library, 2283

James E Van Zandt Veterans Administration Medical Center, Medical Library, 2284

Veterans Administration Hospital, Health Sciences Library, 2287

Veterans Administration Lakeside Medical Center, Library Service, 2289

Veterans Administration Medical Center & Patients' Library, 2293

Veterans Administration Medical Center Learning Resource Center, 2297

Veterans Administration Medical Center Library, 2312

Veterans Administration Medical Center Library, 2317

Veterans Administration Medical Center Library Service, 2325

Veterans Administration Medical Center Library Service, 2326

Veterans Administration Medical Center Library Service, 2331

Veterans Administration Medical Center Library Service, 2333

Veterans Administration Medical Center Library Service, 2336

Veterans Administration Medical Center Library Service, 2340

Veterans Administration Medical Center Library Service, 2344

Veterans Administration Medical Center Library Service, 2345

Veterans Administration Medical Center Library Service, 2349

Veterans Administration Medical Center Library Service, 2352

Veterans Administration Medical Center Library Service, 2357

Veterans Administration Medical Center Library Service, 2366

Veterans Administration Medical Center Library Service, 2370

Veterans Administration Medical Center Library Service, 2371

Veterans Administration Medical Center Library Service, 2374

Veterans Administration Medical Center Library Service, 2375

Veterans Administration Medical Center Library Service, 2376

Veterans Administration Medical Center, Medical Library, 2386

Veterans Administration Medical Center, Medical Library, 2395

Veterans Administration Medical Center, Medical Library, 2396

Veterans Administration Medical Center, Medical Library, 2399

Veterans Administration Medical Center, Medical Library, Library Service, 2412

Veterans Administration Medical Center, Medical & Patient's Library, 2413

Veterans Administration Medical Center, Medical & Patient's Library, 2414

Veterans Administration Medical Center, Medical & Patients' Library, 2417

Veterans Administration Medical Center, Medical & Patients' Library, 2419

Veterans Administration Medical Center, Medical & Patients' Library Wade Park & Brecksville Units, 2423

Veterans Administration Medical Center Patients' Library, 2425

Veterans Administration Medical Center Patients' Library, 2426

Veterans Administration Medical & Regional Office Center Library Service, 2433

Veterans Administration Medical & Regional Office Center Medical Library, 2434

Veterans Administration Medical & Regional Office Center, Medical & Patients' Library, 2436

Veterans Administration Outpatient Clinic Library Service, 2439

Veterans Administration Patients' Library, 2440

Veterans Administration Westside Medical Center Library Service, 2442

Health Statistics

Parklawn Health Library, Prince George's Center Branch, 1351

Helicopters

Corpus Christi Army Depot, Reference & Research Library, 425

Hematology

Letterman Army Institute of Research, Medical Research Library, 586

Veterans Administration Medical & Regional Office Center Library, 2291

Hemingway, Ernest

John F Kennedy Presidential Library, 2074

Hemodialysis

Veterans Administration Medical Center, Health Sciences Library, 2294

Heraldry

The Institute of Heraldry Library, 583

Herbert, Victor

Library of Congress, 9

Hessian Transcripts

Morristown National Historical Park Library, 1737

Hides

USDA, Agricultural Research Service, Eastern Regional Research Center Library, 84

Highland Scots

Moores Creek National Military Park Library, 1736

Highway Maps

Map Library & Information Service Library, 163

Highway Safety

National Highway Traffic Safety Administration, Technical Reference Division, Library, 1940

Highways and Roads

Bureau of Land Management, Roseburg District Office Library, 1514

Department of Transportation Library, 1931

Engineering Technical Information Center, 101

Engineering Technical Information Center, Forest Service, 102

Hispanic Literature

White Sands Missile Range, Post Library, 805

Hispanics

Defense Equal Opportunity Management Institute Library, 1259

Kelly AFB, Base Library/FL 2050, 272

US Commission on Civil Rights, National Clearinghouse Library, 1962

Historic Preservation

Historic American Buildings Survey Library, 1585

National Park Service, Central Compliance Library, 1746

National Register of Historic Places Library, 1589

History

Aberdeen Proving Ground, Ordnance Center & School Library, 398

Armed Forces Staff College Library, 1253

Buffalo National River Library, 1615

Cabrillo National Monument Library, 1616

Carlsbad Caverns & Guadalupe Mountains National Parks Headquarters Library, 1624

Christiansted National Historic Site Library, 1637

Department of Justice Main Library, 1854

Effigy Mounds National Monument Library, 1658

Fossil Butte National Monument Library, 1681

General Accounting Office, Office of Library Services, 5

Hot Springs National Park Library, 1706

Lemoore Naval Air Station Library, 993

Library of Congress, 9

March AFB, Base Library/FL 4664, 287

National Museum of American Art & National Portrait Gallery Library, 2460

National Park Service, Midwest Archeological Center Library, 1748

National Park Service, Western Regional Resources Library, 1752

Naval War College Library, 1095

Pecos National Monument Library, 1763

Philadelphia Naval Hospital, Medical & General Libraries, 1135

Salem Maritime National Historic Site Library, 1783

US Senate Library, 2

Hitchcock-Chase Collection

National Museum of Natural History, Branch Library, 2462

Hobbies

Cubi Point Naval Air Station Library, 1182

Yakima Firing Center, Field Library, 808

Holmes, Oliver Wendell

Library of Congress, 9

Geological Survey, Gerryan Memorial Library, 1563
Geological Survey Library, 1568
Geological Survey, Water Resources Division Library, 1582
NOAA, Great Lakes Environmental Research Laboratory Library, 170
National Weather Service, Central Region Library, 179
National Weather Service, Southern Region Headquarters Library, 180
Nevada Technical Library, Department of Energy, 1311
Northwest Watershed Research Center, 78
US Army Cold Region Research & Engineering Laboratory Library, 656
US Army Corps of Engineers, Buffalo District Technical Library, 661
US Army Corps of Engineers, Ft Worth District, Technical Library, 666
US Army Corps of Engineers, Hydrologic Engineering Center Library, 673
US Army Corps of Engineers, Nashville District Technical Library, 687
US Army Corps of Engineers, New England Division Technical Library, 689
US Army Corps of Engineers, New Orleans District Technical Library, 691
US Army Corps of Engineers, Sacramento District Technical Library, 712
US Army Corps of Engineers, South Pacific Division Technical Library, 722

Hydropower

US Army Corps of Engineers, New England Division Technical Library, 689

Hyperbaric Medicine

Bethesda Naval Medical Research Institute, Information Services Branch, 954

Iceland

US Naval Air Station Library, 1196

Icks, Robert J.

Ft Knox, Emert L Davis Memorial Library, 504

Idaho

Bureau of Land Management, Idaho State Office Library, 1489
Bureau of Mines, Western Field Operations Center Library, 1543
Geological Survey, Public Inquiries Office Library, 1575
Pacific Northwest Regional Library System, 1760

Idaho History

Mountain Home AFB, Base Library/FL 4897, 299

Idaho Law

Economic Development Administration, Seattle Regional Office Library, 146

Ikebana

US National Arboretum Library, 91

Illinois

Indiana Dunes National Lakeshore Library, 1710
St Louis Area Support Center, Recreational Library, 620

Immigration

American Museum of Immigration Library, 1596
Board of Immigration Appeals Library, 1910
Camp Humphreys Legal Center, 817
Foreign Service Institute Library, 1928
Ft Laramie National Historic Site Library, 1670
Immigration & Naturalization Law Library, 1911
Immigration & Naturalization Service Library, 1912
Immigration & Naturalization Service, General Counsel's Library, 1913

Immunology

Bethesda Naval Medical Research Institute, Information Services Branch, 954
National Animal Disease Center Library, 76
Plum Island Animal Disease Center Library, 79
Rocky Mountain Laboratory Library, 1347

Imports

Department of Commerce, District Office Library, 128
US Court of International Trade Library, 60
US Customs Service, New York Region, Library, 1955
US International Trade Commission, Law Library, 2269

Income

Bureau of the Census, Dallas Regional Office Library, 138
Internal Revenue Service, Central Region, Freedom of Information Public Reading Room, 1951

Income Distribution

Social Security Administration, District of Columbia Branch Library, 1352

Independence Hall Association

Independence National Historic Park Library, 1709

Indian Affairs, Bureau of

National Archives & Records Administration, Fort Worth Branch, 2075

Indian Wars

Ft Laramie National Historic Site Library, 1670
Presidio Army Museum Library, 607

Indiana Dunes

Indiana Dunes National Lakeshore Library, 1710

Indiana History

Indiana Dunes National Lakeshore Library, 1710
Lincoln Boyhood National Memorial Library, 1729

Industrial Design

Cooper-Hewitt Museum Library, 2454

Industrial Engineering

Long Beach Naval Shipyard, Technical Library, 995
Redstone Scientific Information Center, 615

Industrial Mobilization

National Defense University Library, 1278

Industrial Pollution

Environmental Protection Agency, National Enforcement Investigation Center, Information Center, 1980

Industrial Psychology

Navy Personnel Research & Development Center, Technical Library, 1110

Industrial Relations

Bureau of Labor Statistics Library, 1920
Department of Labor Library, 1919

Industrial Waste

USDA, Agricultural Research Service, Eastern Regional Research Center Library, 84

Industry

Bureau of Labor Statistics, Regional Office, Reference Library, 1921
Consumer Product Safety Commission Library, 1966
Defense Industrial Supply, Technical Data Repository, 1261
Department of Commerce, District Office Library, 128
Department of Justice Antitrust Library, 1849
Industry & Trade Administration Library, 147
National Defense University Library, 1278
US Army Corps of Engineers, Ft Worth District, Technical Library, 666
US Army Corps of Engineers, St Paul District Technical Library, 714
White Sands Missile Range, Technical Library, 806

Industry Standards

Defense Logistics Agency Headquarters Library, 1267

Infantry

US Army Infantry School, Donovan Technical Library, 740

Infectious Diseases

Bethesda Naval Medical Research Institute, Information Services Branch, 954
Medical Research Institute for Infectious Diseases Library, 597
US Army Medical Research Institute of Infectious Diseases Library, 756

Information Management

Defense Personnel Support Center, Directorate of Medical Material Library, 1272

Information Science

Air Force Engineering & Services Center Technical Library/FL 7050, 196
National Commission on Libraries & Information Science, Library/Information Center, 2450
National Science Foundation Library, 2085
Rome Air Development Center Technical Library/FL 2810, 315
US Army & Air Force Exchange Service, Central Library, 1283
US Department of Education, Office of Educational Research & Improvement Library, 1286

Information Technology

General Accounting Office, Office of Library Services, 5

Inorganic Chemistry

Brookhaven National Laboratory, Research Library, 1293
Geological Survey, National Water Quality Laboratory-Library, 1572
National Institute on Aging, Gerontology Research Center Library, 1343

Insect Repellents

Letterman Army Institute of Research, Medical Research Library, 586

Insignia

The Institute of Heraldry Library, 583

Institute of Aeronautical Sciences

National Air & Space Museum, Branch Library, 2457

Instrumentation

Geological Survey, National Water Quality Laboratory-Library, 1572
NASA Dryden Flight Research Center Library, 2062

Intellectual Property

Department of Justice Civil Library, 1850

Intelligence

Central Intelligence Agency, Law Library, 1960
Central Intelligence Agency Library, 1961

Inter-American Tropical Tuna Commission

Southwest Fisheries Center Library, 188

Interest Rates

Federal Home Loan Bank of Chicago Library, 2015

Intergovernmental Relations

Advisory Commission on Intergovernmental Relations Library, 2444

Interior Department

Bureau of Land Management, Arizona State Office Library, 1466
Bureau of Land Management, New Mexico State Office Central Files/Library, 1504
Department of the Interior, Center for Information & Library Services, Natural Resources Library, Law Branch, 1822

Department of the Interior, Office of the Regional Solicitor, Law Library, 1825
Department of the Interior, Office of the Regional Solicitor, Law Library, 1826
Department of the Interior, Office of the Regional Solicitor, Law Library, 1827

Internal Medicine

Veterans Administration Medical Center Library Service, 2352
Veterans Administration Medical Center Library Service, 2359

Internal Revenue Codes

US Tax Court Library, 62

Internal Revenue Service

Internal Revenue Service, Central Region, Freedom of Information Public Reading Room, 1951
Internal Revenue Service Library, 1952

International Affairs

Armed Forces Staff College Library, 1253
Army Materiel Command Headquarters, Technical Library, 408
Base Library/FL 5531, 355
Base Library/FL 5670, 360
Bergstrom AFB, Base Library/FL 4857, 221
Combined Arms Research Library, 422
Defense Institute of Security Assistance Management Library, 1262
Defense Institute of Security Assistance Management Library/FL 2301, 235
Department of State Library, 1927
El Toro Marine Corps Air Station Library, 1233
Fairchild AFB, Base Library/FL 4620, 247
Fleet Intelligence Center, Europe & Atlantic, Library, 980
Gerald R Ford Library, 2072
Foreign Service Institute Library, 1928
Ft Bragg Command Reference Center & Main Post Library, 447
Ft McPherson, Staff Judge Advocate, 3rd US Army Law Library, 528
Ft George G Meade, Language Training Facility Library, 533
Holloman AFB, Base Library/FL 4801, 264
Langley AFB, Base Library/FL 4800, 277
Library of Congress, 9
Luke AFB, Base Library/FL 4887, 283
March AFB, Base Library/FL 4664, 287
Mather AFB, Base Library/FL 3067, 288
Mildenhall Base Library/FL 5518, 379
Mountain Home AFB, Base Library/FL 4897, 299
National Defense University Library, 1278
Naval Amphibious School Library, 1021
Naval Postgraduate School, Dudley Knox Library, 1062
Navy Department Library, 1106
Office of International Cooperation & Development (OICD), Technical Inquiries, 127
Overseas Private Investment Corporation Library, 2266
Patch Barracks, US Army Library, 875
Patuxent Naval Air Station Library, 1129
Peace Corps Information Services, Division Library, 2090
Pentagon Library, 605
Ramstein Library/FL 5612, 382
US Agency for International Development Water & Sanitation for Health Project Information Center, 2268

US Arms Control & Disarmament Agency Library, 2103
USAREUR Library & Resource Center, 911
US Army John F Kennedy Special Warfare Center, Marquat Memorial Library, 747
US Army War College Library, 790
US Information Agency Library, 2104

International Atomic Energy Agency

Brookhaven National Laboratory, Nuclear Safeguards Library, 1292
Energy Library, 1298
Nuclear Regulatory Commission Library, 2087

International Censuses

Bureau of the Census Library, 143

International Council for the Exploration of the Sea

Woods Hole Laboratory Library, 192

International Law

Department of Commerce, Law Library, 131
Department of State Library, 1927
Naval War College Library, 1095
21st Support Command, Office of Staff Judge Advocate, Law Library, 899
US International Trade Commission, Law Library, 2269

International Standards

National Center for Standards & Certification Information, 156

International Statistics

Bureau of the Census Library, 143

International Studies

Defense Institute of Security Assistance Management Library/FL 2301, 235
Defense Intelligence Agency Library, 1263

International Trade

Department of Commerce, District Office Library, 128
Department of Commerce, Law Library, 131
Department of Commerce, Miami District Office Library, 133
International Trade Administration, Chicago Field Office Library, 148
International Trade Administration District Office, US & FCS Commercial Library, 149
International Trade Administration, International Marketing Center Library, 150
International Trade Administration Library, 151
International Trade Administration Library, 152
International Trade Administration Library, 153
International Trade Administration, Richmond District Office Library, 154
US Court of International Trade Library, 60
US Customs Service, Library & Information Center, 1954
US Customs Service, New York Region, Library, 1955

US Customs Service, Southwest Region, Library & Information Center, 1957

US International Trade Commission, Law Library, 2269

US International Trade Commission Main Library, 2270

International Trade Administration
International Trade Administration District Office, US & FCS Commercial Library, 149

International Whaling Commission
National Marine Mammal Library, 168

Interstate Commerce Act
Interstate Commerce Commission, Regional Library, 2054

Investments
Ft Bliss, Center Library, 445

Iowa
Effigy Mounds National Monument Library, 1658

Iowa History
Effigy Mounds National Monument Library, 1658

Iron Manufacture
Hopewell Furnace National Historic Site Library, 1704

Saugus Iron Works National Historic Site Library, 1789

Iron Works Association
Saugus Iron Works National Historic Site Library, 1789

Irrigation
Lower Colorado Regional Library, 1846

USDA, Agricultural Research Service, Snake River Conservation Research Service, 85

USDA, Agricultural Research Service, Water Conservation Research Library, 86

Water & Power Resources Service, Regional Library, 1847

Islamic Law
Ft McPherson, Staff Judge Advocate, 3rd US Army Law Library, 528

Islands
Cape Lookout National Seashore Library, 1621

Isle Royale National Park
Isle Royale National Park Library, 1711

Italian Language
Camp Darby Post Library, 815

Italian Law
US Army Southern European Task Force & 5th Support Command, Army Law Library, 928

Italy
Base Library/FL 5517, 354

US Navy Support Office Library, 1225

Jackson Aviation Collection
US Army Aviation Center Library, 646

Jacksonian Era
Martin Van Buren National Historic Site Library, 1805

Jamestown
Colonial National Historic Park Library, 1639

Jane's Fighting Ships
Great Lakes Naval Training Station Center Library, 985

Japan
COMFLEACT Library, 1180

Kadena AFB, Base Library/FL 5270, 373

Kami Seya Station Library, 1186

Misawa Base, Overstreet Memorial Library/FL 5205, 380

Torii Station Library, DPCA, MSAD, 897

Zama Library, 943

Japanese Flower Arrangement
National Agricultural Library, 124

Jefferson, Thomas
Library of Congress, 9

Mall Operation Library, 1730

Jesuits
Islesford Historic Museum Library, 1712

Jewel Cave
Jewel Cave National Monument Library, 1714

Jewish Americans
Defense Equal Opportunity Management Institute Library, 1259

John Day Basin
John Day Fossil Beds National Monument Library, 1649

Johnson, Addision
FAA Technical Library, 1936

Johnson, Andrew
Andrew Johnson National Historic Site Library, 1715

Johnson, Lyndon B.
Lyndon B Johnson National Historical Park Library, 1716

Johnstown Flood
Allegheny Portage Railroad National Historic Site Library, 1595

Joint Committee on Atomic Energy
Energy Library, 1298

Jones Collection
Abraham Lincoln Birthplace National Historic Site Library, 1728

Justice Department
Department of Justice Main Library, 1854

Justice Statistics, Bureau of
National Institute of Justice Library, 1856

Juvenile Justice
National Institute of Justice Library, 1856

National Institute of Justice/National Criminal Justice Reference Service, 1857

Juvenile Justice and Delinquency Prevention, Office of
National Institute of Justice Library, 1856

Kansas
McConnell AFB, Base Library/FL 4621, 293

Katmai National Park and Preserve
Katmai National Park & Preserve Library, 1718

Kayenta Indians
Wupatki National Monument Library, 1815

Kellog, Charles E.
National Agricultural Library, 124

Kennedy, John F.
John F Kennedy Presidential Library, 2074

Kennesaw Battlefield
Kennesaw Mountain National Battlefield Park Library, 1719

Kentucky
Environmental Protection Agency, Region 4 Library, 1988

Kentucky History
Abraham Lincoln Birthplace National Historic Site Library, 1728

Kentucky Law
US Army Corps of Engineers, Huntington District Law Library, 669

Kings Canyon
Sequoia & Kings Canyon National Park Library, 1791

Kings Mountain, Battle of
Kings Mountain National Military Park Library, 1720

Korea
HQ 23rd Support Group, Army Library, 851

Misawa Base, Overstreet Memorial Library/FL 5205, 380

Suwon Base Library/FL 5261, 386

Yongsan Library, 942

Korean Language
Camp Red Cloud Army Library, 821
HQ 23rd Support Group, Army Library, 851

Korean War
Presidio Army Museum Library, 607

Kraus, Hans P.
Library of Congress, 9

Krug, Julius A.
National Defense University Library, 1278

Kunz Collection
Geological Survey Library, 1564

Labor
Bureau of Labor Statistics, Regional Office, Reference Library, 1921
Department of Labor Library, 1919
Federal Reserve Bank of Dallas Library, 2032

Labor History
National Labor Relations Board Library, 2084

Labor Law
Equal Employment Opportunity Commission, New Orleans District Office Library, 2001
Federal Labor Relations Authority, Region 5 Library, 2023
Ft Leonard Wood, Office of the Staff Judge Advocate, Army Field Law Library, 568
National Labor Relations Board Library, 2084
Sharpe Army Depot, Law Library, 627
US Army Corps of Engineers, Kansas City District, Office of Counsel Law Library, 677
US Army Corps of Engineers, South Atlantic Division Law Library, 719
US Army Engineer Division, Memphis District, Law Library, 730

Labor Relations
Bureau of Labor Statistics Library, 1920
Bureau of Labor Statistics, Regional Office, Reference Library, 1921
Federal Labor Relations Authority Law Library, 2021
Federal Labor Relations Authority, Region 2 Library, 2022
Federal Labor Relations Authority, Region 5 Library, 2023
National Labor Relations Board Library, 2084

Labor Statistics
Bureau of Labor Statistics Library, 1920
Bureau of Labor Statistics, Regional Office, Reference Library, 1922

Labor Statistics, Bureau of
Bureau of Labor Statistics, Regional Office, Reference Library, 1921

Labor Unions
Department of Labor Library, 1919

Laboratory Medicine
Centers for Disease Control Library, 1327

Lafitte, Jean
Jean Lafitte National Historical Park Library, 1722

Lahm-Chandler Collection
Wright-Patterson AFB, Technical Library/FL 2802, 345

Lake Erie, Battle of
Perry's Victory & International Peace Memorial Library, 1764

Lake Mead
Lake Mead National Recreation Area Library, 1723

Lake Meredith
Lake Meredith Recreation Area Library, 1724

Lake Roosevelt
Coulee Dam National Recreation Area Library, 1642

Lake Superior
Pictured Rocks National Lakeshore Library, 1767

Lakes
Geological Survey, Water Resources Division Library, 1579

Lakota Indians
Crazy Horse School Library-Media Center, 1388

Land Acquisition
Department of Justice Lands Library, 1853

Land Between The Lakes
Tennessee Valley Authority, Land Between The Lakes Library, 2100

Land Claims
Department of the Interior, Center for Information & Library Services, Natural Resources Library, Law Branch, 1820
Department of the Interior, Office of the Solicitor, Law Library, 1841

Land Law
Bureau of Land Management, Fairbanks District Office Library, 1486
Department of the Interior, Office of the Regional Solicitor, Law Library, 1825
Department of the Interior, Office of the Regional Solicitor, Law Library, 1826
Department of the Interior, Office of the Regional Solicitor, Law Library, 1827

Land Management, Bureau of
Bureau of Land Management, Fairbanks District Office Library, 1486

Land Use
Bureau of Land Management, Arizona State Office Library, 1466
Bureau of Land Management, Arizona Strip, District Office Library, 1467

Bureau of Land Management, Bakersfield District Office Library, 1469
Bureau of Land Management, Bishop Resource Area Headquarters Library, 1470
Bureau of Land Management, Branch of Records & Data Management, 1471
Bureau of Land Management, California State Office Library, 1473
Bureau of Land Management, Cedar City District Library, 1474
Bureau of Land Management, Coeur D'Alene District Office Library, 1475
Bureau of Land Management, Colorado State Office Library, 1476
Bureau of Land Management, Colorado State Office Library, 1477
Bureau of Land Management, Coos Bay District Office Library, 1478
Bureau of Land Management, Craig District Office Library, 1479
Bureau of Land Management, District Library, 1480
Bureau of Land Management, District Office Library, 1481
Bureau of Land Management, District Office Library, 1482
Bureau of Land Management, Eastern States Office Library, 1483
Bureau of Land Management, Elko District Office Library, 1484
Bureau of Land Management, Eugene Office Library, 1485
Bureau of Land Management, Fairbanks District Office Library, 1486
Bureau of Land Management, Folsom District Office Library, 1487
Bureau of Land Management, Garnet Resource Area Library, 1488
Bureau of Land Management, Idaho State Office Library, 1489
Bureau of Land Management, Kanab Office Library, 1490
Bureau of Land Management, Lake States Office Library, 1491
Bureau of Land Management, Lakeview District Office Library, 1492
Bureau of Land Management, Las Cruces District Office Library, 1493
Bureau of Land Management, Las Vegas District Office Library, 1494
Bureau of Land Management Library, 1495
Bureau of Land Management Library, 1496
Bureau of Land Management Library, 1498
Bureau of Land Management, Medford District Office Library, 1499
Bureau of Land Management, Minerals Management Service Library, 1501
Bureau of Land Management, Montrose District Office Library, 1503
Bureau of Land Management, New Mexico State Office Central Files/Library, 1504
Bureau of Land Management, New Mexico State Office Library, 1505
Bureau of Land Management, Phillips Resource Area Office Library, 1507
Bureau of Land Management, Phoenix District Office Library, 1508
Bureau of Land Management, Prineville District Office Library, 1509
Bureau of Land Management, Rawlins District Office Library, 1510
Bureau of Land Management, Research Library, 1511
Bureau of Land Management, Richfield Office Library, 1512
Bureau of Land Management, Riverside District Office Library, 1513
Bureau of Land Management, Roswell District Office Library, 1515

Bureau of Land Management, Salem District Office Library, 1517

Bureau of Land Management, Salmon District Office Library, 1518

Bureau of Land Management, Salt Lake City District Office Library, 1519

Bureau of Land Management, San Rafael-Price River Resource Area Library, 1520

Bureau of Land Management, Shoshone District Library, 1521

Bureau of Land Management, Spokane District Office Library, 1522

Bureau of Land Management, Susanville District Office Library, 1523

Bureau of Land Management, Ukiah District Office Library, 1524

Bureau of Land Management, Utah State Office Library, 1525

Bureau of Land Management, Vernal District Office Library, 1526

Bureau of Land Management, Worland District Office Library, 1527

Bureau of Land Management, Wyoming State Office Library, 1528

Bureau of Land Management, Yuma District Office Library, 1529

Department of the Interior, Center for Information & Library Services, Natural Resources Library, Law Branch, 1820

Department of the Interior, Center for Information & Library Services, Natural Resources Library, 1821

Department of the Interior, Office of the Solicitor, Intermountain Region, Library, 1840

Environmental Protection Agency, Robert S Kerr Library, 1975

Environmental Protection Agency, Region 4 Library, 1988

Heritage Conservation & Recreation Service, Northwest Region Office Library, 1584

Mid-Continent Region Library, 1588

National Park Service, Southeast Regional Office Library, 1750

WESTFORNET/FS-INFO Intermountain Research Station, 122

Landauer, Bella

National Air & Space Museum, Branch Library, 2457

Language Instruction

Defense Language Institute, Learning Resource Center, 1265

Foreign Service Institute Library, 1928

Ft Hood, Language Training Facility Library, 480

Ft George G Meade, Language Training Facility Library, 533

Gunter AFB, Base Library/FL 3370, 256

Peace Corps Information Services, Division Library, 2090

Languages

Ft Gordon, Morale Support Activities Library Branch, Patients' Library, 470

Ft George G Meade, Language Training Facility Library, 533

Ft George G Meade, Post Library, 535

Ft Leonard Wood Post Library, 569

Goodfellow AFB, Base Library/FL 3030, 250

Library of Congress, 9

National Security Agency, Central Security Service Libraries, 1279

US Army Library System, Norddeutschland, 922

Large Print Books

Bolling AFB, Base Library/FL 4400, 224

Parris Island, Marine Corps Recruit Depot Station Library, 1242

Harry S Truman Memorial Veterans Hospital, Medical Library, 2283

Veterans Administration Medical Center Library Service, 2356

Veterans Administration Medical Center Library Service, 2357

Lasers

Air Force Weapons Laboratory Technical Library/FL 2809, 209

Bureau of Radiological Health Library, 1329

Letterman Army Institute of Research, Medical Research Library, 586

US Army Strategic Defense Command, Huntsville, Library, 781

Latin America

Peace Corps Information Services, Division Library, 2090

Lava Beds

Lava Beds National Monument Library, 1726

Law

Bonneville Power Administration Library, 1291

Bureau of Land Management, Phoenix District Office Library, 1508

Bureau of Land Management, Utah State Office Library, 1525

Camp Humphreys Legal Center, 817

Coast Guard Law Library, 1941

Command Judge Advocate, Army Law Library, 822

Consumer Product Safety Commission Library, 1966

Department of Commerce, Law Library, 131

HUD, Region 1 Library, 1355

Department of Justice Antitrust Library, 1849

Department of Justice Civil Rights Library, 1851

Department of Justice Criminal Library, 1852

Department of Justice Lands Library, 1853

Department of Justice Main Library, 1854

Department of State Law Library, 1926

Department of the Interior, Office of the Regional Solicitor, Law Library, 1824

Department of the Interior, Office of the Regional Solicitor, Law Library, 1825

Department of the Interior, Office of the Regional Solicitor, Law Library, 1826

Department of the Interior, Office of the Regional Solicitor, Law Library, 1827

Department of the Interior, Office of the Solicitor, Field Solicitor, Law Library, 1836

Department of Transportation Law Library, 1930

Department of Transportation Library, 1931

Environmental Protection Agency, Region 3 Library, 1987

Environmental Protection Agency, Region 6 Library, 1990

Equal Employment Opportunity Commission, Charlotte District Office, Law Library, 1996

Equal Employment Opportunity Commission, Cleveland District Office Library, 1997

Equal Employment Opportunity Commission, Houston District Office, Law Library, 1998

Equal Employment Opportunity Commission Library, 1999

Farm Credit Administration Library, 2003

Federal Election Commission, Law Library, 2008

Federal Energy Regulatory Commission Library, 1318

Federal Law Enforcement Training Center Library, 1950

Federal Trade Commission, Law Library, 2046

Federal Trade Commission Library, 2048

1st Infantry Division Forward, Office of the Judge Advocate, Army Law Library, 834

Ft Hood, Office of the Staff Judge Advocate, HQ III Corps & Ft Hood, Army Law Library, 482

Ft Sam Houston, Office of the Staff Judge Advocate, Army Law Library, 488

Ft Leonard Wood, Office of the Staff Judge Advocate, Army Field Law Library, 568

General Accounting Office, Office of Library Services, 5

General Services Administration Library, 2051

HQ, US Army Japan/9th Corps, Office of the Staff Judge Advocate, Army Field Law Library, 853

Health & Human Services Department Library, 1320

Internal Revenue Service, Office of Chief Counsel, Library, 1953

Karlsruhe Legal Center, US Army Law Library, 858

Library of Congress, 9

Mannheim Law Center, US Army Law Library, 865

Maxwell AFB, Federal Prison Camp Library, 1879

Miami Metropolitan Correctional Center, Inmate Law Library, 1881

Milan Federal Correctional Institution Library, 1882

National Archives & Records Administration, Fort Worth Branch, 2075

National Archives & Records Administration, Philadelphia Branch, 2076

Office of the General Counsel Law Library, Department of Agriculture, 126

Patent & Trademark Office, Law Library, 193

Pension Benefit Guaranty Corporation, Legal Department, Law Library, 2092

Pentagon Law Library, 604

Pentagon Library, 605

Southeastern Power Administration Library, 1315

10A Services Branch Library, 1933

21st Support Command, Office of Staff Judge Advocate, Law Library, 899

US Army Corps of Engineers, Baltimore District Library Branch, 660

US Army Corps of Engineers, Galveston District Technical Library, 667

US Army Corps of Engineers, Huntington District Law Library, 669

US Army Corps of Engineers, Mississippi River Commission Technical Library, 683

US Army Corps of Engineers, Missouri River Division, Omaha District Technical Library, 684

US Army Corps of Engineers, Walla Walla District Technical & Law Library, 725

US Army Engineer Division Europe, Technical Library, 909

US Army Southern European Task Force & 5th Support Command, Army Law Library, 928

US Commission on Civil Rights, National Clearinghouse Library, 1962

US Court of Appeals First Circuit Library, 18

US Court of Appeals for the 5th Circuit Library, 23

US Court of Appeals for the Federal Circuit Library, 53

US Court of Military Appeals Library, 61

US Customs Service, Library & Information Center, 1954

US Customs Service, New York Region, Library, 1955

US District Court Eastern District of New York Library, 54

US Securities & Exchange Commission Library, 2096

US Courts Branch Library, 52

Western Area Power Administration, Office of General Counsel, Law Library, 1317

White House Law Library, 65

Law Enforcement

Horace M Albright Training Center Library, 1594

FBI Academy Library, 1908

Federal Law Enforcement Training Center Library, 1949

Federal Law Enforcement Training Center Library, 1950

National Institute of Justice Library, 1856

National Institute of Justice/National Criminal Justice Reference Service, 1857

Seneca Post Library, 625

US Army Military Police School, Ramsey Library, 759

US Customs Service, Library & Information Center, 1954

Leadership

Air Force Officer Training School Library/FL 3050, 205

Ft Bliss, Valent Learning Resources Center Library, 446

Naval Amphibious School Library, 1021

Naval Amphibious School, John Sidney McCain, Jr Amphibious Warfare Library, 1022

Naval Education & Training Center, Main Library, 1035

US Army Transportation & Aviation Logistics Schools, Information Center, 788

Leather Products

USDA, Agricultural Research Service, Eastern Regional Research Center Library, 84

US International Trade Commission Main Library, 2270

Lee, Robert E.

Arlington House, The Robert E Lee Memorial Library, 1602

Legislation

Bureau of the Census Library, 143

Command Judge Advocate, Army Law Library, 822

Executive Office of the President Library, 64

General Accounting Office, Office of Library Services, 5

Health & Human Services Department Library, 1320

Library of Congress, 9

US Court of Appeals First Circuit Library, 18

US Senate Library, 2

US Tax Court Library, 62

Legislative Histories

Department of Justice Civil Library, 1850

Department of Justice Main Library, 1854

Department of Justice Tax Library, 1855

Department of Transportation Law Library, 1930

FCC Library, 2005

Federal Energy Regulatory Commission Library, 1318

Lemnitzer, Lyman L.

National Defense University Library, 1278

Lewis and Clark Expedition

Ft Clatsop National Memorial Library, 1666

Lewis, Edwin

Independence National Historic Park Library, 1709

Lewis, Ralph H.

Harpers Ferry Center Library, 1699

Library Science

Library of Congress, 9

National Commission on Libraries & Information Science, Library/Information Center, 2450

US Department of Education, Office of Educational Research & Improvement Library, 1286

Life Savings Services

Cape Cod National Seashore Library, 1619

Limnology

NOAA, Great Lakes Environmental Research Laboratory Library, 170

Lin, Maya

Library of Congress, 9

Lincoln, Abraham

Ford's Theatre National Historic Site Library, 1664

Abraham Lincoln Birthplace National Historic Site Library, 1728

Lincoln Boyhood National Memorial Library, 1729

Mall Operation Library, 1730

Lincoln Family

Abraham Lincoln Birthplace National Historic Site Library, 1728

Lincoln Farm Association

Abraham Lincoln Birthplace National Historic Site Library, 1728

Lincoln, Thomas

Abraham Lincoln Birthplace National Historic Site Library, 1728

Linguistics

Foreign Service Institute Library, 1928

Linneaeus, Carl

National Agricultural Library, 124

Literature

Library of Congress, 9

Naval Weapons Station, MenRiv Library, 1099

US Army Russian Institute, Research Library, 927

White Sands Missile Range, Post Library, 805

Litigation

Mainz Detachment, Office of the Staff Judge Advocate, Law Library, 863

Little Bighorn, Battle of

Custer Battlefield National Monument Library, 1647

Livestock

Bureau of Land Management, District Office Library, 1481

Local History

Bureau of Land Management, Elko District Office Library, 1484

Cape Cod National Seashore Library, 1619

Curecanti National Recreation Area Library, 1646

Dinosaur National Monument Library, 1656

Ft Bragg Command Reference Center & Main Post Library, 447

Library of Congress, 9

National Defense University Library, 1278

Timpanogos Cave National Monument Library, 1799

USAREUR Library & Resource Center, 911

US Army Transportation Center, Groninger Library, 789

Veterans Administration Medical Center Library Service, 2348

Logistics

Air Force Institute of Technology Academic Library/FL 3319, 200

Air Force Logistics Management Center, Technical Library, 202

Wright-Patterson AFB, Area A Technical Library, 346

Loosanoff, V. L.

Tiburon Laboratory Library, 190

Lothrop, Harriett M.

Minute Man National Historical Park Library, 1734

Louisiana

Barksdale AFB, Base Library/FL 4608, 219

Louisiana History

Ft Polk, Morale Support Activities Library, 543

Jean Lafitte National Historical Park Library, 1722

Louisiana Law

Ft Polk, Office of the Staff Judge Advocate, HQ, 5th Infantry Division (Mech), Law Library, 544

National Archives & Records Administration, Fort Worth Branch, 2075

US Court of Appeals for the 5th Circuit Library, 23

Lung Diseases

Appalachian Laboratory for Occupational Safety & Health Library, 1325

Machinery

Hull, Machinery & Electrical Technical Library, 987

US International Trade Commission Main Library, 2270

Magnetism

US Naval Academy, Nimitz Library, 1169

Maine History

Islesford Historic Museum Library, 1712
Loring AFB, Base Library/FL 4678, 281

Maine Law

US Court of Appeals First Circuit Library, 18

Mammals

Badlands National Park Library, 1605
Carlsbad Caverns & Guadalupe Mountains National Parks Headquarters Library, 1624

Marine Mammal Commission Library, 2449

National Marine Mammal Library, 168

Mammoth Cave

Mammoth Cave National Park Library, 1731

Management

Aberdeen Proving Ground, Ordnance Center & School Library, 398

Air Force Accounting & Finance Center Library/FL 7040, 195

Air Force Institute of Technology Library, 201

Air Force Officer Training School Library/FL 3050, 205

Air Force Systems Command Technical Information Center, 208

Armament Division Technical Library/FL 2825, 217

Armed Forces Staff College Library, 1253
Army Materiel Command Headquarters, Technical Library, 408

Base Library/FL 5531, 355

Base Library/FL 5670, 360
Bureau of Land Management, Roseburg District Office Library, 1514

Chanute AFB, Base Library/FL 3018, 231
COMFLEACT Library, 1180
Consumer Product Safety Commission Library, 1967

Corpus Christi Army Depot, Reference & Research Library, 425

Defense Equal Opportunity Management Institute Library, 1259

Defense General Supply Center Library, 1260

Defense Logistic Services Center, Learning Resources Center Library, 1266

Defense Logistics Agency Headquarters Library, 1267

Department of Commerce, Miami District Office Library, 133

Department of Energy, Solar Research Institute, Technical Library, 1296

Department of Justice Main Library, 1854
Environmental Protection Agency, Region 3 Library, 1987

FAA Central Regional Library, 1935
Ft Bliss, Center Library, 445
Ft Bliss, Valent Learning Resources Center Library, 446

Ft Sam Houston, Academy of Health Sciences, Stimson Library, 484

Ft George G Meade, Post Library, 535
Ft Monroe, General Library & Intern Training Center, 538

Ft Leonard Wood Post Library, 569
George AFB, Base Library/FL 4812, 249
Grissom AFB, Base Library/FL 4654, 254
Holloman AFB, Base Library/FL 4801, 264
Long Beach Naval Shipyard, Technical Library, 995

March AFB, Base Library/FL 4664, 287
Mather AFB, Base Library/FL 3067, 288
McBride Library/FL 3010, 291
Minerals Management Service Library, 1591

Miramar Naval Air Station Library, 1008
Audie L Murphy Memorial Veterans Hospital, Library Service, 2279

Myrtle Beach AFB, Base Library/FL 4806, 300

NASA Headquarters, S & T Library & Systems Support, 2069

National Mine Health & Safety Academy, Learning Resource Center, 1923

Naval Air Systems Command, Technical Information & Reference Center, 1018

Naval Amphibious School Library, 1021
Naval Amphibious School, John Sidney McCain, Jr Amphibious Warfare Library, 1022

Naval Education & Training Center, Main Library, 1035

Naval Electronic Systems Engineering Center, Portsmouth Electronic Library, 1037

Naval Facilities Engineering Command, Technical Library, 1044

Naval Postgraduate School, Dudley Knox Library, 1061

Naval Postgraduate School, Dudley Knox Library, 1062

Naval School of Health Sciences Library, 1069

Naval Underwater Systems Center, Technical Library, 1094

Navy Personnel Research & Development Center, Technical Library, 1110

Nellis AFB, Base Library/FL 4852, 301
Norton AFB, Base Library/FL 4448, 302
Pentagon Library, 605
Peterson AFB, Base Library/FL 2500, 307

Red River Army Depot, School of Engineering & Logistics, Technical Library, 613

Robins AFB, Base Library/FL 2060, 314
Sheppard AFB Regional Hospital, Medical Library, 322

Space & Naval Warfare Systems Command Library, 1156

Strategic Systems Program Office, Technical Library, 1157

Tennessee Valley Authority, Technical Library, 2101

Tinker AFB, Base Library/FL 2030, 325
US Army Corps of Engineers, Baltimore District Library Branch, 660

US Army Corps of Engineers, Kansas City District, Office of Counsel Law Library, 677

US Army Corps of Engineers, St Louis District Technical Library, 713

US Army Logistics Library, 751
US Army Ordnance Missile & Munitions Center & School, Technical Library, 769

US Army Transportation & Aviation Logistics Schools, Information Center, 788

US Coast Guard Academy Library, 1942
US Department of Education, Office of Educational Research & Improvement Library, 1286

US Office of Personnel Management Library, 2089

Veterans Administration Central Office Library, Library Division, 2285

Veterans Administration Medical Center, Health Sciences Library, 2294

Veterans Administration Medical Center Library Service, 2353

Veterans Administration Medical Center, Medical Library, 2386

Veterans Administration Medical Center, Medical & Patient's Library, 2414

Veterans Administration Medical Center, Carl Vinson Center Library, 2428

White Sands Missile Range, Post Library, 805

Zaragoza Base Library/FL 5571, 394

Manassas Battlefield

Manassas National Battlefield Park Library, 1732

Manhattan Project, Nuclear Weapons

National Atomic Museum Library, 1308

Manufacturers Catalogs

Long Beach Naval Shipyard, Technical Library, 995

Philadelphia Naval Shipyard, Technical Library, 1136

Manufacturing

US Customs Service, Library & Information Center, 1954

US International Trade Commission Main Library, 2270

Manufacturing History

Hopewell Furnace National Historic Site Library, 1704

Saugus Iron Works National Historic Site Library, 1789

Manuscripts

Chickamauga & Chattanooga National Military Park Library, 1635
Independence National Historic Park Library, 1709
Kennesaw Mountain National Battlefield Park Library, 1719
Library of Congress, 9
Abraham Lincoln Birthplace National Historic Site Library, 1728
Marine Corps Historical Center Library, 1237
Morristown National Historical Park Library, 1737
National Agricultural Library, 124
US National Arboretum Library, 91
Yellowstone Association Research Library, 1816

Mapping

Defense Mapping Agency, Aerospace Center Technical Library, 1268
Defense Mapping Agency, Hydrographic/Topographic Center Library, 1269
Geological Survey Library, 1565
Geological Survey, National Mapping Division Applications Assistance Facility Library, 1571
US Army Engineering Topographic Laboratories Scientific & Technical Information Center, 732

Maps

Bureau of Land Management, Elko District Office Library, 1484
Bureau of the Census, Atlanta Regional Office Library, 136
Chesapeake & Ohio Canal National Historic Park Resource Library, 1634
Coastal Zone Information Center, 159
Delaware River Basin Commission Library, 2446
Department of Transportation Library, 1931
Geological Survey Library, 1566
Geological Survey Library, 1568
Geological Survey, Water Resources Division Library, 1580
Library of Congress, 9
Map Library & Information Service Library, 163
National Defense University Library, 1278
NOAA, Coral Gables Center Library, 169
NOAA, National Climatic Data Center Library, 173
US Army Missile & Space Intelligence Center Library, 760
US Army Russian Institute, Research Library, 927
US Army TRADOC Systems Analysis Activity TRASANA, Technical Library, 785

Marad Technical Reports

US Merchant Marine Academy, Schyler Otis Bland Memorial Library, 1939

Marianas Islands

US Navy Public Works Center, Technical Library, 1224

Marine Biology

Auke Bay Fisheries Laboratory Library, 158
Bureau of Land Management, Minerals Management Service Library, 1500

Environmental Protection Agency, Environmental Research Laboratory Library, 1973
Environmental Protection Agency, Research Laboratory Library, 1993
Everglades National Park Research Center Library, 1660
Marine Mammal Commission Library, 2449
Miami Laboratory Library, 164
NOAA, Miami Library, 171
NOAA, Library & Information Services Division, 182
Northwest & Alaska Fisheries Center Library, 183
Office of the Chief of Naval Research Library, 1122
Panama City Laboratory Library, 185
Rice Library, 187
Smithsonian Institution Libraries, Museum Support Center Branch, 2469
Southwest Fisheries Center Library, 188
Lionel A Walford Library, 191

Marine Chemistry

NOAA, Miami Library, 171
NOAA, Seattle Center Library, 175
NOAA, Southeast Fisheries Center, Galveston Laboratory Library, 176

Marine Corps

James Carson Breckinridge Library & Amphibious Warfare Facility, 1227
Doctrine Center Library, 1232
US Marine Band, Music Library, 1243
US Marine Corps Air Ground Combat Center Library, 1244

Marine Corps History

El Toro Marine Corps Air Station Library, 1233
Marine Corps Historical Center Library, 1237

Marine Ecology

Cabrillo National Monument Library, 1616
Environmental Protection Agency, Environmental Research Laboratory Library, 1972

Marine Engineering

Department of Transportation Library, 1931
Long Beach Naval Shipyard, Technical Library, 995
Mare Island Naval Shipyard, Technical Library, 997
Naval Ocean Systems Center, Technical Libraries, 1058
Naval Sea Systems Command, Library Documentation Branch, 1072
Philadelphia Naval Shipyard, Technical Library, 1136
Puget Sound Naval Shipyard, Engineering Library, 1145
David Taylor Naval Ship R&D Center, Technical Information Center, 1166
US Merchant Marine Academy, Schyler Otis Bland Memorial Library, 1939

Marine Mammals

National Marine Mammal Library, 168

Marine Resources

Department of Justice Lands Library, 1853

Marine Science

Buck Island Reef National Monument Library, 1614
Cabrillo National Monument Library, 1616
NOAA, Southeast Fisheries Center, Galveston Laboratory Library, 176
Naval Ocean Systems Center, Technical Libraries, 1058
Naval Postgraduate School, Dudley Knox Library, 1062
Pascagoula Laboratory Library, 186
Tiburon Laboratory Library, 190
US Coast Guard Academy Library, 1942

Marine Transportation

Federal Maritime Commission Library, 2024

Maritime Administration

National Maritime Research Center, Study Center Library, 1938

Maritime History

Cape Lookout National Seashore Library, 1621
Islesford Historic Museum Library, 1712
National Maritime Museum, J Porter Shaw Library, 1745
Salem Maritime National Historic Site Library, 1783

Maritime Law

Department of the Interior, Center for Information & Library Services, Natural Resources Library, Law Branch, 1820

Maritime Legislation

Department of Transportation Law Library, 1930

Maritime Trades

Salem Maritime National Historic Site Library, 1783

Market Surveys

Department of Commerce, District Office Library, 128

Marketing

US Grain Marketing Research Laboratory Library, 90

Marketing, International

Department of Commerce, District Office Library, 128
International Trade Administration, International Marketing Center Library, 150

Maryland

Bureau of the Census, Information Services Program Library, 142
Federal Reserve Bank of Richmond, Baltimore Branch Library, 2039
Federal Reserve Bank of Richmond, Research Library, 2040

Maryland History

Chesapeake & Ohio Canal National Historic Park Resource Library, 1634

Maryland Law

US Army Corps of Engineers, Baltimore District Library Branch, 660

Massachusetts Law

US Court of Appeals First Circuit Library, 18

Materials Science

Air Force Geophysics Laboratory Research Library, 198

Argonne National Laboratory, Technical Information Services Department, 1289

Bureau of Mines, Albany Metallurgy Research Center, 1531

Department of Energy, Solar Research Institute, Technical Library, 1296

Mare Island Naval Shipyard, Technical Library, 997

National Bureau of Standards Research Information Center, 155

National Science Foundation Library, 2085

Sandia National Laboratories, Technical Library, 1314

Tuscaloosa Research Center Library, 1546

Mathematics

Air Force Flight Test Center, Technical Library/FL 2806, 197

Air Force Geophysics Laboratory Research Library, 198

Air Force Human Resources Laboratory, Technical Library/FL 2870, 199

Air Force Office of Scientific Research Library/FL 2819, 204

Armament Division Technical Library/FL 2825, 217

Arnold Engineering Development Center Technical Library/FL 2804, 218

Benet Weapons Laboratory, Technical Library, 416

Brookhaven National Laboratory, Research Library, 1293

Defense Personnel Support Center, Directorate of Medical Material Library, 1272

Memphis Naval Air Station Library, 1004

Myrtle Beach AFB, Base Library/FL 4806, 300

NASA-AMES Research Center Library, 2059

NASA-AMES Research Center, Technical Library, 2061

NASA Goddard Institute for Space Studies Library, 2063

NASA Goddard Space Flight Center Library, 2064

NASA Goddard Space Flight Center, Wallops Flight Facility Library, 2065

NASA Lyndon B Johnson Space Center, Technical Library, 2066

National Bureau of Standards Research Information Center, 155

National Institutes of Health, Division of Computer Research & Technology Library, 1344

NOAA, Miami Library, 171

NOAA, Mountain Administrative Support Center, 172

National Science Foundation Library, 2085

Naval Air Systems Command, Technical Information & Reference Center, 1018

Naval Weapons Center, Technical Library, 1097

NOAA, Library & Information Services Division, 182

Philadelphia Naval Shipyard, Technical Library, 1136

Point Mugu Naval Air Station Library, 1138

Redstone Scientific Information Center, 615

Sandia National Laboratories, Technical Library, 1313

Smithsonian Institution, Astrophysical Observatory Library, 2467

Space & Naval Warfare Systems Command Library, 1156

US Army TRADOC Systems Analysis Activity TRASANA, Technical Library, 785

US Naval Academy, Nimitz Library, 1169

US Naval Observatory Library, 1172

Mathematics History

US Naval Observatory Library, 1172

Meats Research

Roman L Hruska US Meat Animal Research Center Library, 75

Mechanical Engineering

General Services Administration, Design & Construction Division Library, 2050

Naval Facilities Engineering Command, Technical Library, 1044

Naval Ship Systems Engineering Station, Technical Library, 1076

Naval Supervisor of Shipbuilding, Conversion & Repair, Technical Library, 1079

Philadelphia Naval Shipyard, Technical Library, 1136

Redstone Scientific Information Center, 615

US Army Materials & Mechanics Research Center, Technical Library, 753

Medals

The Institute of Heraldry Library, 583

Mediation

Bureau of Land Management, Baker District Office Library, 1468

Medical Catalogs

Center for Devices & Radiological Health Library, 1331

Medical Devices

Center for Devices & Radiological Health Library, 1331

Food & Drug Administration, Medical Library, 1333

Medical Education

Veterans Administration Medical Center Library, 2316

Medical Entomology

Rocky Mountain Laboratory Library, 1347

Smithsonian Institution Libraries, Museum Support Center Branch, 2469

Medical Information Systems

National Institutes of Health, Division of Computer Research & Technology Library, 1344

Medical Malpractice

Ft Shafter, Office of the Staff Judge Advocate, Law Library, 552

Medical Technology

Bureau of Radiological Health Library, 1329

Medicine

Agency for Toxic Substances & Disease Registry Library, 1321

Bethesda Naval Hospital, Edward Rhodes Stitt Library, 953

Bethesda Naval Medical Research Institute, Information Services Branch, 954

Camp Lejeune Naval Hospital, Medical & General Libraries, 957

Camp Pendleton Naval Hospital Library, 959

Center for Devices & Radiological Health Library, 1331

Centers for Disease Control, Chamblee Branch Library, 1326

Centers for Disease Control Library, 1327

Consumer Product Safety Commission Library, 1966

Consumer Product Safety Commission Library, 1967

Darnall Army Community Hospital, Medical Library, 426

Defense Personnel Support Center, Directorate of Medical Material Library, 1272

Directorate of Medical Materiel Library, 1277

Eisenhower Army Medical Center, Health Sciences Library, 436

Food & Drug Administration, Medical Library, 1333

Ft Campbell, Blanchfield Army Community Hospital, Medical Library, 450

Ft Carson, Evans US Army Community Hospital, Medical Library, 453

Ft Dix, Walson Army Community Hospital, Medical Library, 463

Ft Eustis, McDonald US Army Community Hospital, Medical Library, 466

Ft Sam Houston, Brooke Army Medical Center, Medical Library, 485

Ft Sam Houston, Morale Support Activities, Library System, 486

Ft Sam Houston, Office of the Staff Judge Advocate, Army Law Library, 488

Ft Huachuca, Raymond W Bliss Army Community Hospital, Medical Library, 490

Ft Leavenworth, Munson Army Community Hospital, Medical Library, 509

Ft Monmouth, Patterson Army Community Hospital, Medical & Patients' Library, 537

Ft Riley, Irwin Army Hospital, Medical Library, 546

Ft Rucker, Medical Library, 551

Ft Leonard Wood, Gen Leonard Wood Army Community Hospital, Medical Library, 566

Frederick Cancer Research Facility, Scientific Library, 1340

David Grant USAF Medical Center, Medical Library/SGEL, 252

Great Lakes Naval Hospital, Medical Library, 984

James A Haley Veterans Hospital, Library Service, 2272

Royal C Johnson Veterans Memorial Medical Center, Medical & Patient's Library, 2274

Keesler AFB, Medical Library/SGAL, 270

Lackland AFB, Wilford Hall Medical Center Library/FL 2879, 276

Library of Congress, 9

Gillis W Long Hansen's Disease Center, Medical Library, 1348

Los Alamos National Laboratory Libraries, 1303

Los Alamos National Laboratory, Medical Library, 1304

Medical & Health Sciences Division Library, 1306

Memphis Naval Regional Medical Center, General & Medical Libraries, 1005

Karl A Menninger Medical Library, 2276

William S Middleton Memorial Veterans Hospital Library Service, 2277

Audie L Murphy Memorial Veterans Hospital, Library Service, 2279

NASA-AMES Research Center, Life Sciences Library, 2060

NASA Dryden Flight Research Center Library, 2062

National Institutes of Health, Division of Computer Research & Technology Library, 1344

National Institutes of Health Library, 1345

National Library of Medicine, 1346

Naval Health Research Center, Wilkins Biomedical Library, 1046

Naval Hospital, Medical Library, 1050

Naval School of Health Sciences Library, 1069

Navy Disease Vector Ecology & Control Center Library, 1107

Oakland Naval Hospital, Medical Library, 1119

Office of the Chief of Naval Research Library, 1122

Offices of the Surgeons General, US Army - US Air Force, Joint Medical Library, 1280

Orlando Naval Hospital, Medical Library, 1125

Parklawn Health Library, Prince George's Center Branch, 1351

Phoenix Indian Medical Center, Health Sciences Library, 1339

Sheppard AFB Regional Hospital, Medical Library, 322

Uniformed Services University of the Health Services, Learning Resource Center, 1282

US Air Force Regional Hospital, Carswell (SAC), Medical Library, 336

USAF School of Health Care Science, Academic Library/FL 3021, 337

US Army Aeromedical Research Laboratory, Medical Library, 639

US Army Corps of Engineers, Huntington District, Technical Library, 670

US Army, Keller Army Community Hospital Library, 746

US Naval Hospital, Medical, Crews' & Patients' Library, 1208

Veterans Administration Central Office Library, Library Division, 2285

Veterans Administration Hospital, Health Sciences Library, 2287

Veterans Administration Lakeside Medical Center, Library Service, 2289

Veterans Administration Library Service, Edith Nourse Rogers Memorial Veterans Hospital, 2290

Veterans Administration Medical & Regional Office Center Library, 2291

Veterans Administration Medical Center & Patients' Library, 2293

Veterans Administration Medical Center Library, 2303

Veterans Administration Medical Center Library, 2305

Veterans Administration Medical Center Library, 2309

Veterans Administration Medical Center Library, 2312

Veterans Administration Medical Center Library, 2313

Veterans Administration Medical Center Library, 2314

Veterans Administration Medical Center Library, 2316

Veterans Administration Medical Center Library, 2317

Veterans Administration Medical Center Library, 2319

Veterans Administration Medical Center Library-Learning Resources Center, 2322

Veterans Administration Medical Center Library Service, 2327

Veterans Administration Medical Center Library Service, 2329

Veterans Administration Medical Center Library Service, 2331

Veterans Administration Medical Center Library Service, 2332

Veterans Administration Medical Center Library Service, 2333

Veterans Administration Medical Center Library Service, 2337

Veterans Administration Medical Center Library Service, 2339

Veterans Administration Medical Center Library Service, 2345

Veterans Administration Medical Center Library Service, 2348

Veterans Administration Medical Center Library Service, 2349

Veterans Administration Medical Center Library Service, 2352

Veterans Administration Medical Center Library Service, 2353

Veterans Administration Medical Center Library Service, 2362

Veterans Administration Medical Center Library Service, 2363

Veterans Administration Medical Center Library Service, 2365

Veterans Administration Medical Center Library Service, 2366

Veterans Administration Medical Center Library Service, 2372

Veterans Administration Medical Center Library Service, 2373

Veterans Administration Medical Center Library Service, 2377

Veterans Administration Medical Center Library Service, 2378

Veterans Administration Medical Center Library Service, 2383

Veterans Administration Medical Center, Medical Library, 2386

Veterans Administration Medical Center, Medical Library, 2389

Veterans Administration Medical Center, Medical Library, 2391

Veterans Administration Medical Center, Medical Library, 2392

Veterans Administration Medical Center, Medical Library, 2393

Veterans Administration Medical Center, Medical Library, 2395

Veterans Administration Medical Center, Medical Library, 2396

Veterans Administration Medical Center, Medical Library, 2398

Veterans Administration Medical Center, Medical Library, 2400

Veterans Administration Medical Center, Medical Library, 2403

Veterans Administration Medical Center, Medical Library, 2406

Veterans Administration Medical Center, Medical Library, 2410

Veterans Administration Medical Center, Medical Library, Library Service, 2412

Veterans Administration Medical Center, Medical & Patient's Library, 2413

Veterans Administration Medical Center, Medical & Patient's Library, 2414

Veterans Administration Medical Center, Medical & Patients' Library, 2417

Veterans Administration Medical Center, Medical & Patients' Library, 2419

Veterans Administration Medical Center, Medical & Patients' Library Wade Park & Brecksville Units, 2423

Veterans Administration Medical Center, Carl Vinson Center Library, 2428

Veterans Administration Medical Library, 2429

Veterans Administration Medical & Regional Office Center Library Service, 2433

Veterans Administration Medical & Regional Office Center Medical Library, 2434

Veterans Administration Medical & Regional Office Center, Medical & Patients' Library, 2436

Veterans Administration Westside Medical Center Library Service, 2442

Winchester Engineering & Analytical Center Library, 1338

Wright-Patterson AFB, Medical Center Library, 347

Alvin C York Veterans Administration Medical Center, Library Service, 2443

Medicine, History of

Bethesda Naval Hospital, Edward Rhodes Stitt Library, 953

Fitzsimons Army Medical Center, Medical Technical Library, 440

Ft Huachuca, Raymond W Bliss Army Community Hospital, Medical Library, 490

Memory and Cognitive Processes

National Institute on Aging, Gerontology Research Center Library, 1343

Menninger, Karl A.

Karl A Menninger Medical Library, 2276

Mental Health

Ft Carson, Evans US Army Community Hospital, Medical Library, 453

Ft Dix, Walson Army Community Hospital, Medical Library, 463

National Institute of Mental Health Library, Division of Intramural Research Programs, 1322

Parklawn Health Library, 1350

Veterans Administration Medical Center Library Service, 2375

Veterans Administration Medical Center Medical Library, 2398

Veterans Administration Medical Center, Medical Library, 2409

Mesa Verde

Mesa Verde Research Library, 1733

Metallurgical Engineering

Naval Ship Systems Engineering Station, Technical Library, 1076

Metallurgy

Argonne National Laboratory, Argonne-West, Technical Library, 1288
Avondale Research Center Library, 1530
Bureau of Mines, Albany Metallurgy Research Center, 1531
Bureau of Mines, Boulder City Metallurgy Library, 1532
Bureau of Mines, Metallurgy Research Center Library, 1537
Bureau of Mines, Salt Lake City Research Center Library, 1538
Bureau of Mines, Twin Cities Library, 1541
Bureau of Mines, Twin Cities Research Center Library, 1542
Naval Avionics Center, Technical Library, 1024
Reno Metallurgy Research Center Library, 1544
Rolla Metallurgy Research Center, Technical Library, 1545
Sandia National Laboratories, Technical Library, 1313
Tuscaloosa Research Center Library, 1546
US International Trade Commission Main Library, 2270

Meteorology

Air Force Geophysics Laboratory Research Library, 198
Air Weather Service Technical Library/FL 4414, 212
Environmental Protection Agency, Meteorology Division Library, 1979
Geophysical Fluid Dynamics Laboratory Library, 160
NASA Goddard Institute for Space Studies Library, 2063
National Bureau of Standards Research Information Center, 155
NOAA, Coral Gables Center Library, 169
NOAA, Great Lakes Environmental Research Laboratory Library, 170
NOAA, Miami Library, 171
NOAA, Mountain Administrative Support Center, 172
NOAA, Seattle Center Library, 175
National Severe Storms Laboratory Library, 178
National Weather Service, Central Region Library, 179
National Weather Service, Southern Region Headquarters Library, 180
National Weather Service, Weather Service Nuclear Support Office Library, 181
Naval Environmental Prediction Research Facility/Fleet Numerical Oceanography Center Technical Library, 1041
NOAA, Library & Information Services Division, 182
Point Mugu Naval Air Station Library, 1138

Meteorology, History of

National Bureau of Standards Research Information Center, 155

Methanol

Motor Vehicle Emission Laboratory Library, 1994

Metis Indians

Turtle Mountain Community School Media Center, 1455

Mexican-American War

Bent's Old Fort National Historic Site Library, 1607

Michelson, Albert A.

US Naval Academy, Nimitz Library, 1169

Michif Indians

Turtle Mountain Community School Media Center, 1455

Michigan

K I Sawyer AFB, Base Library/FL 4515, 316

Microbiology

Centers for Disease Control Library, 1327
Environmental Protection Agency, Environmental Research Laboratory Library, 1972
Environmental Protection Agency, Environmental Research Laboratory Library, 1973
Food & Drug Administration, Dallas District Library, 1335
National Animal Disease Center Library, 76
National Marine Fisheries Service, Southeast Fisheries Center Library, 167
Plum Island Animal Disease Center Library, 79
Rocky Mountain Laboratory Library, 1347
Russell Research Center Library, 80
USDA, Agricultural Research Service, Water Conservation Research Library, 86
USDA Northern Regional Research Center Library, 87
Western Regional Research Center Library, 92

Microforms

Ft Bragg Command Reference Center & Main Post Library, 447
Geophysical Fluid Dynamics Laboratory Library, 160
Library of Congress, 9
US Army Missile & Space Intelligence Center Library, 760
US Army Russian Institute, Research Library, 927
US Army Support Command, Hawaii Library System, 782
US Navy Public Works Center, Technical Library, 1224

Micronesia

Andersen Base Library/FL 4624, 350
US Naval Hospital, Medical & General Libraries, 1207

Microscopic Slides

Armed Forces Institute of Pathology, Ash Library, 405

Microwaves

Bureau of Radiological Health Library, 1329

Middle East

Ft McPherson, Staff Judge Advocate, 3rd US Army Law Library, 528
MacDill AFB, Base Library/FL 4814, 284

Military Academy

US Military Academy Library, 794

Military Aid

Defense Institute of Security Assistance Management Library/FL 2301, 235
Joint US Military Mission for Aid to Turkey, Library, 372

Military Architecture

Castillo de San Marcos National Monument Library, 1626

Military Aviation

Dover AFB, Base Library/FL 4497, 236
Hanscom AFB, Base Library/FL 2835, 258

Military Contracts

Armed Services Board of Contract Appeals, Law Library, 1254
US Army Engineer Division, Memphis District, Law Library, 730
US Army Legal Services Agency, Law Library, 750

Military Engineering

Castillo de San Marcos National Monument Library, 1626
Thayer Engineering Library, 632
US Army Corps of Engineers, St Paul District Technical Library, 714
US Military Academy Library, 794

Military Equipment

Aberdeen Proving Ground, Ordnance Center & School Library, 398

Military Families

Carlisle Barracks, Post Library, 418
Ft Monroe, General Library & Intern Training Center, 538
Kings Bay Base Library, 991

Military History

Air University Library/FL 3368, 211
Antietam National Battlefield Library, 1598
Base Library/FL 5531, 355
Bent's Old Fort National Historic Site Library, 1607
Big Hole National Battlefield Library, 1609
Bolling AFB, Base Library/FL 4400, 224
James Carson Breckinridge Library & Amphibious Warfare Facility, 1227
Cabrillo National Monument Library, 1616
Camp Red Cloud Army Library, 821
Camp Smith Library, 1230
Columbus AFB, Base Library/FL 3022, 233
Combat Studies Institute Library, 421
El Toro Marine Corps Air Station Library, 1233
Elgin AFB, Base Library/FL 2823/SSL, 242
Elmendorf AFB, Base Library, 244
Fairchild AFB, Base Library/FL 4620, 247
Fitzsimons Army Medical Center, Post-Patients' Library, 442
Ft Bliss, Center Library, 445
Ft Bliss, Valent Learning Resources Center Library, 446
Ft Bragg Command Reference Center & Main Post Library, 447
Ft Campbell, R F Sink Library, 452
Ft Davis National Historic Site Library, 1667

Military Intelligence

Military Justice

Military Law

Military Logistics

Military Medicine

Military Personnel

Military Police

Military Procurement

Military Regulations

Defense Personnel Support Center Library, 1273

General Accounting Office, Office of Library Services, 5

Task Force Judge Advocate Army Law Library, 888

Umatilla Depot Activity, Reference Library, 637

US Army & Air Force Exchange Service, Central Library, 1283

Military Sales

Defense Institute of Security Assistance Management Library, 1262

Defense Institute of Security Assistance Management Library/FL 2301, 235

9th Marine Corps District Library, 1241

Military Science

Aberdeen Proving Ground, Ordnance Center & School Library, 398

Air Force Officer Training School Library/FL 3050, 205

Air Force Space Command Library/FL 2508, 207

Air University Library/FL 3368, 211

Alconbury Base Library/FL 5643, 349

Armed Forces Staff College Library, 1253

Army Materiel Command Headquarters, Technical Library, 408

Beale AFB, Base Library/FL 4686, 220

James Carson Breckinridge Library & Amphibious Warfare Facility, 1227

I G Brown Professional Military Education Center Library/FL 6599, 227

Camp Smith Library, 1230

Combat Studies Institute Library, 421

Combined Arms Research Library, 422

Cubi Point Naval Air Station Library, 1182

Defense General Supply Center Library, 1260

Defense Intelligence Agency Library, 1263

Defense Logistics Agency Headquarters Library, 1267

Defense Personnel Support Center Library, 1273

Department of Transportation Library, 1931

Doctrine Center Library, 1232

Ellsworth AFB, Base Library/FL 4690, 243

Fairchild AFB, Base Library/FL 4620, 247

Fleet Intelligence Center, Europe & Atlantic, Library, 980

Ft Bliss, Valent Learning Resources Center Library, 446

Ft Campbell, R F Sink Library, 452

Ft Devens, Davis Library, 458

Ft Dix, US Army Training Center & Post Library, 462

Ft Gordon, Morale Support Activities Library Branch, Patients' Library, 470

Ft Hamilton, Morale Support Activities, Post Library, 474

Ft Huachuca Library Division, 491

Ft Irwin Post Library, 498

Ft Jackson Thomas E Hall Post Library, 500

Ft McPherson Library System, 526

Ft McPherson, Staff Judge Advocate, 3rd US Army Law Library, 528

Ft George G Meade, Post Library, 535

Ft Myer Post Library, 539

Ft Sheridan Post Library, 555

Ft Sill, Morris Swett Technical Library, 558

Ft Story Post Library, 561

Ft Leonard Wood, Library Service Center, 567

Ft Leonard Wood Post Library, 569

George AFB, Base Library/FL 4812, 249

Goodfellow AFB, Base Library/FL 3030, 250

Hanscom AFB, Base Library/FL 2835, 258

Harpers Ferry Center Library, 1699

HQ US Army Training & Doctrine Command, Technical Library, 581

Holloman AFB, Base Library/FL 4801, 264

Seymour Johnson AFB, Base Library/FL 4809, 268

Kelly AFB, Base Library/FL 2050, 272

Kirtland AFB, Base Library/FL 4469, 273

Little Rock AFB, Base Library/FL 4460, 280

Lowry AFB, Base Library/FL 3059, 282

MacDill AFB, Base Library/FL 4814, 284

Mannheim Community Library, 864

McBride Library/FL 3010, 291

McClellan AFB, Base Library/FL 2040, 292

McConnell AFB, Base Library/FL 4621, 293

Military Airlift Command Library/FL 4401, 296

Minot AFB, Base Library/FL 4528, 297

Miramar Naval Air Station Library, 1008

Myrtle Beach AFB, Base Library/FL 4806, 300

National Defense University Library, 1278

Naval Education & Training Center, Main Library, 1035

Naval Postgraduate School, Dudley Knox Library, 1061

Naval Postgraduate School, Dudley Knox Library, 1062

Naval School of Health Sciences Library, 1069

Naval Security Group Activity Station Library, 1074

Naval Surface Weapons Center, Technical Library, 1087

Naval War College Library, 1095

New River Marine Corps Air Station Library, 1240

Norton AFB, Base Library/FL 4448, 302

Oakland Army Base Post Library, 603

Oceana Naval Air Station Library, 1120

Parris Island, Marine Corps Recruit Depot Station Library, 1242

Patuxent Naval Air Station Library, 1129

Pentagon Library, 605

Philadelphia Naval Hospital, Medical & General Libraries, 1135

Philadelphia Naval Station Library, 1137

Ramstein Library/FL 5612, 382

Redstone Scientific Information Center, 615

Roosevelt Roads Naval Station Library, 1189

St Louis Area Support Center, Recreational Library, 620

Seneca Post Library, 625

US Air Force Academy Library/FL 7000, 331

US Army Chemical School, Fisher Library, 654

US Army Engineer Center & Ft Belvoir, Van Noy Library, 728

USAREUR Library & Resource Center, 911

US Army Infantry School, Donovan Technical Library, 740

US Army Intelligence & Security Command, Post Library, 744

US Army Intelligence School Library, 1284

US Army Logistics Library, 751

US Army Military Police School, Ramsey Library, 759

US Army Operational Test & Evaluation Agency, Technical Library, 767

US Army Ordnance Center & School Library, 768

US Army TRADOC Systems Analysis Activity TRASANA, Technical Library, 785

US Army Training & Doctrine Command, Technical Library, 787

US Army Transportation Center, Groninger Library, 789

US Army War College Library, 790

US Marine Corps Air Ground Combat Center Library, 1244

US Military Academy Library, 794

Yongsan Library, 942

Military Security

Defense Institute of Security Assistance Management Library/FL 2301, 235

Naval Electronic Systems, Security Engineering, Naval Security Station, Technical Library, 1039

Naval Security Group Activity Library, 1188

Naval Security Group Activity, Northwest, General Library, 1073

US Naval Security Group Activity, General Library, 1212

Military Specifications

Defense Logistics Agency Headquarters Library, 1267

Directorate of Medical Materiel Library, 1277

Long Beach Naval Shipyard, Technical Library, 995

Philadelphia Naval Shipyard, Technical Library, 1136

US Army Armament Research & Development Center, Plastics Technical Evaluation Center, 643

US Army Corps of Engineers, Ft Worth District, Technical Library, 666

White Sands Missile Range, Technical Library, 806

Military Standards

Philadelphia Naval Shipyard, Technical Library, 1136

Military Supplies

Aberdeen Proving Ground, Ordnance Center & School Library, 398

Aberdeen Proving Ground, Ordnance Center & School Museum Library, 399

Castillo de San Marcos National Monument Library, 1626

Red River Army Depot, School of Engineering & Logistics, Technical Library, 613

Redstone Scientific Information Center, 615

Sandia National Laboratories, Technical Library, 1314

Springfield Armory National Historic Site Library, 1796

US Army Logistics Library, 751

US Army Ordnance Center & School Library, 768

Military Technology

HQ TRADOC Combined Arms Test Activity (TCATA), Technical Library, 577

Military Training

Doctrine Center Library, 1232

Mills

Rock Creek Nature Center, 1774

Mine Safety

Federal Mine Safety & Health Review Commission Library, 2447
Federal Mine Safety & Health Review Commission Library, 2448

Mine Warfare

Fleet & Mine Warfare Training Center, 976
Naval Coastal Systems Center, Technical Information Services Branch, 1028
Naval Mine Warfare Engineering Activity, Library, 1055

Mineralogy

Avondale Research Center Library, 1530
Bureau of Land Management, Arizona State Office Library, 1466
Bureau of Land Management, Bakersfield District Office Library, 1469
Bureau of Land Management, Bishop Resource Area Headquarters Library, 1470
Bureau of Land Management, Branch of Records & Data Management, 1471
Bureau of Land Management, California State Office Library, 1473
Bureau of Land Management, Cedar City District Library, 1474
Bureau of Land Management, District Office Library, 1481
Bureau of Land Management, District Office Library, 1482
Bureau of Land Management, Eastern States Office Library, 1483
Bureau of Land Management, Elko District Office Library, 1484
Bureau of Land Management, Fairbanks District Office Library, 1486
Bureau of Land Management, Folsom District Office Library, 1487
Bureau of Land Management, Idaho State Office Library, 1489
Bureau of Land Management, Kanab Office Library, 1490
Bureau of Land Management Library, 1497
Bureau of Land Management, Minerals Management Service Library, 1501
Bureau of Land Management, Phillips Resource Area Office Library, 1507
Bureau of Land Management, Phoenix District Office Library, 1508
Bureau of Land Management, Roseburg District Office Library, 1514
Bureau of Land Management, Safford District Office Library, 1516
Bureau of Land Management, Utah State Office Library, 1525
Bureau of Land Management, Wyoming State Office Library, 1528
Bureau of Mines, Albany Metallurgy Research Center, 1531
Bureau of Mines, Section of Administrative Services Library, 1539
Bureau of Mines, Twin Cities Research Center Library, 1542
Geological Survey Library, 1565
Geological Survey, Mineral Resources Library, 1569
Minerals Management Service Library, 1591

National Museum of Natural History, Branch Library, 2462
Tuscaloosa Research Center Library, 1546

Mineralogy, International

Bureau of Mines, Section of Administrative Services Library, 1539

Mines, Bureau of

Bureau of Mines Library, 1534
Bureau of Mines Library, 1536
Bureau of Mines, Spokane Research Center Library, 1540
Morgantown Energy Technology Center, 1307
National Mine Health & Safety Academy, Learning Resource Center, 1923
Reno Metallurgy Research Center Library, 1544
Tuscaloosa Research Center Library, 1546

Mining

Bureau of Land Management, California State Office Library, 1473
Bureau of Land Management, District Office Library, 1481
Bureau of Land Management, New Mexico State Office Central Files/Library, 1504
Bureau of Mines, Charles W Henderson Memorial Library, 1533
Bureau of Mines Library, 1534
Bureau of Mines Library, 1536
Bureau of Mines, Salt Lake City Research Center Library, 1538
Bureau of Mines, Twin Cities Library, 1541
Bureau of Mines, Twin Cities Research Center Library, 1542
Department of Energy, Grand Junction Area Office, Technical Library, 1294
Department of the Interior, Center for Information & Library Services, Natural Resources Library, 1821
Federal Mine Safety & Health Review Commission Library, 2447
Federal Mine Safety & Health Review Commission Library, 2448
National Mine Health & Safety Academy, Learning Resource Center, 1923
Office of Surface Mining Reclamation & Enforcement Library, 1844
Office of Surface Mining Reclamation & Enforcement Library, 1845
Tuscaloosa Research Center Library, 1546

Mining Engineering

Bureau of Mines, Charles W Henderson Memorial Library, 1533
Bureau of Mines Library, 1536
Bureau of Mines, Spokane Research Center Library, 1540
Reno Metallurgy Research Center Library, 1544

Minority Groups

Alameda Naval Air Station Library, 944
American Museum of Immigration Library, 1596
Anacostia Neighborhood Museum Library, 2452
Bergstrom AFB, Base Library/FL 4857, 221
Defense Equal Opportunity Management Institute Library, 1259
US Commission on Civil Rights, National Clearinghouse Library, 1962

Minority Literature

White Sands Missile Range, Post Library, 805

Missiles

Air Force Flight Test Center, Technical Library/FL 2806, 197
Air Force Western Space & Missile Center, Technical Library/FL 2827, 210
Eastern Space & Missile Center Technical Library/FL 2828, 238
Naval Ordnance Station, Library Branch, 1059
Naval Weapons Center, Technical Library, 1097
Navy Fleet Ballistic Missile Submarine Training Center, Technical Publications Library, 1109
Redstone Scientific Information Center, 615
Strategic Systems Program Office, Technical Library, 1157
Trident Refit Facility, Bangor, Library, 1168
US Army Missile & Space Intelligence Center Library, 760
US Army Ordnance Missile & Munitions Center & School, Technical Library, 769
US Army Strategic Defense Command, Huntsville, Library, 781
White Sands Missile Range, Technical Library, 806

Missions

Whitman Mission National Historic Site Library, 1813

Mississippi

Environmental Protection Agency, Region 4 Library, 1988

Mississippi History

Natchez Trace Parkway Library, 1743

Mississippi Law

US Army Engineer Division, Memphis District, Law Library, 730
US Court of Appeals for the 5th Circuit Library, 23

Mississippi River

National Fishery Research Center Library, 1556
US Army Corps of Engineers, Mississippi River Commission Technical Library, 683
US Army Engineer Division, LMV, Technical Library, 729

Missoula Papers

Equipment Development Center Library, 103

Missouri

St Louis Area Support Center, Recreational Library, 620

Missouri History

Mr & Mrs John K Hulston Civil War Research Library, 1708
Jefferson National Expansion Memorial Library, 1713

Missouri Law

Ft Leonard Wood, Office of the Staff Judge Advocate, Army Field Law Library, 568

US Army Engineer Division, Memphis District, Law Library, 730

Missouri River

Ft Union Trading Post National Historic Site Library, 1679

Knife River Indian Villages National Historic Site Library, 1721

Missouri River Basin

Bureau of Land Management, Montana State Office Library, 1502

Mobility Devices

Veterans Administration Office of Technology Transfer-Reference Collection, 2438

Modoc Indians

Lava Beds National Monument Library, 1726

Modoc War

Lava Beds National Monument Library, 1726

Moffett, James

Van Oosten Library, 1560

Molecular Biology

Brookhaven National Laboratory, Research Library, 1293

Plum Island Animal Disease Center Library, 79

Montana

Bureau of Land Management, Montana State Office Library, 1502

Bureau of Mines, Western Field Operations Center Library, 1543

Geological Survey, Public Inquiries Office Library, 1575

Geological Survey, Water Resources Division Library, 1580

Moreell, Ben

Naval School, Civil Engineer Corps Officers, Moreell Library, 1068

Moreell Collection

Naval School, Civil Engineer Corps Officers, Moreell Library, 1068

Mormons

Pipe Springs National Monument Library, 1769

Mortgages

Department of Housing & Urban Development Library, 1354

Federal Home Loan Bank of Atlanta, Research Library, 2014

Federal Home Loan Bank of Chicago Library, 2015

Federal Home Loan Bank of Dallas, Research & Information Library, 2016

Federal Home Loan Bank of New York Library, 2019

Motor Vehicle Safety

National Highway Traffic Safety Administration, Technical Reference Division, Library, 1940

Motor Vehicles

Motor Vehicle Emission Laboratory Library, 1994

Mount McKinley

Denali National Park Library, 1653

Mount Rainier

Mount Rainier National Park Library, 1739

Mount Rushmore

Mount Rushmore National Memorial Library, 1740

Muir, John

John Muir National Historic Site Library, 1741

Muir Woods

Muir Woods National Monument, Eleanor Bello Memorial Research Library, 1742

Multinational Corporations

Overseas Private Investment Corporation Library, 2266

Municipal Pollution

Environmental Protection Agency, National Enforcement Investigation Center, Information Center, 1980

Murray, Samuel

Hirshhorn Museum & Sculpture Garden Library, 2456

Museum Science

Ft Pulaski National Monument Library, 1675

Museums

Death Valley National Monument Research Library, 1651

Grant-Kohrs Ranch National Historic Site Library, 1692

Harpers Ferry Center Library, 1699

National Bureau of Standards Research Information Center, 155

Smithsonian Institution Libraries, Museum Support Center Branch, 2469

Smithsonian Institution, Museum Reference Center, 2470

Martin Van Buren National Historic Site Library, 1805

Music

Library of Congress, 9

National Air & Space Museum, Branch Library, 2457

National Museum of African Art, Branch Library, 2459

US Marine Band, Music Library, 1243

Music Recordings

Institute of American Indian Arts Library, 1405

Mutagenesis

National Institute of Environmental Health Sciences Library, 1342

Natchez Trace Parkway

Natchez Trace Parkway Library, 1743

National Advisory Committee for Aeronautics

NASA Headquarters, S & T Library & Systems Support, 2069

National Aeronautics and Space Administration

NASA Headquarters, S & T Library & Systems Support, 2069

National Bureau of Standards

National Bureau of Standards Research Information Center, 155

National Geographic Society

Map Library & Information Service Library, 163

National Institute of Justice

National Institute of Justice Library, 1856

National Institute of Occupational Safety and Health

US Army Environmental Hygiene Agency Library, 733

National Labor Relations Act

National Labor Relations Board Library, 2084

National Labor Relations Board

National Labor Relations Board Library, 2084

National Ocean Service

Map Library & Information Service Library, 163

National Oceanic and Atmospheric Administration

NOAA, Library & Information Services Division, 182

National Park Service

Apostle Islands National Lakeshore Library, 1599

Bighorn Canyon National Recreation Area Library, 1611

Cabrillo National Monument Library, 1616

Margaret Davis Cate Collection, 1627

Catoctin Mountain Park Library, 1628

Colorado National Monument Library, 1640

De Soto National Memorial Library, 1650

Great Sand Dunes National Monument Library, 1693

Harpers Ferry Center Library, 1699

Horse Bend National Military Park Library, 1705

Sequoia & Kings Canyon National Park Library, 1791

Tonto National Monument Library, 1800

Whiskeytown Unit Library, National Park Service, 1811

Yosemite National Park Research Library, 1817

National Security

National Defense University Library, 1278

National Solar Observatory

National Solar Observatory, Technical Library, 2086

Natural History

Horace M Albright Training Center Library, 1594
Apostle Islands National Lakeshore Library, 1599
Arches National Park Library, 1601
Big Thicket National Preserve Library, 1610
Buffalo National River Library, 1615
Cabrillo National Monument Library, 1616
Canyon de Chelly National Monument Library, 1618
Cape Cod National Seashore Library, 1619
Capitol Reef National Park Library, 1622
Capulin Mountain National Monument Library, 1623
Catoctin Mountain Park Library, 1628
Chaco Culture National Historical Park Reference & Research Library, 1631
Chiricahua National Monument Library, 1636
Colorado National Monument Library, 1640
Cuyahoga Valley National Recreation Area Library, 1648
De Soto National Memorial Library, 1650
Devils Postpile Library, 1654
Devils Tower National Monument Library, 1655
Effigy Mounds National Monument Library, 1658
Ft Clatsop National Memorial Library, 1666
Glen Canyon National Recreation Area Library, 1688
Grand Canyon National Park Research Library, 1689
Great Sand Dunes National Monument Library, 1693
Haleakala National Park, Library, 1697
Isle Royale National Park Library, 1711
Jewel Cave National Monument Library, 1714
Joshua Tree National Monument Library, 1717
Katmai National Park & Preserve Library, 1718
Lake Mead National Recreation Area Library, 1723
Lake Meredith Recreation Area Library, 1724
Mammoth Cave National Park Library, 1731
Moores Creek National Military Park Library, 1736
Mount Rainier National Park Library, 1739
Mount Rushmore National Memorial Library, 1740
National Museum of American History, Branch Library, 2461
National Museum of Natural History, Branch Library, 2462
National Park Service Library, 1747
National Park Service, Southeast Regional Office Library, 1750
National Park Service, Western Regional Resources Library, 1752

North Cascades National Park Library, 1755
Olympic National Park Library, 1757
Organ Pipe Cactus National Monument Library, 1758
Pictured Rocks National Lakeshore Library, 1767
Puuhonua o Honaunau National Historical Park, Library, 1771
Rock Creek Nature Center, 1774
Theodore Roosevelt National Park Library, 1777
Sequoia & Kings Canyon National Park Library, 1791
Sitka National Historic Park Library, 1794
Virgin Islands National Park Reference Library, 1807
Voyageurs National Park Library, 1808
Whiskeytown Unit Library, National Park Service, 1811
White Sands National Monument Library, 1812
Yosemite National Park Research Library, 1817
Zion National Park Library, 1818

Natural Resources

Alaska Resources Library, 1819
Bandelier National Monument Library, 1606
Bureau of Land Management, California State Office Library, 1473
Bureau of Land Management, Colorado State Office Library, 1476
Bureau of Land Management, Colorado State Office Library, 1477
Bureau of Land Management, District Library, 1480
Bureau of Land Management, Fairbanks District Office Library, 1486
Bureau of Land Management, Folsom District Office Library, 1487
Bureau of Land Management, Idaho State Office Library, 1489
Bureau of Land Management, Lake States Office Library, 1491
Bureau of Land Management Library, 1495
Bureau of Land Management, Richfield Office Library, 1512
Bureau of Land Management, Spokane District Office Library, 1522
Bureau of Land Management, Susanville District Office Library, 1523
Bureau of Land Management, Utah State Office Library, 1525
Bureau of Land Management, Wyoming State Office Library, 1528
Bureau of Mines, Metallurgy Research Center Library, 1537
Department of the Interior, Center for Information & Library Services, Natural Resources Library, Law Branch, 1820
Department of the Interior, Center for Information & Library Services, Natural Resources Library, Law Branch, 1822
Environmental Protection Agency, Region 5 Library, 1989
Grand Canyon National Park Research Library, 1689
Heritage Conservation & Recreation Service, Northwest Region Office Library, 1584
Katmai National Park & Preserve Library, 1718
Jean Lafitte National Historical Park Library, 1722
Abraham Lincoln Birthplace National Historic Site Library, 1728

North Central Forest Experiment Station Library, 116
Pacific Southwest Regional Office Library, 1590
Pinnacles National Monument Library, 1768
SOUTHFORNET Science Library, 120
US Army Corps of Engineers, New England Division Technical Library, 689

Naturalization

Immigration & Naturalization Law Library, 1911
Immigration & Naturalization Service Library, 1912

Nautical Cartography

NOAA, Library & Information Services Division, 182

Nautical Charts

Map Library & Information Service Library, 163

Nautical Law

US Coast Guard Academy Library, 1942

Navajo Indians

Aneth Community School Library, 1363
Greasewood Boarding School Library, 1401
Hubbell Trading Post National Historic Site Library, 1707
Navajo National Monument Library, 1753
Sanostee Boarding School Media Center, 1438

Naval Academy

Naval Academy Preparatory School Library, 1011

Naval Air Systems Command

Patuxent Naval Aviation Logistics Center, Technical Library, 1130

Naval Architecture

Long Beach Naval Shipyard, Technical Library, 995
Naval Sea Systems Command, Library Documentation Branch, 1072
Naval Supervisor of Shipbuilding, Conversion & Repair, Technical Library, 1079
Philadelphia Naval Shipyard, Technical Library, 1136
Puget Sound Naval Shipyard, Engineering Library, 1145

Naval Art

Long Beach Naval Shipyard, Technical Library, 995

Naval Aviation

Naval Air Development Center, Scientific & Technical Library Branch, 1014

Naval Construction

Naval Construction Battalion Center Library, 1032

Naval Engineering

Pacific Naval Facilities Engineering Command Library, 1128
Pearl Harbor Naval Shipyard, Technical Library, 1132

Naval Medicine

Naval Submarine Medical Research Laboratory, Medical Library, 1078

Naval Science

Armed Forces Staff College Library, 1253
Naval Audit Service Headquarters Library, 1023
Naval Postgraduate School, Dudley Knox Library, 1062
Naval War College Library, 1095
Navy Department Library, 1106
Oceana Naval Air Station Library, 1120
Office of the Chief of Naval Research Library, 1122
Patuxent Naval Air Station Library, 1129
Pearl Harbor Naval Base Library, 1131
Philadelphia Naval Shipyard, Technical Library, 1136
San Diego Naval Training Center Library, 1153
Space & Naval Warfare Systems Command Library, 1156
US Naval Academy, Nimitz Library, 1169

Naval Shipyards

Charleston Naval Shipyard, Technical Library, 962
Norfolk Naval Shipyard, Technical Library, 1117
Pearl Harbor Naval Shipyard, Technical Library, 1132
Portsmouth Naval Shipyard Library, 1142
Portsmouth Naval Shipyard Museum, Marshall W Butt Library, 1143

Naval Supplies

Naval Explosive Ordnance Disposal Technology Center, Library, 1042
Naval Ordnance Station, Library Branch, 1059
Naval Ordnance Station, Technical Library, 1060
Naval Sea Support Center, Pacific, Library, 1071
Naval Sea Systems Command, Library Documentation Branch, 1072
Naval Supply Center Library, 1080
Naval Supply Center, Technical Division Library, 1081
Naval Supply Corps School Library, 1082
Naval Surface Weapons Center, Technical Library, 1088
Naval Underwater Systems Center, New London Laboratory, Technical Library, 1092
Naval Underwater Systems Center, Technical Library, 1094
Naval Weapons Center, Technical Library, 1097
Navy Supply Center, Inventory Control Department, Technical Library, 1113
Portsmouth Naval Shipyard Museum, Marshall W Butt Library, 1143
Portsmouth Naval Shipyard, Supply Department, Technical Library, 1144
San Diego Naval Supply, Technical Library, 1152
Supervisor of Shipbuilding Conversion & Repair Library, 1159
Supervisor of Shipbuilding, Conversion & Repair, Technical Library, 1165

Naval War College

Beeville Naval Air Station Library, 951

Naval Warfare

Fleet Anti-Submarine Warfare Training Center, Pacific, Technical Library, 977
Fleet Combat Training Center Library, 979
Naval Amphibious School Library, 1021
Naval Mine Warfare Engineering Activity, Library, 1055
Philadelphia Naval Station Library, 1137
Space & Naval Warfare Systems Command Library, 1156

Naval Warfare Publications Library

Fleet Anti-Submarine Warfare Training Center, Pacific, Technical Library, 977

Naval Weapons

Concord Naval Weapons Station Library, 969
Naval Ship Weapons Systems, Engineering Station, Technical Library, 1077
Naval Surface Weapons Center, General Library, 1086
Naval Surface Weapons Center, Technical Library, 1088
Naval Weapons Center Library, 1096
Naval Weapons Center, Technical Library, 1097
Naval Weapons Station Library, 1098
Naval Weapons Station, Seal Beach, Scientific & Technical Library, 1100
Naval Weapons Station, Seal Beach, Scientific & Technical Library, Corona Site, 1101
Naval Weapons Station, Seal Beach, Scientific & Technical Library, Fallbrook Site, 1102
Naval Weapons Station, Technical Services Library, 1103
Naval Weapons Station, WQEC Technical Library, 1104
Naval Weapons Support Center, Technical Library, 1105
Navy Fleet Ballistic Missile Submarine Training Center, Technical Publications Library, 1109
US Navy Atlantic Fleet Weapons Training Facility, 1222

Navigation

Department of Transportation Library, 1931
US Army Corps of Engineers, North Central Division Library, 698
US Army Corps of Engineers, St Paul District Technical Library, 714
US Customs Service, Library & Information Center, 1954
US Naval Observatory Library, 1172

Navigation History

Navy Department Library, 1106
US Naval Observatory Library, 1172

Navy

Cubi Point Naval Air Station Library, 1182
Naval Air Development Center, Scientific & Technical Library Branch, 1014
Naval Amphibious Base Library, 1020
Naval Amphibious School, John Sidney McCain, Jr Amphibious Warfare Library, 1022
Naval Avionics Center, Technical Library, 1024

Naval Intelligence Support Center Library, 1052
Naval Mobile Construction Battalion Center Library, 1056
Naval Regional Library, Groton, 1064
Navy Department Library, 1106
Navy Department Library, 1106
Navy Environmental Health Center Library, 1108
US Naval Institute, Photographic & Reference Library, 1171

Navy Audit Reports

Naval Audit Service Headquarters Library, 1023

Navy Equipment

Naval Electronic Systems Engineering Center, Technical Library, 1038

Navy History

Bangor Naval Submarine Base Library, 948
Cubi Point Naval Air Station Library, 1182
Great Lakes Naval Training Station Center Library, 985
Kingsville Naval Air Station Library, 992
Long Beach Naval Station Library, 996
Mare Island Naval Station, Rodman Library, 998
Mayport Naval Air Station Library, 1000
Mayport Naval Station Library, 1003
Miramar Naval Air Station Library, 1008
Naval Education & Training Center, Main Library, 1035
Naval Postgraduate School, Dudley Knox Library, 1061
Naval Postgraduate School, Dudley Knox Library, 1062
Naval School, Civil Engineer Corps Officers, Moreell Library, 1068
Naval War College Library, 1095
Naval Weapons Station Library, 1098
Navy Department Library, 1106
Oceana Naval Air Station Library, 1120
Pearl Harbor Naval Base Library, 1131
Portsmouth Naval Shipyard Museum, Marshall W Butt Library, 1143
Puget Sound Naval Shipyard, Engineering Library, 1145
Franklin D Roosevelt Library, 2079
Franklin D Roosevelt National Historic Site Library, 1776
US Naval Academy, Nimitz Library, 1169
US Naval Historical Center, Operational Archives Branch, 1170

Navy Hull

Naval Ship Systems Engineering Station, Technical Library, 1076

Navy Regulations

Defense General Supply Center Library, 1260

Navy Seabees

Naval School, Civil Engineer Corps Officers, Moreell Library, 1068

Navy, Secretary of

Portsmouth Naval Shipyard Museum, Marshall W Butt Library, 1143

Navy Ships

Long Beach Naval Station Library, 996
Naval Ship Research & Development Center, W Taylor Library, 1075
Naval Surface Warfare Officers School Library, 1085
Portsmouth Naval Shipyard, Supply Department, Technical Library, 1144

Near Eastern Art

Freer Gallery of Art Library, 2455

Neilson Collection

Saratoga National Historical Park Library, 1788

Netherlands

Camp New Amsterdam, Base Library/FL 5688, 362

Netherlands Law

21st SUPCOM, Law Library, 898

Neurology

Armed Forces Institute of Pathology, Ash Library, 405
Medical Research Institute of Chemical Defense, Wood Technical Library, 598
Karl A Menninger Medical Library, 2276
National Institute of Mental Health Library, Division of Intramural Research Programs, 1322
National Institute on Aging, Gerontology Research Center Library, 1343
Tripler Army Medical Center, Medical Library, 636
Veterans Administration Medical & Regional Office Center Library, 2291
Veterans Administration Medical Center Library Service, 2346
Veterans Administration Medical Center Library Service, 2373

Nevada

Bureau of Mines, Western Field Operations Center Library, 1543
Geological Survey, Public Inquiries Office Library, 1575

Nevada Law

Economic Development Administration, Seattle Regional Office Library, 146

New England

Environmental Protection Agency, Region 1 Library, 1984

New England History

Loring AFB, Base Library/FL 4678, 281
Salem Maritime National Historic Site Library, 1783

New Hampshire Law

US Court of Appeals First Circuit Library, 18

New Jersey

Bureau of the Census, Information Services Program Library, 142
Federal Home Loan Bank of New York Library, 2019

New Mexico

Bureau of Land Management, New Mexico State Office Central Files/Library, 1504
Bureau of Land Management, New Mexico State Office Library, 1505
Geological Survey, Public Inquiries Office Library, 1575
Geological Survey, Water Resources Division Library, 1582

New Mexico History

Chaco Center Archives & Library, Branch of Cultural Research Library, 1630
Salinas National Monument Library, 1784

New Mexico Law

Department of the Interior, Office of the Solicitor, Field Solicitor, Law Library, 1836

New York

Federal Home Loan Bank of New York Library, 2019
Ft Drum Post Library, 465
Plattsburgh AFB, Base Library/FL 4615, 308
Seneca Post Library, 625

New York History

Federal Hall National Memorial Library, 1661
Ft Hamilton, Morale Support Activities, Post Library, 474
Franklin D Roosevelt National Historic Site Library, 1776
West Point Post Library, 803

New York, Port of

US Army Corps of Engineers, New York District Technical Library, 693

Newbery, Caldeco H.

March AFB, Base Library/FL 4664, 287

Newspapers

Ft George G Meade, Language Training Facility Library, 533
Library of Congress, 9
Riverside Indian School Library, 1432

Nez Perce Indians

Big Hole National Battlefield Library, 1609
Nez Perce National Historic Park Library, 1754

Noise

Environmental Protection Agency Library, Region 8, 1978

Nonprint Materials

Royal C Johnson Veterans Memorial Medical Center, Medical & Patient's Library, 2274
Kirtland AFB, Medical Library/SGAL, 274
Library of Congress, 9
National Library Service for the Blind & Physically Handicapped, Library of Congress, 10
Veterans Administration Medical Center & Patients' Library, 2293
Veterans Administration Medical Center, Jefferson Barracks Division, Library Service, 2296

Veterans Administration Medical Center Library Service, 2333
Veterans Administration Medical Center Library Service, 2345
Veterans Administration Medical Center Library Service, 2375
Veterans Administration Medical Center Library Service, 2383
Veterans Administration Westside Medical Center Library Service, 2442

Norfolk Naval Shipyard

Portsmouth Naval Shipyard Museum, Marshall W Butt Library, 1143

North Carolina

Cape Hatteras National Seashore Library, 1620
Environmental Protection Agency, Region 4 Library, 1988
Federal Reserve Bank of Richmond, Research Library, 2040

North Carolina History

Cape Hatteras National Seashore Library, 1620
Moores Creek National Military Park Library, 1736

North, Charles E.

National Agricultural Library, 124

North Dakota

Bureau of Land Management, Montana State Office Library, 1502
Theodore Roosevelt National Park Library, 1777

North Dakota History

Theodore Roosevelt National Park Library, 1777

Northwest

Heritage Conservation & Recreation Service, Northwest Region Office Library, 1584
Pacific Northwest Region Library, 1548
Pacific Northwest Regional Library System, 1760
Sitka National Historic Park Library, 1794
US Army Corps of Engineers, Seattle District Library, 718

Northwestern History

Ft Clatsop National Memorial Library, 1666
Ft Vancouver National Historic Site Library, 1680
Olympic National Park Library, 1757

Nuclear Chemistry

Brookhaven National Laboratory, Research Library, 1293

Nuclear Energy

The Energy Library, Germantown Branch, 1299
Los Alamos National Laboratory Libraries, 1303
Nevada Technical Library, Department of Energy, 1311
Tennessee Valley Authority, Technical Library, 2102

Nuclear Engineering

Argonne National Laboratory, Argonne-West, Technical Library, 1288
Argonne National Laboratory, Technical Information Services Department, 1289
Brookhaven National Laboratory, Research Library, 1293
Mare Island Naval Shipyard, Technical Library, 997

Nuclear Explosives

Nevada Technical Library, Department of Energy, 1311

Nuclear Medicine

Bureau of Radiological Health Library, 1329
Center for Devices & Radiological Health Library, 1330
Medical & Health Sciences Division Library, 1306

Nuclear Nonproliferation

Brookhaven National Laboratory, Nuclear Safeguards Library, 1292

Nuclear Physics

Brookhaven National Laboratory, Research Library, 1293

Nuclear Safety

Brookhaven National Laboratory, Nuclear Safeguards Library, 1292
Sandia National Laboratories, Technical Library, 1314

Nuclear Science

Argonne National Laboratory, Argonne-West, Technical Library, 1288
Argonne National Laboratory, Technical Information Services Department, 1289
National Weather Service, Weather Service Nuclear Support Office Library, 181
Nuclear Regulatory Commission Library, 2087
Redstone Scientific Information Center, 615
Sandia National Laboratories, Technical Library, 1313

Nuclear Waste

Basalt Waste Isolation Project Library, 1290
Nevada Technical Library, Department of Energy, 1311
Sandia National Laboratories, Technical Library, 1314
US Army Corps of Engineers, Buffalo District Technical Library, 661

Nuclear Weapons

Air Force Weapons Laboratory Technical Library/FL 2809, 209
Defense Nuclear Agency, Technical Library Services, 1271
Los Alamos National Laboratory Libraries, 1303
National Atomic Museum Library, Public Document Room, 1309
Sandia National Laboratories, Technical Library, 1314
US Arms Control & Disarmament Agency Library, 2103

Nursery Trade Catalogs

US National Arboretum Library, 91

Nursing

Bethesda Naval Hospital, Edward Rhodes Stitt Library, 953
Camp Lejeune Naval Hospital, Medical & General Libraries, 957
Camp Pendleton Naval Hospital Library, 959
Ft Carson, Evans US Army Community Hospital, Medical Library, 453
Ft Dix, Walson Army Community Hospital, Medical Library, 463
Ft Eustis, McDonald US Army Community Hospital, Medical Library, 466
Ft Sam Houston, Academy of Health Sciences, Stimson Library, 484
Ft Sam Houston, Brooke Army Medical Center, Medical Library, 485
Ft Huachuca, Raymond W Bliss Army Community Hospital, Medical Library, 490
Ft Rucker, Medical Library, 551
David Grant USAF Medical Center, Medical Library/SGEL, 252
James A Haley Veterans Hospital, Library Service, 2272
Royal C Johnson Veterans Memorial Medical Center, Medical & Patient's Library, 2274
Keesler AFB, Medical Library/SGAL, 270
Memphis Naval Regional Medical Center, General & Medical Libraries, 1005
Karl A Menninger Medical Library, 2276
Orlando Naval Hospital, Medical Library, 1125
Franklin Delano Roosevelt Hospital, Veterans Administration Library Service, 2281
Sheppard AFB Regional Hospital, Medical Library, 322
USAF School of Health Care Science, Academic Library/FL 3021, 337
US Army Corps of Engineers, Huntington District, Technical Library, 670
US Army, Keller Army Community Hospital Library, 746
Veterans Administration Hospital, Health Sciences Library, 2287
Veterans Administration Library Service, Edith Nourse Rogers Memorial Veterans Hospital, 2290
Veterans Administration Medical Center, Health Sciences Library, 2294
Veterans Administration Medical Center Learning Resources Center, 2299
Veterans Administration Medical Center Library, 2303
Veterans Administration Medical Center Library, 2314
Veterans Administration Medical Center Library, 2316
Veterans Administration Medical Center Library, 2319
Veterans Administration Medical Center Library-Learning Resources Center, 2322
Veterans Administration Medical Center Library Service, 2325
Veterans Administration Medical Center Library Service, 2332
Veterans Administration Medical Center Library Service, 2333
Veterans Administration Medical Center Library Service, 2334
Veterans Administration Medical Center Library Service, 2341
Veterans Administration Medical Center Library Service, 2344
Veterans Administration Medical Center Library Service, 2345
Veterans Administration Medical Center Library Service, 2348
Veterans Administration Medical Center Library Service, 2349
Veterans Administration Medical Center Library Service, 2352
Veterans Administration Medical Center Library Service, 2362
Veterans Administration Medical Center Library Service, 2363
Veterans Administration Medical Center Library Service, 2365
Veterans Administration Medical Center Library Service, 2366
Veterans Administration Medical Center Library Service, 2371
Veterans Administration Medical Center Library Service, 2373
Veterans Administration Medical Center Library Service, 2383
Veterans Administration Medical Center, Medical Library, 2386
Veterans Administration Medical Center, Medical Library, 2390
Veterans Administration Medical Center, Medical Library, 2391
Veterans Administration Medical Center, Medical Library, 2392
Veterans Administration Medical Center, Medical Library, 2393
Veterans Administration Medical Center, Medical Library, 2395
Veterans Administration Medical Center, Medical Library, 2398
Veterans Administration Medical Center, Medical Library, 2400
Veterans Administration Medical Center, Medical Library, 2403
Veterans Administration Medical Center, Medical Library, 2406
Veterans Administration Medical Center, Medical Library, 2409
Veterans Administration Medical Center, Medical & Patient's Library, 2413
Veterans Administration Medical Center, Medical & Patient's Library, 2414
Veterans Administration Medical Center, Medical & Patients' Library, 2419
Veterans Administration Medical Center, Medical & Patients' Library, 2422
Veterans Administration Medical Center, Medical & Patients' Library Wade Park & Brecksville Units, 2423
Veterans Administration Medical & Regional Office Center Medical Library, 2434

Nursing Homes

Veterans Administration Medical Center Library-Learning Resources Center, 2322

Nutrition

Beltsville Human Nutrition Research Center, 71
Center for Food Safety & Applied Nutrition Library, 1332
Food & Nutrition Information Center, 123
Food & Nutrition Service Reference Center, 97
Roman L Hruska US Meat Animal Research Center Library, 75
Karl A Menninger Medical Library, 2276
National Agricultural Library, 124

National Marine Fisheries Service, Southeast Fisheries Center Library, 167

Southern Regional Research Center Library, 81

Tunison Laboratory of Fish Nutrition Library, 1559

Veterans Administration Medical Center, Medical Library, 2389

Veterans Administration Medical Center, Medical Library, 2393

Veterans Administration Medical & Regional Office Center Medical Library, 2434

Western Regional Research Center Library, 92

Obstetrics

Kirtland AFB, Medical Library/SGAL, 274

Occupational Education

Gunter AFB, Base Library/FL 3370, 256

March AFB, Base Library/FL 4664, 287

Occupational Health and Safety

Air Force Occupational & Environmental Health Laboratory, Technical Library/ FL 2817, 203

Appalachian Laboratory for Occupational Safety & Health Library, 1325

Bureau of Labor Statistics Library, 1920

Bureau of Labor Statistics, Regional Office, Reference Library, 1921

Bureau of Mines, Twin Cities Research Center Library, 1542

Federal Mine Safety & Health Review Commission Library, 2447

Federal Mine Safety & Health Review Commission Library, 2448

Long Beach Naval Shipyard, Technical Library, 995

Mare Island Naval Shipyard, Technical Library, 997

Medical & Health Sciences Division Library, 1306

National Institute for Occupational Safety & Health Library, 1328

National Mine Health & Safety Academy, Learning Resource Center, 1923

Navy Environmental Health Center Library, 1108

Occupational Safety & Health Administration, Region 3, Library, 1924

Occupational Safety & Health Review Commission Library, 2088

Occupational Safety & Health Administration, Technical Data Center, 1925

US Army Environmental Hygiene Agency Library, 733

Occupational Medicine

Occupational Safety & Health Administration, Technical Data Center, 1925

Ocean Thermal Energy

Department of Energy, Solar Research Institute, Technical Library, 1296

Oceanography

Assateague Island National Seashore Library, 1603

Department of Energy, Solar Research Institute, Technical Library, 1296

Environmental Protection Agency, Research Laboratory Library, 1993

Geophysical Fluid Dynamics Laboratory Library, 160

Matthew Fontaine Maury Oceanographic Library, 999

National Museum of Natural History, Branch Library, 2462

NOAA, Great Lakes Environmental Research Laboratory Library, 170

NOAA, Miami Library, 171

NOAA, Mountain Administrative Support Center, 172

NOAA, Seattle Center Library, 175

NOAA, Southeast Fisheries Center, Galveston Laboratory Library, 176

NOAA World Data Center A, Oceanography, 177

National Science Foundation Library, 2085

Naval Civil Engineering Laboratory Library, 1026

Naval Coastal Systems Center, Technical Information Services Branch, 1028

Naval Environmental Prediction Research Facility/Fleet Numerical Oceanography Center Technical Library, 1041

Naval Ocean Research & Development Activity Library, 1057

Naval Ocean Systems Center, Technical Libraries, 1058

NOAA, Library & Information Services Division, 182

Northwest & Alaska Fisheries Center Library, 183

Office of Naval Research, Detachment Boston Library, 1121

Panama City Laboratory Library, 185

Pascagoula Laboratory Library, 186

Rice Library, 187

Southwest Fisheries Center Library, 188

US Coast Guard Academy Library, 1942

Lionel A Walford Library, 191

Oceanography History

NOAA, Library & Information Services Division, 182

Ohio

Cuyahoga Valley National Recreation Area Library, 1648

Wright-Patterson AFB, Base Library/FL 2300, 344

Ohio Canal

Cuyahoga Valley National Recreation Area Library, 1648

Ohio Law

US Army Corps of Engineers, Huntington District Law Library, 669

Oil and Gas Industry

Bureau of Land Management, Elko District Office Library, 1484

Geological Survey, Resource Appraisal Group Library, 1577

National Institute for Petroleum & Energy Research Library, 1310

Oil Shale

Bureau of Mines, Twin Cities Research Center Library, 1542

Okinawa

Kadena AFB, Base Library/FL 5270, 373

Torii Station Library, DPCA, MSAD, 897

Oklahoma

National Archives & Records Administration, Fort Worth Branch, 2075

Oklahoma History

Cherokee Strip Living Museum Library, 1633

Oklahoma Law

National Archives & Records Administration, Fort Worth Branch, 2075

Olympic Peninsula

Olympic National Park Library, 1757

Omaha Exposition

Haskell Indian Junior College, Learning Resource Center, 1403

Operations Research

Naval Postgraduate School, Dudley Knox Library, 1062

Navy Personnel Research & Development Center, Technical Library, 1110

US Army TRADOC Systems Analysis Activity TRASANA, Technical Library, 785

Ophthalmology

Kirtland AFB, Medical Library/SGAL, 274

San Diego Naval Hospital, Thompson Medical Library, 1149

Optics

Arnold Engineering Development Center Technical Library/FL 2804, 218

National Solar Observatory, Technical Library, 2086

Naval Weapons Center, Technical Library, 1097

Office of Naval Research, Detachment Boston Library, 1121

Smithsonian Institution, Astrophysical Observatory Library, 2467

Options Trading

Commodity Futures Trading Commission Library, 1965

Oral History Collections

American Museum of Immigration Library, 1596

Chesapeake & Ohio Canal National Historic Park Resource Library, 1634

Grant-Kohrs Ranch National Historic Site Library, 1692

Lyndon B Johnson National Historical Park Library, 1716

Marine Corps Historical Center Library, 1237

Mount Rushmore National Memorial Library, 1740

National Agricultural Library, 124

National Maritime Museum, J Porter Shaw Library, 1745

National Park Service, Western Regional Resources Library, 1752

Rocky Mountain National Park Library, 1775

US Air Force Historical Research Center, 334

US Naval Academy, Nimitz Library, 1169

Voyageurs National Park Library, 1808

Orchestra Music
US Marine Band, Music Library, 1243

Oregon
Bureau of Mines, Western Field Operations Center Library, 1543
Pacific Northwest Regional Library System, 1760

Oregon Law
Economic Development Administration, Seattle Regional Office Library, 146

Oregon Trail
Scotts Bluff National Monument, Oregon Trail Association Library, 1790

Organic Chemistry
Geological Survey, National Water Quality Laboratory-Library, 1572
USDA Northern Regional Research Center Library, 87

Organized Crime
Department of Justice Criminal Library, 1852

Orient
US Military Academy Library, 794

Origin of Life Collection
NASA-AMES Research Center, Life Sciences Library, 2060

Ornithology
National Museum of Natural History, Branch Library, 2462

Orr, Elison
Effigy Mounds National Monument Library, 1658

Orthopedics
Ft Carson, Evans US Army Community Hospital, Medical Library, 453
Kirtland AFB, Medical Library/SGAL, 274
Veterans Administration Medical Center Library Service, 2341
Veterans Administration Office of Technology Transfer-Reference Collection, 2438

Ozark History
Mr & Mrs John K Hulston Civil War Research Library, 1708

Ozark Riverways
Ozark National Scenic Riverways Library, 1759

Ozarks
Buffalo National River Library, 1615

Pacific Basin
Federal Reserve Bank of San Francisco, Research Library, 2042

Pacific Islands
Andersen Base Library/FL 4624, 350
Peace Corps Information Services, Division Library, 2090
Schofield Barracks, Sgt Yano Library, 622

Packaging
US Army Natick Research, Development, & Engineering Center, Technical Library, 766

Padre Island
Padre Island National Seashore Library, 1761

Painting
Archives of American Art, 2453
Hirshhorn Museum & Sculpture Garden Library, 2456

Pajarito Plateau
Bandelier National Monument Library, 1606

Paleobiology
National Museum of Natural History, Branch Library, 2462

Paleontology
Badlands National Park Library, 1605
Carlsbad Caverns & Guadalupe Mountains National Parks Headquarters Library, 1624
John Day Fossil Beds National Monument Library, 1649
Dinosaur National Monument Library, 1656
Fossil Butte National Monument Library, 1681
Lake Mead National Recreation Area Library, 1723

Paleopathology
Fossil Butte National Monument Library, 1681

Panama
Ft Clayton Post Library, 838

Panama Canal
Ft Clayton Post Library, 838

Papago Literature
San Simon Media Center, 1437
Santa Rosa Elementary School Library, 1441

Parachutes
Naval Weapons Center, Technical Library, 1097

Park Administration
Wind Cave National Park Library, 1814

Park History
Cabrillo National Monument Library, 1616
Harpers Ferry Center Library, 1699
Lake Meredith Recreation Area Library, 1724
Rocky Mountain National Park Library, 1775
Western Archeological & Conservation Center Library, 1810
Whiskeytown Unit Library, National Park Service, 1811
Wind Cave National Park Library, 1814

Parks
Horace M Albright Training Center Library, 1594
Bighorn Canyon National Recreation Area Library, 1611
Carlsbad Caverns & Guadalupe Mountains National Parks Headquarters Library, 1624
Commission of Fine Arts Library, 1964
Cuyahoga Valley National Recreation Area Library, 1648
Department of the Interior, Center for Information & Library Services, Natural Resources Library, 1821
Everglades National Park Research Center Library, 1660
Harpers Ferry Center Library, 1699
Isle Royale National Park Library, 1711
Moores Creek National Military Park Library, 1736
Mound City Group National Monument Library, 1738
Muir Woods National Monument, Eleanor Bello Memorial Research Library, 1742
National Capital Parks-East Library, 1744
National Park Service, Central Compliance Library, 1746
National Park Service Library, 1747
National Park Service Midwest Regional Library, 1749
National Park Service, Southeast Regional Office Library, 1750
National Park Service, Western Regional Resources Library, 1752
Olympic National Park Library, 1757
Pacific Northwest Regional Library System, 1760
Pinnacles National Monument Library, 1768
Wind Cave National Park Library, 1814

Parole
US Parole Commission Library, 1918

Pastoral Care
Bethesda Naval Hospital, Edward Rhodes Stitt Library, 953
Edison National Historic Site, 1657
Naval Chaplains' School Library, 1025

Patents
Bureau of Land Management, Eastern States Office Library, 1483
Patent & Trademark Office, Law Library, 193
Patent & Trademark Office Scientific Library, 194
US Army Legal Services Agency, Law Library, 750
US Court of Appeals for the Federal Circuit Library, 53
US International Trade Commission, Law Library, 2269

Pathobiology
Oxford Laboratory Library, 184

Pathology
Armed Forces Institute of Pathology, Ash Library, 405
Armed Forces Institute of Pathology, Ash Library, 1252
National Zoological Park Library Branch, 2463
US Army Aeromedical Research Laboratory, Medical Library, 639

US National Arboretum Library, 91
US Naval Academy, Nimitz Library, 1169
US Naval Institute, Photographic & Reference Library, 1171
Western Archeological & Conservation Center Library, 1810

Photography

Lowry AFB, Base Library/FL 3059, 282

Photovoltaics

Department of Energy, Solar Research Institute, Technical Library, 1296

Physical Sciences

Air Force Weapons Laboratory Technical Library/FL 2809, 209
Benet Weapons Laboratory, Technical Library, 416
Bureau of Mines, Metallurgy Research Center Library, 1537
Los Alamos National Laboratory Libraries, 1303
NASA Goddard Space Flight Center, Wallops Flight Facility Library, 2065
NASA Headquarters, S & T Library & Systems Support, 2069
National Science Foundation Library, 2085
Naval Research Laboratory, Ruth H Hooker Technical Library, 1066
Office of the Chief of Naval Research Library, 1122
Patuxent Naval Air Station Library, 1129
Smithsonian Institution Libraries, 2468
US Coast Guard Academy Library, 1942
Wright-Patterson AFB, Technical Library/FL 2802, 345

Physical Therapy

Ft Carson, Evans US Army Community Hospital, Medical Library, 453
Ft Sam Houston, Academy of Health Sciences, Stimson Library, 484

Physics

Air Force Flight Test Center, Technical Library/FL 2806, 197
Air Force Geophysics Laboratory Research Library, 198
Air Force Office of Scientific Research Library/FL 2819, 204
Argonne National Laboratory, Technical Information Services Department, 1289
Armament Division Technical Library/FL 2825, 217
Arnold Engineering Development Center Technical Library/FL 2804, 218
Brookhaven National Laboratory, Research Library, 1293
Bureau of Mines, Albany Metallurgy Research Center, 1531
Defense Personnel Support Center, Directorate of Medical Material Library, 1272
Department of Energy, Grand Junction Area Office, Technical Library, 1294
Department of Energy, Solar Research Institute, Technical Library, 1296
Directorate of Medical Materiel Library, 1277
Environmental Measurements Laboratory Library, 1300
Fermi National Accelerator Laboratory Library, 1301
Library & Information Services Division, Camp Springs Center, 162
NASA Goddard Institute for Space Studies Library, 2063

NASA Goddard Space Flight Center Library, 2064
NASA Lyndon B Johnson Space Center, Technical Library, 2066
National Bureau of Standards Research Information Center, 155
NOAA, Mountain Administrative Support Center, 172
National Solar Observatory, Technical Library, 2086
Naval Ocean Systems Center, Technical Libraries, 1058
Naval Research Laboratory, USRD, 1067
Naval Surface Weapons Center, Technical Library, 1087
Naval Weapons Center, Technical Library, 1097
Redstone Scientific Information Center, 615
Sandia National Laboratories, Technical Library, 1313
Smithsonian Institution, Astrophysical Observatory Library, 2467
US Army Environmental Hygiene Agency Library, 733
US Army Ordnance Missile & Munitions Center & School, Technical Library, 769
US Army Strategic Defense Command, Huntsville, Library, 781
US Naval Academy, Nimitz Library, 1169
US Naval Observatory Library, 1172
White Sands Missile Range, Technical Library, 806
Winchester Engineering & Analytical Center Library, 1338

Physiology

Auke Bay Fisheries Laboratory Library, 158
National Institute on Aging, Gerontology Research Center Library, 1343
National Institutes of Health Library, 1345
NOAA, Southeast Fisheries Center, Galveston Laboratory Library, 176

Pima Indians

Casa Blanca Day School Library, 1373

Pinchot, Gifford

Equipment Development Center Library, 103

Pioneers

Chiricahua National Monument Library, 1636
Cumberland Gap National Historic Park Library, 1645
Homestead National Monument Library, 1702
Jefferson National Expansion Memorial Library, 1713
Lincoln Boyhood National Memorial Library, 1729

Pipelines

Bureau of Land Management, District Office Library, 1481
Bureau of Reclamation, Engineering & Research Center Library, 1547
Department of Transportation Library, 1931
Heritage Conservation & Recreation Service, Northwest Region Office Library, 1584

Plains Indians

Glacier National Park, George C. Ruhle Library, 1687
Knife River Indian Villages National Historic Site Library, 1721

Planning

Department of Housing & Urban Development Library, 1354

Plastic Surgery

Veterans Administration Office of Technology Transfer-Reference Collection, 2438

Plastics

US Army Armament Research & Development Center, Plastics Technical Evaluation Center, 643

Plymouth Records

Cape Cod National Seashore Library, 1619

Point Reyes National Seashore

Point Reyes National Seashore Library, 1770

Polar Bears

Marine Mammal Commission Library, 2449

Polar Regions

NOAA, Seattle Center Library, 175
National Science Foundation Library, 2085
Naval Civil Engineering Laboratory Library, 1026

Policy

Congressional Research Service, Library of Congress, 7

Policy Analysis

Office of Technology Assessment Information Center, 11

Political Science

Armed Forces Staff College Library, 1253
Defense Institute of Security Assistance Management Library/FL 2301, 235
Department of Justice Main Library, 1854
Department of State Library, 1927
Dwight D Eisenhower Library, 2071
Executive Office of the President Library, 64
Gerald R Ford Library, 2072
Herbert Hoover Presidential Library, 2073
John F Kennedy Presidential Library, 2074
Library of Congress, 9
National Defense University Library, 1278
National Endowment for the Humanities Library, 2083
National Labor Relations Board Library, 2084
Franklin D Roosevelt National Historic Site Library, 1776
Sagamore Hill National Historic Site Library, 1779
Harry S Truman Library, 2080
US Army Engineer Center & Ft Belvoir, Van Noy Library, 728
US Army John F Kennedy Special Warfare Center, Marquat Memorial Library, 747
US Information Agency Library, 2104
US Senate Library, 2

Pollution

Arnold Engineering Development Center Technical Library/FL 2804, 218
Atmospheric Turbulence & Diffusion Laboratory Library, 157
Bureau of Mines, Metallurgy Research Center Library, 1537
Department of Justice Lands Library, 1853
Environmental Protection Agency, Corvallis Environmental Research Library, 1971
Environmental Protection Agency, National Enforcement Investigation Center, Information Center, 1980
Environmental Protection Agency, Region 2, Field Office Library, 1985
Environmental Protection Agency, Region 2 Library, 1986
NOAA, Seattle Center Library, 175
Patuxent Wildlife Research Center Library, 1558
USDA, Agricultural Research Service, Snake River Conservation Research Service, 85

Polymers

USDA, Agricultural Research Service, Eastern Regional Research Center Library, 84

Population Census

Bureau of the Census, Atlanta Regional Office Library, 136
Bureau of the Census, Charlotte Regional Office Library, 137
Bureau of the Census, Dallas Regional Office Library, 138
Bureau of the Census, New York Regional Office Library, 144

Postal Law

US Postal Service Library, 2271

Postal Rate Commission

Postal Rate Commission Library, 2093

Poultry

National Agricultural Library, 124

Poverty

Bureau of the Census, Dallas Regional Office Library, 138
Food & Nutrition Service Reference Center, 97
Social Security Administration, District of Columbia Branch Library, 1352

Powell, Ralph L.

National Defense University Library, 1278

Prairie Ecosystems

Wind Cave National Park Library, 1814

Prairies

Homestead National Monument Library, 1702

Precipitation

Northwest Watershed Research Center, 78

Prehistoric America

Navajo National Monument Library, 1753
Petrified Forest National Park Library, 1766
Salinas National Monument Library, 1784
Wupatki National Monument Library, 1815

Preservation Programs

Historic American Buildings Survey Library, 1585
National Park Service, Central Compliance Library, 1746
National Register of Historic Places Library, 1589
Smithsonian Institution Libraries, Museum Support Center Branch, 2469
Martin Van Buren National Historic Site Library, 1805

Presidency

Adams National Historic Site, Stone Library, 1593
Jimmy Carter Library, 2070
Dwight D Eisenhower Library, 2071
Executive Office of the President Library, 64
Gerald R Ford Library, 2072
Ford's Theatre National Historic Site Library, 1664
Herbert Hoover Presidential Library, 2073
Andrew Johnson National Historic Site Library, 1715
John F Kennedy Presidential Library, 2074
Library of Congress, 9
Sagamore Hill National Historic Site Library, 1779
Harry S Truman Library, 2080
White House Library & Research Center, 66

Presidio of Monterey

US Army Museum Library, 764

Preventive Medicine

Centers for Disease Control Library, 1327
Ft Campbell, Blanchfield Army Community Hospital, Medical Library, 450
Ft Dix, Walson Army Community Hospital, Medical Library, 463
Ft Monmouth, Patterson Army Community Hospital, Medical & Patients' Library, 537
Navy Environmental Health Center Library, 1108

Prince Family Nursery

National Agricultural Library, 124

Printing

Library of Congress, 9

Prisoners of War

Andersonville National Historic Site Library, 1597
Survival Training Reference Library/FL 3061, 324

Prisons

Federal Prison System Library, 1870

Prisons, Bureau of

Milan Federal Correctional Institution Library, 1882

Procurement

Aviation Systems Command, Library & Information Center, 411
Department of Commerce, Law Library, 131
General Accounting Office, Office of Library Services, 5
General Services Administration Library, 2051
Pentagon Law Library, 604
US Army Logistics Library, 751
Western Area Power Administration, Office of General Counsel, Law Library, 1317

Productivity

Bureau of Labor Statistics Library, 1920
Bureau of Labor Statistics, Regional Office, Reference Library, 1921
Bureau of Labor Statistics, Regional Office, Reference Library, 1922

Prohibition

Bureau of Alcohol, Tobacco & Firearms Reference Library, 1947

Project Warrior

Alconbury Base Library/FL 5643, 349
Andersen Base Library/FL 4624, 350
Barksdale AFB, Base Library/FL 4608, 219
Base Library/FL 5543, 357
Eielson AFB, Base Library/FL 5004, 240
Elmendorf AFB, Base Library, 244
Hanscom AFB, Base Library/FL 2835, 258
Homestead AFB, Base Library/FL 4829, 266
Seymour Johnson AFB, Base Library/FL 4809, 268
Kadena AFB, Base Library/FL 5270, 373
Kelly AFB, Base Library/FL 2050, 272
Lowry AFB, Base Library/FL 3059, 282
Luke AFB, Base Library/FL 4887, 283
McClellan AFB, Base Library/FL 2040, 292
McConnell AFB, Base Library/FL 4621, 293
Military Airlift Command Library/FL 4401, 296
Minot AFB, Base Library/FL 4528, 297
Mountain Home AFB, Base Library/FL 4897, 299
Myrtle Beach AFB, Base Library/FL 4806, 300
Osan Base Library/FL 5294, 381
Thule Base Library/FL 2507, 388
Warrior Preparation Center, Library/FL 5649, 392
Whiteman AFB, Base Library/FL 4625, 342
Wright-Patterson AFB, Base Library/FL 2300, 344

Propellants

Naval Ordnance Station, Library Branch, 1059
Naval Weapons Center, Technical Library, 1097
Scientific & Technical Information Division Library, 623

Propulsion

Air Force Flight Test Center, Technical Library/FL 2806, 197
Arnold Engineering Development Center Technical Library/FL 2804, 218

Naval Air Propulsion Center, Technical Library, 1016

Naval Weapons Center, Technical Library, 1097

Redstone Scientific Information Center, 615

Wright-Patterson AFB, Technical Library/FL 2802, 345

Prosthetics

Veterans Administration Office of Technology Transfer-Reference Collection, 2438

Psychiatry

Fort Worth Federal Correctional Institute Library Services, 1871

Karl A Menninger Medical Library, 2276

Mirsky Medical Library, Brentwood Division, Veterans Administration Medical Center West, Los Angeles, 2278

National Institute of Mental Health Library, Division of Intramural Research Programs, 1322

Parklawn Health Library, 1350

Franklin Delano Roosevelt Hospital, Veterans Administration Library Service, 2281

St Elizabeth's Hospital, Health Sciences Library, 1324

Tripler Army Medical Center, Medical Library, 636

Veterans Administration Medical Center Learning Resources Center, 2299

Veterans Administration Medical Center Learning Resources Service, 2300

Veterans Administration Medical Center Library-Learning Resources Center, 2322

Veterans Administration Medical Center Library Service, 2325

Veterans Administration Medical Center Library Service, 2329

Veterans Administration Medical Center Library Service, 2332

Veterans Administration Medical Center Library Service, 2334

Veterans Administration Medical Center Library Service, 2336

Veterans Administration Medical Center Library Service, 2338

Veterans Administration Medical Center Library Service, 2343

Veterans Administration Medical Center Library Service, 2346

Veterans Administration Medical Center Library Service, 2347

Veterans Administration Medical Center Library Service, 2349

Veterans Administration Medical Center Library Service, 2352

Veterans Administration Medical Center Library Service, 2362

Veterans Administration Medical Center Library Service, 2367

Veterans Administration Medical Center Library Service, 2373

Veterans Administration Medical Center Library Service, 2374

Veterans Administration Medical Center Library Service, 2375

Veterans Administration Medical Center Library Service, 2377

Veterans Administration Medical Center Library Service, 2378

Veterans Administration Medical Center Library Service, 2380

Veterans Administration Medical Center, Medical Library, 2386

Veterans Administration Medical Center, Medical Library, 2391

Veterans Administration Medical Center, Medical Library, 2392

Veterans Administration Medical Center, Medical Library, 2408

Veterans Administration Medical Center, Medical Library, 2409

Veterans Administration Medical Center, Medical & Patient's Library, 2413

Veterans Administration Medical Center, Medical & Patients' Library, 2422

Veterans Administration Medical Center, Medical & Patients' Library Wade Park & Brecksville Units, 2423

Veterans Administration Medical Center Patients' Library, 2427

Veterans Administration Outpatient Clinic Library Service, 2439

Alvin C York Veterans Administration Medical Center, Library Service, 2443

Psychology

Air Force Human Resources Laboratory, Technical Library/FL 2870, 199

Ft Bliss, Valent Learning Resources Center Library, 446

Ft Sam Houston, Academy of Health Sciences, Stimson Library, 484

Fort Worth Federal Correctional Institute Library Services, 1871

Lemoore Naval Air Station Library, 993

Karl A Menninger Medical Library, 2276

Mirsky Medical Library, Brentwood Division, Veterans Administration Medical Center West, Los Angeles, 2278

National Institute on Aging, Gerontology Research Center Library, 1343

Naval Amphibious School Library, 1021

Naval Health Research Center, Wilkins Biomedical Library, 1046

Navy Personnel Research & Development Center, Technical Library, 1110

New River Marine Corps Air Station Library, 1240

Office of the Chief of Naval Research Library, 1122

Parklawn Health Library, 1350

Franklin Delano Roosevelt Hospital, Veterans Administration Library Service, 2281

St Elizabeth's Hospital, Health Sciences Library, 1324

US Army Laboratory Command, Human Engineering Laboratory Library, 748

US Army Military Police School, Ramsey Library, 759

US Army Ordnance Missile & Munitions Center & School, Technical Library, 769

US Army Research Institute, Technical Information Center, 773

US Department of Education, Office of Educational Research & Improvement Library, 1286

Veterans Administration Library Service, Edith Nourse Rogers Memorial Veterans Hospital, 2290

Veterans Administration Medical Center Learning Resources Center, 2299

Veterans Administration Medical Center Learning Resources Service, 2300

Veterans Administration Medical Center Library Service, 2325

Veterans Administration Medical Center Library Service, 2334

Veterans Administration Medical Center Library Service, 2343

Veterans Administration Medical Center Library Service, 2344

Veterans Administration Medical Center Library Service, 2347

Veterans Administration Medical Center Library Service, 2349

Veterans Administration Medical Center Library Service, 2358

Veterans Administration Medical Center Library Service, 2362

Veterans Administration Medical Center Library Service, 2364

Veterans Administration Medical Center Library Service, 2367

Veterans Administration Medical Center Library Service, 2373

Veterans Administration Medical Center Library Service, 2378

Veterans Administration Medical Center Library Service, 2380

Veterans Administration Medical Center, Medical Library, 2392

Veterans Administration Medical Center, Medical & Patients' Library, 2422

Veterans Administration Medical Center, Medical & Patients' Library Wade Park & Brecksville Units, 2423

Veterans Administration Medical Center Patients' Library, 2427

Wright-Patterson AFB, Medical Center Library, 347

Public Administration

Castle AFB, Baker Library/FL 4672, 230

Department of Justice Main Library, 1854

Elgin AFB, Base Library/FL 2823/SSL, 242

Executive Office of the President Library, 64

Ft Myer Post Library, 539

General Accounting Office, Office of Library Services, 5

NASA Headquarters, S & T Library & Systems Support, 2069

US Office of Personnel Management Library, 2089

Zaragoza Base Library/FL 5571, 394

Public Affairs

Gerald R Ford Library, 2072

National Endowment for the Humanities Library, 2083

Naval Weapons Station, MenRiv Library, 1099

US Army Intelligence School Library, 1284

US Information Agency Library, 2104

Public Health

Bureau of Radiological Health Library, 1329

Centers for Disease Control Library, 1327

Ft Sam Houston, Academy of Health Sciences, Stimson Library, 484

US Agency for International Development Water & Sanitation for Health Project Information Center, 2268

Public Lands

Bureau of Land Management, New Mexico State Office Central Files/Library, 1504

Bureau of Land Management, Salt Lake City District Office Library, 1519

Department of the Interior, Center for Information & Library Services, Natural Resources Library, Law Branch, 1822

Public Policy

Congressional Research Service, Library of Congress, 7

Public Relations

Ft Benjamin Harrison, Soldiers' Support Center Library, 479

Public Utilities

US Army Legal Services Agency, Law Library, 750

US Securities & Exchange Commission Library, 2096

Public Welfare

Health & Human Services Department Library, 1320

Social Security Administration, District of Columbia Branch Library, 1352

Public Works

Department of Justice Lands Library, 1853

US Army Corps of Engineers, North Central Division Library, 698

Pueblo Indians

Navajo National Monument Library, 1753

Puerto Rico

Federal Home Loan Bank of New York Library, 2019

Puerto Rico Law

US Court of Appeals First Circuit Library, 18

Put-in-Bay

Perry's Victory & International Peace Memorial Library, 1764

Pyrotechnics

Scientific & Technical Information Division Library, 623

Quality Control

Geological Survey, National Water Quality Laboratory-Library, 1572

Race Relations

Bergstrom AFB, Base Library/FL 4857, 221

Radar

Air Force Systems Command Technical Information Center, 208

Air Force Western Space & Missile Center, Technical Library/FL 2827, 210

National Severe Storms Laboratory Library, 178

Naval Explosive Ordnance Disposal Technology Center, Library, 1042

Pacific Missile Test Center, Technical Library, 1127

US Army Strategic Defense Command, Huntsville, Library, 781

Radford, Arthur

National Defense University Library, 1278

Radiation

Bureau of Radiological Health Library, 1329

Center for Devices & Radiological Health Library, 1330

Environmental Protection Agency Library, Region 8, 1978

Environmental Protection Agency, Region 5 Library, 1989

Environmental Protection Agency, Region 7 Library, 1991

Medical & Health Sciences Division Library, 1306

National Weather Service, Weather Service Nuclear Support Office Library, 181

Nevada Technical Library, Department of Energy, 1311

Nuclear Regulatory Commission Library, 2087

Smithsonian Environmental Research Center Library, Rockville Branch, 2465

Radiation Chemistry

Brookhaven National Laboratory, Research Library, 1293

Radiation Effects

Defense Nuclear Agency, National Naval Medical Center Library, 1270

Radiation Medicine

Center for Devices & Radiological Health Library, 1330

Radiation Safety

Air Force Occupational & Environmental Health Laboratory, Technical Library/FL 2817, 203

Radio

FCC Library, 2005

Naval Radio Station Library, 1063

Radio Science

NOAA, Mountain Administrative Support Center, 172

Radio Stations

FCC Chicago District Office Library, 2004

Radiobiology

Bureau of Radiological Health Library, 1329

Radiocarbon Dating

Smithsonian Environmental Research Center Library, Rockville Branch, 2465

Radiography

Bureau of Radiological Health Library, 1329

Radiology

Air Force School of Aerospace Medicine, Strughold Aeromedical Library/FL 2855, 206

Bureau of Radiological Health Library, 1329

Navy Environmental Health Center Library, 1108

Winchester Engineering & Analytical Center Library, 1338

Railroads

Allegheny Portage Railroad National Historic Site Library, 1595

Department of Transportation Library, 1931

Ranches

Grant-Kohrs Ranch National Historic Site Library, 1692

Pipe Springs National Monument Library, 1769

Range Lands

Bureau of Land Management, Arizona State Office Library, 1466

Bureau of Land Management, Arizona Strip, District Office Library, 1467

Bureau of Land Management, Bakersfield District Office Library, 1469

Bureau of Land Management, Bishop Resource Area Headquarters Library, 1470

Bureau of Land Management, California State Office Library, 1473

Bureau of Land Management, Cedar City District Library, 1474

Bureau of Land Management, District Library, 1480

Bureau of Land Management, District Office Library, 1482

Bureau of Land Management, Elko District Office Library, 1484

Bureau of Land Management, Folsom District Office Library, 1487

Bureau of Land Management, Kanab Office Library, 1490

Bureau of Land Management Library, 1495

Bureau of Land Management Library, 1497

Bureau of Land Management, Montana State Office Library, 1502

Bureau of Land Management, Phillips Resource Area Office Library, 1507

Bureau of Land Management, Phoenix District Office Library, 1508

Bureau of Land Management, Roseburg District Office Library, 1514

Bureau of Land Management, Safford District Office Library, 1516

Bureau of Land Management, Susanville District Office Library, 1523

WESTFORNET/FS-INFO Intermountain Research Station, 122

Rare Books

Air University Library/FL 3368, 211

Federal Hall National Memorial Library, 1661

Ft Sill, Morris Swett Technical Library, 558

Interstate Commerce Commission Library, 2053

Library of Congress, 9

National Agricultural Library, 124

National Air & Space Museum, Branch Library, 2457

National Bureau of Standards Research Information Center, 155

Navajo National Monument Library, 1753

Naval War College Library, 1095

NOAA, Library & Information Services Division, 182

Stewart Boarding School Library-Media Center, 1449

Thayer Engineering Library, 632

US Army Legal Services Agency, Law Library, 750

US Department of Education, Office of Educational Research & Improvement Library, 1286

US Naval Observatory Library, 1172

Yellowstone Association Research Library, 1816

Rayleigh Collection
Air Force Geophysics Laboratory Research Library, 198

Reactor Physics
Brookhaven National Laboratory, Research Library, 1293

Reading
US Department of Education, Office of Educational Research & Improvement Library, 1286

Real Estate
Bureau of Land Management, Burns District Office Library, 1472
Federal Home Loan Bank Board, Research Library, 2013
Federal Home Loan Bank of Chicago Library, 2015
US Army Corps of Engineers, New England Division Technical Library, 689
US Army Real Estate Agency Europe, Office of the Staff Judge Advocate, Army Law Library, 926

Reclamation
Western Area Power Administration, Office of General Counsel, Law Library, 1317

Reclamation, Bureau of
Water & Power Resources Service, Regional Library, 1847

Records Management
National Archives & Records Center, Kansas City Branch, 2077
National Archives Library, 2078

Recreation
Buffalo National River Library, 1615
Bureau of Land Management, Arizona State Office Library, 1466
Bureau of Land Management, Arizona Strip, District Office Library, 1467
Bureau of Land Management, Bakersfield District Office Library, 1469
Bureau of Land Management, California State Office Library, 1473
Bureau of Land Management, Cedar City District Library, 1474
Bureau of Land Management, District Library, 1480
Bureau of Land Management, District Office Library, 1481
Bureau of Land Management, District Office Library, 1482
Bureau of Land Management, Elko District Office Library, 1484
Bureau of Land Management, Eugene Office Library, 1485
Bureau of Land Management, Fairbanks District Office Library, 1486
Bureau of Land Management, Folsom District Office Library, 1487
Bureau of Land Management, Kanab Office Library, 1490
Bureau of Land Management, Phillips Resource Area Office Library, 1507
Bureau of Land Management, Phoenix District Office Library, 1508
Bureau of Land Management, Roseburg District Office Library, 1514

Bureau of Land Management, Wyoming State Office Library, 1528
Bureau of Land Management, Yuma District Office Library, 1529
Department of the Interior, Center for Information & Library Services, Natural Resources Library, 1821
Forestry Sciences Laboratory Library, 113
Heritage Conservation & Recreation Service, Northwest Region Office Library, 1584
Isle Royale National Park Library, 1711
Lake Central Regional Office Library, 1587
Lake Mead National Recreation Area Library, 1723
Mid-Continent Region Library, 1588
National Park Service Library, 1747
National Park Service, Southeast Regional Office Library, 1750
Pacific Southwest Regional Office Library, 1590
Tennessee Valley Authority, Land Between The Lakes Library, 2100
US Army Corps of Engineers, St Louis District Technical Library, 713
WESTFORNET/FS-INFO Intermountain Research Station, 122

Recreational Reading
Big Spring Federal Prison Camp Library, 1862
Camp Smith Library, 1230
Ft Dix, US Army Training Center & Post Library, 462
Mayport Naval Hospital, Crew's Library, 1001
Naval Regional Library, Groton, 1064
Scott AFB, Base Library/FL 4407, 318
Tinker AFB, Base Library/FL 2030, 325
US Army Intelligence & Security Command, Post Library, 744
Veterans Administration Medical Center Library, 2312
Veterans Administration Medical Center, Medical & Patient's Library, 2414

Recycling
Environmental Protection Agency, Region 5 Library, 1989

Redwood National Park
Redwood National Park Library, 1772

Redwoods
Muir Woods National Monument, Eleanor Bello Memorial Research Library, 1742

Regional Planning
National Park Service Library, 1747

Regulations
General Accounting Office, Office of Library Services, 5

Rehabilitation
Architectural & Transportation Barriers Compliance Board, Technical Library, 2445
Veterans Administration Medical Center, Hospital & Patients' Library, 2295
Veterans Administration Medical Center Learning Resources Service, 2300
Veterans Administration Medical Center Library, 2317
Veterans Administration Medical Center Library Service, 2325

Veterans Administration Medical Center Library Service, 2373
Veterans Administration Medical Center, Medical Library, 2389

Religion
Bethesda Naval Hospital, Edward Rhodes Stitt Library, 953
Edison National Historic Site, 1657
Naval Chaplains' School Library, 1025

Remote Sensing
Environmental Monitoring & Systems Laboratory Library, 1968
Matthew Fontaine Maury Oceanographic Library, 999
NASA Goddard Institute for Space Studies Library, 2063
NASA Goddard Space Flight Center Library, 2064
NASA-National Space Technology Laboratories, Research Library, 2068
Naval Ocean Systems Center, Technical Libraries, 1058
US Army Engineering Topographic Laboratories Scientific & Technical Information Center, 732
USDA, Agricultural Research Service, Water Conservation Research Library, 86

Remoting Sensing
EROS Data Center, Technical Reference Unit, 1561

Reproductive Biology
Roman L Hruska US Meat Animal Research Center Library, 75
The National Family Planning Information Clearinghouse Library, 1349
Russell Research Center Library, 80

Retirement
Pension Benefit Guaranty Corporation, Legal Department, Law Library, 2092
Railroad Retirement Board Library, 2094
Social Security Administration, District of Columbia Branch Library, 1352

Revolutionary War
George Rogers Clark National Historical Park Library, 1638
Federal Hall National Memorial Library, 1661
Ft Sumter National Monument Library, 1677
Guilford Courthouse National Military Park Library, 1695
Kings Mountain National Military Park Library, 1720
Minute Man National Historical Park Library, 1734
Moores Creek National Military Park Library, 1736
Morristown National Historical Park Library, 1737
Saratoga National Historical Park Library, 1788
Valley Forge National Historical Park, Horace "Vox" Willcox Library, 1804

Revolutionary Way
Salem Maritime National Historic Site Library, 1783

Science

Benet Weapons Laboratory, Technical Library, 416
Bureau of Land Management, New Orleans Outer-Continental Shelf Office Library, 1506
Consumer Product Safety Commission Library, 1967
Darnall Army Community Hospital, Medical Library, 426
Eastern Space & Missile Center Technical Library/FL 2828, 238
Effigy Mounds National Monument Library, 1658
FAA Central Regional Library, 1935
Food & Drug Administration Library, 1336
Ft Greely Post Library, 473
Geophysical Fluid Dynamics Laboratory Library, 160
Library & Information Services Division, Camp Springs Center, 162
Library of Congress, 9
March AFB, Base Library/FL 4664, 287
NASA Goddard Space Flight Center, Wallops Flight Facility Library, 2065
NOAA, Scientific Services Division, 174
National Science Foundation Library, 2085
Naval Intelligence Support Center Library, 1052
Naval Postgraduate School, Dudley Knox Library, 1061
Naval Postgraduate School, Dudley Knox Library, 1062
Patent & Trademark Office Scientific Library, 194
Smithsonian Institution Libraries, 2468
US Army Chemical School, Fisher Library, 654
US Army Corps of Engineers, Baltimore District Library Branch, 660
US Army Missile & Space Intelligence Center Library, 760
US Army Operational Test & Evaluation Agency, Technical Library, 767
US Army Ordnance Center & School Library, 768
US Army Strategic Defense Command, Huntsville, Library, 781
US Coast Guard Academy Library, 1942
US Court of International Trade Library, 60
US Customs Service, Library & Information Center, 1954
US Military Academy Library, 794
US Naval Academy, Nimitz Library, 1169

Science History

Air Force Geophysics Laboratory Research Library, 198
National Archives Library, 2078
National Museum of American History, Branch Library, 2461
National Museum of Natural History, Branch Library, 2462
Smithsonian Institution Archives, 2466
Smithsonian Institution Libraries, 2468
US Naval Observatory Library, 1172

Science, International

US Army Missile & Space Intelligence Center Library, 760

Science Policy

National Science Foundation Library, 2085
Office of Technology Assessment Information Center, 11

Sculpture

Archives of American Art, 2453
Commission of Fine Arts Library, 1964
Hirshhorn Museum & Sculpture Garden Library, 2456
National Museum of African Art, Branch Library, 2459

Sea Lions

National Marine Mammal Library, 168

Seals

National Marine Mammal Library, 168

Seashore

Assateague Island National Seashore Library, 1603
Canaveral National Seashore Park Library, 1617
Cape Cod National Seashore Library, 1619
Cape Hatteras National Seashore Library, 1620
Cape Lookout National Seashore Library, 1621
Fire Island National Seashore Library, 1662
Gulf Islands National Seashore Library, 1696
Padre Island National Seashore Library, 1761
Point Reyes National Seashore Library, 1770

Sebald, William

US Naval Academy, Nimitz Library, 1169

Securities

Federal Home Loan Bank Board, Law Library, 2012

Security

Office of Chief Counsel Legal Law Library, Savannah River Operations Office, 1312

Security Assistance

Defense Institute of Security Assistance Management Library/FL 2301, 235

Sedimentation

NOAA, Great Lakes Environmental Research Laboratory Library, 170
Northwest Watershed Research Center, 78
US Army Corps of Engineers, Omaha District Library, 702
USDA Sedimentation Laboratory Library, 88

Seed Catalogs

National Agricultural Library, 124
US National Arboretum Library, 91

Senate

US Senate Library, 2

Sensory Aids

Veterans Administration Office of Technology Transfer-Reference Collection, 2438

Sequoias

Sequoia & Kings Canyon National Park Library, 1791

Sewage

USDA, Agricultural Research Service, Water Conservation Research Library, 86

Sex Discrimination

US Commission on Civil Rights, National Clearinghouse Library, 1962

Sharks

Tiburon Laboratory Library, 190

Shellfish

National Marine Fisheries Service, Southeast Fisheries Center Library, 167
Tiburon Laboratory Library, 190

Shenandoah National Park

Shenandoah National Park Library, 1792

Sherman, Augustus F.

American Museum of Immigration Library, 1596

Shiloh Battlefield

Shiloh National Monument Park Library, 1793

Ship Repair

Long Beach Naval Shipyard, Technical Library, 995
Naval Sea Support Center, Pacific, Library, 1071
Portsmouth Naval Shipyard, Supply Department, Technical Library, 1144
Supervisor of Shipbuilding Conversion & Repair Library, 1159
Supervisor of Shipbuilding Conversion & Repair Library, 1160
Supervisor of Shipbuilding Conversion & Repair Library, 1162
Supervisor of Shipbuilding, Conversion & Repair, Technical Library, 1164
Supervisor of Shipbuilding, Conversion & Repair, Technical Library, 1165

Ship Systems

Naval Ship Systems Engineering Station, Technical Library, 1076

Shipbuilding

Long Beach Naval Shipyard, Technical Library, 995
Mare Island Naval Shipyard, Technical Library, 997
National Maritime Research Center, Study Center Library, 1938
Naval Sea Support Center, Pacific, Library, 1071
Naval Supervisor of Shipbuilding, Conversion & Repair, Technical Library, 1079
Pearl Harbor Naval Shipyard, Technical Library, 1132
Portsmouth Naval Shipyard, Supply Department, Technical Library, 1144
Supervisor of Shipbuilding Conversion & Repair Library, 1159
Supervisor of Shipbuilding Conversion & Repair Library, 1160
Supervisor of Shipbuilding, Conversion & Repair Library, 1161
Supervisor of Shipbuilding Conversion & Repair Library, 1162

Solar Radiation

Smithsonian Environmental Research Center Library, Rockville Branch, 2465

Solar System

National Solar Observatory, Technical Library, 2086

Solid Waste

Avondale Research Center Library, 1530
Environmental Protection Agency Library, Region 8, 1978
Environmental Protection Agency, Region 1 Library, 1984
Environmental Protection Agency, Region 5 Library, 1989
Environmental Protection Agency, Region 7 Library, 1991

Solid-State Physics

Department of Energy, Solar Research Institute, Technical Library, 1296
Sandia National Laboratories, Technical Library, 1314

Sonar

Naval Sea Systems Command, Library Documentation Branch, 1072

Sonoran Desert

Organ Pipe Cactus National Monument Library, 1758

Sousa, John Phillip

US Marine Band, Music Library, 1243

South Carolina

Environmental Protection Agency, Region 4 Library, 1988
Federal Reserve Bank of Richmond, Research Library, 2040
Myrtle Beach AFB, Base Library/FL 4806, 300
Parris Island, Marine Corps Recruit Depot Station Library, 1242

South Dakota

Bureau of Land Management, Montana State Office Library, 1502

South Dakota History

Badlands National Park Library, 1605
Mount Rushmore National Memorial Library, 1740
Veterans Administration Medical Center Library, 2309

Southeast

Department of the Interior, Office of the Regional Solicitor, Law Library, 1824
Environmental Protection Agency, Region 4 Library, 1988

Southeastern History

Ocmulgee National Monument Library, 1756
Southeast Archeological Center Library, 1795

Southern History

Ocmulgee National Monument Library, 1756

Southwest

Bandelier National Monument Library, 1606
Cedar Breaks National Monument Library, 1629
Chinle Boarding School Library, 1382
Dennehotso Boarding School Library, 1392
Federal Reserve Bank of Dallas Library, 2032
Ft Huachuca Library Division, 491
Geological Survey, Water Resources Division Library, 1582
Greyhills High School Library, 1402
Holloman AFB, Base Library/FL 4801, 264
Kirtland AFB, Base Library/FL 4469, 273
Navajo National Monument Library, 1753
Pacific Southwest Regional Office Library, 1590
Tonto National Monument Library, 1800
USDA, Agricultural Research Service, Water Conservation Research Library, 86
Wingate Elementary School Library, 1462
Wingate High School Library-Media Center, 1463

Southwestern History

Aztec Ruins National Monument Library, 1604
Bandelier National Monument Library, 1606
El Morro National Monument Library, 1659
Ft Bliss, Center Library, 445
Ft Union National Monument Library, 1678
Hubbell Trading Post National Historic Site Library, 1707
Mesa Verde Research Library, 1733
Navajo National Monument Library, 1753
Petrified Forest National Park Library, 1766
Pipe Springs National Monument Library, 1769
Tumacacori National Monument Library, 1802
Western Archeological & Conservation Center Library, 1810
Wupatki National Monument Library, 1815

Southwestern Literature

White Sands Missile Range, Post Library, 805

Spain

Torrejon Base Library/FL 5573, 389
Zaragoza Base Library/FL 5571, 394

Spanish Archives

Castillo de San Marcos National Monument Library, 1626

Spanish Civil Law

US Court of Appeals First Circuit Library, 18

Spanish Colonies

Tumacacori National Monument Library, 1802

Spanish Exploration

Castillo de San Marcos National Monument Library, 1626
Coronado National Memorial Library, 1641

De Soto National Memorial Library, 1650

Spanish Florida

Castillo de San Marcos National Monument Library, 1626

Spanish History

San Juan National Historic Site, Division of Visitors Services—Library, 1786
Torrejon Base Library/FL 5573, 389

Spanish Language

Torrejon Base Library/FL 5573, 389

Spanish Literature

White Sands Missile Range, Post Library, 805

Spanish-American History

Library of Congress, 9

Spanish-American War

Presidio Army Museum Library, 607
US Army Military History Institute Library, 757

Special Education

Gallaudet University Library, 1285

Spectroscopy

Environmental Protection Agency, Environmental Research Laboratory Library, 1973

Speech and Hearing Disorders

Gallaudet University Library, 1285

Spinal Cord Injuries

Veterans Administration Medical Center Library Service, 2372
Veterans Administration Medical Center, Medical Library, 2389
Veterans Administration Office of Technology Transfer-Reference Collection, 2438

Sports

New River Marine Corps Air Station Library, 1240
Twin Buttes School Library, 1456

Sports Medicine

US Army, Keller Army Community Hospital Library, 746

Spotsylvania Battlefield

Fredericksburg & Spotsylvania National Military Park Library, 1682

St. Croix Riverway

St Croix National Scenic Riverway Library, 1781

St. Vrain, Ceran

Bent's Old Fort National Historic Site Library, 1607

Standards

Consumer Product Safety Commission Library, 1967
Directorate of Medical Materiel Library, 1277

National Center for Standards & Certification Information, 156

Philadelphia Naval Shipyard, Technical Library, 1136

Portsmouth Naval Shipyard, Supply Department, Technical Library, 1144

Stanford Ocean Research Laboratory

Southwest Fisheries Center Library, 188

Star Spangled Banner

Ft McHenry National Monument & Historic Shrine Library, 1672

State Banking

Federal Deposit Insurance Corporation Library, 2007

Federal Reserve Bank of Richmond, Research Library, 2040

State Codes

Economic Development Administration, Seattle Regional Office Library, 146

US Army Corps of Engineers, Huntington District Law Library, 669

State Disaster Planning

Federal Emergency Management Agency Library, 2010

State Finances

Bureau of the Census Library, 143

State Law

Command Judge Advocate, Army Law Library, 822

Department of Justice Main Library, 1854

Ft Polk, Office of the Staff Judge Advocate, HQ, 5th Infantry Division (Mech), Law Library, 544

Ft Leonard Wood, Office of the Staff Judge Advocate, Army Field Law Library, 568

US Army Corps of Engineers, Ft Worth District, Technical Library, 666

US Army Corps of Engineers, Huntington District Law Library, 669

US Army Engineer Division, Memphis District, Law Library, 730

US Court of Appeals First Circuit Library, 18

US District Court Eastern District of New York Library, 54

State Maps

Coastal Zone Information Center, 159

Department of Transportation Library, 1931

Map Library & Information Service Library, 163

State Taxation

21st Support Command, Office of Staff Judge Advocate, Law Library, 899

Statistical Methodology

Bureau of the Census Library, 143

Statistics

Air Force Accounting & Finance Center Library/FL 7040, 195

Air Force Human Resources Laboratory, Technical Library/FL 2870, 199

Bureau of Economic Analysis, Research Resource Center, 145

Bureau of Labor Statistics, Regional Office, Reference Library, 1921

Bureau of Land Management, Utah State Office Library, 1525

Bureau of Mines, Section of Administrative Services Library, 1539

Bureau of the Census, Atlanta Regional Office Library, 136

Bureau of the Census, Charlotte Regional Office Library, 137

Bureau of the Census, Dallas Regional Office Library, 138

Bureau of the Census, Denver Regional Office Reference Center, 139

Bureau of the Census, Information Service Program, Boston Regional Office, 140

Bureau of the Census, Information Services Program, Detroit Regional Office Information Center, 141

Bureau of the Census, Information Services Program Library, 142

Bureau of the Census Library, 143

Bureau of the Census, New York Regional Office Library, 144

Department of Commerce, District Office Library, 128

Federal Reserve Bank of Chicago Library, 2030

Federal Reserve Bank of Kansas City, Research Library, 2033

Geological Survey, Resource Appraisal Group Library, 1577

Health & Human Services Department Library, 1320

Internal Revenue Service, Central Region, Freedom of Information Public Reading Room, 1951

International Trade Administration District Office, US & FCS Commercial Library, 149

Interstate Commerce Commission Library, 2053

National Bureau of Standards Research Information Center, 155

National Institute of Justice Library, 1856

National Institutes of Health, Division of Computer Research & Technology Library, 1344

Parklawn Health Library, Prince George's Center Branch, 1351

Patuxent Wildlife Research Center Library, 1558

Social Security Administration, District of Columbia Branch Library, 1352

US Army TRADOC Systems Analysis Activity TRASANA, Technical Library, 785

US Department of Education, Office of Educational Research & Improvement Library, 1286

US International Trade Commission Main Library, 2270

Statue of Liberty

American Museum of Immigration Library, 1596

Steichen Photography Collection

US Naval Academy, Nimitz Library, 1169

Stock Market

US Securities & Exchange Commission Library, 2096

Stones River, Battle of

Stones River National Battlefield Library, 1797

Storms

National Severe Storms Laboratory Library, 178

Strategic Arms Limitation Talks

US Arms Control & Disarmament Agency Library, 2103

Streams

Geological Survey Library, 1568

Stress

Veterans Administration Medical Center Library Service, 2375

Structural Engineering

Naval Facilities Engineering Command, Technical Library, 1044

David Taylor Naval Ship R&D Center, Technical Information Center, 1166

US Army Corps of Engineers, New England Division Technical Library, 689

Strughold, Hubertus

Air Force School of Aerospace Medicine, Strughold Aeromedical Library/FL 2855, 206

Studer Collection

Lake Meredith Recreation Area Library, 1724

Stupka Collection

Great Smoky Mountains National Park, Sugarlands Visitor Center Library, 1694

Submarines

Fleet Anti-Submarine Warfare Training Center, Pacific, Technical Library, 977

Nautilus Memorial/Submarine Force Library & Museum, 1010

Naval Regional Library, Groton, 1064

Naval Submarine Medical Research Laboratory, Medical Library, 1078

Navy Fleet Ballistic Missile Submarine Training Center, Technical Publications Library, 1109

Subtropical Products

US Citrus & Subtropical Products Laboratory Library, 83

Supplemental Security Income

Social Security Administration, District of Columbia Branch Library, 1352

Supreme Court

Department of Justice Main Library, 1854

HQ, US Army Japan/9th Corps, Office of the Staff Judge Advocate, Army Field Law Library, 853

Supreme Court of the United States Library, 13

US Army Corps of Engineers, Huntington District Law Library, 669

Surface Water

Geological Survey, Water Resources Division Library, 1579

Surgery

Bethesda Naval Hospital, Edward Rhodes Stitt Library, 953
Bethesda Naval Medical Research Institute, Information Services Branch, 954
Camp Lejeune Naval Hospital, Medical & General Libraries, 957
Darnall Army Community Hospital, Medical Library, 426
Ft Dix, Walson Army Community Hospital, Medical Library, 463
Kirtland AFB, Medical Library/SGAL, 274
Karl A Menninger Medical Library, 2276
William S Middleton Memorial Veterans Hospital Library Service, 2277
Oakland Naval Hospital, Medical Library, 1119
Orlando Naval Hospital, Medical Library, 1125
Sheppard AFB Regional Hospital, Medical Library, 322
US Air Force Regional Hospital, Carswell (SAC), Medical Library, 336
US Army Institute of Surgical Research, Library Branch, 742
Veterans Administration Hospital, Health Sciences Library, 2287
Veterans Administration Medical Center Library, 2314
Veterans Administration Medical Center Library, 2316
Veterans Administration Medical Center Library, 2319
Veterans Administration Medical Center Library-Learning Resources Center, 2322
Veterans Administration Medical Center Library Service, 2327
Veterans Administration Medical Center Library Service, 2329
Veterans Administration Medical Center Library Service, 2333
Veterans Administration Medical Center Library Service, 2348
Veterans Administration Medical Center Library Service, 2352
Veterans Administration Medical Center Library Service, 2362
Veterans Administration Medical Center Library Service, 2363
Veterans Administration Medical Center Library Service, 2377
Veterans Administration Medical Center Library Service, 2378
Veterans Administration Medical Center, Medical Library, 2386
Veterans Administration Medical Center, Medical Library, 2398
Veterans Administration Medical Center, Medical Library, 2400
Veterans Administration Medical Center, Medical & Patient's Library, 2414
Veterans Administration Medical Center, Medical & Patients' Library Wade Park & Brecksville Units, 2423
Veterans Administration Medical & Regional Office Center Medical Library, 2434
Veterans Administration Medical & Regional Office Center, Medical & Patients' Library, 2436
Veterans Administration Office of Technology Transfer-Reference Collection, 2438

Survey Methodology

Bureau of the Census Library, 143

Surveying

NOAA, Library & Information Services Division, 182

Survival Training

Survival Training Reference Library/FL 3061, 324

Symbolism

The Institute of Heraldry Library, 583

Systems Engineering

Bureau of Mines, Twin Cities Research Center Library, 1542

Taft, William Howard

William Howard Taft National Historic Site Library, 1798

Talking Books

Bolling AFB, Base Library/FL 4400, 224
National Library Service for the Blind & Physically Handicapped, Library of Congress, 10
Harry S Truman Memorial Veterans Hospital, Medical Library, 2283
Veterans Administration Medical Center Library Service, 2356
Veterans Administration Patients' Library, 2440
Zaragoza Base Library/FL 5571, 394

Tariffs

US Customs Service, Library & Information Center, 1954
US International Trade Commission, Law Library, 2269
US International Trade Commission Main Library, 2270

Tax History

Internal Revenue Service, Office of Chief Counsel, Library, 1953

Tax Law

Department of Justice Tax Library, 1855
HQ, 10th Area Support Group (Prov), Office of the Staff Judge Advocate, Army Law Library, 849
HQ, US Army Japan/9th Corps, Office of the Staff Judge Advocate, Army Field Law Library, 853
Internal Revenue Service, Office of Chief Counsel, Library, 1953
US Tax Court Library, 62

Taxation

Internal Revenue Service, Central Region, Freedom of Information Public Reading Room, 1951
Internal Revenue Service Library, 1952
Internal Revenue Service, Office of Chief Counsel, Library, 1953
21st Support Command, Office of Staff Judge Advocate, Law Library, 899
US Court of Appeals for the Federal Circuit Library, 53
US Tax Court Library, 62

Taylor, Maxwell

National Defense University Library, 1278

Teacher Training

Canoncito Community School, Resource Center, 1372
Laguna Elementary School Library, 1413
Oglala Community Elementary School, 1424
Wide Ruins School Library, 1461

Technology

Air Force Institute of Technology Library, 201
Air Force Officer Training School Library/FL 3050, 205
Bureau of Labor Statistics Library, 1920
Consumer Product Safety Commission Library, 1967
Drug Enforcement Administration Library, 1907
Geophysical Fluid Dynamics Laboratory Library, 160
Library & Information Services Division, Camp Springs Center, 162
Library of Congress, 9
March AFB, Base Library/FL 4664, 287
National Science Foundation Library, 2085
Naval Education & Training Center, Main Library, 1035
Naval Intelligence Support Center Library, 1052
Naval Postgraduate School, Dudley Knox Library, 1061
Naval Sea Support Center, Atlantic, Technical Library, 1070
Patent & Trademark Office Scientific Library, 194
Shiprock Boarding School Library, 1445
Southwestern Indian Polytechnic Institute Instructional Media Center, 1447
US Army Air Defense Artillery School Library, 641
US Army Corps of Engineers, Baltimore District Library Branch, 660
US Army Missile & Space Intelligence Center Library, 760
US Army Operational Test & Evaluation Agency, Technical Library, 767
US Army Ordnance Center & School Library, 768
US Army Ordnance Missile & Munitions Center & School, Technical Library, 769
US Army Strategic Defense Command, Huntsville, Library, 781
US Coast Guard Academy Library, 1942
US Court of International Trade Library, 60
US Customs Service, Library & Information Center, 1954
US Naval Academy, Nimitz Library, 1169

Technology Forecasting

Office of Technology Assessment Information Center, 11

Technology History

National Museum of American History, Branch Library, 2461
National Museum of Natural History, Branch Library, 2462
Smithsonian Institution Libraries, 2468

Technology, International

Foreign Technology Division Technical Library/FL 2830, 248
US Army Missile & Space Intelligence Center Library, 760

Department of Commerce, Office of Field Services Library, 134
Department of Commerce, St Louis District Office Library, 135
Eximbank Library, 2002
Federal Trade Commission, Cleveland Regional Office Library, 2044
Federal Trade Commission, San Francisco Regional Office Library, 2049
Industry & Trade Administration Library, 147
National Museum of American History, Branch Library, 2461
US International Trade Commission, Law Library, 2269

Trade Catalogs

National Museum of Natural History, Branch Library, 2462

Trade Policy

US International Trade Commission Main Library, 2270

Trade Regulations

Federal Trade Commission, Dallas Regional Office Library, 2045
Federal Trade Commission Library, 2047

Trade Standards

National Center for Standards & Certification Information, 156

Trade Statistics

US International Trade Commission Main Library, 2270

Trade Unions

Department of Labor Library, 1919

Trademarks

Patent & Trademark Office, Law Library, 193
Patent & Trademark Office Scientific Library, 194
US Court of Appeals for the Federal Circuit Library, 53
US International Trade Commission, Law Library, 2269

Trading Posts

Ft Union Trading Post National Historic Site Library, 1679
Hubbell Trading Post National Historic Site Library, 1707

Traffic Engineering

Department of Transportation Library, 1931

Traffic Safety

National Highway Traffic Safety Administration, Technical Reference Division, Library, 1940

Training

Department of Energy, Solar Research Institute, Technical Library, 1296
Doctrine Center Library, 1232
Manpower, Education, Research, & Training (MERT) Division Library, 1305
Naval Education & Training Center, Main Library, 1035
Naval Training Systems Center, 1091

Navy Personnel Research & Development Center, Technical Library, 1110

Translations

National Soil Dynamics Laboratory Library, 77
Northwest & Alaska Fisheries Center Library, 183

Transplantation Medicine

Bethesda Naval Medical Research Institute, Information Services Branch, 954

Transportation

Architectural & Transportation Barriers Compliance Board, Technical Library, 2445
Department of Transportation Library, 1931
Department of Transportation, Technical Reference Center, 1932
10A Services Branch Library, 1933
US Army & Air Force Exchange Service, Central Library, 1283
US Army Transportation & Aviation Logistics Schools, Information Center, 788
US Army Transportation Center, Groninger Library, 789

Transportation History

Chesapeake & Ohio Canal National Historic Park Resource Library, 1634
Interstate Commerce Commission Library, 2053

Transportation Law

Department of Transportation Law Library, 1930
Interstate Commerce Commission Library, 2053

Travel

Base Library, 353
Base Library/FL 5670, 360
Loring AFB, Base Library/FL 4678, 281
McClellan AFB, Base Library/FL 2040, 292
Mildenhall Base Library/FL 5518, 379
Robinson Barracks, US Army Library, 878
US Army Library System, Norddeutschland, 922
US Naval Air Station, Sigonella, Base Library, 1198
US Navy Support Office Library, 1225

Treasury Department

Department of the Treasury Library, 1945

Treaties

US Arms Control & Disarmament Agency Library, 2103

Trees

Muir Woods National Monument, Eleanor Bello Memorial Research Library, 1742

Trespassing

Bureau of Land Management, Bakersfield District Office Library, 1469

Trident Missile

Trident Refit Facility, Bangor, Library, 1168

Tropical Forestry

Institute of Tropical Forestry Library, 114

Tropical Meteorology

NOAA, Miami Library, 171

Tropics

NOAA, Coral Gables Center Library, 169
US Army Tropic Test Center, Technical Information Center, 930

Truman, Harry S

Harry S Truman Library, 2080

Tuna

Southwest Fisheries Center Library, 188

Tupelo National Battlefield

Natchez Trace Parkway Library, 1743

Turkey

Base Library, 353
Base Library/FL 5531, 355
Incirlik Base Library/FL 5685, 370
Joint US Military Mission for Aid to Turkey, Library, 372

Underwater Acoustics

NOAA, Miami Library, 171
Naval Coastal Systems Center, Technical Information Services Branch, 1028
Naval Research Laboratory, USRD, 1067
Naval Underwater Systems Center, New London Laboratory, Technical Library, 1092
Naval Underwater Systems Center, Technical Library, 1094

Unemployment

Bureau of Labor Statistics Library, 1920
Bureau of Labor Statistics, Regional Office, Reference Library, 1921

Uniforms

The Institute of Heraldry Library, 583

United Nations

Drug Enforcement Administration Library, 1907
National Agricultural Library, 124
US Arms Control & Disarmament Agency Library, 2103

United States History

Base Library/FL 5670, 360
Bent's Old Fort National Historic Site Library, 1607
Cumberland Gap National Historic Park Library, 1645
De Soto National Memorial Library, 1650
Department of Justice Main Library, 1854
Dwight D Eisenhower Library, 2071
El Toro Marine Corps Air Station Library, 1233
Gerald R Ford Library, 2072
Ford's Theatre National Historic Site Library, 1664
Ft Point National Historic Site Library, 1674
Ft Stanwix National Monument Library, 1676
Ft Union National Monument Library, 1678

General Accounting Office, Office of Library Services, 5
Harpers Ferry Center Library, 1699
Herbert Hoover National Historic Site, 1703
Herbert Hoover Presidential Library, 2073
Joshua Tree National Monument Library, 1717
John F Kennedy Presidential Library, 2074
Library of Congress, 9
Abraham Lincoln Birthplace National Historic Site Library, 1728
Minute Man National Historical Park Library, 1734
National Archives Library, 2078
National Capital Parks-East Library, 1744
National Museum of American History, Branch Library, 2461
National Park Service Library, 1747
National Park Service, Southeast Regional Office Library, 1750
National Register of Historic Places Library, 1589
Naval School, Civil Engineer Corps Officers, Moreell Library, 1068
Naval Weapons Station Library, 1098
Navy Department Library, 1106
Presidio Army Museum Library, 607
Franklin D Roosevelt National Historic Site Library, 1776
Roosevelt Roads Naval Station Library, 1189
Saugus Iron Works National Historic Site Library, 1789
Sitka National Historic Park Library, 1794
Thayer Engineering Library, 632
Travertine Nature Center Library, 1801
Harry S Truman Library, 2080
US Army Military History Institute Library, 757
US Information Agency Library, 2104
US Naval Academy, Nimitz Library, 1169
US Senate Library, 2
White Sands Missile Range, Post Library, 805

United States Information Agency
US Information Agency Library, 2104

Uranium
Department of Energy, Grand Junction Area Office, Technical Library, 1294

Uranium Mill Tailings Remedial Action
National Atomic Museum Library, 1308
National Atomic Museum Library, Public Document Room, 1309

Urban Affairs
Department of Housing & Urban Development Library, 1354

Urban Planning
HUD, Region 1 Library, 1355
HUD, Region 2 Library, 1356
HUD, Region 3 Library, 1357
HUD, Region 5 Library, 1359
HUD, Region 7 Library, 1360
HUD, Region 8 Library, 1361
HUD Region 9 Library, 1362
US Army Corps of Engineers, St Louis District Technical Library, 713

Urban Recreation
Heritage Conservation & Recreation Service, Northwest Region Office Library, 1584

Urban Transportation
Department of Transportation Library, 1931

Urology
Tripler Army Medical Center, Medical Library, 636

USSR
Ft George G Meade, Language Training Facility Library, 533
Library of Congress, 9
Naval Intelligence Support Center Library, 1052
Sitka National Historic Park Library, 1794
US Army Russian Institute, Research Library, 927

Utah
Bureau of Land Management, Salt Lake City District Office Library, 1519
Bureau of Land Management, Utah State Office Library, 1525
Geological Survey, Public Inquiries Office Library, 1575

Utah History
Arches National Park Library, 1601
Capitol Reef National Park Library, 1622
Glen Canyon National Recreation Area Library, 1688

Valley Forge
Valley Forge National Historical Park, Horace "Vox" Willcox Library, 1804

Van Buren, Martin
Martin Van Buren National Historic Site Library, 1805

Van Oosten, John
Van Oosten Library, 1560

Vector-Borne Disease
Navy Disease Vector Ecology & Control Center Library, 1107

Vegetables
Western Regional Research Center Library, 92

Venture Capital
Small Business Administration, Reference Library, 2098

Veterans
Veterans Administration Central Office Library, Library Division, 2285
Veterans Administration Medical Center, Health Sciences Library, 2294
Veterans Administration Medical Center Library Service, 2342
Veterans Administration Medical Center, Medical/General Library, 2385
Veterans Administration Medical Center, Medical & Patient's Library, 2413
Veterans Administration Office of General Counsel, Law Library, 2437

Veterinary Medicine
Food & Drug Administration, Medical Library, 1333
Ft Campbell, Blanchfield Army Community Hospital, Medical Library, 450
Ft Carson, Evans US Army Community Hospital, Medical Library, 453
Ft Huachuca, Raymond W Bliss Army Community Hospital, Medical Library, 490
Ft Rucker, Medical Library, 551
Letterman Army Institute of Research, Medical Research Library, 586
National Animal Disease Center Library, 76
National Zoological Park Library Branch, 2463
Plum Island Animal Disease Center Library, 79
Sheppard AFB Regional Hospital, Medical Library, 322
US Army Aeromedical Research Laboratory, Medical Library, 639
Wright-Patterson AFB, Medical Center Library, 347

Veterinary Science
Animal Science Institute Library, 70
Roman L Hruska US Meat Animal Research Center Library, 75
Russell Research Center Library, 80

Vicksburg Campaign
Vicksburg National Military Park Library, 1806

Victims of Crime
National Institute of Justice/National Criminal Justice Reference Service, 1857

Video Tapes
Department of Energy, Office of General Counsel, Law Library, 1295
Ft Leonard Wood, Library Service Center, 567
Institute of American Indian Arts Library, 1405
John F Kennedy Center Performing Arts Library, 8
Nellis AFB, Base Library/FL 4852, 301
US Army Missile & Space Intelligence Center Library, 760
US Army Support Command, Hawaii Library System, 782
Zaragoza Base Library/FL 5571, 394

Vietnam Memorial
Library of Congress, 9

Vietnam Veterans
Veterans Administration Medical Center, Health Sciences Library, 2294
Veterans Administration Medical Center Library Service, 2342
Veterans Administration Medical Center, Medical & Patient's Library, 2413

Vietnam War
Lemoore Naval Air Station Library, 993
Presidio Army Museum Library, 607
US Army Military History Institute Library, 757
Veterans Administration Medical Center Library Service, 2342

Veterans Administration Medical Center, Medical Library, 2394
Veterans Administration Medical Center, Medical & Patients' Library, 2417

Virgin Islands
Christiansted National Historic Site Library, 1637
Virgin Islands National Park Reference Library, 1807

Virginia
Federal Reserve Bank of Richmond, Research Library, 2040

Virginia History
Appomattox Court House National Historic Park Library, 1600
Colonial National Historic Park Library, 1639
Fredericksburg & Spotsylvania National Military Park Library, 1682
Harpers Ferry National Historic Park Library, 1700
Petersburg National Battlefield Library, 1765

Virology
Centers for Disease Control Library, 1327
Plum Island Animal Disease Center Library, 79
Rocky Mountain Laboratory Library, 1347

Visual Impairment
Bolling AFB, Base Library/FL 4400, 224
National Library Service for the Blind & Physically Handicapped, Library of Congress, 10
Veterans Administration Patients' Library, 2440

Vivian Archives
Chaco Center Archives & Library, Branch of Cultural Research Library, 1630

Vocational Education
Ft Story Post Library, 561
Intermountain Inter-Tribal School Library, 1406
Shiprock Boarding School Library, 1445

Volcanoes
Craters of the Moon National Monument Library, 1644
Hawaii Volcanoes National Park Library, 1701
Lassen Volcanic National Park Library, 1725

Voyageurs National Park
Voyageurs National Park Library, 1808

Wages
Bureau of Labor Statistics Library, 1920
Bureau of Labor Statistics, Regional Office, Reference Library, 1921
Bureau of Labor Statistics, Regional Office, Reference Library, 1922

War Department
Ft George G Meade, Language Training Facility Library, 533
US Army Center of Military History Library, 652

War of 1812
George Rogers Clark National Historical Park Library, 1638
Ft McHenry National Monument & Historic Shrine Library, 1672
Horse Bend National Military Park Library, 1705
Perry's Victory & International Peace Memorial Library, 1764

Ward, J. Carlton Jr.
National Defense University Library, 1278

Warfare
James Carson Breckinridge Library & Amphibious Warfare Facility, 1227
Combat Developments Experimentation Center, Technical Information Center, 420
Dugway Proving Ground, Technical Library, 431
El Toro Marine Corps Air Station Library, 1233
Electronic Security Command, General Library/FL 7046, 241
Electronic Warfare Department, Tactical Publication Library, 974
Fleet & Mine Warfare Training Center, 976
Fleet Anti-Submarine Warfare Training Center, Pacific, Technical Library, 977
Fleet Combat Training Center Library, 979
Ft Sill, Morris Swett Technical Library, 558
Marine Corps Historical Center Library, 1237
McBride Library/FL 3010, 291
Naval Amphibious Base Library, 1020
Naval Amphibious School Library, 1021
Naval Amphibious School, John Sidney McCain, Jr Amphibious Warfare Library, 1022
Naval Coastal Systems Center, Technical Information Services Branch, 1028
Naval Mine Warfare Engineering Activity, Library, 1055
Naval Support Activity Library, 1083
Naval Surface Warfare Officers School Library, 1085
Philadelphia Naval Station Library, 1137
Space & Naval Warfare Systems Command Library, 1156
US Army Armor School Library, 644
US Army Intelligence School Library, 1284
US Army John F Kennedy Special Warfare Center, Marquat Memorial Library, 747

Washington
Bureau of Mines, Western Field Operations Center Library, 1543
Pacific Northwest Regional Library System, 1760

Washington, Booker T.
Booker T Washington National Monument Library, 1809

Washington, George
Federal Hall National Memorial Library, 1661
Ft Necessity National Battlefield Library, 1673
George Washington Birthplace National Monument Library, 1684
Mall Operation Library, 1730

Washington History
Ft Vancouver National Historic Site Library, 1680
Olympic National Park Library, 1757

Washington Law
Economic Development Administration, Seattle Regional Office Library, 146

Waste Isolation Pilot Plant
National Atomic Museum Library, 1308
National Atomic Museum Library, Public Document Room, 1309

Waste Management
Avondale Research Center Library, 1530
Basalt Waste Isolation Project Library, 1290
Department of Justice Lands Library, 1853
Environmental Monitoring & Systems Laboratory Library, 1968
Environmental Protection Agency, Andrew W Breidenbach Library, 1969
Environmental Protection Agency, Corvallis Environmental Research Library, 1971
Environmental Protection Agency Headquarters Library, 1974
Environmental Protection Agency, Robert S Kerr Library, 1975
Environmental Protection Agency Library, Region 8, 1978
Environmental Protection Agency, Region 1 Library, 1984
Environmental Protection Agency, Region 4 Library, 1988
Environmental Protection Agency, Region 5 Library, 1989
Environmental Protection Agency, Region 6 Library, 1990
Environmental Protection Agency, Region 7 Library, 1991
Nevada Technical Library, Department of Energy, 1311
Sandia National Laboratories, Technical Library, 1314
US Army Corps of Engineers, Buffalo District Technical Library, 661
US Army Environmental Hygiene Agency Library, 733
USDA, Agricultural Research Service, Eastern Regional Research Center Library, 84

Water Law
Department of the Interior, Office of the Field Solicitor, Law Library, 1823
Department of the Interior, Office of the Solicitor, Field Solicitor, Law Library, 1836

Water Pollution
Auke Bay Fisheries Laboratory Library, 158
Columbia National Fisheries Research Library, 1549
Delaware River Basin Commission Library, 2446
Environmental Protection Agency, Andrew W Breidenbach Library, 1969
Environmental Protection Agency, Robert S Kerr Library, 1975
Environmental Protection Agency Library, Region 8, 1978

Naval Weapons Station, Technical Services Library, 1103
Naval Weapons Station, WQEC Technical Library, 1104
Naval Weapons Support Center, Technical Library, 1105
Point Mugu Naval Air Station Library, 1138
Scientific & Technical Information Division Library, 623
Strategic Weapons Facility, Pacific, Library, 1158
US Arms Control & Disarmament Agency Library, 2103
US Army Armament Research & Development Center, Plastics Technical Evaluation Center, 643
US Army Strategic Defense Command, Huntsville, Library, 781
US Navy Atlantic Fleet Weapons Training Facility, 1222
Weapons Quality Engineering Center Library, 1175

Webster University

Ft Sill, Nye Library, 556

Weed Control

Bureau of Reclamation, Engineering & Research Center Library, 1547

Well Logs

Bureau of Land Management, Elko District Office Library, 1484

West

Geological Survey, Public Inquiries Office Library, 1574
Naval Weapons Center Library, 1096
Theodore Roosevelt National Park Library, 1777
WESTFORNET/FS-INFO Intermountain Research Station, 122

West Indies History

Christiansted National Historic Site Library, 1637

West Point

US Military Academy Library, 794
West Point Post Library, 803

West Virginia

Bureau of the Census, Information Services Program Library, 142
Federal Reserve Bank of Richmond, Research Library, 2040

West Virginia Law

US Army Corps of Engineers, Huntington District Law Library, 669

Western Expansion

Ft Laramie National Historic Site Library, 1670
Scotts Bluff National Monument, Oregon Trail Association Library, 1790

Western History

Cherokee Strip Living Museum Library, 1633
Ft Bowie National Historic Site Library, 1683
Grand Teton National Park Library, 1691

Grant-Kohrs Ranch National Historic Site Library, 1692
Pipe Springs National Monument Library, 1769
Presidio Army Museum Library, 607
Scotts Bluff National Monument, Oregon Trail Association Library, 1790
Tumacacori National Monument Library, 1802

Western Solar Utilization Network

Bonneville Power Administration Library, 1291

Westward Expansion

Homestead National Monument Library, 1702
Jefferson National Expansion Memorial Library, 1713

Wetlands

Environmental Protection Agency, Region 3 Library, 1987
Geological Survey, Water Resources Division Library, 1579

Whales

National Marine Mammal Library, 168

White Collar Crime

Department of Justice Criminal Library, 1852
National Institute of Justice/National Criminal Justice Reference Service, 1857

White Sands

White Sands National Monument Library, 1812

White, Theodore

Dinosaur National Monument Library, 1656

White, William Alanson

St Elizabeth's Hospital, Health Sciences Library, 1324

Whitman, Walt

Library of Congress, 9

Wildlife

Bureau of Land Management, Arizona State Office Library, 1466
Bureau of Land Management, Arizona Strip, District Office Library, 1467
Bureau of Land Management, Bakersfield District Office Library, 1469
Bureau of Land Management, Bishop Resource Area Headquarters Library, 1470
Bureau of Land Management, Branch of Records & Data Management, 1471
Bureau of Land Management, California State Office Library, 1473
Bureau of Land Management, Cedar City District Library, 1474
Bureau of Land Management, District Library, 1480
Bureau of Land Management, District Office Library, 1481
Bureau of Land Management, District Office Library, 1482

Bureau of Land Management, Eastern States Office Library, 1483
Bureau of Land Management, Elko District Office Library, 1484
Bureau of Land Management, Eugene Office Library, 1485
Bureau of Land Management, Idaho State Office Library, 1489
Bureau of Land Management, Kanab Office Library, 1490
Bureau of Land Management Library, 1497
Bureau of Land Management, Montana State Office Library, 1502
Bureau of Land Management, Phillips Resource Area Office Library, 1507
Bureau of Land Management, Phoenix District Office Library, 1508
Bureau of Land Management, Roseburg District Office Library, 1514
Bureau of Land Management, Safford District Office Library, 1516
Bureau of Land Management, Salt Lake City District Office Library, 1519
Bureau of Land Management, Susanville District Office Library, 1523
Bureau of Land Management, Utah State Office Library, 1525
Denver Wildlife Research Center, 95
Department of Justice Lands Library, 1853
Department of the Interior, Center for Information & Library Services, Natural Resources Library, 1821
Everglades National Park Research Center Library, 1660
Fish & Wildlife Service Library, 1551
Fish & Wildlife Service, Science Reference Library, 1552
Forestry Sciences Laboratory Library, 113
National Zoological Park Library Branch, 2463
North Central Forest Experiment Station Library, 116
Northern Prairie Wildlife Research Center Library, 1557
Pacific Southwest Forest & Range Experiment Station Library, 117
Patuxent Wildlife Research Center Library, 1558
Saguaro National Monument Library, 1780
US Army Corps of Engineers, Jacksonville District Technical Library, 675
US Army Corps of Engineers, New England Division Technical Library, 689
US Army Corps of Engineers, St Louis District Technical Library, 713
US Army Corps of Engineers, Walla Walla District Technical & Law Library, 725
WESTFORNET/FS-INFO Intermountain Research Station, 122

William Copepoda Collection

National Museum of Natural History, Branch Library, 2462

Wind Cave

Wind Cave National Park Library, 1814

Wind Energy

Department of Energy, Solar Research Institute, Technical Library, 1296

Wisconsin History

Grand Portage National Monument Library, 1690

RADICAL,
FUNNY, AND
INSPIRING
WRITING BY
WOMEN

THE FUTURE IS FEMINIST

INTRODUCTION BY
JESSICA VALENTI

EDITED BY
MALLORY FARRUGIA

CHRONICLE BOOKS
SAN FRANCISCO

Library of Congress Cataloging-in-Publication Data available.

ISBN: 978-1-4521-6833-3

Manufactured in China.

Designed by Allison Weiner

10 9 8 7 6 5 4 3 2 1

Chronicle books and gifts are available at special quantity discounts to corporations, professional associations, literacy programs, and other organizations. For details and discount information, please contact our premiums department at corporatesales@ chroniclebooks.com or at 1-800-759-0190.

Chronicle Books LLC
680 Second Street
San Francisco, California 94107
www.chroniclebooks.com

CONTENTS

INTRODUCTION

JESSICA VALENTI

The fascinating and difficult thing about feminism is how much things have both changed *and* remained the same over the last few decades.

Women are still fighting for many of the same basic rights and causes that they were in the '60s and '70s; equal pay, full reproductive rights, and racial justice are still not fully realized. But we've also seen an explosion in the cultural power and relevance of feminism—largely thanks to feminist blogs and social media, which have completely shifted the way we think about activism and identity online and off.

It seems paradoxical, but the truth is that this particular conflicting feminist moment is likely the movement's most important. Feminism has both the most power we've seen in decades and arguably the most work to do. What we do next could change everything for women.

That's part of why this anthology is so exciting—and so vital.

So much of the time we spend engaging with feminist work these days happens online—we follow a link through Twitter or find out about a new women's video series on Instagram. The actions we take mostly happen online, too.

In many ways, this has been an incredible gift to the movement: The speed with which we can move from space to space, article to activism, has been an incredible mobilizer for a new generation of feminists. But something is lost, too, when the vast majority of our work lives in ephemeral moments. Hashtags and tweets, podcasts and viral stories are all talked about and consumed—but only for as long as someone shares them.

What we read and watch online tells a story, to be sure, but only the one we've created for ourselves. The wondrous thing about anthologies—this one, in particular—is the story they tell.

The Future Is Feminist forms a cohesive narrative about feminism, politics, gender, and power. And it's a story that we all need to hear.

From hallmarks of the feminist canon to "resting bitch face," from beauty culture to sexual assault—these writings give us a full sense of where feminism has been, where it is, and where it's going.

This tremendous story is by no means one singular narrative. The diversity of voices highlights one of the most important theories of feminism: that true feminism is intersectional, interlocking, and forward-thinking.

It's unclear what the future holds for feminism. It's unclear what we'll do with this moment—as confusing and powerful and important as it is. What is clear, though—what is inevitable—is that we have the blueprint. We have the ideas, the energy, and the voices to bring feminism where it needs to be. They're all here, on the page. Waiting for us.

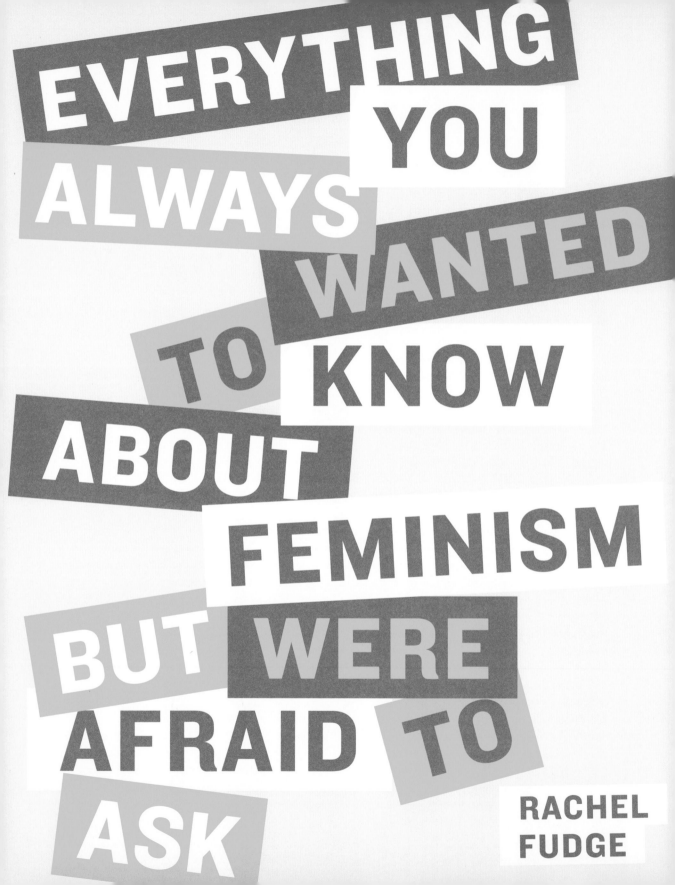

Originally published in *Bitch* magazine
2006

t's a natural, normal part of life. But people hesitate to talk openly about their needs, their desires, and their concerns because they are so fearful of what others might think. But we all have urges, and we all have questions, and the more we can talk about them, the happier and more fulfilled we all will be. It should be a joyful, tender, and esteem-building part of life, not a source of confusion or shame. Yet it's hard to get a handle on it, because although there's a lot of information out there, much of it is judgmental, misinformed, or quite simply false. I'm speaking, of course, about feminism.

Although we can all agree on the most basic dictionary definition of feminism (the theory of the political, economic, and social equality of the sexes), it is rarely ever that simple or straightforward. Despite 150 years of activism in pursuit of women's rights, and nearly 40 years of modern feminism, "feminism" is still considered by many to be a dirty word. In the mainstream media, when feminism is discussed at all, it's most often talked about in negative or pessimistic terms: *TIME*'s "Is

Feminism Dead?" cover stories; the recent series of *New York Times* articles detailing how feminism has "failed" because upper-middle-class white women are still struggling with the work/family dilemma; any number of hand-wringing articles about why young women aren't embracing the label; and so forth. Movie and TV starlets who portray assertive, confident, feminist-leaning characters routinely reject the word—Sarah Michelle Gellar, Drew Barrymore, I'm lookin' at you—as do female musicians whose work is infused with gender play (Polly Jean Harvey, Patti Smith, Björk). It's not that these women aren't into equality: It's because they, like many people, are afraid of what the word implies to the rest of the world. Like the current slanderous usage of "liberal," "feminist" has long been wielded as an epithet—hence many women's discomfort in adopting it.

You wouldn't know it from the blanket terms used to talk about feminism, but the movement's rich history (and current practice) encompasses a slew of ideologies, offshoots, and internal disagreements: radical feminism, cultural feminism, liberal

11

feminism, antiporn feminism, pro-sex feminism, third-wave feminism, womanism—but what does it all mean? A brief primer on the etiology of feminism is sorely needed. The following is hardly exhaustive, and only barely objective, and I must mention that many of the nuances and linguistic turns are still up for debate by and among feminists. So leave your preconceptions behind and join me in this exciting exploration of one of life's most basic urges: feminism.

LIBERAL FEMINISM, A.K.A. JUST PLAIN FEMINISM

Unless you're reading academic treatises about the history or political philosophies of feminism, you almost never hear the term "liberal feminism"—despite the fact that it's the most accurate descriptor for almost all of the mainstream institutional and legislative feminism at work in the United States today. Want to level the playing field? Break the glass ceiling? Make room for women at the table of power? Then you're espousing liberal feminism. Campaigns for legislative-based gender equity—from the ERA to Title IX to *Roe v. Wade* to the Violence Against Women Act to landmark sexual harassment suits like the one detailed in the recent film *North Country*—all arise out of liberal feminism.

The "liberal" part refers not to today's muddled characterizations of Democrats, progressives, or granolas in general but rather to the 300-year-old political philosophy detailing the natural rights of

"man": inalienable rights to government, property, the development of powers, and gratification of desire—in other words, life, liberty, the pursuit of happiness, and the right to vote and to shop.

Today, liberal feminism is at work in the countless local, state, and federal bills that attempt to codify the seemingly no-duh stance that gender should not be a factor in education, employment, housing, or anything else.

Derogatory terms: Well, there's "victim feminism," which is often wielded by the cabal of notorious antifeminist "feminists" (e.g., Camille Paglia, Katie Roiphe, Daphne Patai) who argue that if women really want equal rights, they shouldn't ask for special treatment. And then there's "feminazi"—a choice turn of phrase coined by that bastion of reason Rush Limbaugh that conjures the image of fascist gender terrorists who seek to control and police all aspects of men's lives.

SUFFRAGE

The centuries-long fight for women's right to vote was not just about ballot-casting, but about securing women's right to participate as full citizens: to hold property, keep their own wages, have guardianship of their children, and, yes, vote. While these rights are all direct outgrowths of classic liberalism, it's worth noting that when, in the mid-1800s, Elizabeth Cady Stanton argued that suffrage must be added to the platform of the nascent women's rights campaign, she was considered by many of her supporters—let alone her detractors—to be ridiculous, if not dangerously radical. And subsequent suffrage campaigners like Alice Paul truly were militant activists, engaging in acts of civil disobedience to the disdain of more conservative suffragists like Carrie Chapman Catt, whose tactics centered more on discreet but steady lobbying. (This time is also known retrospectively as the first wave of feminism.)

EQUAL RIGHTS AMENDMENT (ERA)

The liberal feminist holy grail. In one stroke, it declares: "Equality of rights under the law shall not be denied or abridged by the United States or by any state on account of sex." First drafted and proposed by Alice Paul and the National Woman's Party in 1923, the ERA was introduced in every session of Congress until it finally passed in 1972, thanks to the nationwide energy generated by second-wave feminism, sending it to the states for ratification. In one year, 22 of the required 38 states had ratified it, but then the campaign slowed down. Despite an extension—and thanks to the admittedly impressive (if unhinged) efforts of Phyllis Schlafly, whose STOP ERA campaign played on public fears of women getting drafted and unisex bathrooms—it fizzled out. The ERA, or a differently named version of it, has been introduced—unsuccessfully—in every subsequent Congress. So ladies, the next time you hear someone say, "Didn't all that feminist stuff get solved in the '80s?" remind them that, in the eyes of the US Constitution, women are still not equal to men.

NATIONAL ORGANIZATION FOR WOMEN (NOW)

The liberal feminist organization of record was established in 1966 by Betty Friedan, among others, to "take action to bring women into full participation in the mainstream of American society now, exercising all privileges and responsibilities thereof in truly equal partnership with men." Its mission statement today has evolved into a less classically liberal position: "NOW is dedicated to making legal, political, social, and economic change in our society in order to achieve our goal, which is to eliminate sexism and end all oppression."

WOMANISM; BLACK FEMINISM

Black women like Cellestine Ware, Pauli Murray, and Shirley Chisholm, to name just a few, were an integral part of the early women's liberation movement, especially the branches that arose out of women's experiences in the civil rights movement. But early efforts to characterize a universal female experience were largely informed by a white American middle-class perspective, and were thus problematic. The National Black Feminist Organization, created in 1973, is one of the groups that were established to broaden the black liberation struggle to include women's concerns and to stake black women's claim to the women's liberation movement. Concerned that feminists were overly singular in their focus on gender as a unifying caste, black feminist theorists and activists (like Michelle Wallace, Patricia Hill Collins, Gloria Hull, Patricia Bell-Scott, and bell hooks) embarked on the task of formulating an approach to female liberation that took into account the double jeopardy of race and gender. In her 1983 book, *In Search of Our Mothers' Gardens*, Alice Walker coined the term "womanism" to describe black feminism.

Black feminists have been joined by Chicana feminists like Gloria Anzuldúa and Cherríe Moraga and other women of color to broaden the scope of feminism beyond a white middle-class perspective and to explore the intersections of ethnicity, race, class, and gender—exemplified by the anthologies *This Bridge Called My Back* (1981), *This Bridge We Call Home* (2002), and *Colonize This!* (2002).

EQUITY FEMINISM

This is a sly attempt by antifeminist "feminists"—such as Christina Hoff Sommers, author of *Who Stole Feminism?* (1994), and the freaky neocon think tank called the Independent Women's Forum—to appeal to the sentient public that by and large agrees with concepts like equal pay for equal work without actually acknowledging that sexism still exists. (Who can argue with equity?) But as

wielded by Hoff Sommers, the IWF, and others, it's really just another word for antifeminism, unchecked capitalism, corporate welfare, and neoconservatism.

RADICAL FEMINISM

I hate to break it to you, but contrary to popular belief, it takes more than a bad attitude, hairy armpits, or lack of a sense of humor to be a radical feminist. Read on . . .

PART I: DEFINITION

Radical feminism arose in the late 1960s as a political movement that identified the oppression of women, as a sex-based class or caste, as the most pernicious oppression of them all. The "radical" part came from its proponents' background in the student left, civil rights, and antiwar movements, and was coupled with "feminist" to formulate a radical approach to women's liberation. Radical feminists wanted not for women to share power with men but to abolish the notion of power itself—starting with the sex roles that establish power relations between genders. They led direct actions like the 1968 protest against the Miss America pageant and a sit-in at *Ladies' Home Journal*; held speakouts about once-unmentionable topics like abortion and rape; tackled the myth of the vaginal orgasm; questioned the nuclear family; and encouraged women to point out oppression wherever they saw it. Classic texts of radical feminism include, to name just a few, Shulamith Firestone's *The Dialectic* of Sex, Ti-Grace Atkinson's *Amazon Odyssey*, Kate Millett's *Sexual Politics*, Cellestine Ware's *Woman Power*, Susan Brownmiller's *Against Our Will*, and the anthologies *Sisterhood Is Powerful* (edited by Robin Morgan), *Radical Feminism* (edited by Anne Koedt and Ellen Levine), and especially the manifestos, diatribes, and position papers collected in the zine-like *Notes from the First Year* and *Notes from the Second Year*, which are available on microfilm.

In groups like New York Radical Women, Cell 16, Redstockings, The Feminists, and W.I.T.C.H., radical feminists declared the personal to be political and pioneered the now-classic feminist strategy of consciousness-raising: using the sharing of personal experience as the first step toward political consciousness. (Some radical feminists, in looking at the overwhelming reach of patriarchy, advocated female separatism as an antidote—helping create the enduring myth that feminists are man-haters.)

Radical feminism in all its glory was a short-lived phenomenon (lasting from roughly 1968 to 1972), but its influence is immeasurable: Radical feminists spread the idea of women's liberation across the U.S., reframed the language of the feminist debate, and pushed liberal feminism to be more radical.

PART 2: CONFUSION

Today, the term "radical feminism" is wielded equally—and equally incorrectly—by outraged conservatives and self-proclaimed feminists alike.

What other term would be used to describe both Bush toadie/erstwhile Supreme Court nominee Harriet Miers *and* lifelong activist Andrea Dworkin? But it's true: According to the radically antifeminist Concerned Women for America, Miers once gave a speech that "indicate[s] a radical feminist worldview"—by which the ladies of CWA seem to mean such "sex-baiting comments" as "We all know that Congress and of course the Senate are vastly male-dominated. . . . You can muse about what the reason for this is and I have to conclude that a large factor is the control of financial resources." (I know: How radical!)

Other common recipients of the "radical feminist" epithet include the oh-so-extremist Senators and Congresspeople who support the Violence Against Women Act (which states, simply enough, that domestic and sexual violence hurt women and children, and perpetrators should be punished), UNICEF (for suggesting that the well-being of children is integrally linked to the well-being of their mothers), that man-hating gender terrorist Hillary Clinton, and, of course, pro-choice activists. This usage of "radical" is a deliberate attempt to discredit otherwise modest expressions of concern for women's most basic civil rights.

But it isn't just far-right wackos who miswield the term: More moderate folks who aren't well versed in feminist history or theory tend to associate any outspoken expression of feminist leanings as "radical,"

15

so that any instance of speaking up, even softly, becomes associated with the word. Valerie Solanas, the author of the satiric 1967 *S.C.U.M. Manifesto* that advocated destroying "the male sex" (along with capitalism), is frequently labeled a radical feminist, despite the fact that she was never a part of any organized feminist group, and her public feminist efforts were limited to the manifesto. At the other end of the spectrum, we have the bubblegum-pink "radical feminist" T-shirt sold by the Feminist Majority Foundation, which, while hardly the most egregious offense, still largely misses the point: Radical feminism has a rich history and complex etiology of its own that goes beyond *Grrrr! I'm a feisty femme(inist) and you better not mess with me!*

Which brings us to Andrea Dworkin, perhaps the best-known radical in feminism's back pages. In the public mind, Dworkin was radical because she was extreme, and there's no denying that she made incendiary claims and proposals. But she was also willing to push the idea of gender oppression to its limit, and make sweeping pronouncements that bulldozed a path for more tempered discussion. Her unwavering antiporn stance is also closely allied, within both the feminist movement and the public at large, with the idea of radical feminism, although that in itself is a bone of contention among feminists. (Some contemporary feminists—including the publishers of the storied feminist newsjournal *Off Our Backs* and the webzine *Feminista!*—maintain a strict definition of radical feminism as antiporn.

Others, however—like Judith Levine, Susie Bright, and Ellen Willis—combine a radical feminist outlook with a sex-radical perspective, although they are more likely to self-identify as sex radicals and feminists, or simply as feminists, than as radical feminists.)

Derogatory terms: libbers, hairy-legged man-haters, feminazis, "radical feminists," bra-burners. This seems like a good place to point out that no bras were ever actually burned. At the 1968 No More Miss America protest in Atlantic City organized by New York Radical Women, feminists hoped to burn oppressive instruments of femininity (girdles, high heels, curlers, etc.) in a "freedom trashcan," but they couldn't get a fire permit. They did, however, crown a live sheep Miss America. Still, the titillating "feminists = bra burners" equation has been impressively enduring.

ANTIPORN FEMINISM

Are porn, prostitution, and sex work always and inherently bad for women? For more than two decades, this debate has raged among feminists of all stripes.

Often conflated with radical feminism, antiporn feminism grew out of radical feminism in the late '70s and early '80s—as did its counterpart, prosex feminism. The feminist porn wars of the '80s are largely forgotten to the general public by now, but at the time they were heated, divisive, and intensely personal. In 1982, Barnard College's Center for Research on Women held a conference called "Towards a Politics of Sexuality," which was picketed by antiporn feminists for including explorations of s&m and overall pro-sex viewpoints along with discussions of race and sexuality as well as sexual history (many of which were published in the 1983 anthology *Powers of Desire: The Politics of Sexuality*).

Leading the charge on the anti side were Women Against Pornography (a loosely organized group whose supporters at one point or another included Andrea Dworkin, attorney/legal theorist Catharine MacKinnon, Susan Brownmiller, and Gloria Steinem) who rallied behind Robin Morgan's famous declaration that "porn is the theory, rape is the practice," and argued that the misogynist images in pornography were harmful to women and girls. WAP picketed strip clubs and adult video stores in Times Square, while Dworkin and MacKinnon wrote and campaigned for legislation positing that pornography is a violation of women's civil rights (none of which has ever been adopted). They were countered by anticensorship feminists like Ellen Willis, Nadine Strossen, and Carole Vance, who argued that eliminating pornography wouldn't eliminate the rape and battery of women, and that policing sexual desire and prohibiting free expression weren't good for anyone. (See also: pro-sex feminism.)

Although porn and sexual imagery are even more pervasive in popular culture than they were in the '80s, WAP's legacy can be seen throughout mainstream culture, most clearly in the popular myth that all feminists are against pornography, and even against sex itself.

LESBIAN FEMINISM

To hear Pat Roberston tell it, "lesbian feminism" is redundant (remember: "Feminism encourages women to leave their husbands, kill their children, practice witchcraft, destroy capitalism, and become lesbians"), but it's a lot more complicated than that. In the early '70s, some feminists asserted that lesbianism was the natural extension of feminism, and that until the patriarchy was overthrown, sleeping with men was tantamount to treason. Other groups, like Ti-Grace Atkinson's The Feminists, instituted membership quotas: Only one-third of members could be married to or living with men. Around the same time, in response to NOW's unfortunate flirtation with homophobia (leaders were concerned about the potential PR fallout from an alleged "lavender menace" within NOW's ranks), lesbian feminists—like Rita Mae Brown, Jill Johnston, Charlotte Bunch, Audre Lorde, and groups like Radicalesbians and the Lavender Menace—not only encouraged activism on behalf of gay women but also developed a body of theory and writings on the interconnections between feminism and female homosexuality. Adrienne Rich's landmark 1980 essay "Compulsory Heterosexuality and Lesbian Existence" helped give shape both to lesbian feminism and to the strain of cultural feminism aligned with women-born-women-only spaces like the Michigan Womyn's Music Festival.

In the late '80s and '90s, with the rise of queer theory and identity (articulated by folks like Judith Butler, Michel Foucault, and Eve Kosofsky Sedgwick, who argued that sex and gender are socially constructed, not inborn), a newer breed of lesbian feminism (now generally dubbed queer feminism) emerged. This more fluid approach to sexual orientation involves more questioning of gender itself, from the binary gender system to the essentialist feminist notions of female behavior, and has also yielded groundbreaking theoretical work on female masculinity by scholars like Judith Halberstam, Joan Nestle, and Kate Bornstein.

CULTURAL FEMINISM, A.K.A. ESSENTIALIST FEMINISM, A.K.A. DIFFERENCE FEMINISM

A commonly held objection to the term "feminism" is that, linguistically, it seems to elevate women over men—a point of view that is reinforced by the cultural/essentialist strains of feminism positing that women are naturally, biologically different (and often better) than men.

This pro-woman branch of feminism grew out of '70s-era radical feminism, much to the frustration of many radicals, who argued not for the elevation of femalekind but for the obliteration of all socially determined gender roles. The retreat into cultural feminism is understandable, especially for women who had been on the front lines of feminism for years, but its conflation with radical feminism has unfortunately obscured the histories of both branches. Today, there's a wide range of expressions of cultural feminism, from the gyno-centric spirituality of Mary Daly to *Women Who Run with the Wolves*–style New Ageism to the women-as-peacemakers exhortations of Code Pink.

Difference (or essentialist) feminism is the most common contemporary application of cultural feminism, in its scientific grounding of differences between men and women, such as those identified by Carol Gilligan in her classic text, *In a Different Voice*. Difference feminism holds that women are naturally more maternal and nurturing, hence better parents and more likely to be peacemakers; more moral, hence better social gatekeepers and more ethical politicians or leaders; better communicators; less violent; less competitive; and just generally Venusian.

Derogatory terms: Antifeminist crusader Christina Hoff Sommers likes the confusing moniker "gender feminism."

THIRD-WAVE FEMINISM

When the media takes a moment off from ponderously declaring feminism dead or irrelevant to have a look around at contemporary feminists, all it seems to find are third-wavers: If you're under 40 and you're a feminist, then you're a third-wave feminist—regardless of your politics.

GIRLIE FEMINISM

Jennifer Baumgardner and Amy Richards coined this term in their 2000 book *Manifesta: Young Women, Feminism, and the Future* to describe the pro-femininity line of young feminists, most notably expressed by *Bust*. The reclamation of makeup and other girly accoutrements, and the validation of traditionally female activities like cooking, crafting, and talking about sex, they concluded, is a valid way to express the desire for equality—valuing the inherently female aspects of life, rather than trying to erase them. Unfortunately, the tenets of girlie feminism—that women's work is valuable; that crafts are a powerful link to female history; that sexual experimentation is a potent means of feminist expression—have been easily co-opted by market forces and, in many cases, diluted by the resulting slew of consumer products.

PRO-SEX FEMINISM

The pro-sex line of feminism was born out of the '80s porn wars, in reaction to both the feminist antiporn crusades and the sexual repression of the early Reagan years, and owes its name to a *Village Voice* article by Ellen Willis titled "Lust Horizons: Is the Women's Movement Pro-Sex?" What began as an exploration of the power politics of sexuality by women like Willis, Gayle Rubin, and Betty Dodson evolved during the '90s into an explicit sex-positive approach to feminism. (In a distinct nod to the complicated identity of radical feminism, some sex-positive feminists also use the term "sex radical" to describe themselves.) Proponents run the gamut from theorists like bell hooks and Patrick Califia to erotica-and-criticism writers like Susie Bright and Rachel Kramer Bussel to performance artists like Annie Sprinkle.

Derogatory terms: "Do-me feminism," coined by *Esquire* in 1994, in startled response to the supposed emergence of photogenic, unabashedly sexual feminists like Susie Bright, Elizabeth Wurtzel, and Naomi Wolf; sexually suggestive female musicians like Liz Phair and Courtney Love; and professional sex educators like Tristan Taormino and Nina Hartley. Also: "Lipstick feminism."

I'M NOT A FEMINIST BUT . . . FEMINISM

I'm not a feminist, but I support a woman's right to have an abortion. I'm not a feminist, but I believe in equal pay for equal work. I'm not a feminist, but I organized a campaign against sexual harassment at my school. And so it goes, the litany of statements in support of feminist issues, accompanied by the stark disclaimer. A major project of contemporary feminism is encouraging "I'm not . . . but" feminists to embrace the label wholeheartedly, while also recognizing that in many ways the word is less important than the actions or ethos.

POSTFEMINISM

Current readers of the *New York Times* might not be surprised to learn that as early as 1981 the paper of record was already signaling the death knell of feminism: "Voices from the Post-Feminist Generation" (October 1981) reads a whole lot like "Many Women at Elite Colleges Set Career Path to Motherhood" (September 2005). Postfeminism is the notion that the feminist movement has outlived its usefulness, because, after all, we have a few female Senators, it's illegal to discriminate against women in job hiring, there's a women's pro basketball league, and record numbers of women are attending college. Of course, if you want to get all Lacanian about it, postfeminism also derives from the postmodern theories of destabilizing identities, deconstruction, and intertextuality. This primer, however, is long enough already. Put down your torches, gals, 'cause the struggle is over!

While such sentiments do point to feminism's far-reaching success, they also tend to re-personalize the political by assigning any continuing gender-related struggles to individual circumstances. And that, my friends, isn't good for anybody. The truth is, painting ours as a postfeminist world gets everyone in power off the hook; it pretends that everything is peachy and suggests that if, for you, it isn't, then the problem lies with you and your personal choices, not with any larger systems of, oh, let's say patriarchy or capitalism or racism or classism.

Despite the fact that more people than ever embrace feminist causes, the word itself still suffers from image problems. Because feminism suggests that everything isn't hunky-dory, it forces people to acknowledge the problems that plague us. But rather than positioning all women as helpless victims, as many antifeminists claim, feminism offers women a sense of agency, history, and solidarity. It provides a structural framework for making sense of thorny personal issues, and it offers a shared commitment to resolve these issues. Instructive bumper-sticker slogan: "I'll be post-feminist in the post-patriarchy."

I'M A FEMINIST AND . . .

Feminism is, as bell hooks famously put, for everybody, whether or not you need to append an adjective to make it feel like it belongs to you. In the end, it doesn't really matter which labels you choose or reject. What matters is your commitment to challenging the notion that a person's gender should, by law or by rote, be an obstacle to civil and personal liberties. It's important to have a sense of feminism's complex history, but it's also crucial to know—and help others understand—that feminism isn't something that happened to your mother or grandmother and is now over. It's living, breathing, and evolving.

So, how can you talk to your friends, family, and other concerned people about feminism? First of all, remember that many people do have these misconceptions, or have never received any adequate education on the topic. Start with the facts: Feminism is the theory of the political, economic, and social equality of the sexes. Hard to argue with, right? Then you can slowly introduce more complex issues, as questions arise. Be patient: Not everyone takes to feminism right away. Some people, like the *New York Times*'s Maureen Dowd or the always incendiary Camille Paglia, will insist on referring to "the feminists" as if they are one big indistinguishable lump. Others will insist on modifying their own identification as feminist with a sentence like "But I don't hate men or anything." But just keep talking, and encourage others you know to do the same. And in time, you'll make feminism a normal, everyday part of your life and the lives of those around you.

12 THINGS ABOUT BEING A WOMAN THAT WOMEN WON'T TELL YOU

CAITLIN MORAN

Originally published on Esquire.co.uk
2016

Hey, I'm not going to womansplain feminism to the readers of *Esquire*! That's not happening on my watch! You're sophisticated, twenty-first-century men with a copy of the *El Bulli* cookbook, a timeless pair of investment brogues, and a couple of Joni Mitchell albums—for when you want to sit in your leather armchair, and have a little, noble, necessary man-cry.

You don't need me lecturing you—because you're not hanging out the back of a bus shouting "CLUNGE!" at a bunch of terrified 15-year-old girls. You've got sisters, mothers, lovers—female friends and colleagues—and you've never once gone up to any of them shouting, "Blimey! You don't get many of those to the pahnd!" while honking on their breasts, in the manner of Sid James. You're down with the sisterhood. You've got eyes. You know what's going on out there. You've noted that while society's happy for a famous man to age, and become distinguished, and generally wander around looking like a fucking wizard, the women generally still seem to be 20 years younger, and

standing there on the cover of magazines, all like, "Oh! My clothes . . . they fell off!" EVEN IF IT'S DAME JUDI DENCH.

You know the pay disparity; still 20 percent less for women in this country, and not a single prosecution, even though it's literally illegal. You know babies come out of vaginas and it fucking stings, and that the vaginas are having a hard time anyway, what with all the waxing they get. (That's £20 a pop, my friend. Every single month. Just to feel normal. It's basically VAT on your minge. Imagine if you had to get your bum-hole stripped every 30 days—lest the mean girls at school corner you on the bus home and go, "I've heard you're like Catweazle down there. Someone who fingered you said it was like diddling a Gonk. Ugh.")

You've seen Amy Schumer's brilliant, edgy sketches on contraception and rape, and laughed along with them. You've called Donald Trump "a twat" for his sexist comments about a female news anchor being on her period. You've watched the whole Caitlyn Jenner trans thing unfold and gone, "You know

23

what—this all seems fair enough. I am down with the trans thing."

So, no. I'm not going to womansplain feminism to you. It's the twenty-first century and you are, most assuredly, not a dick. You like women being equal to men—which is all that feminism means. Not all the penises being burned in a Penis Bonfire. Just women being equal to men. You are like my friend John, when he talks about dating alpha-women: "Feel intimidated by them? Christ, no. Dating and marrying powerful women is like big game hunting. I fuck tigers and panthers. Not . . . chihuahuas."

No. You get feminism. You don't need Tits McGee here to take you through it one more time. So, what I am going to do, instead, is tell you 12 things about women that women are usually too embarrassed to tell you themselves. Because I am a chronic over-sharer, and incapable of keeping secrets. I'm like that other Deep Throat. The chatty Watergate one. That's the Deep Throat I am.

1

NO MUMBLING Like you, we feel a bit embarrassed about saying the word "feminism." It's the same as when you say the word "environment." They both have that slight implication of, "I'm now going to

launch into a speech that's basically about what a great person I am."

Unfortunately, in both cases, the entire future of the world does rest on people being able to say those words properly, and not mumbling "femernism," or "envibeoment."

You just have to shut yourself in a cupboard and say them over and over again—"FEMINISM! ENVIRONMENT! FEMINISM! ENVIRONMENT!"— until they feel as normal as saying "piña colada," or "Michael Fassbender." Which are both, when you think about it, much odder-sounding.

"THE MAN" So, when women talk about "The Man," we're not talking about you. You're just a man. You're not The Man. Similarly, when we talk about the patriarchy, that's not you, either. You're not the patriarchy. You're just . . . Patrick. When we're doing those "MEN!" chats, we're just identifying the general locus of the problem, i.e., most of the power and influence being held by a small amount of men.

Because remember that patriarchy's bumming you as hard as it's bumming us. We're bulimic, objec-tified, and under-promoted. You, meanwhile, are unable to talk about your feelings lest you get punched in the nuts by "a lad" telling you not to be "a bender." You are unlikely to get custody of your kids, and are three times more likely to commit suicide. Feminism's about sorting all this stuff out. Because it's about equality. Not burning the penises. I can't emphasize enough how much it's not about burning penises. No burnt penises here.

3

PERIODS We're still pretty traumatized about our periods, even though we're now 40. Being a woman doesn't make "being a woman" any easier. All that womb-shit is nuts. It's like having an exploding, insane blood-bag of pain up in your business end—nothing really prepares you for when it all kicks off. One day, you're just a kid on your bike. The next, you're suddenly having to wedge a tiny Barbie mattress in your knickers, crying while you watch *Bergerac*, and eating Nurofen Plus like they're Tic Tacs.

Men, imagine if, sometime around your 12th birthday, some manner of viscous liquid—let's say gravy—suddenly appeared in your pants, in the middle of a maths lesson. And then it turned up every month for the next 30 years. You'd be all like "NO!" and "WTF?!?!" and "SRSLY??? THIS????" That's what we're like, too. We're not wise, or in touch with nature, or down with it. We're just people with

a whole load more laundry issues than you. Have you ever tried to scrub blood out of a Premier Inn sheet at 6 a.m., using just travel shampoo and your toothbrush? It's one of the defining aspects of being a woman.

ABORTION Likewise, imagine accidentally getting pregnant at 16, then having to run past a barrage of anti-abortion protesters outside your local clinic, all holding up pictures of dead foetuses. We're not dealing with this in a special, noble lady-way. We're like, "THIS IS ALREADY A REALLY, REALLY SHIT DAY. I PRESUME YOUR CONCERN FOR THE WELFARE OF CHILDREN EXTENDS INTO A LIFE SPENT VOLUNTEERING IN CARE HOMES, FOSTERING, AND DONATING YOUR WAGES TO THE NSPCC—AND DOESN'T SOLELY REST ON HARASSING AND ABUSING TEARFUL, POSSIBLY RAPED WOMEN WHO ARE TRYING TO GET A SAFE, LEGAL MEDICAL PROCEDURE SO THEY DON'T FUCK UP THE REST OF THEIR LIVES."

Here's another thing we're too embarrassed to say: we'd love it if a big bunch of pro-choice men turned up at these clinics, and helped escort the scared women in. That would be some top bro solidarity.

5

TALKING In the last year or so, we saw this study, from America, and it broke our hearts a bit, because it explains so much: in a mixed-gender group, when women talk 25 percent of the time or less, it's seen as being "equally balanced." And if women talk 25 to 50 percent of the time, they're seen as "dominating the conversation."

And we remembered all the times on social media, or in conversations, an angry man has said, "Women are WINNING now. Women are EVERYWHERE. It is MEN who are being silenced," and it all made sense.

FEAR We're scared. We don't want to mention it, because it's kind of a bummer, chat-wise, and we'd really like to talk about stuff that makes us happy, like look at our daughters—and we can't help but think, "Which one of us? And when?" We walk down the street at night with our keys clutched between our fingers, as a weapon. We move in packs—because it's safer. We talk to each other for hours on the phone—to share knowledge. But we don't want to go on about it to you, because that would be morbid. We just feel anxious. We're scared. Given the figures, we can't sometimes help but feel we're just . . . waiting for the bad thing to come.

Because that would be a realistic thing to think, and we like to be prepared. Awfully, horribly, fearfully prepared.

TIRED We're tired. So, so tired. From the moment we grew our tits, we've been catcalled in the street; commented on by relatives ("Ooooh, she's big-boned"; "Well, you'll be a heartbreaker") as if we weren't standing there in front of them, hearing all this. We've seen our biggest female role models and icons shamed in the press, over and over: computers hacked and nude pictures released; sex tapes released. So we know even success, and money, will not protect us from the humiliation of simply being a woman. We know we must have our babies when we're young—the eggs are running out!—but we must also work for less money, as discussed above. So that makes us tired.

This is why, maybe, women can become suddenly furious—why online discussions about feminism suddenly ignite into rage. Tired, scared people are apt to lash out. Anger is just fear, brought to the boil.

8

WANKING We masturbate as much as you do. One of the few times I have been personally offended was when Martin Amis commented on a column I wrote about female masturbation. "Christ," Amis said, "that's sort of lad's mag talk—sort of more male than male."

Obviously, I am noble enough to recognize that Amis is from an older generation—one whose women, by and large, did not feel comfortable discussing their sexuality in any great detail. But it does seem amazing that a clever, well-traveled man, whose job it is to examine the human condition, and who had a pretty steamy relationship with Germaine Greer at one point, has never realized that women can be just as driven by their desire as men.

I'm gonna be honest with you—for the first five years of my adult life, most of my decisions were made by the contents of my pants. My vagina was—by way of Audrey II in *Little Shop of Horrors*—constantly shouting "Feed me!," and breaking into musical numbers when I was trying to listen to my brain instead. If I had not discovered masturbation, I would have spent the majority of my time sitting on shed roofs, like a cat in heat, yowling at the moon. If a young woman isn't to go mad, then masturbation is a needful hobby, as vital as going on long country walks, to get a bit of air in your lungs, and pursuing the revolution. And what a hobby it is! It doesn't cost anything, it doesn't make you fat, you can knock it off in five minutes flat if you think

about Han Solo, or some monkeys "doing it" on an Attenborough documentary, and it means you can face the world with a kind of stoned, postcoital cheerfulness that would otherwise require Valium, or constant spa breaks.

There's a reason why God designed our bodies so that, when we lie down in bed, our hands naturally come to rest on our genitals. It's the Lord's way of saying, "Go on, have a fiddle. Find out how you work. And then, when you go out into the world, you won't be waiting for some bloke to come along and have sex on you. You'll be in the sex, too. It'll be like this . . . joint endeavor? A thing you can do together? That was kind of how I planned it all along, TBH. So, my Eleventh Commandment is 'Thou Shalt Buff Your Fnuh.' That's official. Signed, God."

CLOTHES You know when we stand in front of a full wardrobe and say, "I don't have anything to wear!"? Obviously we have things to wear. You can see all the shit from where you are standing, fully dressed, ready to leave the house. What we mean is, "I don't have anything to wear for who I need to be today." What women wear is incredibly important and not just because we live in a society with a

$1.5 trillion fashion industry, and spend most of our spare time looking at cut-price Marc Jacobs handbags on Theoutnet.com.

As we are the half of the world that still doesn't get to say as much as men (see stats earlier), how we look works by way of our opening paragraph in any social setting. Think of all the different kinds of looks women can have, depending on their clothes, hair, and makeup: "Slutty." "Ball-busting." "Mumsy." "Manic Pixie Dream Girl." "Gym-bunny." "Mutton." "Nerdy." "Unfuckable."

Now think of all the ways men can dress. It's basically "some trousers." Ninety percent of what men wear is "some trousers." You're just getting up in the morning, putting on your trousers, and getting on with stuff.

And we fret about all this—appearance, clothes—because it matters. If we're still getting talked over at meetings, is it because we're not dressing powerfully enough? If we're getting sexually harassed, is it because we're wearing the wrong skirt? In 2008, a rape case was overturned because the judge decided the alleged victim must have consented to sex, because her jeans were "too tight" for the accused to remove on his own. This is what we're thinking about, when we stand in front of the wardrobe. Will this outfit define the rest of today? Will it, if I am very unlucky, affect my life? Is this going to be the subject of a court case? Could I run for my life in these shoes? Do I have anything for who I need to be today?

10

MALE FEMINISTS We're embarrassed when other women say, "Men can't be feminists!" We don't want to get into an argument, but we just can't see the logic in it. Feminism can only work if men are feminists, too—because the only index by which feminism will succeed is based on how many people believe in it, support it, and want it to happen. By definition, it has to be a populist movement. There's no point in only 27 percent of people believing in equality because the math, very obviously, shows that you won't be equal if 73 percent of people think you're not. You can't go and . . . hide the feminism in a special secret place, and only let certain people have access to it. Besides, as discussed above, men need feminism almost as badly as women do. So, lady-balls to "men can't be feminists." We disbelieve that. In our vaginas.

11

CARBS Our ultimate aim, when it comes to men, is to find an amusing mate we can have sex with, then sit on the sofa with, watching reruns of *Seinfeld* and eating a baked potato. Discount all that Christian Grey/abs of steel/"bad boy" shit. Our priorities are: 1) Kindness; 2) Jokes; 3) High tolerance of carbs.

TRAINERS It actually was us that threw those horrible old trainers of yours away. That story about how a time portal opened up, and they were stolen away by your own teenaged self? That was a lie.

THE BEAUTY BRIDGE

JIA TOLENTINO

Originally published in *The Hairpin*
2014

M y best girl friend in the Peace Corps was an energetic, super-hot French whirl of a person who spoke five languages, taught me how to make pie crust, and wore consistently excellent winged eyeliner even as we fended off wild dogs and pooped in the woods. One day I was poking around her room and opened a drawer that sprang forth with colorful, lacy, perfectly kept bras. "How many of these did you bring?" I asked her. She shrugged and said a dozen or something. I thought about my own suitcase and told her that I'd maybe brought like a couple bras, a couple sports bras too?

"For two years?" she said, genuinely and innocently surprised. I felt ashamed, but only vaguely. Those were gross times in general, and one must always pick and choose one's areas of interest: fancy underwear will never be up my alley in any sense, so to speak. So it had been a while, let's say, since my last purchase when I found myself on American Eagle's lingerie website a few weeks ago, looking to pick up a few clearance bralettes in a pleasingly abrasive shade of lace.

The Aerie brand is aimed at teenagers, but I've never stopped shopping there. Occasionally the website will remind me that I'm not in their main market, especially for the bras I tend to order, which have reviews like "This is PERFECT for under your school uniform!!" Once I accidentally ordered the wrong style (the "Ella" instead of the "Emma") and the sculpted padding ("from Perky to Double Whoa") was fully two inches thick; the reviews, which I checked before returning it, were sprinkled with complaints from girls who had hoped to coax "better cleavage :/" out of their AA chests. So much of teenage girldom is about learning to perform your gender, to exude sex in preparation for having it; it can take much too long before you realize you don't have to do a thing that you don't naturally take to, and this website, while cheery and nonsensational, will sometimes give me a bit of weird.

Like the image to the right [image from #aerieREAL campaign that shows a lingerie model and reads, "These girls are *not* retouched"]: it made me feel a little predatory. *Stare as close as you want, my friend, these chicks are 100% real.* I took a screenshot, filed it away, and then forgot about it until a few days later Jezebel offered money for unretouched photos and featured this exact campaign, saying to Aerie "nicely done." Then Aerie's campaign started to get some heat. *Adweek* called it "revolutionary," the brand gave a proud statement about "challenging super-model standards," and we, the audience, responded: one *Refinery29* article on why the campaign is "so important" has almost 50,000 likes on Facebook.

I will probably be buying my underwear from Aerie for the next decade, and it's lovely to see what they're doing with stomach texture and slight moves toward diversity. Their campaign is already very successful, and it's named, simply, "Real." The Dove version, where women in various iterations are told that they are actually more beautiful than they had suspected, is called "Real Beauty."

———

Many people acknowledge that these are just baby steps; nearly everyone calls them a step in the right direction, which they are, but only if we think the best we can do for women is try and shuffle a bunch more of us into "hot" from "not," if we'd rather constantly redefine beautiful than reject it as one whole gender's teleology at large.

The way these campaigns use the word "real" here is exactly wrong in an important way, a way that has led to the particular fetish value of the "real" in America. We have a national attraction to authenticity, or the signification of authenticity; we heap enormous amounts of meaning and economic power on things that appear to be whole and true. We authenticate people, too, of course, fussing about whether movie stars, rappers, and politicians have an ethos that matches their history that matches their face that matches their words. With women, our attention goes immediately to the body: when a woman is famous enough, her face and figure must be examined for alterations. Remember all that fuss about Britney in her tight white crop top, or Courtney Stodden when she had her brief moment: this authenticity fervor always comes out most strongly when the woman's body itself is her moneymaker. Searching "Kim Kardashian plastic surgery," in quotes, pulls up 900,000 hits.

Both Kardashian and Stodden have gone so far as to X-ray their bodies on television, but the desire to expose a non-effortless beauty is pervasive. "Kim Kardashian Needs to Come Clean About Her Surgery," scolds a headline on a website called CafeMom. This is America; if we're paying for it, for her—even just with our attention—we want to know that it's "real."

———

In the 1870s, economist David Wells wrote a tract called *Robinson Crusoe's Money*, a rewritten narrative in which the natives on Crusoe's island accidentally discover gold. Recognizing the substance as an "object of universal desire," they immediately lose their barter economy; gold "acquired spontaneously a universal purchasing power, and from that moment on, became Money." These natives get along quite well like this until they start printing fiat currency, mistaking paper (the "representative of a thing") with gold, which is the thing itself.

In this framework, gold's beauty is evidence of its goodness. Its face evinces and is identical to its monetary value; its worth is incontrovertible and fixed. This is the same fantasy we have about the conventional American beauty standard, which shares many qualities with the gold bar: an "all-American beauty" is sleek, blonde, expensive-looking, devoid of complicating layers. We have a fantasy of literal face value, which is why pageants keep trying to force an organic connection between beauty and goodness, why you can pick up a magazine in a checkout line and immediately find before-and-after noses, accusatory arrows, the falseness in every beauty ferreted out.

———

Historian Walter Benn Michaels wrote about *Robinson Crusoe's Money* that its real point is "to show that nothing ever acquires value, that no money can become

good and true unless it already is good and true." This, to me, was the ideological backbone of the Lena Dunham bounty. It is deeply bothersome to us to see women printing money if they don't have enough gold to back it up. It is disturbing to see women acquiring any sort of beauty-value that their bodies and faces can't trade on. Dunham's *Vogue* photos were fiat currency, divorced from the goods that were supposed to be backing them; they were the representative of the thing, when we were looking for the thing itself.

Now, Aerie is attempting to play their models off as the thing itself. But a campaign about "real girls," asserting that "the real you is sexy," hews exactly to the proposition it appears to subvert. I expect that for a long time we will continue to see these baby-soft, often obviously stupid ideas masquerading as empowerment, these ideas that push women around each other on the narrow, precarious beauty bridge rather than suggesting we just howl like animals and jump right off.

———

Later in David Wells's *Crusoe*, the islanders begin to understand representation and mimesis: they hire an artist to paint "the finest and most fashionable patterns" on a poor person's clothing, rather than giving the man "real" new clothes. The end result, with "jewelry and fancy buttons to match," looked so much like actual fancy clothing that the islanders happily ran with it, allowing "the shadow of wealth [to] supply the place of its substance."

To Wells, this storyline provided another argument against the validity of paper currency, whose intentional representation of value was supplanting the accidental representation of value, which "made warfare against the beneficence of the Almighty" and provided for "the survival of the unfittest."

But why shouldn't the islanders paint on some buttons? Not everyone's born rich, born uptown, born to win. I take a lot of personal enjoyment in sometimes using makeup to put a fancy face on my plain face, and that is because I feel comfortable knowing what game I'm playing, and know that I am playing, and by my own criteria, rather than fundamentally attempting to fool.

BEAUTY HAS ALWAYS BEEN A MATTER OF WHERE YOU HAPPEN TO FALL IN THE CROSS-SECTION OF GENES, MONEY, PRIORITIES, PASSING FASHIONS, LASTING DISCRIMINATIONS;

BEAUTY IN THE TWENTY-FIRST CENTURY CAN REALLY BE BOILED DOWN TO A COMBINATION OF TECHNOLOGY AND TIME.

But we keep effacing this. Like goldbugs, we are seduced by aesthetic pleasure into creating a fantasy of absolute value; we are refusing to recognize the incredible amount of meaning that is constructed in the space between appearance and worth.

Two years ago, the GOP officially considered the possibility of returning the national economy to the gold standard. The fantasy of "certainty, natural law, and stable meanings" is as powerful as it is socially bankrupt; on a human scale it walks in lockstep with deep historical prejudice. Beauty, like gold, is valued as we choose to value it. We can print so much more paper, and perhaps just to burn it; there's no reason not to wildly, transgressively inflate our ideas of beauty, or better yet, cease to care.

———

When I was Aerie-aged and deeply concerned with what a teenage boy might rate my face and body on a scale from 1 to 10, I was never intimidated by the women I saw in magazines. What cowed me was how tremendously beautiful my friends were. It was a good lesson, maybe, from growing up in Texas: even when girls got plastic surgery or went full All-American, as blonde as can be—some are getting Botox now, at 27! Do your thing, you arrestingly lovely nuts—their "altered" beauty was, to me and to them and to everyone else around us, wholly and powerfully real.

To suggest that there is moral value in accidental beauty because it is accidental is to insist on an essentialism that erases the real complexity of what performing beauty and gender and sexuality means to the millions of people who are invested, for tremendously different reasons, in doing so. Policing and fetishizing authenticity in female beauty is a distraction, a politically blind one when nearly half of transgender people in this country attempt suicide, 87 percent of LGBTQ homicide victims are people of color, and on and on and on. It is useless to either erase the labor of being beautiful or punish it. The search for the "real" under these definitions will always turn up an answer that is fundamentally meaningless, leaving beauty as the primary mover, chasing turtles all the way down.

UGLY

WARSAN SHIRE

Originally published in
Teaching My Mother How to Give Birth
2011

Your daughter is ugly.
She knows loss intimately,
carries whole cities in her
belly.

As a child, relatives wouldn't hold her.
She was splintered wood and sea water.
She reminded them of the war.

On her fifteenth birthday you taught her
how to tie her hair like rope
and smoke it over burning frankincense.

You made her gargle rosewater
and while she coughed, said
*macaanto girls like you shouldn't smell
of lonely or empty.*

You are her mother.
Why did you not warn her,
hold her like a rotting boat
and tell her that men will not love her
if she is covered in continents,
if her teeth are small colonies,
if her stomach is an island
if her thighs are borders?

What man wants to lie down
and watch the world burn
in his bedroom?

Your daughter's face is a small riot,
her hands are a civil war,
a refugee camp behind each ear,
a body littered with ugly things.

But God,
doesn't she wear
the world well?

A WOMAN
SHOPPING

ANNE BOYER

Originally published in *Garments Against Women*
2016

I will soon write a long, sad book called *A Woman Shopping*. It will be a book about what we are required to do and also a book about what we are hated for doing. It will be a book about envy and a book about barely visible things. This book would be a book also about the history of literature and literature's uses against women, also against literature and for it, also against shopping and for it. The flâneur is a poet is an agent free of purses, but a woman is not a woman without a strap over her shoulder or a clutch in her hand.

The back matter of the book will only say this: *If a woman has no purse, we will imagine one for her.*

These would be the chapters:

On a woman shopping
On men shopping, with and without women
On children with women as they shop
On the barely moving lips of the calculating and poor

On attempting to open doors for the elderly and in the process of this, touching their arms
On the acquiring of arms in action movies
On Daniel Defoe
On the time I saw a homeless man murdered for shoplifting
On whether it is better to want nothing or steal everything
On how many of my hours are gone now because I have had to shop
On how I wish I could shop for hours instead

There would be more: lavish descriptions of lavish descriptions of the perverse or decadently feminized marketplace, some long sentences concerning the shipping and distribution of alterity, an entire chapter about *Tender Buttons* in which each sentence is only a question. And from where did that mutton, that roast beef, that carafe come?

But who would publish this book and who, also would shop for it? And how could it be literature if it is not coyly against literature but sincerely against it, as it is also against ourselves?

THE
LIES WE
TELL
PREGNANT
WOMEN

SOFIA JAWED-WESSEL

We're going to share a lot of secrets today, you and I. And in doing so, I hope that we can lift some of the shame many of us feel about sex.

How many here have ever been catcalled by a stranger? Lots of women. For me, the time I remember best is when that stranger was a student of mine. He came up to me after class that night, and his words confirmed what I already knew. "I'm so sorry, professor, if I had known it was you, I would never have said those things." I wasn't a person to him, until I was *his* professor. This concept, called objectification, is the foundation of sexism, and we see it reinforced through all facets of our lives. We see it in advertisements. How many of you have seen an advertisement that uses a woman's breasts to sell an entirely unrelated product? Or movie after movie after movie that portrays women as only love interests? These examples might seem inconsequential and harmless, but they're insidious, slowly building into a culture that refuses to see women as people. We see this in the school that sends home a ten-year-old girl because her clothes were a distraction to boys trying to learn. Or the government that refuses to adequately punish men for raping women, over and over and over. Or the woman who was killed because she asked a man to stop grinding on her on the dance floor.

Media plays a large role in perpetuating the objectification of women. Let's consider the classic romantic comedy. We're typically introduced to two kinds of women in these movies—two kinds of desirable women anyway. The first is the sexy bombshell. This is the unbelievably gorgeous woman with the perfect body. Our leading man has no trouble identifying her and even less trouble having sex with her. The second is our leading lady, the beautiful but demure woman our leading man falls in love with, despite not noticing her at first or not liking her if he did. The first is the slut—highly sexually desirable, but too available. She is to be consumed and forgotten. The other is sexy enough to still be desirable, but modest, and therefore, worthy of having our leading man's future babies—marriage material. These caricatures of women let us in on another little secret: We actually see women as having two purposes.

OH, HOW GENEROUS OF SOCIETY! NOT ONLY DO WE EXIST FOR THE SEXUAL PLEASURE OF MEN, WE ALSO EXIST TO REPRODUCE AND RAISE CHILDREN. BUT THESE TWO PURPOSES HAVE A VERY DIFFICULT TIME COEXISTING WITHIN THE SAME WOMAN.

On the rare occasion that I share with a new acquaintance that I study sex—if they don't end the conversation right then, they're usually pretty intrigued. "Oh, tell me more." So I do. "I'm really interested in studying the sexual behavior of pregnant and postpartum couples." At this point, I

usually get a different kind of response. "Oh, huh. Do pregnant people even have sex? Have you thought about studying sexual desire? Or orgasms? That would be interesting—and sexy." Even though we insist women are sexual objects, our culture either desexualizes or fetishizes pregnant women and mothers—on either end, the message is clear: it's not "normal" to find them sexy.

Tell me, what are the first words that come to mind when you picture a pregnant woman? I asked this question in a survey of over five hundred adults and most responded with "belly" or "round" and "cute." This didn't surprise me too much. What else do we label as cute? Babies. Puppies. Kittens. The elderly. When we label an adult as cute, though, we take away a lot of their intelligence, their complexity. We reduce them to childlike qualities. I also asked heterosexual men to imagine a woman that they're partnered with as pregnant, and I asked women to imagine that they are pregnant, and then tell me the first words that come to mind when they imagine having sex. Most of the responses were negative. "Gross," "awkward," "not sexy," "odd," "uncomfortable," "how?" "not worth the trouble," "not worth the risk." That last one really stuck with me. We might think that because we divorce pregnant women and moms from sexuality, that we're removing the constraints of sexual objectification. They experience less sexism, right? Not exactly. What happens instead is a different kind of objectification.

In my efforts to explain this to others, one conversation led to the Venus of Willendorf, a Paleolithic figurine scholars assumed was a goddess of love and beauty, hence the name Venus. This theory was later revised, though, when scholars noted the sculptor's obvious focus on the figurine's reproductive features. Large breasts, considered ideal for nursing. A round, possibly pregnant belly. The remnants of red dye, alluding to menstruation or birth. They also assumed that she was meant to be held or lying down, because her tiny feet don't allow her to be freestanding. She also had no face. For this reason it was assumed that she was a representation of fertility, not a person. She was an object. In the history of her interpretation she went from object of ideal beauty and love to object of reproduction. I think this transition speaks more about the scholars who have interpreted her purpose than the actual purpose of the figurine herself.

When a woman becomes pregnant, according to society, she leaves the realm of men's sexual desire and slides into her reproductive and child-rearing role. In doing so, she also becomes the property of the community, considered very important, but only because she's pregnant. I've taken to calling this the Willendorf effect. And once again, we see this reinforced in many aspects of her life. Has anyone here ever been visibly pregnant? So how many of you ever had a stranger touch your belly during pregnancy? Maybe even without your permission first. Or been told what you can and

cannot eat by somebody who's not your doctor, your medical provider? Or asked questions about your birth plan? And then told why those choices are all wrong? Yeah, me too. Or had a server refuse to bring you a glass of wine? Now this one might give you pause, but stay with me. This is a huge secret. There is actually little evidence to support that drinking in moderation during pregnancy is not safe. Many of us don't know this because doctors don't trust pregnant women with this secret. Especially if she's less educated or a woman of color. What this tells us is that the Willendorf effect is also classist and racist. It's present when the government reminds women with every new anti-choice bill that the contents of her uterus are not her own. Or when an ob-gyn says, "Well it's safe to have sex during pregnancy but sometimes you never know; better safe than sorry, right?" She's denied basic privacy and bodily autonomy under the guise of "be a good mother." We don't trust her to make her own decisions. She's "cute," remember?

When we tell women that sex isn't "worth the risk" during pregnancy, what we're telling her is that her sexual pleasure doesn't matter. So what we're telling her is that she doesn't matter. Even though the needs of her fetus are not at odds with her own needs. Similar to alcohol during pregnancy, over 50 years of rigorous science has found no evidence sex during pregnancy leads to negative obstetric events such as miscarriage or premature birth. Medical providers, such as the American College of Obstetricians and Gynecologists, have the opportunity to educate about the safety of sex during pregnancy. So what do the experts say? ACOG actually has no public official statement about the safety of sex during pregnancy. Guidance from the Mayo Clinic is generally positive but presented with a caveat: "Although most women can safely have sex throughout pregnancy, sometimes it's best to be cautious." Some women don't want to have sex during pregnancy, and that's ok. Some women do want to have sex during pregnancy, and that's ok, too. What needs to stop is society telling women what they can and cannot do with their bodies. Pregnant women are not faceless, identity-less vessels of reproduction who can't stand on their own two feet.

But the truth is, the real secret is, we tell all women that their sexual pleasure doesn't matter. We refuse to even acknowledge that women who have sex with women or women who don't want children even exist. "Oh, it's just a phase . . . she just needs the right man to come along." Every time a woman has sex simply because it feels good, it is revolutionary. She is revolutionary. She is pushing back against society's insistence that she exist simply for men's pleasure or for reproduction. This is why comprehensive sex education is so scary to many. We're not afraid teenage boys will have sex: *"They're becoming men!"* We're also not afraid teenage girls will start having sex—they're already having

sex, we're just shaming and punishing them for it. We're afraid teenage girls will be given the tools to have safe, consensual, PLEASURABLE sex. That she will become a woman who prioritizes her sexual needs without fear of being labeled a slut.

A woman who prioritizes her sexual needs is scary, because a woman who prioritizes her sexual needs prioritizes herself. That is a woman demanding that she be treated as an equal. That is a woman who insists that you make room for her at the table of power, and that is the most terrifying of all because we can't make room for her without some of us giving up the extra space we hold.

I have one last secret for you. I am the mother of two boys and we could use your help. Even though my boys hear me say regularly that it's important for men to recognize women as equals and they see their father modeling this, we need what happens in the world to reinforce what happens in our home. This is not a men's problem or a women's problem. This is everyone's problem, and we all play a role in dismantling systems of inequality. For starters, we have got to stop telling women what they can and cannot do with their bodies. This includes not treating pregnant women like community property. If you don't know her, don't even ask to touch her belly. You wouldn't anybody else. Don't tell her what she can and cannot eat. Don't ask her private details about her medical decisions. This also includes understanding that even if you are personally against abortion, you can still fight for a woman's right to choose. When it comes to women's equality, the two need not oppose one another. If you're somebody who has sex with women, prioritize her pleasure. If you don't know how, ask. If you have children—have conversations about sex as early as possible, because kids don't look up s-e-x in the dictionary anymore. They look it up on the internet. And when you're having those conversations about sex, don't center them on reproduction only. People have sex for many reasons, some because they want a baby, but most of us have sex because it feels good. Admit it. And regardless of whether you have children or not, support comprehensive sex education that doesn't shame our teenagers. Nothing positive comes from shaming teens for their sexual desires, behaviors, other than positive STD and pregnancy tests. Every single day, we are all given the opportunity to disrupt patterns of inequality. I think we can all agree that it's worth the trouble to do so.

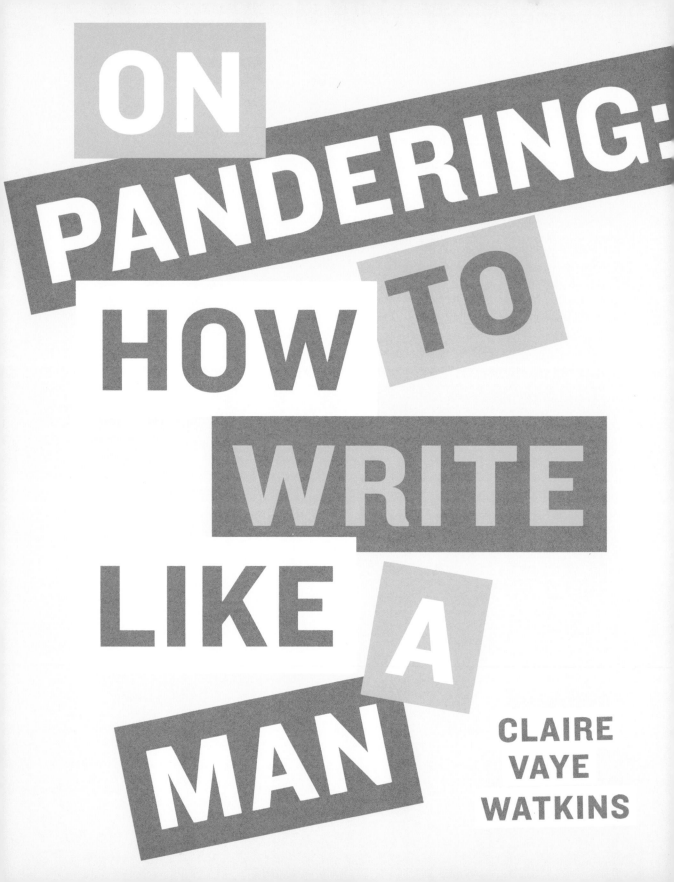

Remarks delivered at the
Tin House Writer's Workshop
2015

SOME EXPOSITION

Until recently I was a professor at a private liberal arts university in Lewisburg, Pennsylvania, a little town located at the exact point of overlap of a three-part Venn diagram. Draw one in your mind: label circle #1 Amish country, label circle #2 coal country, label circle #3 fracking country.

The towns near Lewisburg have names like Shamokin Dam, Frackville, Minersville, and Coal Township. You might have heard of a place called Centralia, a modern-day ghost town thanks to a vein of coal that has been burning beneath the ground since 1962, belching up smoke and carbon monoxide, forcing people to flee their homes and poisoning those who refuse. That vein, by the way, is expected to continue burning for another 250 years. So if you haven't visited Centralia, there's still time. Centralia is about forty miles from my old house, and people from the Buffalo Valley, where I lived, often took day-trips there. So basically all you need to know about this particular region of central Pennsylvania is that we went to Centralia—a smoldering village of noxious fumes—on vacation.

The Buffalo Valley smells like pig shit, puppy mills, or burning garbage, depending on which way the wind blows. It is not uncommon, when hiking, to come across a tarry black field where old-growth forest has been recently clear-cut, the ground still soaked with diesel. This all sounds pretty bleak, and it was, even to me, a person with a high tolerance for bleakness and an affection for abused landscapes. Living there, I can admit now that I've fled, corroded a part of my soul. Driving to a neighboring town for a prenatal checkup felt like driving through Capote's *In Cold Blood*. During the time I lived in central Pennsylvania the adjective I used most to describe the place to faraway friends was "murdersome."

And yet the little town of Lewisburg, where this expensive private university is located, is actually quite pleasant. The houses are gingerbread Victorians and stately brick colonials, all turrets, stained glass, and sleeping porches. Market Street is lined with parks and bed-and-breakfasts and small local businesses from another era—a shoe repair shop, a butcher, a vacuum cleaner repairman, a chocolatier, an independent bookstore, a single-screen art deco movie theater where they put real melted butter on the popcorn. The town square boasts a Christmas tree in the winter, scarecrows in the autumn, and alfresco concerts and community theater in the summer. Every street is lit by old-fashioned globe lampposts, the proud town's icon. It is a place, as residents often insist, that time forgot.

In short, Lewisburg looks almost nothing like its neighbors in coal-Amish-fracking country, which time has remembered all too well. Obviously, this has everything to do with the university—one year spent at this college, located about three hours from New York City, costs $62,368. Generally speaking, the campus can be fairly characterized by the setting of Frederick Busch's wonderful short story "Ralph the Duck," a "northeastern camp for the overindulged." Money from the school, its faculty, its students, and their parents props up the local economy. Simple enough.

But the true relationship between the town and the university did not occur to me until one of my students, from Youngstown, Ohio, described how much her mother loved coming to Lewisburg, how each time she visited her mother would say, "Look at that adorable chocolate shop, look at those gleaming lampposts. I just love Lewisburg!" My student, sharper than we give Millennials credit for, told her mother, "Of course you love it. It's for you."

What she meant, I think, is that Lewisburg, Pennsylvania, is a town in coal country the way Disney's Celebration, Florida, is a suburb of Orlando. Lewisburg, and countless other so-called college towns like it, is Bedford Falls in loco parentis. It's a country-mouse theme park for young people wanting the illusion of distance, wanting the sense of being away on a journey and all the self-discovery that promises. It's for them, and it's for their parents, who will tolerate this distance and this freaky looming self-discovery, so long as it comes with the quaintness of the country, the control of a company town, and all the safety that $62,368 can buy.

All to say that for the past four years, I lived in a landscape of pandering.

STEPHEN ELLIOTT COMES TO TOWN

Let's segue into one of my favorite subgenres of literary gossip: writers behaving badly. What writers' conference would be complete without it?

It is the fall of 2009 and I'm in the final year of my three-year MFA program. The program is hosting a reading by the writer and P. T. Barnum figure Stephen Elliott, who, in addition to being a novelist and memoirist, is editor in chief of the online literary magazine *The Rumpus*. The university does not provide him accommodations, so our program director passes along his request that someone put him up for the night. I volunteer. Kyle Minor, another writer and an alumnus of the program, fetches Stephen from the airport. Stephen, Kyle, and I have lunch, where we talk about Denis Johnson, our works in progress, and our agents. I'd landed a hotshot agent six months earlier, am still freaked out by how, when I Google her, names like Junot Díaz and Jonathan Safran Foer appear. I have a story coming out in *Granta*, a collection in the homestretch, and I'm eager to talk about all this with writers who've been there. After lunch, Stephen takes a nap at my house while I go teach. I come back and take him to his reading, then to a bar with the other grad students, then to get donuts on our way home. Stephen flirts with me all night and back at my apartment he attempts, with what I'll graciously term considerable persistence, to convince me to let him sleep in my bed rather than on the air mattress I've inflated for him in the other room. I decline several times before he relents, doing so only after I tell him I'm seeing someone. He sleeps on the air mattress, and in the morning we have breakfast and then I drive him to the airport.

Later that day, a friend forwards me the *Daily Rumpus* e-newsletter, which Stephen wrote in the airport and sent to his subscribers, allegedly a few thousand readers, writers, and fans of his site. Its subject line is "Overheard in Columbus." Of the visit Stephen wrote:

> It was really a great time, though I can't put my finger on exactly why. It might have been the ride from the airport with Kyle Miner [sic] who's living the post MFA life with a book of stories out, a couple of kids, teaching classes up in Toledo, finishing what sounds like a fantastic novel, and contemplating law school. Or it might have been Claire, the student I stayed with. Or the walk for donuts at 10:30 on a Wednesday night, which felt late in that town, especially on the strip.
>
> I tried to get in Claire's bed. It was a big, comfortable bed. She said no, how would she explain it to the boy she was getting to know. I said there was nothing to explain to the boy, nothing's going to happen. It's like sleeping with your gay friend. But she wasn't so sure. She had been drinking and I don't drink. I slept on the air mattress in the other room.

Now, I realize I'm not a special snowflake, that every woman who writes has a handbag full of stories like this. There is probably an entire teeming sub-subgenre titled "Stephen Elliott Comes to Town." I offer this here partly because it was my very first personal run-in with overtly misogynistic behavior from a male writer, and so perhaps my most instructive. I learned a lot from that *Daily Rumpus* e-mail (which is a sentence that has never before been uttered). I want to stress that I'm not presenting Stephen Elliott as a rogue figure, but as utterly emblematic. I want to show you how, via his compulsive stream-of-consciousness monologue e-mailed to a few thousand readers, I was given a glass-bottom-boat tour of a certain type of male writer's mind.

I scrolled up and down, reading and rereading, and through that glass-bottom boat saw a world where Kyle Minor was Kyle Minor, a writer "with a book of stories out, a couple of kids, teaching classes up in Toledo, finishing what sounds like a fantastic novel, and contemplating law school." Whereas I was Claire, no last name, "the student," owner of a big, comfortable bed. Until my friend forwarded that e-mail to me, I'd been under the impression that since I wrote, I was a writer, period. If I wrote bad I was a bad writer, if I wrote good I was a good writer. Simple as that. I was, I knew, every bit as ambitious as Kyle Minor and Stephen Elliott. I loved books just as much as Kyle and Stephen did, read as much as they did, and worked just as hard to get the right words in the right order. But now I was confronted with Google Groups listserv proof that, to Stephen, Kyle was a writer and I was a drunk girl.

But fuck 'em, right? What did Tina Fey say about sexists in the workplace: over, under, and through. The problem with responding to sexism with *Sesame Street* is that if you read that e-mail as I read that e-mail, as I was being trained to read—that is, carefully and curiously, over and over—you'll see something more than the story Stephen told himself about me as a writer or, in this case, not a writer. I saw, in the form of paragraphs and sentences, my area of expertise, how it took only a few lines to go from professional dismissal to sexual entitlement to being treated as property to gaslighting.

———

Now, I don't know about you, but I tend to think professional sexism via artistic infantilization is a bummer, frustrating, disappointing, but distinct and apart from those violent expressions of misogyny widely agreed upon as horrific: domestic violence, sex slavery, rape. Stephen Elliott did not rape me, did not attempt to rape me. I am not anywhere close to implying that he did. I am saying a sexist negation, a refusal to acknowledge a female writer as a writer, as a peer, as a person, is of a piece with sexual entitlement. No, more than of a piece, it is practically a prerequisite. Humans are wide, open vessels, capable of almost anything—if you read you know this—but you cannot beat the mother of your children, or rape your childhood friend while she's unconscious, or walk up to a sorority outside Santa Barbara and start shooting without first convincing yourself and allowing our culture to convince you that those women are less than human.

I know that's an intense analogy. I intend it to be.

Here, Stephen Elliot handily provides a clear illustration of an idea most recently proposed by Rebecca Solnit in her important essay collection *Men Explain Things to Me*: these things exist on a continuum. Sexist dismissal of women as artists and the assumption of sexual entitlement over them that is necessary to make something like rape okay in our culture—and it very much is okay in our culture—are not separated by vast chasms of principles. Look here, they are two paragraphs of the same story, separated by only a keystroke.

When I said, *I'm a writer*, Stephen heard, *I'm a girl*. And, because I was a girl, when I said, *No, you cannot sleep in my bed*, he heard someone who "wasn't so sure." I continued, in his mind, to be unsure, and only the man I was dating—in Stephen's infantilizing phrase "the boy she was getting to know"—could be sure for me. The story Stephen told himself went: "She had been drinking and I don't drink." Because I was not a writer, not a person, I was easily made into a drunk girl unable to tell her own story.

That is, until now.

WATCHING BOYS DO STUFF

~~But you know all this, even~~ if you haven't heard it recently, even if you haven't heard it out loud. I am not interested in why Stephen did what he did. I was a women's studies minor, I get it. What I'm curious about is what I did with what he did.

For years, I thought this encounter was formative. I described it as I have above, a kind of revelation. These days I think, if only. After all, it's so much gentler to be presented with an ugliness of which you'd been previously completely and honestly oblivious than one you were trying to pretend didn't exist. The truth is, the fact that our culture considers male writers more serious than me was not a revelation. I'd been getting the messages of Stephen's e-mail long before my friend forwarded it to me— all women do. We live in a culture that hates us. We get that. Misogyny is the water we swim in.

To wit:

As a young woman I had one and only one intense and ceaseless pastime, though that's not the right word, though neither is *hobby* or *passion*. I have practiced this activity with religious devotion and for longer than I can remember. I have been trying to give it up recently, since moving away from Bedford Falls, since around the time my daughter was born. But nearly all of my life has been arranged around this activity. I've filled my days doing this, spent all my free time and a great amount of time that was not free doing it. That hobby, that interest, that passion was this: watching boys do stuff.

I've watched boys play the drums, guitar, sing, watched them play football, baseball, soccer, pool, Dungeons and Dragons, and Magic: The Gathering. I've watched them golf. Just the other day I watched them play a kind of sweaty, book-nerd version of basketball. I've watched them work on their trucks and work on their master's theses. I've watched boys build things: halfpipes, bookshelves, screenplays, careers. I've watched boys skateboard, snowboard, act, bike, box, paint, fight, and drink. I could probably write my own series of six virtuosic autobiographical novels based solely on the years I spent watching boys play Resident Evil and Tony Hawk's ProSkater. I watched boys in my leisure time, I watched boys in my love life, and I watched boys in my education. I watched Melville, I watched Salinger, watched Ford, Flaubert, Díaz, Dickens, watched even when I didn't particularly like what I saw—especially then, because it proved there was something wrong with me, something I wanted to fix. So I watched Nabokov, watched Thomas Hardy, watched Raymond Carver. I read women (some, but not enough) but I didn't watch them. I didn't give them megaphones in my mind. The writers with megaphones in my mind were not Mary Austin, or Louise Erdrich, or Joan Didion, or Joy Williams, or Toni Morrison, though all have been as important to me as any of the male writers I mentioned, or more. Still, I watched the boys, watched to learn. I wanted to write something Cormac McCarthy would like, something Thomas Pynchon would come out of hiding to endorse, something David Foster Wallace would blurb from beyond the grave.

I have been reenacting in my artmaking the undying pastime of my girlhood: watching boys, emulating them, trying to catch the attention of the ones who have no idea I exist.

ON INVISIBILITY

Speaking of things that are invisible: picture me in New Mexico, where I've come to teach for a week. Marijuana's just been legalized in Colorado and a friend from there gifts me a joint. I approach another writer, this one down from Alaska, who is standing alone beside the glowing hotel pool. I make small talk:

I say, So, how long have you lived in Alaska?

She says, Well, I'm an Eskimo, so . . .

I ask if she wants to share the joint. She looks circumspect, which is puzzling to me. I've heard her mention Mary Jane before and I'm pretty sure we're of the same mind about it.

Right here? she asks.

Yeah, I say, looking around for what's bothering her. It's dark, only the pool lights glowing, and we're the only ones outside. The stars overhead are staggering.

She says, But weed's not legal here.

I note that it's legal in Colorado, and that Colorado touches New Mexico.

What if someone calls the cops?

They won't call the cops! Are you crazy? We're guests of the hotel.

What if we get arrested?

At this point we're both super puzzled, not understanding each other at all. I'm thinking, *Lighten up.* People smoke weed in city parks, at music festivals, on hiking trails. The last time I smoked was at a wedding in Maine.

I say, Come on, they're not going to arrest us for one tiny joint. We're professors for fuck's sake!

Okay, she says finally, lighting up. But if they call the cops you better hide me under your invisible cloak of white privilege.

At moments like this, when my whiteness materializes in front of me and I can see it, I am so embarrassed of it and also so angry at myself for not being always as aware of it as I am there in that awkward, painful, absurd, essential moment. I want to unsee it, make it invisible again, and usually I do, because it feels better. I have that privilege.

Others don't.

I have watched writers go brown right before my eyes. My husband, half Cuban but made much more so on a job interview, is told by a white male scholar specializing in African American literature that his inventing and imagining aspects of Cuba in his novel was "problematic" and that according to this white professor, he got things about Cuba "wrong."

My best friend, a Basque American, publishes a book set in the Spanish Basque country and *Publishers Weekly* lauds it "just exotic enough." My iBooks library categorizes Joshua Cohen as "Literary" and Toni Morrison as "African American." Think about that for a second: it's either/or. Meaning, according to iBooks, you cannot be African American and Literary. And it was only two years ago that, over on Wikipedia, American authors whom editors suspected of being in possession of a pussy were removed from the category "American

novelists" and relocated to "American women novelists." These categories—writer or student, writer or girl, woman novelist, Eskimo, Latino, Literary or African American—matter. As Sontag told Mailer, "Words matter, Norman." They affect the way we live—whether we can smoke a joint beside a hotel pool in New Mexico without fear of being arrested; whether someone will hear no when we say it— and they affect the way we write.

On Pandering: How to Write Like a Man

THE "LITTLE WHITE MAN DEEP INSIDE OF ALL OF US"

It was Toni Morrison who pointed out that Tolstoy was not writing for her, who said she was writing toward black women. It makes you wonder, Who am I writing for? Who am I writing toward?

Myself, I have been writing to impress old white men. Countless decisions I've made about what to write and how to write it have been in acquiescence to the opinions of the white male literati. Not only acquiescence but a beseeching, approval seeking, people pleasing.

But whom do I mean when I say white male literati? Sounds like a conspiracy theory, one of my favorite genres of American storytelling. I mean the people and voices real and imagined in the positions of power (or at least influence) in writing and publishing, but mostly I mean the man in my mind. James Baldwin wrote of the "little white man deep inside of all of us" but mine is tall. He's a white-haired chain smoker from New Mexico, the short story writer called "Cheever's true heir." It is Lee K. Abbot I hear in my mind. This has little to do with Lee himself, a mentor I admire, a writer I adore, whose encouragement has helped land me before you, whose support I treasure. I am not talking about Lee K. Abbot who once turned to me in a workshop when I was a first-year MFA with a dead mom, a desert rat without a proper winter coat and in bad need of a thumbs-up, and asked me, because I'd turned in a story he liked, "Claire, who are the great Nevada writers?" And when I sputtered something about Robert Laxalt and Mark Twain he stopped me and said, "No. You are." I am speaking not of Lee Kitteridge Abbott the man but what he represents. Or rather I am talking about them both, about the representation and the man himself, for didn't I know he would like that story, about an old prospector who finds a nubile young girl left for dead in the desert?

Glad you like it, Lee. It's *for you.*

I am talking about this reading I gave in Montana in the fall when it was so beautiful I almost never went home, where a late-middle-aged white cowboy—let's call him the Old Sumbitch—waited in my signing line, among the brown-haired girls with glasses, and when he got to me said, "I usually don't read stuff like this but Tom McGuane said you were all right." I am talking about being at once grateful for the friendship and encouragement offered me by Tom McGuane but also angry and exhausted by the fact that I need it. The Old Sumbitch would not have read me if Tom

hadn't said I was all right. I am hiding under Tom's invisible cloak of male privilege. At issue is not Tom McGuane or Lee K. Abbott or Jeffrey Eugenides or Christopher Coake or Chang-Rae Lee, all of whom have offered me guidance and friendship for which I'm tremendously grateful. But why should their voices be louder in my head than that of Karen Russell, a beyond generous certified genius and, with any luck, my future sister-wife? Why should they be louder than Antonya Nelson, who wrote the most illuminating review of *Battleborn* I've ever read? Why should they be louder than Erin McGraw, who read *Battleborn* in its every incarnation, who taught me how to get a job and keep it, who's written me about a hundred letters of recommendation and done every-thing short of hand me this microphone today?

The stunning truth is that I am asking, deep down, as I write, What would Philip Roth think of this? What would Jonathan Franzen think of this? When the answer is probably: nothing. More staggering is the question of why I am trying to prove myself to writers whose work, in many cases, I don't particu-larly admire? I recently finished Roth's *Indignation* with nothing more lasting than a sincere curiosity as to whether Roth is aware that these days even nice girls give blow jobs.

I am trying to understand a phenomenon that hap-pens in my head, and maybe in yours too, whereby the white supremacist patriarchy determines what I write.

I wrote *Battleborn* for white men, toward them. If you hold the book to a certain light, you'll see it as an exercise in self-hazing, a product of working-class madness, the female strain. So, natural then that *Battleborn* was well-received by the white male lit establishment: it was written *for them*. The whole book's a pander. *Look*, I said with my stories: *I can write old men, I can write sex, I can write abortion. I can write hard, unflinching, unsentimental. I can write an old man getting a boner!*

Here are the lampposts, here is the single-screen movie theater. It's all an architecture of pandering. It's *for them*.

She can write like a man, they said, by which they meant, *She can write*.

"A lot of young women (not to mention this WM) loved that book. Should I tell them to disregard their reading experience?"

If you like my book I'm grateful. But I remind you that people at the periphery will travel to accept and even love things not made for or toward them: we have been trained to do so our entire lives. I'm not trying to talk anyone out of their readerly response, only to confess to what went on in my mind when I made the book, to assemble an honest inventory of people I have not been writing toward (though I thought I was): women, young women,

people of color, the rural poor, the American West, my dead mother.

This is frightening on its face, but manyfold scarier because I thought I was doing this for myself. I was under the impression that artmaking was apart from all the rottenness of our culture, when in fact it's not apart from it. It is made of it.

THE PRECEDING

is either an aesthetic/artistic/personal epiphany or my ritualistic prepublication freak-out; perhaps a little of column A, a little of column B. I'll tell you this: I have not written anything of consequence since my daughter was born. It's easy to say, *You had a baby, you're busy, it gets better*, and I'm really glad to hear from those of you who have said as much. But I wonder if part of the reason I have not been writing is because I have not been seeing. My gaze is no longer an artist's gaze.

Why would that be? I think it has something to do with the fact that I don't wander in the desert much anymore. I spend my days with a baby and that, patriarchy says, is not the stuff of art. Once again I am a girl and not a writer. No one said this. No one has to. I am saying it to myself. That's the terrible efficiency of gaslighting.

After watching *Girls* for the first time my friend Annie McGreevy says, "That was my experience, too, but I didn't know it was okay to make art about it." And maybe it's still not okay. After doing an event with

Miranda July, Lena Dunham tweets this quote from Lorrie Moore, writing on July in the *New York Review of Books*, "When one googles 'Wes Anderson' and 'fey' one gets a lot of pictures of him and Tina Fey."

**ABOUT A YEAR AGO
I HAD A BABY,**

and while my life was suddenly more intense, more frightening, more beautiful, more difficult, and more profound than it had ever been, I found myself with nothing to write about.

"Nothing's happening to me," I bemoan to Annie. "I need to go shoot an elephant."

Annie replies, in her late-night Lebowskian cadence, "Dude, you're a mother. You've had a child. You're struggling to make your marriage work, man. You are trying, against your nature and circumstance, to be decent. That's your elephant!" Yet when I write some version of this down it seems quaint or worse. I thought I had enough material for a novel but when it came out it was a short story, and one that felt unserious. I tried a story in the form of a post-partum-depression questionnaire and it felt quaint. Domestic. For women. Motherhood has softened me. I have a tighter valve on what I'll read and what I'll watch. I don't want to write like a man anymore. I don't want to be praised for being "unflinching." I want to flinch. I want to be wide open.

I am trying to write something urgent, trying to be vulnerable and honest, trying to listen, trying to identify and articulate my innermost feelings, trying to make you feel them too, trying a kind of telepathy, all of which is really fucking hard in the first place and, in a culture wherein women are subject to infantilization and gaslighting, in a culture that says your "telepathic heart" (that's Moore on July) is dumb and delicate and boring and frippery and for girls, I sometimes wonder if it's even possible.

I have built a working miniature replica of the patriarchy in my mind. I would like very much to bust it up or burn it down. But I am afraid I don't know how. Though I do have some ideas.

SOME IDEAS:

Let's punch up.

Let us not make people at the margins into scouts or spies for the mainstream. Let us stop asking people to speak for the entire cacophonic segment of humanity that shares their pigmentation, genitalia, or turn-ons.

Let us spend more time in those uncomfortable moments when our privilege is showing. Let us reflect there, let us linger, rather than recoil into the status quo.

Let us continue to count, and talk, and think about the numbers.

Let us name those things that are nameless, as Solnit describes, the way "mansplaining" or "rape culture" or "sexual harassment" were nameless before feminists named them. Let those names sing.

Let us hear the stories we are telling ourselves about ourselves. Let us remember that we become the stories we tell. An illustration: I was talking with the writer Elissa Schappell about how much we are both anticipating Carrie Brownstein's new book. I asked Elissa what she made of this new trend of memoirs by badass women: Carrie Brownstein, Kim Gordon, Sally Mann, Amy Poehler. Was this trend the result of Patti Smith winning the National Book Award five years ago? Was the trend indicative of a new wave of feminism? Elissa interrupted me. "You keep using that word," she said. "Trend. It's not a trend. We are here now. We're not going anywhere. *We are here now.*"

Let us embrace a do-it-yourself canon, wherein we each make our own canon filled with what we love to read, what speaks to us and challenges us and opens us up, wherein we can each determine our artistic lineages for ourselves, with curiosity and vigor, rather than trying to shoehorn ourselves into a canon ready-made and gifted us by some white fucks at Oxford.

(I will start us off by spending no more of my living breath apologizing for the fact that no, actually, even though I write about the American West, Cormac McCarthy is not a major influence of mine.)

Let us use our words and our gazes to make the invisible visible. Let us tell the truth.

Let us, each of us, write things that are uncategorizable, rather than something that panders to and condones and codifies those categories.

Let us burn this motherfucking system to the ground and build something better.

HARVEY WEINSTEIN IS MY MONSTER TOO

SALMA
HAYEK

Originally published in the *New York Times*
2017

Harvey Weinstein was a passionate cinephile, a risk taker, a patron of talent in film, a loving father, and a monster.

For years, he was my monster.

This fall, I was approached by reporters, through different sources, including my dear friend Ashley Judd, to speak about an episode in my life that, although painful, I thought I had made peace with.

I had brainwashed myself into thinking that it was over and that I had survived; I hid from the responsibility to speak out with the excuse that enough people were already involved in shining a light on my monster. I didn't consider my voice important, nor did I think it would make a difference.

In reality, I was trying to save myself the challenge of explaining several things to my loved ones: Why, when I had casually mentioned that I had been bullied like many others by Harvey, I had excluded a couple of details. And why, for so many years, we have been cordial to a man who hurt me so deeply. I had been proud of my capacity for forgiveness, but the mere fact that I was ashamed to describe the details of what I had forgiven made me wonder if that chapter of my life had really been resolved.

When so many women came forward to describe what Harvey had done to them, I had to confront my cowardice and humbly accept that my story, as important as it was to me, was nothing but a drop in an ocean of sorrow and confusion. I felt that by now nobody would care about my pain—maybe this was an effect of the many times I was told, especially by Harvey, that I was nobody.

We are finally becoming conscious of a vice that has been socially accepted and has insulted and humiliated millions of girls like me, for in every woman there is a girl. I am inspired by those who had the courage to speak out, especially in a society that elected a president who has been accused of sexual harassment and assault by more than a dozen women and whom we have all heard make a statement about how a man in power can do anything he wants to women.

Well, not anymore.

In the fourteen years that I stumbled from schoolgirl to Mexican soap star to an extra in a few American films to catching a couple of lucky breaks in *Desperado* and *Fools Rush In*, Harvey Weinstein had become the wizard of a new wave of cinema that took original content into the mainstream. At the same time, it was unimaginable for a Mexican actress to aspire to a place in Hollywood. And even though I had proven them wrong, I was still a nobody.

One of the forces that gave me the determination to pursue my career was the story of Frida Kahlo, who in the golden age of the Mexican muralists would do small intimate paintings that everybody looked down on. She had the courage to express herself while disregarding skepticism. My greatest ambition was to tell her story. It became my mission to portray the life of this extraordinary artist and to show my native Mexico in a way that combated stereotypes.

The Weinstein empire, which was then Miramax, had become synonymous with quality, sophistication, and risk taking—a haven for artists who were complex and defiant. It was everything that Frida was to me and everything I aspired to be.

I had started a journey to produce the film with a different company, but I fought to get it back to take it to Harvey.

I knew him a little bit through my relationship with the director Robert Rodriguez and the producer Elizabeth Avellan, who was then his wife, with whom I had done several films and who had taken me under their wing. All I knew of Harvey at the time was that he had a remarkable intellect, he was a loyal friend and a family man.

Knowing what I know now, I wonder if it wasn't my friendship with them—and Quentin Tarantino and George Clooney—that saved me from being raped.

The deal we made initially was that Harvey would pay for the rights of work I had already developed. As an actress, I would be paid the minimum Screen Actors Guild scale plus 10 percent. As a producer, I would receive a credit that would not yet be defined, but no payment, which was not that rare for a female producer in the '90s. He also demanded a signed deal for me to do several other films with Miramax, which I thought would cement my status as a leading lady.

I did not care about the money; I was so excited to work with him and that company. In my naïveté, I thought my dream had come true. He had validated the last fourteen years of my life. He had taken a chance on me—a nobody. He had said yes.

Little did I know it would become my turn to say no.

No to opening the door to him at all hours of the night, hotel after hotel, location after location, where he would show up unexpectedly, including one location where I was doing a movie he wasn't even involved with.

No to me taking a shower with him.

No to letting him watch me take a shower.

No to letting him give me a massage.

No to letting a naked friend of his give me a massage.

No to letting him give me oral sex.

No to my getting naked with another woman.

No, no, no, no, no . . .

And with every refusal came Harvey's Machiavellian rage.

I don't think he hated anything more than the word "no." The absurdity of his demands went from getting a furious call in the middle of the night asking me to fire my agent for a fight he was having with him about a different movie with a different client to physically dragging me out of the opening gala of the Venice Film Festival, which was in honor of *Frida*, so I could hang out at his private party with

him and some women I thought were models but I was told later were high-priced prostitutes.

The range of his persuasion tactics went from sweet-talking me to that one time when, in an attack of fury, he said the terrifying words, "I will kill you, don't think I can't."

When he was finally convinced that I was not going to earn the movie the way he had expected, he told me he had offered my role and my script with my years of research to another actress.

In his eyes, I was not an artist. I wasn't even a person. I was a thing: not a nobody, but a body.

At that point, I had to resort to using lawyers, not by pursuing a sexual harassment case, but by claiming "bad faith," as I had worked so hard on a movie that he was not intending to make or sell back to me. I tried to get it out of his company.

He claimed that my name as an actress was not big enough and that I was incompetent as a producer, but to clear himself legally, as I understood it, he gave me a list of impossible tasks with a tight deadline:

1. Get a rewrite of the script, with no additional payment.

2. Raise $10 million to finance the film.

3. Attach an A-list director.

4. Cast four of the smaller roles with prominent actors.

Much to everyone's amazement, not least my own, I delivered, thanks to a phalanx of angels who came to my rescue, including Edward Norton, who beautifully rewrote the script several times and appallingly never got credit, and my friend Margaret Perenchio, a first-time producer, who put up the money. The brilliant Julie Taymor agreed to direct, and from then on she became my rock. For the other roles, I recruited my friends Antonio Banderas, Edward Norton, and my dear Ashley Judd. To this day, I don't know how I convinced Geoffrey Rush, whom I barely knew at the time.

Now Harvey Weinstein was not only rejected but also about to do a movie he did not want to do.

Ironically, once we started filming, the sexual harassment stopped but the rage escalated. We paid the price for standing up to him nearly every day of shooting. Once, in an interview he said Julie and I were the biggest ball busters he had ever encountered, which we took as a compliment.

Halfway through shooting, Harvey turned up on set and complained about Frida's "unibrow." He insisted that I eliminate the limp and berated my performance. Then he asked everyone in the room to step out except for me. He told me that the only thing I had going for me was my sex appeal and that there was none of that in this movie. So he told me

he was going to shut down the film because no one would want to see me in that role.

It was soul crushing because, I confess, lost in the fog of a sort of Stockholm syndrome, I wanted him to see me as an artist: not only as a capable actress but also as somebody who could identify a compelling story and had the vision to tell it in an original way.

I was hoping he would acknowledge me as a producer, who on top of delivering his list of demands shepherded the script and obtained the permits to use the paintings. I had negotiated with the Mexican government, and with whomever I had to, to get locations that had never been given to anyone in the past—including Frida Kahlo's houses and the murals of Kahlo's husband, Diego Rivera, among others.

But all of this seemed to have no value. The only thing he noticed was that I was not sexy in the movie. He made me doubt if I was any good as an actress, but he never succeeded in making me think that the film was not worth making.

He offered me one option to continue. He would let me finish the film if I agreed to do a sex scene with another woman. And he demanded full-frontal nudity.

He had been constantly asking for more skin, for more sex. Once before, Julie Taymor got him to settle for a tango ending in a kiss instead of the lovemaking scene he wanted us to shoot between the character Tina Modotti, played by Ashley Judd, and Frida.

But this time, it was clear to me he would never let me finish this movie without him having his fantasy one way or another. There was no room for negotiation.

I had to say yes. By now so many years of my life had gone into this film. We were about five weeks into shooting, and I had convinced so many talented people to participate. How could I let their magnificent work go to waste?

I had asked for so many favors, I felt an immense pressure to deliver and a deep sense of gratitude for all those who did believe in me and followed me into this madness. So I agreed to do the senseless scene.

I arrived on the set the day we were to shoot the scene that I believed would save the movie. And for the first and last time in my career, I had a nervous breakdown: My body began to shake uncontrollably, my breath was short and I began to cry and cry, unable to stop, as if I were throwing up tears.

Since those around me had no knowledge of my history of Harvey, they were very surprised by my struggle that morning. It was not because I would be naked with another woman. It was because I would be naked with her for Harvey Weinstein. But I could not tell them then.

My mind understood that I had to do it, but my body wouldn't stop crying and convulsing. At that point, I started throwing up while a set frozen still waited to shoot. I had to take a tranquilizer, which eventually stopped the crying but made the vomiting worse. As you can imagine, this was not sexy, but it was the only way I could get through the scene.

By the time the filming of the movie was over, I was so emotionally distraught that I had to distance myself during the postproduction.

When Harvey saw the cut film, he said it was not good enough for a theatrical release and that he would send it straight to video.

This time Julie had to fight him without me and got him to agree to release the film in one movie theater in New York if we tested it to an audience and we scored at least an 80.

Less than 10 percent of films achieve that score on a first screening.

I didn't go to the test. I anxiously awaited to receive the news. The film scored 85.

And again, I heard Harvey raged. In the lobby of a theater after the screening, he screamed at Julie. He balled up one of the scorecards and threw it at her. It bounced off her nose. Her partner, the film's composer Elliot Goldenthal, stepped in, and Harvey physically threatened him.

Once he calmed down, I found the strength to call Harvey to ask him also to open the movie in a theater in Los Angeles, which made a total of two theaters. And without much ado, he gave me that. I have to say sometimes he was kind, fun, and witty—and that was part of the problem: You just never knew which Harvey you were going to get.

Months later, in October 2002, this film, about my hero and inspiration—this Mexican artist who never truly got acknowledged in her time with her limp and her unibrow—this film that Harvey never wanted to do, gave him a box office success that no one could have predicted, and despite his lack of support, added six Academy Award nominations to his collection, including best actress.

Even though *Frida* eventually won him two Oscars, I still didn't see any joy. He never offered me a starring role in a movie again. The films that I was obliged to do under my original deal with Miramax were all minor supporting roles.

Years later, when I ran into him at an event, he pulled me aside and told me he had stopped smoking and he had had a heart attack. He said he'd fallen in love and married Georgina Chapman, and that he was a changed man. Finally, he said to me: "You did well with *Frida*; we did a beautiful movie."

I believed him. Harvey would never know how much those words meant to me. He also would never know how much he hurt me. I never showed Harvey how terrified I was of him. When I saw him socially, I'd smile and try to remember the good things about him, telling myself that I went to war and I won.

BUT WHY DO SO MANY OF US, AS FEMALE ARTISTS, HAVE TO GO TO WAR TO TELL OUR STORIES WHEN WE HAVE SO MUCH TO OFFER? WHY DO WE HAVE TO FIGHT TOOTH AND NAIL TO MAINTAIN OUR DIGNITY?

I think it is because we, as women, have been devalued artistically to an indecent state, to the point where the film industry stopped making an effort to find out what female audiences wanted to see and what stories we wanted to tell.

According to a recent study, between 2007 and 2016, only 4 percent of directors were female and 80 percent of those got the chance to make only one film. In 2016, another study found, only 27 percent of words spoken in the biggest movies were spoken by women. And people wonder why you didn't hear our voices sooner. I think the statistics are self-explanatory—our voices are not welcome.

Until there is equality in our industry, with men and women having the same value in every aspect of it, our community will continue to be a fertile ground for predators.

I am grateful for everyone who is listening to our experiences. I hope that adding my voice to the chorus of those who are finally speaking out will shed light on why it is so difficult, and why so many of us have waited so long. Men sexually harassed because they could. Women are talking today because, in this new era, we finally can.

WHEN A WOMAN DELETES A MAN'S COMMENT ONLINE

IJEOMA OLUO

Originally published in *The Establishment*

2017

I spent a fair amount of time this weekend in mixed states of amusement, frustration, anger, and confusion as a grown man threw a fit in my online spaces. It had started on Facebook, with multiple comments left on my page, the same screenshots posted over and over. He then looked up my Twitter handle and railed against me there, trying to drag in a celebrity, his followers, and one of my employers. According to him, I was a fatwa-issuing Nazi (I'm not making this word choice up) of no journalistic integrity who was censoring the public. And the world needed to know.

Why had a man spent two days on a mission to tell the entire world that I was a journalism-destroying fascist? Because I deleted his comment on my personal Facebook page.

If this shocks you, you are likely not a semi-prominent woman on the internet, because this happens, to greater or lesser severity, about once a week.

I used to love debate. I believed in testing ideas and theories, and in the power of discourse. And I thought that debate, the back and forth of ideas, was instrumental to that. This love carried me through my Political Science degree. But I've found that there are two types of debate. There's the debate of ideas represented in new vs. old schools of thought, nuanced critique, new study, and the progression of circumstance and ideas. And then there's the patriarchal sport of debate now given new life in the age of the internet.

The latter is harmful, distracting bullshit.

Many Western debates have had a strong element of privilege running throughout their history. To be able to imbibe at a salon, stand at a podium, or sit at a roundtable while sparring about the minutiae of important issues requires a surplus of time, a dispassionate objectivity, and a platform that many don't have the luxury of possessing around issues that can be life or death. We live in a world where the most hotly debated issues surround questions of women's rights, health care, racism and racial oppression, immigration, trans rights, reproductive rights, and religious discrimination. To be able to take issues fundamental to the health and safety of millions of people and turn them into sport where winners and losers are decided by talking points requires some level of insulation from the negative impacts of the outcome in order to enjoy participating.

It is no surprise to me that online debate has become the international sport of cis white men. Those who are least likely to be negatively impacted by the outcomes of discussions regarding the rights of marginalized people, who are driven by little more than ego and the risk of slight discomfort if society is made more equal, can gleefully jump from post to post, forum to forum, challenging the heartfelt pleas of those most at risk. "Well actuallys" are flung at those working for justice and equality like drive-bys of apathy. And those who are fighting for their lives are then forced to battle each challenger bearing advanced degrees in Google and entitlement in order to prevent the outright dismissal of their lived experience.

But as much as I hate this sort of debate, as much as I make it known I hate this sort of debate, many men are more than happy to completely ignore that and challenge me—even if I'm a complete stranger to them—to a debate about basically any social issue I dare post about. I do not get mad at the challenge, even if the predictability and mundanity of it all does try my patience. I do get mad at the continued insistence of it. I used to just say, "I don't debate this here," when random strangers would find their way to my Twitter feed or personal Facebook page. But that boundary put in place on my personal page is almost never respected, and others jump in to argue on my behalf, and my online space is inevitably full of debate over the basic humanity of marginalized people that does nothing but remind the marginalized people watching that they are not valued or safe.

These sorts of archaic anti-progress/anti-rights opinions already have a platform from which to shout

their side of the debate on issues we should not still be debating. In this white supremacist, transphobic, ableist, misogynistic, hyper-Christian society, the majority of our speech platforms were built off the loud espousals of hatred that still hurt so many today. There is no lack of space for a white man who thinks that Mike Brown was a thug who deserved to die. There is no lack of space for a Midwestern white woman who lives thousands of miles away from anywhere that could be a target of tourism, let alone terrorism, and yet wants to spread fear of Muslim extremism. That side of the debate is heard in deafeningly loud decibels, to the detriment of the rest of us.

And honestly, these are not subjects that should still be up for debate to begin with. Whether or not a woman deserves the same pay as a man should not be up for debate. Whether or not a cop should be able to shoot an unarmed black man in the street without consequence should not be up for debate. Whether or not trans people should be able to use the restrooms that match their gender identity in safety should not be up for debate. Whether or not sick people and many disabled people should be allowed to suffer and die without medical coverage in the richest country in the world should not be up for debate.

And if you, in 2017, think that these issues should be up for debate, it is because you've willfully ignored or dismissed the fact that these debates have been had for decades, if not centuries, and progress and general human decency have already shown the fatal flaws of your arguments. There is no debate right now that will convince a flat-earther that the earth is round. If you think the earth is flat in 2017, it is because you are determined to think the earth is flat in 2017, not because you haven't seen enough evidence. You are choosing to climb up on a cross of archaic bullshit, and I certainly have no intention of climbing up with you.

And so, I just do not have these useless, outdated, repetitive, one-on-one debates. When a comment about how "illegals need to get out" is left on my post voicing concern over families being torn apart over this country's xenophobia, I just delete it. I don't have time to debate something so backward, and I don't have time to explain. My page is my part of the debate at large, this is true. But I'm not debating those who show up wedded to bigotry, I'm debating those who are instead wedded to the inertia of inaction and ignorance.

It has been really freeing, as a woman, to not have to ask permission or apologize for deleting a comment that I do not want. At first I just said no to really blatant hate. But now I delete whatever minimizes, distracts, obfuscates, or annoys—if I feel like it. It's my house and you will get kicked out if you smash my windows, and you also don't get to track mud all over my floors or change my radio station. It has been really freeing, as a woman of color, to be both public and to be able to say, "no, not here in my space." It has been empowering to know that yes, I could exist in the world and retain my right to refuse to engage with those who would force their way into my proximity. I don't have to fight each individual foot soldier of oppression; I can keep my focus on the big picture and my fight on where it could be most effective.

And also, fuck those dudes.

But for my audacity, some men have tried their hardest to make sure that I pay. They have plastered my page with comment after comment, some hundreds a day. They have written about me in blogs and forums. They have written to my employers demanding that I be fired. They have sent me DMs and e-mails. Sometimes the harassment lasts a few hours, sometimes a few days, sometimes it will go on for a week, disappear, and then start up again a few months later—hate renewed over my continued, unbothered existence.

Sometimes I block these dudes—a lot of people tell me to. But I usually don't. My personal Facebook page (I don't have a professional one) and my Twitter account are mine. I mean, I know technically they belong to the social media companies themselves, but my followers and my friends—that is a community that I built. And I should be able to say "go away" when somebody insists, uninvited, on my time and attention. I shouldn't have to block them, and lower my voice, in order to not be harassed. Other people in similar situations choose for good reason to deal with this sort of harassment differently, and many see my decision to repeatedly erase these demands instead of just blocking and moving on as impractical stubbornness. But the walls that I build for my safety because my "no" was not enough may eventually be the box that I am stuck in where my "no" can no longer be heard.

Whether or not a black woman has a right to decline conversation from a white man is not something that should be up for debate. So I won't.

I'M NOT MAD. THAT'S JUST MY RBF.

JESSICA BENNETT

Originally published in the *New York Times*

2015

I didn't think much about it at the time: I was appearing in a short television segment and had quickly brushed my hair, then slapped on some concealer. I figured my glasses would cover the circles under my eyes.

Only later did I behold what I looked like—and it was terrifying. It wasn't that I was disheveled; it was the actual face that looked back at me in the frozen screen shot.

LIPS WERE A LITTLE PURSED. MY EYES AIMED FORWARD IN A DEADPAN STARE.

MY MOUTH CURLED SLIGHTLY DOWNWARD, MY BROWS WERE FURROWED, MY

I LOOKED SIMULTANEOUSLY BORED, MAD, AND SKEPTICAL.

I was basically saying to the newscaster: Die.

In that moment, I joined the ranks of a tribe of women who suffer from the scourge known as "resting bitch face" or, increasingly, just RBF.

If you're up on your internet memes, perhaps you've heard of its linguistic predecessor: "bitchy resting face," which emerged from a parody Public Service Announcement.

For those who need a review, RBF is a face that, when at ease, is perceived as angry, irritated, or simply . . . expressionless. It's the kind a person may make when thinking hard about something— or perhaps when they're not thinking at all.

"Is there a filter on Instagram that fixes Bitchy Resting Face? I'm asking for a friend," the actress Anna Kendrick tweeted, explaining recently to the late-show host James Corden that, "When some-body takes a photo and I'm in the background of it, I think, like, 'Oh my God, what's wrong with me?!'"

Other celebrities caught in serious repose: January Jones, whose "absolutely miserable" face made headlines this month at a ComicCon event; Tyra Banks, who has famously advised women to "smize" (smile with your eyes); Victoria Beckham; Kristen Stewart; and Anna Paquin, who has defined RBF as "you are kind of caught off guard and you're not smiling, and it means you look really angry all the

time, or like you want to kill people." (Also, in the less-chronicled male RBF category: Kanye.)

Now, it's safe to assume that humans have always made The Face. (Doesn't the Mona Lisa sort of have it?) And it does have its uses. It is great for staring down Greenpeace solicitors on the street, or glaring at men who catcall you on the subway.

At a crowded bar, the expression can serve as a kind of armor against unwanted pickup artists (better, as one young woman put it, "than a fake engagement ring").

And, as Tanya Tarr, a 36-year-old professional coach, described it: When engaged correctly, it can part a crowd of tourists on a busy street "like the Red Sea."

But it is also a problem (and, like the word "bitch" itself, one that seems to predominantly affect one-half of the gender equation).

RBF is now the topic of multiple "communities" on Facebook, dominated by women.

Plastic surgeons say they are fielding a growing number of requests from those who want to surgi-cally correct their "permafrowns" (again, primarily from women).

The country star Kacey Musgraves recently helped Buzzfeed create a list of 17 more accurate names for RBF (among them, Resting "this wouldn't bother you if I was a guy" face).

A New Jersey business journal, *NJBIZ*, even published a special report on the topic.

"Yes, we've asked ourselves the questions you might be asking yourself right now: What relevance does this have in the workplace? Is this topic sexist? Should we write this story at all?" the publication wrote, noting the seeming absurdity of a business publication tackling RBF.

"But, after calling around the state asking more than a dozen C-suite women in multiple industries to weigh in on the subject, we noticed one thing: No one ever scoffed or even asked, 'Why would this matter?'"

Yes, the tyranny of RBF is real.

For Nora Long, a 22-year-old intern at a Florida law firm, the struggle began in kindergarten, when her school's headmaster summoned her to his office "because he thought I looked unhappy." "From that day on until he left the school when I was in the seventh grade," Ms. Long said, "he would say 'Smile, Nora!' every time he saw me."

Morra Aarons-Mele, a small-business owner in Los Angeles, said she "Botoxed away" her "congenital frown line" so that people would stop asking, "Are you mad?" "Then people were warmer to me—I swear," she said.

Ms. Tarr, after being told by a mentor that her scowl was "setting her back" at work, began taking pictures of her face so she could try to look more cheerful. "I have since trained myself on what my face feels like," she said.

There is some science behind it. Dr. Anthony Youn, a cosmetic surgeon in Detroit, said that as we age, the corners of our mouths droop, causing us to look a little more grumpy—a natural response to gravity and genetics.

In mild cases, this has the capacity to make a person look less cheerful when their face is resting. But in "severe cases," said Dr. Youn, it can cause the face to look "mean, angry, and give people a false perception of what our mood is."

"The mouth tends to denote a lot of expression," said Dr. Scot Bradley Glasberg, the president of the American Society of Plastic Surgeons.

But RBF is not a problem merely of the old. It matters at all ages because, as science has long proved, humans make judgments based on facial cues. Studies have found that people are less likely to find friendly-looking faces guilty of crimes; people who look "happy" are generally deemed more trustworthy, too.

And yet: men do not experience RBF, at least not by name.

"When a man looks stern, or serious, or grumpy, it's simply the default," said Rachel Simmons, an author and leadership consultant at Smith College. "We don't inherently judge the moodiness of a male face. But as women, we are almost expected to put on a smile. So if we don't, it's deemed 'bitchy.'"

"I like RBF," Ms. Simmons said. "I think it's fun to say. I think it can be empowering to own a serious face. But the problem with it lies with the fact that there is no male equivalent."

For many years, studies have determined that women do tend to smile more than men, but not necessarily because they're happier (in fact, they suffer higher rates of depression). Nancy Henley, a cognitive psychologist, has theorized that women's frequent smiling stems from their lower social status (she called the smile a "badge of appeasement"). Still others have pointed out that women are more likely to work in the service sector, where smiling is an asset.

And yet there is also a kind of ingrained association between women and the friendly face. The

phrase "Stop telling women to smile" has become a rallying cry for the movement against street harassment. Studies have found that smiling babies are more likely to be labeled female, while men view serious women as less sexually attractive than those who look friendly (the opposite of how women view men).

"One of my biggest pet peeves is when people come up to me in a social setting, where I am having fun, and ask, 'Are you O.K.?'" said Talia Cuddeback, a junior at Barnard who suffers from RBF and wonders why she has to smile all the time just to show she isn't angry.

Meredith Fineman, a 28-year-old founder of a public relations firm in New York, said she has perfected the art of her business smile during meetings "so that I come across authoritative but also accessible," she said. "I'm also very careful of not smiling too much," she said, "as I am often afraid of seeming cloying or ditsy."

Dr. Sherelle Laifer-Narin, a radiology professor at Columbia University Medical Center, said that she has mastered the art of the emphatic smile, which she plasters across her face during staff meetings to avoid the question: "Is everything O.K.?"

"During the first lecture of the year for my residents, I make sure to let all the first years know that I don't bite, just bark, even if my facial expressions might indicate otherwise," she said.

And then there are those who rebuff the concept altogether.

"It doesn't make me feel like I'm unhappy, un-fun, or unpleasant," said Noelle Wyman, 19, a junior at Columbia. "My RBF makes me feel serious, pensive, and reserved, like someone who only engages those who deserve it."

Who has the energy to smile to strangers all day, anyway?

NOT HERE TO MAKE FRIENDS

ROXANE GAY

Originally published in *Buzzfeed*
2014

"MY MEMORY OF MEN IS NEVER LIT UP AND ILLUMINATED LIKE MY MEMORY OF WOMEN."
—MARGUERITE DURAS, *THE LOVER*

In my high school yearbook there is a note from a girl who wrote, "I like you even though you are very mean." I do not remember the girl who wrote this note. I do not remember being mean to her, or anyone for that matter. I do remember I was feral in high school, socially awkward, emotionally closed off, completely lost.

Or maybe I don't want to remember being mean because I've changed in the 20 years between now and then. Around my junior year, I went from being quiet and withdrawn to being mean where mean was saying exactly what I thought and making sarcastic comments, relentlessly. Sincerity was dead to me.

I had so few friends it didn't really matter how I behaved. I had nothing to lose. I had no idea what it meant to be likable though I was surrounded by generally likable people, or I suppose, I was surrounded by people who were very invested in projecting a likable façade, people who were willing to play by the rules. I had likable parents and brothers. I was the anomaly as a social outcast, but even from a young age, I understood that when a girl is unlikable, a girl is a problem. I also understood that I wasn't being intentionally mean. I was being honest (admittedly, without tact), and I was being human. It is either a blessing or a curse that those are rarely likable qualities in a woman.

Inevitably on every reality-television program, someone will boldly declare, "I'm not here to make friends." They do so to establish that they are on a given program to win the nebulous prize or the bachelor's heart or get the exposure they need to begin their unsteady rise to a modicum of fame. These people make this declaration by way of explaining their unlikability or the inevitably unkind edit they're going to receive from the show's producers. It isn't that they are terrible, you see. It's simply that they are not participating in the show to make friends. They are freeing themselves from the burden of likability or they are, perhaps, freeing us from the burden of guilt for the dislike and eventual contempt we might hold for them.

In the movie *Young Adult*, Charlize Theron stars as Mavis Gary. Nearly every review of the movie raises her character's unlikability, painting her with a bright scarlet U. Based on this character's critical reception, an unlikable woman embodies any number of unpleasing but entirely human characteristics. Mavis is beautiful, cold, calculating, self-absorbed, full of odd tics, insensitive, and largely dysfunctional in nearly every aspect of her life. These are, apparently, unacceptable traits for a woman, particularly given the sheer number working in concert. Some reviews go so far as to suggest that Mavis is mentally ill because there's nothing more reliable than armchair diagnosis by disapproving critics. In his review, Roger Ebert lauds *Young Adult* screenwriter Diablo Cody for making Mavis an alcoholic

because, "without such a context, Mavis would simply be insane." Ebert, and many others, require an explanation for Mavis's behavior. They require a diagnosis for her unlikability in order to tolerate her. The simplest explanation, of Mavis as human, will not suffice.

In many ways, likability is a very elaborate lie, a performance, a code of conduct dictating the proper way to be. Characters who don't follow this code become unlikable. Critics who fault a character's unlikability cannot necessarily be faulted. They are merely expressing a wider cultural malaise with all things unpleasant, all things that dare to breach the norm of social acceptability.

Why is likability even a question? Why are we so concerned with, whether in fact or fiction, someone is likable? Unlikable is a fluid designation that can be applied to any character who doesn't behave in a way the reader finds palatable. Lionel Shriver notes in an essay for *The Financial Times*, "This 'liking' business has two components: moral approval and affection." We need characters to be lovable while doing right.

Some might suggest this likability question is a by-product of an online culture where we reflexively like or favorite every status update and bit of personal trivia shared on social networks. Certainly, online there is a culture of relentless affirmation, but it would be shortsighted to believe that this desire to be liked, this desire to express what or whom we like, begins or ends with the internet. I have no doubt that Abraham Maslow has some ideas on this persistent desire, in so many of us, to be liked and, in turn, to belong, to have our deftness at following the proper code of conduct affirmed.

As a writer and a person who has struggled with likability—being likable, wanting to be liked, wanting to belong—I have spent a great deal of time thinking about likability in the stories I read and those I write. I am often drawn to unlikable characters, to those who behave in socially unacceptable ways and say whatever is on their mind and do what they want with varying levels of regard for the consequences. I want characters to do bad things and get away with their misdeeds. I want characters to think ugly thoughts and make ugly decisions. I want characters to make mistakes and put themselves first without apologizing for it.

I don't even mind unlikable characters whose behavior is psychopathic or sociopathic. This is not to say I condone, for example, murder, but *American Psycho*'s Patrick Bateman is a very interesting man. There is a psychiatric diagnosis for his unlikability, a deviant pathology, but he has his charms, particularly in his scathing self-awareness. Serial killers are people too, and sometimes they are funny. My

conscience, Bateman thinks in the novel, my pity, my hopes disappeared a long time ago (probably at Harvard) if they ever did exist.

I want characters to do the things I am afraid to do for fear of making myself more unlikable than I may already be. I want characters to be the most honest of all things—human.

———

That the question of likability even exists in literary conversations is odd. It implies we are engaging in a courtship. When characters are unlikable, they don't meet our mutable, varying standards. Certainly, we can find kinship in fiction, but literary merit shouldn't be dictated by whether or not we want to be friends or lovers with those about whom we read.

Frankly, I find "good," purportedly likable characters, rather unbearable. Take May Welland in Edith Wharton's *Age of Innocence*. May's likability is, to be fair, deliberate, a choice Wharton has made so Newland Archer's passion for Countess Olenska is ever more fraught and bittersweet. Still, May is the kind of woman who always does everything right, everything that is expected of her. She is a perfect society lady. She knows how to keep up appearances. Meanwhile, everyone looks down on May's unspoken rival and cousin, the Countess Olenska, a woman who dares to defy social conventions, who dares to not tolerate a terrible marriage, who dares to want real passion in her life even if that passion is found with an unsuitable man.

We're not supposed to like her, but Countess Olenska intrigues me because she is interesting. She stands apart from the blur of social conformity. We're supposed to like, or at least respect, May for being the proper and sweet innocent she carries herself as, but in Wharton's skilled hands, we eventually see that May Welland is as human, and therefore unlikable, as anyone else. This question of likability would be far more tolerable if all writers were as talented as Edith Wharton, but alas.

Far more pernicious than the characters whose likability serves a greater purpose within a narrative are the characters who are flatly likable. It's a bit silly, but I spend a great deal of time, even now, lamenting the perfection of one Elizabeth Wakefield, one of the two golden twins prominently featured in the popular *Sweet Valley High* young adult series. Elizabeth is the good girl who always makes the right choices, even when she has to sacrifice her own happiness. She gets good grades. She's a good daughter, sister, and girlfriend. It's boring. Elizabeth's likability is downright loathsome. I am Team Jessica. I prefer Nellie Olsen to Laura Ingalls Wilder.

This matter of likability is largely a futile one. Oftentimes, a likable character is simply designed as such to show that he or she is one who knows how to play-by the rules and cares to be seen as playing by the rules. The likable character, like the unlikable character, is generally used to make some greater narrative point.

————

Writers are often told a character isn't likable as literary criticism, as if a character's likability is directly proportional to the quality of a novel's writing. This is particularly true for women in fiction. In literature as in life, the rules are all too often different for girls. There are many instances where an unlikable man is billed as an anti-hero, earning a special term to explain those ways in which he deviates from the norm, the traditionally likable. Beginning with Holden Caulfield in *Catcher in the Rye*, the list is long. An unlikable man is inscrutably interesting, dark, or tormented but ultimately compelling even when he might behave in distasteful ways. This is the only explanation I can come up with for the popularity of, say, the novels of Philip Roth who is one hell of a writer, but also a writer who practically revels in the unlikability of his men, their neuroses and self-loathing (and, of course humanity) boldly on display from one page to the next.

When women are unlikable, it becomes a point of obsession in critical conversations by professional and amateur critics alike. Why are these women daring to flaunt convention? Why aren't they making themselves likable (and therefore acceptable) to polite society? In a *Publisher's Weekly* interview with Claire Messud about her recent novel *The Woman*

Upstairs, which features a rather "unlikable" protagonist named Nora who is bitter, bereft, and downright angry about what her life has become, the interviewer said, "I wouldn't want to be friends with Nora, would you? Her outlook is almost unbearably grim." And there we have it. A reader was here to make friends with the characters in a book and she didn't like what she found.

Messud, for her part, had a sharp response for her interviewer. "For heaven's sake, what kind of question is that? Would you want to be friends with Humbert Humbert? Would you want to be friends with Mickey Sabbath? Saleem Sinai? Hamlet? Krapp? Oedipus? Oscar Wao? Antigone? Raskolnikov? Any of the characters in *The Corrections*? Any of the characters in *Infinite Jest*? Any of the characters in anything Pynchon has ever written? Or Martin Amis? Or Orhan Pamuk? Or Alice Munro, for that matter? If you're reading to find friends, you're in deep trouble. We read to find life, in all its possibilities. The relevant question isn't 'Is this a potential friend for me?' but 'Is this character alive?'"

Perhaps, then, unlikable characters, the ones who are the most human, are also the ones who are the most alive. Perhaps this intimacy makes us uncomfortable because we don't dare be so alive.

———

In *How Fiction Works*, James Wood says, "A great deal of nonsense is written every day about characters in fiction—from the side of those who believe too much in character and from the side of those who believe too little. Those who believe too much have an iron set of prejudices about what characters are: We should get to 'know' them; they should 'grow' and 'develop'; and they should be nice. So they should be pretty much like us." Wood is correct, in part, but the ongoing question of character likability leaves the impression that what we're looking for in fiction is an ideal world where people behave in ideal ways. The question suggests that characters should be reflections not of us, but of our better selves.

Wood also says, "There is nothing harder than the creation of fictional character." I can attest to this difficulty though with, perhaps, less hyperbole. I have, indeed, found several other tasks harder over the years. Regardless, characters are hard to create because we need to develop people who are interesting enough to hold a reader's attention. We need to ensure that they are some measure of credible. We need to make them distinct from ourselves (and in the best of all worlds, from those in our lives, unless of course, there is a need to settle scores). Somehow they need to be well developed enough to carry a plot or carry a narrative without a plot or endure the tribulations we writers tend to throw at them with alacrity. It's no wonder so many characters are unlikable given what they have to put up with.

It is a seductive position a writer puts the reader in when they create an interesting, unlikable character—they make you complicit, in ways that are both uncomfortable and intriguing.

———

If people with messy lives are the point of certain narratives, if unlikable women are the point of certain narratives, novels like *Gone Girl*, *Treasure Island!!!*, *Dare Me*, *Magnificence*, and many others exhibit a delightful excess of purpose with stories filled with women who are deemed unlikable because they make so-called bad choices, describe the world exactly as they see it, and are, ultimately, honest and breathtakingly alive.

These novels depict women who are clearly not participating in their narratives to make friends and whose characters are the better for it. Freed from the constraints of likability, they are able to exist on and beyond the page as fully realized, interesting, and realistic characters. There is the saying that the truth hurts, and perhaps this is what lies at the heart of worrying over likability or the lack thereof: how much of the truth we're willing to subject ourselves to, how much we are willing to hurt, when we immerse ourselves in the safety of a fictional world.

Sara Levine's *Treasure Island!!!* features a narrator who is unlikable in curious ways. She is utterly self-obsessed, acts without considering consequences, and always makes choices that will benefit herself over others. She is intensely preoccupied with the book *Treasure Island*, and sets out to live her life by the book's core values: BOLDNESS, RESOLUTION, INDEPENDENCE, and HORN-BLOWING. As she careens from one self-created disaster to another, the narrator is unrepentant. There is no redemption or lesson learned from misdeeds. There is no apology or moral to the story, and that makes an already incisive and intelligent novel even more compelling.

When you think about it, these core values the narrator in *Treasure Island!!!* seeks to live by—BOLDNESS, RESOLUTION, INDEPENDENCE, and HORN-BLOWING—are characteristics that define how many unlikable women lead their fictional lives.

In Pamela Ribon's *You Take It From Here*, a woman, Smidge, is dying of lung cancer and wants her best friend Danielle to essentially finish the job of raising her daughter and being her husband's companion in grief. The book's premise is an interesting one, but what really stands out is how deeply unlikable Smidge is. She is the kind of person who, it might seem, shouldn't have any friends. She's bossy, intense, controlling, unrepentant, and manipulative. And yet. She has a best friend, a daughter, a husband, and a community of people who will deeply mourn her when she is gone. Ribon's steadfastness in this character's lack of likability is admirable. She never panders by making Smidge somehow have some kind of epiphany of character simply because she is dying. Ribon is unwavering in what she shows us of Smidge and the novel is the better for it.

A customer review of *You Take It From Here* on Amazon from Danae Savitri states, "I never warmed up to Smidge as a character, thought she suffered from borderline personality disorder, common among people who are charismatic narcissistics, who alternately bully, manipulate, and charm others around them." Instead of judging the book, it is a woman's likability that comes into question. Again, there is an armchair diagnosis of mental disease. It is an almost Pavlovian response to pathologize the unlikable in fictional characters.

Dare Me by Megan Abbott is a book about high school cheerleaders, but it's nothing like what you might expect. Populated by women who act with boldness, resolve, independence, and a prioritizing of the self—these mighty principles from *Treasure Island!!!—Dare Me* is both engaging and terrifying because it reveals the fraught intimacy between girls. It's a novel about bodies and striving for perfection and ambition and desire so naked, so palpable, you cannot help but want the deeply flawed women in the book to get what they want no matter how terribly they go about getting it. The young women at the center of the novel, Beth and Addy, are friends as much as they are enemies. They betray each other and they betray themselves. They commit wrongs, and still, they are each other's gravitational center.

On the phone, after a drunken night, Beth asks Addy if she remembers "how we used to hang on the monkey bars, hooking our legs around each other, and how strong we got and how no one could ever beat us, and we could never beat each other, but we'd agree to each release our hands at the count of three, and that she always cheated, and I always let her, standing beneath, looking up at her and grinning my gap-toothed pre-orthodontic grin." It is a moment that shows us how Addy has always seen Beth plainly and understood her and loved her nonetheless. Throughout the novel, Beth and Addy remain unlikable, remain flawed to an extent, but there is no explanation for it, no clear trajectory between cause and effect. Traditional parameters of likability are deftly avoided throughout the novel in moments as honest and no less poignant as these.

Susan Lindley, a widow, has to move on after her husband's tragic death in Lydia Millet's *Magnificence*. From the outset we know she was unfaithful to her husband. She inherits her uncle's mansion, filled with a rotting taxidermy collection, and sets about making some kind of order, both in the mansion and in her own life. She has a daughter involved with her boss and a boyfriend who is married to another woman. She feels responsible for her husband's death but is matter of fact in reconciling this. "Was she relieved, slut that she was?" Susan thinks to herself. "Was there something in her that was relieved by any of this? If anyone could admit such a thing, she should be able to. She was not only a slut but a killer." Susan does go on to acknowledge she feels a profound absence in the loss of her husband, a "freedom of nothing," and throughout the novel, she indulges in this freedom; she embraces it.

So much of *Magnificence* is grounded solely in Susan's experiences, her awkward perceptions of the world she has created and continues to create for herself. We also have the pleasure of seeing a woman in her late forties as a deeply sexual being who is equally unashamed in her want for material things as she becomes more and more attached to the mansion she has inherited. Though the prose often gives over to lush excess and meditation, what remains compelling is this woman who reveals little remorse for her infidelities and the ways she tends to fail the people in her life. In a lesser novel, such remorse would be the primary narrative thrust, but in *Magnificence*, we see how a woman, one deemed unlikable by many, is able to exist and be part of a story that expands far beyond remorse and the kinds of entrapments that could hold likable characters back. We are able to see just what the freedom of nothing looks like.

The short story collection *Battleborn* by Claire Vaye Watkins contains many stories with seemingly unlikable women. As much as the stories are about place, all set, in some form, in the desert of the American West, several stories are about women and their strength, where their strength comes from and how that strength can fail in unbearably human ways. The phrase "battle born" is, in fact, Nevada's state motto—meant to represent the state's strength, forged from struggle. In perhaps the most powerful story "Rondine Al Nido," there is an epigraph at the beginning. Normally, I do not care for epigraphs. I don't want my reading of a story to be framed by the writer in such an overt way. This story's epigraph, though, is from the Bhagavad Gita and reads, "Now I am become Death, the destroyer of worlds." From the outset, we know only ruin lies ahead and the story becomes a matter of learning just how that ruin comes about. We learn of a woman who "walks out on a man who in the end, she'll decide, didn't love her enough, though he in fact did love her, but his love wrenched something inside him, and this caused him to hurt her." Really, though, this is a story about when the woman was a girl, 16, with a friend, Lena, the kind who would follow the narrator, "our girl," wherever she went. There is an evening in Las Vegas, and an incident in a hotel room with some boys the girls meet, one that will irrevocably change the friendship, one that could be avoided if a flawed young woman didn't make the wrong choice, the choice that makes the story everything.

Perhaps the most unlikable woman in recent fictional memory is Amy in Gillian Flynn's *Gone Girl*, a woman who goes to extraordinary lengths—faking her own murder and framing her husband Nick, to punish his infidelity—and keep him within her grasp. Amy was so excessively unlikable, so unrepentant, so shameless, that at times, this book is intensely uncomfortable. Flynn engages in a clever manipulation where we learn more and more about both Nick and Amy, in small moments so that we never quite know how to feel about them. We never quite know if they are likable or unlikable and then we do know that they are both flawed, both terrible, and stuck together in many ways and it is exhilarating to see a writer who doesn't blink, who doesn't pull back.

There is a line of anger that runs throughout *Gone Girl*, and for Amy, that anger is borne of the unreasonable burdens women are so often forced to bear. The novel is a psychological thriller but it is also an exquisite character study. Amy is, by all accounts, a woman people should like. She's "a smart, pretty, nice girl, with so many interests and enthusiasms, a cool job, a loving family. And let's say it: money." Even with all these assets, Amy finds herself single at 32, and then she finds Nick.

The most uncomfortable aspect of *Gone Girl* is the book's honesty and how desperately similar many of us likely are to Nick and Amy the ways they love and hate each other. The truth hurts. It hurts, it hurts, it hurts. When we finally begin to see the truth of Amy, she says, of the night she met Nick, "That night at the Brooklyn party, I was playing the girl who was in style, the girl a man like Nick wants: the Cool Girl. Men always say that as the defining compliment, don't they? She's a cool girl. Being the Cool Girl means I am a hot, brilliant, funny woman who adores football, poker, dirty jokes, and burping, who plays video games, drinks cheap beer, loves threesomes and anal sex, and jams hot dogs into her mouth like she's hosting the world's biggest culinary gang bang while somehow maintaining a size 2, because Cool Girls are above all hot. Hot and understanding . . . Men actually think this girl exists. Maybe they're fooled because so many women are willing to pretend to be this girl."

This is what is so rarely said about unlikable women in fiction—that they aren't pretending, that they won't or can't pretend to be someone they are not. They have neither the energy for it, nor the desire. They don't have the willingness of a May Welland to play the part demanded of her. In *Gone Girl*, Amy talks about the temptation of being the woman a man wants but ultimately she doesn't give in to that temptation to be "the girl who likes every fucking thing he likes and doesn't ever complain." Unlikable women refuse to give in to that temptation. They are, instead, themselves. They accept the consequences of their choices and those consequences become stories worth reading.

TYPES OF WOMEN IN ROMANTIC COMEDIES WHO DO NOT EXIST

MINDY KALING

Originally published in
Is Everyone Hanging Out Without Me?
2014

When I was a kid, Christmas vacation meant renting VHS copies of romantic comedies from Blockbuster and watching them with my parents at home. *Sleepless in Seattle* was big, and so was *When Harry Met Sally*. I laughed along with everyone else at the scene where Meg Ryan fakes an orgasm at the restaurant without even knowing what an orgasm was. In my mind, she was just being kind of loud and silly at a diner, and that was hilarious enough for me.

I love romantic comedies. I feel almost sheepish writing that, because the genre has been so degraded in the past twenty years or so that admitting you like these movies is essentially an admission of mild stupidity. But that has not stopped me from watching them. I enjoy watching people fall in love on-screen so much that I can suspend my disbelief for the contrived situations that only happen in the heightened world of romantic comedies. I have come to enjoy the moment when the normal lead guy, say, slips and falls right on top of the hideously expensive wedding cake. I actually feel robbed when the female lead's dress doesn't get torn open at a baseball game while the JumboTron is on her. I simply regard romantic comedies as a

subgenre of sci-fi, in which the world created therein has different rules than my regular human world. Then I just lap it up. There is no difference between Ripley from *Alien* and any Katherine Heigl character. They're all participating in the same level of made-up awesomeness, and I enjoy every second of it.

So it makes sense that in this world there are many specimens of women who I do not think exist in real life, like Vulcans or UFO people or whatever. They are:

THE KLUTZ

When a beautiful actress is in a movie, executives wrack their brains to find some kind of flaw in her that still allows her to be palatable. She can't be overweight or not perfect-looking, because who would want to see that? A not 100-percent-perfect-looking-in-every-way female? You might as well film a dead squid decaying on a beach somewhere for two hours.

So they make her a Klutz.

The 100-percent-perfect-looking female is perfect in every way, except that she constantly falls down. She bonks her head on things. She trips and falls and spills soup on her affable date. (Josh Lucas. Is that his name? I know it's two first names. Josh George? Brad Mike? Fred Tom? Yes, it's Fred Tom.) Our Klutz clangs into Stop signs while riding a bike, and knocks over giant displays of expensive fine china. Despite being five foot nine and weighing 110 pounds, she is basically like a drunk buffalo who has never been a part of human society. But Fred Tom loves her anyway.

THE ETHEREAL WEIRDO

The smart and funny writer Nathan Rabin coined the term *Manic Pixie Dream Girl* to describe a version of this archetype after seeing Kirsten Dunst in the movie *Elizabethtown*. This girl can't be pinned down and may or may not show up when you make concrete plans. She wears gauzy blouses and braids. She decides to dance in the rain and weeps uncontrollably if she sees a sign for a missing dog or cat. She spins a globe, places her finger on a random spot, and decides to move there. This ethereal weirdo abounds in movies, but nowhere else. If she were from real life, people would think she was a homeless woman and would cross the street to avoid her, but she is essential to the male fantasy that even if a guy is boring, he deserves a woman who will find him fascinating and pull him out of himself by forcing him to go skinny-dipping in a stranger's pool.

THE WOMAN WHO IS OBSESSED WITH HER CAREER AND IS NO FUN AT ALL

I, Mindy Kaling, basically have two full-time jobs. I regularly work sixteen hours a day. But like most of the other people I know who are similarly busy,

I think I'm a pleasant, pretty normal person. I am slightly offended by the way busy working women my age are presented in film. I'm not, like, always barking orders into my hands-free phone device and telling people constantly, "I have no time for this!" I didn't completely forget how to be nice or feminine because I have a career. Also, since when does having a job necessitate women having their hair pulled back in a severe, tight bun? Often this uptight woman has to "re-learn" how to seduce a man because her estrogen leaked out of her from leading so many board meetings, and she has to do all sorts of crazy, unnecessary crap, like eat a hot dog in a libidinous way or something. Having a challenging job in movies means the compassionate, warm, or sexy side of your brain has fallen out.

THE FORTY-TWO-YEAR-OLD MOTHER OF THE THIRTY-YEAR-OLD MALE LEAD

If you think about the backstory of a typical mother character in a romantic comedy, you realize this: when "Mom" was an adolescent, the very month she started to menstruate she was impregnated with a baby who would grow up to be the movie's likable brown-haired leading man. I am fascinated by Mom's sordid early life. I would rather see this movie than the one I bought a ticket for.

I am so brainwashed by the young-mom phenomenon that when I saw a poster for *The Proposal* I wondered for a second if the proposal in the movie was Ryan Reynolds suggesting that he send his mother, Sandra Bullock, to an old-age home.

THE SASSY BEST FRIEND

You know that really horny and hilarious best friend who is always asking about your relationship and has nothing really going on in her own life? She always wants to meet you in coffee shops or wants to go to Bloomingdale's to sample perfumes? She runs a chic dildo store in the West Village? Nope? Okay, that's this person.

THE SKINNY WOMAN WHO IS BEAUTIFUL AND TONED BUT ALSO GLUTTONOUS AND DISGUSTING

Again, I am more than willing to suspend my disbelief during a romantic comedy for good set decoration alone. One pristine kitchen from a Nancy Meyers movie like in *It's Complicated* is worth five Diane Keatons being caught half-clad in a topiary or whatever situation her character has found herself in.

But sometimes even my suspended disbelief isn't enough. I am speaking of the gorgeous and skinny heroine who is also a disgusting pig when it comes to food. And everyone in the movie—her parents, her friends, her boss—are all complicit in this huge lie. They are constantly telling her to stop eating and being such a glutton. And this actress, this poor skinny actress who so clearly lost weight to play the likable lead, has to say things like "Shut up you guys! I love cheesecake! If I want to eat an entire cheesecake, I will!" If you look closely, you can see this woman's ribs through the dress she's wearing— that's how skinny she is, this cheesecake-loving cow.

You wonder, as you sit and watch this movie, what the characters would do if they were confronted by an actual average American woman. They would all kill themselves, which would actually be kind of an interesting movie.

THE WOMAN WHO WORKS IN AN ART GALLERY

How many freakin' art galleries are out there? Are people buying visual art on a daily basis? This posh, smart, classy profession is a favorite in movies. It's in the same realm as kindergarten teacher or children's book illustrator in terms of accessibility: guys don't really get it, but it is likable and nonthreatening.

ART GALLERY WOMAN: Dust off the Warhol. You know, that Campbell's Soup one in the crazy color! We have an important buyer coming into town and this is a really big deal for my career. I have no time for this!

The gallery worker character is the rare female movie archetype that has a male counterpart. Whenever you meet a handsome, charming, successful man in a romantic comedy, the heroine's friend always says the same thing. "He's really successful—he's . . .

(say it with me)

. . . an architect!"

There are like nine people in the entire world who are architects, and one of them is my dad. None of them looks like Patrick Dempsey.

OBSERVATIONS ON THE STATE OF DEGRADATION TO WHICH WOMAN IS REDUCED BY VARIOUS CAUSES

MARY WOLLSTONECRAFT

Originally published in
A Vindication of the Rights of Women
1792

T hat woman is naturally weak, or degraded by a concurrence of circumstances is, I think, clear. But this position I shall simply contrast with a conclusion, which I have frequently heard fall from sensible men in favor of an aristocracy: that the mass of mankind cannot be any thing, or the obsequious slaves, who patiently allow themselves to be penned up, would feel their own consequence, and spurn their chains. Men, they further observe, submit every where to oppression, when they have only to lift up their heads to throw off the yoke; yet, instead of asserting their birthright, they quietly lick the dust, and say, let us eat and drink, for tomorrow we die. Women, I argue from analogy, are degraded by the same propensity to enjoy the present moment; and, at last, despise the freedom which they have not sufficient virtue to struggle to attain. But I must be more explicit.

With respect to the culture of the heart, it is unanimously allowed that sex is out of the question; but the line of subordination in the mental powers is never to be passed over.

ONLY "ABSOLUTE IN LOVELINESS," THE PORTION OF RATIONALITY GRANTED TO WOMAN IS, INDEED, VERY SCANTY; FOR, DENYING HER GENIUS AND JUDGMENT, IT IS SCARCELY POSSIBLE TO DIVINE WHAT REMAINS TO CHARACTERIZE INTELLECT.

The stamina of immortality, if I may be allowed the phrase, is the perfectibility of human reason; for, was man created perfect, or did a flood of knowledge break in upon him, when he arrived at maturity, that precluded error, I should doubt whether his existence would be continued after the dissolution of the body. But in the present state of things, every difficulty in morals, that escapes from human discussion, and equally baffles the investigation of profound thinking, and the lightning glance of genius, is an argument on which I build my belief of the immortality of the soul. Reason is, consequentially, the simple power of improvement; or, more properly speaking, of discerning truth. Every individual is in this respect a world in itself. More or less may be conspicuous in one being than other; but the nature of reason must be the same in all, if it be an emanation of divinity, the tie that connects the creature with the Creator; for, can that soul be stamped with the heavenly image, that is not perfected by the exercise of its own reason? Yet outwardly ornamented with elaborate care, and so adorned to delight man, "that with honor he may love," (Vide Milton) the soul of woman is not allowed to have this distinction, and man, ever placed between her and reason, she is always represented as only created to see through a gross medium, and to take things on trust. But, dismissing these fanciful theories, and considering woman as a whole, let it be what it will, instead of a part of man, the inquiry is, whether she has reason or not. If she has, which, for a moment, I will take

for granted, she was not created merely to be the solace of man, and the sexual should not destroy the human character.

Into this error men have, probably, been led by viewing education in a false light; not considering it as the first step to form a being advancing gradually toward perfection; (This word is not strictly just, but I cannot find a better.) but only as a preparation for life. On this sensual error, for I must call it so, has the false system of female manners been reared, which robs the whole sex of its dignity, and classes the brown and fair with the smiling flowers that only adorn the land. This has ever been the language of men, and the fear of departing from a supposed sexual character, has made even women of superior sense adopt the same sentiments. Thus understanding, strictly speaking, has been denied to woman; and instinct, sublimated into wit and cunning, for the purposes of life, has been substituted in its stead.

The power of generalizing ideas, of drawing comprehensive conclusions from individual observations, is the only acquirement for an immortal being, that really deserves the name of knowledge. Merely to observe, without endeavoring to account for any thing, may, (in a very incomplete manner) serve as the common sense of life; but where is the store laid up that is to clothe the soul when it leaves the body?

This power has not only been denied to women; but writers have insisted that it is inconsistent, with a few exceptions, with their sexual character. Let men prove this, and I shall grant that woman only exists for man. I must, however, previously remark, that the power of generalizing ideas, to any great extent, is not very common amongst men or women. But this exercise is the true cultivation of the understanding; and every thing conspires to render the cultivation of the understanding more difficult in the female than the male world.

I am naturally led by this assertion to the main subject of the present chapter, and shall now attempt to point out some of the causes that degrade the sex, and prevent women from generalizing their observations.

I shall not go back to the remote annals of antiquity to trace the history of woman; it is sufficient to allow, that she has always been either a slave or a despot, and to remark, that each of these situations equally retards the progress of reason. The grand source of female folly and vice has ever appeared to me to arise from narrowness of mind; and the very constitution of civil governments has put almost insuperable obstacles in the way to prevent the cultivation of the female understanding: yet virtue can be built on no other foundation! The same obstacles are thrown in the way of the rich, and the same consequences ensue.

Necessity has been proverbially termed the mother of invention; the aphorism may be extended to virtue. It is an acquirement, and an acquirement to which pleasure must be sacrificed, and who sacrifices pleasure when it is within the grasp, whose mind has not been opened and strengthened by adversity, or the pursuit of knowledge goaded on by necessity? Happy is it when people have the cares of life to struggle with; for these struggles prevent their becoming a prey to enervating vices, merely from idleness! But, if from their birth men and women are placed in a torrid zone, with the meridian sun of pleasure darting directly upon them, how can they sufficiently brace their minds to discharge the duties of life, or even to relish the affections that carry them out of themselves?

Pleasure is the business of a woman's life, according to the present modification of society, and while it continues to be so, little can be expected from such weak beings. Inheriting, in a lineal descent from the first fair defect in nature, the sovereignty of beauty, they have, to maintain their power, resigned their natural rights, which the exercise of reason, might have procured them, and chosen rather to be short-lived queens than labor to attain the sober pleasures that arise from equality. Exalted by their inferiority (this sounds like a contradiction) they constantly demand homage as women, though experience should teach them that the men who pride themselves upon paying this arbitrary insolent respect to the sex, with the most

93

scrupulous exactness, are most inclined to tyrannize over, and despise the very weakness they cherish. Often do they repeat Mr. Hume's sentiments; when comparing the French and Athenian character, he alludes to women. "But what is more singular in this whimsical nation, say I to the Athenians, is, that a frolic of yours during the Saturnalia, when the slaves are served by their masters, is seriously continued by them through the whole year, and through the whole course of their lives; accompanied too with some circumstances, which still further augment the absurdity and ridicule. Your sport only elevates for a few days, those whom fortune has thrown down, and whom she too, in sport, may really elevate forever above you. But this nation gravely exalts those, whom nature has subjected to them, and whose inferiority and infirmities are absolutely incurable. The women, though without virtue, are their masters and sovereigns."

Ah! why do women, I write with affectionate solicitude, condescend to receive a degree of attention and respect from strangers, different from that reciprocation of civility which the dictates of humanity, and the politeness of civilization authorize between man and man? And why do they not discover, when "in the noon of beauty's power," that they are treated like queens only to be deluded by hollow respect, till they are led to resign, or not assume, their natural prerogatives? Confined then in cages, like the feathered race, they have nothing to do but to plume themselves, and stalk with

mock-majesty from perch to perch. It is true, they are provided with food and raiment, for which they neither toil nor spin; but health, liberty, and virtue are given in exchange. But, where, amongst mankind has been found sufficient strength of mind to enable a being to resign these adventitious prerogatives; one who rising with the calm dignity of reason above opinion, dared to be proud of the privileges inherent in man? and it is vain to expect it whilst hereditary power chokes the affections, and nips reason in the bud.

The passions of men have thus placed women on thrones; and, till mankind become more reasonable, it is to be feared that women will avail themselves of the power which they attain with the least exertion, and which is the most indisputable. They will smile, yes, they will smile, though told that—

> "In beauty's empire is no mean,
> And woman either slave or queen,
> Is quickly scorn'd when not ador'd."

But the adoration comes first, and the scorn is not anticipated.

Lewis the XIVth, in particular, spread factitious manners, and caught in a specious way, the whole nation in his toils; for establishing an artful chain of despotism, he made it the interest of the people at large, individually to respect his station, and support his power. And women, whom he flattered by a puerile attention to the whole sex, obtained in his reign that prince-like distinction so fatal to reason and virtue.

A king is always a king, and a woman always a woman: (And a wit, always a wit, might be added; for the vain fooleries of wits and beauties to obtain attention, and make conquests, are much upon a par.) his authority and her sex, ever stand between them and rational converse. With a lover, I grant she should be so, and her sensibility will naturally lead her to endeavor to excite emotion, not to gratify her vanity but her heart. This I do not allow to be coquetry, it is the artless impulse of nature, I only exclaim against the sexual desire of conquest, when the heart is out of the question.

This desire is not confined to women; "I have endeavored," says Lord Chesterfield, "to gain the hearts of twenty women, whose persons I would not have given a fig for." The libertine who in a gust of passion, takes advantage of unsuspecting tenderness, is a saint when compared with this cold-hearted rascal; for I like to use significant words. Yet only taught to please, women are always on the watch to please, and with true heroic ardor endeavor to gain hearts merely to resign, or spurn them, when the victory is decided, and conspicuous.

I must descend to the minutiae of the subject.

I lament that women are systematically degraded by receiving the trivial attentions, which men think it manly to pay to the sex, when, in fact, they are insultingly supporting their own superiority. It is not condescension to bow to an inferior. So ludicrous, in fact, do these ceremonies appear to me, that I scarcely am able to govern my muscles, when I see a man start with eager, and serious solicitude to lift a handkerchief, or shut a door, when the LADY could have done it herself, had she only moved a pace or two.

A wild wish has just flown from my heart to my head, and I will not stifle it though it may excite a horse laugh. I do earnestly wish to see the distinction of sex confounded in society, unless where love animates the behavior. For this distinction is, I am firmly persuaded, the foundation of the weakness of character ascribed to woman; is the cause why the understanding is neglected, whilst accomplishments are acquired with sedulous care: and the same cause accounts for their preferring the graceful before the heroic virtues.

Mankind, including every description, wish to be loved and respected for SOMETHING; and the common herd will always take the nearest road to the completion of their wishes. The respect paid to wealth and beauty is the most certain and unequivocal; and of course, will always attract the vulgar eye of common minds. Abilities and virtues are absolutely necessary to raise men from the middle rank of life into notice; and the natural consequence is notorious, the middle rank contains most virtue and abilities. Men have thus, in one station, at least, an opportunity of exerting themselves with dignity, and of rising by the exertions which really improve a rational creature; but the whole female sex are, till their character is formed, in the same condition as the rich: for they are born, I now speak of a state of civilization, with certain sexual privileges, and whilst they are gratuitously granted them, few will ever think of works of supererogation, to obtain the esteem of a small number of superior people.

When do we hear of women, who starting out of obscurity, boldly claim respect on account of their great abilities or daring virtues? Where are they to be found? "To be observed, to be attended to, to be taken notice of with sympathy, complacency, and approbation, are all the advantages which they seek." True! my male readers will probably exclaim; but let them, before they draw any conclusion, recollect, that this was not written originally as descriptive of women, but of the rich. In Dr. Smith's *Theory of Moral Sentiments*, I have found a general character of people of rank and fortune, that in my opinion, might with the greatest propriety be applied to the female sex. I refer the sagacious reader to the whole comparison; but must be allowed to quote a passage to enforce an argument that I mean to insist on, as the one most conclusive against a sexual character. For if, excepting warriors, no great men of any denomination, have ever appeared amongst the nobility, may it not be fairly inferred, that their local situation swallowed up the man, and produced a character similar to that of women, who are

LOCALIZED, if I may be allowed the word, by the rank they are placed in, by COURTESY? Women, commonly called Ladies, are not to be contradicted in company, are not allowed to exert any manual strength; and from them the negative virtues only are expected, when any virtues are expected, patience, docility, good-humor, and flexibility; virtues incompatible with any vigorous exertion of intellect. Besides by living more with each other, and to being seldom absolutely alone, they are more under the influence of sentiments than passions. Solitude and reflection are necessary to give to wishes the force of passions, and enable the imagination to enlarge the object and make it the most desirable. The same may be said of the rich; they do not sufficiently deal in general ideas, collected by impassionate thinking, or calm investigation, to acquire that strength of character, on which great resolves are built. But hear what an acute observer says of the great.

"Do the great seem insensible of the easy price at which they may acquire the public admiration? or do they seem to imagine, that to them, as to other men, it must be the purchase either of sweat or of blood? By what important accomplishments is the young nobleman instructed to support the dignity of his rank, and to render himself worthy of that superiority over his fellow citizens, to which the virtue of his ancestors had raised them? Is it by knowledge, by industry, by patience, by self-denial, or by virtue of any kind? As all his words, as all his motions are attended to, he learns an habitual regard for every circumstance of ordinary behavior, and studies to perform all those small duties with the most exact propriety. As he is conscious how much he is observed, and how much mankind are disposed to favor all his inclinations, he acts, upon the most indifferent occasions, with that freedom and elevation which the thought of this naturally inspires. His air, his manner, his deportment all mark that elegant and graceful sense of his own superiority, which those who are born to an inferior station can hardly ever arrive at. These are the arts by which he proposes to make mankind more easily submit to his authority, and to govern their inclinations according to his own pleasure: and in this he is seldom disappointed. These arts, supported by rank and pre-eminence, are, upon ordinary occasions, sufficient to govern the world. Lewis XIV, during the greater part of his reign, was regarded, not only in France, but over all Europe, as the most perfect model of a great prince. But what were the talents and virtues, by which he acquired this great reputation? Was it by the scrupulous and inflexible justice of all his undertakings, by the immense dangers and difficulties with which they were attended, or by the unwearied and unrelenting application with which he pursued them? Was it by his extensive knowledge, by his exquisite judgment, or by his heroic valor? It was by none of these qualities. But he was, first of all, the most powerful prince in Europe, and consequently held the highest rank among kings; and then, says his

historian, 'he surpassed all his courtiers in the gracefulness of his shape, and the majestic beauty of his features. The sound of his voice noble and affecting, gained those hearts which his presence intimidated. He had a step and a deportment, which could suit only him and his rank, and which would have been ridiculous in any other person. The embarrassment which he occasioned to those who spoke to him, flattered that secret satisfaction with which he felt his own superiority.' These frivolous accomplishments, supported by his rank, and, no doubt, too, by a degree of other talents and virtues, which seems, however, not to have been much above mediocrity, established this prince in the esteem of his own age, and have drawn even from posterity, a good deal of respect for his memory. Compared with these, in his own times, and in his own presence, no other virtue, it seems, appeared to have any merit. Knowledge, industry, valor, and beneficence, trembling, were abashed, and lost all dignity before them."

Woman, also, thus "in herself complete," by possessing all these FRIVOLOUS accomplishments, so changes the nature of things,

—"That what she wills to do or say
Seems wisest, virtuousest, discreetest, best;
All higher knowledge in HER PRESENCE falls
Degraded. Wisdom in discourse with her
Loses discountenanc'd, and like folly shows;
Authority and reason on her wait."—

And all this is built on her loveliness!

In the middle rank of life, to continue the comparison, men, in their youth, are prepared for professions, and marriage is not considered as the grand feature in their lives; whilst women, on the contrary, have no other scheme to sharpen their faculties. It is not business, extensive plans, or any of the excursive flights of ambition, that engross their attention; no, their thoughts are not employed in rearing such noble structures. To rise in the world, and have the liberty of running from pleasure to pleasure, they must marry advantageously, and to this object their time is sacrificed, and their persons often legally prostituted. A man, when he enters any profession, has his eye steadily fixed on some future advantage (and the mind gains great strength by having all its efforts directed to one point) and, full of his business, pleasure is considered as mere relaxation; whilst women seek for pleasure as the main purpose of existence. In fact, from the education which they receive from society, the love of pleasure may be said to govern them all; but does this prove that there is a sex in souls? It would be just as rational to declare, that the courtiers in France, when a destructive system of despotism had formed their character, were not men, because liberty, virtue, and humanity, were sacrificed to pleasure and vanity. Fatal passions, which have ever domineered over the WHOLE race!

The same love of pleasure, fostered by the whole tendency of their education, gives a trifling turn to the conduct of women in most circumstances: for instance, they are ever anxious about secondary things; and on the watch for adventures, instead of being occupied by duties.

A man, when he undertakes a journey, has, in general the end in view; a woman thinks more of the incidental occurrences, the strange things that may possibly occur on the road; the impression that she may make on her fellow travelers; and, above all, she is anxiously intent on the care of the finery that she carries with her, which is more than ever a part of herself, when going to figure on a new scene; when, to use an apt French turn of expression, she is going to produce a sensation. Can dignity of mind exist with such trivial cares?

In short, women, in general, as well as the rich of both sexes, have acquired all the follies and vices of civilization, and missed the useful fruit. It is not necessary for me always to premise, that I speak of the condition of the whole sex, leaving exceptions out of the question. Their senses are inflamed, and their understandings neglected; consequently they become the prey of their senses, delicately termed sensibility, and are blown about by every momentary gust of feeling. They are, therefore, in a much worse condition than they would be in, were they in a state nearer to nature. Ever restless and anxious, their over exercised sensibility not only renders them uncomfortable themselves, but troublesome, to use a soft phrase, to others. All their thoughts turn on things calculated to excite emotion; and, feeling, when they should reason, their conduct is unstable, and their opinions are wavering, not the wavering produced by deliberation or progressive views, but by contradictory emotions. By fits and starts they are warm in many pursuits; yet this warmth, never concentrated into perseverance, soon exhausts itself; exhaled by its own heat, or meeting with some other fleeting passion, to which reason has never given any specific gravity, neutrality ensues. Miserable, indeed, must be that being whose cultivation of mind has only tended to inflame its passions! A distinction should be made between inflaming and strengthening them. The passions thus pampered, whilst the judgment is left unformed, what can be expected to ensue? Undoubtedly, a mixture of madness and folly!

I WANT A WIFE

JUDY BRADY

Originally published in *Ms.* magazine
1971

1

I belong to that classification of people known as wives. I am A Wife. And, not altogether incidentally, I am a mother.

2

Not too long ago a male friend of mine appeared on the scene fresh from a recent divorce. He had one child, who is, of course, with his ex-wife. He is looking for another wife. As I thought about him while I was ironing one evening, it suddenly occurred to me that I, too, would like to have a wife. Why do I want a wife?

3

I would like to go back to school so that I can become economically independent, support myself, and, if need be, support those dependent upon me. I want a wife who will work and send me to school.

And while I am going to school, I want a wife to take care of my children. I want a wife to keep track of the children's doctor and dentist appointments. And to keep track of mine, too. I want a wife to make sure my children eat properly and are kept clean. I want a wife who will wash the children's clothes and keep them mended. I want a wife who is a good nurturant attendant to my children, who arranges for their schooling, makes sure that they have an adequate social life with their peers, takes them to the park, the zoo, etc. I want a wife who takes care of the children when they are sick, a wife who arranges to be around when the children need special care, because, of course, I cannot miss classes at school. My wife must arrange to lose time at work and not lose the job. It may mean a small cut in my wife's income from time to time, but I guess I can tolerate that. Needless to say, my wife will arrange and pay for the care of the children while my wife is working.

4

I want a wife who will take care of my physical needs. I want a wife who will keep my house clean. A wife who will pick up after my children, a wife who will pick up after me. I want a wife who will keep my clothes clean, ironed, mended, replaced when need be, and who will see to it that my personal things are kept in their proper place so that I can find what I need the minute I need it. I want a wife who cooks the meals, a wife who is a good cook. I want a wife who will plan the menus, do the necessary grocery shopping, prepare the meals, serve them pleasantly, and then do the cleaning up while I do my studying. I want a wife who will care for me when I am sick and sympathize with my pain and loss of time from school. I want a wife to go along when our family takes a vacation so that someone can continue to care for me and my children when I need a rest and change of scene.

6

I want a wife who will take care of the details of my social life. When my wife and I are invited out by my friends, I want a wife who will take care of the baby-sitting arrangements. When I meet people at school that I like and want to entertain, I want a wife who will have the house clean, will prepare a special meal, serve it to me and my friends, and not interrupt when I talk about things that interest me and my friends. I want a wife who will have arranged that the children are fed and ready for bed before my guests arrive so that the children do not bother us. I want a wife who takes care of the needs of my guests so that they feel comfortable, who makes sure that they have an ashtray, that they are passed the hors d'oeuvres, that they are offered a second helping of the food, that their wine glasses are replenished when necessary, that their coffee is served to them as they like it. And I want a wife who knows that sometimes I need a night out by myself.

5

I want a wife who will not bother me with rambling complaints about a wife's duties. But I want a wife who will listen to me when I feel the need to explain a rather difficult point I have come across in my course studies. And I want a wife who will type my papers for me when I have written them.

7

I want a wife who is sensitive to my sexual needs, a wife who makes love passionately and eagerly when I feel like it, a wife who makes sure that I am satisfied. And, of course, I want a wife who will not demand sexual attention when I am not in the mood for it. I want a wife who assumes the complete responsibility for birth control, because

I do not want more children. I want a wife who will remain sexually faithful to me so that I do not have to clutter up my intellectual life with jealousies. And I want a wife who understands that my sexual needs may entail more than strict adherence to monogamy. I must, after all, be able to relate to people as fully as possible.

When I am through with school and have a job, I want my wife to quit working and remain at home so that my wife can more fully and completely take care of a wife's duties.

My God, who wouldn't want a wife?

If, by chance, I find another person more suitable as a wife than the wife I already have, I want the liberty to replace my present wife with another one. Naturally, I will expect a fresh, new life; my wife will take the children and be solely responsible for them so that I am left free.

GENDER, STATUS, AND FEELING

ARLIE
RUSSELL
HOCHSCHILD

Originally published in *The Managed Heart:*
The Commercialization of Human Feeling
1983

EMOTIONAL.
2. *subject to or easily affected by emotion:* SHE is an emotional woman, easily upset by any disturbance.

COGITATION.
1. *meditation, contemplation:* After hours of cogitation HE came up with a new proposal.
2. *the faculty of thinking:* SHE was not a serious student and seemed to lack the power of cogitation.
—*Random House Dictionary of the English Language*

More emotion management goes on in the families and jobs of the upper classes than in those of the lower classes. That is, in the class system, social conditions conspire to make it more prevalent at the top. In the gender system, on the other hand, the reverse is true: social conditions make it more prevalent, and prevalent in different ways, for those at the bottom—women. In what sense is this so? And why?

Both men and women do emotion work, in private life and at work. In all kinds of ways, men as well as women get into the spirit of the party, try to escape the grip of hopeless love, try to pull themselves out of depression, try to allow grief. But in the whole realm of emotional experience, is emotion work as important for men as it is for women? And is it important in the same ways? I believe that the answer to both questions is No. The reason, at bottom, is the fact that women in general have far less independent access to money, power, authority, or status in society. They are a subordinate social stratum, and this has four consequences.

First, lacking other resources, women make a resource out of feeling and offer it to men as a gift in return for the more material resources they lack. (For example, in 1980 only 6 percent of women but 50 percent of men earned over $15,000 a year.) Thus their capacity to manage feeling and to do "relational" work is for them a more important resource.

Second, emotion work is important in different ways for men and for women. This is because each gender tends to be called on to do different kinds of this work. On the whole, women tend to specialize in the flight attendant side of emotional labor, men in the bill collection side of it. This specialization of emotional labor in the marketplace rests on the different childhood training of the heart that is given to girls and to boys. ("What are little girls made of? Sugar and spice and everything nice. What are little boys made of? Snips and snails and puppy dog tails.") Moreover, each specialization presents men and women with different emotional tasks. Women are more likely to be presented with the task of mastering anger and aggression in the service of "being nice." To men, the socially assigned task of aggressing against those that break rules of various sorts creates the private task of mastering fear and vulnerability.

Third, and less noticed, the general subordination of women leaves every individual woman with a weaker "status shield" against the displaced feelings of others. For example, female flight attendants found themselves easier targets for verbal abuse from passengers so that male attendants often found themselves called upon to handle unwarranted aggression against them.

The fourth consequence of the power difference between the sexes is that for each gender a different portion of the managed heart is enlisted for commercial use. Women often react to subordination by

making defensive use of sexual beauty, charm, and relational skills. For them, it is these capacities that become most vulnerable to commercial exploitation, and so it is these capacities that they are most likely to become estranged from. For male workers in "male" jobs it is more often the capacity to wield anger and make threats that is delivered over to the company, and so it is this sort of capacity that they are more likely to feel estranged from. After the great transmutation, then, men and women come to experience emotion work in different ways. In the previous chapter we focused on the social stratum in which emotion work is most prominent—the middle class. Here we shall focus on the gender for which it has the greatest importance—women.

WOMEN AS EMOTION MANAGERS

Middle-class American women, tradition suggests, feel emotion more than men do. The definitions of "emotional" and "cogitation" in the *Random House Dictionary of the English Language* reflect a deeply rooted cultural idea. Yet women are also thought to command "feminine wiles," to have the capacity to premeditate a sigh, an outburst of tears, or a flight of joy. In general, they are thought to manage expression and feeling not only better but more often than men do. How much the conscious feelings of women and men may differ is an issue I leave aside here.*

* Nancy Chodorow, a neo-Freudian theorist, suggests that women are, in fact, more likely to have access to their emotions. With Freud, she argues that in early childhood boys but not girls must relinquish their primary identification with the mother. To achieve this difficult task, the boy (but not the

girl) must repress feelings associated with the mother in the difficult effort to establish himself as "not like mother," as a boy. The consequence is a repression of feeling generally. The girl, on the other hand, because she enters a social and sexual category the same as that of her mother, does not have

However, the evidence seems clear that women do more emotion managing than men. And because the well-managed feeling has an outside resemblance to spontaneous feeling, it is possible to confuse the condition of being "more easily affected by emotion" with the action of willfully managing emotion when the occasion calls for it.

Especially in the American middle class, women tend to manage feeling more because in general they depend on men for money, and one of the various ways of repaying their debt is to do extra emotion work—*especially emotion work that affirms, enhances, and celebrates the well-being and status of others*. When the emotional skills that children learn and practice at home move into the marketplace, the emotional labor of women becomes more prominent because men in general have not been trained to make their emotions a resource and are therefore less likely to develop their capacity for managing feeling.

There is also a difference in the kind of emotion work that men and women tend to do. Many studies have told us that women adapt more to the needs of others and cooperate more than men do.[1] These studies often imply the existence of gender-specific

characteristics that are inevitable if not innate.[2] But do these characteristics simply exist passively in women? Or are they signs of a social work that women *do*—the work of affirming, enhancing, and celebrating the well-being and status of others? I believe that much of the time, the adaptive, cooperative woman is actively working at showing deference. This deference requires her to make an outward display of what Leslie Fiedler has called the "seriously" good girl in her and to support this effort by evoking feelings that make the "nice" display seem natural.† Women who want to put their own feelings less at the service of others must still confront the idea that if they do so, they will be considered less "feminine."

What it takes to be more "adaptive" is suggested in a study of college students by William Kephart (1967). Students were asked: "If a boy or girl had all the other qualities you desire, would you marry this person if you were not in love with him/her?" In response, 64 percent of the men but only 24 percent of the women said No. Most of the women answered that they "did not know." As one put it: "I don't know, if he were that good, maybe I could *bring myself around* to loving him."‡ In my own study

---

to relinquish identification with her or sacrifice her access to feelings through repression. If this interpretation is valid (and I find it plausible) we might expect women to be more in touch with their feelings, which are, as a consequence, more available for conscious management. See Chodorow (1980). Men may manage feelings more by subconscious repressing, women more by conscious suppressing.

† Fiedler (1960) suggests that girls are trained to be "seriously" good and to be ashamed of being bad whereas boys are asked to be good in formalistic ways but covertly invited to be ashamed of being "too" good. Oversocialization into "sugar-and-spice" demeanor produces feminine skills in delivering deference.

‡ Other researchers have found men to have a more "romantic" orientation to love, women a more "realistic"

(1975), women more often than men described themselves as "trying to make myself love," "talking myself into not caring," or "trying to convince myself." A content analysis of 260 protocols showed that more women than men (33 percent versus 18 percent) spontaneously used the language of emotion work to describe their emotions. The image of women as "more emotional," more subject to uncontrolled feelings, has also been challenged by a study of 250 students at UCLA, in which only 20 percent of the men but 45 percent of the women said that they deliberately show emotion to get their way.[*] As one woman put it: "I pout, frown, and say something to make the other person feel bad, such as 'You don't love me, you don't care what happens to me.' I'm not the type to come right out with what I want; I'll usually hint around. It's all hope and a lot of beating around the bush."[3]

The emotional arts that women have cultivated are analogous to the art of feigning that Lionel Trilling has noted among those whose wishes outdistance their opportunities for class advancement. As for many others of lower status, it has been in the woman's interest to be the better actor.[†] As the psychologists would say, the techniques of deep acting

have unusually high "secondary gains." Yet these skills have long been mislabeled "natural," a part of woman's "being" rather than something of her own making.

Sensitivity to nonverbal communication and to the micropolitical significance of feeling gives women something like an ethnic language, which men can speak too, but on the whole less well. It is a language women share offstage in their talk "about feelings." This talk is not, as it is for men offstage, the score-keeping of conquistadors. It is the talk of the artful prey, the language of tips on how to make him want her, how to psyche him out, how to put him on or turn him off. Within the traditional female subculture, subordination at close quarters is understood, especially in adolescence, as a "fact of life." Women accommodate, then, but not passively. They actively adapt feeling to a need or a purpose at hand, and they do it so that it *seems* to express a passive state of agreement, the chance occurrence of coinciding needs. Being becomes a way of doing. Acting is the needed art, and emotion work is the tool.

The emotion work of enhancing the status and well-being of others is a form of what Ivan Illich

---

orientation. That is, males may find cultural support for a passive construction of love, for seeing themselves as "falling head over heels," or "walking on air." According to Kephart, "the female is not pushed hither and yon by her romantic compulsions. On the contrary, she seems to have a greater measure of rational control over her romantic inclinations than the male" (1967, p. 473).

[*] This pattern is also socially reinforced. When women sent direct messages (persuading by logic, reason, or an onslaught of

information), they were later rated as more aggressive than men who did the same thing (Johnson and Goodchilds 1976, p. 70).

[†] The use of feminine wiles (including flattery) is felt to be a psychopolitical style of the subordinate; it is therefore disapproved of by women who have gained a foothold in the man's world and can afford to disparage what they do not need to use.

has called "shadow labor," an unseen effort which, like housework, does not quite count as labor but is nevertheless crucial to getting other things done. As with doing housework well, the trick is to erase any evidence of effort, to offer only the clean house and the welcoming smile.

We have a simple word for the product of this shadow labor: "nice." Niceness is a necessary and important lubricant to any civil exchange, and men make themselves nice, too. It keeps the social wheels turning. As one flight attendant said, "I'll make comments like 'Nice jacket you have on'—that sort of thing, something to make them feel good. Or I'll laugh at their jokes. It makes them feel relaxed and amusing." Beyond the smaller niceties are larger ones of doing a favor, offering a service. Finally, there is the moral or spiritual sense of being seriously nice, in which we embrace the needs of another person as more important than our own.

Each way of being "nice" adds a dimension to deference. Deference is more than the offering of cold respect, the formal bow of submission, the distant smile of politeness; it can also have a warm face and offer gestures small and large that show support for the well-being and status of others.[4]

Almost everyone does the emotion work that produces what we might, broadly speaking, call

deference. But women are expected to do more of it. A study by Wikler (1976) comparing male with female university professors found that students expected women professors to be warmer and more supportive than male professors; given these expectations, proportionally more women professors were perceived as cold. In another study, Braverman, Braverman, and Clarkson (1970) asked clinically trained psychologists, psychiatrists, and social workers to match various characteristics with "normal adult men" and "normal adult women"; they more often associated "very tactful, very gentle, and very aware of feelings of others" with their ideas of the normal adult woman. In being adaptive, cooperative, and helpful, the woman is on a private stage behind the public stage, and as a consequence she is often seen as less good at arguing, telling jokes, and teaching than she is at expressing appreciation of these activities.‡ She is the conversational cheerleader. She actively enhances other people—usually men, but also other women to whom she plays woman. The more she seems natural at it, the more her labor does not show as labor, the more successfully it is disguised as the *absence* of other, more prized qualities. As a *woman* she may be praised for out-enhancing the best enhancer, but as a *person* in comparison with comics, teachers, and argument-builders, she usually lives outside the climate of enhancement that men tend to inhabit. Men, of course, pay court to certain other men and women

‡ Celebrating male humor or enhancing male status often involves the use of what Suzanne Langer has called non-discursive symbols, "symbols which are not verifiable, do not have dictionary meanings or socially defined syntax and order" (Langer 1951, 1967).

and thus also do the emotion work that keeps deference sincere. The difference between men and women is a difference in the psychological effects of having or not having power.[5]

Racism and sexism share this general pattern, but the two systems differ in the avenues available for the translation of economic inequality into private terms. The white manager and the black factory worker leave work and go home, one to a generally white neighborhood and family and the other to a generally black neighborhood and family. But in the case of women and men, the larger economic inequality is filtered into the intimate daily exchanges between wife and husband. Unlike other subordinates, women seek *primary* ties with a supplier. In marriage, the principle of reciprocity applies to wider arenas of each self: there is more to choose from in how we pay and are paid, and the paying between economically unequal parties goes on morning, noon, and night. The larger inequities find intimate expression.

Wherever it goes, the bargain of wages-for-other-things travels in disguise. Marriage both bridges and obscures the gap between the resources available to men and those available to women.[6] Because men and women do try to love one another—to cooperate in making love, making babies, and making a life together—the very closeness of the bond they accept calls for some disguise of subordination.

There will be talk in the "we" mode, joint bank accounts and joint decisions, and the idea among women that they are equal in the ways that "really count." But underlying this pattern will be *different potential futures outside the marriage* and the effect of that on the patterning of life.* The woman may thus become especially active in certain limited domains, in order to experience a sense of equality that is missing from the overall relationship.

Women who understand their ultimate disadvantage and feel that their position cannot change may jealously guard the covertness of their traditional emotional resources in the understandable fear that if the secret were told, their immediate situation would get worse. For to confess that their social charms are the product of secret work might make them less valuable, just as the sexual revolution has made sexual contact less "valuable" by lowering its bargaining power without promoting the advance of women into better-paying jobs. In fact, of course, when we redefine "adaptability" and "cooperativeness" as a form of shadow labor, we are pointing to a hidden cost for which some recompense is due and suggesting that a general reordering of female-male relationships is desirable.

There is one further reason why women may offer more emotion work of this sort than men: more women at all class levels do unpaid labor of a highly interpersonal sort. They nurture, manage, and

---

* Zick Rubin's study of young men and women in love relationships (generally middle-class persons of about the same age) found that the women tended to admire their male loved ones more than they were, in turn, admired by them. The women also felt "more like" their loved ones than the men did. (See Rubin 1970; Reiss 1960.)

befriend children. More "adaptive" and "cooperative," they address themselves better to the needs of those who are not yet able to adapt and cooperate much themselves. Then, according to Jourard (1968), because they are seen as members of the category from which mothers come, women in general are asked to look out for psychological needs more than men are. The world turns to women for mothering, and this fact silently attaches itself to many a job description.

WOMEN AT WORK

With the growth of large organizations calling for skills in personal relations, the womanly art of status enhancement and the emotion work that it requires has been made more public, more systematized, and more standardized. It is performed by largely middle-class women in largely public contact jobs. As indicated in Chapter Seven (and Appendix C), jobs involving emotional labor comprise over a third of all jobs. But they form only a *quarter* of all jobs that men do, and over *half* of all jobs that women do.

Many of the jobs that call for public contact also call for giving service to the public. Richard Sennett and Jonathan Cobb, in *The Hidden Injuries of Class*, comment on how people tend to rank service jobs in relation to other kinds of jobs: "At the bottom end of the scale are found not factory jobs but service jobs where the individual has to perform personally for someone else. A bartender is listed below a coal miner, a taxi driver below a truck driver; we believe this occurs because their functions *are felt to be more dependent on and more at the mercy of others*" [my emphasis].[7] Because there are more women than men in service jobs (21 percent compared with 9 percent), there are "hidden injuries" of gender attached to those of class.

Once women are at work in public-contact jobs, a new pattern unfolds: they receive less basic deference. That is, although some women are still elbow-guided through doors, chauffeured in cars, and protected from rain puddles, they are not shielded from one fundamental consequence of their lower status: their feelings are accorded less weight than the feelings of men.

As a result of this status effect, flight attending is one sort of job for a woman and another sort of job for a man. For a man the principal hidden task is to maintain his identity as a man in a "woman's occupation" and occasionally to cope with tough passengers "for" female flight attendants. For a woman, the principal hidden task is to deal with the status effect: the absence of a social shield against the displaced anger and frustration of passengers.

How then does a woman's lower status influence how she is treated by others? More basically, what is the prior link between status and the treatment of feeling? High-status people tend to enjoy the privilege of having their feelings noticed and considered important. The lower one's status the more one's feelings are not noticed or treated as inconsequential. H. E. Dale, in *The Higher Civil Service of Great Britain*, reports the existence of a "doctrine of feelings":

> The doctrine of feelings was expounded to me many years ago by a very eminent civil servant. . . . He explained that the importance of feelings varies in close correspondence with the importance of the person who feels. If the public interest requires that a junior clerk should be removed from his post, no regard need be paid to his feelings; if it is the case of an assistant secretary, they must be carefully considered, within reason; if it is a permanent secretary, feelings are a principal element in the situation, and only imperative public interest can override their requirements.[8]

Working women are to working men as junior clerks are to permanent secretaries. Between executive and secretary, doctor and nurse, psychiatrist and social worker, dentist and dental assistant, a power difference is reflected as a gender difference. The "doctrine of feelings" is another double standard between the two sexes.*

The feelings of the lower-status party may be discounted in two ways: by considering them rational

but unimportant or by considering them irrational and hence dismissable. An article entitled "On Aggression in Politics: Are Women Judged by a Double Standard?" presented the results of a survey of female politicians. All those surveyed said they believed there was an affective double standard. As Frances Farenthold, the president of Wells College in Aurora, New York, put it: "You certainly see to it that you don't throw any tantrums. Henry Kissinger can have his scenes—remember the way he acted in Salzburg? But for women, we're still in the stage that if you don't hold in your emotions, you're pegged as emotional, unstable, and all those terms that have always been used to describe women."[9] These women in public life were agreed on the following points. When a man expresses anger, it is deemed "rational" or understandable anger, anger that indicates not weakness of character but deeply held conviction. When women express an equivalent degree of anger, it is more likely to be interpreted as a sign of personal instability. It is believed that women are more emotional, and this very belief is used to invalidate their feelings. That is, the women's feelings are seen not as a response to real events but as reflections of themselves as "emotional" women.

Here we discover a corollary of the "doctrine of feelings": the lower our status, the more our manner of seeing and feeling is subject to being discredited,

---

* The code of chivalry is said to require protection of the weaker by the stronger. Yet a boss may bring flowers to his secretary or open the door for her only to make up for the fact that he gets openly angry at her more often than he does at a male equal or superior, and more often than she does at him. The flowers symbolize redress, even as they obscure the basic maldistribution of respect and its psychic cost.

and the less believable it becomes.[10] An "irrational" feeling is the twin of an invalidated perception. A person of lower status has a weaker claim to the right to define what is going on; less trust is placed in her judgments; and less respect is accorded to what she feels. Relatively speaking, it more often becomes the burden of women, as with other lower-status persons, to uphold a minority viewpoint, a discredited opinion.

Medical responses to male and female illness provide a case in point. One study of how doctors respond to the physical complaints of back pain, headache, dizziness, chest pain, and fatigue—symptoms for which a doctor must take the patient's word—showed that among fifty-two married couples, the complaints of the husbands elicited more medical response than those of the wives. The authors conclude: "The data may bear out . . . that the physicians . . . tend to take illness more seriously in men than in women."† Another study of physician interactions with 184 male and 130 female patients concluded that "doctors were more likely to consider the psychological component of the patient's illness important when the patient was a woman."[11] The female's assertion that she was physically sick was more likely to be invalidated as something "she just imagined," something "subjective," not a response to anything real.

To make up for either way of weighing the feelings of the two sexes unequally, many women urge their feelings forward, trying to express them with more force, so as to get them treated with seriousness. But from there the spiral moves down. For the harder women try to oppose the "doctrine of feeling" by expressing their feelings more, the more they come to fit the image awaiting them as "emotional." Their efforts are discounted as one more example of emotionalism. The only way to counter the doctrine of feelings is to eliminate the more fundamental tie between gender and status.[12]

---

† More women than men go to doctors, and this might seem to explain why doctors take them less seriously. But here it is hard to tell cause from effect, for if a woman's complaints are not taken seriously, she may have to make several visits to doctors before a remedy is found (Armitage et al. 1979).

1. The research literature reflects a contradiction. According to paper and pencil tests, women record a feeling of greater helplessness: what they do, they think, affects their fate less. On the other hand, at least one study indicates that women take blame for things more. Jackson and Getzels's study (1959) of boys' and girls' attitudes toward school found that boys tended to blame problems on the school whereas girls tended to place blame on themselves. To blame oneself, one must have some sense of responsibility, and beneath that, some sense of control. One possible explanation of this apparent contradiction is that women develop a compensatory sense of affective agency. The more one lacks a sense of control in the world, the more one compensates for this by turning control onto the self in relation to feeling. Those who lack a sense of control over the world do not lack control entirely. Rather, their sense of control turns inward; it goes "downstairs." Women have also been found to be more field-dependent—that is, more reliant on external cues and less on internal cues—than men. See Maccoby (1972), Tyler (1965), MacArthur (1967), Vaught (1965), and Witkins et al. (1967).

2. For example, one author writes: "Masculine thinking is oriented more in terms of the self, while feminine thinking is oriented more in terms of the environment. Masculine thinking anticipates rewards and punishments determined more as a result of the adequacy or inadequacy of the self, while feminine thinking anticipates rewards and punishments determined more as a result of the friendship or hostility of the environment. But the question to ask about 'masculine thinking' and 'feminine thinking' is not what innate natures they issue from but what ranks in life they go with" (Tyler 1965, pp. 259–260). See also Rotter (1966), and Brannigan and Toler (1971).

3. Johnson and Goodchilds (1976), p. 69.

4. I am focusing on the warm face of deference and on the deferential aspect of nurturance. This is not to confuse all expressions of nurturance with those of deference. See Kemper (1978), especially the last two chapters on love as status conferral.

5. Societies vary in just *how* women are eliminated from competition for income, opportunity, and occupational status. Some eliminate women by physical segregation. Others allow and even encourage females to compete with men for jobs but they train females to develop traits not favored in economic competition. These traits can be understood at the psychodynamic, emotion management, and behavioral-display levels. At the psychodynamic level, Chodorow (1980) argues that girls learn to want to mother in ways that boys do not learn to want to father, which suits girls for unpaid work. At the level of emotion management, girls learn to manage emotion in ways that adapt them to males outside the "male" competitive arena. Finally, at the level of display, girls learn "feminine" head-tilting, smiling, conversational cheerleading, and other deference displays. On all three levels, women are encouraged to develop traits that disadvantage them in a "male" arena of competition, governed by male rules of competition.

6. Because women have less access to money and status than their male class peers do, they are more motivated than men to marry in order to win access to a much higher "male wage." Wedding cartoons tell the story at this class level, depicting as they do the "official experience." The groom is happy but caught, eager for love but mindful of lost freedoms and burdensome obligations. The bride, on the other hand, almost regardless of age, personality, beauty, or intelligence, is shown as triumphant and lucky to get any man because he provides access to resources otherwise unavailable to her. See Hartmann (1976) for a superb article on economic relations between men and women.

The bargain of wages-for-other-things holds not only for the traditional breadwinner and housewife but also for the working wife, whose earnings from full-time work provide, on the average, less than a third of the family income. Working or not, the basic economic dependence of married women leaves them "owing" something to make it even. But there are class variations.

The higher up the class ladder one goes, the wider the income gap between husband and wife and the more prevalent this sort of bargain is likely to be. Lower down the class ladder, the income gap narrows; more women work and find themselves married to men who earn little more than women do. By reducing male privilege at the bottom, the bargain between the sexes is somewhat evened. Yet the lower-income couples in which both partners work are subjected to cultural images of men and women that originated among the upper-middle classes in the late eighteenth century. It is against this anachronistic class-based measure of what a woman owes a man that lower-class men decide what is owing to them and try to get it, sometimes in physical ways.

7. Sennett and Cobb (1973), p. 236.

8. Quoted in Goffman (1967), p. 10.

9. *New York Times*, February 12, 1979.

10. This conclusion is supported in Hovland et al. (1953).

11. Wallens et al. (1979), p. 143.

12. There seems to be another tie between status and the treatment of feeling. The lower the status, the less acceptable is the expression of open anger. Also, men classically have more license to swear and fight than women do. (Unless the woman has a class advantage or some other sanction, she can be openly aggressive only at some risk to her reputation.) On the other hand, women more than men seem to express "subordinate" feelings. The scream of terror as Dracula or King Kong advances generally comes from a female. Even when the heroine is brave, it is the same. When Nancy Drew, girl detective, becomes the nonemotional (masculinized) doer, another girl is assigned what Goffman has called (and perhaps misunderstood as) "freak-out privileges" (1967, p. 26). Consider this passage from *The Message in the Hollow Oak* (Carolyn Keene, Nancy Drew Series, 1972): "In a sudden lurch he [a large dog] leaped on Nancy. She lost her balance, stumbled backward, and fell into the quarry. Julie Anne screamed. She and the boys watched horror-stricken, as Nancy hit the water and disappeared. Ned started down the steep embankment, while Art yanked a coil of wire from a pocket. Using it as a whip, he finally drove off the attacking dog. As it ran away, whimpering, Nancy's head appeared above the water. 'Oh, Nancy. Thank goodness,' cried Julie Anne. She was near tears" (p. 147). Julie Anne really does fear for Nancy and the boys. Not all women play Julie Anne, but we judge whether a woman is expressive or not according to this female standard; it is part of our cultural understanding of femininity, and therefore also of masculinity. In my view, this culturally mandated expressiveness is not so much a privilege as a job.

WE HAVE A PROBLEM WITH WOMEN SUPPORTING WOMEN

CHELSEA HANDLER

Originally published on *Thrive Global*
2016

n November 2016, 135 million Americans cast their presidential ballots and the final vote count (as of Dec. 9) was:

- 65,746,544, or 48.2%, for Hillary Clinton

- 62,904,682, or 46.2%, for Donald Trump

- 7,645,378, or 5.6%, for Gary Johnson, Jill Stein, Captain Kangaroo, Easter Bunny, etc.

94% of black women voted for Hillary Clinton, because unlike white women, black women don't take their rights, liberties, or justice for granted. They honor how hard people fought for them, and they are fully committed to honoring the very people who risked, and in many cases lost, their lives fighting for the ability to count. They understand how fragile our democracy is and they show up again and again, because they know firsthand how fragile democracy and civilization are.

Another 96 million eligible American voters—or 41% of eligible voters—didn't register and/or didn't vote for president.

And oddly in these United States of Russia, the popular votes aren't worth the ballots they're cast on thanks to America's infamous Electoral College.

So here we are, with President-elect Donald Trump and his Vice President-elect Mike Pence—who as the governor of Indiana spent most of his free time signing Christian Shariah forced pregnancy laws—ready to lead the United States of America starting January 20, 2017, at precisely high noon.

But let's return to the scene of the November 8 election itself, which had a lot of other poisonous ingredients aside from the Electoral College.

One of the saddest things about November 8, aside from the very presence of Donald Trump on the ballot as a major party American presidential candidate, were the women of America who somehow managed to vote for Donald Trump, specifically the

53% percent of all white female voters who chose Mr. Trump.

We don't just have a problem with men supporting women in this country; we have a problem with women supporting women.

America is a free country, and we are free to differ on public policy, but what kind of a woman votes for a white, entitled rich guy who has spent his entire life working the system for excess personal profit while insatiably groping strange women for personal pleasure while Hillary Clinton—arguably the most qualified presidential candidate in modern American history—was standing right there in her pleated pantsuit waiting to lift America up out of its 240-year "winning streak" of male dominance and patriarchy?

American women had a unique chance to vote for Hillary Clinton, the woman who started her career at the Children's Defense Fund defending the least among us—the woman who was the guiding intellectual and compassionate light behind the 1997 creation of the federal Children's Health Insurance Program (CHIP) that provides health care coverage to more than 8 million American children—that very same CHIP of which the late Senator Ted Kennedy said, "The children's health program wouldn't be in existence today if we didn't have Hillary pushing for it from the other end of Pennsylvania Avenue."

And yet, when Hillary Clinton—with her long, accomplished record of public service who left the office of Secretary of State with a 69% approval rating just a few years ago—presented herself on the presidential ballot, white women of America reactivated their prehistoric Pavlovian reflexes and fell obediently as they reincarnated the great female penchant for self-mutilation so brilliantly articulated by H. L. Mencken: "Misogynist: A man who hates women as much as women hate one another."

Ladies, we can do better than this. We can eliminate the competitiveness that has been imposed upon us because we are treated as a minority and have been taught to tackle, rather than climb.

We can wake up America and American women to do a better job going forward; to create an activist fire under women to start treating other women and our America with more respect than we have obsequiously shown for our traditional male dominators.

We need to rise up and use our votes to help ourselves, and to stop hurting ourselves.

Forget the jealousy. Forget the competitiveness. We are stronger together. Find a woman you have nothing in common with and give her a hug. Then hug yourself. Then roll up your sleeves and stop looking in the mirror.

Look around. Get away from yourself. Find women to support. Throw your weight behind them. Get involved.

We are better than this. We have got to get behind each other. We have to stop ourselves from the snide comments that come easily and out of jealousy that are simply a projection of our own insecurities.

Let's stop it with the dialogue about how women look or what they wear, or if they've gained or lost weight. We are more guilty of this with each other than most men are.

It's time to get focused on what really matters. Find women that are different than you and figure out the things you have in common. We have a whole generation of girls who are looking at us to see how we treat each other. Let's show them what the power of being a woman really looks like. Let's open our arms to each other, and to them.

We can do better than this, ladies, and we will during the next four years as we stand up for women, children, the majority vote, and American justice against the Trumpian whitemare. I know I can do better, and I will. It starts now.

In the words of a female much greater than me who stood up to the patriarchic Taliban:

"I RAISE UP MY VOICE — NOT SO I CAN SHOUT, BUT SO THAT THOSE WITHOUT A VOICE CAN BE HEARD . . . WE CANNOT SUCCEED WHEN HALF OF US ARE HELD BACK."
—MALALA YOUSAFZAI

AIN'T I A WOMAN?

SOJOURNER TRUTH

Well, children, where there is so much racket there must be something out of kilter. I think that 'twixt the negroes of the South and the women at the North, all talking about rights, the white men will be in a fix pretty soon. But what's all this here talking about?

That man over there says that women need to be helped into carriages, and lifted over ditches, and to have the best place everywhere. Nobody ever helps me into carriages, or over mud-puddles, or gives me any best place! And ain't I a woman? Look at me! Look at my arm! I have ploughed and planted, and gathered into barns, and no man could head me! And ain't I a woman? I could work as much and eat as much as a man—when I could get it—and bear the lash as well! And ain't I a woman? I have borne thirteen children, and seen most all sold off to slavery, and when I cried out with my mother's grief, none but Jesus heard me! And ain't I a woman?

Then they talk about this thing in the head; what's this they call it? [A member of audience whispers, "intellect."] That's it, honey. What's that got to do with women's rights or negroes' rights? If my cup won't hold but a pint, and yours holds a quart, wouldn't you be mean not to let me have my little half measure full?

Then that little man in black there, he says women can't have as much rights as men, 'cause Christ wasn't a woman! Where did your Christ come from? Where did your Christ come from? From God and a woman! Man had nothing to do with Him.

If the first woman God ever made was strong enough to turn the world upside down all alone, these women together ought to be able to turn it back, and get it right side up again! And now they is asking to do it, the men better let them.

Obliged to you for hearing me, and now old Sojourner ain't got nothing more to say.

A STORY

OF A

FUCK

OFF

FUND

**PAULETTE
PERHACH**

You're telling your own story: You graduated college and you're a grown-ass woman now. Tina Fey is your hero; Beyoncé, your preacher.

You know how to take care of you. You've learned self-defense. If any man ever hit you, you'd rip his eyes out. You've seen *Mad Men*, and if anyone ever sexually harassed you at work, you'd tell him to fuck right off, throw your coffee in his face, and wave two middle fingers as you marched out the door.

You get your first internship. You get your first credit card. You get to walk into Nordstrom, where your mom would never take you, and congratulate yourself with one fabulous black leather skirt, and the heels to match.

Your car? It's the car of a college student. You get a lease, graduate from the rusted Civic to last year's Accord.

You get your first student loan bill, and look at all those numbers.

Your life turns into a stock photo tagged "young professionals": you and your new work friends, hanging out at the bar across the street from the office. The cocktails cost twice as much as you paid when you still measured time by semesters and nights by cans of PBR.

The college boyfriend gets serious. You move into his place, spruce it up by buying your first coffee table together. Ikea lets you put half on your newest credit card.

Your internship ends before you find a permanent job. You pay minimum payments, then max out your cards again buying two days' worth of groceries and filling your gas tank halfway.

Your bank app upgrades to a new feature that combines all your balances—the shiny Nordstrom card with the Visa and the Chase Freedom you were only supposed to use for emergencies—and tells you that somehow you owe people seven thousand dollars.

Your boyfriend offers to cover the rent for a while. You get a job a few months later, but you're that many loan payments behind. Your first paycheck feels like a breath of air that gets sucked right out of your lungs.

Your new boss, who seems nice, calls you in his office, shows you a picture of his kids. He jokes about his son, then as you're laughing, he puts his hand on your arm, gives you a little squeeze. You smile it off.

You wait to pay the electric bill while you're gathering up the half you owe, and the lights go out. On your phone you see the e-mail about the $50 late fee. Your boyfriend asks how you could be so stupid. "I am not stupid," you say. You would never be with someone who called you names, but you would never be able to make first, last, and deposit right now, either.

You say yes to payday P.F. Chang's with your new co-workers, because you want to make friends, your turkey sandwich sounds boring, and what's one more charge? You buy a halter dress you know you can't afford, because it makes you look like the successful young woman you want everyone to think you are.

Your boss tells you that you look nice in that dress, asks you to do a spin. Just to get the moment over with, you do.

Your boyfriend asks you how much you paid for it, says it makes you look chubby. You lock yourself in the bathroom until he bangs on the door so hard you think he must have hurt himself. After he falls asleep, you search Craigslist for places, and can't

believe how expensive rent's gotten around town. You erase your internet history and go to sleep.

A few weeks later, your boss calls a one-on-one in his office, walks up behind you, and stands too close. His breath fogs your neck. His hand crawls up your new dress. You squirm away. He says, "Sorry, I thought . . . "

You know what to do. You're just shocked to find you're not doing it. You are not telling him to fuck off. You are not storming out. All you're doing is math. You have $159 in the bank and your car payment and your maxed out credit cards and you'll die before you ask your dad for a loan again and it all equals one thought: I need this job.

"It's ok," you hear your voice saying. "Just forget it." You scurry out of the room, survey the office half full of women, and wonder how many of them have secrets like the one you're about to keep.

At the apartment, your best guy friend calls. After you hang up, your boyfriend says you laugh too much with him, that you're flirting with him, probably sleeping with him. You say it's not like that. You yell, he yells. You try to leave, he blocks your way. When you struggle to get by, he grabs your wrist in the exact way they pretended to in self-defense class, and you know to go for the eyes, but you don't know how to go for his eyes. He yanks you back until you fall and crack the coffee table.

He seems so sorry, cries, even, so that night you lie down in the same bed. You stare up at the dark and try to calculate how long it would take you to save up the cash to move out. Telling yourself that he's sorry, convincing yourself it was an accident, discounting this one time because he didn't hit you, exactly, seems much more feasible than finding the money, with what you owe every month. The next time you go out as a couple, his arm around your shoulders, you look at all the other girlfriends and imagine finger-sized bruises under their long sleeves.

Wait. This story sucks. If it were one of those Choose Your Own Adventures, here's where you'd want to flip back, start over, rewrite what happens to you.

You graduated college and you're a grown-ass woman now. Tina Fey is your hero. Beyoncé, your preacher.

If any man ever hit you, if anyone ever sexually harassed you, you'd tell him to fuck right off. You want to be, no, you will be the kind of woman who can tell anyone to fuck off if a fuck off is deserved, so naturally you start a Fuck Off Fund.

To build this account, you keep living like you lived as a broke student. Drive the decade-old Civic even after the fender falls off. Buy the thrift store clothes. You waitress on Saturdays, even though you work Monday through Friday. You make do with the garage sale coffee table. It's hard, your loan payments suck, but you make girl's night an at-home thing and do tacos potluck.

You save up a Fuck Off Fund of $1,000, $2,000, $3,000, then enough to live half a year without

anyone else's help. So when your boss tells you that you look nice, asks you to do a spin, you say, "Is there some way you need my assistance in the professional capacity or can I go back to my desk now?"

When your boyfriend calls you stupid, you say if he ever says that again, you're out of there, and it's not hard to imagine how you'll accomplish your getaway.

When your boss attempts to grope you, you say, "Fuck off, you creep!" You wave two middle fingers in the air, and march over to HR. Whether the system protects you or fails you, you will be able to take care of yourself.

When your boyfriend pounds the door, grabs your wrist, you see it as the red flag it is, leave a post-it in the night that says, "Fuck off, lunatic douche!" You stay up in a fancy hotel drinking room service champagne, shopping for apartments, and swiping around on Tinder.

Once your Fuck Off Fund is built back up, with your new, better job, you pay cash for the most bad ass black leather skirt you can find, upgrade to the used but nicer convertible you've always wanted, and start saving to go to Thailand with your best friend the next summer.

Yes, that's a better story.

It's a story no one ever told me.

It's the kind I'd hope for you.

THE TRANSFORMATION OF SILENCE INTO LANGUAGE AND ACTION

AUDRE LORDE

Originally published in *Sister Outsider*
1984

I have come to believe over and over again that what is most important to me must be spoken, made verbal and shared, even at the risk of having it bruised or misunderstood. That the speaking profits me, beyond any other effect. I am standing here as a Black lesbian poet, and the meaning of all that waits upon the fact that I am still alive, and might not have been. Less than two months ago I was told by two doctors, one female and one male, that I would have to have breast surgery, and that there was a 60 to 80 percent chance that the tumor was malignant. Between that telling and the actual surgery, there was a three week period of the agony of an involuntary reorganization of my entire life. The surgery was completed, and the growth was benign.

But within those three weeks, I was forced to look upon myself and my living with a harsh and urgent clarity that has left me still shaken but much stronger. This is a situation faced by many women, by some of you here today. Some of what I experienced during that time has helped elucidate for me much of what I feel concerning the transformation of silence into language and action.

In becoming forcibly and essentially aware of my mortality, and of what I wished and wanted for my life, however short it might be, priorities and omissions became strongly etched in a merciless light, and what I most regretted were my silences. Of what had I ever been afraid? To question or to speak as I believed could have meant pain, or death. But we all hurt in so many different ways, all the time, and pain will either change or end. Death, on the other hand, is the final silence. And that might be coming quickly, now, without regard for whether I had ever spoken what needed to be said, or had only betrayed myself into small silences, while I planned someday to speak, or waited for someone else's words. And I began to recognize a source of power within myself that comes from the knowledge that while it is most desirable not to be afraid, learning to put fear into a perspective gave me great strength.

I was going to die, if not sooner then later, whether or not I had ever spoken myself. My silences had not protected me. Your silence will not protect you. But for every real word spoken, for every attempt I had ever made to speak those truths for which I am still seeking, I had made contact with other women while we examined the words to fit a world in which we all believed, bridging our differences. And it was the concern and caring of all those women which gave me strength and enabled me to scrutinize the essentials of my living.

The women who sustained me through that period were Black and white, old and young, lesbian, bisexual, and heterosexual, and we all shared a war against the tyrannies of silence. They all gave me a strength and concern without which I could not have survived intact. Within those weeks of acute fear came the knowledge—within the war we are all waging with the forces of death, subtle and otherwise, conscious or not—I am not only a casualty, I am also a warrior.

What are the words you do not yet have? What do you need to say? What are the tyrannies you swallow day by day and attempt to make your own, until you will sicken and die of them, still in silence? Perhaps for some of you here today, I am the face of one of your fears. Because I am woman, because I am Black, because I am lesbian, because I am myself—a Black woman warrior poet doing my work—come to ask you, are you doing yours?

And of course I am afraid, because the transformation of silence into language and action is an act of self-revelation, and that always seems fraught with danger. But my daughter, when I told her of our topic and my difficulty with it, said, "Tell them about how you're never really a whole person if you remain silent, because there's always that one little piece inside you that wants to be spoken out, and if you keep ignoring it, it gets madder and madder and hotter and hotter,

and if you don't speak it out one day it will just up and punch you in the mouth from the inside."

In the cause of silence, each of us draws the face of her own fear—fear of contempt, of censure, or some judgment, or recognition, of challenge, of annihilation. But most of all, I think, we fear the visibility without which we cannot truly live. Within this country where racial difference creates a constant, if unspoken, distortion of vision, Black women have on one hand always been highly visible, and so, on the other hand, have been rendered invisible through the depersonalization of racism. Even within the women's movement, we have had to fight, and still do, for that very visibility which also renders us most vulnerable, our Blackness. For to survive in the mouth of this dragon we call america, we have had to learn this first and most vital lesson—that we were never meant to survive. Not as human beings. And neither were most of you here today, Black or not. And that visibility which makes us most vulnerable is that which also is the source of our greatest strength. Because the machine will try to grind you into dust anyway, whether or not we speak. We can sit in our corners mute forever while our sisters and our selves are wasted while our children are distorted and destroyed, while our earth is poisoned; we can sit in our safe corners mute as bottles, and we will still be no less afraid.

In my house this year we are celebrating the feast of Kwanza, the African-American festival of harvest which begins the day after Christmas and lasts for seven days. There are seven principles of Kwanza, one for each day. The first principle is Umoja, which means unity, the decision to strive for and maintain unity in self and community. The principle for yesterday, the second day, was Kujichagulia—self-determination—the decision to define ourselves, name ourselves, and speak for ourselves, instead of being defined and spoken for by others. Today is the third day of Kwanza, and the principle for today is Ujima—collective work and responsibility—the decision to build and maintain ourselves and our communities together and to recognize and solve our problems together.

Each of us is here now because in one way or another we share a commitment to language and to the power of language, and to the reclaiming of that language which has been made to work against us. In the transformation of silence into language and action, it is vitally necessary for each one of us to establish or examine her function in that transformation and to recognize her role as vital within that transformation. For those of us who write, it is necessary to scrutinize not only the truth of what we speak, but the truth of that language by which we speak it. For others, it is to share and spread also those words that are meaningful to us. But primarily for us all, it is necessary to teach by living and speaking those truths which we believe and know beyond understanding. Because in this way alone we can survive, by taking part in a process of life that is creative and continuing, that is growth.

And it is never without fear—of visibility, of the harsh light of scrutiny and perhaps judgment, of pain, of death. But we have lived through all of those already, in silence, except death. And I remind myself all the

time now that if I were to have been born mute, or had maintained an oath of silence my whole life long for safety, I would still have suffered, and I would still die. It is very good for establishing perspective. And where the words of women are crying to be heard, we must each of us recognize our responsibility to seek those words out, to read them and share them and examine them in their pertinence to our lives. That we not hide behind the mockeries of separations that have been imposed upon us and which so often we accept as our own. For instance, "I can't possibly teach Black women's writing—their experience is so different from mine." Yet how many years have you spent teaching Plato and Shakespeare and Proust? Or another, "She's a white woman and what could she possibly have to say to me?" Or, "She's a lesbian, what would my husband say, or my chairman?" Or again, "This woman writes of her sons and I have no children." And all the other endless ways in which we rob ourselves of ourselves and each other.

We can learn to work and speak when we are afraid in the same way we have learned to work and speak when we are tired. For we have been socialized to respect fear more than our own needs for language and definition, and while we wait in silence for that final luxury of fearlessness, the weight of that silence will choke us.

The fact that we are here and that I speak these words is an attempt to break that silence and bridge some of those differences between us, for it is not difference which immobilizes us, but silence. And there are so many silences to be broken.

FEMINISM SHOULD NOT BE AN EXCLUSIVE PARTY

CHIMAMANDA NGOZI ADICHIE

I'm truly, truly happy to be here today, so happy, in fact, that when I found out your class color was yellow, I decided I would wear yellow eye shadow. But on second thoughts, I realized that as much as I admire Wellesley, even yellow eye shadow was a bit too much of a gesture. So I dug out this yellow—yellowish—headwrap instead.

Speaking of eye shadow, I wasn't very interested in makeup until I was in my twenties, which is when I began to wear makeup. Because of a man. A loud, unpleasant man. He was one of the guests at a friend's dinner party. I was also a guest. I was about 23, but people often told me I looked 12. The conversation at dinner was about traditional Igbo culture, about the custom that allows only men to break the kola nut, and the kola nut is a deeply symbolic part of Igbo cosmology. I argued that it would be better if that honor were based on achievement rather than gender, and he looked at me and said, dismissively, "You don't know what you are talking about, you're a small girl."

I wanted him to disagree with the substance of my argument, but by looking at me, young and female, it was easy for him to dismiss what I said. So I decided to try to look older. So I thought lipstick might help. And eyeliner. And I am grateful to that man because I have since come to love makeup, and its wonderful possibilities for temporary transformation. So, I have not told you this anecdote as a way to illustrate my discovery of gender injustice. If anything, it's really just an ode to makeup. It's really just to say that this, your graduation, is a good time to buy some lipsticks—if makeup is your sort of thing—because a good shade of lipstick can always put you in a slightly better mood on dark days.

It's not about my discovering gender injustice because of course I had discovered it years before then. From childhood. From watching the world. I already knew that the world does not extend to women the many small courtesies that it extends to men. I also knew that victimhood is not a virtue. That being discriminated against does not make you somehow morally better. And I knew that men were not inherently bad or evil. They were merely privileged. And I knew that privilege blinds because it is the nature of privilege to blind. I knew from this personal experience, from the class privilege I had of growing up in an educated family, that it sometimes blinded me, that I was not always as alert to the nuances of people who were different from me.

And you, because you now have your beautiful Wellesley degree, have become privileged, no matter what your background. That degree, and the experience of being here, is a privilege. Don't let it blind you too often. Sometimes you will need to push it aside in order to see clearly.

———

I bring greetings to you from my mother. She's a big admirer of Wellesley, and she wishes she could be here. She called me yesterday to ask how the speech-writing was going and to tell me to remember to use a lot of lotion on my legs today so they would not look ashy. My mother is 73 and she retired as the first female registrar of the University of Nigeria—which was quite a big deal at the time.

My mother likes to tell a story of the first university meeting she chaired. It was in a large conference room, and at the head of the table was a sign that said CHAIRMAN. My mother was about to get seated there when a clerk came over and made to remove the sign. All the past meetings had of course been chaired by men, and somebody had forgotten to replace the CHAIRMAN with a new sign that

said CHAIRPERSON. The clerk apologized and told her he would find the new sign, since she was not a chairman. My mother said no. Actually, she said, she WAS a chairman. She wanted the sign left exactly where it was. The meeting was about to begin. She didn't want anybody to think that what she was doing in that meeting at that time on that day was in any way different from what a CHAIRMAN would have done.

I always liked this story, and admired what I thought of as my mother's fiercely feminist choice. I once told the story to a friend, a card carrying feminist, and I expected her to say bravo to my mother, but she was troubled by it. "Why would your mother want to be called a chairman, as though she needed the MAN part to validate her?" my friend asked.

In some ways, I saw my friend's point. Because if there were a Standard Handbook published annually by the Secret Society of Certified Feminists, then that handbook would certainly say that a woman should not be called, nor want to be called, a CHAIRMAN. But gender is always about context and circumstance. If there is a lesson in this anecdote, apart from just telling you a story about my mother to make her happy that I spoke about her at Wellesley, then it is this: Your standardized ideologies will not always fit your life. Because life is messy.

———

When I was growing up in Nigeria I was expected, as every student who did well was expected, to become a doctor. Deep down I knew that what I really wanted to do was to write stories. But I did what I was supposed to do and I went into medical school. I told myself that I would tough it out and become a psychiatrist and that way I could use my patients' stories for my fiction. But after one year of medical school I fled. I realized I would be a very unhappy doctor and I really did not want to be responsible for the inadvertent death of my patients. Leaving medical school was a very unusual decision, especially in Nigeria where it is very difficult to get into medical school.

Later, people told me that it had been very courageous of me, but I did not feel courageous at all.

What I felt then was not courage but a desire to make an effort. To try. I could either stay and study something that was not right for me. Or I could try and do something different. I decided to try. I took the American exams and got a scholarship to come to the U.S. where I could study something else that was not related to medicine. Now it might not have worked out. I might not have been given an American scholarship. My writing might not have ended up being successful. But the point is that I tried.

We cannot always bend the world into the shapes we want but we can try, we can make a concerted and real and true effort. And you are privileged that, because of your education here, you have already

been given many of the tools that you will need to try. Always just try. Because you never know.

And so as you graduate, as you deal with your excitement and your doubts today, I urge you to try and create the world you want to live in. Minister to the world in a way that can change it. Minister radically in a real, active, practical, get your hands dirty way. Wellesley will open doors for you. Walk through those doors and make your strides long and firm and sure.

Write television shows in which female strength is not depicted as remarkable but merely normal.

Teach your students to see that vulnerability is a human rather than a female trait.

Commission magazine articles that teach men how to keep a woman happy. Because there are already too many articles that tell women how to keep a man happy. And in media interviews make sure fathers are asked how they balance family and work. In this age of "parenting as guilt," please spread the guilt equally. Make fathers feel as bad as mothers. Make fathers share in the glory of guilt.

Campaign and agitate for paid paternity leave everywhere in America.

Hire more women where there are few. But remember that a woman you hire doesn't have to be exceptionally good. Like a majority of the men who get hired, she just needs to be good enough.

Recently a feminist organization kindly nominated me for an important prize in a country that will remain unnamed. I was very pleased. I've been fortunate to have received a few prizes so far and I quite like them, especially when they come with shiny presents. To get this prize, I was required to talk about how important a particular European feminist woman writer had been to me. Now the truth was that I had never managed to finish this feminist writer's book. It did not speak to me. It would have been a lie to claim that she had any major influence on my thinking. The truth is that I learned so much more about feminism from watching the women traders in the market in Nsukka where I grew up, than from reading any seminal feminist text. I could have said that this woman was important to me, and I could have talked the talk, and I could have been given the prize and a shiny present.

But I didn't. Because I had begun to ask myself what it really means to wear this "feminist" label so publicly. Just as I asked myself after excerpts of my feminism speech were used in a song by a talented musician whom I think some of you might know. I thought it was a very good thing that the word "feminist" would be introduced to a new generation. But I was startled by how many people, many of whom were academics, saw something troubling, even menacing, in this. It was as though feminism was supposed to be an elite little cult, with esoteric rites of membership. But it shouldn't. Feminism should be an inclusive party. Feminism should be a party full of different feminisms.

And so, class of 2015, please go out there and make feminism a big raucous inclusive party.

———

The past three weeks have been the most emotionally difficult of my life. My father is 83 years old, a retired professor of statistics, a lovely kind man. I am an absolute Daddy's girl. Three weeks ago, he was kidnapped near his home in Nigeria. And for a number of days, my family and I went through the kind of emotional pain that I have never known in my life. We were talking to threatening strangers on the phone, begging and negotiating for my father's safety and we were not always sure if my father was alive. He was released after we paid a ransom. He is well, in fairly good shape and in his usual lovely way, is very keen to reassure us all that he is fine.

I am still not sleeping well, I still wake up many times at night, in panic, worried that something else has gone wrong, I still cannot look at my father without fighting tears, without feeling this profound relief and gratitude that he is safe, but also rage that he had to undergo such an indignity to his body and to his spirit. And the experience has made me re-think many things, what truly matters, and what doesn't. What I value, and what I don't.

And as you graduate today, I urge you to think about that a little more. Think about what really matters to you. Think about what you want to really matter to you.

I read about your rather lovely tradition of referring to older students as "big sisters" and younger ones as "little sisters." And I read about the rather strange thing about being thrown into the pond—and I didn't really get that—but I would very much like to be your honorary big sister today. Which means that I would like to give you bits of advice as your big sister: All over the world, girls are raised to make themselves likable, to twist themselves into shapes that suit other people. Please do not twist yourself into shapes to please. Don't do it. If someone likes that version of you, that version of you that is false and holds back, then they actually just like that twisted shape, and not you. And the world is such a gloriously multifaceted, diverse place that there are people in the world who will like you, the real you, as you are.

I am lucky that my writing has given me a platform that I choose to use to talk about things that I care about, and I have said a few things that have not been so popular with a number of people. I have been told to shut up about certain things—such as my position on the equal rights of gay people on the continent of Africa, such as my deeply held belief that men and women are completely equal. I don't speak to provoke. I speak because I think our time on earth is short and each moment that we are not our truest selves, each moment we pretend to be what we are not, each moment we say what we do not mean because we imagine that is what some-body wants us to say, then we are wasting our time on earth. I don't mean to sound precious but please

don't waste your time on earth. But there is one exception. The only acceptable way of wasting your time on earth is online shopping.

One last thing about my mother. My mother and I do not agree on many things regarding gender. There are certain things my mother believes a person should do, for the simple reason that said person is a woman. Such as: nod occasionally and smile even when smiling is the last thing one wants to do. Such as: strategically give in to certain arguments, espe-cially when arguing with a non-female. Such as get married and have children. I can think of fairly good reasons for doing any of these. But "because you are a woman" is not one of them. And so, Class of 2015, never ever accept "because you are a woman" as a reason for doing or not doing anything.

And, finally I would like to end with a final note on the most important thing in the world: love.

Now girls are often raised to see love only as giving. Women are praised for their love when that love is an act of giving. But to love is to give and to take.

Please love by giving and by taking. Give and be given. If you are only giving and not taking, you'll know. You'll know from that small and true voice inside you that we females are so often socialized to silence.

Don't silence that voice. Dare to take.

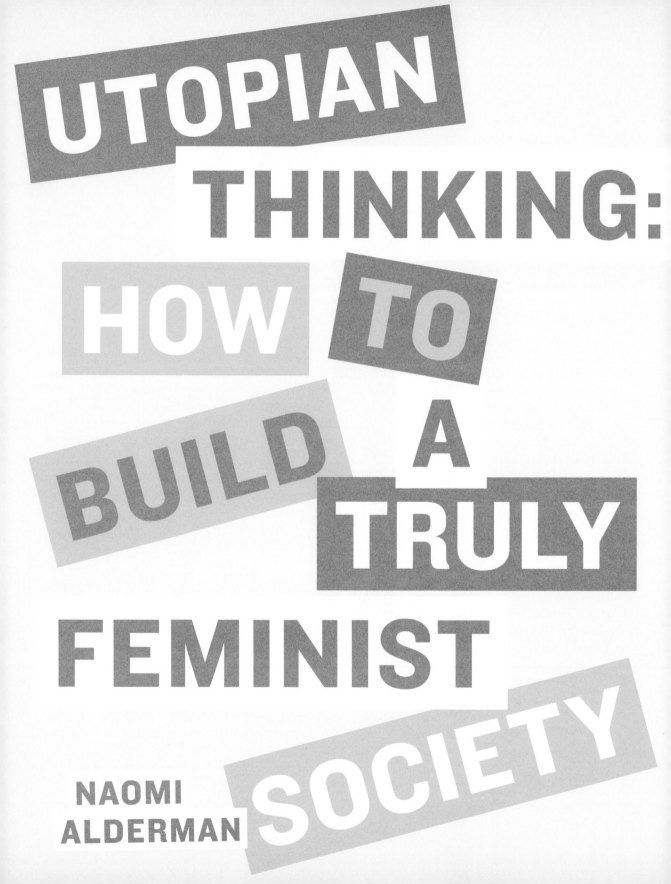

UTOPIAN THINKING: HOW TO BUILD A TRULY FEMINIST SOCIETY

NAOMI ALDERMAN

Originally published in *The Guardian*

2017

Sometimes over the past few decades it's seemed as if we're slowly, inch by inch, getting closer to a gender-equal utopia. And sometimes, as for instance with the election of a "pussy-grabbing" women's-hotness-rating misogynist as "the leader of the free world," it does feel as if we're getting further away from living in a feminist paradise. The worldwide women's marches against Trump were a way of saying how much of a step back his inauguration feels.

So it might be good to think about where we're hoping to get to. Here's what a feminist utopia is for me: a world where your genitals, hormonal arrangements, or gender identification matter not a whit. Where no emotions are gendered: everyone gets to be both vulnerable and tough, aggressive and nurturing, effortlessly confident and inclusively consensus-building, compassionate and dominant. Each by turn, just as it exists in us: no part of our rich, human selves cut off or excised because "boys don't cry" or "girls aren't funny."

It's a world where there are no "boys' toys" and "girls' toys." No women's jobs and men's jobs. No insistent drumbeat of culture keeping us in order. No one kicking us if we step out of our assigned lines. It's a world where—among many many other things—there are no specific men's clothes or women's clothes, but everyone gets to play in the dressing-up box exactly as they like. If all you want is to wear overalls: fair enough. If you want to wear a suit one day and a floaty dress another, what's the problem?

What I want is a world where neither gender nor sex are destiny. Where no child is ever told there's anything they can't do, or must do, "because you're a boy" or "because you're a girl." It's not a world where anything is "taken" from anyone—it's one where everyone's possibilities are enlarged.

We are very far from that world today. So how do we get from here to there? A million steps, large and small. But here are a few ideas. We urgently need to address the assumption bound up in our employment laws and custody arrangements that women are the "natural child carers" and men don't really want much to do with their children. In the UK, it's possible to share parental leave, but the way the law is framed means that if a heterosexual couple chooses to, the man's time at home with his baby is deducted from the woman's. If we take the need for fathers in children's lives seriously—and I do—we must ringfence time for both parents to spend with their children: at least three months for each parent. Of course the father might choose not to use it, but then it'd be lost, not just shunted over to the mother.

We also need the idea of "shared parenting" after divorce—perhaps one week on, one week off—to become the expected norm, rather than a rarity. And we badly need mandatory creche facilities at large companies—and incentives and resources for smaller companies to set up shared, local childcare for their employees.

Girls and boys wouldn't grow up with their father a rare visitor while their mother is constantly present—my hunch is that this would make a massive difference in the emotional lives of children and the adults they become, perhaps altering the dynamics of adult relationships profoundly.

And employers would have even less reason to wonder whether they should take on a woman who might be about to start a family—and more of a reason to apply the same thinking to men, improving the gender pay gap. While we're on that subject, let's introduce public gender pay audits for larger companies

(say, those with over 50 or 100 staff), not revealing individual salaries but aggregating salaries of similar jobs. Then let the conversation surrounding those pay audits do its work.

In discussions in homes across the nation, when perfectly reasonable people have a think about "which of us should go part time to be there for pick-up after school," that perfectly reasonable conversation will—if women are paid 86% of men's salaries, as the Fawcett Society has found—go one way almost every time. So men are deprived of time with their children; women are deprived of economic independence. The cycle goes on. Let's commit to ending it.

And, talking of endless cycles, in the UK men are about 22 times more likely to be sent to prison than women are. Men are more likely than women to both perpetrate, and be a victim of, violence. I don't happen to think men are "naturally" more criminal or violent. But even if there are some hormonal differences involved, I think we're failing boys and men: failing to teach them that there are answers that don't involve violence, that violence says nothing about how "manly" you are, that aggression isn't the best answer to most situations. We need to change our cultural conversation around that, quickly.

Let's teach boys at school the personally and economically valuable skills of self-expression and emotional intelligence, of mediation and problem-solving. It would introduce the expectation that disputes are to be solved with words, thinking, and kindness, not a half-brick to the head. Men are more often the victims of male violence; sorting this out would benefit more men than women.

Which is not to say it wouldn't benefit women too. Three women a week are killed by men in England and Wales. Women are given a litany of supposedly "preventive" measures, the effect of which is just that some other woman, not them, is the victim of the wandering sadist on the street: don't walk on the streets after dark; don't wear tight clothing. How about this? Teach every girl self-defense at school, from the age of five to 16. It's infinitely more important than netball. Give these lessons at least some of the time in the curriculum devoted to team sports. The skills of hurting a larger opponent enough to buy you time to get away should be second nature to all women by the time they leave school.

And, on the subject of women being raped, I've given up watching any television that includes a posed female corpse or starts with a naked, bruised woman—ruling out a surprisingly large number of shows. I wouldn't censor; creators must be free to create, and we viewers can make our own choices.

But I've heard people defend shows such as *Game of Thrones* for showing women being raped on the grounds that this "would happen" in their pseudo-medieval worlds of constant warfare.

Well, fine. But estimates are that in one in six rapes the victim is a man. If we're talking about what "just would happen" in war . . . Jaime, Tyrion, and Theon would have been raped, as would many male characters in other shows. Sometimes men have responded to my pointing this out by saying, "Oh, but symbolically these characters are raped." But women don't get to have "symbolism" in these shows. They get the real thing. Either be "realistic" or don't. But let's not pretend that women are always beautiful victims and men can never be.

That's the essence of it all, really, and why I started by talking about emotions. In so many areas, we still insist that women are "weak" and men "strong." Men work and women care. Women are kind and men are violent. Personality, inner life, and life experiences don't divide neatly into "boys" and "girls." Denying that simple truth hurts us all, in a million ways, and we need to meticulously unpick each and every one of them.

TEXT CREDITS

THE AUTHORS

CHIMAMANDA NGOZI ADICHIE is a multi-award-winning author and feminist. Her 2012 talk "We Should All Be Feminists" earned international renown, and in 2013 her book *Americanah* was named by the *New York Times* as one of the top ten books of the year.

NAOMI ALDERMAN is an award-winning author and professor of creative writing. She was mentored by Margaret Atwood and her novel *The Power* was one of President Barack Obama's favorite books of 2017.

JESSICA BENNETT is an award-winning journalist and author of the book *Feminist Fight Club: A Survival Manual for a Sexist Workplace*. In 2017 she was appointed as the inaugural gender editor of the *New York Times*.

ANNE BOYER is a poet, essayist, and professor at the Kansas City Art Institute. In 2018, she was the inaugural winner of the Cy Twombly Award for Poetry from the Foundation for Contemporary Arts.

JUDY BRADY was a writer and figure in the Women's Liberation movement. She was an activist on topics ranging from abortion to cancer to gentrification.

RACHEL FUDGE is a former editor of *Bitch*. She currently serves on *Bitch Media*'s National Advisory Board.

ROXANE GAY is an author whose books include the *New York Times* bestsellers *Bad Feminist* and *Hunger*. She is also a regular contributing opinion writer for the *New York Times*.

CHELSEA HANDLER is a comedian, actor, producer, writer, and activist. She has authored five *New York Times* bestsellers.

SALMA HAYEK is an actress and producer. She earned an Academy Award nomination for her portrayal of Frida Kahlo in *Frida*.

ARLIE RUSSELL HOCHSCHILD is a writer, sociologist, and professor at the University of California, Berkeley. Her book *Strangers in Their Own Land: Anger and Mourning on the American Right* was a finalist for the National Book Award.

SOFIA JAWED-WESSEL is an Assistant Professor in the School of Health, Physical Education and Recreation at the University of Nebraska at Omaha, and the Associate Director of the Midlands Sexual Health Research Collaborative. She teaches a sex-positive approach to providing medically accurate sex education.

MINDY KALING is an actor, producer, writer, and director. She currently writes, stars in, and executive produces *The Mindy Project*. She has also written two *New York Times* bestsellers and was named one of *Glamour*'s women of the year in 2014.

AUDRE LORDE was a Civil Rights and LGBTQ+ activist, a feminist, and a writer. She was a prominent member of the Black Arts Movement and the cofounder of the first press for women of color in the United States.

CAITLIN MORAN is a British columnist and the author of the international bestseller *How to Be a Woman*. She has won multiple awards for her journalism, and was named one of Britain's most influential women by the BBC in 2014.

IJEOMA OLUO is a writer whose work has been featured in *TIME, NY Magazine, The Guardian,* and *The Establishment.*

PAULETTE PERHACH is a journalist whose writing on women and personal finance has appeared in the *New York Times, Elle,* and other publications.

WARSAN SHIRE is a poet and activist. In 2014, she was named the first Young Poet Laureate for London, and in 2016 her poetry was featured in Beyonce's visual album *Lemonade.*

JIA TOLENTINO is a staff writer for the *New Yorker*. Previously, she served as deputy editor of *Jezebel* and contributing editor of *The Hairpin.*

SOJOURNER TRUTH, née Isabella Baumfree, was born into slavery in 1797. She escaped to freedom in 1826 and became an advocate for abolition and women's rights.

JESSICA VALENTI is a Brooklyn-based writer and founder of the award-winning website Feministing.com. Her memoir *Sex Object* was a *New York Times* bestseller.

CLAIRE VAYE WATKINS is the author of the novel *Gold, Fame, Citrus* and the award-winning short story collection *Battleborn*, and she is an Assistant Professor of writing at the University of Michigan. In 2012, she was named one of the National Book Foundation's "5 under 35."

MARY WOLLSTONECRAFT, born in in 1759, was a writer and advocate of women's rights. She passed away at age 38, due to complications after giving birth to a daughter—writer Mary Shelley.

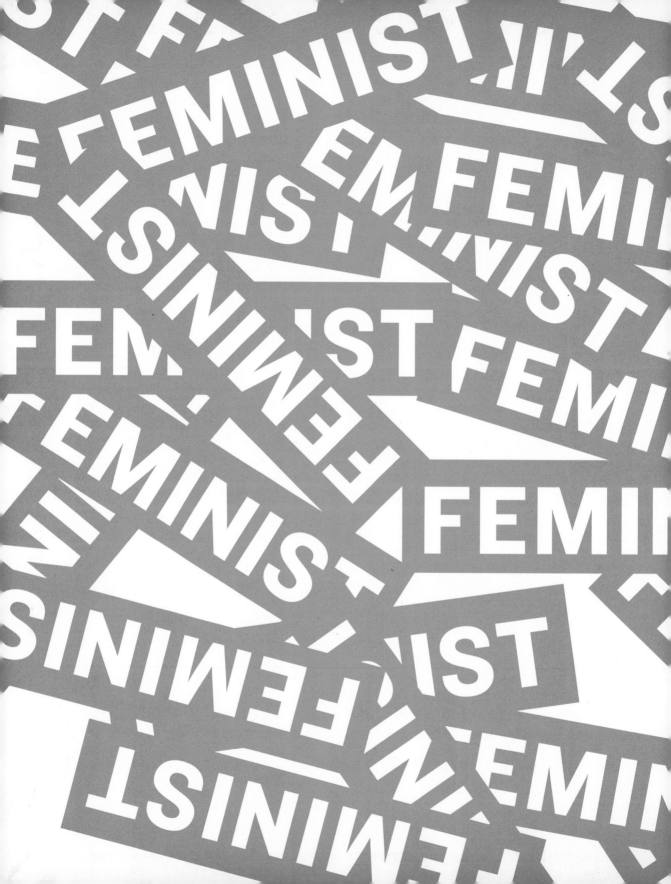